STAR WARS®

OMNIBUS

THE COMPLETE SAGA

EPISODES I THROUGH VI

STAR WARS
OMNIBUS
THE COMPLETE SAGA
EPISODES I THROUGH VI

DARK HORSE BOOKS®

cover illustration Tsuneo Sanda
president and publisher Mike Richardson
series editors Lynn Adair, Bob Cooper, Dave Land, Edward Martin III, Randy Stradley,
and Suzanne Taylor, with assistance from Jeremy Barlow and Philip Simon
collection editor Randy Stradley
collection assistant editor Freddye Lins
collection designer Kat Larson

special thanks to Jann Moorhead, David Anderman, Troy Alders, Leland Chee, Sue Rostoni, and Carol Roeder at
Lucas Licensing

Star Wars® Omnibus: The Complete Saga—Episodes I through VI

This volume collects *Star Wars:* Episode I *The Phantom Menace* #1–#4; *Star Wars:* Episode II *Attack of the Clones*
#1–#4; *Star Wars:* Episode III *Revenge of the Sith* #1–#4; *Star Wars: A New Hope Special Edition* #1–#4; Marvel's
Star Wars #39–#44, remastered as *Star Wars: The Empire Strikes Back Special Edition*; and Marvel's *Star Wars:
Return of the Jedi* #1–#4, remastered as *Star Wars: Return of the Jedi Special Edition*.

Published by Dark Horse Books
A division of Dark Horse Comics, Inc.
10956 SE Main Street
Milwaukie, OR 97222

DarkHorse.com | StarWars.com

To find a comics shop in your area, call the Comic Shop Locator Service toll-free at 1-888-266-4226

executive vice president Neil Hankerson • chief financial officer Tom Weddle • vice president of publishing Randy Stradley • vice
president of book trade sales Michael Martens • vice president of business affairs Anita Nelson • vice president of marketing Micha
Hershman • vice president of product development David Scroggy • vice president of information technology Dale LaFountain •
senior director of print, design, and production Darlene Vogel • general counsel Ken Lizzi • editorial director Davey Estrada • senior
managing editor Scott Allie • senior books editor Chris Warner • executive editor Diana Schutz • director of print and development
Cary Grazzini • art director Lia Ribacchi • director of scheduling Cara Niece

Printed at 1010 Printing International, Ltd., Guangdong Province, China

First edition: October 2011
ISBN 978-1-59582-832-3

10 9 8 7 6 5 4 3 2 1

CONTENTS

BASED ON THE GEORGE LUCAS FILMS

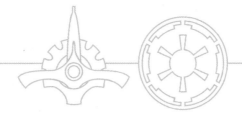

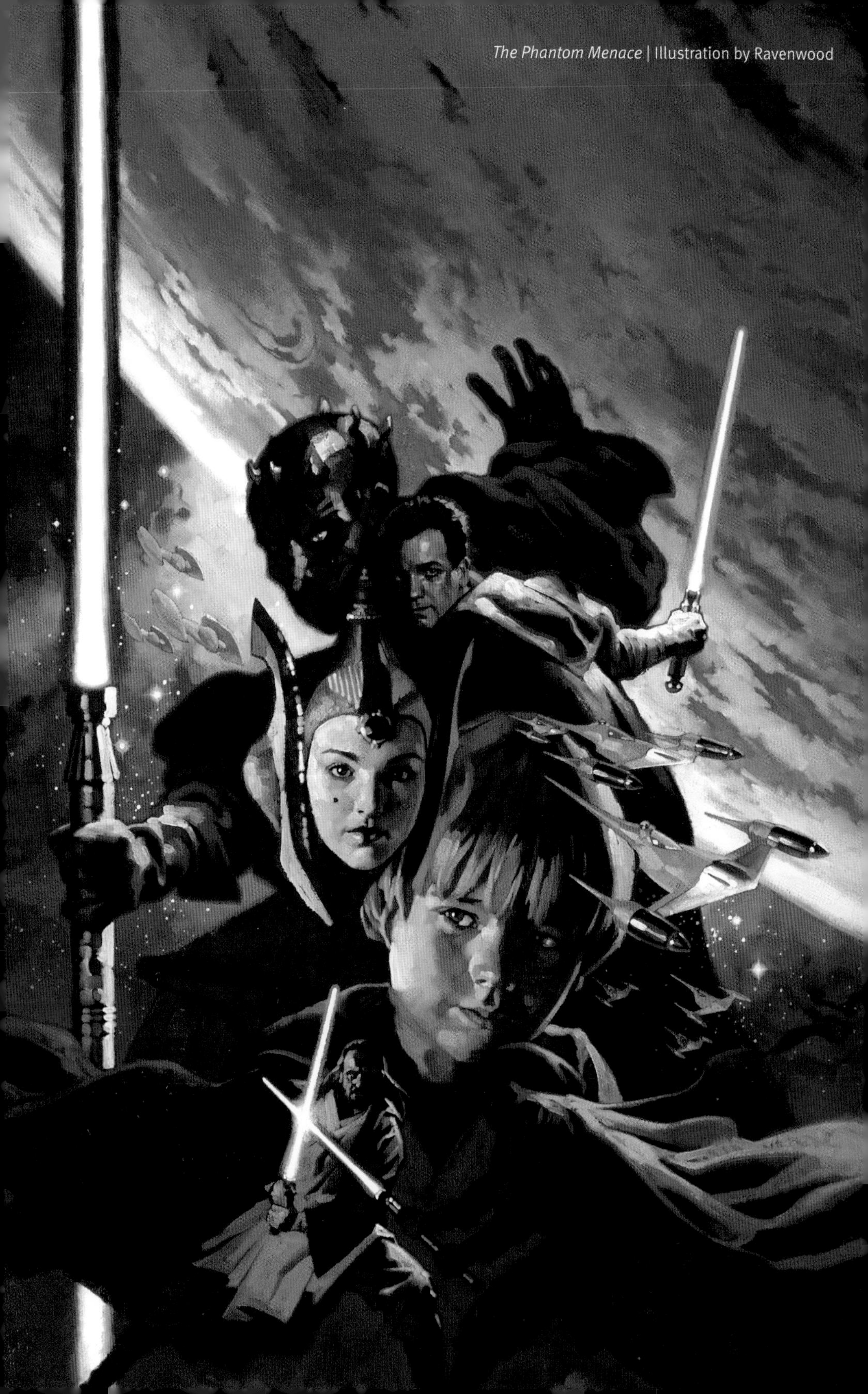

The Phantom Menace | Illustration by Ravenwood

Turmoil has engulfed the Galactic Republic. The taxation of trade routes to outlying star systems is in dispute.

Hoping to resolve the matter with a blockade of deadly battleships, the greedy Trade Federation has stopped all shipping to the small planet of Naboo.

While the Congress of the Republic endlessly debates the alarming chain of events, the Supreme Chancellor has secretly dispatched two Jedi Knights, the guardians of peace and justice in the galaxy, to settle the conflict. . . .

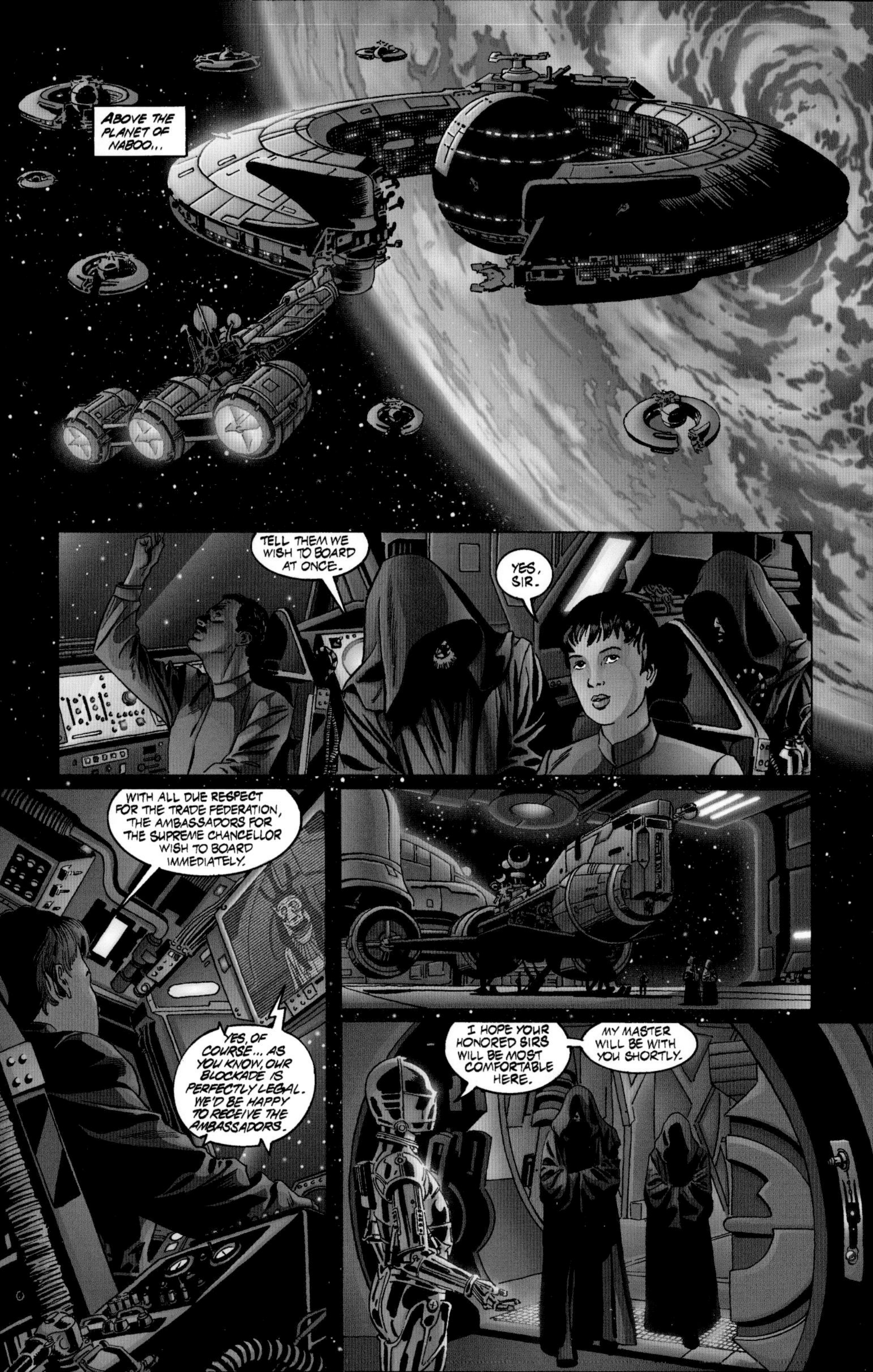
ABOVE THE PLANET OF NABOO...
TELL THEM WE WISH TO BOARD AT ONCE.
YES, SIR.
WITH ALL DUE RESPECT FOR THE TRADE FEDERATION, THE AMBASSADORS FOR THE SUPREME CHANCELLOR WISH TO BOARD IMMEDIATELY.
YES, OF COURSE... AS YOU KNOW, OUR BLOCKADE IS PERFECTLY LEGAL. WE'D BE HAPPY TO RECEIVE THE AMBASSADORS.
I HOPE YOUR HONORED SIRS WILL BE MOST COMFORTABLE HERE.
MY MASTER WILL BE WITH YOU SHORTLY.

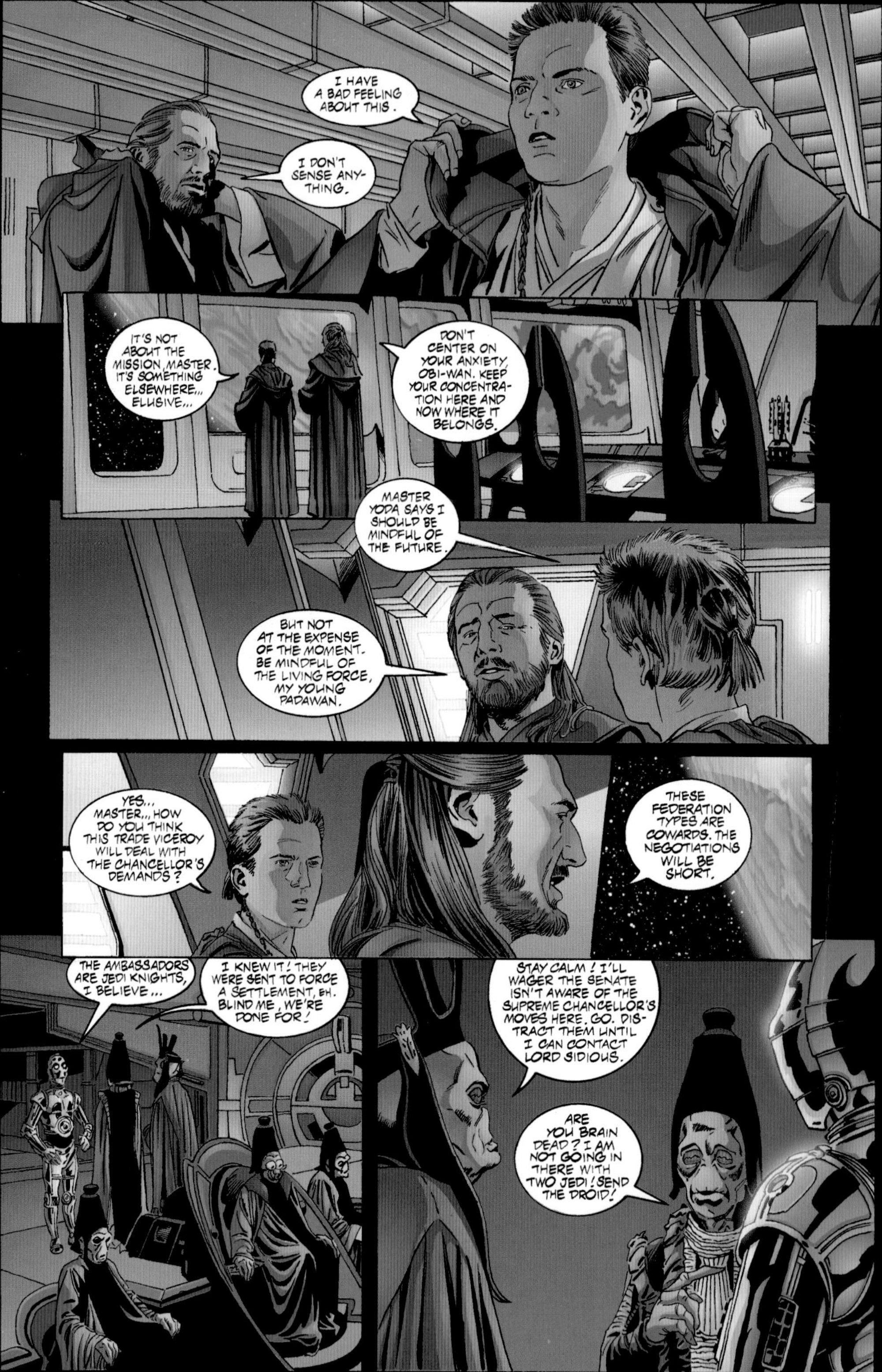
I HAVE A BAD FEELING ABOUT THIS.
I DON'T SENSE ANYTHING.
IT'S NOT ABOUT THE MISSION, MASTER. IT'S SOMETHING ELSEWHERE... ELUSIVE...
DON'T CENTER ON YOUR ANXIETY, OBI-WAN. KEEP YOUR CONCENTRATION HERE AND NOW WHERE IT BELONGS.
MASTER YODA SAYS I SHOULD BE MINDFUL OF THE FUTURE.
BUT NOT AT THE EXPENSE OF THE MOMENT. BE MINDFUL OF THE LIVING FORCE, MY YOUNG PADAWAN.
YES... MASTER... HOW DO YOU THINK THIS TRADE VICEROY WILL DEAL WITH THE CHANCELLOR'S DEMANDS?
THESE FEDERATION TYPES ARE COWARDS. THE NEGOTIATIONS WILL BE SHORT.
THE AMBASSADORS ARE JEDI KNIGHTS, I BELIEVE...
I KNEW IT! THEY WERE SENT TO FORCE A SETTLEMENT, EH. BLIND ME, WE'RE DONE FOR!
STAY CALM! I'LL WAGER THE SENATE ISN'T AWARE OF THE SUPREME CHANCELLOR'S MOVES HERE. GO. DISTRACT THEM UNTIL I CAN CONTACT LORD SIDIOUS.
ARE YOU BRAIN DEAD? I AM NOT GOING IN THERE WITH TWO JEDI! SEND THE DROID!

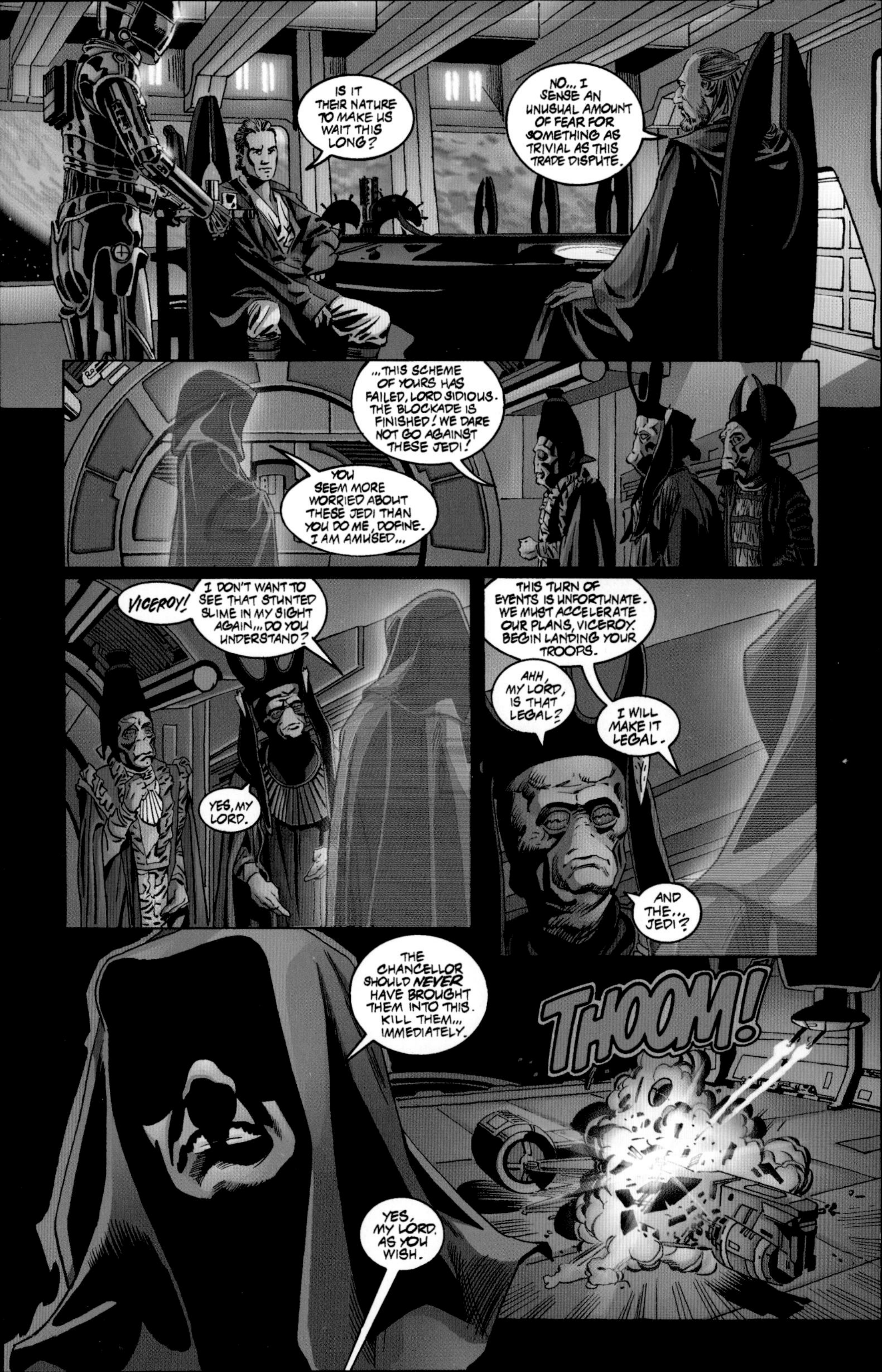
IS IT THEIR NATURE TO MAKE US WAIT THIS LONG?
NO... I SENSE AN UNUSUAL AMOUNT OF FEAR FOR SOMETHING AS TRIVIAL AS THIS TRADE DISPUTE.
...THIS SCHEME OF YOURS HAS FAILED, LORD SIDIOUS. THE BLOCKADE IS FINISHED! WE DARE NOT GO AGAINST THESE JEDI!
YOU SEEM MORE WORRIED ABOUT THESE JEDI THAN YOU DO ME, DOFINE. I AM AMUSED...
VICEROY!
I DON'T WANT TO SEE THAT STUNTED SLIME IN MY SIGHT AGAIN... DO YOU UNDERSTAND?
YES, MY LORD.
THIS TURN OF EVENTS IS UNFORTUNATE. WE MUST ACCELERATE OUR PLANS, VICEROY. BEGIN LANDING YOUR TROOPS.
AHH, MY LORD, IS THAT LEGAL?
I WILL MAKE IT LEGAL.
AND THE... JEDI?
THE CHANCELLOR SHOULD NEVER HAVE BROUGHT THEM INTO THIS. KILL THEM... IMMEDIATELY.
YES, MY LORD. AS YOU WISH.
THOOM!

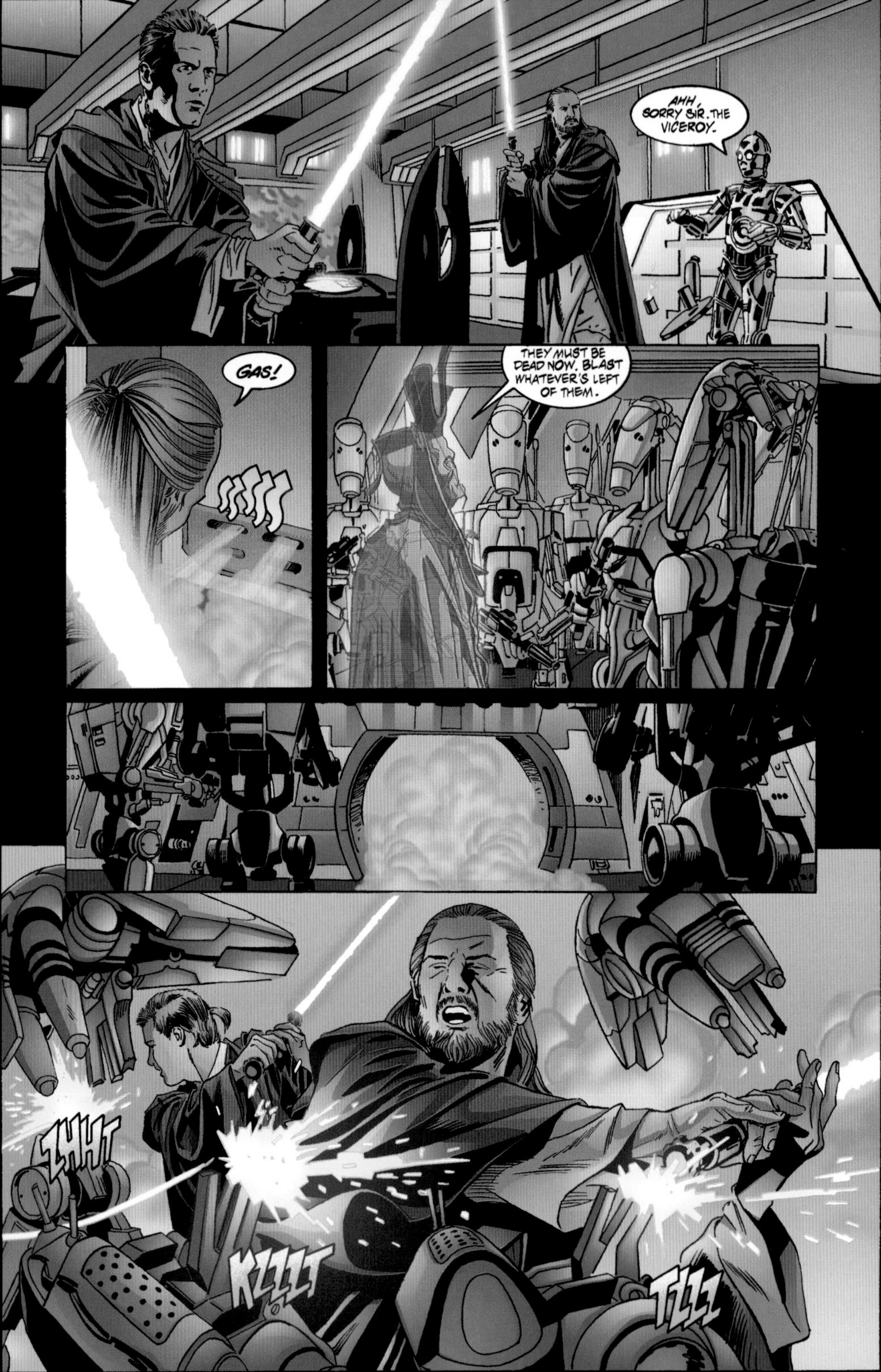
AHH, SORRY SIR. THE VICEROY.
GAS!
SSSS
THEY MUST BE DEAD NOW. BLAST WHATEVER'S LEFT OF THEM.
ZHHT
KZZZT
TZZZ

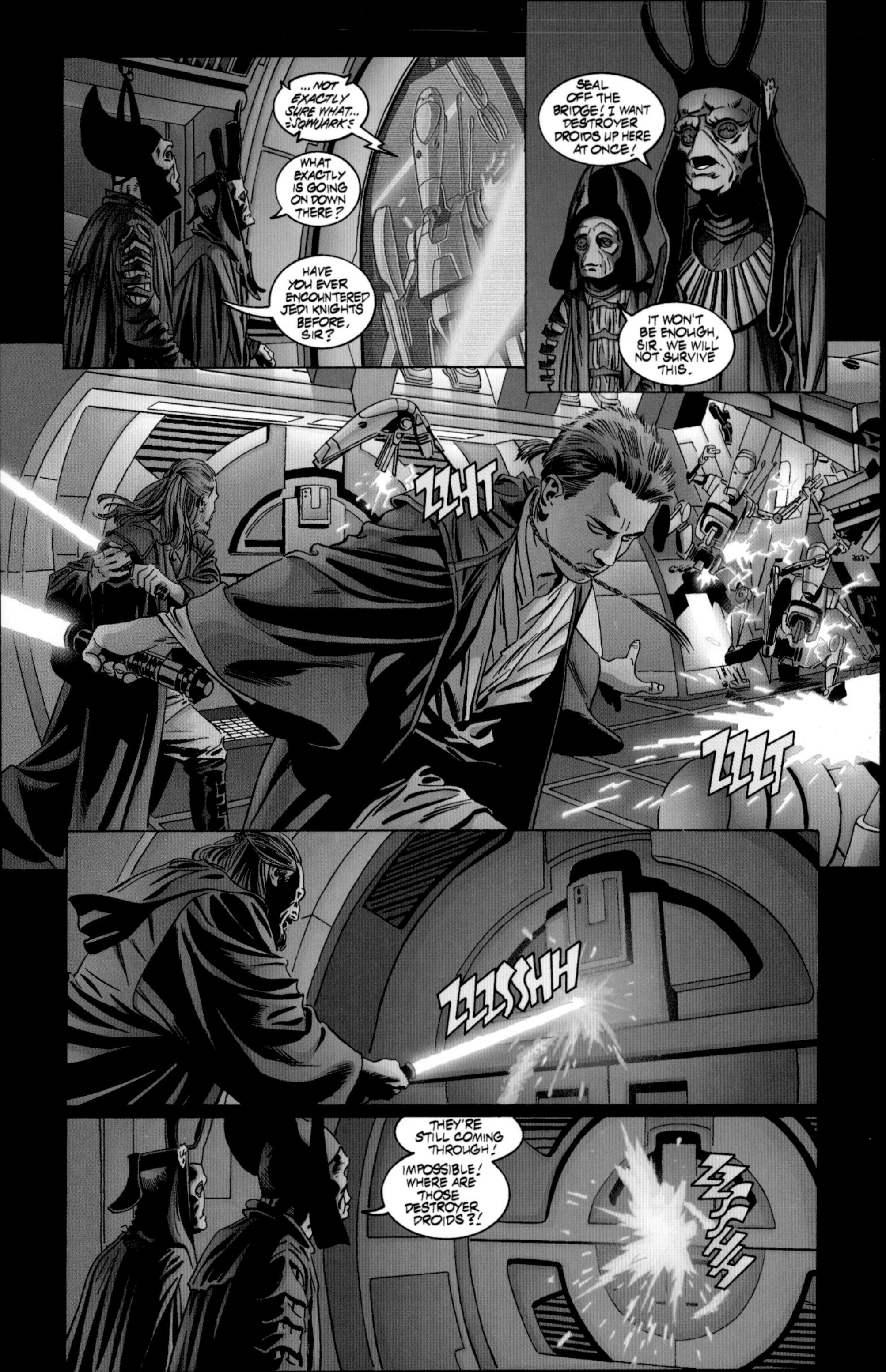
...NOT EXACTLY SURE WHAT... =SQWUARK=
WHAT EXACTLY IS GOING ON DOWN THERE?
HAVE YOU EVER ENCOUNTERED JEDI KNIGHTS BEFORE, SIR?
SEAL OFF THE BRIDGE! I WANT DESTROYER DROIDS UP HERE AT ONCE!
IT WON'T BE ENOUGH, SIR. WE WILL NOT SURVIVE THIS.
ZZHT
ZZZT
ZZZSSHH
THEY'RE STILL COMING THROUGH!
IMPOSSIBLE! WHERE ARE THOSE DESTROYER DROIDS?!
ZZSHHH

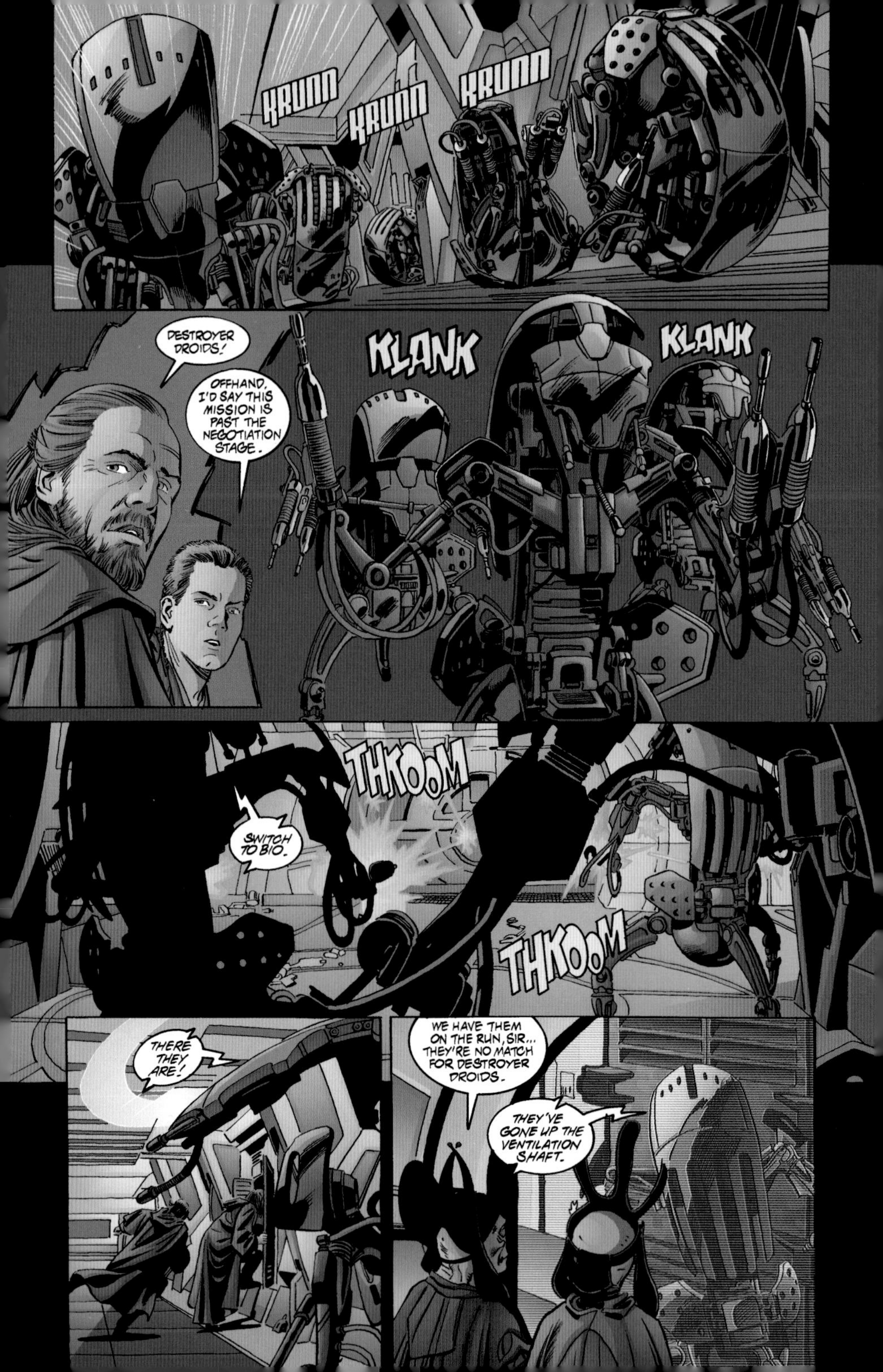
KRUNN
KRUNN
KRUNN
DESTROYER DROIDS!
OFFHAND, I'D SAY THIS MISSION IS PAST THE NEGOTIATION STAGE.
KLANK
KLANK
THKOOM
SWITCH TO BIO.
THKOOM
THERE THEY ARE!
WE HAVE THEM ON THE RUN, SIR... THEY'RE NO MATCH FOR DESTROYER DROIDS.
THEY'VE GONE UP THE VENTILATION SHAFT.

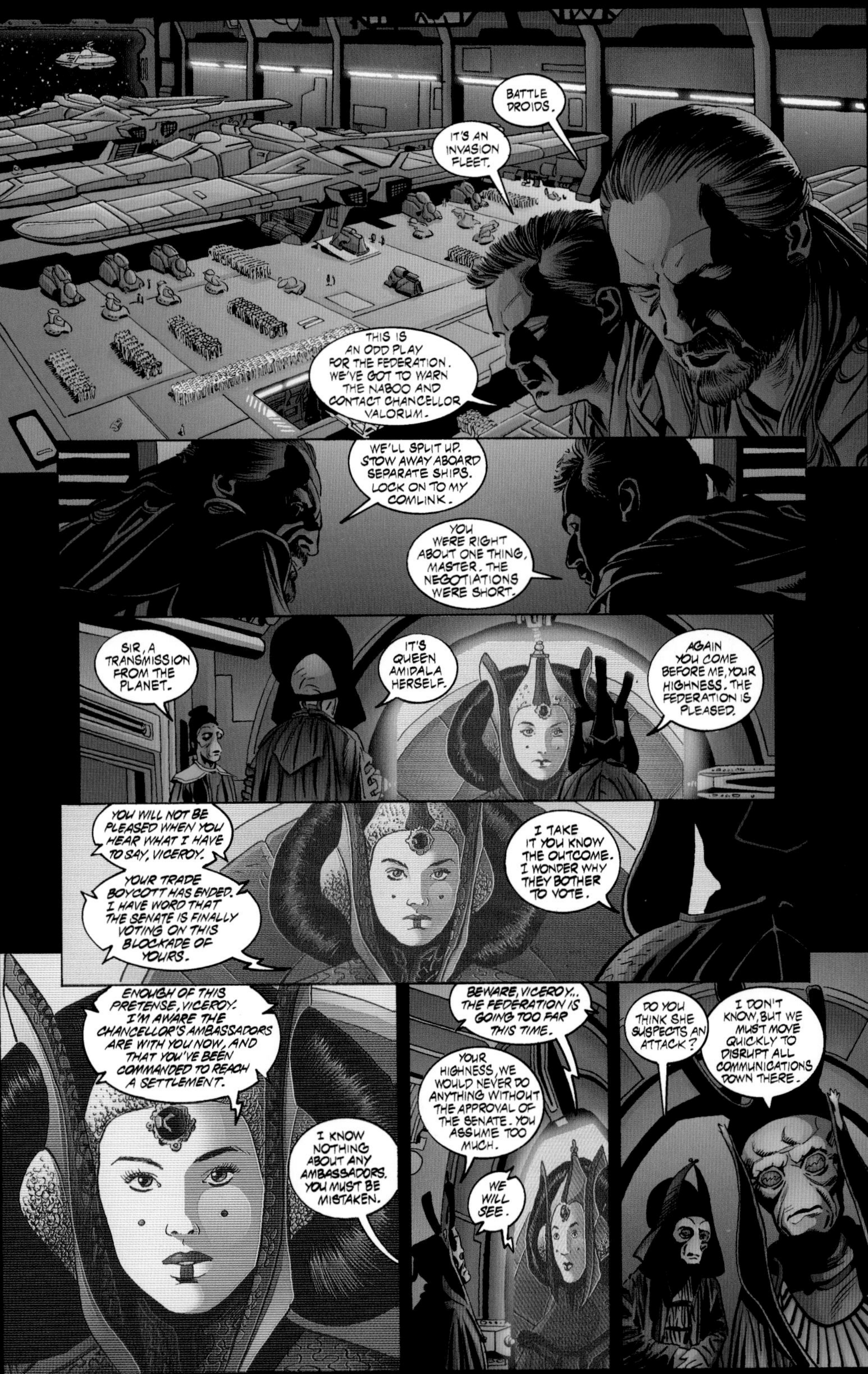
BATTLE DROIDS.
IT'S AN INVASION FLEET.
THIS IS AN ODD PLAY FOR THE FEDERATION. WE'VE GOT TO WARN THE NABOO AND CONTACT CHANCELLOR VALORUM.
WE'LL SPLIT UP. STOW AWAY ABOARD SEPARATE SHIPS. LOCK ON TO MY COMLINK.
YOU WERE RIGHT ABOUT ONE THING, MASTER. THE NEGOTIATIONS WERE SHORT.
SIR, A TRANSMISSION FROM THE PLANET.
IT'S QUEEN AMIDALA HERSELF.
AGAIN YOU COME BEFORE ME, YOUR HIGHNESS. THE FEDERATION IS PLEASED.
YOU WILL NOT BE PLEASED WHEN YOU HEAR WHAT I HAVE TO SAY, VICEROY.
YOUR TRADE BOYCOTT HAS ENDED. I HAVE WORD THAT THE SENATE IS FINALLY VOTING ON THIS BLOCKADE OF YOURS.
I TAKE IT YOU KNOW THE OUTCOME. I WONDER WHY THEY BOTHER TO VOTE.
ENOUGH OF THIS PRETENSE, VICEROY. I'M AWARE THE CHANCELLOR'S AMBASSADORS ARE WITH YOU NOW, AND THAT YOU'VE BEEN COMMANDED TO REACH A SETTLEMENT.
I KNOW NOTHING ABOUT ANY AMBASSADORS. YOU MUST BE MISTAKEN.
BEWARE, VICEROY... THE FEDERATION IS GOING TOO FAR THIS TIME.
YOUR HIGHNESS, WE WOULD NEVER DO ANYTHING WITHOUT THE APPROVAL OF THE SENATE. YOU ASSUME TOO MUCH.
WE WILL SEE.
DO YOU THINK SHE SUSPECTS AN ATTACK?
I DON'T KNOW, BUT WE MUST MOVE QUICKLY TO DISRUPT ALL COMMUNICATIONS DOWN THERE.

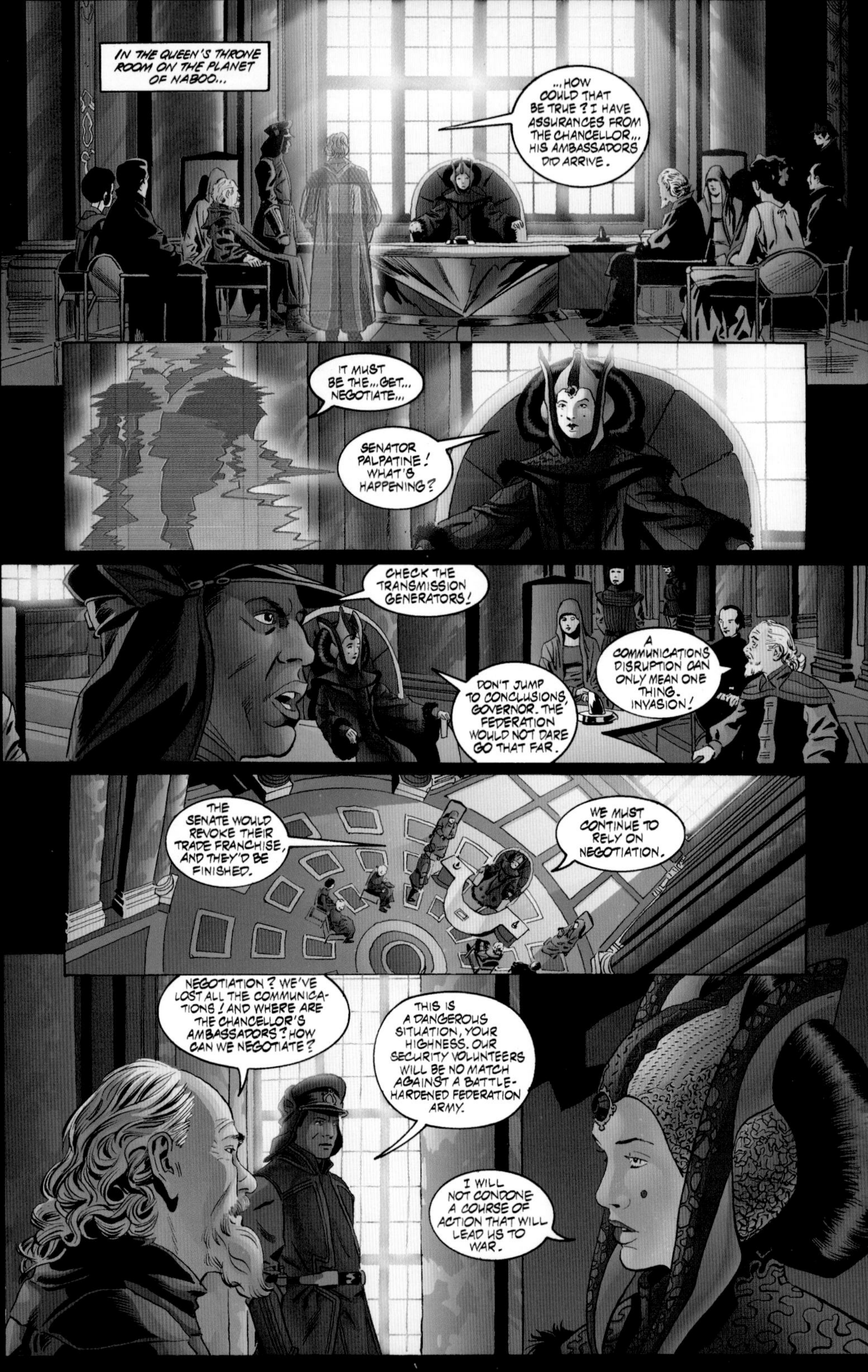

IN THE QUEEN'S THRONE ROOM ON THE PLANET OF NABOO...
...HOW COULD THAT BE TRUE? I HAVE ASSURANCES FROM THE CHANCELLOR... HIS AMBASSADORS DID ARRIVE.
IT MUST BE THE...GET... NEGOTIATE...
SENATOR PALPATINE! WHAT'S HAPPENING?
CHECK THE TRANSMISSION GENERATORS!
A COMMUNICATIONS DISRUPTION CAN ONLY MEAN ONE THING. INVASION!
DON'T JUMP TO CONCLUSIONS, GOVERNOR. THE FEDERATION WOULD NOT DARE GO THAT FAR.
THE SENATE WOULD REVOKE THEIR TRADE FRANCHISE, AND THEY'D BE FINISHED.
WE MUST CONTINUE TO RELY ON NEGOTIATION.
NEGOTIATION? WE'VE LOST ALL THE COMMUNICATIONS! AND WHERE ARE THE CHANCELLOR'S AMBASSADORS? HOW CAN WE NEGOTIATE?
THIS IS A DANGEROUS SITUATION, YOUR HIGHNESS. OUR SECURITY VOLUNTEERS WILL BE NO MATCH AGAINST A BATTLE-HARDENED FEDERATION ARMY.
I WILL NOT CONDONE A COURSE OF ACTION THAT WILL LEAD US TO WAR.

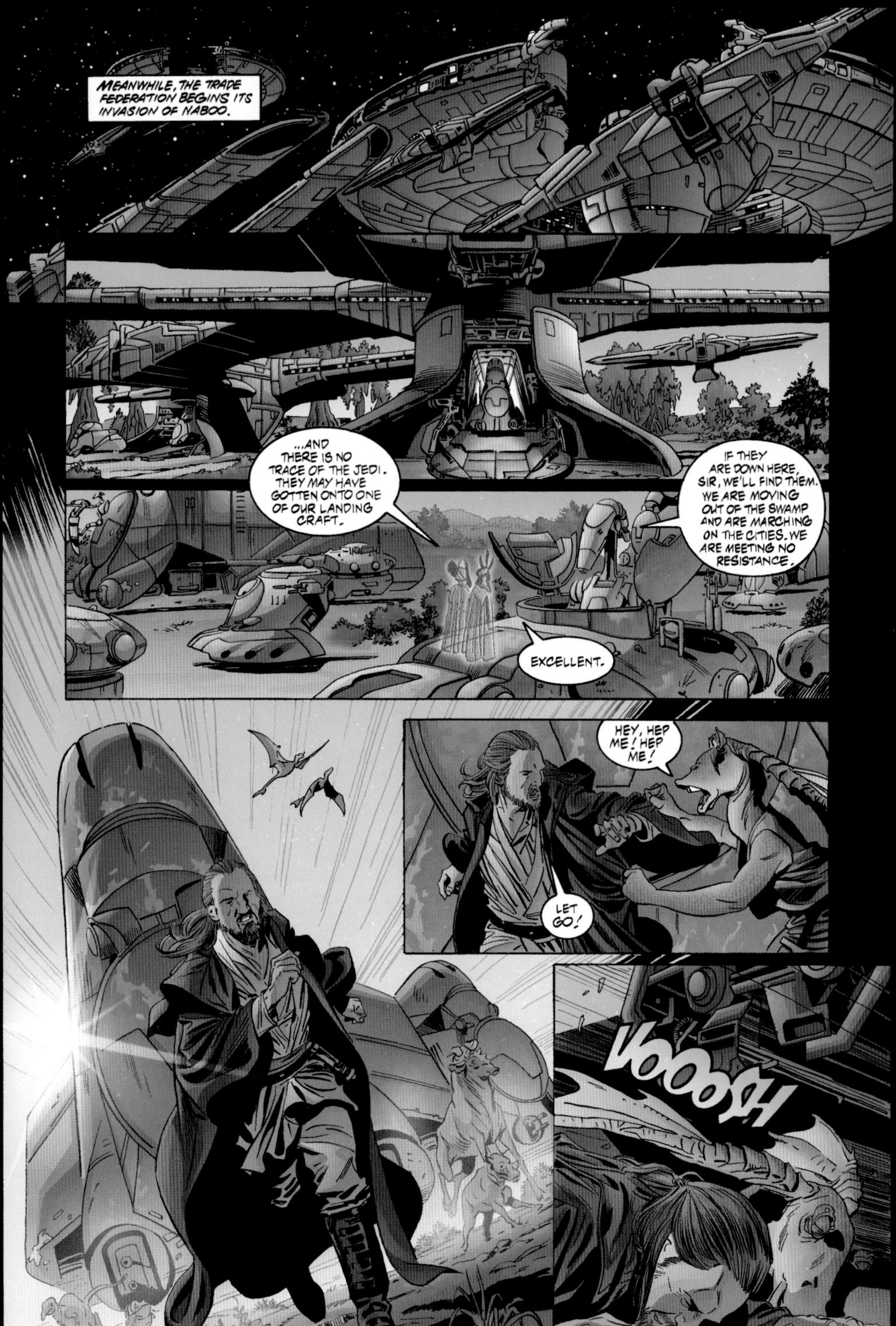
MEANWHILE, THE TRADE FEDERATION BEGINS ITS INVASION OF NABOO.
...AND THERE IS NO TRACE OF THE JEDI. THEY MAY HAVE GOTTEN ONTO ONE OF OUR LANDING CRAFT.
IF THEY ARE DOWN HERE, SIR, WE'LL FIND THEM. WE ARE MOVING OUT OF THE SWAMP AND ARE MARCHING ON THE CITIES. WE ARE MEETING NO RESISTANCE.
EXCELLENT.
HEY, HEP ME! HEP ME!
LET GO!
VOOOSH

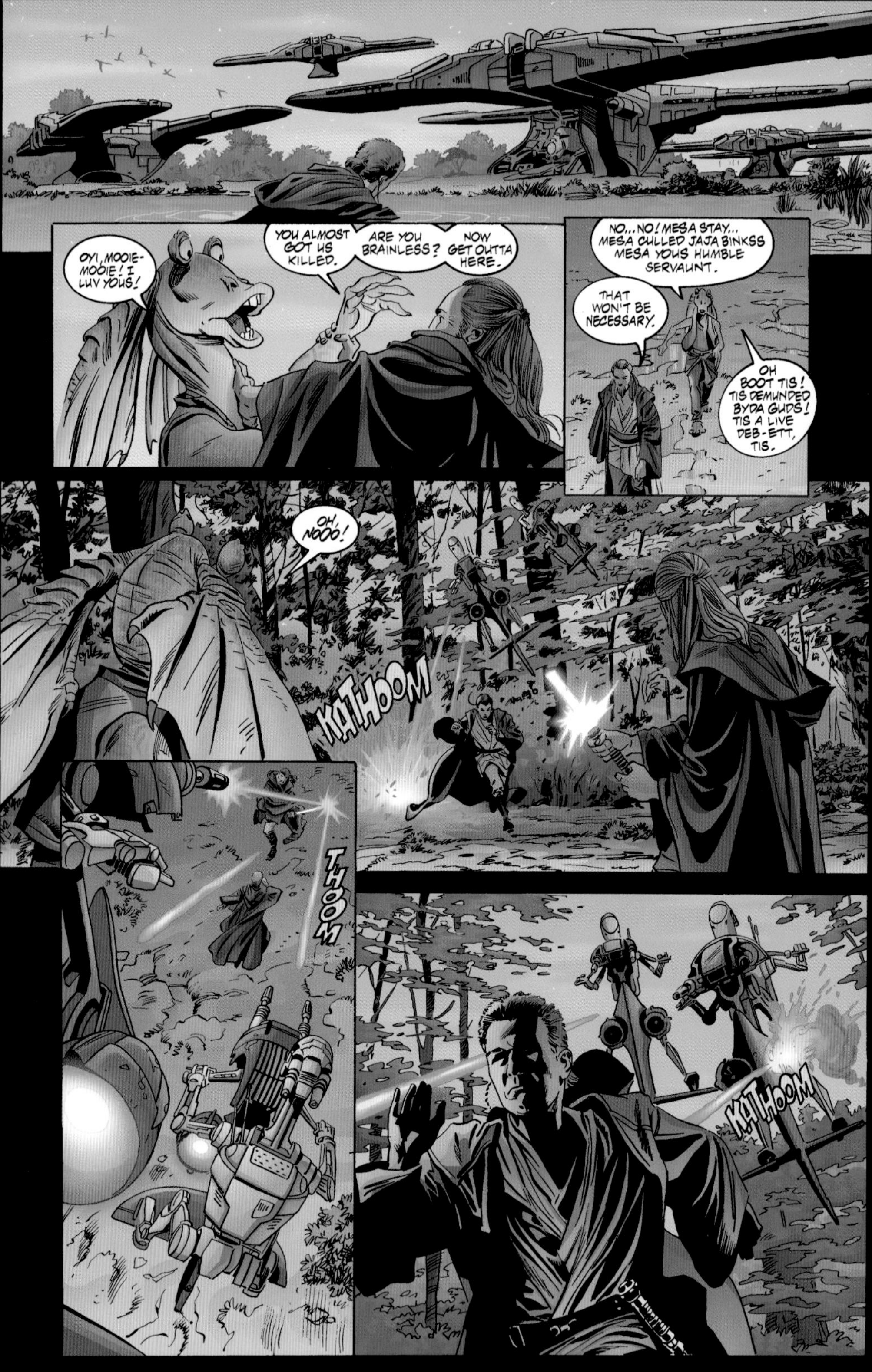
OY! MOOIE-MOOIE! I LUV YOUS!
YOU ALMOST GOT US KILLED.
ARE YOU BRAINLESS?
NOW GET OUTTA HERE.
NO...NO! MESA STAY... MESA CULLED JAJA BINKSS MESA YOUS HUMBLE SERVAUNT.
THAT WON'T BE NECESSARY.
OH BOOT TIS! TIS DEMUNDED BYDA GUDS! TIS A LIVE DEB-ETT, TIS.
OH, NOOO!
KATHOOM
THOOM
KATHOOM

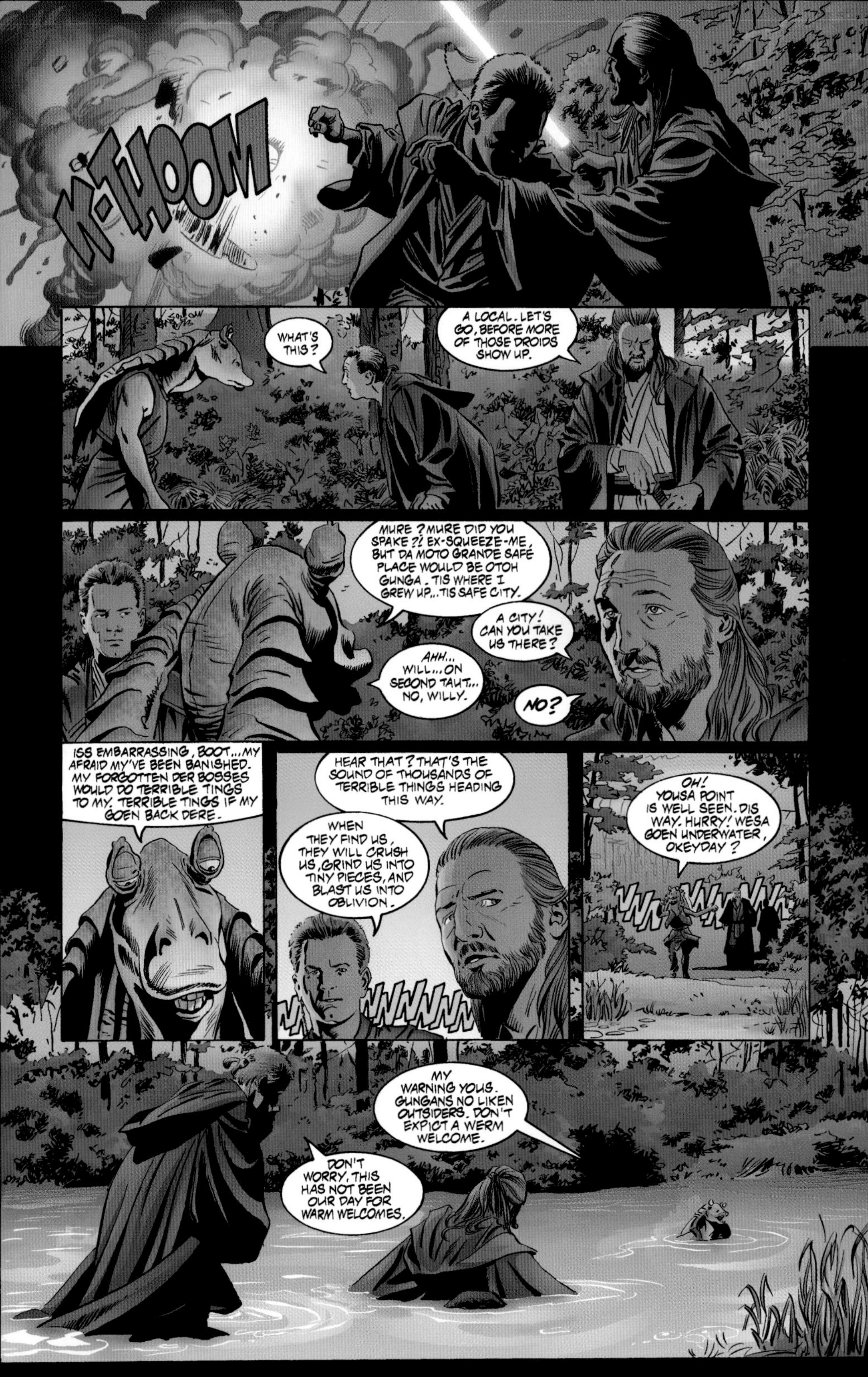
K-THOOM
WHAT'S THIS?
A LOCAL. LET'S GO, BEFORE MORE OF THOSE DROIDS SHOW UP.
MURE? MURE DID YOU SPAKE?! EX-SQUEEZE-ME, BUT DA MOTO GRANDE SAFE PLACE WOULD BE OTOH GUNGA. TIS WHERE I GREW UP... TIS SAFE CITY.
A CITY! CAN YOU TAKE US THERE?
AHH... WILL... ON SECOND TAUT... NO, WILLY.
NO?
ISS EMBARRASSING, BOOT... MY AFRAID MY'VE BEEN BANISHED. MY FORGOTTEN DER BOSSES WOULD DO TERRIBLE TINGS TO MY. TERRIBLE TINGS IF MY GOEN BACK DERE.
HEAR THAT? THAT'S THE SOUND OF THOUSANDS OF TERRIBLE THINGS HEADING THIS WAY.
WHEN THEY FIND US, THEY WILL CRUSH US, GRIND US INTO TINY PIECES, AND BLAST US INTO OBLIVION.
NNNNNNN
OH! YOUSA POINT IS WELL SEEN. DIS WAY. HURRY! WESA GOEN UNDERWATER, OKEYDAY?
MY WARNING YOUS. GUNGANS NO LIKEN OUTSIDERS. DON'T EXPICT A WERM WELCOME.
DON'T WORRY. THIS HAS NOT BEEN OUR DAY FOR WARM WELCOMES.

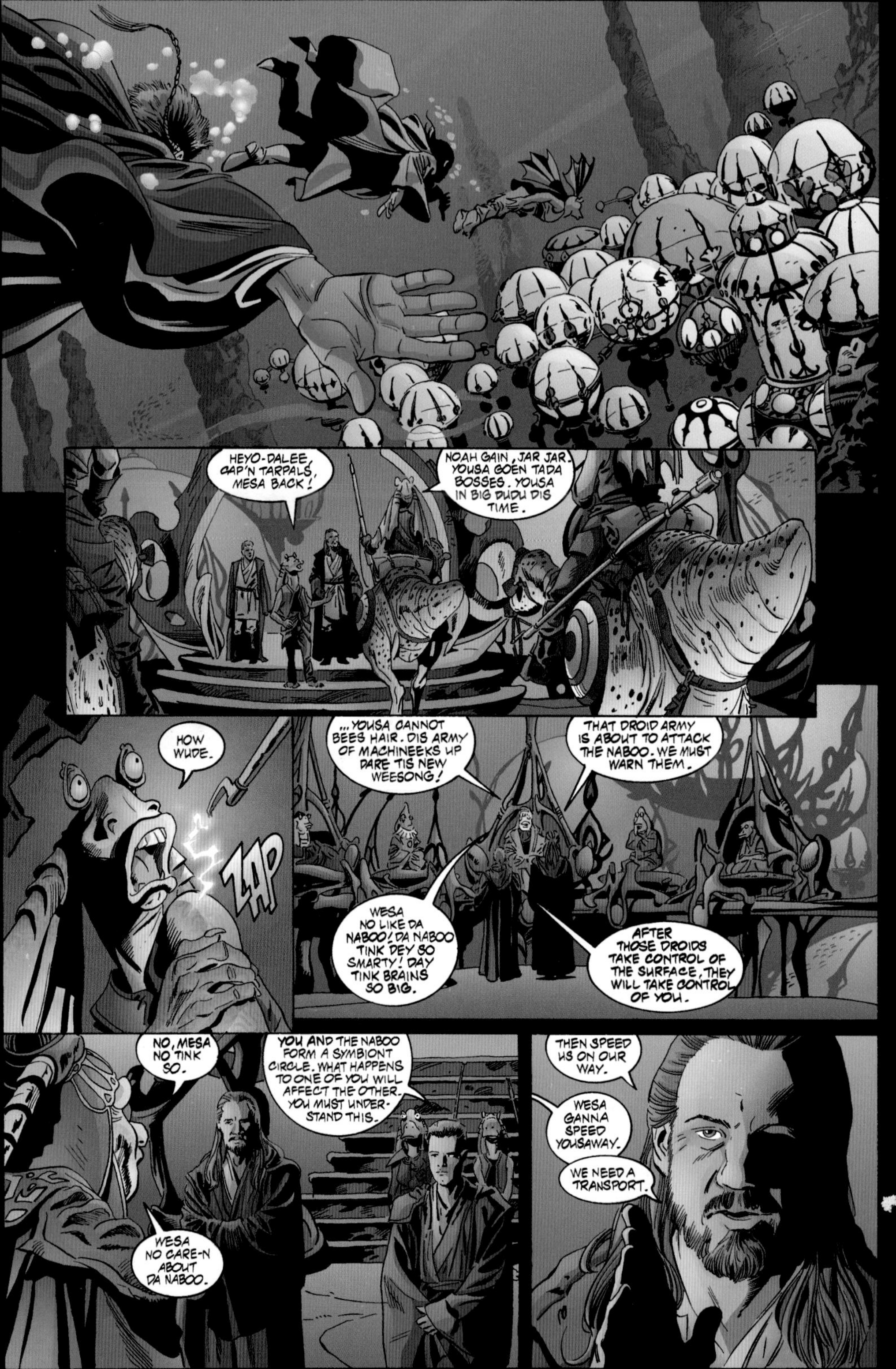

HEYO-DALEE, CAP'N TARPALS, MESA BACK!
NOAH GAIN, JAR JAR. YOUSA GOEN TADA BOSSES. YOUSA IN BIG DUDU DIS TIME.
HOW WUDE.
ZAP
...YOUSA CANNOT BEES HAIR. DIS ARMY OF MACHINEEKS UP DARE TIS NEW WEESONG!
THAT DROID ARMY IS ABOUT TO ATTACK THE NABOO. WE MUST WARN THEM.
WESA NO LIKE DA NABOO! DA NABOO TINK DEY SO SMARTY! DAY TINK BRAINS SO BIG.
AFTER THOSE DROIDS TAKE CONTROL OF THE SURFACE, THEY WILL TAKE CONTROL OF YOU.
NO, MESA NO TINK SO.
YOU AND THE NABOO FORM A SYMBIONT CIRCLE. WHAT HAPPENS TO ONE OF YOU WILL AFFECT THE OTHER. YOU MUST UNDER-STAND THIS.
WESA NO CARE-N ABOUT DA NABOO.
THEN SPEED US ON OUR WAY.
WESA GANNA SPEED YOUSAWAY.
WE NEED A TRANSPORT.

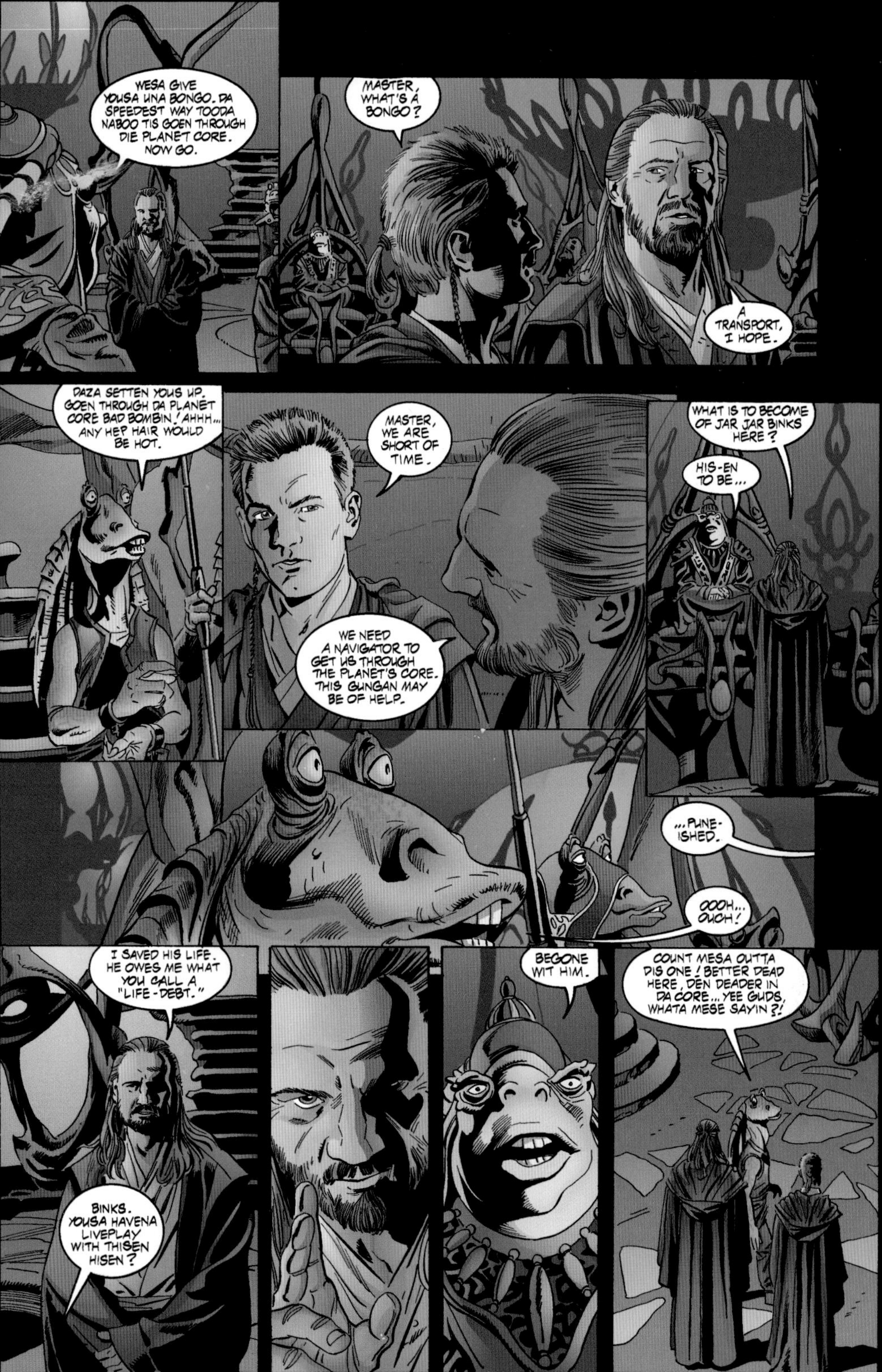
WESA GIVE YOUSA UNA BONGO. DA SPEEDEST WAY TOODA NABOO TIS GOEN THROUGH DIE PLANET CORE. NOW GO.
MASTER, WHAT'S A BONGO?
A TRANSPORT, I HOPE.
DAZA SETTEN YOUS UP. GOEN THROUGH DA PLANET CORE BAD BOMBIN! AHHH... ANY HEP HAIR WOULD BE HOT.
MASTER, WE ARE SHORT OF TIME.
WE NEED A NAVIGATOR TO GET US THROUGH THE PLANET'S CORE. THIS GUNGAN MAY BE OF HELP.
WHAT IS TO BECOME OF JAR JAR BINKS HERE?
HIS-EN TO BE...
...PUNE-ISHED.
OOOH... OUCH!
I SAVED HIS LIFE. HE OWES ME WHAT YOU CALL A "LIFE-DEBT."
BINKS. YOUSA HAVENA LIVEPLAY WITH THISEN HISEN?
BEGONE WIT HIM.
COUNT MESA OUTTA DIS ONE! BETTER DEAD HERE, DEN DEADER IN DA CORE... YEE GUDS, WHATA MESE SAYIN?!

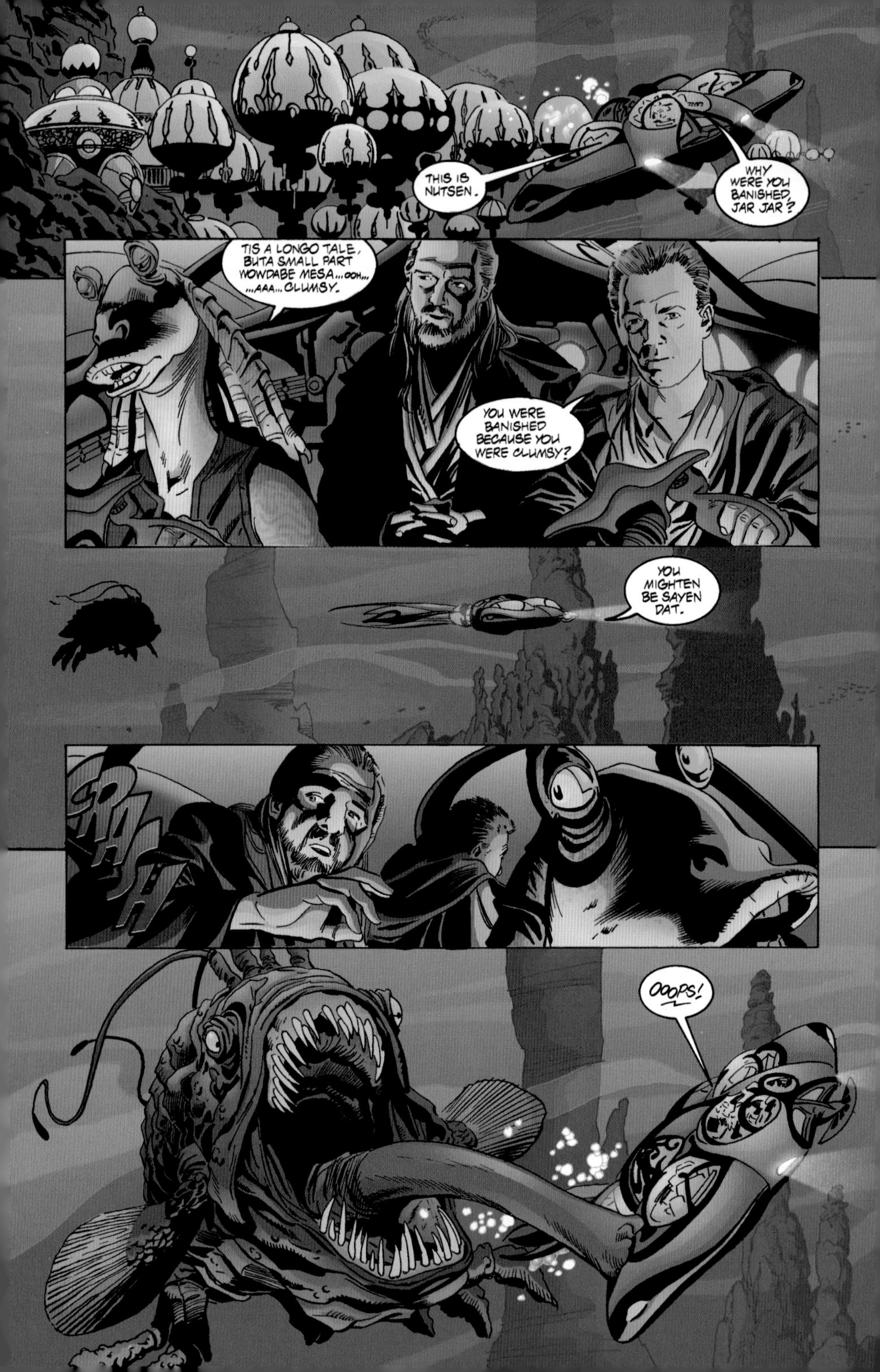
THIS IS NUTSEN.
WHY WERE YOU BANISHED, JAR JAR?
TIS A LONGO TALE, BUTA SMALL PART WOWDABE MESA...OOH... ...AAA...CLUMSY.
YOU WERE BANISHED BECAUSE YOU WERE CLUMSY?
YOU MIGHTEN BE SAYEN DAT.
OOOPS!

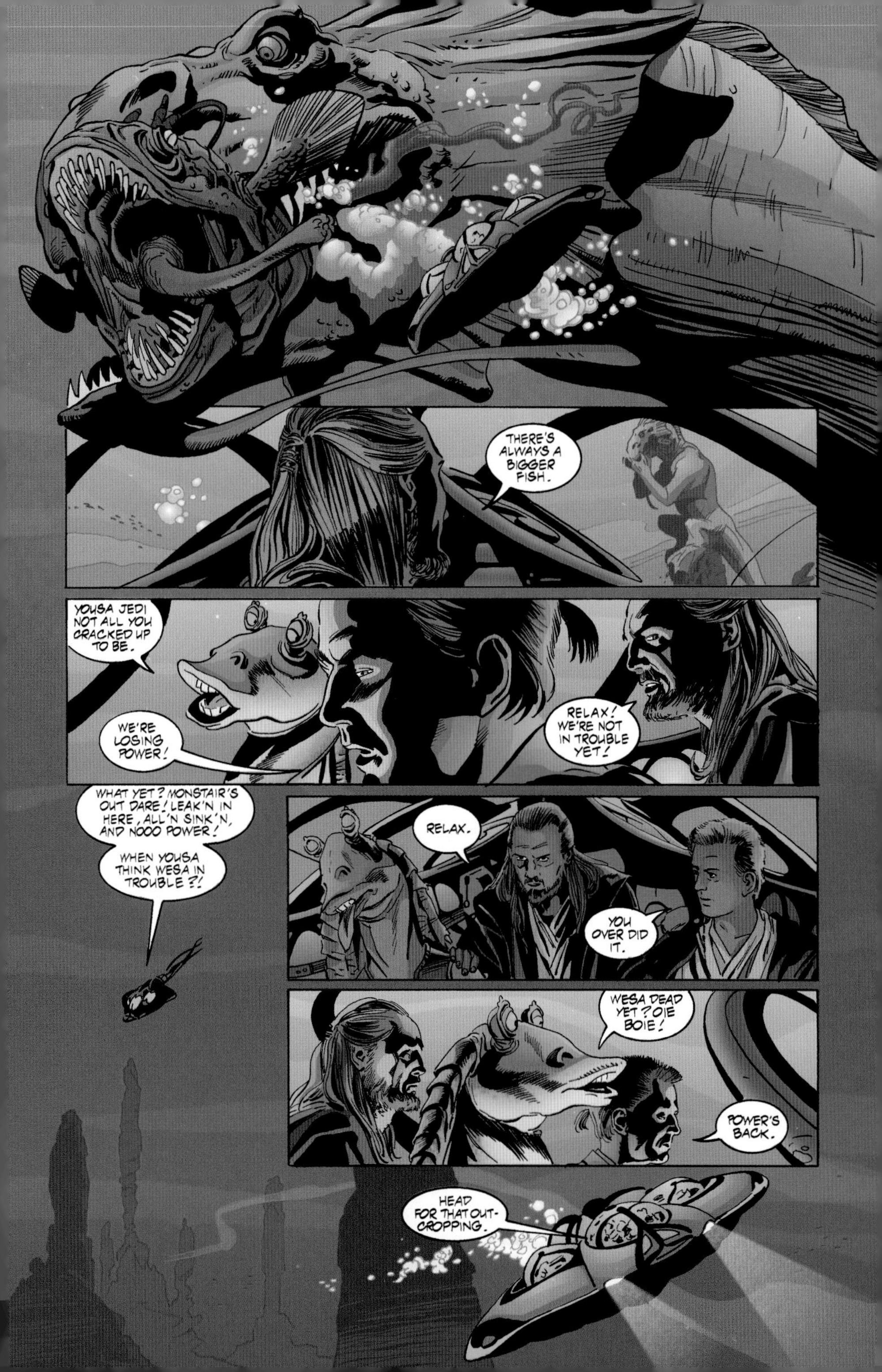

THERE'S ALWAYS A BIGGER FISH.
YOUSA JEDI NOT ALL YOU CRACKED UP TO BE.
WE'RE LOSING POWER!
RELAX! WE'RE NOT IN TROUBLE YET!
WHAT YET? MONSTAIR'S OUT DARE! LEAK'N IN HERE, ALL'N SINK'N, AND NOOO POWER!
WHEN YOUSA THINK WESA IN TROUBLE?!
RELAX.
YOU OVER DID IT.
WESA DEAD YET? OIE BOIE!
POWER'S BACK.
HEAD FOR THAT OUT-CROPPING.

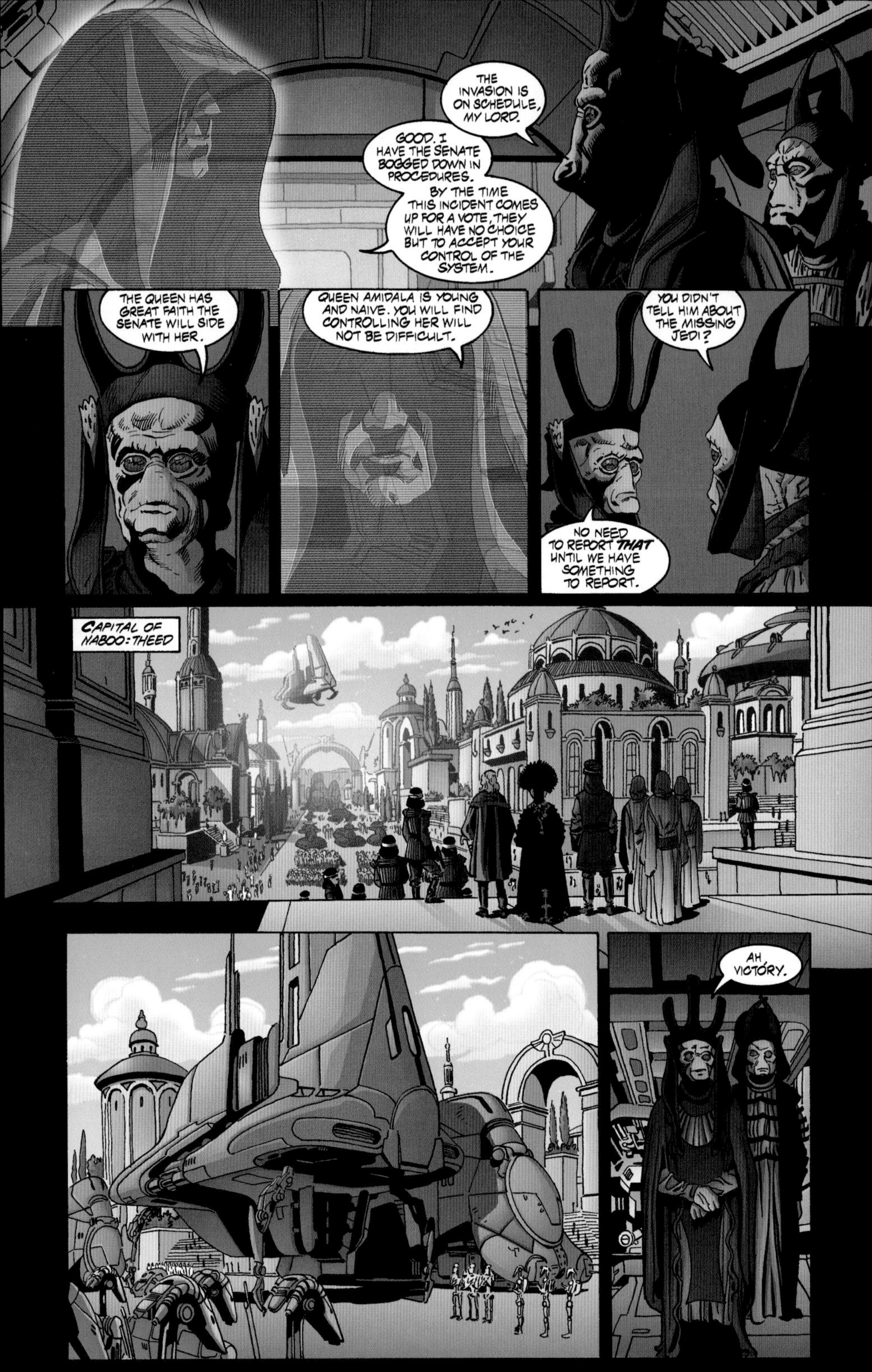
THE INVASION IS ON SCHEDULE, MY LORD.
GOOD. I HAVE THE SENATE BOGGED DOWN IN PROCEDURES.
BY THE TIME THIS INCIDENT COMES UP FOR A VOTE, THEY WILL HAVE NO CHOICE BUT TO ACCEPT YOUR CONTROL OF THE SYSTEM.
THE QUEEN HAS GREAT FAITH THE SENATE WILL SIDE WITH HER.
QUEEN AMIDALA IS YOUNG AND NAIVE. YOU WILL FIND CONTROLLING HER WILL NOT BE DIFFICULT.
YOU DIDN'T TELL HIM ABOUT THE MISSING JEDI?
NO NEED TO REPORT THAT UNTIL WE HAVE SOMETHING TO REPORT.
CAPITAL OF NABOO: THEED
AH, VICTORY.

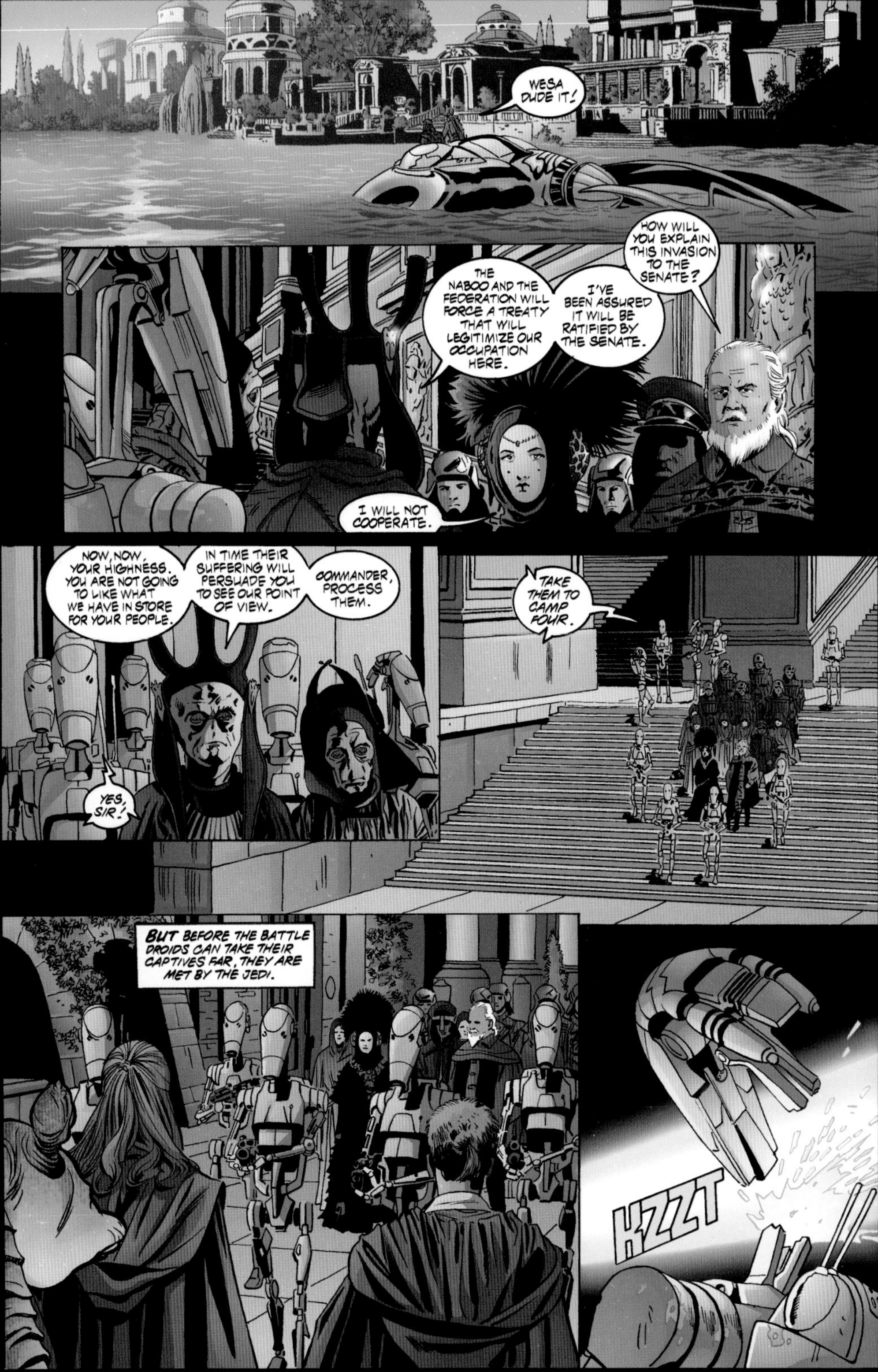
WESA DUDE IT!
THE NABOO AND THE FEDERATION WILL FORCE A TREATY THAT WILL LEGITIMIZE OUR OCCUPATION HERE.
I'VE BEEN ASSURED IT WILL BE RATIFIED BY THE SENATE.
HOW WILL YOU EXPLAIN THIS INVASION TO THE SENATE?
I WILL NOT COOPERATE.
NOW, NOW, YOUR HIGHNESS. YOU ARE NOT GOING TO LIKE WHAT WE HAVE IN STORE FOR YOUR PEOPLE.
IN TIME THEIR SUFFERING WILL PERSUADE YOU TO SEE OUR POINT OF VIEW.
COMMANDER, PROCESS THEM.
YES, SIR!
TAKE THEM TO CAMP FOUR.
BUT BEFORE THE BATTLE DROIDS CAN TAKE THEIR CAPTIVES FAR, THEY ARE MET BY THE JEDI.
HZZT

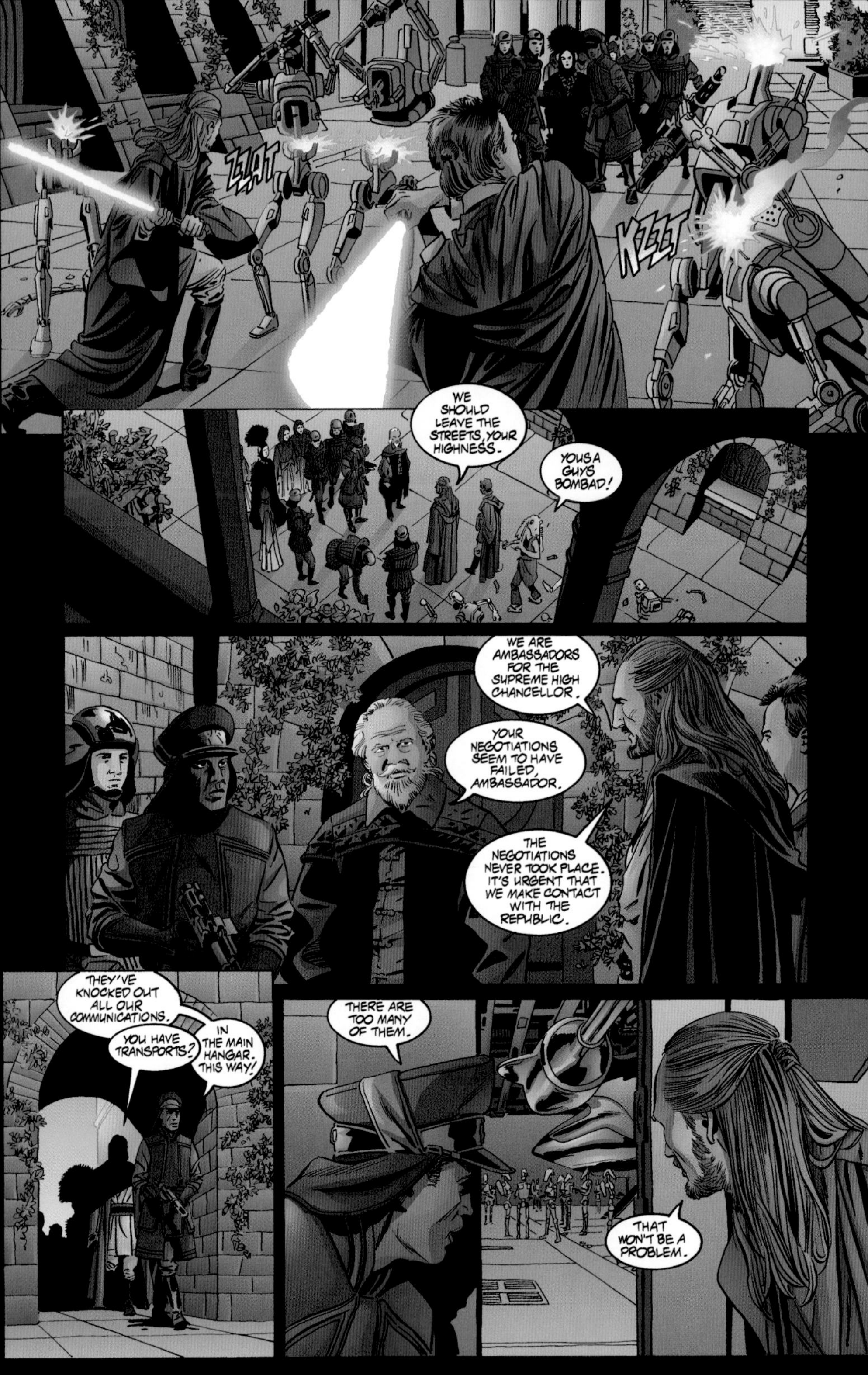
ZZAT
KZZT
WE SHOULD LEAVE THE STREETS, YOUR HIGHNESS.
YOUSA GUYS BOMBAD!
WE ARE AMBASSADORS FOR THE SUPREME HIGH CHANCELLOR.
YOUR NEGOTIATIONS SEEM TO HAVE FAILED, AMBASSADOR.
THE NEGOTIATIONS NEVER TOOK PLACE. IT'S URGENT THAT WE MAKE CONTACT WITH THE REPUBLIC.
THEY'VE KNOCKED OUT ALL OUR COMMUNICATIONS.
YOU HAVE TRANSPORTS?
IN THE MAIN HANGAR. THIS WAY!
THERE ARE TOO MANY OF THEM.
THAT WON'T BE A PROBLEM.

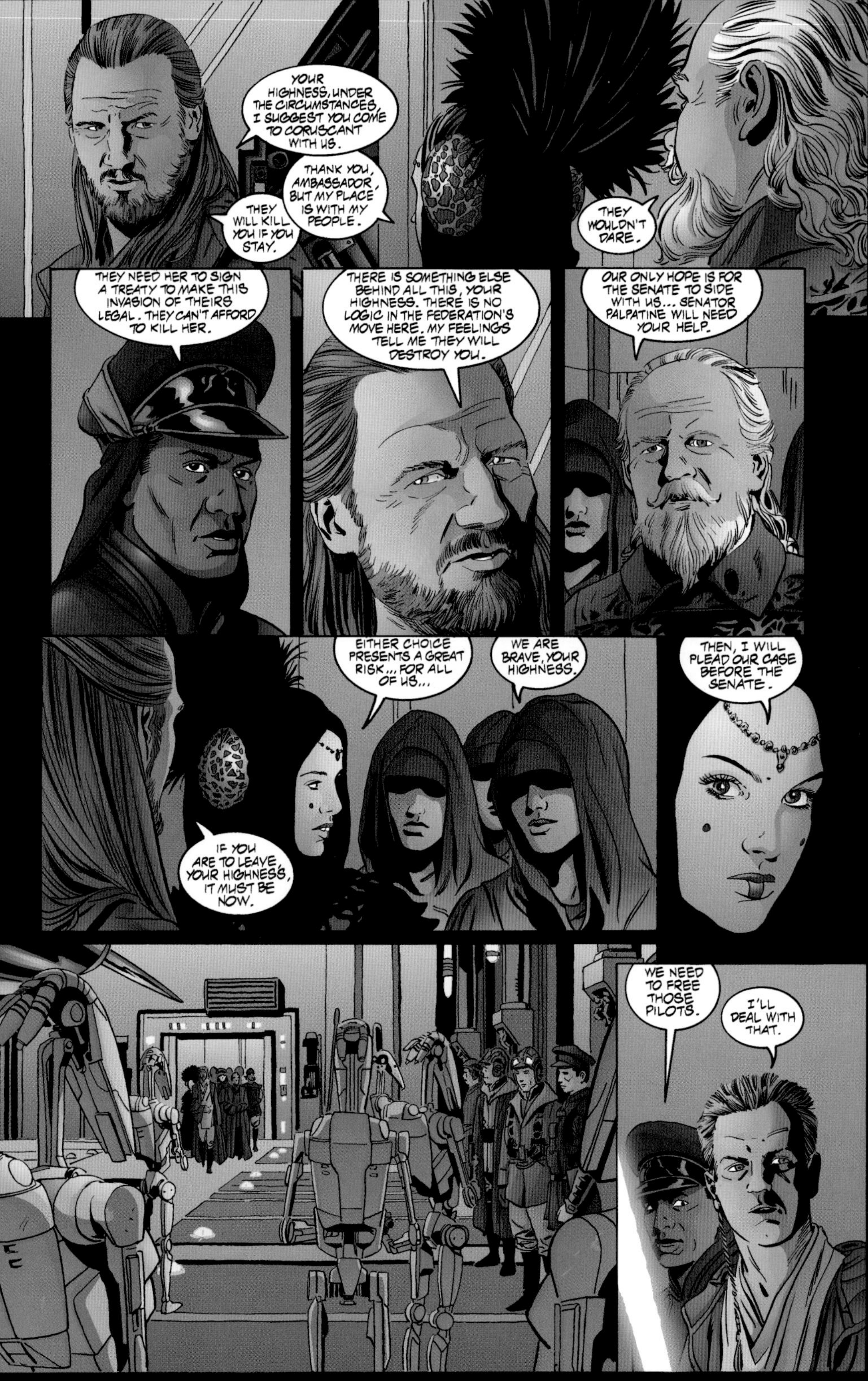
YOUR HIGHNESS, UNDER THE CIRCUMSTANCES, I SUGGEST YOU COME TO CORUSCANT WITH US.
THANK YOU, AMBASSADOR, BUT MY PLACE IS WITH MY PEOPLE.
THEY WILL KILL YOU IF YOU STAY.
THEY WOULDN'T DARE.
THEY NEED HER TO SIGN A TREATY TO MAKE THIS INVASION OF THEIRS LEGAL. THEY CAN'T AFFORD TO KILL HER.
THERE IS SOMETHING ELSE BEHIND ALL THIS, YOUR HIGHNESS. THERE IS NO LOGIC IN THE FEDERATION'S MOVE HERE. MY FEELINGS TELL ME THEY WILL DESTROY YOU.
OUR ONLY HOPE IS FOR THE SENATE TO SIDE WITH US... SENATOR PALPATINE WILL NEED YOUR HELP.
IF YOU ARE TO LEAVE, YOUR HIGHNESS, IT MUST BE NOW.
EITHER CHOICE PRESENTS A GREAT RISK... FOR ALL OF US...
WE ARE BRAVE, YOUR HIGHNESS.
THEN, I WILL PLEAD OUR CASE BEFORE THE SENATE.
WE NEED TO FREE THOSE PILOTS.
I'LL DEAL WITH THAT.

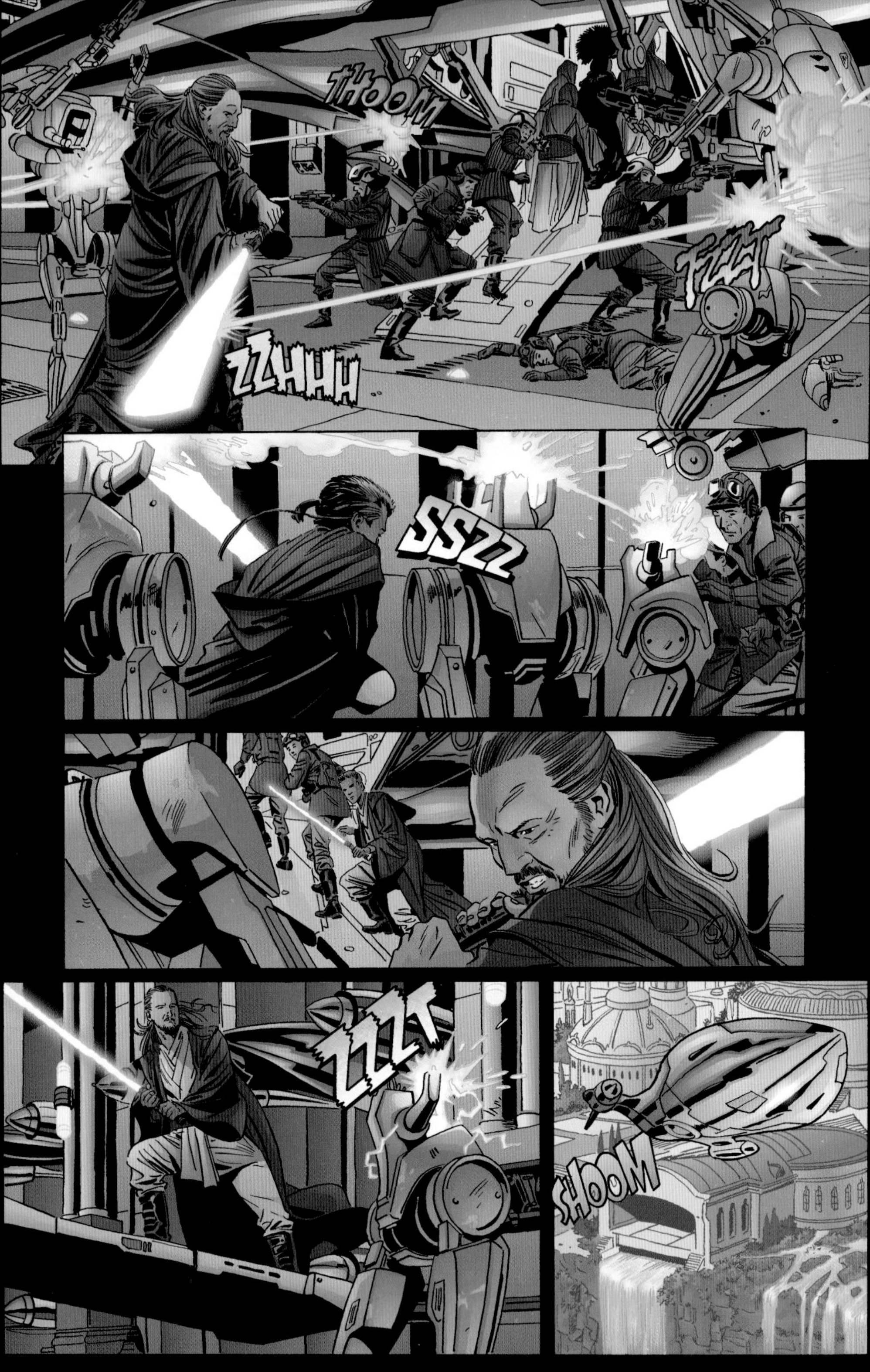
THOOM
FZZT
ZZHHH
SSZZ
ZZZT
SHOOM

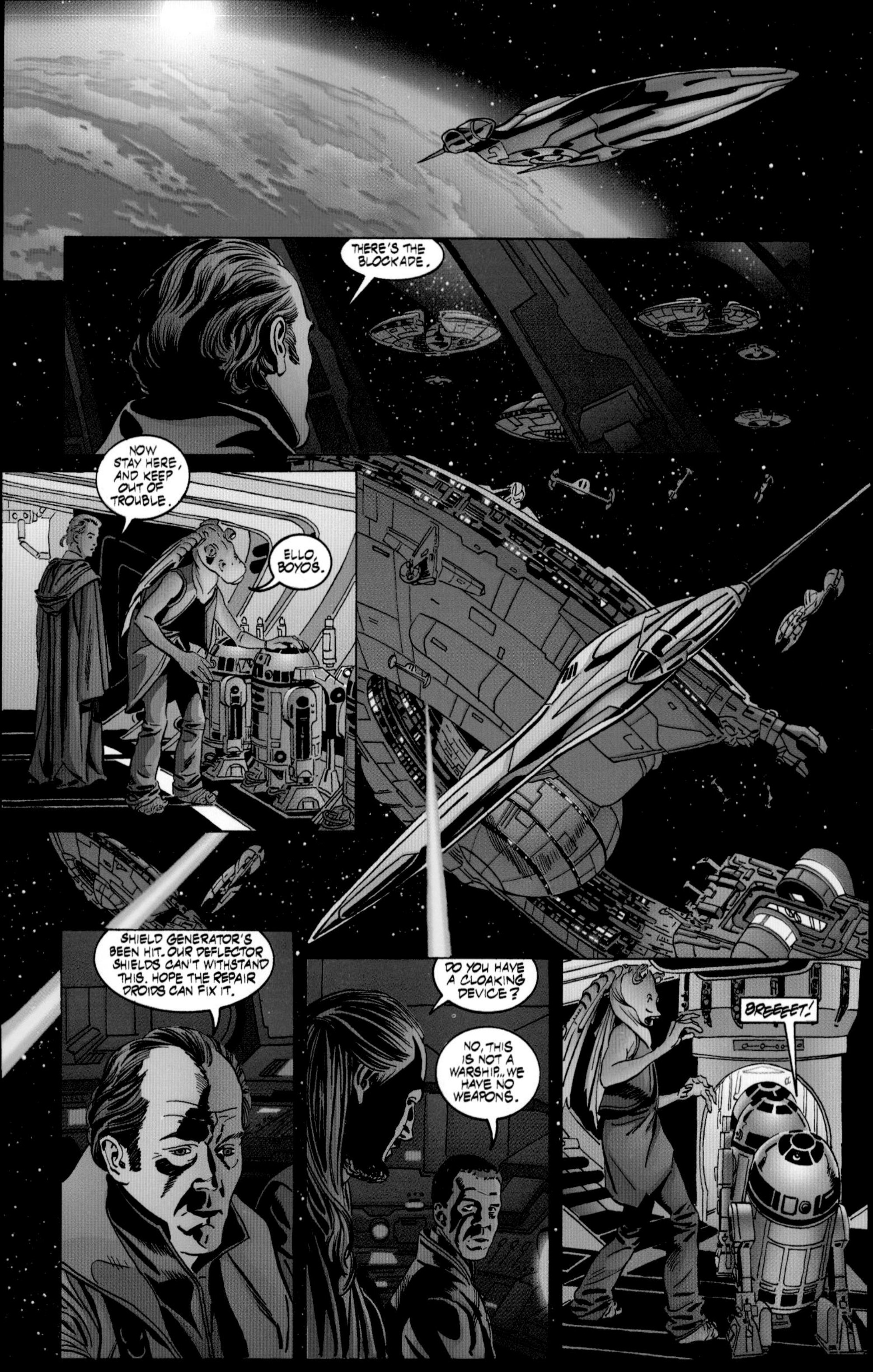
THERE'S THE BLOCKADE.
NOW STAY HERE, AND KEEP OUT OF TROUBLE.
ELLO, BOYOS.
SHIELD GENERATOR'S BEEN HIT. OUR DEFLECTOR SHIELDS CAN'T WITHSTAND THIS. HOPE THE REPAIR DROIDS CAN FIX IT.
DO YOU HAVE A CLOAKING DEVICE?
NO, THIS IS NOT A WARSHIP... WE HAVE NO WEAPONS.
BREEEET!

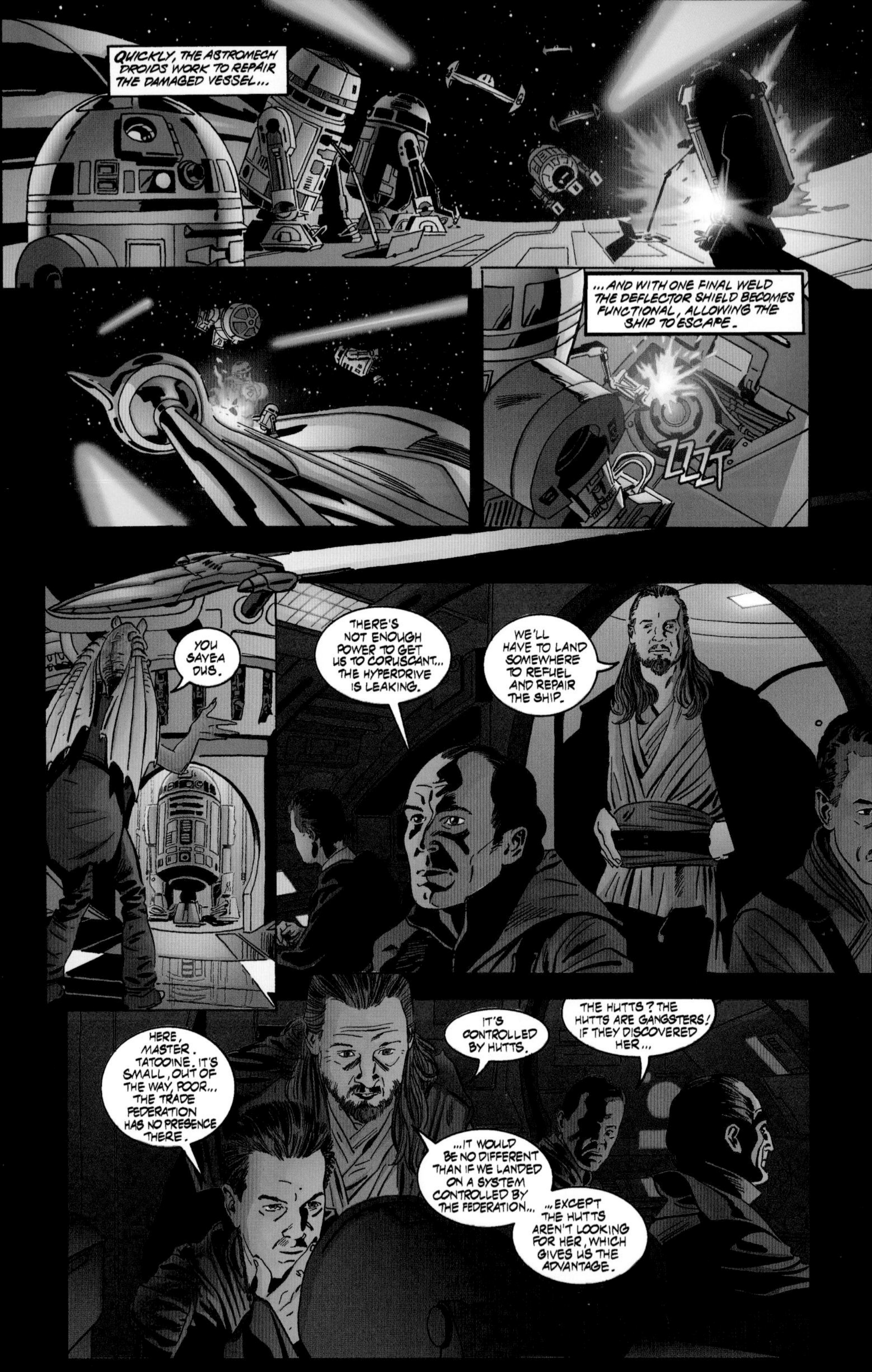
QUICKLY, THE ASTROMECH DROIDS WORK TO REPAIR THE DAMAGED VESSEL...
...AND WITH ONE FINAL WELD THE DEFLECTOR SHIELD BECOMES FUNCTIONAL, ALLOWING THE SHIP TO ESCAPE.
ZZZT
YOU SAYEA DUS.
THERE'S NOT ENOUGH POWER TO GET US TO CORUSCANT... THE HYPERDRIVE IS LEAKING.
WE'LL HAVE TO LAND SOMEWHERE TO REFUEL AND REPAIR THE SHIP.
HERE, MASTER. TATOOINE. IT'S SMALL, OUT OF THE WAY, POOR... THE TRADE FEDERATION HAS NO PRESENCE THERE.
IT'S CONTROLLED BY HUTTS.
THE HUTTS? THE HUTTS ARE GANGSTERS! IF THEY DISCOVERED HER...
...IT WOULD BE NO DIFFERENT THAN IF WE LANDED ON A SYSTEM CONTROLLED BY THE FEDERATION...
...EXCEPT THE HUTTS AREN'T LOOKING FOR HER, WHICH GIVES US THE ADVANTAGE.

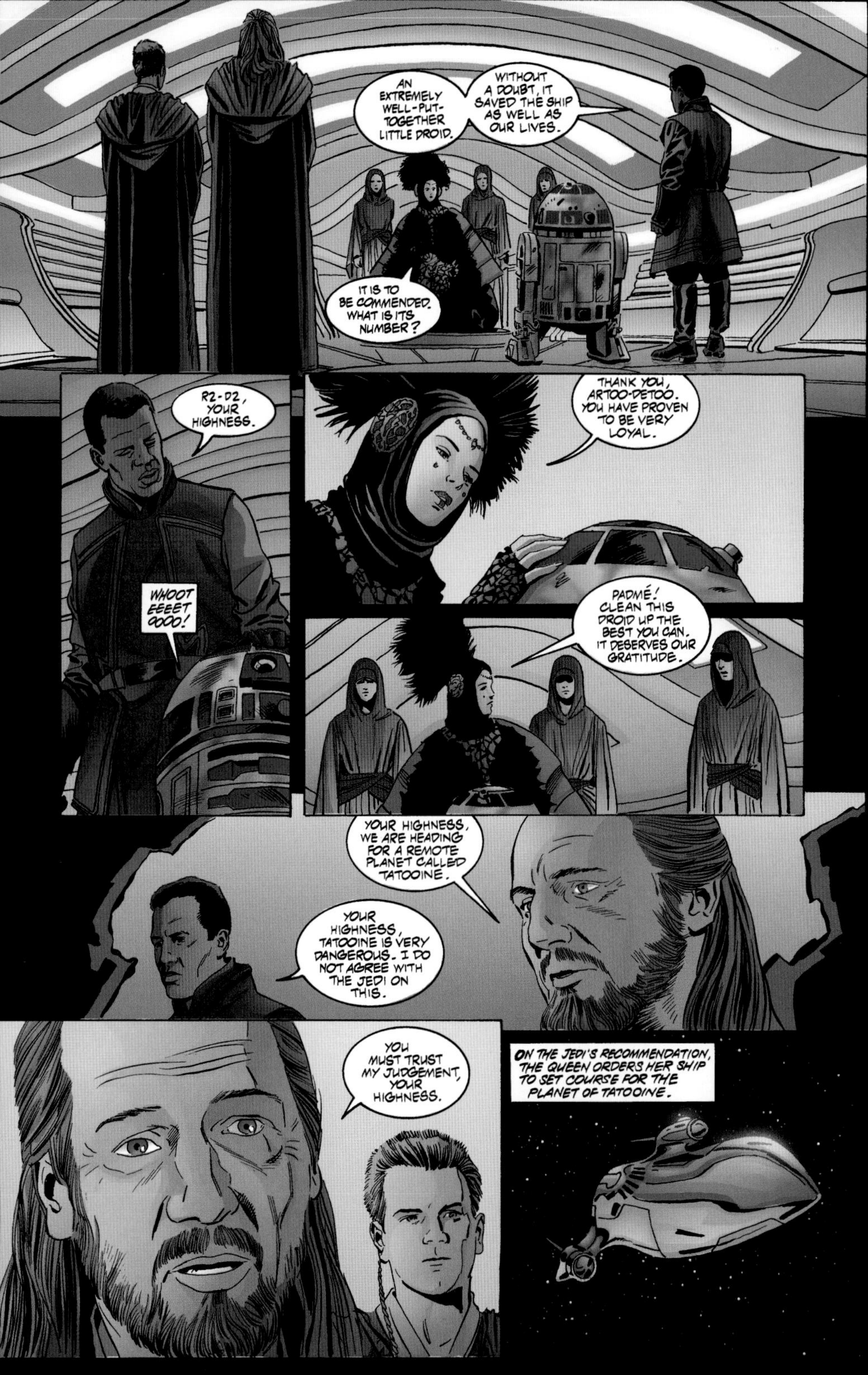
AN EXTREMELY WELL-PUT-TOGETHER LITTLE DROID.
WITHOUT A DOUBT, IT SAVED THE SHIP AS WELL AS OUR LIVES.
IT IS TO BE COMMENDED. WHAT IS ITS NUMBER?
R2-D2, YOUR HIGHNESS.
WHOOT EEEET OOOO!
THANK YOU, ARTOO-DETOO. YOU HAVE PROVEN TO BE VERY LOYAL.
PADMÉ! CLEAN THIS DROID UP THE BEST YOU CAN. IT DESERVES OUR GRATITUDE.
YOUR HIGHNESS, WE ARE HEADING FOR A REMOTE PLANET CALLED TATOOINE.
YOUR HIGHNESS, TATOOINE IS VERY DANGEROUS. I DO NOT AGREE WITH THE JEDI ON THIS.
YOU MUST TRUST MY JUDGEMENT, YOUR HIGHNESS.
ON THE JEDI'S RECOMMENDATION, THE QUEEN ORDERS HER SHIP TO SET COURSE FOR THE PLANET OF TATOOINE.

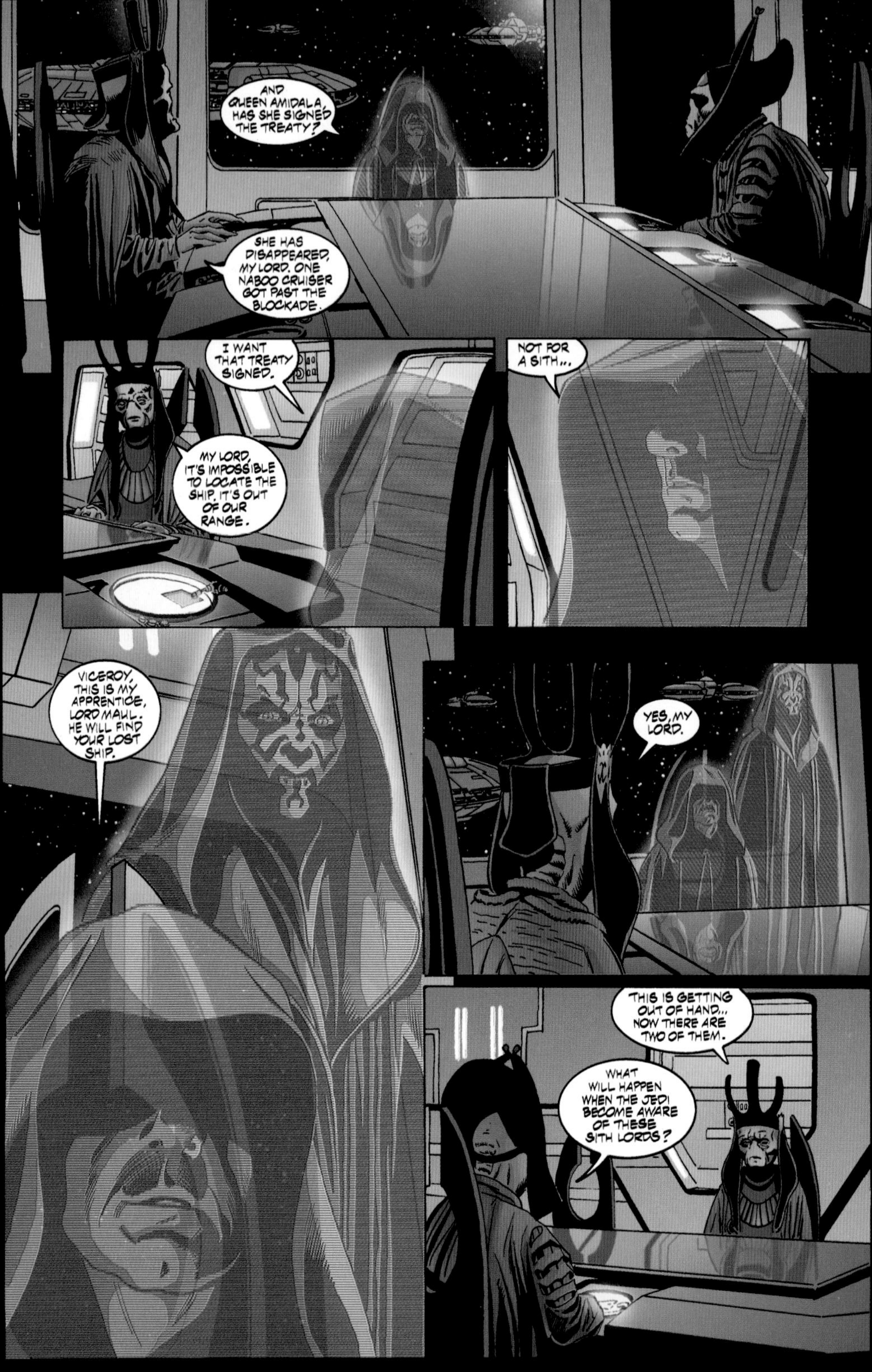
AND QUEEN AMIDALA, HAS SHE SIGNED THE TREATY?
SHE HAS DISAPPEARED, MY LORD. ONE NABOO CRUISER GOT PAST THE BLOCKADE.
I WANT THAT TREATY SIGNED.
MY LORD, IT'S IMPOSSIBLE TO LOCATE THE SHIP. IT'S OUT OF OUR RANGE.
NOT FOR A SITH...
VICEROY, THIS IS MY APPRENTICE, LORD MAUL. HE WILL FIND YOUR LOST SHIP.
YES, MY LORD.
THIS IS GETTING OUT OF HAND... NOW THERE ARE TWO OF THEM.
WHAT WILL HAPPEN WHEN THE JEDI BECOME AWARE OF THESE SITH LORDS?

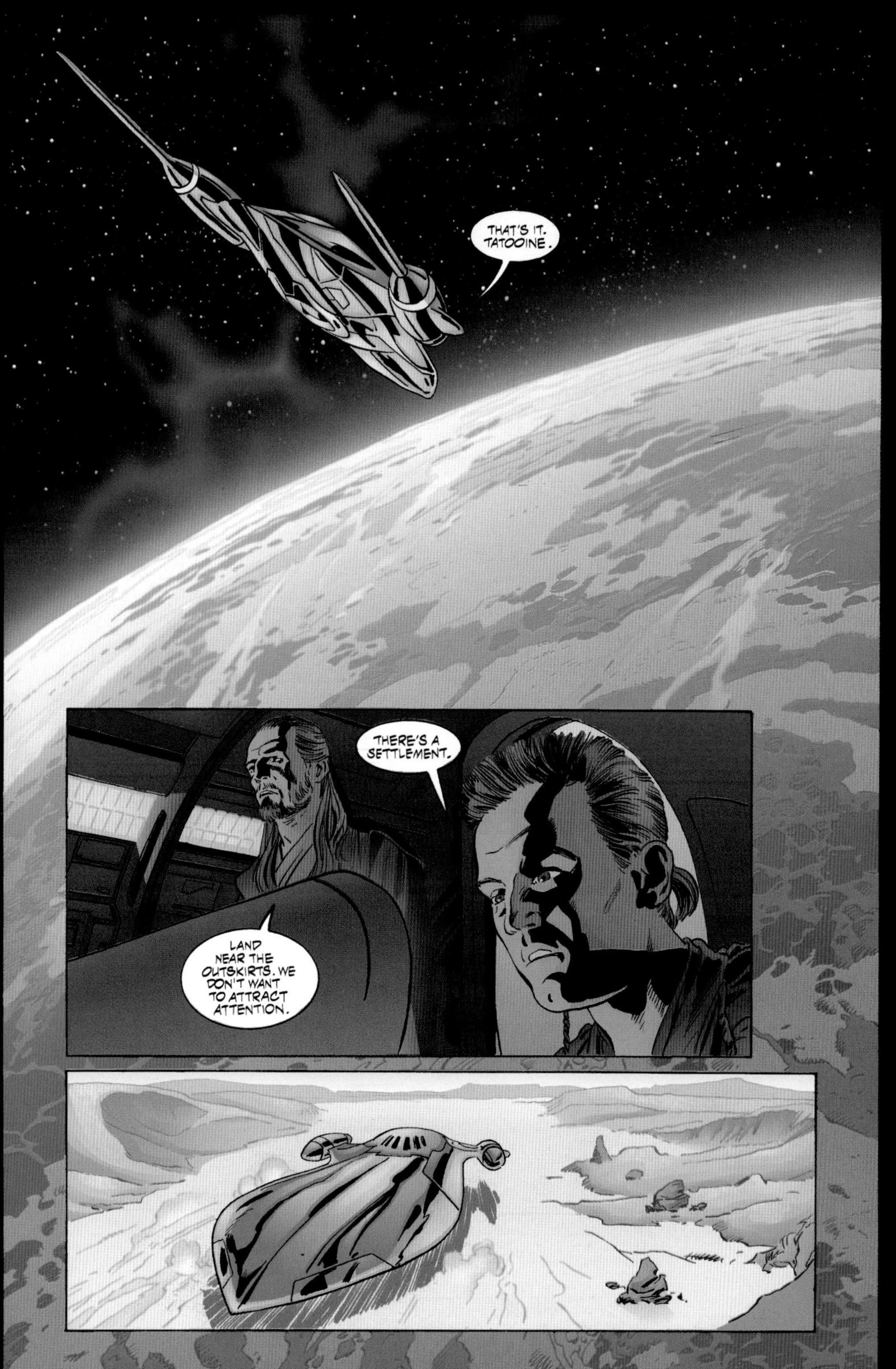
THAT'S IT. TATOOINE.
THERE'S A SETTLEMENT.
LAND NEAR THE OUTSKIRTS. WE DON'T WANT TO ATTRACT ATTENTION.

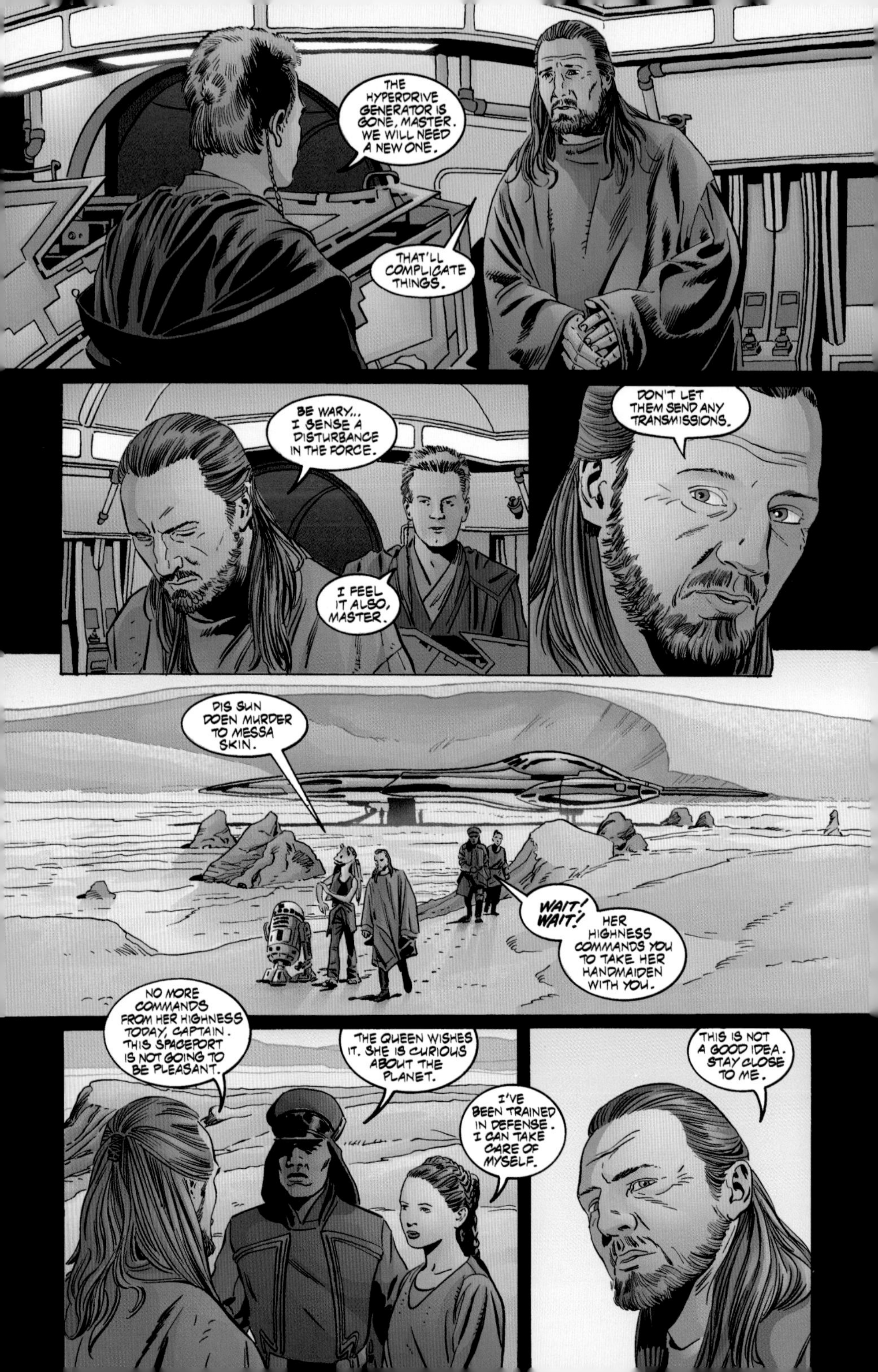
THE HYPERDRIVE GENERATOR IS GONE, MASTER. WE WILL NEED A NEW ONE.
THAT'LL COMPLICATE THINGS.
BE WARY... I SENSE A DISTURBANCE IN THE FORCE.
I FEEL IT ALSO, MASTER.
DON'T LET THEM SEND ANY TRANSMISSIONS.
DIS SUN DOEN MURDER TO MESSA SKIN.
WAIT! WAIT!
HER HIGHNESS COMMANDS YOU TO TAKE HER HANDMAIDEN WITH YOU.
NO MORE COMMANDS FROM HER HIGHNESS TODAY, CAPTAIN. THIS SPACEPORT IS NOT GOING TO BE PLEASANT.
THE QUEEN WISHES IT. SHE IS CURIOUS ABOUT THE PLANET.
I'VE BEEN TRAINED IN DEFENSE. I CAN TAKE CARE OF MYSELF.
THIS IS NOT A GOOD IDEA. STAY CLOSE TO ME.

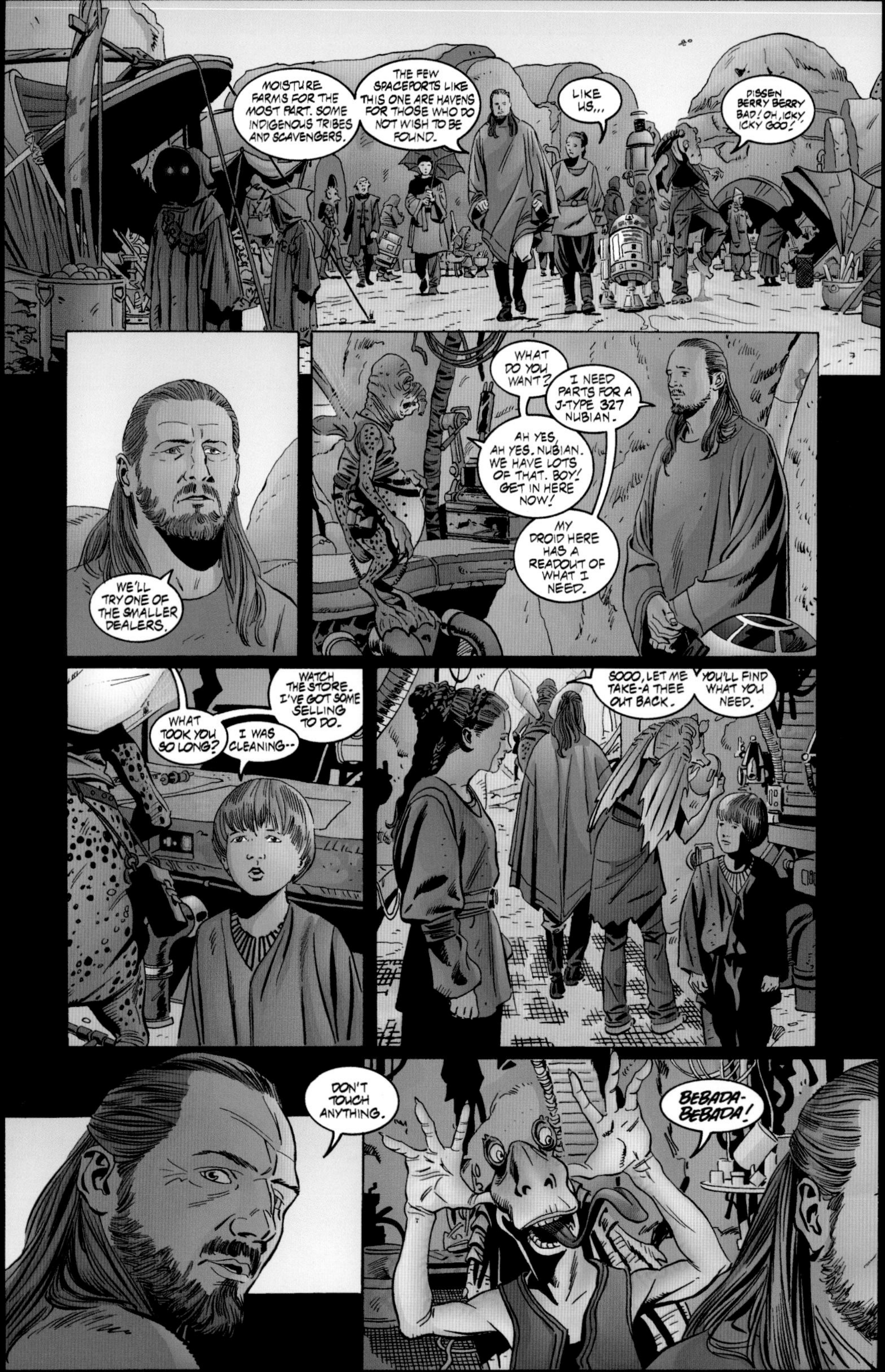
MOISTURE FARMS FOR THE MOST PART. SOME INDIGENOUS TRIBES AND SCAVENGERS.
THE FEW SPACEPORTS LIKE THIS ONE ARE HAVENS FOR THOSE WHO DO NOT WISH TO BE FOUND.
LIKE US...
DISSEN BERRY BERRY BAD! OH, ICKY, ICKY GOO!
WE'LL TRY ONE OF THE SMALLER DEALERS.
WHAT DO YOU WANT?
I NEED PARTS FOR A J-TYPE 327 NUBIAN.
AH YES, AH YES. NUBIAN. WE HAVE LOTS OF THAT. BOY! GET IN HERE NOW!
MY DROID HERE HAS A READOUT OF WHAT I NEED.
WHAT TOOK YOU SO LONG?
I WAS CLEANING--
WATCH THE STORE. I'VE GOT SOME SELLING TO DO.
SOOO, LET ME TAKE-A THEE OUT BACK.
YOU'LL FIND WHAT YOU NEED.
DON'T TOUCH ANYTHING.
BEBADA-BEBADA!

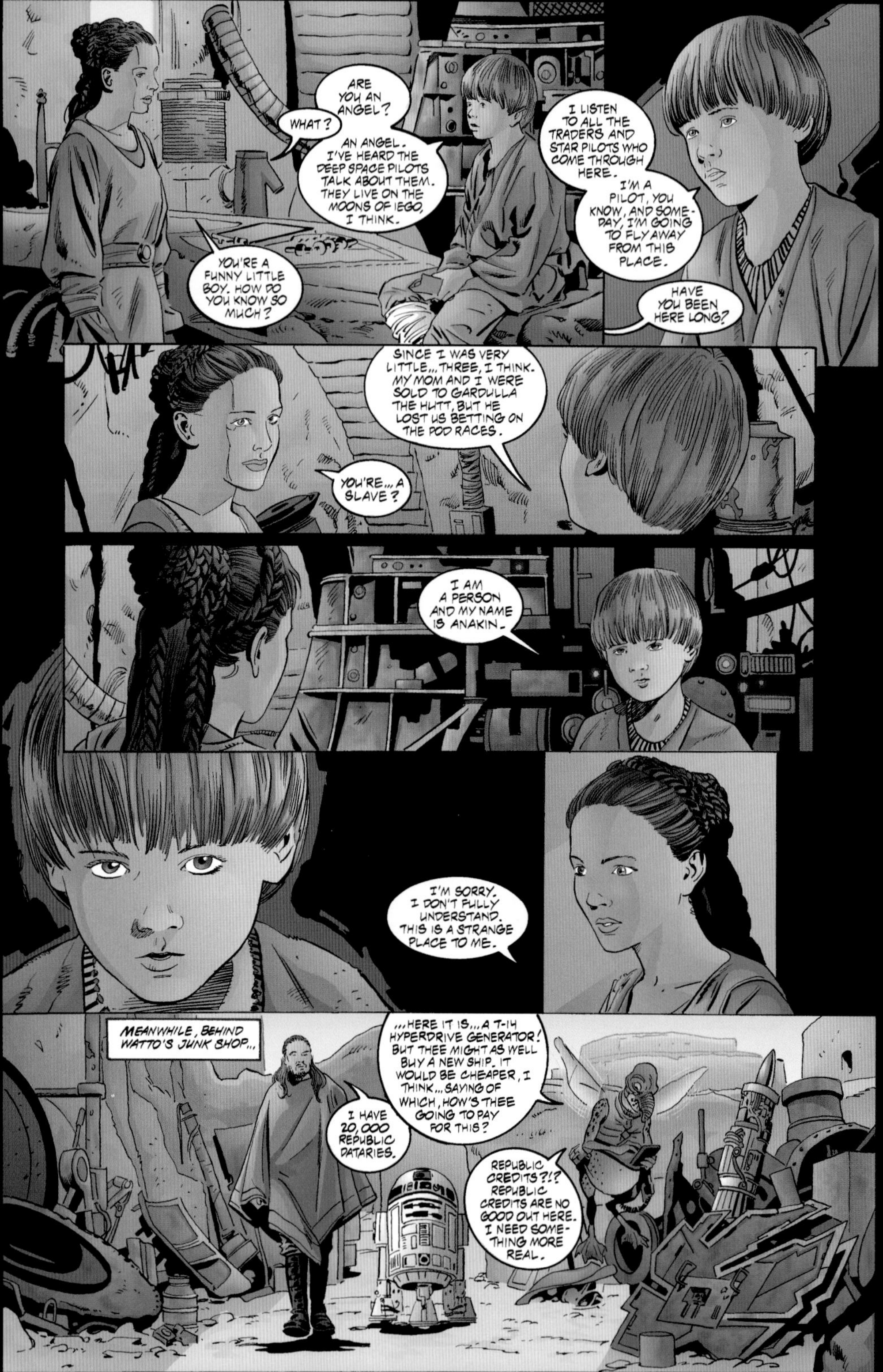

ARE YOU AN ANGEL?
WHAT?
AN ANGEL. I'VE HEARD THE DEEP SPACE PILOTS TALK ABOUT THEM. THEY LIVE ON THE MOONS OF IEGO, I THINK.
YOU'RE A FUNNY LITTLE BOY. HOW DO YOU KNOW SO MUCH?
I LISTEN TO ALL THE TRADERS AND STAR PILOTS WHO COME THROUGH HERE.
I'M A PILOT, YOU KNOW, AND SOMEDAY, I'M GOING TO FLY AWAY FROM THIS PLACE.
HAVE YOU BEEN HERE LONG?
SINCE I WAS VERY LITTLE... THREE, I THINK. MY MOM AND I WERE SOLD TO GARDULLA THE HUTT, BUT HE LOST US BETTING ON THE POD RACES.
YOU'RE... A SLAVE?
I AM A PERSON AND MY NAME IS ANAKIN.
I'M SORRY. I DON'T FULLY UNDERSTAND. THIS IS A STRANGE PLACE TO ME.
MEANWHILE, BEHIND WATTO'S JUNK SHOP...
...HERE IT IS... A T-14 HYPERDRIVE GENERATOR! BUT THEE MIGHT AS WELL BUY A NEW SHIP. IT WOULD BE CHEAPER, I THINK... SAYING OF WHICH, HOW'S THEE GOING TO PAY FOR THIS?
I HAVE 20,000 REPUBLIC DATARIES.
REPUBLIC CREDITS?!? REPUBLIC CREDITS ARE NO GOOD OUT HERE. I NEED SOMETHING MORE REAL.

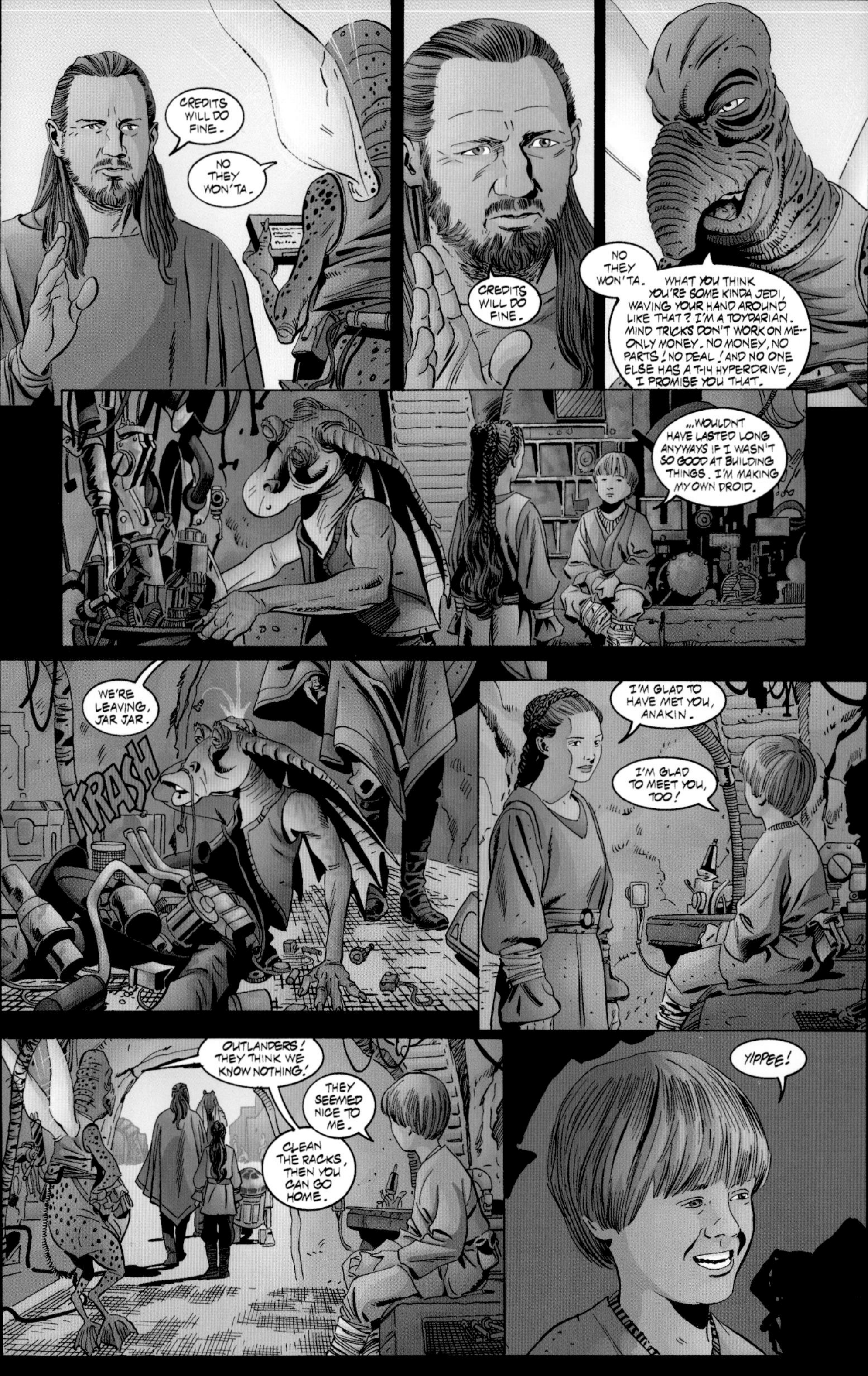
CREDITS WILL DO FINE.
NO THEY WON'TA.
CREDITS WILL DO FINE.
NO THEY WON'TA.
WHAT YOU THINK YOU'RE SOME KINDA JEDI, WAVING YOUR HAND AROUND LIKE THAT? I'M A TOYDARIAN. MIND TRICKS DON'T WORK ON ME-- ONLY MONEY. NO MONEY, NO PARTS! NO DEAL! AND NO ONE ELSE HAS A T-14 HYPERDRIVE, I PROMISE YOU THAT.
...WOULDNT HAVE LASTED LONG ANYWAYS IF I WASN'T SO GOOD AT BUILDING THINGS. I'M MAKING MY OWN DROID.
WE'RE LEAVING, JAR JAR.
KRASH
I'M GLAD TO HAVE MET YOU, ANAKIN.
I'M GLAD TO MEET YOU, TOO!
OUTLANDERS! THEY THINK WE KNOW NOTHING!
THEY SEEMED NICE TO ME.
CLEAN THE RACKS, THEN YOU CAN GO HOME.
YIPPEE!

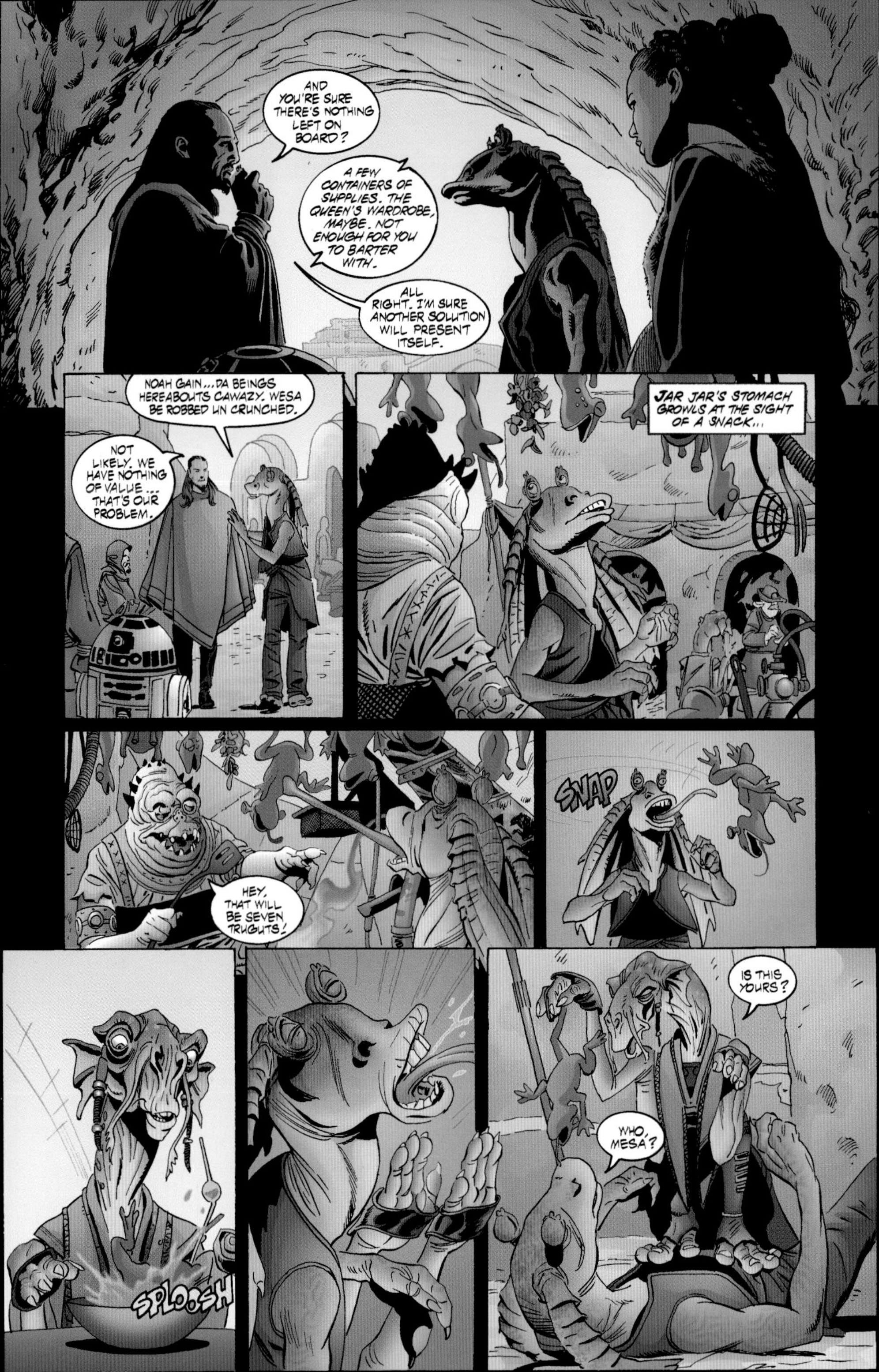
AND YOU'RE SURE THERE'S NOTHING LEFT ON BOARD?
A FEW CONTAINERS OF SUPPLIES. THE QUEEN'S WARDROBE, MAYBE. NOT ENOUGH FOR YOU TO BARTER WITH.
ALL RIGHT. I'M SURE ANOTHER SOLUTION WILL PRESENT ITSELF.
NOAH GAIN...DA BEINGS HEREABOUTS CAWAZY. WESA BE ROBBED UN CRUNCHED.
NOT LIKELY. WE HAVE NOTHING OF VALUE... THAT'S OUR PROBLEM.
JAR JAR'S STOMACH GROWLS AT THE SIGHT OF A SNACK...
HEY, THAT WILL BE SEVEN TRUGUTS!
SNAP
SPLOOSH
IS THIS YOURS?
WHO, MESA?

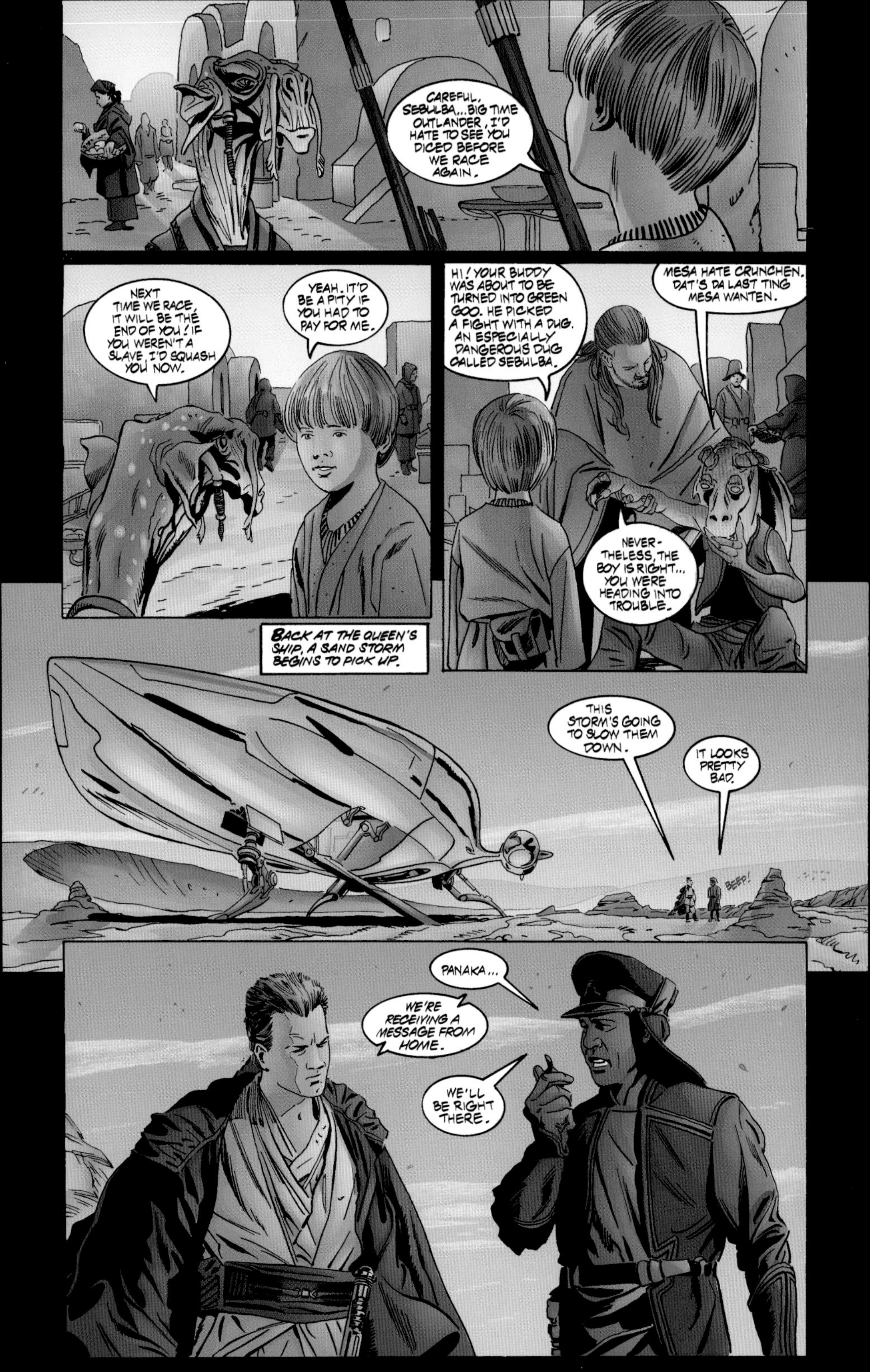
CAREFUL, SEBULBA... BIG TIME OUTLANDER, I'D HATE TO SEE YOU DICED BEFORE WE RACE AGAIN.
NEXT TIME WE RACE, IT WILL BE THE END OF YOU! IF YOU WEREN'T A SLAVE, I'D SQUASH YOU NOW.
YEAH. IT'D BE A PITY IF YOU HAD TO PAY FOR ME.
HI! YOUR BUDDY WAS ABOUT TO BE TURNED INTO GREEN GOO. HE PICKED A FIGHT WITH A DUG. AN ESPECIALLY DANGEROUS DUG CALLED SEBULBA.
MESA HATE CRUNCHEN. DAT'S DA LAST TING MESA WANTEN.
NEVER-THELESS, THE BOY IS RIGHT... YOU WERE HEADING INTO TROUBLE.
BACK AT THE QUEEN'S SHIP, A SAND STORM BEGINS TO PICK UP.
THIS STORM'S GOING TO SLOW THEM DOWN.
IT LOOKS PRETTY BAD.
BEEP!
PANAKA...
WE'RE RECEIVING A MESSAGE FROM HOME.
WE'LL BE RIGHT THERE.

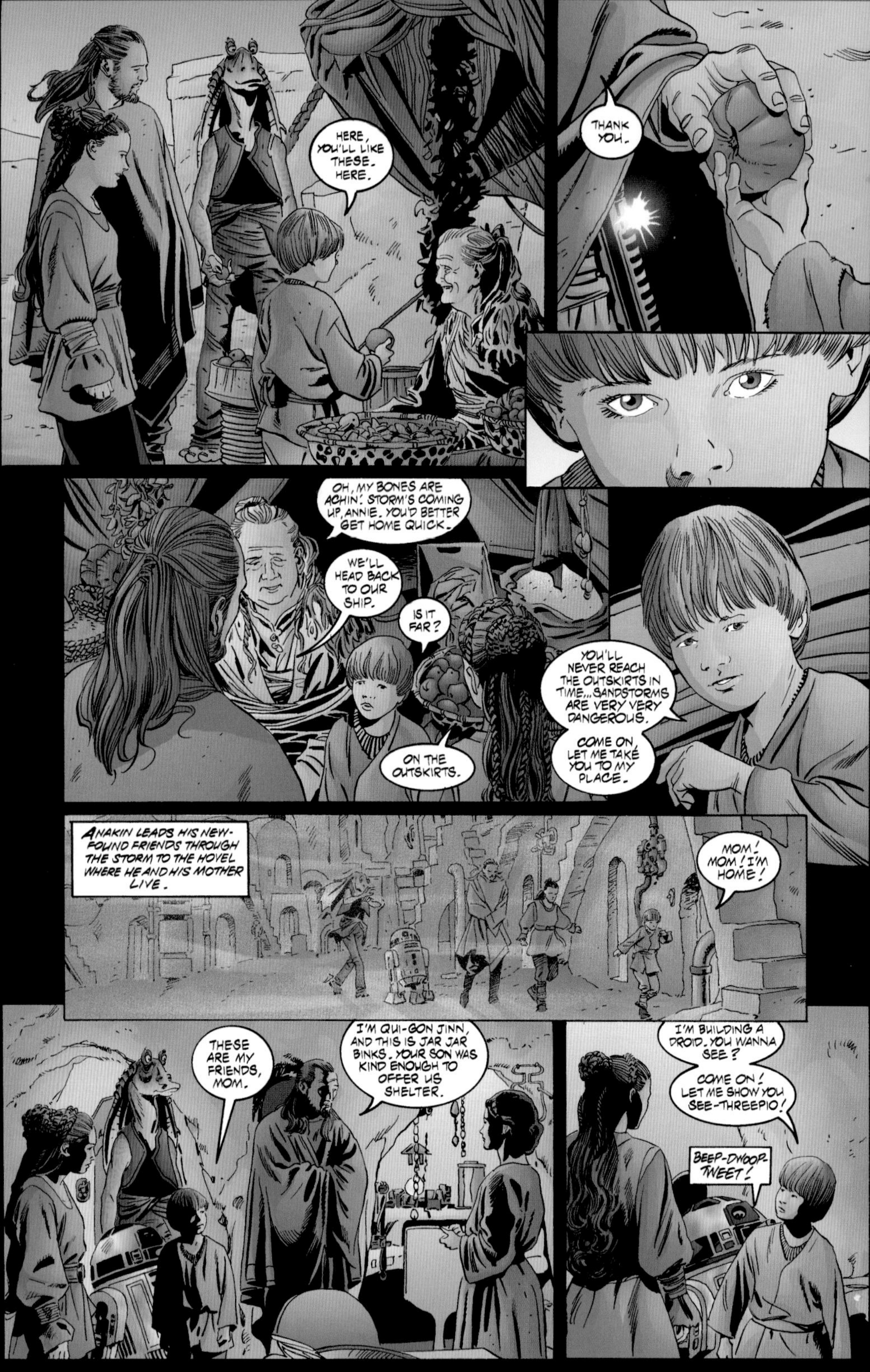
HERE, YOU'LL LIKE THESE. HERE.
THANK YOU.
OH, MY BONES ARE ACHIN'. STORM'S COMING UP, ANNIE. YOU'D BETTER GET HOME QUICK.
WE'LL HEAD BACK TO OUR SHIP.
IS IT FAR?
ON THE OUTSKIRTS.
YOU'LL NEVER REACH THE OUTSKIRTS IN TIME... SANDSTORMS ARE VERY VERY DANGEROUS.
COME ON, LET ME TAKE YOU TO MY PLACE.
ANAKIN LEADS HIS NEW-FOUND FRIENDS THROUGH THE STORM TO THE HOVEL WHERE HE AND HIS MOTHER LIVE.
MOM! MOM! I'M HOME!
THESE ARE MY FRIENDS, MOM.
I'M QUI-GON JINN, AND THIS IS JAR JAR BINKS. YOUR SON WAS KIND ENOUGH TO OFFER US SHELTER.
I'M BUILDING A DROID. YOU WANNA SEE?
COME ON! LET ME SHOW YOU SEE-THREEPIO!
BEEP-DWOOP TWEET!

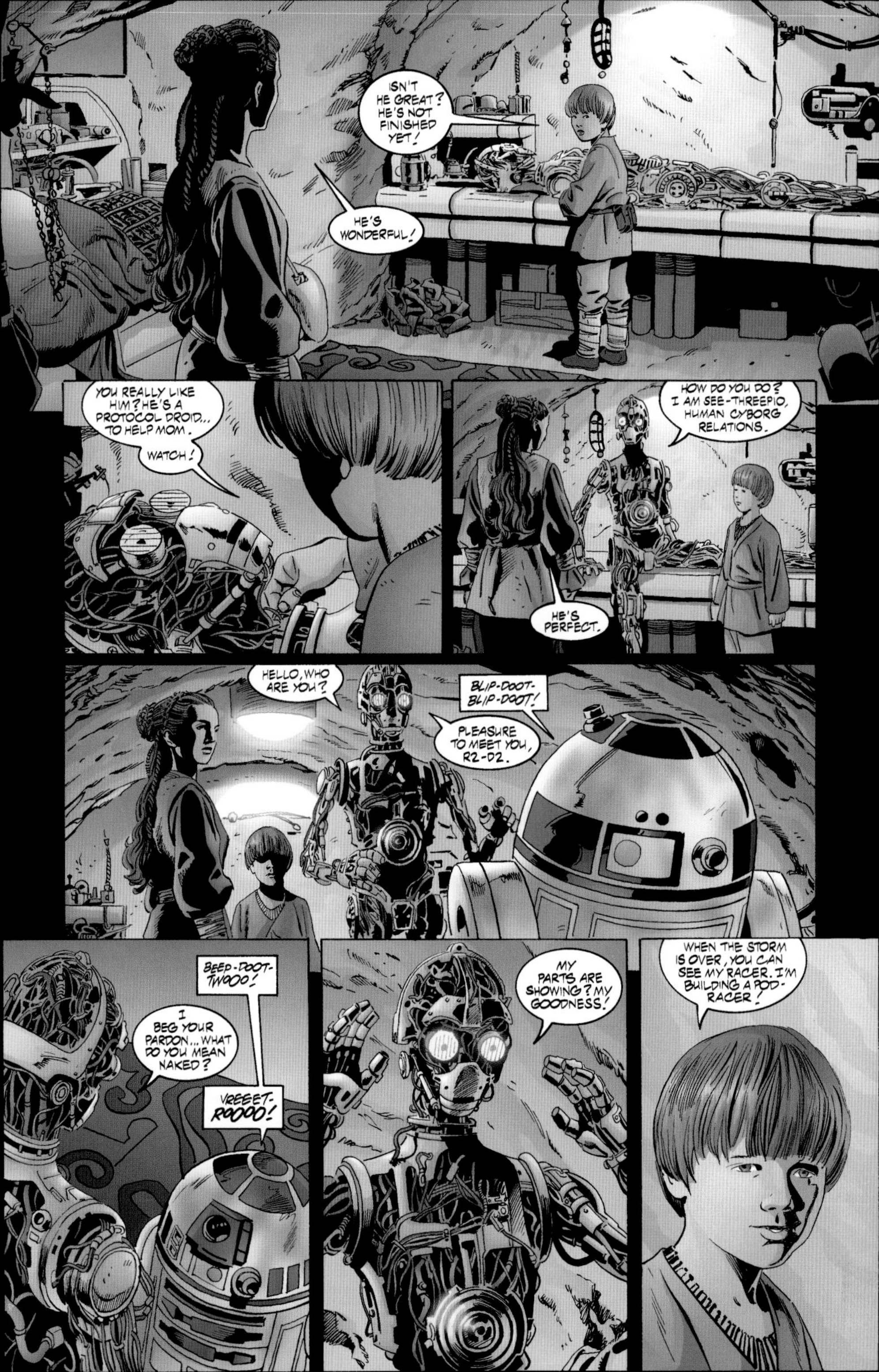
ISN'T HE GREAT? HE'S NOT FINISHED YET!
HE'S WONDERFUL!
YOU REALLY LIKE HIM? HE'S A PROTOCOL DROID... TO HELP MOM.
WATCH!
HOW DO YOU DO? I AM SEE-THREEPIO, HUMAN CYBORG RELATIONS.
HE'S PERFECT.
HELLO, WHO ARE YOU?
BLIP-DOOT-BLIP-DOOT!
PLEASURE TO MEET YOU, R2-D2.
BEEP-DOOT-TWOOO!
I BEG YOUR PARDON... WHAT DO YOU MEAN NAKED?
VREEET-ROOOO!
MY PARTS ARE SHOWING? MY GOODNESS!
WHEN THE STORM IS OVER, YOU CAN SEE MY RACER. I'M BUILDING A POD-RACER!

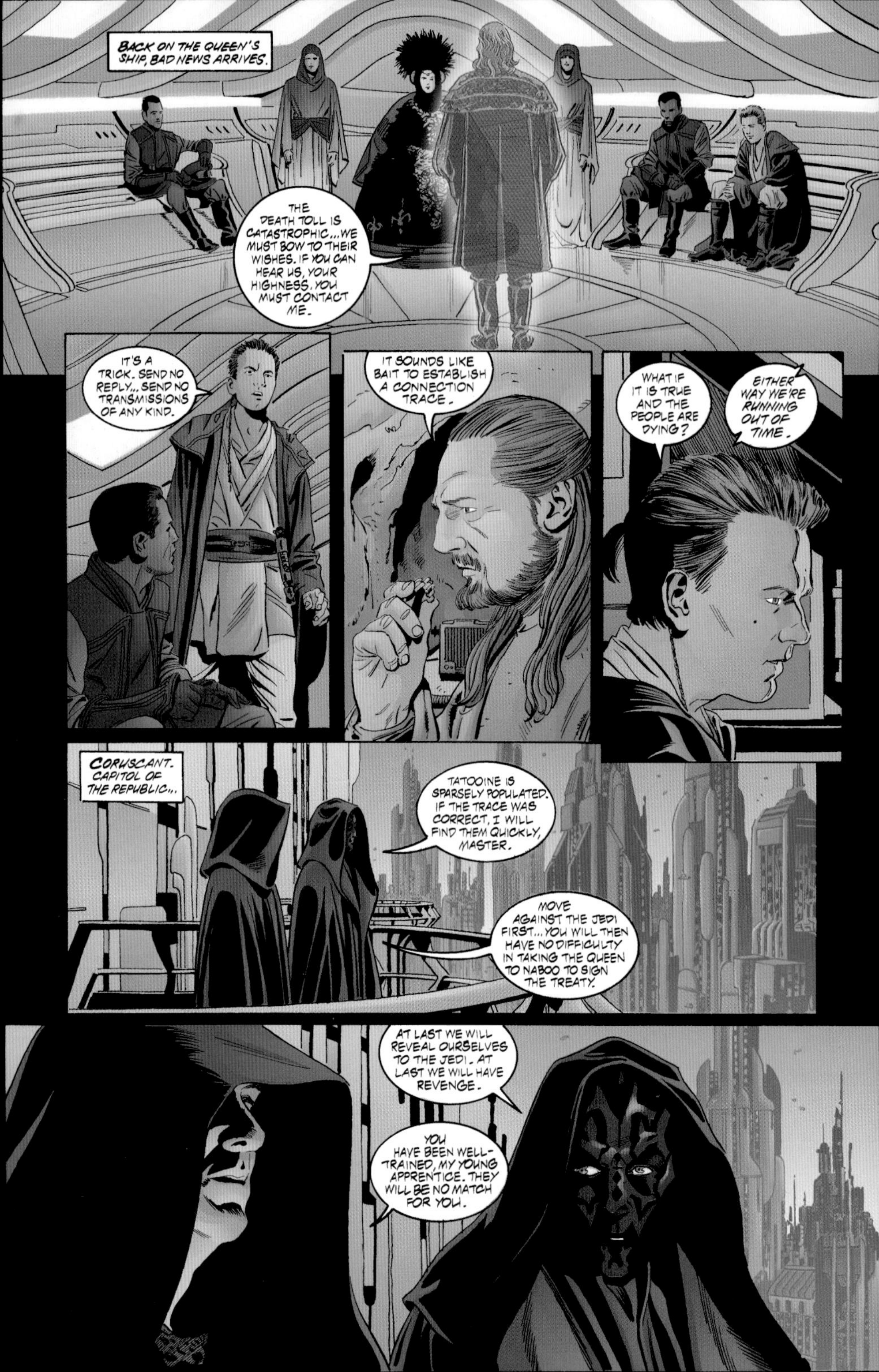
BACK ON THE QUEEN'S SHIP, BAD NEWS ARRIVES.
THE DEATH TOLL IS CATASTROPHIC...WE MUST BOW TO THEIR WISHES. IF YOU CAN HEAR US, YOUR HIGHNESS, YOU MUST CONTACT ME.
IT'S A TRICK. SEND NO REPLY... SEND NO TRANSMISSIONS OF ANY KIND.
IT SOUNDS LIKE BAIT TO ESTABLISH A CONNECTION TRACE.
WHAT IF IT IS TRUE AND THE PEOPLE ARE DYING?
EITHER WAY WE'RE RUNNING OUT OF TIME.
CORUSCANT. CAPITOL OF THE REPUBLIC...
TATOOINE IS SPARSELY POPULATED. IF THE TRACE WAS CORRECT, I WILL FIND THEM QUICKLY, MASTER.
MOVE AGAINST THE JEDI FIRST... YOU WILL THEN HAVE NO DIFFICULTY IN TAKING THE QUEEN TO NABOO TO SIGN THE TREATY.
AT LAST WE WILL REVEAL OURSELVES TO THE JEDI. AT LAST WE WILL HAVE REVENGE.
YOU HAVE BEEN WELL-TRAINED, MY YOUNG APPRENTICE. THEY WILL BE NO MATCH FOR YOU.

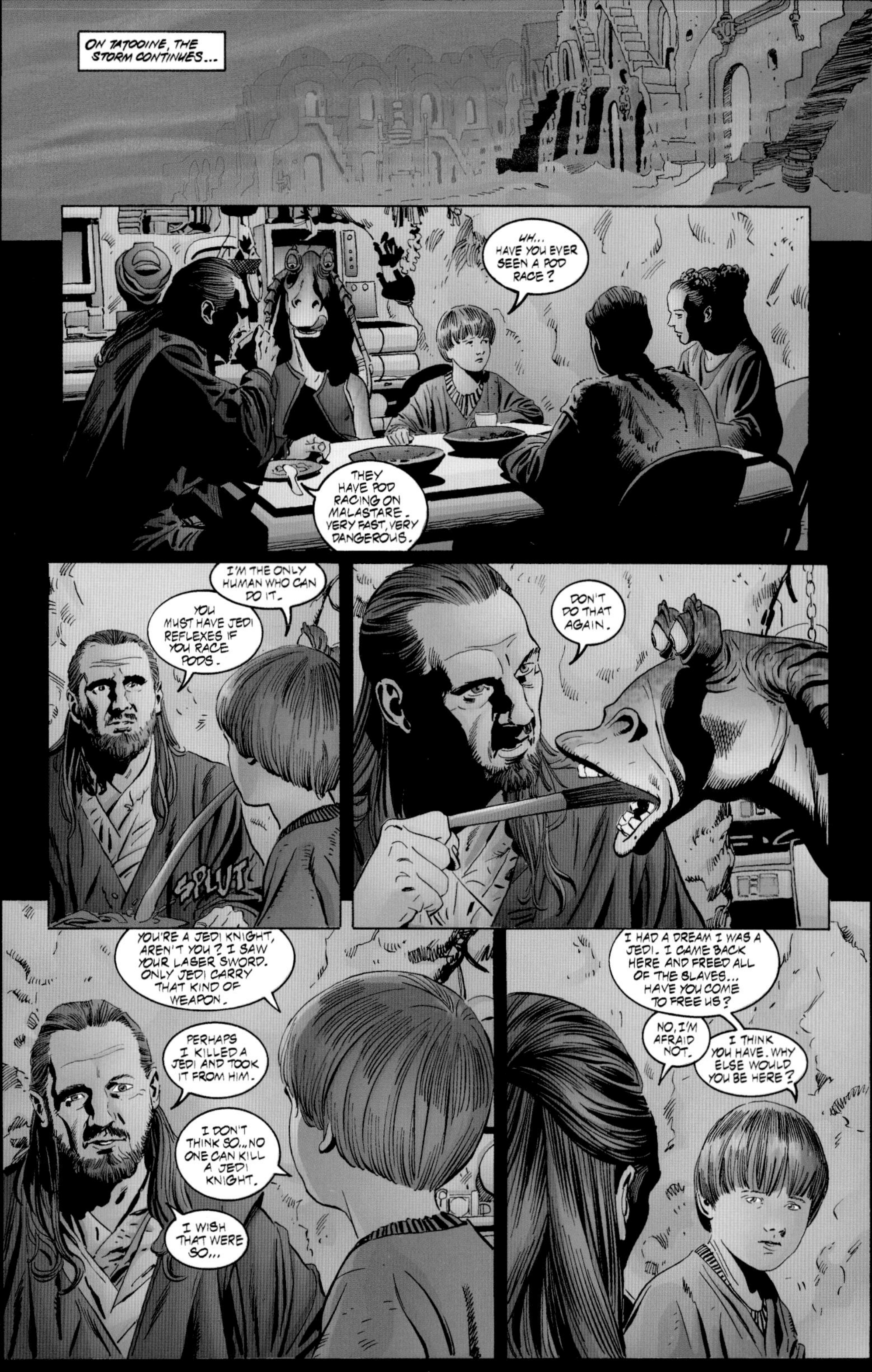
ON TATOOINE, THE STORM CONTINUES...
UH... HAVE YOU EVER SEEN A POD RACE?
THEY HAVE POD RACING ON MALASTARE. VERY FAST, VERY DANGEROUS.
YOU MUST HAVE JEDI REFLEXES IF YOU RACE PODS.
I'M THE ONLY HUMAN WHO CAN DO IT.
SPLUT
DON'T DO THAT AGAIN.
YOU'RE A JEDI KNIGHT, AREN'T YOU? I SAW YOUR LASER SWORD. ONLY JEDI CARRY THAT KIND OF WEAPON.
PERHAPS I KILLED A JEDI AND TOOK IT FROM HIM.
I DON'T THINK SO... NO ONE CAN KILL A JEDI KNIGHT.
I WISH THAT WERE SO...
I HAD A DREAM I WAS A JEDI. I CAME BACK HERE AND FREED ALL OF THE SLAVES... HAVE YOU COME TO FREE US?
NO, I'M AFRAID NOT.
I THINK YOU HAVE. WHY ELSE WOULD YOU BE HERE?

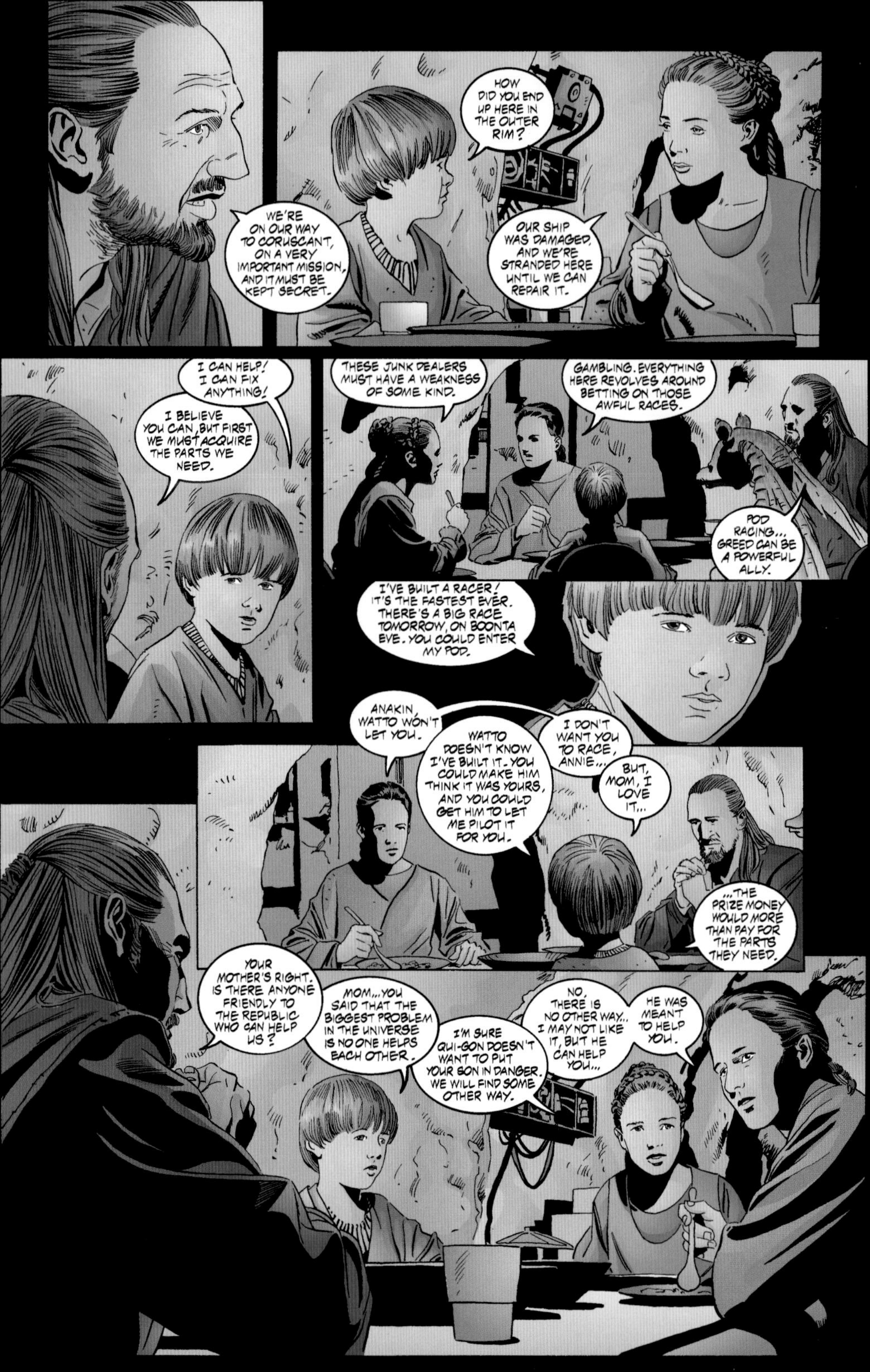
HOW DID YOU END UP HERE IN THE OUTER RIM?
WE'RE ON OUR WAY TO CORUSCANT, ON A VERY IMPORTANT MISSION, AND IT MUST BE KEPT SECRET.
OUR SHIP WAS DAMAGED, AND WE'RE STRANDED HERE UNTIL WE CAN REPAIR IT.
I CAN HELP! I CAN FIX ANYTHING!
I BELIEVE YOU CAN, BUT FIRST WE MUST ACQUIRE THE PARTS WE NEED.
THESE JUNK DEALERS MUST HAVE A WEAKNESS OF SOME KIND.
GAMBLING. EVERYTHING HERE REVOLVES AROUND BETTING ON THOSE AWFUL RACES.
POD RACING... GREED CAN BE A POWERFUL ALLY.
I'VE BUILT A RACER! IT'S THE FASTEST EVER. THERE'S A BIG RACE TOMORROW, ON BOONTA EVE. YOU COULD ENTER MY POD.
ANAKIN, WATTO WON'T LET YOU.
WATTO DOESN'T KNOW I'VE BUILT IT. YOU COULD MAKE HIM THINK IT WAS YOURS, AND YOU COULD GET HIM TO LET ME PILOT IT FOR YOU.
I DON'T WANT YOU TO RACE, ANNIE...
BUT, MOM, I LOVE IT...
...THE PRIZE MONEY WOULD MORE THAN PAY FOR THE PARTS THEY NEED.
YOUR MOTHER'S RIGHT. IS THERE ANYONE FRIENDLY TO THE REPUBLIC WHO CAN HELP US?
MOM... YOU SAID THAT THE BIGGEST PROBLEM IN THE UNIVERSE IS NO ONE HELPS EACH OTHER.
I'M SURE QUI-GON DOESN'T WANT TO PUT YOUR SON IN DANGER. WE WILL FIND SOME OTHER WAY.
NO, THERE IS NO OTHER WAY... I MAY NOT LIKE IT, BUT HE CAN HELP YOU...
HE WAS MEANT TO HELP YOU.

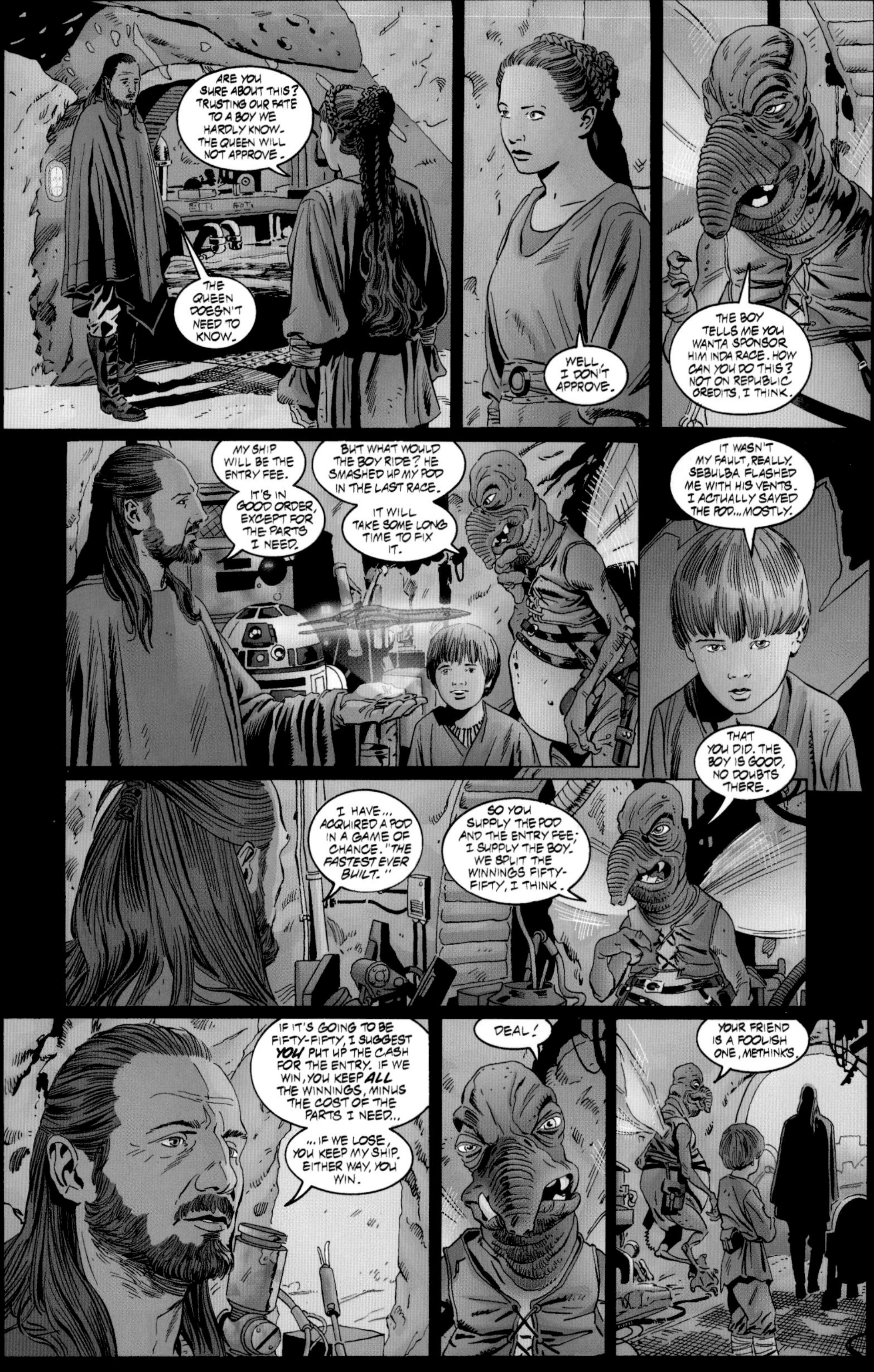
ARE YOU SURE ABOUT THIS? TRUSTING OUR FATE TO A BOY WE HARDLY KNOW. THE QUEEN WILL NOT APPROVE.
THE QUEEN DOESN'T NEED TO KNOW.
WELL, I DON'T APPROVE.
THE BOY TELLS ME YOU WANTA SPONSOR HIM INDA RACE. HOW CAN YOU DO THIS? NOT ON REPUBLIC CREDITS, I THINK.
MY SHIP WILL BE THE ENTRY FEE.
IT'S IN GOOD ORDER, EXCEPT FOR THE PARTS I NEED.
BUT WHAT WOULD THE BOY RIDE? HE SMASHED UP MY POD IN THE LAST RACE.
IT WILL TAKE SOME LONG TIME TO FIX IT.
IT WASN'T MY FAULT, REALLY. SEBULBA FLASHED ME WITH HIS VENTS. I ACTUALLY SAVED THE POD... MOSTLY.
THAT YOU DID. THE BOY IS GOOD, NO DOUBTS THERE.
I HAVE... ACQUIRED A POD IN A GAME OF CHANCE. "THE FASTEST EVER BUILT."
SO YOU SUPPLY THE POD AND THE ENTRY FEE; I SUPPLY THE BOY. WE SPLIT THE WINNINGS FIFTY-FIFTY, I THINK.
IF IT'S GOING TO BE FIFTY-FIFTY, I SUGGEST YOU PUT UP THE CASH FOR THE ENTRY. IF WE WIN, YOU KEEP ALL THE WINNINGS, MINUS THE COST OF THE PARTS I NEED...
...IF WE LOSE, YOU KEEP MY SHIP. EITHER WAY, YOU WIN.
DEAL!
YOUR FRIEND IS A FOOLISH ONE, METHINKS.

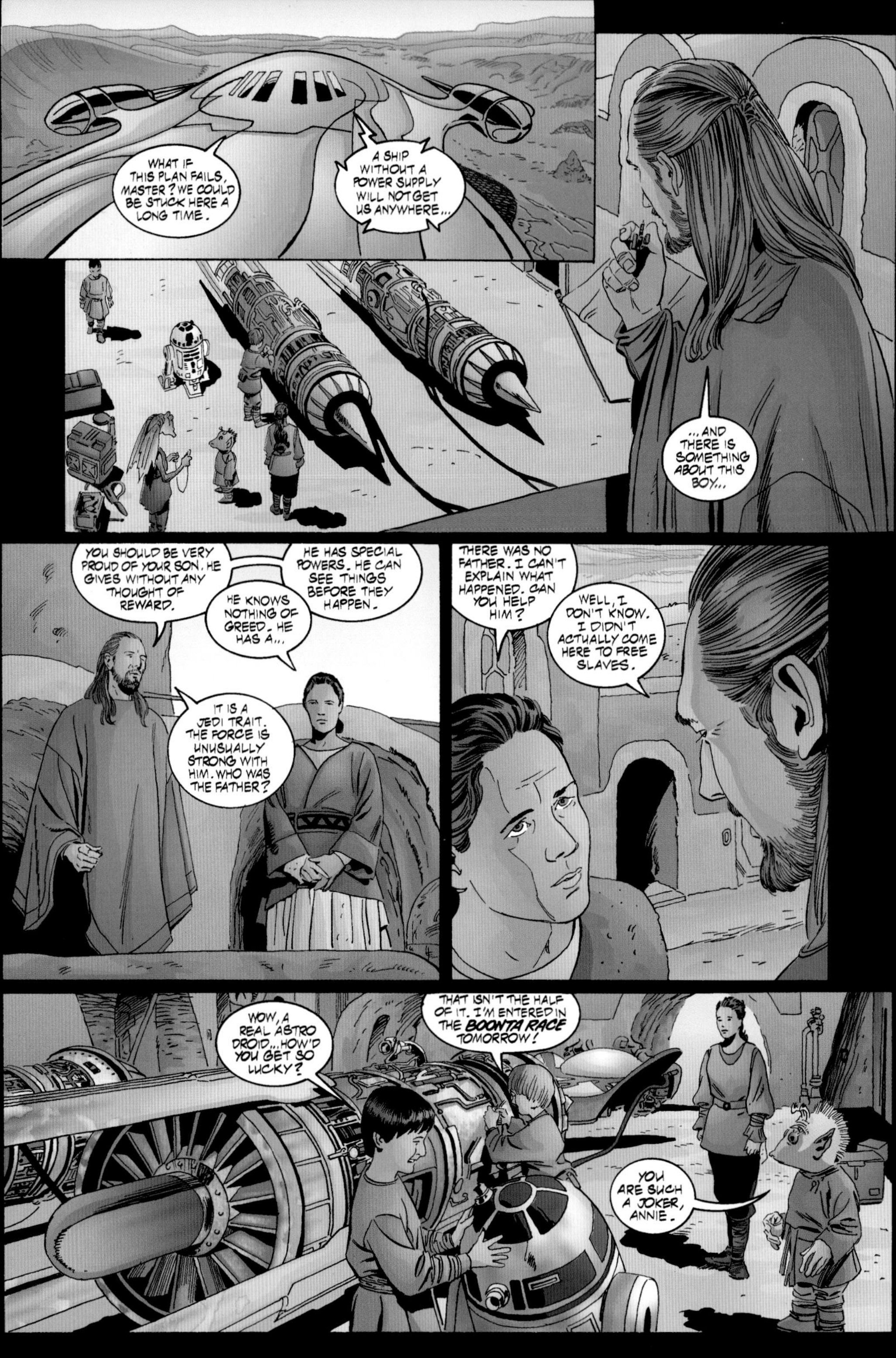
WHAT IF THIS PLAN FAILS, MASTER? WE COULD BE STUCK HERE A LONG TIME.
A SHIP WITHOUT A POWER SUPPLY WILL NOT GET US ANYWHERE...
...AND THERE IS SOMETHING ABOUT THIS BOY...
YOU SHOULD BE VERY PROUD OF YOUR SON. HE GIVES WITHOUT ANY THOUGHT OF REWARD.
HE KNOWS NOTHING OF GREED. HE HAS A...
HE HAS SPECIAL POWERS. HE CAN SEE THINGS BEFORE THEY HAPPEN.
IT IS A JEDI TRAIT. THE FORCE IS UNUSUALLY STRONG WITH HIM. WHO WAS THE FATHER?
THERE WAS NO FATHER. I CAN'T EXPLAIN WHAT HAPPENED. CAN YOU HELP HIM?
WELL, I DON'T KNOW. I DIDN'T ACTUALLY COME HERE TO FREE SLAVES.
WOW, A REAL ASTRO DROID...HOW'D YOU GET SO LUCKY?
THAT ISN'T THE HALF OF IT. I'M ENTERED IN THE BOONTA RACE TOMORROW!
YOU ARE SUCH A JOKER, ANNIE.

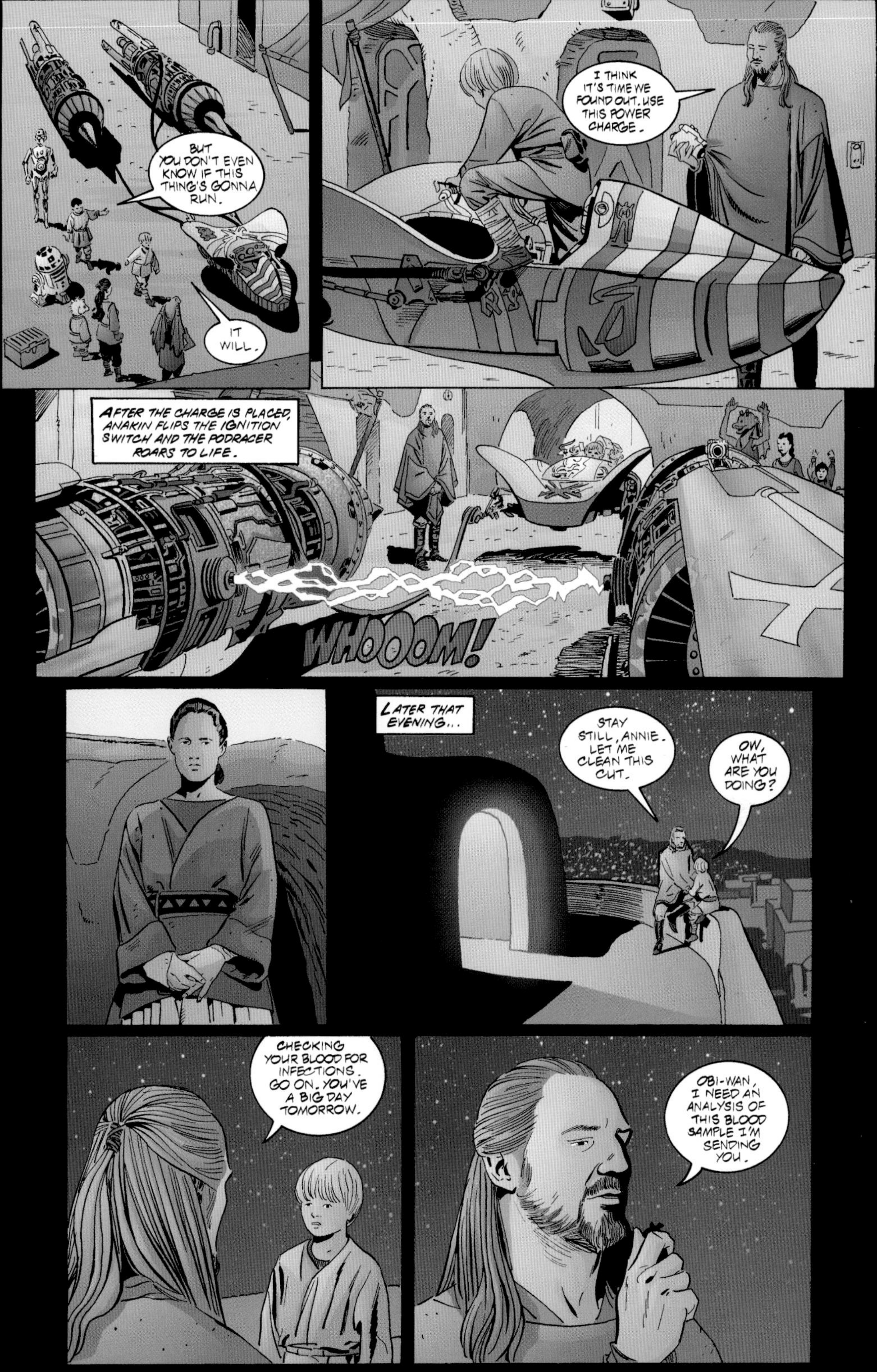

BUT YOU DON'T EVEN KNOW IF THIS THING'S GONNA RUN.
IT WILL.
I THINK IT'S TIME WE FOUND OUT. USE THIS POWER CHARGE.
AFTER THE CHARGE IS PLACED, ANAKIN FLIPS THE IGNITION SWITCH AND THE PODRACER ROARS TO LIFE.
WHOOOM!
LATER THAT EVENING...
STAY STILL, ANNIE. LET ME CLEAN THIS CUT.
OW, WHAT ARE YOU DOING?
CHECKING YOUR BLOOD FOR INFECTIONS. GO ON. YOU'VE A BIG DAY TOMORROW.
OBI-WAN, I NEED AN ANALYSIS OF THIS BLOOD SAMPLE I'M SENDING YOU.

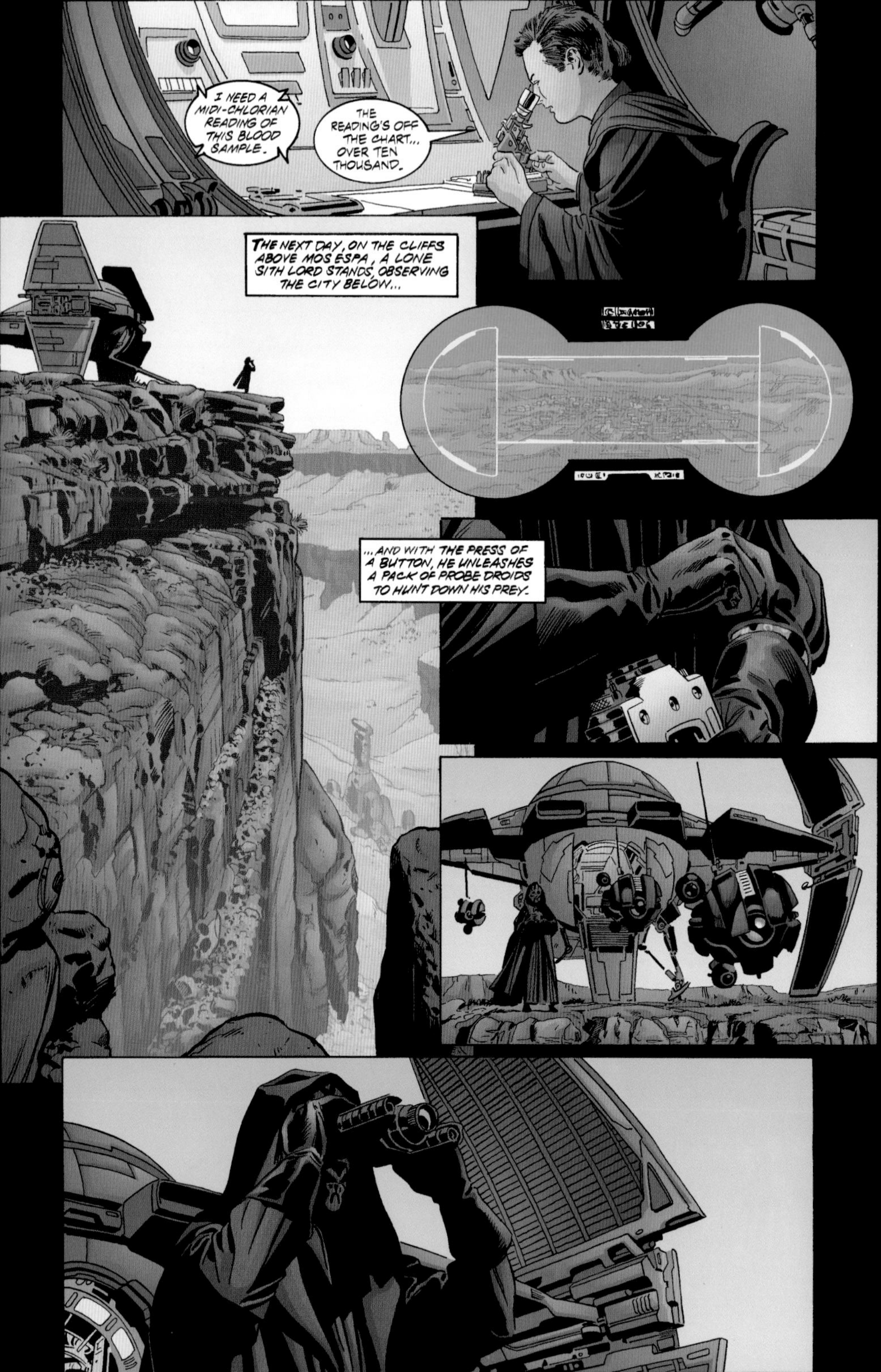

I NEED A MIDI-CHLORIAN READING OF THIS BLOOD SAMPLE.
THE READING'S OFF THE CHART... OVER TEN THOUSAND.
THE NEXT DAY, ON THE CLIFFS ABOVE MOS ESPA, A LONE SITH LORD STANDS, OBSERVING THE CITY BELOW...
...AND WITH THE PRESS OF A BUTTON, HE UNLEASHES A PACK OF PROBE DROIDS TO HUNT DOWN HIS PREY.

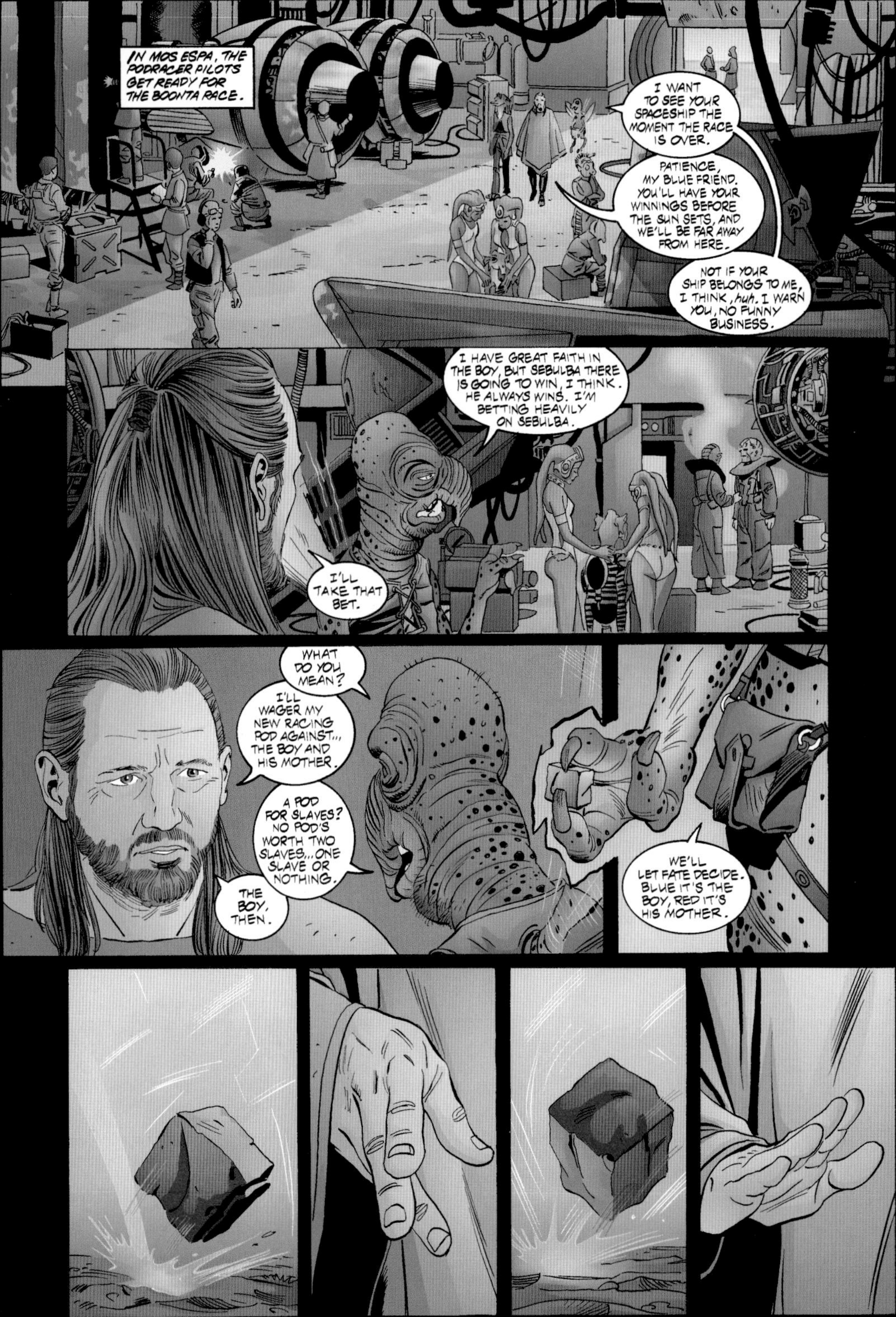
IN MOS ESPA, THE PODRACER PILOTS GET READY FOR THE BOONTA RACE.
I WANT TO SEE YOUR SPACESHIP THE MOMENT THE RACE IS OVER.
PATIENCE, MY BLUE FRIEND. YOU'LL HAVE YOUR WINNINGS BEFORE THE SUN SETS, AND WE'LL BE FAR AWAY FROM HERE.
NOT IF YOUR SHIP BELONGS TO ME, I THINK, huh. I WARN YOU, NO FUNNY BUSINESS.
I HAVE GREAT FAITH IN THE BOY, BUT SEBULBA THERE IS GOING TO WIN, I THINK. HE ALWAYS WINS. I'M BETTING HEAVILY ON SEBULBA.
I'LL TAKE THAT BET.
WHAT DO YOU MEAN?
I'LL WAGER MY NEW RACING POD AGAINST... THE BOY AND HIS MOTHER.
A POD FOR SLAVES? NO POD'S WORTH TWO SLAVES... ONE SLAVE OR NOTHING.
THE BOY, THEN.
WE'LL LET FATE DECIDE. BLUE IT'S THE BOY, RED IT'S HIS MOTHER.

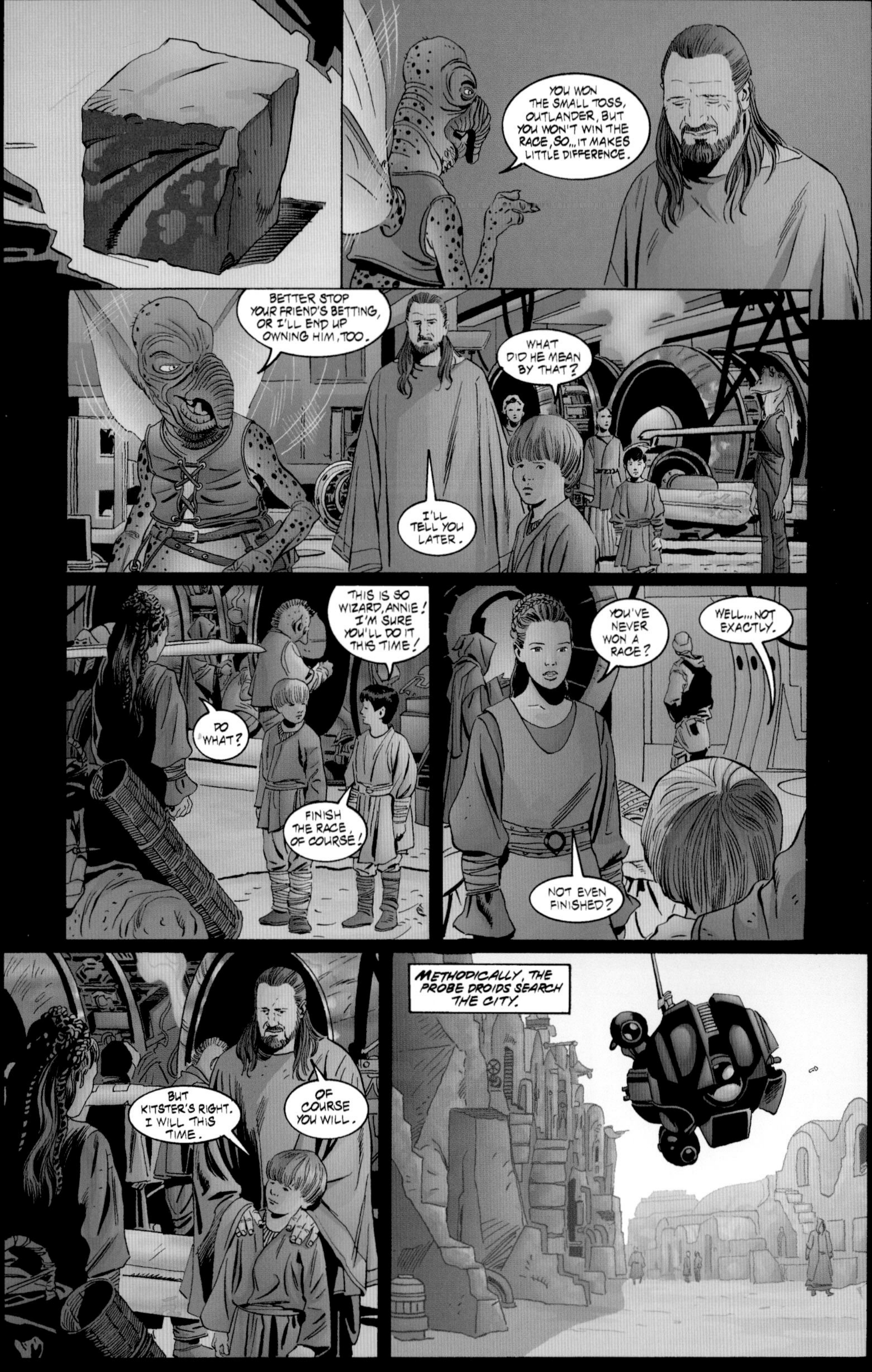
YOU WON THE SMALL TOSS, OUTLANDER, BUT YOU WON'T WIN THE RACE, SO... IT MAKES LITTLE DIFFERENCE.
BETTER STOP YOUR FRIEND'S BETTING, OR I'LL END UP OWNING HIM, TOO.
WHAT DID HE MEAN BY THAT?
I'LL TELL YOU LATER.
THIS IS SO WIZARD, ANNIE! I'M SURE YOU'LL DO IT THIS TIME!
DO WHAT?
FINISH THE RACE, OF COURSE!
YOU'VE NEVER WON A RACE?
WELL... NOT EXACTLY.
NOT EVEN FINISHED?
BUT KITSTER'S RIGHT. I WILL THIS TIME.
OF COURSE YOU WILL.
METHODICALLY, THE PROBE DROIDS SEARCH THE CITY.

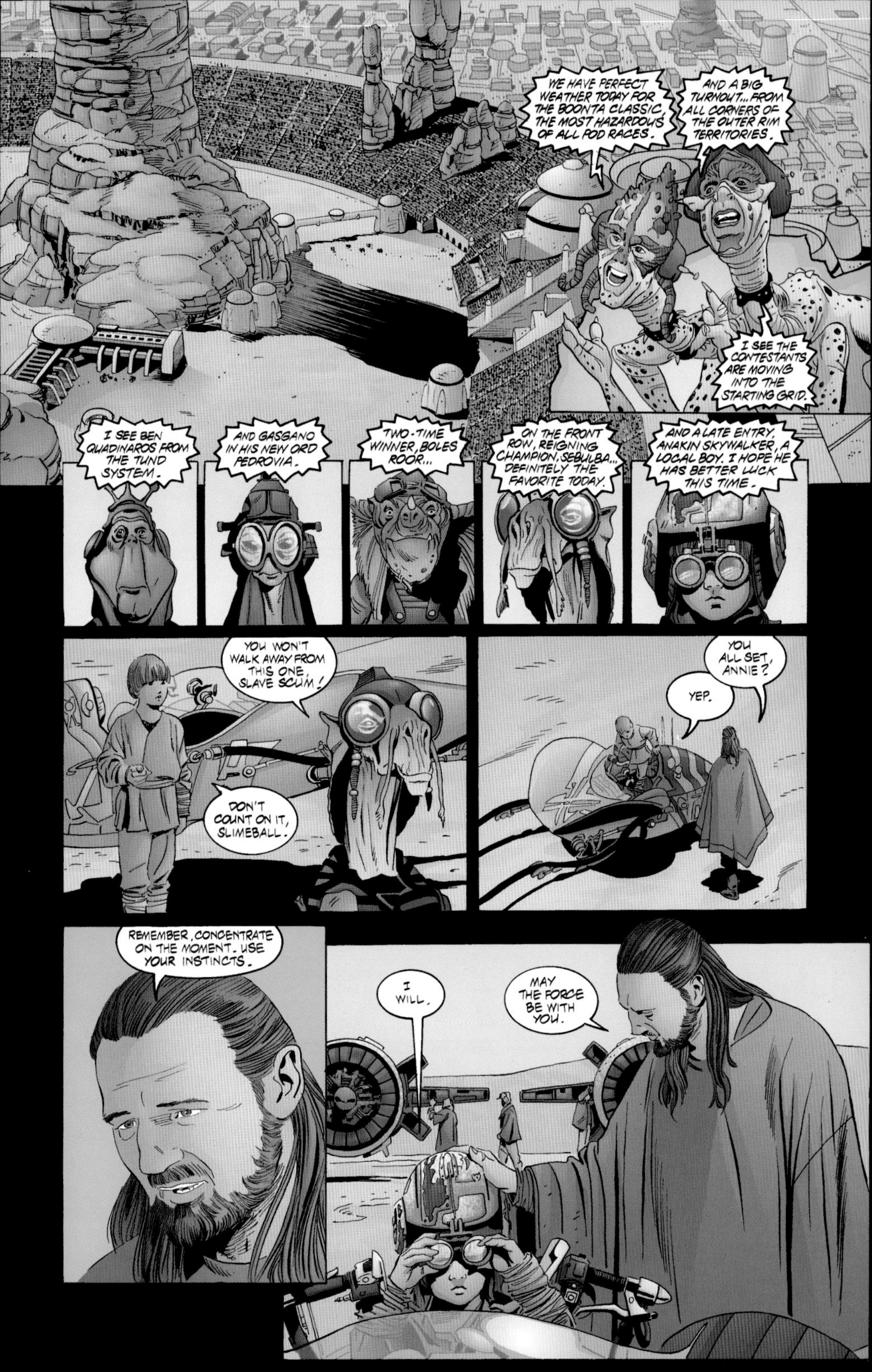
WE HAVE PERFECT WEATHER TODAY FOR THE BOONTA CLASSIC, THE MOST HAZARDOUS OF ALL POD RACES.
AND A BIG TURNOUT... FROM ALL CORNERS OF THE OUTER RIM TERRITORIES.
I SEE THE CONTESTANTS ARE MOVING INTO THE STARTING GRID.
I SEE BEN QUADINAROS FROM THE TUND SYSTEM.
AND GASGANO IN HIS NEW ORD PEDROVIA.
TWO-TIME WINNER, BOLES ROOR...
ON THE FRONT ROW, REIGNING CHAMPION, SEBULBA... DEFINITELY THE FAVORITE TODAY.
AND A LATE ENTRY, ANAKIN SKYWALKER, A LOCAL BOY. I HOPE HE HAS BETTER LUCK THIS TIME.
YOU WON'T WALK AWAY FROM THIS ONE, SLAVE SCUM!
DON'T COUNT ON IT, SLIMEBALL.
YOU ALL SET, ANNIE?
YEP.
REMEMBER, CONCENTRATE ON THE MOMENT. USE YOUR INSTINCTS.
I WILL.
MAY THE FORCE BE WITH YOU.

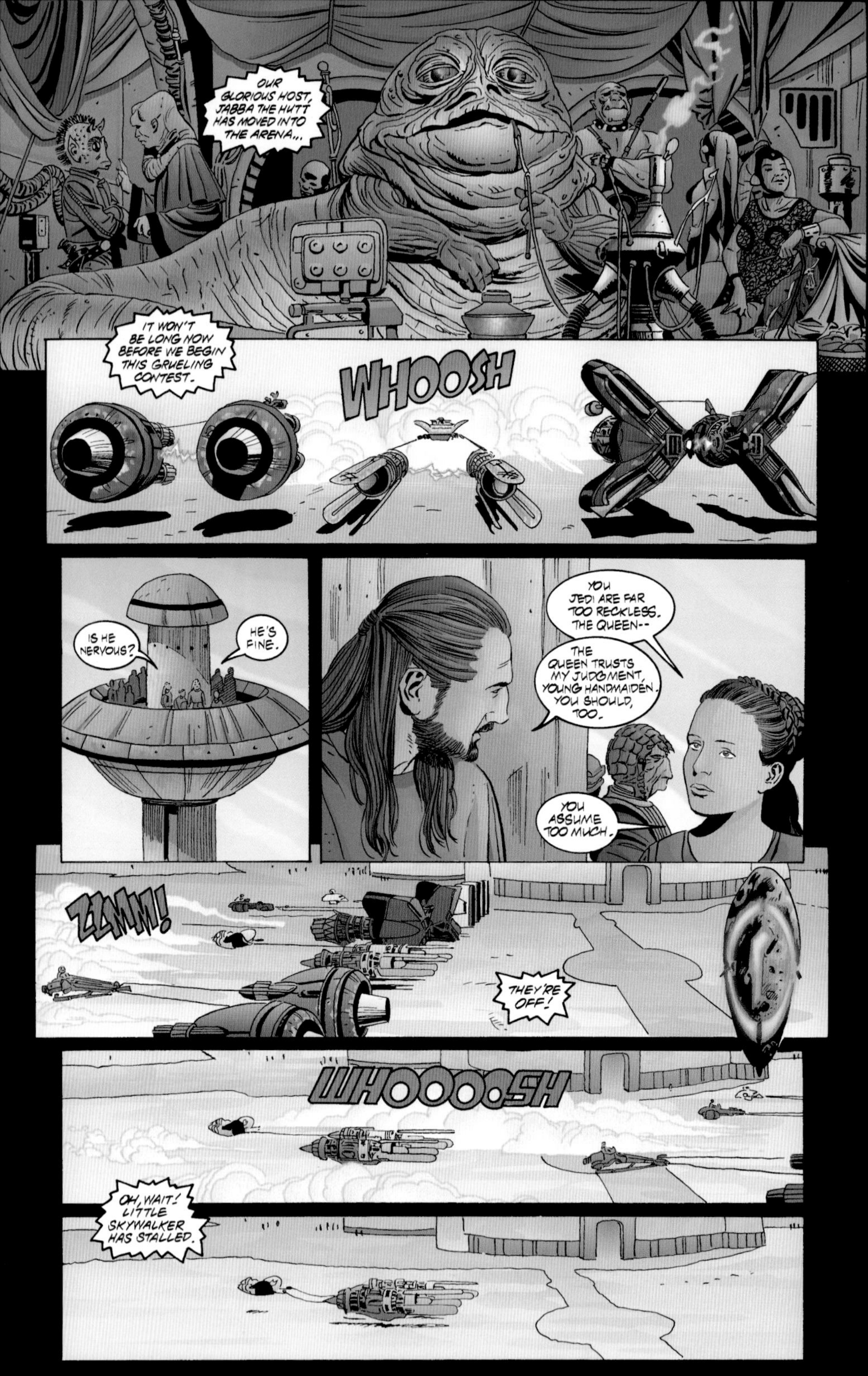
OUR GLORIOUS HOST, JABBA THE HUTT HAS MOVED INTO THE ARENA...
IT WON'T BE LONG NOW BEFORE WE BEGIN THIS GRUELING CONTEST.
WHOOSH
IS HE NERVOUS?
HE'S FINE.
YOU JEDI ARE FAR TOO RECKLESS. THE QUEEN--
THE QUEEN TRUSTS MY JUDGMENT, YOUNG HANDMAIDEN. YOU SHOULD, TOO.
YOU ASSUME TOO MUCH.
ZZMMM!
THEY'RE OFF!
WHOOOOSH
OH, WAIT! LITTLE SKYWALKER HAS STALLED.

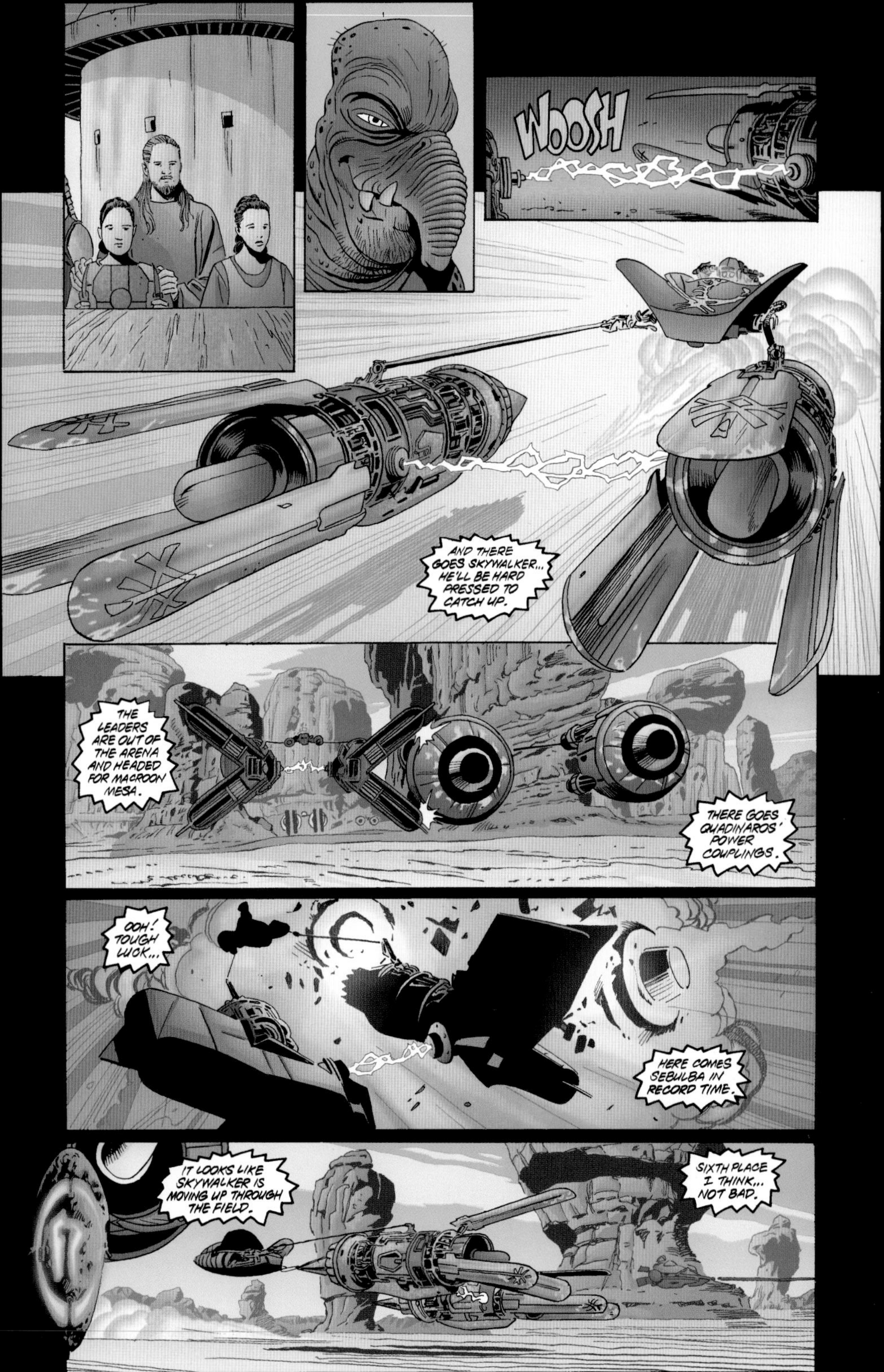
WOOSH
AND THERE GOES SKYWALKER... HE'LL BE HARD PRESSED TO CATCH UP.
THE LEADERS ARE OUT OF THE ARENA AND HEADED FOR MACROON MESA.
THERE GOES QUADINAROS' POWER COUPLINGS.
OOH! TOUGH LUCK...
HERE COMES SEBULBA IN RECORD TIME.
IT LOOKS LIKE SKYWALKER IS MOVING UP THROUGH THE FIELD.
SIXTH PLACE I THINK... NOT BAD.

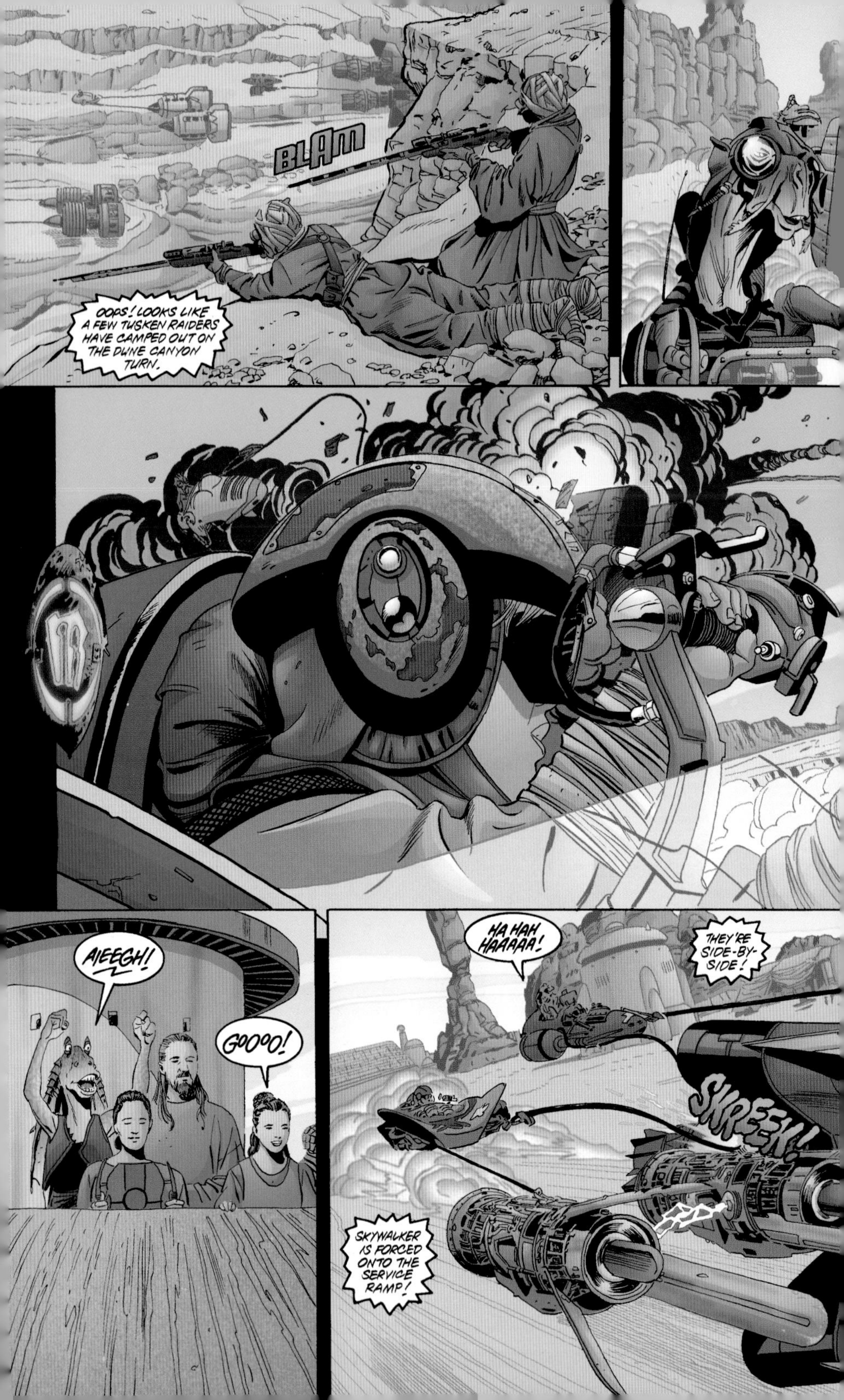
BLAM
OOPS! LOOKS LIKE A FEW TUSKEN RAIDERS HAVE CAMPED OUT ON THE DUNE CANYON TURN.
AIEEGH!
GOOOO!
HA HAH HAAAAA!
THEY'RE SIDE-BY-SIDE!
SKREEK!
SKYWALKER IS FORCED ONTO THE SERVICE RAMP!

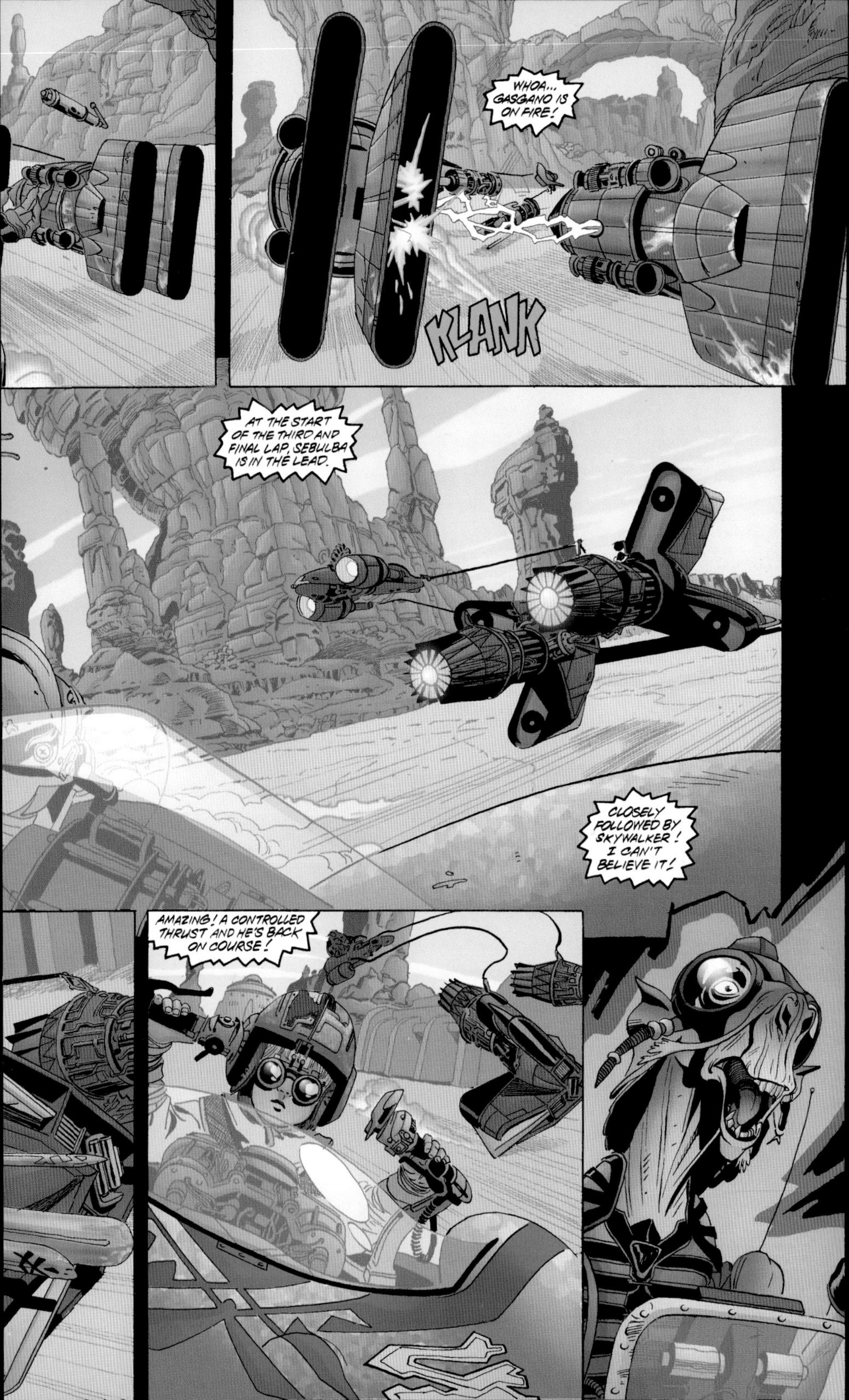
WHOA... GASGANO IS ON FIRE!
KLANK
AT THE START OF THE THIRD AND FINAL LAP, SEBULBA IS IN THE LEAD.
CLOSELY FOLLOWED BY SKYWALKER! I CAN'T BELIEVE IT!
AMAZING! A CONTROLLED THRUST AND HE'S BACK ON COURSE!

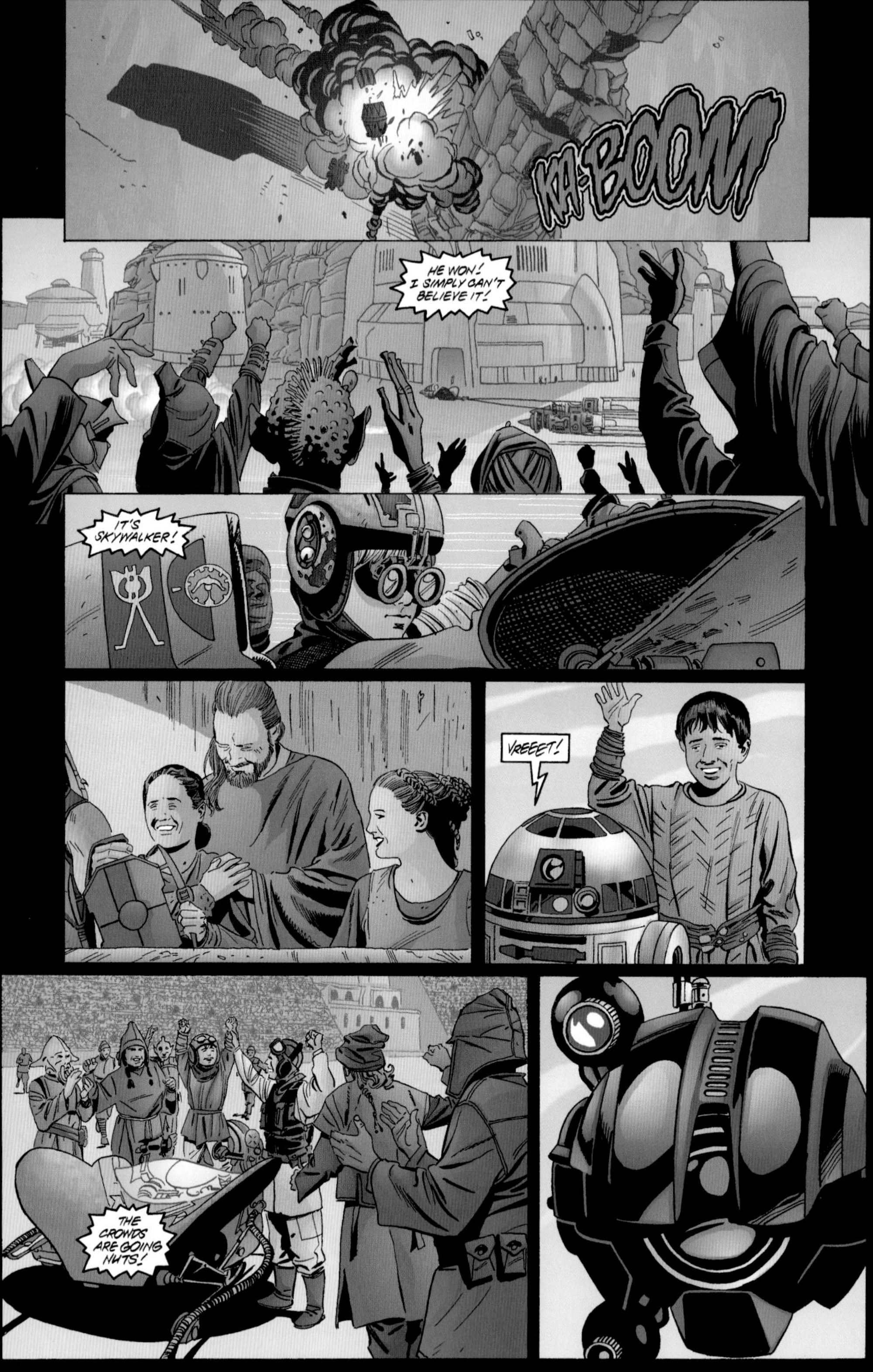
KA-BOOM!
HE WON! I SIMPLY CAN'T BELIEVE IT!
IT'S SKYWALKER!
VREEET!
THE CROWDS ARE GOING NUTS!

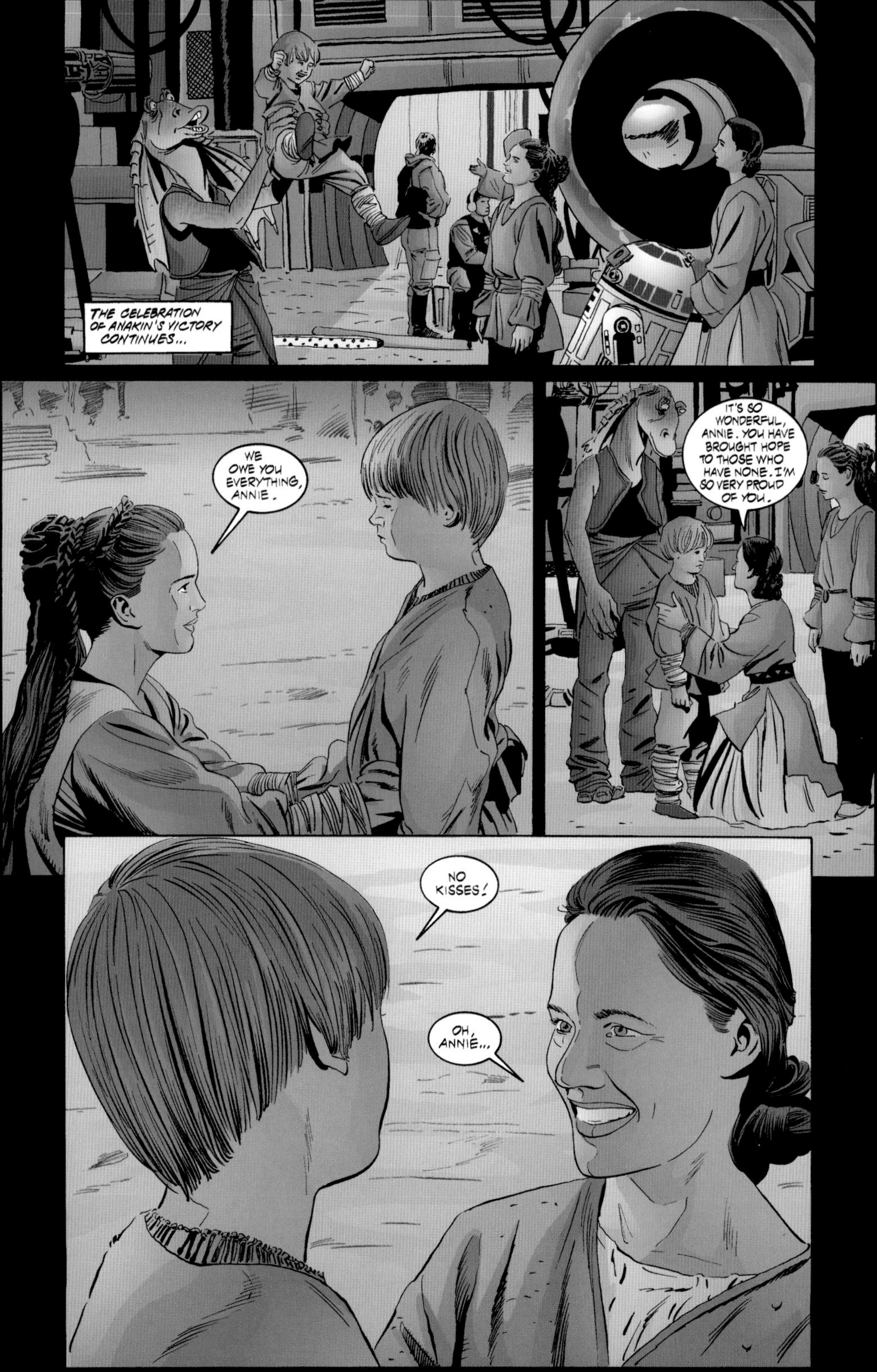
THE CELEBRATION OF ANAKIN'S VICTORY CONTINUES...
WE OWE YOU EVERYTHING, ANNIE.
IT'S SO WONDERFUL, ANNIE. YOU HAVE BROUGHT HOPE TO THOSE WHO HAVE NONE. I'M SO VERY PROUD OF YOU.
NO KISSES!
OH, ANNIE...

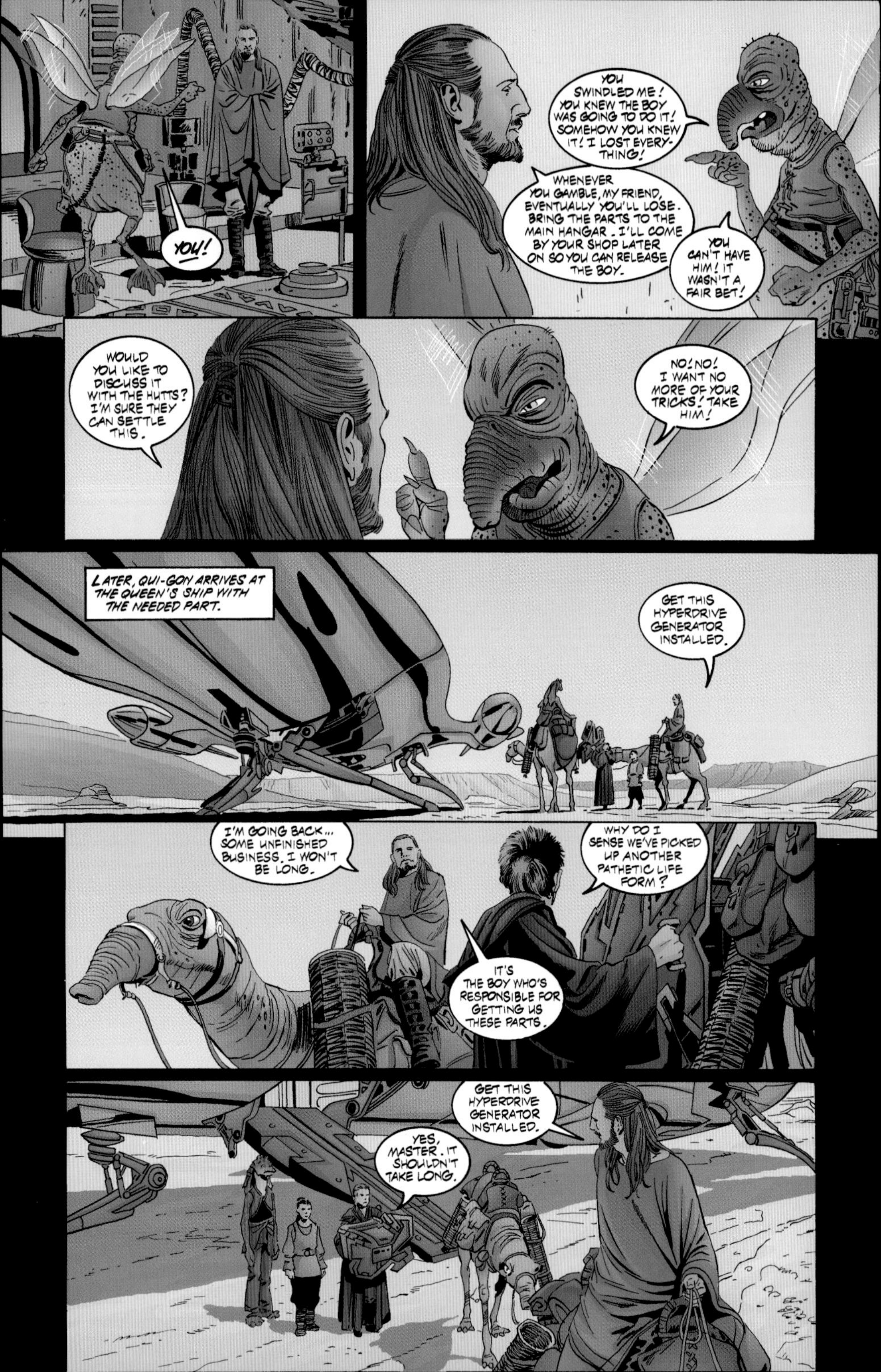
YOU!
YOU SWINDLED ME! YOU KNEW THE BOY WAS GOING TO DO IT! SOMEHOW YOU KNEW IT! I LOST EVERYTHING!
WHENEVER YOU GAMBLE, MY FRIEND, EVENTUALLY YOU'LL LOSE. BRING THE PARTS TO THE MAIN HANGAR. I'LL COME BY YOUR SHOP LATER ON SO YOU CAN RELEASE THE BOY.
YOU CAN'T HAVE HIM! IT WASN'T A FAIR BET!
WOULD YOU LIKE TO DISCUSS IT WITH THE HUTTS? I'M SURE THEY CAN SETTLE THIS.
NO! NO! I WANT NO MORE OF YOUR TRICKS! TAKE HIM!
LATER, QUI-GON ARRIVES AT THE QUEEN'S SHIP WITH THE NEEDED PART.
GET THIS HYPERDRIVE GENERATOR INSTALLED.
I'M GOING BACK... SOME UNFINISHED BUSINESS. I WON'T BE LONG.
WHY DO I SENSE WE'VE PICKED UP ANOTHER PATHETIC LIFE FORM?
IT'S THE BOY WHO'S RESPONSIBLE FOR GETTING US THESE PARTS.
GET THIS HYPERDRIVE GENERATOR INSTALLED.
YES, MASTER. IT SHOULDN'T TAKE LONG.

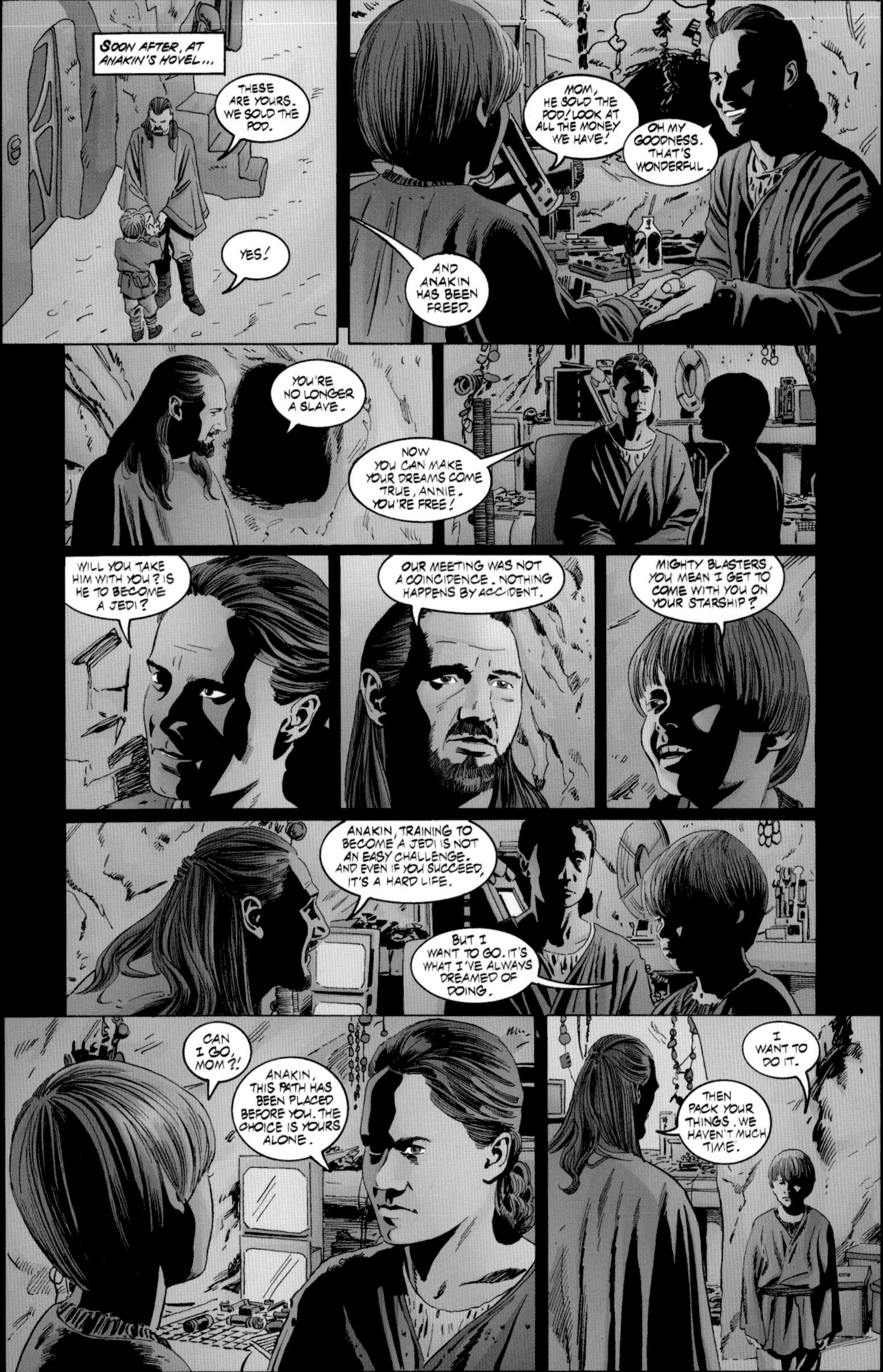
SOON AFTER, AT ANAKIN'S HOVEL...
THESE ARE YOURS. WE SOLD THE POD.
YES!
MOM, HE SOLD THE POD! LOOK AT ALL THE MONEY WE HAVE!
OH MY GOODNESS. THAT'S WONDERFUL.
AND ANAKIN HAS BEEN FREED.
YOU'RE NO LONGER A SLAVE.
NOW YOU CAN MAKE YOUR DREAMS COME TRUE, ANNIE. YOU'RE FREE!
WILL YOU TAKE HIM WITH YOU? IS HE TO BECOME A JEDI?
OUR MEETING WAS NOT A COINCIDENCE. NOTHING HAPPENS BY ACCIDENT.
MIGHTY BLASTERS, YOU MEAN I GET TO COME WITH YOU ON YOUR STARSHIP?
ANAKIN, TRAINING TO BECOME A JEDI IS NOT AN EASY CHALLENGE. AND EVEN IF YOU SUCCEED, IT'S A HARD LIFE.
BUT I WANT TO GO. IT'S WHAT I'VE ALWAYS DREAMED OF DOING.
CAN I GO, MOM?!
ANAKIN, THIS PATH HAS BEEN PLACED BEFORE YOU. THE CHOICE IS YOURS ALONE.
I WANT TO DO IT.
THEN PACK YOUR THINGS. WE HAVEN'T MUCH TIME.

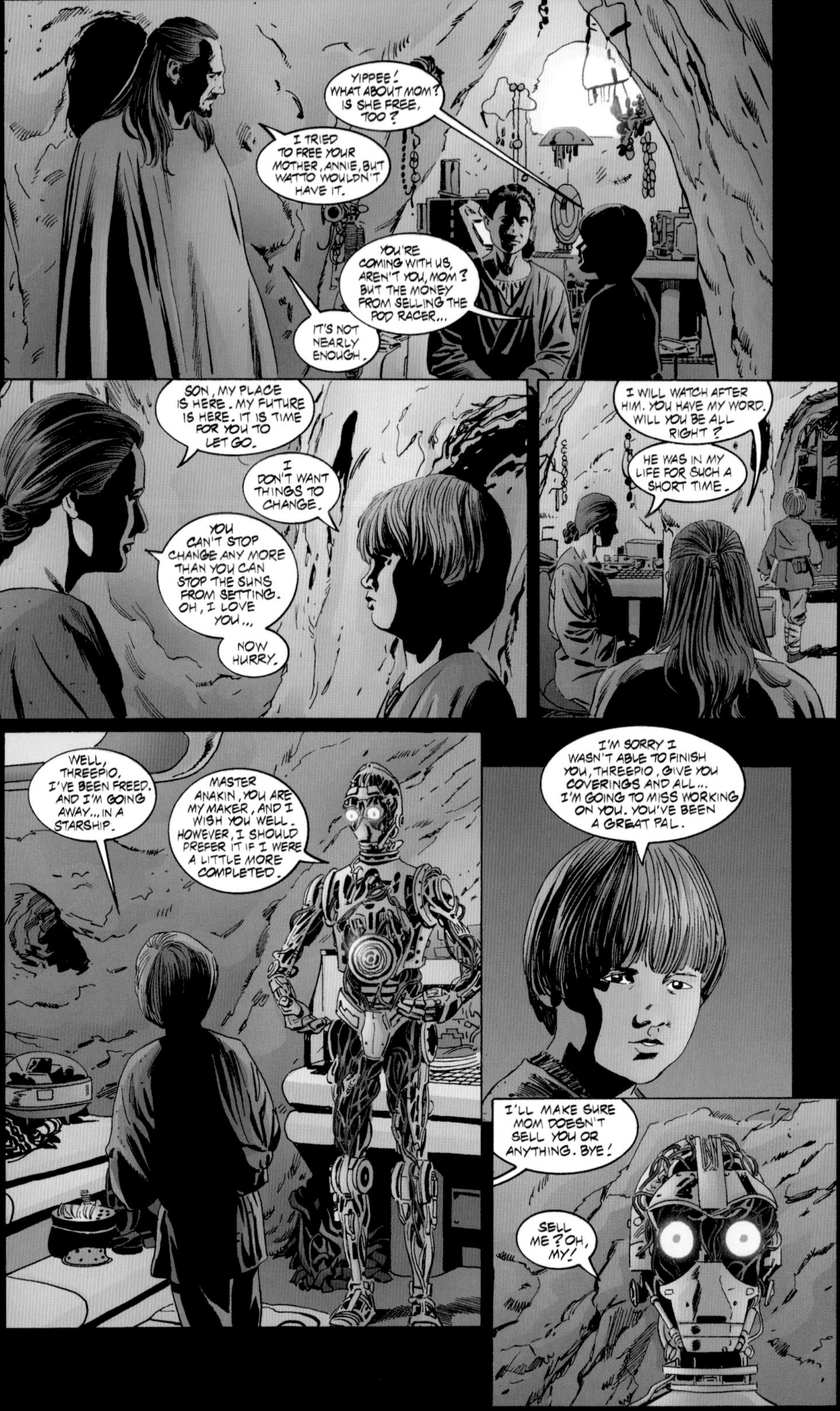
YIPPEE! WHAT ABOUT MOM? IS SHE FREE, TOO?
I TRIED TO FREE YOUR MOTHER, ANNIE, BUT WATTO WOULDN'T HAVE IT.
YOU'RE COMING WITH US, AREN'T YOU, MOM? BUT THE MONEY FROM SELLING THE POD RACER...
IT'S NOT NEARLY ENOUGH.
SON, MY PLACE IS HERE. MY FUTURE IS HERE. IT IS TIME FOR YOU TO LET GO.
I DON'T WANT THINGS TO CHANGE.
YOU CAN'T STOP CHANGE ANY MORE THAN YOU CAN STOP THE SUNS FROM SETTING. OH, I LOVE YOU...
NOW HURRY.
I WILL WATCH AFTER HIM. YOU HAVE MY WORD. WILL YOU BE ALL RIGHT?
HE WAS IN MY LIFE FOR SUCH A SHORT TIME.
WELL, THREEPIO, I'VE BEEN FREED. AND I'M GOING AWAY... IN A STARSHIP.
MASTER ANAKIN, YOU ARE MY MAKER, AND I WISH YOU WELL. HOWEVER, I SHOULD PREFER IT IF I WERE A LITTLE MORE COMPLETED.
I'M SORRY I WASN'T ABLE TO FINISH YOU, THREEPIO, GIVE YOU COVERINGS AND ALL... I'M GOING TO MISS WORKING ON YOU. YOU'VE BEEN A GREAT PAL.
I'LL MAKE SURE MOM DOESN'T SELL YOU OR ANYTHING. BYE!
SELL ME? OH, MY!

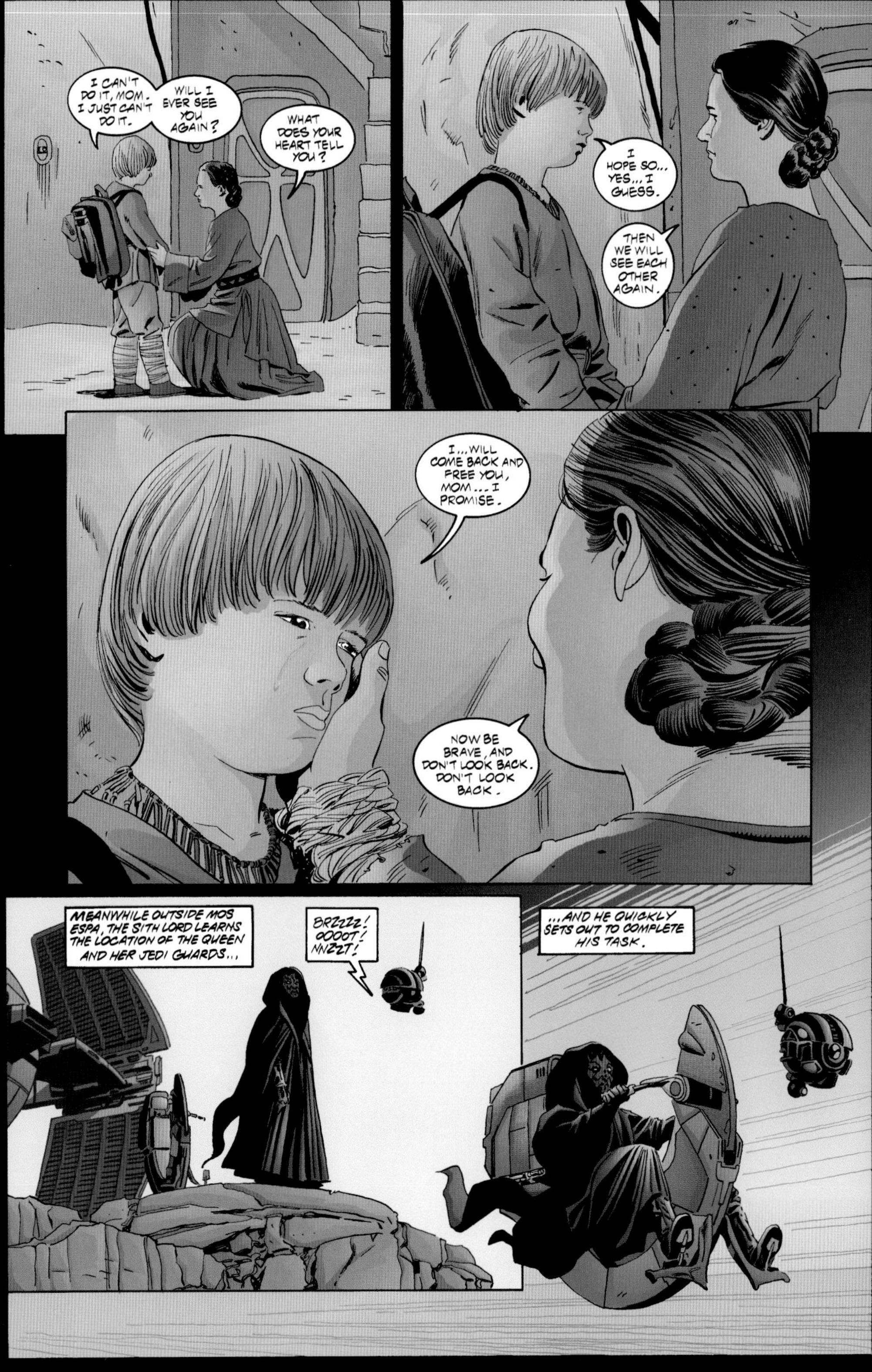
I CAN'T DO IT, MOM. I JUST CAN'T DO IT.
WILL I EVER SEE YOU AGAIN?
WHAT DOES YOUR HEART TELL YOU?
I HOPE SO... YES... I GUESS.
THEN WE WILL SEE EACH OTHER AGAIN.
I...WILL COME BACK AND FREE YOU, MOM... I PROMISE.
NOW BE BRAVE, AND DON'T LOOK BACK. DON'T LOOK BACK.
MEANWHILE OUTSIDE MOS ESPA, THE SITH LORD LEARNS THE LOCATION OF THE QUEEN AND HER JEDI GUARDS...
BRZZZZ! OOOOT! NNZZT!
...AND HE QUICKLY SETS OUT TO COMPLETE HIS TASK.

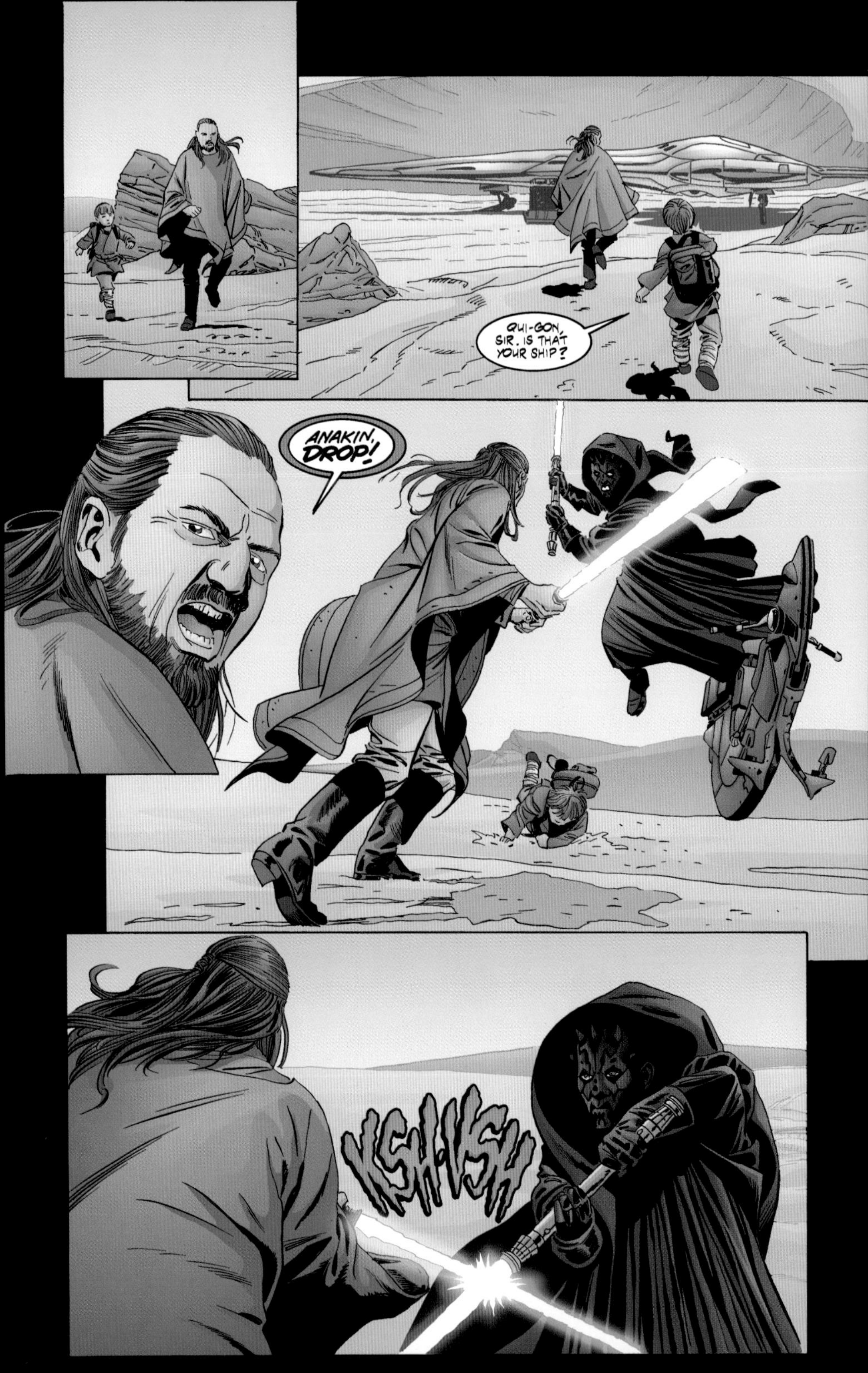
QUI-GON, SIR. IS THAT YOUR SHIP?
ANAKIN, DROP!
KSH-VSH

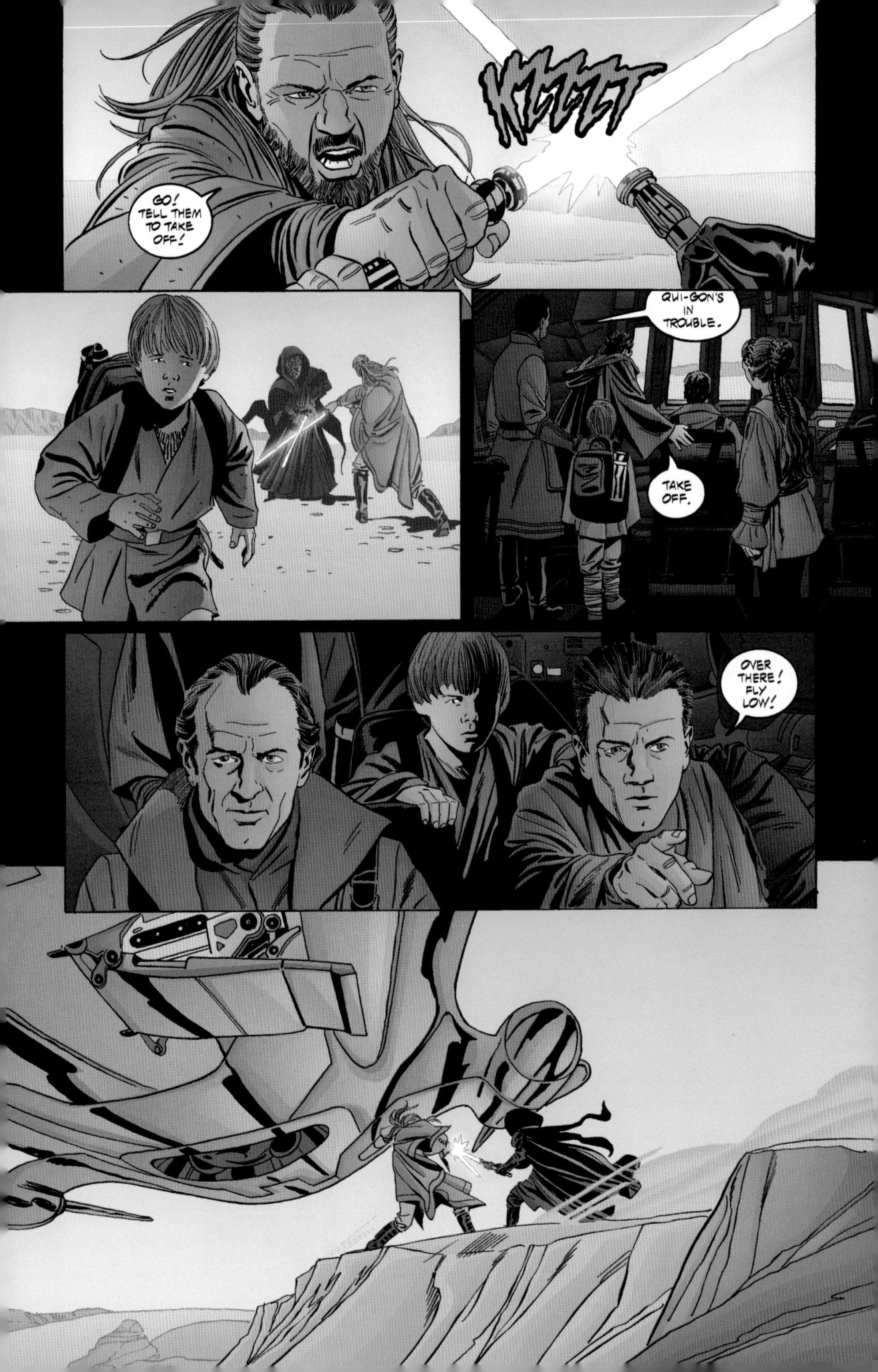
KZZZT
GO! TELL THEM TO TAKE OFF!
QUI-GON'S IN TROUBLE.
TAKE OFF.
OVER THERE! FLY LOW!

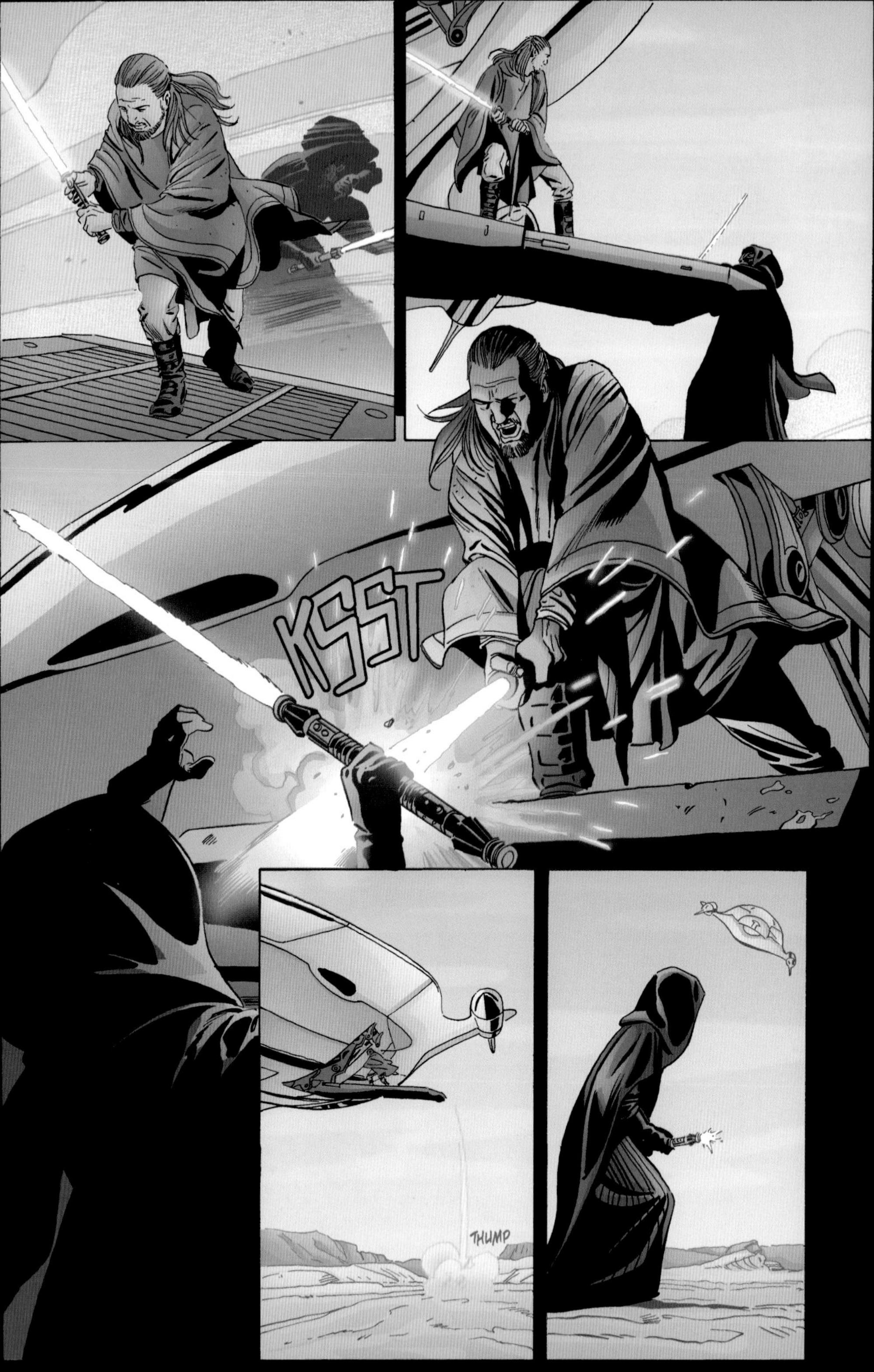
KSST
THUMP

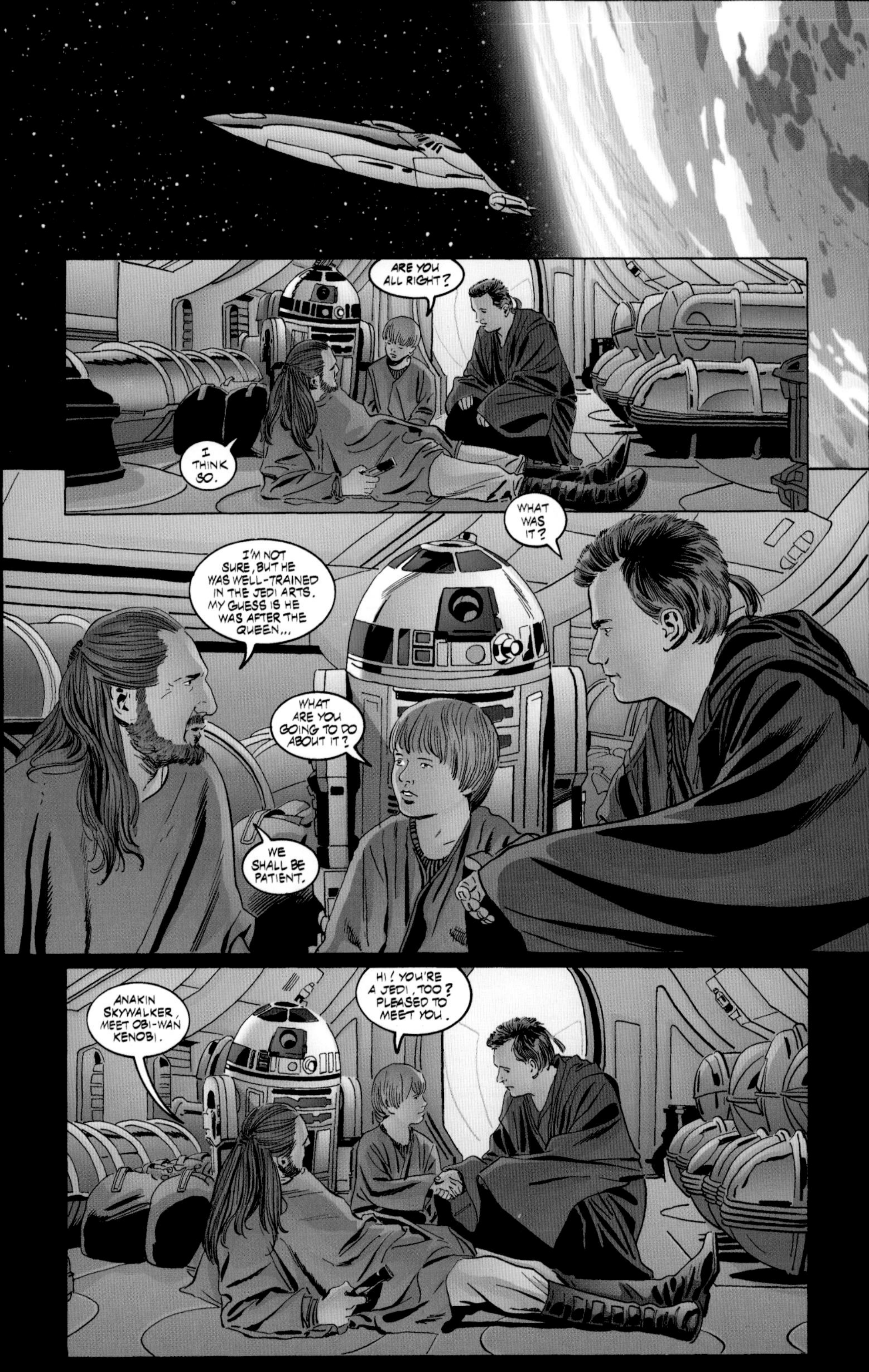
ARE YOU ALL RIGHT?
I THINK SO.
WHAT WAS IT?
I'M NOT SURE, BUT HE WAS WELL-TRAINED IN THE JEDI ARTS. MY GUESS IS HE WAS AFTER THE QUEEN...
WHAT ARE YOU GOING TO DO ABOUT IT?
WE SHALL BE PATIENT.
ANAKIN SKYWALKER, MEET OBI-WAN KENOBI.
HI! YOU'RE A JEDI, TOO? PLEASED TO MEET YOU.

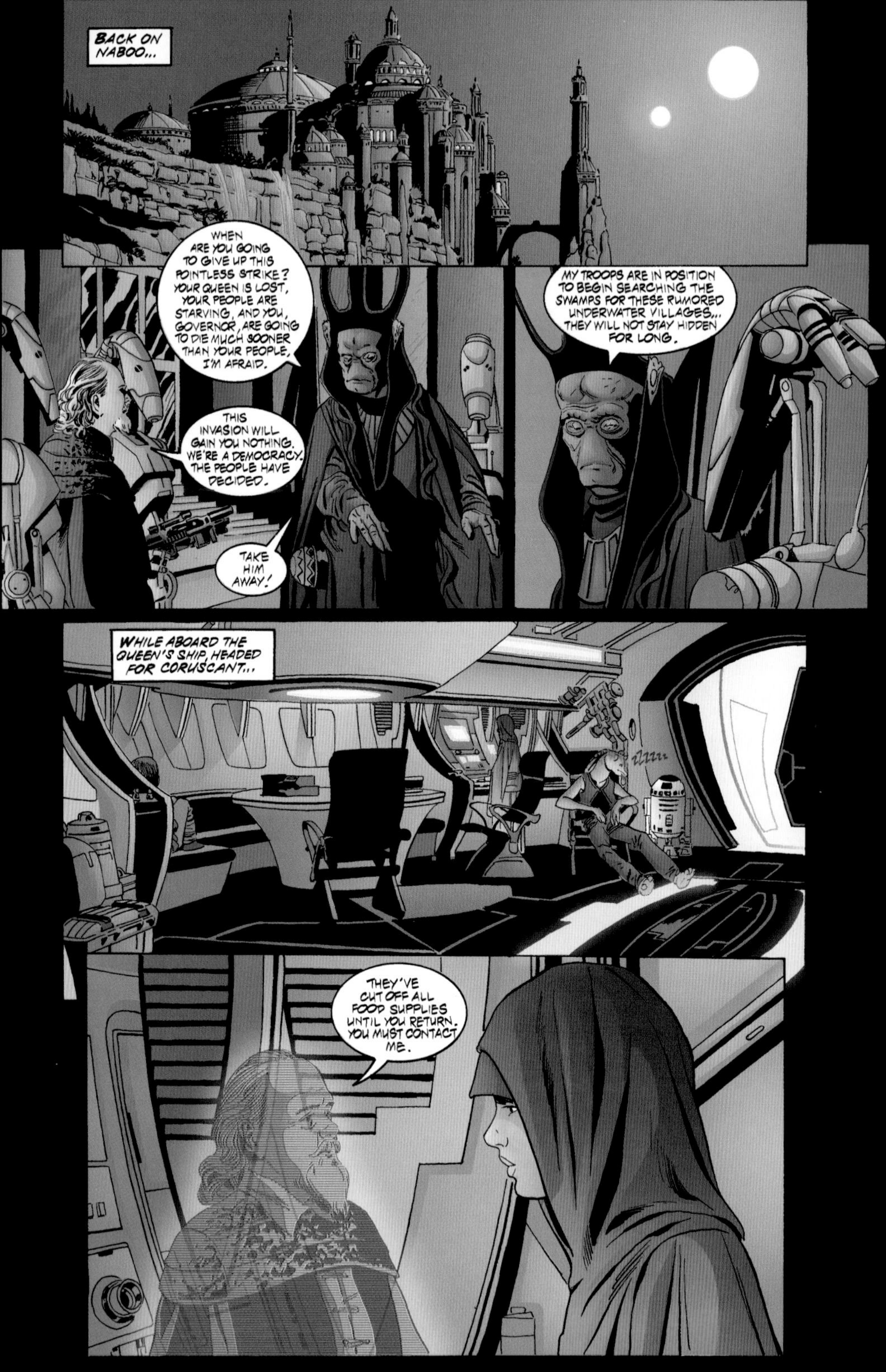
BACK ON NABOO...
WHEN ARE YOU GOING TO GIVE UP THIS POINTLESS STRIKE? YOUR QUEEN IS LOST, YOUR PEOPLE ARE STARVING, AND YOU, GOVERNOR, ARE GOING TO DIE MUCH SOONER THAN YOUR PEOPLE, I'M AFRAID.
THIS INVASION WILL GAIN YOU NOTHING. WE'RE A DEMOCRACY. THE PEOPLE HAVE DECIDED.
TAKE HIM AWAY!
MY TROOPS ARE IN POSITION TO BEGIN SEARCHING THE SWAMPS FOR THESE RUMORED UNDERWATER VILLAGES... THEY WILL NOT STAY HIDDEN FOR LONG.
WHILE ABOARD THE QUEEN'S SHIP, HEADED FOR CORUSCANT...
ZZZZZ
THEY'VE CUT OFF ALL FOOD SUPPLIES UNTIL YOU RETURN. YOU MUST CONTACT ME.

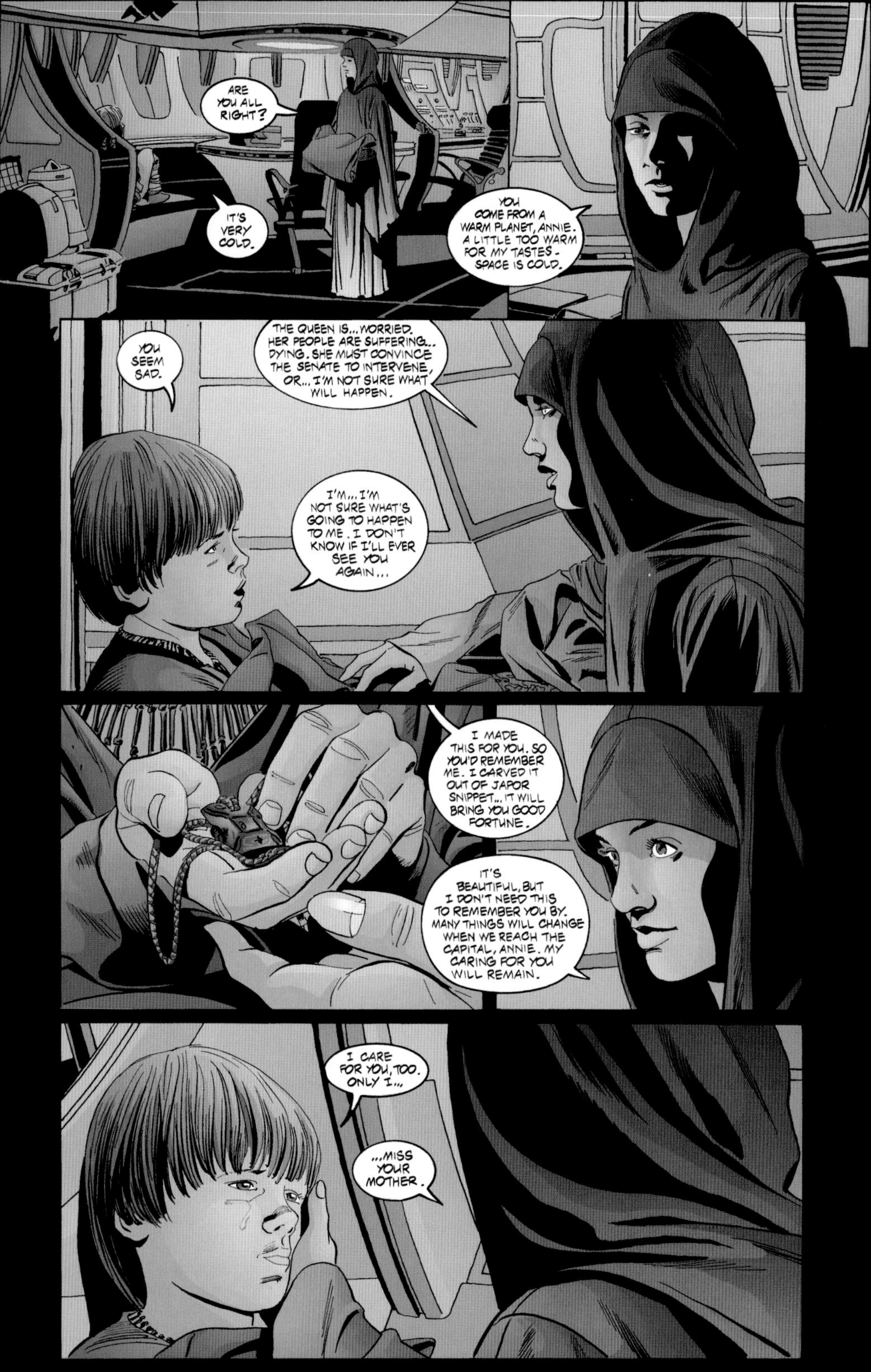
ARE YOU ALL RIGHT?
IT'S VERY COLD.
YOU COME FROM A WARM PLANET, ANNIE. A LITTLE TOO WARM FOR MY TASTES. SPACE IS COLD.
YOU SEEM SAD.
THE QUEEN IS... WORRIED. HER PEOPLE ARE SUFFERING... DYING. SHE MUST CONVINCE THE SENATE TO INTERVENE, OR... I'M NOT SURE WHAT WILL HAPPEN.
I'M... I'M NOT SURE WHAT'S GOING TO HAPPEN TO ME. I DON'T KNOW IF I'LL EVER SEE YOU AGAIN...
I MADE THIS FOR YOU. SO YOU'D REMEMBER ME. I CARVED IT OUT OF JAPOR SNIPPET... IT WILL BRING YOU GOOD FORTUNE.
IT'S BEAUTIFUL, BUT I DON'T NEED THIS TO REMEMBER YOU BY. MANY THINGS WILL CHANGE WHEN WE REACH THE CAPITAL, ANNIE. MY CARING FOR YOU WILL REMAIN.
I CARE FOR YOU, TOO. ONLY I...
...MISS YOUR MOTHER.

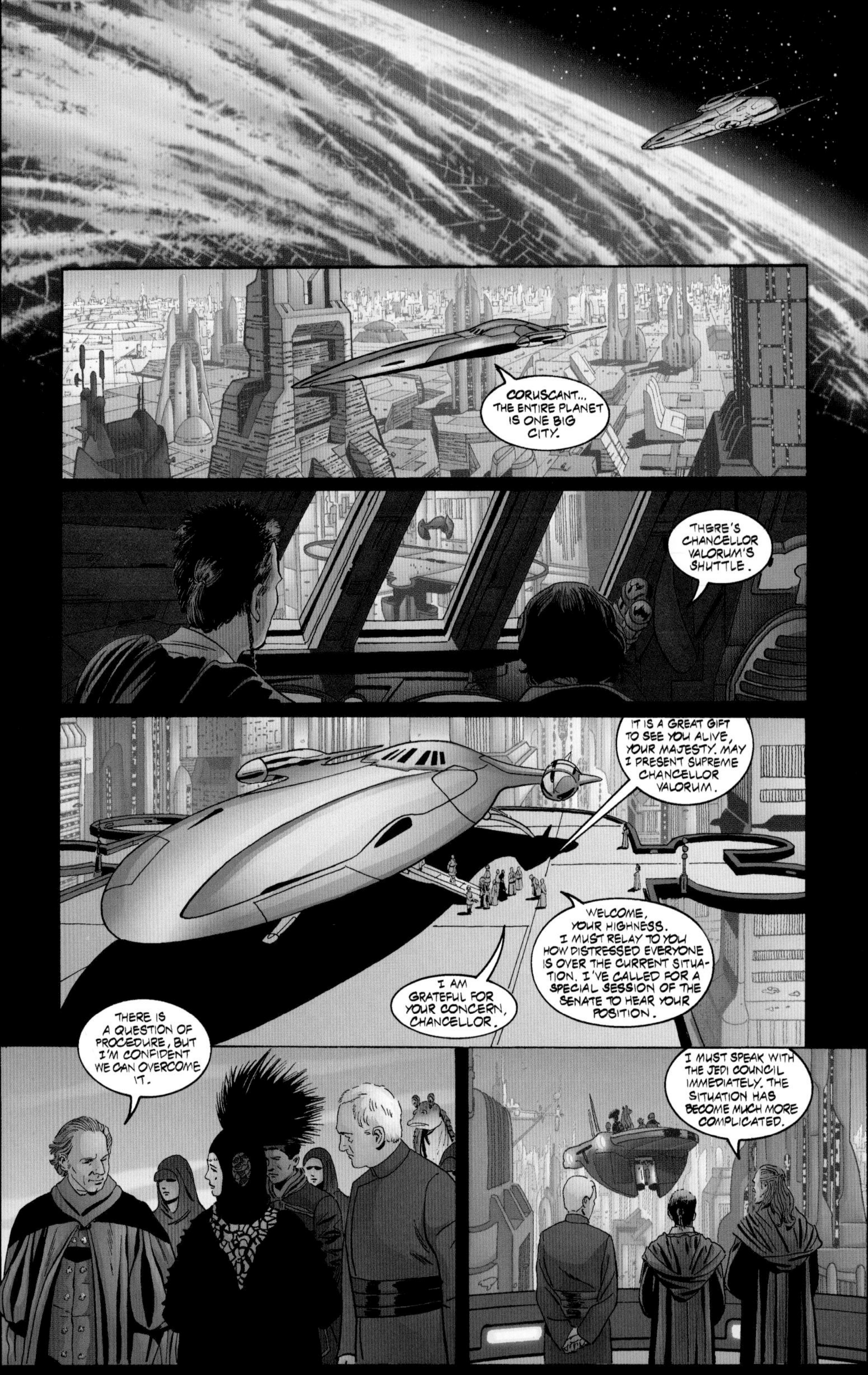
CORUSCANT... THE ENTIRE PLANET IS ONE BIG CITY.
THERE'S CHANCELLOR VALORUM'S SHUTTLE.
IT IS A GREAT GIFT TO SEE YOU ALIVE, YOUR MAJESTY. MAY I PRESENT SUPREME CHANCELLOR VALORUM.
WELCOME, YOUR HIGHNESS. I MUST RELAY TO YOU HOW DISTRESSED EVERYONE IS OVER THE CURRENT SITUA-TION. I'VE CALLED FOR A SPECIAL SESSION OF THE SENATE TO HEAR YOUR POSITION.
I AM GRATEFUL FOR YOUR CONCERN, CHANCELLOR.
THERE IS A QUESTION OF PROCEDURE, BUT I'M CONFIDENT WE CAN OVERCOME IT.
I MUST SPEAK WITH THE JEDI COUNCIL IMMEDIATELY. THE SITUATION HAS BECOME MUCH MORE COMPLICATED.

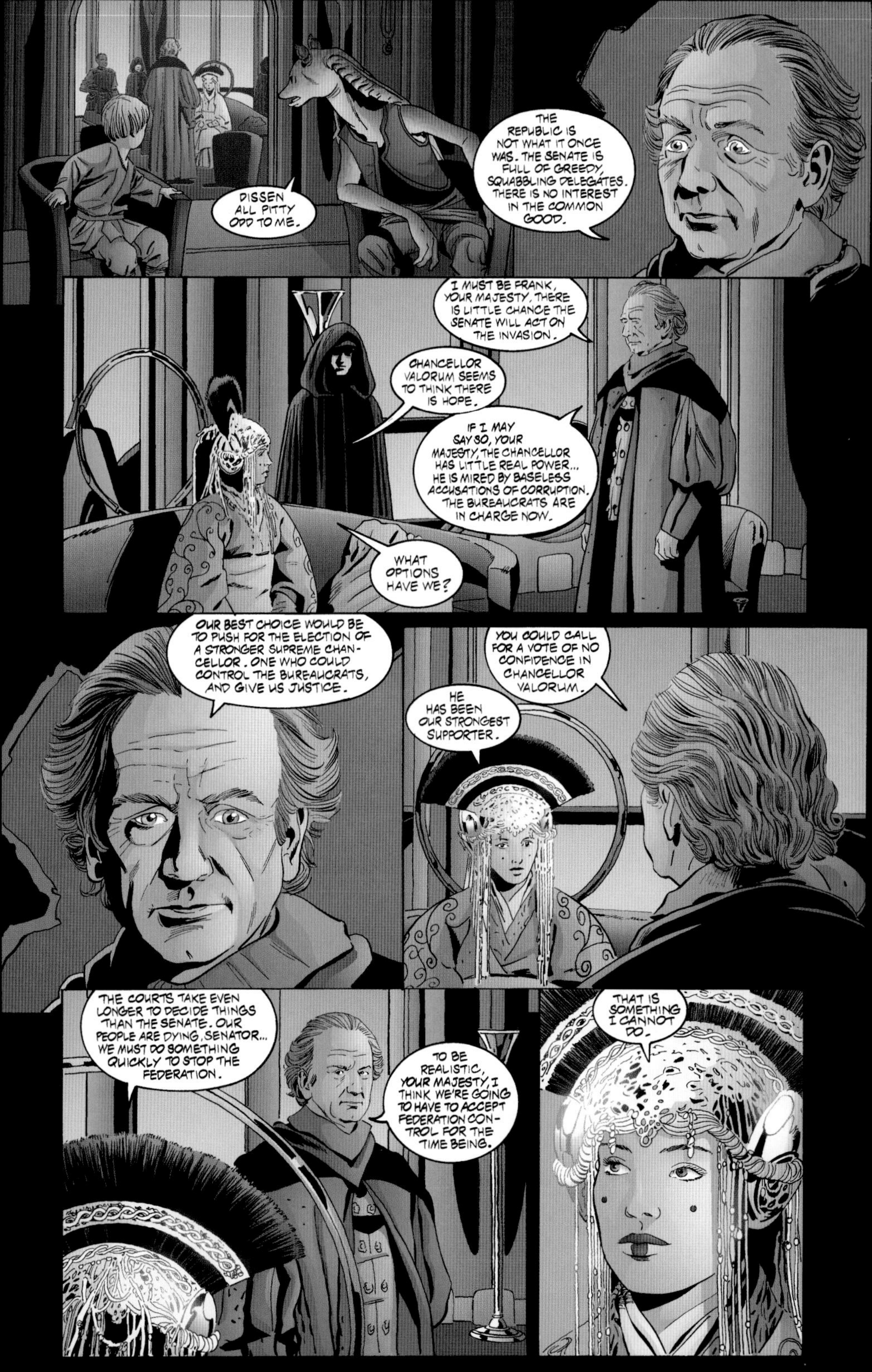
DISSEN ALL PITTY ODD TO ME.
THE REPUBLIC IS NOT WHAT IT ONCE WAS. THE SENATE IS FULL OF GREEDY, SQUABBLING DELEGATES. THERE IS NO INTEREST IN THE COMMON GOOD.
I MUST BE FRANK, YOUR MAJESTY, THERE IS LITTLE CHANCE THE SENATE WILL ACT ON THE INVASION.
CHANCELLOR VALORUM SEEMS TO THINK THERE IS HOPE.
IF I MAY SAY SO, YOUR MAJESTY, THE CHANCELLOR HAS LITTLE REAL POWER... HE IS MIRED BY BASELESS ACCUSATIONS OF CORRUPTION. THE BUREAUCRATS ARE IN CHARGE NOW.
WHAT OPTIONS HAVE WE?
OUR BEST CHOICE WOULD BE TO PUSH FOR THE ELECTION OF A STRONGER SUPREME CHAN-CELLOR. ONE WHO COULD CONTROL THE BUREAUCRATS, AND GIVE US JUSTICE.
YOU COULD CALL FOR A VOTE OF NO CONFIDENCE IN CHANCELLOR VALORUM.
HE HAS BEEN OUR STRONGEST SUPPORTER.
THE COURTS TAKE EVEN LONGER TO DECIDE THINGS THAN THE SENATE. OUR PEOPLE ARE DYING, SENATOR... WE MUST DO SOMETHING QUICKLY TO STOP THE FEDERATION.
TO BE REALISTIC, YOUR MAJESTY, I THINK WE'RE GOING TO HAVE TO ACCEPT FEDERATION CON-TROL FOR THE TIME BEING.
THAT IS SOMETHING I CANNOT DO.

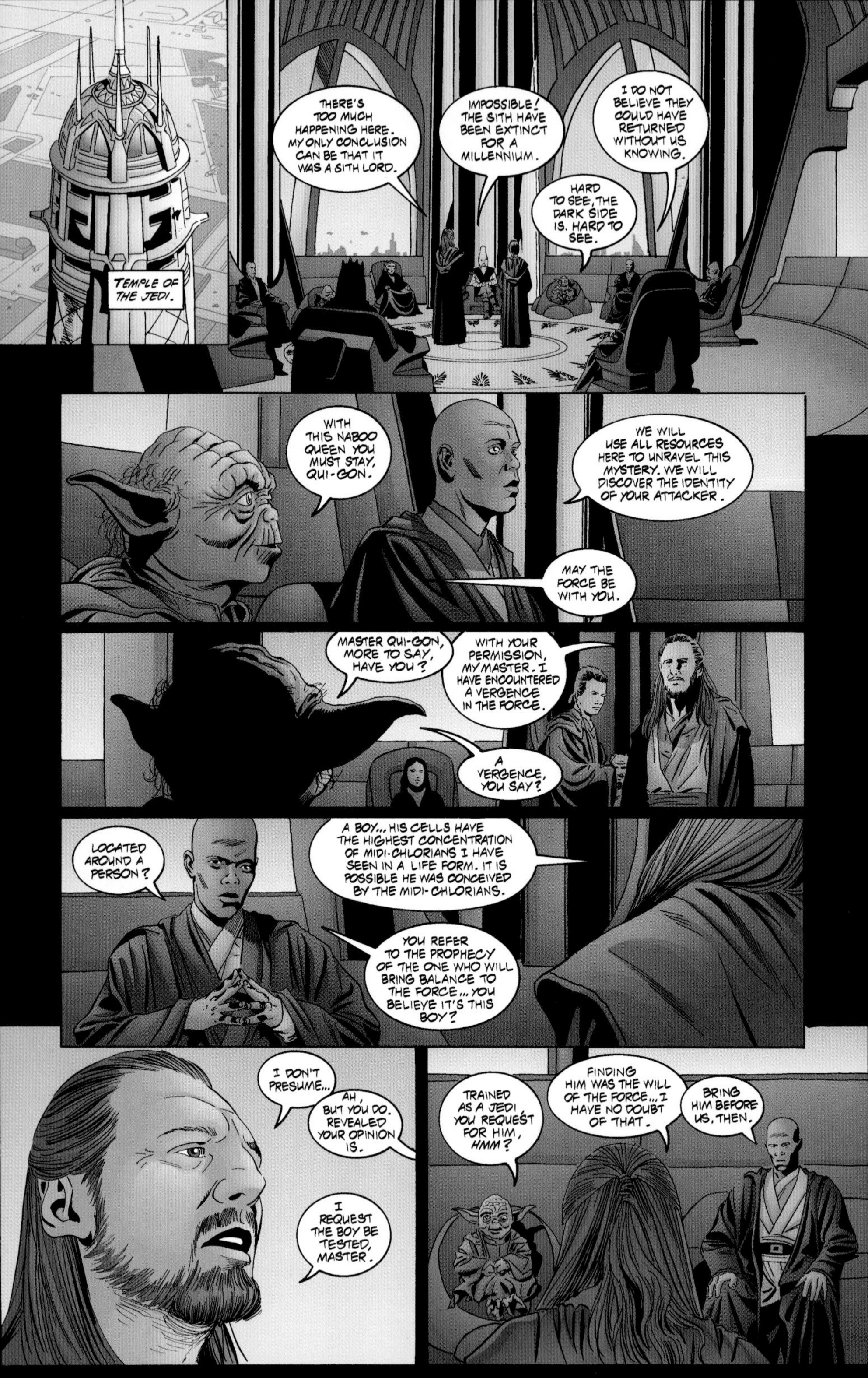
TEMPLE OF THE JEDI.
THERE'S TOO MUCH HAPPENING HERE. MY ONLY CONCLUSION CAN BE THAT IT WAS A SITH LORD.
IMPOSSIBLE! THE SITH HAVE BEEN EXTINCT FOR A MILLENNIUM.
I DO NOT BELIEVE THEY COULD HAVE RETURNED WITHOUT US KNOWING.
HARD TO SEE, THE DARK SIDE IS. HARD TO SEE.
WITH THIS NABOO QUEEN YOU MUST STAY, QUI-GON.
WE WILL USE ALL RESOURCES HERE TO UNRAVEL THIS MYSTERY. WE WILL DISCOVER THE IDENTITY OF YOUR ATTACKER.
MAY THE FORCE BE WITH YOU.
MASTER QUI-GON, MORE TO SAY, HAVE YOU?
WITH YOUR PERMISSION, MY MASTER. I HAVE ENCOUNTERED A VERGENCE IN THE FORCE.
A VERGENCE, YOU SAY?
LOCATED AROUND A PERSON?
A BOY... HIS CELLS HAVE THE HIGHEST CONCENTRATION OF MIDI-CHLORIANS I HAVE SEEN IN A LIFE FORM. IT IS POSSIBLE HE WAS CONCEIVED BY THE MIDI-CHLORIANS.
YOU REFER TO THE PROPHECY OF THE ONE WHO WILL BRING BALANCE TO THE FORCE... YOU BELIEVE IT'S THIS BOY?
I DON'T PRESUME...
AH, BUT YOU DO. REVEALED YOUR OPINION IS.
I REQUEST THE BOY BE TESTED, MASTER.
TRAINED AS A JEDI YOU REQUEST FOR HIM, HMM?
FINDING HIM WAS THE WILL OF THE FORCE... I HAVE NO DOUBT OF THAT.
BRING HIM BEFORE US, THEN.

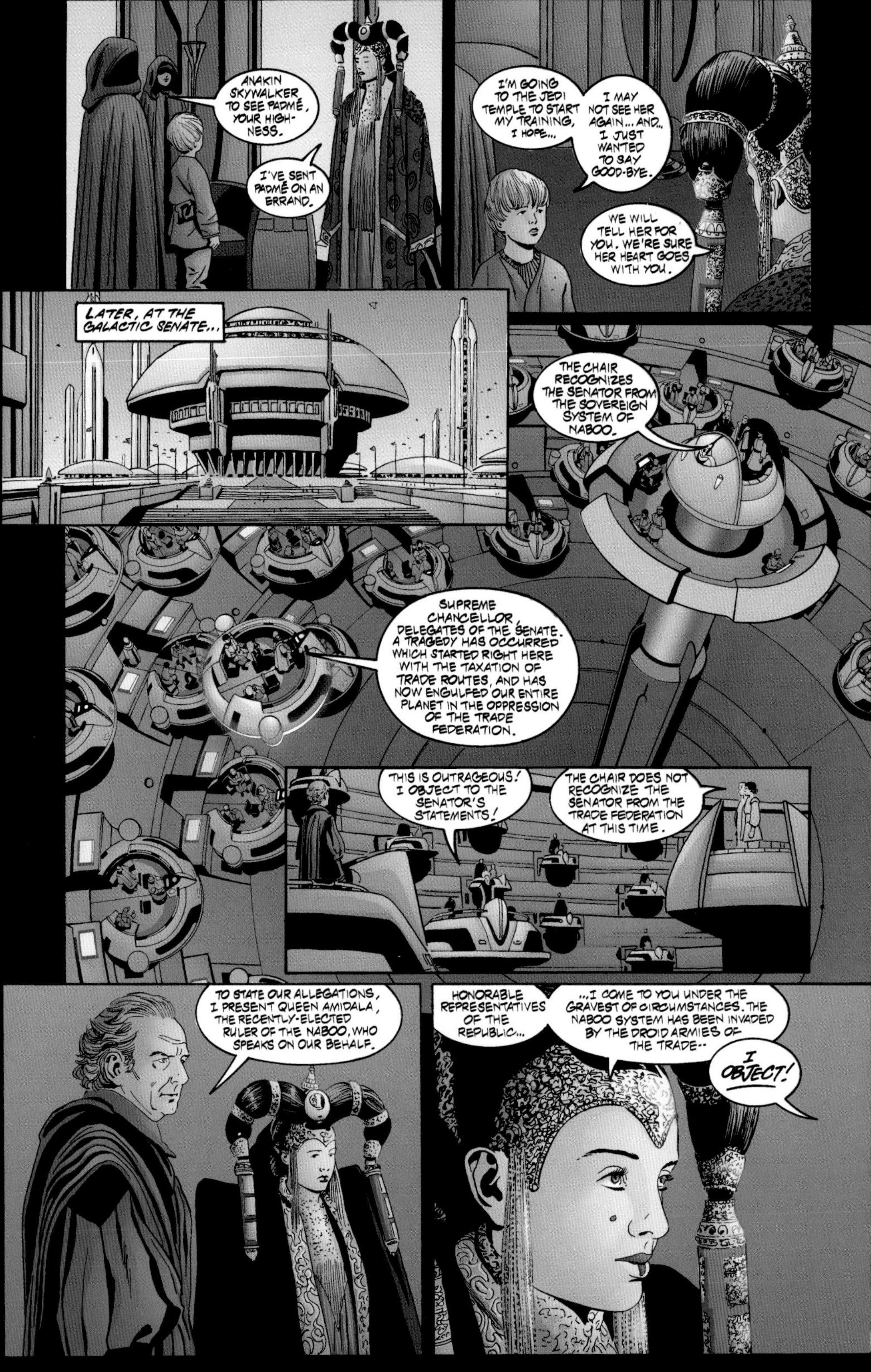
ANAKIN SKYWALKER TO SEE PADMÉ, YOUR HIGHNESS.
I'VE SENT PADMÉ ON AN ERRAND.
I'M GOING TO THE JEDI TEMPLE TO START MY TRAINING, I HOPE...
I MAY NOT SEE HER AGAIN... AND... I JUST WANTED TO SAY GOOD-BYE.
WE WILL TELL HER FOR YOU. WE'RE SURE HER HEART GOES WITH YOU.
LATER, AT THE GALACTIC SENATE...
THE CHAIR RECOGNIZES THE SENATOR FROM THE SOVEREIGN SYSTEM OF NABOO.
SUPREME CHANCELLOR, DELEGATES OF THE SENATE. A TRAGEDY HAS OCCURRED WHICH STARTED RIGHT HERE WITH THE TAXATION OF TRADE ROUTES, AND HAS NOW ENGULFED OUR ENTIRE PLANET IN THE OPPRESSION OF THE TRADE FEDERATION.
THIS IS OUTRAGEOUS! I OBJECT TO THE SENATOR'S STATEMENTS!
THE CHAIR DOES NOT RECOGNIZE THE SENATOR FROM THE TRADE FEDERATION AT THIS TIME.
TO STATE OUR ALLEGATIONS, I PRESENT QUEEN AMIDALA, THE RECENTLY-ELECTED RULER OF THE NABOO, WHO SPEAKS ON OUR BEHALF.
HONORABLE REPRESENTATIVES OF THE REPUBLIC...
...I COME TO YOU UNDER THE GRAVEST OF CIRCUMSTANCES. THE NABOO SYSTEM HAS BEEN INVADED BY THE DROID ARMIES OF THE TRADE--
I OBJECT!

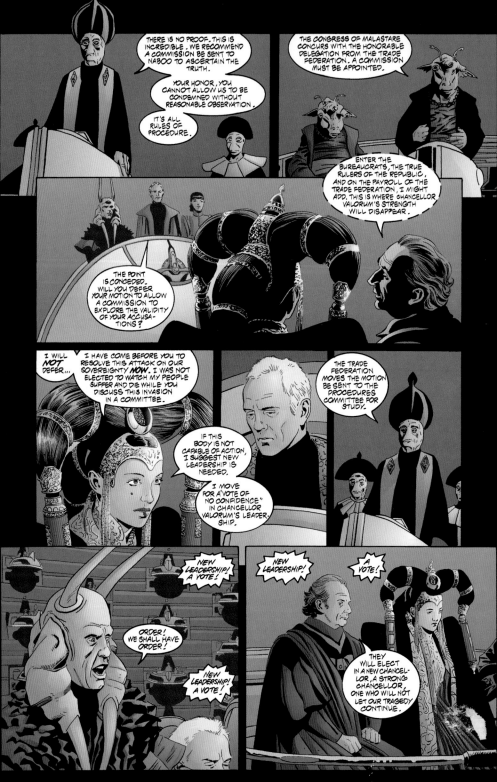

THERE IS NO PROOF. THIS IS INCREDIBLE. WE RECOMMEND A COMMISSION BE SENT TO NABOO TO ASCERTAIN THE TRUTH.

YOUR HONOR, YOU CANNOT ALLOW US TO BE CONDEMNED WITHOUT REASONABLE OBSERVATION.

IT'S ALL RULES OF PROCEDURE.

THE CONGRESS OF MALASTARE CONCURS WITH THE HONORABLE DELEGATION FROM THE TRADE FEDERATION. A COMMISSION MUST BE APPOINTED.

ENTER THE BUREAUCRATS, THE TRUE RULERS OF THE REPUBLIC, AND ON THE PAYROLL OF THE TRADE FEDERATION, I MIGHT ADD. THIS IS WHERE CHANCELLOR VALORUM'S STRENGTH WILL DISAPPEAR.

THE POINT IS CONCEDED. WILL YOU DEFER YOUR MOTION TO ALLOW A COMMISSION TO EXPLORE THE VALIDITY OF YOUR ACCUSA- TIONS?

I WILL *NOT* DEFER...

I HAVE COME BEFORE YOU TO RESOLVE THIS ATTACK ON OUR SOVEREIGNTY *NOW*. I WAS NOT ELECTED TO WATCH MY PEOPLE SUFFER AND DIE WHILE YOU DISCUSS THIS INVASION IN A COMMITTEE.

IF THIS BODY IS NOT CAPABLE OF ACTION, I SUGGEST NEW LEADERSHIP IS NEEDED.

I MOVE FOR A "VOTE OF NO CONFIDENCE" IN CHANCELLOR VALORUM'S LEADER- SHIP.

THE TRADE FEDERATION MOVES THE MOTION BE SENT TO THE PROCEDURES COMMITTEE FOR STUDY.

NEW LEADERSHIP! A VOTE!

ORDER! WE SHALL HAVE ORDER!

NEW LEADERSHIP! A VOTE!

NEW LEADERSHIP!

A VOTE!

THEY WILL ELECT IN A NEW CHANCEL- LOR, A STRONG CHANCELLOR, ONE WHO WILL NOT LET OUR TRAGEDY CONTINUE.

72

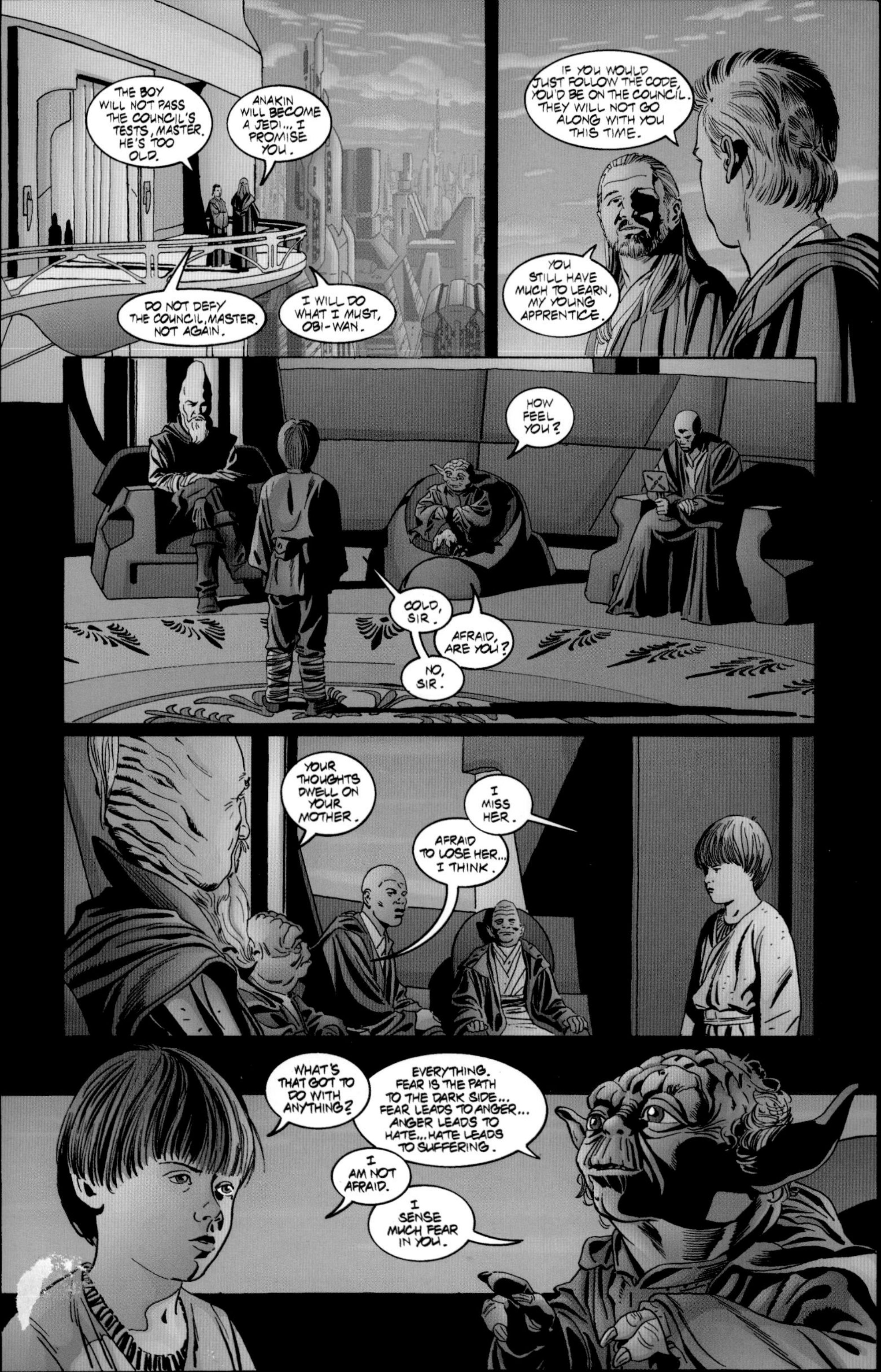
THE BOY WILL NOT PASS THE COUNCIL'S TESTS, MASTER. HE'S TOO OLD.
ANAKIN WILL BECOME A JEDI... I PROMISE YOU.
DO NOT DEFY THE COUNCIL, MASTER. NOT AGAIN.
I WILL DO WHAT I MUST, OBI-WAN.
IF YOU WOULD JUST FOLLOW THE CODE, YOU'D BE ON THE COUNCIL. THEY WILL NOT GO ALONG WITH YOU THIS TIME.
YOU STILL HAVE MUCH TO LEARN, MY YOUNG APPRENTICE.
HOW FEEL YOU?
COLD, SIR.
AFRAID, ARE YOU?
NO, SIR.
YOUR THOUGHTS DWELL ON YOUR MOTHER.
I MISS HER.
AFRAID TO LOSE HER... I THINK.
WHAT'S THAT GOT TO DO WITH ANYTHING?
EVERYTHING. FEAR IS THE PATH TO THE DARK SIDE... FEAR LEADS TO ANGER... ANGER LEADS TO HATE... HATE LEADS TO SUFFERING.
I AM NOT AFRAID.
I SENSE MUCH FEAR IN YOU.

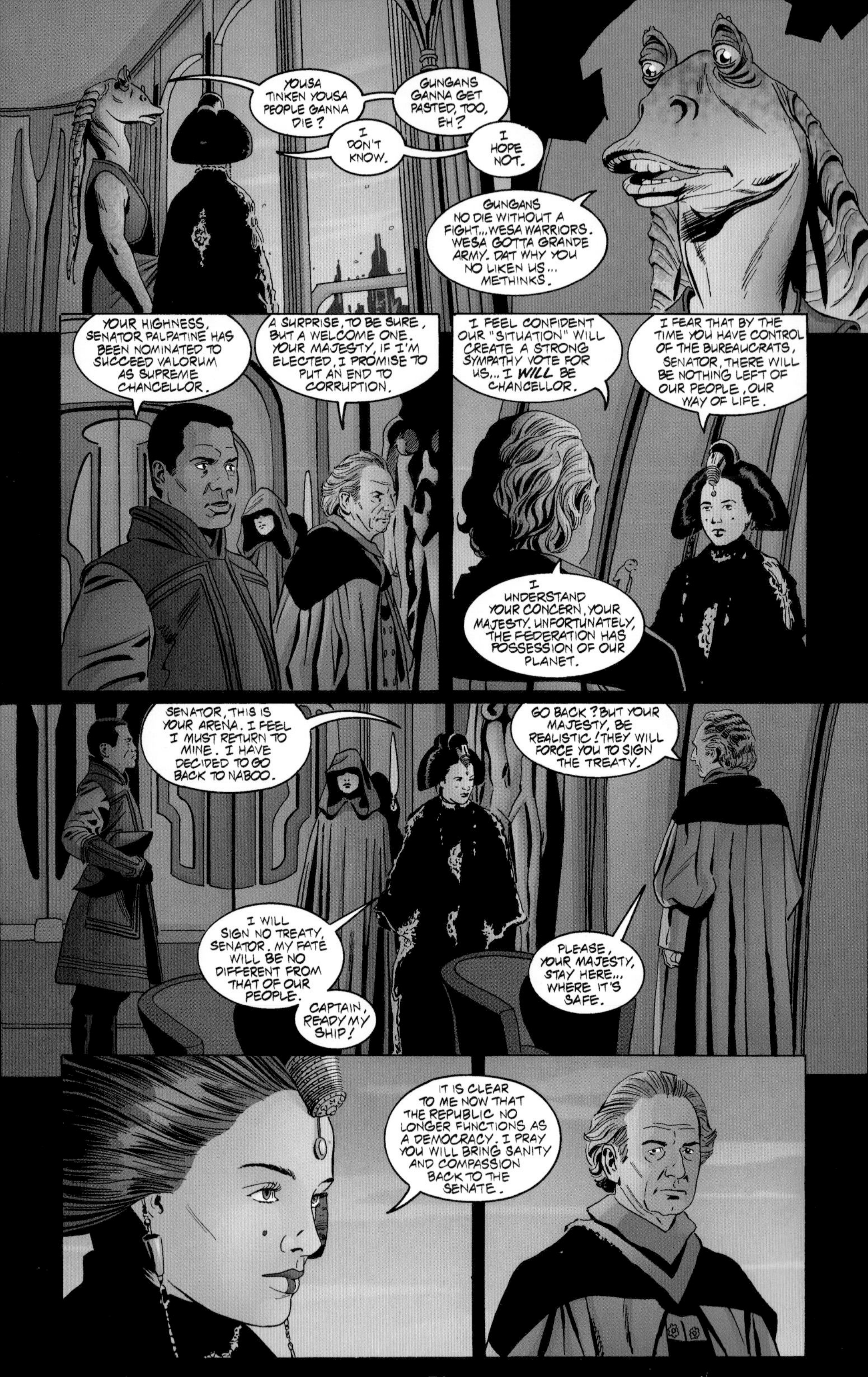
YOUSA TINKEN YOUSA PEOPLE GANNA DIE?
GUNGANS GANNA GET PASTED, TOO, EH?
I DON'T KNOW.
I HOPE NOT.
GUNGANS NO DIE WITHOUT A FIGHT... WESA WARRIORS. WESA GOTTA GRANDE ARMY. DAT WHY YOU NO LIKEN US... METHINKS.
YOUR HIGHNESS, SENATOR PALPATINE HAS BEEN NOMINATED TO SUCCEED VALORUM AS SUPREME CHANCELLOR.
A SURPRISE, TO BE SURE, BUT A WELCOME ONE. YOUR MAJESTY, IF I'M ELECTED, I PROMISE TO PUT AN END TO CORRUPTION.
I FEEL CONFIDENT OUR "SITUATION" WILL CREATE A STRONG SYMPATHY VOTE FOR US... I **WILL** BE CHANCELLOR.
I FEAR THAT BY THE TIME YOU HAVE CONTROL OF THE BUREAUCRATS, SENATOR, THERE WILL BE NOTHING LEFT OF OUR PEOPLE, OUR WAY OF LIFE.
I UNDERSTAND YOUR CONCERN, YOUR MAJESTY. UNFORTUNATELY, THE FEDERATION HAS POSSESSION OF OUR PLANET.
SENATOR, THIS IS YOUR ARENA. I FEEL I MUST RETURN TO MINE. I HAVE DECIDED TO GO BACK TO NABOO.
GO BACK? BUT YOUR MAJESTY, BE REALISTIC! THEY WILL FORCE YOU TO SIGN THE TREATY.
I WILL SIGN NO TREATY, SENATOR. MY FATE WILL BE NO DIFFERENT FROM THAT OF OUR PEOPLE.
CAPTAIN, READY MY SHIP!
PLEASE, YOUR MAJESTY, STAY HERE... WHERE IT'S SAFE.
IT IS CLEAR TO ME NOW THAT THE REPUBLIC NO LONGER FUNCTIONS AS A DEMOCRACY. I PRAY YOU WILL BRING SANITY AND COMPASSION BACK TO THE SENATE.

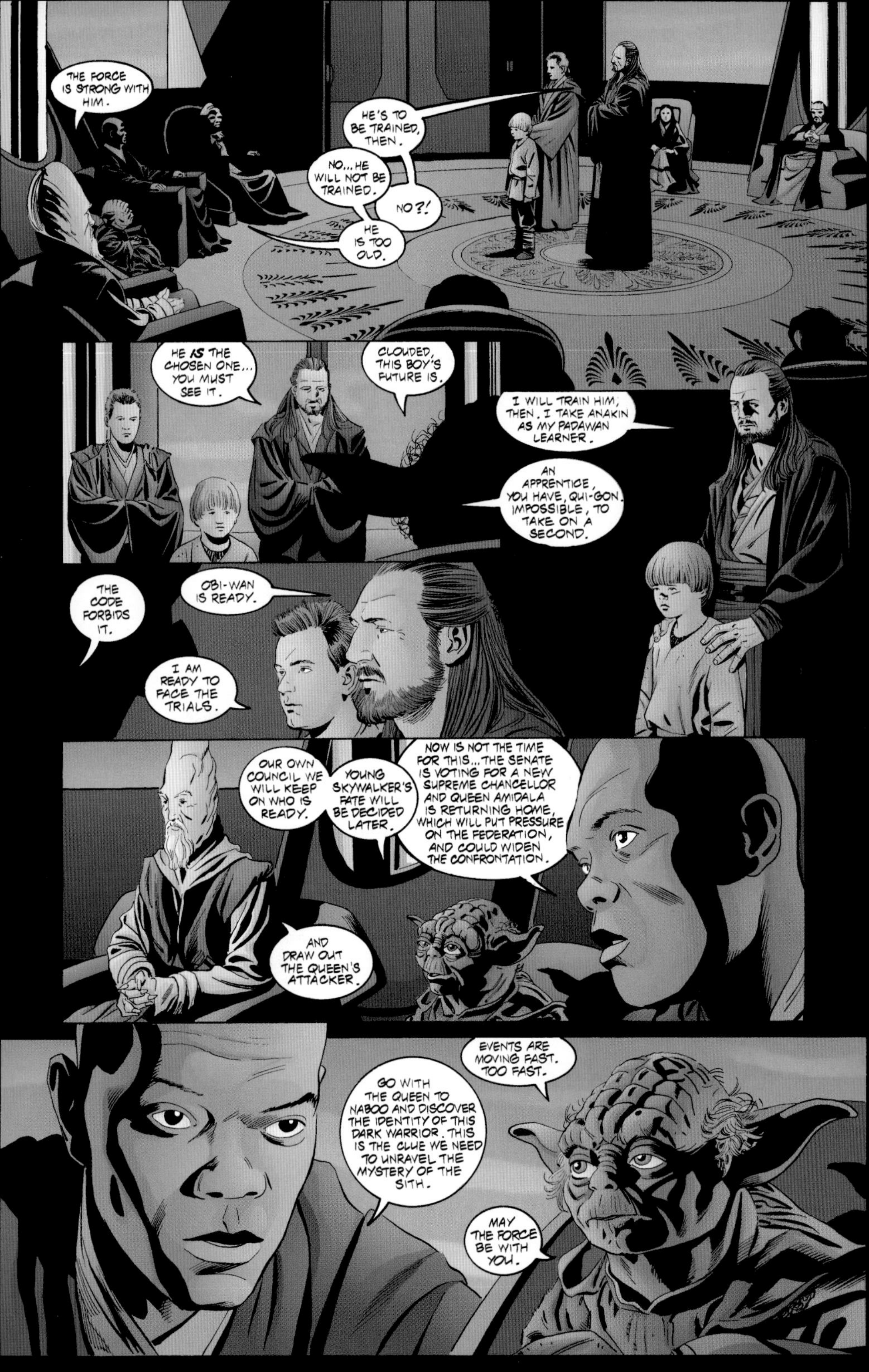
THE FORCE IS STRONG WITH HIM.
HE'S TO BE TRAINED, THEN.
NO... HE WILL NOT BE TRAINED.
NO?!
HE IS TOO OLD.
HE *IS* THE CHOSEN ONE... YOU MUST SEE IT.
CLOUDED, THIS BOY'S FUTURE IS.
I WILL TRAIN HIM, THEN. I TAKE ANAKIN AS MY PADAWAN LEARNER.
AN APPRENTICE, YOU HAVE, QUI-GON. IMPOSSIBLE, TO TAKE ON A SECOND.
THE CODE FORBIDS IT.
OBI-WAN IS READY.
I AM READY TO FACE THE TRIALS.
OUR OWN COUNCIL WE WILL KEEP ON WHO IS READY.
YOUNG SKYWALKER'S FATE WILL BE DECIDED LATER.
NOW IS NOT THE TIME FOR THIS... THE SENATE IS VOTING FOR A NEW SUPREME CHANCELLOR AND QUEEN AMIDALA IS RETURNING HOME, WHICH WILL PUT PRESSURE ON THE FEDERATION, AND COULD WIDEN THE CONFRONTATION.
AND DRAW OUT THE QUEEN'S ATTACKER.
EVENTS ARE MOVING FAST. TOO FAST.
GO WITH THE QUEEN TO NABOO AND DISCOVER THE IDENTITY OF THIS DARK WARRIOR. THIS IS THE CLUE WE NEED TO UNRAVEL THE MYSTERY OF THE SITH.
MAY THE FORCE BE WITH YOU.

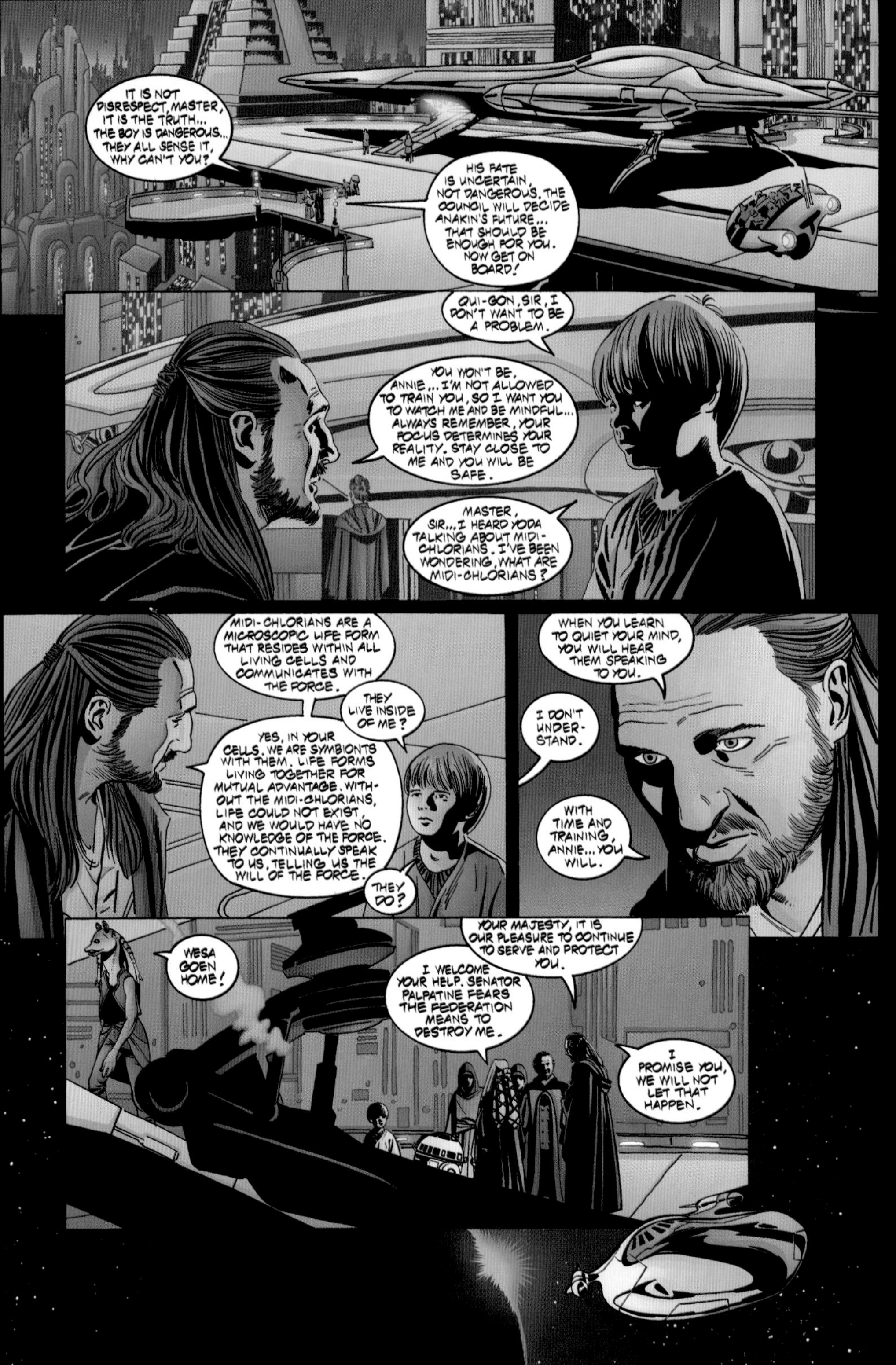
IT IS NOT DISRESPECT, MASTER, IT IS THE TRUTH... THE BOY IS DANGEROUS... THEY ALL SENSE IT, WHY CAN'T YOU?
HIS FATE IS UNCERTAIN, NOT DANGEROUS. THE COUNCIL WILL DECIDE ANAKIN'S FUTURE... THAT SHOULD BE ENOUGH FOR YOU. NOW GET ON BOARD!
QUI-GON, SIR, I DON'T WANT TO BE A PROBLEM.
YOU WON'T BE, ANNIE... I'M NOT ALLOWED TO TRAIN YOU, SO I WANT YOU TO WATCH ME AND BE MINDFUL... ALWAYS REMEMBER, YOUR FOCUS DETERMINES YOUR REALITY. STAY CLOSE TO ME AND YOU WILL BE SAFE.
MASTER, SIR... I HEARD YODA TALKING ABOUT MIDI-CHLORIANS. I'VE BEEN WONDERING, WHAT ARE MIDI-CHLORIANS?
MIDI-CHLORIANS ARE A MICROSCOPIC LIFE FORM THAT RESIDES WITHIN ALL LIVING CELLS AND COMMUNICATES WITH THE FORCE.
THEY LIVE INSIDE OF ME?
YES, IN YOUR CELLS. WE ARE SYMBIONTS WITH THEM. LIFE FORMS LIVING TOGETHER FOR MUTUAL ADVANTAGE. WITHOUT THE MIDI-CHLORIANS, LIFE COULD NOT EXIST, AND WE WOULD HAVE NO KNOWLEDGE OF THE FORCE. THEY CONTINUALLY SPEAK TO US, TELLING US THE WILL OF THE FORCE.
THEY DO?
WHEN YOU LEARN TO QUIET YOUR MIND, YOU WILL HEAR THEM SPEAKING TO YOU.
I DON'T UNDERSTAND.
WITH TIME AND TRAINING, ANNIE... YOU WILL.
WESA GOEN HOME!
YOUR MAJESTY, IT IS OUR PLEASURE TO CONTINUE TO SERVE AND PROTECT YOU.
I WELCOME YOUR HELP. SENATOR PALPATINE FEARS THE FEDERATION MEANS TO DESTROY ME.
I PROMISE YOU, WE WILL NOT LET THAT HAPPEN.

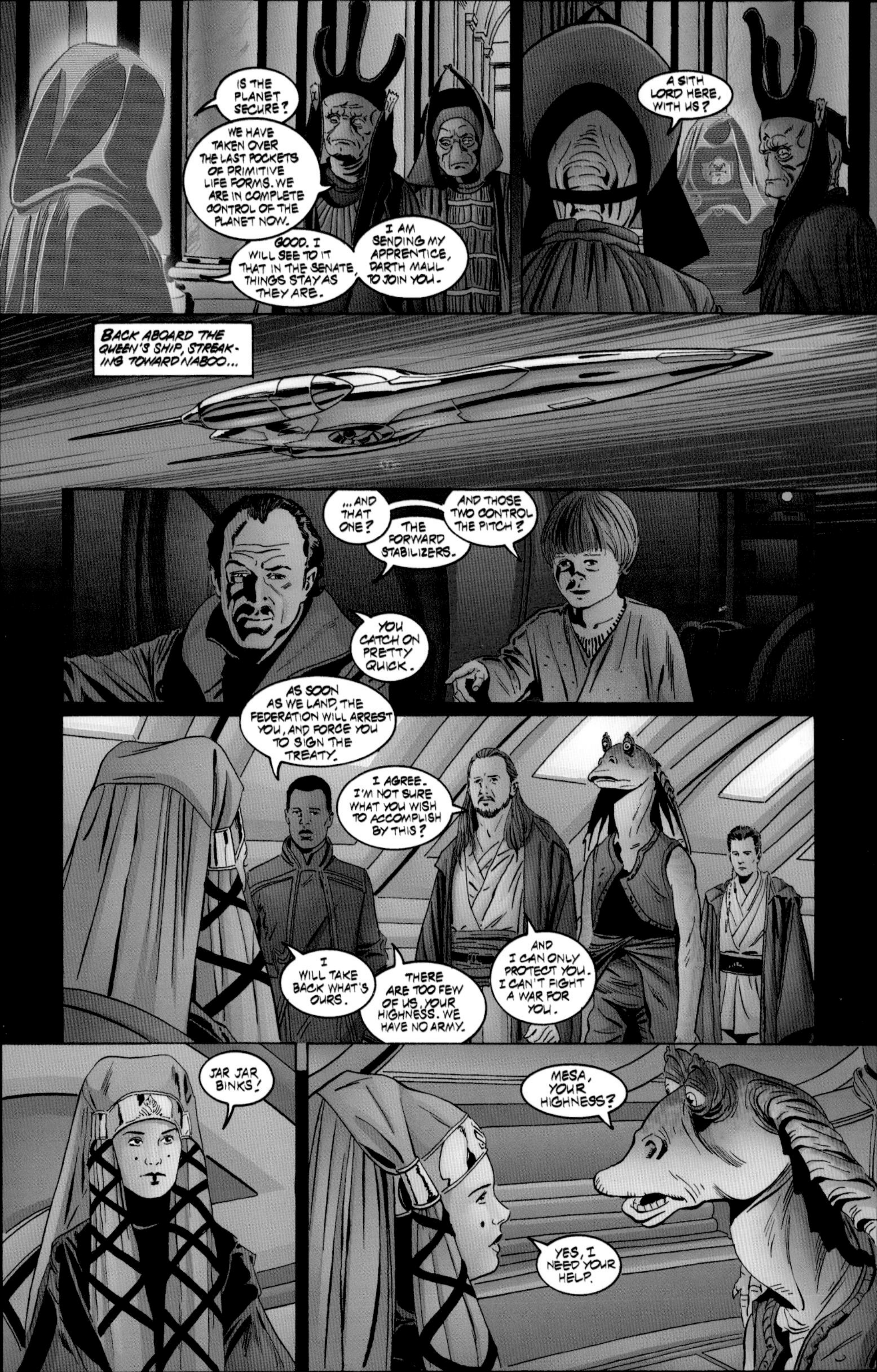
IS THE PLANET SECURE?
WE HAVE TAKEN OVER THE LAST POCKETS OF PRIMITIVE LIFE FORMS. WE ARE IN COMPLETE CONTROL OF THE PLANET NOW.
GOOD. I WILL SEE TO IT THAT IN THE SENATE, THINGS STAY AS THEY ARE.
I AM SENDING MY APPRENTICE, DARTH MAUL TO JOIN YOU.
A SITH LORD HERE, WITH US?
BACK ABOARD THE QUEEN'S SHIP, STREAKING TOWARD NABOO...
...AND THAT ONE?
THE FORWARD STABILIZERS.
AND THOSE TWO CONTROL THE PITCH?
YOU CATCH ON PRETTY QUICK.
AS SOON AS WE LAND, THE FEDERATION WILL ARREST YOU, AND FORCE YOU TO SIGN THE TREATY.
I AGREE. I'M NOT SURE WHAT YOU WISH TO ACCOMPLISH BY THIS?
I WILL TAKE BACK WHAT'S OURS.
THERE ARE TOO FEW OF US, YOUR HIGHNESS. WE HAVE NO ARMY.
AND I CAN ONLY PROTECT YOU. I CAN'T FIGHT A WAR FOR YOU.
JAR JAR BINKS!
MESA, YOUR HIGHNESS?
YES, I NEED YOUR HELP.

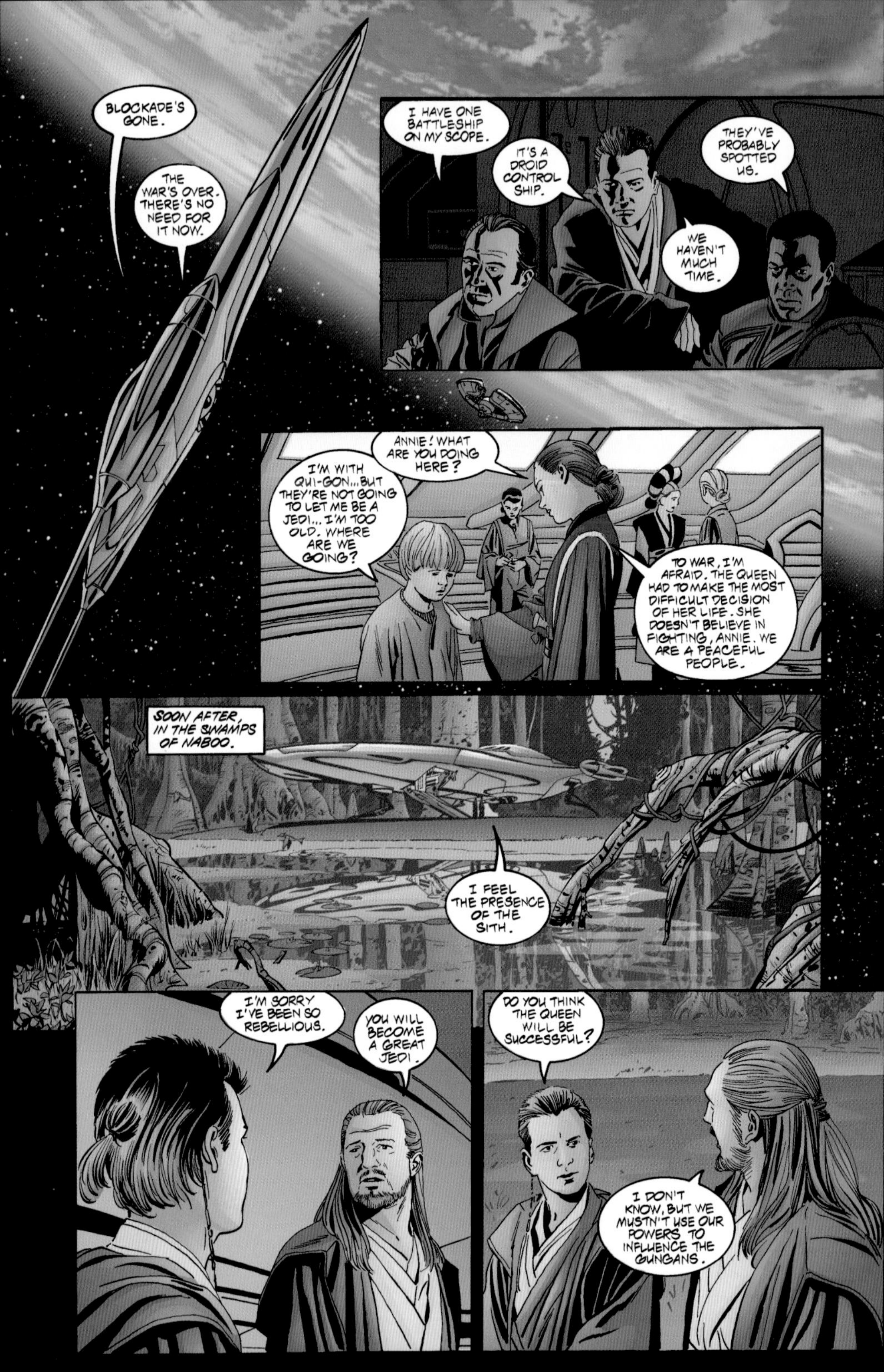
BLOCKADE'S GONE.
THE WAR'S OVER. THERE'S NO NEED FOR IT NOW.
I HAVE ONE BATTLESHIP ON MY SCOPE.
IT'S A DROID CONTROL SHIP.
THEY'VE PROBABLY SPOTTED US.
WE HAVEN'T MUCH TIME.
ANNIE! WHAT ARE YOU DOING HERE?
I'M WITH QUI-GON...BUT THEY'RE NOT GOING TO LET ME BE A JEDI... I'M TOO OLD. WHERE ARE WE GOING?
TO WAR, I'M AFRAID. THE QUEEN HAD TO MAKE THE MOST DIFFICULT DECISION OF HER LIFE. SHE DOESN'T BELIEVE IN FIGHTING, ANNIE. WE ARE A PEACEFUL PEOPLE.
SOON AFTER, IN THE SWAMPS OF NABOO.
I FEEL THE PRESENCE OF THE SITH.
I'M SORRY I'VE BEEN SO REBELLIOUS.
YOU WILL BECOME A GREAT JEDI.
DO YOU THINK THE QUEEN WILL BE SUCCESSFUL?
I DON'T KNOW, BUT WE MUSTN'T USE OUR POWERS TO INFLUENCE THE GUNGANS.

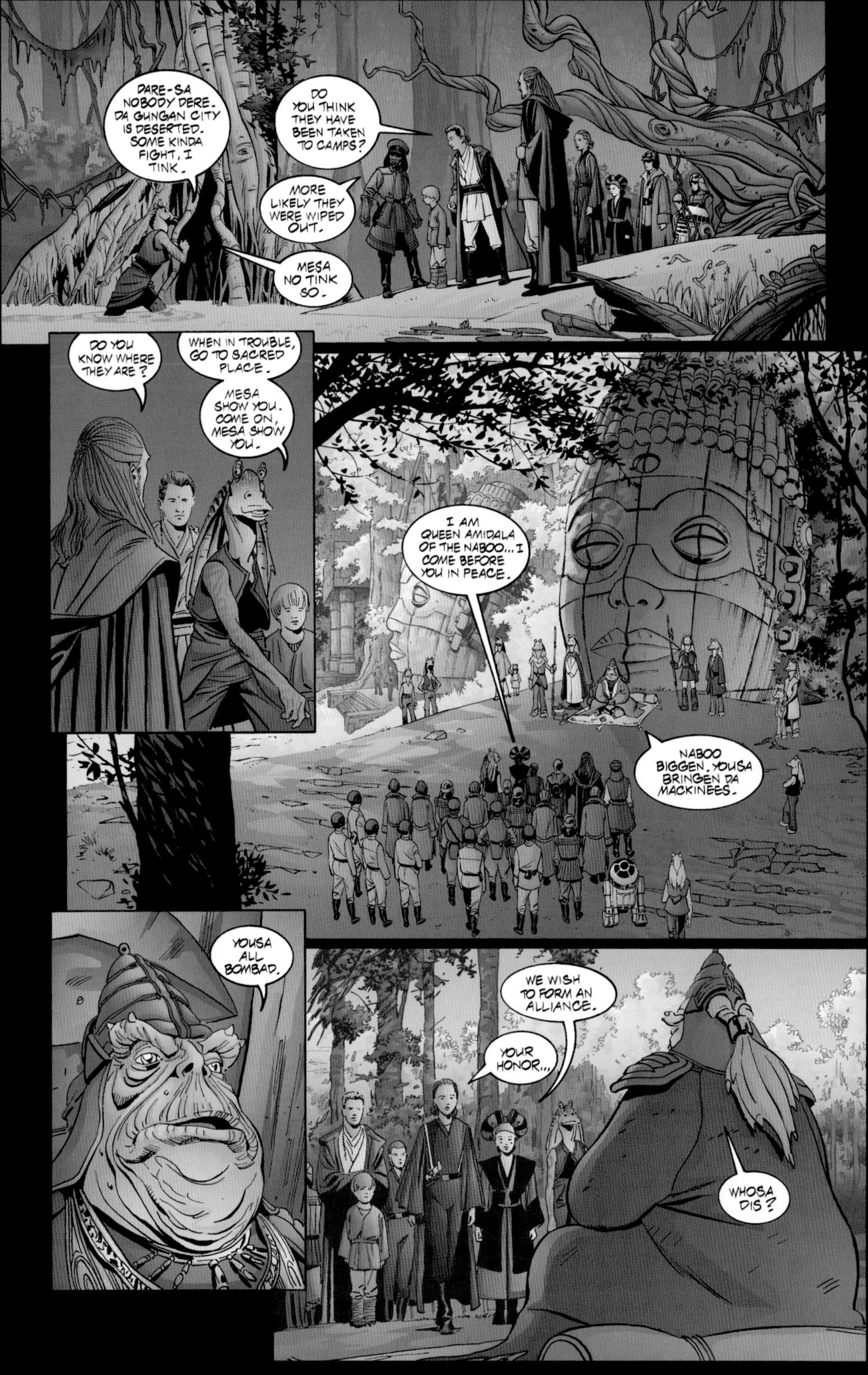
DARE-SA NOBODY DERE. DA GUNGAN CITY IS DESERTED. SOME KINDA FIGHT, I TINK.
DO YOU THINK THEY HAVE BEEN TAKEN TO CAMPS?
MORE LIKELY THEY WERE WIPED OUT.
MESA NO TINK SO.
DO YOU KNOW WHERE THEY ARE?
WHEN IN TROUBLE, GO TO SACRED PLACE.
MESA SHOW YOU. COME ON, MESA SHOW YOU.
I AM QUEEN AMIDALA OF THE NABOO... I COME BEFORE YOU IN PEACE.
NABOO BIGGEN. YOUSA BRINGEN DA MACKINEES.
YOUSA ALL BOMBAD.
WE WISH TO FORM AN ALLIANCE.
YOUR HONOR...
WHOSA DIS?

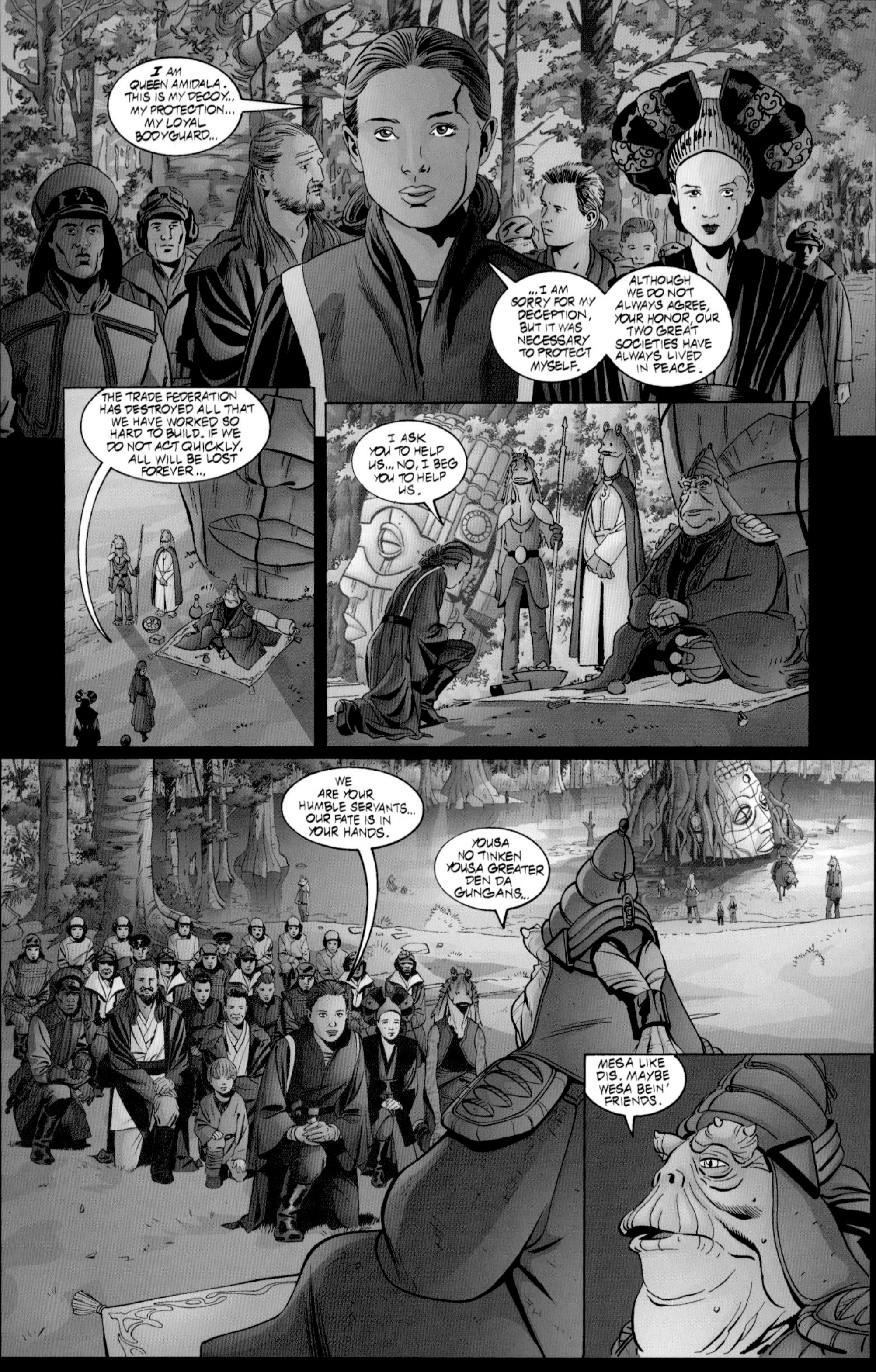
I AM QUEEN AMIDALA. THIS IS MY DECOY... MY PROTECTION... MY LOYAL BODYGUARD...
...I AM SORRY FOR MY DECEPTION, BUT IT WAS NECESSARY TO PROTECT MYSELF.
ALTHOUGH WE DO NOT ALWAYS AGREE, YOUR HONOR, OUR TWO GREAT SOCIETIES HAVE ALWAYS LIVED IN PEACE.
THE TRADE FEDERATION HAS DESTROYED ALL THAT WE HAVE WORKED SO HARD TO BUILD. IF WE DO NOT ACT QUICKLY, ALL WILL BE LOST FOREVER...
I ASK YOU TO HELP US... NO, I BEG YOU TO HELP US.
WE ARE YOUR HUMBLE SERVANTS... OUR FATE IS IN YOUR HANDS.
YOUSA NO TINKEN YOUSA GREATER DEN DA GUNGANS...
MESA LIKE DIS. MAYBE WESA BEIN' FRIENDS.

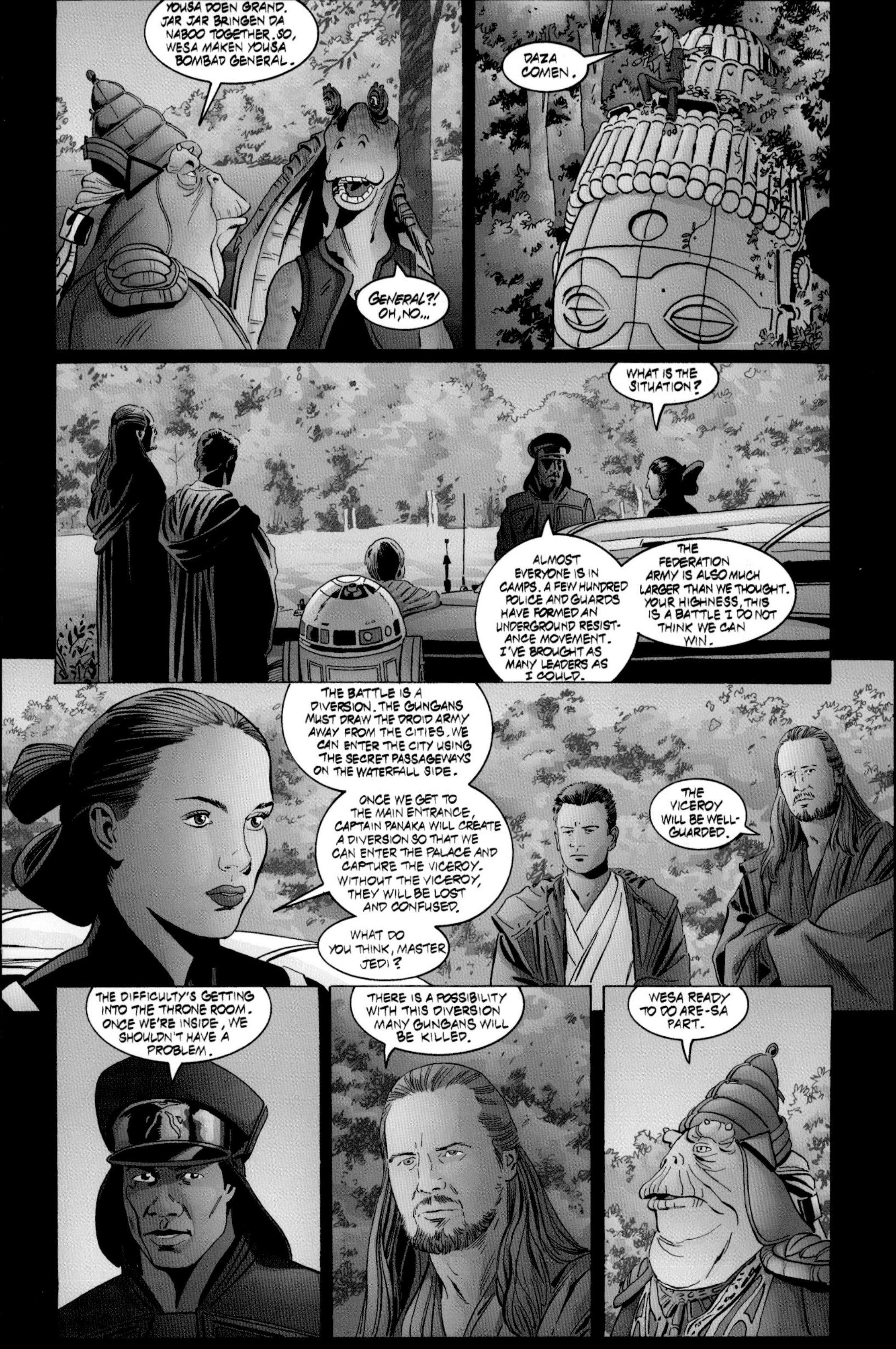
YOUSA DOEN GRAND. JAR JAR BRINGEN DA NABOO TOGETHER. SO, WESA MAKEN YOUSA BOMBAD GENERAL.
GENERAL?! OH, NO...
DAZA COMEN.
WHAT IS THE SITUATION?
ALMOST EVERYONE IS IN CAMPS. A FEW HUNDRED POLICE AND GUARDS HAVE FORMED AN UNDERGROUND RESISTANCE MOVEMENT. I'VE BROUGHT AS MANY LEADERS AS I COULD.
THE FEDERATION ARMY IS ALSO MUCH LARGER THAN WE THOUGHT. YOUR HIGHNESS, THIS IS A BATTLE I DO NOT THINK WE CAN WIN.
THE BATTLE IS A DIVERSION. THE GUNGANS MUST DRAW THE DROID ARMY AWAY FROM THE CITIES. WE CAN ENTER THE CITY USING THE SECRET PASSAGEWAYS ON THE WATERFALL SIDE.
ONCE WE GET TO THE MAIN ENTRANCE, CAPTAIN PANAKA WILL CREATE A DIVERSION SO THAT WE CAN ENTER THE PALACE AND CAPTURE THE VICEROY. WITHOUT THE VICEROY, THEY WILL BE LOST AND CONFUSED.
WHAT DO YOU THINK, MASTER JEDI?
THE VICEROY WILL BE WELL-GUARDED.
THE DIFFICULTY'S GETTING INTO THE THRONE ROOM. ONCE WE'RE INSIDE, WE SHOULDN'T HAVE A PROBLEM.
THERE IS A POSSIBILITY WITH THIS DIVERSION MANY GUNGANS WILL BE KILLED.
WESA READY TO DO ARE-SA PART.

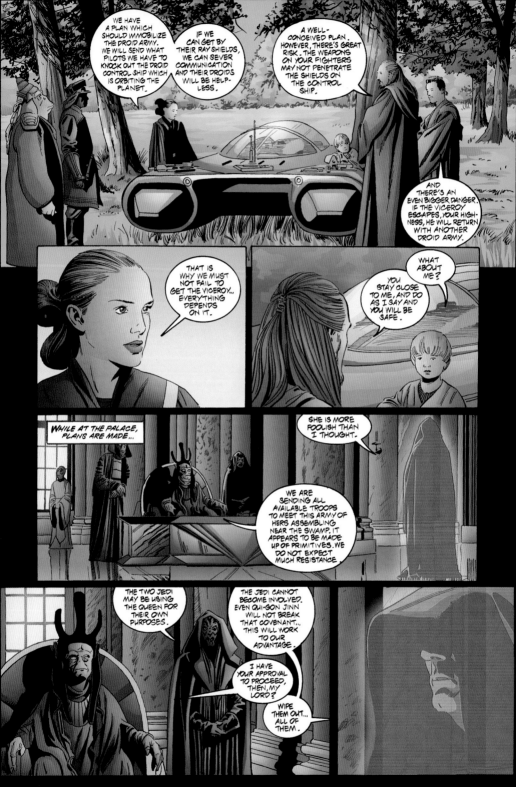

WE HAVE A PLAN WHICH SHOULD IMMOBILIZE THE DROID ARMY. WE WILL SEND WHAT PILOTS WE HAVE TO KNOCK OUT THE DROID CONTROL SHIP WHICH IS ORBITING THE PLANET.

IF WE CAN GET BY THEIR RAY SHIELDS, WE CAN SEVER COMMUNICATION AND THEIR DROIDS WILL BE HELPLESS.

A WELL-CONCEIVED PLAN. HOWEVER, THERE'S GREAT RISK. THE WEAPONS ON YOUR FIGHTERS MAY NOT PENETRATE THE SHIELDS ON THE CONTROL SHIP.

AND THERE'S AN EVEN BIGGER DANGER. IF THE VICEROY ESCAPES, YOUR HIGHNESS, HE WILL RETURN WITH ANOTHER DROID ARMY.

THAT IS WHY WE MUST NOT FAIL TO GET THE VICEROY... EVERYTHING DEPENDS ON IT.

WHAT ABOUT ME?

YOU STAY CLOSE TO ME, AND DO AS I SAY AND YOU WILL BE SAFE.

WHILE AT THE PALACE, PLANS ARE MADE...

SHE IS MORE FOOLISH THAN I THOUGHT.

WE ARE SENDING ALL AVAILABLE TROOPS TO MEET THIS ARMY OF HERS ASSEMBLING NEAR THE SWAMP. IT APPEARS TO BE MADE UP OF PRIMITIVES. WE DO NOT EXPECT MUCH RESISTANCE.

THE TWO JEDI MAY BE USING THE QUEEN FOR THEIR OWN PURPOSES.

THE JEDI CANNOT BECOME INVOLVED. EVEN QUI-GON JINN WILL NOT BREAK THAT COVENANT... THIS WILL WORK TO OUR ADVANTAGE.

I HAVE YOUR APPROVAL TO PROCEED, THEN, MY LORD?

WIPE THEM OUT... ALL OF THEM.

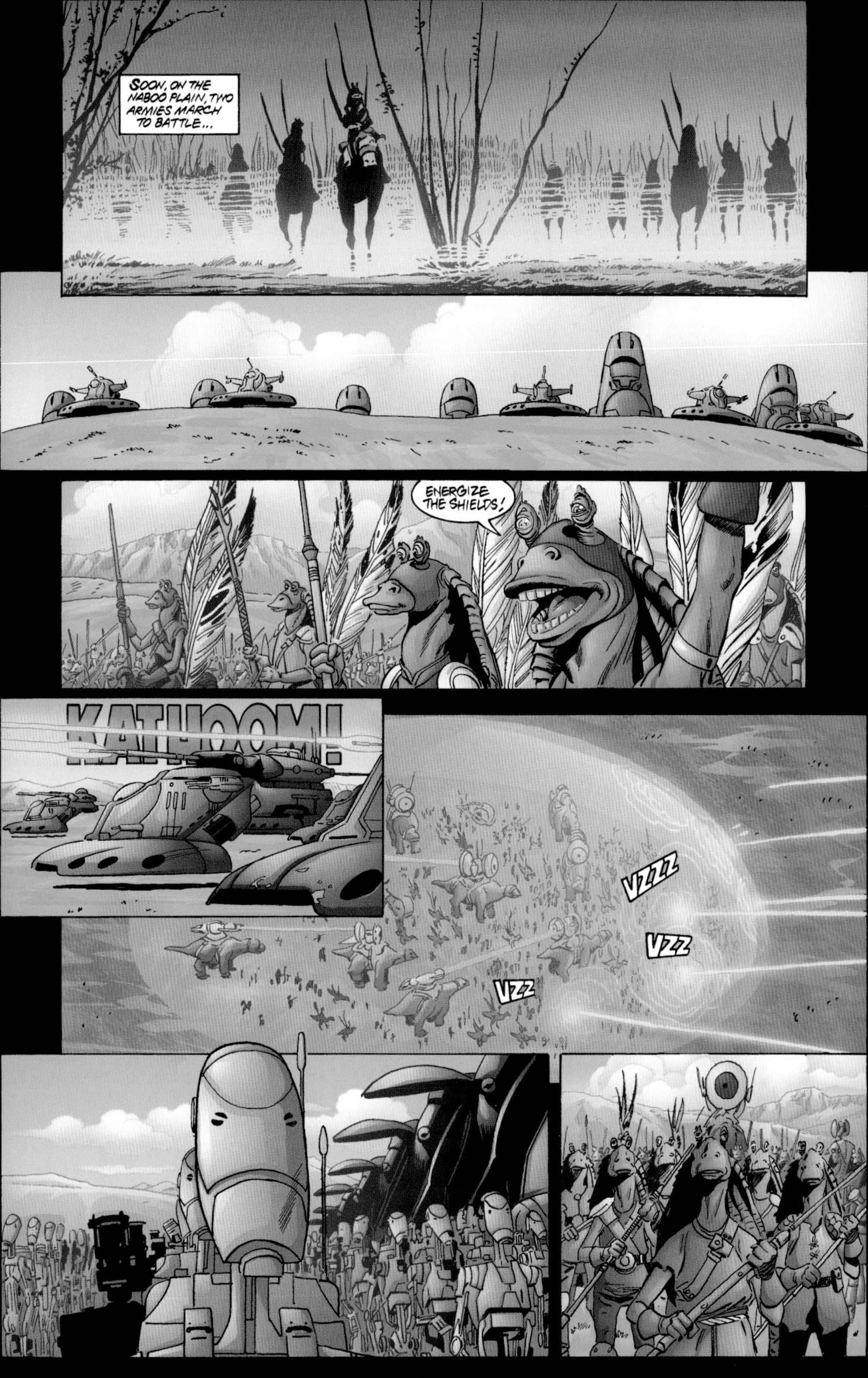
SOON, ON THE NABOO PLAIN, TWO ARMIES MARCH TO BATTLE...
ENERGIZE THE SHIELDS!
KATHOOM!
VZZZ
VZZ
VZZ

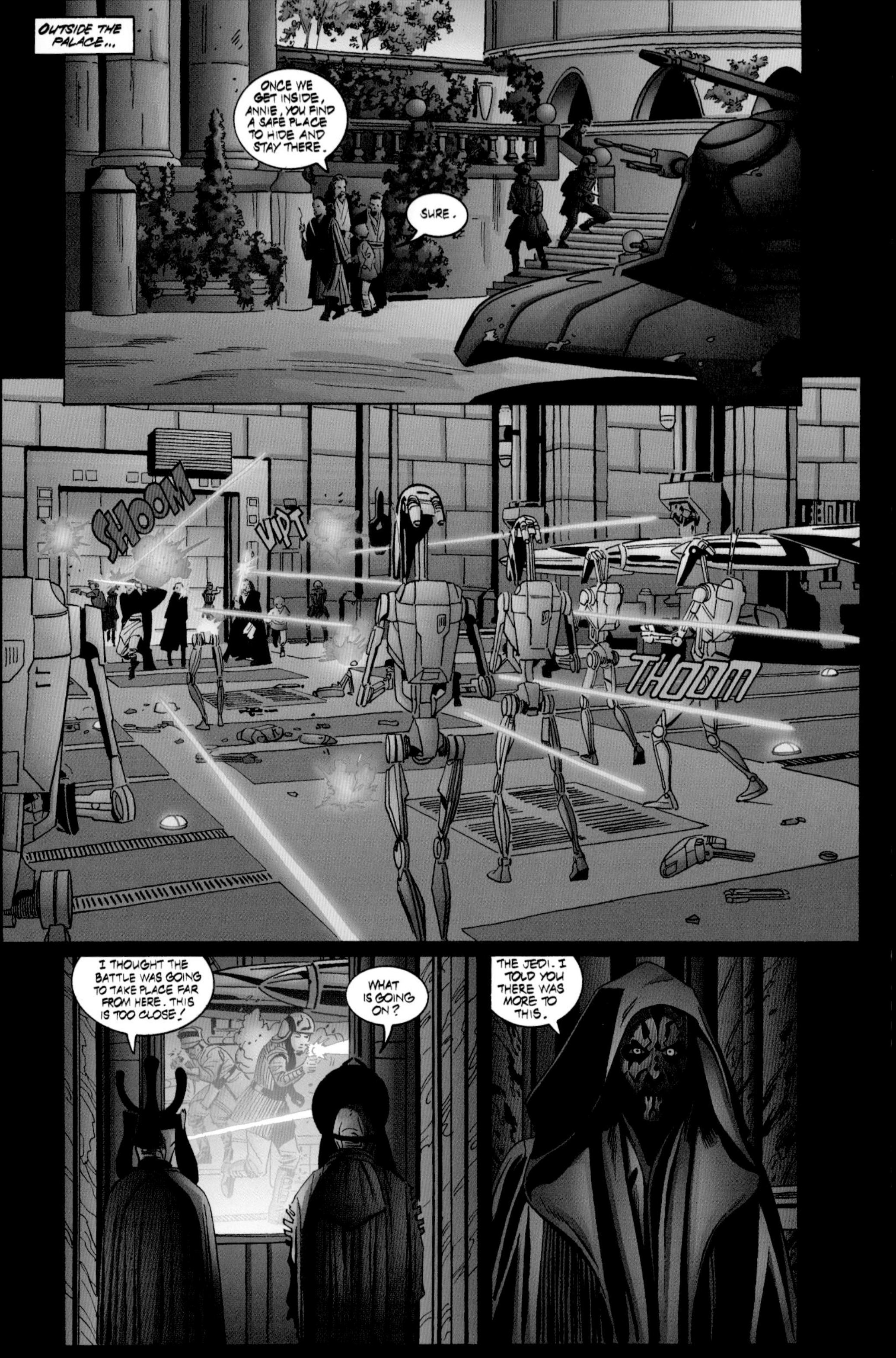

OUTSIDE THE PALACE...
ONCE WE GET INSIDE, ANNIE, YOU FIND A SAFE PLACE TO HIDE AND STAY THERE.
SURE.
SHOOM
VIPT
THOOM
I THOUGHT THE BATTLE WAS GOING TO TAKE PLACE FAR FROM HERE. THIS IS TOO CLOSE!
WHAT IS GOING ON?
THE JEDI. I TOLD YOU THERE WAS MORE TO THIS.

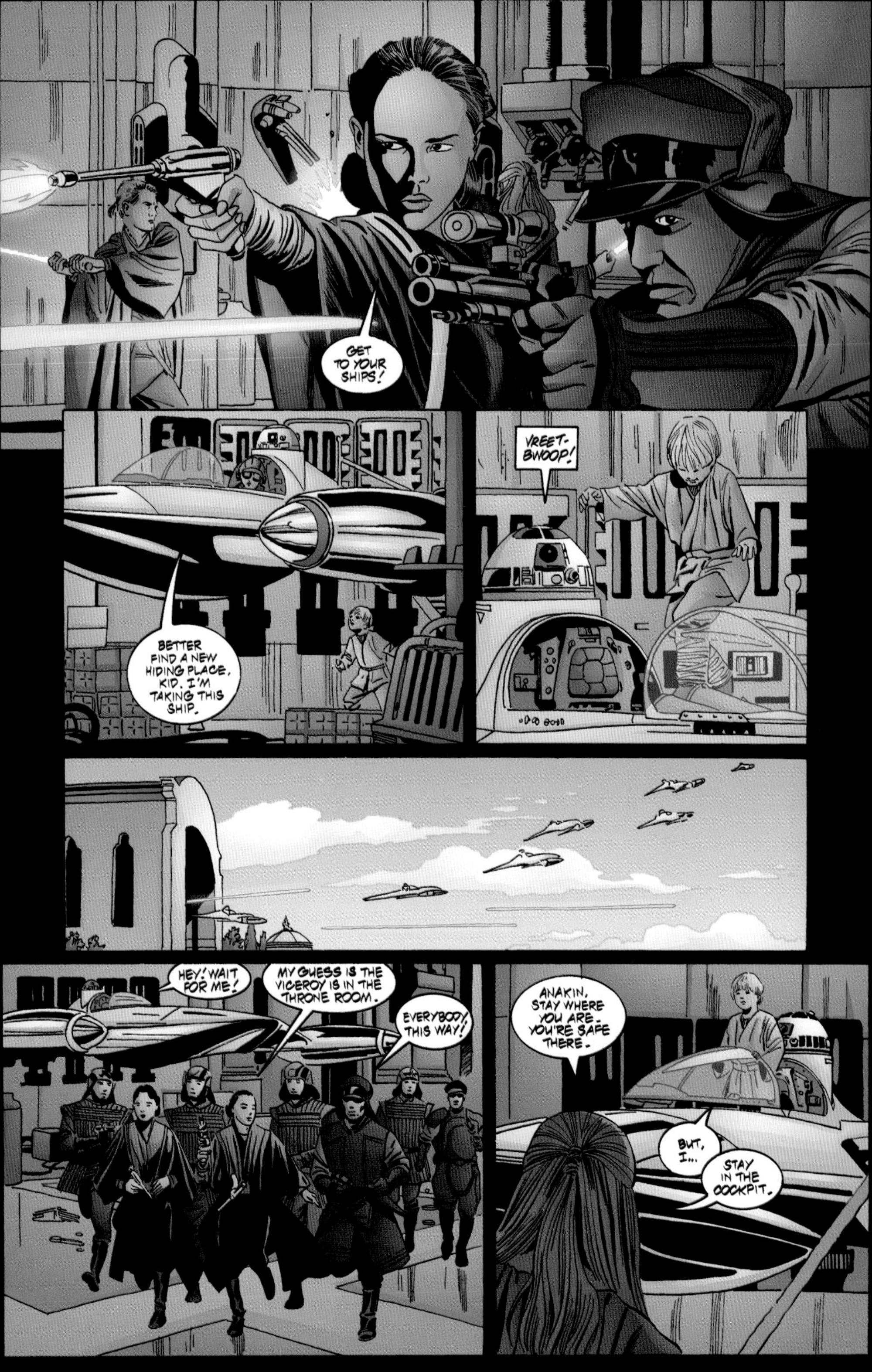
GET TO YOUR SHIPS!
BETTER FIND A NEW HIDING PLACE, KID. I'M TAKING THIS SHIP.
VREET-BWOOP!
HEY! WAIT FOR ME!
MY GUESS IS THE VICEROY IS IN THE THRONE ROOM.
EVERYBODY, THIS WAY!
ANAKIN, STAY WHERE YOU ARE. YOU'RE SAFE THERE.
BUT, I...
STAY IN THE COCKPIT.

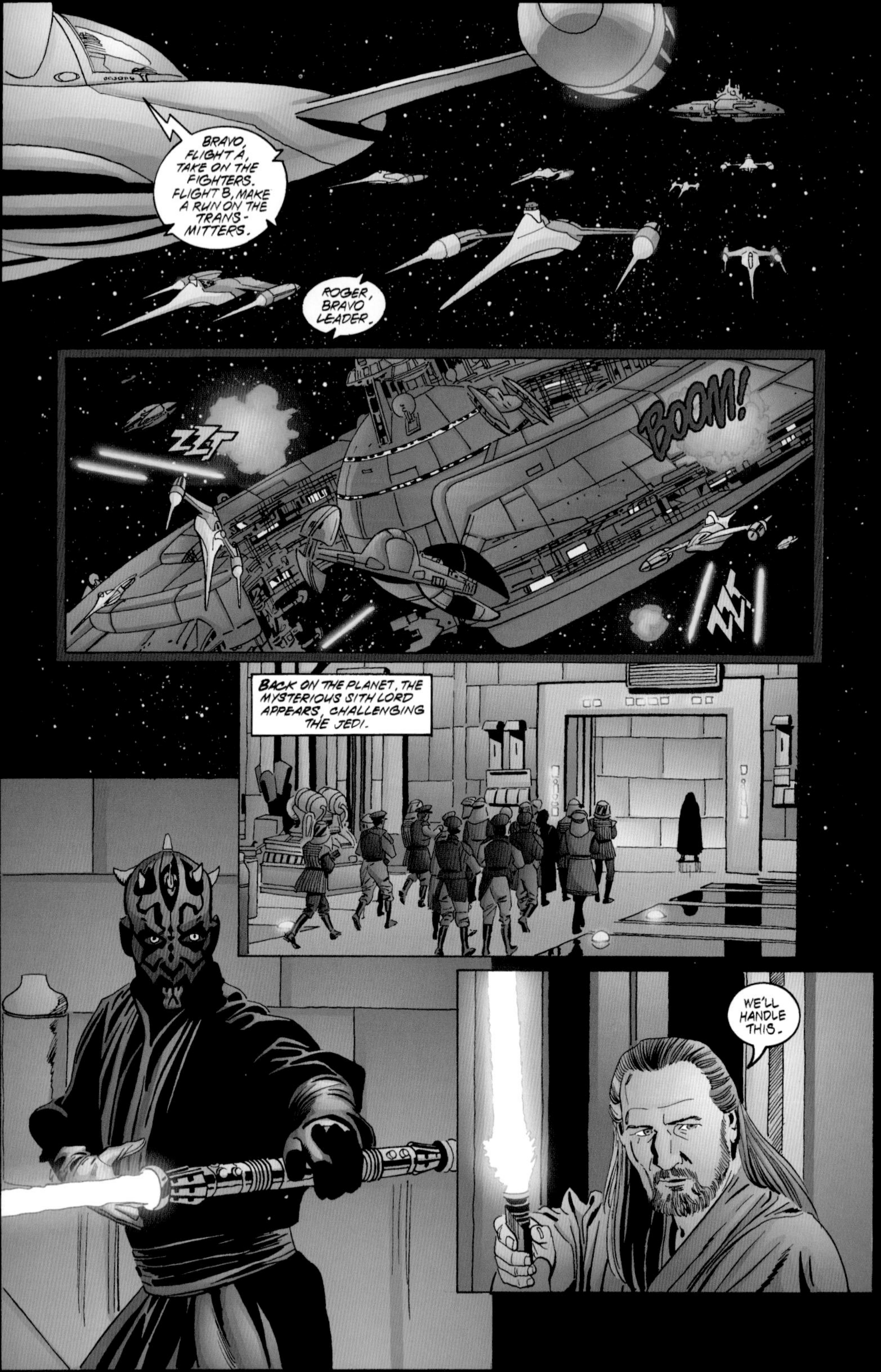
BRAVO, FLIGHT A, TAKE ON THE FIGHTERS. FLIGHT B, MAKE A RUN ON THE TRANS-MITTERS.
ROGER, BRAVO LEADER.
ZZZT
BOOM!
ZZZT
BACK ON THE PLANET, THE MYSTERIOUS SITH LORD APPEARS, CHALLENGING THE JEDI.
WE'LL HANDLE THIS.

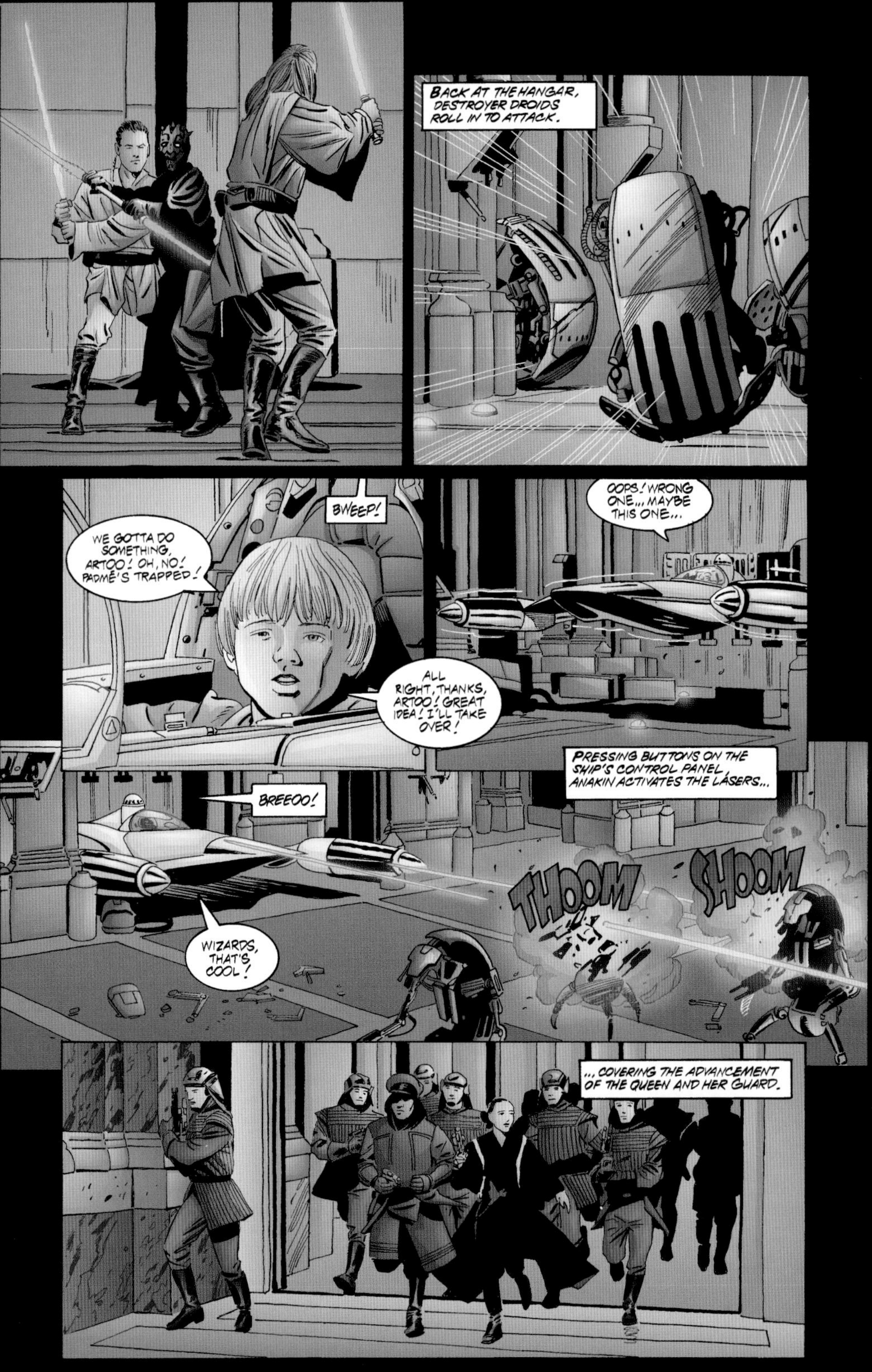
BACK AT THE HANGAR, DESTROYER DROIDS ROLL IN TO ATTACK.
BWEEP!
WE GOTTA DO SOMETHING, ARTOO! OH, NO! PADMÉ'S TRAPPED!
ALL RIGHT, THANKS, ARTOO! GREAT IDEA! I'LL TAKE OVER!
OOPS! WRONG ONE... MAYBE THIS ONE...
PRESSING BUTTONS ON THE SHIP'S CONTROL PANEL, ANAKIN ACTIVATES THE LASERS...
BREEOO!
WIZARDS, THAT'S COOL!
THOOM
SHOOM
...COVERING THE ADVANCEMENT OF THE QUEEN AND HER GUARD.

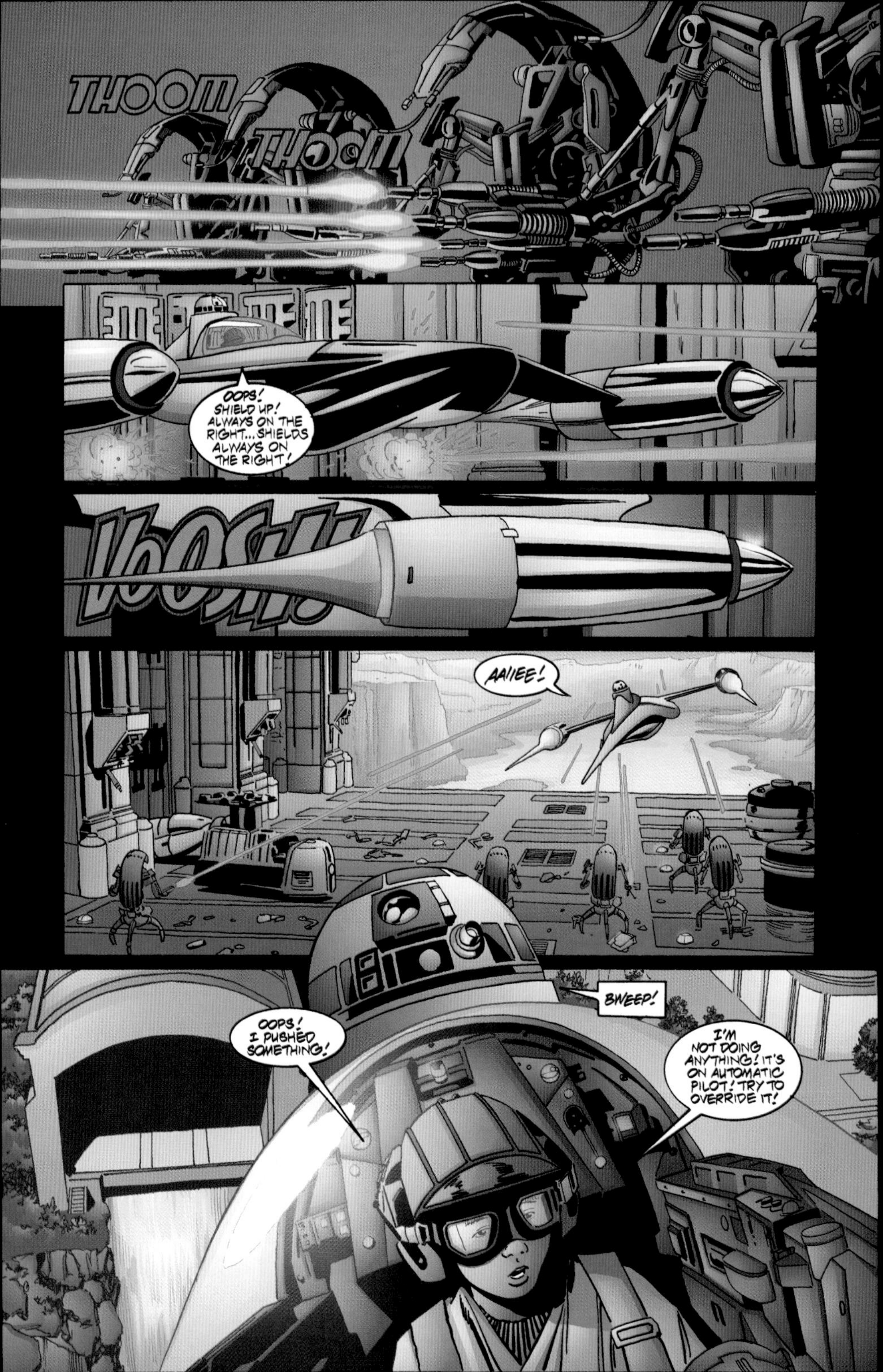
THOOM
THOOM
OOPS! SHIELD UP! ALWAYS ON THE RIGHT...SHIELDS ALWAYS ON THE RIGHT!
AAIIEE!
BWEEP!
OOPS! I PUSHED SOMETHING!
I'M NOT DOING ANYTHING! IT'S ON AUTOMATIC PILOT! TRY TO OVERRIDE IT!

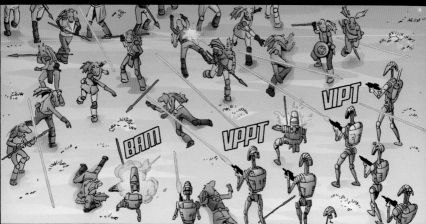

BAM

VPPT

VIPT

WHILE AT THE PALACE...

WE DON'T HAVE TIME FOR THIS, CAPTAIN.

ABOVE NABOO...

WHOO, BOY! THIS IS TENSE! ARTOO, GET US OFF AUTO-PILOT!

BWEEP?

YES, I'VE GOT CONTROL. YOU DID IT, ARTOO!

VREET-DOOP!

GO BACK?! QUI-GON TOLD ME TO STAY IN THIS COCKPIT AND THAT'S WHAT I'M GONNA DO. NOW C'MON!

BACK ON THE NABOO PLAIN THE BATTLE RAGES.
OH, NO...
BWAM
WAM
VVZ
TRYING TO ESCAPE THE BATTLE, JAR JAR JUMPS ON THE BACK OF A RETREATING WAGON, ACCIDENTALLY FREEING ITS DEADLY CARGO...
OOOPS.

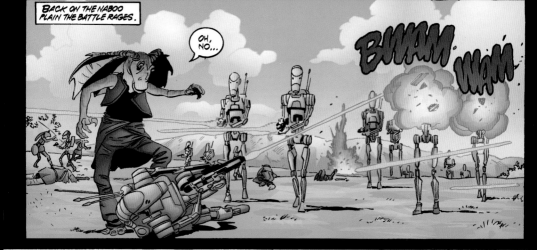

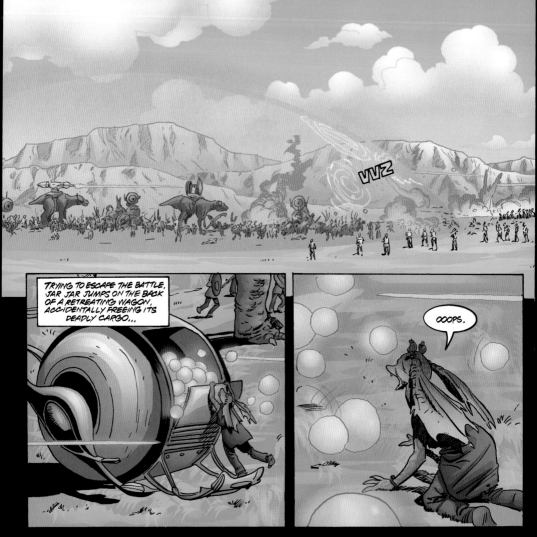

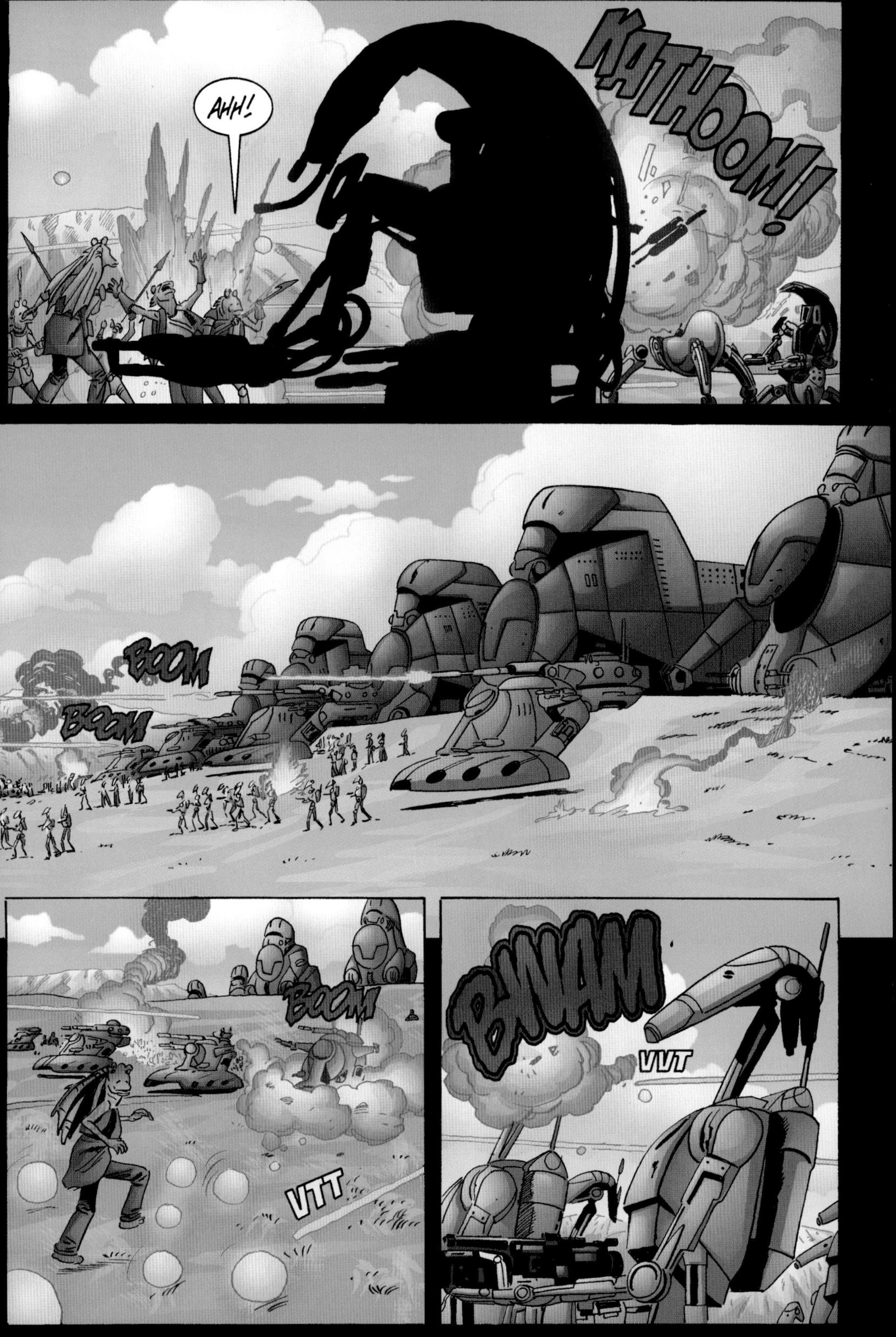
AHH!
KATHOOM!
BOOM
BOOM
BOOM
VTT
BWAM
VVT

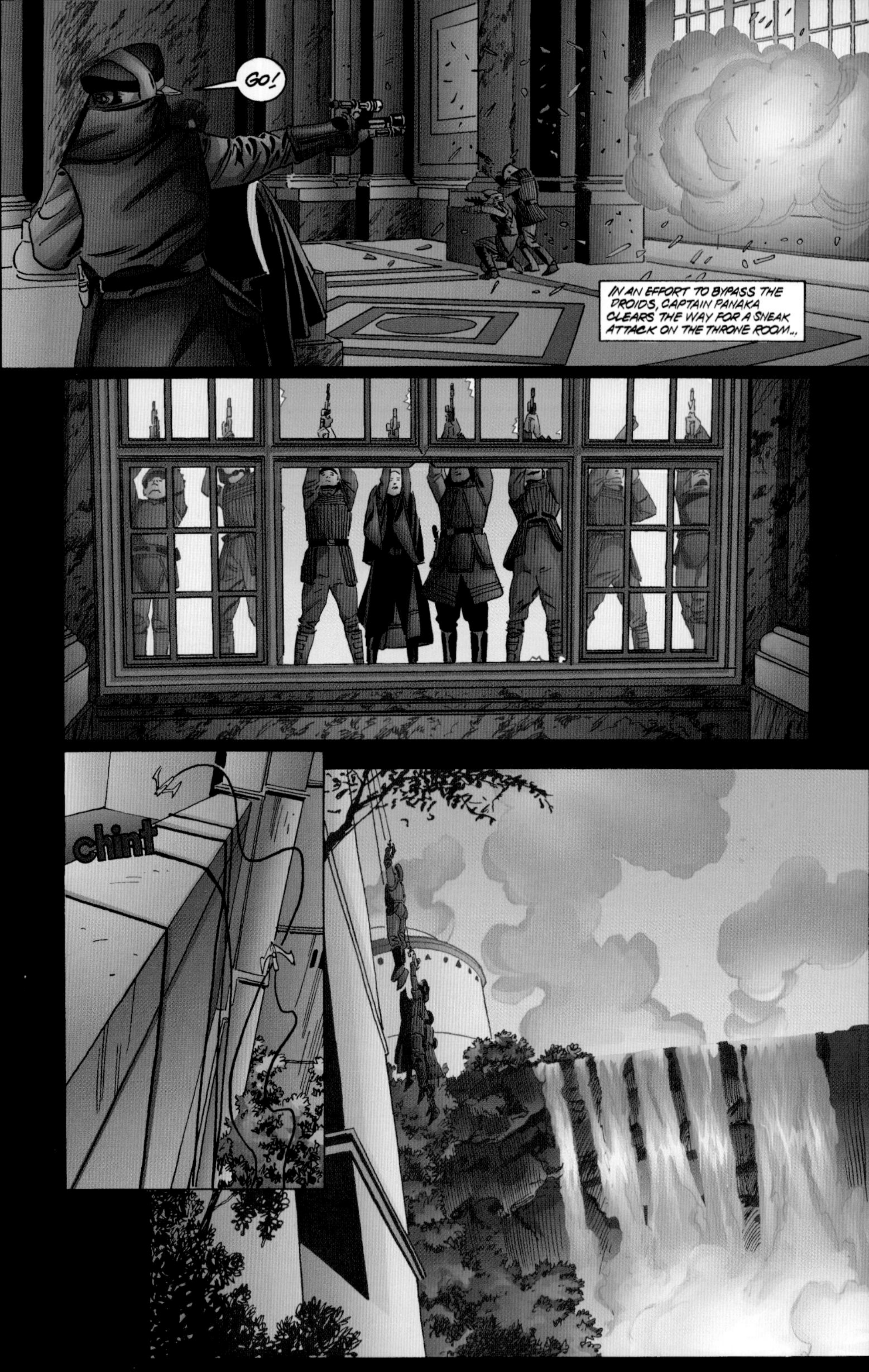
GO!
IN AN EFFORT TO BYPASS THE DROIDS, CAPTAIN PANAKA CLEARS THE WAY FOR A SNEAK ATTACK ON THE THRONE ROOM...
chint

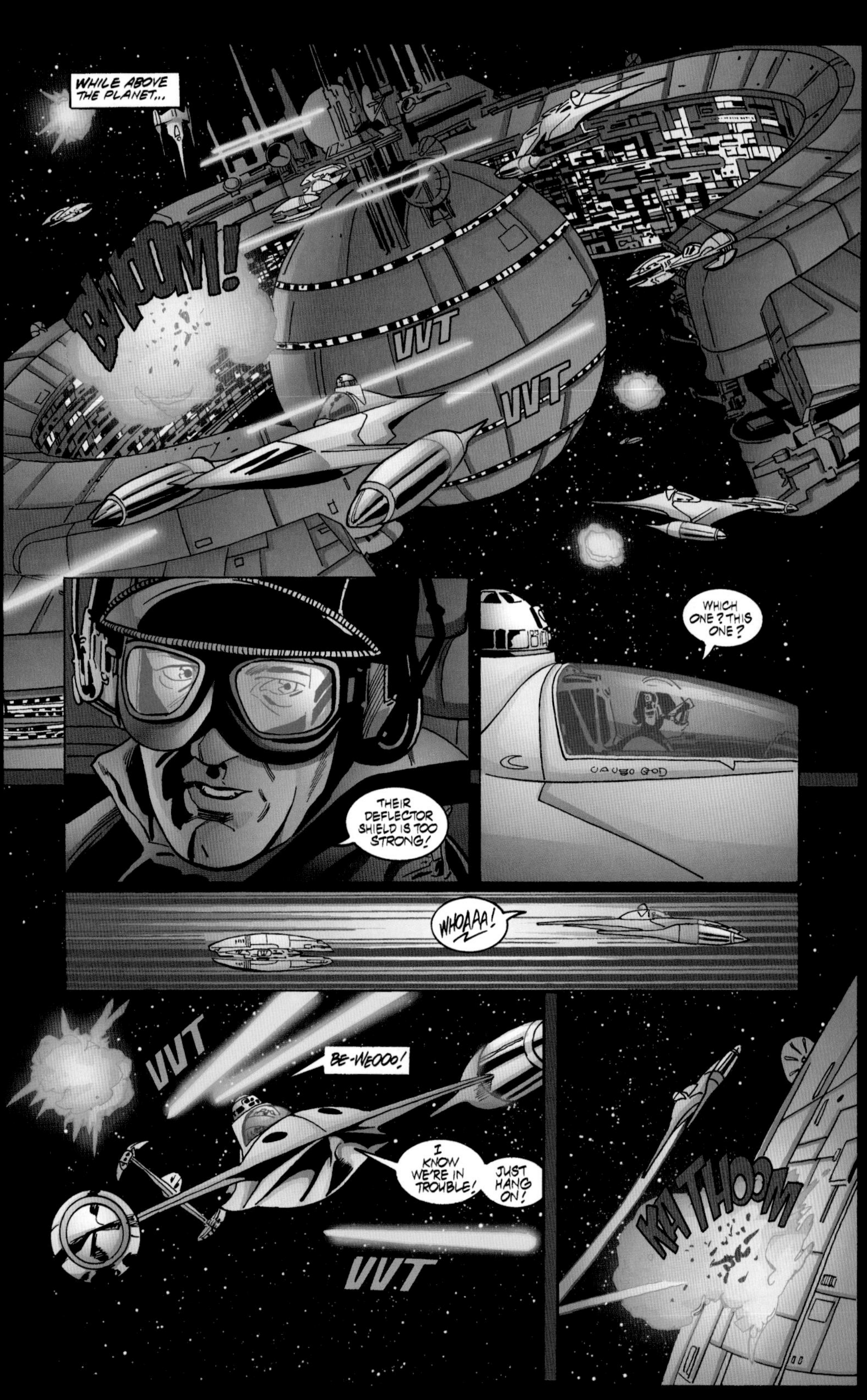
WHILE ABOVE THE PLANET...
BAROOM!
VVT
VVT
WHICH ONE? THIS ONE?
THEIR DEFLECTOR SHIELD IS TOO STRONG!
WHOAAA!
VVT
BE-WEOOO!
I KNOW WE'RE IN TROUBLE!
JUST HANG ON!
VVT
KA THOOM

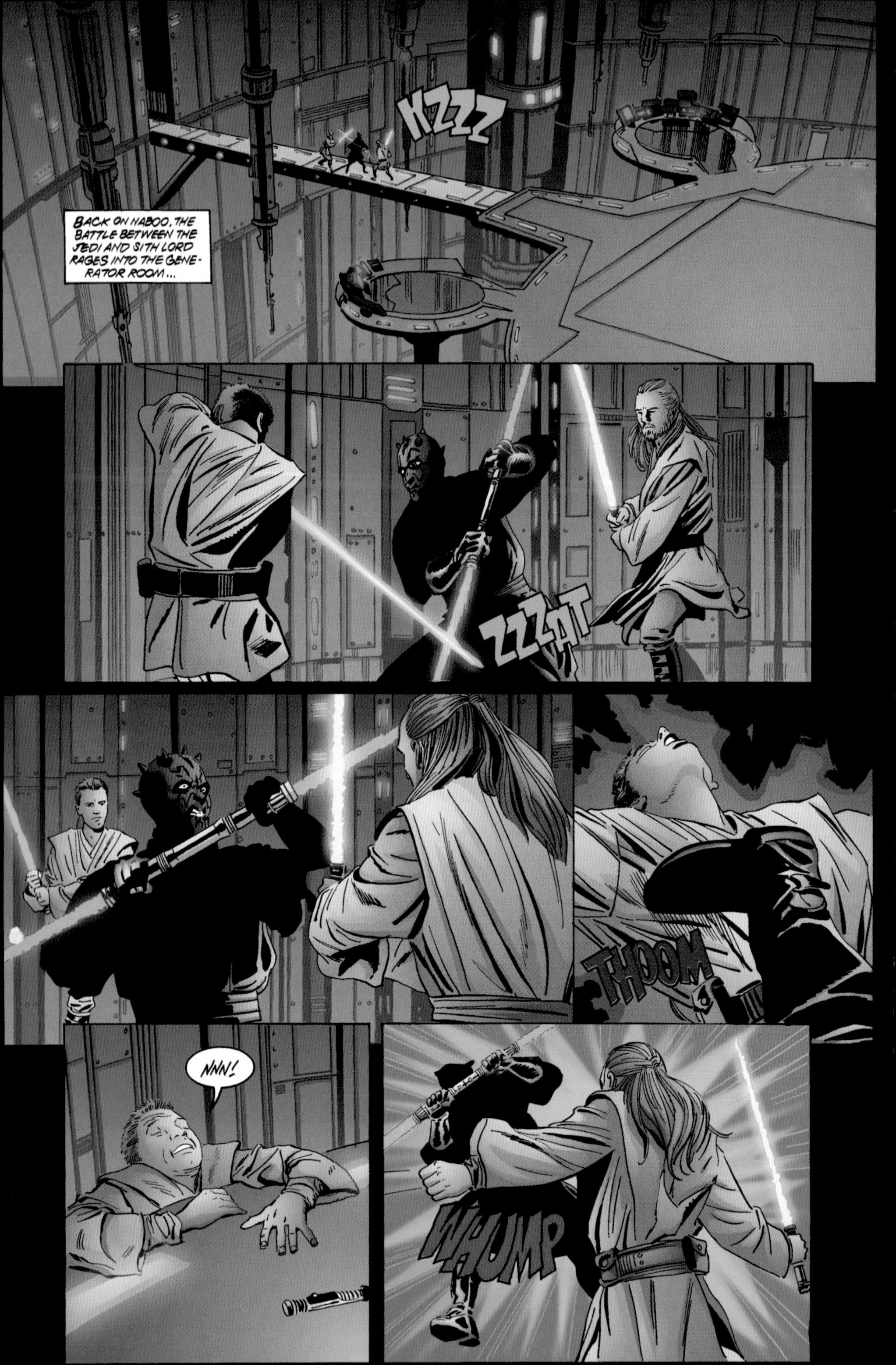
HZZZ
BACK ON NABOO, THE BATTLE BETWEEN THE JEDI AND SITH LORD RAGES INTO THE GENERATOR ROOM...
ZZZAT
THOOM
NNN!
WHUMP

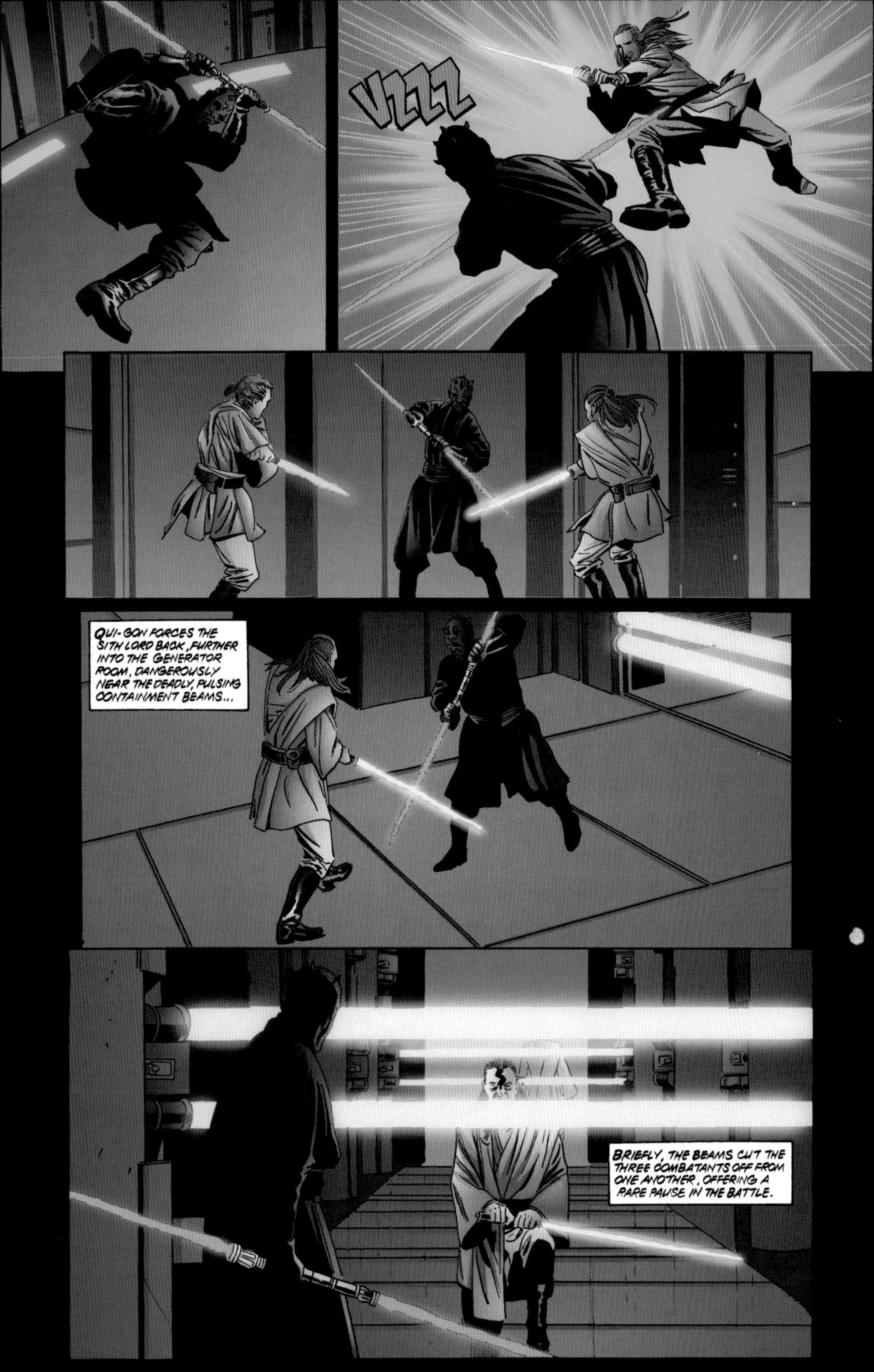
VZZZ
QUI-GON FORCES THE SITH LORD BACK, FURTHER INTO THE GENERATOR ROOM, DANGEROUSLY NEAR THE DEADLY, PULSING CONTAINMENT BEAMS...
BRIEFLY, THE BEAMS CUT THE THREE COMBATANTS OFF FROM ONE ANOTHER, OFFERING A RARE PAUSE IN THE BATTLE.

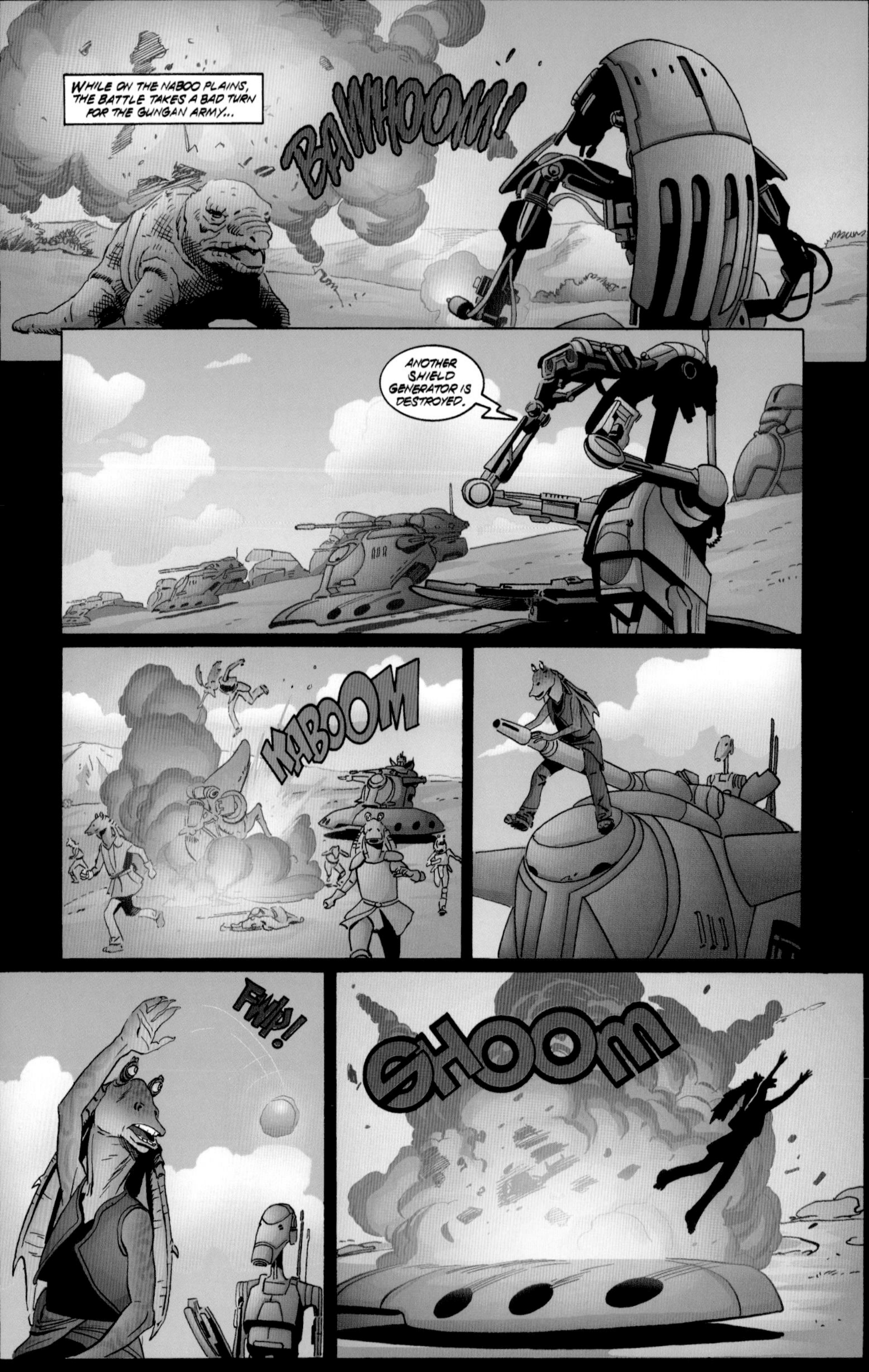
WHILE ON THE NABOO PLAINS, THE BATTLE TAKES A BAD TURN FOR THE GUNGAN ARMY...
BAWHOOM!
ANOTHER SHIELD GENERATOR IS DESTROYED.
KABOOM
FWIP!
SHOOM

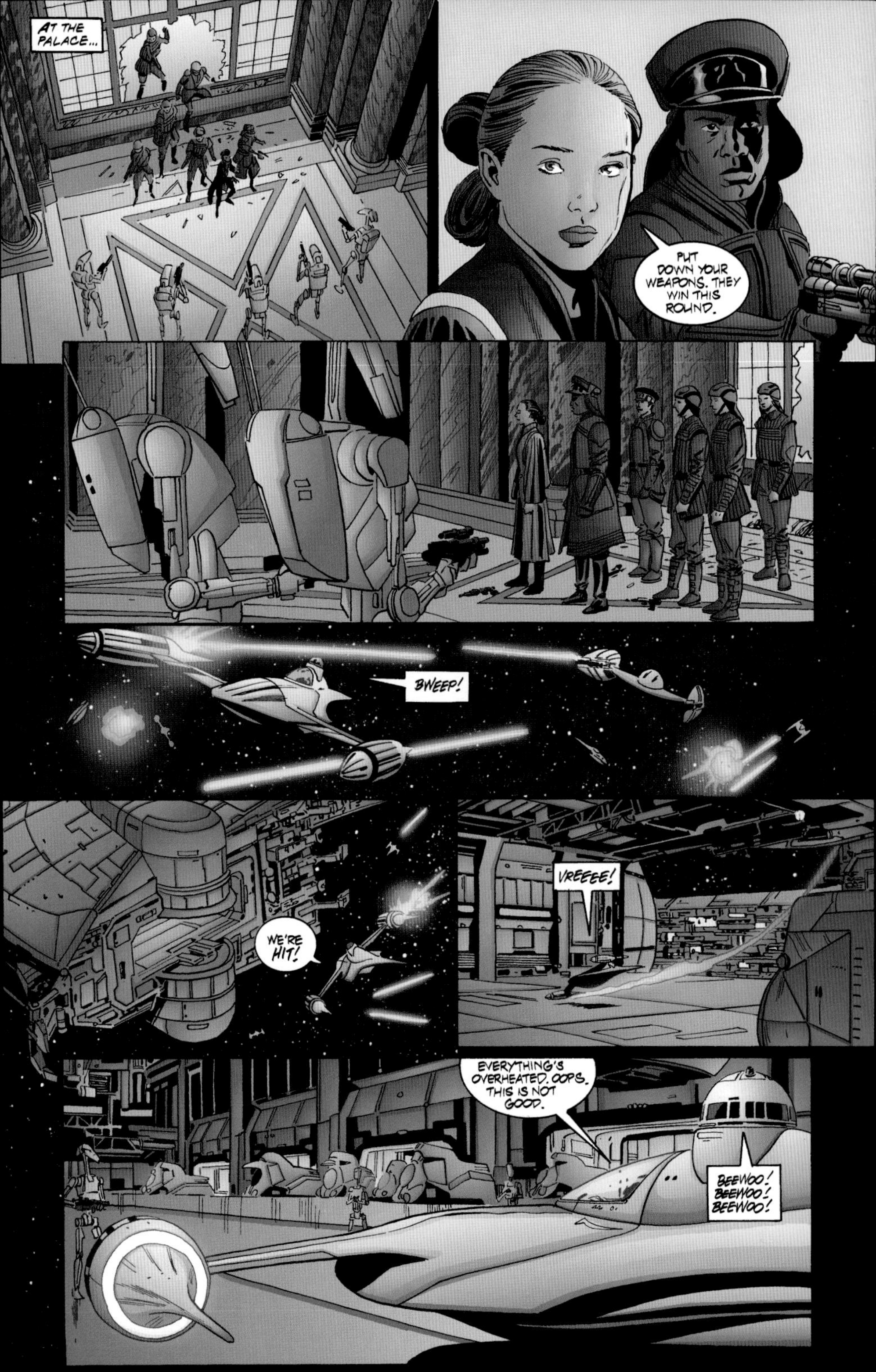

AT THE PALACE...
PUT DOWN YOUR WEAPONS. THEY WIN THIS ROUND.
BWEEP!
WE'RE HIT!
VREEEE!
EVERYTHING'S OVERHEATED. OOPS. THIS IS NOT GOOD.
BEEWOO! BEEWOO! BEEWOO!

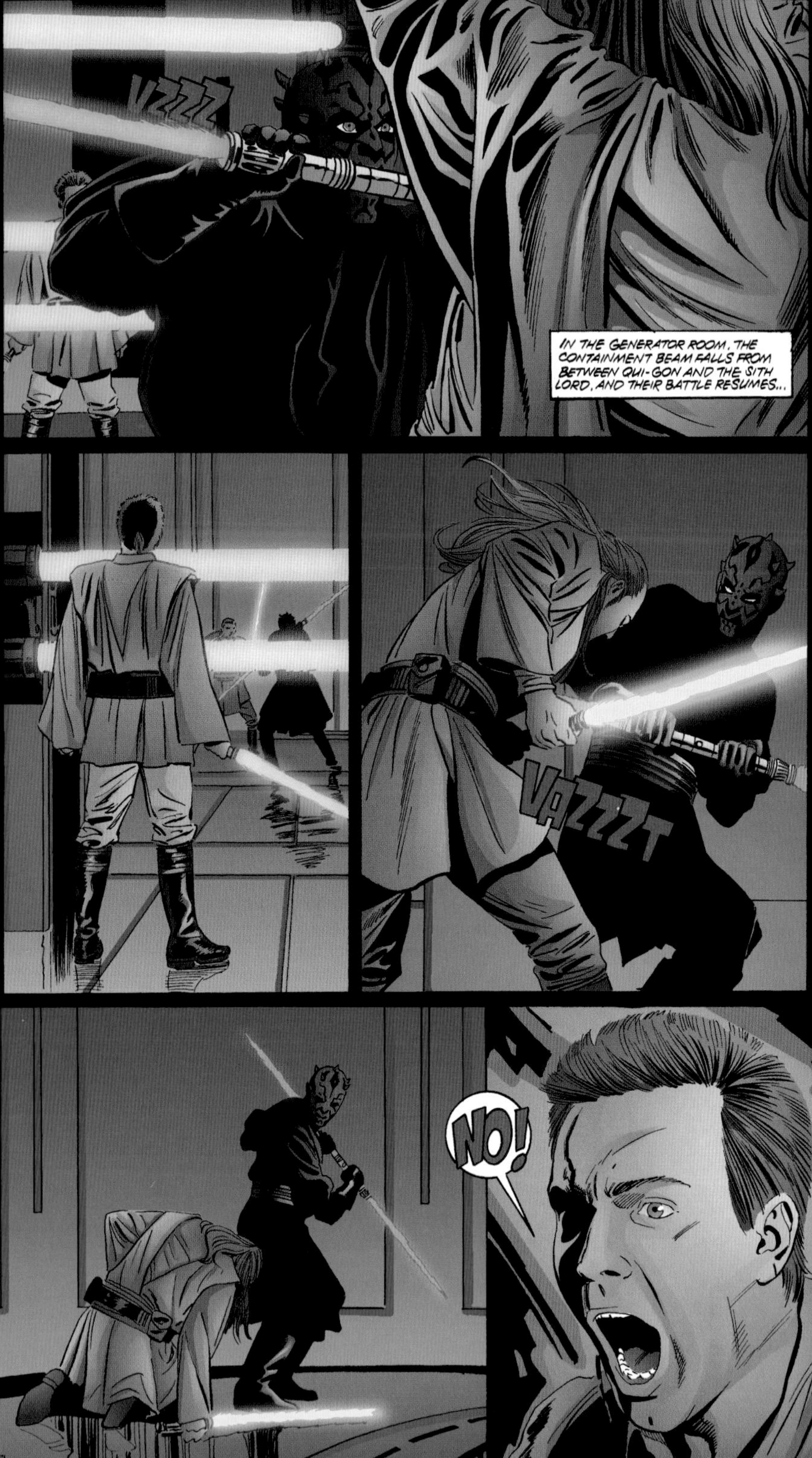
VZZZZ
IN THE GENERATOR ROOM, THE CONTAINMENT BEAM FALLS FROM BETWEEN QUI-GON AND THE SITH LORD, AND THEIR BATTLE RESUMES...
VAZZZT
NO!

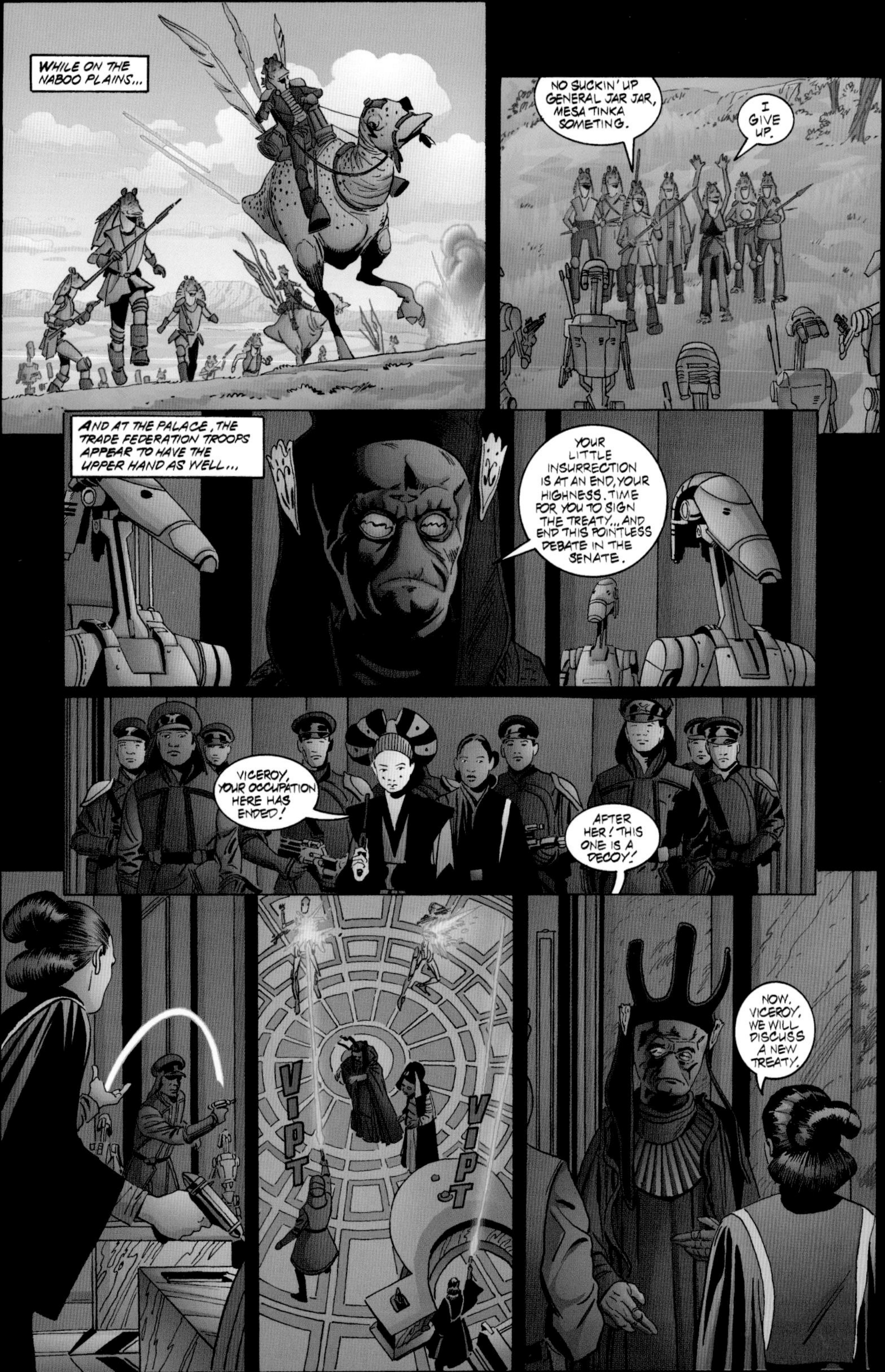
WHILE ON THE NABOO PLAINS...
NO SUCKIN' UP GENERAL JAR JAR, MESA TINKA SOMETING.
I GIVE UP.
AND AT THE PALACE, THE TRADE FEDERATION TROOPS APPEAR TO HAVE THE UPPER HAND AS WELL...
YOUR LITTLE INSURRECTION IS AT AN END, YOUR HIGHNESS. TIME FOR YOU TO SIGN THE TREATY... AND END THIS POINTLESS DEBATE IN THE SENATE.
VICEROY, YOUR OCCUPATION HERE HAS ENDED!
AFTER HER! THIS ONE IS A DECOY!
VIPT
VIPT
NOW, VICEROY, WE WILL DISCUSS A NEW TREATY.

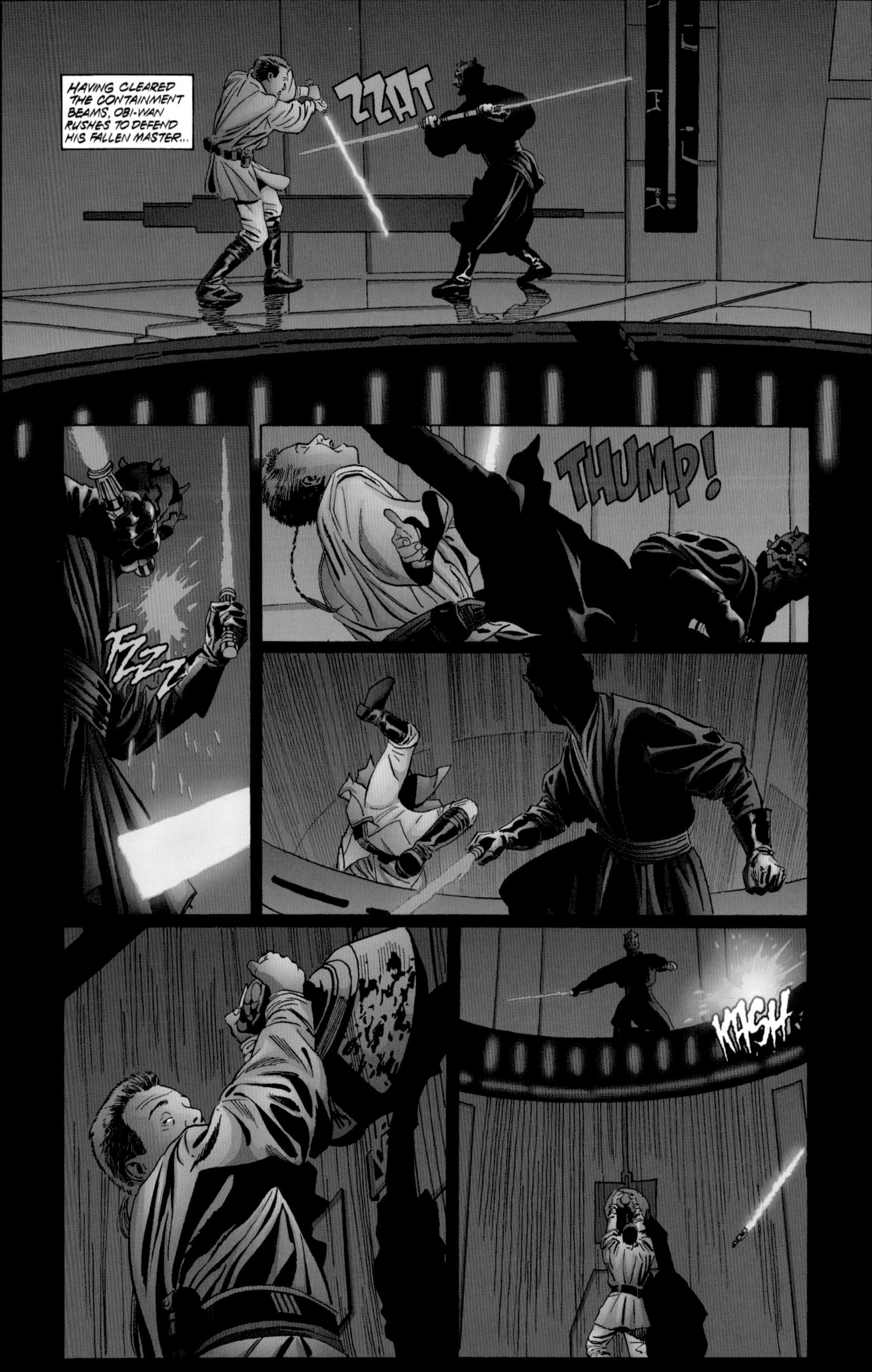
HAVING CLEARED THE CONTAINMENT BEAMS, OBI-WAN RUSHES TO DEFEND HIS FALLEN MASTER...
ZZAT
THUMP!
FZZZZ
KASH

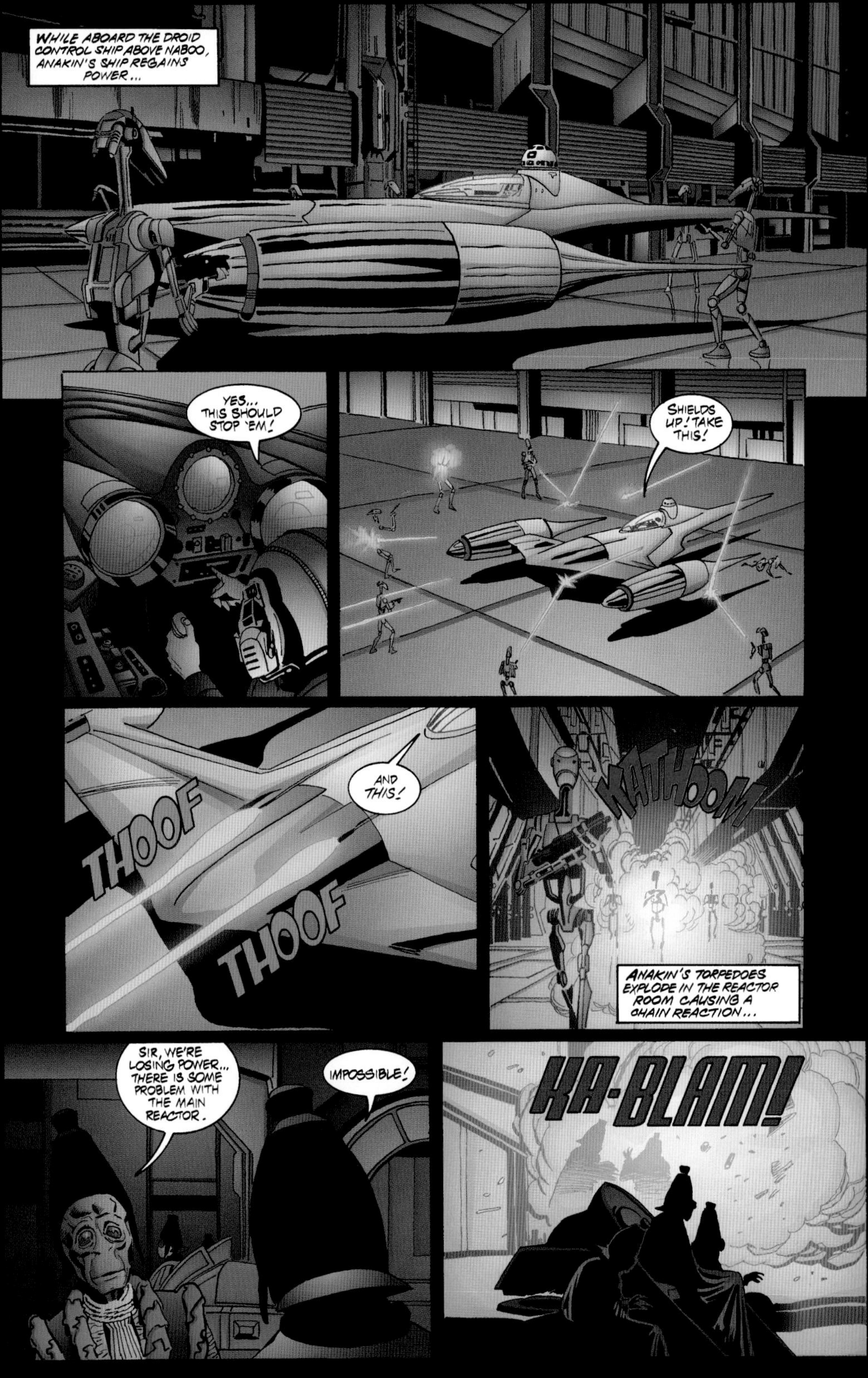
WHILE ABOARD THE DROID CONTROL SHIP ABOVE NABOO, ANAKIN'S SHIP REGAINS POWER...
YES... THIS SHOULD STOP 'EM!
SHIELDS UP! TAKE THIS!
THOOF
THOOF
AND THIS!
KATHOOM
ANAKIN'S TORPEDOES EXPLODE IN THE REACTOR ROOM CAUSING A CHAIN REACTION...
SIR, WE'RE LOSING POWER... THERE IS SOME PROBLEM WITH THE MAIN REACTOR.
IMPOSSIBLE!
KA-BLAM!

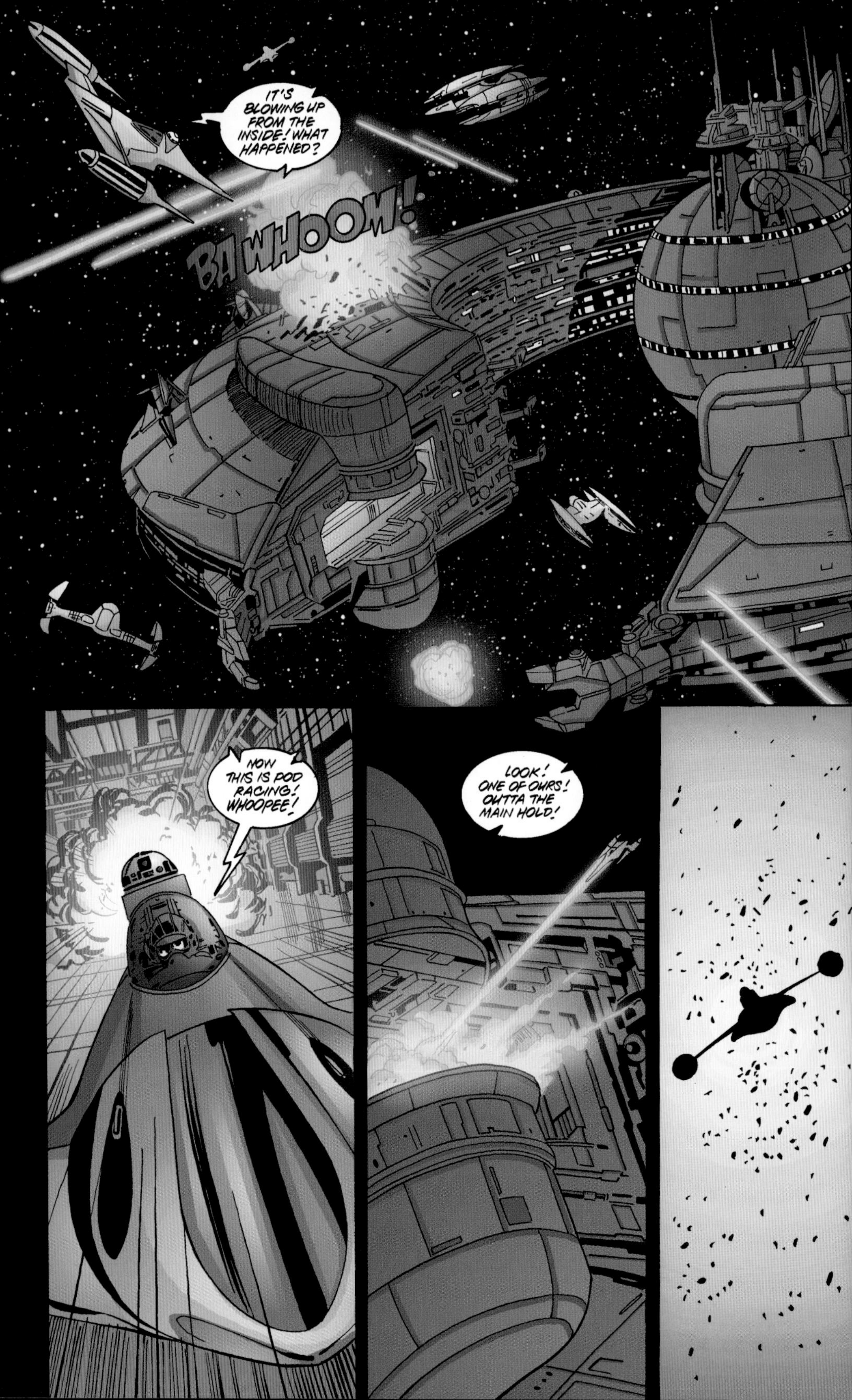
IT'S BLOWING UP FROM THE INSIDE! WHAT HAPPENED?
BAWHOOM!
NOW THIS IS POD RACING! WHOOPEE!
LOOK! ONE OF OURS! OUTTA THE MAIN HOLD!

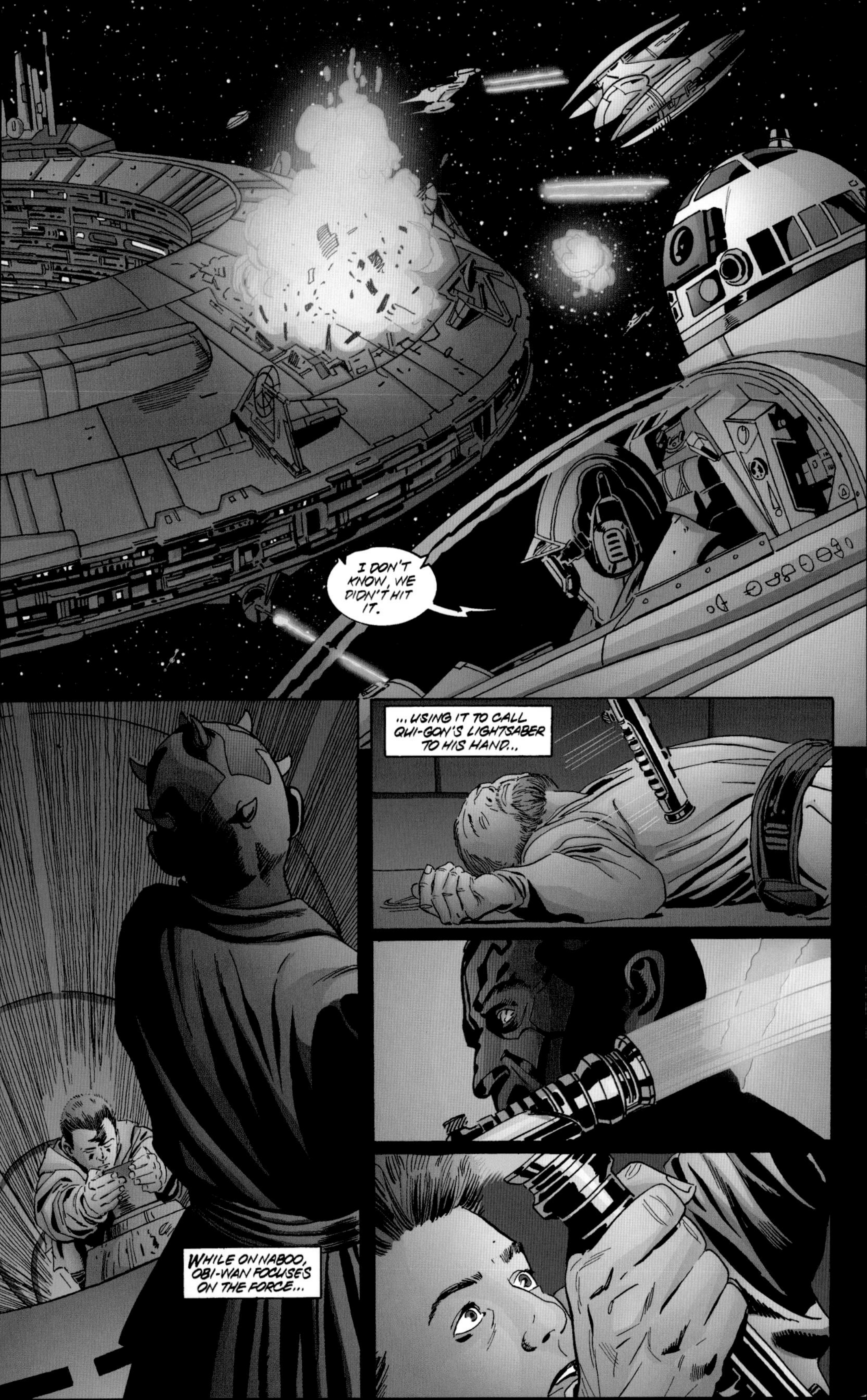
I DON'T KNOW, WE DIDN'T HIT IT.
WHILE ON NABOO, OBI-WAN FOCUSES ON THE FORCE...
...USING IT TO CALL QUI-GON'S LIGHTSABER TO HIS HAND...

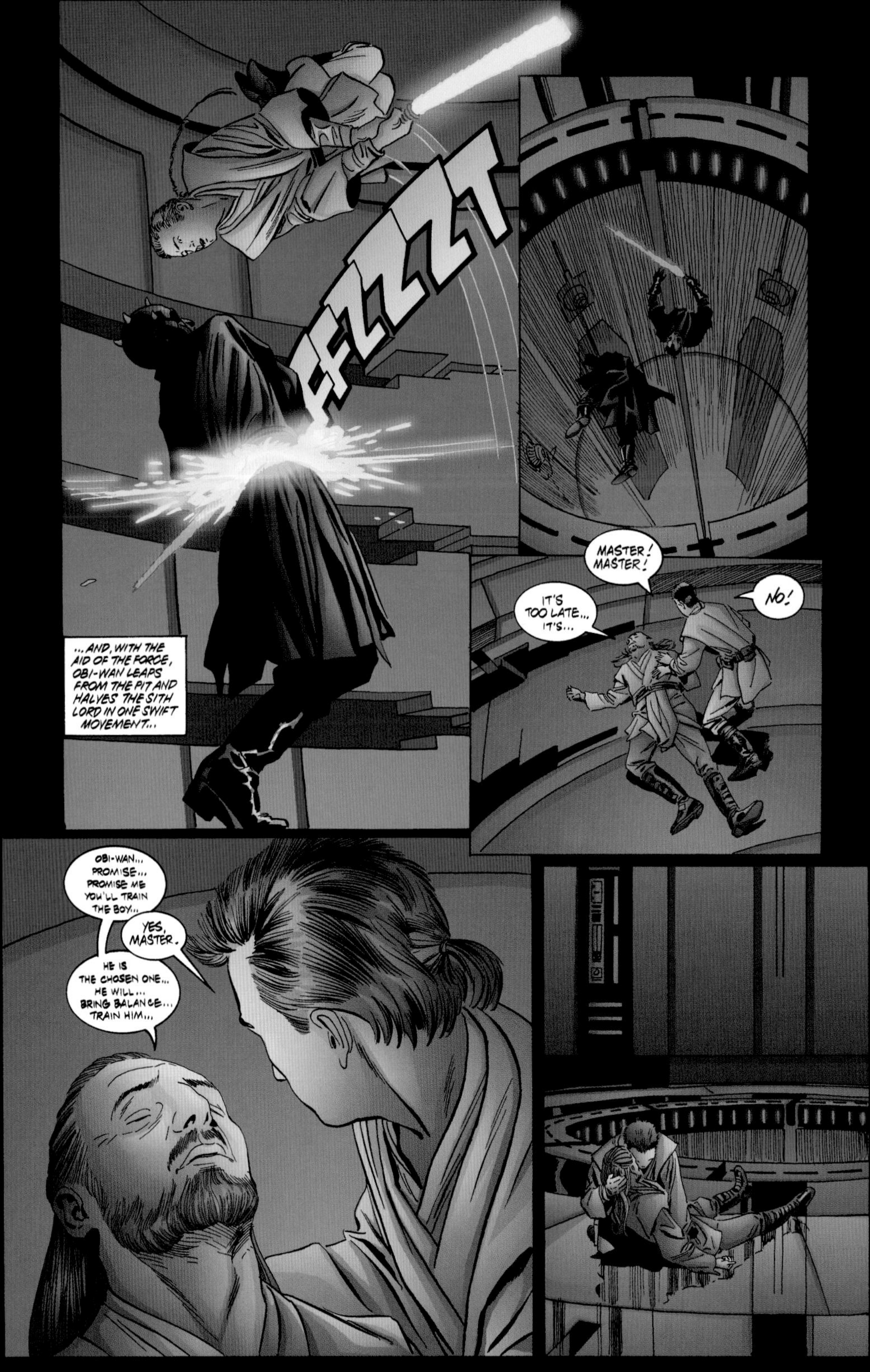
FZZZT
...AND, WITH THE AID OF THE FORCE, OBI-WAN LEAPS FROM THE PIT AND HALVES THE SITH LORD IN ONE SWIFT MOVEMENT...
MASTER! MASTER!
NO!
IT'S TOO LATE... IT'S...
OBI-WAN... PROMISE... PROMISE ME YOU'LL TRAIN THE BOY...
YES, MASTER.
HE IS THE CHOSEN ONE... HE WILL... BRING BALANCE... TRAIN HIM...

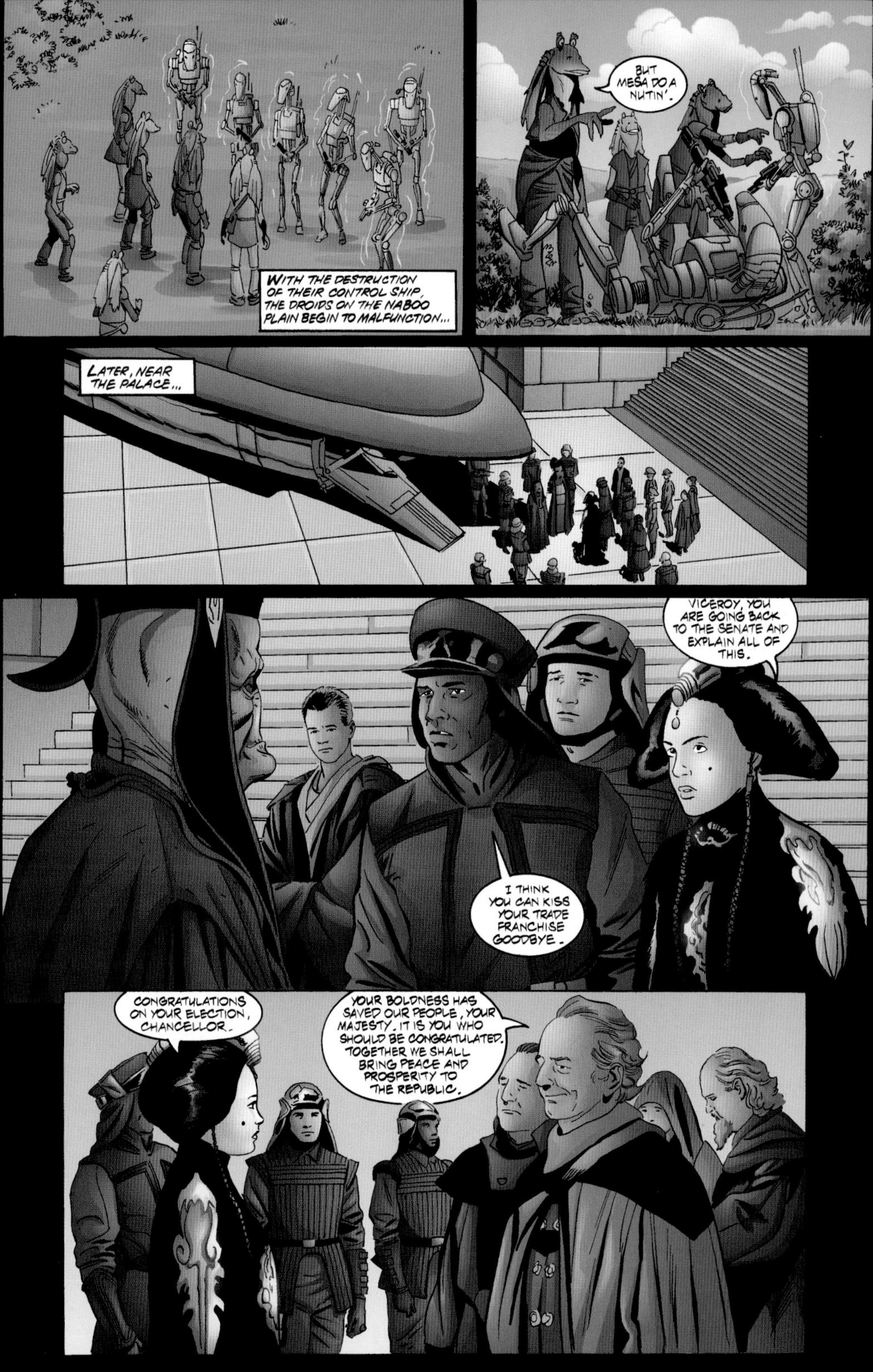
WITH THE DESTRUCTION OF THEIR CONTROL SHIP, THE DROIDS ON THE NABOO PLAIN BEGIN TO MALFUNCTION...
BUT MESA DO A NUTIN'.
LATER, NEAR THE PALACE...
VICEROY, YOU ARE GOING BACK TO THE SENATE AND EXPLAIN ALL OF THIS.
I THINK YOU CAN KISS YOUR TRADE FRANCHISE GOODBYE.
CONGRATULATIONS ON YOUR ELECTION, CHANCELLOR.
YOUR BOLDNESS HAS SAVED OUR PEOPLE, YOUR MAJESTY. IT IS YOU WHO SHOULD BE CONGRATULATED. TOGETHER WE SHALL BRING PEACE AND PROSPERITY TO THE REPUBLIC.

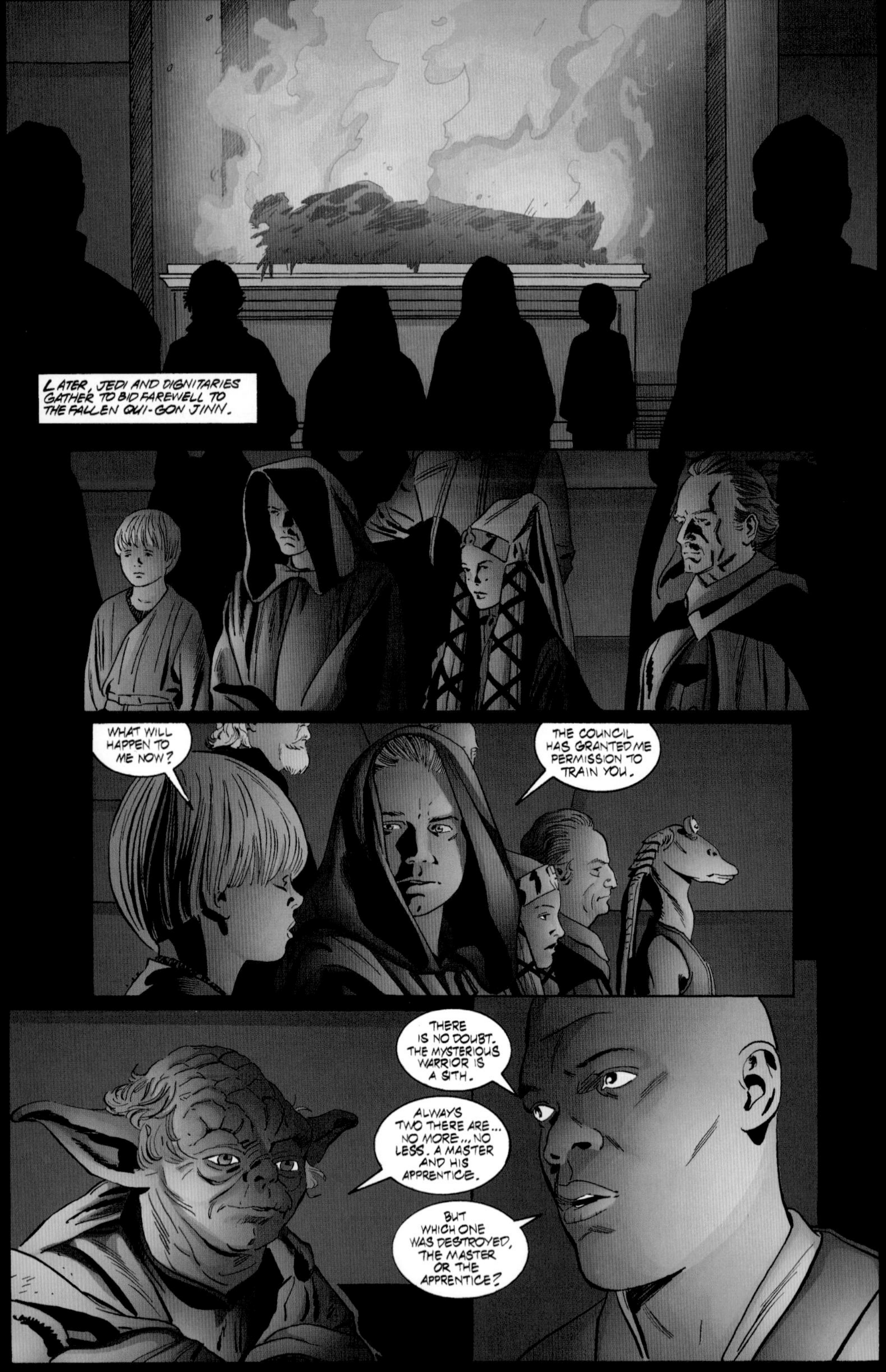
LATER, JEDI AND DIGNITARIES GATHER TO BID FAREWELL TO THE FALLEN QUI-GON JINN.
WHAT WILL HAPPEN TO ME NOW?
THE COUNCIL HAS GRANTED ME PERMISSION TO TRAIN YOU.
THERE IS NO DOUBT. THE MYSTERIOUS WARRIOR IS A SITH.
ALWAYS TWO THERE ARE... NO MORE... NO LESS. A MASTER AND HIS APPRENTICE.
BUT WHICH ONE WAS DESTROYED, THE MASTER OR THE APPRENTICE?

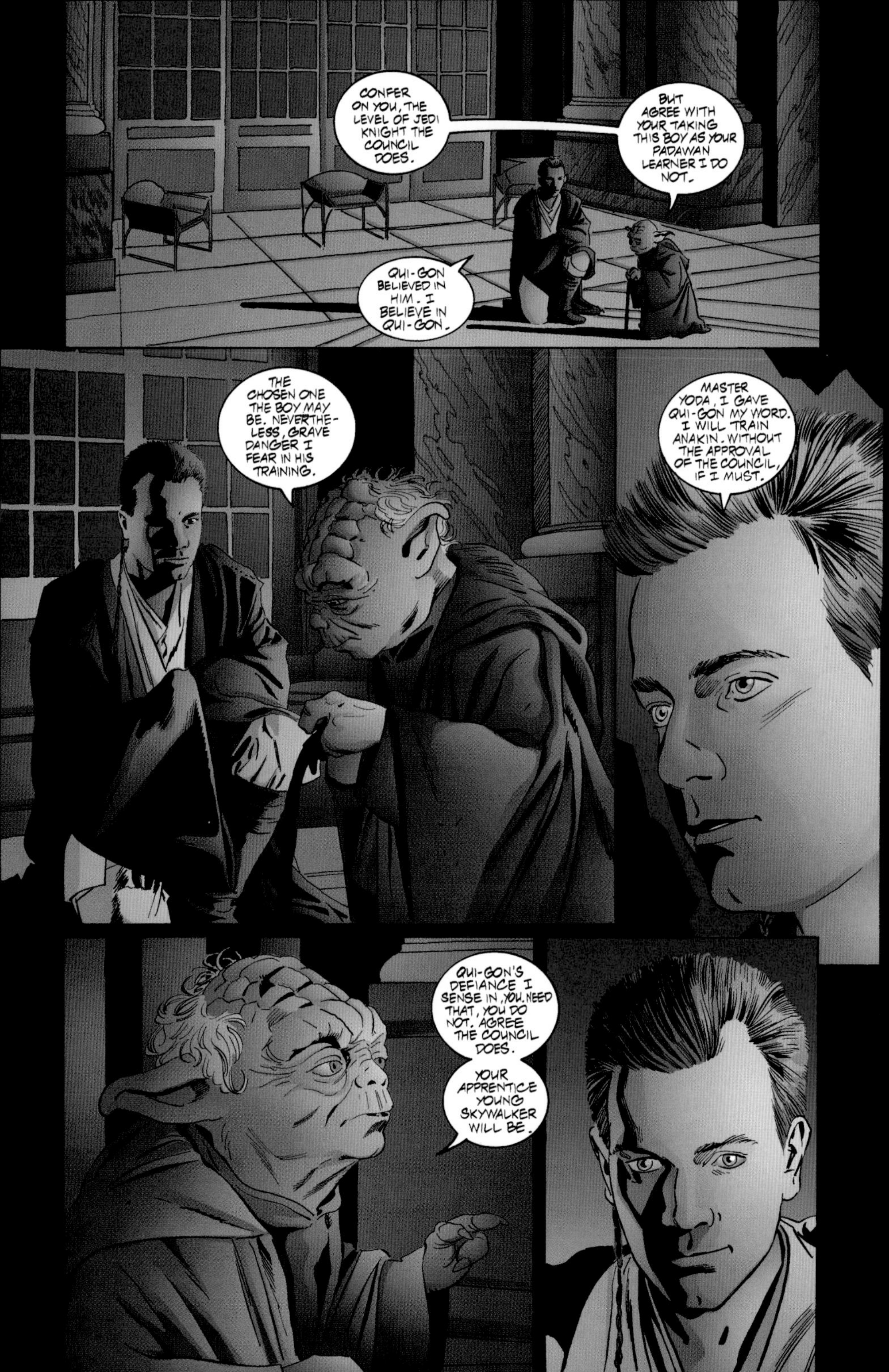
CONFER ON YOU, THE LEVEL OF JEDI KNIGHT THE COUNCIL DOES.
BUT AGREE WITH YOUR TAKING THIS BOY AS YOUR PADAWAN LEARNER I DO NOT.
QUI-GON BELIEVED IN HIM. I BELIEVE IN QUI-GON.
THE CHOSEN ONE THE BOY MAY BE. NEVERTHELESS, GRAVE DANGER I FEAR IN HIS TRAINING.
MASTER YODA, I GAVE QUI-GON MY WORD. I WILL TRAIN ANAKIN. WITHOUT THE APPROVAL OF THE COUNCIL, IF I MUST.
QUI-GON'S DEFIANCE I SENSE IN YOU. NEED THAT, YOU DO NOT. AGREE THE COUNCIL DOES.
YOUR APPRENTICE YOUNG SKYWALKER WILL BE.

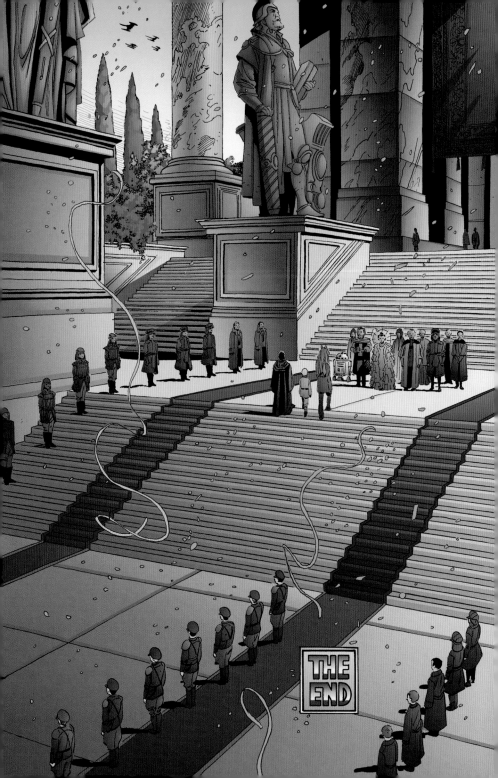

THE END

Attack of the Clones | Illustration by Drew Struzan

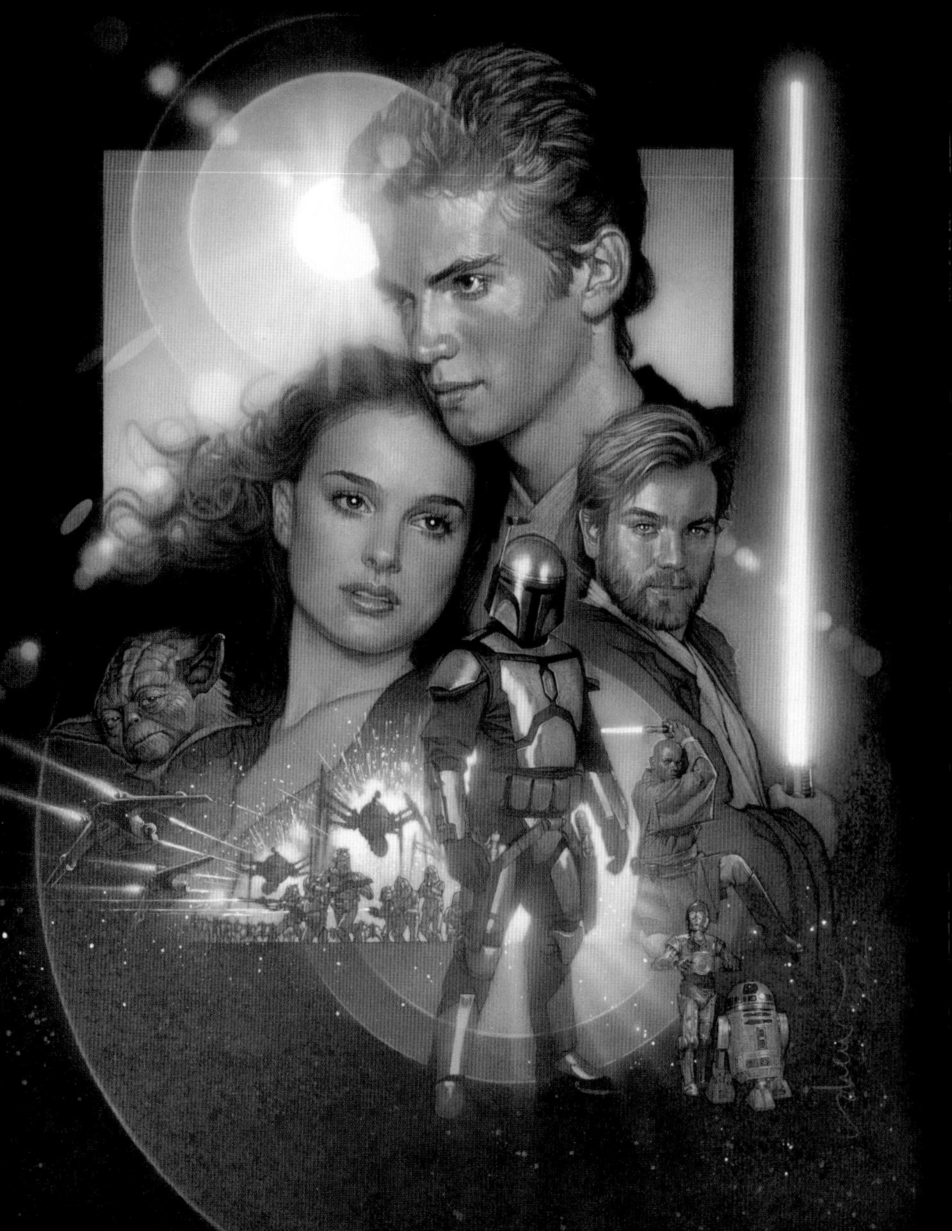

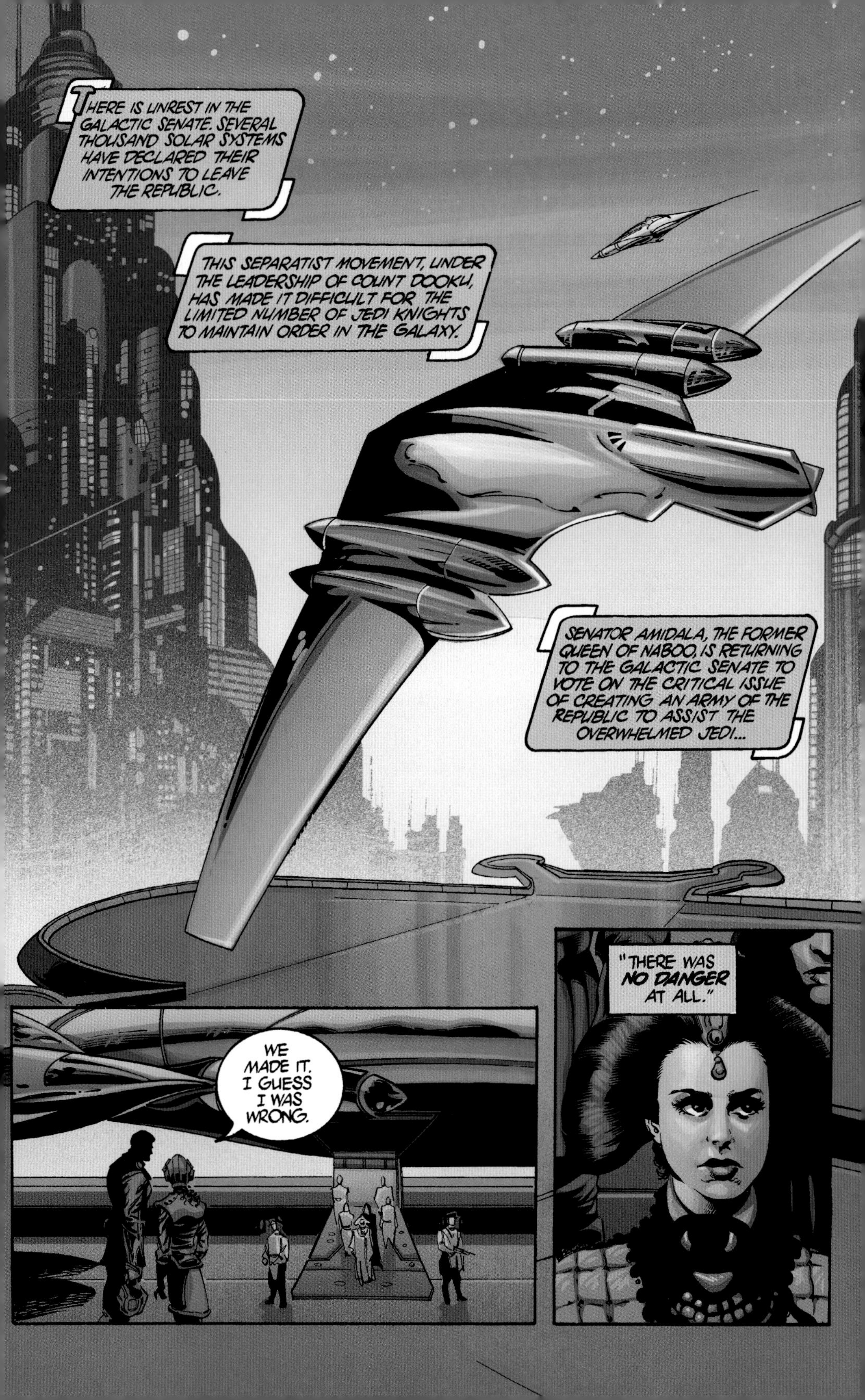
THERE IS UNREST IN THE GALACTIC SENATE. SEVERAL THOUSAND SOLAR SYSTEMS HAVE DECLARED THEIR INTENTIONS TO LEAVE THE REPUBLIC.
THIS SEPARATIST MOVEMENT, UNDER THE LEADERSHIP OF COUNT DOOKU, HAS MADE IT DIFFICULT FOR THE LIMITED NUMBER OF JEDI KNIGHTS TO MAINTAIN ORDER IN THE GALAXY.
SENATOR AMIDALA, THE FORMER QUEEN OF NABOO, IS RETURNING TO THE GALACTIC SENATE TO VOTE ON THE CRITICAL ISSUE OF CREATING AN ARMY OF THE REPUBLIC TO ASSIST THE OVERWHELMED JEDI...
WE MADE IT. I GUESS I WAS WRONG.
"THERE WAS NO DANGER AT ALL."

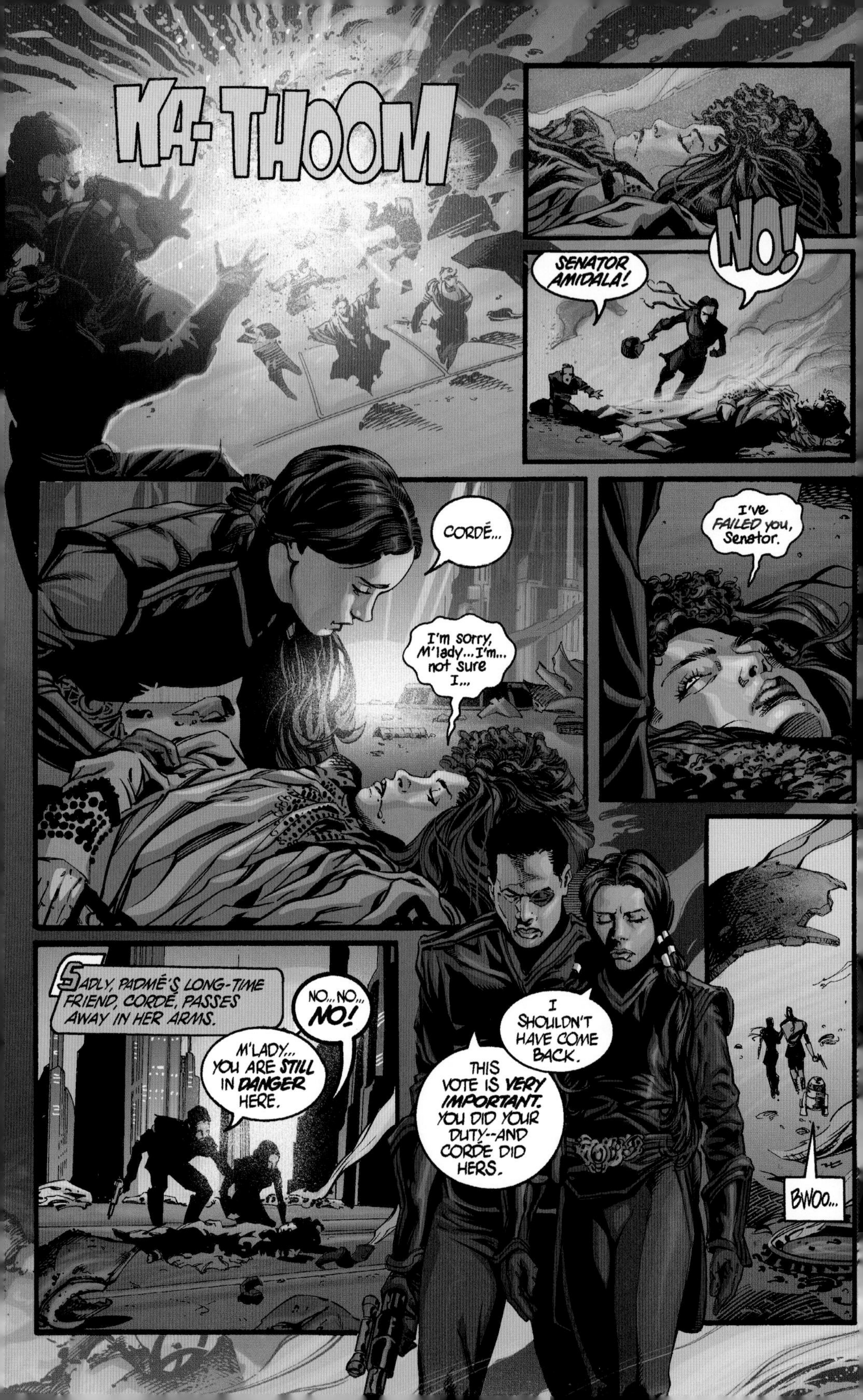

KA-THOOM
NO!
SENATOR AMIDALA!
CORDÉ...
I'm sorry, M'lady... I'm... not sure I...
I've FAILED you, Senator.
SADLY, PADMÉ'S LONG-TIME FRIEND, CORDÉ, PASSES AWAY IN HER ARMS.
NO... NO... NO!
M'LADY... YOU ARE STILL IN DANGER HERE.
I SHOULDN'T HAVE COME BACK.
THIS VOTE IS VERY IMPORTANT. YOU DID YOUR DUTY--AND CORDÉ DID HERS.
BWOO...

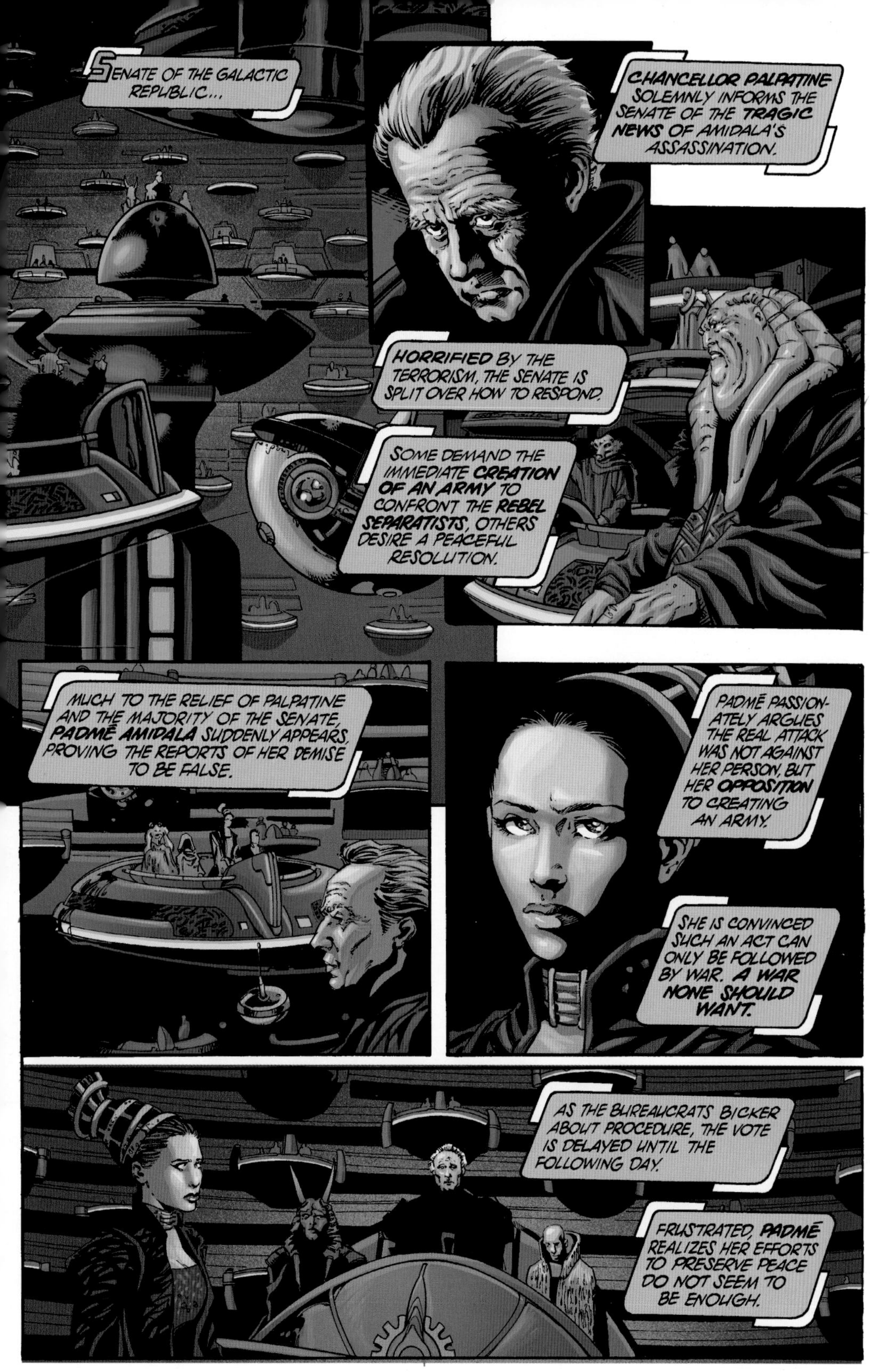
SENATE OF THE GALACTIC REPUBLIC...
CHANCELLOR PALPATINE SOLEMNLY INFORMS THE SENATE OF THE TRAGIC NEWS OF AMIDALA'S ASSASSINATION.
HORRIFIED BY THE TERRORISM, THE SENATE IS SPLIT OVER HOW TO RESPOND.
SOME DEMAND THE IMMEDIATE CREATION OF AN ARMY TO CONFRONT THE REBEL SEPARATISTS, OTHERS DESIRE A PEACEFUL RESOLUTION.
MUCH TO THE RELIEF OF PALPATINE AND THE MAJORITY OF THE SENATE, PADMÉ AMIDALA SUDDENLY APPEARS, PROVING THE REPORTS OF HER DEMISE TO BE FALSE.
PADMÉ PASSIONATELY ARGUES THE REAL ATTACK WAS NOT AGAINST HER PERSON, BUT HER OPPOSITION TO CREATING AN ARMY.
SHE IS CONVINCED SUCH AN ACT CAN ONLY BE FOLLOWED BY WAR. A WAR NONE SHOULD WANT.
AS THE BUREAUCRATS BICKER ABOUT PROCEDURE, THE VOTE IS DELAYED UNTIL THE FOLLOWING DAY.
FRUSTRATED, PADMÉ REALIZES HER EFFORTS TO PRESERVE PEACE DO NOT SEEM TO BE ENOUGH.

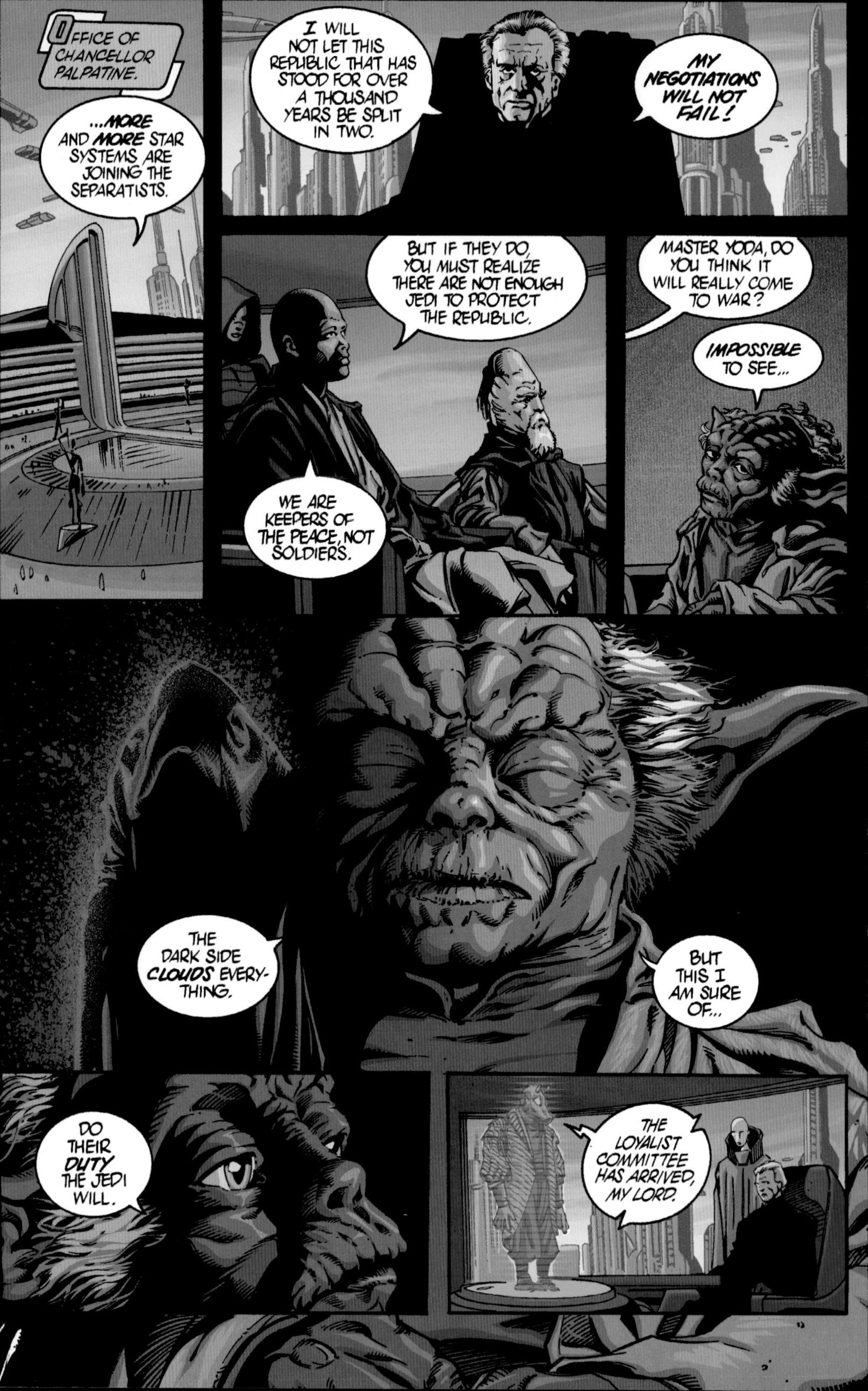
Office of Chancellor Palpatine.
...MORE AND MORE STAR SYSTEMS ARE JOINING THE SEPARATISTS.
I WILL NOT LET THIS REPUBLIC THAT HAS STOOD FOR OVER A THOUSAND YEARS BE SPLIT IN TWO.
MY NEGOTIATIONS WILL NOT FAIL!
BUT IF THEY DO, YOU MUST REALIZE THERE ARE NOT ENOUGH JEDI TO PROTECT THE REPUBLIC.
WE ARE KEEPERS OF THE PEACE, NOT SOLDIERS.
MASTER YODA, DO YOU THINK IT WILL REALLY COME TO WAR?
IMPOSSIBLE TO SEE...
THE DARK SIDE CLOUDS EVERY-THING.
BUT THIS I AM SURE OF...
DO THEIR DUTY THE JEDI WILL.
THE LOYALIST COMMITTEE HAS ARRIVED, MY LORD.

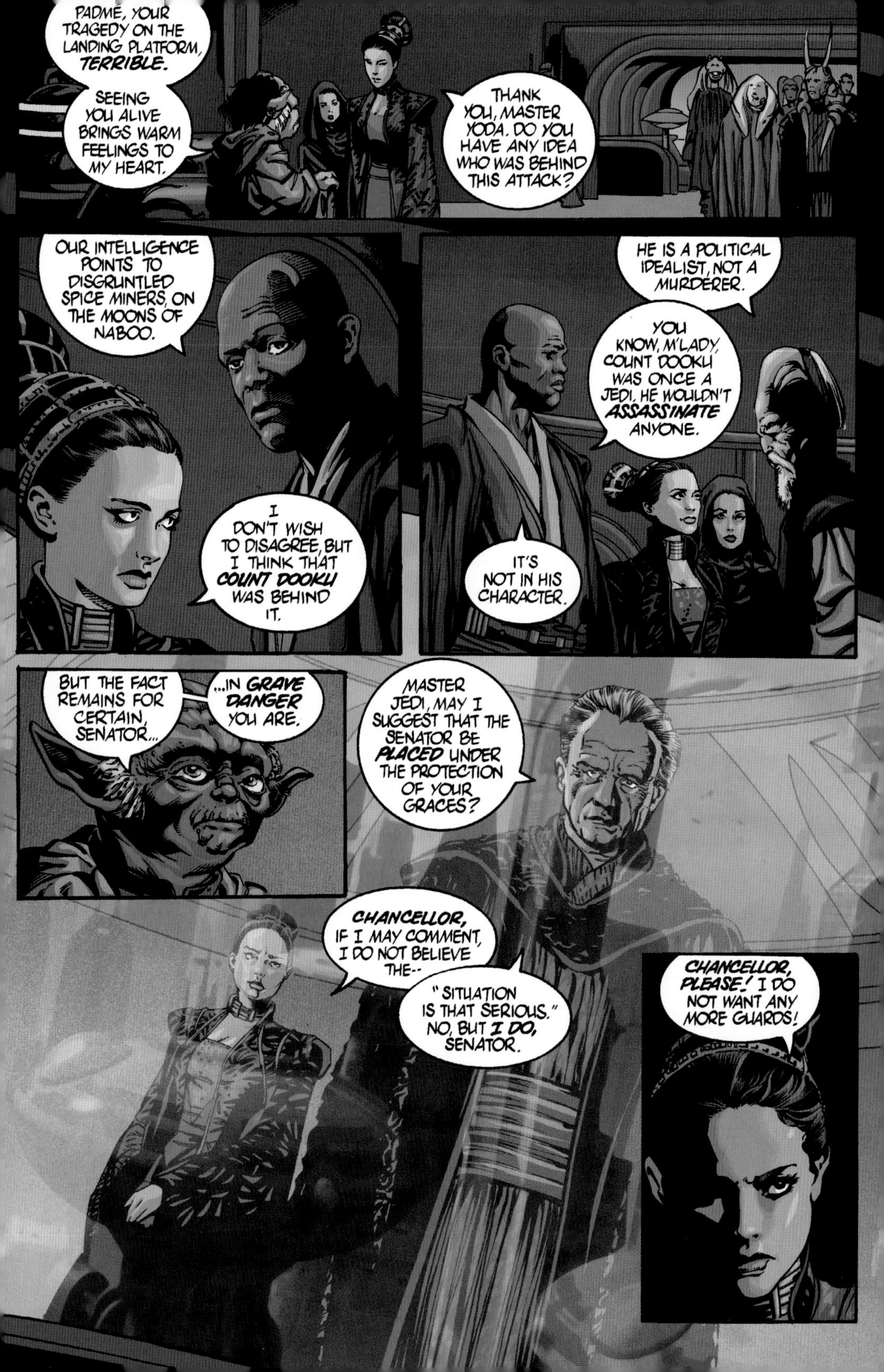
PADME, YOUR TRAGEDY ON THE LANDING PLATFORM, TERRIBLE.
SEEING YOU ALIVE BRINGS WARM FEELINGS TO MY HEART.
THANK YOU, MASTER YODA. DO YOU HAVE ANY IDEA WHO WAS BEHIND THIS ATTACK?
OUR INTELLIGENCE POINTS TO DISGRUNTLED SPICE MINERS, ON THE MOONS OF NABOO.
I DON'T WISH TO DISAGREE, BUT I THINK THAT COUNT DOOKU WAS BEHIND IT.
HE IS A POLITICAL IDEALIST, NOT A MURDERER.
YOU KNOW, M'LADY, COUNT DOOKU WAS ONCE A JEDI. HE WOULDN'T ASSASSINATE ANYONE.
IT'S NOT IN HIS CHARACTER.
BUT THE FACT REMAINS FOR CERTAIN, SENATOR...
...IN GRAVE DANGER YOU ARE.
MASTER JEDI, MAY I SUGGEST THAT THE SENATOR BE PLACED UNDER THE PROTECTION OF YOUR GRACES?
CHANCELLOR, IF I MAY COMMENT, I DO NOT BELIEVE THE--
"SITUATION IS THAT SERIOUS." NO, BUT I DO, SENATOR.
CHANCELLOR, PLEASE! I DO NOT WANT ANY MORE GUARDS!

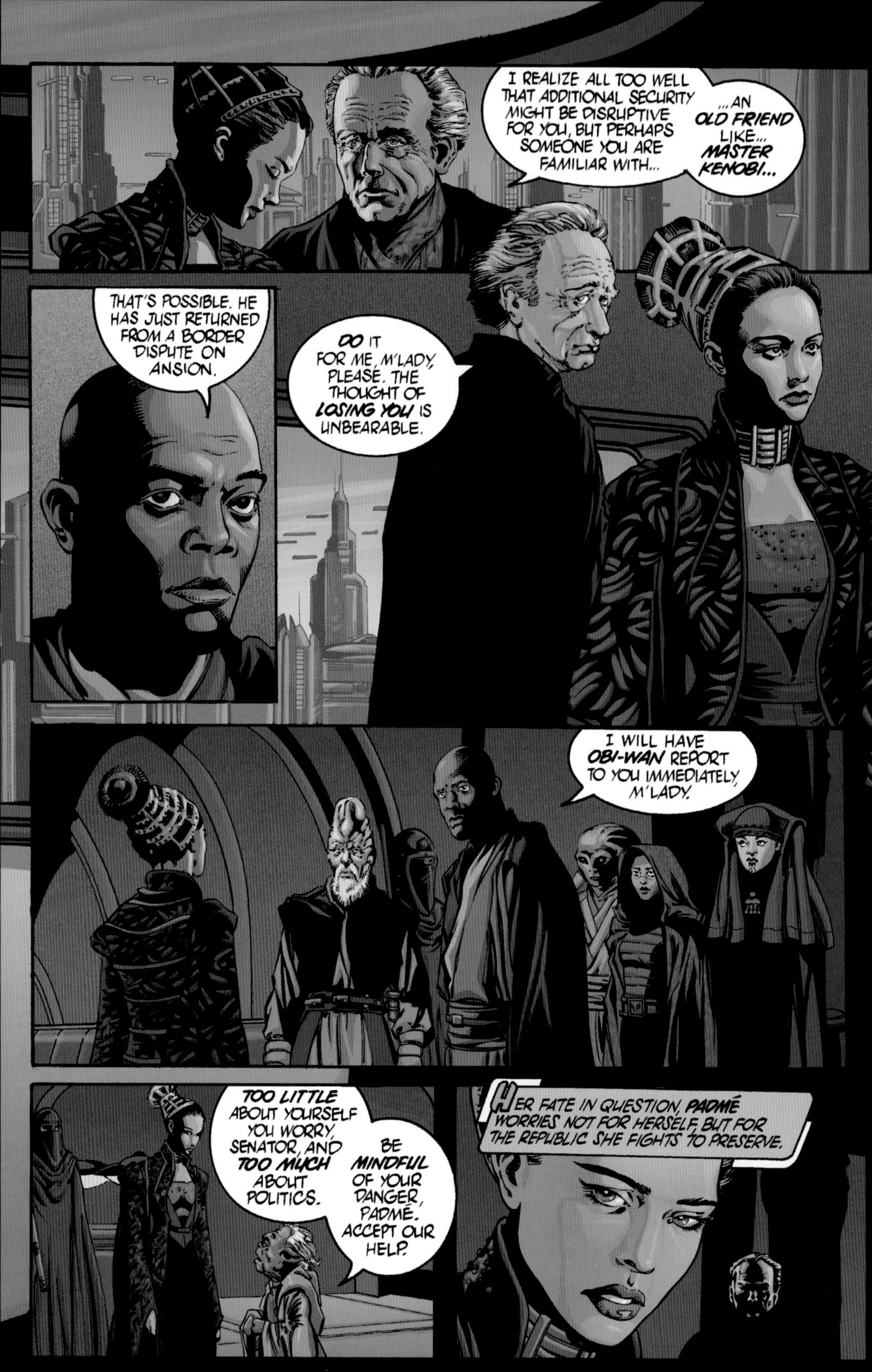
I REALIZE ALL TOO WELL THAT ADDITIONAL SECURITY MIGHT BE DISRUPTIVE FOR YOU, BUT PERHAPS SOMEONE YOU ARE FAMILIAR WITH...
...AN OLD FRIEND LIKE... MASTER KENOBI...
THAT'S POSSIBLE. HE HAS JUST RETURNED FROM A BORDER DISPUTE ON ANSION.
DO IT FOR ME, M'LADY, PLEASE. THE THOUGHT OF LOSING YOU IS UNBEARABLE.
I WILL HAVE OBI-WAN REPORT TO YOU IMMEDIATELY, M'LADY.
TOO LITTLE ABOUT YOURSELF YOU WORRY, SENATOR, AND TOO MUCH ABOUT POLITICS.
BE MINDFUL OF YOUR DANGER, PADMÉ. ACCEPT OUR HELP.
HER FATE IN QUESTION, PADMÉ WORRIES NOT FOR HERSELF, BUT FOR THE REPUBLIC SHE FIGHTS TO PRESERVE.

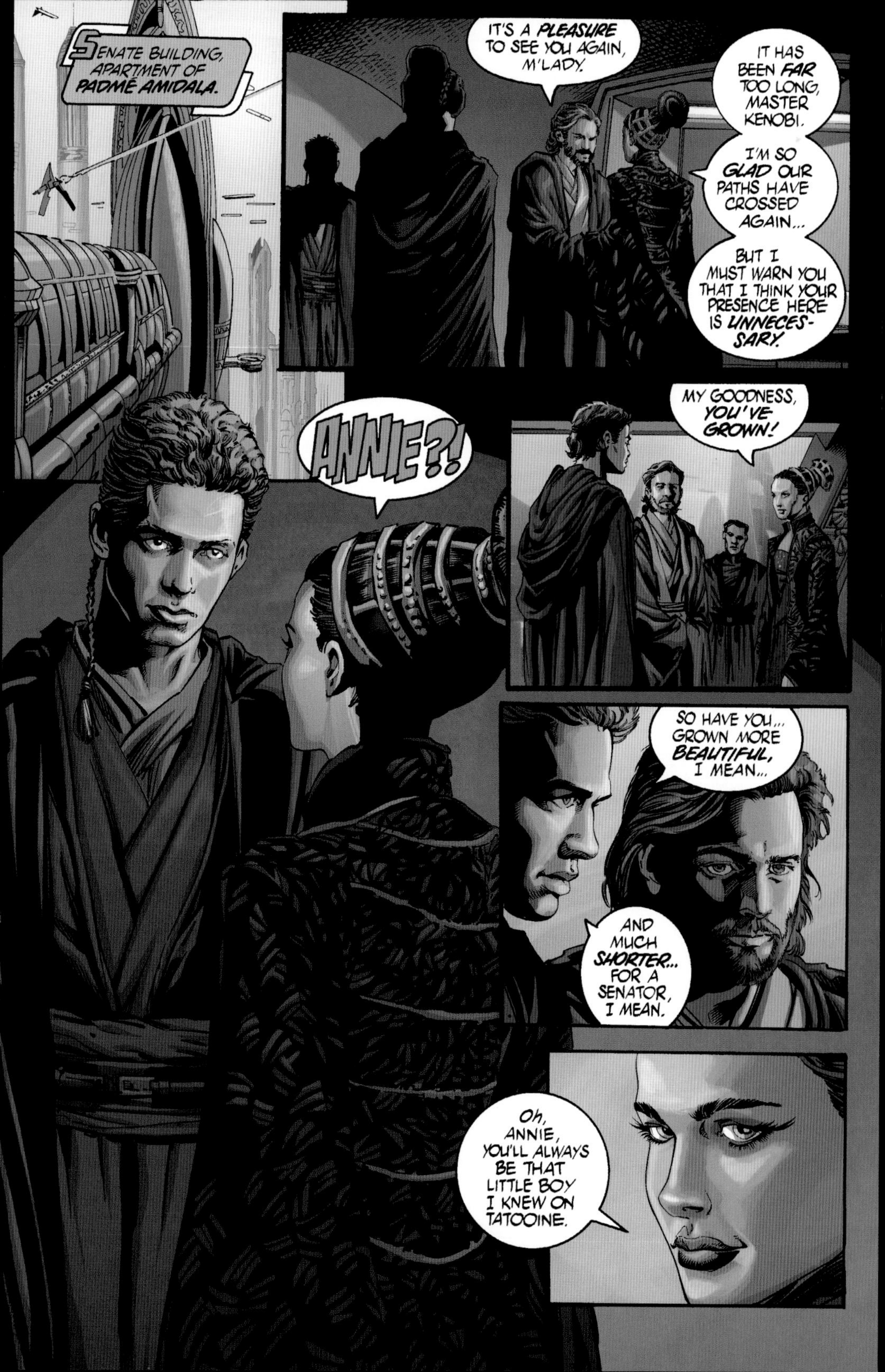
SENATE BUILDING, APARTMENT OF PADMÉ AMIDALA.
IT'S A PLEASURE TO SEE YOU AGAIN, M'LADY.
IT HAS BEEN FAR TOO LONG, MASTER KENOBI.
I'M SO GLAD OUR PATHS HAVE CROSSED AGAIN...
BUT I MUST WARN YOU THAT I THINK YOUR PRESENCE HERE IS UNNECES-SARY.
ANNIE?!
MY GOODNESS, YOU'VE GROWN!
SO HAVE YOU... GROWN MORE BEAUTIFUL, I MEAN...
AND MUCH SHORTER... FOR A SENATOR, I MEAN.
Oh, ANNIE, YOU'LL ALWAYS BE THAT LITTLE BOY I KNEW ON TATOOINE.

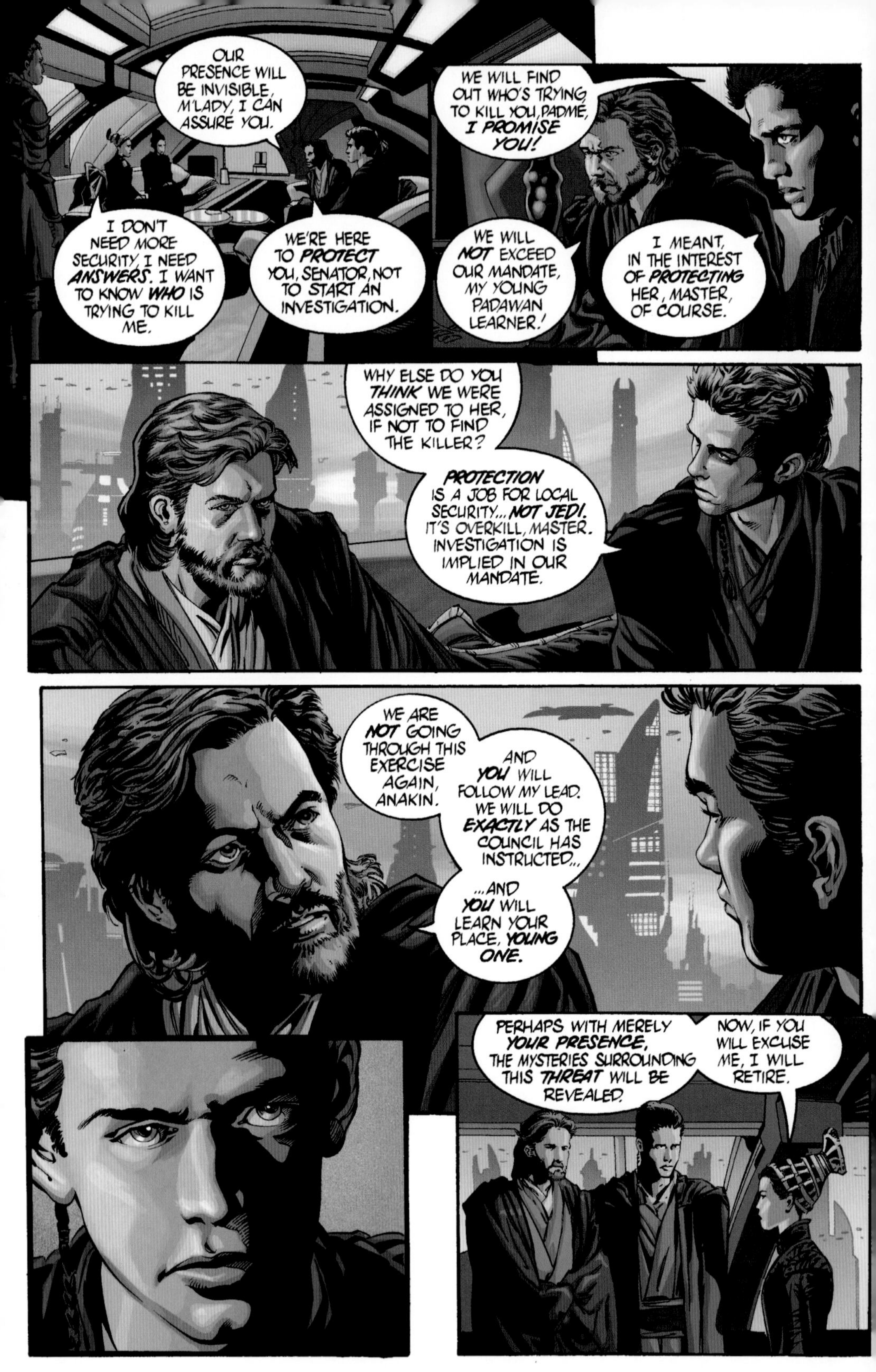
OUR PRESENCE WILL BE INVISIBLE, M'LADY, I CAN ASSURE YOU.
I DON'T NEED MORE SECURITY, I NEED ANSWERS. I WANT TO KNOW WHO IS TRYING TO KILL ME.
WE'RE HERE TO PROTECT YOU, SENATOR, NOT TO START AN INVESTIGATION.
WE WILL FIND OUT WHO'S TRYING TO KILL YOU, PADMÉ, I PROMISE YOU!
WE WILL NOT EXCEED OUR MANDATE, MY YOUNG PADAWAN LEARNER!
I MEANT, IN THE INTEREST OF PROTECTING HER, MASTER, OF COURSE.
WHY ELSE DO YOU THINK WE WERE ASSIGNED TO HER, IF NOT TO FIND THE KILLER?
PROTECTION IS A JOB FOR LOCAL SECURITY... NOT JEDI. IT'S OVERKILL, MASTER. INVESTIGATION IS IMPLIED IN OUR MANDATE.
WE ARE NOT GOING THROUGH THIS EXERCISE AGAIN, ANAKIN.
AND YOU WILL FOLLOW MY LEAD. WE WILL DO EXACTLY AS THE COUNCIL HAS INSTRUCTED...
...AND YOU WILL LEARN YOUR PLACE, YOUNG ONE.
PERHAPS WITH MERELY YOUR PRESENCE, THE MYSTERIES SURROUNDING THIS THREAT WILL BE REVEALED.
NOW, IF YOU WILL EXCUSE ME, I WILL RETIRE.

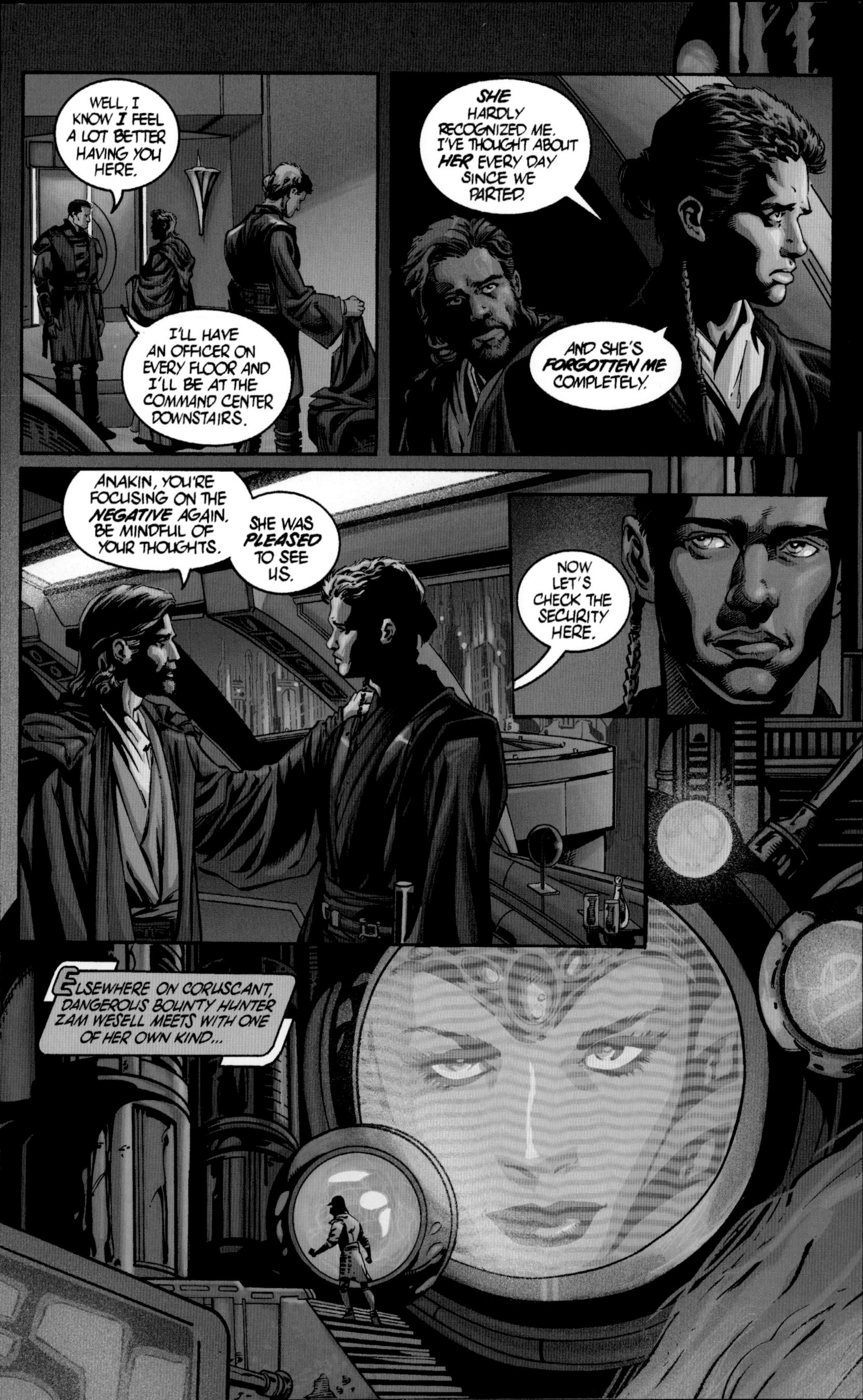
WELL, I KNOW I FEEL A LOT BETTER HAVING YOU HERE.
I'LL HAVE AN OFFICER ON EVERY FLOOR AND I'LL BE AT THE COMMAND CENTER DOWNSTAIRS.
SHE HARDLY RECOGNIZED ME. I'VE THOUGHT ABOUT HER EVERY DAY SINCE WE PARTED.
AND SHE'S FORGOTTEN ME COMPLETELY.
ANAKIN, YOU'RE FOCUSING ON THE NEGATIVE AGAIN. BE MINDFUL OF YOUR THOUGHTS.
SHE WAS PLEASED TO SEE US.
NOW LET'S CHECK THE SECURITY HERE.
ELSEWHERE ON CORUSCANT, DANGEROUS BOUNTY HUNTER ZAM WESELL MEETS WITH ONE OF HER OWN KIND...

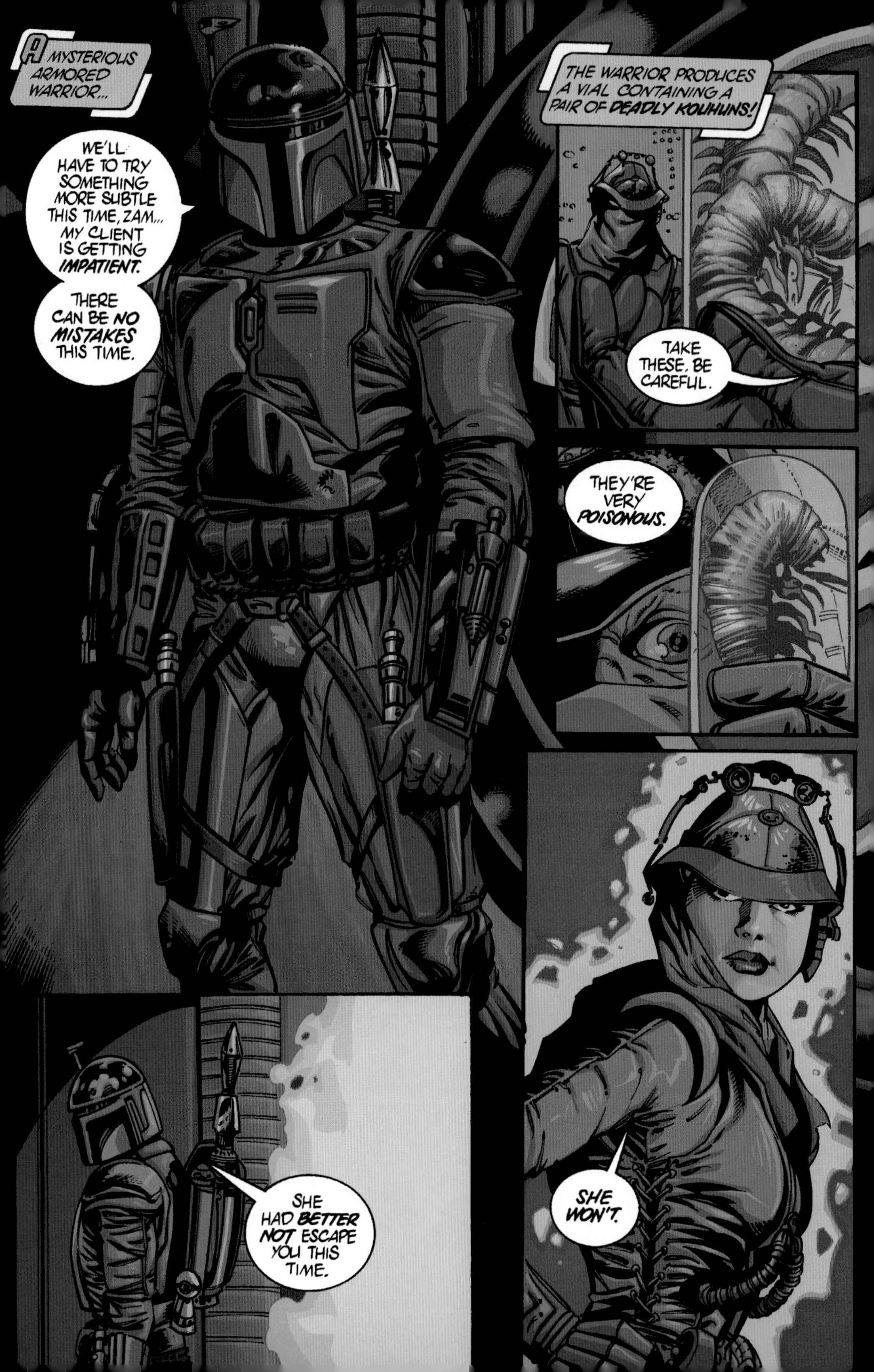
A MYSTERIOUS ARMORED WARRIOR...
WE'LL HAVE TO TRY SOMETHING MORE SUBTLE THIS TIME, ZAM... MY CLIENT IS GETTING IMPATIENT.
THERE CAN BE NO MISTAKES THIS TIME.
THE WARRIOR PRODUCES A VIAL CONTAINING A PAIR OF DEADLY KOUHUNS!
TAKE THESE. BE CAREFUL.
THEY'RE VERY POISONOUS.
SHE HAD BETTER NOT ESCAPE YOU THIS TIME.
SHE WON'T.

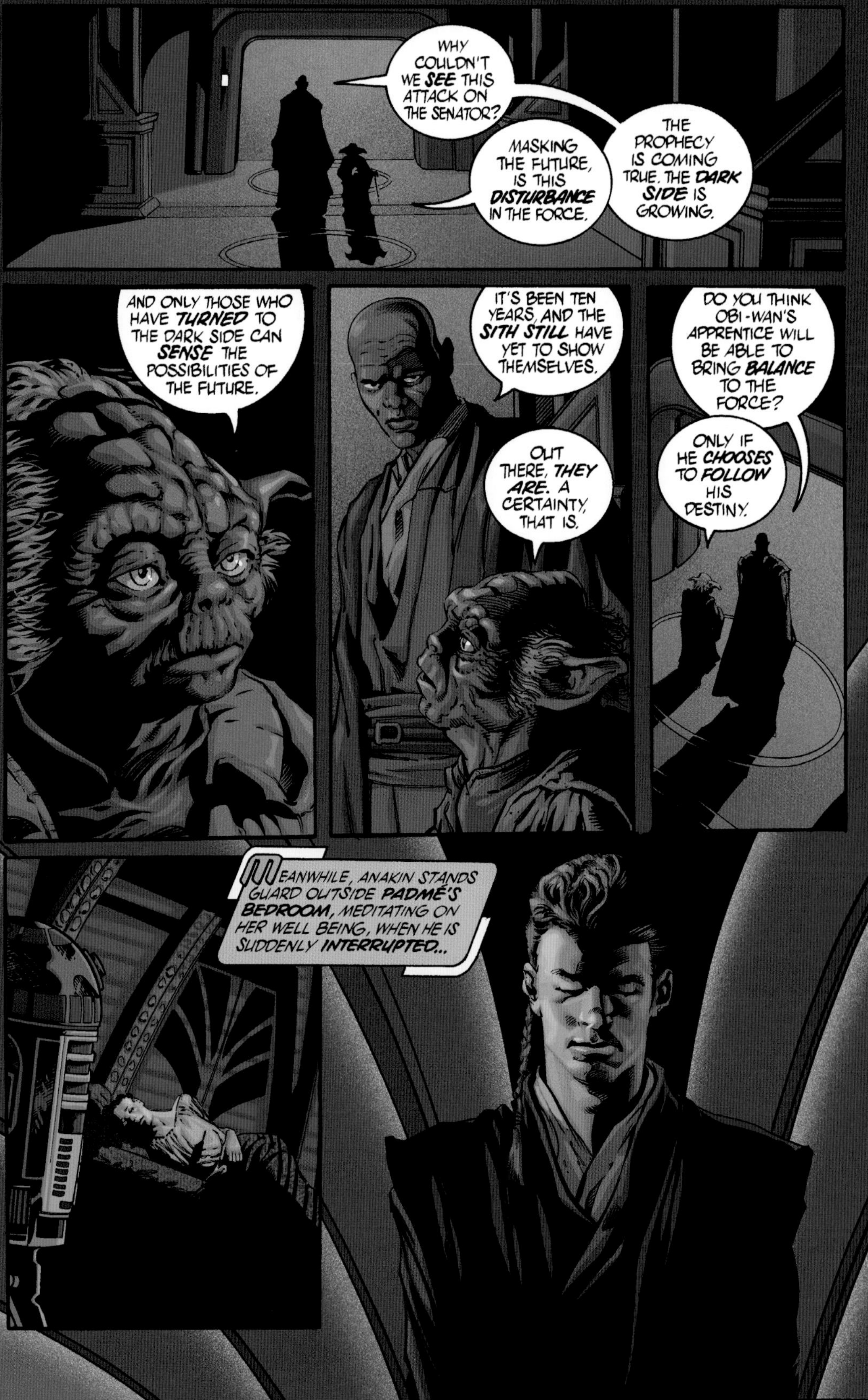
WHY COULDN'T WE SEE THIS ATTACK ON THE SENATOR?
MASKING THE FUTURE, IS THIS DISTURBANCE IN THE FORCE.
THE PROPHECY IS COMING TRUE. THE DARK SIDE IS GROWING.
AND ONLY THOSE WHO HAVE TURNED TO THE DARK SIDE CAN SENSE THE POSSIBILITIES OF THE FUTURE.
IT'S BEEN TEN YEARS, AND THE SITH STILL HAVE YET TO SHOW THEMSELVES.
OUT THERE, THEY ARE. A CERTAINTY, THAT IS.
DO YOU THINK OBI-WAN'S APPRENTICE WILL BE ABLE TO BRING BALANCE TO THE FORCE?
ONLY IF HE CHOOSES TO FOLLOW HIS DESTINY.
MEANWHILE, ANAKIN STANDS GUARD OUTSIDE PADMÉ'S BEDROOM, MEDITATING ON HER WELL BEING, WHEN HE IS SUDDENLY INTERRUPTED...

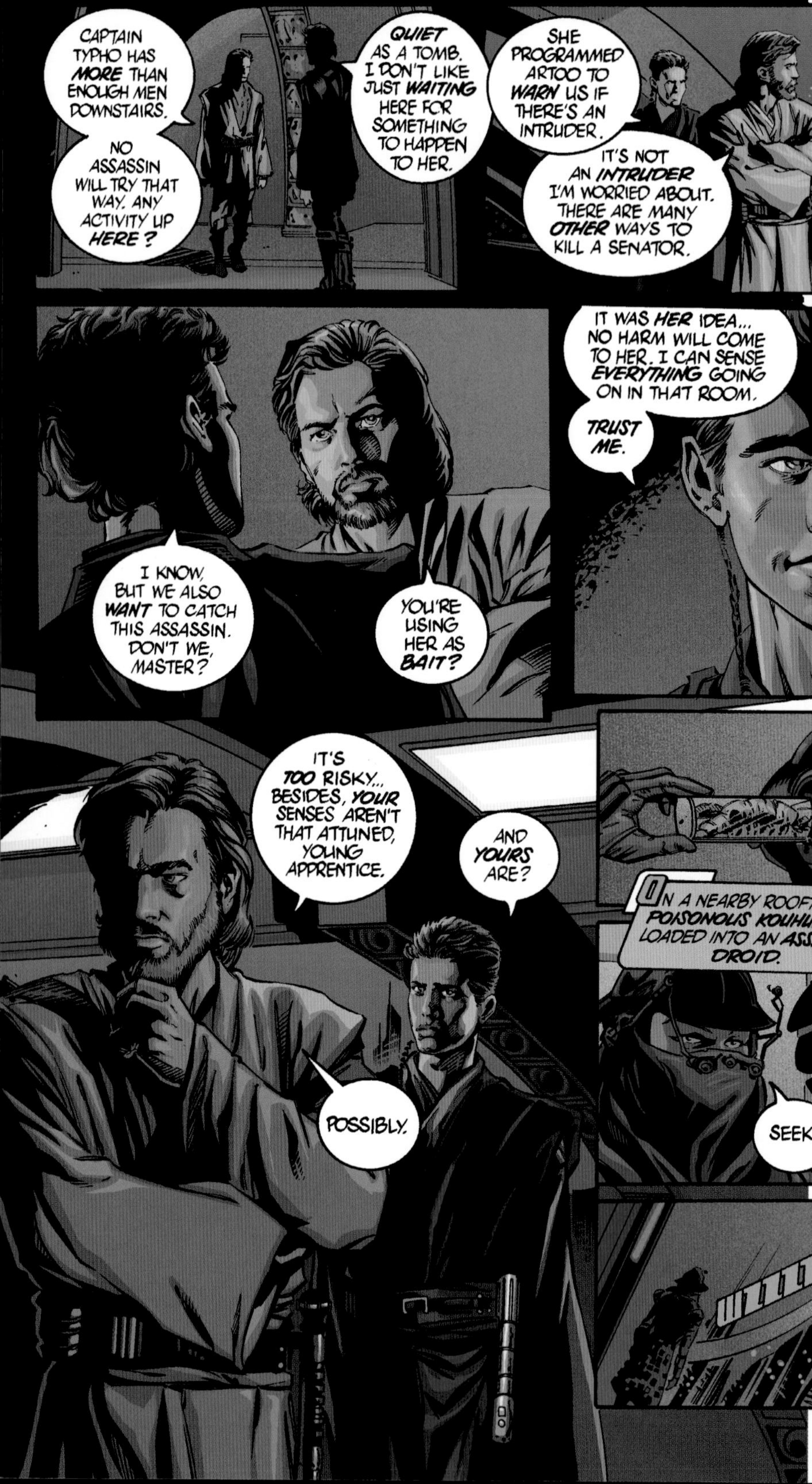
CAPTAIN TYPHO HAS MORE THAN ENOUGH MEN DOWNSTAIRS.
NO ASSASSIN WILL TRY THAT WAY. ANY ACTIVITY UP HERE?
QUIET AS A TOMB. I DON'T LIKE JUST WAITING HERE FOR SOMETHING TO HAPPEN TO HER.
SHE PROGRAMMED ARTOO TO WARN US IF THERE'S AN INTRUDER.
IT'S NOT AN INTRUDER I'M WORRIED ABOUT. THERE ARE MANY OTHER WAYS TO KILL A SENATOR.
I KNOW, BUT WE ALSO WANT TO CATCH THIS ASSASSIN. DON'T WE, MASTER?
YOU'RE USING HER AS BAIT?
IT WAS HER IDEA... NO HARM WILL COME TO HER. I CAN SENSE EVERYTHING GOING ON IN THAT ROOM.
TRUST ME.
IT'S TOO RISKY... BESIDES, YOUR SENSES AREN'T THAT ATTUNED, YOUNG APPRENTICE.
AND YOURS ARE?
POSSIBLY.
ON A NEARBY ROOFTOP, THE POISONOUS KOUHUNS ARE LOADED INTO AN ASSASSIN DROID.
SEEK.
WZZZZ

UNAWARE OF THE APPROACHING DANGER, *ANAKIN* AND *OBI-WAN* CONVERSE...

I DON'T SLEEP WELL ANYMORE.

BECAUSE OF YOUR *MOTHER?*

I DON'T KNOW WHY I KEEP *DREAMING* ABOUT HER NOW. I HAVEN'T SEEN *HER* SINCE I WAS LITTLE.

DREAMS PASS IN TIME.

I'D RATHER DREAM OF *PADMÉ.* JUST BEING AROUND HER AGAIN IS...

INTOXI-CATING.

MIND YOUR THOUGHTS, ANAKIN, THEY *BETRAY* YOU.

YOU'VE MADE A COMMITMENT TO THE JEDI ORDER... A *COMMITMENT* NOT EASILY BROKEN.

AND THEY *FORGET THE NICETIES* OF DEMOCRACY TO GET THOSE FUNDS.

AND DON'T FORGET SHE'S A POLITICIAN. THEY'RE *NOT* TO BE TRUSTED.

IT'S BEEN MY EXPERIENCE THAT SENATORS ARE ONLY FOCUSED ON *PLEASING THOSE* WHO FUND THEIR CAMPAIGNS.

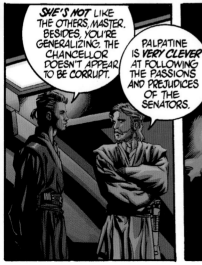

SHE'S NOT LIKE THE OTHERS, MASTER. BESIDES, YOU'RE GENERALIZING. THE CHANCELLOR DOESN'T APPEAR TO BE CORRUPT.

PALPATINE IS *VERY CLEVER* AT FOLLOWING THE PASSIONS AND PREJUDICES OF THE SENATORS.

I *THINK* HE IS A GOOD MAN. MY INSTINCTS ARE VERY *POSITIVE* ABOUT HIM.

MASTER...

I SENSE IT, TOO!

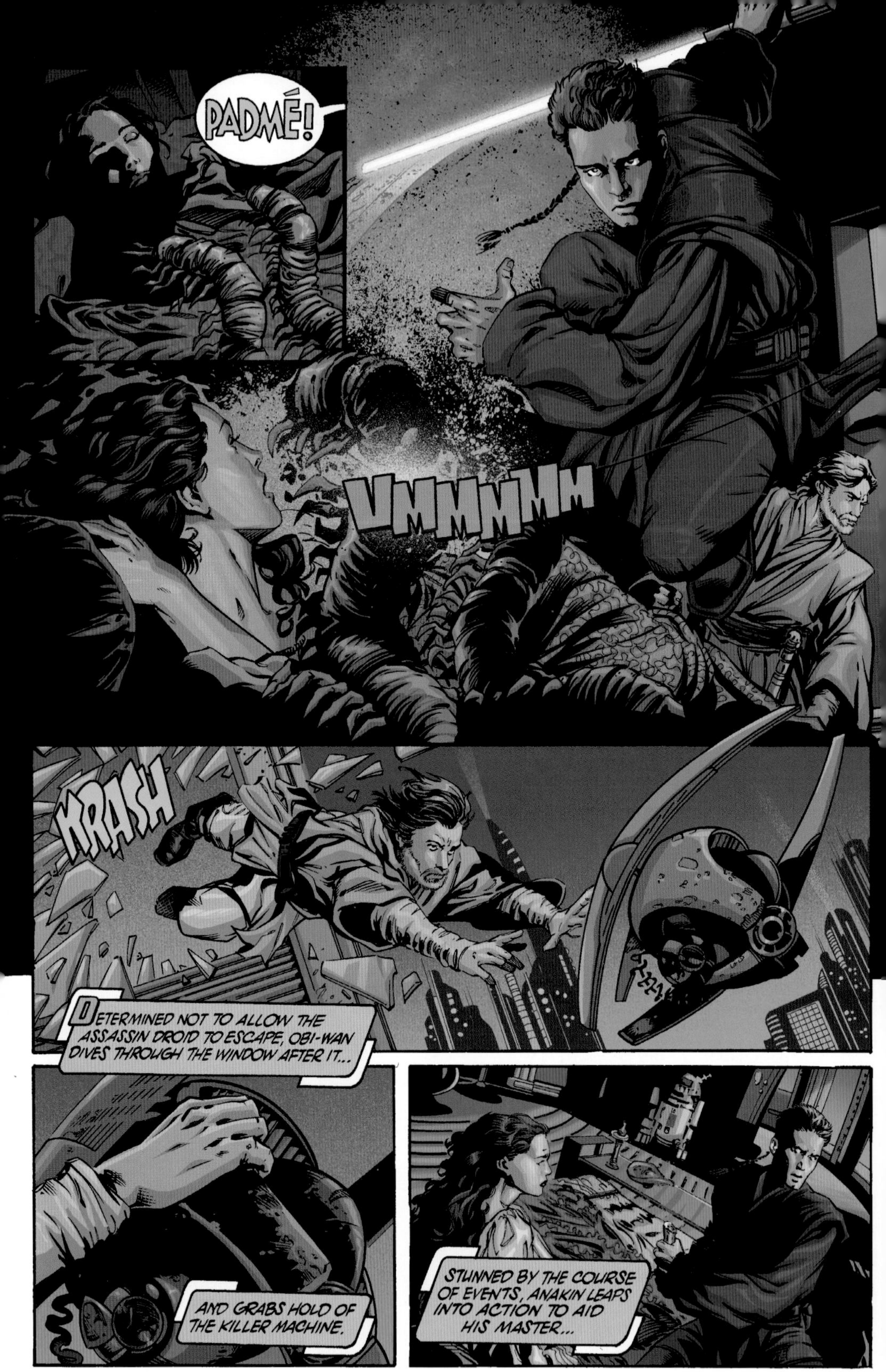
PADMÉ!
UMMMMMM
KRASH
DETERMINED NOT TO ALLOW THE ASSASSIN DROID TO ESCAPE, OBI-WAN DIVES THROUGH THE WINDOW AFTER IT...
AND GRABS HOLD OF THE KILLER MACHINE.
STUNNED BY THE COURSE OF EVENTS, ANAKIN LEAPS INTO ACTION TO AID HIS MASTER...

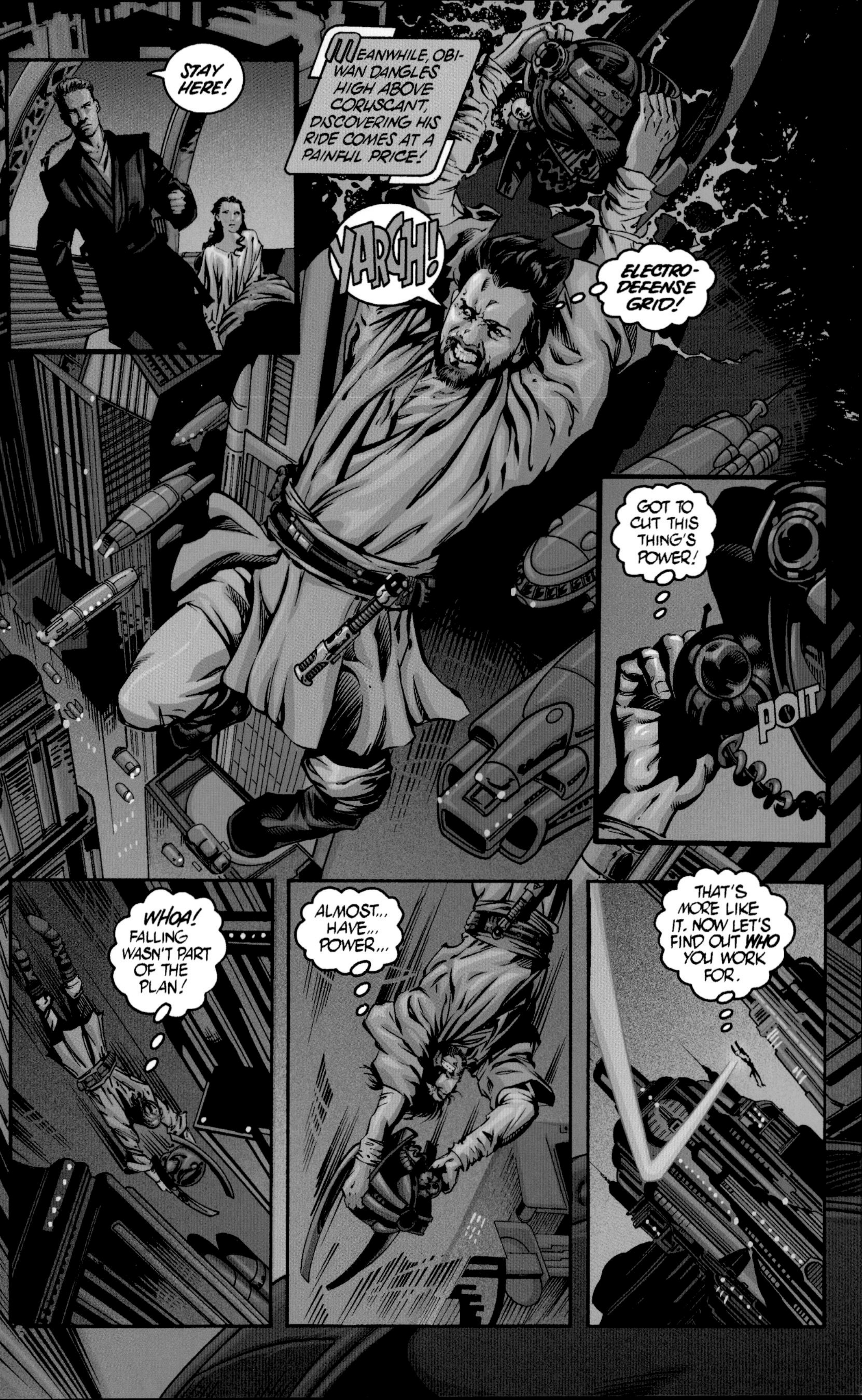
STAY HERE!
MEANWHILE, OBI-WAN DANGLES HIGH ABOVE CORUSCANT, DISCOVERING HIS RIDE COMES AT A PAINFUL PRICE!
YARGH!
ELECTRO-DEFENSE GRID!
GOT TO CUT THIS THING'S POWER!
POIT
WHOA! FALLING WASN'T PART OF THE PLAN!
ALMOST... HAVE... POWER...
THAT'S MORE LIKE IT. NOW LET'S FIND OUT WHO YOU WORK FOR.

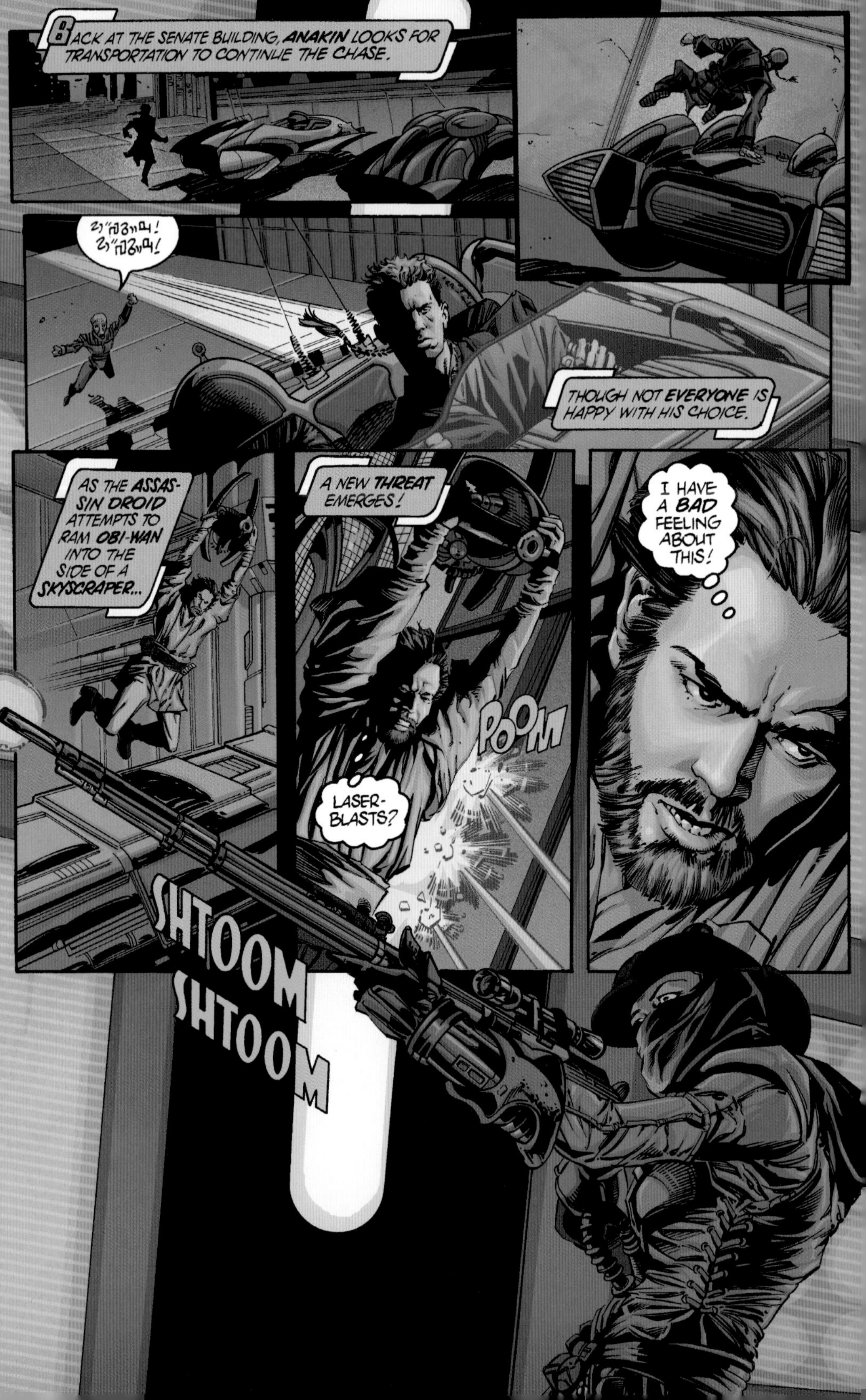
BACK AT THE SENATE BUILDING, ANAKIN LOOKS FOR TRANSPORTATION TO CONTINUE THE CHASE.
THOUGH NOT EVERYONE IS HAPPY WITH HIS CHOICE.
AS THE ASSASSIN DROID ATTEMPTS TO RAM OBI-WAN INTO THE SIDE OF A SKYSCRAPER...
A NEW THREAT EMERGES!
POOM
LASER-BLASTS?
I HAVE A BAD FEELING ABOUT THIS!
SHTOOM
SHTOOM

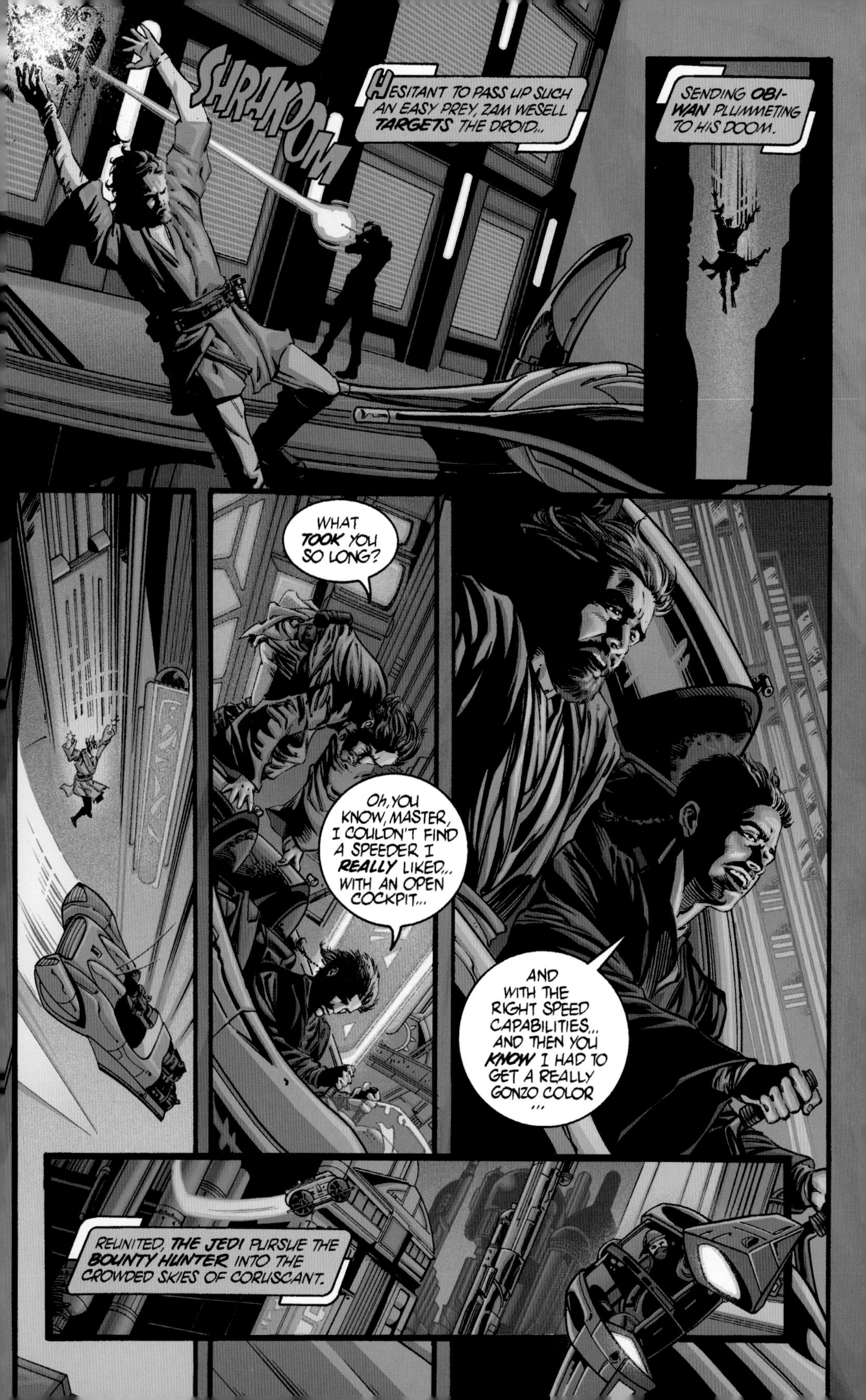
SHRAKOOM
HESITANT TO PASS UP SUCH AN EASY PREY, ZAM WESELL TARGETS THE DROID...
SENDING OBI-WAN PLUMMETING TO HIS DOOM.
WHAT TOOK YOU SO LONG?
Oh, YOU KNOW, MASTER, I COULDN'T FIND A SPEEDER I REALLY LIKED... WITH AN OPEN COCKPIT...
AND WITH THE RIGHT SPEED CAPABILITIES... AND THEN YOU KNOW I HAD TO GET A REALLY GONZO COLOR ...
REUNITED, THE JEDI PURSUE THE BOUNTY HUNTER INTO THE CROWDED SKIES OF CORUSCANT.

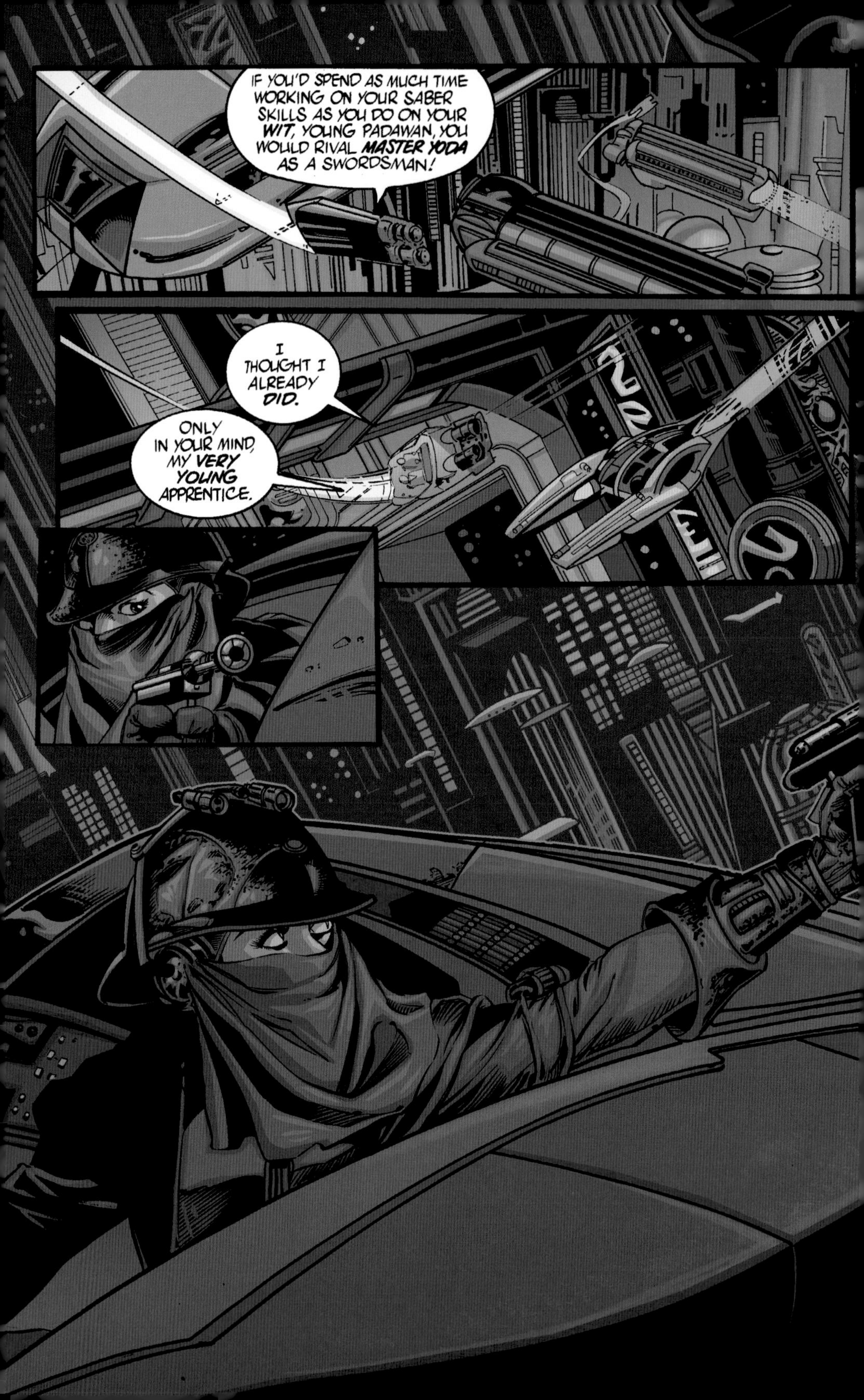
IF YOU'D SPEND AS MUCH TIME WORKING ON YOUR SABER SKILLS AS YOU DO ON YOUR *WIT,* YOUNG PADAWAN, YOU WOULD RIVAL ***MASTER YODA*** AS A SWORDSMAN!
I THOUGHT I ALREADY ***DID.***
ONLY IN YOUR MIND, MY ***VERY YOUNG*** APPRENTICE.

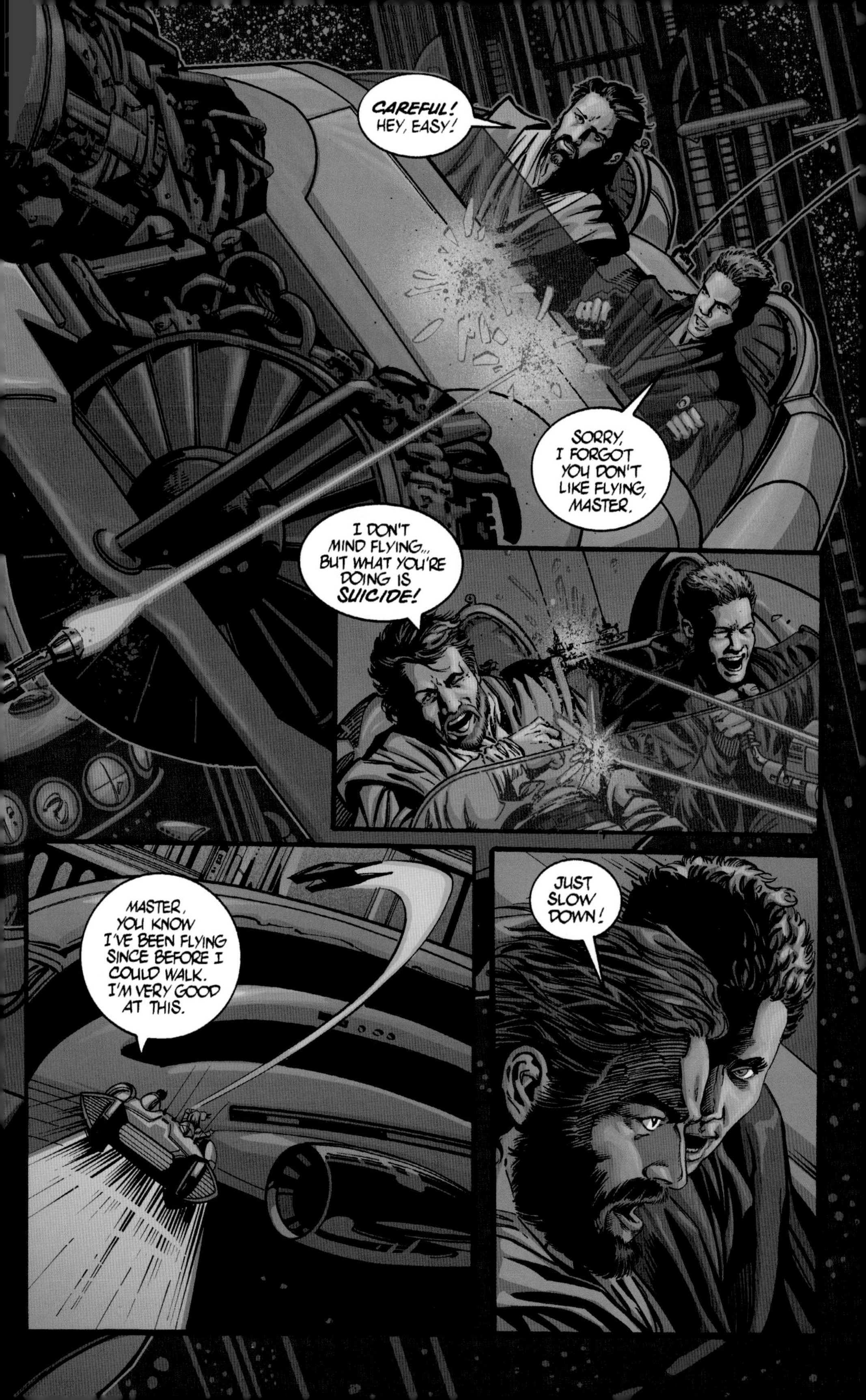
CAREFUL! HEY, EASY!
SORRY, I FORGOT YOU DON'T LIKE FLYING, MASTER.
I DON'T MIND FLYING... BUT WHAT YOU'RE DOING IS SUICIDE!
MASTER, YOU KNOW I'VE BEEN FLYING SINCE BEFORE I COULD WALK. I'M VERY GOOD AT THIS.
JUST SLOW DOWN!

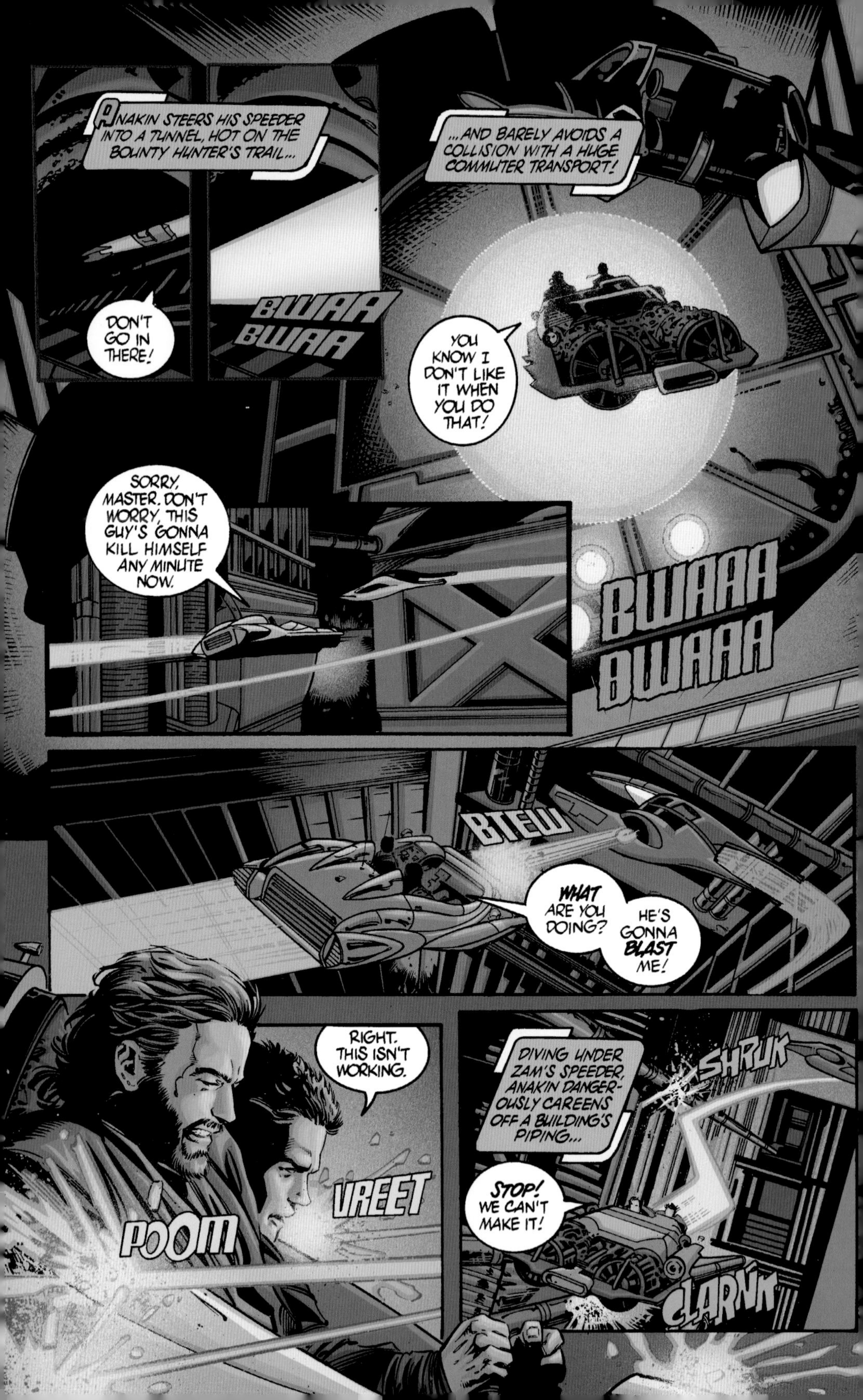
ANAKIN STEERS HIS SPEEDER INTO A TUNNEL, HOT ON THE BOUNTY HUNTER'S TRAIL...
DON'T GO IN THERE!
BWAA BWAA
...AND BARELY AVOIDS A COLLISION WITH A HUGE COMMUTER TRANSPORT!
YOU KNOW I DON'T LIKE IT WHEN YOU DO THAT!
SORRY, MASTER. DON'T WORRY, THIS GUY'S GONNA KILL HIMSELF ANY MINUTE NOW.
BWAAA BWAAA
BTEW
WHAT ARE YOU DOING?
HE'S GONNA BLAST ME!
RIGHT. THIS ISN'T WORKING.
VREET
POOM
DIVING UNDER ZAM'S SPEEDER, ANAKIN DANGEROUSLY CAREENS OFF A BUILDING'S PIPING...
SHRUK
STOP! WE CAN'T MAKE IT!
CLARNK

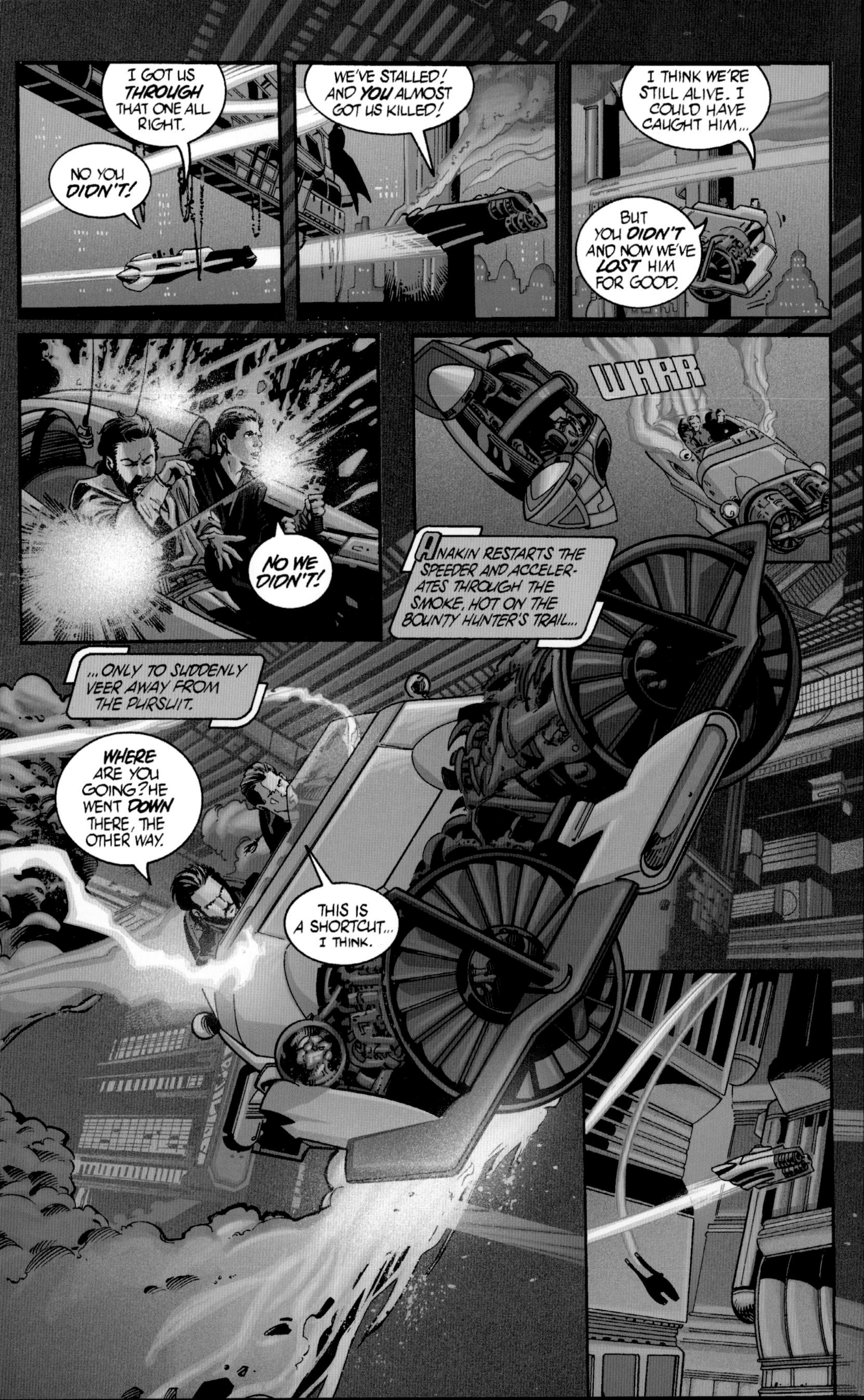
I GOT US THROUGH THAT ONE ALL RIGHT.
NO YOU DIDN'T!
WE'VE STALLED! AND YOU ALMOST GOT US KILLED!
I THINK WE'RE STILL ALIVE. I COULD HAVE CAUGHT HIM...
BUT YOU DIDN'T AND NOW WE'VE LOST HIM FOR GOOD.
NO WE DIDN'T!
WHRR
ANAKIN RESTARTS THE SPEEDER AND ACCELERATES THROUGH THE SMOKE, HOT ON THE BOUNTY HUNTER'S TRAIL...
...ONLY TO SUDDENLY VEER AWAY FROM THE PURSUIT.
WHERE ARE YOU GOING? HE WENT DOWN THERE, THE OTHER WAY.
THIS IS A SHORTCUT... I THINK.

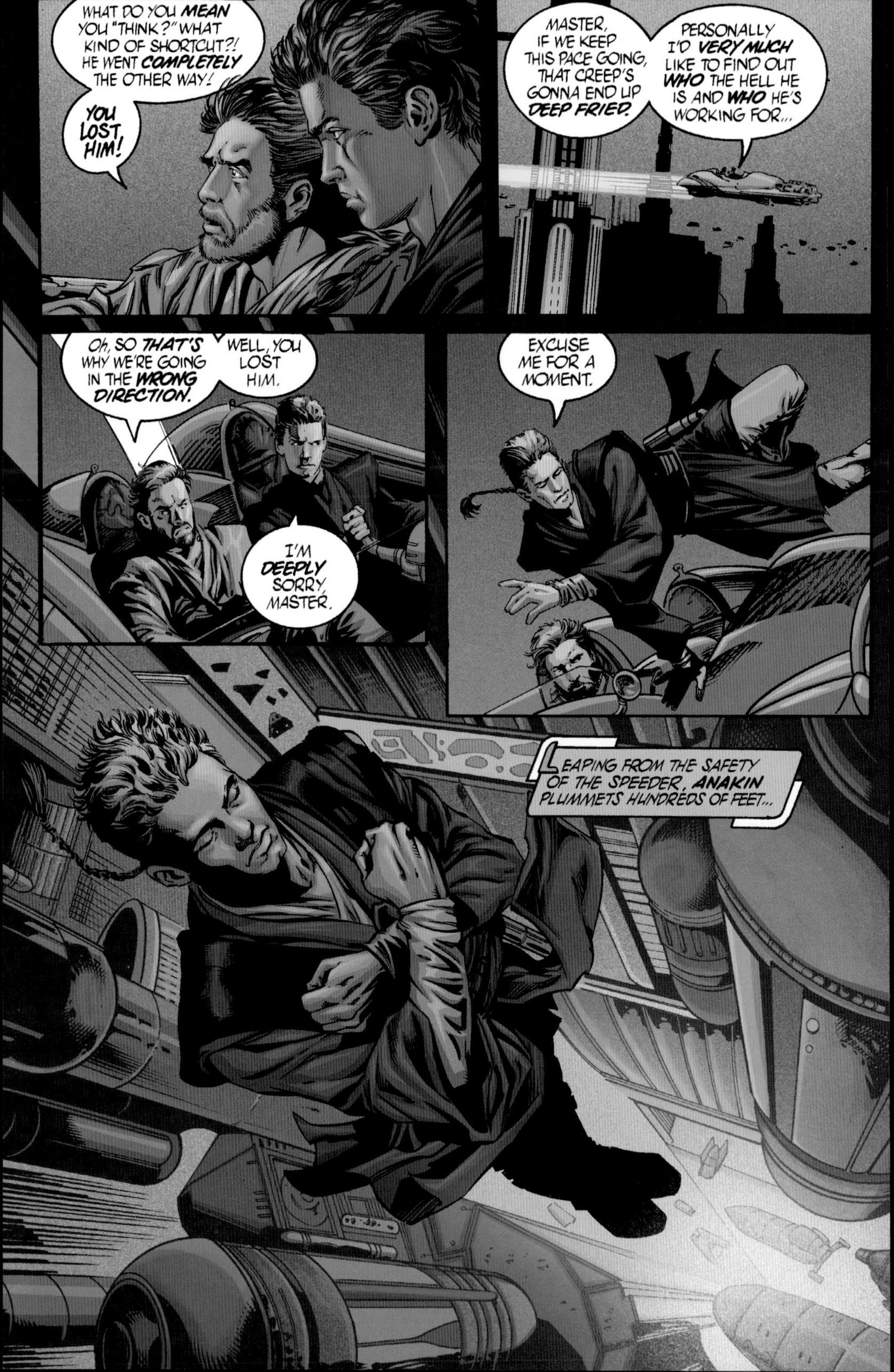

WHAT DO YOU **MEAN** YOU "THINK?" WHAT KIND OF SHORTCUT?! HE WENT **COMPLETELY** THE OTHER WAY!
YOU LOST HIM!
MASTER, IF WE KEEP THIS PACE GOING, THAT CREEP'S GONNA END UP **DEEP FRIED.**
PERSONALLY I'D **VERY MUCH** LIKE TO FIND OUT **WHO** THE HELL HE IS AND **WHO** HE'S WORKING FOR...
Oh, SO **THAT'S** WHY WE'RE GOING IN THE **WRONG DIRECTION**.
WELL, YOU LOST HIM.
I'M **DEEPLY** SORRY, MASTER.
EXCUSE ME FOR A MOMENT.
LEAPING FROM THE SAFETY OF THE SPEEDER, **ANAKIN** PLUMMETS HUNDREDS OF FEET...

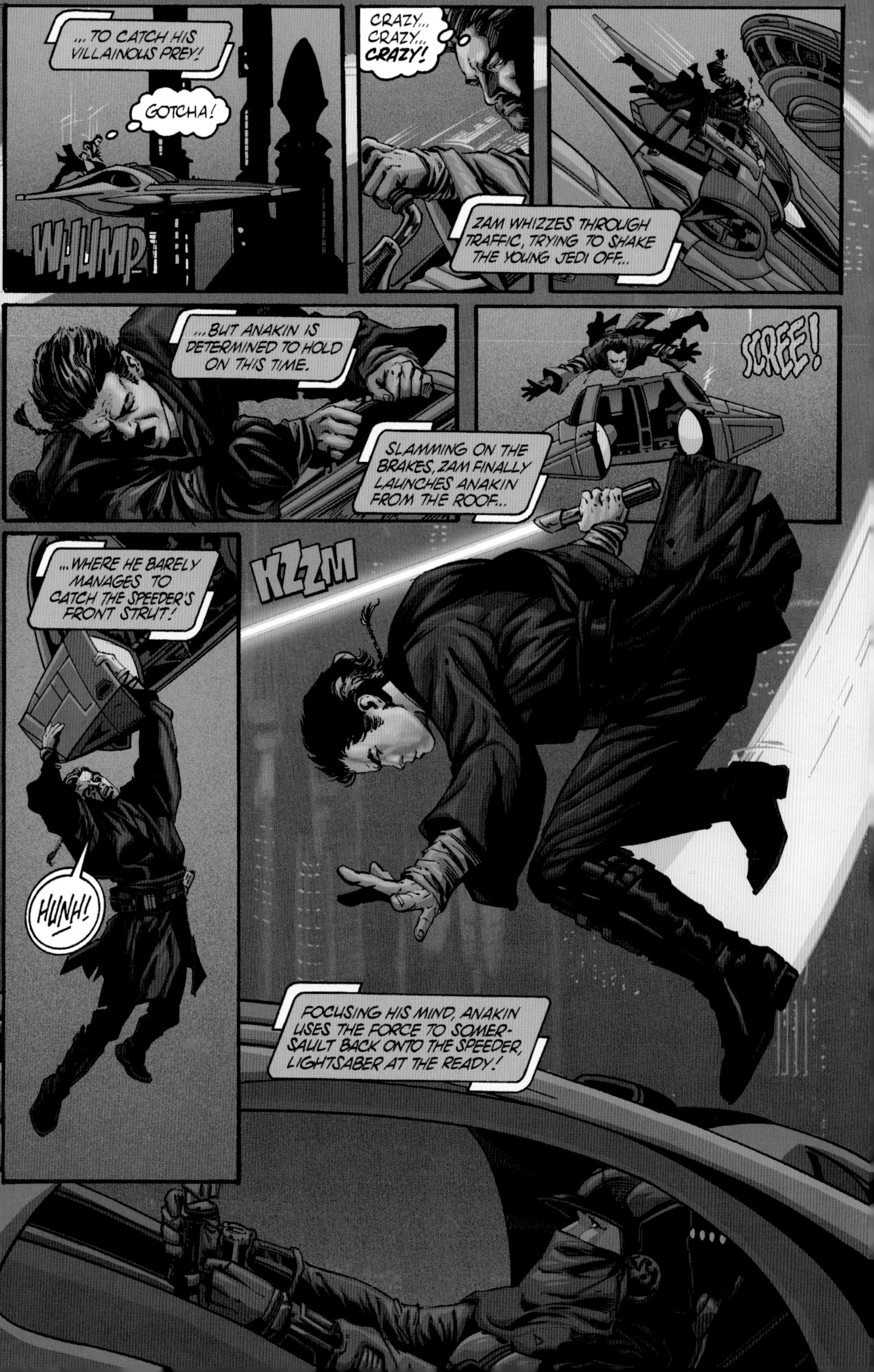
...TO CATCH HIS VILLAINOUS PREY!
GOTCHA!
WHUMP
CRAZY... CRAZY... CRAZY!
ZAM WHIZZES THROUGH TRAFFIC, TRYING TO SHAKE THE YOUNG JEDI OFF...
...BUT ANAKIN IS DETERMINED TO HOLD ON THIS TIME.
SCREE!
SLAMMING ON THE BRAKES, ZAM FINALLY LAUNCHES ANAKIN FROM THE ROOF...
...WHERE HE BARELY MANAGES TO CATCH THE SPEEDER'S FRONT STRUT!
HZZM
HUNH!
FOCUSING HIS MIND, ANAKIN USES THE FORCE TO SOMER-SAULT BACK ONTO THE SPEEDER, LIGHTSABER AT THE READY!

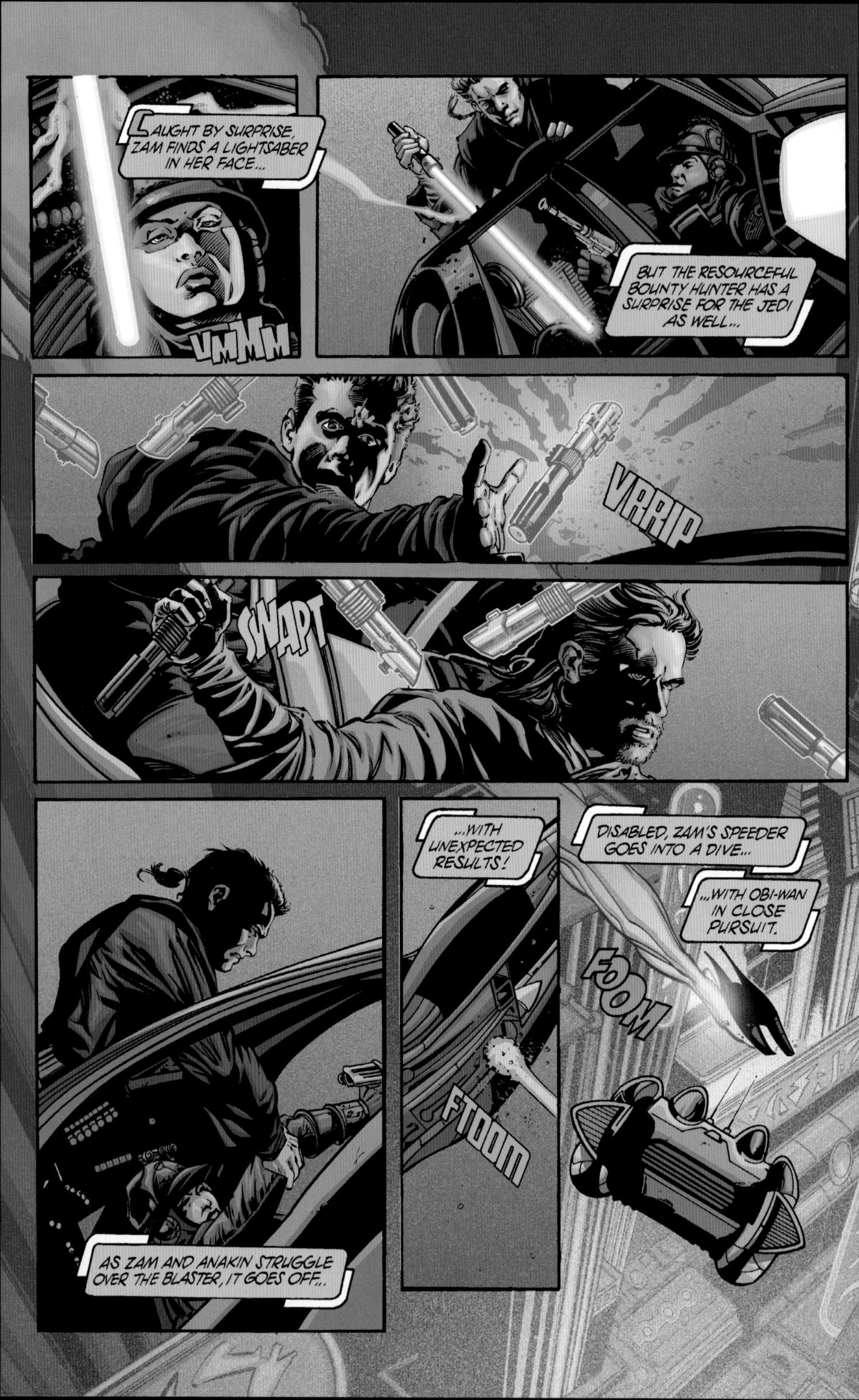
CAUGHT BY SURPRISE, ZAM FINDS A LIGHTSABER IN HER FACE...
UMMM
BUT THE RESOURCEFUL BOUNTY HUNTER HAS A SURPRISE FOR THE JEDI AS WELL...
VRRIP
SWAPT
AS ZAM AND ANAKIN STRUGGLE OVER THE BLASTER, IT GOES OFF...
...WITH UNEXPECTED RESULTS!
FTOOM
DISABLED, ZAM'S SPEEDER GOES INTO A DIVE...
...WITH OBI-WAN IN CLOSE PURSUIT.
FOOM

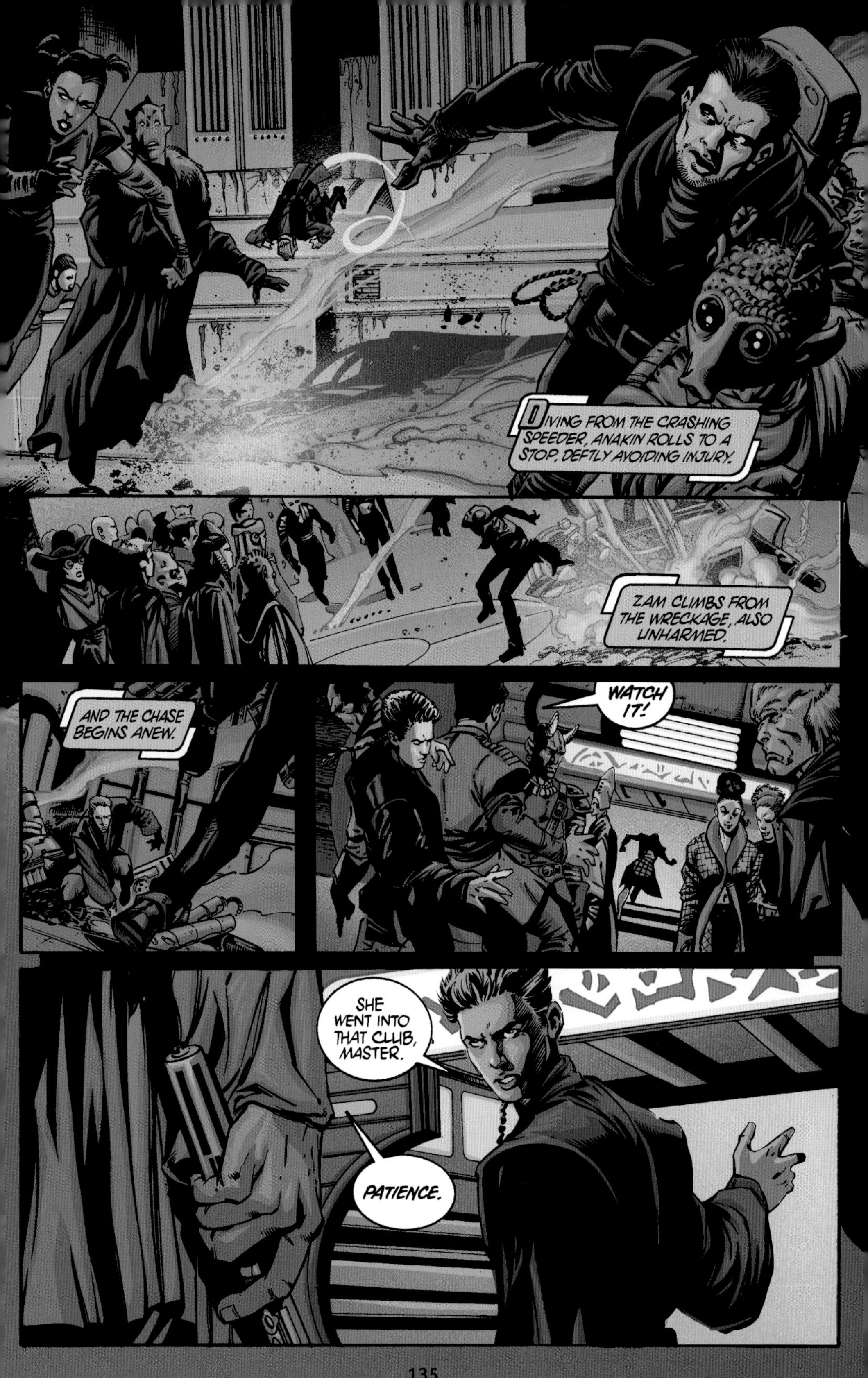
DIVING FROM THE CRASHING SPEEDER, ANAKIN ROLLS TO A STOP, DEFTLY AVOIDING INJURY.
ZAM CLIMBS FROM THE WRECKAGE, ALSO UNHARMED.
AND THE CHASE BEGINS ANEW.
WATCH IT!
SHE WENT INTO THAT CLUB, MASTER.
PATIENCE.

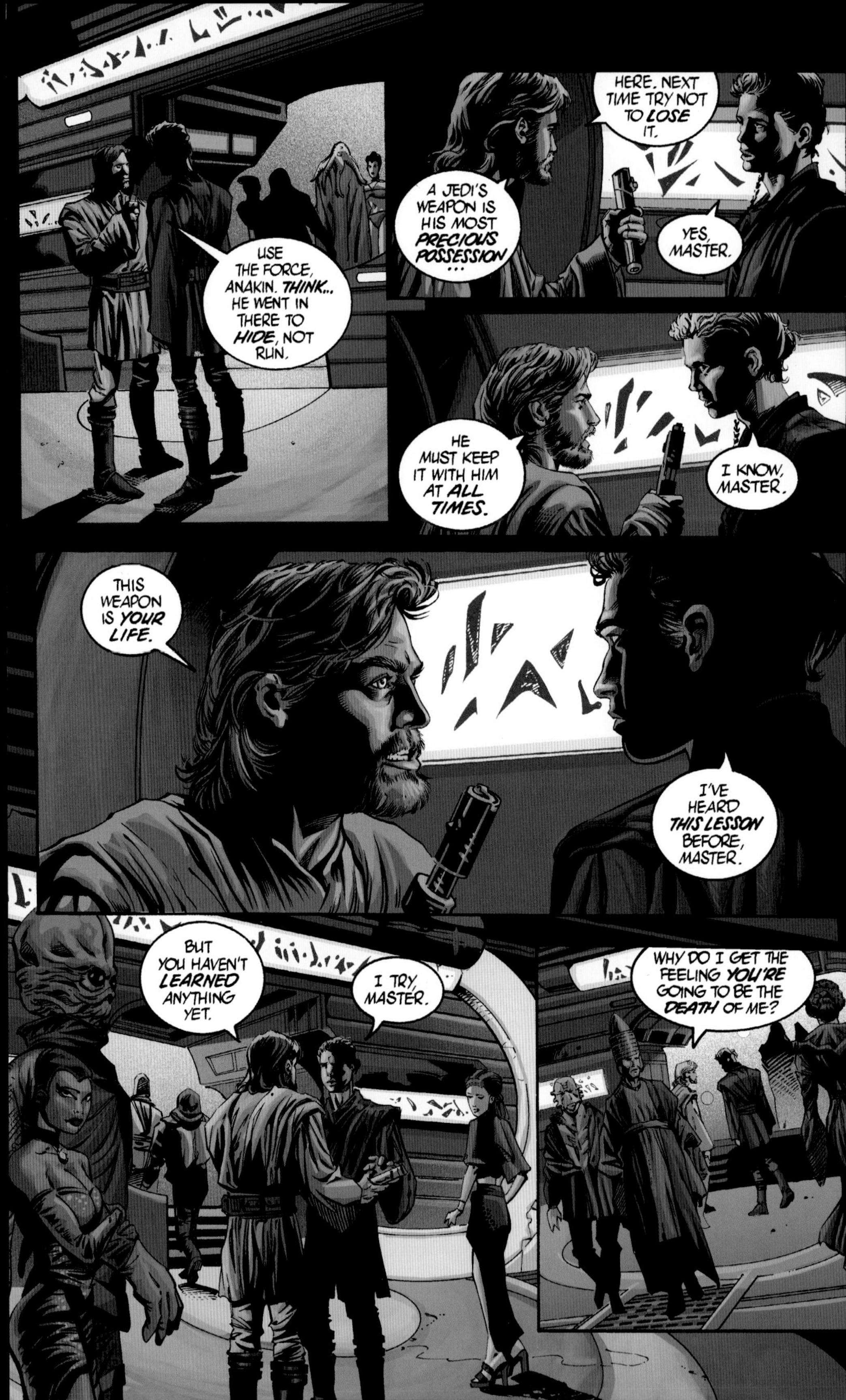
USE THE FORCE, ANAKIN. THINK... HE WENT IN THERE TO HIDE, NOT RUN.
HERE. NEXT TIME TRY NOT TO LOSE IT.
A JEDI'S WEAPON IS HIS MOST PRECIOUS POSSESSION...
YES, MASTER.
HE MUST KEEP IT WITH HIM AT ALL TIMES.
I KNOW, MASTER.
THIS WEAPON IS YOUR LIFE.
I'VE HEARD THIS LESSON BEFORE, MASTER.
BUT YOU HAVEN'T LEARNED ANYTHING YET.
I TRY, MASTER.
WHY DO I GET THE FEELING YOU'RE GOING TO BE THE DEATH OF ME?

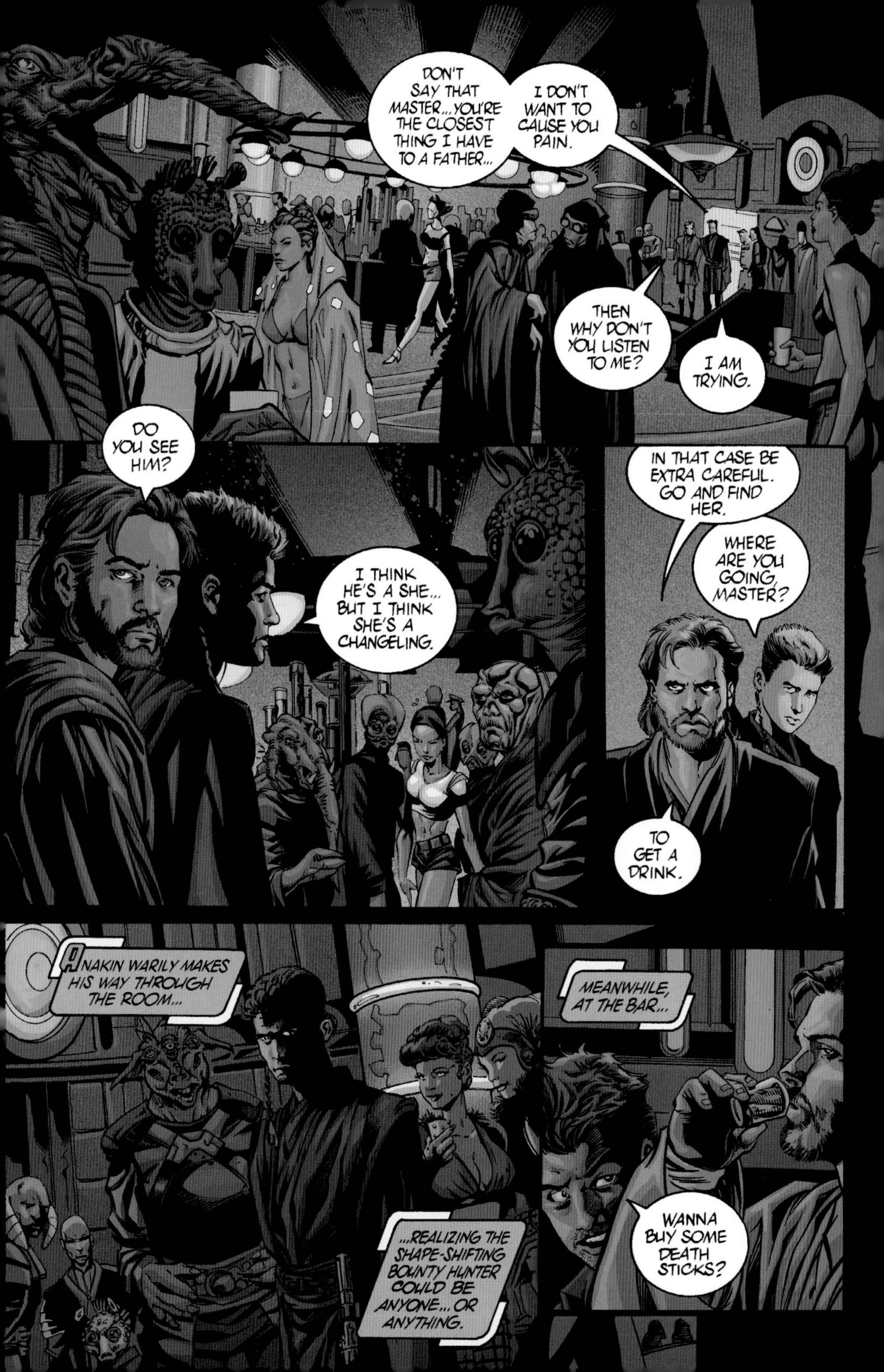
DON'T SAY THAT MASTER... YOU'RE THE CLOSEST THING I HAVE TO A FATHER...
I DON'T WANT TO CAUSE YOU PAIN.
THEN WHY DON'T YOU LISTEN TO ME?
I AM TRYING.
DO YOU SEE HIM?
I THINK HE'S A SHE... BUT I THINK SHE'S A CHANGELING.
IN THAT CASE BE EXTRA CAREFUL. GO AND FIND HER.
WHERE ARE YOU GOING, MASTER?
TO GET A DRINK.
ANAKIN WARILY MAKES HIS WAY THROUGH THE ROOM...
...REALIZING THE SHAPE-SHIFTING BOUNTY HUNTER COULD BE ANYONE... OR ANYTHING.
MEANWHILE, AT THE BAR...
WANNA BUY SOME DEATH STICKS?

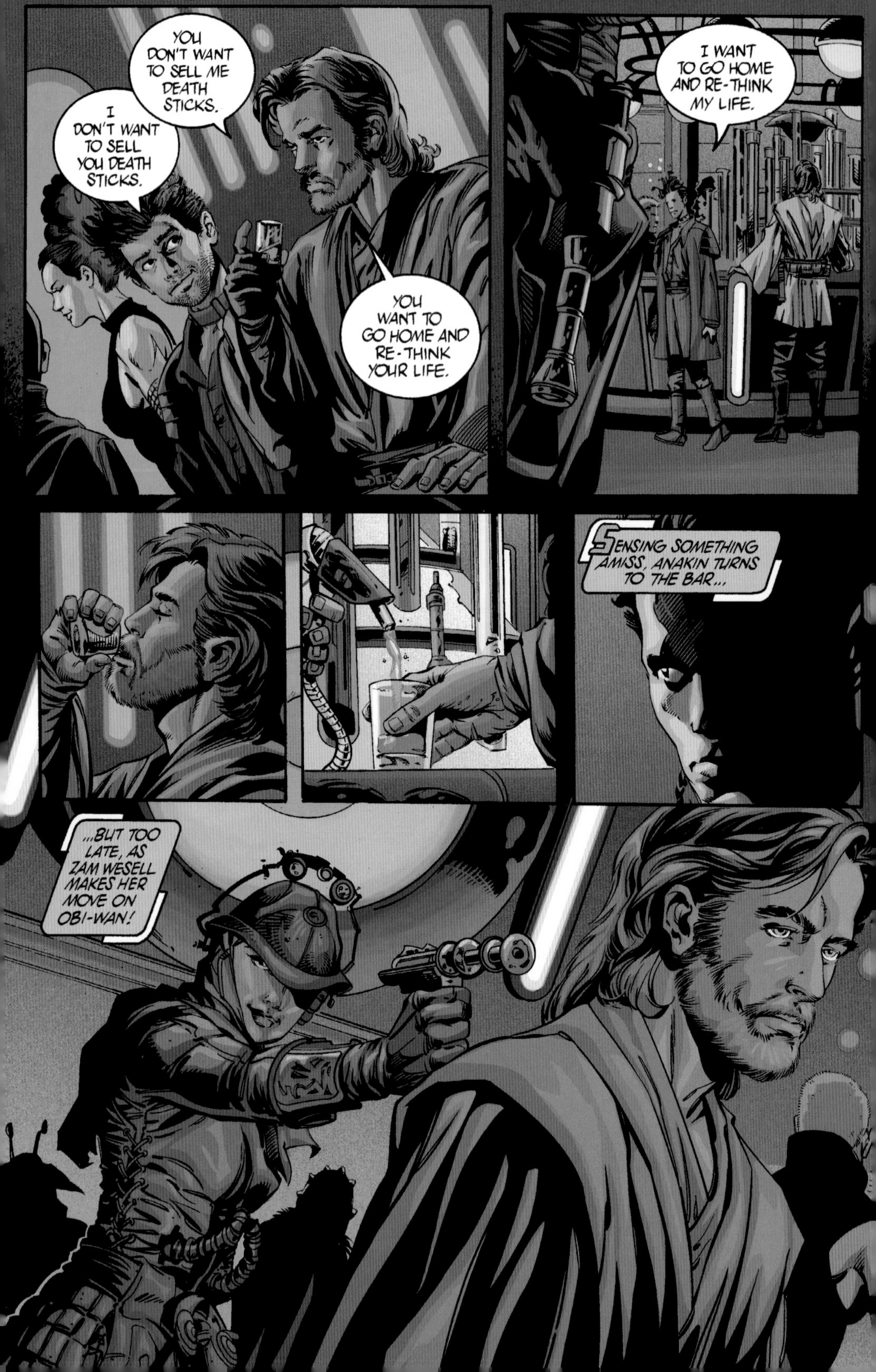
YOU DON'T WANT TO SELL ME DEATH STICKS.
I DON'T WANT TO SELL YOU DEATH STICKS.
YOU WANT TO GO HOME AND RE-THINK YOUR LIFE.
I WANT TO GO HOME AND RE-THINK MY LIFE.
SENSING SOMETHING AMISS, ANAKIN TURNS TO THE BAR...
...BUT TOO LATE, AS ZAM WESELL MAKES HER MOVE ON OBI-WAN!

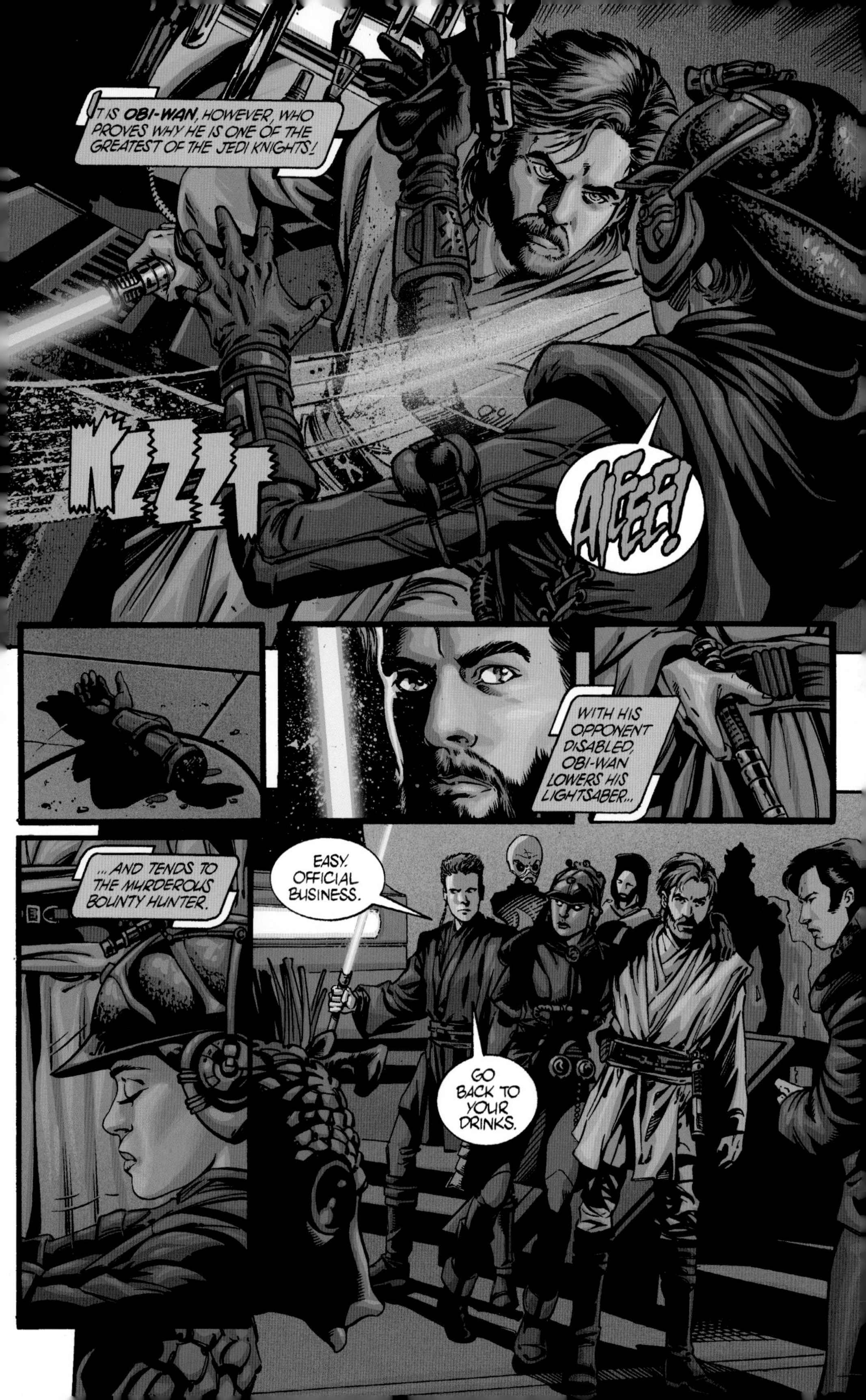
IT IS OBI-WAN, HOWEVER, WHO PROVES WHY HE IS ONE OF THE GREATEST OF THE JEDI KNIGHTS!
KZZZT
AIEEE!
WITH HIS OPPONENT DISABLED, OBI-WAN LOWERS HIS LIGHTSABER...
...AND TENDS TO THE MURDEROUS BOUNTY HUNTER.
EASY. OFFICIAL BUSINESS.
GO BACK TO YOUR DRINKS.

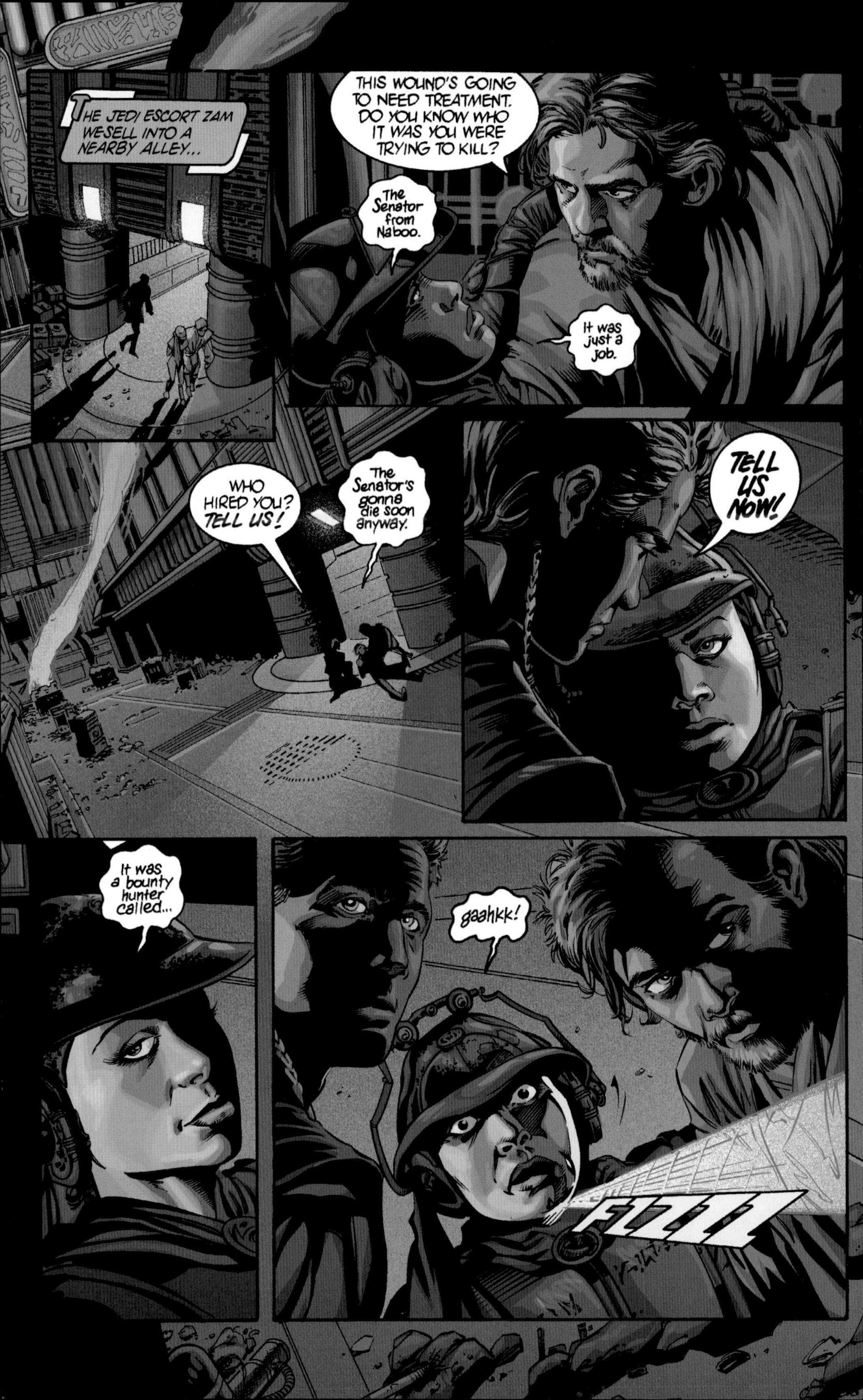
THE JEDI ESCORT ZAM WESELL INTO A NEARBY ALLEY...
THIS WOUND'S GOING TO NEED TREATMENT. DO YOU KNOW WHO IT WAS YOU WERE TRYING TO KILL?
The Senator from Naboo.
It was just a job.
WHO HIRED YOU? TELL US!
The Senator's gonna die soon anyway.
TELL US NOW!
It was a bounty hunter called...
gaahkk!
FZZZ

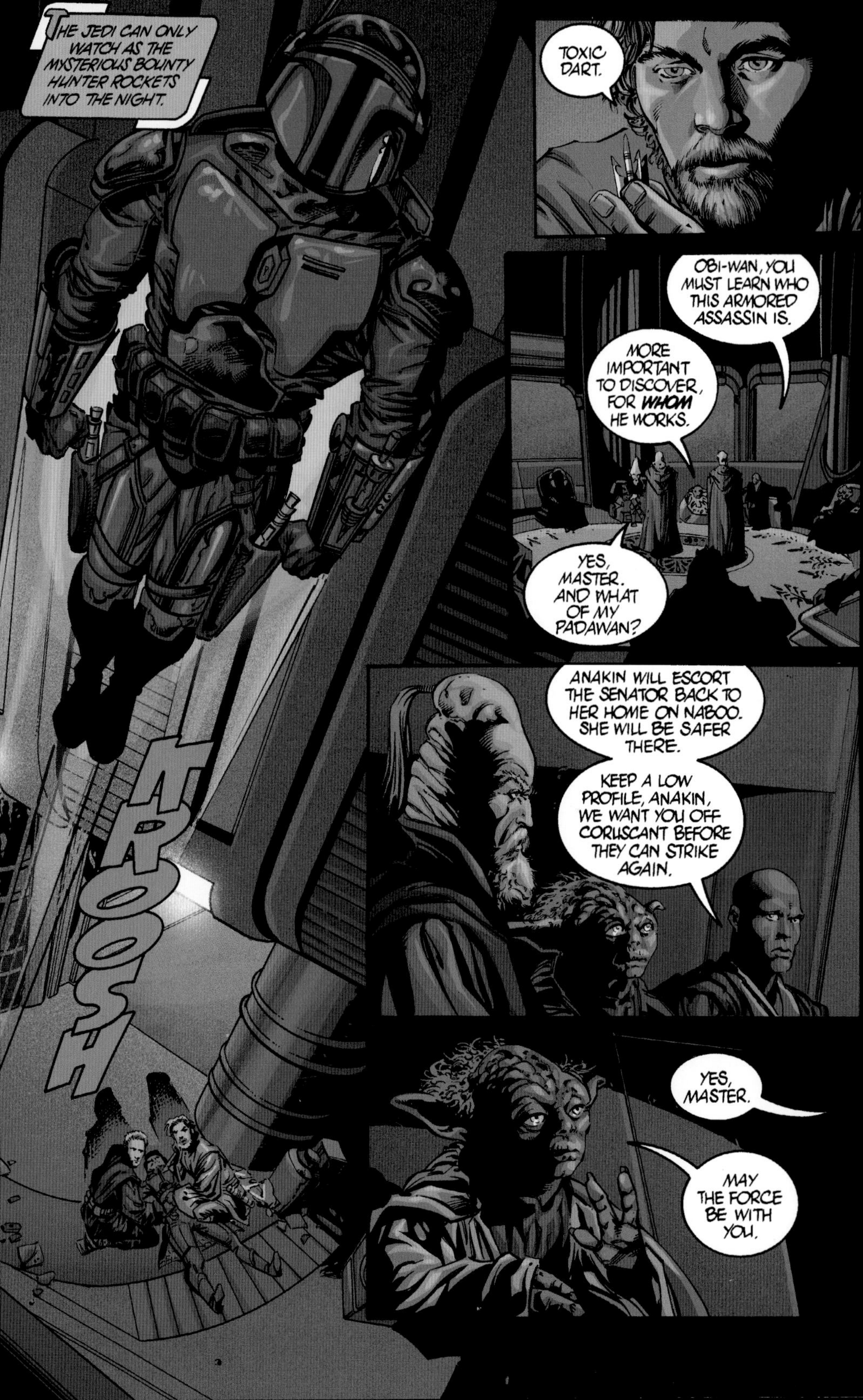
THE JEDI CAN ONLY WATCH AS THE MYSTERIOUS BOUNTY HUNTER ROCKETS INTO THE NIGHT.
KROOOSH
TOXIC DART.
OBI-WAN, YOU MUST LEARN WHO THIS ARMORED ASSASSIN IS.
MORE IMPORTANT TO DISCOVER, FOR WHOM HE WORKS.
YES, MASTER. AND WHAT OF MY PADAWAN?
ANAKIN WILL ESCORT THE SENATOR BACK TO HER HOME ON NABOO. SHE WILL BE SAFER THERE.
KEEP A LOW PROFILE, ANAKIN, WE WANT YOU OFF CORUSCANT BEFORE THEY CAN STRIKE AGAIN.
YES, MASTER.
MAY THE FORCE BE WITH YOU.

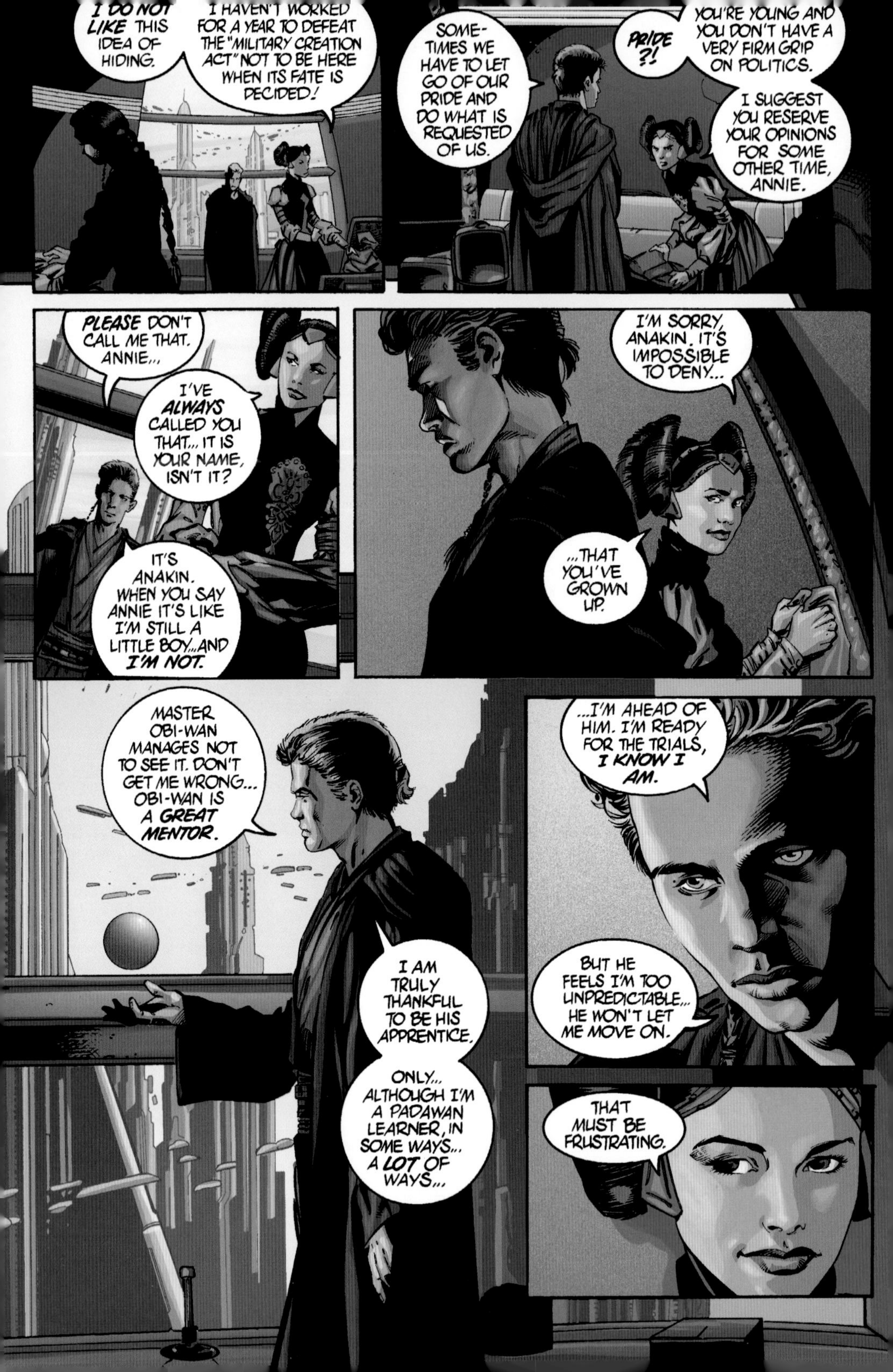

I DO NOT LIKE THIS IDEA OF HIDING.
I HAVEN'T WORKED FOR A YEAR TO DEFEAT THE "MILITARY CREATION ACT" NOT TO BE HERE WHEN ITS FATE IS DECIDED!
SOME-TIMES WE HAVE TO LET GO OF OUR PRIDE AND DO WHAT IS REQUESTED OF US.
PRIDE?!
YOU'RE YOUNG AND YOU DON'T HAVE A VERY FIRM GRIP ON POLITICS.
I SUGGEST YOU RESERVE YOUR OPINIONS FOR SOME OTHER TIME, ANNIE.
PLEASE DON'T CALL ME THAT. ANNIE...
I'VE ALWAYS CALLED YOU THAT... IT IS YOUR NAME, ISN'T IT?
IT'S ANAKIN. WHEN YOU SAY ANNIE IT'S LIKE I'M STILL A LITTLE BOY...AND I'M NOT.
I'M SORRY, ANAKIN. IT'S IMPOSSIBLE TO DENY...
...THAT YOU'VE GROWN UP.
MASTER OBI-WAN MANAGES NOT TO SEE IT. DON'T GET ME WRONG... OBI-WAN IS A GREAT MENTOR.
I AM TRULY THANKFUL TO BE HIS APPRENTICE.
ONLY... ALTHOUGH I'M A PADAWAN LEARNER, IN SOME WAYS... A LOT OF WAYS...
...I'M AHEAD OF HIM. I'M READY FOR THE TRIALS, I KNOW I AM.
BUT HE FEELS I'M TOO UNPREDICTABLE... HE WON'T LET ME MOVE ON.
THAT MUST BE FRUSTRATING.

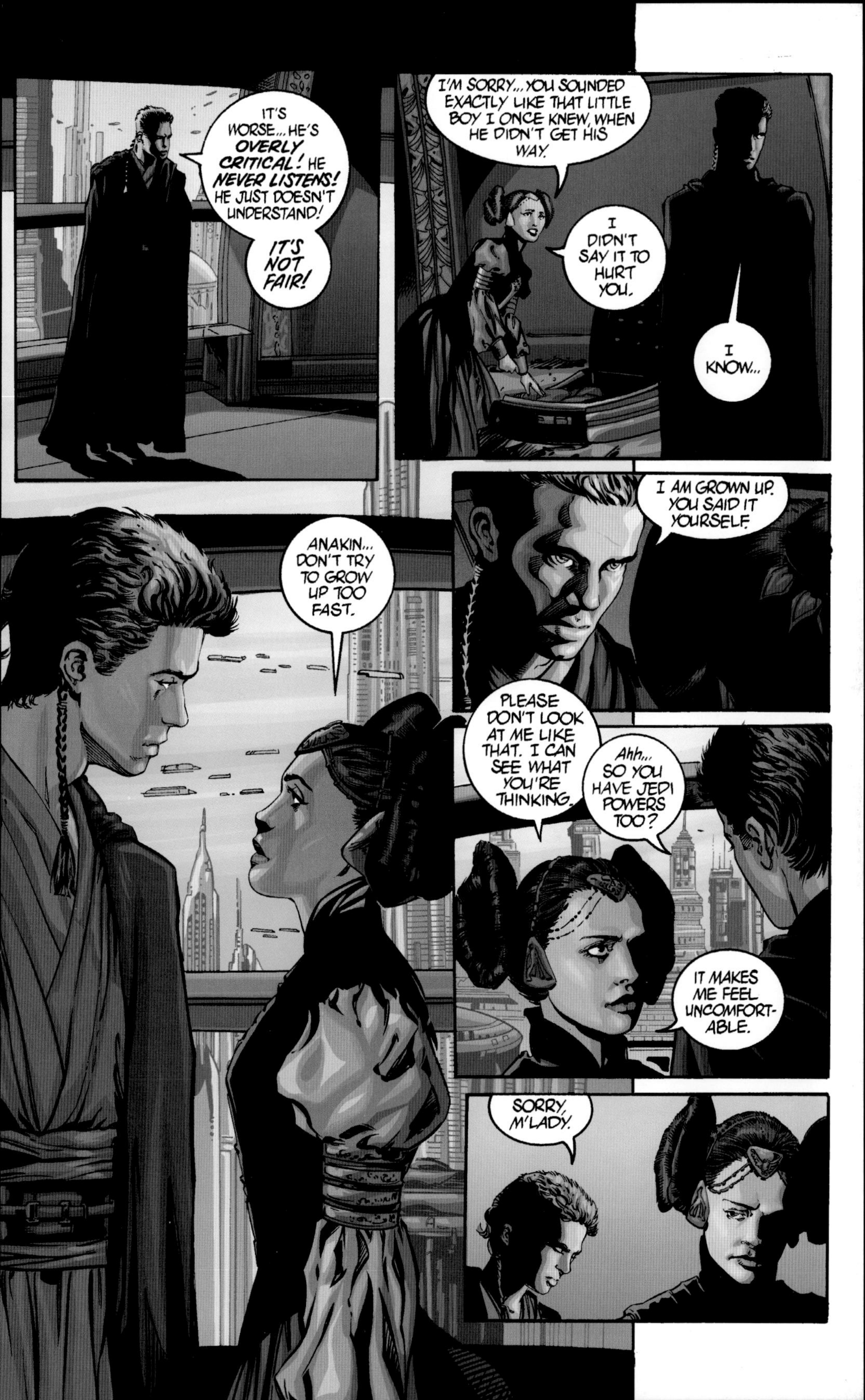
IT'S WORSE... HE'S OVERLY CRITICAL! HE NEVER LISTENS! HE JUST DOESN'T UNDERSTAND!
IT'S NOT FAIR!
I'M SORRY... YOU SOUNDED EXACTLY LIKE THAT LITTLE BOY I ONCE KNEW, WHEN HE DIDN'T GET HIS WAY.
I DIDN'T SAY IT TO HURT YOU.
I KNOW...
ANAKIN... DON'T TRY TO GROW UP TOO FAST.
I AM GROWN UP. YOU SAID IT YOURSELF.
PLEASE DON'T LOOK AT ME LIKE THAT. I CAN SEE WHAT YOU'RE THINKING.
Ahh... SO YOU HAVE JEDI POWERS TOO?
IT MAKES ME FEEL UNCOMFORT-ABLE.
SORRY, M'LADY.

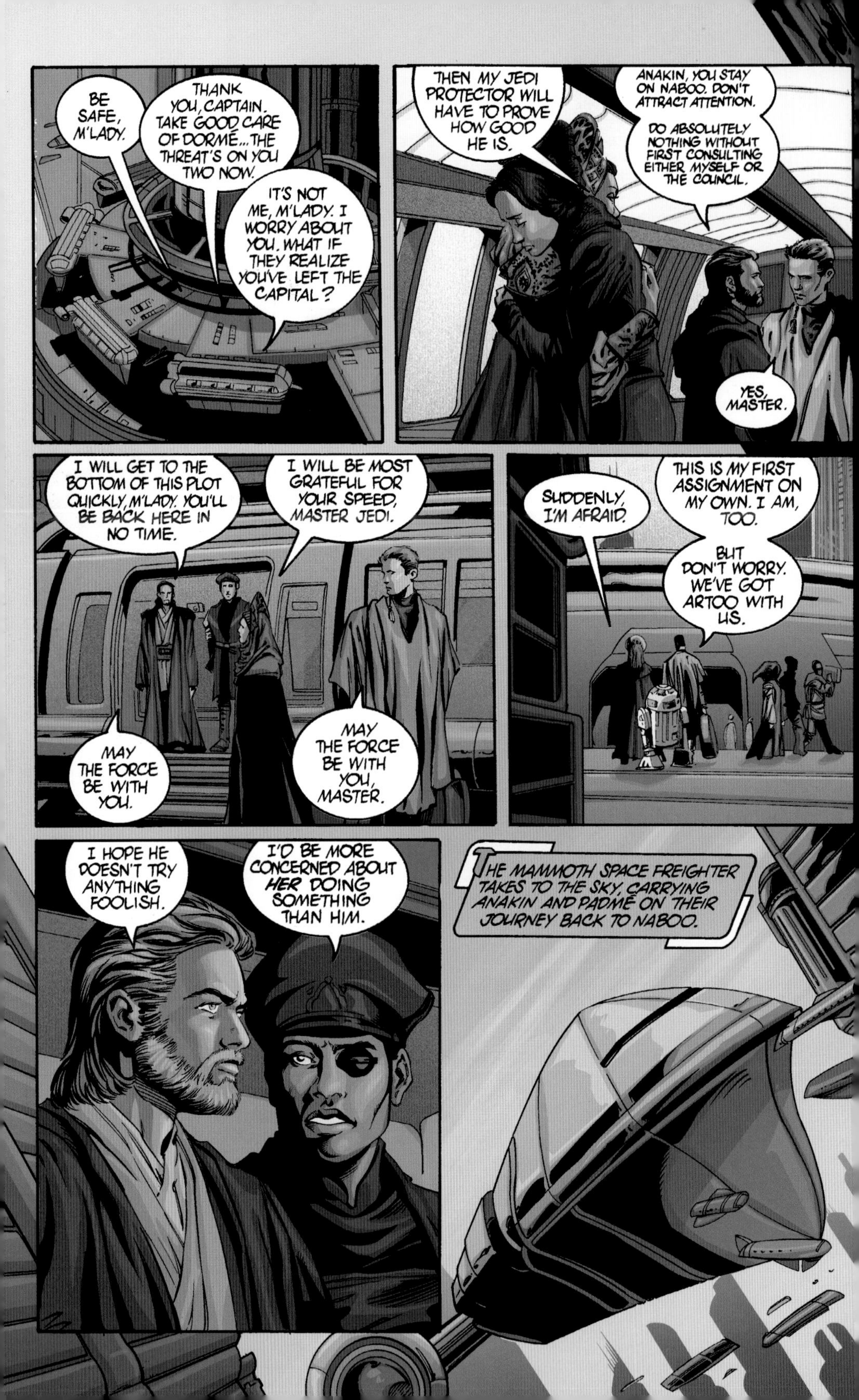
BE SAFE, M'LADY.
THANK YOU, CAPTAIN. TAKE GOOD CARE OF DORMÉ... THE THREAT'S ON YOU TWO NOW.
IT'S NOT ME, M'LADY. I WORRY ABOUT YOU. WHAT IF THEY REALIZE YOU'VE LEFT THE CAPITAL?
THEN MY JEDI PROTECTOR WILL HAVE TO PROVE HOW GOOD HE IS.
ANAKIN, YOU STAY ON NABOO. DON'T ATTRACT ATTENTION.
DO ABSOLUTELY NOTHING WITHOUT FIRST CONSULTING EITHER MYSELF OR THE COUNCIL.
YES, MASTER.
I WILL GET TO THE BOTTOM OF THIS PLOT QUICKLY, M'LADY. YOU'LL BE BACK HERE IN NO TIME.
I WILL BE MOST GRATEFUL FOR YOUR SPEED, MASTER JEDI.
MAY THE FORCE BE WITH YOU.
MAY THE FORCE BE WITH YOU, MASTER.
SUDDENLY, I'M AFRAID.
THIS IS MY FIRST ASSIGNMENT ON MY OWN. I AM, TOO.
BUT DON'T WORRY. WE'VE GOT ARTOO WITH US.
I HOPE HE DOESN'T TRY ANYTHING FOOLISH.
I'D BE MORE CONCERNED ABOUT HER DOING SOMETHING THAN HIM.
THE MAMMOTH SPACE FREIGHTER TAKES TO THE SKY, CARRYING ANAKIN AND PADMÉ ON THEIR JOURNEY BACK TO NABOO.

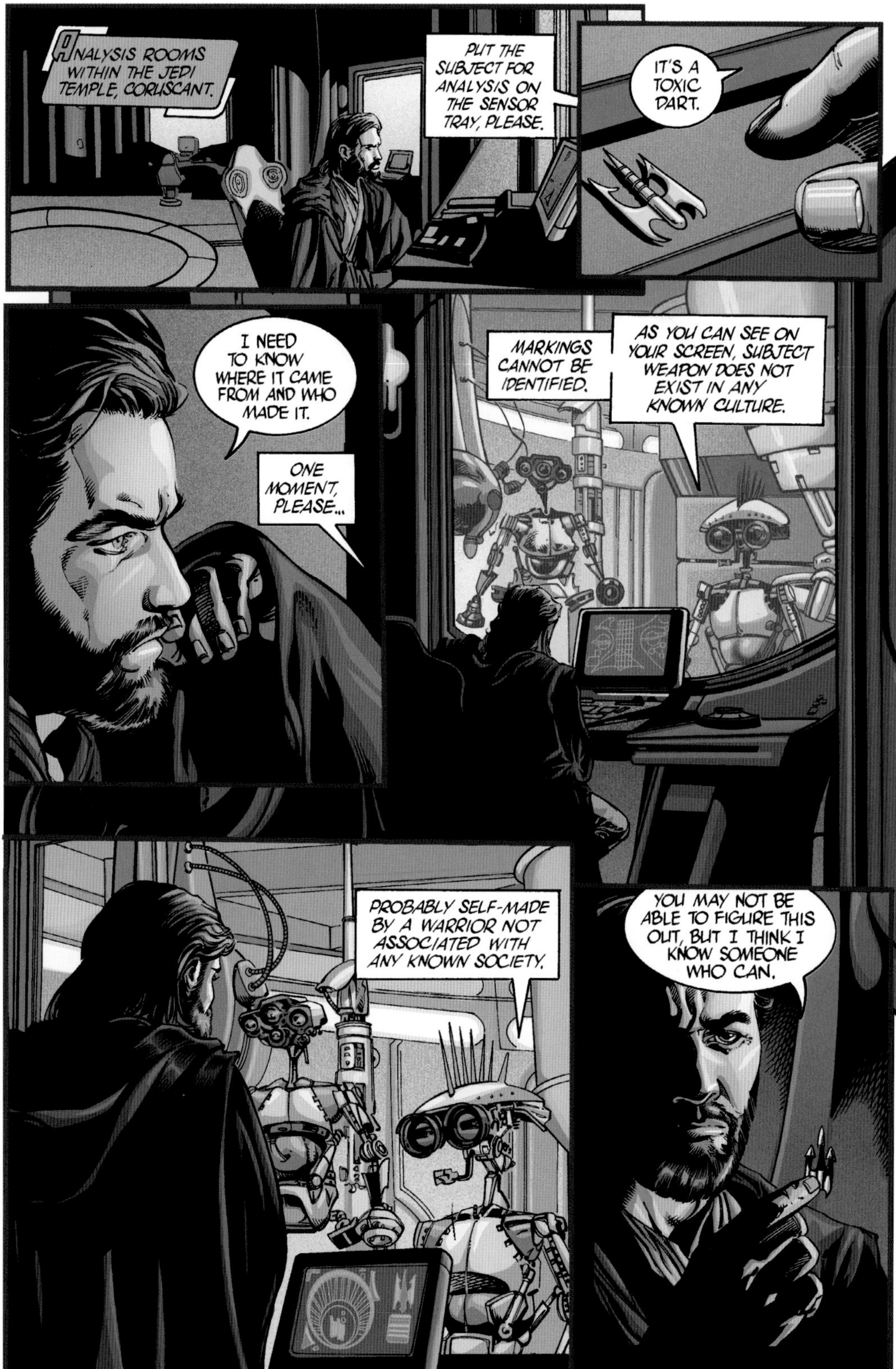
ANALYSIS ROOMS WITHIN THE JEDI TEMPLE, CORUSCANT.
PUT THE SUBJECT FOR ANALYSIS ON THE SENSOR TRAY, PLEASE.
IT'S A TOXIC DART.
I NEED TO KNOW WHERE IT CAME FROM AND WHO MADE IT.
ONE MOMENT, PLEASE...
MARKINGS CANNOT BE IDENTIFIED.
AS YOU CAN SEE ON YOUR SCREEN, SUBJECT WEAPON DOES NOT EXIST IN ANY KNOWN CULTURE.
PROBABLY SELF-MADE BY A WARRIOR NOT ASSOCIATED WITH ANY KNOWN SOCIETY.
YOU MAY NOT BE ABLE TO FIGURE THIS OUT, BUT I THINK I KNOW SOMEONE WHO CAN.

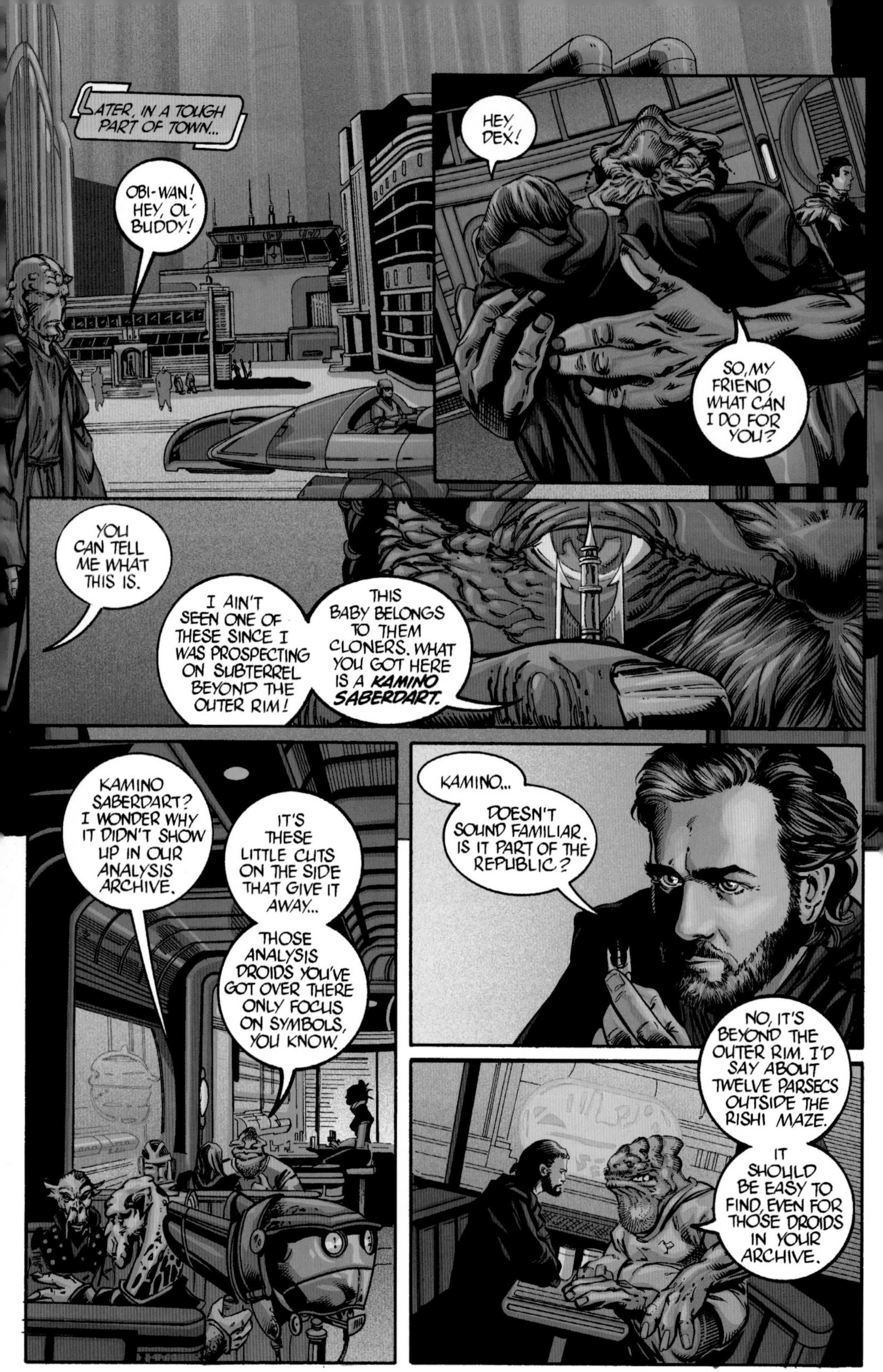

LATER, IN A TOUGH PART OF TOWN...
OBI-WAN! HEY, OL' BUDDY!
HEY, DEX!
SO, MY FRIEND, WHAT CAN I DO FOR YOU?
YOU CAN TELL ME WHAT THIS IS.
I AIN'T SEEN ONE OF THESE SINCE I WAS PROSPECTING ON SUBTERREL BEYOND THE OUTER RIM!
THIS BABY BELONGS TO THEM CLONERS. WHAT YOU GOT HERE IS A KAMINO SABERDART.
KAMINO SABERDART? I WONDER WHY IT DIDN'T SHOW UP IN OUR ANALYSIS ARCHIVE.
IT'S THESE LITTLE CUTS ON THE SIDE THAT GIVE IT AWAY...
THOSE ANALYSIS DROIDS YOU'VE GOT OVER THERE ONLY FOCUS ON SYMBOLS, YOU KNOW.
KAMINO...
DOESN'T SOUND FAMILIAR. IS IT PART OF THE REPUBLIC?
NO, IT'S BEYOND THE OUTER RIM. I'D SAY ABOUT TWELVE PARSECS OUTSIDE THE RISHI MAZE.
IT SHOULD BE EASY TO FIND, EVEN FOR THOSE DROIDS IN YOUR ARCHIVE.

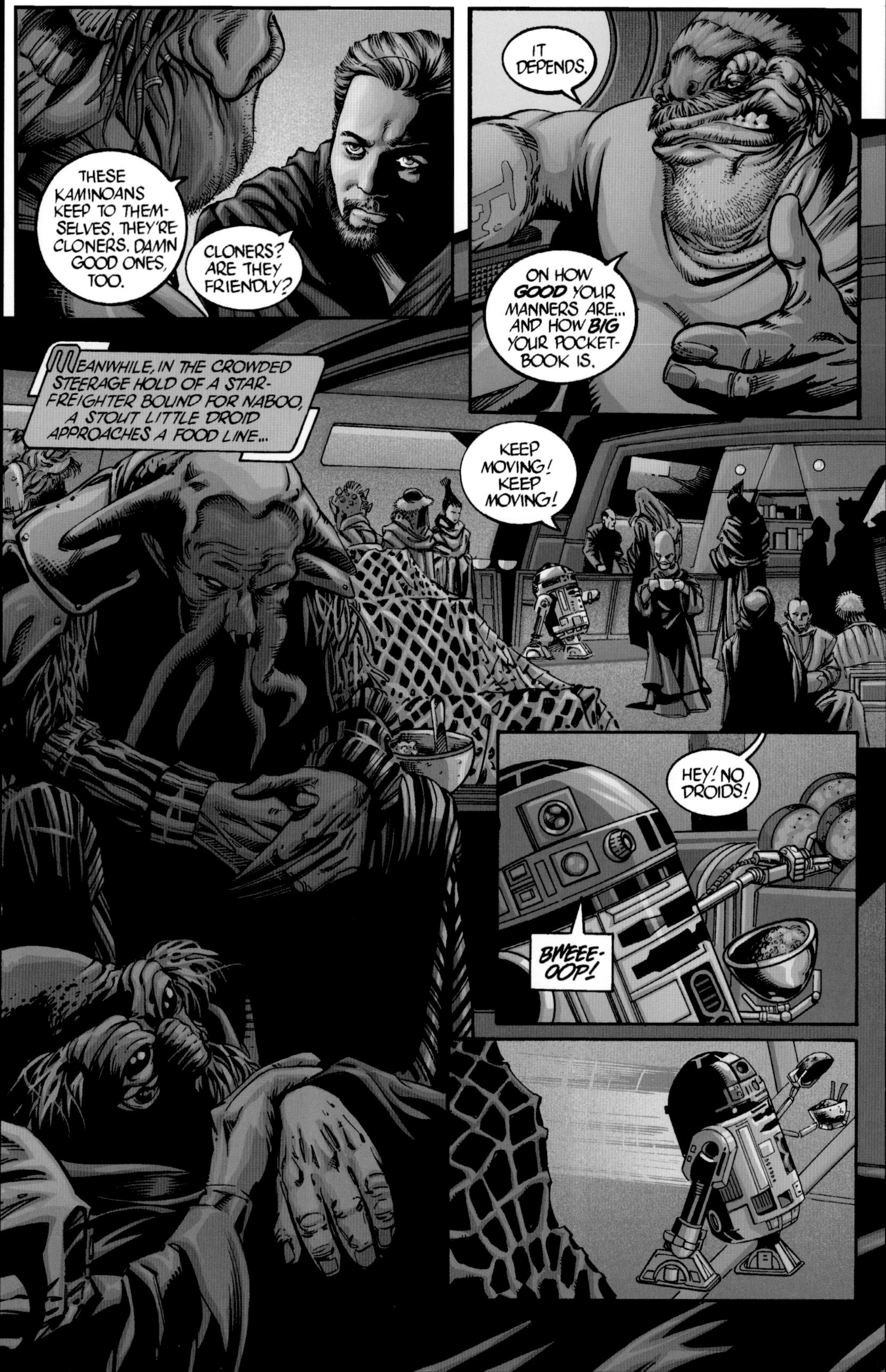
THESE KAMINOANS KEEP TO THEM-SELVES. THEY'RE CLONERS. DAMN GOOD ONES, TOO.
CLONERS? ARE THEY FRIENDLY?
IT DEPENDS.
ON HOW GOOD YOUR MANNERS ARE... AND HOW BIG YOUR POCKET-BOOK IS.
MEANWHILE, IN THE CROWDED STEERAGE HOLD OF A STAR-FREIGHTER BOUND FOR NABOO, A STOUT LITTLE DROID APPROACHES A FOOD LINE...
KEEP MOVING! KEEP MOVING!
HEY! NO DROIDS!
BWEEE-OOP!

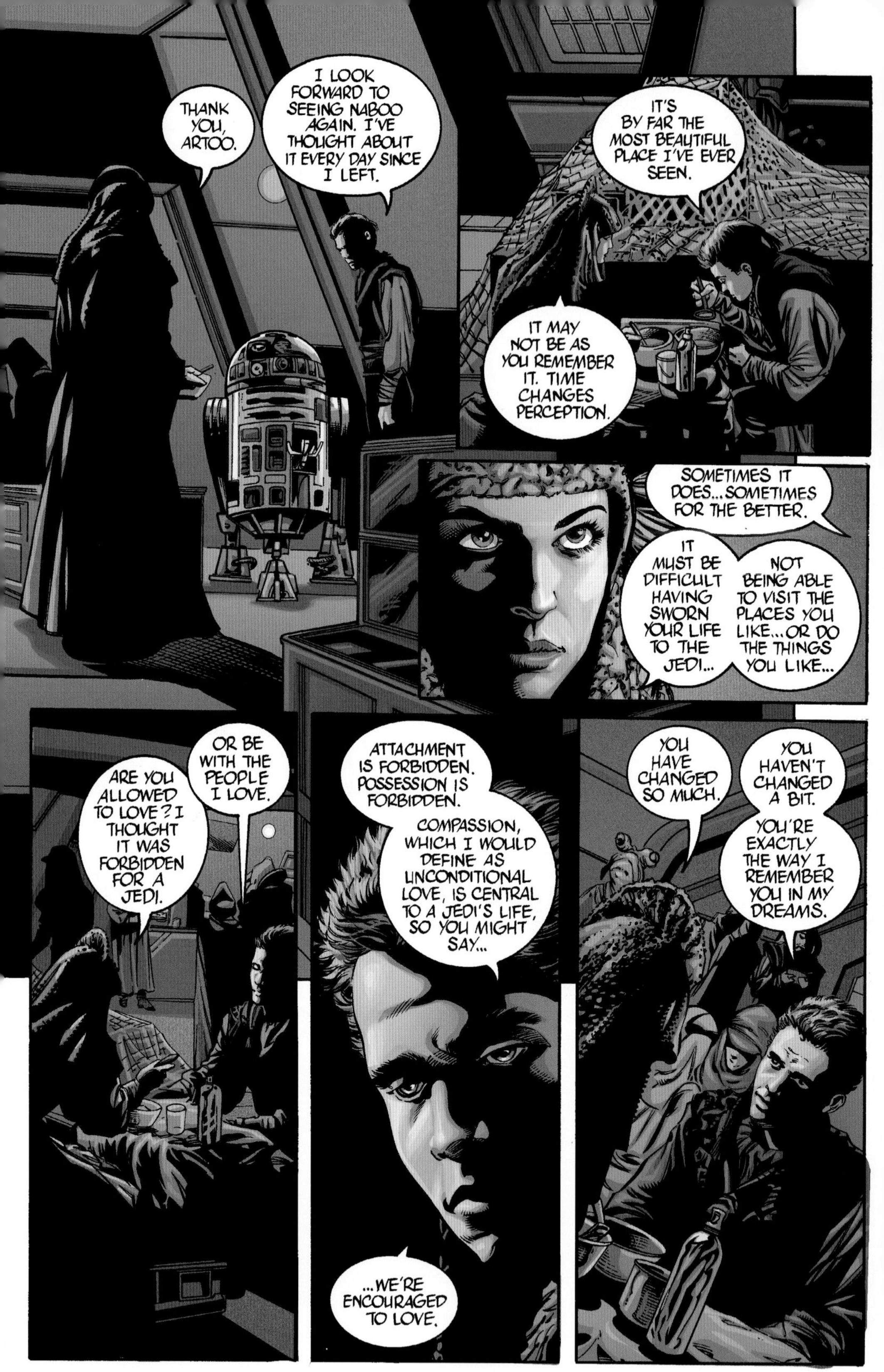
THANK YOU, ARTOO.
I LOOK FORWARD TO SEEING NABOO AGAIN. I'VE THOUGHT ABOUT IT EVERY DAY SINCE I LEFT.
IT'S BY FAR THE MOST BEAUTIFUL PLACE I'VE EVER SEEN.
IT MAY NOT BE AS YOU REMEMBER IT. TIME CHANGES PERCEPTION.
SOMETIMES IT DOES...SOMETIMES FOR THE BETTER.
IT MUST BE DIFFICULT HAVING SWORN YOUR LIFE TO THE JEDI...
NOT BEING ABLE TO VISIT THE PLACES YOU LIKE...OR DO THE THINGS YOU LIKE...
OR BE WITH THE PEOPLE I LOVE.
ARE YOU ALLOWED TO LOVE? I THOUGHT IT WAS FORBIDDEN FOR A JEDI.
ATTACHMENT IS FORBIDDEN. POSSESSION IS FORBIDDEN.
COMPASSION, WHICH I WOULD DEFINE AS UNCONDITIONAL LOVE, IS CENTRAL TO A JEDI'S LIFE, SO YOU MIGHT SAY...
...WE'RE ENCOURAGED TO LOVE.
YOU HAVE CHANGED SO MUCH.
YOU HAVEN'T CHANGED A BIT.
YOU'RE EXACTLY THE WAY I REMEMBER YOU IN MY DREAMS.

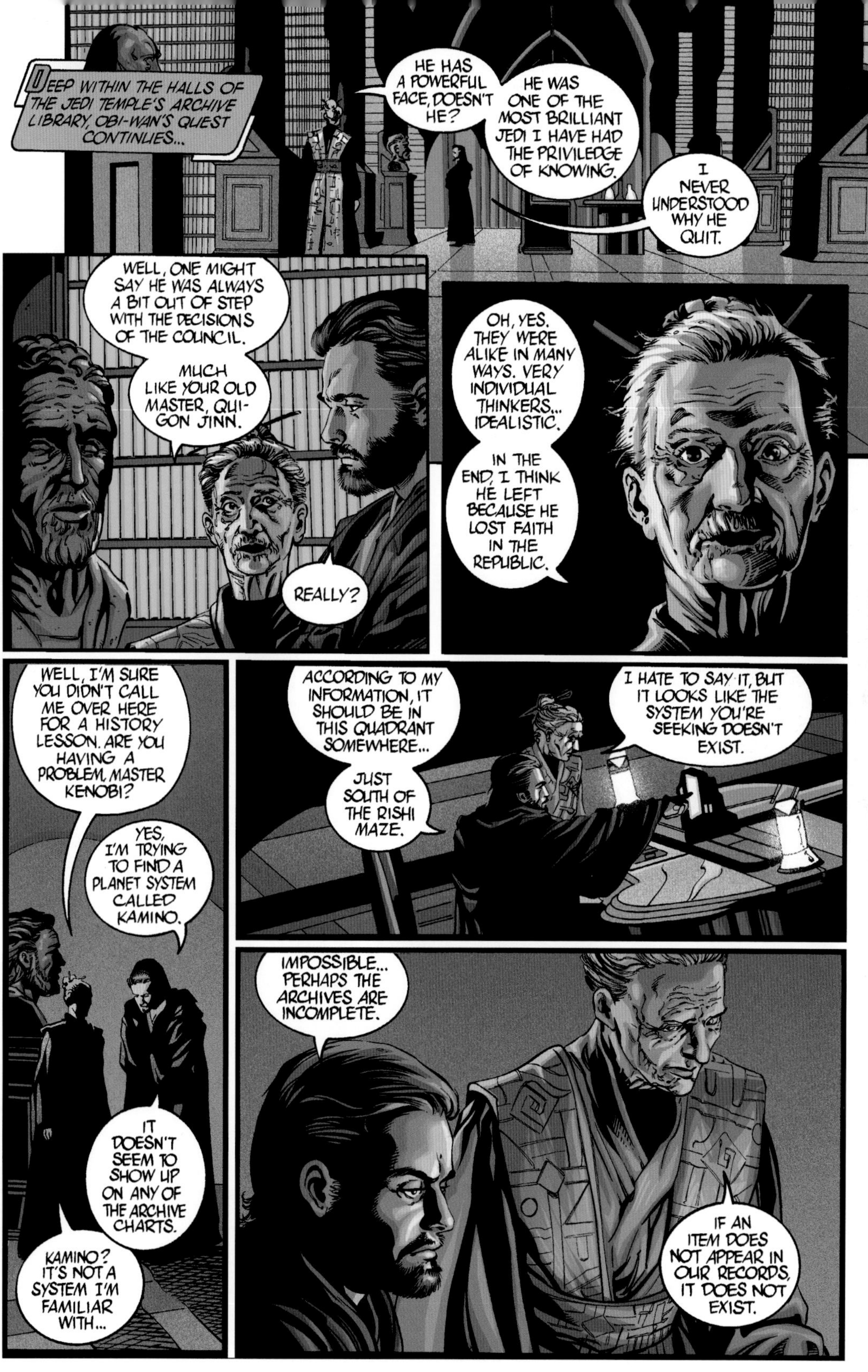
DEEP WITHIN THE HALLS OF THE JEDI TEMPLE'S ARCHIVE LIBRARY, OBI-WAN'S QUEST CONTINUES...
HE HAS A POWERFUL FACE, DOESN'T HE?
HE WAS ONE OF THE MOST BRILLIANT JEDI I HAVE HAD THE PRIVILEDGE OF KNOWING.
I NEVER UNDERSTOOD WHY HE QUIT.
WELL, ONE MIGHT SAY HE WAS ALWAYS A BIT OUT OF STEP WITH THE DECISIONS OF THE COUNCIL.
MUCH LIKE YOUR OLD MASTER, QUI-GON JINN.
REALLY?
OH, YES. THEY WERE ALIKE IN MANY WAYS. VERY INDIVIDUAL THINKERS... IDEALISTIC.
IN THE END, I THINK HE LEFT BECAUSE HE LOST FAITH IN THE REPUBLIC.
WELL, I'M SURE YOU DIDN'T CALL ME OVER HERE FOR A HISTORY LESSON. ARE YOU HAVING A PROBLEM, MASTER KENOBI?
YES, I'M TRYING TO FIND A PLANET SYSTEM CALLED KAMINO.
IT DOESN'T SEEM TO SHOW UP ON ANY OF THE ARCHIVE CHARTS.
KAMINO? IT'S NOT A SYSTEM I'M FAMILIAR WITH...
ACCORDING TO MY INFORMATION, IT SHOULD BE IN THIS QUADRANT SOMEWHERE...
JUST SOUTH OF THE RISHI MAZE.
I HATE TO SAY IT, BUT IT LOOKS LIKE THE SYSTEM YOU'RE SEEKING DOESN'T EXIST.
IMPOSSIBLE... PERHAPS THE ARCHIVES ARE INCOMPLETE.
IF AN ITEM DOES NOT APPEAR IN OUR RECORDS, IT DOES NOT EXIST.

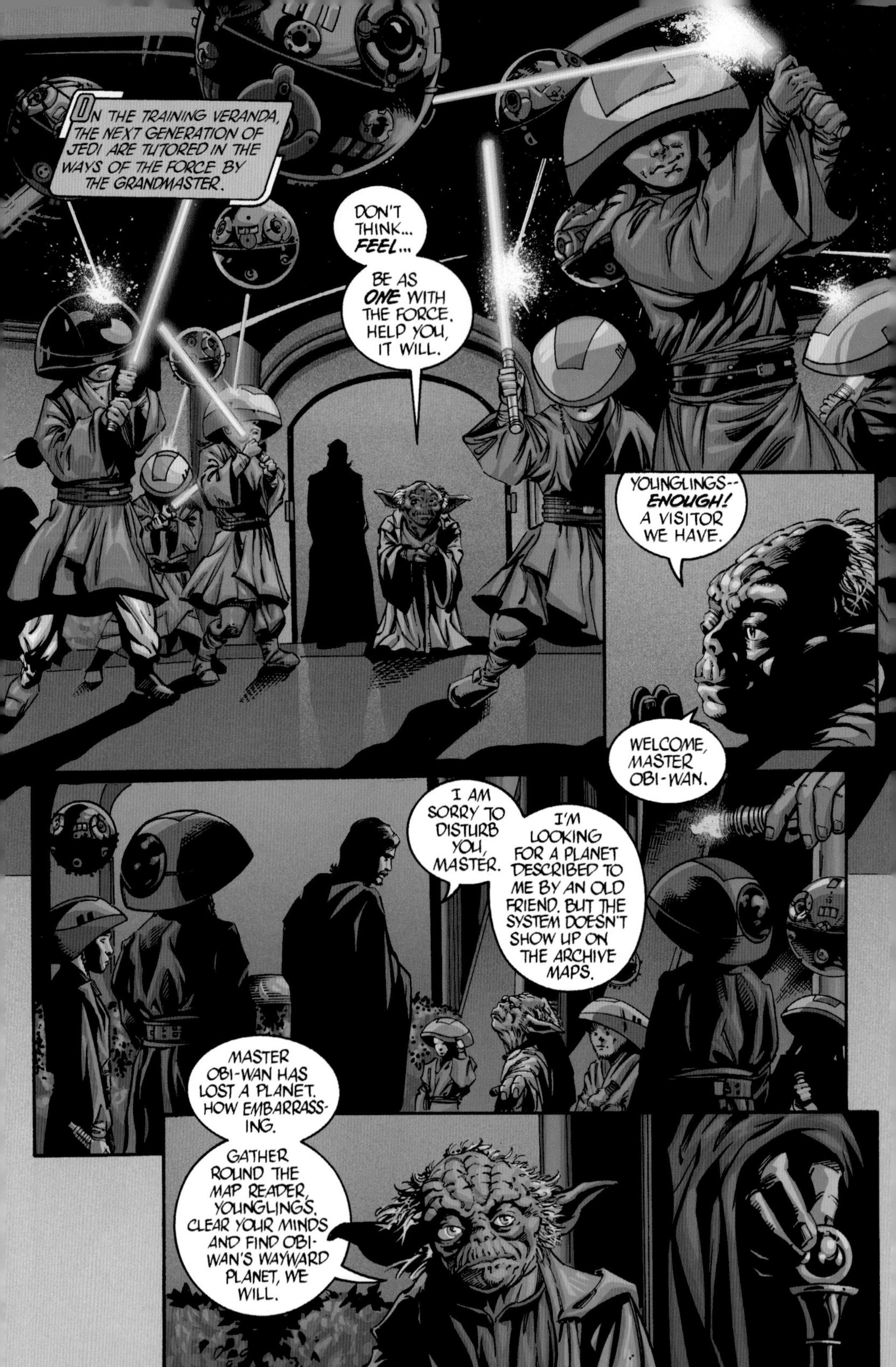
ON THE TRAINING VERANDA, THE NEXT GENERATION OF JEDI ARE TUTORED IN THE WAYS OF THE FORCE BY THE GRANDMASTER.
DON'T THINK... FEEL...
BE AS ONE WITH THE FORCE. HELP YOU, IT WILL.
YOUNGLINGS--ENOUGH! A VISITOR WE HAVE.
WELCOME, MASTER OBI-WAN.
I AM SORRY TO DISTURB YOU, MASTER.
I'M LOOKING FOR A PLANET DESCRIBED TO ME BY AN OLD FRIEND. BUT THE SYSTEM DOESN'T SHOW UP ON THE ARCHIVE MAPS.
MASTER OBI-WAN HAS LOST A PLANET. HOW EMBARRASS-ING.
GATHER ROUND THE MAP READER, YOUNGLINGS. CLEAR YOUR MINDS AND FIND OBI-WAN'S WAYWARD PLANET, WE WILL.

THIS IS WHERE IT OUGHT TO BE... BUT IT ISN'T. GRAVITY IS PULLING ALL THE STARS IN THIS AREA INWARD TO THIS SPOT.

THERE SHOULD BE A STAR HERE... BUT THERE ISN'T.

MOST INTERESTING.

GRAVITY'S SILHOUETTE REMAINS, BUT THE STAR AND ALL OF ITS PLANETS HAVE DISAPPEARED.

HOW CAN THIS BE?

BECAUSE SOMEONE ERASED IT FROM THE ARCHIVE MEMORY.

TRULY WONDERFUL, THE MIND OF A CHILD IS. UNCLUTTERED.

TO THE CENTER OF THE PULL OF GRAVITY GO, AND FIND YOUR PLANET YOU WILL.

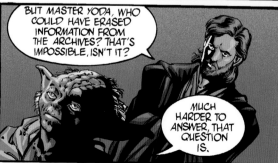

BUT MASTER YODA, WHO COULD HAVE ERASED INFORMATION FROM THE ARCHIVES? THAT'S IMPOSSIBLE, ISN'T IT?

MUCH HARDER TO ANSWER, THAT QUESTION IS.

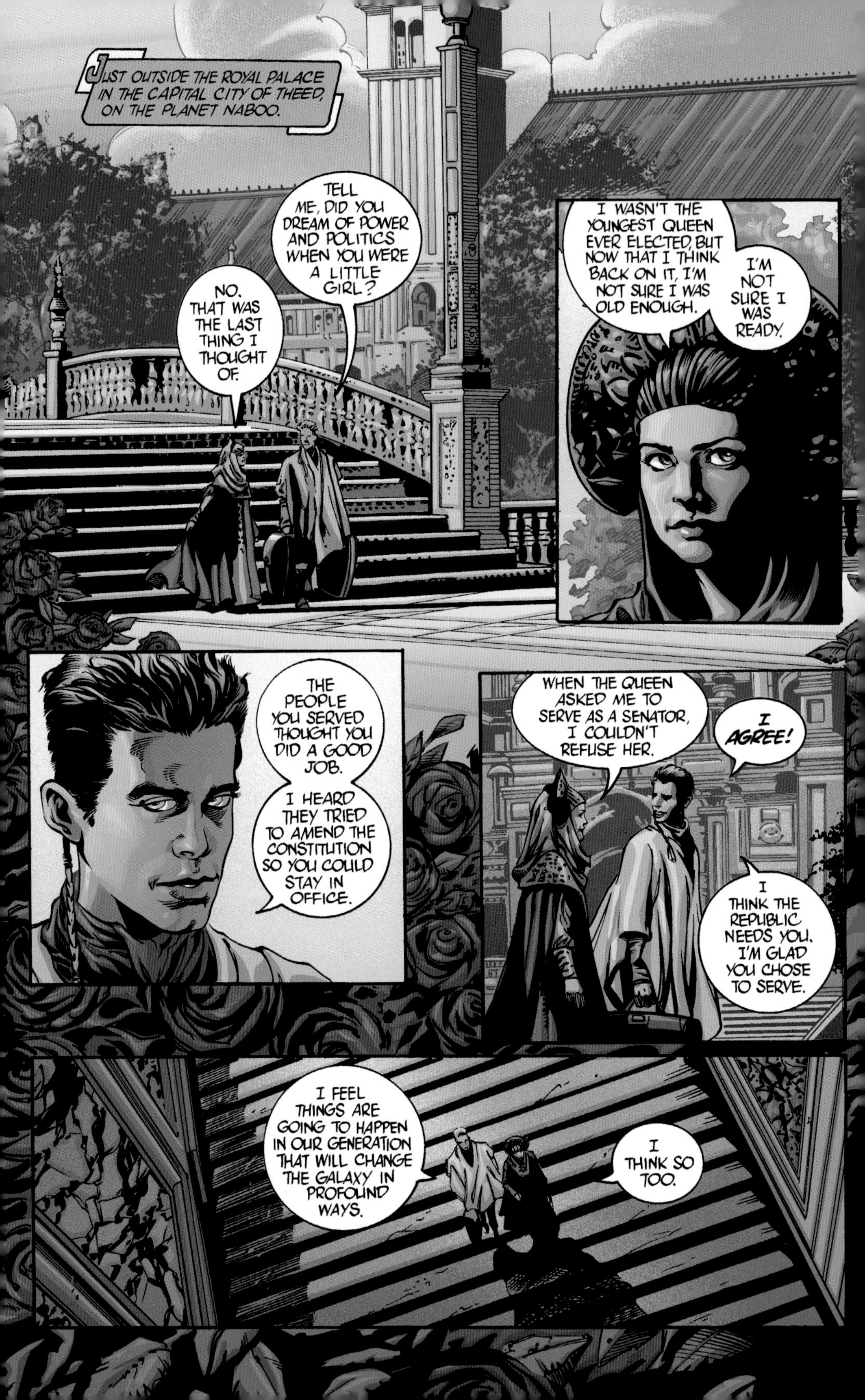
JUST OUTSIDE THE ROYAL PALACE IN THE CAPITAL CITY OF THEED, ON THE PLANET NABOO.
TELL ME, DID YOU DREAM OF POWER AND POLITICS WHEN YOU WERE A LITTLE GIRL?
NO. THAT WAS THE LAST THING I THOUGHT OF.
I WASN'T THE YOUNGEST QUEEN EVER ELECTED, BUT NOW THAT I THINK BACK ON IT, I'M NOT SURE I WAS OLD ENOUGH.
I'M NOT SURE I WAS READY.
THE PEOPLE YOU SERVED THOUGHT YOU DID A GOOD JOB.
I HEARD THEY TRIED TO AMEND THE CONSTITUTION SO YOU COULD STAY IN OFFICE.
WHEN THE QUEEN ASKED ME TO SERVE AS A SENATOR, I COULDN'T REFUSE HER.
I AGREE!
I THINK THE REPUBLIC NEEDS YOU. I'M GLAD YOU CHOSE TO SERVE.
I FEEL THINGS ARE GOING TO HAPPEN IN OUR GENERATION THAT WILL CHANGE THE GALAXY IN PROFOUND WAYS.
I THINK SO TOO.

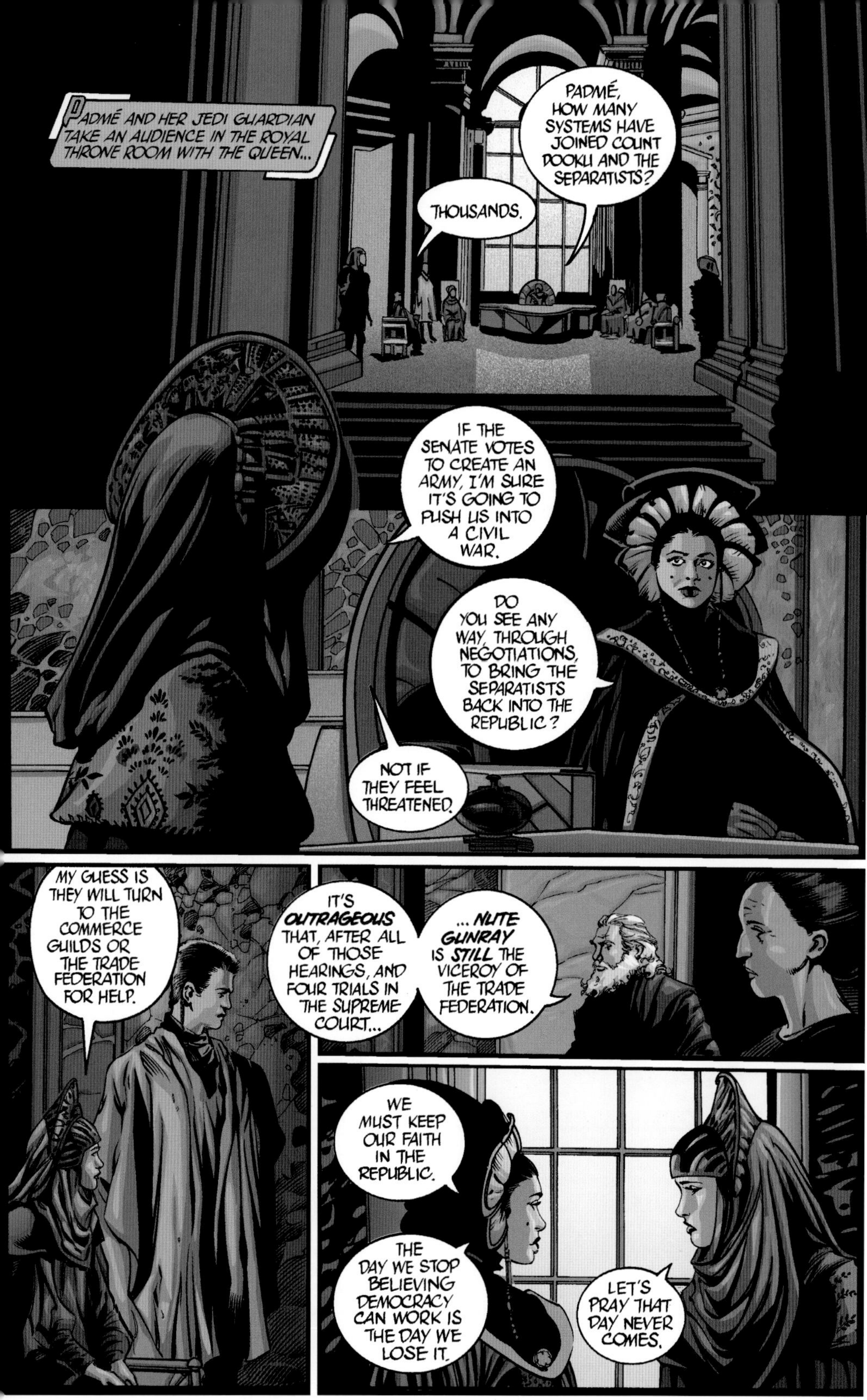
PADMÉ AND HER JEDI GUARDIAN TAKE AN AUDIENCE IN THE ROYAL THRONE ROOM WITH THE QUEEN...
PADMÉ, HOW MANY SYSTEMS HAVE JOINED COUNT DOOKU AND THE SEPARATISTS?
THOUSANDS.
IF THE SENATE VOTES TO CREATE AN ARMY, I'M SURE IT'S GOING TO PUSH US INTO A CIVIL WAR.
DO YOU SEE ANY WAY, THROUGH NEGOTIATIONS, TO BRING THE SEPARATISTS BACK INTO THE REPUBLIC?
NOT IF THEY FEEL THREATENED.
MY GUESS IS THEY WILL TURN TO THE COMMERCE GUILDS OR THE TRADE FEDERATION FOR HELP.
IT'S OUTRAGEOUS THAT, AFTER ALL OF THOSE HEARINGS, AND FOUR TRIALS IN THE SUPREME COURT...
...NUTE GUNRAY IS STILL THE VICEROY OF THE TRADE FEDERATION.
WE MUST KEEP OUR FAITH IN THE REPUBLIC.
THE DAY WE STOP BELIEVING DEMOCRACY CAN WORK IS THE DAY WE LOSE IT.
LET'S PRAY THAT DAY NEVER COMES.

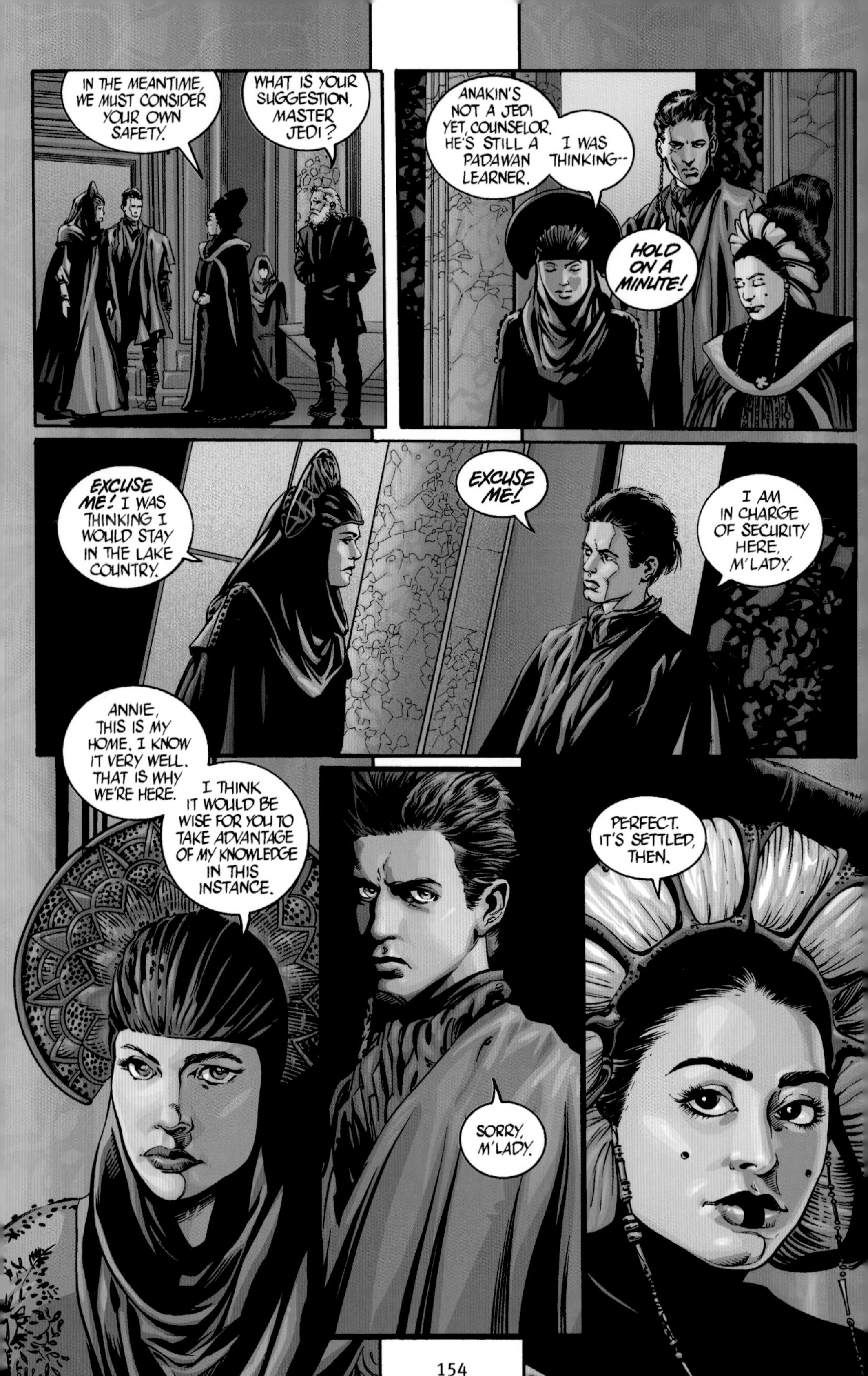

IN THE MEANTIME, WE MUST CONSIDER YOUR OWN SAFETY.
WHAT IS YOUR SUGGESTION, MASTER JEDI?
ANAKIN'S NOT A JEDI YET, COUNSELOR. HE'S STILL A PADAWAN LEARNER.
I WAS THINKING--
HOLD ON A MINUTE!
EXCUSE ME! I WAS THINKING I WOULD STAY IN THE LAKE COUNTRY.
EXCUSE ME!
I AM IN CHARGE OF SECURITY HERE, M'LADY.
ANNIE, THIS IS MY HOME. I KNOW IT VERY WELL. THAT IS WHY WE'RE HERE.
I THINK IT WOULD BE WISE FOR YOU TO TAKE ADVANTAGE OF MY KNOWLEDGE IN THIS INSTANCE.
SORRY, M'LADY.
PERFECT. IT'S SETTLED, THEN.

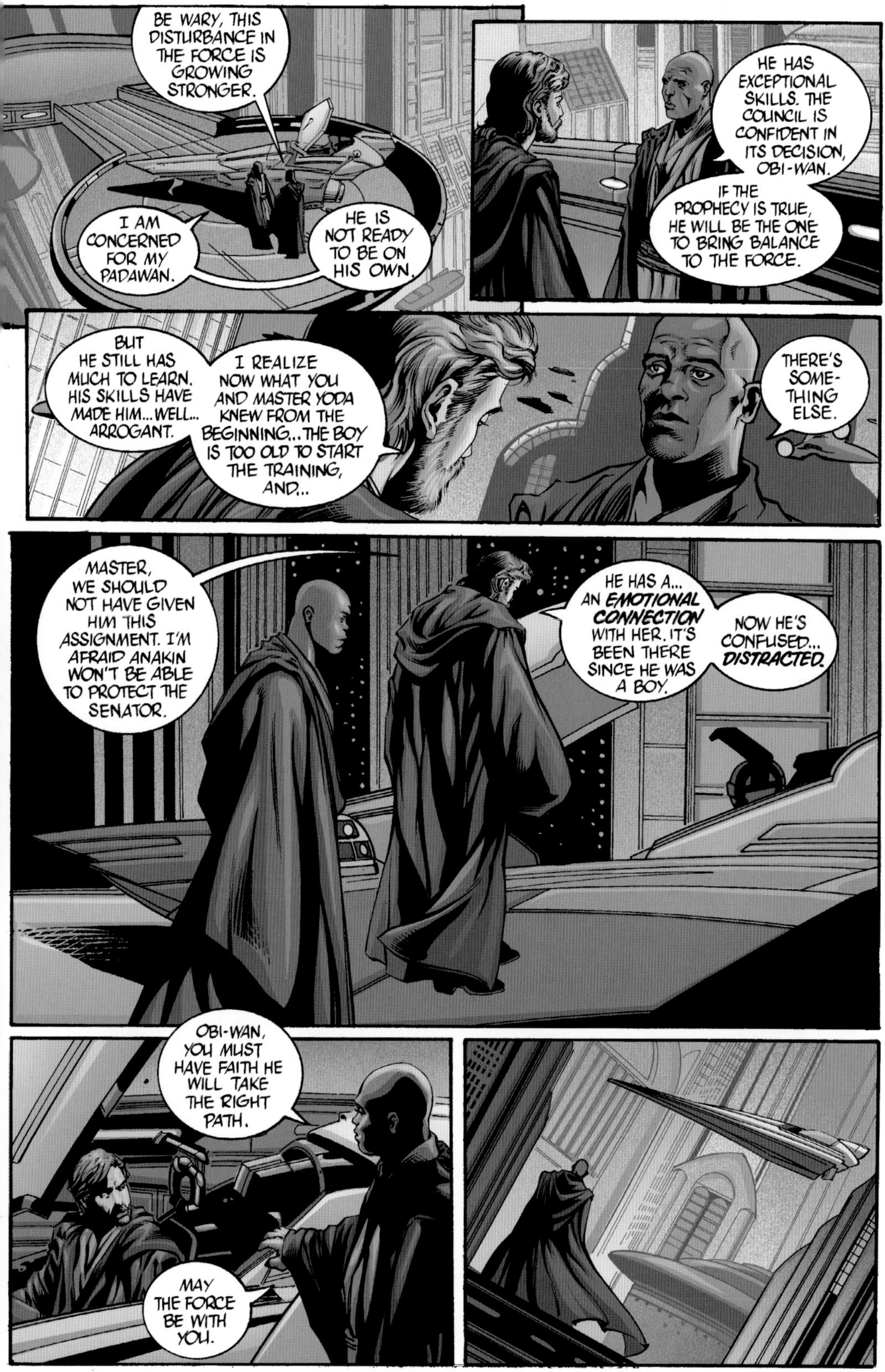
BE WARY, THIS DISTURBANCE IN THE FORCE IS GROWING STRONGER.
I AM CONCERNED FOR MY PADAWAN.
HE IS NOT READY TO BE ON HIS OWN.
HE HAS EXCEPTIONAL SKILLS. THE COUNCIL IS CONFIDENT IN ITS DECISION, OBI-WAN.
IF THE PROPHECY IS TRUE, HE WILL BE THE ONE TO BRING BALANCE TO THE FORCE.
BUT HE STILL HAS MUCH TO LEARN. HIS SKILLS HAVE MADE HIM...WELL... ARROGANT.
I REALIZE NOW WHAT YOU AND MASTER YODA KNEW FROM THE BEGINNING...THE BOY IS TOO OLD TO START THE TRAINING, AND...
THERE'S SOME-THING ELSE.
MASTER, WE SHOULD NOT HAVE GIVEN HIM THIS ASSIGNMENT. I'M AFRAID ANAKIN WON'T BE ABLE TO PROTECT THE SENATOR.
HE HAS A... AN EMOTIONAL CONNECTION WITH HER. IT'S BEEN THERE SINCE HE WAS A BOY.
NOW HE'S CONFUSED... DISTRACTED.
OBI-WAN, YOU MUST HAVE FAITH HE WILL TAKE THE RIGHT PATH.
MAY THE FORCE BE WITH YOU.

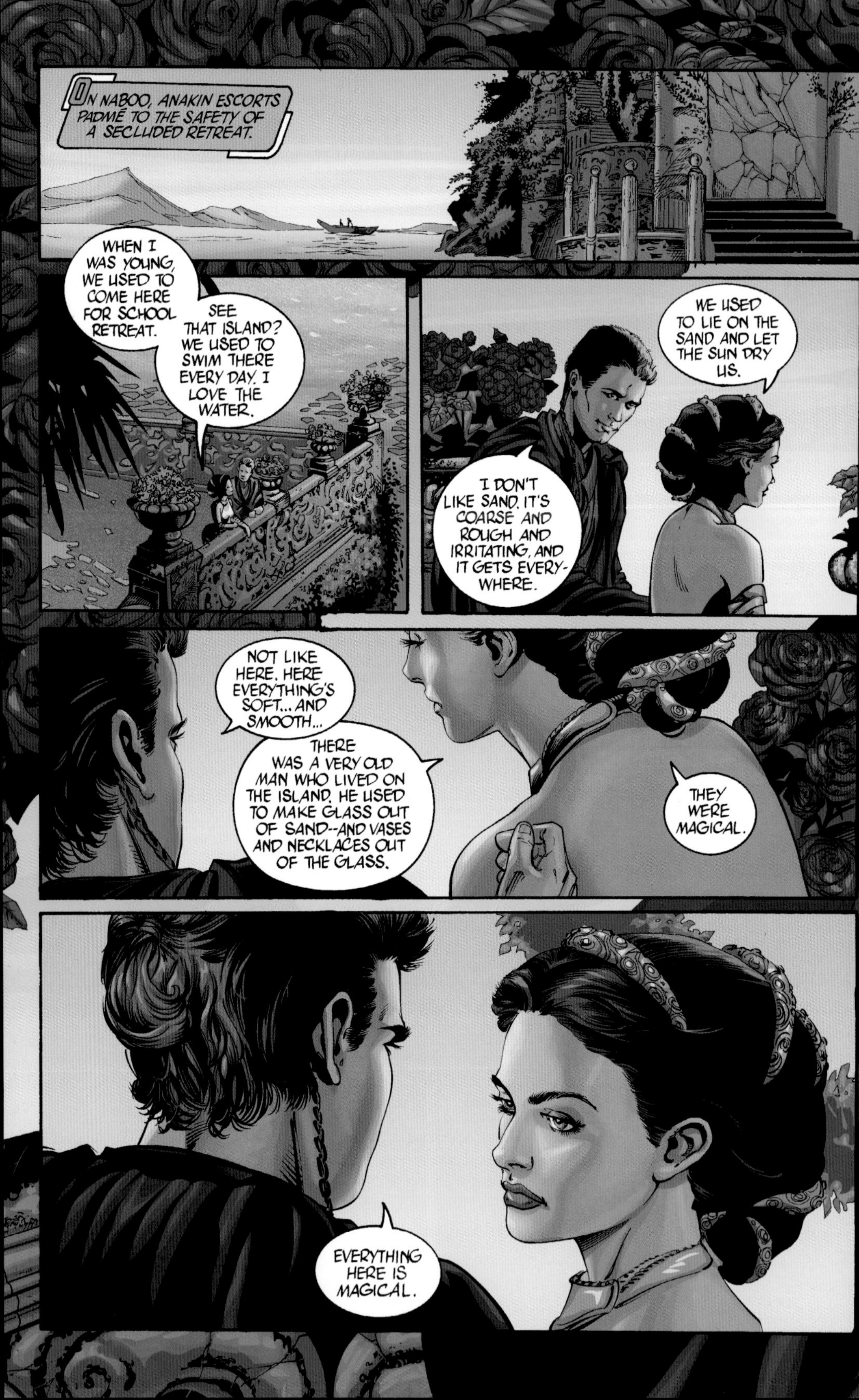
ON NABOO, ANAKIN ESCORTS PADMÉ TO THE SAFETY OF A SECLUDED RETREAT.
WHEN I WAS YOUNG, WE USED TO COME HERE FOR SCHOOL RETREAT.
SEE THAT ISLAND? WE USED TO SWIM THERE EVERY DAY. I LOVE THE WATER.
WE USED TO LIE ON THE SAND AND LET THE SUN DRY US.
I DON'T LIKE SAND. IT'S COARSE AND ROUGH AND IRRITATING, AND IT GETS EVERY-WHERE.
NOT LIKE HERE. HERE EVERYTHING'S SOFT... AND SMOOTH...
THERE WAS A VERY OLD MAN WHO LIVED ON THE ISLAND. HE USED TO MAKE GLASS OUT OF SAND--AND VASES AND NECKLACES OUT OF THE GLASS.
THEY WERE MAGICAL.
EVERYTHING HERE IS MAGICAL.

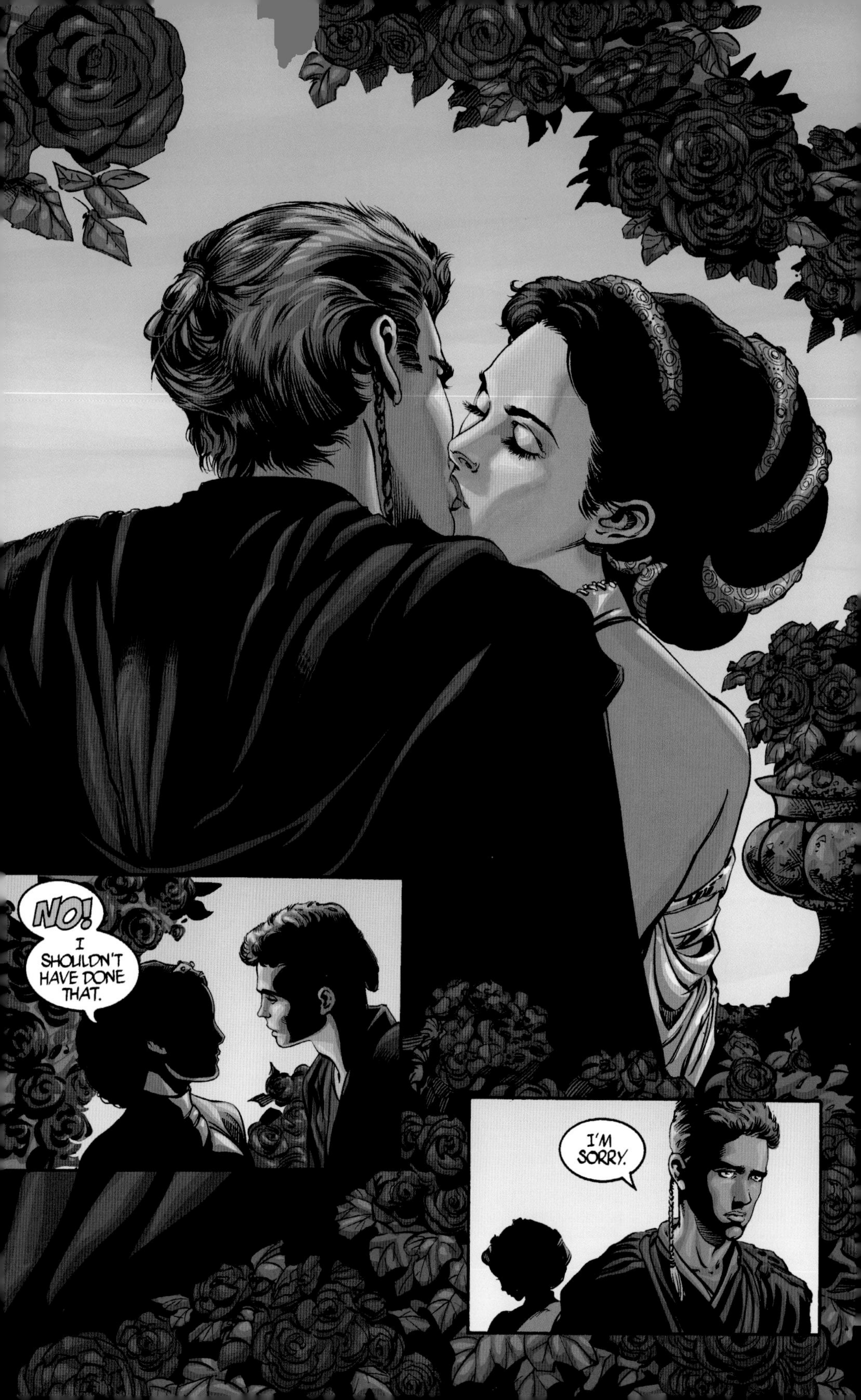
NO! I SHOULDN'T HAVE DONE THAT.
I'M SORRY.

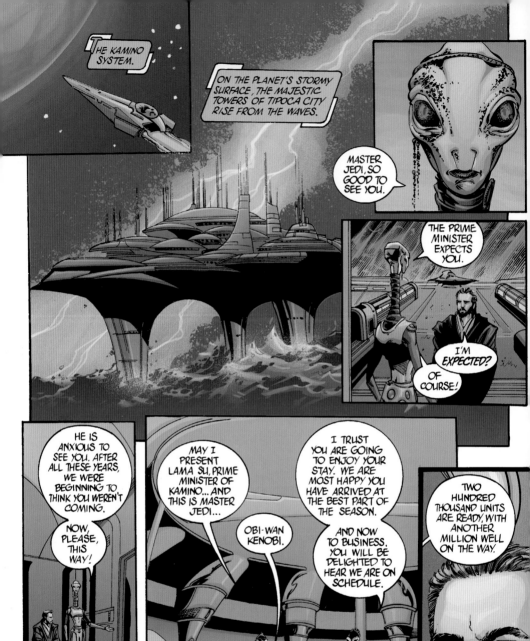

THE KAMINO SYSTEM.

ON THE PLANET'S STORMY SURFACE, THE MAJESTIC TOWERS OF TIPOCA CITY RISE FROM THE WAVES.

MASTER JEDI, SO GOOD TO SEE YOU.

THE PRIME MINISTER EXPECTS YOU.

I'M EXPECTED?

OF COURSE!

HE IS ANXIOUS TO SEE YOU. AFTER ALL THESE YEARS, WE WERE BEGINNING TO THINK YOU WEREN'T COMING.

NOW, PLEASE, THIS WAY!

MAY I PRESENT LAMA SU, PRIME MINISTER OF KAMINO... AND THIS IS MASTER JEDI...

OBI-WAN KENOBI.

I TRUST YOU ARE GOING TO ENJOY YOUR STAY. WE ARE MOST HAPPY YOU HAVE ARRIVED AT THE BEST PART OF THE SEASON.

AND NOW TO BUSINESS. YOU WILL BE DELIGHTED TO HEAR WE ARE ON SCHEDULE.

TWO HUNDRED THOUSAND UNITS ARE READY, WITH ANOTHER MILLION WELL ON THE WAY.

THAT IS...GOOD NEWS.

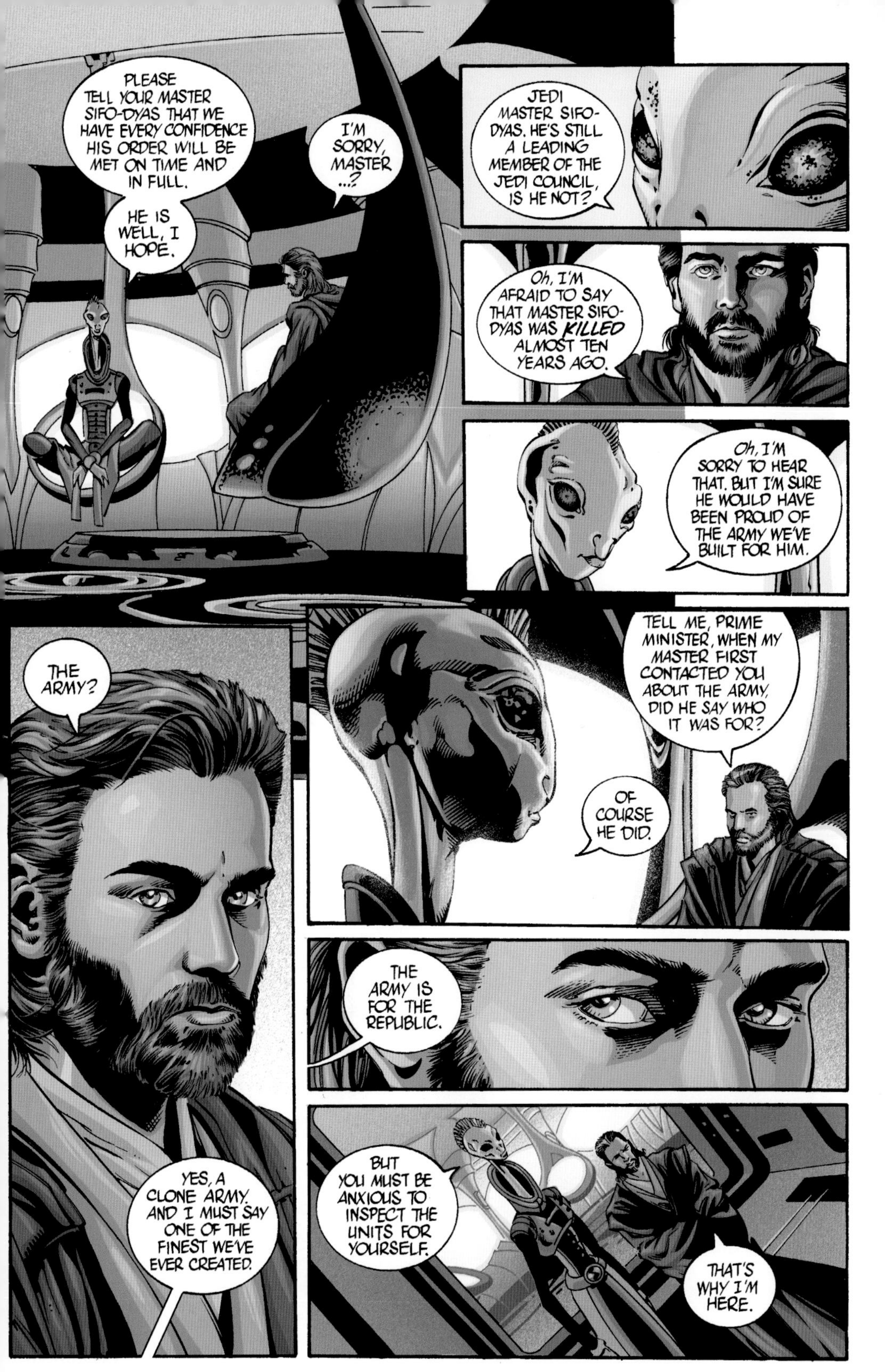
PLEASE TELL YOUR MASTER SIFO-DYAS THAT WE HAVE EVERY CONFIDENCE HIS ORDER WILL BE MET ON TIME AND IN FULL.
HE IS WELL, I HOPE.
I'M SORRY, MASTER ...?
JEDI MASTER SIFO-DYAS. HE'S STILL A LEADING MEMBER OF THE JEDI COUNCIL, IS HE NOT?
Oh, I'M AFRAID TO SAY THAT MASTER SIFO-DYAS WAS KILLED ALMOST TEN YEARS AGO.
Oh, I'M SORRY TO HEAR THAT. BUT I'M SURE HE WOULD HAVE BEEN PROUD OF THE ARMY WE'VE BUILT FOR HIM.
THE ARMY?
YES, A CLONE ARMY. AND I MUST SAY ONE OF THE FINEST WE'VE EVER CREATED.
TELL ME, PRIME MINISTER, WHEN MY MASTER FIRST CONTACTED YOU ABOUT THE ARMY, DID HE SAY WHO IT WAS FOR?
OF COURSE HE DID.
THE ARMY IS FOR THE REPUBLIC.
BUT YOU MUST BE ANXIOUS TO INSPECT THE UNITS FOR YOURSELF.
THAT'S WHY I'M HERE.

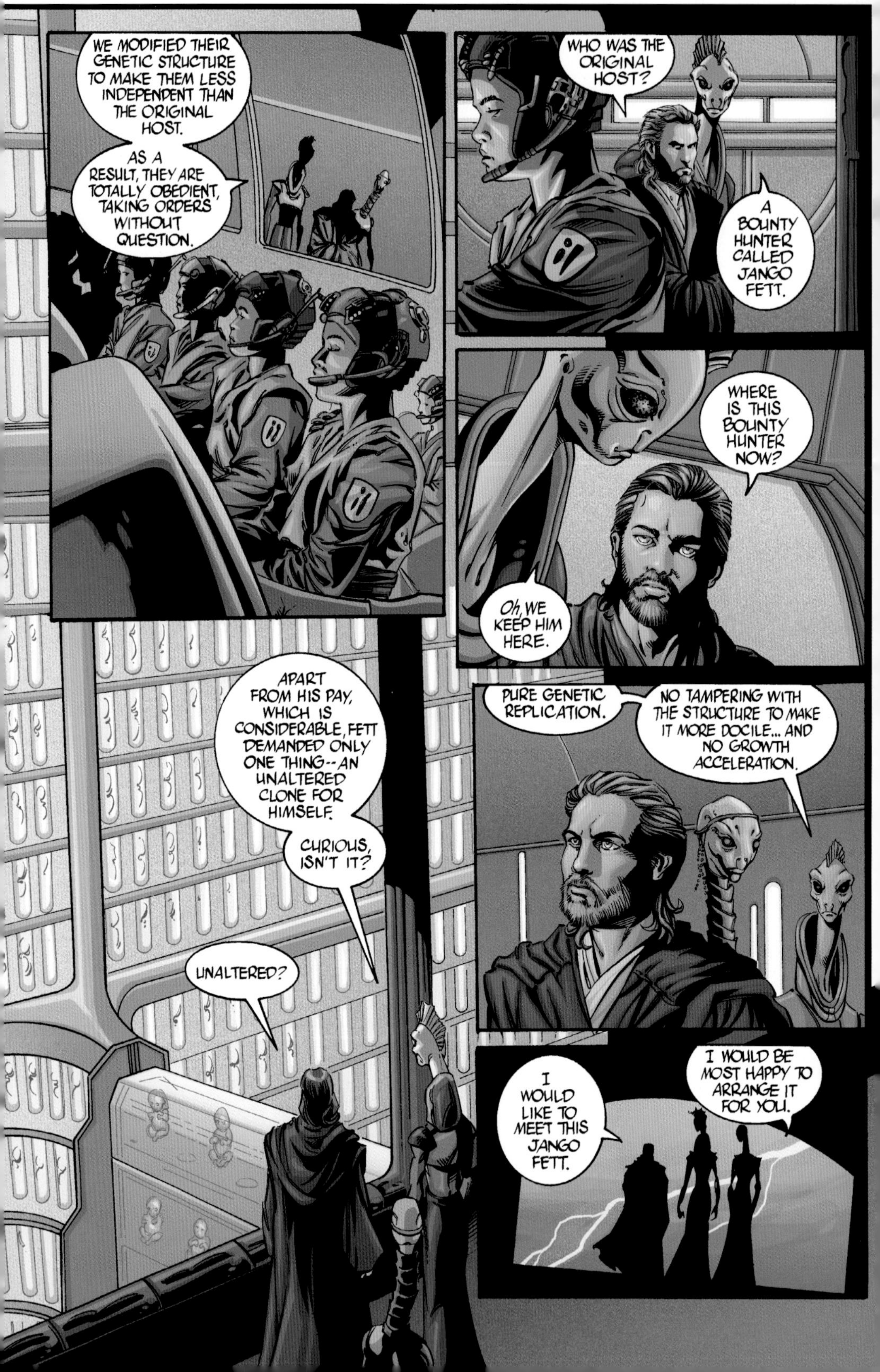
WE MODIFIED THEIR GENETIC STRUCTURE TO MAKE THEM LESS INDEPENDENT THAN THE ORIGINAL HOST.
AS A RESULT, THEY ARE TOTALLY OBEDIENT, TAKING ORDERS WITHOUT QUESTION.
WHO WAS THE ORIGINAL HOST?
A BOUNTY HUNTER CALLED JANGO FETT.
WHERE IS THIS BOUNTY HUNTER NOW?
Oh, WE KEEP HIM HERE.
APART FROM HIS PAY, WHICH IS CONSIDERABLE, FETT DEMANDED ONLY ONE THING--AN UNALTERED CLONE FOR HIMSELF.
CURIOUS, ISN'T IT?
UNALTERED?
PURE GENETIC REPLICATION.
NO TAMPERING WITH THE STRUCTURE TO MAKE IT MORE DOCILE... AND NO GROWTH ACCELERATION.
I WOULD LIKE TO MEET THIS JANGO FETT.
I WOULD BE MOST HAPPY TO ARRANGE IT FOR YOU.

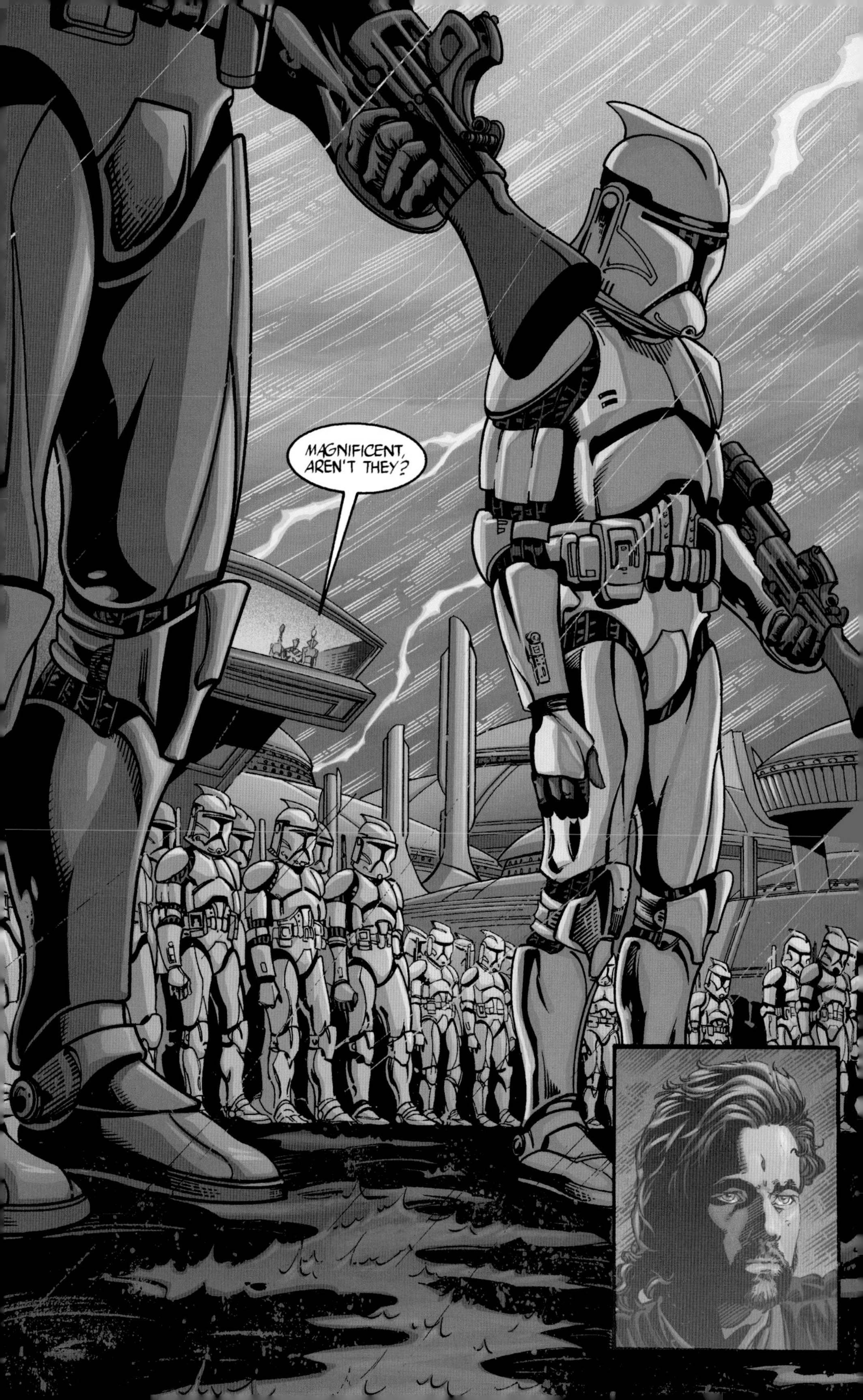
MAGNIFICENT, AREN'T THEY?

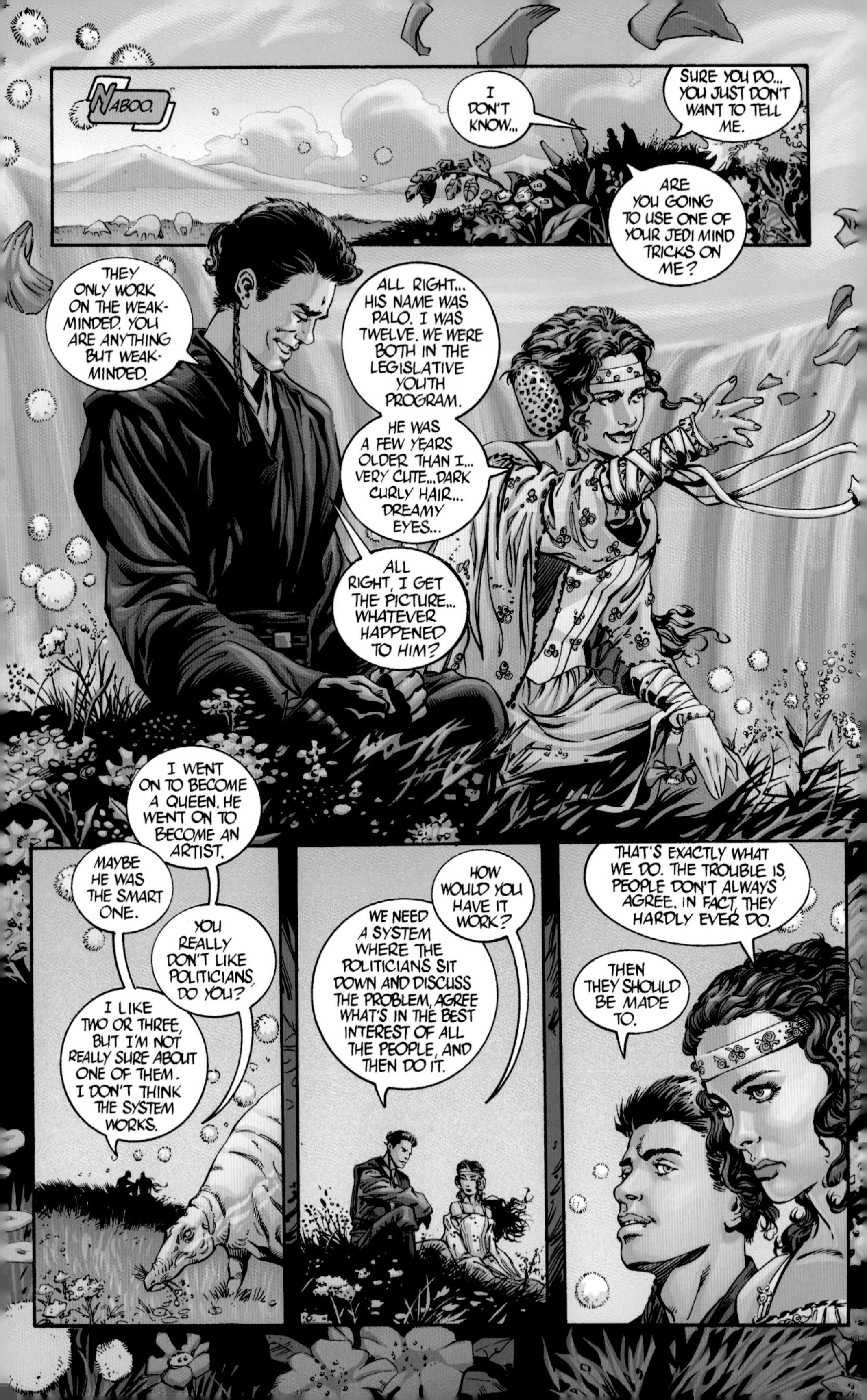
NABOO.
I DON'T KNOW...
SURE YOU DO... YOU JUST DON'T WANT TO TELL ME.
ARE YOU GOING TO USE ONE OF YOUR JEDI MIND TRICKS ON ME?
THEY ONLY WORK ON THE WEAK-MINDED. YOU ARE ANYTHING BUT WEAK-MINDED.
ALL RIGHT... HIS NAME WAS PALO. I WAS TWELVE. WE WERE BOTH IN THE LEGISLATIVE YOUTH PROGRAM.
HE WAS A FEW YEARS OLDER THAN I... VERY CUTE...DARK CURLY HAIR... DREAMY EYES...
ALL RIGHT, I GET THE PICTURE... WHATEVER HAPPENED TO HIM?
I WENT ON TO BECOME A QUEEN. HE WENT ON TO BECOME AN ARTIST.
MAYBE HE WAS THE SMART ONE.
YOU REALLY DON'T LIKE POLITICIANS, DO YOU?
I LIKE TWO OR THREE, BUT I'M NOT REALLY SURE ABOUT ONE OF THEM. I DON'T THINK THE SYSTEM WORKS.
HOW WOULD YOU HAVE IT WORK?
WE NEED A SYSTEM WHERE THE POLITICIANS SIT DOWN AND DISCUSS THE PROBLEM, AGREE WHAT'S IN THE BEST INTEREST OF ALL THE PEOPLE, AND THEN DO IT.
THAT'S EXACTLY WHAT WE DO. THE TROUBLE IS, PEOPLE DON'T ALWAYS AGREE. IN FACT, THEY HARDLY EVER DO.
THEN THEY SHOULD BE MADE TO.

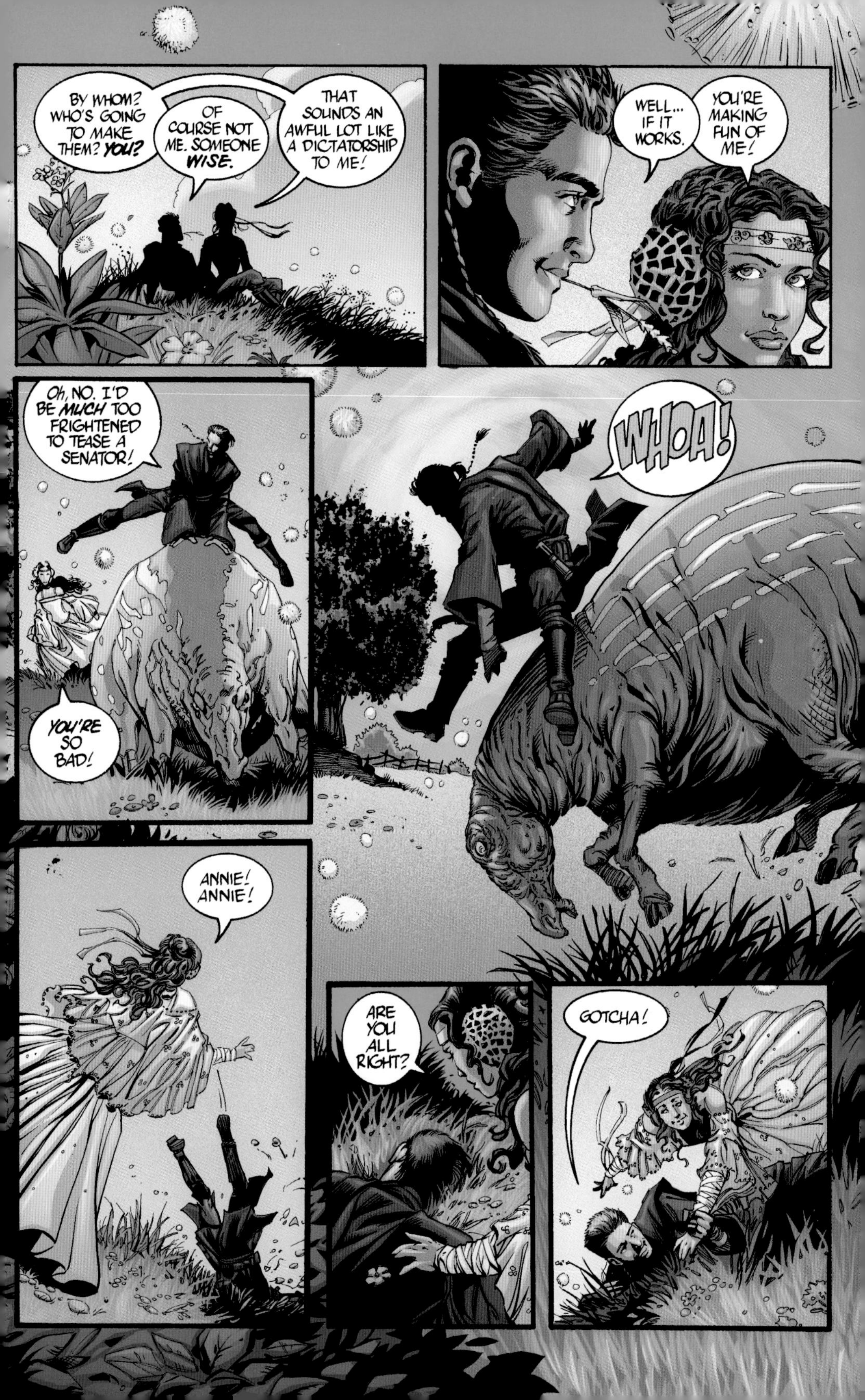
BY WHOM? WHO'S GOING TO MAKE THEM? YOU?
OF COURSE NOT ME. SOMEONE WISE.
THAT SOUNDS AN AWFUL LOT LIKE A DICTATORSHIP TO ME!
YOU'RE MAKING FUN OF ME!
WELL... IF IT WORKS.
Oh, NO. I'D BE MUCH TOO FRIGHTENED TO TEASE A SENATOR!
YOU'RE SO BAD!
WHOA!
ANNIE! ANNIE!
ARE YOU ALL RIGHT?
GOTCHA!

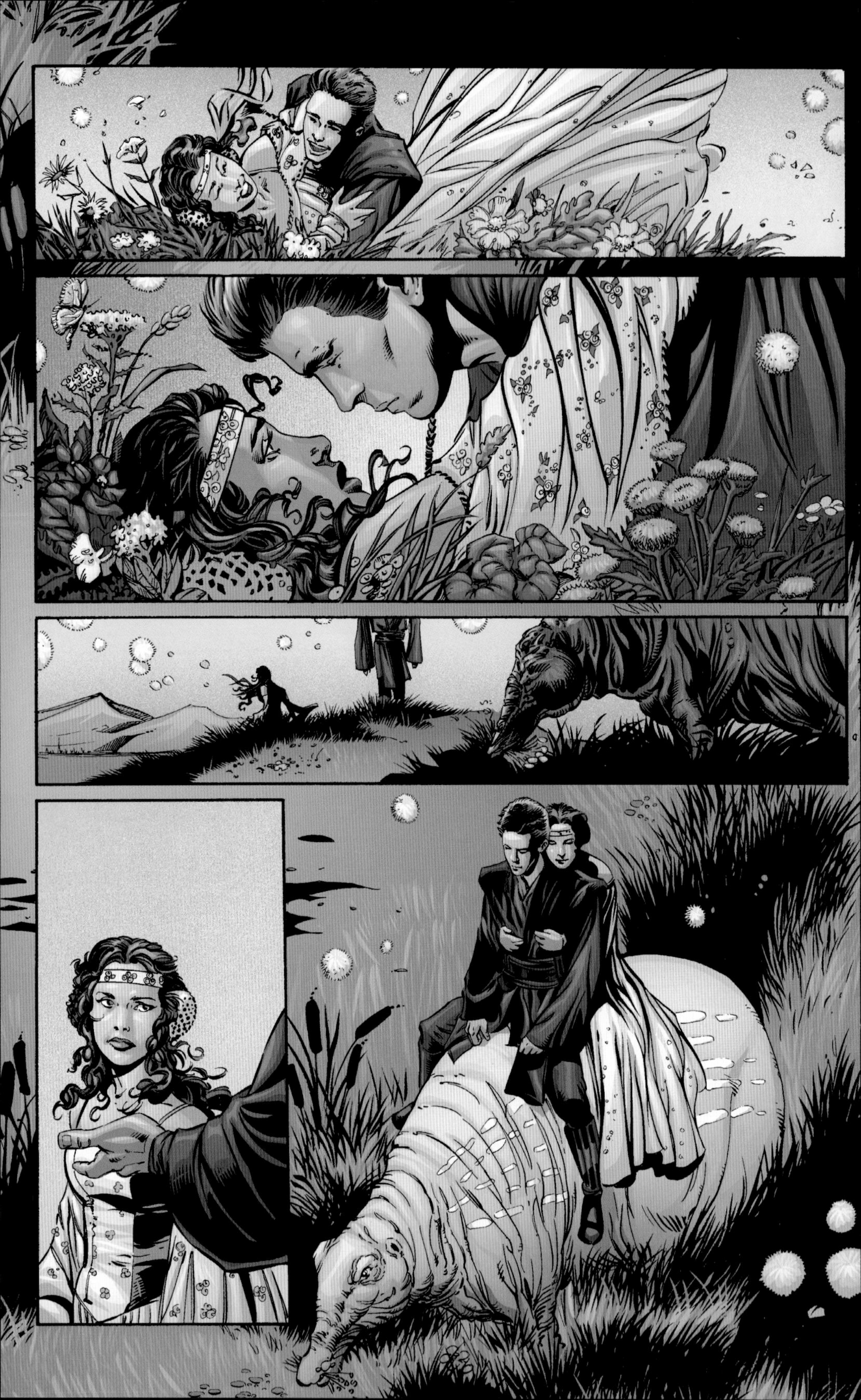

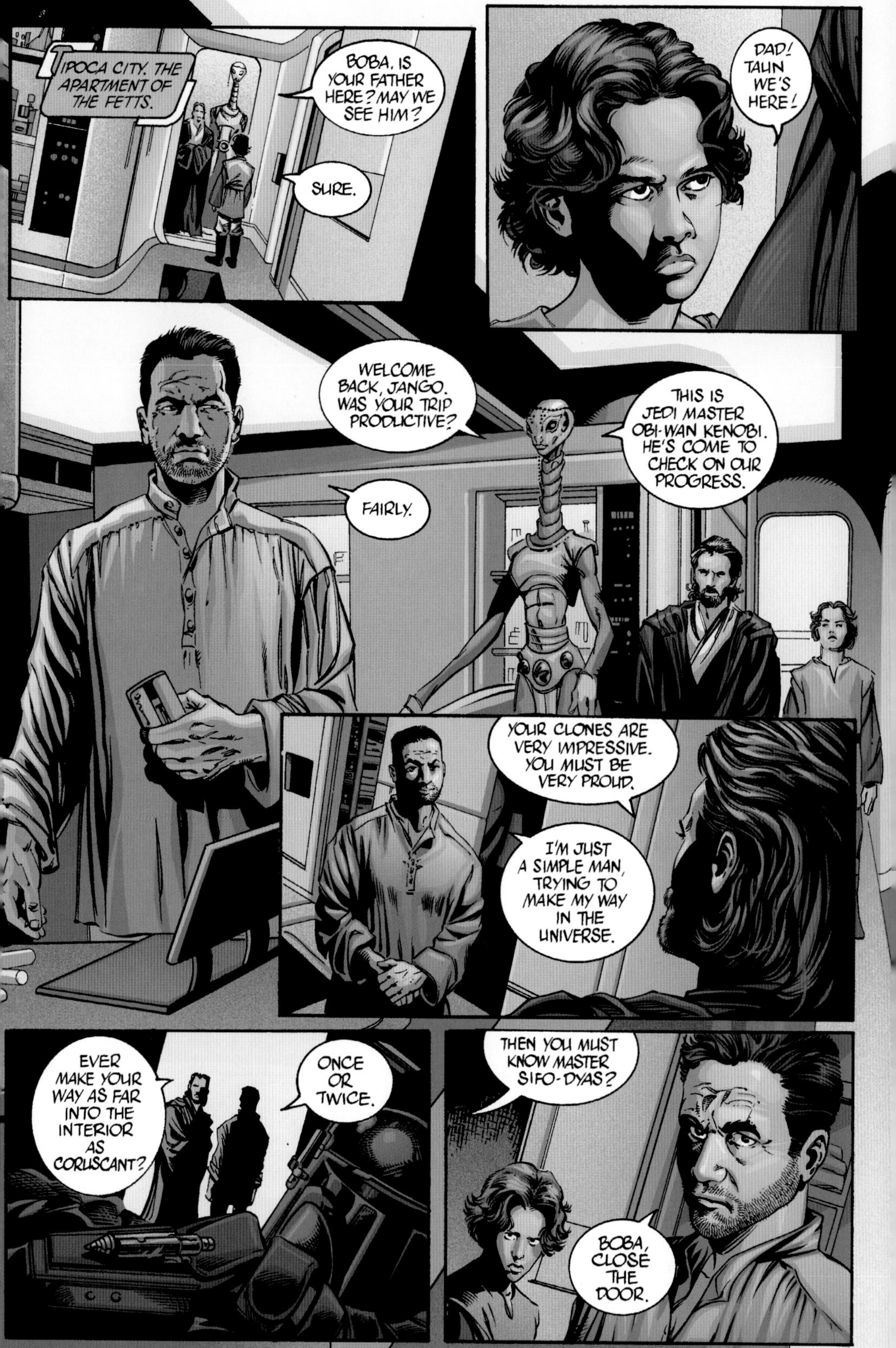
TIPOCA CITY. THE APARTMENT OF THE FETTS.
BOBA, IS YOUR FATHER HERE? MAY WE SEE HIM?
SURE.
DAD! TAUN WE'S HERE!
WELCOME BACK, JANGO. WAS YOUR TRIP PRODUCTIVE?
FAIRLY.
THIS IS JEDI MASTER OBI-WAN KENOBI. HE'S COME TO CHECK ON OUR PROGRESS.
YOUR CLONES ARE VERY IMPRESSIVE. YOU MUST BE VERY PROUD.
I'M JUST A SIMPLE MAN, TRYING TO MAKE MY WAY IN THE UNIVERSE.
EVER MAKE YOUR WAY AS FAR INTO THE INTERIOR AS CORUSCANT?
ONCE OR TWICE.
THEN YOU MUST KNOW MASTER SIFO-DYAS?
BOBA, CLOSE THE DOOR.

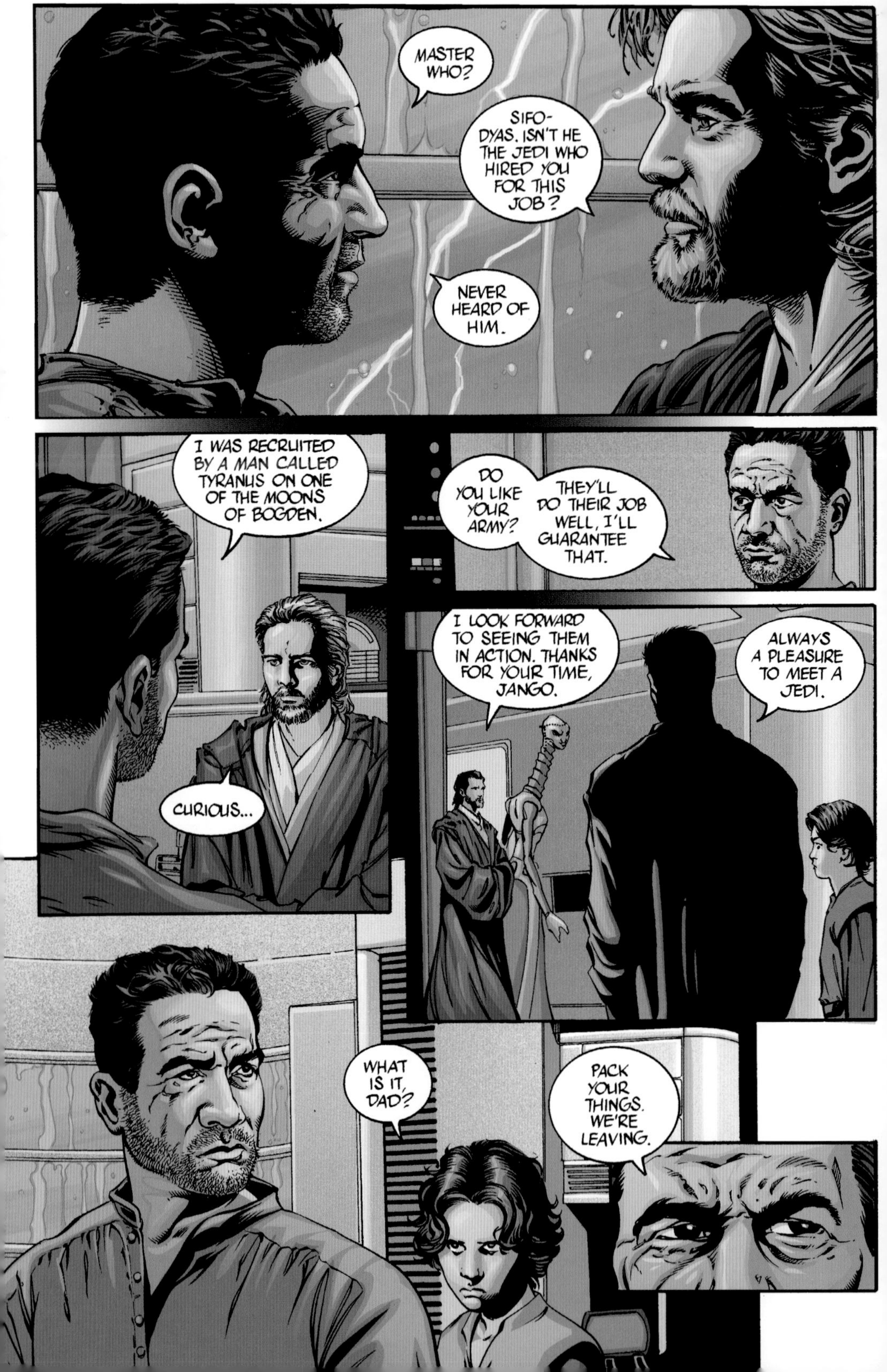
MASTER WHO?
SIFO-DYAS. ISN'T HE THE JEDI WHO HIRED YOU FOR THIS JOB?
NEVER HEARD OF HIM.
I WAS RECRUITED BY A MAN CALLED TYRANUS ON ONE OF THE MOONS OF BOGDEN.
CURIOUS...
DO YOU LIKE YOUR ARMY?
THEY'LL DO THEIR JOB WELL, I'LL GUARANTEE THAT.
I LOOK FORWARD TO SEEING THEM IN ACTION. THANKS FOR YOUR TIME, JANGO.
ALWAYS A PLEASURE TO MEET A JEDI.
WHAT IS IT, DAD?
PACK YOUR THINGS. WE'RE LEAVING.

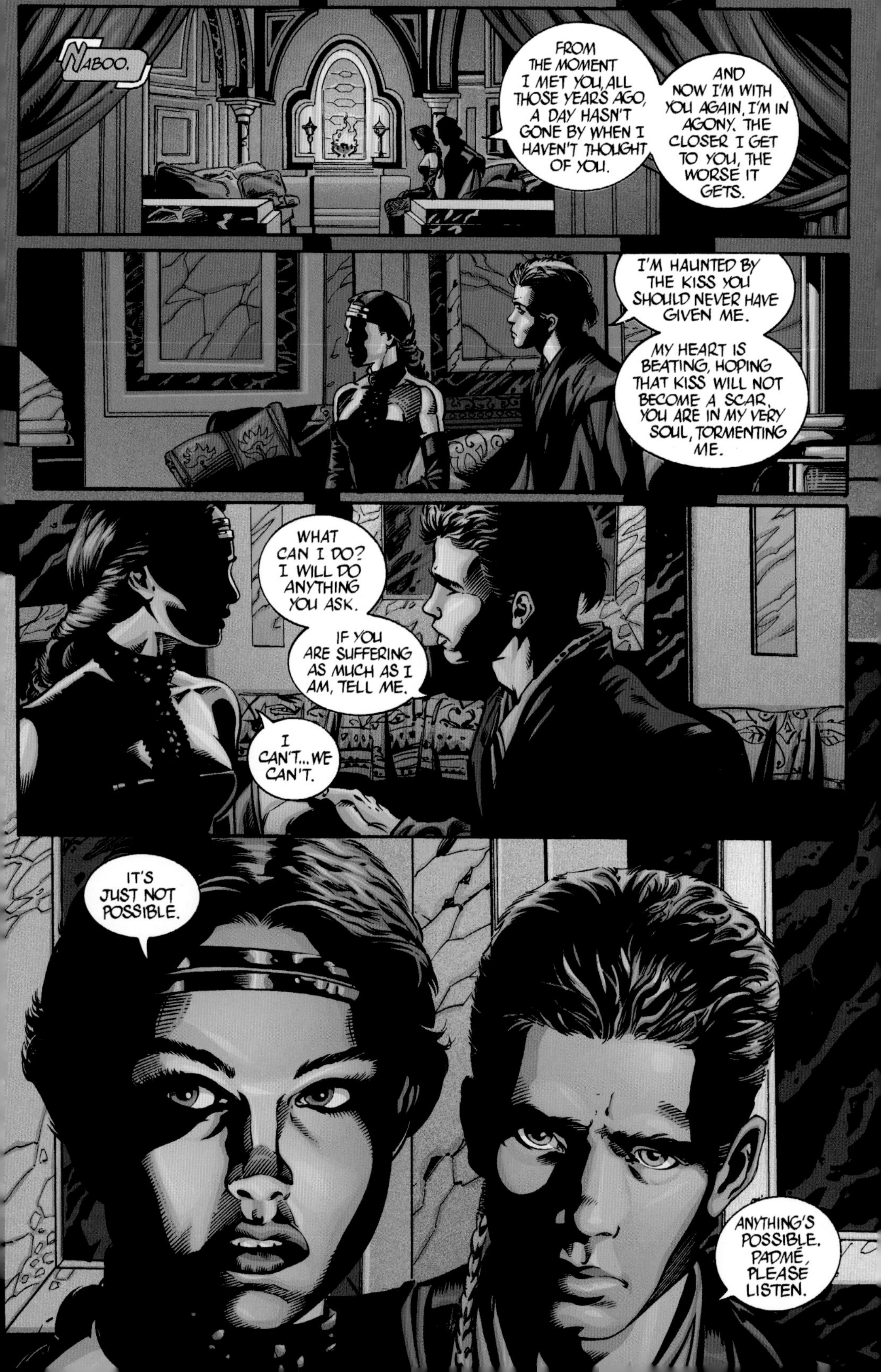
NABOO.
FROM THE MOMENT I MET YOU, ALL THOSE YEARS AGO, A DAY HASN'T GONE BY WHEN I HAVEN'T THOUGHT OF YOU.
AND NOW I'M WITH YOU AGAIN, I'M IN AGONY. THE CLOSER I GET TO YOU, THE WORSE IT GETS.
I'M HAUNTED BY THE KISS YOU SHOULD NEVER HAVE GIVEN ME.
MY HEART IS BEATING, HOPING THAT KISS WILL NOT BECOME A SCAR. YOU ARE IN MY VERY SOUL, TORMENTING ME.
WHAT CAN I DO? I WILL DO ANYTHING YOU ASK.
IF YOU ARE SUFFERING AS MUCH AS I AM, TELL ME.
I CAN'T...WE CAN'T.
IT'S JUST NOT POSSIBLE.
ANYTHING'S POSSIBLE. PADMÉ, PLEASE LISTEN.

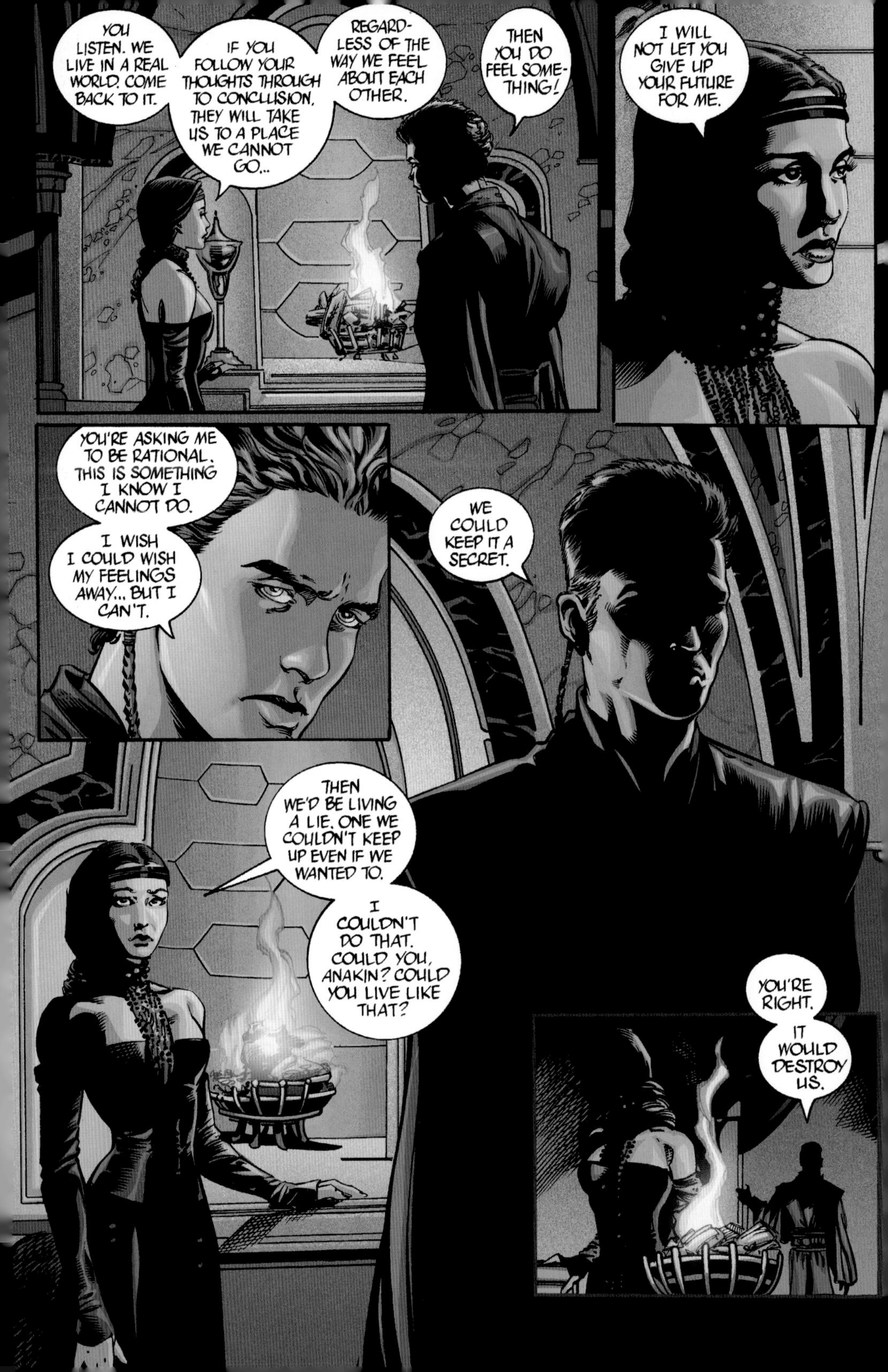
YOU LISTEN. WE LIVE IN A REAL WORLD. COME BACK TO IT.
IF YOU FOLLOW YOUR THOUGHTS THROUGH TO CONCLUSION, THEY WILL TAKE US TO A PLACE WE CANNOT GO...
REGARDLESS OF THE WAY WE FEEL ABOUT EACH OTHER.
THEN YOU DO FEEL SOME-THING!
I WILL NOT LET YOU GIVE UP YOUR FUTURE FOR ME.
YOU'RE ASKING ME TO BE RATIONAL. THIS IS SOMETHING I KNOW I CANNOT DO.
I WISH I COULD WISH MY FEELINGS AWAY... BUT I CAN'T.
WE COULD KEEP IT A SECRET.
THEN WE'D BE LIVING A LIE. ONE WE COULDN'T KEEP UP EVEN IF WE WANTED TO.
I COULDN'T DO THAT. COULD YOU, ANAKIN? COULD YOU LIVE LIKE THAT?
YOU'RE RIGHT.
IT WOULD DESTROY US.

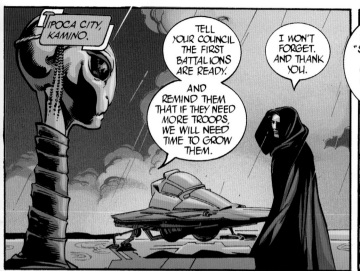

TIPOCA CITY, KAMINO.

TELL YOUR COUNCIL THE FIRST BATTALIONS ARE READY.

AND REMIND THEM THAT IF THEY NEED MORE TROOPS, WE WILL NEED TIME TO GROW THEM.

I WON'T FORGET. AND THANK YOU.

ARFOUR, RELAY THIS, "SCRAMBLE CODE FIVE," TO CORUSCANT-- CARE OF "THE OLD FOLKS' HOME."

I HAVE SUCCESSFULLY MADE CONTACT WITH THE PRIME MINISTER OF KAMINO.

THEY ARE USING A BOUNTY HUNTER NAMED JANGO FETT TO CREATE A CLONE ARMY FOR THE REPUBLIC.

I HAVE A STRONG FEELING THIS BOUNTY HUNTER IS THE ASSASSIN WE'RE LOOKING FOR.

DO YOU THINK THESE CLONERS ARE INVOLVED IN THE PLOT TO ASSASSINATE SENATOR AMIDALA?

NO, MASTER. THERE APPEARS TO BE NO MOTIVE.

DO NOT ASSUME ANYTHING, OBI-WAN. CLEAR YOUR MIND MUST BE IF YOU ARE TO DISCOVER THE REAL VILLAIN BEHIND THIS PLOT.

YES, MASTER.

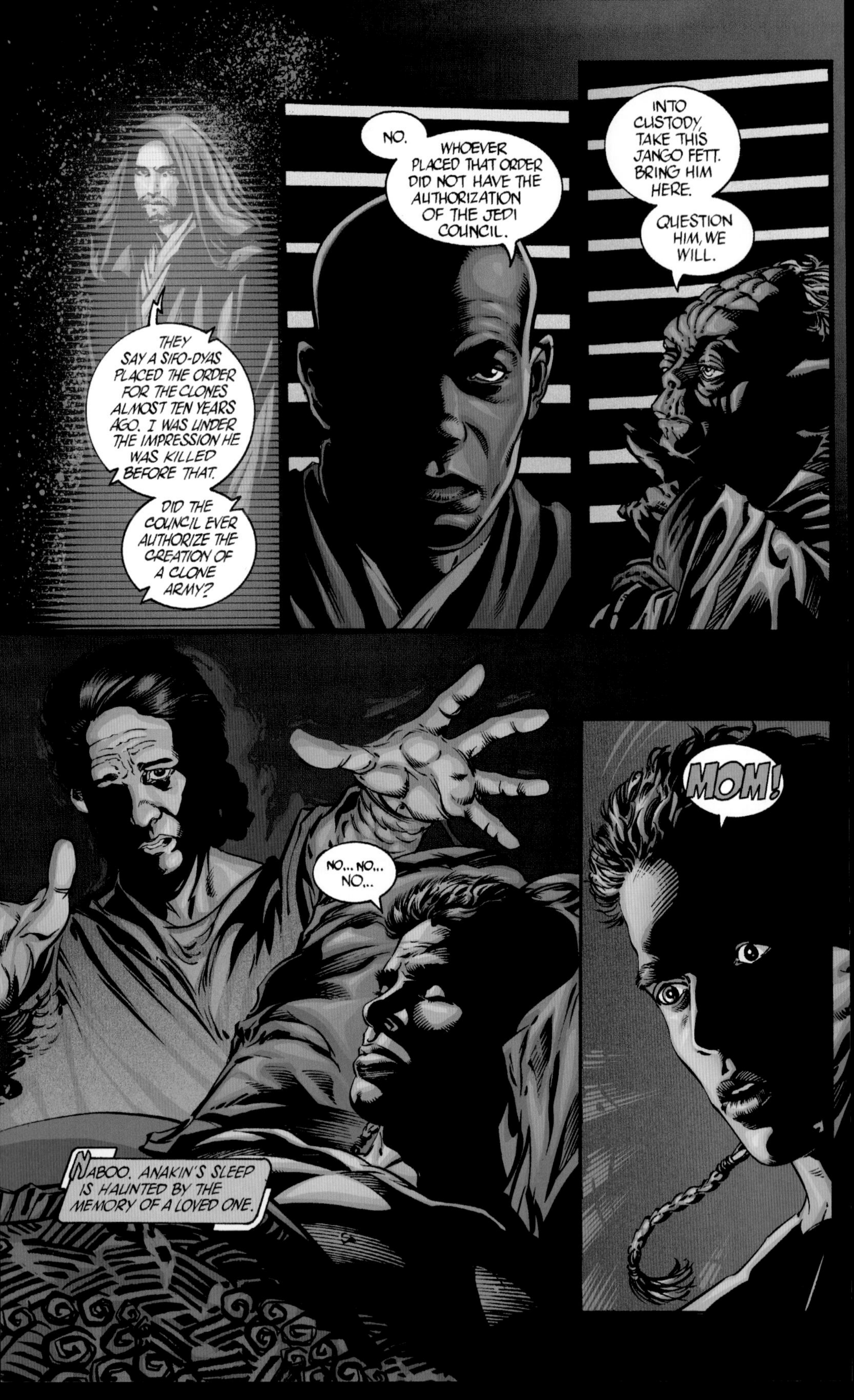
THEY SAY A SIFO-DYAS PLACED THE ORDER FOR THE CLONES ALMOST TEN YEARS AGO. I WAS UNDER THE IMPRESSION HE WAS KILLED BEFORE THAT.
DID THE COUNCIL EVER AUTHORIZE THE CREATION OF A CLONE ARMY?
NO.
WHOEVER PLACED THAT ORDER DID NOT HAVE THE AUTHORIZATION OF THE JEDI COUNCIL.
INTO CUSTODY, TAKE THIS JANGO FETT. BRING HIM HERE.
QUESTION HIM, WE WILL.
NABOO. ANAKIN'S SLEEP IS HAUNTED BY THE MEMORY OF A LOVED ONE.
NO... NO... NO...
MOM!

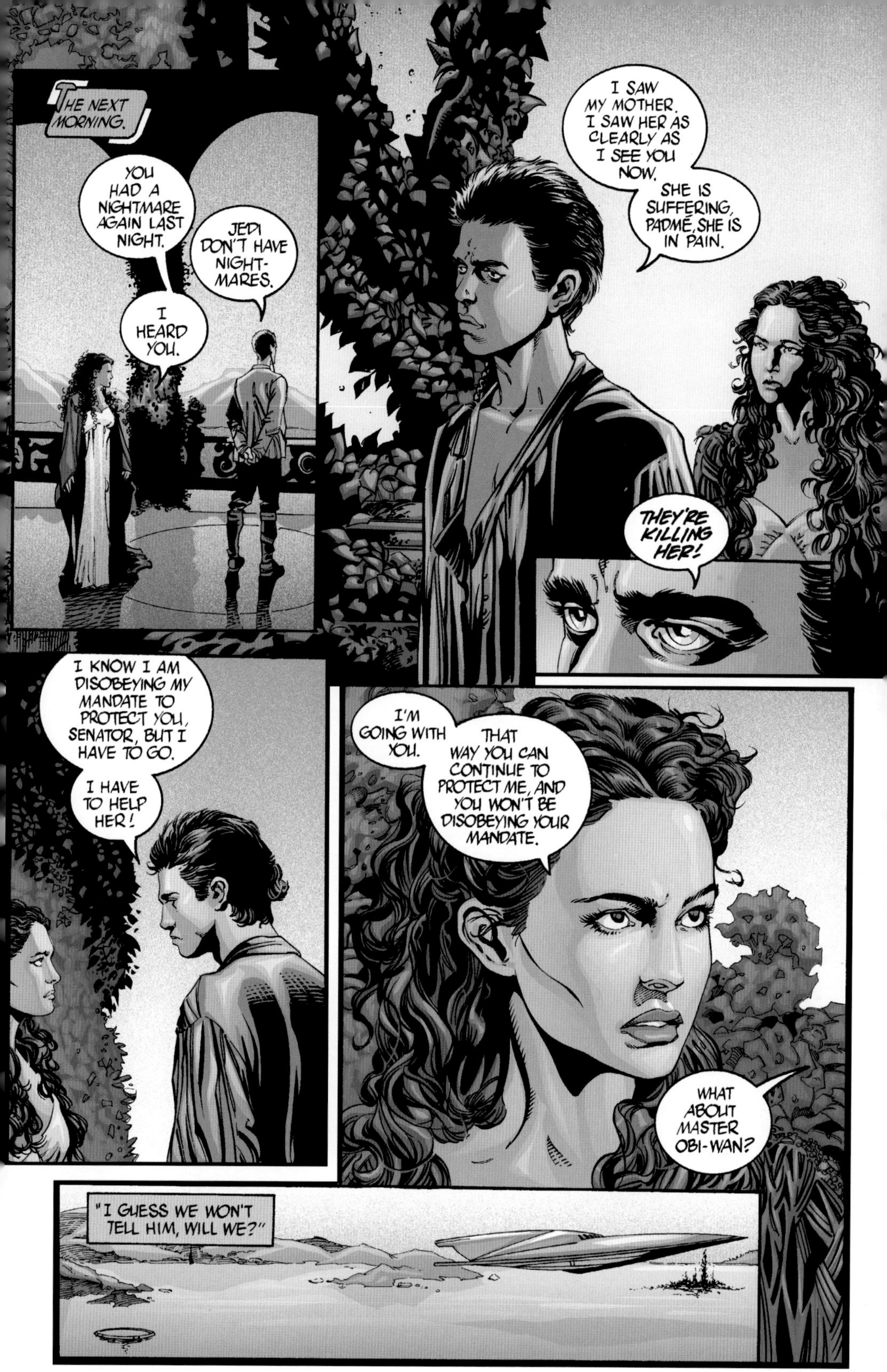
THE NEXT MORNING.
YOU HAD A NIGHTMARE AGAIN LAST NIGHT.
JEDI DON'T HAVE NIGHT-MARES.
I HEARD YOU.
I SAW MY MOTHER. I SAW HER AS CLEARLY AS I SEE YOU NOW.
SHE IS SUFFERING, PADMÉ, SHE IS IN PAIN.
THEY'RE KILLING HER!
I KNOW I AM DISOBEYING MY MANDATE TO PROTECT YOU, SENATOR, BUT I HAVE TO GO.
I HAVE TO HELP HER!
I'M GOING WITH YOU.
THAT WAY YOU CAN CONTINUE TO PROTECT ME, AND YOU WON'T BE DISOBEYING YOUR MANDATE.
WHAT ABOUT MASTER OBI-WAN?
"I GUESS WE WON'T TELL HIM, WILL WE?"

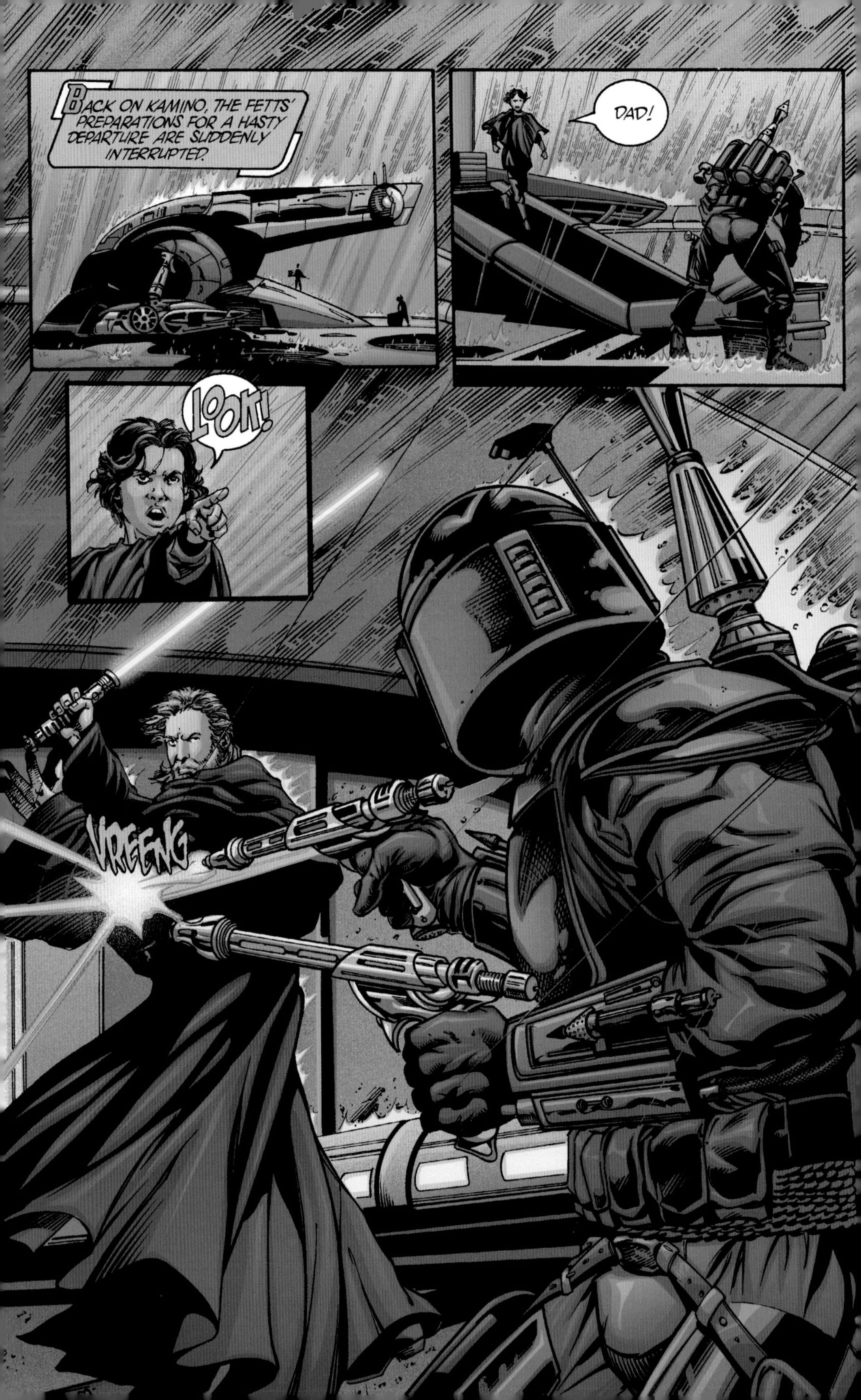
BACK ON KAMINO, THE FETTS' PREPARATIONS FOR A HASTY DEPARTURE ARE SUDDENLY INTERRUPTED.
DAD!
LOOK!
VREENG

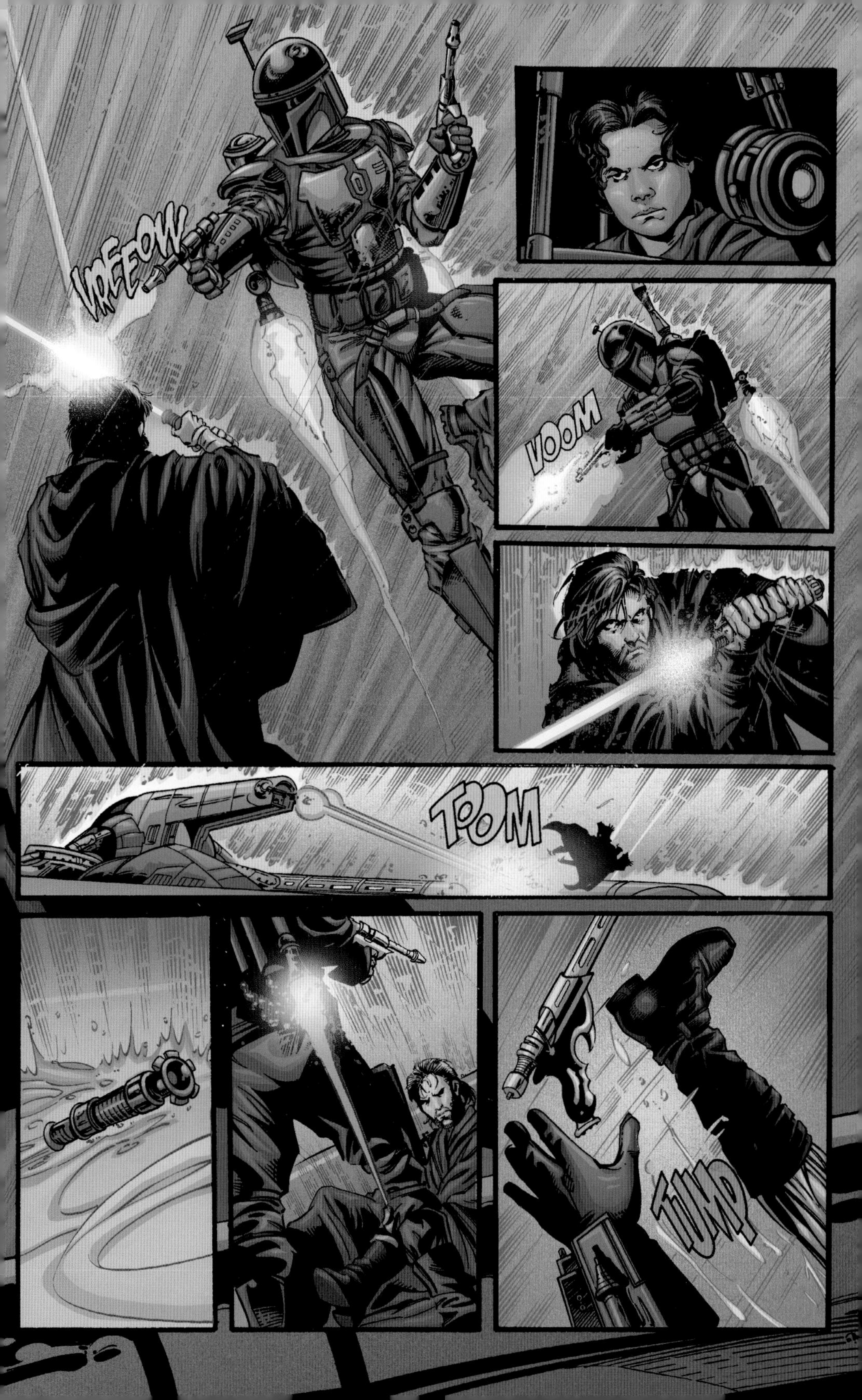
VREEOW
VOOM
TOOM
TUMP

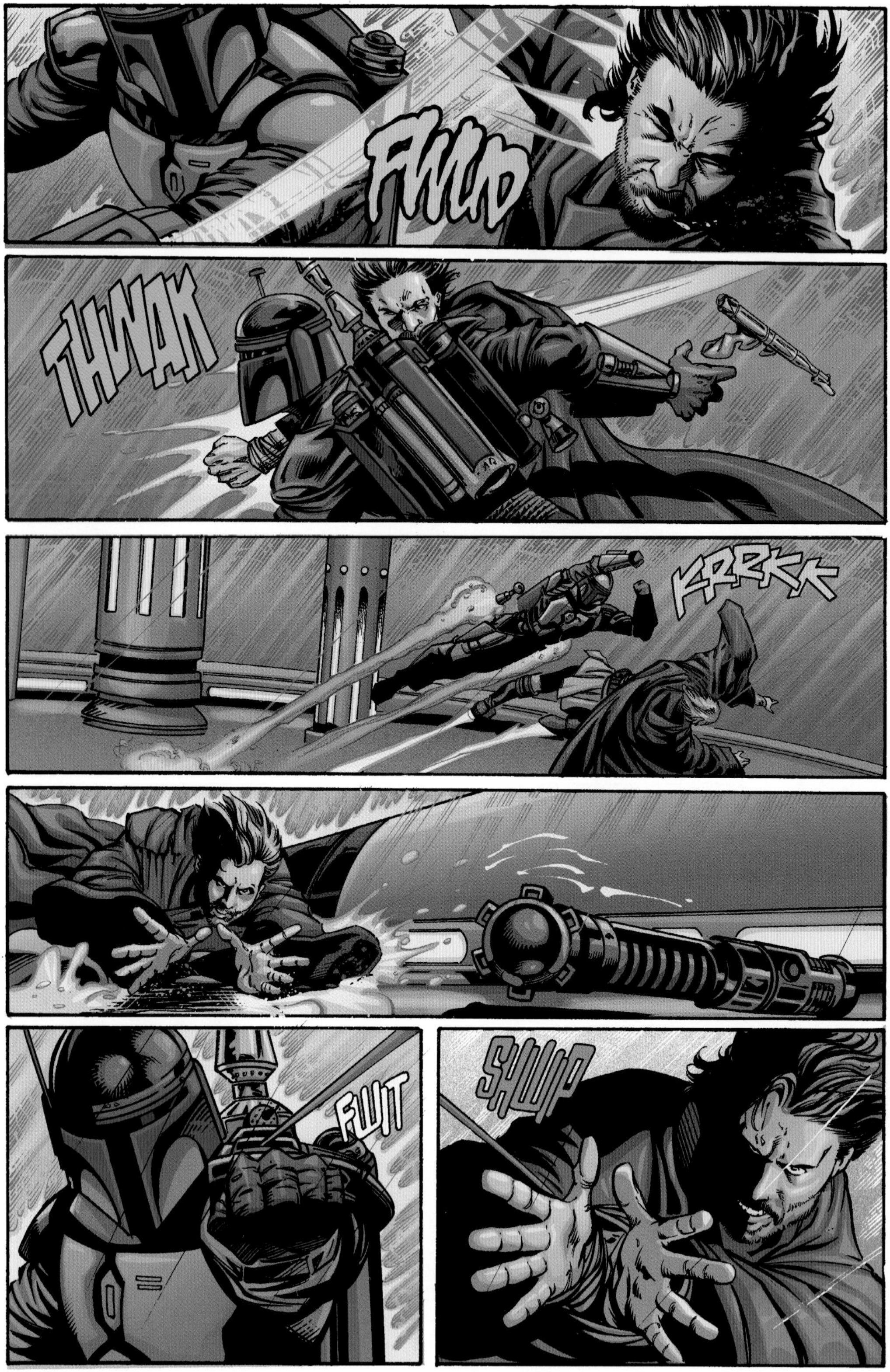
FWUD
THWAK
KRRKK
FWIT
SHWIP

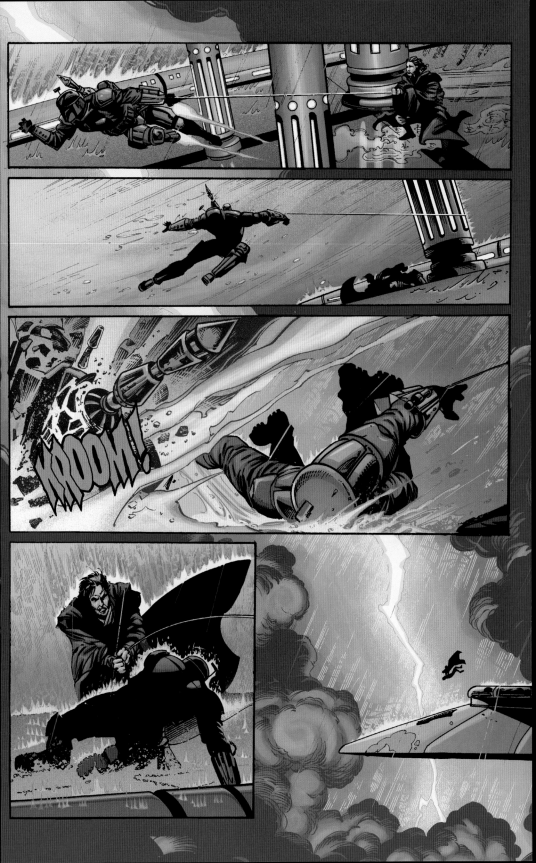

KROOM!

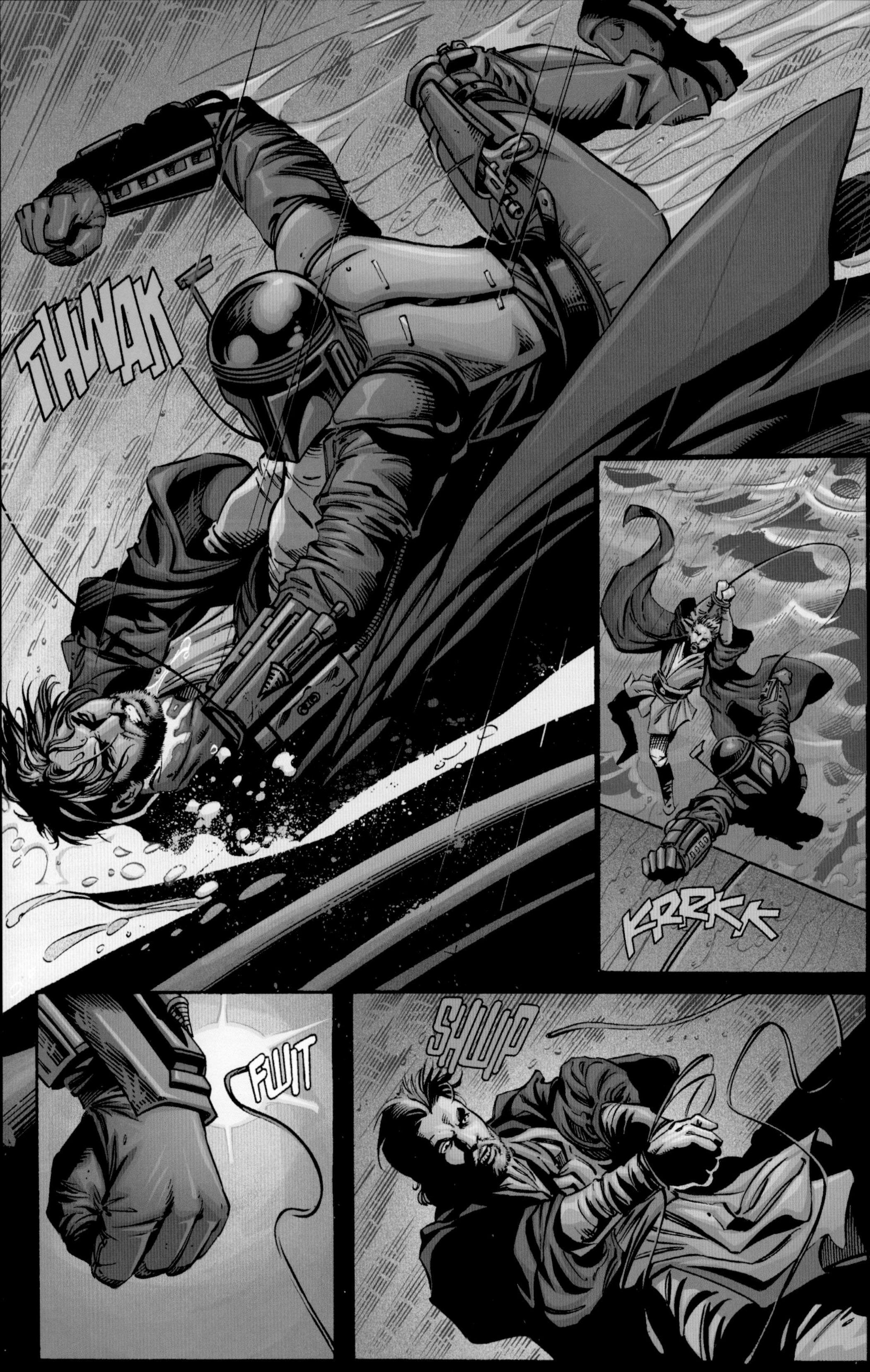
THWAK
KRRKK
FWIT
SHWIP

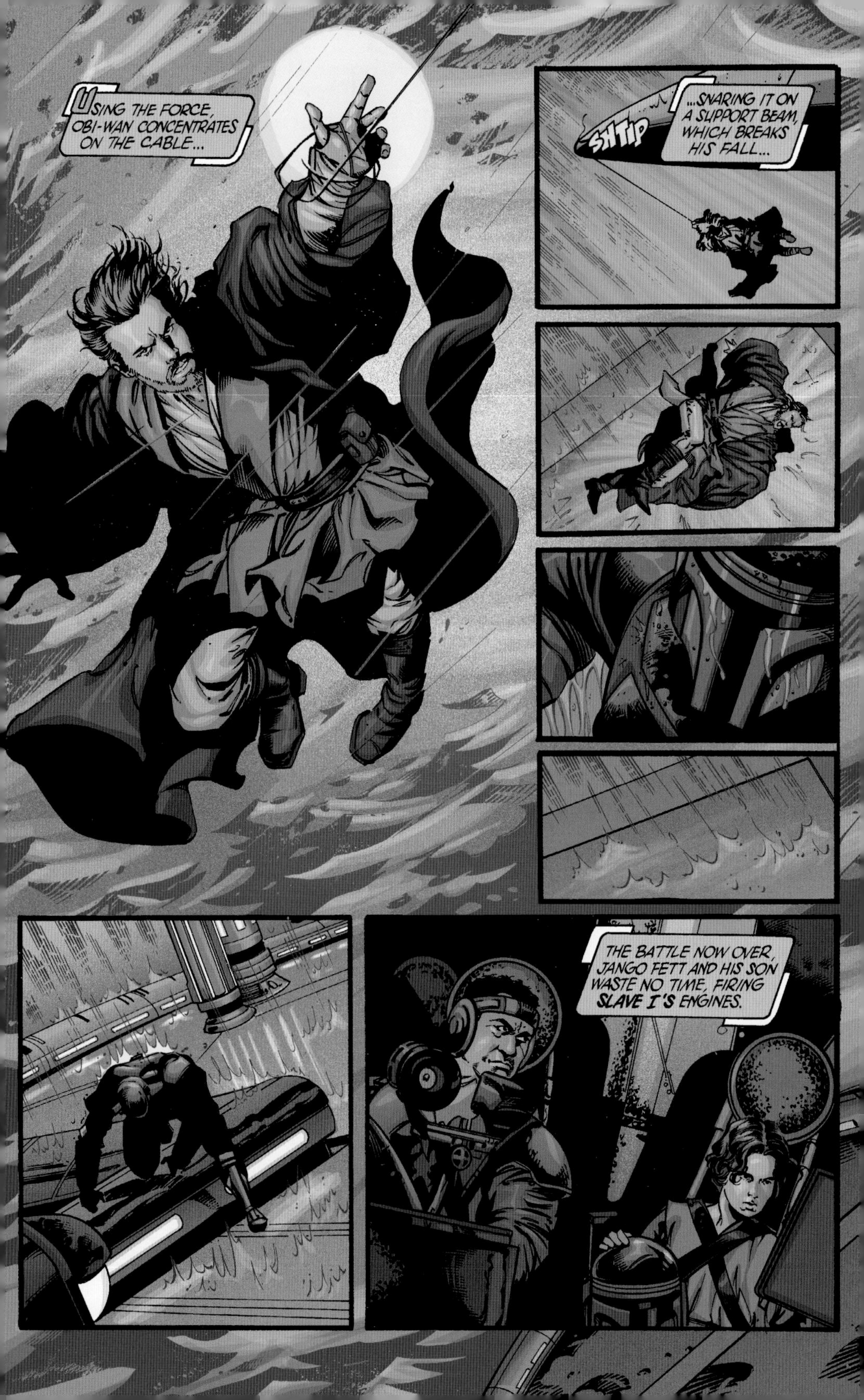
USING THE FORCE, OBI-WAN CONCENTRATES ON THE CABLE...
SHTIP
...SNARING IT ON A SUPPORT BEAM, WHICH BREAKS HIS FALL...
THE BATTLE NOW OVER, JANGO FETT AND HIS SON WASTE NO TIME, FIRING SLAVE I'S ENGINES.

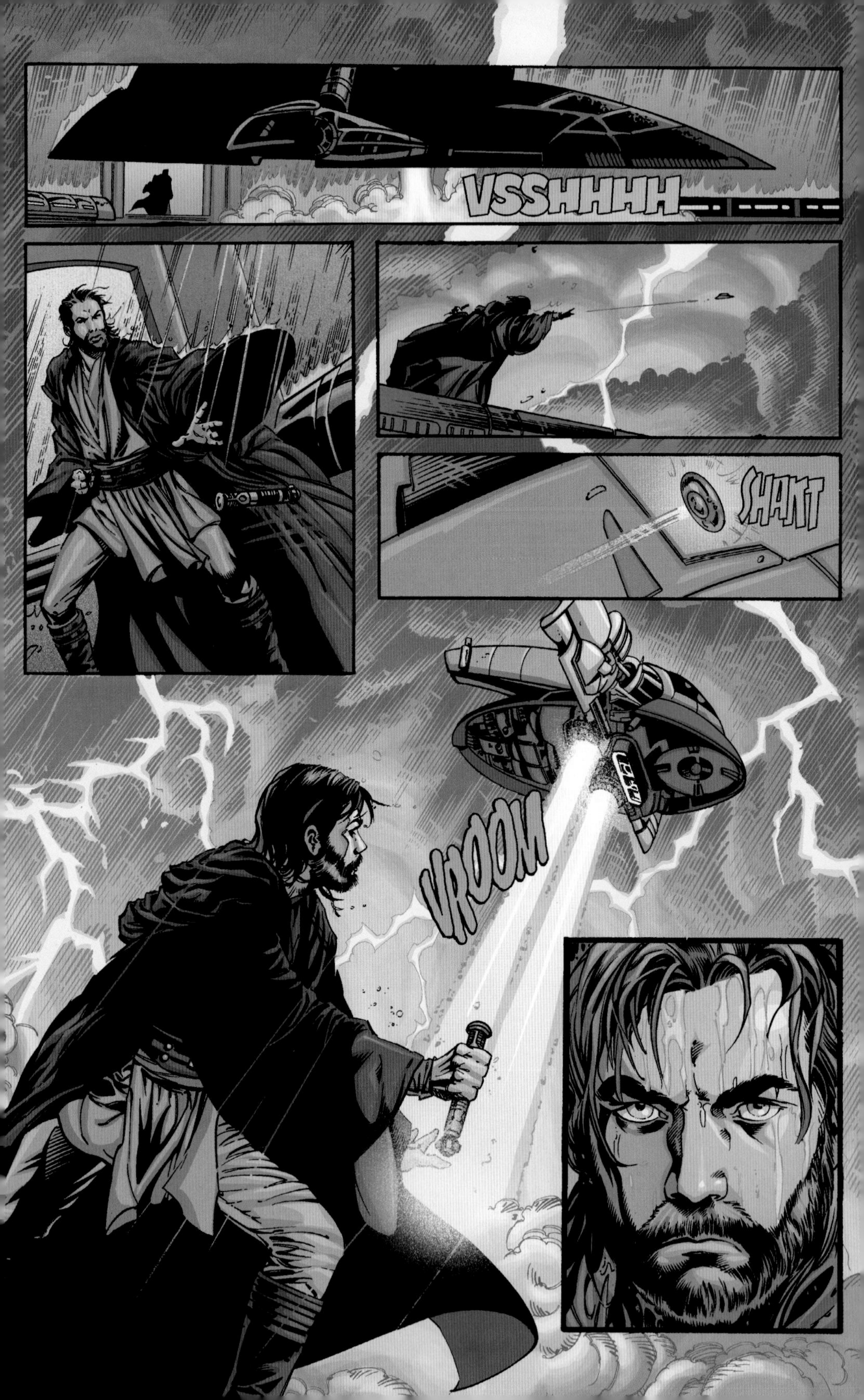
VSSHHHH
SHAKT
VROOM

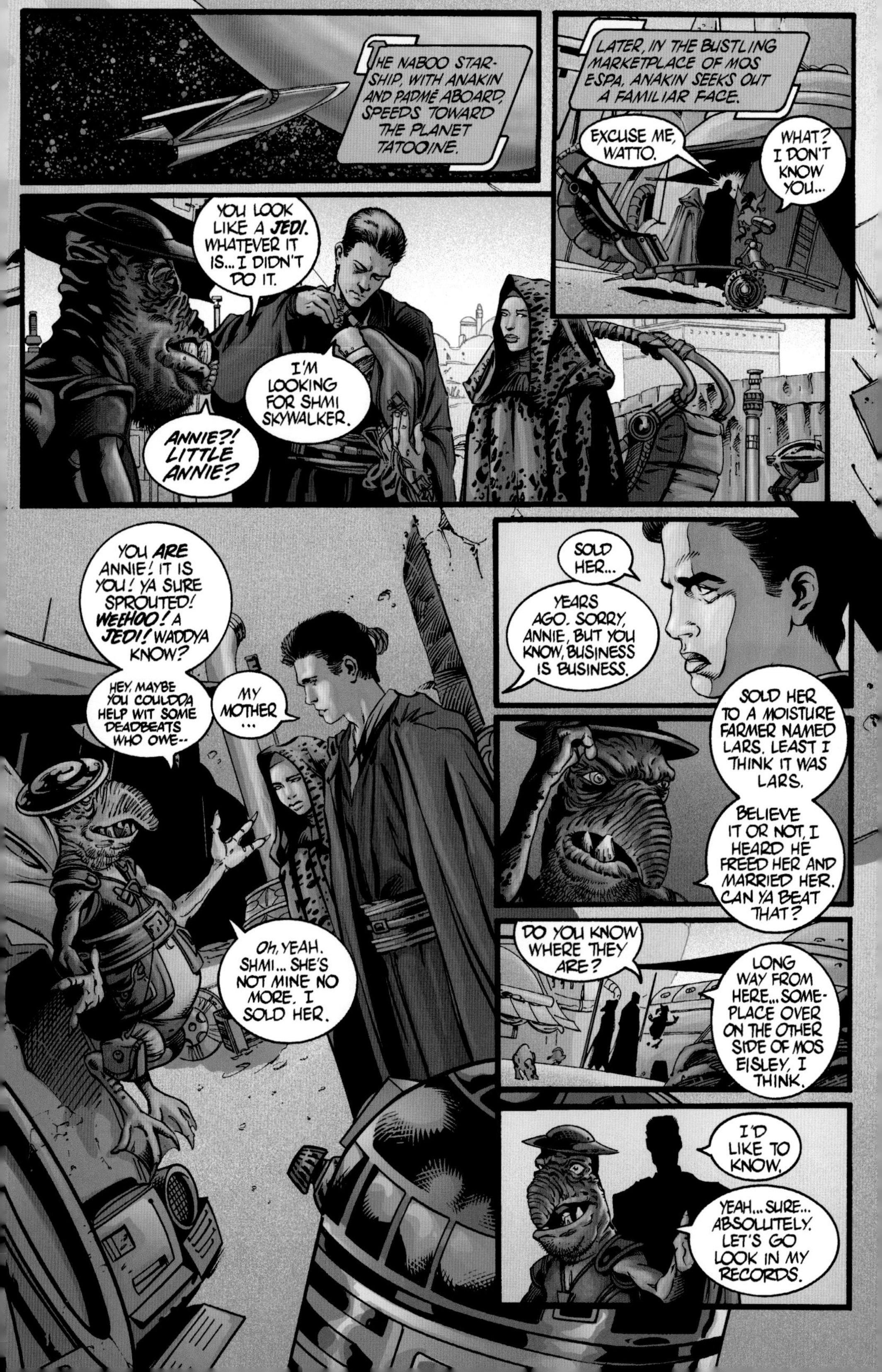
THE NABOO STARSHIP, WITH ANAKIN AND PADMÉ ABOARD, SPEEDS TOWARD THE PLANET TATOOINE.
LATER, IN THE BUSTLING MARKETPLACE OF MOS ESPA, ANAKIN SEEKS OUT A FAMILIAR FACE.
EXCUSE ME, WATTO.
WHAT? I DON'T KNOW YOU...
YOU LOOK LIKE A JEDI. WHATEVER IT IS... I DIDN'T DO IT.
I'M LOOKING FOR SHMI SKYWALKER.
ANNIE?! LITTLE ANNIE?
YOU ARE ANNIE! IT IS YOU! YA SURE SPROUTED! WEEHOO! A JEDI! WADDYA KNOW?
HEY, MAYBE YOU COULDDA HELP WIT SOME DEADBEATS WHO OWE--
MY MOTHER ...
OH, YEAH. SHMI... SHE'S NOT MINE NO MORE. I SOLD HER.
SOLD HER...
YEARS AGO. SORRY, ANNIE, BUT YOU KNOW, BUSINESS IS BUSINESS.
SOLD HER TO A MOISTURE FARMER NAMED LARS. LEAST I THINK IT WAS LARS.
BELIEVE IT OR NOT, I HEARD HE FREED HER AND MARRIED HER. CAN YA BEAT THAT?
DO YOU KNOW WHERE THEY ARE?
LONG WAY FROM HERE... SOMEPLACE OVER ON THE OTHER SIDE OF MOS EISLEY, I THINK.
I'D LIKE TO KNOW.
YEAH... SURE... ABSOLUTELY. LET'S GO LOOK IN MY RECORDS.

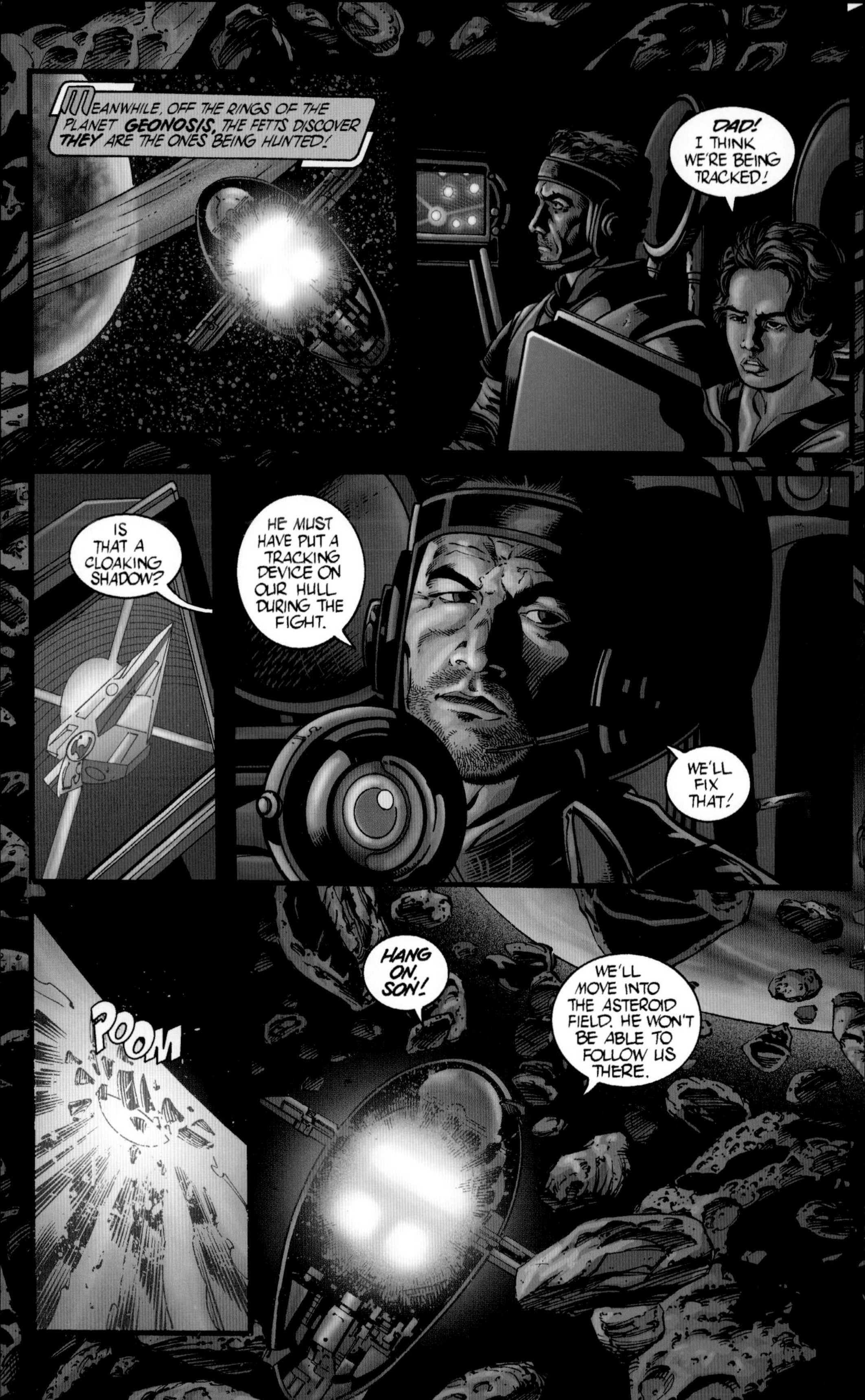
MEANWHILE, OFF THE RINGS OF THE PLANET GEONOSIS, THE FETTS DISCOVER THEY ARE THE ONES BEING HUNTED!
DAD! I THINK WE'RE BEING TRACKED!
IS THAT A CLOAKING SHADOW?
HE MUST HAVE PUT A TRACKING DEVICE ON OUR HULL DURING THE FIGHT.
WE'LL FIX THAT!
POOM
HANG ON, SON!
WE'LL MOVE INTO THE ASTEROID FIELD. HE WON'T BE ABLE TO FOLLOW US THERE.

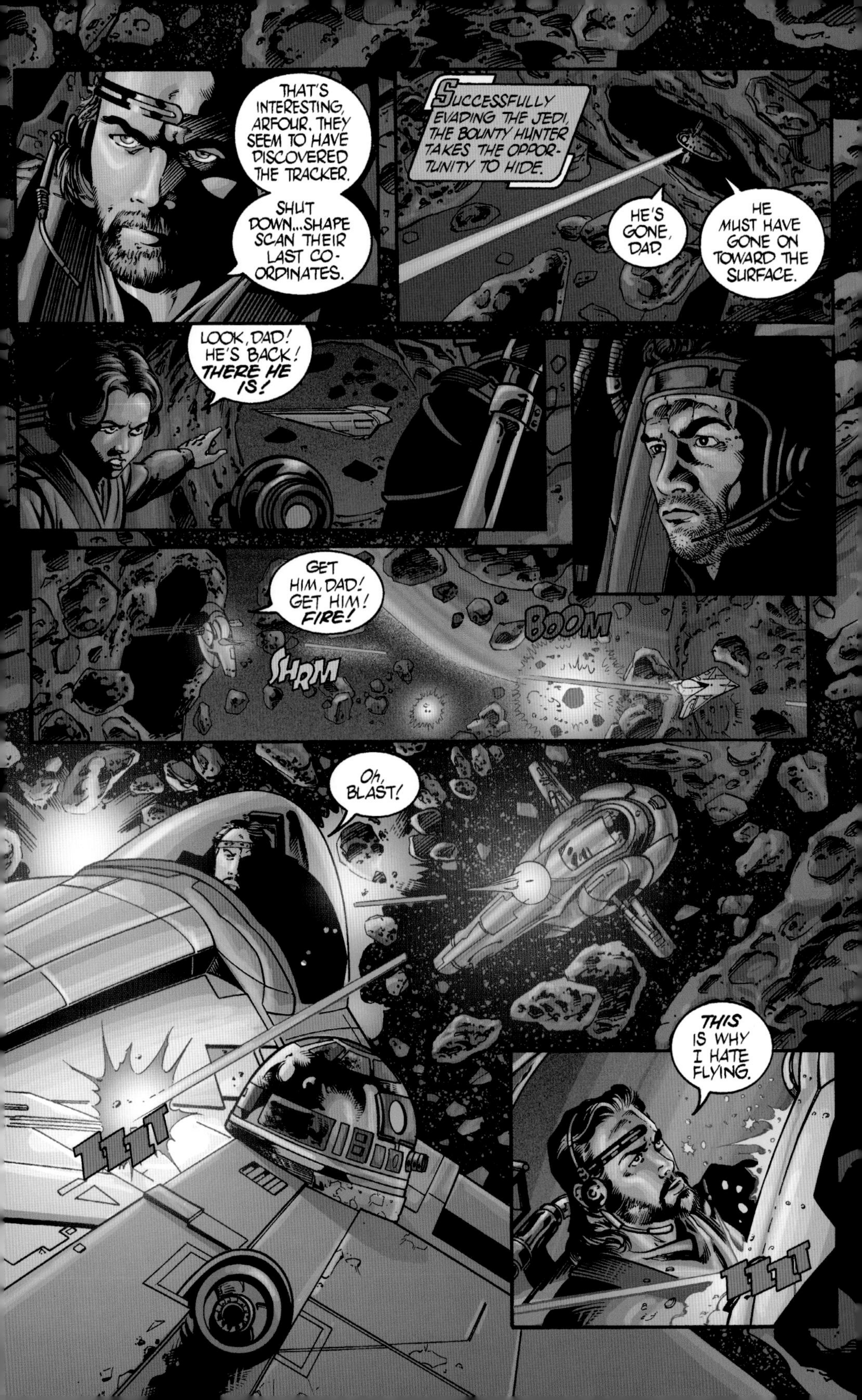
THAT'S INTERESTING, ARFOUR. THEY SEEM TO HAVE DISCOVERED THE TRACKER.
SHUT DOWN...SHAPE SCAN THEIR LAST CO-ORDINATES.
SUCCESSFULLY EVADING THE JEDI, THE BOUNTY HUNTER TAKES THE OPPORTUNITY TO HIDE.
HE'S GONE, DAD.
HE MUST HAVE GONE ON TOWARD THE SURFACE.
LOOK, DAD! HE'S BACK! THERE HE IS!
GET HIM, DAD! GET HIM! FIRE!
BOOM
SHRM
Oh, BLAST!
THIS IS WHY I HATE FLYING.

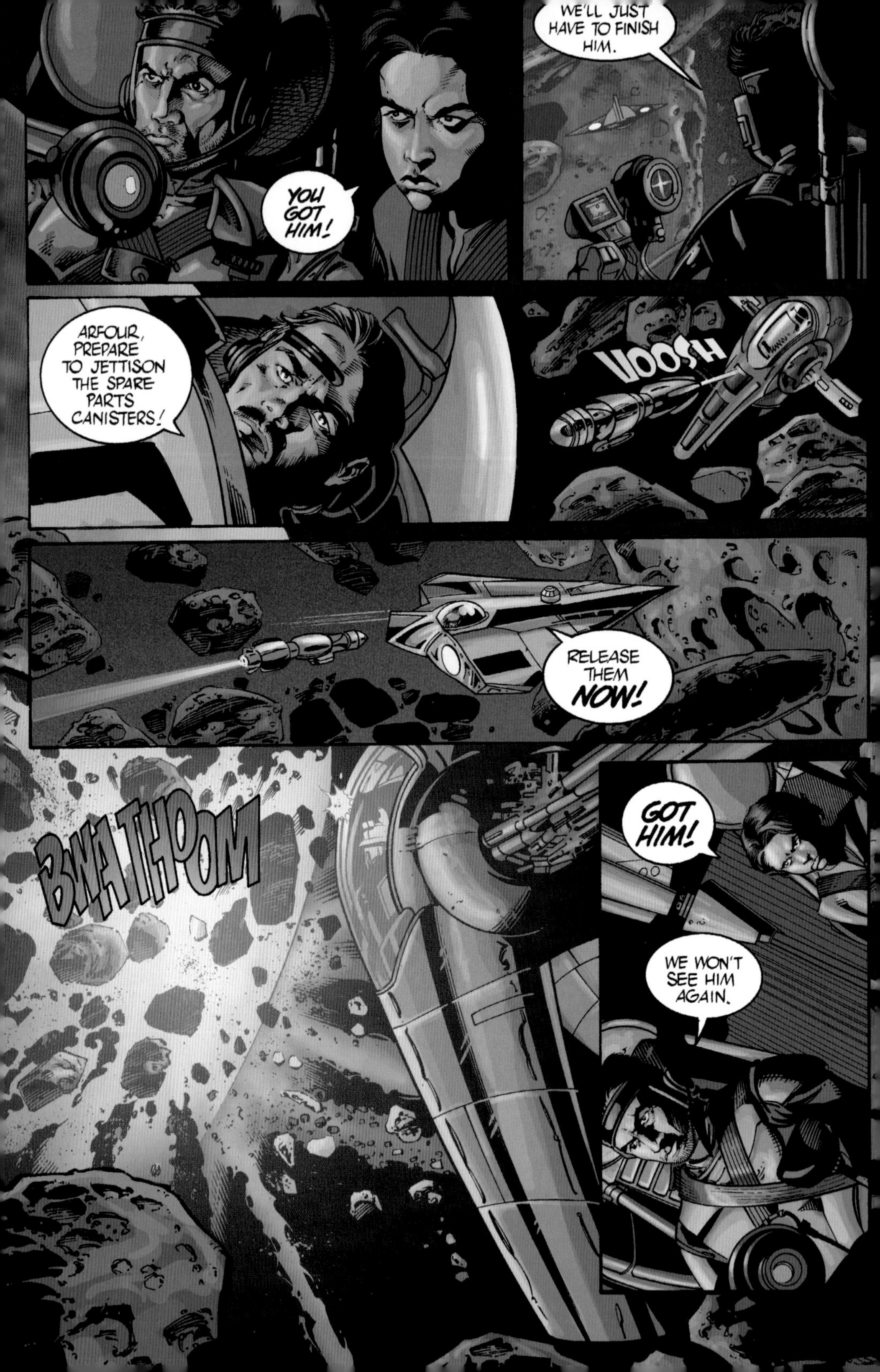
YOU GOT HIM!
WE'LL JUST HAVE TO FINISH HIM.
ARFOUR, PREPARE TO JETTISON THE SPARE PARTS CANISTERS!
VOOSH
RELEASE THEM NOW!
BWATHOOM
GOT HIM!
WE WON'T SEE HIM AGAIN.

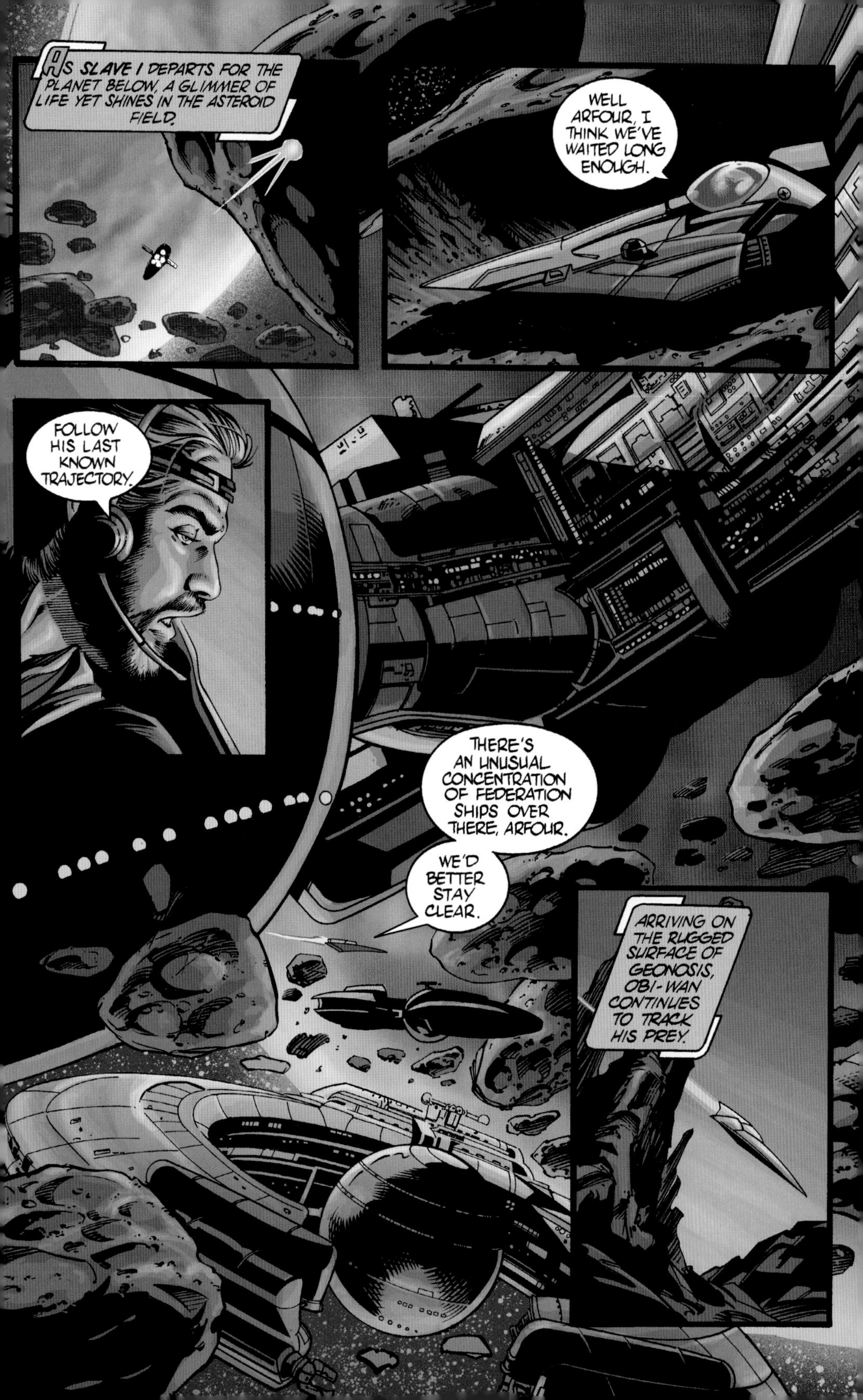
AS SLAVE I DEPARTS FOR THE PLANET BELOW, A GLIMMER OF LIFE YET SHINES IN THE ASTEROID FIELD.
WELL ARFOUR, I THINK WE'VE WAITED LONG ENOUGH.
FOLLOW HIS LAST KNOWN TRAJECTORY.
THERE'S AN UNUSUAL CONCENTRATION OF FEDERATION SHIPS OVER THERE, ARFOUR.
WE'D BETTER STAY CLEAR.
ARRIVING ON THE RUGGED SURFACE OF GEONOSIS, OBI-WAN CONTINUES TO TRACK HIS PREY.

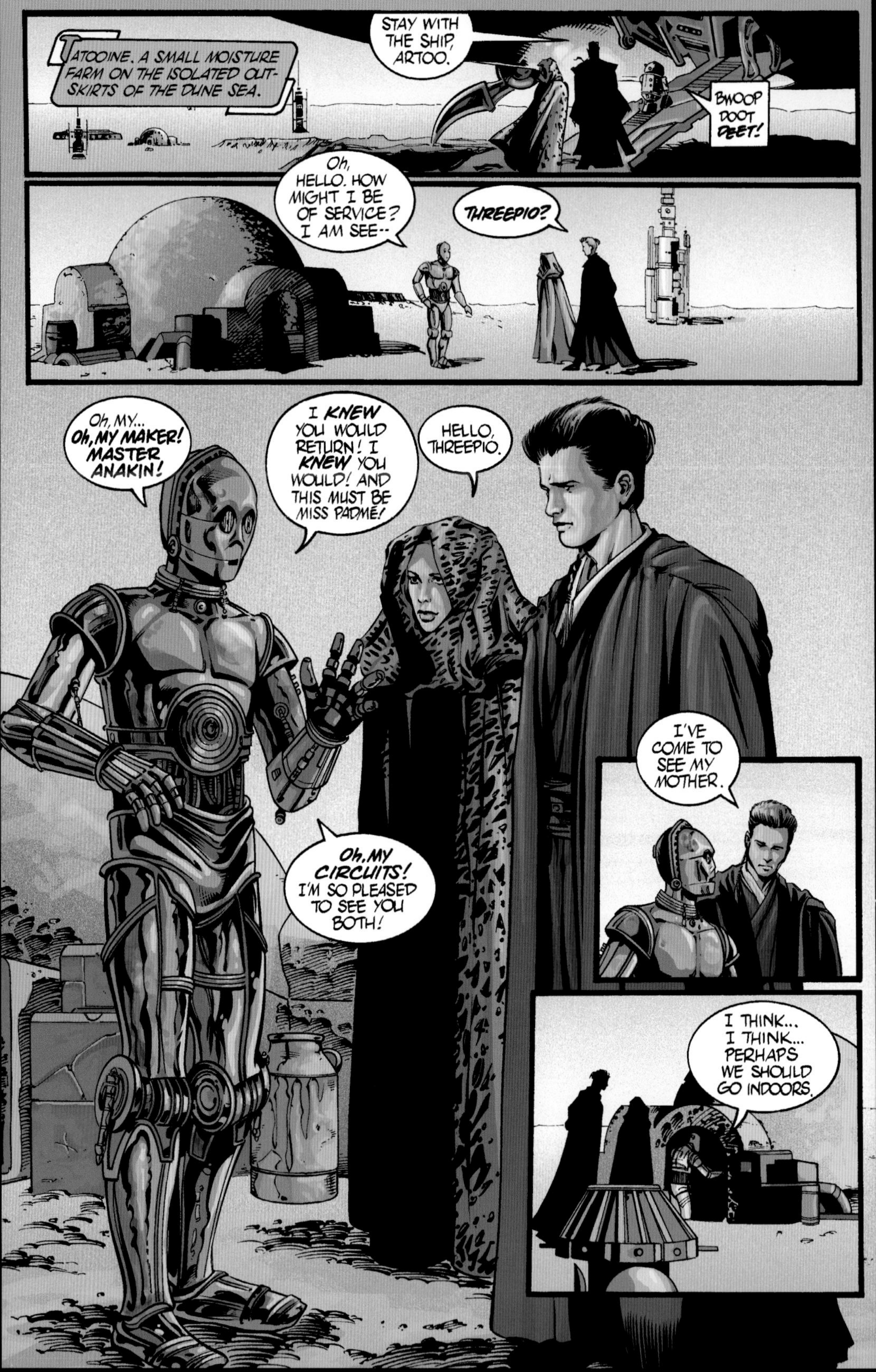
TATOOINE. A SMALL MOISTURE FARM ON THE ISOLATED OUT-SKIRTS OF THE DUNE SEA.
STAY WITH THE SHIP, ARTOO.
BWOOP DOOT DEET!
OH, HELLO. HOW MIGHT I BE OF SERVICE? I AM SEE--
THREEPIO?
OH, MY... OH, MY MAKER! MASTER ANAKIN!
I KNEW YOU WOULD RETURN! I KNEW YOU WOULD! AND THIS MUST BE MISS PADMÉ!
HELLO, THREEPIO.
OH, MY CIRCUITS! I'M SO PLEASED TO SEE YOU BOTH!
I'VE COME TO SEE MY MOTHER.
I THINK... I THINK... PERHAPS WE SHOULD GO INDOORS.

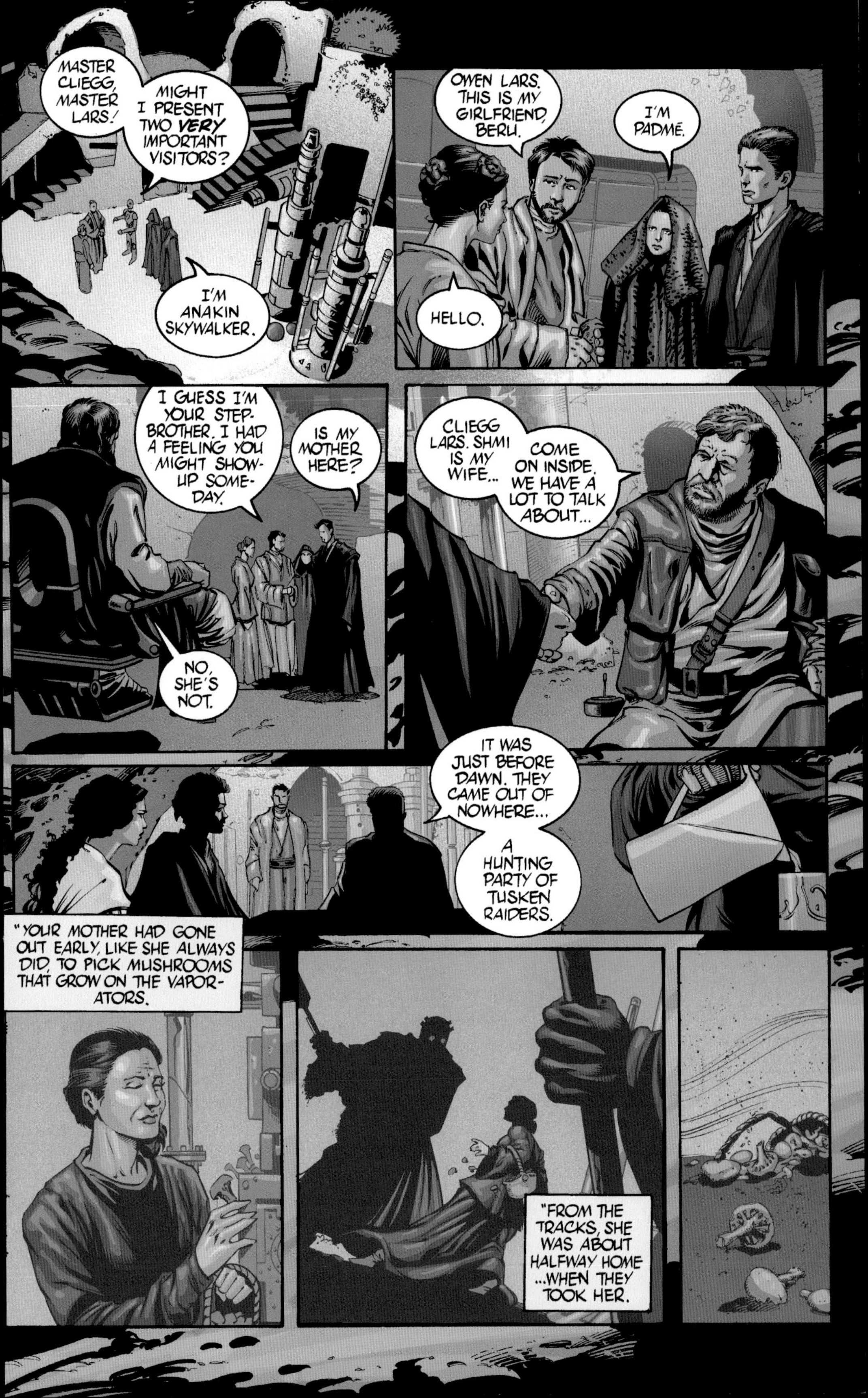
MASTER CLIEGG, MASTER LARS!
MIGHT I PRESENT TWO VERY IMPORTANT VISITORS?
I'M ANAKIN SKYWALKER.
OWEN LARS. THIS IS MY GIRLFRIEND, BERU.
I'M PADMÉ.
HELLO.
I GUESS I'M YOUR STEP-BROTHER. I HAD A FEELING YOU MIGHT SHOW-UP SOME-DAY.
IS MY MOTHER HERE?
NO, SHE'S NOT.
CLIEGG LARS. SHMI IS MY WIFE...
COME ON INSIDE. WE HAVE A LOT TO TALK ABOUT...
IT WAS JUST BEFORE DAWN. THEY CAME OUT OF NOWHERE...
A HUNTING PARTY OF TUSKEN RAIDERS.
"YOUR MOTHER HAD GONE OUT EARLY, LIKE SHE ALWAYS DID, TO PICK MUSHROOMS THAT GROW ON THE VAPOR-ATORS.
"FROM THE TRACKS, SHE WAS ABOUT HALFWAY HOME ...WHEN THEY TOOK HER.

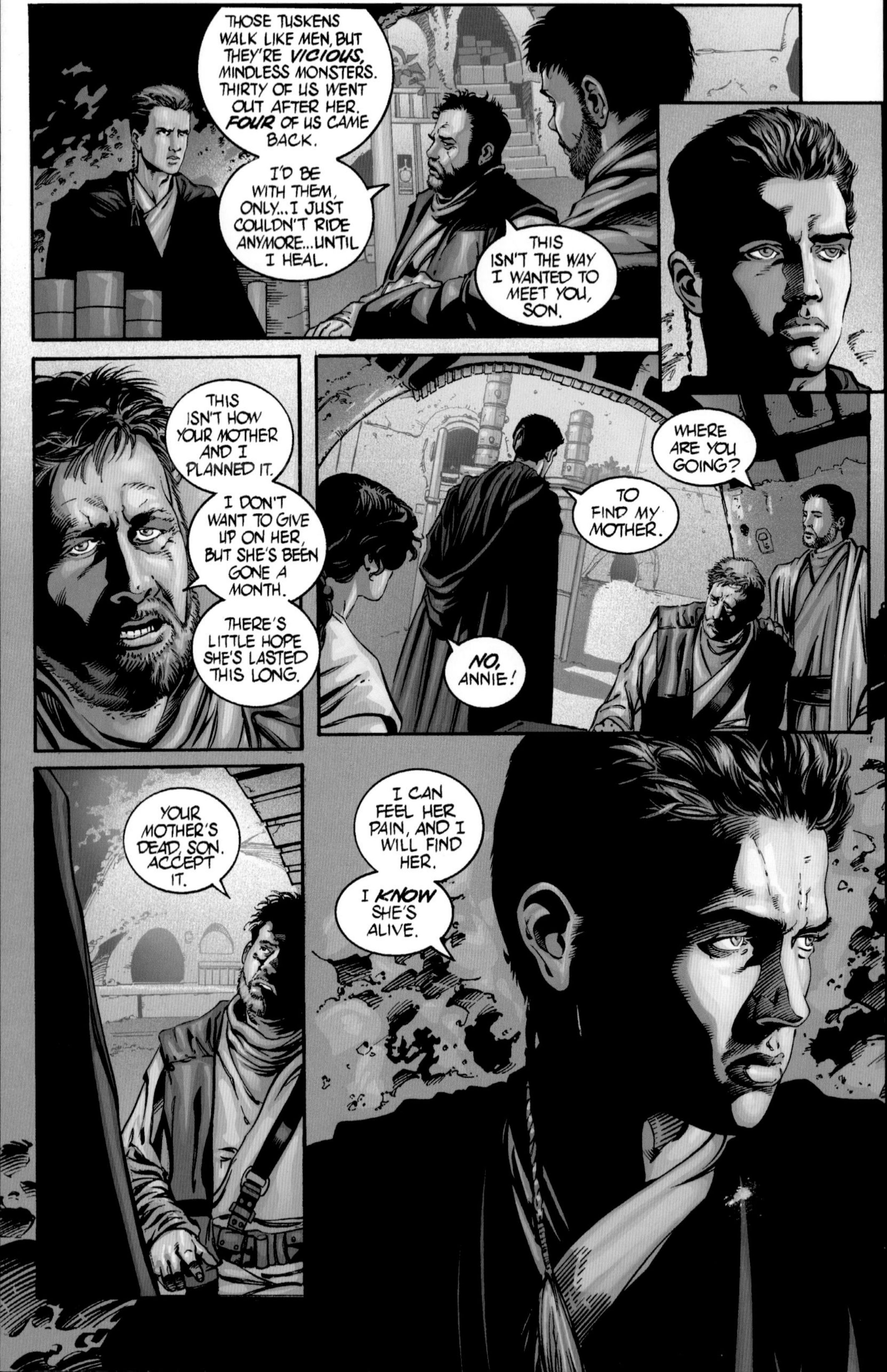
THOSE TUSKENS WALK LIKE MEN, BUT THEY'RE VICIOUS, MINDLESS MONSTERS. THIRTY OF US WENT OUT AFTER HER. FOUR OF US CAME BACK.
I'D BE WITH THEM, ONLY... I JUST COULDN'T RIDE ANYMORE... UNTIL I HEAL.
THIS ISN'T THE WAY I WANTED TO MEET YOU, SON.
THIS ISN'T HOW YOUR MOTHER AND I PLANNED IT.
I DON'T WANT TO GIVE UP ON HER, BUT SHE'S BEEN GONE A MONTH.
THERE'S LITTLE HOPE SHE'S LASTED THIS LONG.
WHERE ARE YOU GOING?
TO FIND MY MOTHER.
NO, ANNIE!
YOUR MOTHER'S DEAD, SON. ACCEPT IT.
I CAN FEEL HER PAIN, AND I WILL FIND HER.
I KNOW SHE'S ALIVE.

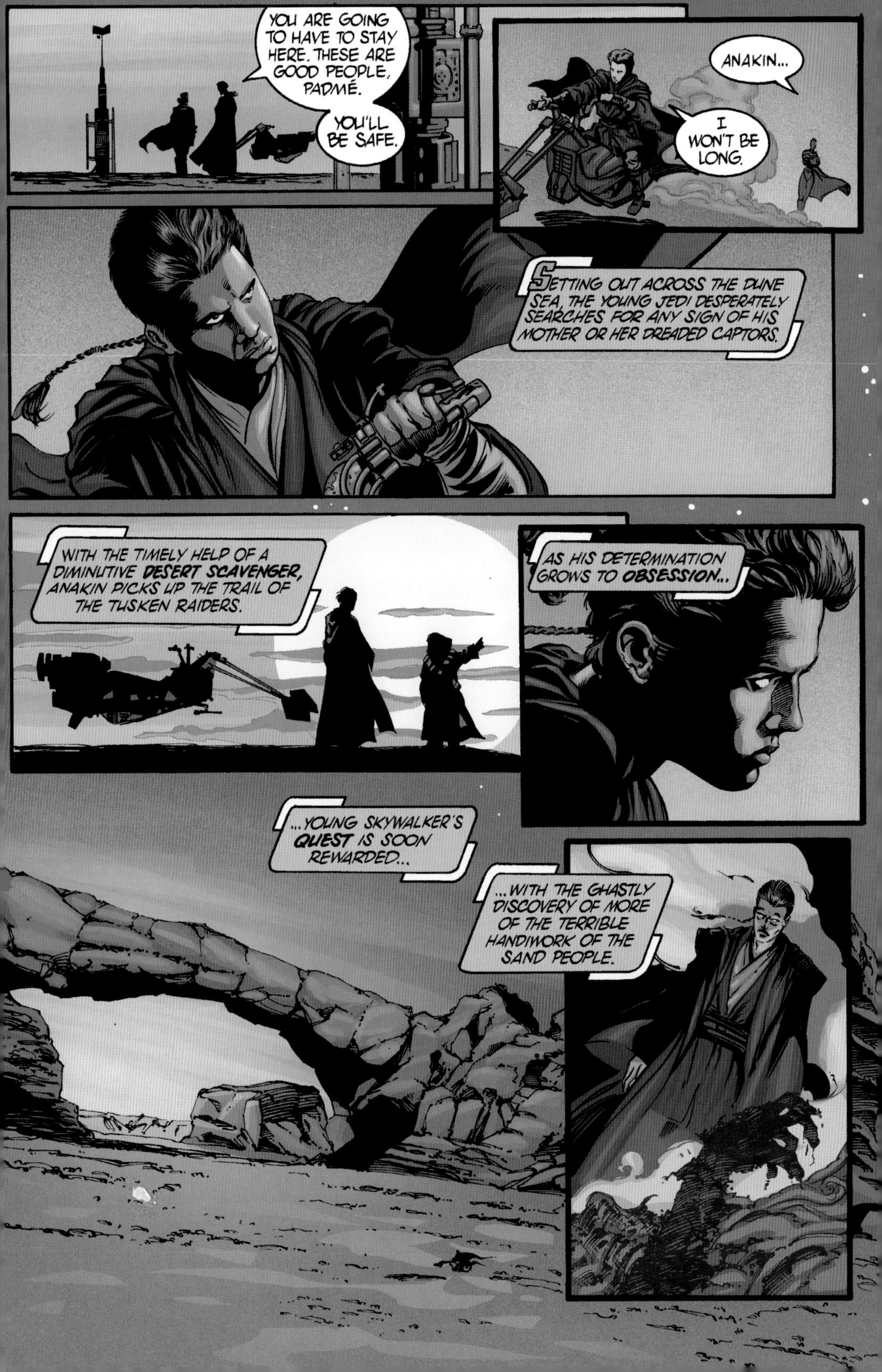
YOU ARE GOING TO HAVE TO STAY HERE. THESE ARE GOOD PEOPLE, PADMÉ.
YOU'LL BE SAFE.
ANAKIN...
I WON'T BE LONG.
SETTING OUT ACROSS THE DUNE SEA, THE YOUNG JEDI DESPERATELY SEARCHES FOR ANY SIGN OF HIS MOTHER OR HER DREADED CAPTORS.
WITH THE TIMELY HELP OF A DIMINUTIVE DESERT SCAVENGER, ANAKIN PICKS UP THE TRAIL OF THE TUSKEN RAIDERS.
AS HIS DETERMINATION GROWS TO OBSESSION...
...YOUNG SKYWALKER'S QUEST IS SOON REWARDED...
...WITH THE GHASTLY DISCOVERY OF MORE OF THE TERRIBLE HANDIWORK OF THE SAND PEOPLE.

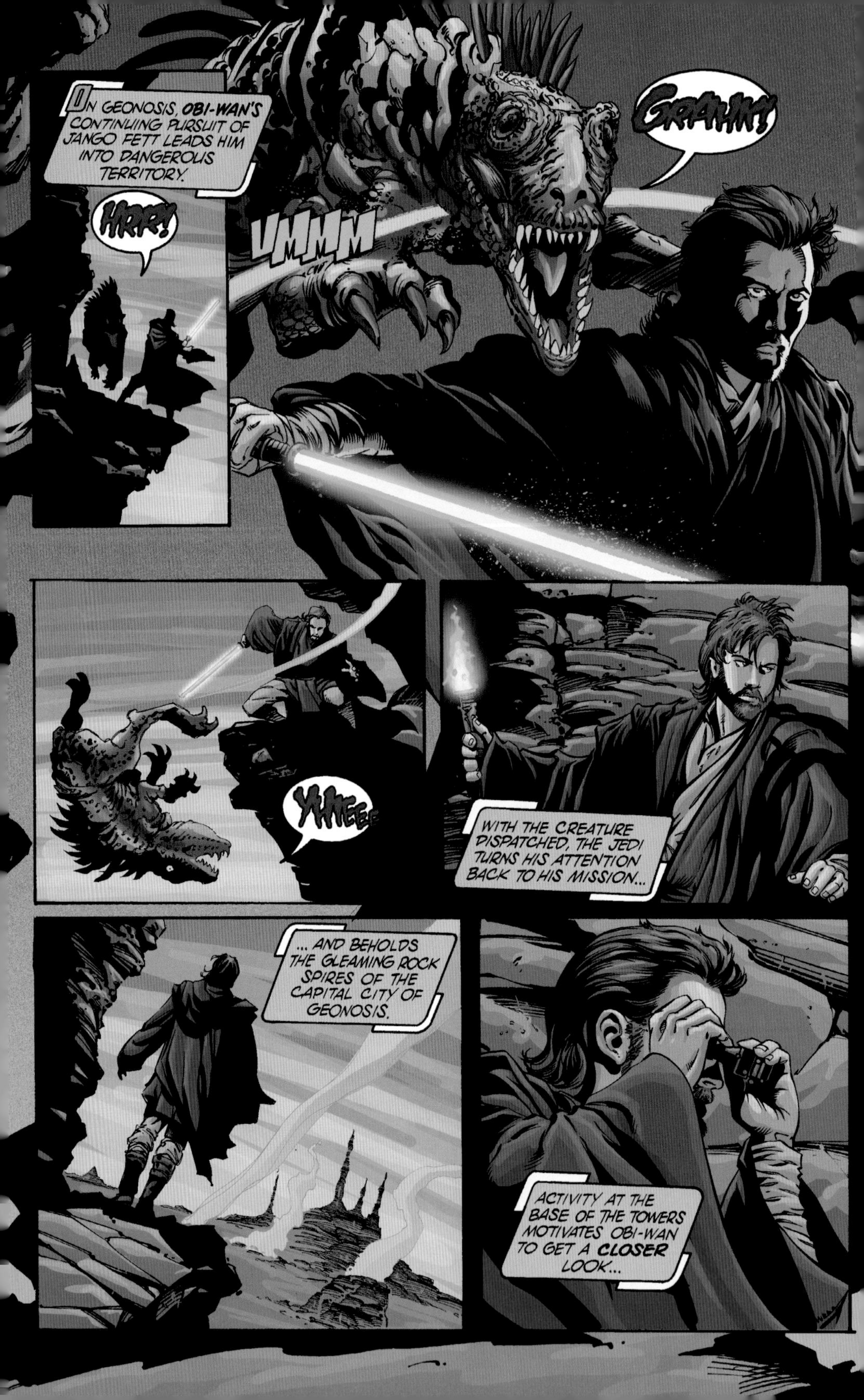
ON GEONOSIS, OBI-WAN'S CONTINUING PURSUIT OF JANGO FETT LEADS HIM INTO DANGEROUS TERRITORY.
HRR!
GRAHH!
UMMM
YHHEEE
WITH THE CREATURE DISPATCHED, THE JEDI TURNS HIS ATTENTION BACK TO HIS MISSION...
... AND BEHOLDS THE GLEAMING ROCK SPIRES OF THE CAPITAL CITY OF GEONOSIS.
ACTIVITY AT THE BASE OF THE TOWERS MOTIVATES OBI-WAN TO GET A CLOSER LOOK...

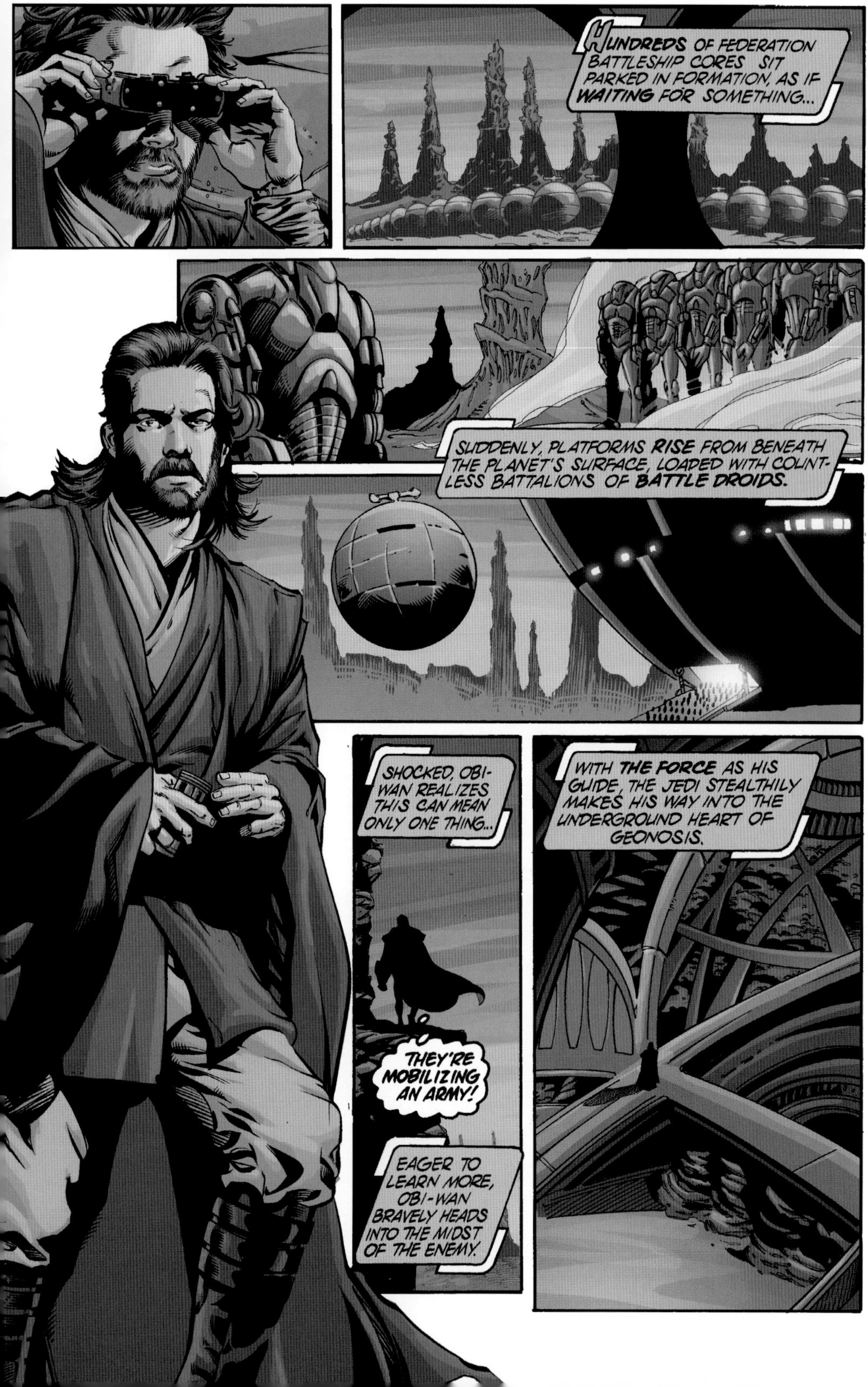
HUNDREDS OF FEDERATION BATTLESHIP CORES SIT PARKED IN FORMATION, AS IF WAITING FOR SOMETHING...
SUDDENLY, PLATFORMS RISE FROM BENEATH THE PLANET'S SURFACE, LOADED WITH COUNTLESS BATTALIONS OF BATTLE DROIDS.
SHOCKED, OBI-WAN REALIZES THIS CAN MEAN ONLY ONE THING...
THEY'RE MOBILIZING AN ARMY!
EAGER TO LEARN MORE, OBI-WAN BRAVELY HEADS INTO THE MIDST OF THE ENEMY.
WITH THE FORCE AS HIS GUIDE, THE JEDI STEALTHILY MAKES HIS WAY INTO THE UNDERGROUND HEART OF GEONOSIS.

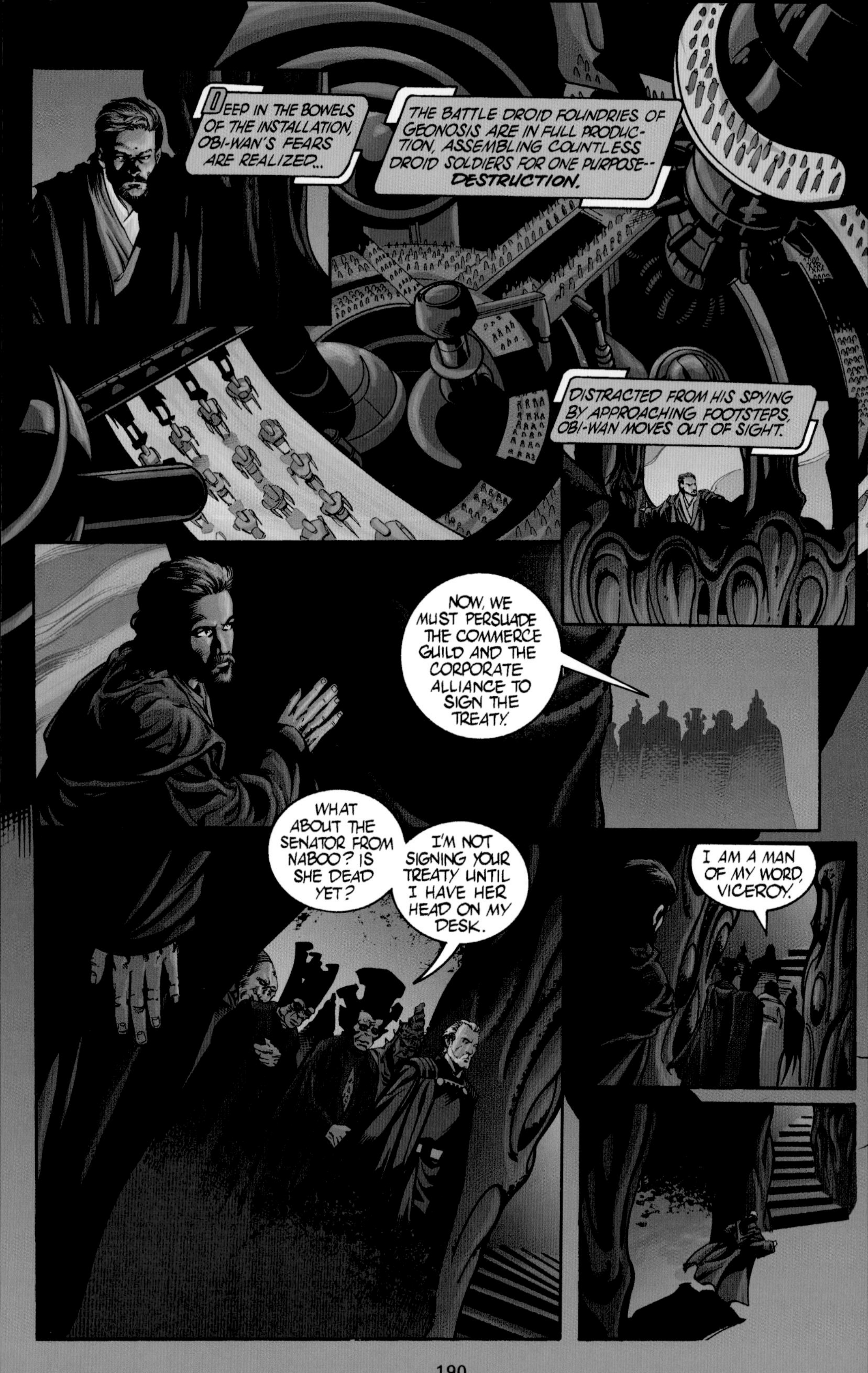
DEEP IN THE BOWELS OF THE INSTALLATION, OBI-WAN'S FEARS ARE REALIZED...
THE BATTLE DROID FOUNDRIES OF GEONOSIS ARE IN FULL PRODUCTION, ASSEMBLING COUNTLESS DROID SOLDIERS FOR ONE PURPOSE-- DESTRUCTION.
DISTRACTED FROM HIS SPYING BY APPROACHING FOOTSTEPS, OBI-WAN MOVES OUT OF SIGHT.
NOW, WE MUST PERSUADE THE COMMERCE GUILD AND THE CORPORATE ALLIANCE TO SIGN THE TREATY.
WHAT ABOUT THE SENATOR FROM NABOO? IS SHE DEAD YET?
I'M NOT SIGNING YOUR TREATY UNTIL I HAVE HER HEAD ON MY DESK.
I AM A MAN OF MY WORD, VICEROY.

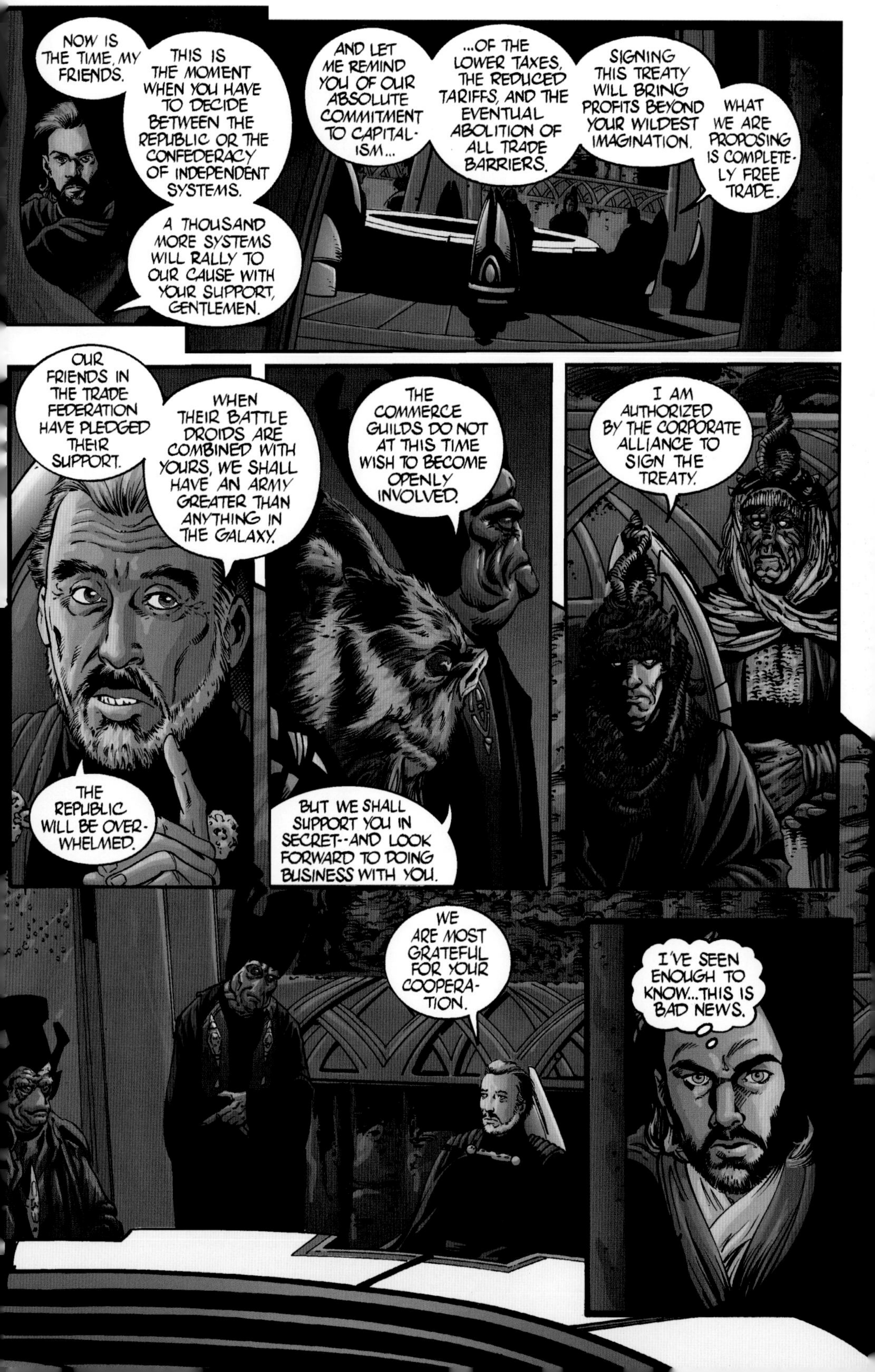
NOW IS THE TIME, MY FRIENDS.
THIS IS THE MOMENT WHEN YOU HAVE TO DECIDE BETWEEN THE REPUBLIC OR THE CONFEDERACY OF INDEPENDENT SYSTEMS.
A THOUSAND MORE SYSTEMS WILL RALLY TO OUR CAUSE WITH YOUR SUPPORT, GENTLEMEN.
AND LET ME REMIND YOU OF OUR ABSOLUTE COMMITMENT TO CAPITAL-ISM...
...OF THE LOWER TAXES, THE REDUCED TARIFFS, AND THE EVENTUAL ABOLITION OF ALL TRADE BARRIERS.
SIGNING THIS TREATY WILL BRING PROFITS BEYOND YOUR WILDEST IMAGINATION.
WHAT WE ARE PROPOSING IS COMPLETE-LY FREE TRADE.
OUR FRIENDS IN THE TRADE FEDERATION HAVE PLEDGED THEIR SUPPORT.
WHEN THEIR BATTLE DROIDS ARE COMBINED WITH YOURS, WE SHALL HAVE AN ARMY GREATER THAN ANYTHING IN THE GALAXY.
THE REPUBLIC WILL BE OVER-WHELMED.
THE COMMERCE GUILDS DO NOT AT THIS TIME WISH TO BECOME OPENLY INVOLVED.
BUT WE SHALL SUPPORT YOU IN SECRET--AND LOOK FORWARD TO DOING BUSINESS WITH YOU.
I AM AUTHORIZED BY THE CORPORATE ALLIANCE TO SIGN THE TREATY.
WE ARE MOST GRATEFUL FOR YOUR COOPERA-TION.
I'VE SEEN ENOUGH TO KNOW...THIS IS BAD NEWS.

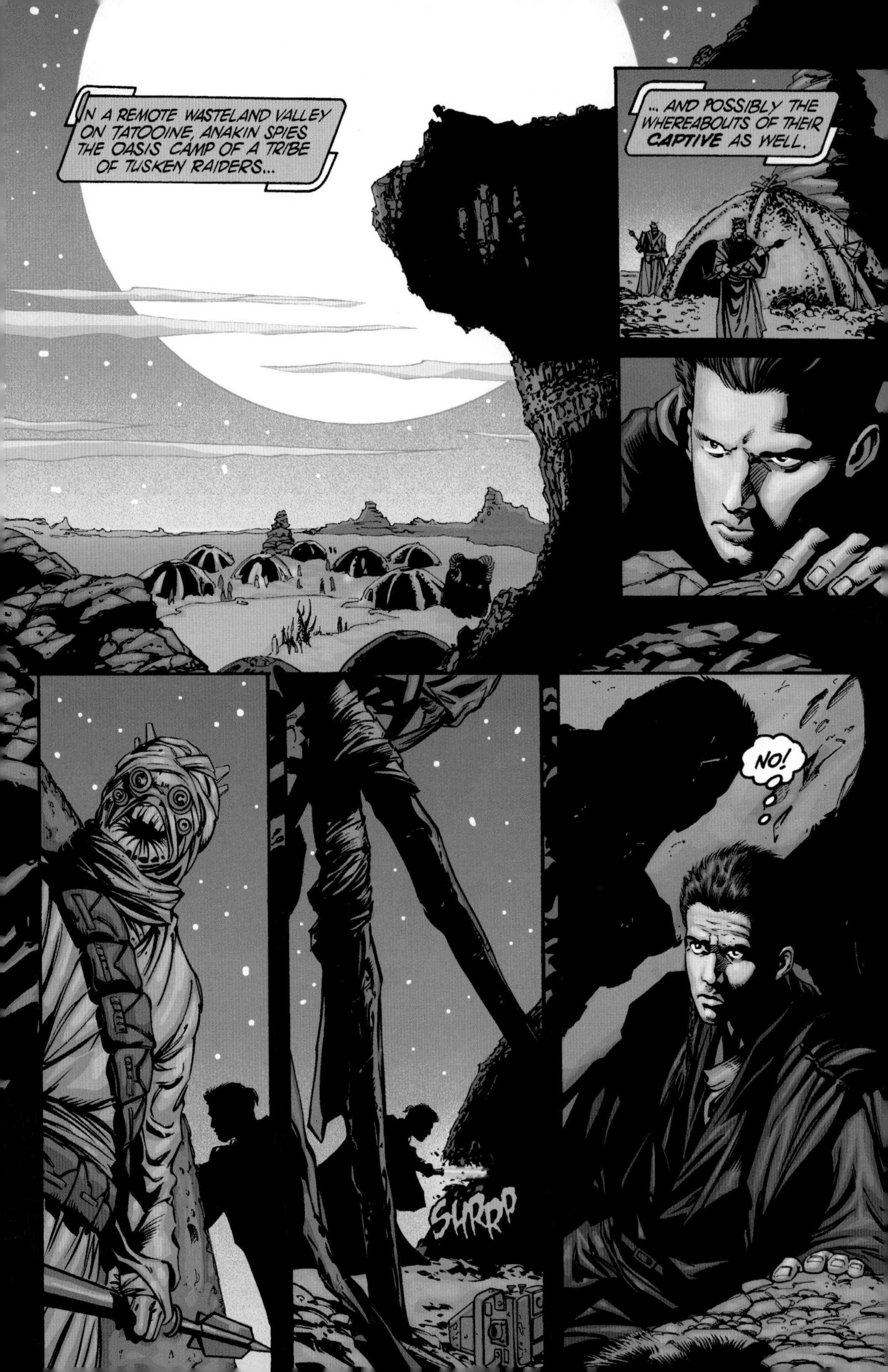
IN A REMOTE WASTELAND VALLEY ON TATOOINE, ANAKIN SPIES THE OASIS CAMP OF A TRIBE OF TUSKEN RAIDERS...
... AND POSSIBLY THE WHEREABOUTS OF THEIR CAPTIVE AS WELL.
SHRRP
NO!

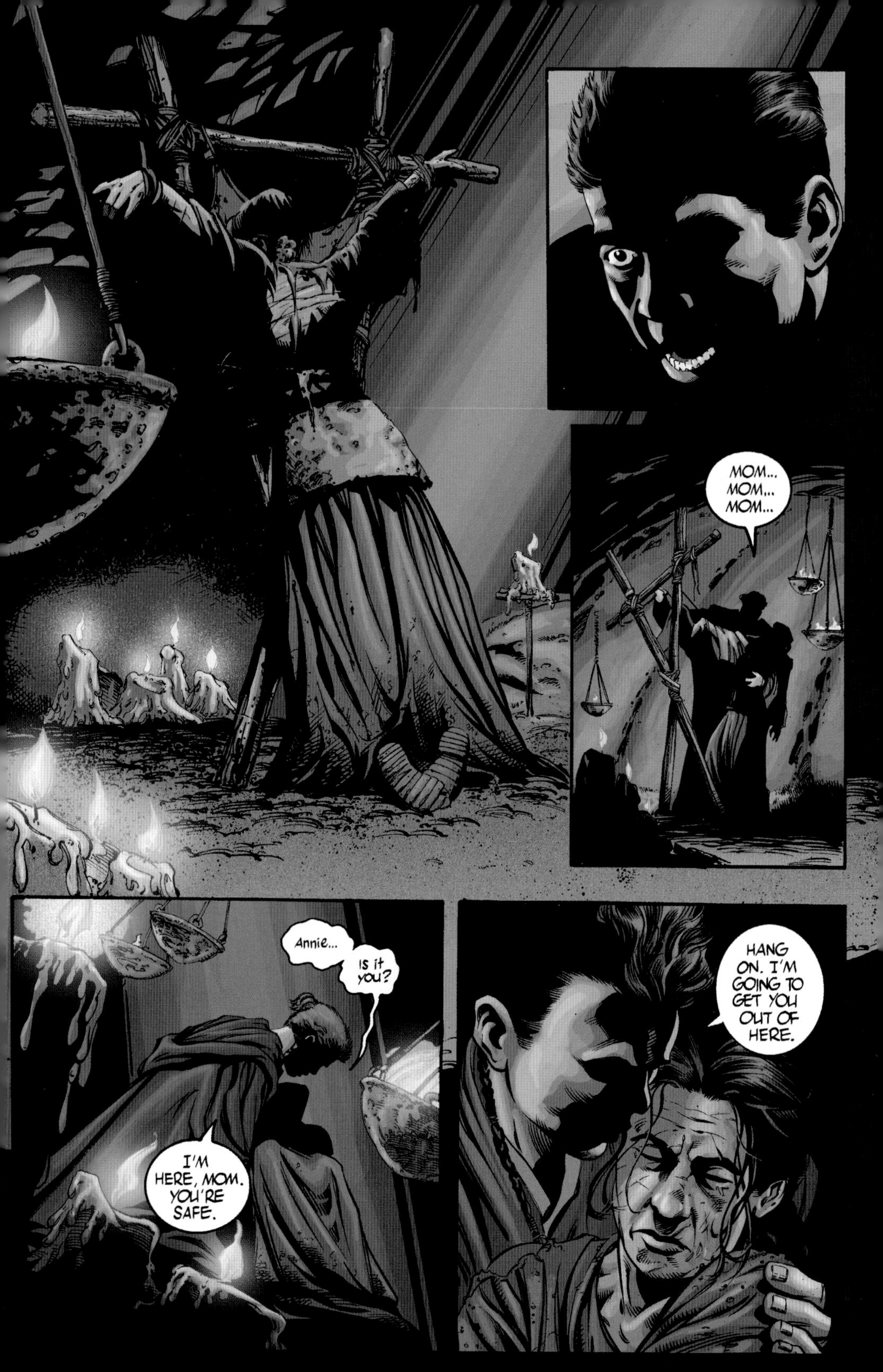
MOM... MOM... MOM...
Annie...
Is it you?
I'M HERE, MOM. YOU'RE SAFE.
HANG ON. I'M GOING TO GET YOU OUT OF HERE.

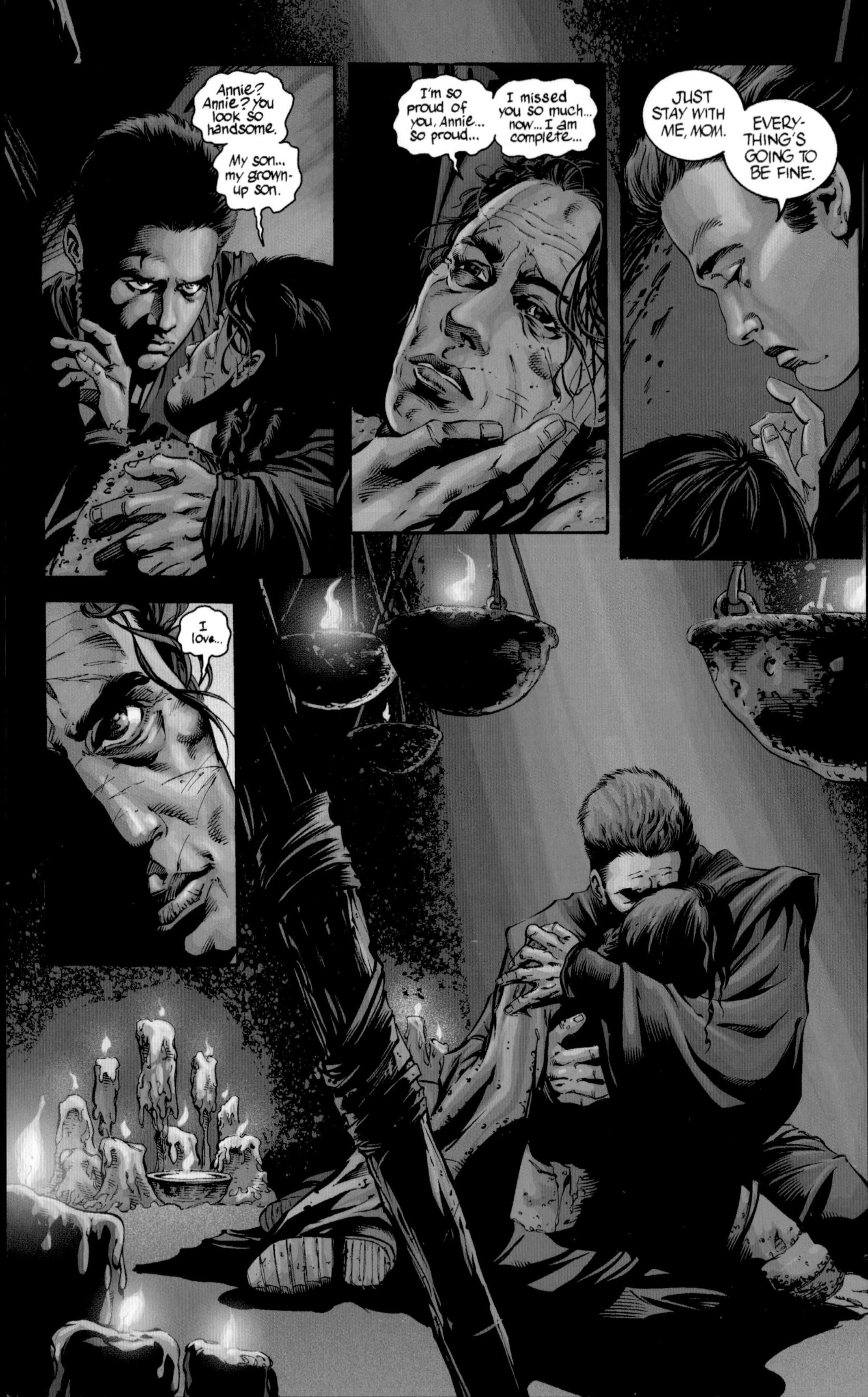
Annie? Annie? you look so handsome.
My son... my grown-up son.
I'm so proud of you, Annie... so proud...
I missed you so much... now... I am complete...
JUST STAY WITH ME, MOM.
EVERY-THING'S GOING TO BE FINE.
I love...

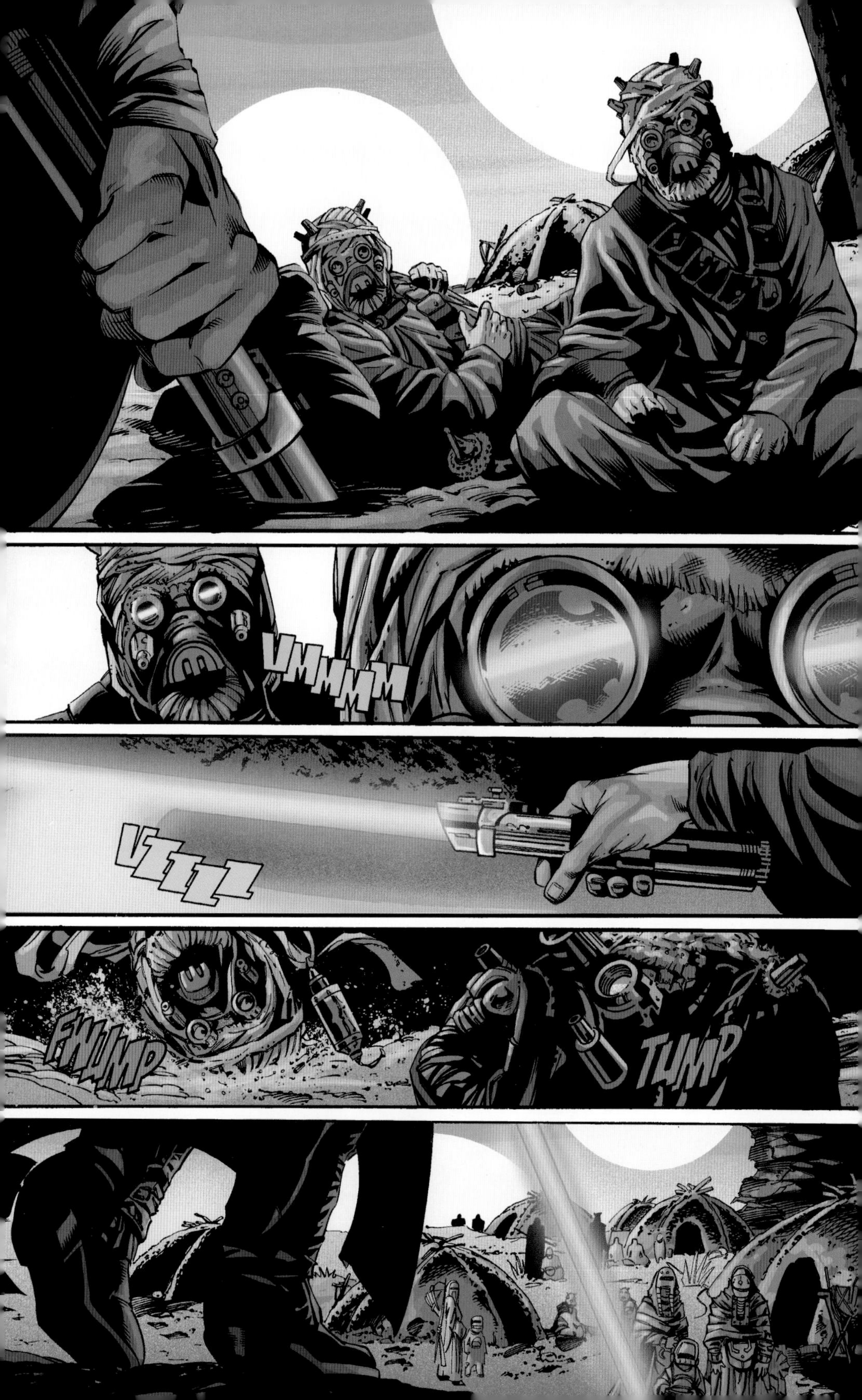

UMMMMM
VZZZZ
FWUMP
TUMP

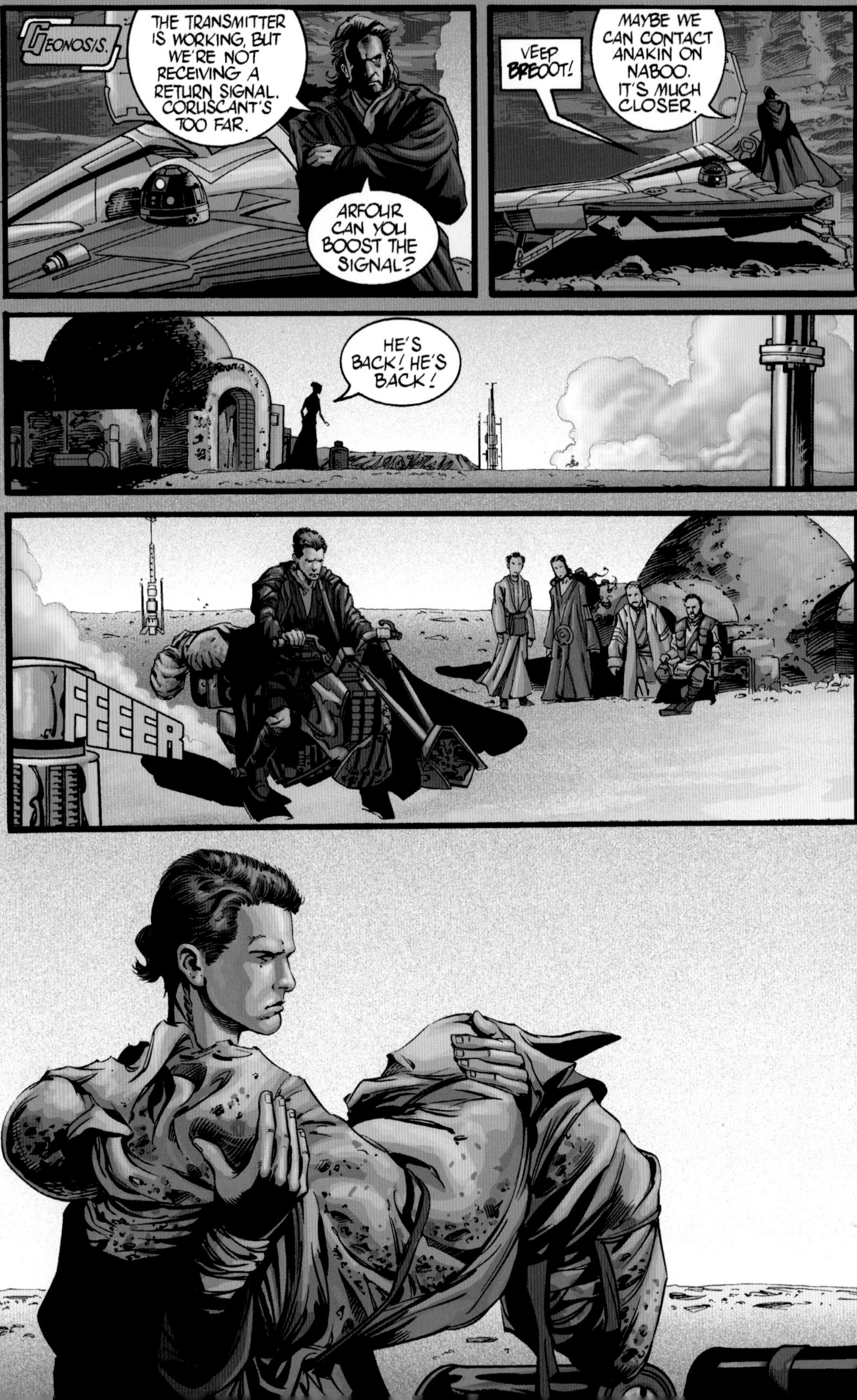
GEONOSIS.
THE TRANSMITTER IS WORKING, BUT WE'RE NOT RECEIVING A RETURN SIGNAL. CORUSCANT'S TOO FAR.
ARFOUR CAN YOU BOOST THE SIGNAL?
VEEP BREOOT!
MAYBE WE CAN CONTACT ANAKIN ON NABOO. IT'S MUCH CLOSER.
HE'S BACK! HE'S BACK!
FEEER

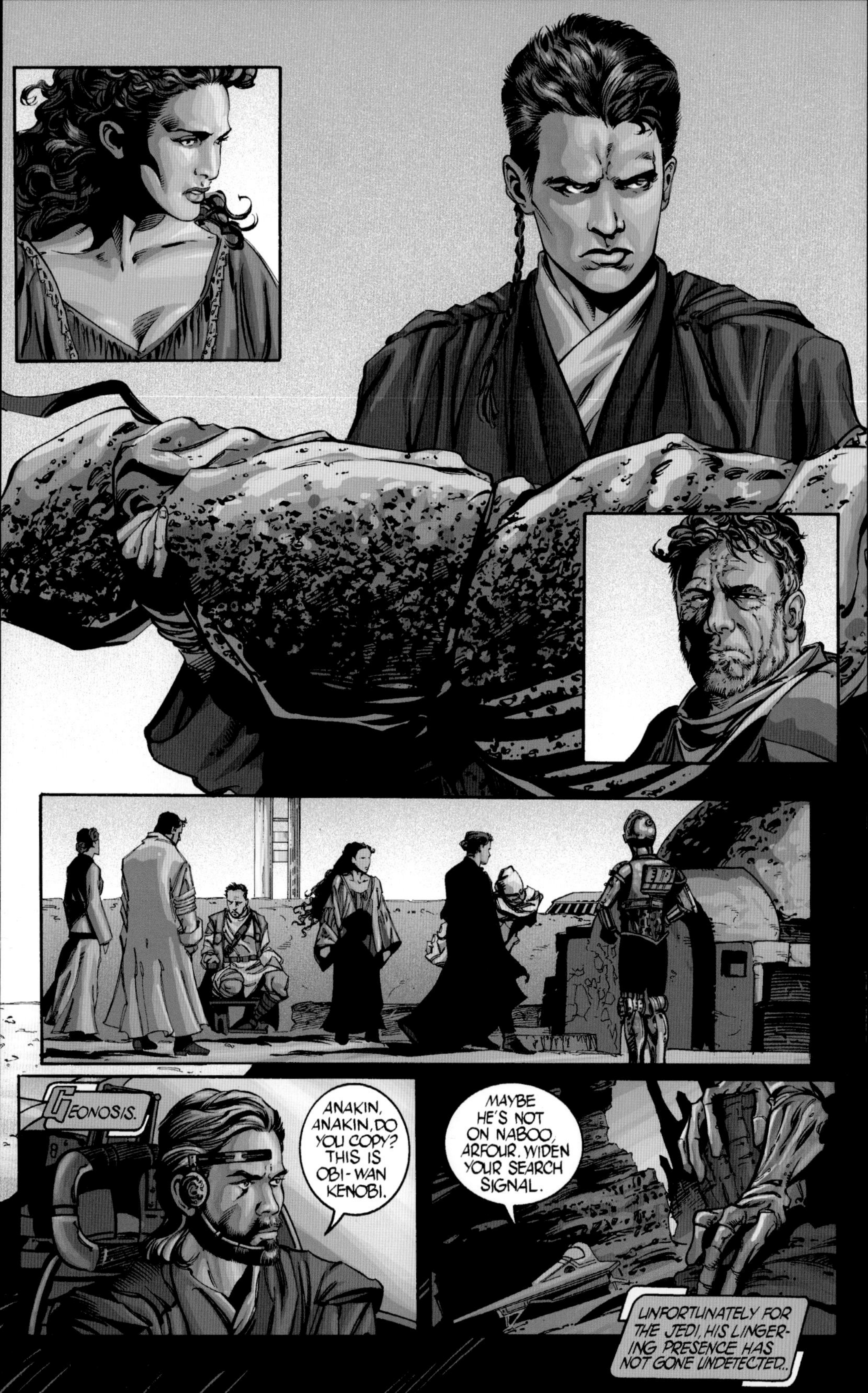
GEONOSIS.
ANAKIN, ANAKIN, DO YOU COPY? THIS IS OBI-WAN KENOBI.
MAYBE HE'S NOT ON NABOO, ARFOUR. WIDEN YOUR SEARCH SIGNAL.
UNFORTUNATELY FOR THE JEDI, HIS LINGER-ING PRESENCE HAS NOT GONE UNDETECTED...

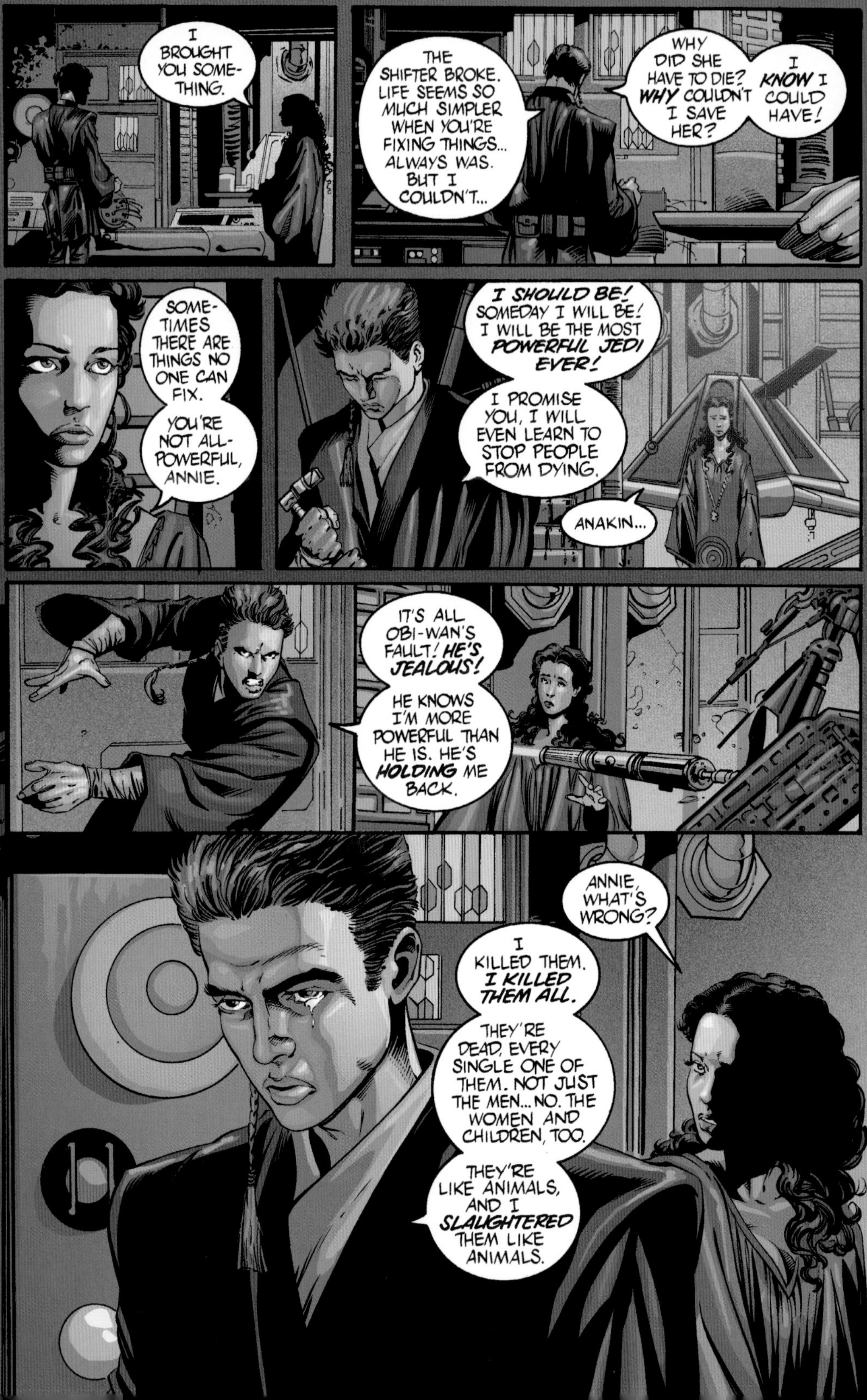
I BROUGHT YOU SOMETHING.
THE SHIFTER BROKE. LIFE SEEMS SO MUCH SIMPLER WHEN YOU'RE FIXING THINGS... ALWAYS WAS. BUT I COULDN'T...
WHY DID SHE HAVE TO DIE? WHY COULDN'T I SAVE HER?
I KNOW I COULD HAVE!
SOMETIMES THERE ARE THINGS NO ONE CAN FIX.
YOU'RE NOT ALL-POWERFUL, ANNIE.
I SHOULD BE! SOMEDAY I WILL BE! I WILL BE THE MOST POWERFUL JEDI EVER!
I PROMISE YOU, I WILL EVEN LEARN TO STOP PEOPLE FROM DYING.
ANAKIN...
IT'S ALL OBI-WAN'S FAULT! HE'S JEALOUS!
HE KNOWS I'M MORE POWERFUL THAN HE IS. HE'S HOLDING ME BACK.
ANNIE, WHAT'S WRONG?
I KILLED THEM. I KILLED THEM ALL.
THEY'RE DEAD, EVERY SINGLE ONE OF THEM. NOT JUST THE MEN... NO. THE WOMEN AND CHILDREN, TOO.
THEY'RE LIKE ANIMALS, AND I SLAUGHTERED THEM LIKE ANIMALS.

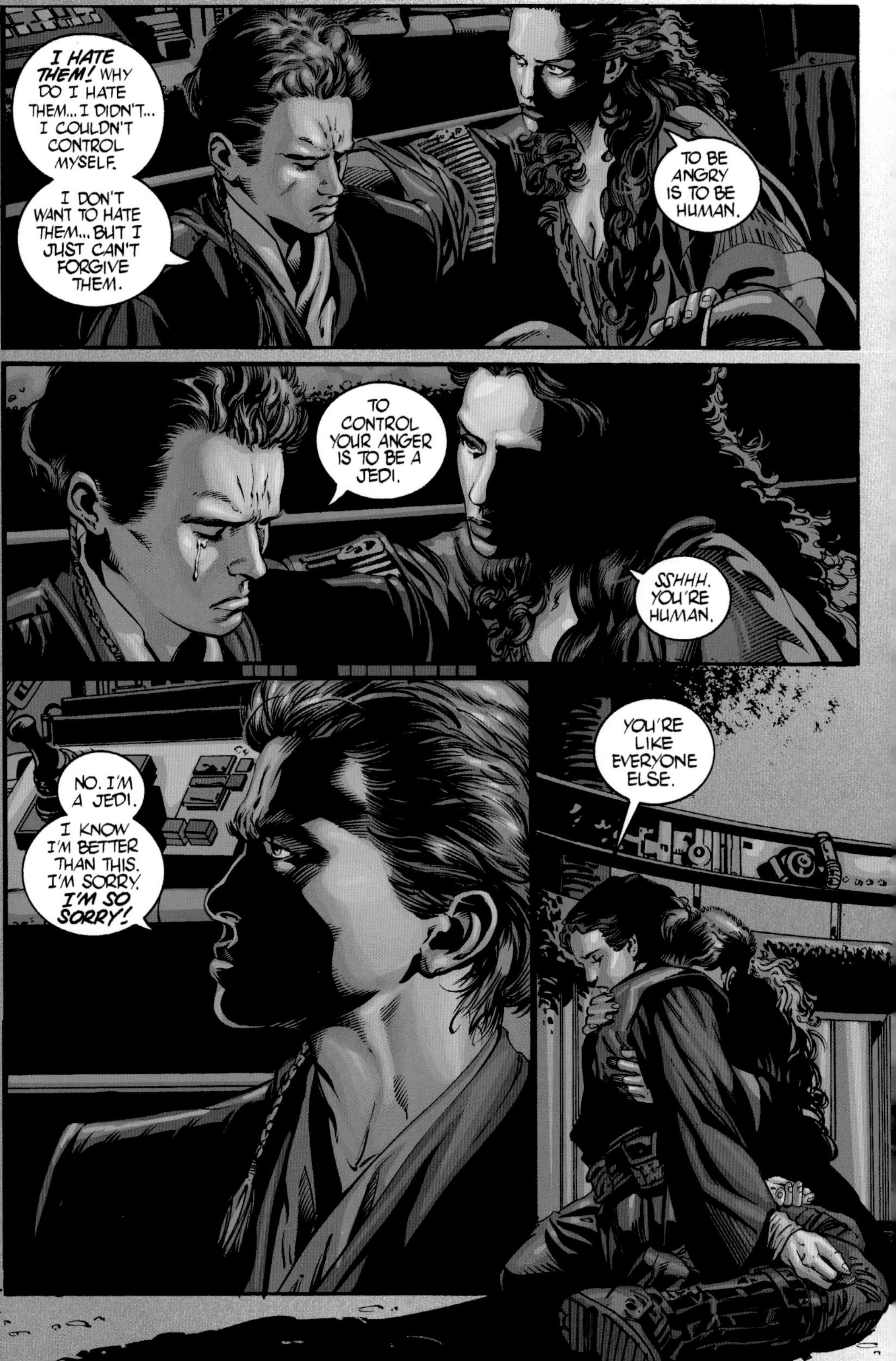

I HATE THEM! WHY DO I HATE THEM... I DIDN'T... I COULDN'T CONTROL MYSELF.
I DON'T WANT TO HATE THEM... BUT I JUST CAN'T FORGIVE THEM.
TO BE ANGRY IS TO BE HUMAN.
TO CONTROL YOUR ANGER IS TO BE A JEDI.
SSHHH. YOU'RE HUMAN.
NO. I'M A JEDI.
I KNOW I'M BETTER THAN THIS. I'M SORRY. I'M SO SORRY!
YOU'RE LIKE EVERYONE ELSE.

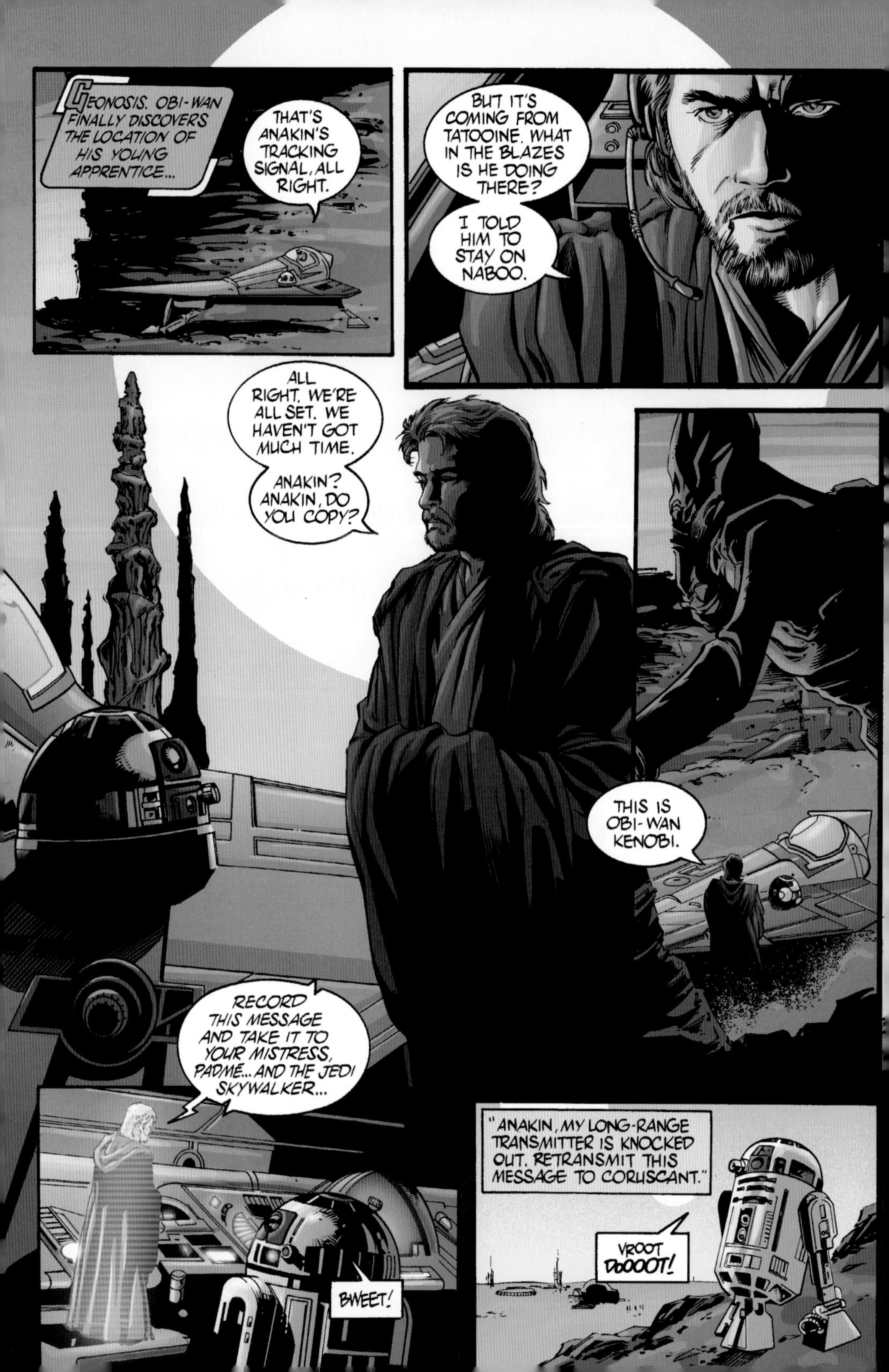
GEONOSIS. OBI-WAN FINALLY DISCOVERS THE LOCATION OF HIS YOUNG APPRENTICE...
THAT'S ANAKIN'S TRACKING SIGNAL, ALL RIGHT.
BUT IT'S COMING FROM TATOOINE. WHAT IN THE BLAZES IS HE DOING THERE?
I TOLD HIM TO STAY ON NABOO.
ALL RIGHT. WE'RE ALL SET. WE HAVEN'T GOT MUCH TIME.
ANAKIN? ANAKIN, DO YOU COPY?
THIS IS OBI-WAN KENOBI.
RECORD THIS MESSAGE AND TAKE IT TO YOUR MISTRESS, PADMÉ... AND THE JEDI SKYWALKER...
BWEET!
"ANAKIN, MY LONG-RANGE TRANSMITTER IS KNOCKED OUT. RETRANSMIT THIS MESSAGE TO CORUSCANT."
VROOT DOOOOT!

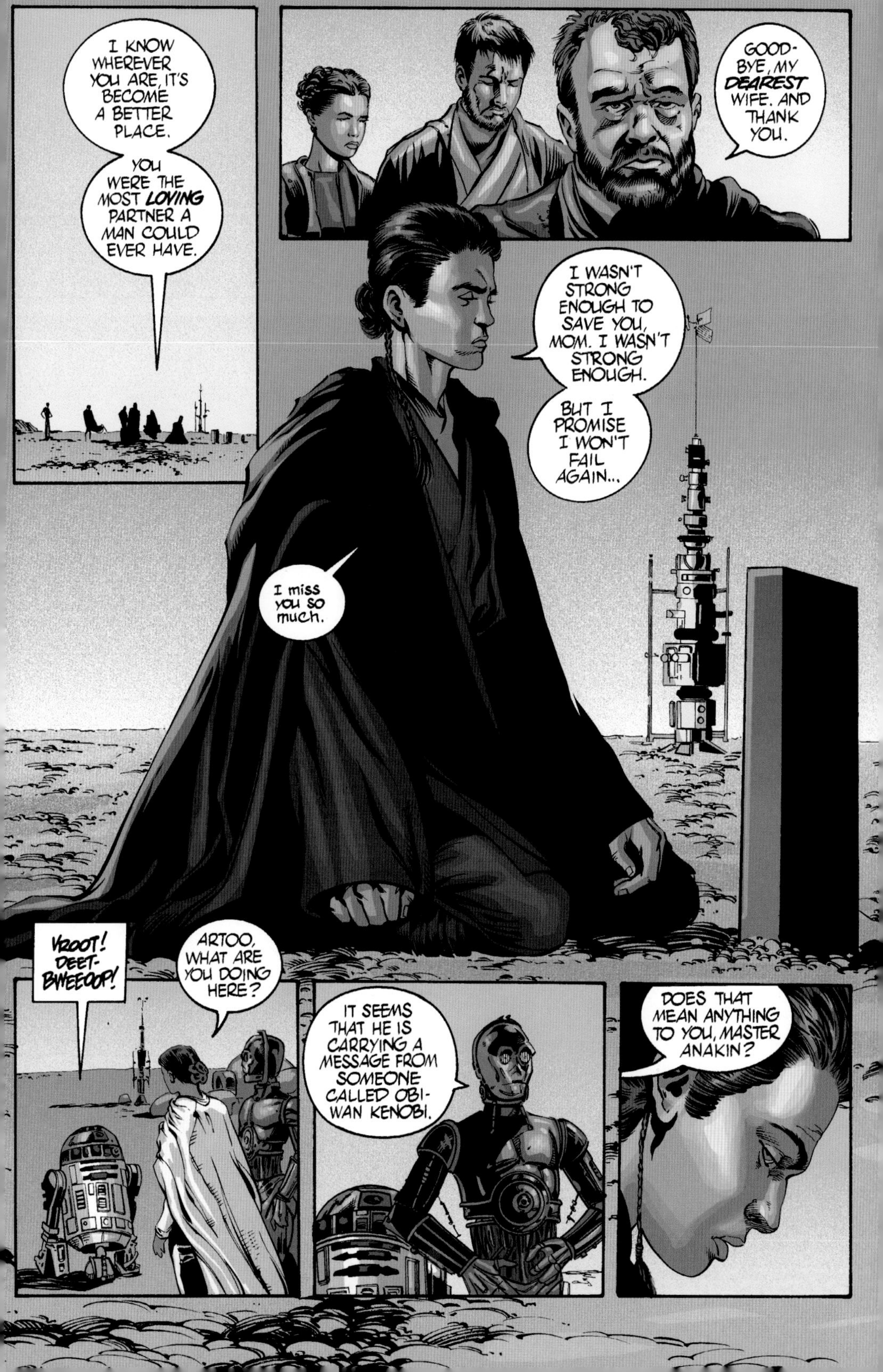
I KNOW WHEREVER YOU ARE, IT'S BECOME A BETTER PLACE.
YOU WERE THE MOST LOVING PARTNER A MAN COULD EVER HAVE.
GOOD-BYE, MY DEAREST WIFE. AND THANK YOU.
I WASN'T STRONG ENOUGH TO SAVE YOU, MOM. I WASN'T STRONG ENOUGH.
BUT I PROMISE I WON'T FAIL AGAIN...
I miss you so much.
VROOT! DEET-BWEEOOP!
ARTOO, WHAT ARE YOU DOING HERE?
IT SEEMS THAT HE IS CARRYING A MESSAGE FROM SOMEONE CALLED OBI-WAN KENOBI.
DOES THAT MEAN ANYTHING TO YOU, MASTER ANAKIN?

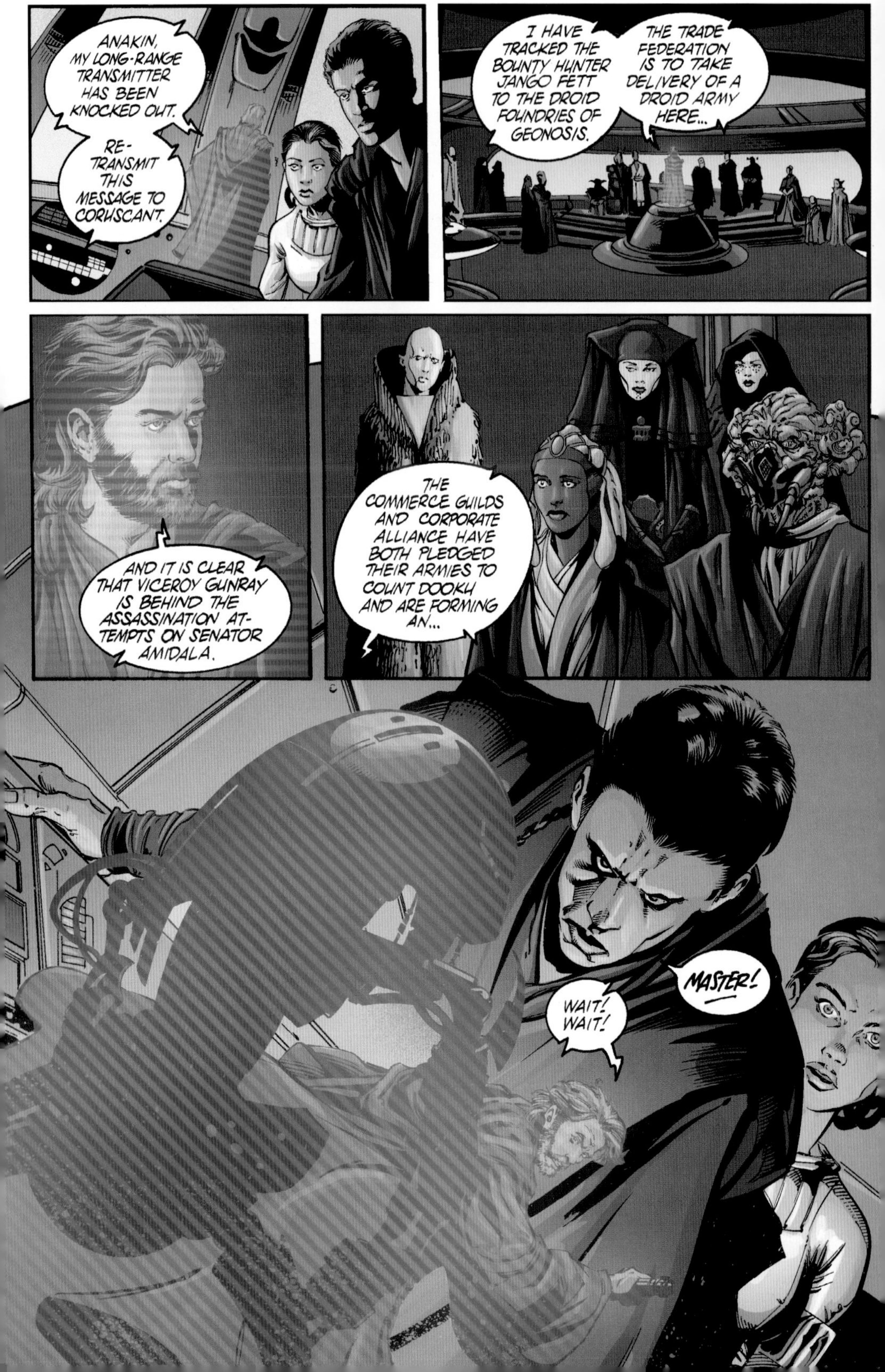
ANAKIN, MY LONG-RANGE TRANSMITTER HAS BEEN KNOCKED OUT.
RE-TRANSMIT THIS MESSAGE TO CORUSCANT.
I HAVE TRACKED THE BOUNTY HUNTER JANGO FETT TO THE DROID FOUNDRIES OF GEONOSIS.
THE TRADE FEDERATION IS TO TAKE DELIVERY OF A DROID ARMY HERE...
AND IT IS CLEAR THAT VICEROY GUNRAY IS BEHIND THE ASSASSINATION AT-TEMPTS ON SENATOR AMIDALA.
THE COMMERCE GUILDS AND CORPORATE ALLIANCE HAVE BOTH PLEDGED THEIR ARMIES TO COUNT DOOKU AND ARE FORMING AN...
MASTER!
WAIT! WAIT!

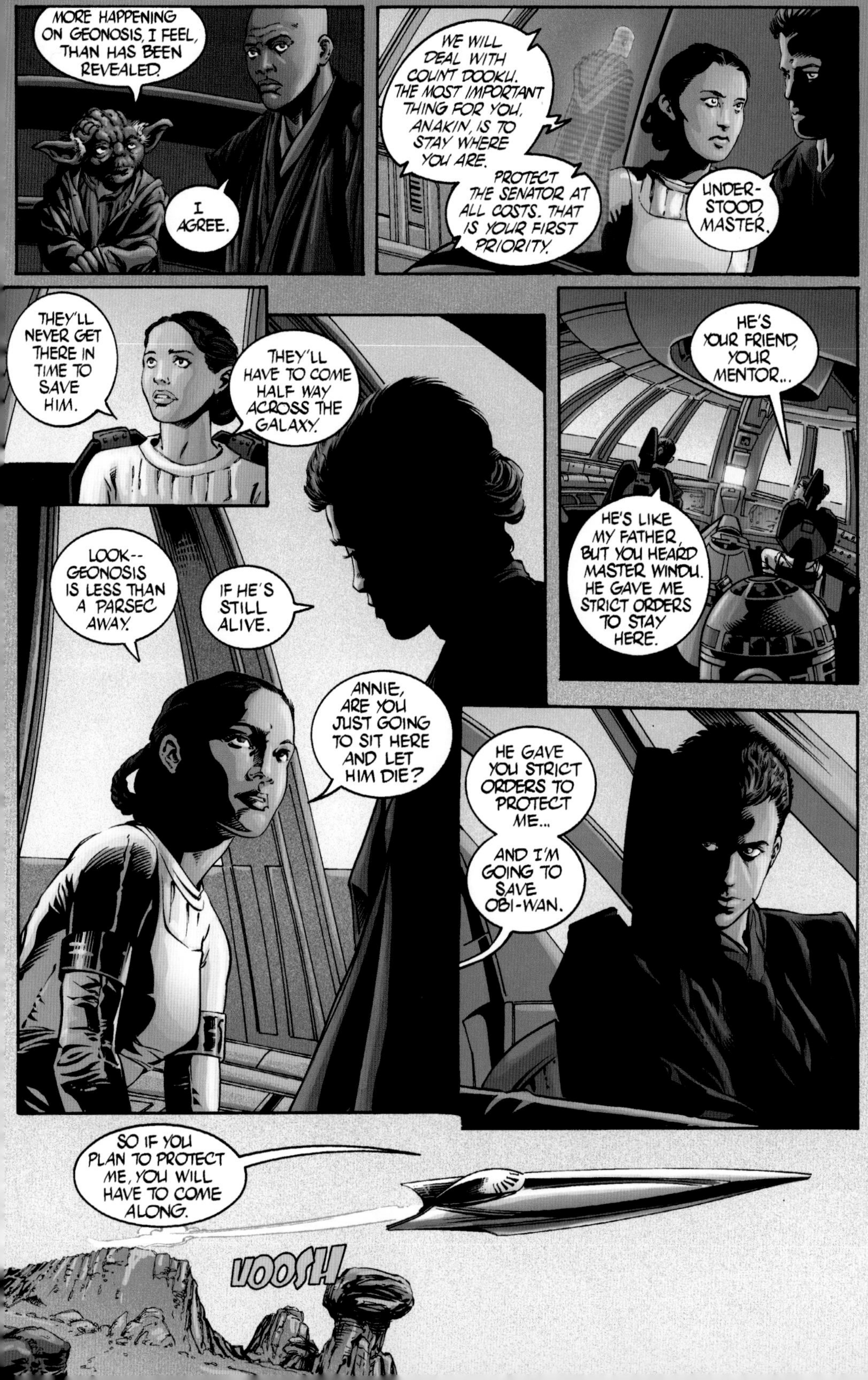
MORE HAPPENING ON GEONOSIS, I FEEL, THAN HAS BEEN REVEALED.
I AGREE.
WE WILL DEAL WITH COUNT DOOKU. THE MOST IMPORTANT THING FOR YOU, ANAKIN, IS TO STAY WHERE YOU ARE.
PROTECT THE SENATOR AT ALL COSTS. THAT IS YOUR FIRST PRIORITY.
UNDER-STOOD, MASTER.
THEY'LL NEVER GET THERE IN TIME TO SAVE HIM.
THEY'LL HAVE TO COME HALF WAY ACROSS THE GALAXY.
HE'S YOUR FRIEND, YOUR MENTOR...
HE'S LIKE MY FATHER, BUT YOU HEARD MASTER WINDU. HE GAVE ME STRICT ORDERS TO STAY HERE.
LOOK-- GEONOSIS IS LESS THAN A PARSEC AWAY.
IF HE'S STILL ALIVE.
ANNIE, ARE YOU JUST GOING TO SIT HERE AND LET HIM DIE?
HE GAVE YOU STRICT ORDERS TO PROTECT ME...
AND I'M GOING TO SAVE OBI-WAN.
SO IF YOU PLAN TO PROTECT ME, YOU WILL HAVE TO COME ALONG.
VOOSH

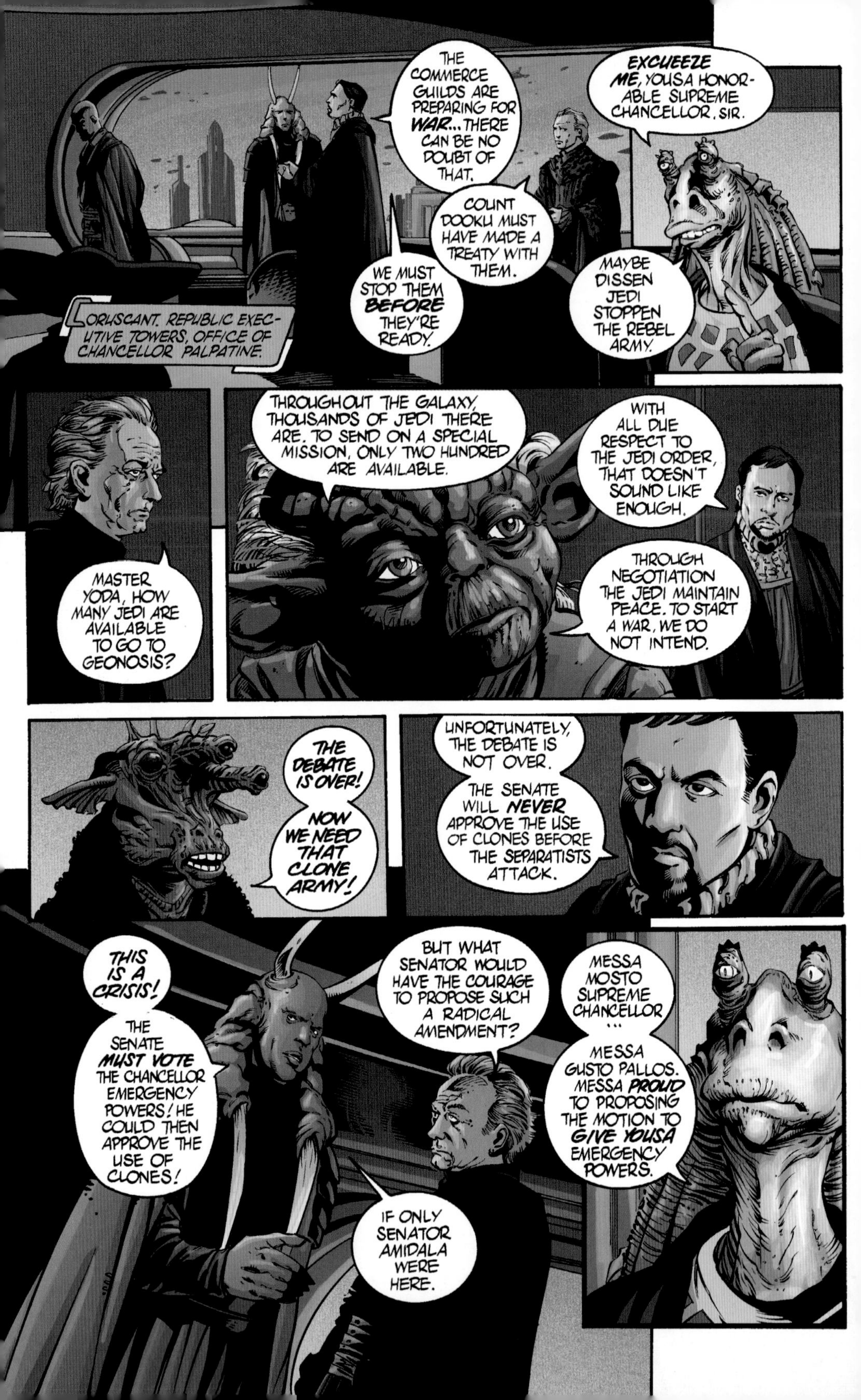
CORUSCANT. REPUBLIC EXECUTIVE TOWERS, OFFICE OF CHANCELLOR PALPATINE.
THE COMMERCE GUILDS ARE PREPARING FOR WAR... THERE CAN BE NO DOUBT OF THAT.
COUNT DOOKU MUST HAVE MADE A TREATY WITH THEM.
WE MUST STOP THEM BEFORE THEY'RE READY.
EXCUEEZE ME, YOUSA HONORABLE SUPREME CHANCELLOR, SIR.
MAYBE DISSEN JEDI STOPPEN THE REBEL ARMY.
MASTER YODA, HOW MANY JEDI ARE AVAILABLE TO GO TO GEONOSIS?
THROUGHOUT THE GALAXY, THOUSANDS OF JEDI THERE ARE. TO SEND ON A SPECIAL MISSION, ONLY TWO HUNDRED ARE AVAILABLE.
WITH ALL DUE RESPECT TO THE JEDI ORDER, THAT DOESN'T SOUND LIKE ENOUGH.
THROUGH NEGOTIATION THE JEDI MAINTAIN PEACE. TO START A WAR, WE DO NOT INTEND.
THE DEBATE IS OVER!
NOW WE NEED THAT CLONE ARMY!
UNFORTUNATELY, THE DEBATE IS NOT OVER.
THE SENATE WILL NEVER APPROVE THE USE OF CLONES BEFORE THE SEPARATISTS ATTACK.
THIS IS A CRISIS!
THE SENATE MUST VOTE THE CHANCELLOR EMERGENCY POWERS! HE COULD THEN APPROVE THE USE OF CLONES!
BUT WHAT SENATOR WOULD HAVE THE COURAGE TO PROPOSE SUCH A RADICAL AMENDMENT?
IF ONLY SENATOR AMIDALA WERE HERE.
MESSA MOSTO SUPREME CHANCELLOR...
MESSA GUSTO PALLOS. MESSA PROUD TO PROPOSING THE MOTION TO GIVE YOUSA EMERGENCY POWERS.

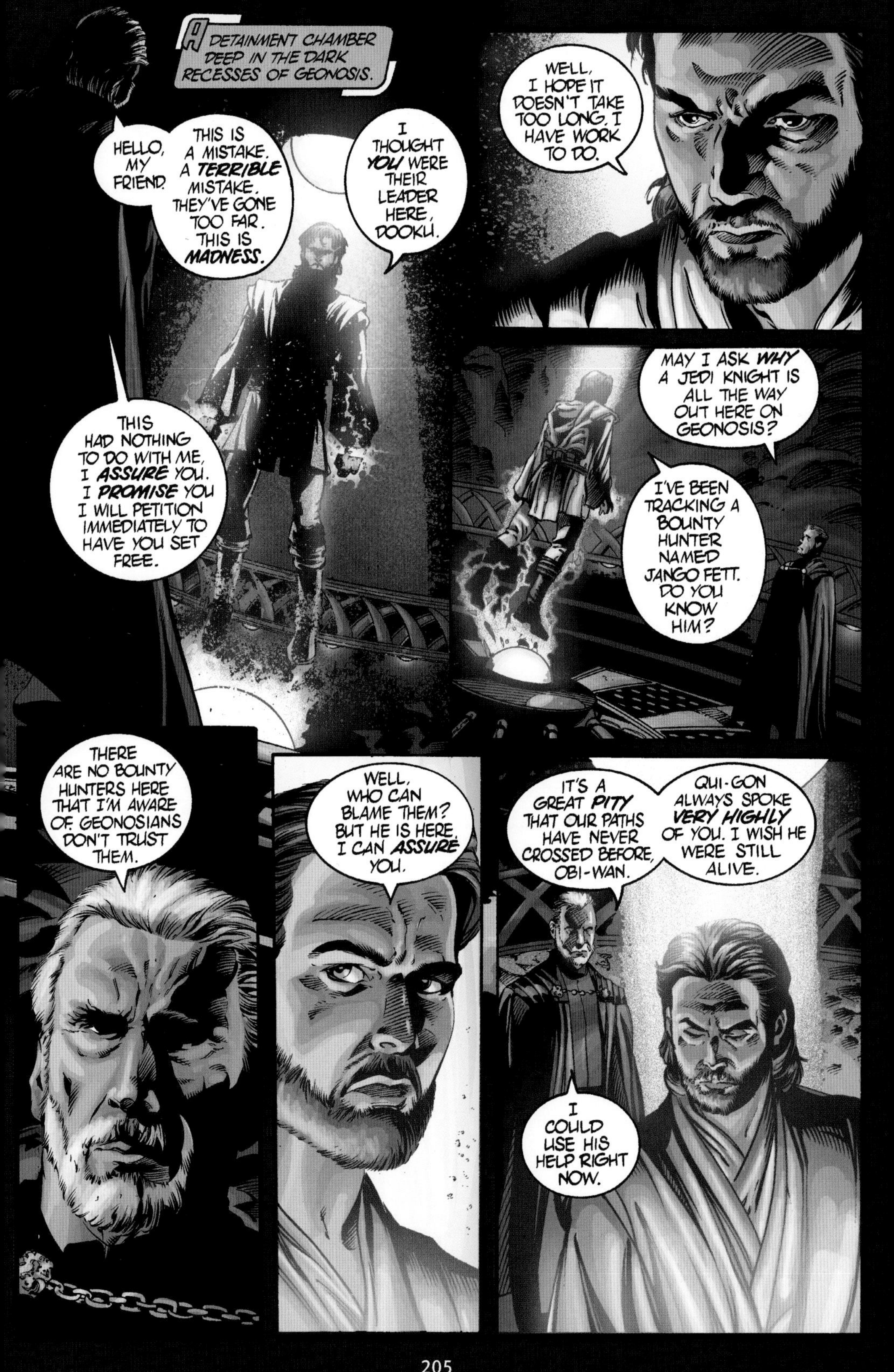

A DETAINMENT CHAMBER DEEP IN THE DARK RECESSES OF GEONOSIS.
HELLO, MY FRIEND.
THIS IS A MISTAKE. A TERRIBLE MISTAKE. THEY'VE GONE TOO FAR. THIS IS MADNESS.
I THOUGHT YOU WERE THEIR LEADER HERE, DOOKU.
THIS HAD NOTHING TO DO WITH ME, I ASSURE YOU. I PROMISE YOU I WILL PETITION IMMEDIATELY TO HAVE YOU SET FREE.
WELL, I HOPE IT DOESN'T TAKE TOO LONG. I HAVE WORK TO DO.
MAY I ASK WHY A JEDI KNIGHT IS ALL THE WAY OUT HERE ON GEONOSIS?
I'VE BEEN TRACKING A BOUNTY HUNTER NAMED JANGO FETT. DO YOU KNOW HIM?
THERE ARE NO BOUNTY HUNTERS HERE THAT I'M AWARE OF. GEONOSIANS DON'T TRUST THEM.
WELL, WHO CAN BLAME THEM? BUT HE IS HERE, I CAN ASSURE YOU.
IT'S A GREAT PITY THAT OUR PATHS HAVE NEVER CROSSED BEFORE, OBI-WAN.
QUI-GON ALWAYS SPOKE VERY HIGHLY OF YOU. I WISH HE WERE STILL ALIVE.
I COULD USE HIS HELP RIGHT NOW.

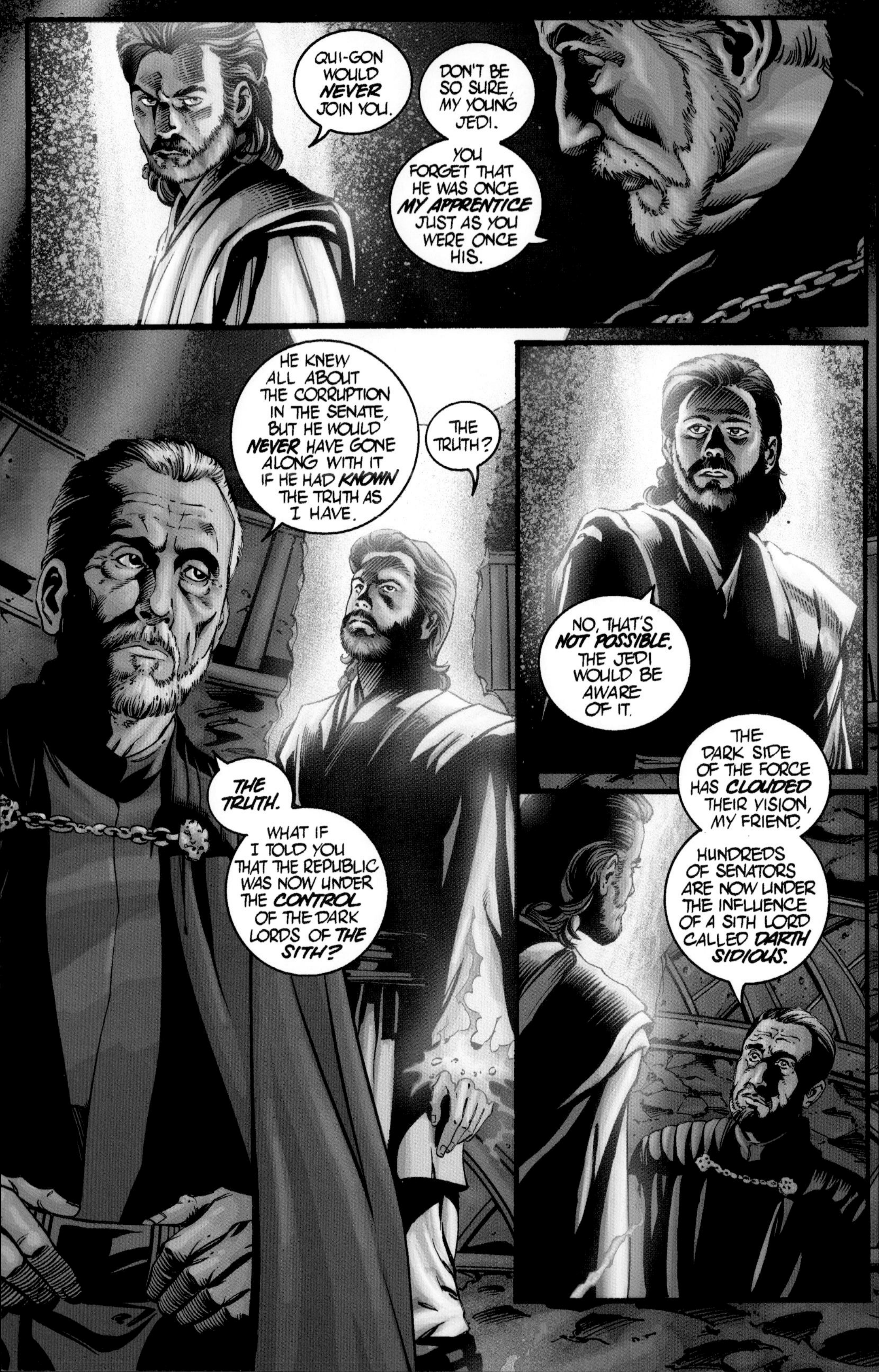
QUI-GON WOULD NEVER JOIN YOU.
DON'T BE SO SURE, MY YOUNG JEDI.
YOU FORGET THAT HE WAS ONCE MY APPRENTICE JUST AS YOU WERE ONCE HIS.
HE KNEW ALL ABOUT THE CORRUPTION IN THE SENATE, BUT HE WOULD NEVER HAVE GONE ALONG WITH IT IF HE HAD KNOWN THE TRUTH AS I HAVE.
THE TRUTH?
THE TRUTH.
WHAT IF I TOLD YOU THAT THE REPUBLIC WAS NOW UNDER THE CONTROL OF THE DARK LORDS OF THE SITH?
NO, THAT'S NOT POSSIBLE. THE JEDI WOULD BE AWARE OF IT.
THE DARK SIDE OF THE FORCE HAS CLOUDED THEIR VISION, MY FRIEND.
HUNDREDS OF SENATORS ARE NOW UNDER THE INFLUENCE OF A SITH LORD CALLED DARTH SIDIOUS.

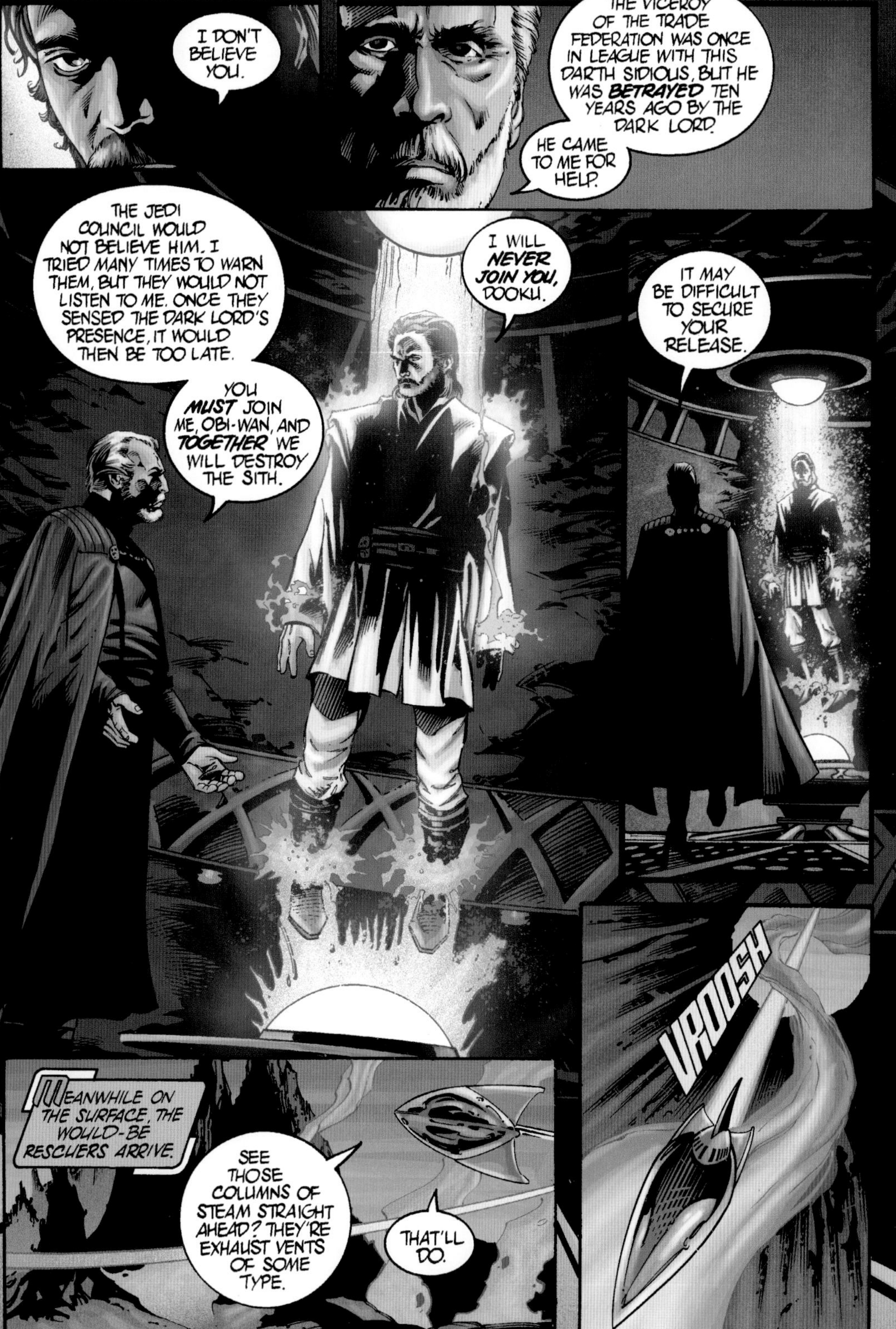
I DON'T BELIEVE YOU.
THE VICEROY OF THE TRADE FEDERATION WAS ONCE IN LEAGUE WITH THIS DARTH SIDIOUS, BUT HE WAS BETRAYED TEN YEARS AGO BY THE DARK LORD.
HE CAME TO ME FOR HELP.
THE JEDI COUNCIL WOULD NOT BELIEVE HIM. I TRIED MANY TIMES TO WARN THEM, BUT THEY WOULD NOT LISTEN TO ME. ONCE THEY SENSED THE DARK LORD'S PRESENCE, IT WOULD THEN BE TOO LATE.
YOU MUST JOIN ME, OBI-WAN, AND TOGETHER WE WILL DESTROY THE SITH.
I WILL NEVER JOIN YOU, DOOKU.
IT MAY BE DIFFICULT TO SECURE YOUR RELEASE.
MEANWHILE ON THE SURFACE, THE WOULD-BE RESCUERS ARRIVE.
SEE THOSE COLUMNS OF STEAM STRAIGHT AHEAD? THEY'RE EXHAUST VENTS OF SOME TYPE.
THAT'LL DO.
VROOSH

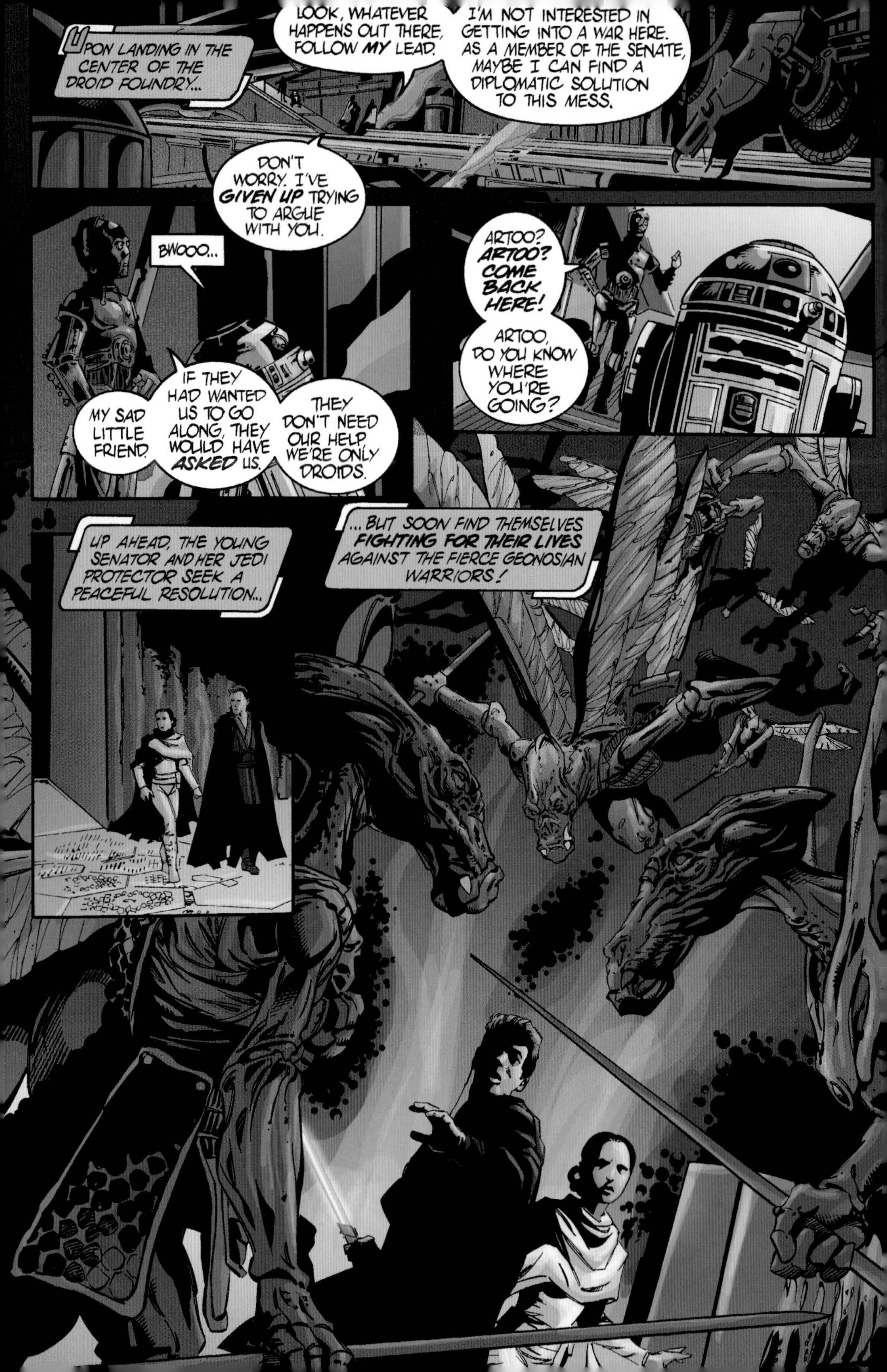
UPON LANDING IN THE CENTER OF THE DROID FOUNDRY...
LOOK, WHATEVER HAPPENS OUT THERE, FOLLOW MY LEAD.
I'M NOT INTERESTED IN GETTING INTO A WAR HERE. AS A MEMBER OF THE SENATE, MAYBE I CAN FIND A DIPLOMATIC SOLUTION TO THIS MESS.
DON'T WORRY. I'VE GIVEN UP TRYING TO ARGUE WITH YOU.
BWOOO...
MY SAD LITTLE FRIEND.
IF THEY HAD WANTED US TO GO ALONG, THEY WOULD HAVE ASKED US.
THEY DON'T NEED OUR HELP. WE'RE ONLY DROIDS.
ARTOO? ARTOO? COME BACK HERE!
ARTOO, DO YOU KNOW WHERE YOU'RE GOING?
UP AHEAD, THE YOUNG SENATOR AND HER JEDI PROTECTOR SEEK A PEACEFUL RESOLUTION...
...BUT SOON FIND THEMSELVES FIGHTING FOR THEIR LIVES AGAINST THE FIERCE GEONOSIAN WARRIORS!

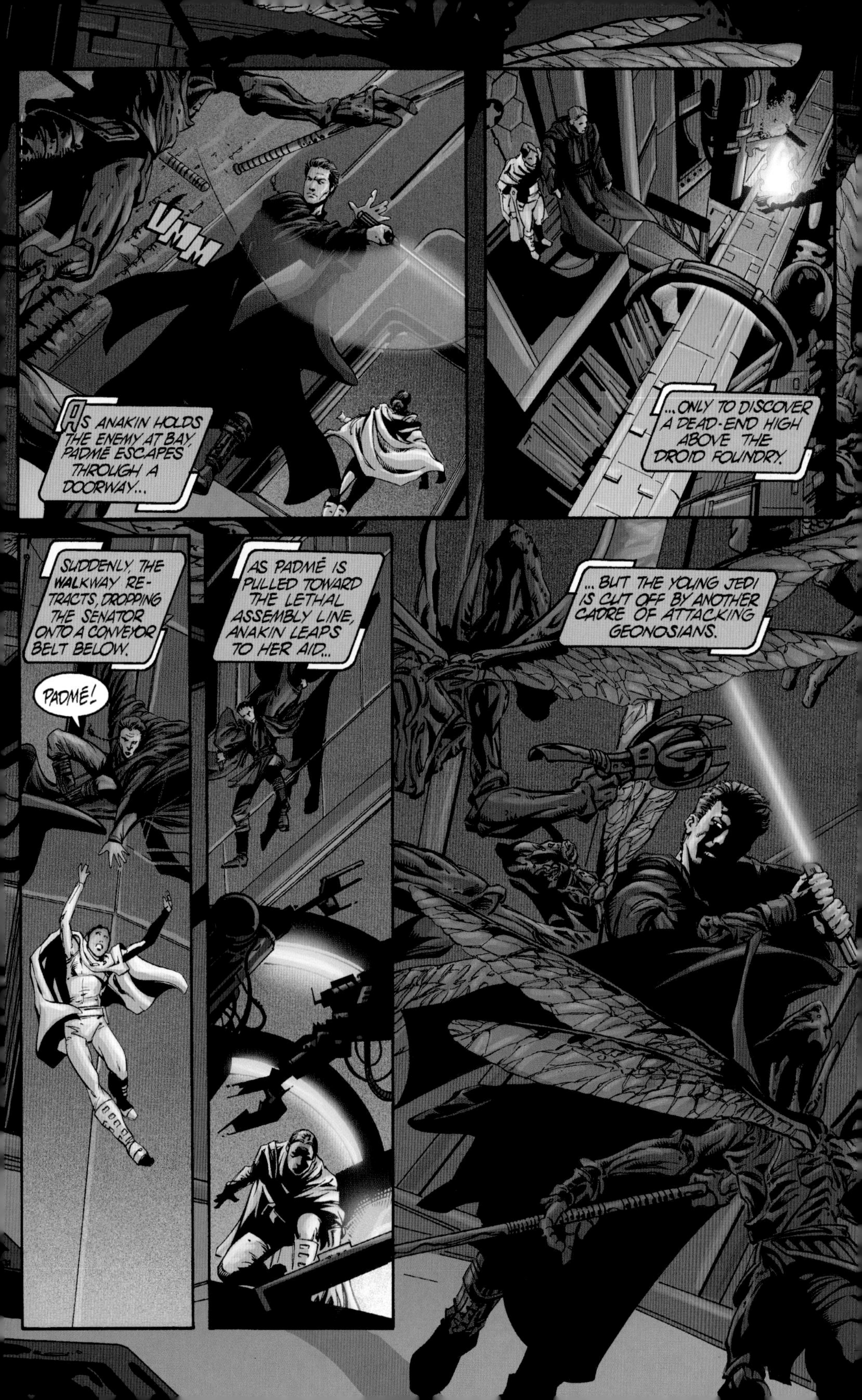
UMM
AS ANAKIN HOLDS THE ENEMY AT BAY, PADMÉ ESCAPES THROUGH A DOORWAY...
...ONLY TO DISCOVER A DEAD-END HIGH ABOVE THE DROID FOUNDRY.
SUDDENLY, THE WALKWAY RETRACTS, DROPPING THE SENATOR ONTO A CONVEYOR BELT BELOW.
PADMÉ!
AS PADMÉ IS PULLED TOWARD THE LETHAL ASSEMBLY LINE, ANAKIN LEAPS TO HER AID...
...BUT THE YOUNG JEDI IS CUT OFF BY ANOTHER CADRE OF ATTACKING GEONOSIANS.

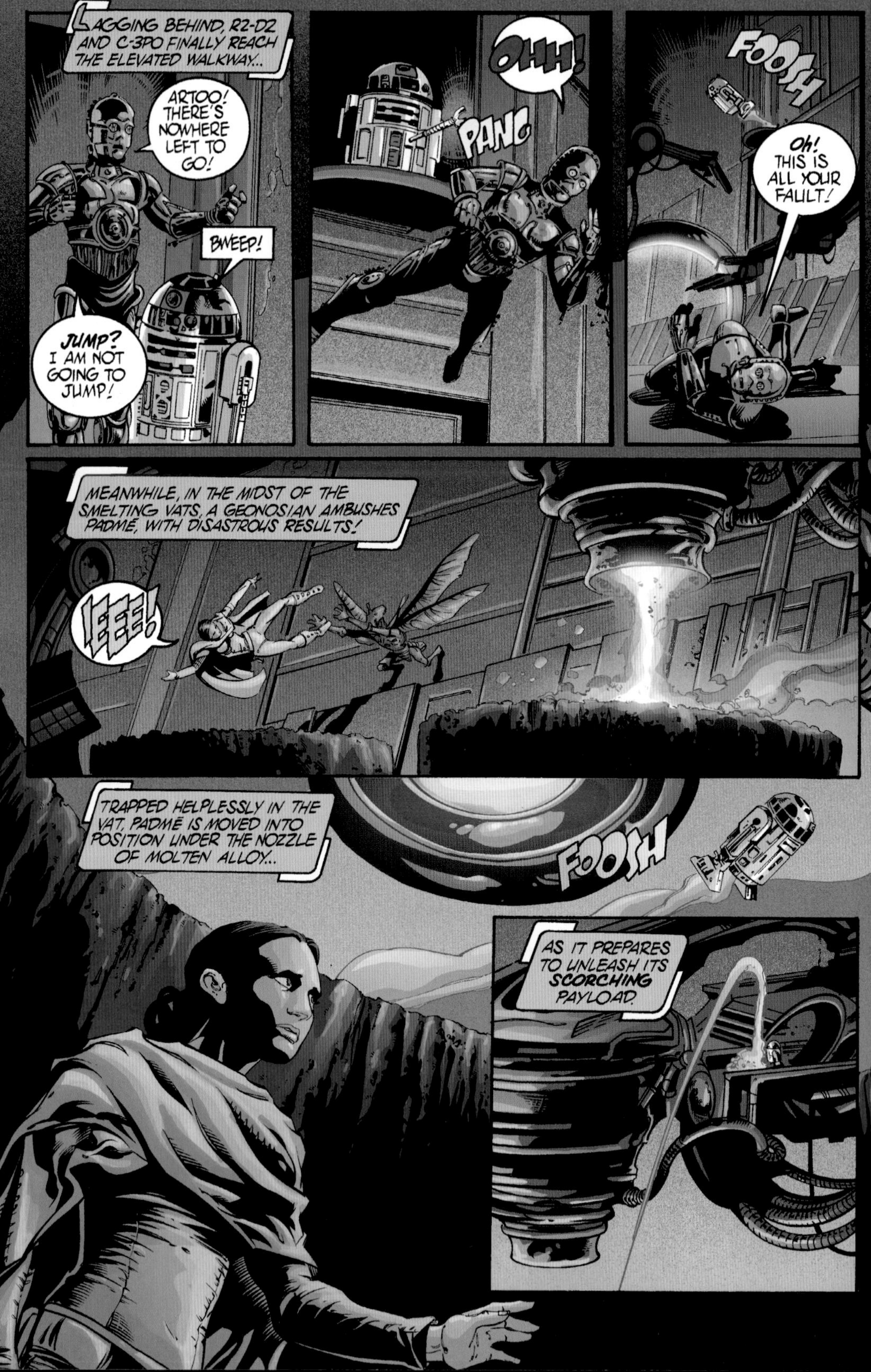
LAGGING BEHIND, R2-D2 AND C-3PO FINALLY REACH THE ELEVATED WALKWAY...
ARTOO! THERE'S NOWHERE LEFT TO GO!
BWEEP!
JUMP? I AM NOT GOING TO JUMP!
OHH!
PANG
FOOSH
Oh! THIS IS ALL YOUR FAULT!
MEANWHILE, IN THE MIDST OF THE SMELTING VATS, A GEONOSIAN AMBUSHES PADMÉ, WITH DISASTROUS RESULTS!
IEEEE!
TRAPPED HELPLESSLY IN THE VAT, PADMÉ IS MOVED INTO POSITION UNDER THE NOZZLE OF MOLTEN ALLOY...
FOOSH
AS IT PREPARES TO UNLEASH ITS SCORCHING PAYLOAD.

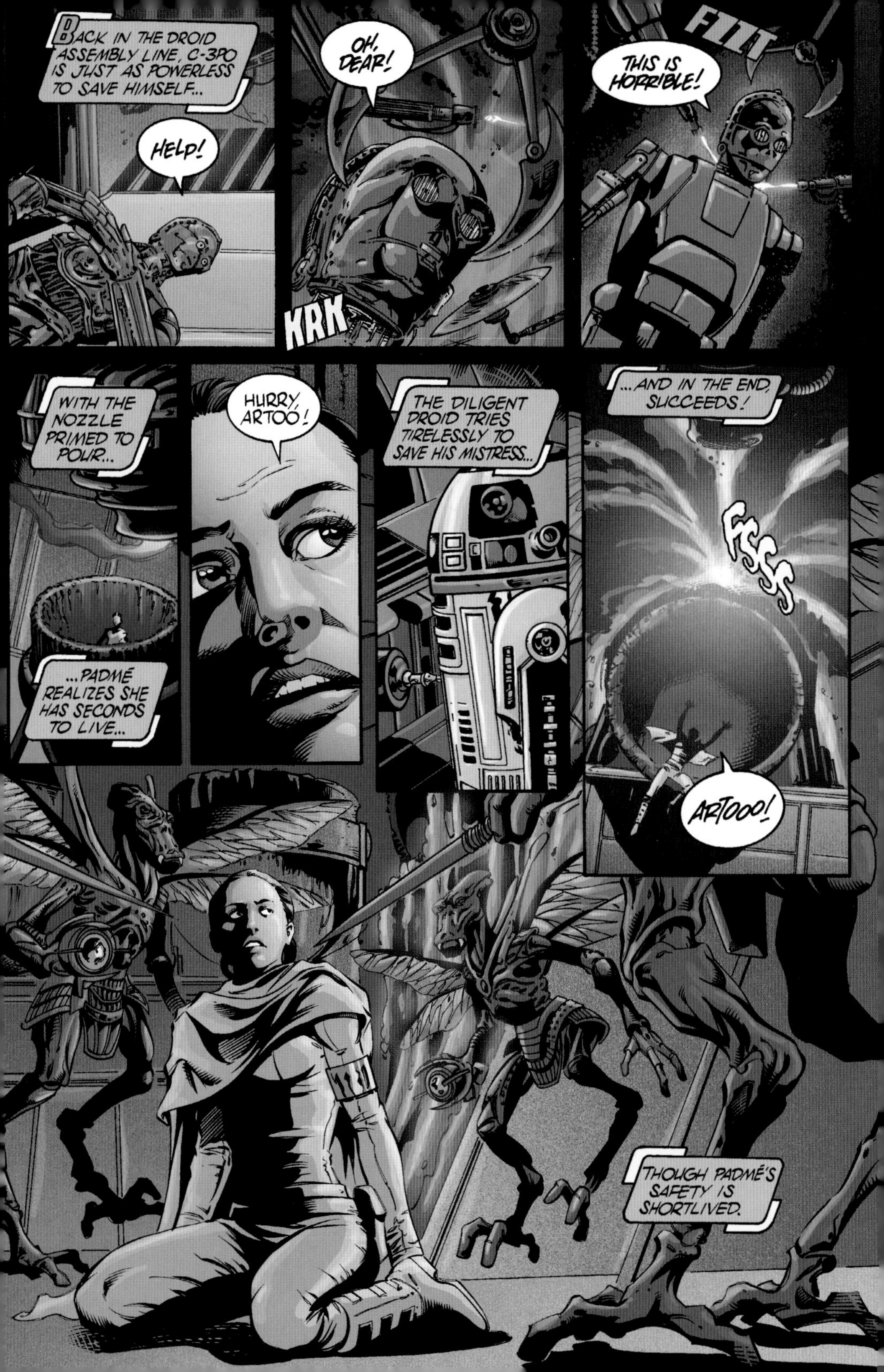
BACK IN THE DROID ASSEMBLY LINE, C-3PO IS JUST AS POWERLESS TO SAVE HIMSELF...
HELP!
OH, DEAR!
KRK
FZZT
THIS IS HORRIBLE!
WITH THE NOZZLE PRIMED TO POUR...
...PADMÉ REALIZES SHE HAS SECONDS TO LIVE...
HURRY, ARTOO!
THE DILIGENT DROID TRIES TIRELESSLY TO SAVE HIS MISTRESS...
...AND IN THE END, SUCCEEDS!
FSSS
ARTOOO!
THOUGH PADMÉ'S SAFETY IS SHORTLIVED.

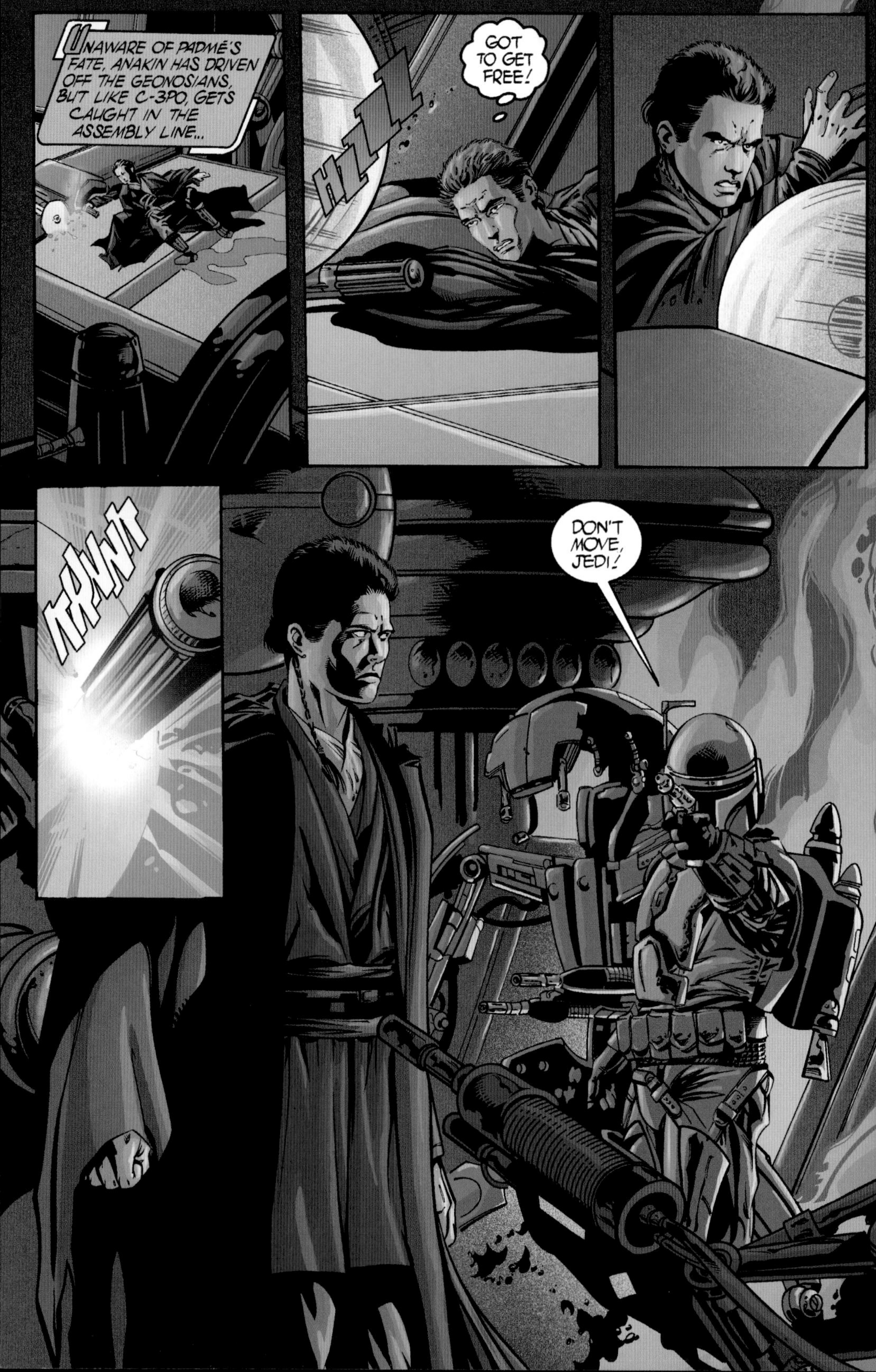
UNAWARE OF PADMÉ'S FATE, ANAKIN HAS DRIVEN OFF THE GEONOSIANS, BUT LIKE C-3PO, GETS CAUGHT IN THE ASSEMBLY LINE...
HZZZ
GOT TO GET FREE!
KRUNT
DON'T MOVE, JEDI!

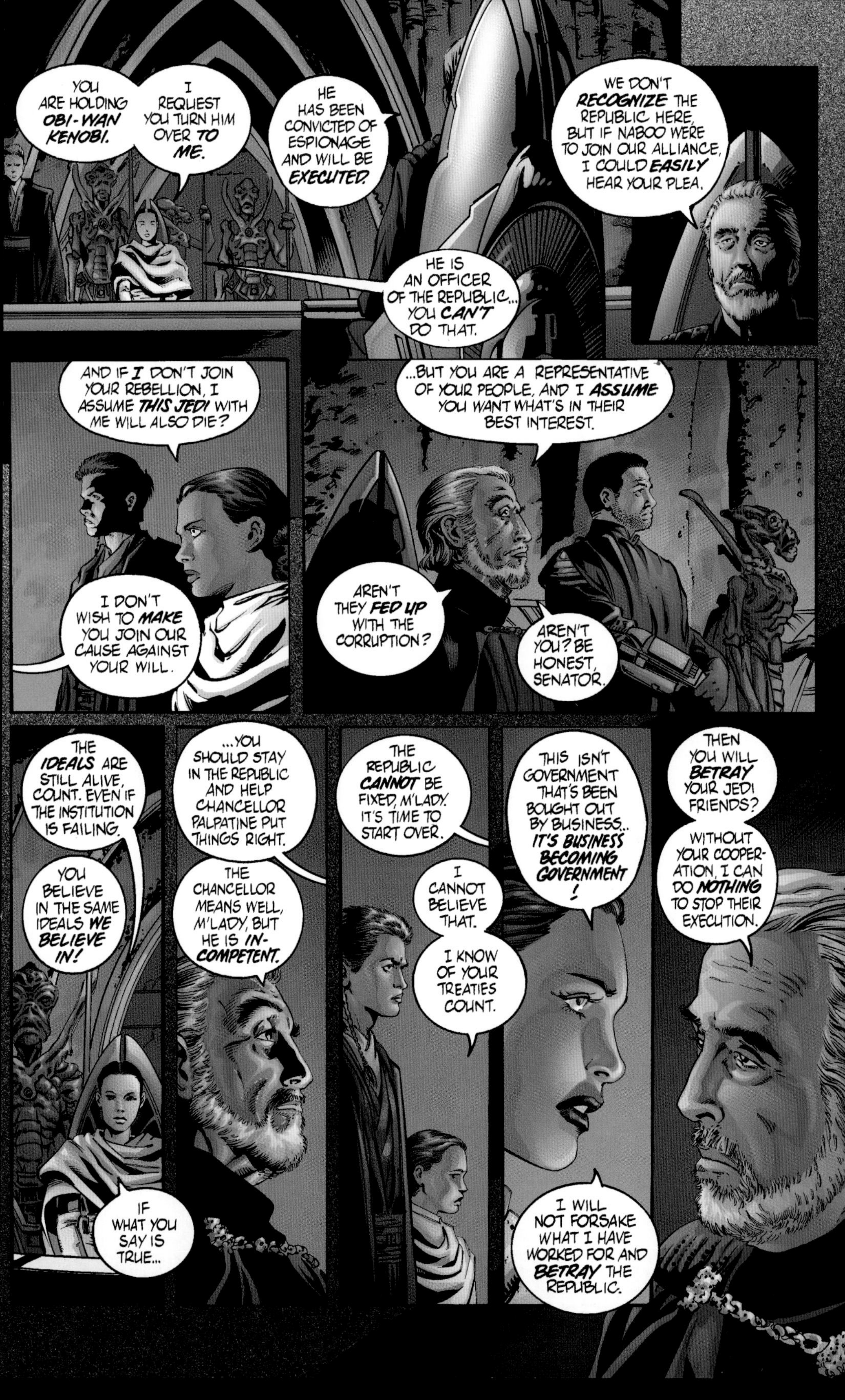
YOU ARE HOLDING OBI-WAN KENOBI.
I REQUEST YOU TURN HIM OVER TO ME.
HE HAS BEEN CONVICTED OF ESPIONAGE AND WILL BE EXECUTED.
HE IS AN OFFICER OF THE REPUBLIC... YOU CAN'T DO THAT.
WE DON'T RECOGNIZE THE REPUBLIC HERE, BUT IF NABOO WERE TO JOIN OUR ALLIANCE, I COULD EASILY HEAR YOUR PLEA.
AND IF I DON'T JOIN YOUR REBELLION, I ASSUME THIS JEDI WITH ME WILL ALSO DIE?
I DON'T WISH TO MAKE YOU JOIN OUR CAUSE AGAINST YOUR WILL.
...BUT YOU ARE A REPRESENTATIVE OF YOUR PEOPLE, AND I ASSUME YOU WANT WHAT'S IN THEIR BEST INTEREST.
AREN'T THEY FED UP WITH THE CORRUPTION?
AREN'T YOU? BE HONEST, SENATOR.
THE IDEALS ARE STILL ALIVE, COUNT. EVEN IF THE INSTITUTION IS FAILING.
YOU BELIEVE IN THE SAME IDEALS WE BELIEVE IN!
IF WHAT YOU SAY IS TRUE...
...YOU SHOULD STAY IN THE REPUBLIC AND HELP CHANCELLOR PALPATINE PUT THINGS RIGHT.
THE CHANCELLOR MEANS WELL, M'LADY, BUT HE IS IN-COMPETENT.
THE REPUBLIC CANNOT BE FIXED, M'LADY. IT'S TIME TO START OVER.
I CANNOT BELIEVE THAT.
I KNOW OF YOUR TREATIES COUNT.
THIS ISN'T GOVERNMENT THAT'S BEEN BOUGHT OUT BY BUSINESS... IT'S BUSINESS BECOMING GOVERNMENT!
I WILL NOT FORSAKE WHAT I HAVE WORKED FOR AND BETRAY THE REPUBLIC.
THEN YOU WILL BETRAY YOUR JEDI FRIENDS?
WITHOUT YOUR COOPER-ATION, I CAN DO NOTHING TO STOP THEIR EXECUTION.

AND WHAT ABOUT ME? AM *I* TO BE EXECUTED ALSO?

I WOULDN'T THINK OF SUCH AN OFFENSE, BUT THERE ARE INDIVIDUALS WHO HAVE A *STRONG INTEREST* IN YOUR DEMISE, M'LADY!

WITHOUT YOUR COOPERATION, I'VE DONE *ALL* I CAN FOR YOU.

TAKE THEM AWAY.

ON CORUSCANT, THE SENATE FURIOUSLY DEBATES HOW TO RESPOND TO THE SEPARATISTS...

‹PEACE IS THE ANSWER!›

WE NEED PROTECTION!

THE REPUBLIC MUST PREPARE FOR WAR!

ORDER! ORDER!

IN THE REGRETTABLE ABSENCE OF SENATOR AMIDALA, THE CHAIR RECOGNIZES THE SENIOR REPRESENTATIVE OF NABOO...

...JAR JAR BINKS.

SENATORS, DELLOW FELEGATES...

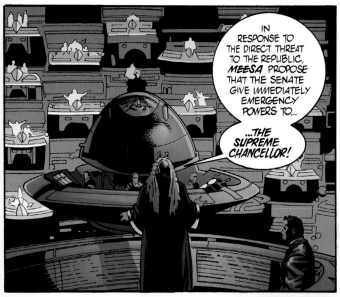

IN RESPONSE TO THE DIRECT THREAT TO THE REPUBLIC, *MEESA* PROPOSE THAT THE SENATE GIVE IMMEDIATELY EMERGENCY POWERS TO...

...THE *SUPREME CHANCELLOR!*

JAR JAR'S SURPRISING PROPOSITION IS MET WITH WILD APPROVAL BY THE SENATE...

AT LAST! WE'RE SAVED!

... MUCH TO THE GUNGAN DIPLOMAT'S DELIGHT.

IT IS WITH GREAT RELUCTANCE THAT I HAVE AGREED TO THIS CALLING. I LOVE DEMOCRACY... I LOVE THE REPUBLIC.

BUT I AM MILD BY NATURE, AND I DO NOT DESIRE TO SEE THE *DESTRUCTION* OF DEMOCRACY.

THE POWER YOU GIVE ME I WILL LAY DOWN WHEN THIS CRISIS HAS ABATED, *I PROMISE YOU.*

AND AS MY FIRST ACT WITH THIS NEW AUTHORITY...

...I WILL CREATE A GRAND ARMY OF THE REPUBLIC TO COUNTER THE INCREASING THREATS OF THE SEPARATISTS.

IT IS DONE, THEN.

I WILL TAKE THE JEDI WE HAVE LEFT AND GO TO GEONOSIS AND HELP OBI-WAN.

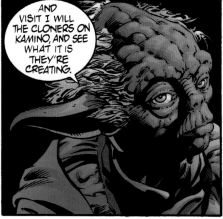

AND VISIT I WILL THE CLONERS ON KAMINO, AND SEE WHAT IT IS THEY'RE CREATING.

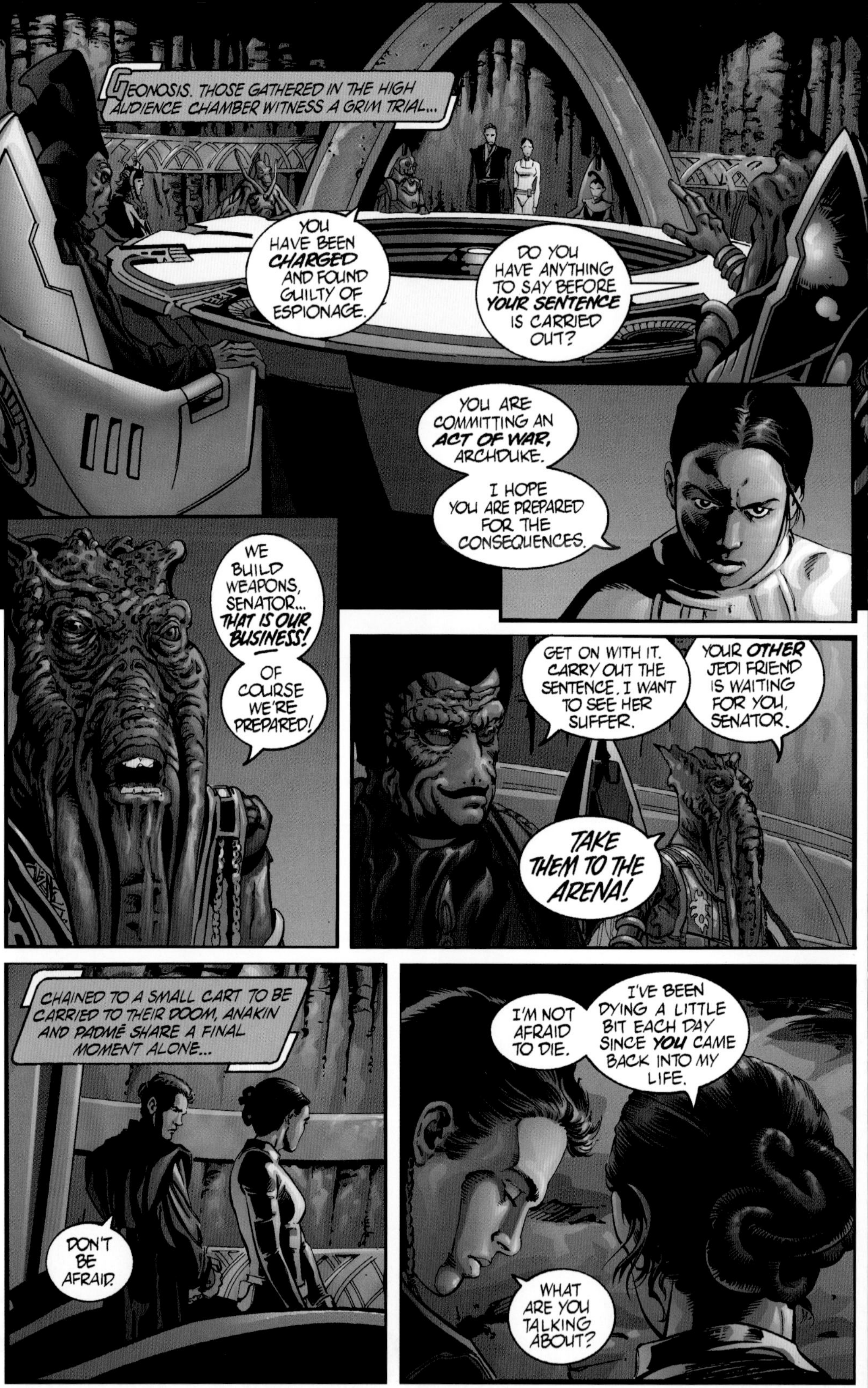
GEONOSIS. THOSE GATHERED IN THE HIGH AUDIENCE CHAMBER WITNESS A GRIM TRIAL...
YOU HAVE BEEN CHARGED AND FOUND GUILTY OF ESPIONAGE.
DO YOU HAVE ANYTHING TO SAY BEFORE YOUR SENTENCE IS CARRIED OUT?
YOU ARE COMMITTING AN ACT OF WAR, ARCHDUKE.
I HOPE YOU ARE PREPARED FOR THE CONSEQUENCES.
WE BUILD WEAPONS, SENATOR... THAT IS OUR BUSINESS!
OF COURSE WE'RE PREPARED!
GET ON WITH IT. CARRY OUT THE SENTENCE. I WANT TO SEE HER SUFFER.
YOUR OTHER JEDI FRIEND IS WAITING FOR YOU, SENATOR.
TAKE THEM TO THE ARENA!
CHAINED TO A SMALL CART TO BE CARRIED TO THEIR DOOM, ANAKIN AND PADMÉ SHARE A FINAL MOMENT ALONE...
DON'T BE AFRAID.
I'M NOT AFRAID TO DIE.
I'VE BEEN DYING A LITTLE BIT EACH DAY SINCE YOU CAME BACK INTO MY LIFE.
WHAT ARE YOU TALKING ABOUT?

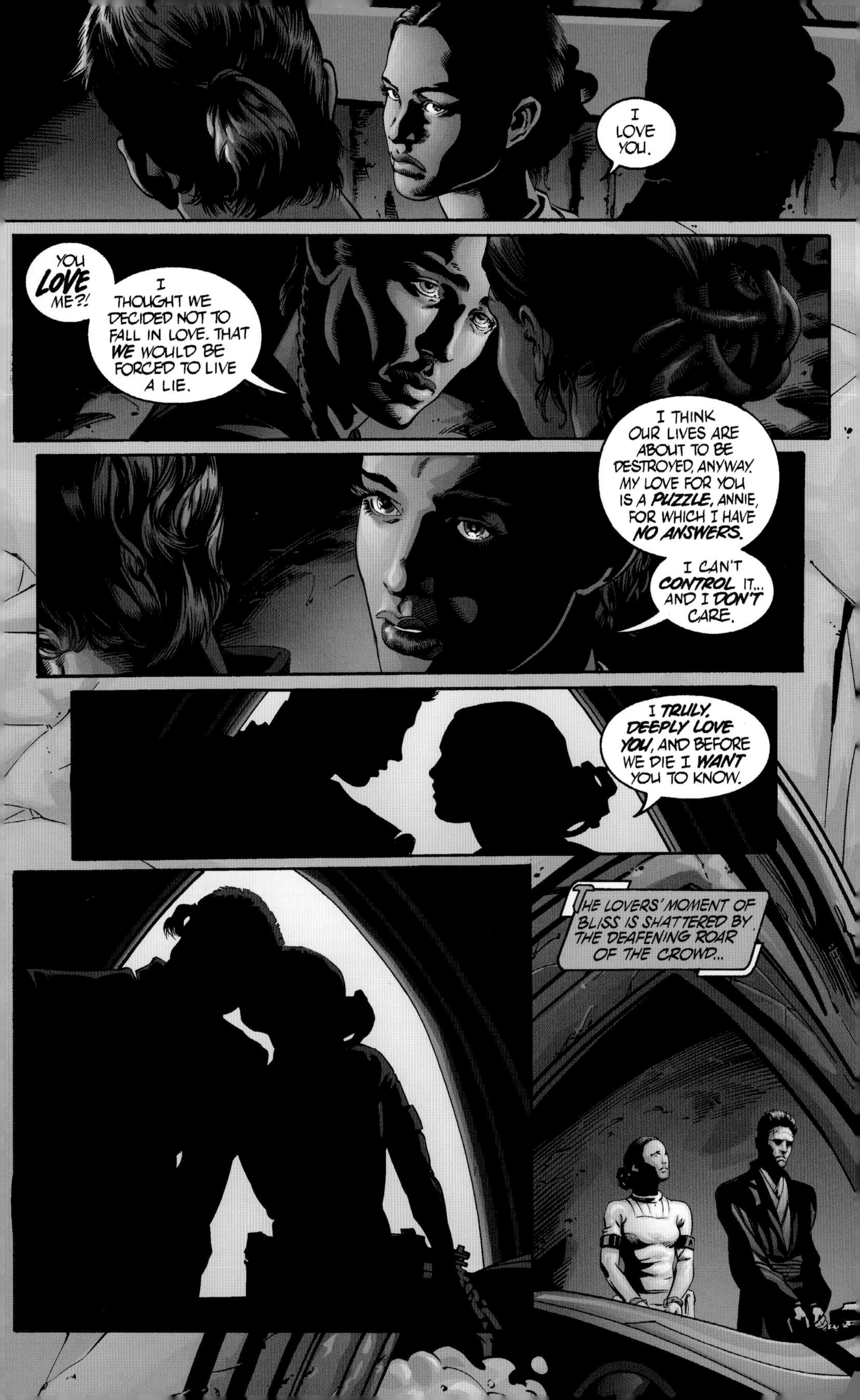

I LOVE YOU.
YOU LOVE ME?!
I THOUGHT WE DECIDED NOT TO FALL IN LOVE. THAT WE WOULD BE FORCED TO LIVE A LIE.
I THINK OUR LIVES ARE ABOUT TO BE DESTROYED, ANYWAY. MY LOVE FOR YOU IS A PUZZLE, ANNIE, FOR WHICH I HAVE NO ANSWERS.
I CAN'T CONTROL IT... AND I DON'T CARE.
I TRULY, DEEPLY LOVE YOU, AND BEFORE WE DIE I WANT YOU TO KNOW.
THE LOVERS' MOMENT OF BLISS IS SHATTERED BY THE DEAFENING ROAR OF THE CROWD...

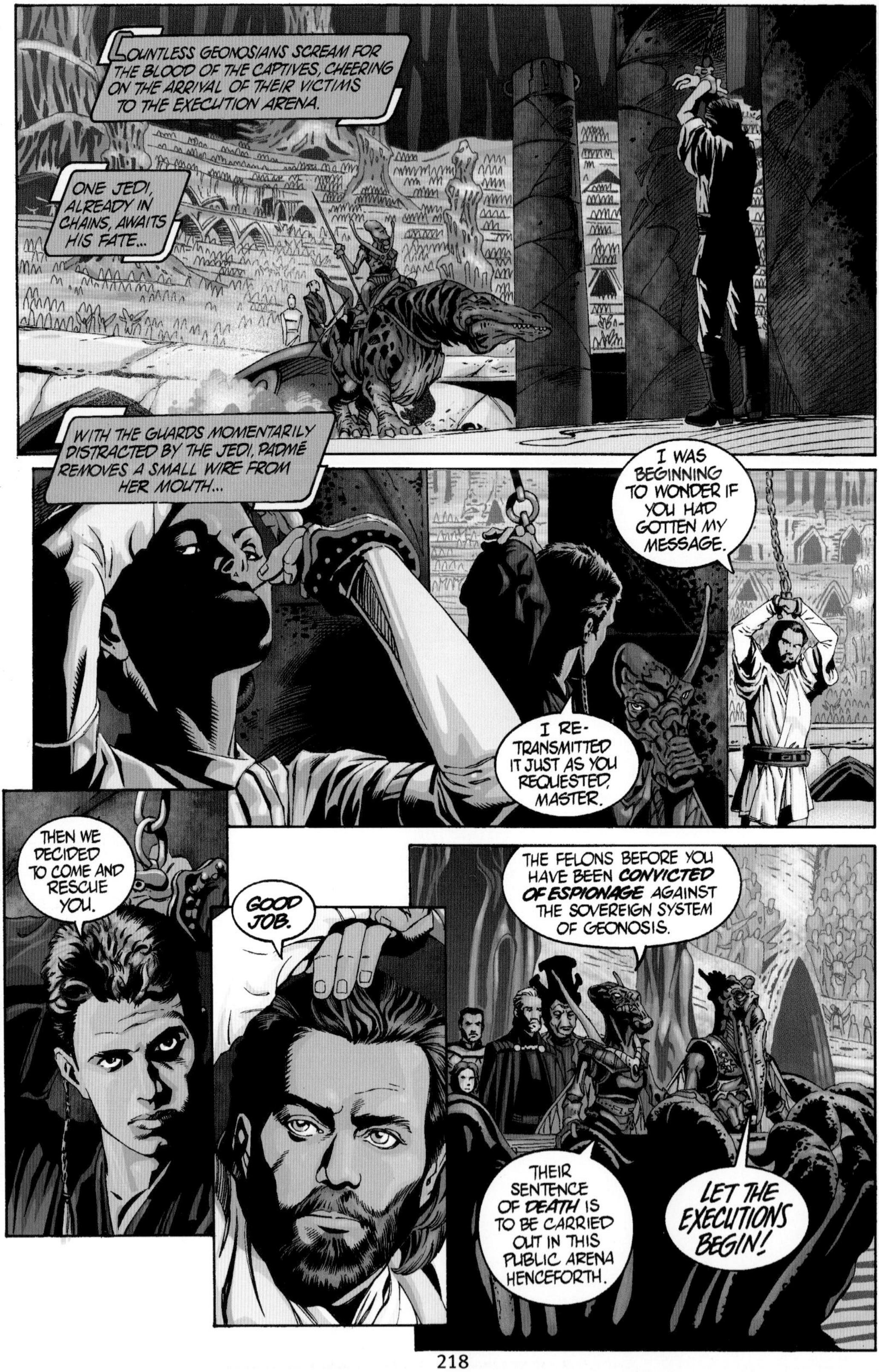
COUNTLESS GEONOSIANS SCREAM FOR THE BLOOD OF THE CAPTIVES, CHEERING ON THE ARRIVAL OF THEIR VICTIMS TO THE EXECUTION ARENA.
ONE JEDI, ALREADY IN CHAINS, AWAITS HIS FATE...
WITH THE GUARDS MOMENTARILY DISTRACTED BY THE JEDI, PADMÉ REMOVES A SMALL WIRE FROM HER MOUTH...
I WAS BEGINNING TO WONDER IF YOU HAD GOTTEN MY MESSAGE.
I RE-TRANSMITTED IT JUST AS YOU REQUESTED, MASTER.
THEN WE DECIDED TO COME AND RESCUE YOU.
GOOD JOB.
THE FELONS BEFORE YOU HAVE BEEN CONVICTED OF ESPIONAGE AGAINST THE SOVEREIGN SYSTEM OF GEONOSIS.
THEIR SENTENCE OF DEATH IS TO BE CARRIED OUT IN THIS PUBLIC ARENA HENCEFORTH.
LET THE EXECUTIONS BEGIN!

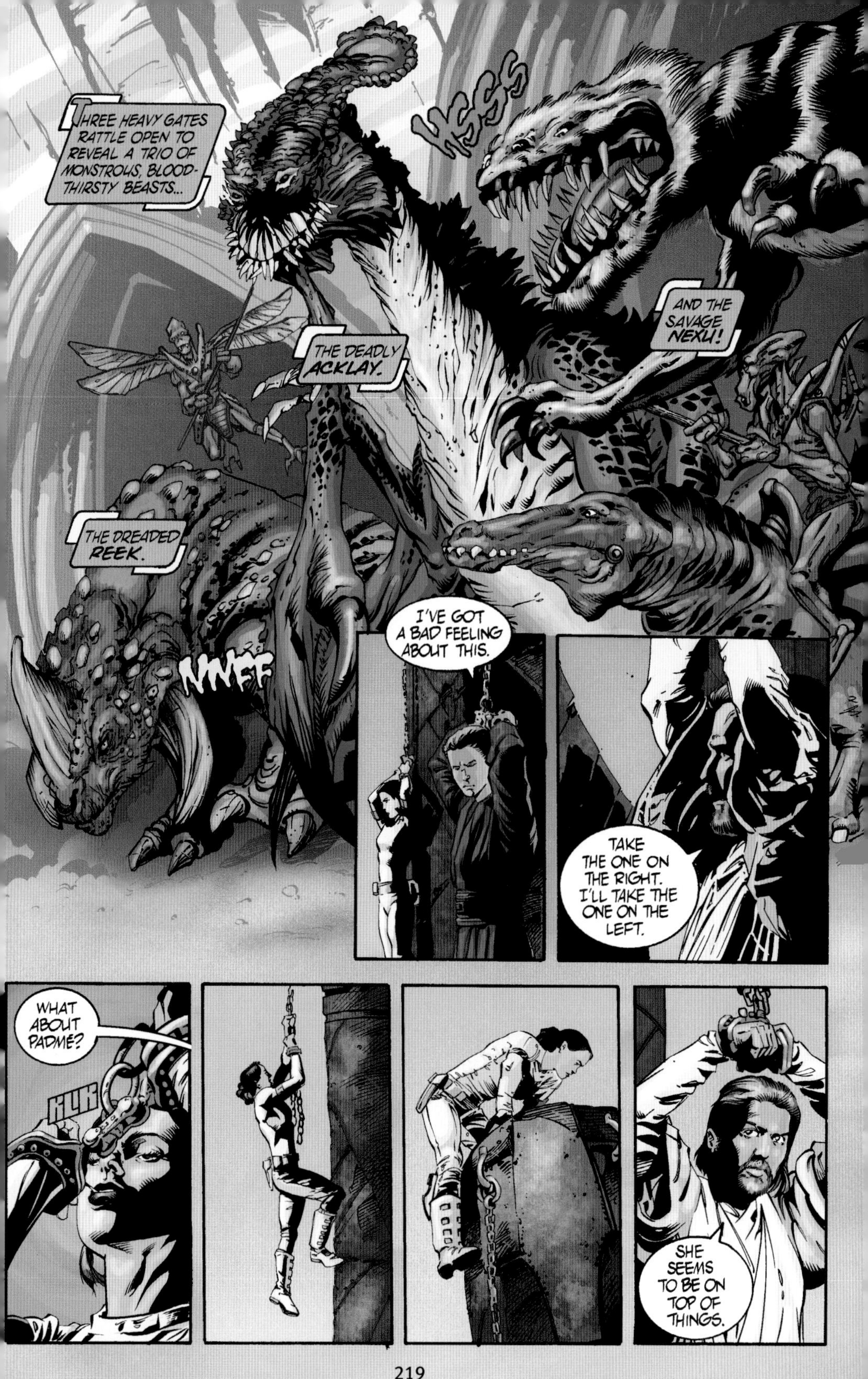
THREE HEAVY GATES RATTLE OPEN TO REVEAL A TRIO OF MONSTROUS, BLOOD-THIRSTY BEASTS...
HSSS
THE DEADLY ACKLAY.
AND THE SAVAGE NEXU!
THE DREADED REEK.
NNFF
I'VE GOT A BAD FEELING ABOUT THIS.
TAKE THE ONE ON THE RIGHT. I'LL TAKE THE ONE ON THE LEFT.
WHAT ABOUT PADMÉ?
KLIK
SHE SEEMS TO BE ON TOP OF THINGS.

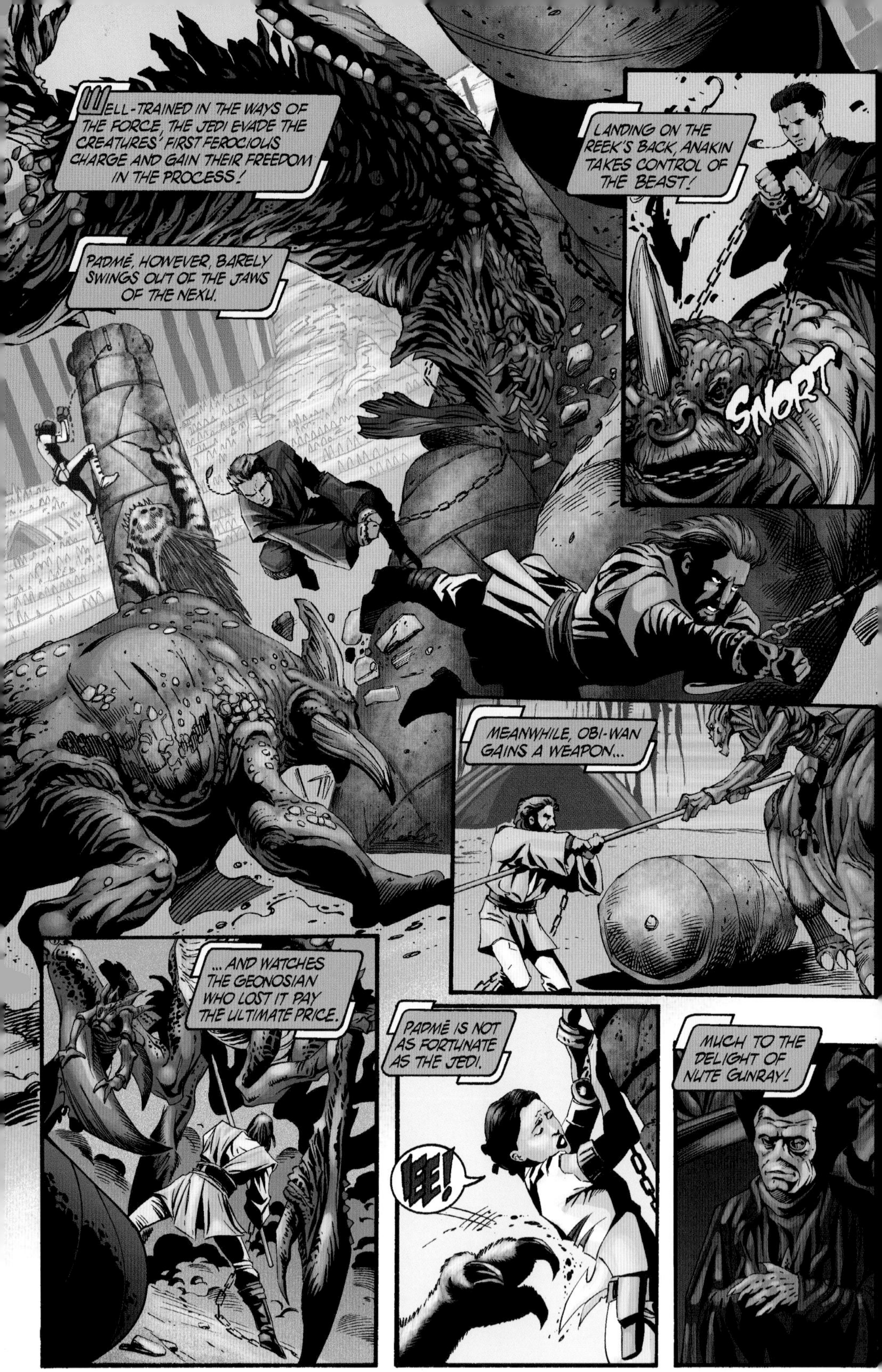
WELL-TRAINED IN THE WAYS OF THE FORCE, THE JEDI EVADE THE CREATURES' FIRST FEROCIOUS CHARGE AND GAIN THEIR FREEDOM IN THE PROCESS!
LANDING ON THE REEK'S BACK, ANAKIN TAKES CONTROL OF THE BEAST!
PADMÉ, HOWEVER, BARELY SWINGS OUT OF THE JAWS OF THE NEXU.
SNORT
MEANWHILE, OBI-WAN GAINS A WEAPON...
... AND WATCHES THE GEONOSIAN WHO LOST IT PAY THE ULTIMATE PRICE.
PADMÉ IS NOT AS FORTUNATE AS THE JEDI.
IEEE!
MUCH TO THE DELIGHT OF NUTE GUNRAY!

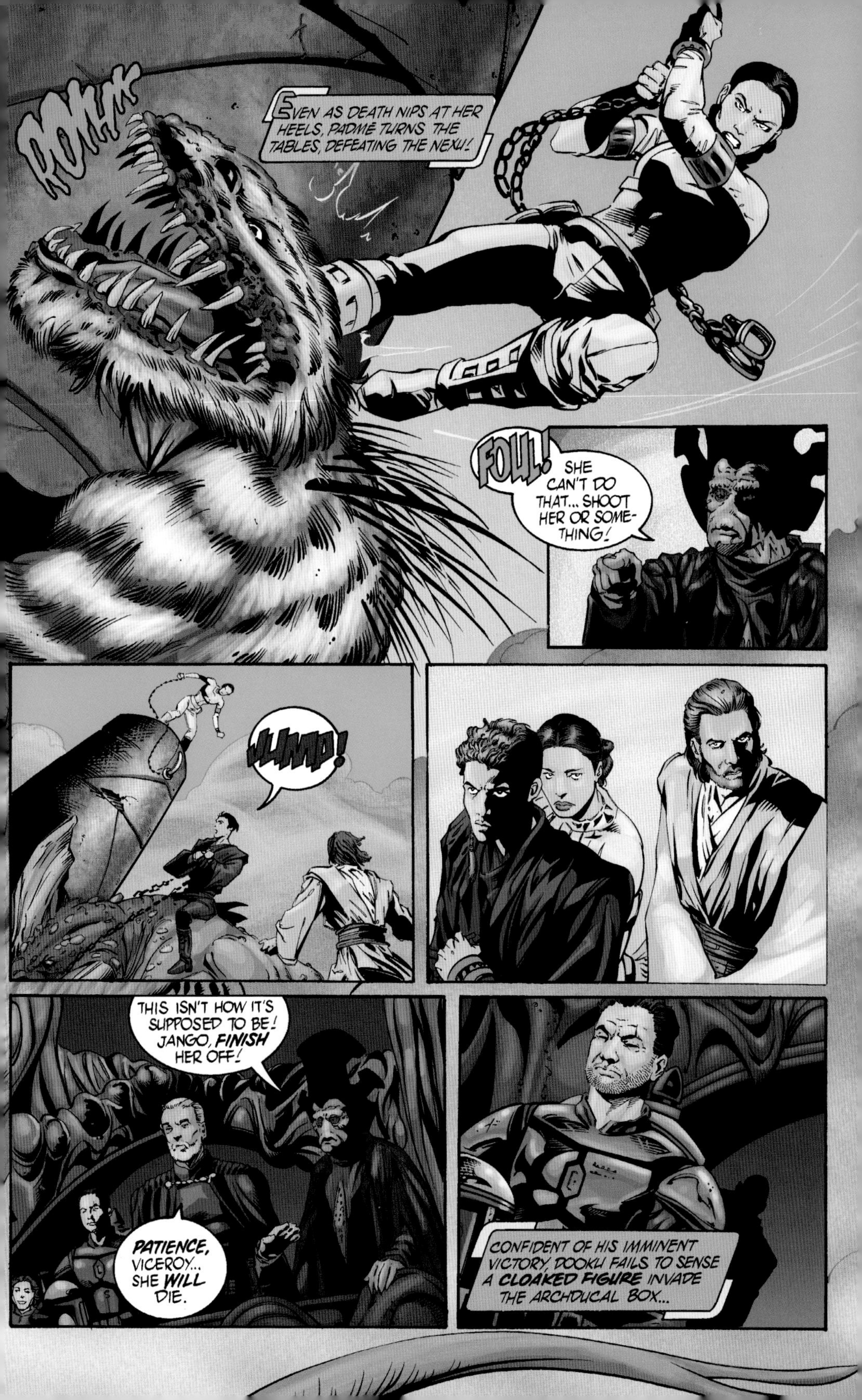
ROWR
EVEN AS DEATH NIPS AT HER HEELS, PADMÉ TURNS THE TABLES, DEFEATING THE NEXU!
FOUL!
SHE CAN'T DO THAT... SHOOT HER OR SOME-THING!
JUMP!
THIS ISN'T HOW IT'S SUPPOSED TO BE! JANGO, FINISH HER OFF!
PATIENCE, VICEROY... SHE WILL DIE.
CONFIDENT OF HIS IMMINENT VICTORY, DOOKU FAILS TO SENSE A CLOAKED FIGURE INVADE THE ARCHDUCAL BOX...

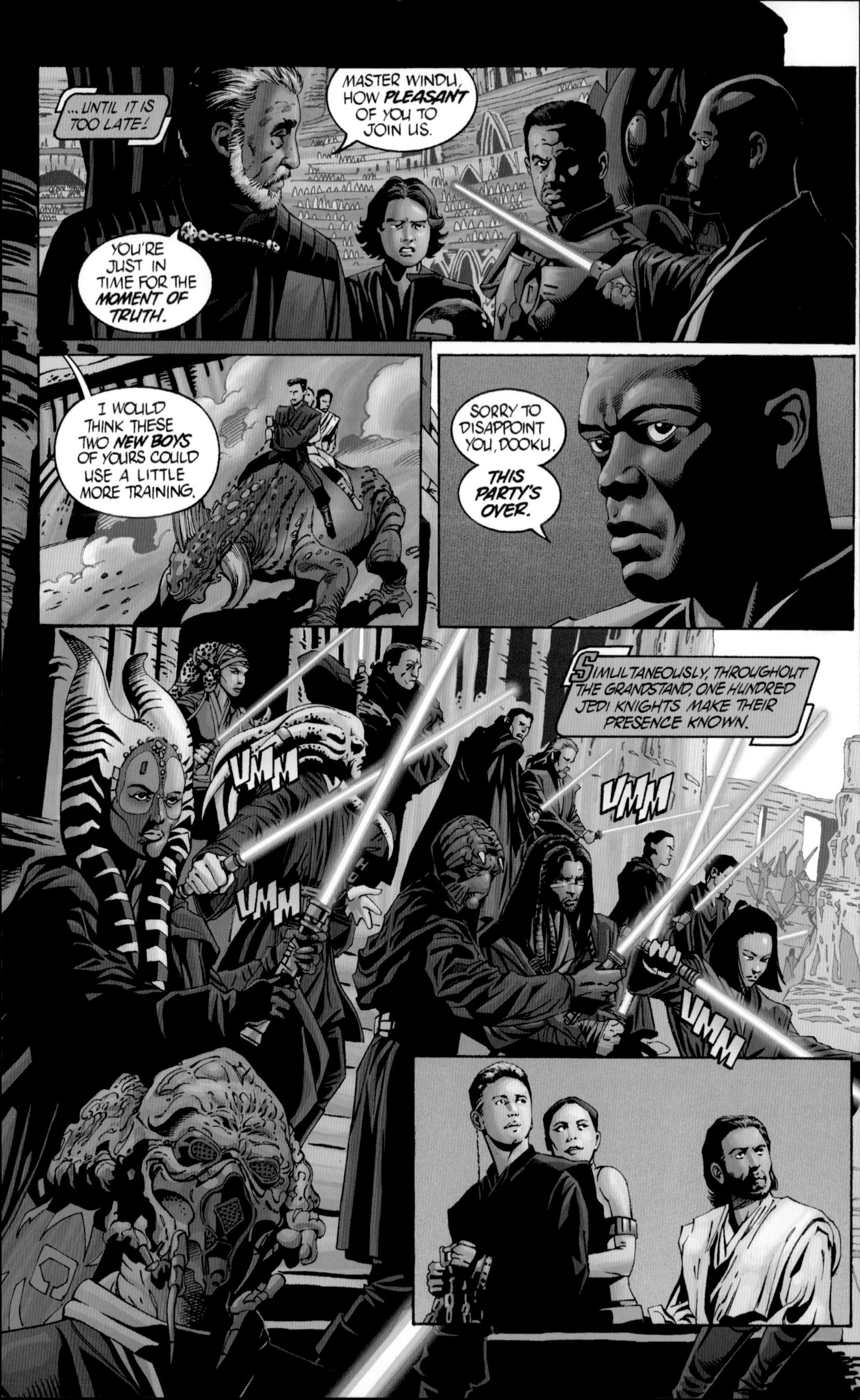
...UNTIL IT IS TOO LATE!
MASTER WINDU, HOW *PLEASANT* OF YOU TO JOIN US.
YOU'RE JUST IN TIME FOR THE *MOMENT OF TRUTH.*
I WOULD THINK THESE TWO *NEW BOYS* OF YOURS COULD USE A LITTLE MORE TRAINING.
SORRY TO DISAPPOINT YOU, DOOKU.
THIS PARTY'S OVER.
SIMULTANEOUSLY, THROUGHOUT THE GRANDSTAND, ONE HUNDRED JEDI KNIGHTS MAKE THEIR PRESENCE KNOWN.
UMM
UMM
UMM
UMM

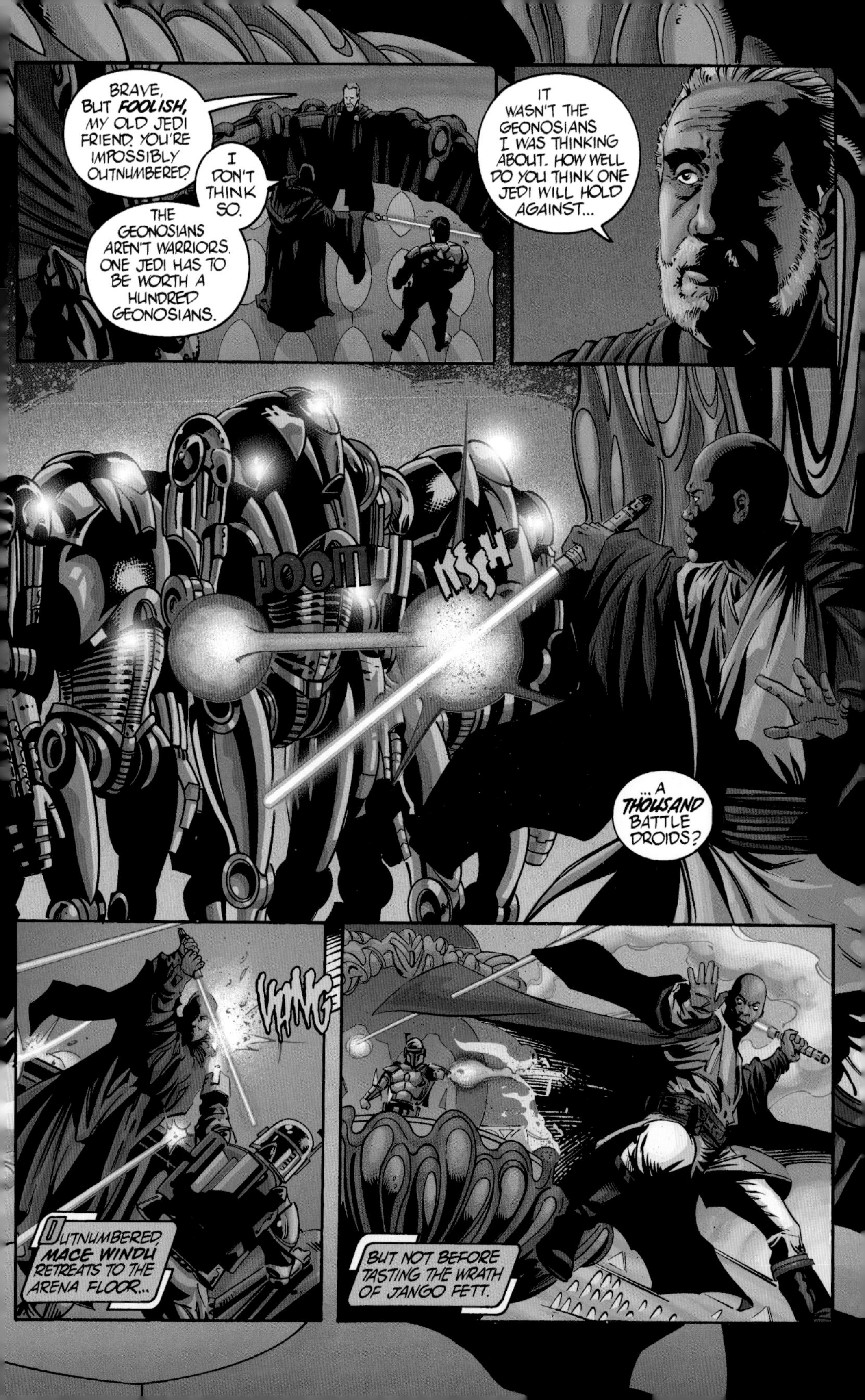
BRAVE, BUT FOOLISH, MY OLD JEDI FRIEND. YOU'RE IMPOSSIBLY OUTNUMBERED.
I DON'T THINK SO.
THE GEONOSIANS AREN'T WARRIORS. ONE JEDI HAS TO BE WORTH A HUNDRED GEONOSIANS.
IT WASN'T THE GEONOSIANS I WAS THINKING ABOUT. HOW WELL DO YOU THINK ONE JEDI WILL HOLD AGAINST...
POOM
KSSH
...A THOUSAND BATTLE DROIDS?
VWANG
OUTNUMBERED, MACE WINDU RETREATS TO THE ARENA FLOOR...
BUT NOT BEFORE TASTING THE WRATH OF JANGO FETT.

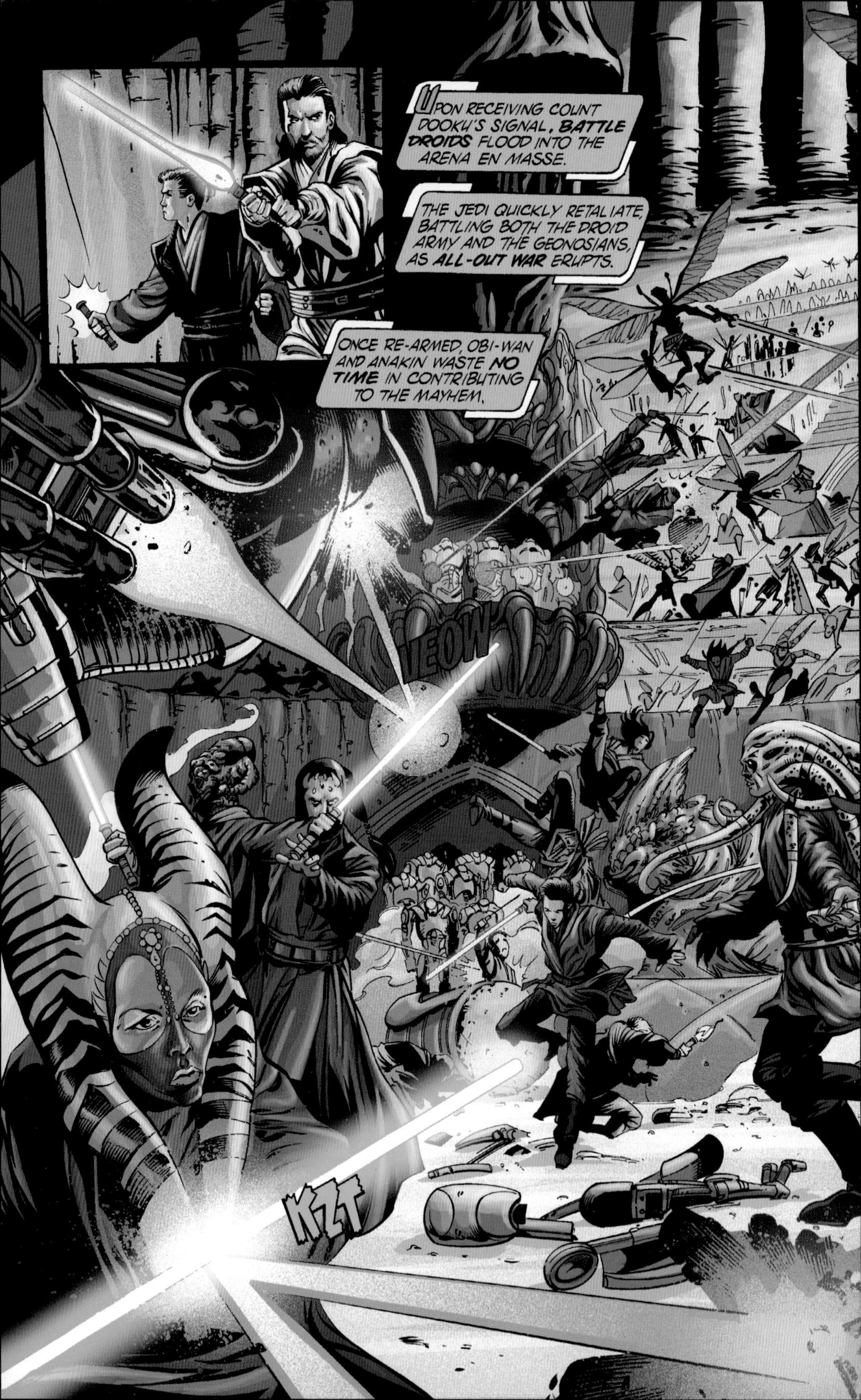
UPON RECEIVING COUNT DOOKU'S SIGNAL, BATTLE DROIDS FLOOD INTO THE ARENA EN MASSE.
THE JEDI QUICKLY RETALIATE, BATTLING BOTH THE DROID ARMY AND THE GEONOSIANS, AS ALL-OUT WAR ERUPTS.
ONCE RE-ARMED, OBI-WAN AND ANAKIN WASTE NO TIME IN CONTRIBUTING TO THE MAYHEM.
VEOW
KZT

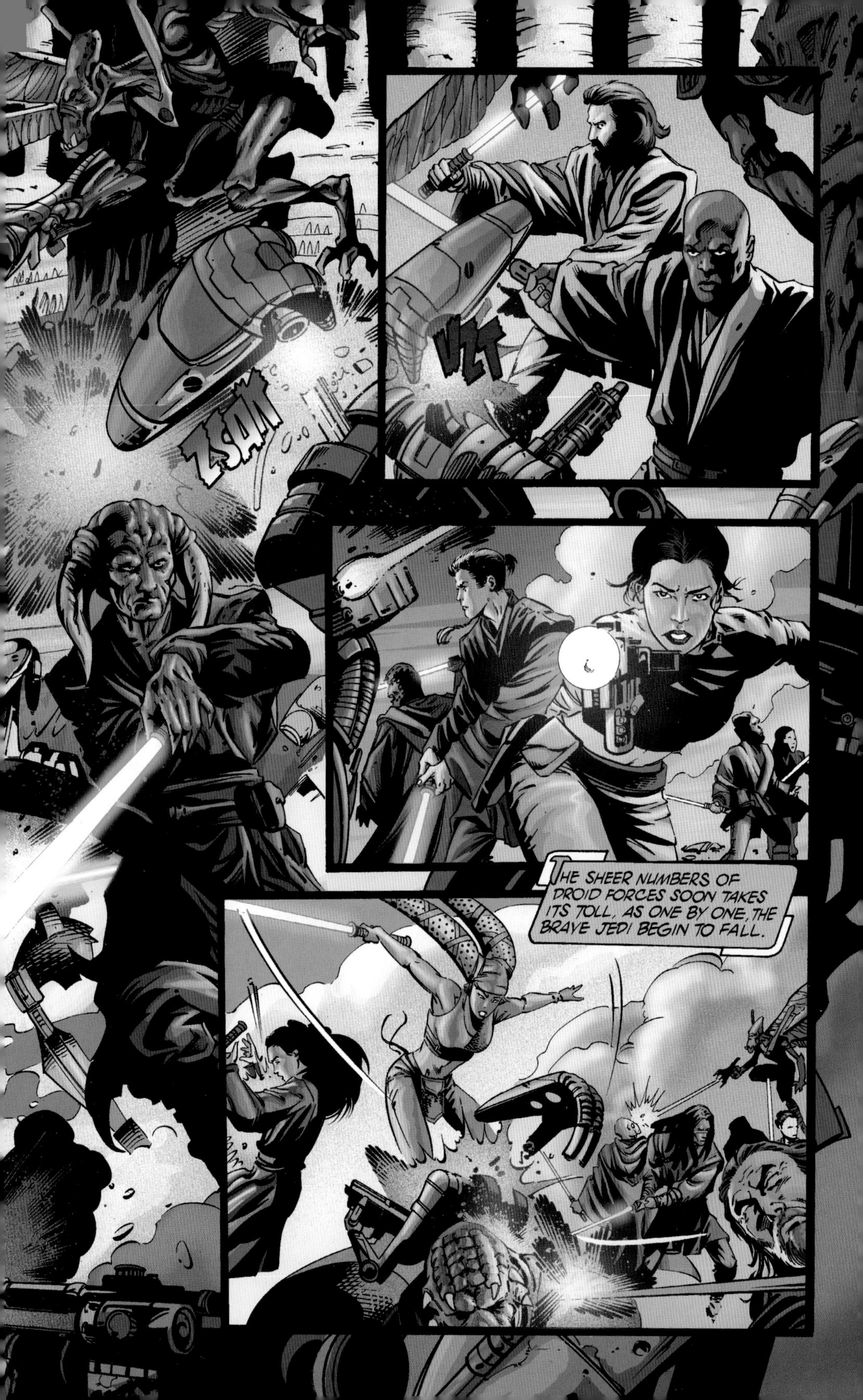
ZSAK
VZT
THE SHEER NUMBERS OF DROID FORCES SOON TAKES ITS TOLL, AS ONE BY ONE, THE BRAVE JEDI BEGIN TO FALL.

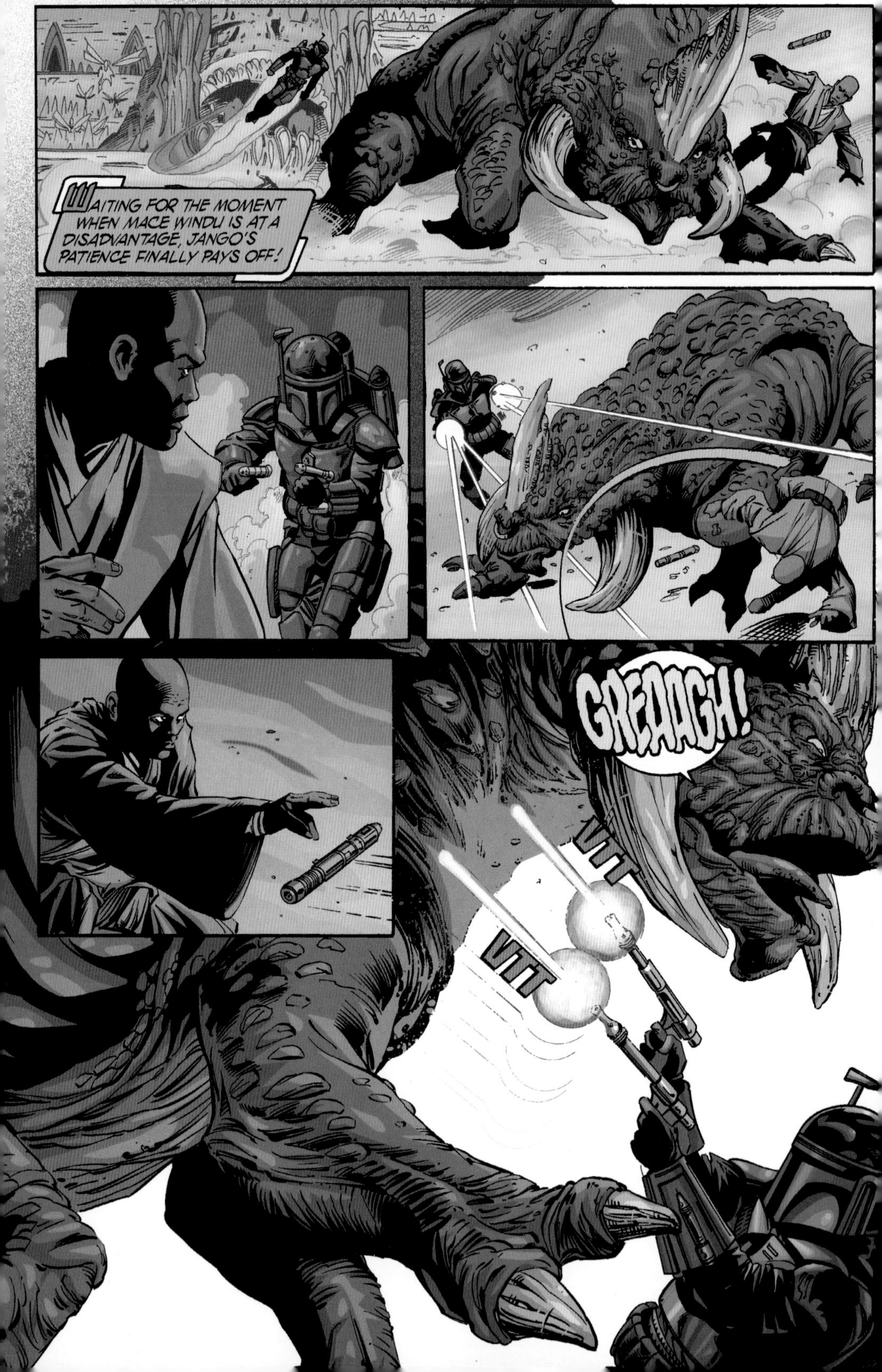
WAITING FOR THE MOMENT WHEN MACE WINDU IS AT A DISADVANTAGE, JANGO'S PATIENCE FINALLY PAYS OFF!
GREAAGH!
VIT
VIT

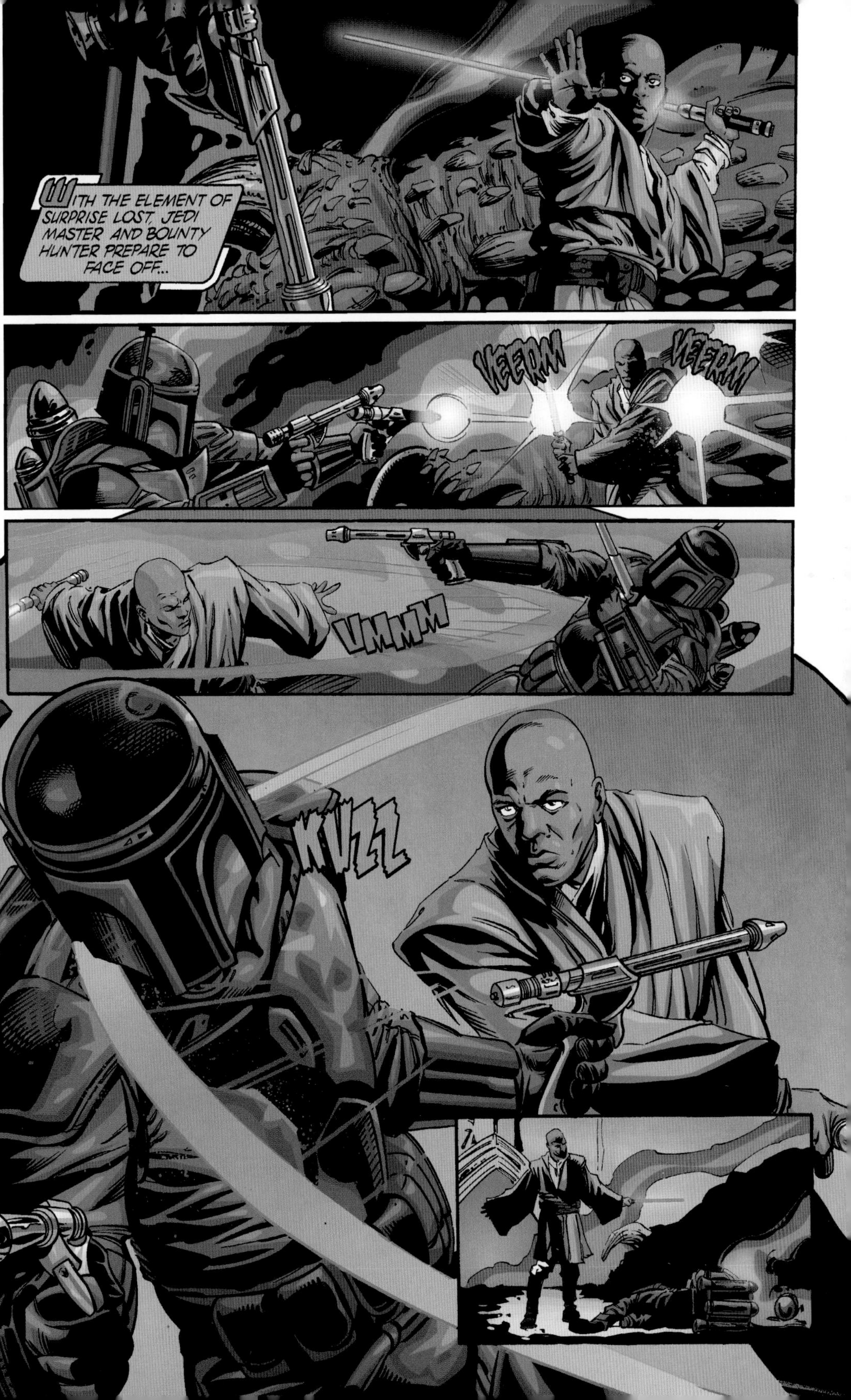
WITH THE ELEMENT OF SURPRISE LOST, JEDI MASTER AND BOUNTY HUNTER PREPARE TO FACE OFF...
VEEERM
VEEERM
UMMM
KVZZ

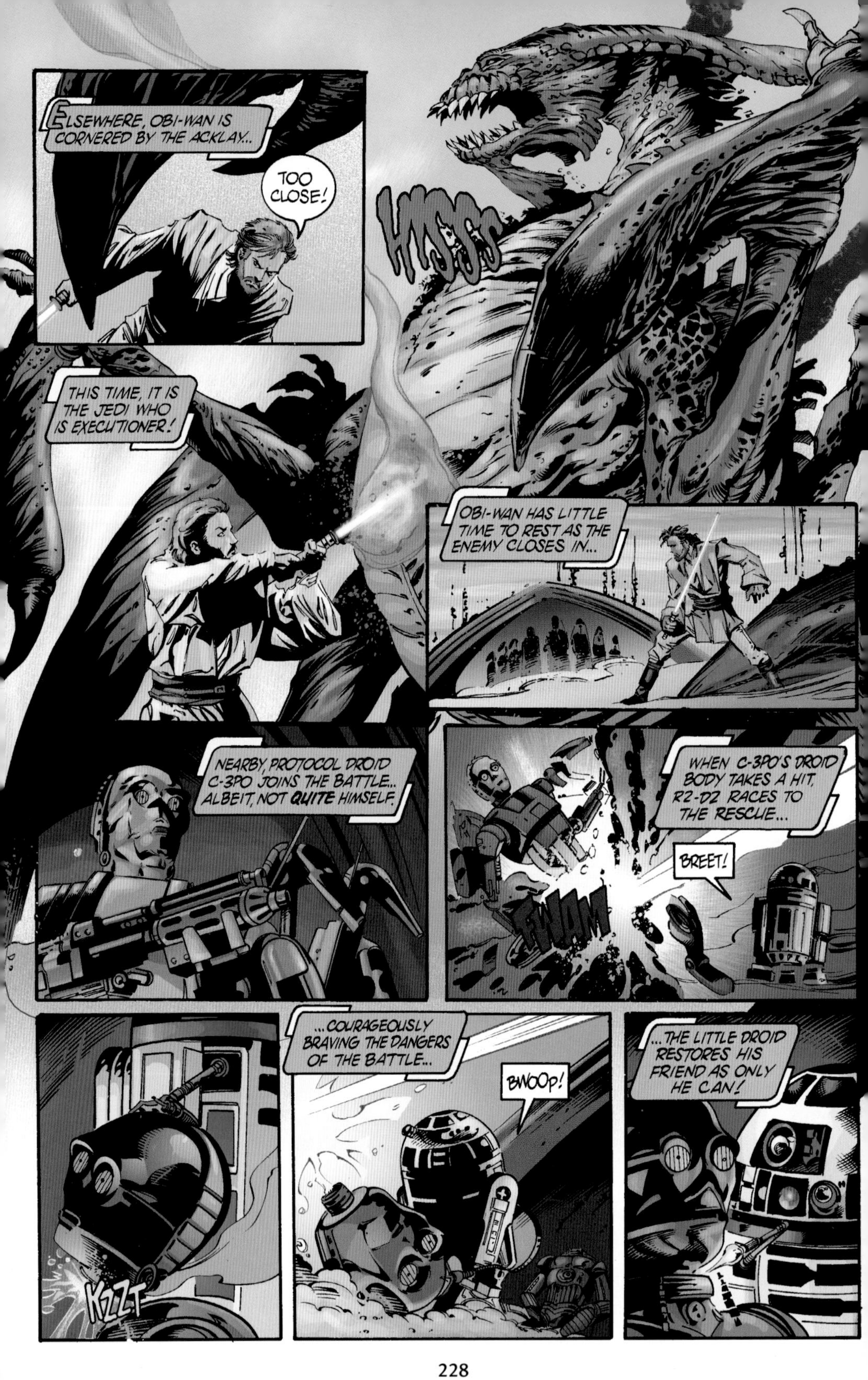
ELSEWHERE, OBI-WAN IS CORNERED BY THE ACKLAY...
TOO CLOSE!
HISSSS
THIS TIME, IT IS THE JEDI WHO IS EXECUTIONER!
OBI-WAN HAS LITTLE TIME TO REST AS THE ENEMY CLOSES IN...
NEARBY, PROTOCOL DROID C-3PO JOINS THE BATTLE... ALBEIT, NOT QUITE HIMSELF.
WHEN C-3PO'S DROID BODY TAKES A HIT, R2-D2 RACES TO THE RESCUE...
BREET!
FWAM
KZZT
...COURAGEOUSLY BRAVING THE DANGERS OF THE BATTLE...
BWOOP!
...THE LITTLE DROID RESTORES HIS FRIEND AS ONLY HE CAN!

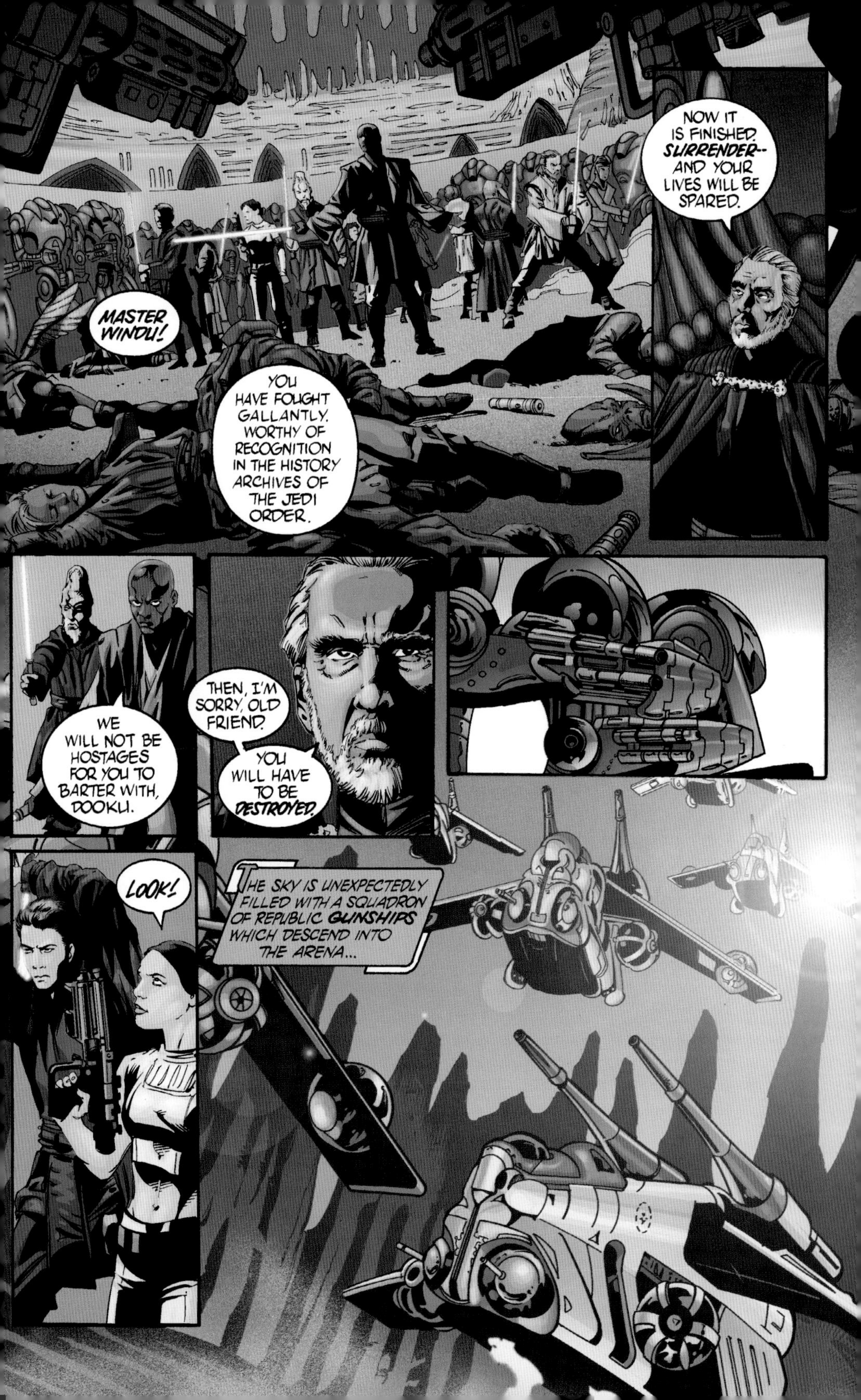
NOW IT IS FINISHED. SURRENDER-- AND YOUR LIVES WILL BE SPARED.
MASTER WINDU!
YOU HAVE FOUGHT GALLANTLY. WORTHY OF RECOGNITION IN THE HISTORY ARCHIVES OF THE JEDI ORDER.
WE WILL NOT BE HOSTAGES FOR YOU TO BARTER WITH, DOOKU.
THEN, I'M SORRY, OLD FRIEND.
YOU WILL HAVE TO BE DESTROYED.
LOOK!
THE SKY IS UNEXPECTEDLY FILLED WITH A SQUADRON OF REPUBLIC GUNSHIPS WHICH DESCEND INTO THE ARENA...

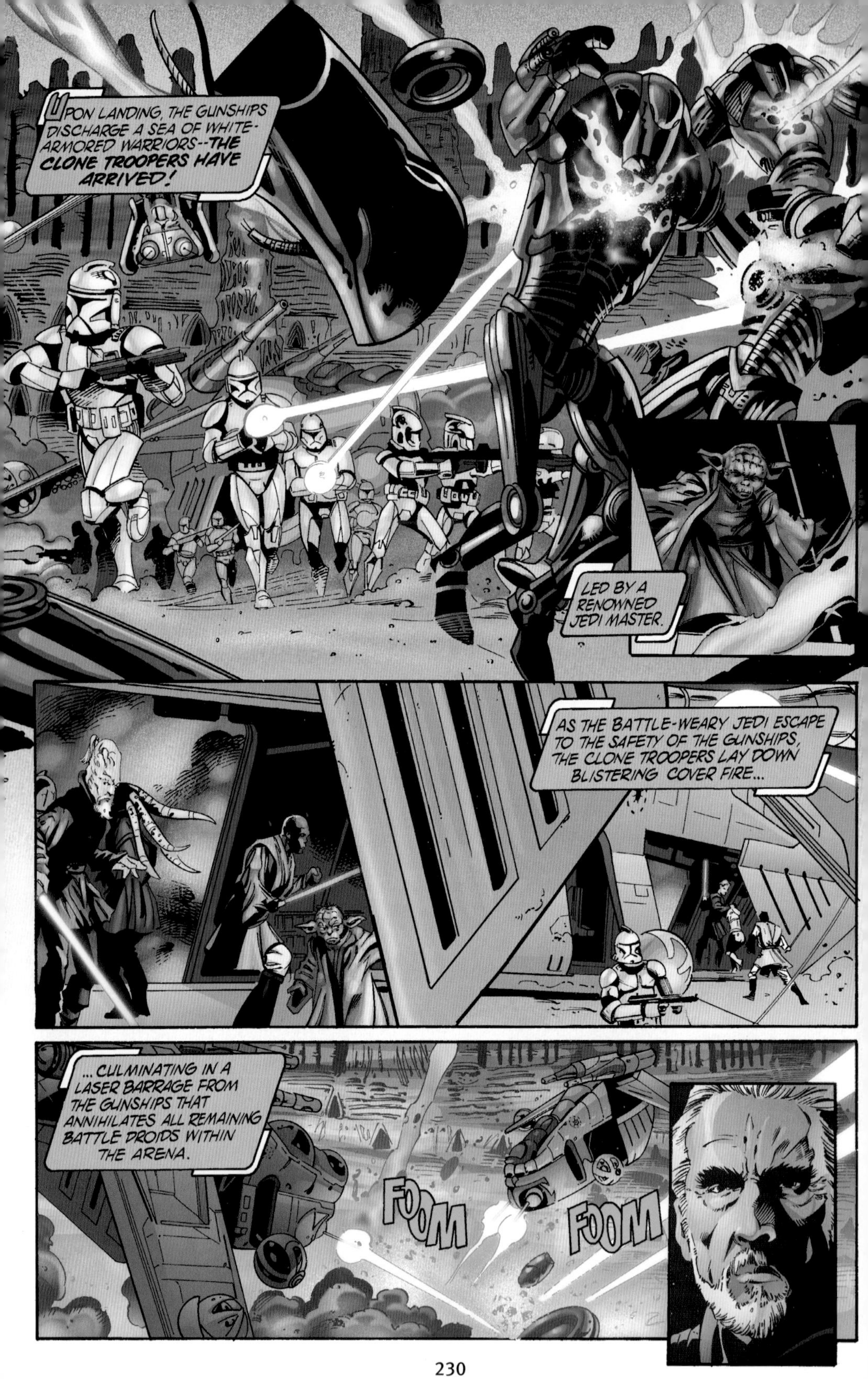
UPON LANDING, THE GUNSHIPS DISCHARGE A SEA OF WHITE-ARMORED WARRIORS--THE CLONE TROOPERS HAVE ARRIVED!
LED BY A RENOWNED JEDI MASTER.
AS THE BATTLE-WEARY JEDI ESCAPE TO THE SAFETY OF THE GUNSHIPS, THE CLONE TROOPERS LAY DOWN BLISTERING COVER FIRE...
...CULMINATING IN A LASER BARRAGE FROM THE GUNSHIPS THAT ANNIHILATES ALL REMAINING BATTLE DROIDS WITHIN THE ARENA.
FOOM
FOOM

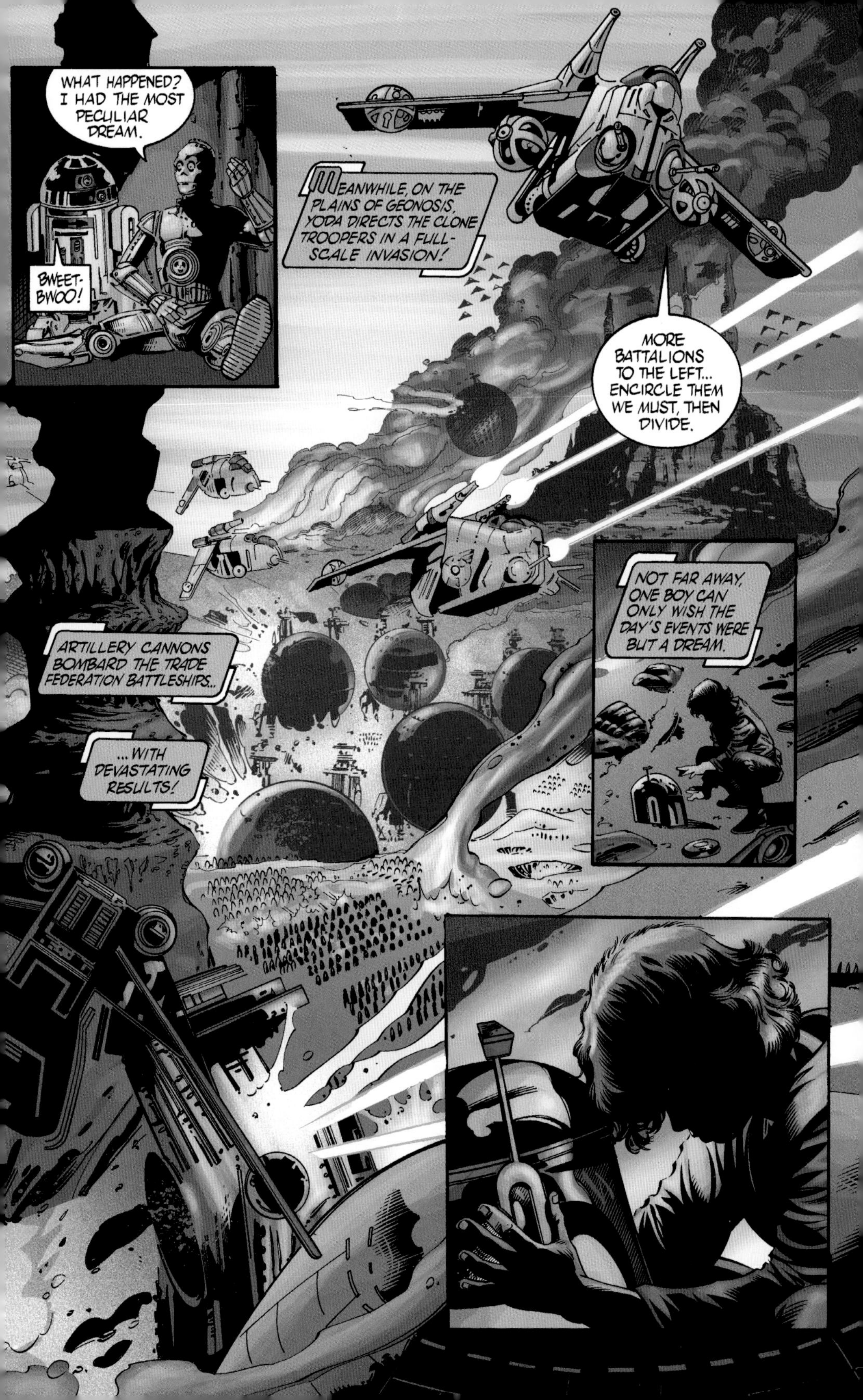
WHAT HAPPENED? I HAD THE MOST PECULIAR DREAM.
BWEET-BWOO!
MEANWHILE, ON THE PLAINS OF GEONOSIS, YODA DIRECTS THE CLONE TROOPERS IN A FULL-SCALE INVASION!
MORE BATTALIONS TO THE LEFT... ENCIRCLE THEM WE MUST, THEN DIVIDE.
ARTILLERY CANNONS BOMBARD THE TRADE FEDERATION BATTLESHIPS...
...WITH DEVASTATING RESULTS!
NOT FAR AWAY, ONE BOY CAN ONLY WISH THE DAY'S EVENTS WERE BUT A DREAM.

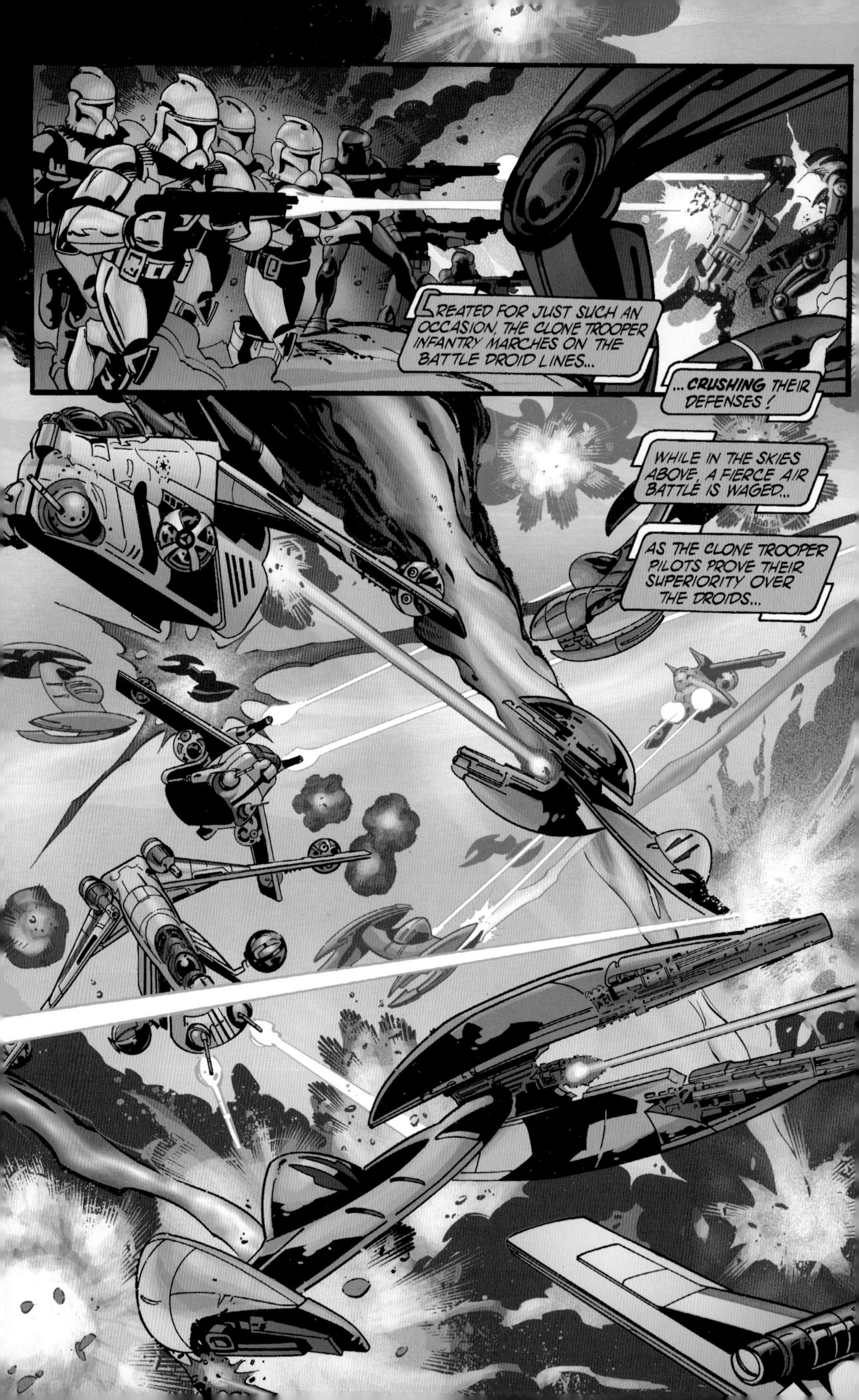
CREATED FOR JUST SUCH AN OCCASION, THE CLONE TROOPER INFANTRY MARCHES ON THE BATTLE DROID LINES...
...CRUSHING THEIR DEFENSES!
WHILE IN THE SKIES ABOVE, A FIERCE AIR BATTLE IS WAGED...
AS THE CLONE TROOPER PILOTS PROVE THEIR SUPERIORITY OVER THE DROIDS...

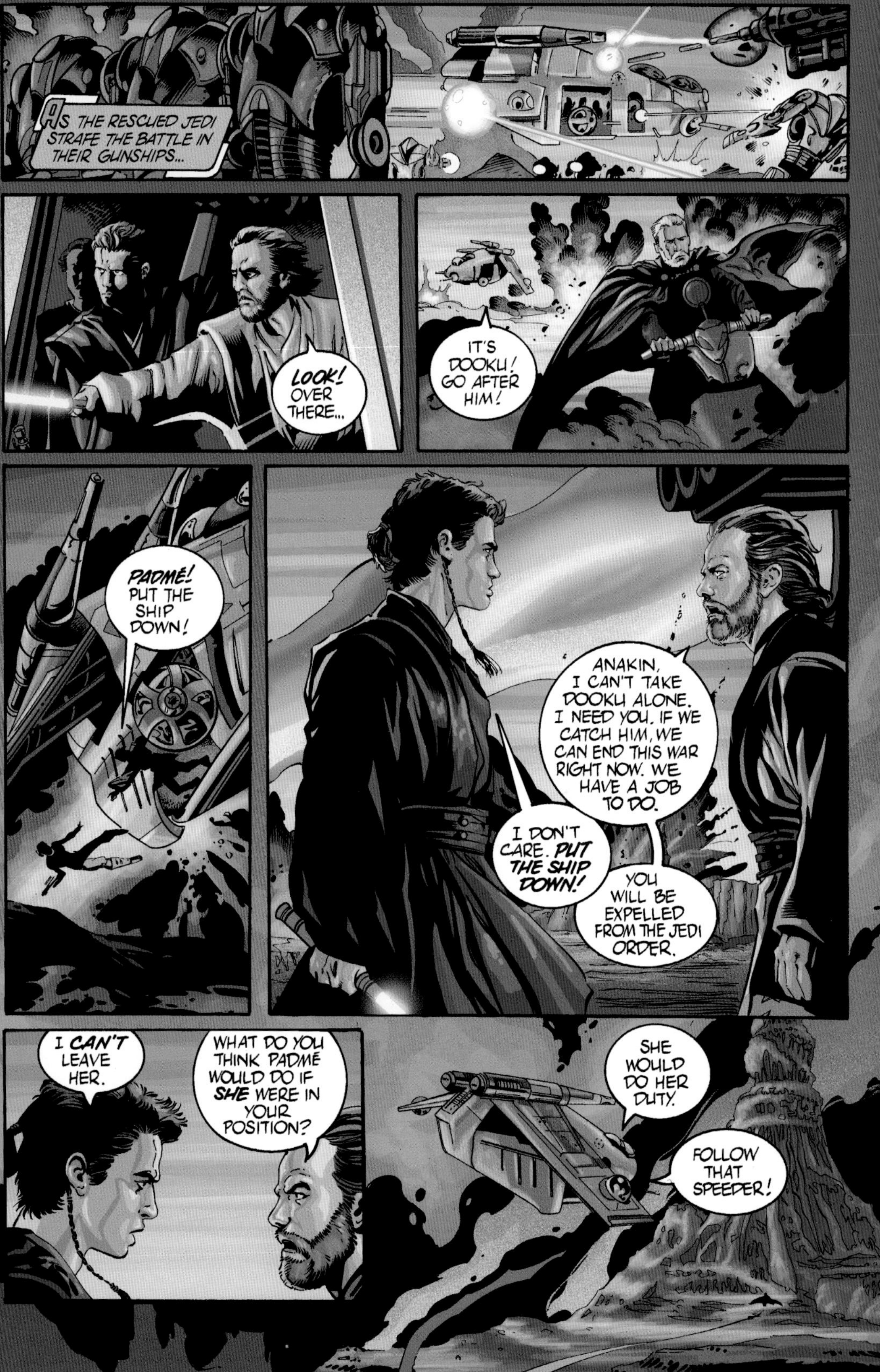
AS THE RESCUED JEDI STRAFE THE BATTLE IN THEIR GUNSHIPS...
LOOK! OVER THERE...
IT'S DOOKU! GO AFTER HIM!
PADMÉ! PUT THE SHIP DOWN!
ANAKIN, I CAN'T TAKE DOOKU ALONE. I NEED YOU. IF WE CATCH HIM, WE CAN END THIS WAR RIGHT NOW. WE HAVE A JOB TO DO.
I DON'T CARE. PUT THE SHIP DOWN!
YOU WILL BE EXPELLED FROM THE JEDI ORDER.
I CAN'T LEAVE HER.
WHAT DO YOU THINK PADMÉ WOULD DO IF SHE WERE IN YOUR POSITION?
SHE WOULD DO HER DUTY.
FOLLOW THAT SPEEDER!

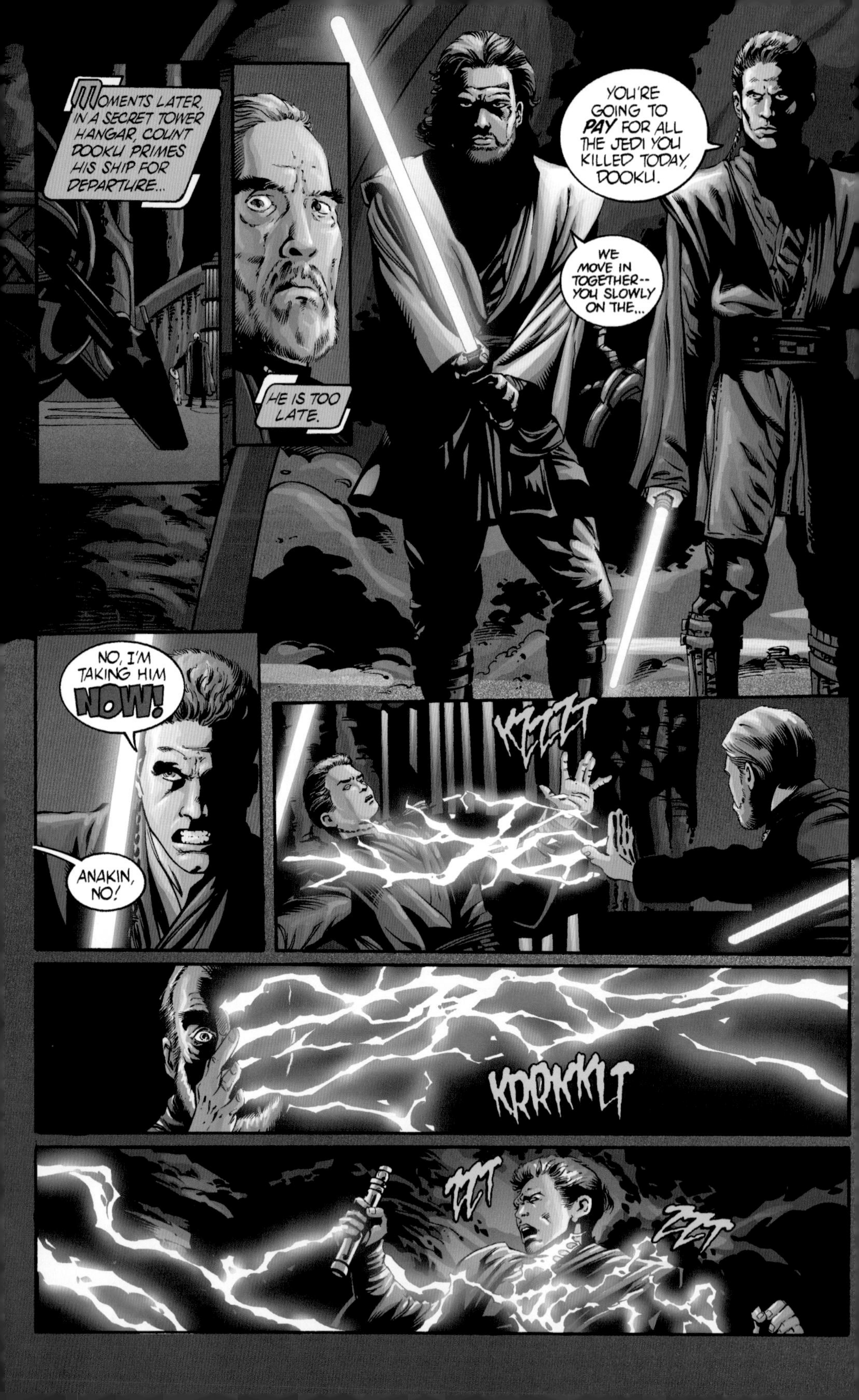
MOMENTS LATER, IN A SECRET TOWER HANGAR, COUNT DOOKU PRIMES HIS SHIP FOR DEPARTURE...
HE IS TOO LATE.
YOU'RE GOING TO PAY FOR ALL THE JEDI YOU KILLED TODAY, DOOKU.
WE MOVE IN TOGETHER-- YOU SLOWLY ON THE...
NO, I'M TAKING HIM NOW!
ANAKIN, NO!
KZZZT
KRRKKLT
ZZZT
ZZZT

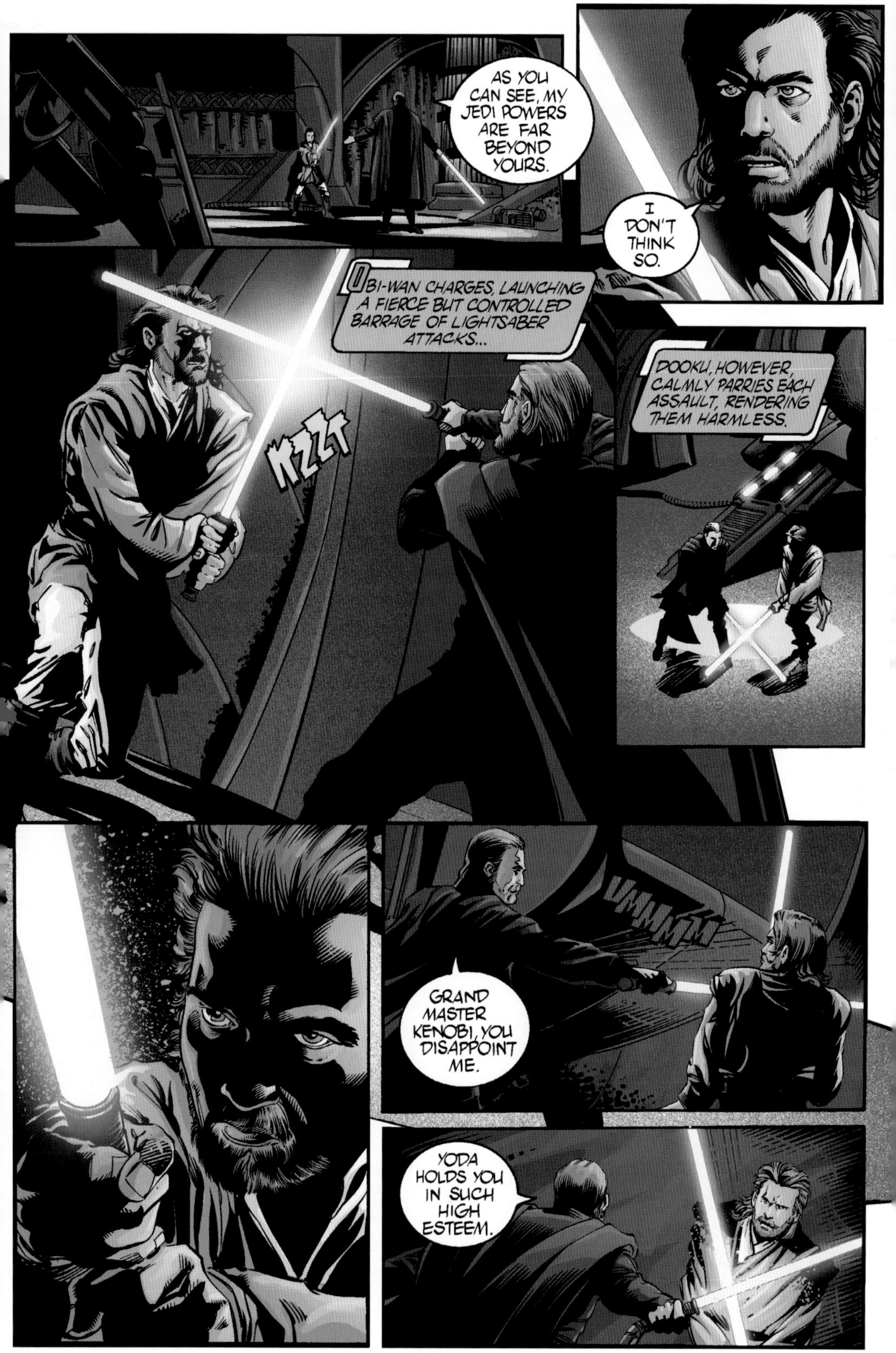

AS YOU CAN SEE, MY JEDI POWERS ARE FAR BEYOND YOURS.
I DON'T THINK SO.
OBI-WAN CHARGES, LAUNCHING A FIERCE BUT CONTROLLED BARRAGE OF LIGHTSABER ATTACKS...
KZZT
DOOKU, HOWEVER, CALMLY PARRIES EACH ASSAULT, RENDERING THEM HARMLESS.
VMMMM
GRAND MASTER KENOBI, YOU DISAPPOINT ME.
YODA HOLDS YOU IN SUCH HIGH ESTEEM.

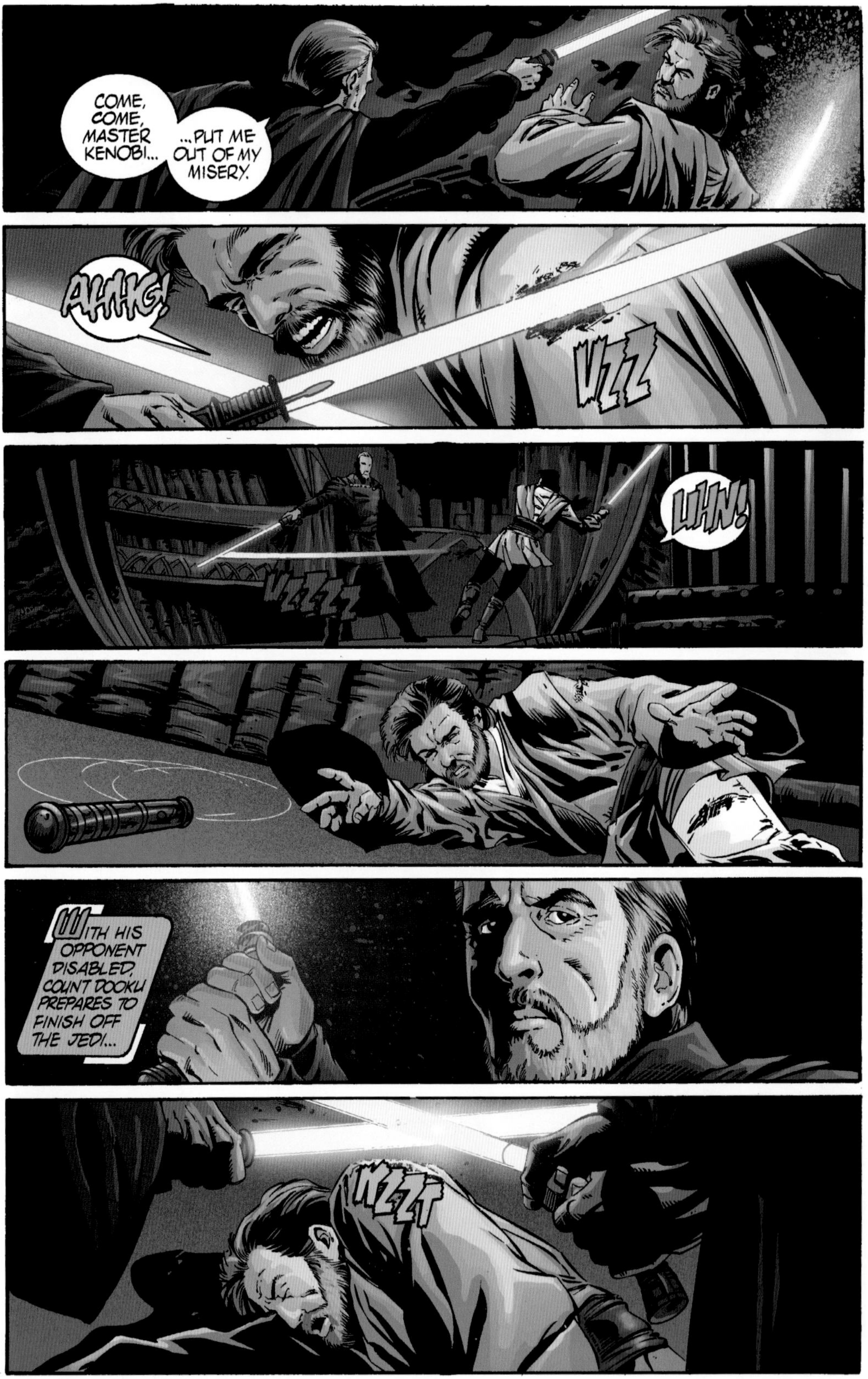
COME, COME, MASTER KENOBI...
...PUT ME OUT OF MY MISERY.
AHHG!
VZZ
UHN!
VZZZZ
WITH HIS OPPONENT DISABLED, COUNT DOOKU PREPARES TO FINISH OFF THE JEDI...
TKZZT

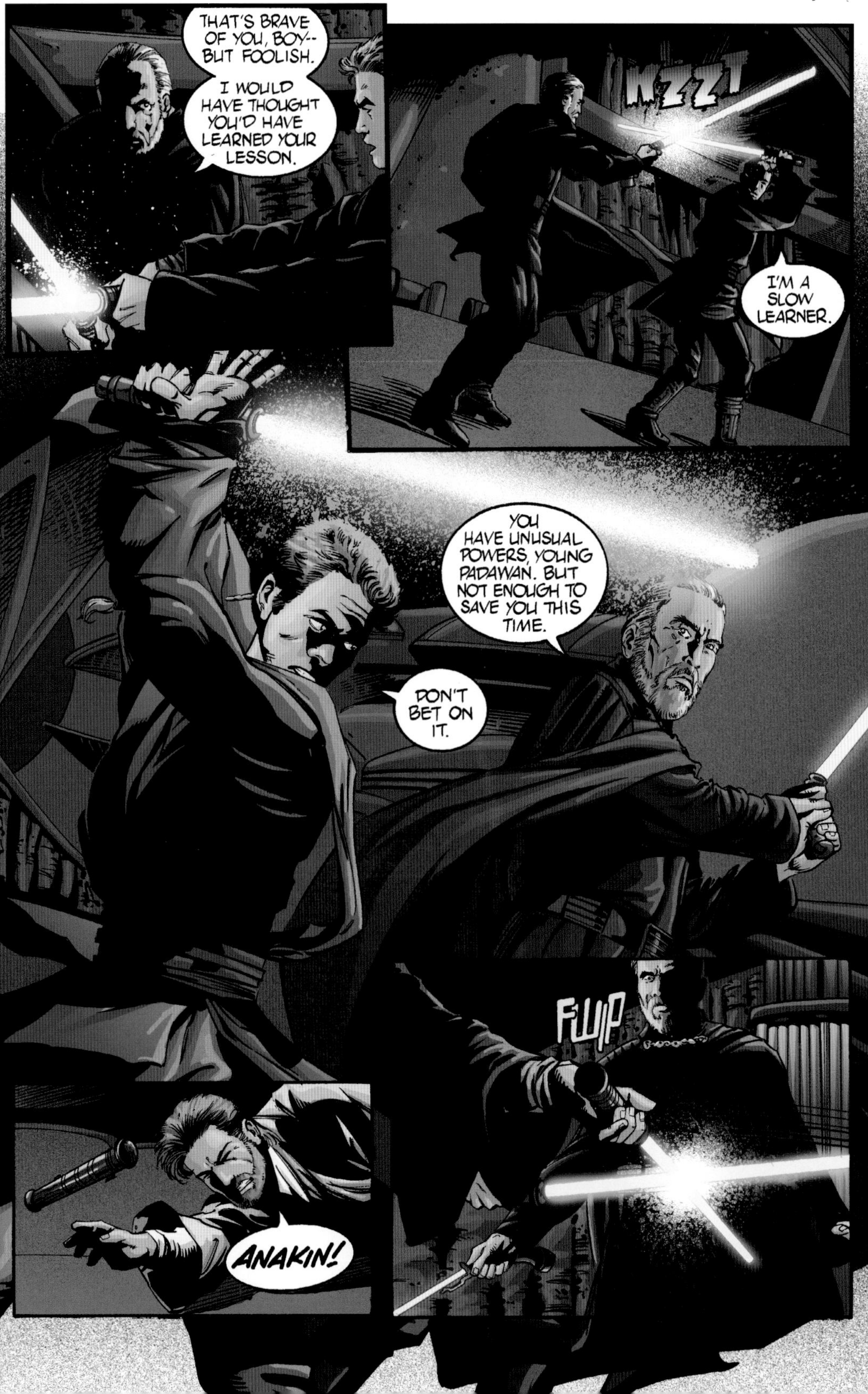
THAT'S BRAVE OF YOU, BOY-- BUT FOOLISH.
I WOULD HAVE THOUGHT YOU'D HAVE LEARNED YOUR LESSON.
NZZT
I'M A SLOW LEARNER.
YOU HAVE UNUSUAL POWERS, YOUNG PADAWAN. BUT NOT ENOUGH TO SAVE YOU THIS TIME.
DON'T BET ON IT.
FWIP
ANAKIN!

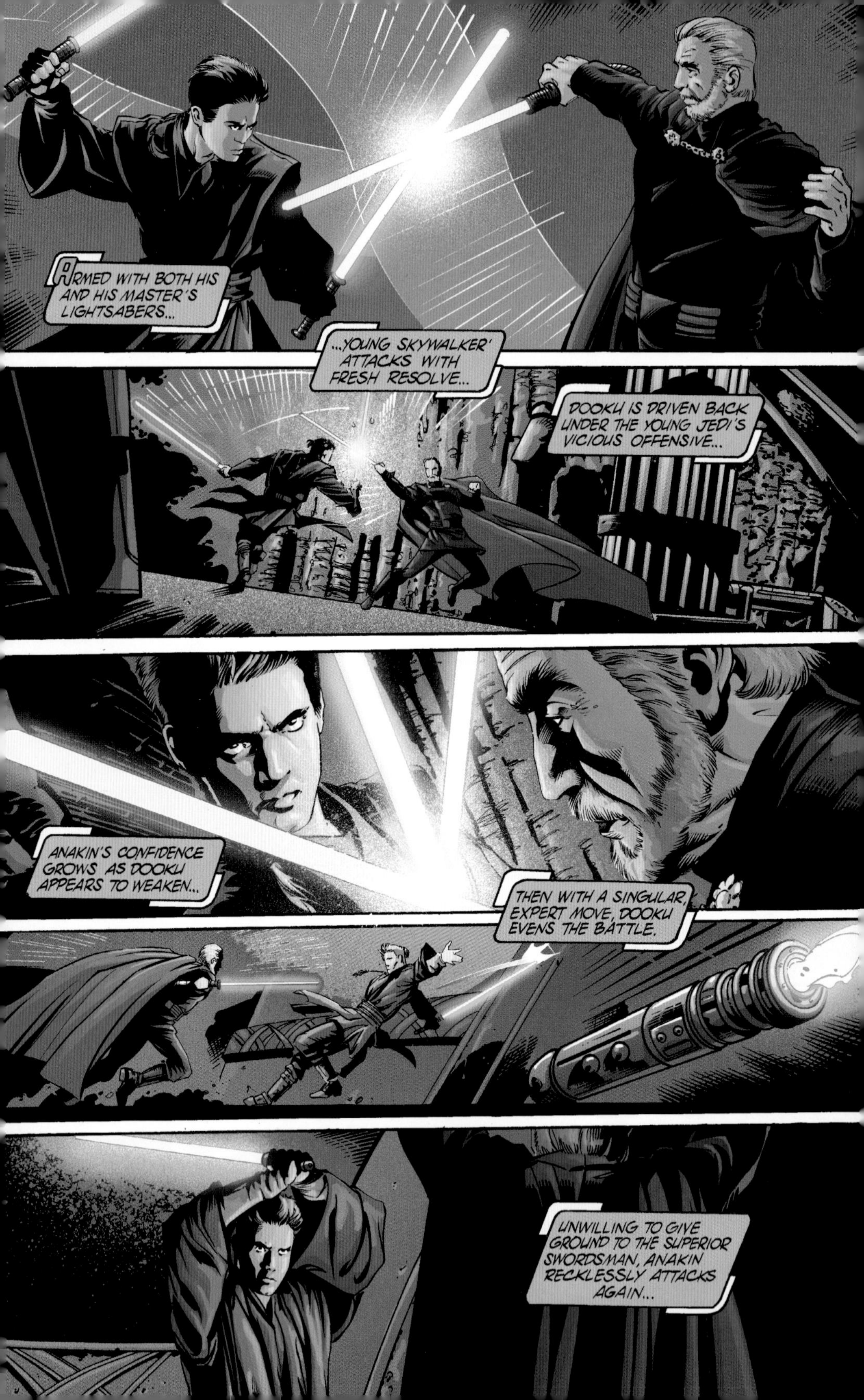
ARMED WITH BOTH HIS AND HIS MASTER'S LIGHTSABERS...
...YOUNG SKYWALKER' ATTACKS WITH FRESH RESOLVE...
DOOKU IS DRIVEN BACK UNDER THE YOUNG JEDI'S VICIOUS OFFENSIVE...
ANAKIN'S CONFIDENCE GROWS AS DOOKU APPEARS TO WEAKEN...
THEN WITH A SINGULAR, EXPERT MOVE, DOOKU EVENS THE BATTLE.
UNWILLING TO GIVE GROUND TO THE SUPERIOR SWORDSMAN, ANAKIN RECKLESSLY ATTACKS AGAIN...

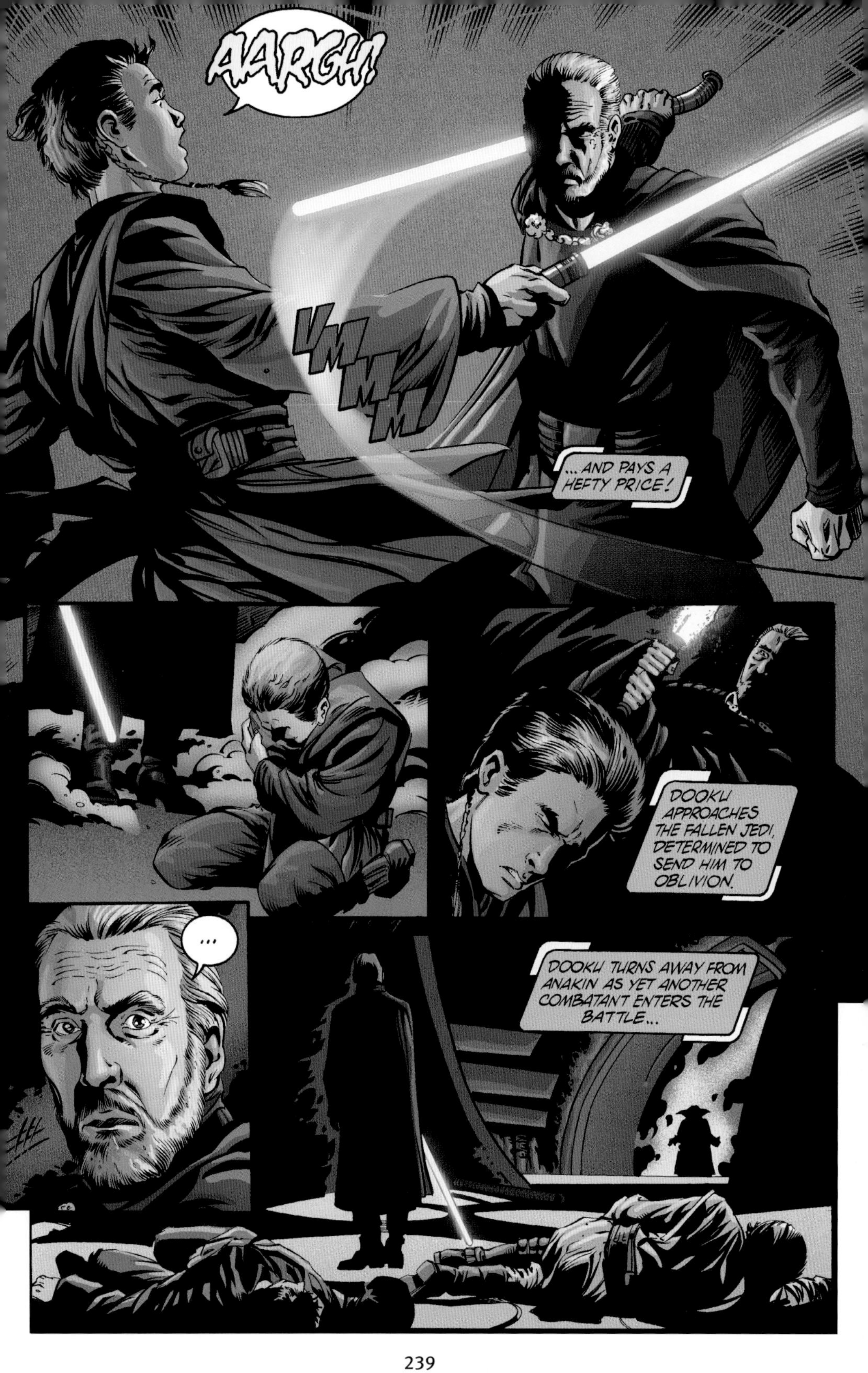
AARGH!
VMMMM
...AND PAYS A HEFTY PRICE!
DOOKU APPROACHES THE FALLEN JEDI, DETERMINED TO SEND HIM TO OBLIVION.
...
DOOKU TURNS AWAY FROM ANAKIN AS YET ANOTHER COMBATANT ENTERS THE BATTLE...

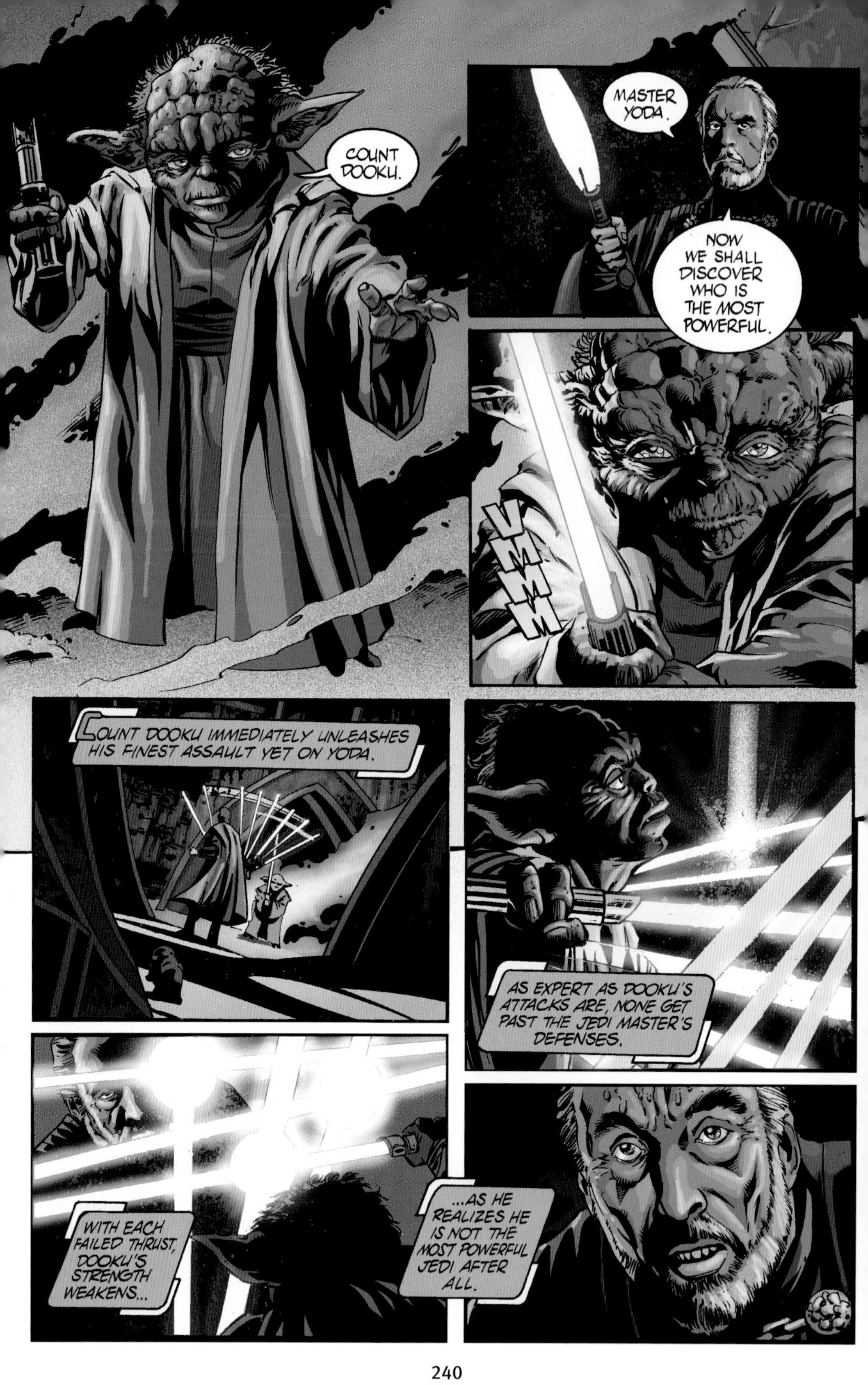
COUNT DOOKU.
MASTER YODA.
NOW WE SHALL DISCOVER WHO IS THE MOST POWERFUL.
VMMMM
COUNT DOOKU IMMEDIATELY UNLEASHES HIS FINEST ASSAULT YET ON YODA.
AS EXPERT AS DOOKU'S ATTACKS ARE, NONE GET PAST THE JEDI MASTER'S DEFENSES.
WITH EACH FAILED THRUST, DOOKU'S STRENGTH WEAKENS...
...AS HE REALIZES HE IS NOT THE MOST POWERFUL JEDI AFTER ALL.

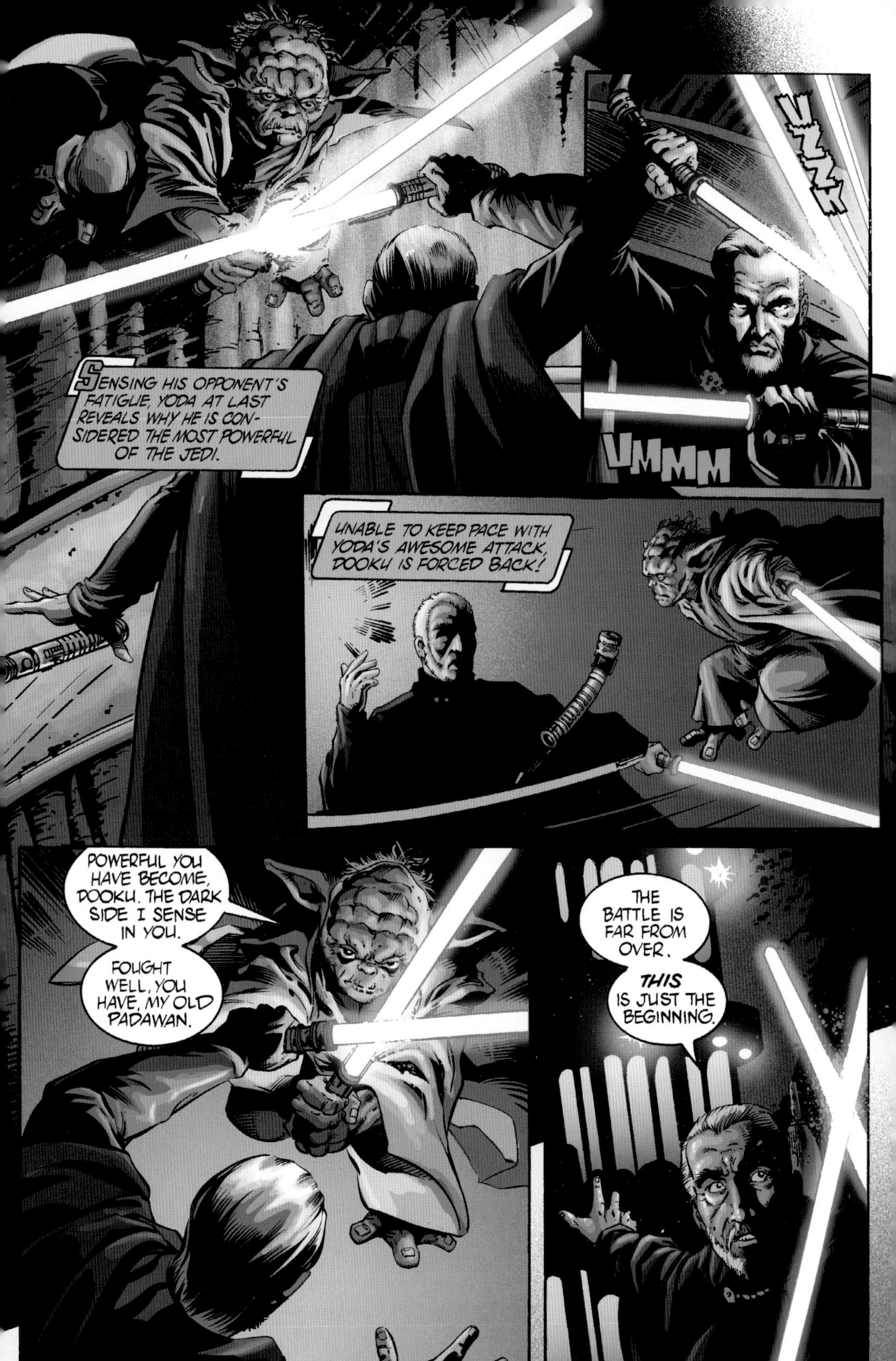
VNNK
SENSING HIS OPPONENT'S FATIGUE, YODA AT LAST REVEALS WHY HE IS CONSIDERED THE MOST POWERFUL OF THE JEDI.
UMMM
UNABLE TO KEEP PACE WITH YODA'S AWESOME ATTACK, DOOKU IS FORCED BACK!
POWERFUL YOU HAVE BECOME, DOOKU. THE DARK SIDE I SENSE IN YOU.
FOUGHT WELL, YOU HAVE, MY OLD PADAWAN.
THE BATTLE IS FAR FROM OVER.
THIS IS JUST THE BEGINNING.

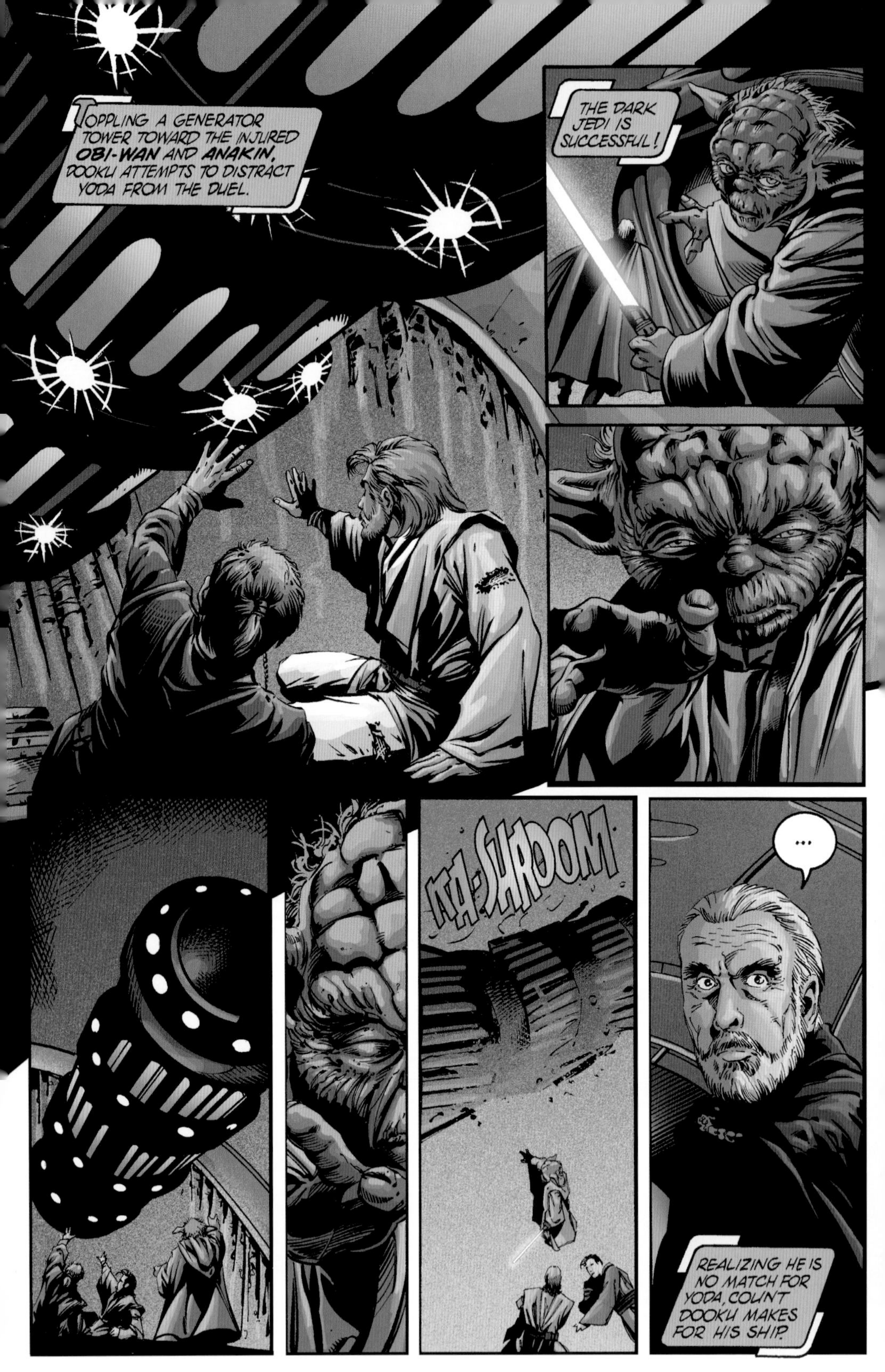
TOPPLING A GENERATOR TOWER TOWARD THE INJURED **OBI-WAN** AND **ANAKIN**, DOOKU ATTEMPTS TO DISTRACT YODA FROM THE DUEL.
THE DARK JEDI IS SUCCESSFUL!
KA-SHROOM
...
REALIZING HE IS NO MATCH FOR YODA, COUNT DOOKU MAKES FOR HIS SHIP.

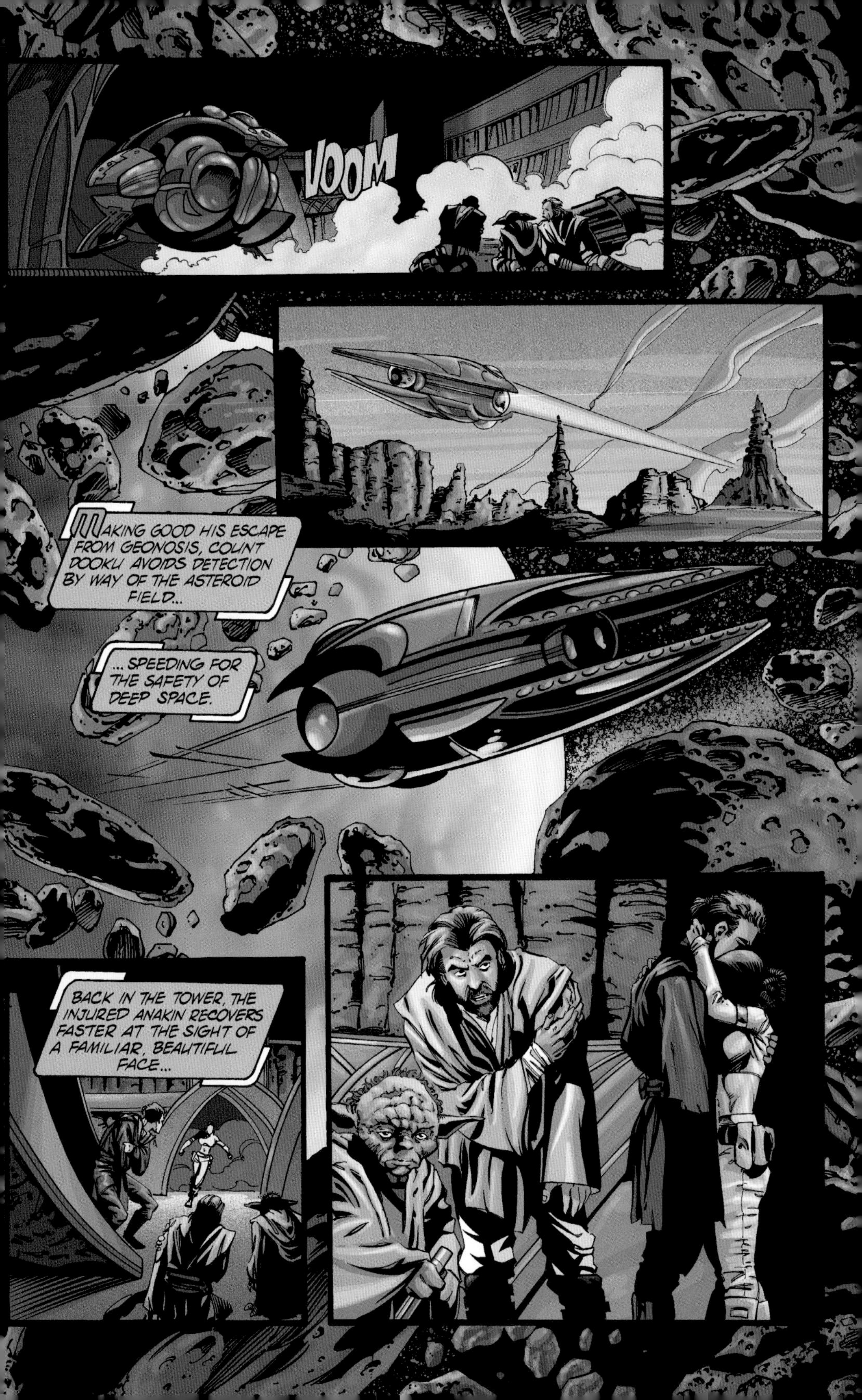
VOOM
MAKING GOOD HIS ESCAPE FROM GEONOSIS, COUNT DOOKU AVOIDS DETECTION BY WAY OF THE ASTEROID FIELD...
...SPEEDING FOR THE SAFETY OF DEEP SPACE.
BACK IN THE TOWER, THE INJURED ANAKIN RECOVERS FASTER AT THE SIGHT OF A FAMILIAR, BEAUTIFUL FACE...

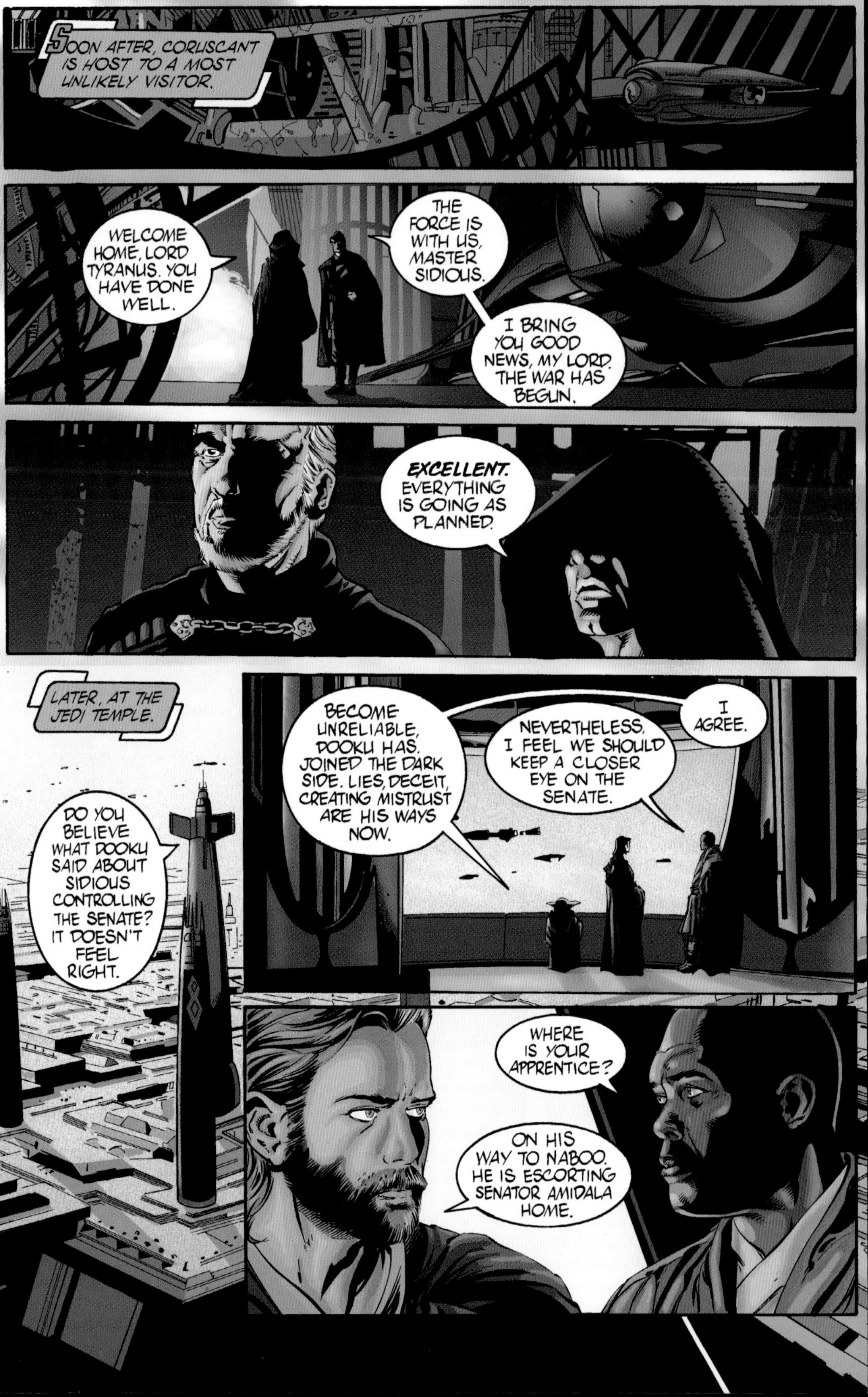
SOON AFTER, CORUSCANT IS HOST TO A MOST UNLIKELY VISITOR.
WELCOME HOME, LORD TYRANUS. YOU HAVE DONE WELL.
THE FORCE IS WITH US, MASTER SIDIOUS.
I BRING YOU GOOD NEWS, MY LORD. THE WAR HAS BEGUN.
EXCELLENT. EVERYTHING IS GOING AS PLANNED.
LATER, AT THE JEDI TEMPLE.
DO YOU BELIEVE WHAT DOOKU SAID ABOUT SIDIOUS CONTROLLING THE SENATE? IT DOESN'T FEEL RIGHT.
BECOME UNRELIABLE, DOOKU HAS. JOINED THE DARK SIDE. LIES, DECEIT, CREATING MISTRUST ARE HIS WAYS NOW.
NEVERTHELESS, I FEEL WE SHOULD KEEP A CLOSER EYE ON THE SENATE.
I AGREE.
WHERE IS YOUR APPRENTICE?
ON HIS WAY TO NABOO. HE IS ESCORTING SENATOR AMIDALA HOME.

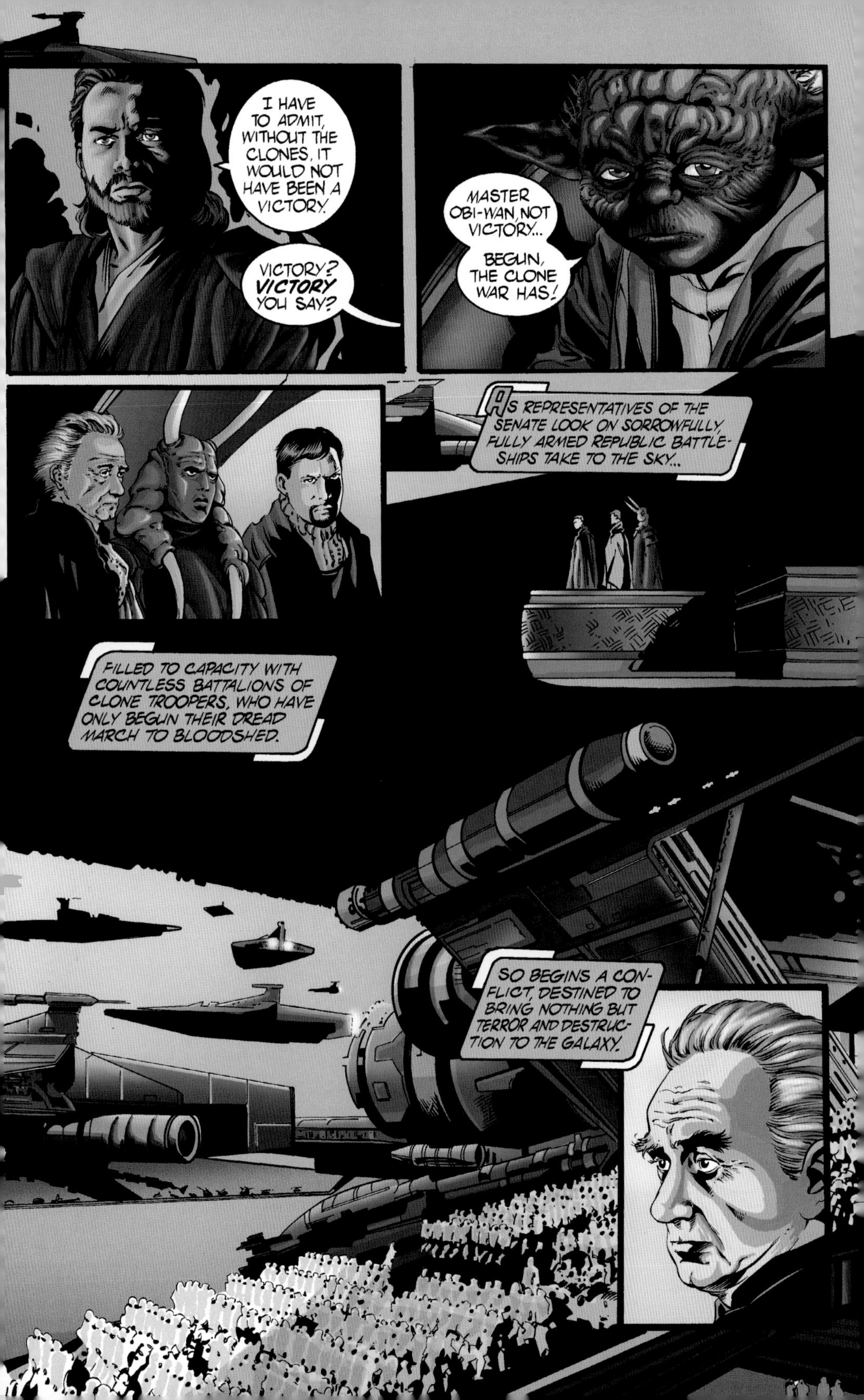
I HAVE TO ADMIT, WITHOUT THE CLONES, IT WOULD NOT HAVE BEEN A VICTORY.
VICTORY? VICTORY YOU SAY?
MASTER OBI-WAN, NOT VICTORY...
BEGUN, THE CLONE WAR HAS!
AS REPRESENTATIVES OF THE SENATE LOOK ON SORROWFULLY, FULLY ARMED REPUBLIC BATTLE-SHIPS TAKE TO THE SKY...
FILLED TO CAPACITY WITH COUNTLESS BATTALIONS OF CLONE TROOPERS, WHO HAVE ONLY BEGUN THEIR DREAD MARCH TO BLOODSHED.
SO BEGINS A CONFLICT, DESTINED TO BRING NOTHING BUT TERROR AND DESTRUCTION TO THE GALAXY.

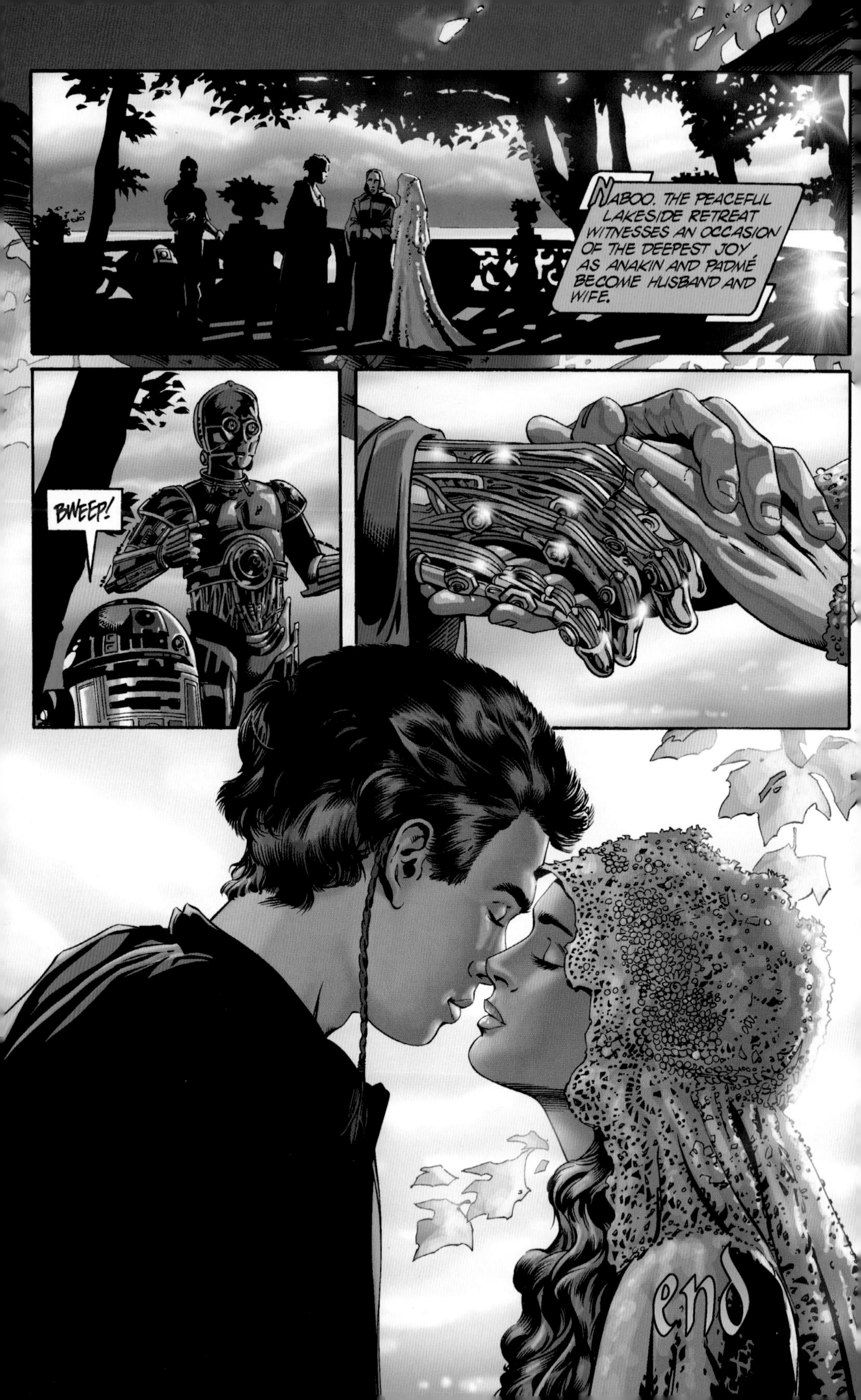
NABOO. THE PEACEFUL LAKESIDE RETREAT WITNESSES AN OCCASION OF THE DEEPEST JOY AS ANAKIN AND PADMÉ BECOME HUSBAND AND WIFE.
BWEEP!
end

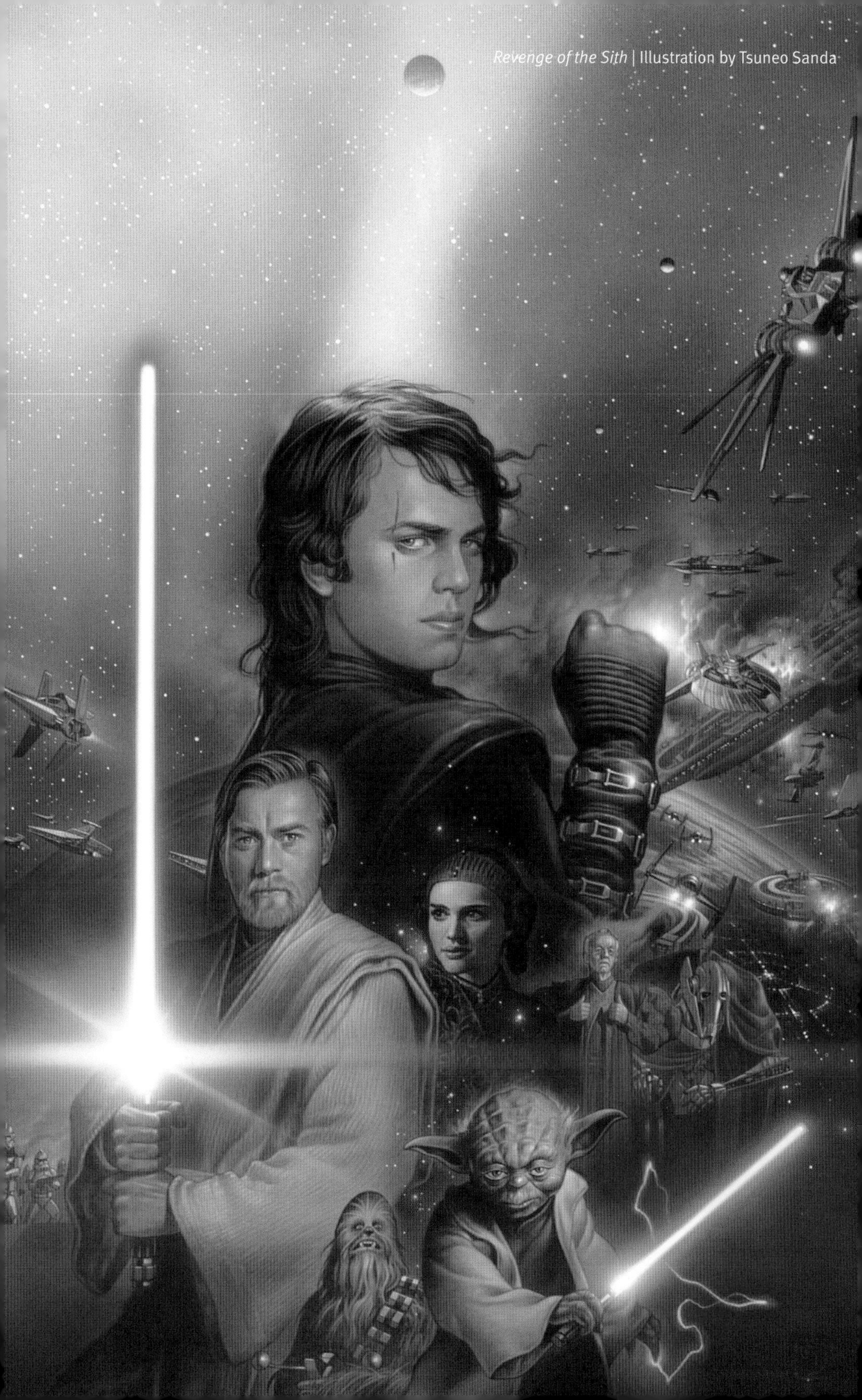

Revenge of the Sith | Illustration by Tsuneo Sanda

War! The Republic is crumbling under attacks by the Separatist leader, Count Dooku. There are heroes on both sides. Evil is everywhere.

In a stunning move, the fiendish droid leader, General Grievous, has swept into the Republic capital and kidnapped Chancellor Palpatine, leader of the Galactic Senate.

As the Separatist Droid Army attempts to flee the besieged capital with their valuable hostage, two Jedi Knights lead a desperate mission to rescue the captive Chancellor....

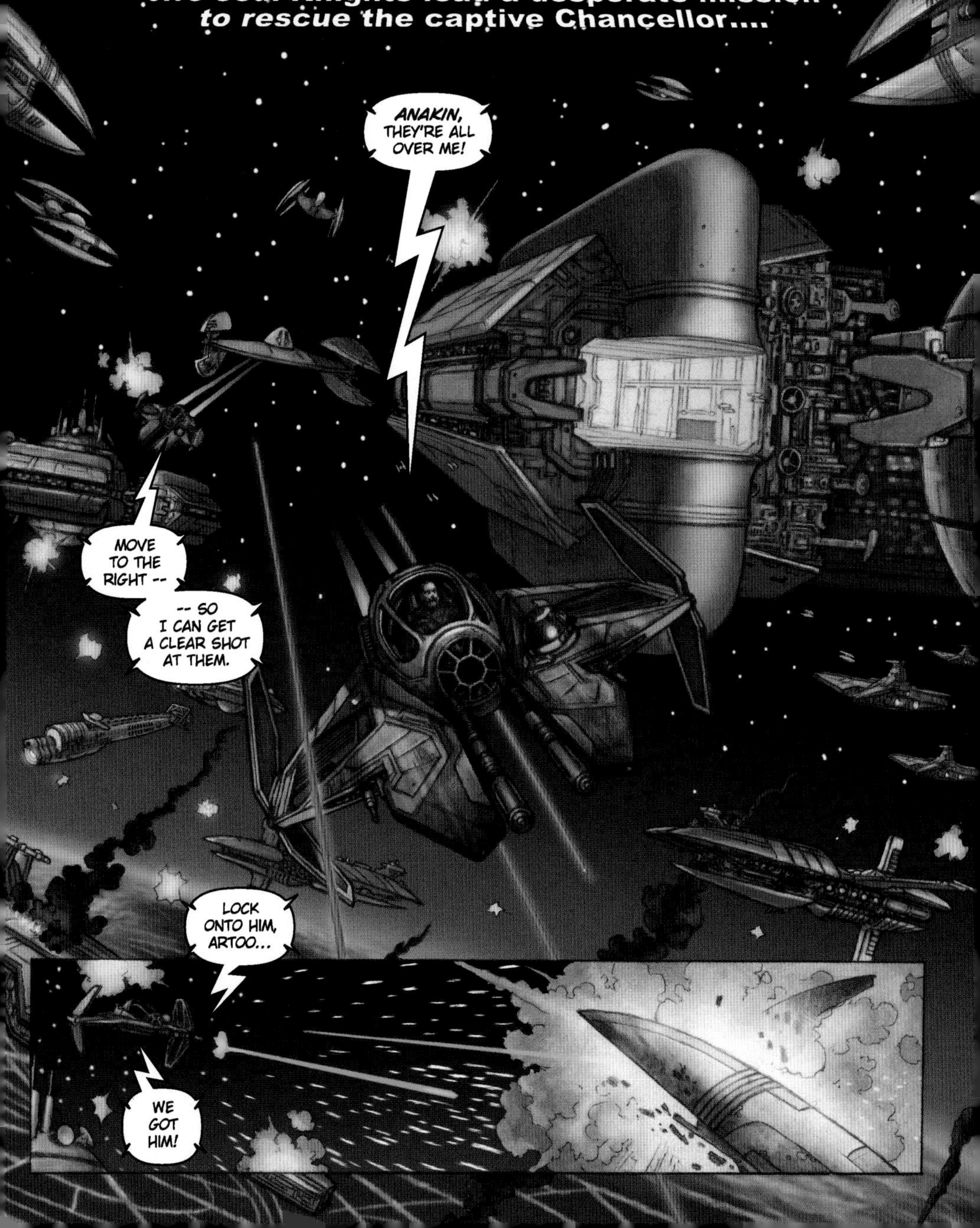
ANAKIN, THEY'RE ALL OVER ME!
MOVE TO THE RIGHT --
-- SO I CAN GET A CLEAR SHOT AT THEM.
LOCK ONTO HIM, ARTOO...
WE GOT HIM!

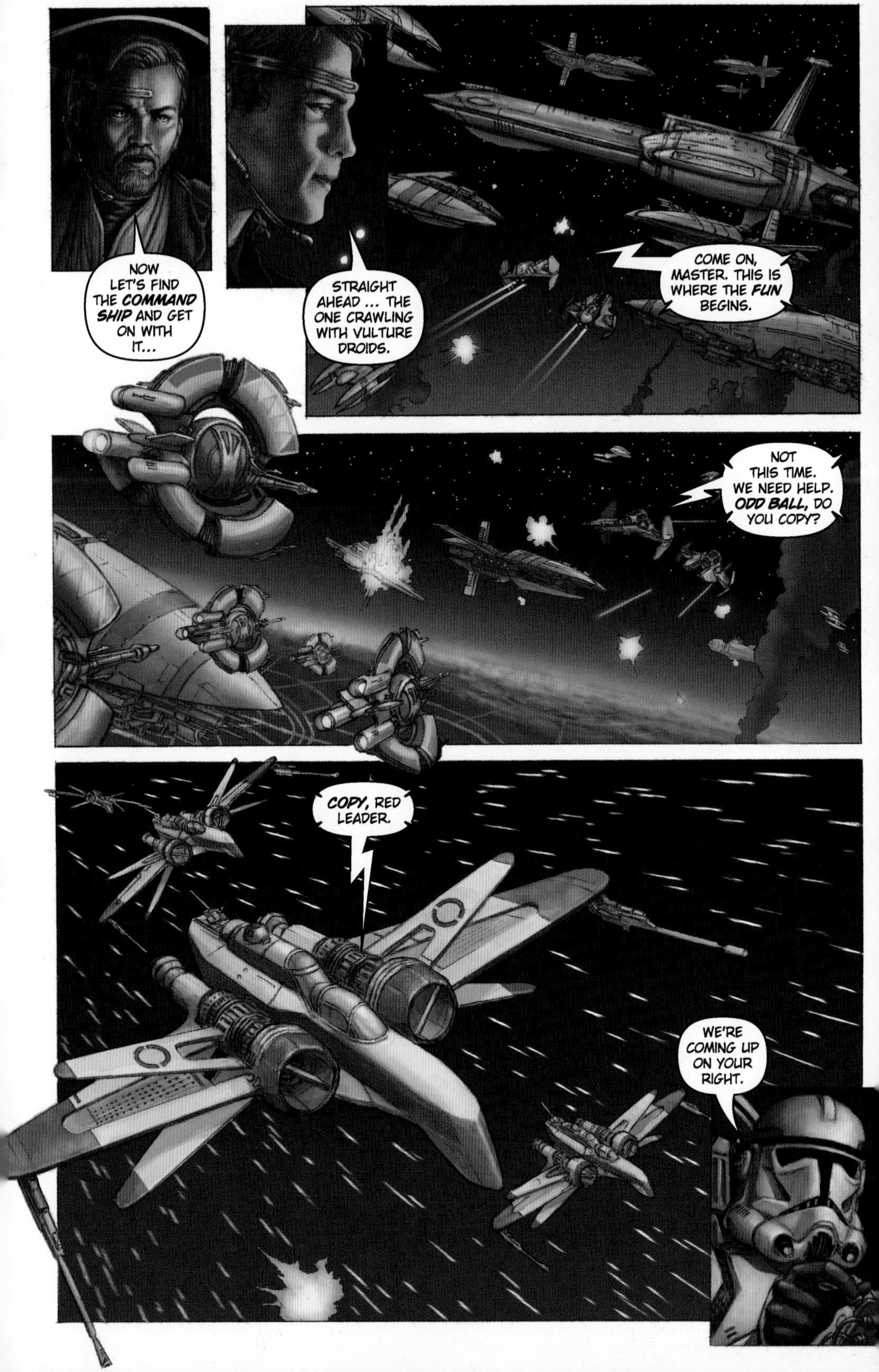
NOW LET'S FIND THE ***COMMAND SHIP*** AND GET ON WITH IT...
STRAIGHT AHEAD ... THE ONE CRAWLING WITH VULTURE DROIDS.
COME ON, MASTER. THIS IS WHERE THE ***FUN*** BEGINS.
NOT THIS TIME. WE NEED HELP. ***ODD BALL,*** DO YOU COPY?
COPY, RED LEADER.
WE'RE COMING UP ON YOUR RIGHT.

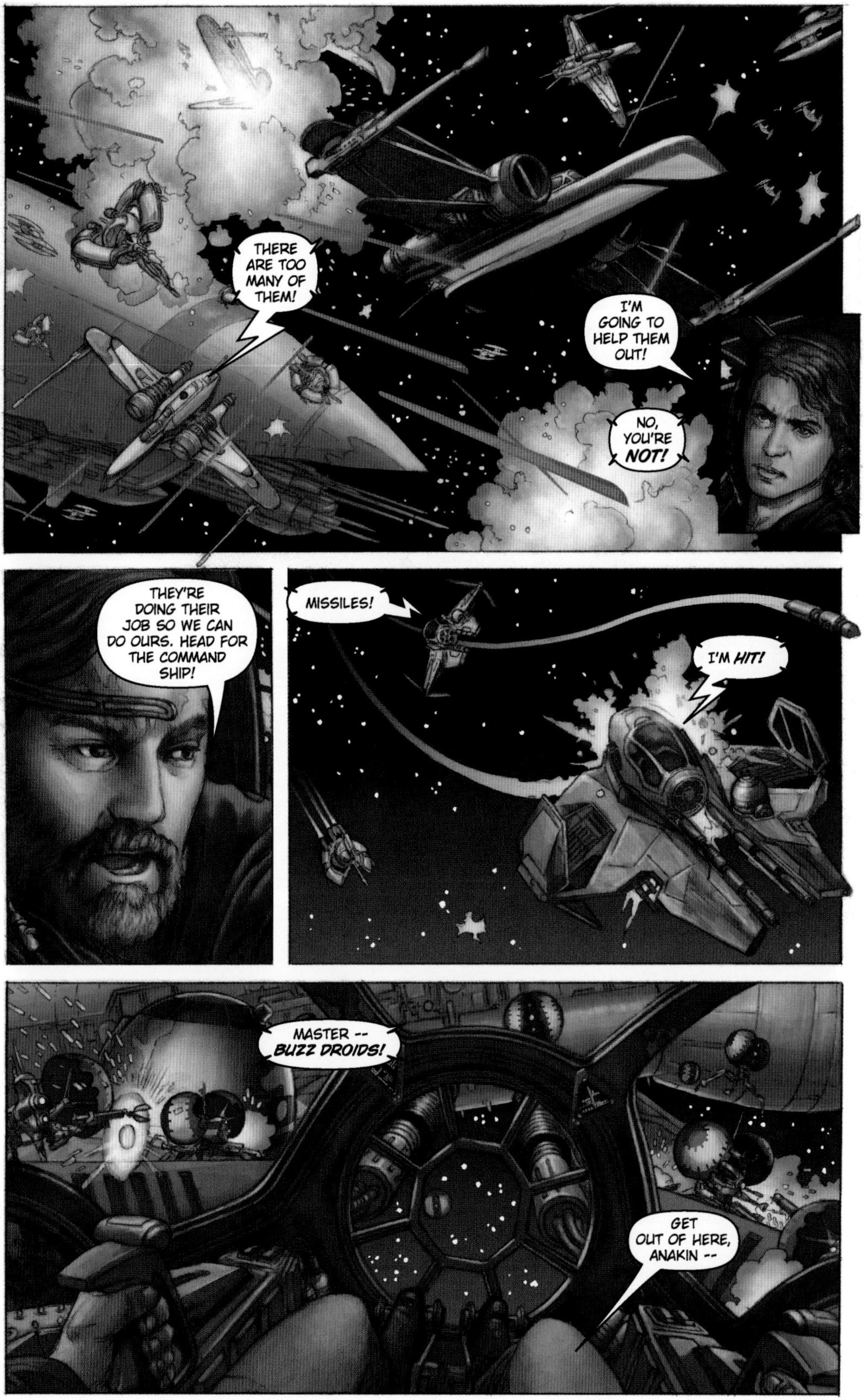
THERE ARE TOO MANY OF THEM!
I'M GOING TO HELP THEM OUT!
NO, YOU'RE NOT!
THEY'RE DOING THEIR JOB SO WE CAN DO OURS. HEAD FOR THE COMMAND SHIP!
MISSILES!
I'M HIT!
MASTER -- BUZZ DROIDS!
GET OUT OF HERE, ANAKIN --

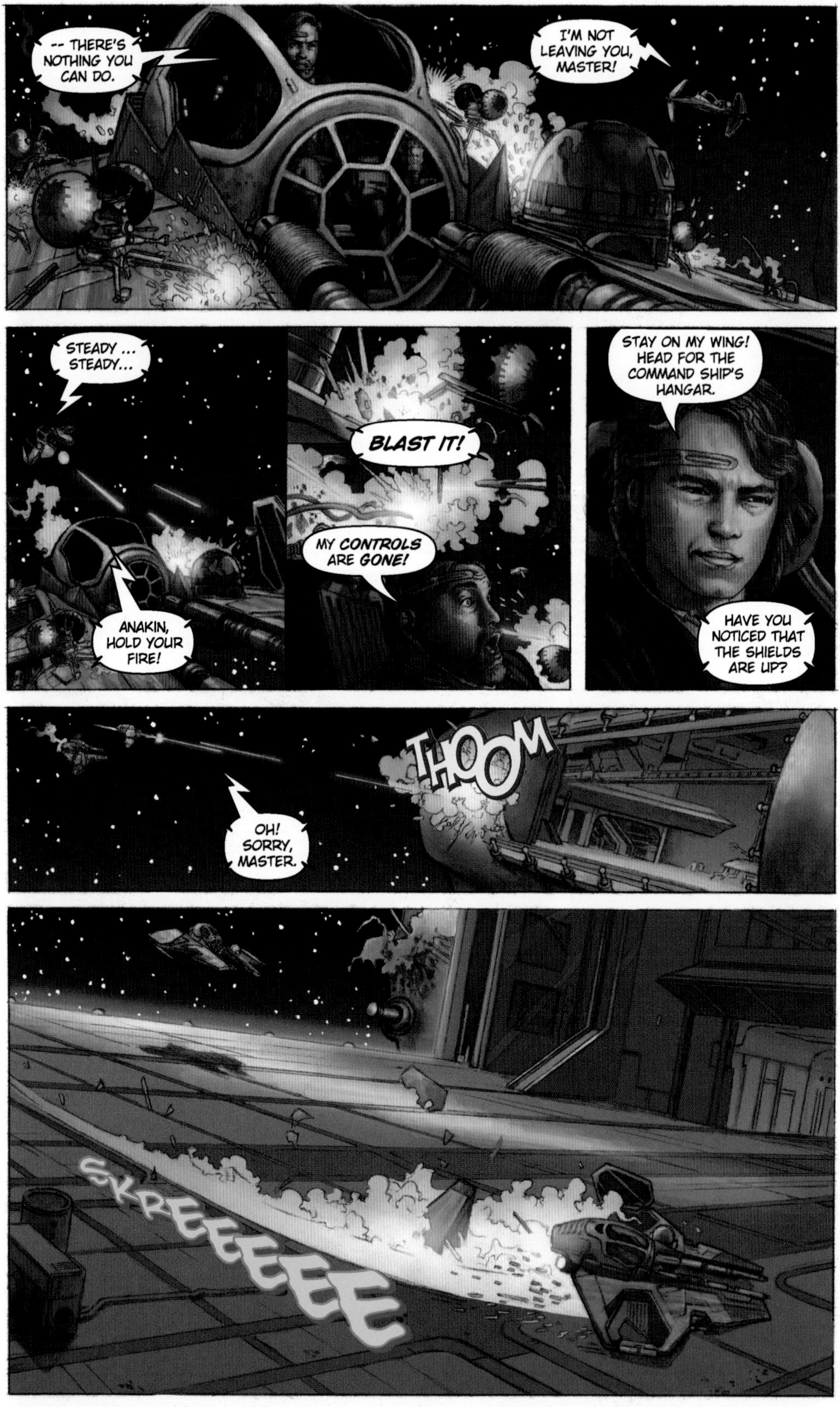
-- THERE'S NOTHING YOU CAN DO.
I'M NOT LEAVING YOU, MASTER!
STEADY ... STEADY...
ANAKIN, HOLD YOUR FIRE!
BLAST IT!
MY CONTROLS ARE GONE!
STAY ON MY WING! HEAD FOR THE COMMAND SHIP'S HANGAR.
HAVE YOU NOTICED THAT THE SHIELDS ARE UP?
THOOM
OH! SORRY, MASTER.
SKREEEEEEE

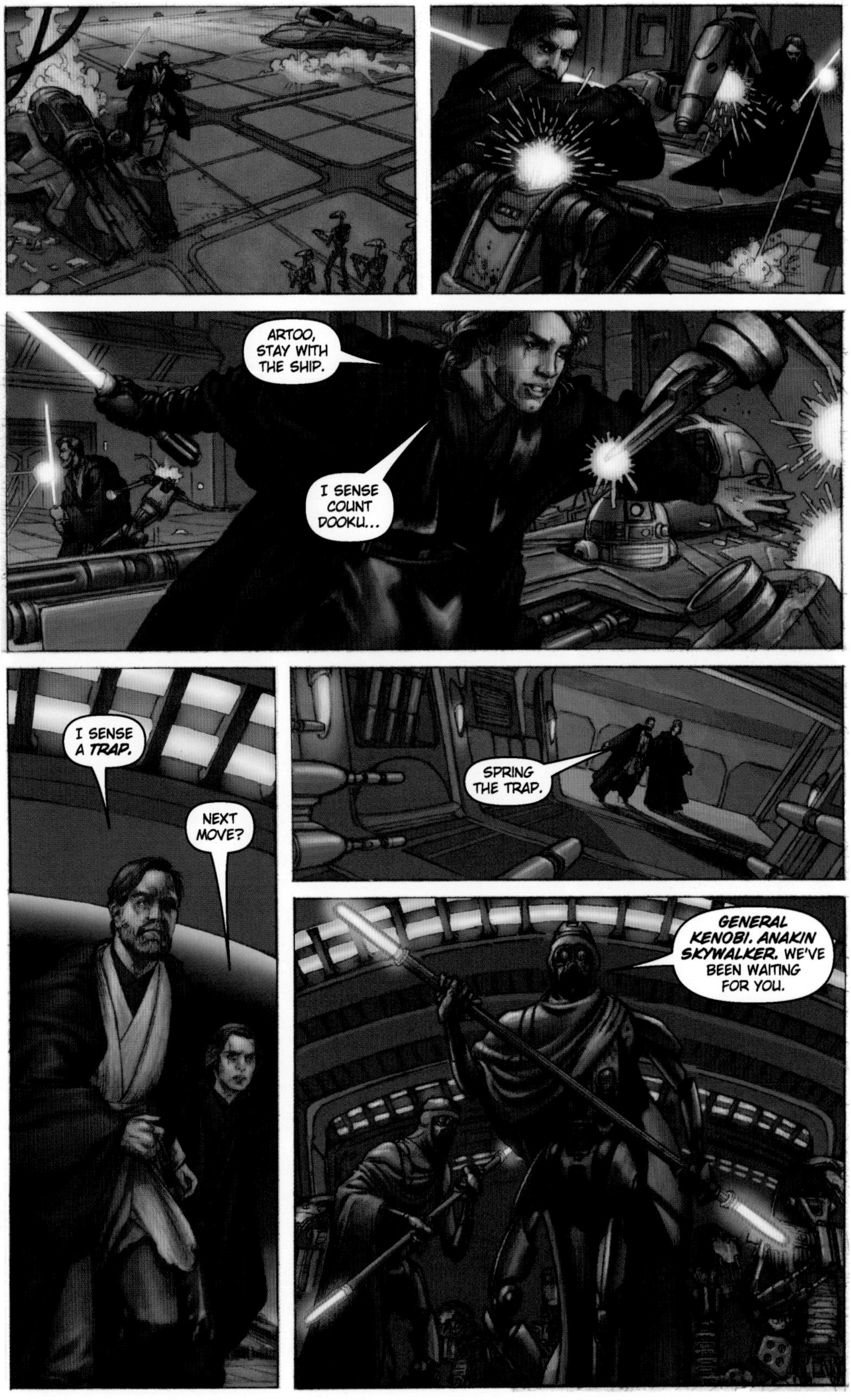
ARTOO, STAY WITH THE SHIP.
I SENSE COUNT DOOKU...
I SENSE A *TRAP*.
NEXT MOVE?
SPRING THE TRAP.
GENERAL KENOBI. ANAKIN SKYWALKER. WE'VE BEEN WAITING FOR YOU.

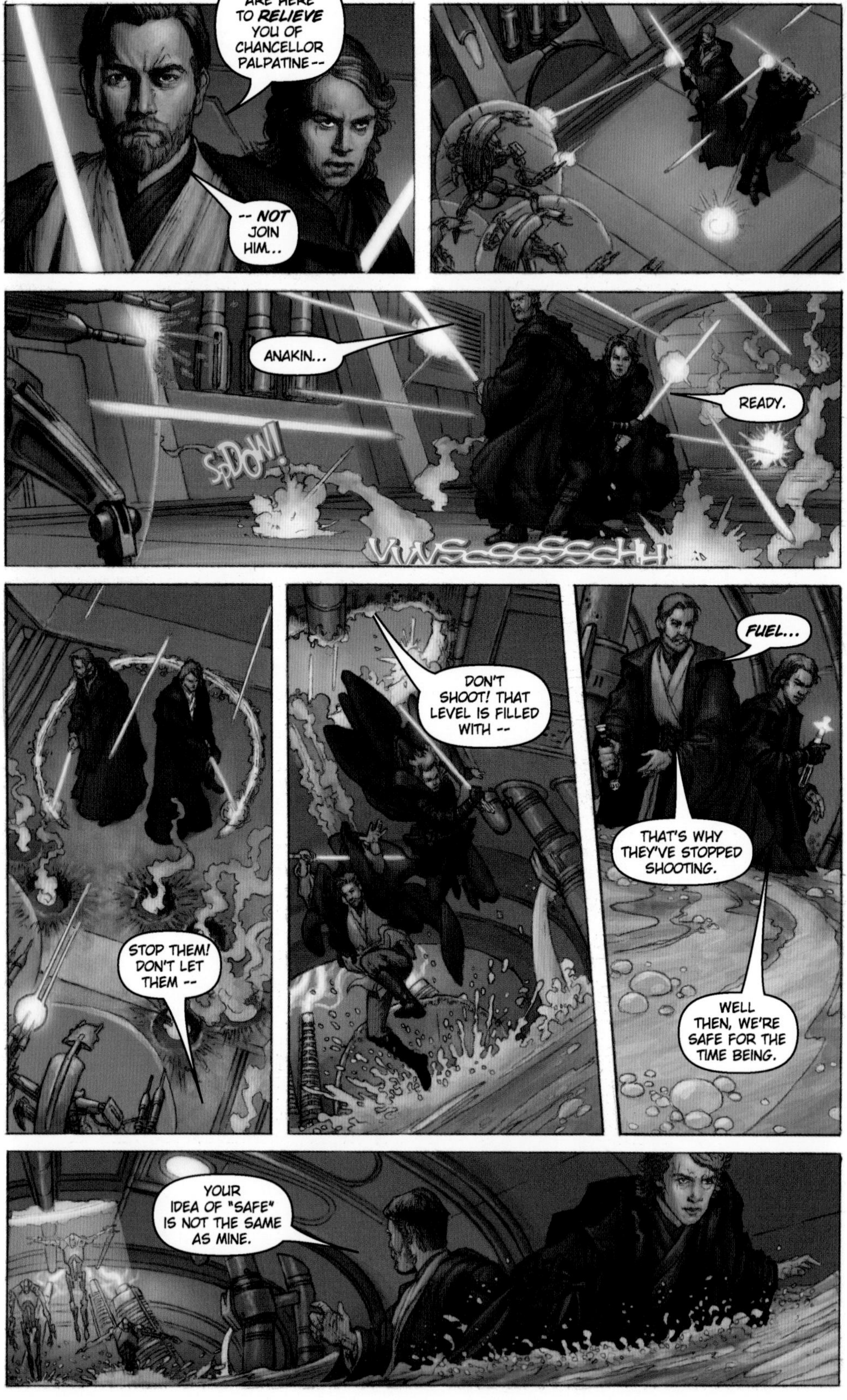
WE ARE HERE TO RELIEVE YOU OF CHANCELLOR PALPATINE --
-- NOT JOIN HIM...
ANAKIN...
READY.
SPDOW!
VWSSSSSSSHH
STOP THEM! DON'T LET THEM --
DON'T SHOOT! THAT LEVEL IS FILLED WITH --
FUEL...
THAT'S WHY THEY'VE STOPPED SHOOTING.
WELL THEN, WE'RE SAFE FOR THE TIME BEING.
YOUR IDEA OF "SAFE" IS NOT THE SAME AS MINE.

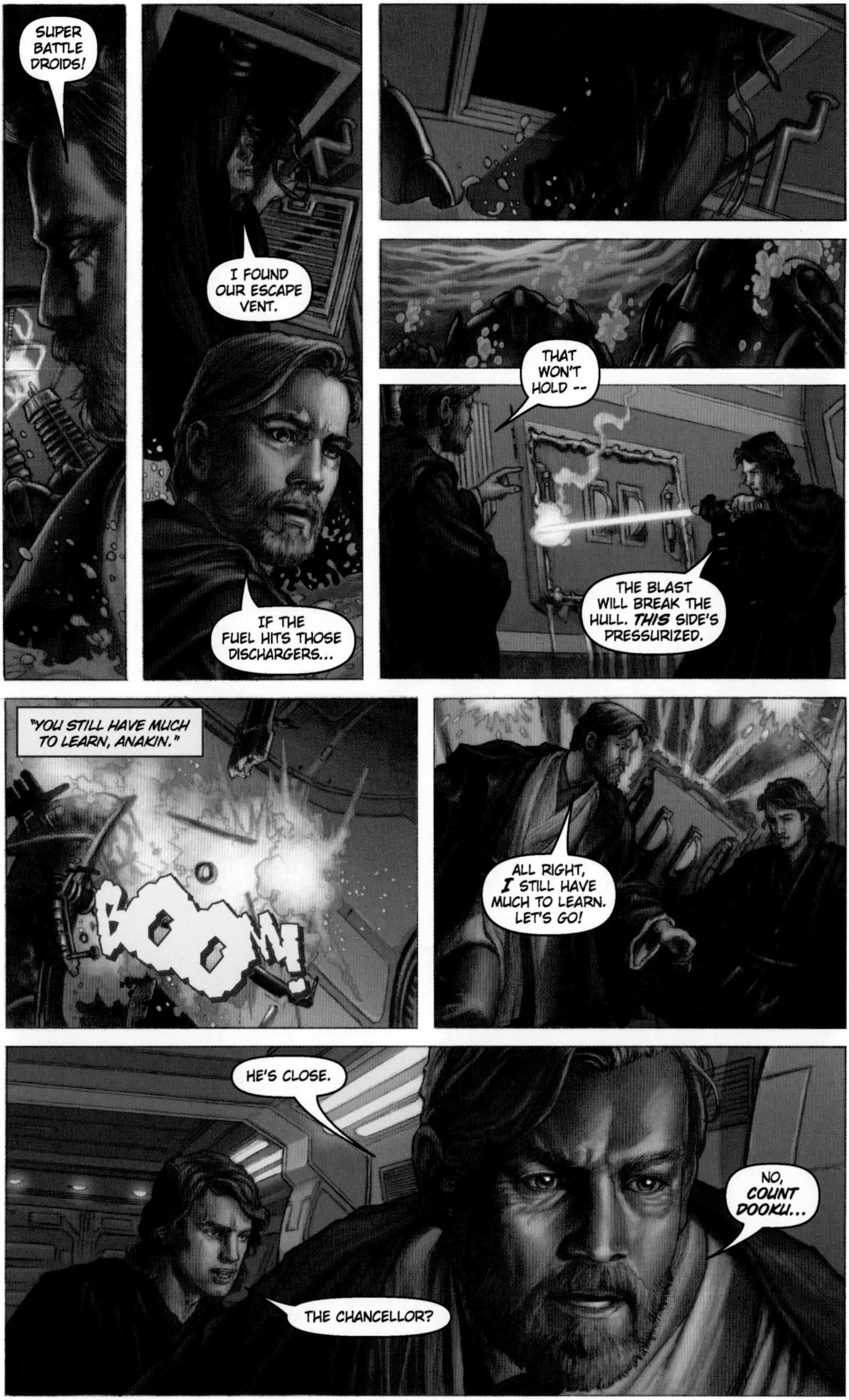
SUPER BATTLE DROIDS!
I FOUND OUR ESCAPE VENT.
IF THE FUEL HITS THOSE DISCHARGERS...
THAT WON'T HOLD --
THE BLAST WILL BREAK THE HULL. *THIS* SIDE'S PRESSURIZED.
"YOU STILL HAVE MUCH TO LEARN, ANAKIN."
BOOM!
ALL RIGHT, *I* STILL HAVE MUCH TO LEARN. LET'S GO!
HE'S CLOSE.
THE CHANCELLOR?
NO, *COUNT DOOKU*...

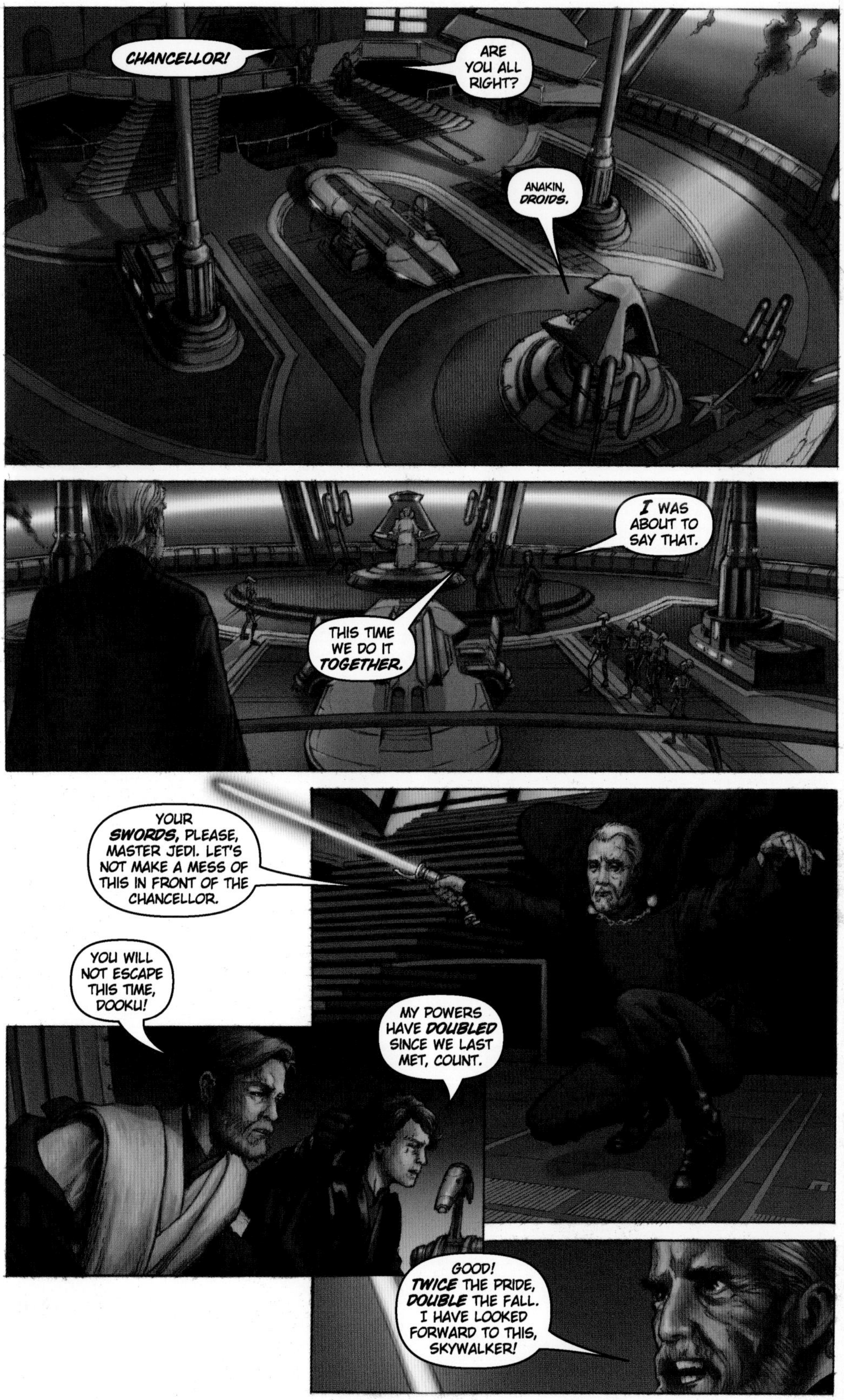
CHANCELLOR!
ARE YOU ALL RIGHT?
ANAKIN, DROIDS.
I WAS ABOUT TO SAY THAT.
THIS TIME WE DO IT TOGETHER.
YOUR SWORDS, PLEASE, MASTER JEDI. LET'S NOT MAKE A MESS OF THIS IN FRONT OF THE CHANCELLOR.
YOU WILL NOT ESCAPE THIS TIME, DOOKU!
MY POWERS HAVE DOUBLED SINCE WE LAST MET, COUNT.
GOOD! TWICE THE PRIDE, DOUBLE THE FALL. I HAVE LOOKED FORWARD TO THIS, SKYWALKER!

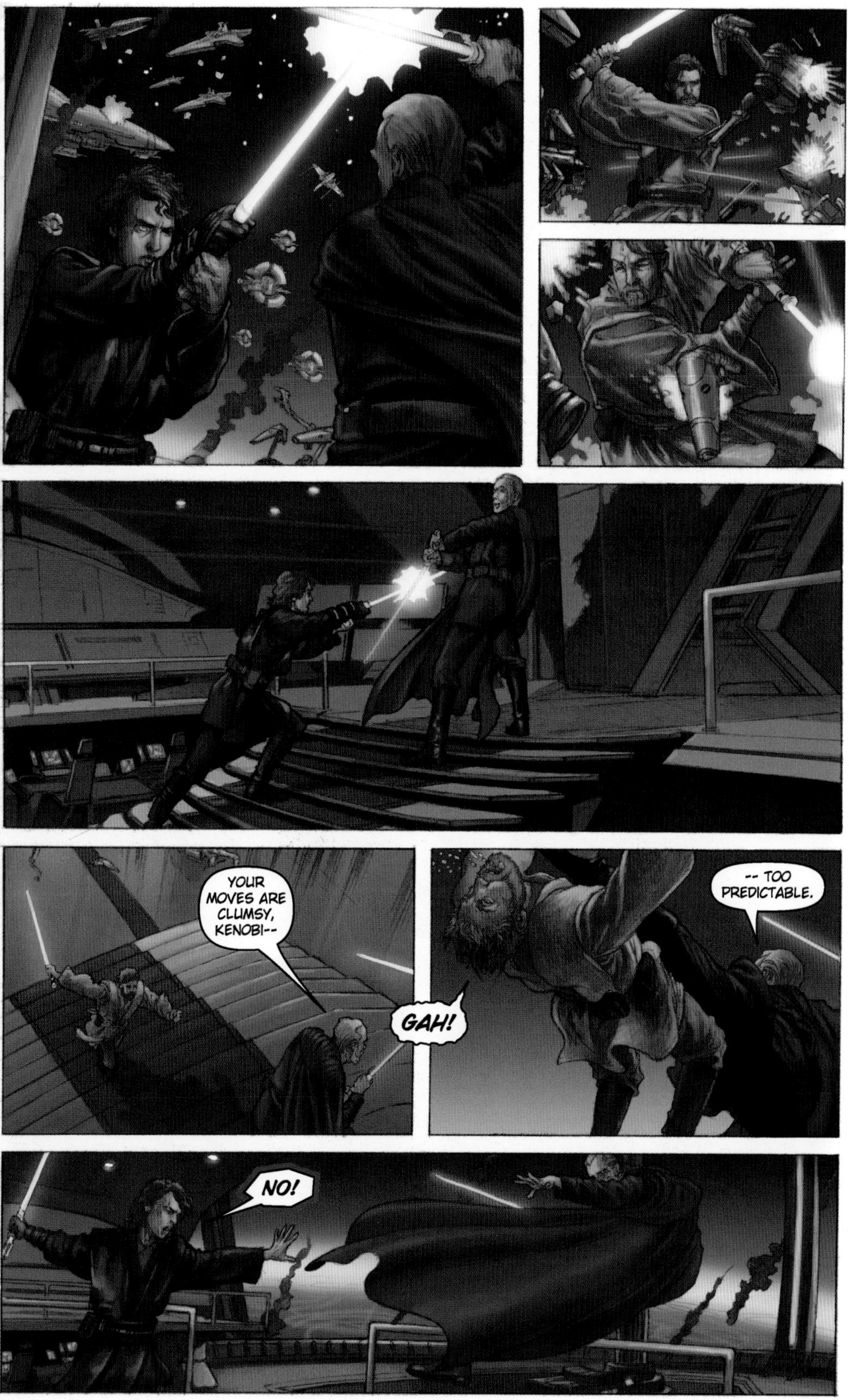
YOUR MOVES ARE CLUMSY, KENOBI--
GAH!
-- TOO PREDICTABLE.
NO!

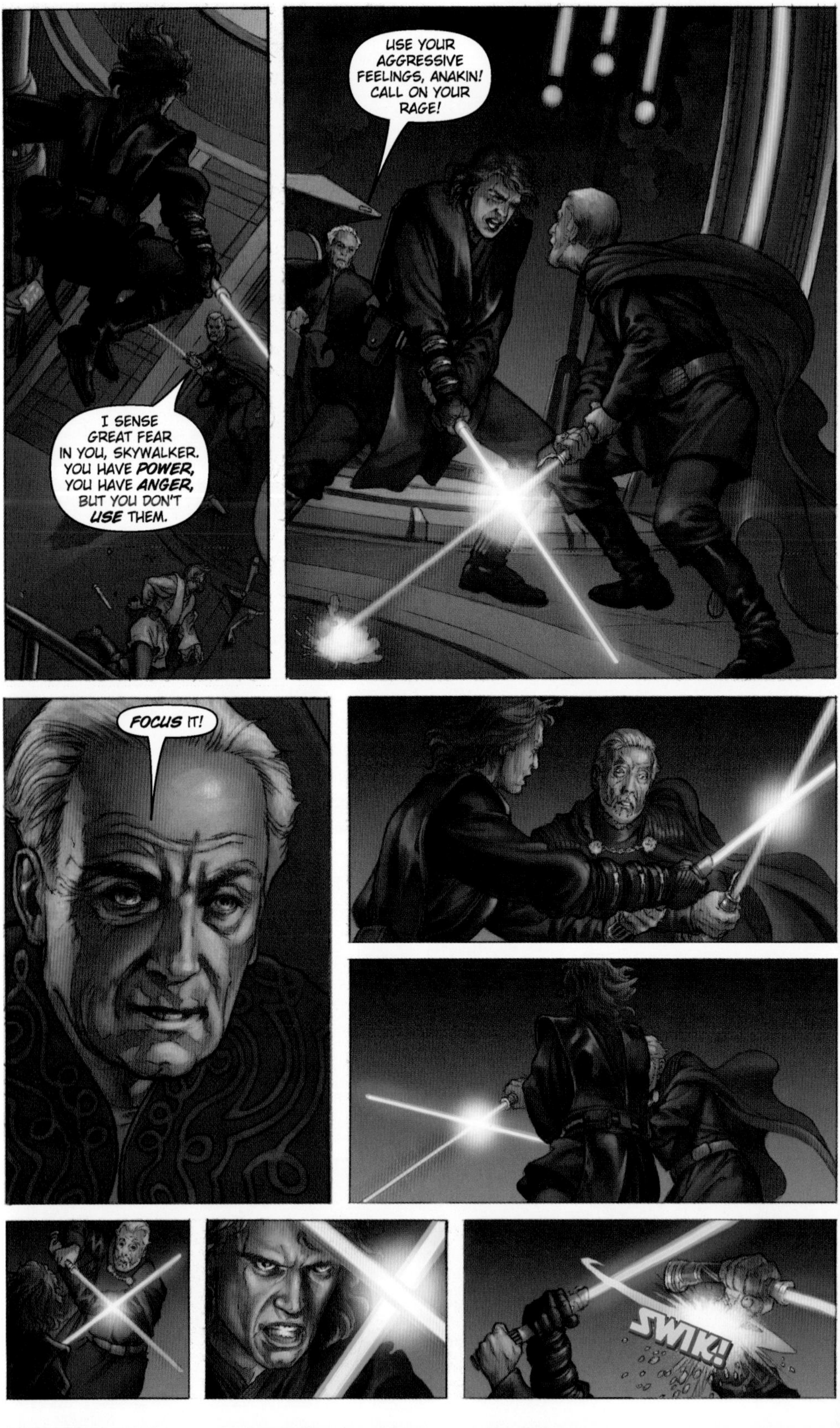
USE YOUR AGGRESSIVE FEELINGS, ANAKIN! CALL ON YOUR RAGE!
I SENSE GREAT FEAR IN YOU, SKYWALKER. YOU HAVE POWER, YOU HAVE ANGER, BUT YOU DON'T USE THEM.
FOCUS IT!
SWIK!

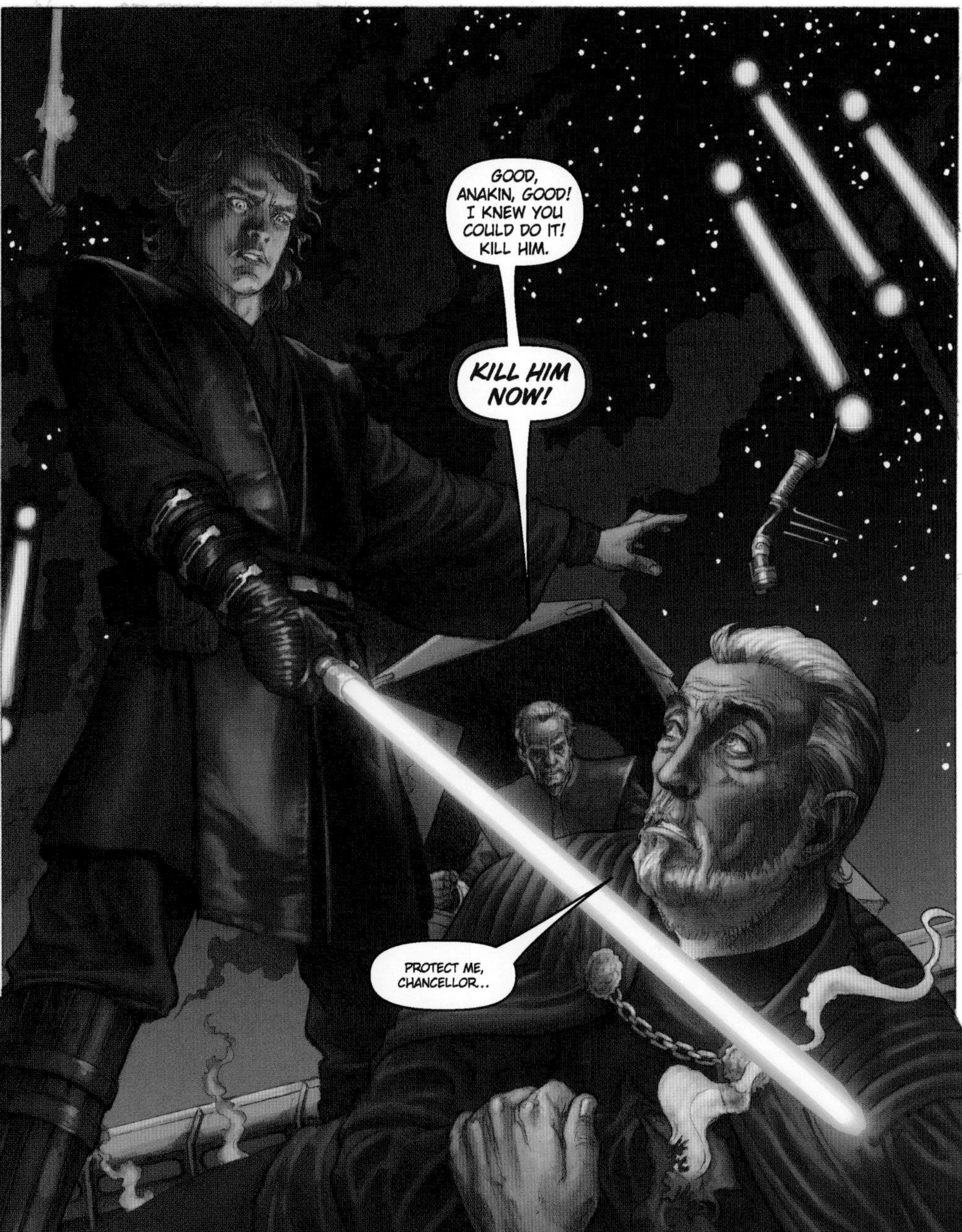
GOOD, ANAKIN, GOOD! I KNEW YOU COULD DO IT! KILL HIM.
KILL HIM NOW!
PROTECT ME, CHANCELLOR...
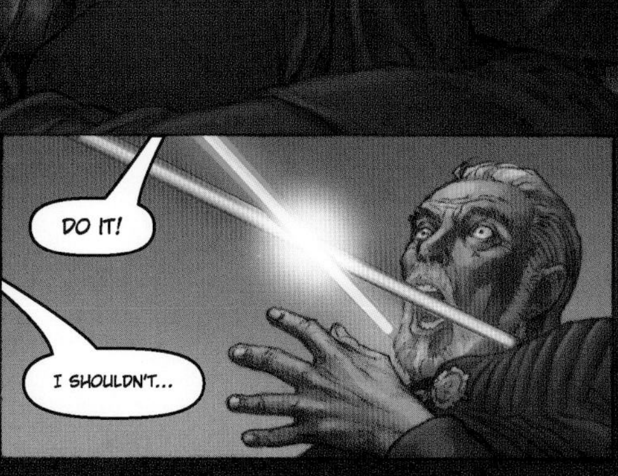
DO IT!
I SHOULDN'T...
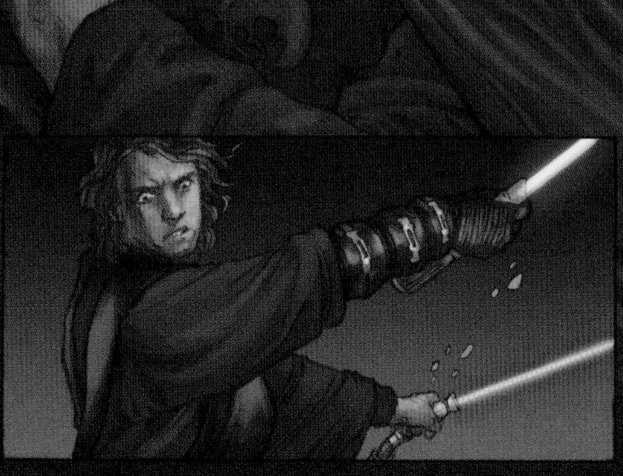

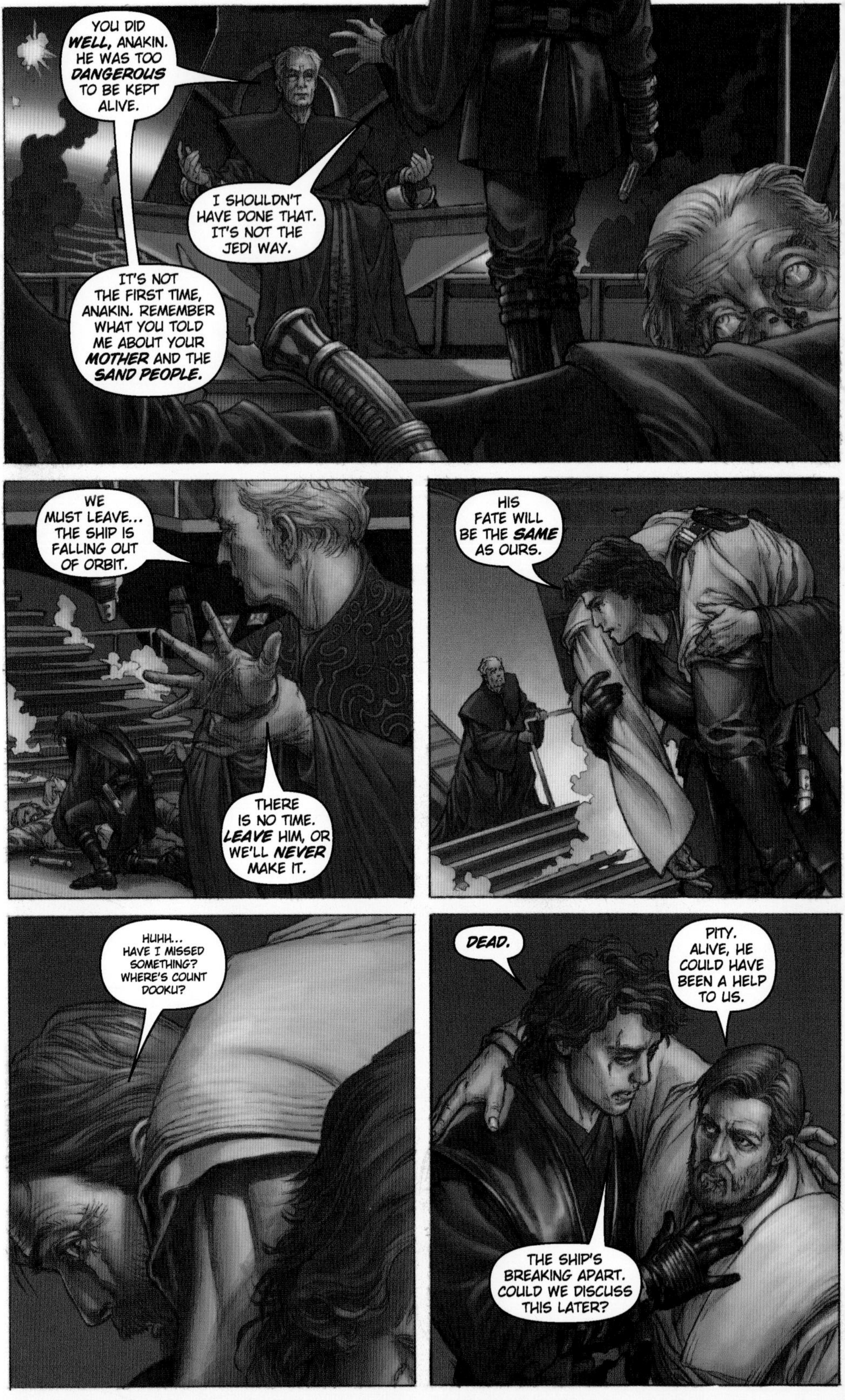
YOU DID WELL, ANAKIN. HE WAS TOO DANGEROUS TO BE KEPT ALIVE.
I SHOULDN'T HAVE DONE THAT. IT'S NOT THE JEDI WAY.
IT'S NOT THE FIRST TIME, ANAKIN. REMEMBER WHAT YOU TOLD ME ABOUT YOUR MOTHER AND THE SAND PEOPLE.
WE MUST LEAVE... THE SHIP IS FALLING OUT OF ORBIT.
THERE IS NO TIME. LEAVE HIM, OR WE'LL NEVER MAKE IT.
HIS FATE WILL BE THE SAME AS OURS.
HUHH... HAVE I MISSED SOMETHING? WHERE'S COUNT DOOKU?
DEAD.
PITY. ALIVE, HE COULD HAVE BEEN A HELP TO US.
THE SHIP'S BREAKING APART. COULD WE DISCUSS THIS LATER?

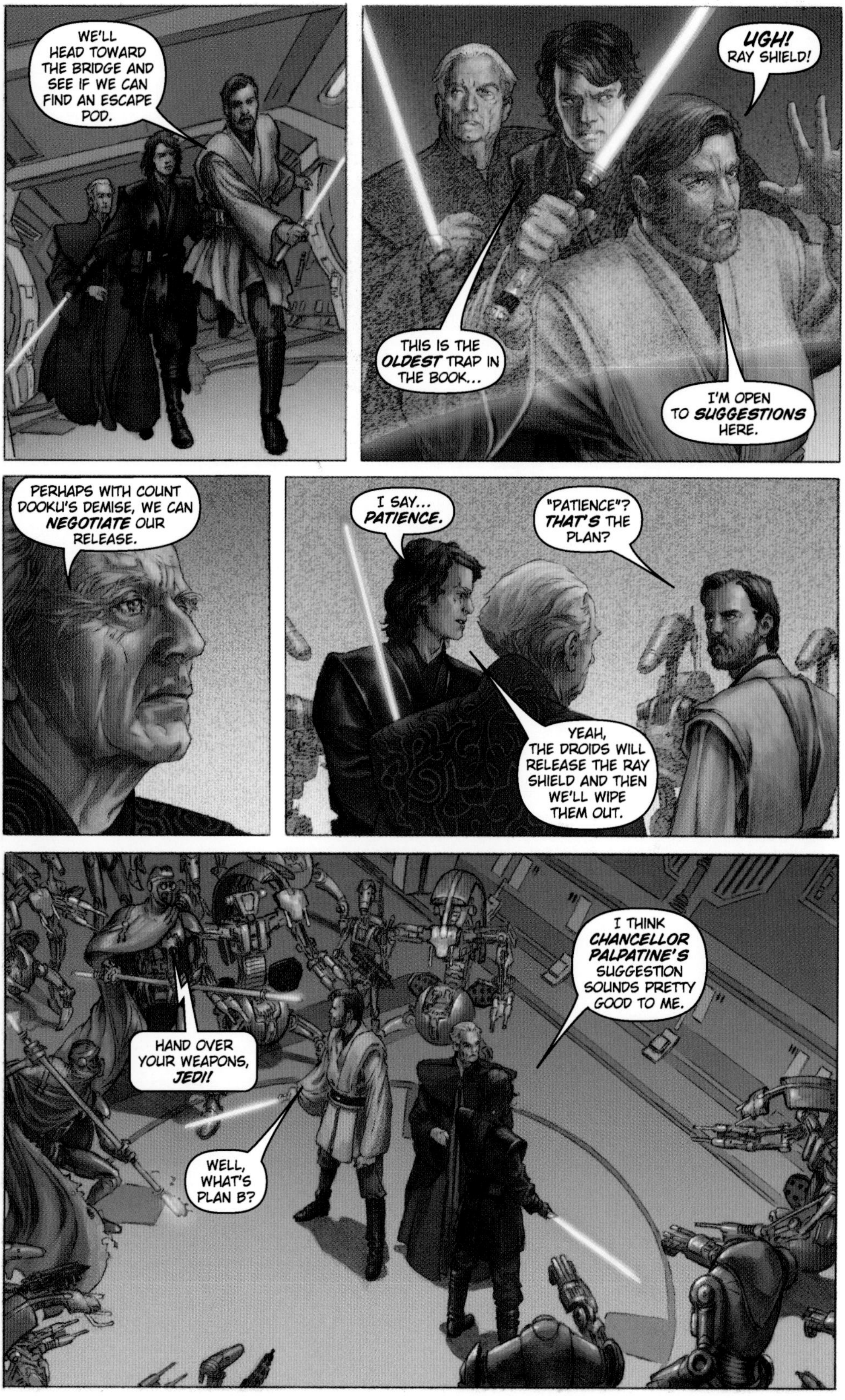

WE'LL HEAD TOWARD THE BRIDGE AND SEE IF WE CAN FIND AN ESCAPE POD.
UGH! RAY SHIELD!
THIS IS THE OLDEST TRAP IN THE BOOK...
I'M OPEN TO SUGGESTIONS HERE.
PERHAPS WITH COUNT DOOKU'S DEMISE, WE CAN NEGOTIATE OUR RELEASE.
I SAY... PATIENCE.
"PATIENCE"? THAT'S THE PLAN?
YEAH, THE DROIDS WILL RELEASE THE RAY SHIELD AND THEN WE'LL WIPE THEM OUT.
HAND OVER YOUR WEAPONS, JEDI!
I THINK CHANCELLOR PALPATINE'S SUGGESTION SOUNDS PRETTY GOOD TO ME.
WELL, WHAT'S PLAN B?

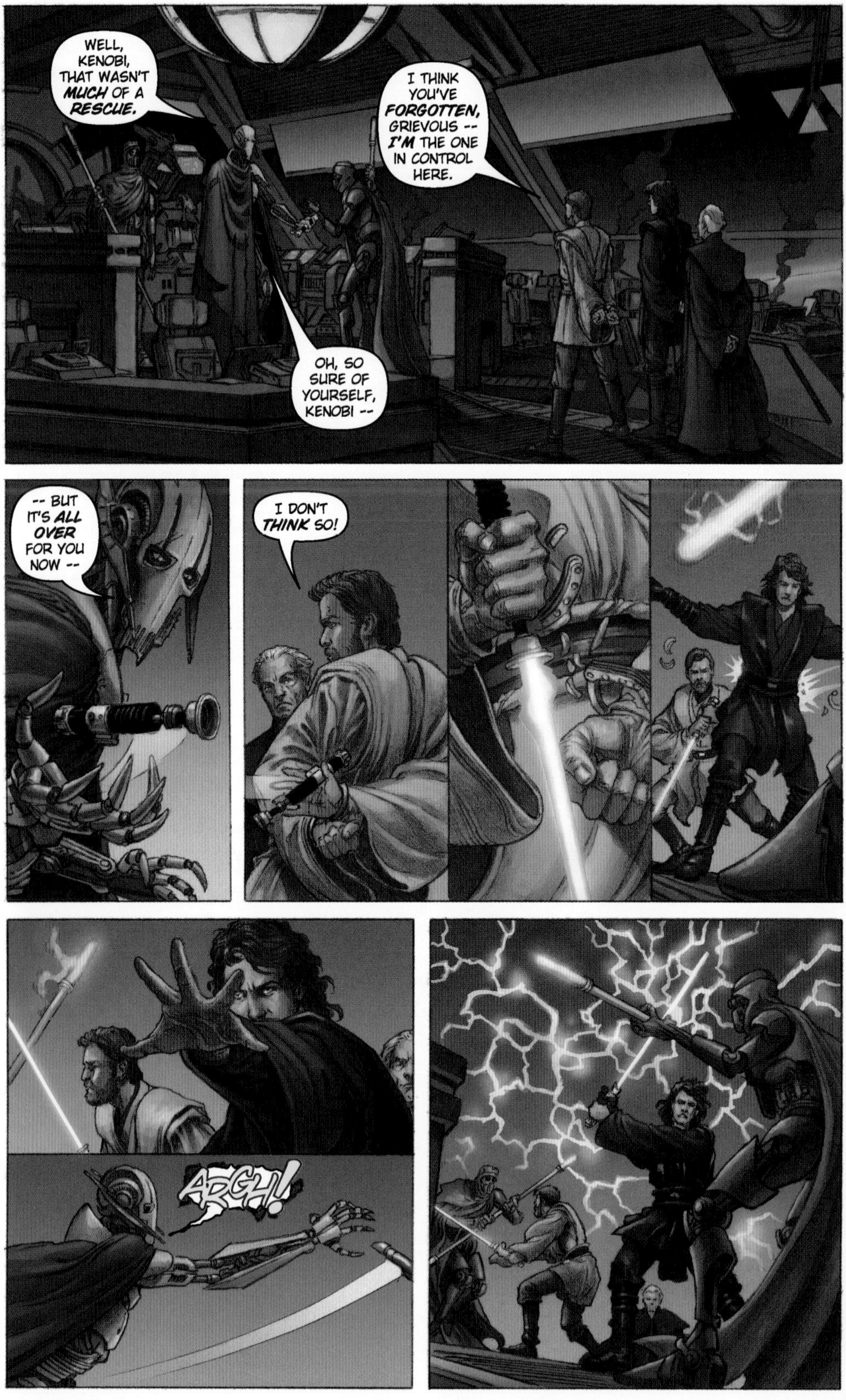
WELL, KENOBI, THAT WASN'T *MUCH* OF A *RESCUE.*
I THINK YOU'VE *FORGOTTEN,* GRIEVOUS -- *I'M* THE ONE IN CONTROL HERE.
OH, SO SURE OF YOURSELF, KENOBI --
-- BUT IT'S *ALL OVER* FOR YOU NOW --
I DON'T *THINK* SO!
ARGH!

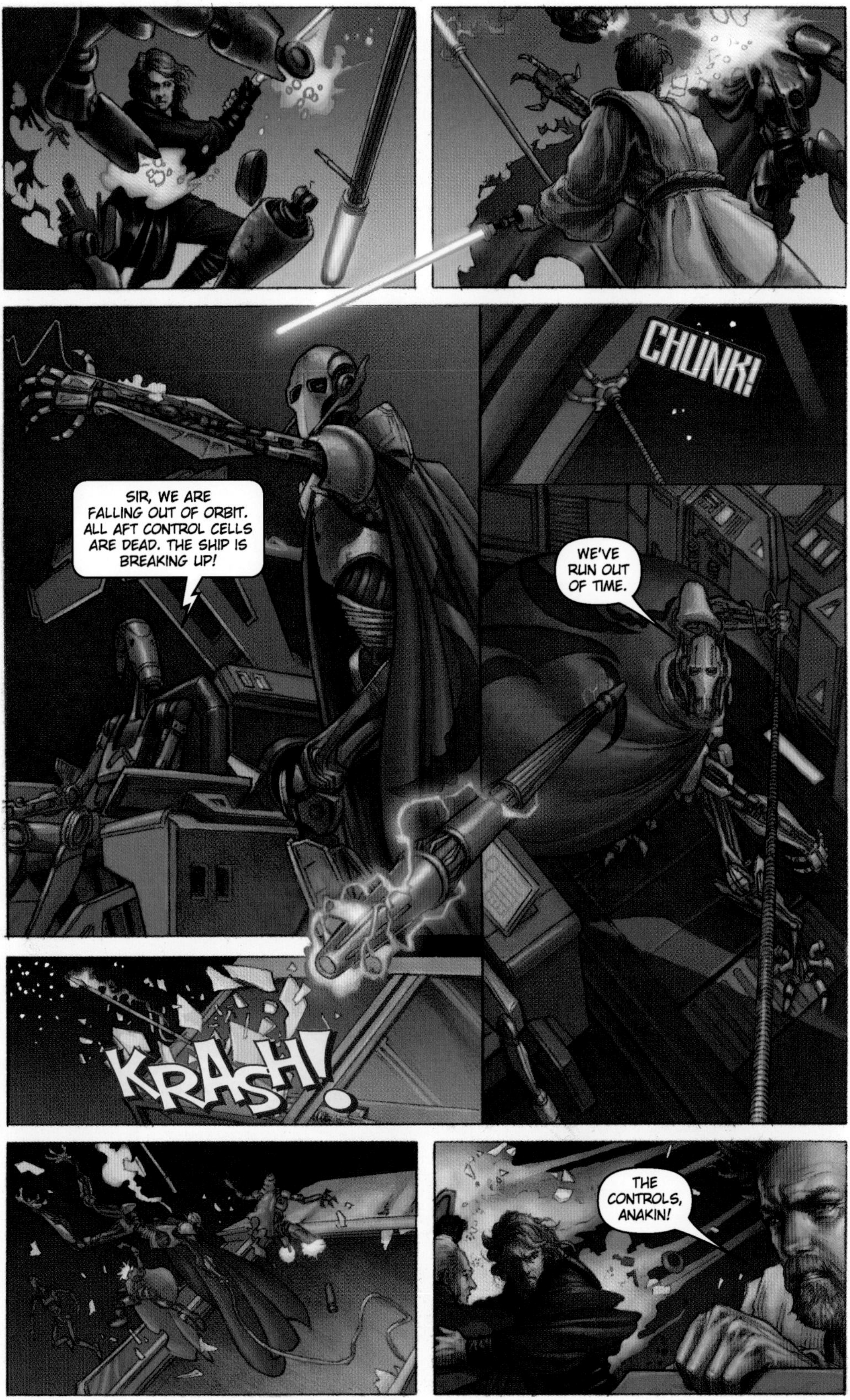
CHUNK!
SIR, WE ARE FALLING OUT OF ORBIT. ALL AFT CONTROL CELLS ARE DEAD. THE SHIP IS BREAKING UP!
WE'VE RUN OUT OF TIME.
KRASH!
THE CONTROLS, ANAKIN!

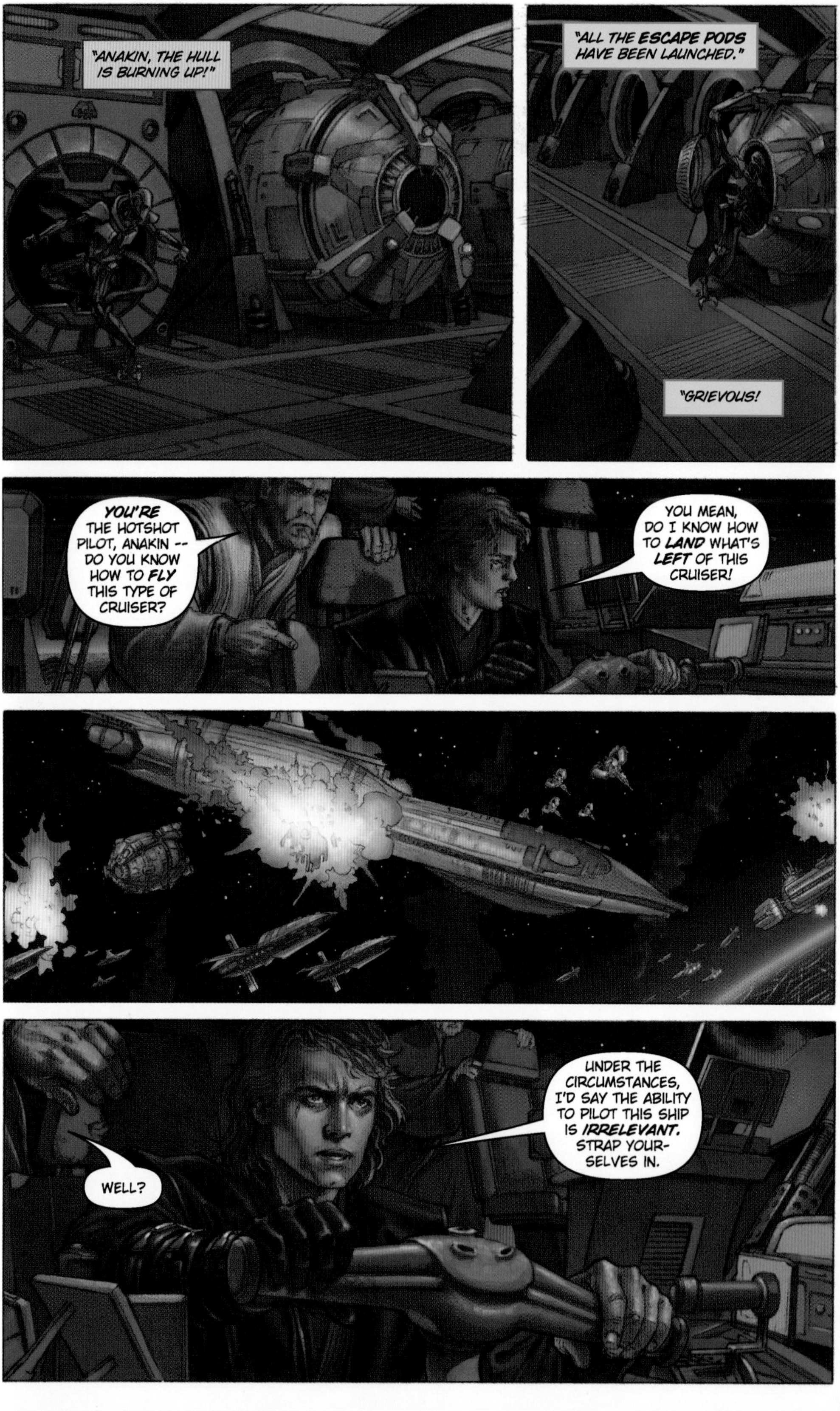
"ANAKIN, THE HULL IS BURNING UP!"
"ALL THE ESCAPE PODS HAVE BEEN LAUNCHED."
"GRIEVOUS!
YOU'RE THE HOTSHOT PILOT, ANAKIN -- DO YOU KNOW HOW TO FLY THIS TYPE OF CRUISER?
YOU MEAN, DO I KNOW HOW TO LAND WHAT'S LEFT OF THIS CRUISER!
WELL?
UNDER THE CIRCUMSTANCES, I'D SAY THE ABILITY TO PILOT THIS SHIP IS IRRELEVANT. STRAP YOURSELVES IN.

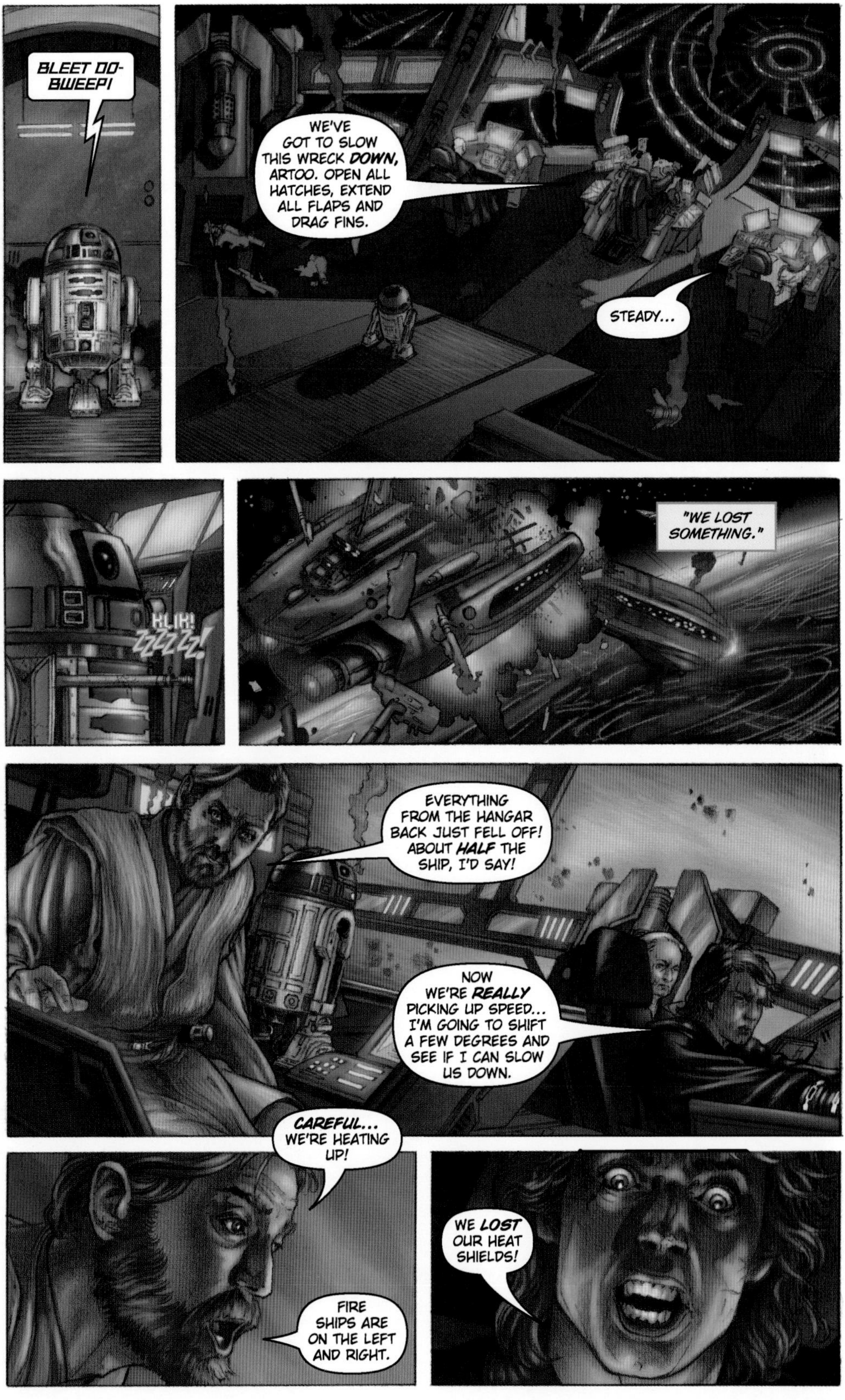
BLEET DO-BWEEP!
WE'VE GOT TO SLOW THIS WRECK DOWN, ARTOO. OPEN ALL HATCHES, EXTEND ALL FLAPS AND DRAG FINS.
STEADY...
KLIK! ZZZZZZ!
"WE LOST SOMETHING."
EVERYTHING FROM THE HANGAR BACK JUST FELL OFF! ABOUT HALF THE SHIP, I'D SAY!
NOW WE'RE REALLY PICKING UP SPEED... I'M GOING TO SHIFT A FEW DEGREES AND SEE IF I CAN SLOW US DOWN.
CAREFUL... WE'RE HEATING UP!
FIRE SHIPS ARE ON THE LEFT AND RIGHT.
WE LOST OUR HEAT SHIELDS!

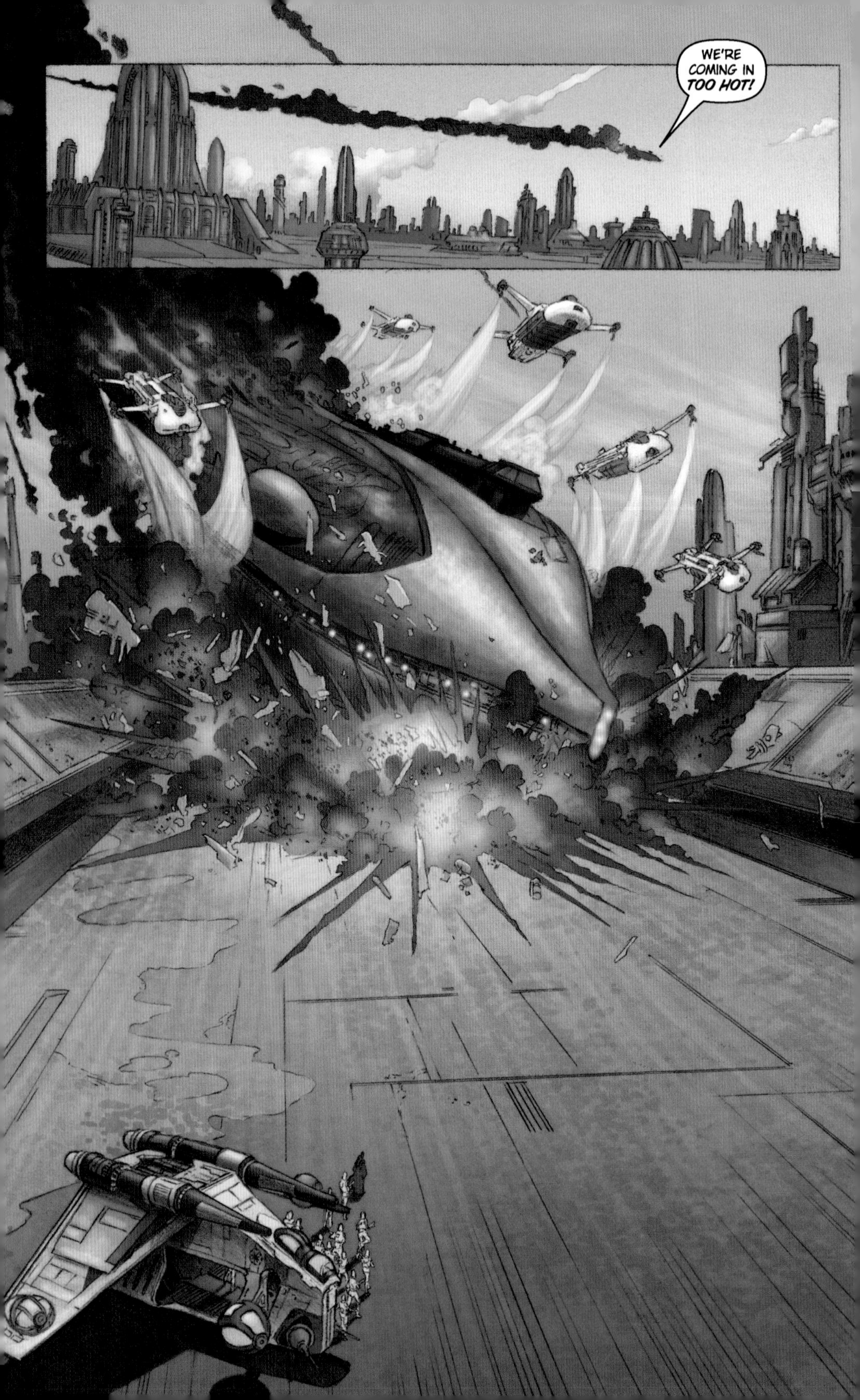
WE'RE COMING IN TOO HOT!

CHANCELLOR, ARE YOU ALL RIGHT?

I AM -- THANKS TO *THESE* TWO.

I KILLED COUNT DOOKU.

UNFORTUNATELY, GENERAL GRIEVOUS ESCAPED.

AND SO THE WAR WILL *CONTINUE.*

WITHOUT COUNT DOOKU THE SEPARATISTS ARE *LEADERLESS. NOW* IS THE TIME TO SUE FOR *PEACE.*

NONSENSE, MASTER WINDU! WITH GRIEVOUS STILL ALIVE, THEIR ABILITY TO WAGE WAR HAS NEVER BEEN *STRONGER.*

THEN WE WILL TRACK DOWN GRIEVOUS AND *DESTROY* HIM. THIS WAR *MUST* END!

WHAT IF MASTER YODA'S FEELINGS ARE *CORRECT,* AND COUNT DOOKU WAS MERELY THE *APPRENTICE* TO THE SITH LORD?

MY JEDI FRIENDS --

THAT'S A QUESTION ONLY TIME WILL REVEAL.

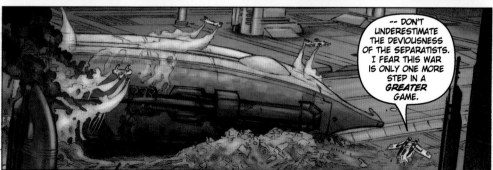

-- DON'T UNDERESTIMATE THE DEVIOUSNESS OF THE SEPARATISTS. I FEAR THIS WAR IS ONLY ONE MORE STEP IN A *GREATER* GAME.

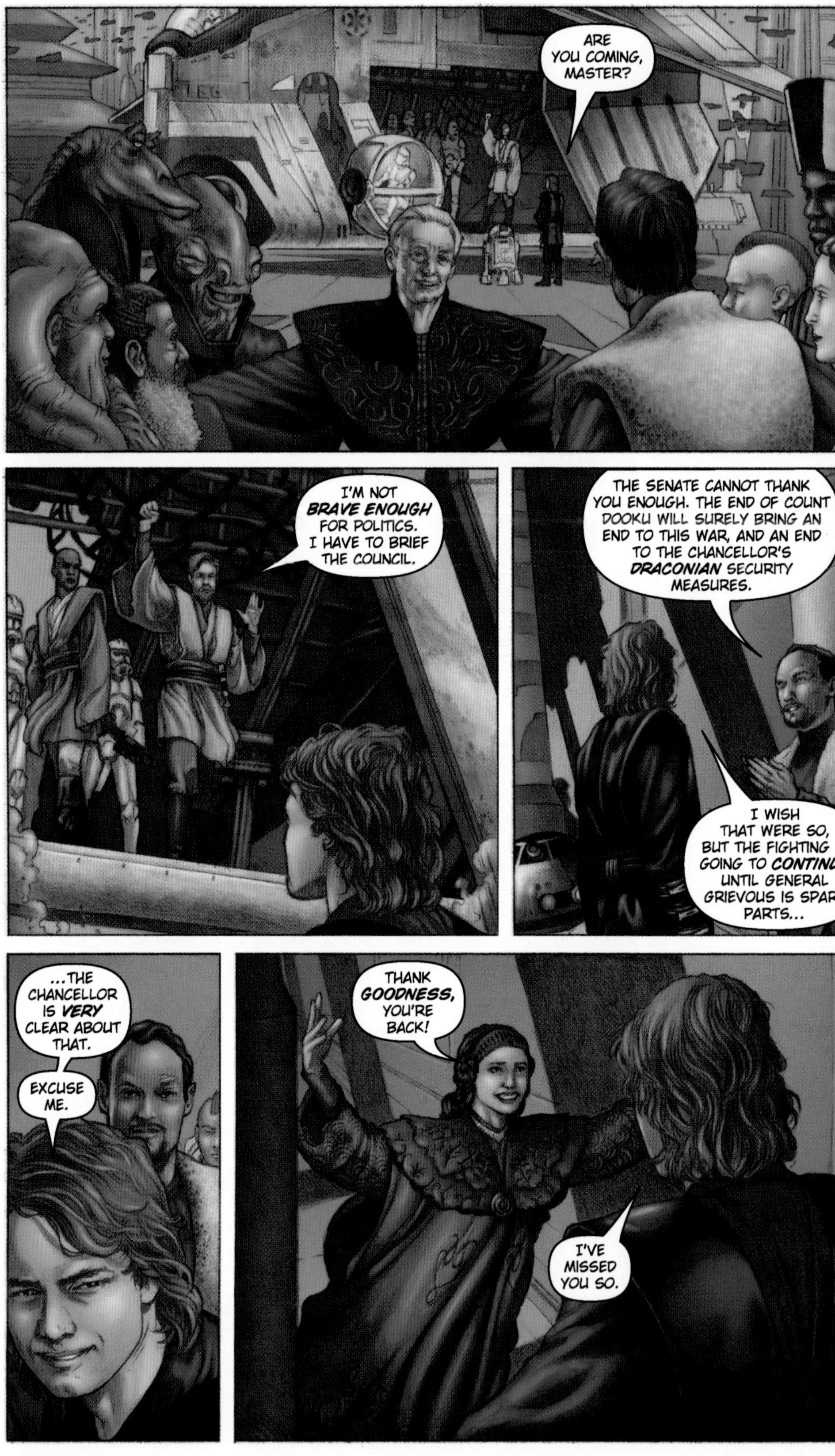

ARE YOU COMING, MASTER?
I'M NOT BRAVE ENOUGH FOR POLITICS. I HAVE TO BRIEF THE COUNCIL.
THE SENATE CANNOT THANK YOU ENOUGH. THE END OF COUNT DOOKU WILL SURELY BRING AN END TO THIS WAR, AND AN END TO THE CHANCELLOR'S DRACONIAN SECURITY MEASURES.
I WISH THAT WERE SO, BUT THE FIGHTING IS GOING TO CONTINUE UNTIL GENERAL GRIEVOUS IS SPARE PARTS...
...THE CHANCELLOR IS VERY CLEAR ABOUT THAT.
EXCUSE ME.
THANK GOODNESS, YOU'RE BACK!
I'VE MISSED YOU SO.

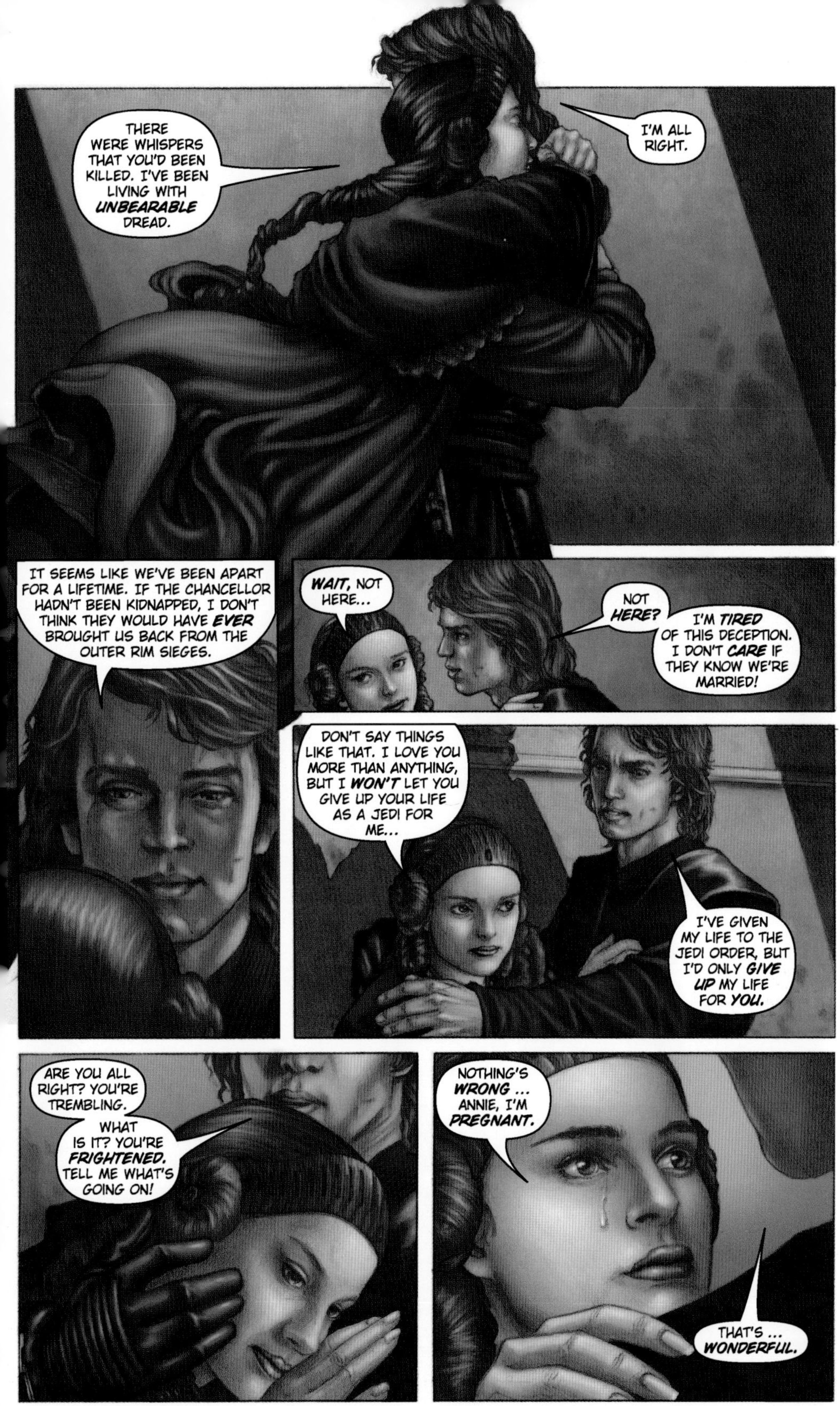
THERE WERE WHISPERS THAT YOU'D BEEN KILLED. I'VE BEEN LIVING WITH UNBEARABLE DREAD.
I'M ALL RIGHT.
IT SEEMS LIKE WE'VE BEEN APART FOR A LIFETIME. IF THE CHANCELLOR HADN'T BEEN KIDNAPPED, I DON'T THINK THEY WOULD HAVE EVER BROUGHT US BACK FROM THE OUTER RIM SIEGES.
WAIT, NOT HERE...
NOT HERE?
I'M TIRED OF THIS DECEPTION. I DON'T CARE IF THEY KNOW WE'RE MARRIED!
DON'T SAY THINGS LIKE THAT. I LOVE YOU MORE THAN ANYTHING, BUT I WON'T LET YOU GIVE UP YOUR LIFE AS A JEDI FOR ME...
I'VE GIVEN MY LIFE TO THE JEDI ORDER, BUT I'D ONLY GIVE UP MY LIFE FOR YOU.
ARE YOU ALL RIGHT? YOU'RE TREMBLING.
WHAT IS IT? YOU'RE FRIGHTENED. TELL ME WHAT'S GOING ON!
NOTHING'S WRONG ... ANNIE, I'M PREGNANT.
THAT'S ... WONDERFUL.

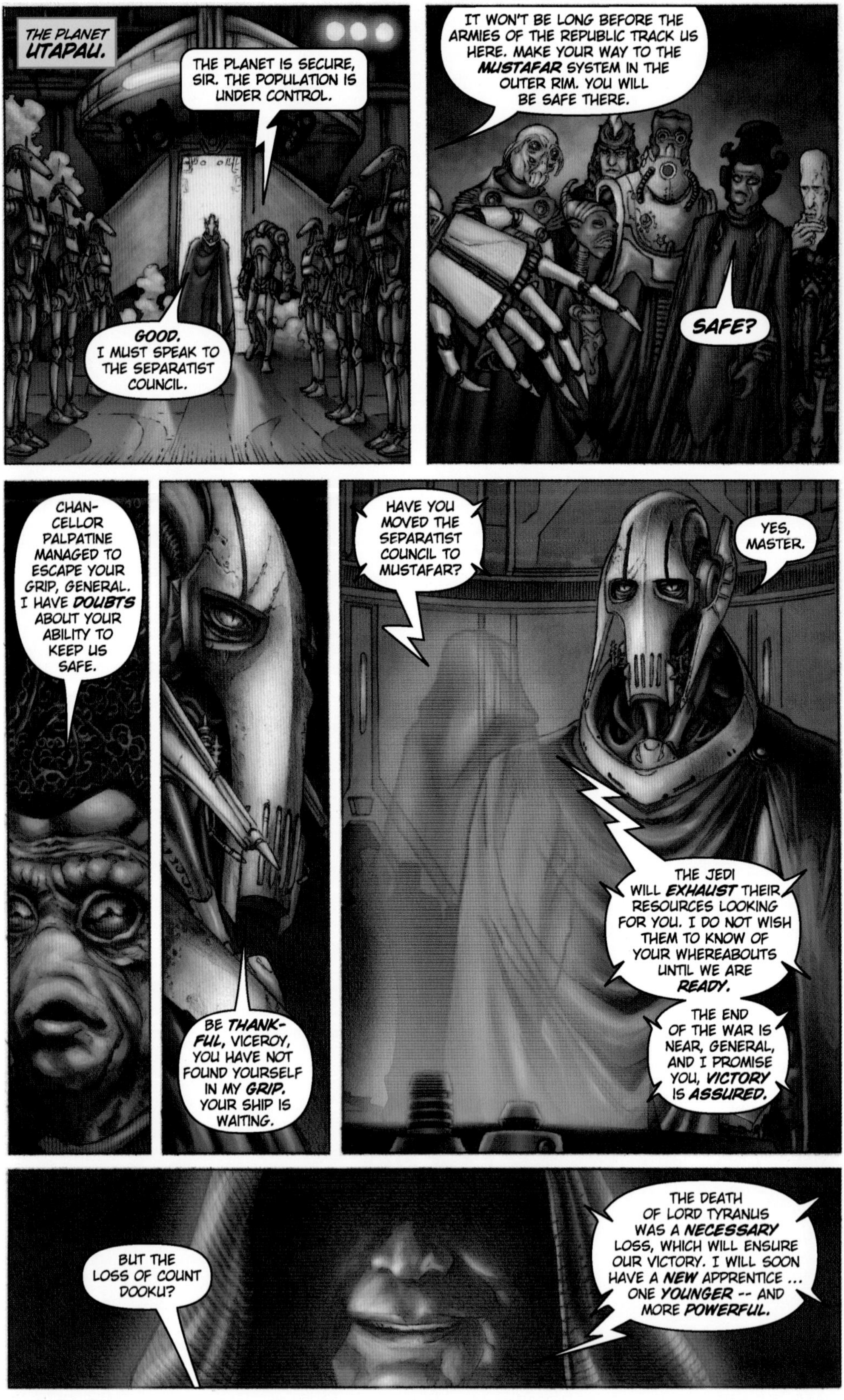
THE PLANET UTAPAU.
THE PLANET IS SECURE, SIR. THE POPULATION IS UNDER CONTROL.
GOOD. I MUST SPEAK TO THE SEPARATIST COUNCIL.
IT WON'T BE LONG BEFORE THE ARMIES OF THE REPUBLIC TRACK US HERE. MAKE YOUR WAY TO THE MUSTAFAR SYSTEM IN THE OUTER RIM. YOU WILL BE SAFE THERE.
SAFE?
CHAN-CELLOR PALPATINE MANAGED TO ESCAPE YOUR GRIP, GENERAL. I HAVE DOUBTS ABOUT YOUR ABILITY TO KEEP US SAFE.
BE THANK-FUL, VICEROY, YOU HAVE NOT FOUND YOURSELF IN MY GRIP. YOUR SHIP IS WAITING.
HAVE YOU MOVED THE SEPARATIST COUNCIL TO MUSTAFAR?
YES, MASTER.
THE JEDI WILL EXHAUST THEIR RESOURCES LOOKING FOR YOU. I DO NOT WISH THEM TO KNOW OF YOUR WHEREABOUTS UNTIL WE ARE READY.
THE END OF THE WAR IS NEAR, GENERAL, AND I PROMISE YOU, VICTORY IS ASSURED.
BUT THE LOSS OF COUNT DOOKU?
THE DEATH OF LORD TYRANUS WAS A NECESSARY LOSS, WHICH WILL ENSURE OUR VICTORY. I WILL SOON HAVE A NEW APPRENTICE ... ONE YOUNGER -- AND MORE POWERFUL.

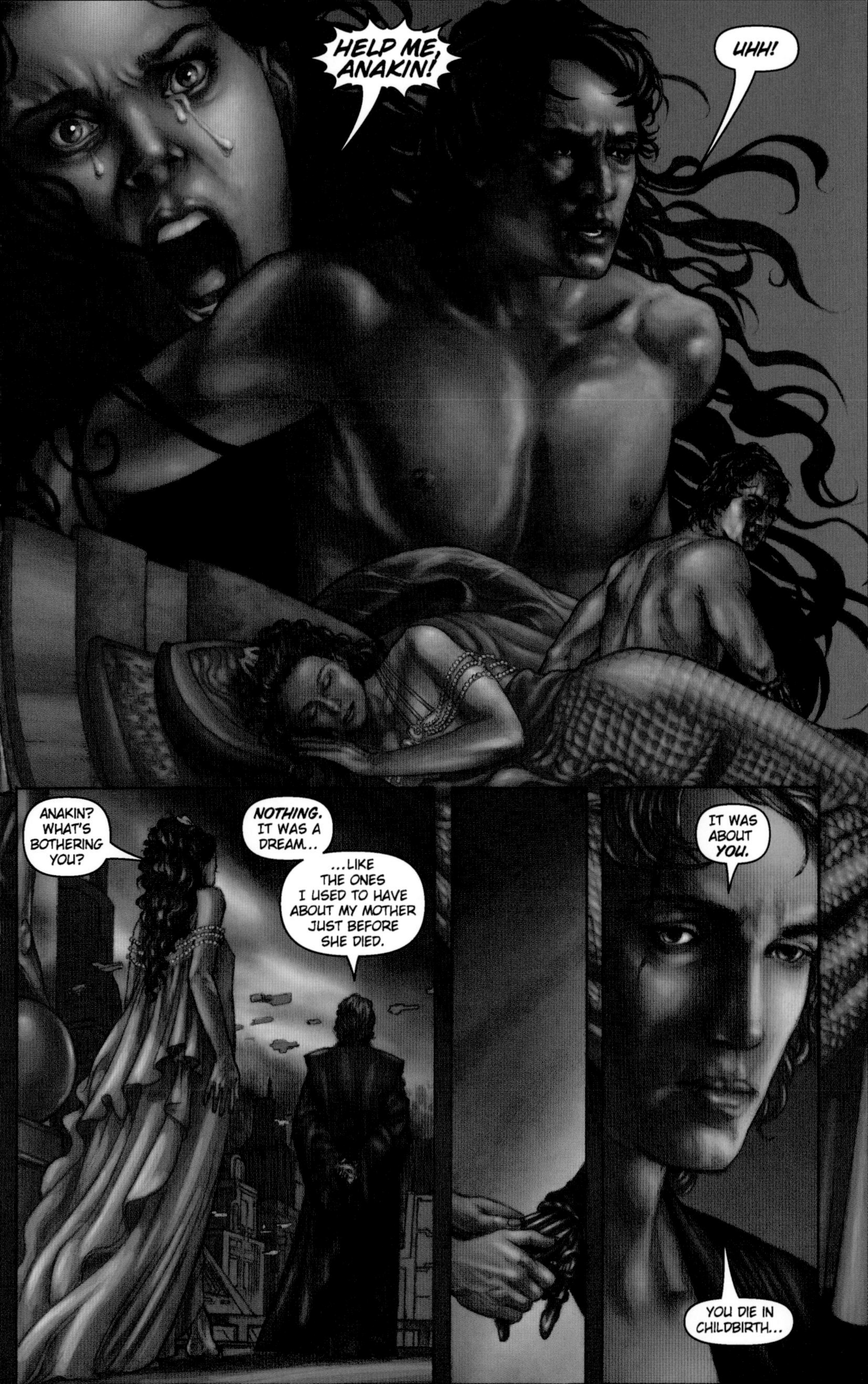
HELP ME, ANAKIN!
UHH!
ANAKIN? WHAT'S BOTHERING YOU?
NOTHING. IT WAS A DREAM...
...LIKE THE ONES I USED TO HAVE ABOUT MY MOTHER JUST BEFORE SHE DIED.
IT WAS ABOUT YOU.
YOU DIE IN CHILDBIRTH...

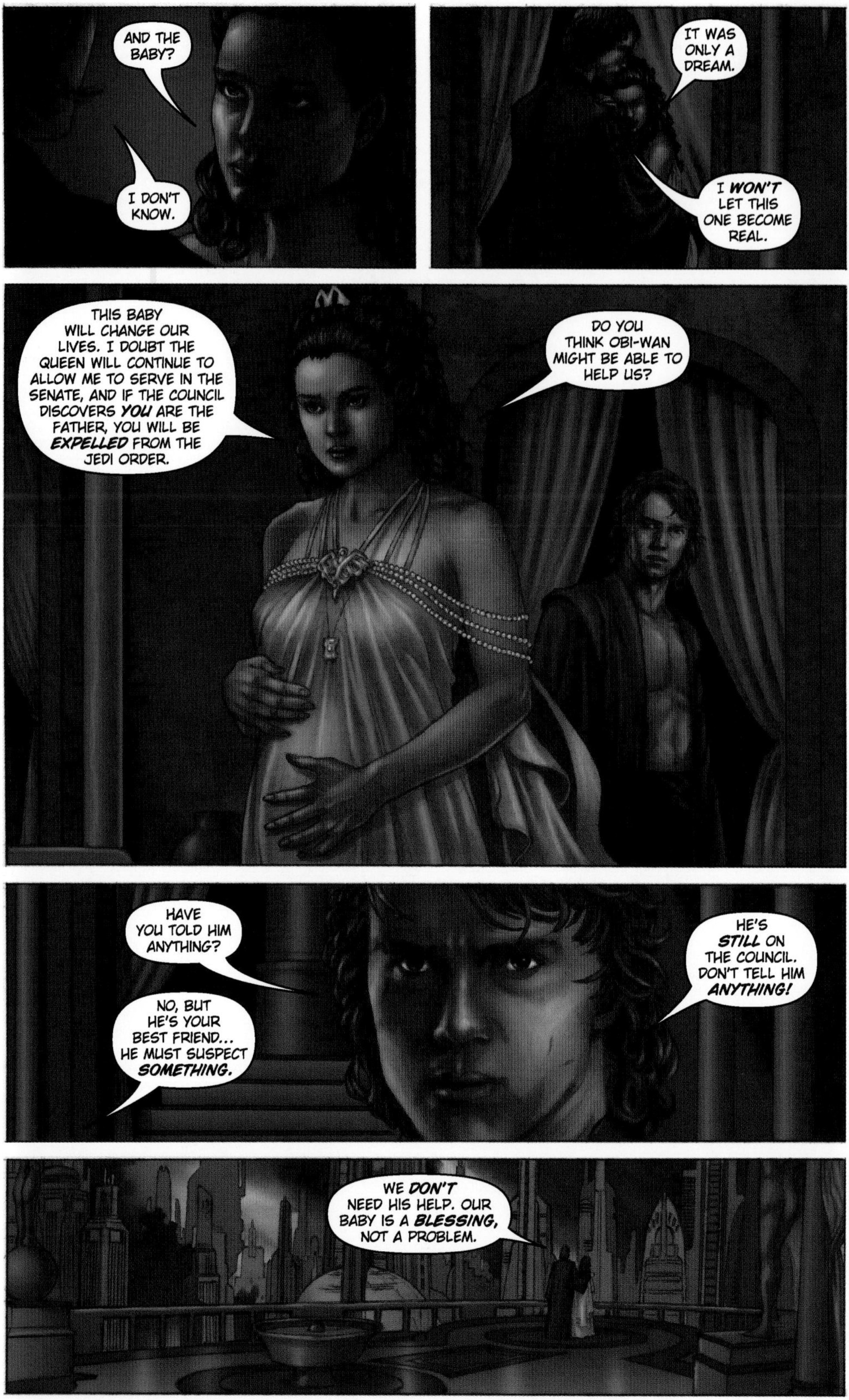
AND THE BABY?
I DON'T KNOW.
IT WAS ONLY A DREAM.
I WON'T LET THIS ONE BECOME REAL.
THIS BABY WILL CHANGE OUR LIVES. I DOUBT THE QUEEN WILL CONTINUE TO ALLOW ME TO SERVE IN THE SENATE, AND IF THE COUNCIL DISCOVERS YOU ARE THE FATHER, YOU WILL BE EXPELLED FROM THE JEDI ORDER.
DO YOU THINK OBI-WAN MIGHT BE ABLE TO HELP US?
HAVE YOU TOLD HIM ANYTHING?
NO, BUT HE'S YOUR BEST FRIEND... HE MUST SUSPECT SOMETHING.
HE'S STILL ON THE COUNCIL. DON'T TELL HIM ANYTHING!
WE DON'T NEED HIS HELP. OUR BABY IS A BLESSING, NOT A PROBLEM.

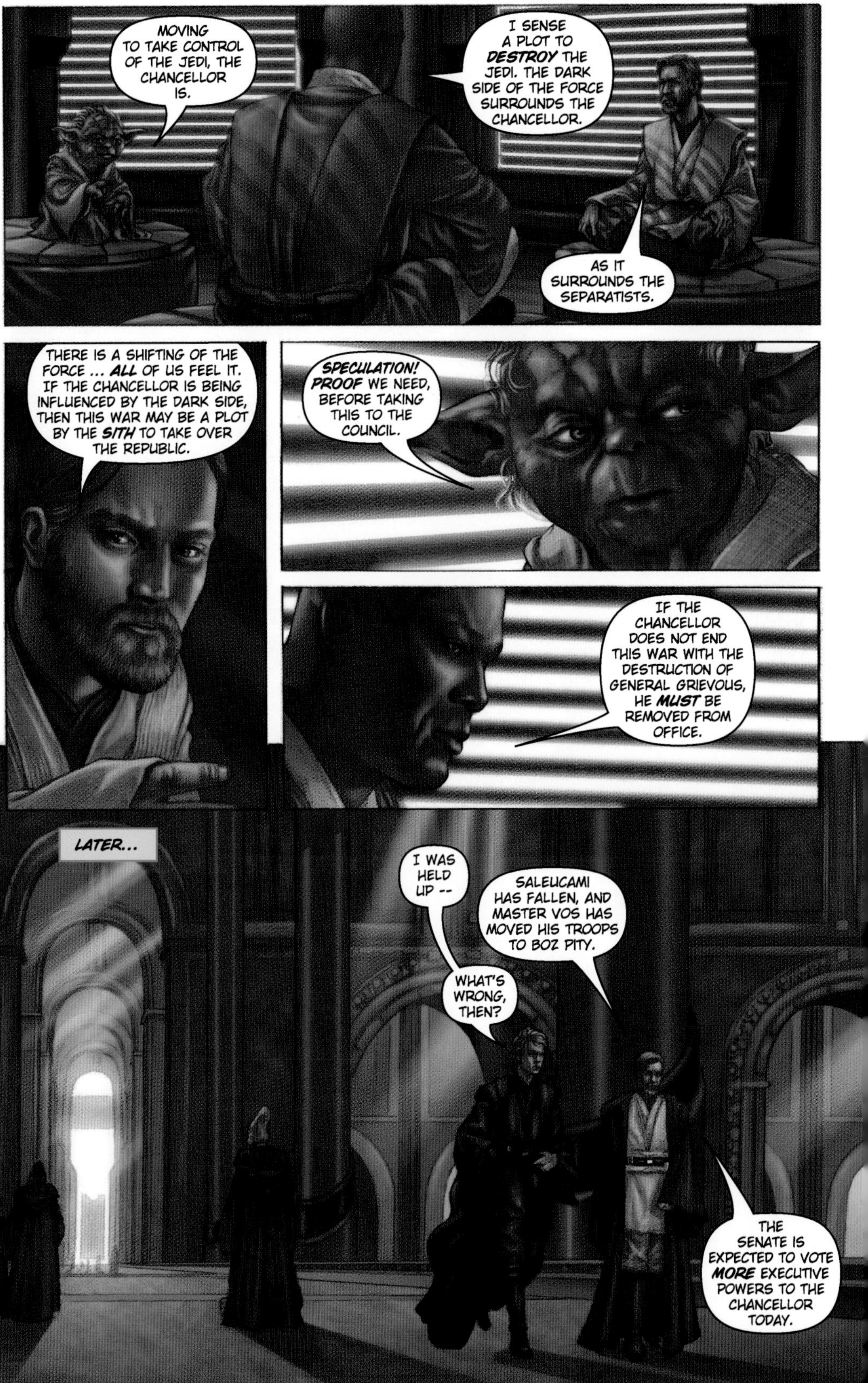
MOVING TO TAKE CONTROL OF THE JEDI, THE CHANCELLOR IS.
I SENSE A PLOT TO DESTROY THE JEDI. THE DARK SIDE OF THE FORCE SURROUNDS THE CHANCELLOR.
AS IT SURROUNDS THE SEPARATISTS.
THERE IS A SHIFTING OF THE FORCE ... ALL OF US FEEL IT. IF THE CHANCELLOR IS BEING INFLUENCED BY THE DARK SIDE, THEN THIS WAR MAY BE A PLOT BY THE SITH TO TAKE OVER THE REPUBLIC.
SPECULATION! PROOF WE NEED, BEFORE TAKING THIS TO THE COUNCIL.
IF THE CHANCELLOR DOES NOT END THIS WAR WITH THE DESTRUCTION OF GENERAL GRIEVOUS, HE MUST BE REMOVED FROM OFFICE.
LATER...
I WAS HELD UP --
SALEUCAMI HAS FALLEN, AND MASTER VOS HAS MOVED HIS TROOPS TO BOZ PITY.
WHAT'S WRONG, THEN?
THE SENATE IS EXPECTED TO VOTE MORE EXECUTIVE POWERS TO THE CHANCELLOR TODAY.

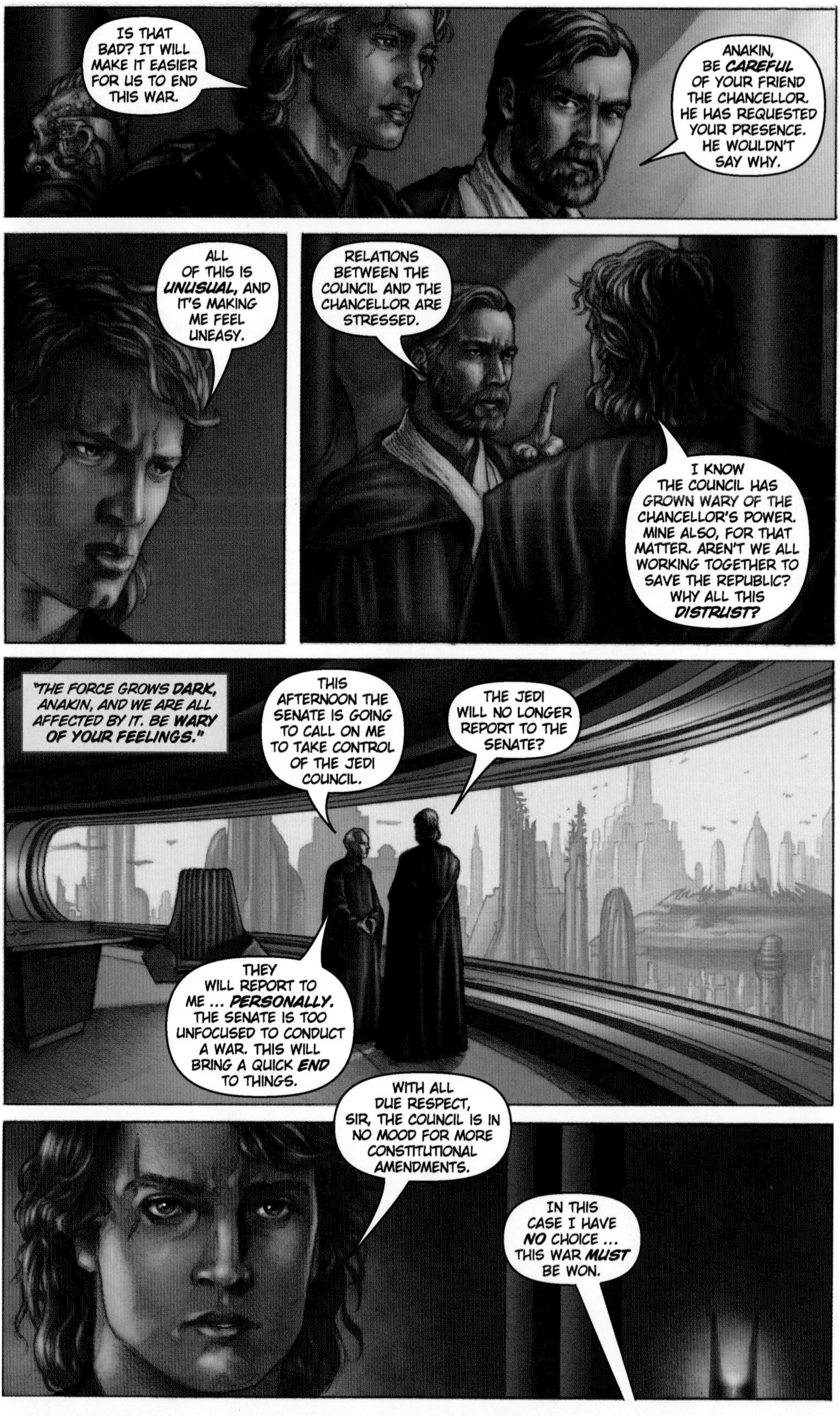
IS THAT BAD? IT WILL MAKE IT EASIER FOR US TO END THIS WAR.
ANAKIN, BE ***CAREFUL*** OF YOUR FRIEND THE CHANCELLOR. HE HAS REQUESTED YOUR PRESENCE. HE WOULDN'T SAY WHY.
ALL OF THIS IS ***UNUSUAL,*** AND IT'S MAKING ME FEEL UNEASY.
RELATIONS BETWEEN THE COUNCIL AND THE CHANCELLOR ARE STRESSED.
I KNOW THE COUNCIL HAS GROWN WARY OF THE CHANCELLOR'S POWER. MINE ALSO, FOR THAT MATTER. AREN'T WE ALL WORKING TOGETHER TO SAVE THE REPUBLIC? WHY ALL THIS ***DISTRUST?***
*"THE FORCE GROWS **DARK**, ANAKIN, AND WE ARE ALL AFFECTED BY IT. BE **WARY OF YOUR FEELINGS.**"*
THIS AFTERNOON THE SENATE IS GOING TO CALL ON ME TO TAKE CONTROL OF THE JEDI COUNCIL.
THE JEDI WILL NO LONGER REPORT TO THE SENATE?
THEY WILL REPORT TO ME ... ***PERSONALLY.*** THE SENATE IS TOO UNFOCUSED TO CONDUCT A WAR. THIS WILL BRING A QUICK ***END*** TO THINGS.
WITH ALL DUE RESPECT, SIR, THE COUNCIL IS IN NO MOOD FOR MORE CONSTITUTIONAL AMENDMENTS.
IN THIS CASE I HAVE ***NO*** CHOICE ... THIS WAR ***MUST*** BE WON.

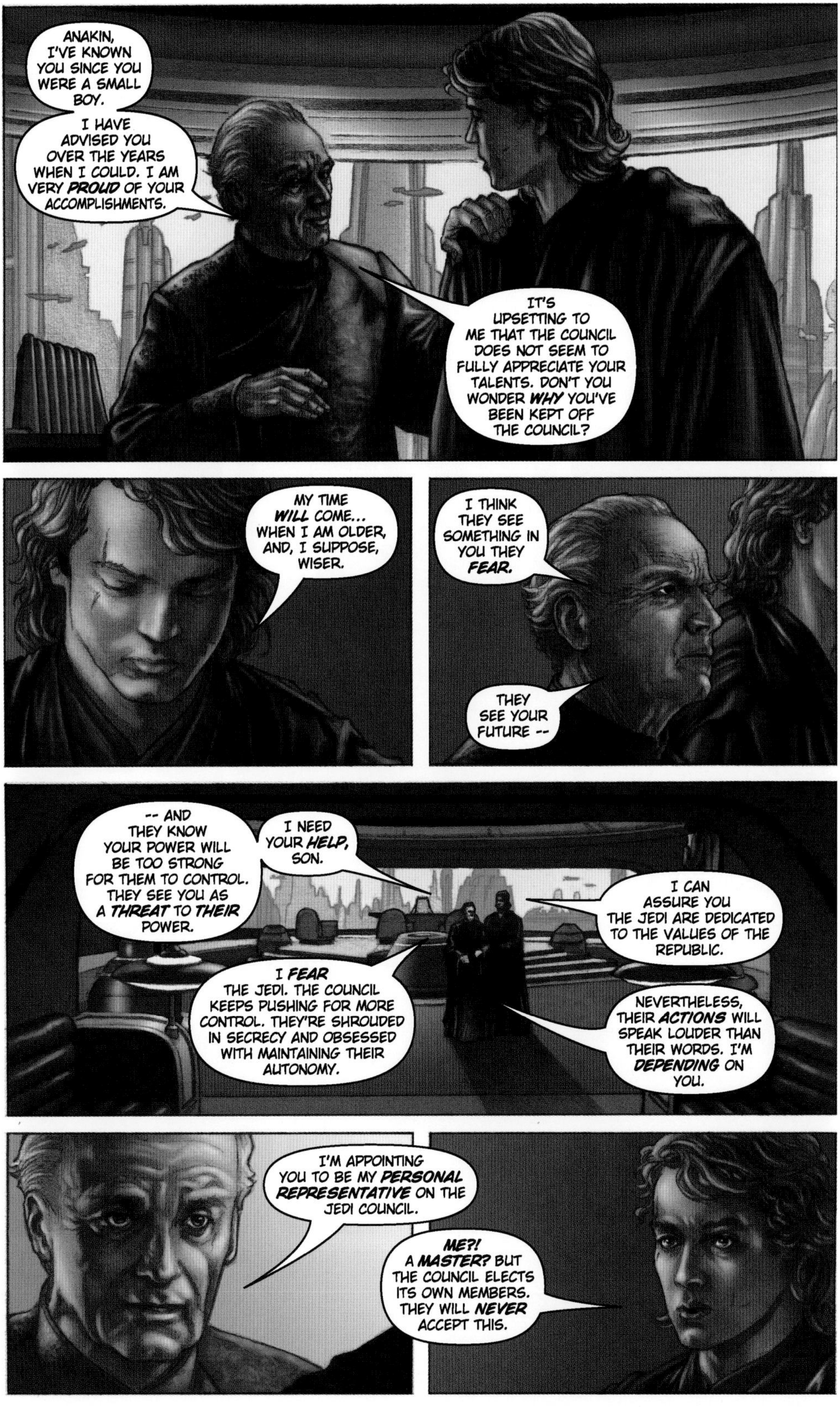

ANAKIN, I'VE KNOWN YOU SINCE YOU WERE A SMALL BOY.
I HAVE ADVISED YOU OVER THE YEARS WHEN I COULD. I AM VERY *PROUD* OF YOUR ACCOMPLISHMENTS.
IT'S UPSETTING TO ME THAT THE COUNCIL DOES NOT SEEM TO FULLY APPRECIATE YOUR TALENTS. DON'T YOU WONDER *WHY* YOU'VE BEEN KEPT OFF THE COUNCIL?
MY TIME *WILL* COME... WHEN I AM OLDER, AND, I SUPPOSE, WISER.
I THINK THEY SEE SOMETHING IN YOU THEY *FEAR.*
THEY SEE YOUR FUTURE --
-- AND THEY KNOW YOUR POWER WILL BE TOO STRONG FOR THEM TO CONTROL. THEY SEE YOU AS A *THREAT* TO *THEIR* POWER.
I NEED YOUR *HELP,* SON.
I CAN ASSURE YOU THE JEDI ARE DEDICATED TO THE VALUES OF THE REPUBLIC.
I *FEAR* THE JEDI. THE COUNCIL KEEPS PUSHING FOR MORE CONTROL. THEY'RE SHROUDED IN SECRECY AND OBSESSED WITH MAINTAINING THEIR AUTONOMY.
NEVERTHELESS, THEIR *ACTIONS* WILL SPEAK LOUDER THAN THEIR WORDS. I'M *DEPENDING* ON YOU.
I'M APPOINTING YOU TO BE MY *PERSONAL REPRESENTATIVE* ON THE JEDI COUNCIL.
ME?! A *MASTER?* BUT THE COUNCIL ELECTS ITS OWN MEMBERS. THEY WILL *NEVER* ACCEPT THIS.

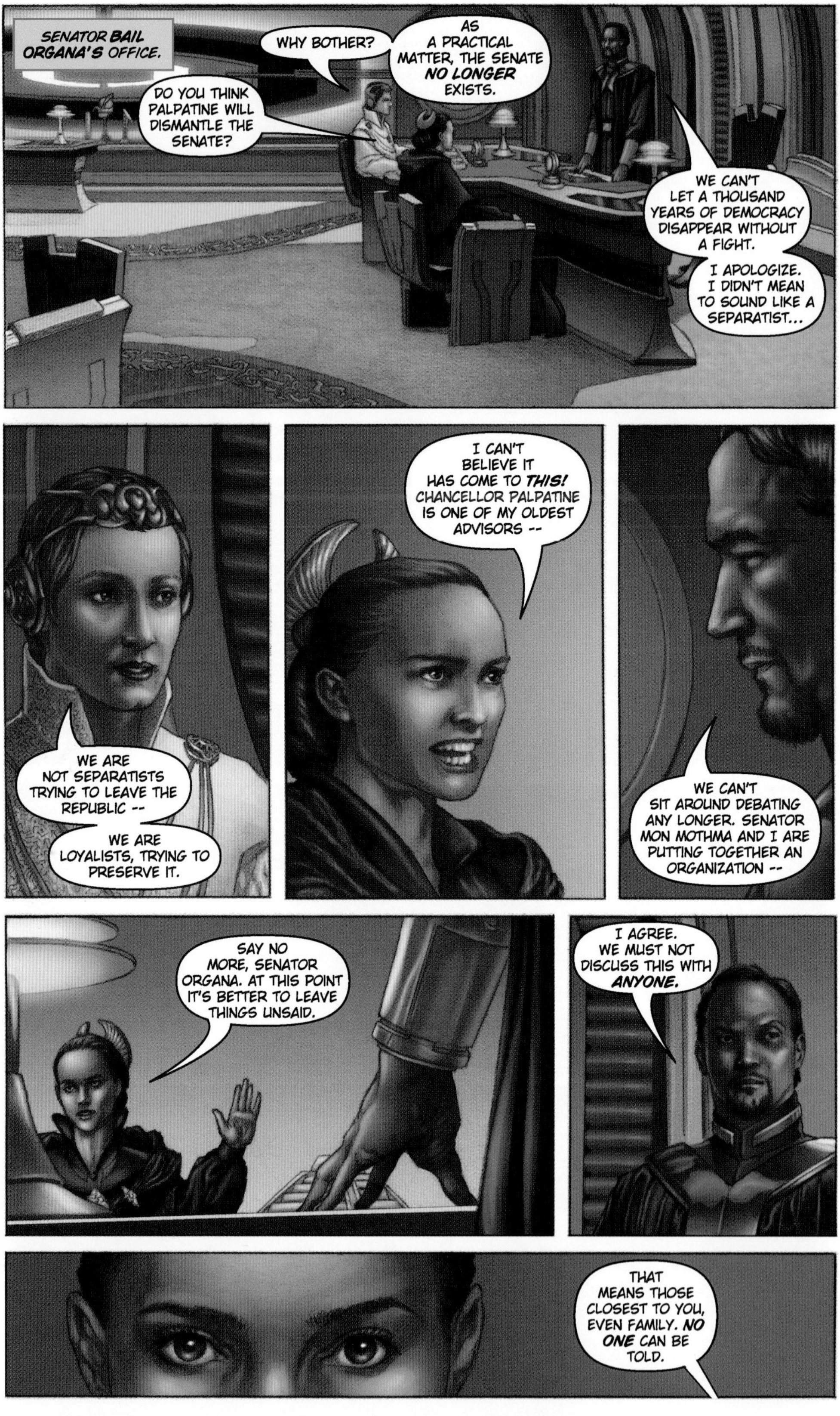
SENATOR BAIL ORGANA'S OFFICE.
DO YOU THINK PALPATINE WILL DISMANTLE THE SENATE?
WHY BOTHER?
AS A PRACTICAL MATTER, THE SENATE NO LONGER EXISTS.
WE CAN'T LET A THOUSAND YEARS OF DEMOCRACY DISAPPEAR WITHOUT A FIGHT.
I APOLOGIZE. I DIDN'T MEAN TO SOUND LIKE A SEPARATIST...
WE ARE NOT SEPARATISTS TRYING TO LEAVE THE REPUBLIC --
WE ARE LOYALISTS, TRYING TO PRESERVE IT.
I CAN'T BELIEVE IT HAS COME TO THIS! CHANCELLOR PALPATINE IS ONE OF MY OLDEST ADVISORS --
WE CAN'T SIT AROUND DEBATING ANY LONGER. SENATOR MON MOTHMA AND I ARE PUTTING TOGETHER AN ORGANIZATION --
SAY NO MORE, SENATOR ORGANA. AT THIS POINT IT'S BETTER TO LEAVE THINGS UNSAID.
I AGREE. WE MUST NOT DISCUSS THIS WITH ANYONE.
THAT MEANS THOSE CLOSEST TO YOU, EVEN FAMILY. NO ONE CAN BE TOLD.

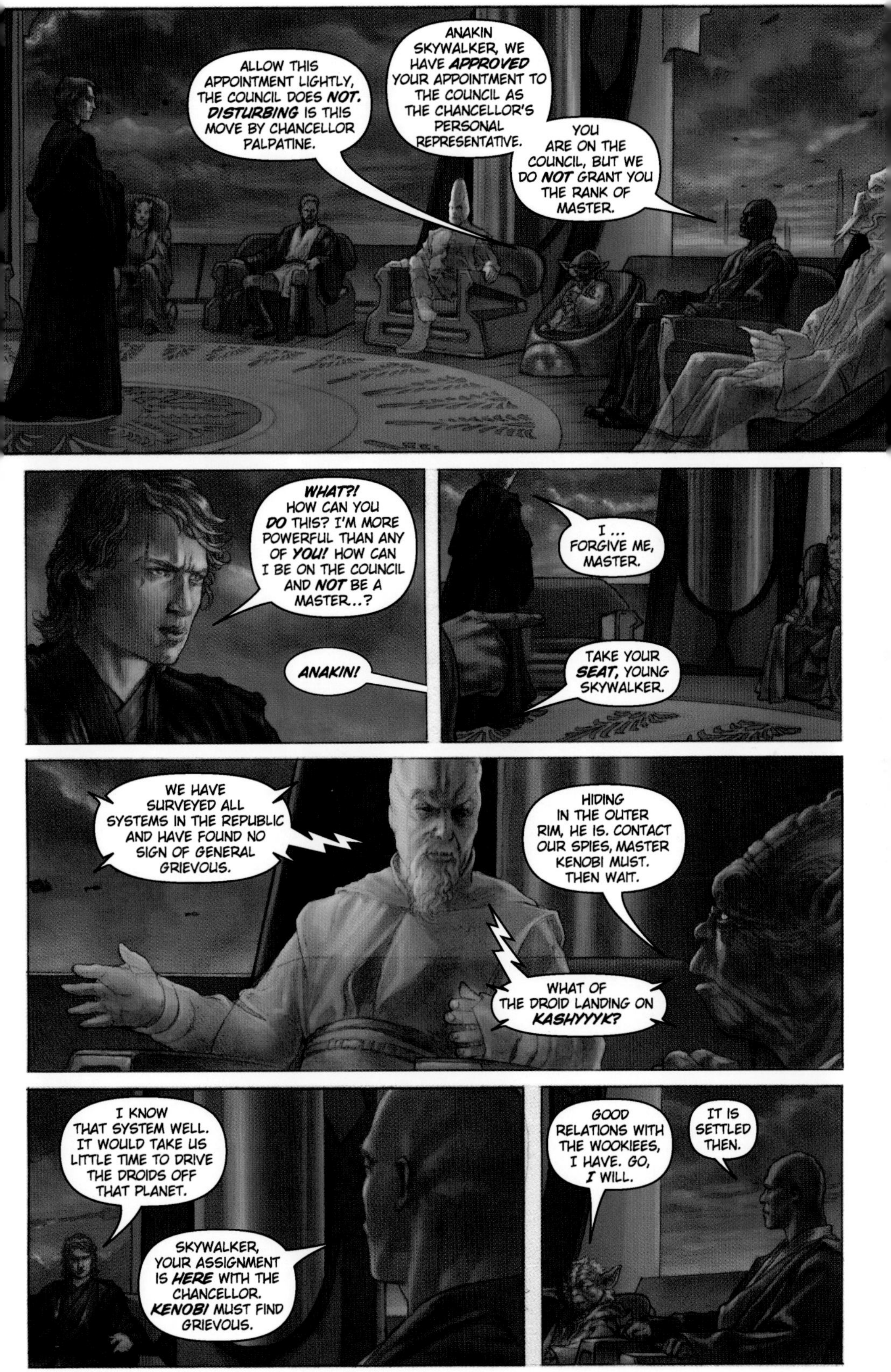
ALLOW THIS APPOINTMENT LIGHTLY, THE COUNCIL DOES NOT. DISTURBING IS THIS MOVE BY CHANCELLOR PALPATINE.
ANAKIN SKYWALKER, WE HAVE APPROVED YOUR APPOINTMENT TO THE COUNCIL AS THE CHANCELLOR'S PERSONAL REPRESENTATIVE.
YOU ARE ON THE COUNCIL, BUT WE DO NOT GRANT YOU THE RANK OF MASTER.
WHAT?! HOW CAN YOU DO THIS? I'M MORE POWERFUL THAN ANY OF YOU! HOW CAN I BE ON THE COUNCIL AND NOT BE A MASTER..?
ANAKIN!
I ... FORGIVE ME, MASTER.
TAKE YOUR SEAT, YOUNG SKYWALKER.
WE HAVE SURVEYED ALL SYSTEMS IN THE REPUBLIC AND HAVE FOUND NO SIGN OF GENERAL GRIEVOUS.
HIDING IN THE OUTER RIM, HE IS. CONTACT OUR SPIES, MASTER KENOBI MUST. THEN WAIT.
WHAT OF THE DROID LANDING ON KASHYYYK?
I KNOW THAT SYSTEM WELL. IT WOULD TAKE US LITTLE TIME TO DRIVE THE DROIDS OFF THAT PLANET.
SKYWALKER, YOUR ASSIGNMENT IS HERE WITH THE CHANCELLOR. KENOBI MUST FIND GRIEVOUS.
GOOD RELATIONS WITH THE WOOKIEES, I HAVE. GO, I WILL.
IT IS SETTLED THEN.

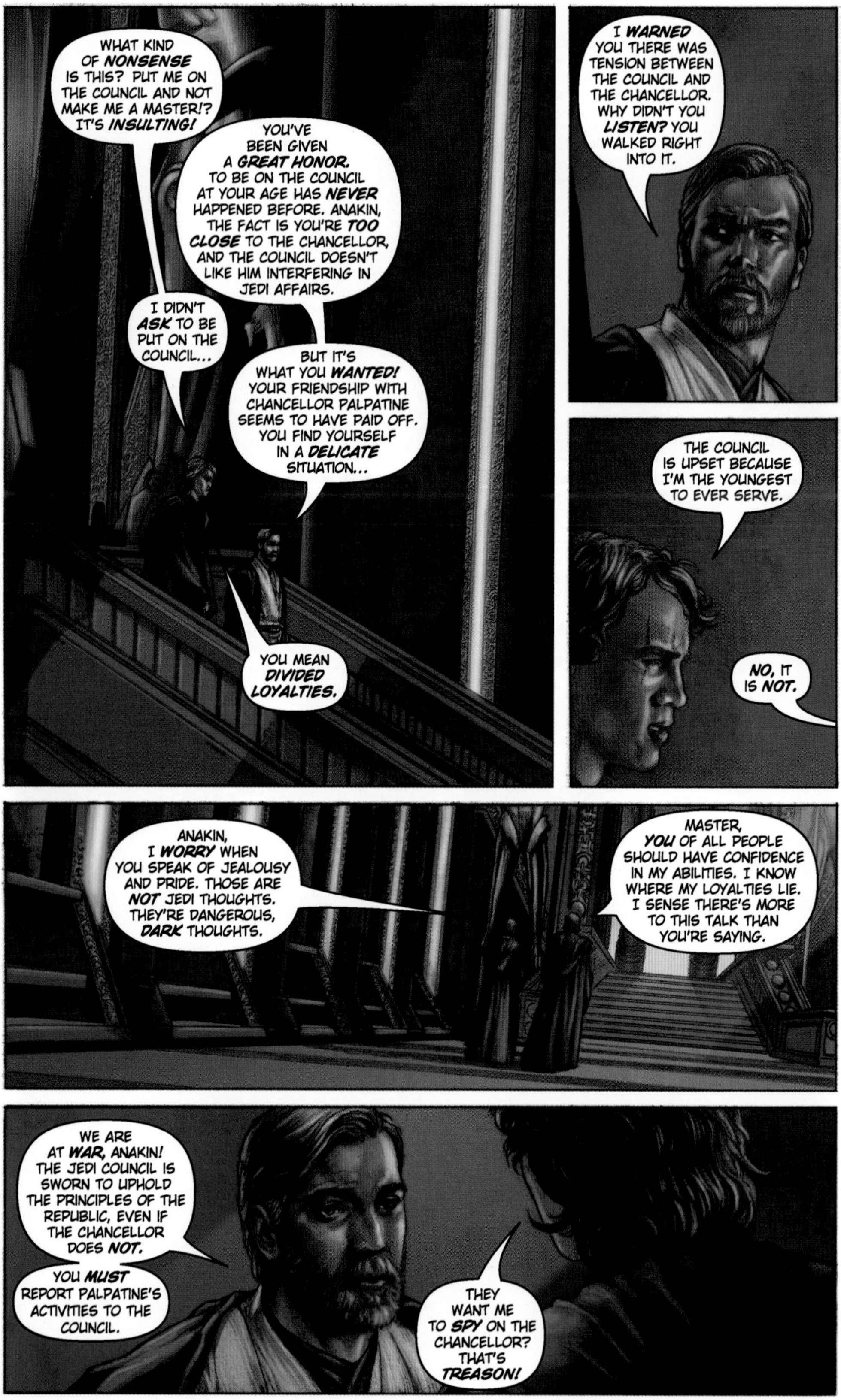
WHAT KIND OF NONSENSE IS THIS? PUT ME ON THE COUNCIL AND NOT MAKE ME A MASTER!? IT'S INSULTING!
YOU'VE BEEN GIVEN A GREAT HONOR. TO BE ON THE COUNCIL AT YOUR AGE HAS NEVER HAPPENED BEFORE. ANAKIN, THE FACT IS YOU'RE TOO CLOSE TO THE CHANCELLOR, AND THE COUNCIL DOESN'T LIKE HIM INTERFERING IN JEDI AFFAIRS.
I DIDN'T ASK TO BE PUT ON THE COUNCIL...
BUT IT'S WHAT YOU WANTED! YOUR FRIENDSHIP WITH CHANCELLOR PALPATINE SEEMS TO HAVE PAID OFF. YOU FIND YOURSELF IN A DELICATE SITUATION...
YOU MEAN DIVIDED LOYALTIES.
I WARNED YOU THERE WAS TENSION BETWEEN THE COUNCIL AND THE CHANCELLOR. WHY DIDN'T YOU LISTEN? YOU WALKED RIGHT INTO IT.
THE COUNCIL IS UPSET BECAUSE I'M THE YOUNGEST TO EVER SERVE.
NO, IT IS NOT.
ANAKIN, I WORRY WHEN YOU SPEAK OF JEALOUSY AND PRIDE. THOSE ARE NOT JEDI THOUGHTS. THEY'RE DANGEROUS, DARK THOUGHTS.
MASTER, YOU OF ALL PEOPLE SHOULD HAVE CONFIDENCE IN MY ABILITIES. I KNOW WHERE MY LOYALTIES LIE. I SENSE THERE'S MORE TO THIS TALK THAN YOU'RE SAYING.
WE ARE AT WAR, ANAKIN! THE JEDI COUNCIL IS SWORN TO UPHOLD THE PRINCIPLES OF THE REPUBLIC, EVEN IF THE CHANCELLOR DOES NOT.
YOU MUST REPORT PALPATINE'S ACTIVITIES TO THE COUNCIL.
THEY WANT ME TO SPY ON THE CHANCELLOR? THAT'S TREASON!

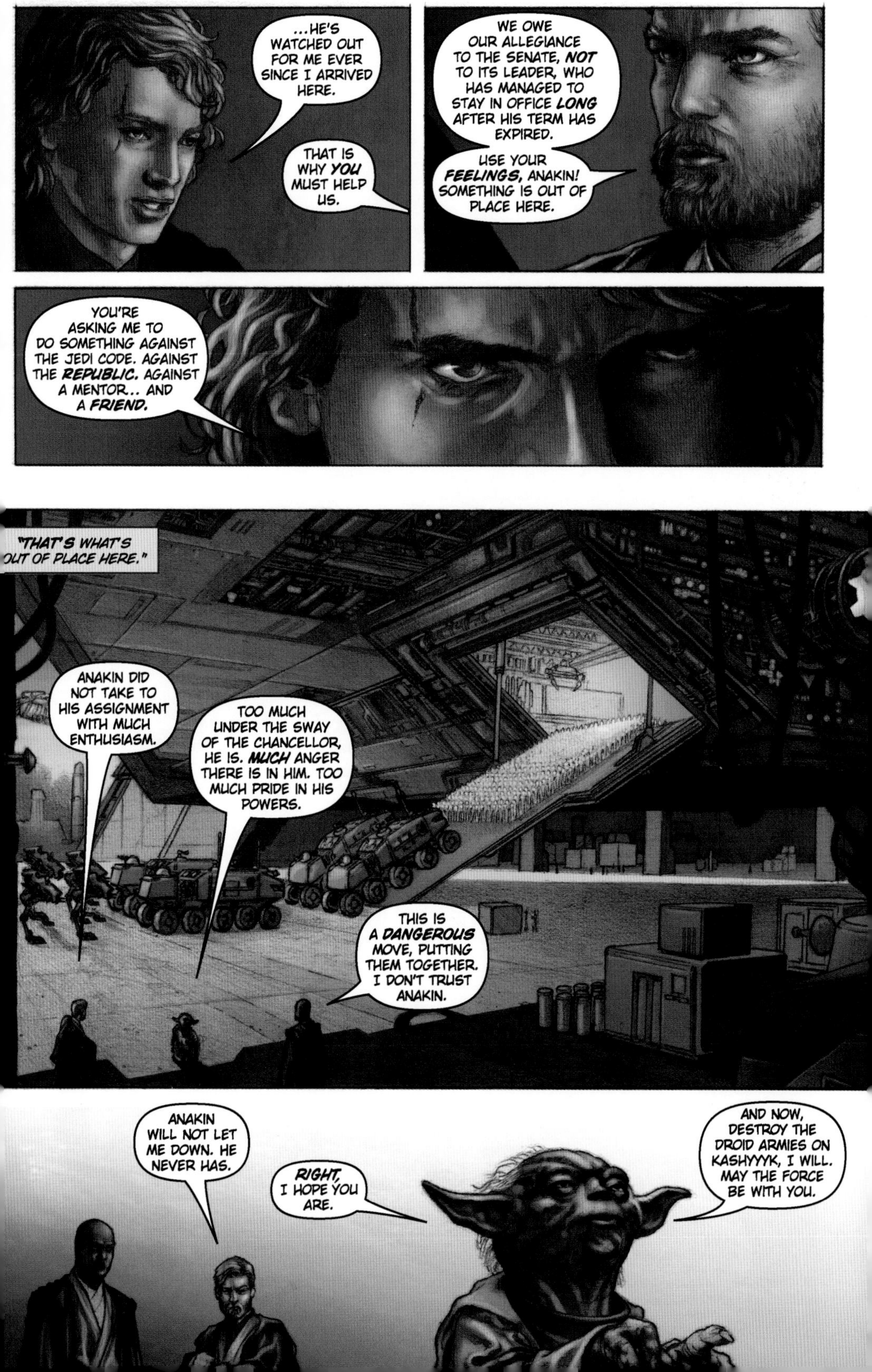
...HE'S WATCHED OUT FOR ME EVER SINCE I ARRIVED HERE.
THAT IS WHY YOU MUST HELP US.
WE OWE OUR ALLEGIANCE TO THE SENATE, NOT TO ITS LEADER, WHO HAS MANAGED TO STAY IN OFFICE LONG AFTER HIS TERM HAS EXPIRED.
USE YOUR FEELINGS, ANAKIN! SOMETHING IS OUT OF PLACE HERE.
YOU'RE ASKING ME TO DO SOMETHING AGAINST THE JEDI CODE. AGAINST THE REPUBLIC. AGAINST A MENTOR... AND A FRIEND.
"THAT'S WHAT'S OUT OF PLACE HERE."
ANAKIN DID NOT TAKE TO HIS ASSIGNMENT WITH MUCH ENTHUSIASM.
TOO MUCH UNDER THE SWAY OF THE CHANCELLOR, HE IS. MUCH ANGER THERE IS IN HIM. TOO MUCH PRIDE IN HIS POWERS.
THIS IS A DANGEROUS MOVE, PUTTING THEM TOGETHER. I DON'T TRUST ANAKIN.
ANAKIN WILL NOT LET ME DOWN. HE NEVER HAS.
RIGHT, I HOPE YOU ARE.
AND NOW, DESTROY THE DROID ARMIES ON KASHYYYK, I WILL. MAY THE FORCE BE WITH YOU.

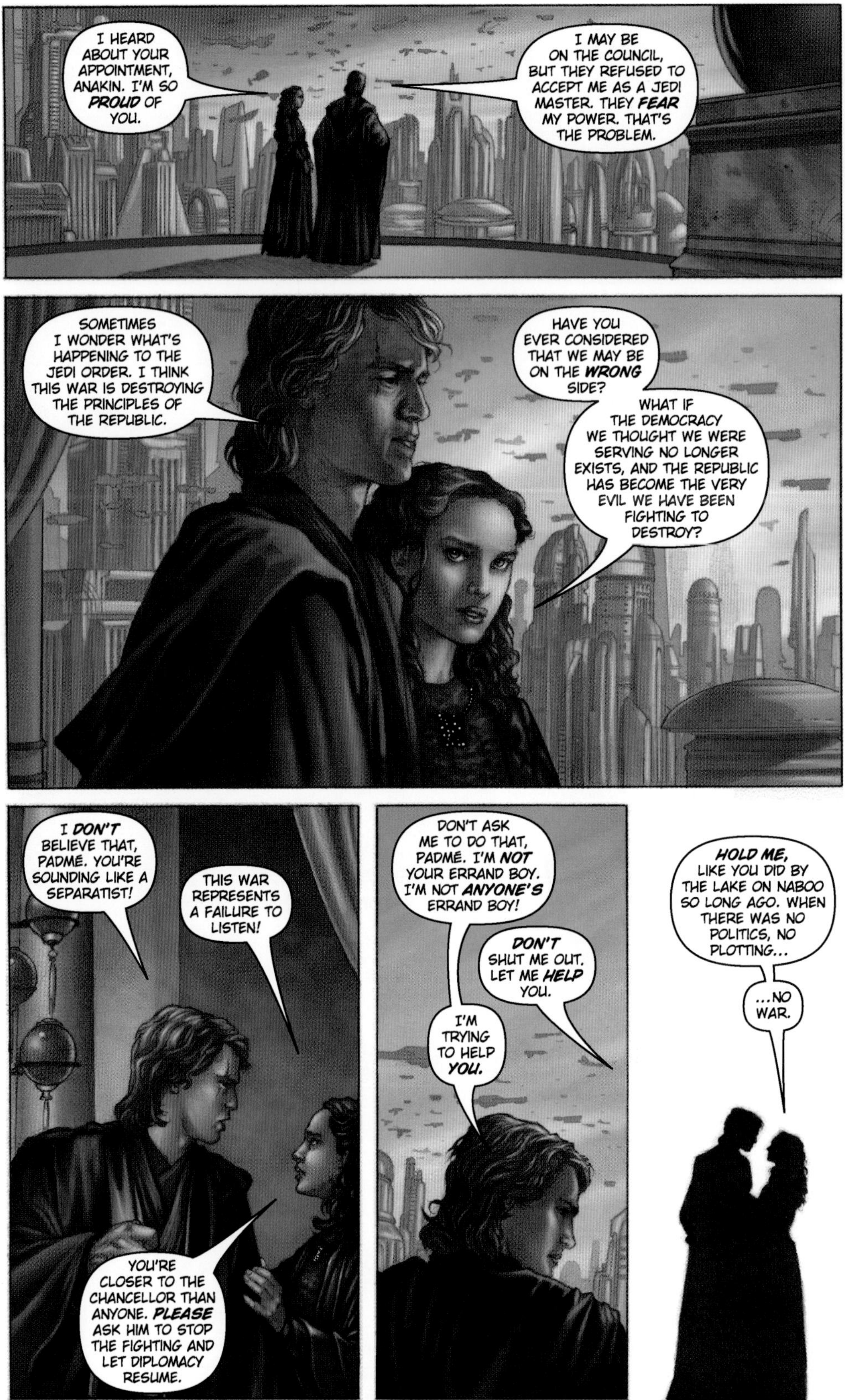
I HEARD ABOUT YOUR APPOINTMENT, ANAKIN. I'M SO PROUD OF YOU.
I MAY BE ON THE COUNCIL, BUT THEY REFUSED TO ACCEPT ME AS A JEDI MASTER. THEY FEAR MY POWER. THAT'S THE PROBLEM.
SOMETIMES I WONDER WHAT'S HAPPENING TO THE JEDI ORDER. I THINK THIS WAR IS DESTROYING THE PRINCIPLES OF THE REPUBLIC.
HAVE YOU EVER CONSIDERED THAT WE MAY BE ON THE WRONG SIDE?
WHAT IF THE DEMOCRACY WE THOUGHT WE WERE SERVING NO LONGER EXISTS, AND THE REPUBLIC HAS BECOME THE VERY EVIL WE HAVE BEEN FIGHTING TO DESTROY?
I DON'T BELIEVE THAT, PADMÉ. YOU'RE SOUNDING LIKE A SEPARATIST!
THIS WAR REPRESENTS A FAILURE TO LISTEN!
YOU'RE CLOSER TO THE CHANCELLOR THAN ANYONE. PLEASE ASK HIM TO STOP THE FIGHTING AND LET DIPLOMACY RESUME.
DON'T ASK ME TO DO THAT, PADMÉ. I'M NOT YOUR ERRAND BOY. I'M NOT ANYONE'S ERRAND BOY!
DON'T SHUT ME OUT. LET ME HELP YOU.
I'M TRYING TO HELP YOU.
HOLD ME, LIKE YOU DID BY THE LAKE ON NABOO SO LONG AGO. WHEN THERE WAS NO POLITICS, NO PLOTTING...
...NO WAR.

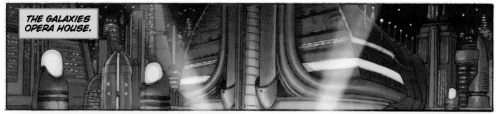

THE GALAXIES OPERA HOUSE.

YOU WANTED TO SEE ME, CHANCELLOR?

YES, ANAKIN. YOU KNOW I'M NOT ABLE TO RELY ON THE JEDI COUNCIL. YOU MUST SENSE WHAT I'VE COME TO SUSPECT...

THE JEDI COUNCIL WANTS CONTROL OF THE REPUBLIC. THEY'RE PLANNING TO *BETRAY* ME.

YOU *KNOW*, DON'T YOU?

I KNOW THEY DON'T TRUST YOU.

THEY ASKED YOU TO *SPY* ON ME, DIDN'T THEY?

"ALL THOSE WHO GAIN POWER ARE AFRAID TO LOSE IT." EVEN THE *JEDI*.

THE JEDI USE THEIR POWER FOR *GOOD*.

GOOD IS A POINT OF VIEW, ANAKIN. THE JEDI POINT OF VIEW IS NOT THE *ONLY* VALID ONE. THE DARK LORDS OF THE SITH BELIEVE IN SECURITY AND JUSTICE ALSO, YET THEY ARE CONSIDERED BY THE JEDI TO BE --

EVIL.

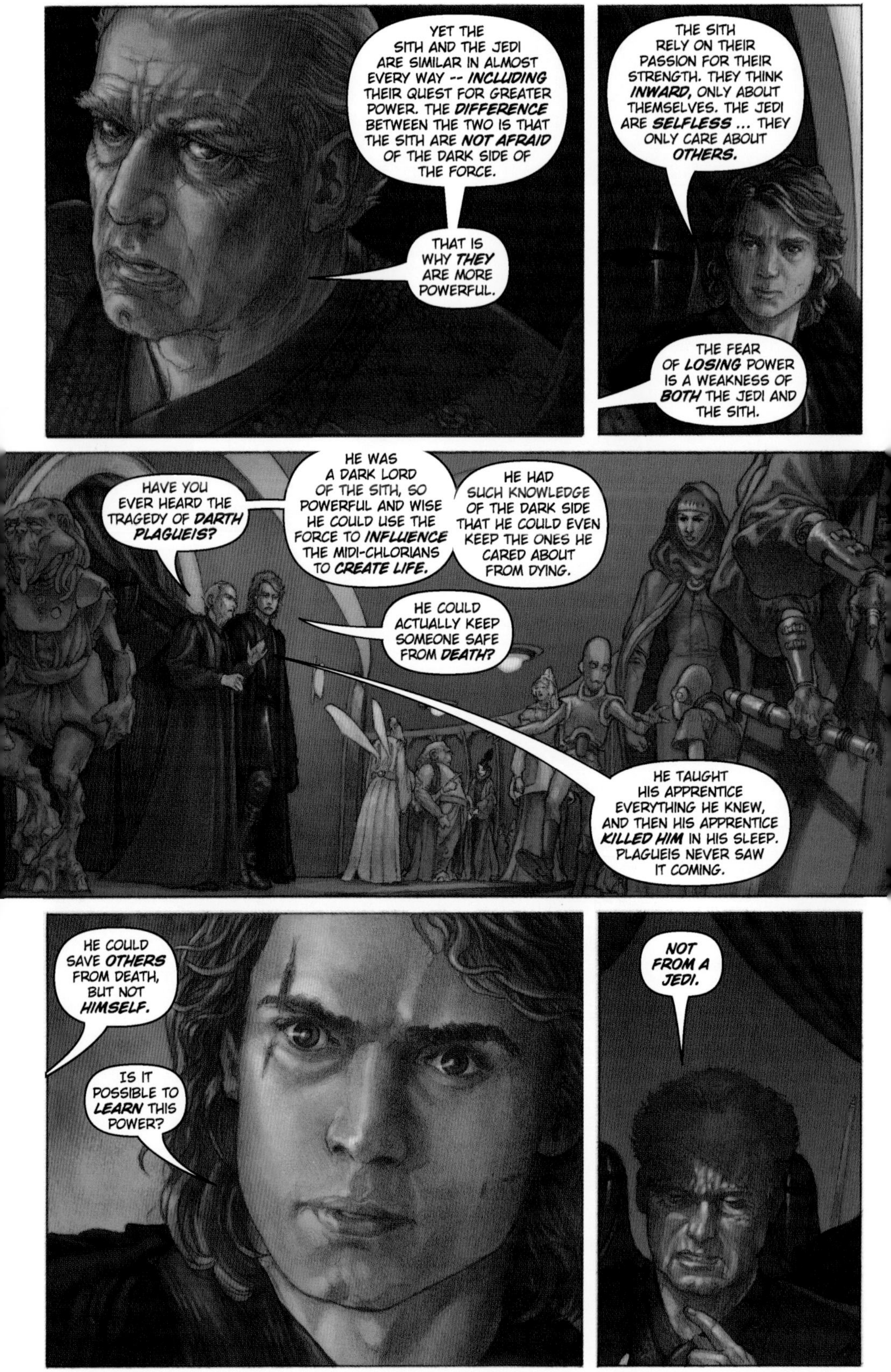
YET THE SITH AND THE JEDI ARE SIMILAR IN ALMOST EVERY WAY -- INCLUDING THEIR QUEST FOR GREATER POWER. THE DIFFERENCE BETWEEN THE TWO IS THAT THE SITH ARE NOT AFRAID OF THE DARK SIDE OF THE FORCE.
THAT IS WHY THEY ARE MORE POWERFUL.
THE SITH RELY ON THEIR PASSION FOR THEIR STRENGTH. THEY THINK INWARD, ONLY ABOUT THEMSELVES. THE JEDI ARE SELFLESS ... THEY ONLY CARE ABOUT OTHERS.
THE FEAR OF LOSING POWER IS A WEAKNESS OF BOTH THE JEDI AND THE SITH.
HAVE YOU EVER HEARD THE TRAGEDY OF DARTH PLAGUEIS?
HE WAS A DARK LORD OF THE SITH, SO POWERFUL AND WISE HE COULD USE THE FORCE TO INFLUENCE THE MIDI-CHLORIANS TO CREATE LIFE.
HE HAD SUCH KNOWLEDGE OF THE DARK SIDE THAT HE COULD EVEN KEEP THE ONES HE CARED ABOUT FROM DYING.
HE COULD ACTUALLY KEEP SOMEONE SAFE FROM DEATH?
HE TAUGHT HIS APPRENTICE EVERYTHING HE KNEW, AND THEN HIS APPRENTICE KILLED HIM IN HIS SLEEP. PLAGUEIS NEVER SAW IT COMING.
HE COULD SAVE OTHERS FROM DEATH, BUT NOT HIMSELF.
IS IT POSSIBLE TO LEARN THIS POWER?
NOT FROM A JEDI.

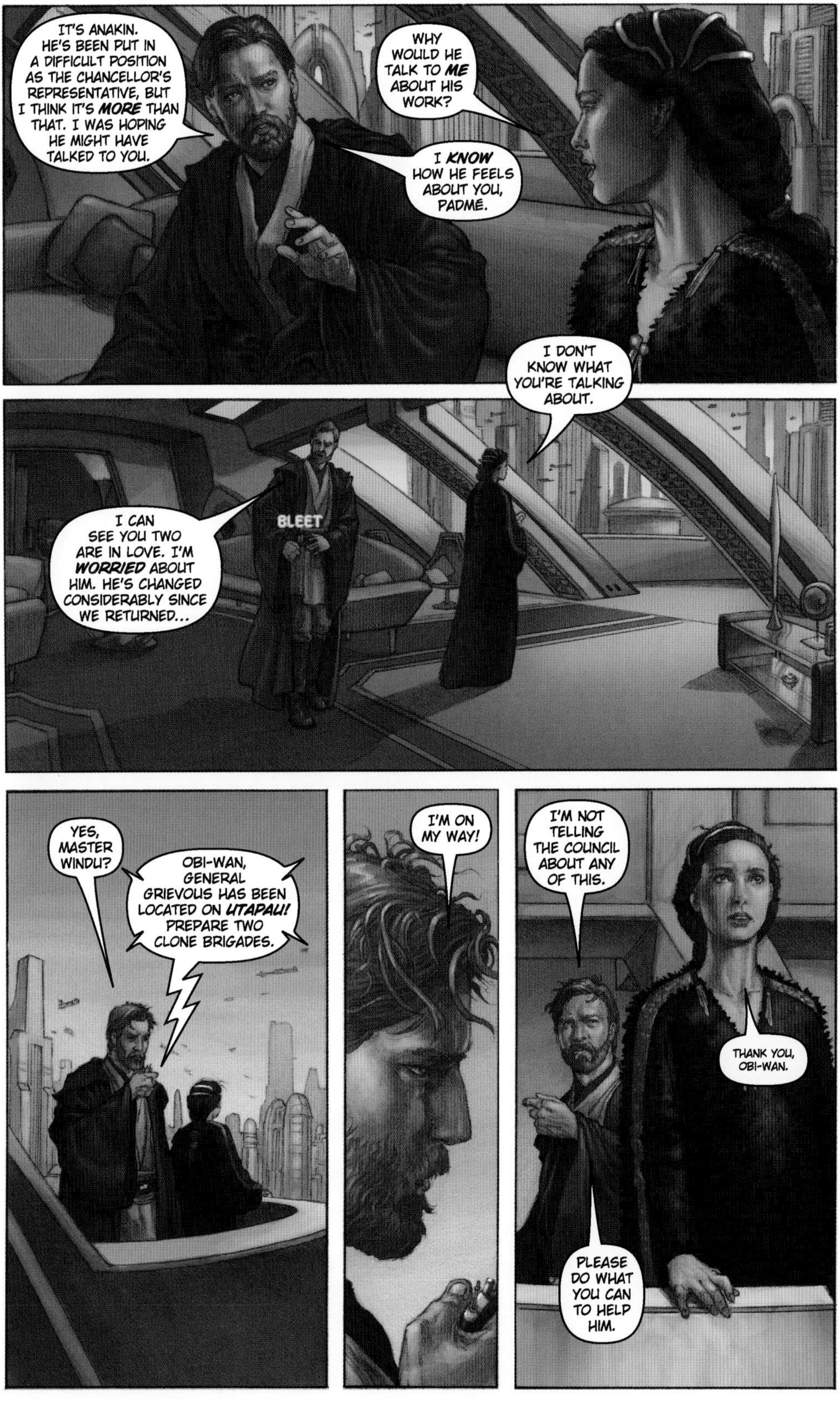
IT'S ANAKIN. HE'S BEEN PUT IN A DIFFICULT POSITION AS THE CHANCELLOR'S REPRESENTATIVE, BUT I THINK IT'S MORE THAN THAT. I WAS HOPING HE MIGHT HAVE TALKED TO YOU.
WHY WOULD HE TALK TO ME ABOUT HIS WORK?
I KNOW HOW HE FEELS ABOUT YOU, PADMÉ.
I DON'T KNOW WHAT YOU'RE TALKING ABOUT.
I CAN SEE YOU TWO ARE IN LOVE. I'M WORRIED ABOUT HIM. HE'S CHANGED CONSIDERABLY SINCE WE RETURNED...
BLEET
YES, MASTER WINDU?
OBI-WAN, GENERAL GRIEVOUS HAS BEEN LOCATED ON UTAPAU! PREPARE TWO CLONE BRIGADES.
I'M ON MY WAY!
I'M NOT TELLING THE COUNCIL ABOUT ANY OF THIS.
THANK YOU, OBI-WAN.
PLEASE DO WHAT YOU CAN TO HELP HIM.

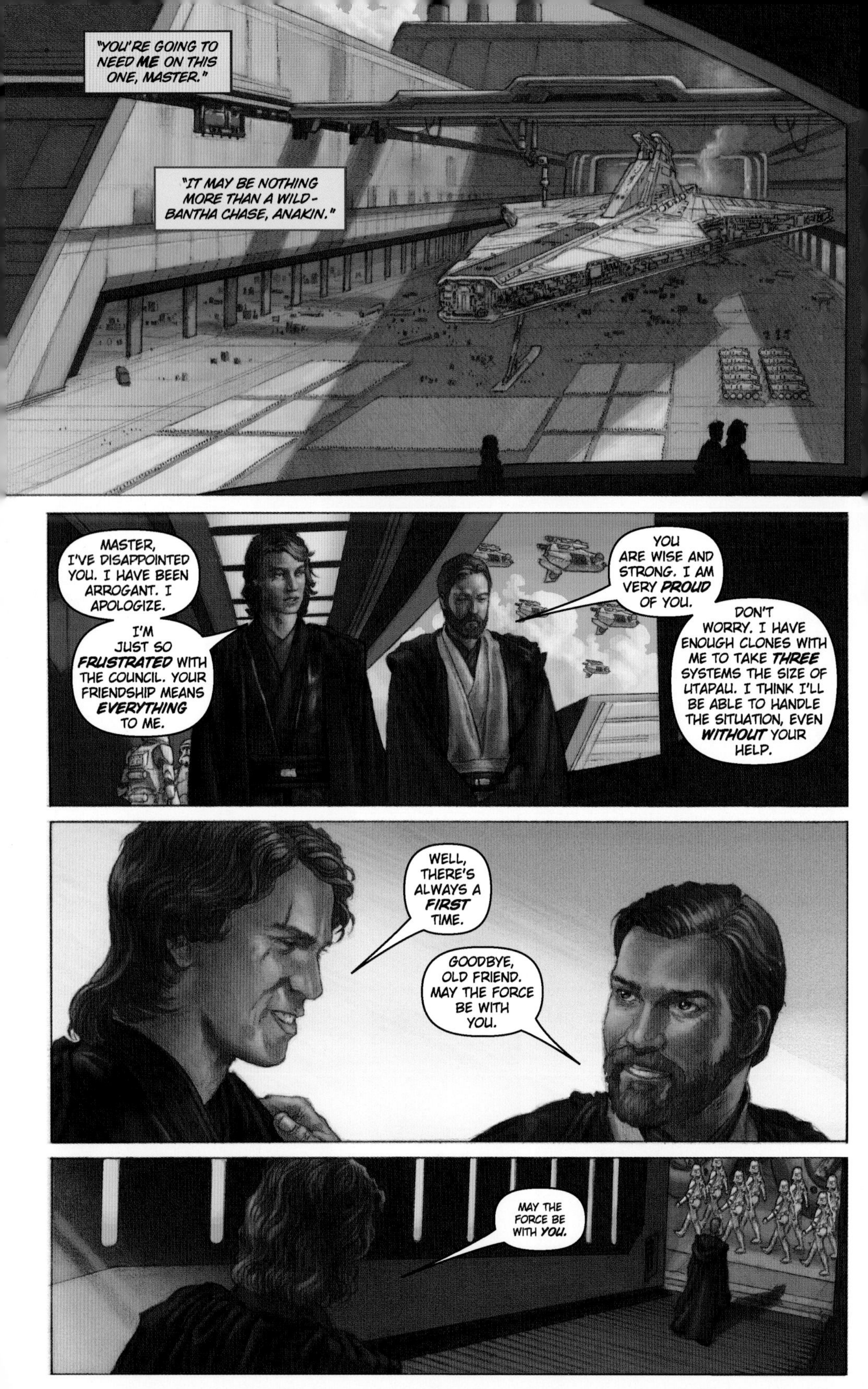
"YOU'RE GOING TO NEED ME ON THIS ONE, MASTER."
"IT MAY BE NOTHING MORE THAN A WILD-BANTHA CHASE, ANAKIN."
MASTER, I'VE DISAPPOINTED YOU. I HAVE BEEN ARROGANT. I APOLOGIZE.
I'M JUST SO FRUSTRATED WITH THE COUNCIL. YOUR FRIENDSHIP MEANS EVERYTHING TO ME.
YOU ARE WISE AND STRONG. I AM VERY PROUD OF YOU.
DON'T WORRY. I HAVE ENOUGH CLONES WITH ME TO TAKE THREE SYSTEMS THE SIZE OF UTAPAU. I THINK I'LL BE ABLE TO HANDLE THE SITUATION, EVEN WITHOUT YOUR HELP.
WELL, THERE'S ALWAYS A FIRST TIME.
GOODBYE, OLD FRIEND. MAY THE FORCE BE WITH YOU.
MAY THE FORCE BE WITH YOU.

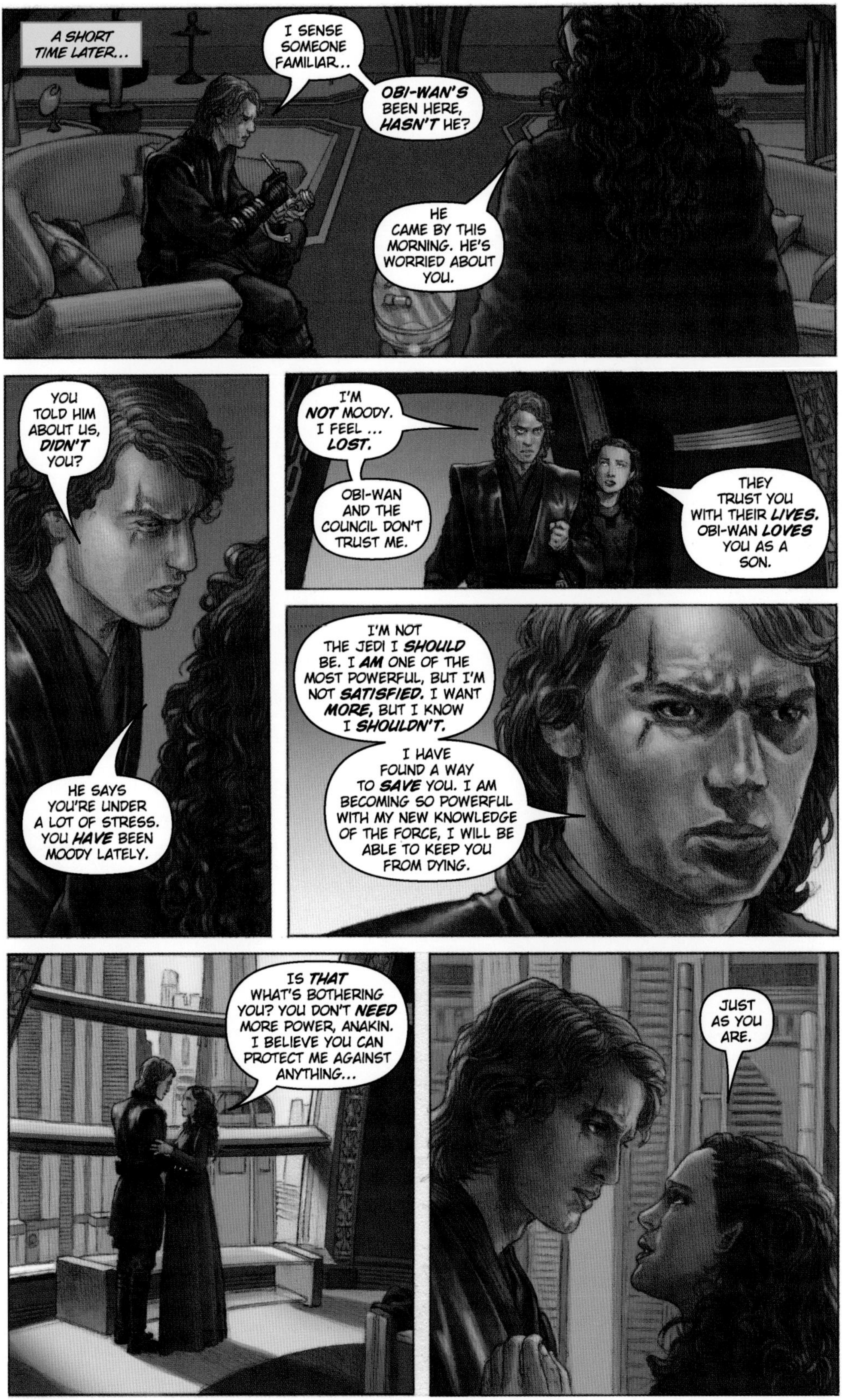
A SHORT TIME LATER...
I SENSE SOMEONE FAMILIAR...
OBI-WAN'S BEEN HERE, HASN'T HE?
HE CAME BY THIS MORNING. HE'S WORRIED ABOUT YOU.
YOU TOLD HIM ABOUT US, DIDN'T YOU?
HE SAYS YOU'RE UNDER A LOT OF STRESS. YOU HAVE BEEN MOODY LATELY.
I'M NOT MOODY. I FEEL ... LOST.
OBI-WAN AND THE COUNCIL DON'T TRUST ME.
THEY TRUST YOU WITH THEIR LIVES. OBI-WAN LOVES YOU AS A SON.
I'M NOT THE JEDI I SHOULD BE. I AM ONE OF THE MOST POWERFUL, BUT I'M NOT SATISFIED. I WANT MORE, BUT I KNOW I SHOULDN'T.
I HAVE FOUND A WAY TO SAVE YOU. I AM BECOMING SO POWERFUL WITH MY NEW KNOWLEDGE OF THE FORCE, I WILL BE ABLE TO KEEP YOU FROM DYING.
IS THAT WHAT'S BOTHERING YOU? YOU DON'T NEED MORE POWER, ANAKIN. I BELIEVE YOU CAN PROTECT ME AGAINST ANYTHING...
JUST AS YOU ARE.

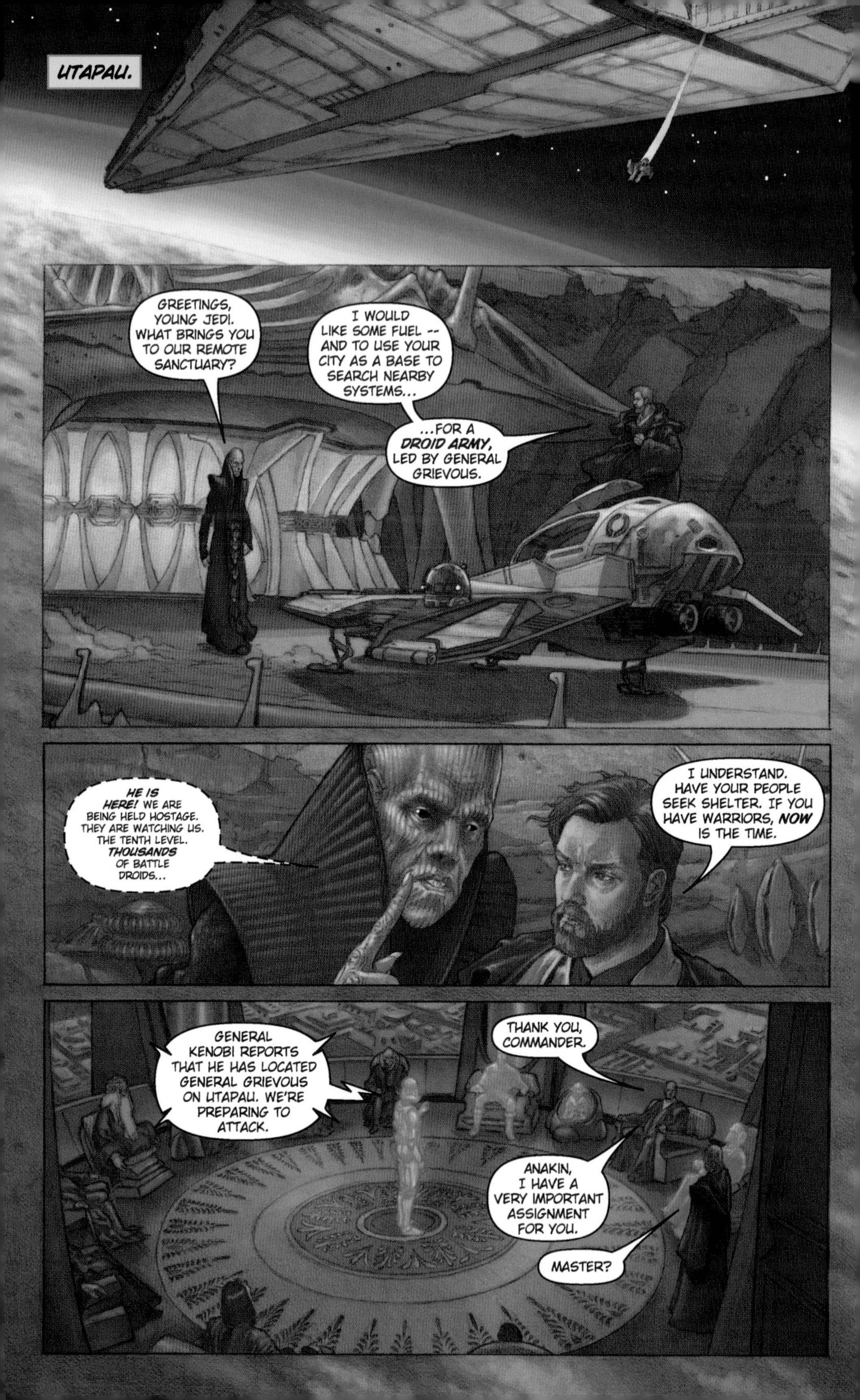
UTAPAU.
GREETINGS, YOUNG JEDI. WHAT BRINGS YOU TO OUR REMOTE SANCTUARY?
I WOULD LIKE SOME FUEL -- AND TO USE YOUR CITY AS A BASE TO SEARCH NEARBY SYSTEMS...
...FOR A DROID ARMY, LED BY GENERAL GRIEVOUS.
HE IS HERE! WE ARE BEING HELD HOSTAGE. THEY ARE WATCHING US. THE TENTH LEVEL. THOUSANDS OF BATTLE DROIDS...
I UNDERSTAND. HAVE YOUR PEOPLE SEEK SHELTER. IF YOU HAVE WARRIORS, NOW IS THE TIME.
GENERAL KENOBI REPORTS THAT HE HAS LOCATED GENERAL GRIEVOUS ON UTAPAU. WE'RE PREPARING TO ATTACK.
THANK YOU, COMMANDER.
ANAKIN, I HAVE A VERY IMPORTANT ASSIGNMENT FOR YOU.
MASTER?

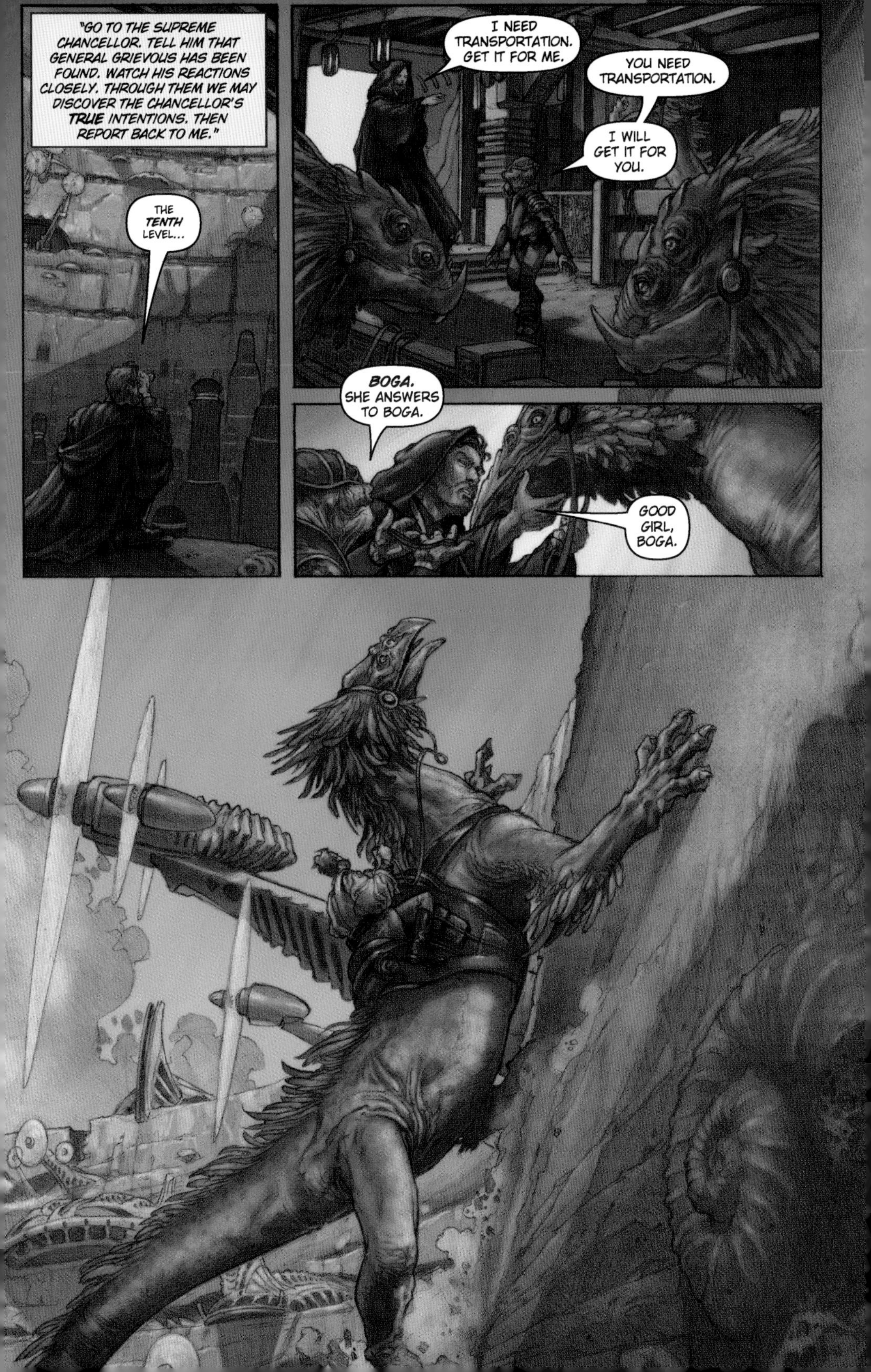
"GO TO THE SUPREME CHANCELLOR. TELL HIM THAT GENERAL GRIEVOUS HAS BEEN FOUND. WATCH HIS REACTIONS CLOSELY. THROUGH THEM WE MAY DISCOVER THE CHANCELLOR'S **TRUE** INTENTIONS. THEN REPORT BACK TO ME."
THE *TENTH* LEVEL...
I NEED TRANSPORTATION. GET IT FOR ME.
YOU NEED TRANSPORTATION.
I WILL GET IT FOR YOU.
BOGA. SHE ANSWERS TO BOGA.
GOOD GIRL, BOGA.

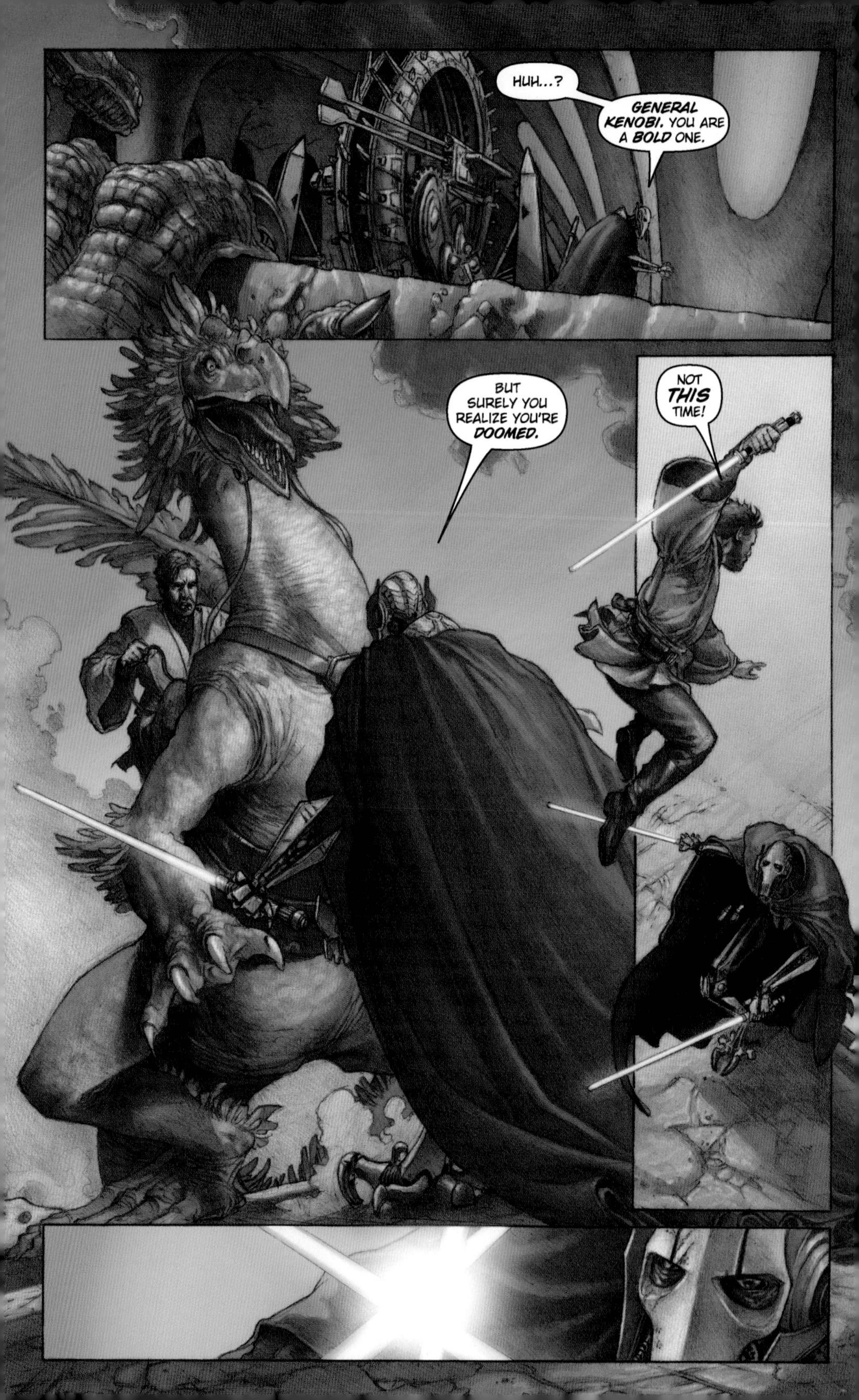
HUH...?
GENERAL KENOBI. YOU ARE A BOLD ONE.
BUT SURELY YOU REALIZE YOU'RE DOOMED.
NOT THIS TIME!

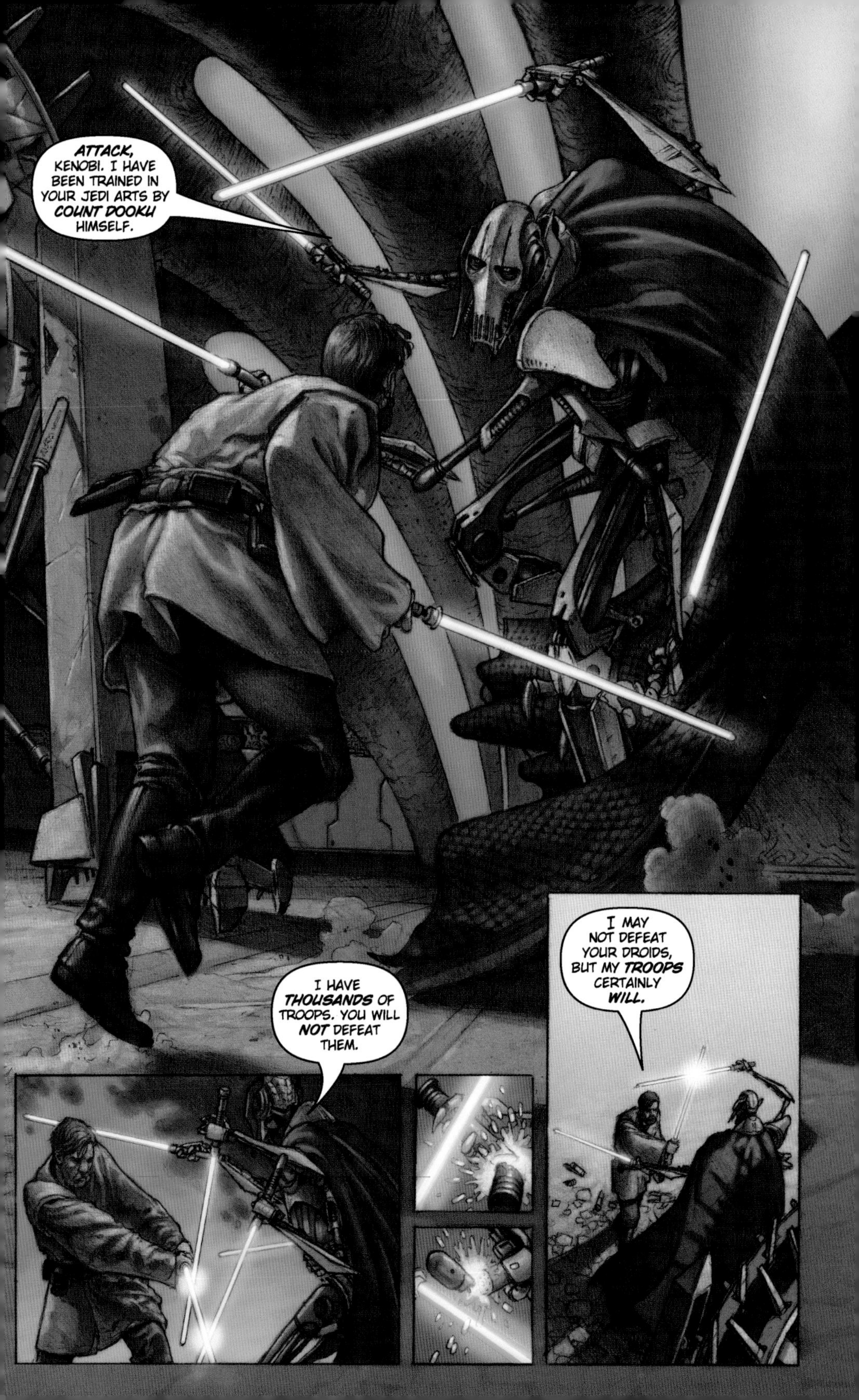
ATTACK, KENOBI. I HAVE BEEN TRAINED IN YOUR JEDI ARTS BY COUNT DOOKU HIMSELF.
I HAVE THOUSANDS OF TROOPS. YOU WILL NOT DEFEAT THEM.
I MAY NOT DEFEAT YOUR DROIDS, BUT MY TROOPS CERTAINLY WILL.

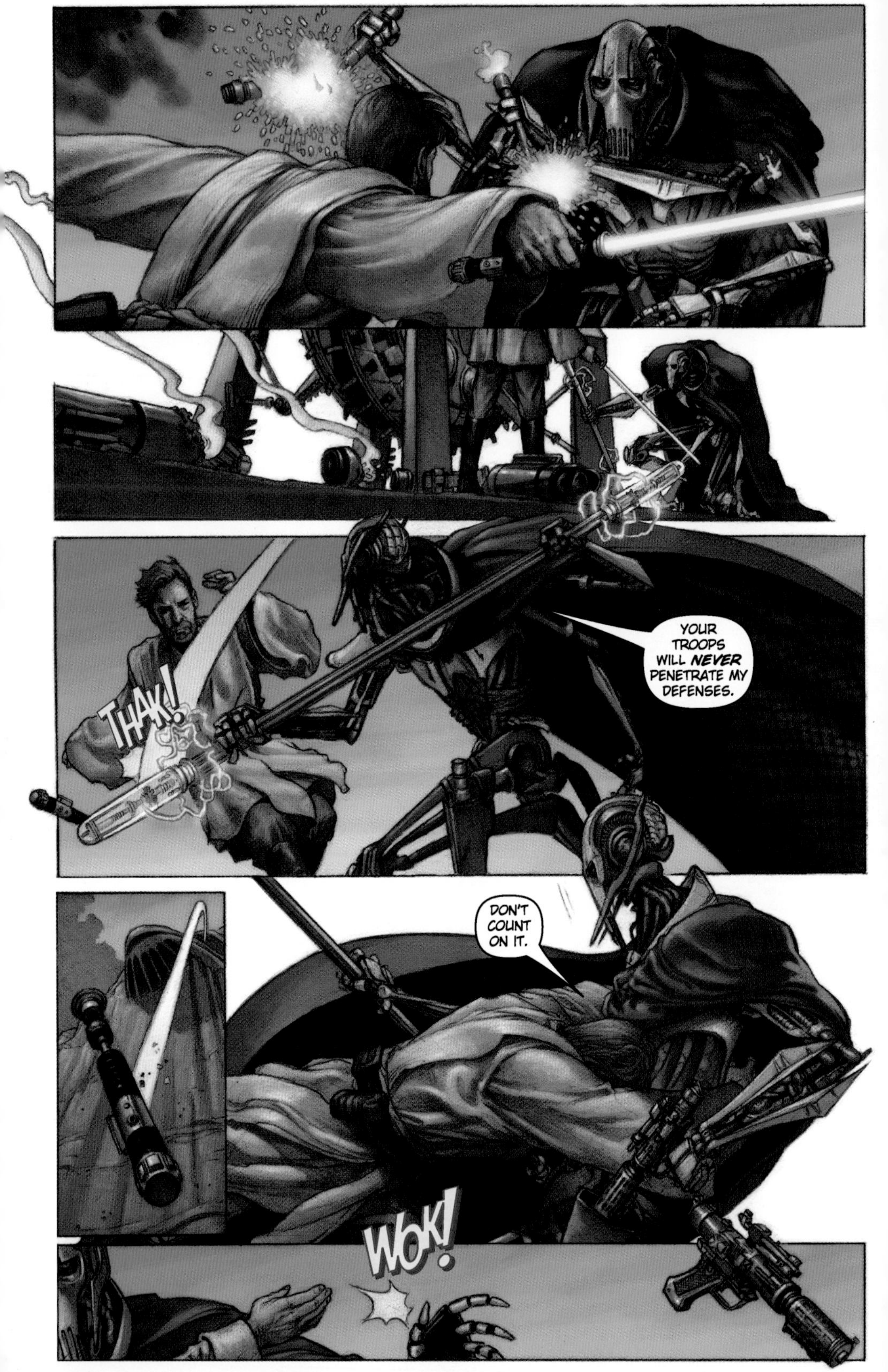
THAK!
YOUR TROOPS WILL NEVER PENETRATE MY DEFENSES.
DON'T COUNT ON IT.
WOK!

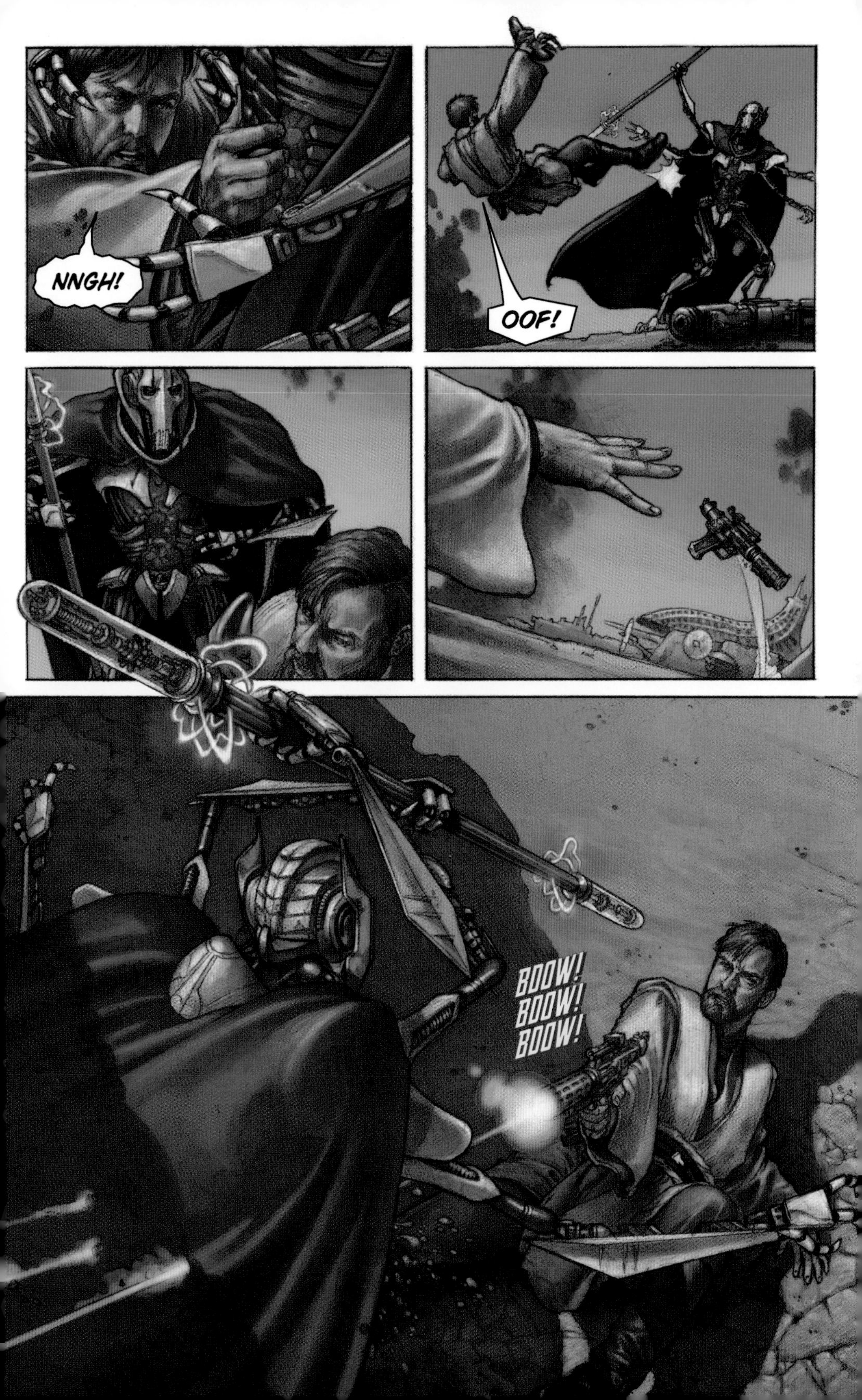
NNGH!
OOF!
BOOW!
BOOW!
BOOW!

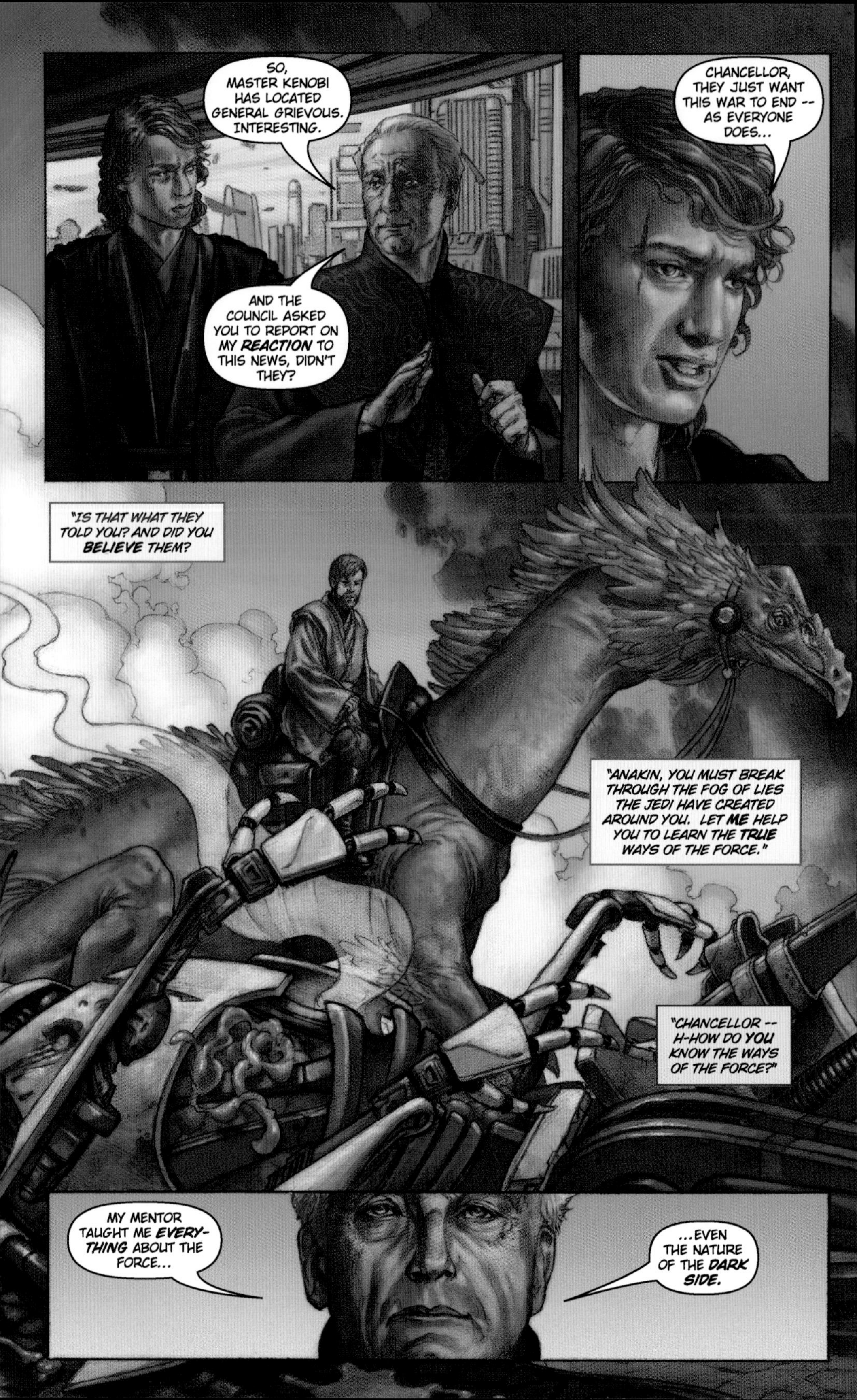
SO, MASTER KENOBI HAS LOCATED GENERAL GRIEVOUS. INTERESTING.
AND THE COUNCIL ASKED YOU TO REPORT ON MY **REACTION** TO THIS NEWS, DIDN'T THEY?
CHANCELLOR, THEY JUST WANT THIS WAR TO END -- AS EVERYONE DOES...
"IS THAT WHAT THEY TOLD YOU? AND DID YOU **BELIEVE** THEM?
"ANAKIN, YOU MUST BREAK THROUGH THE FOG OF LIES THE JEDI HAVE CREATED AROUND YOU. LET **ME** HELP YOU TO LEARN THE **TRUE** WAYS OF THE FORCE."
"CHANCELLOR -- H-HOW DO **YOU** KNOW THE WAYS OF THE FORCE?"
MY MENTOR TAUGHT ME **EVERYTHING** ABOUT THE FORCE...
...EVEN THE NATURE OF THE **DARK SIDE.**

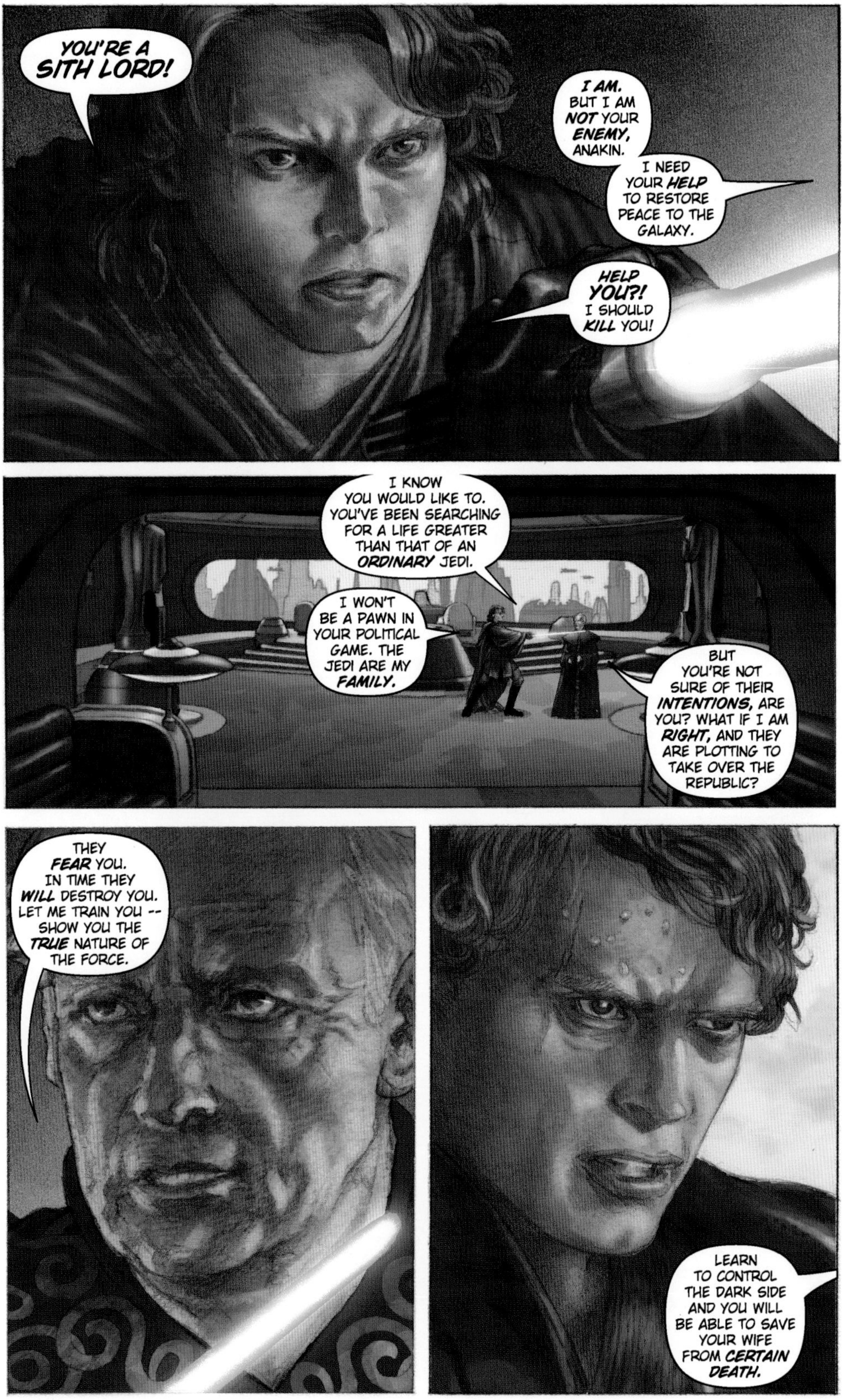
YOU'RE A SITH LORD!
I AM. BUT I AM NOT YOUR ENEMY, ANAKIN.
I NEED YOUR HELP TO RESTORE PEACE TO THE GALAXY.
HELP YOU?! I SHOULD KILL YOU!
I KNOW YOU WOULD LIKE TO. YOU'VE BEEN SEARCHING FOR A LIFE GREATER THAN THAT OF AN ORDINARY JEDI.
I WON'T BE A PAWN IN YOUR POLITICAL GAME. THE JEDI ARE MY FAMILY.
BUT YOU'RE NOT SURE OF THEIR INTENTIONS, ARE YOU? WHAT IF I AM RIGHT, AND THEY ARE PLOTTING TO TAKE OVER THE REPUBLIC?
THEY FEAR YOU. IN TIME THEY WILL DESTROY YOU. LET ME TRAIN YOU -- SHOW YOU THE TRUE NATURE OF THE FORCE.
LEARN TO CONTROL THE DARK SIDE AND YOU WILL BE ABLE TO SAVE YOUR WIFE FROM CERTAIN DEATH.

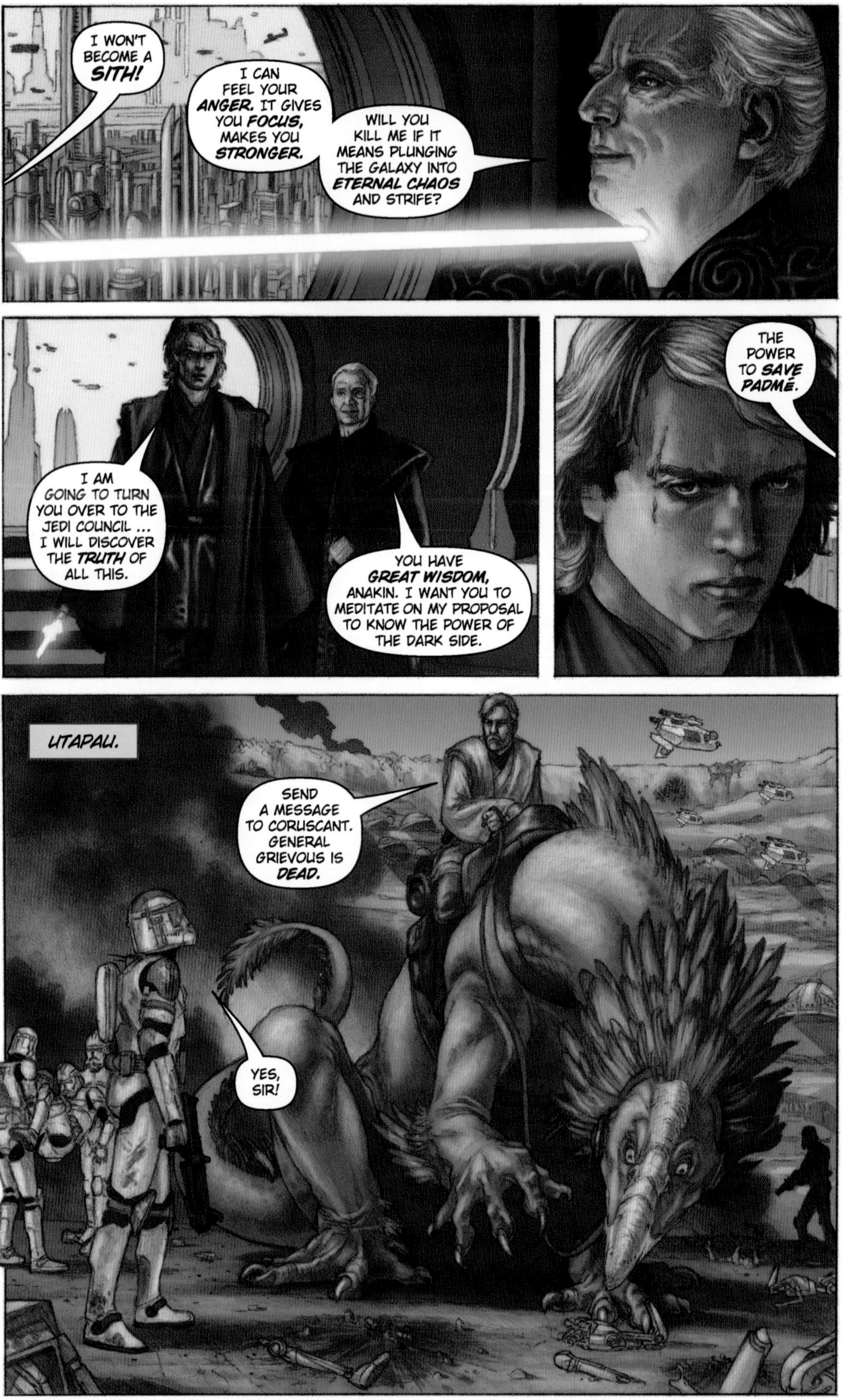
I WON'T BECOME A SITH!
I CAN FEEL YOUR ANGER. IT GIVES YOU FOCUS, MAKES YOU STRONGER.
WILL YOU KILL ME IF IT MEANS PLUNGING THE GALAXY INTO ETERNAL CHAOS AND STRIFE?
I AM GOING TO TURN YOU OVER TO THE JEDI COUNCIL ... I WILL DISCOVER THE TRUTH OF ALL THIS.
YOU HAVE GREAT WISDOM, ANAKIN. I WANT YOU TO MEDITATE ON MY PROPOSAL TO KNOW THE POWER OF THE DARK SIDE.
THE POWER TO SAVE PADMÉ.
UTAPAU.
SEND A MESSAGE TO CORUSCANT. GENERAL GRIEVOUS IS DEAD.
YES, SIR!

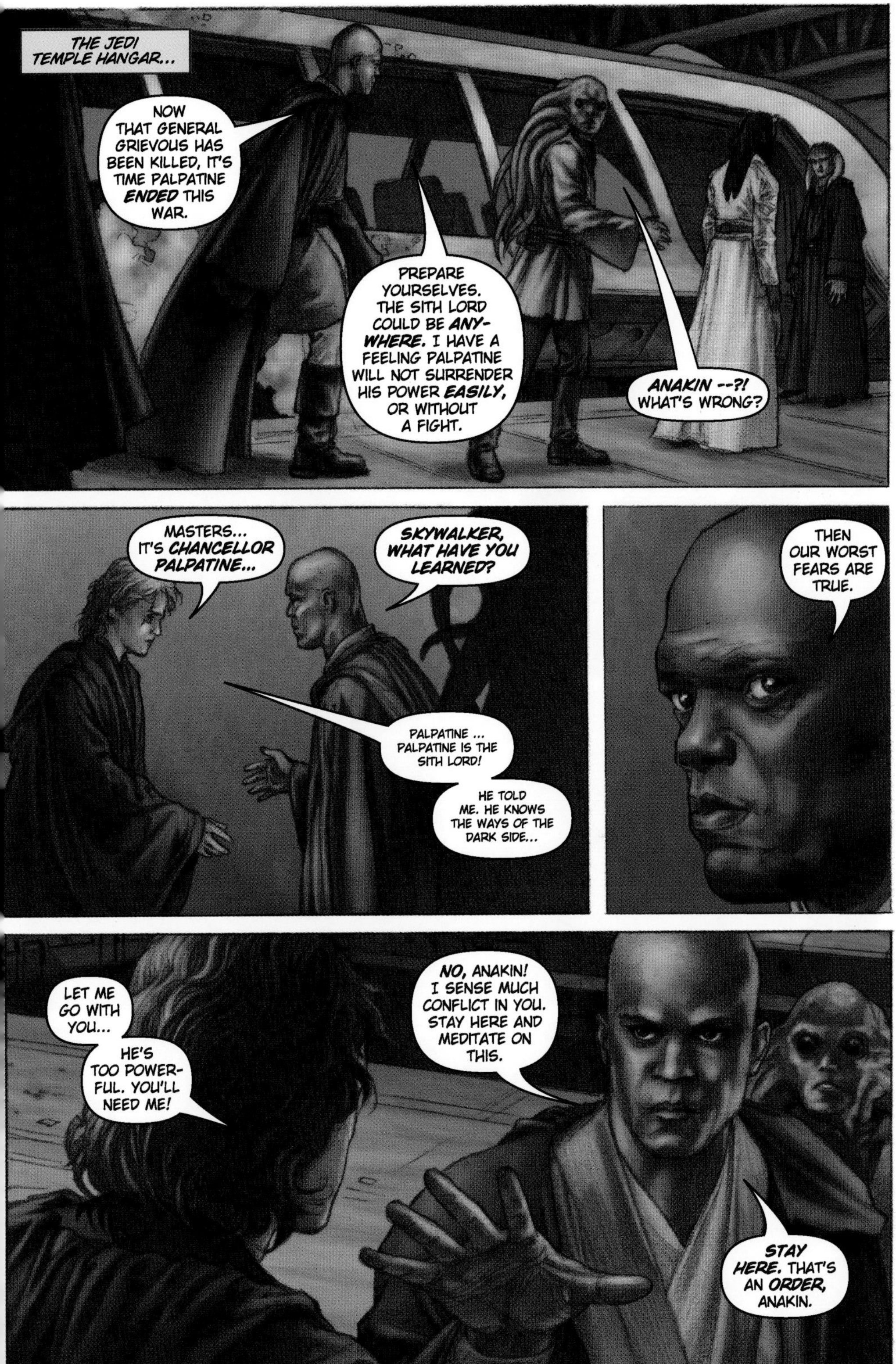
THE JEDI TEMPLE HANGAR...
NOW THAT GENERAL GRIEVOUS HAS BEEN KILLED, IT'S TIME PALPATINE ENDED THIS WAR.
PREPARE YOURSELVES. THE SITH LORD COULD BE ANY-WHERE. I HAVE A FEELING PALPATINE WILL NOT SURRENDER HIS POWER EASILY, OR WITHOUT A FIGHT.
ANAKIN --?! WHAT'S WRONG?
MASTERS... IT'S CHANCELLOR PALPATINE...
SKYWALKER, WHAT HAVE YOU LEARNED?
PALPATINE ... PALPATINE IS THE SITH LORD!
HE TOLD ME. HE KNOWS THE WAYS OF THE DARK SIDE...
THEN OUR WORST FEARS ARE TRUE.
LET ME GO WITH YOU...
HE'S TOO POWER-FUL. YOU'LL NEED ME!
NO, ANAKIN! I SENSE MUCH CONFLICT IN YOU. STAY HERE AND MEDITATE ON THIS.
STAY HERE. THAT'S AN ORDER, ANAKIN.

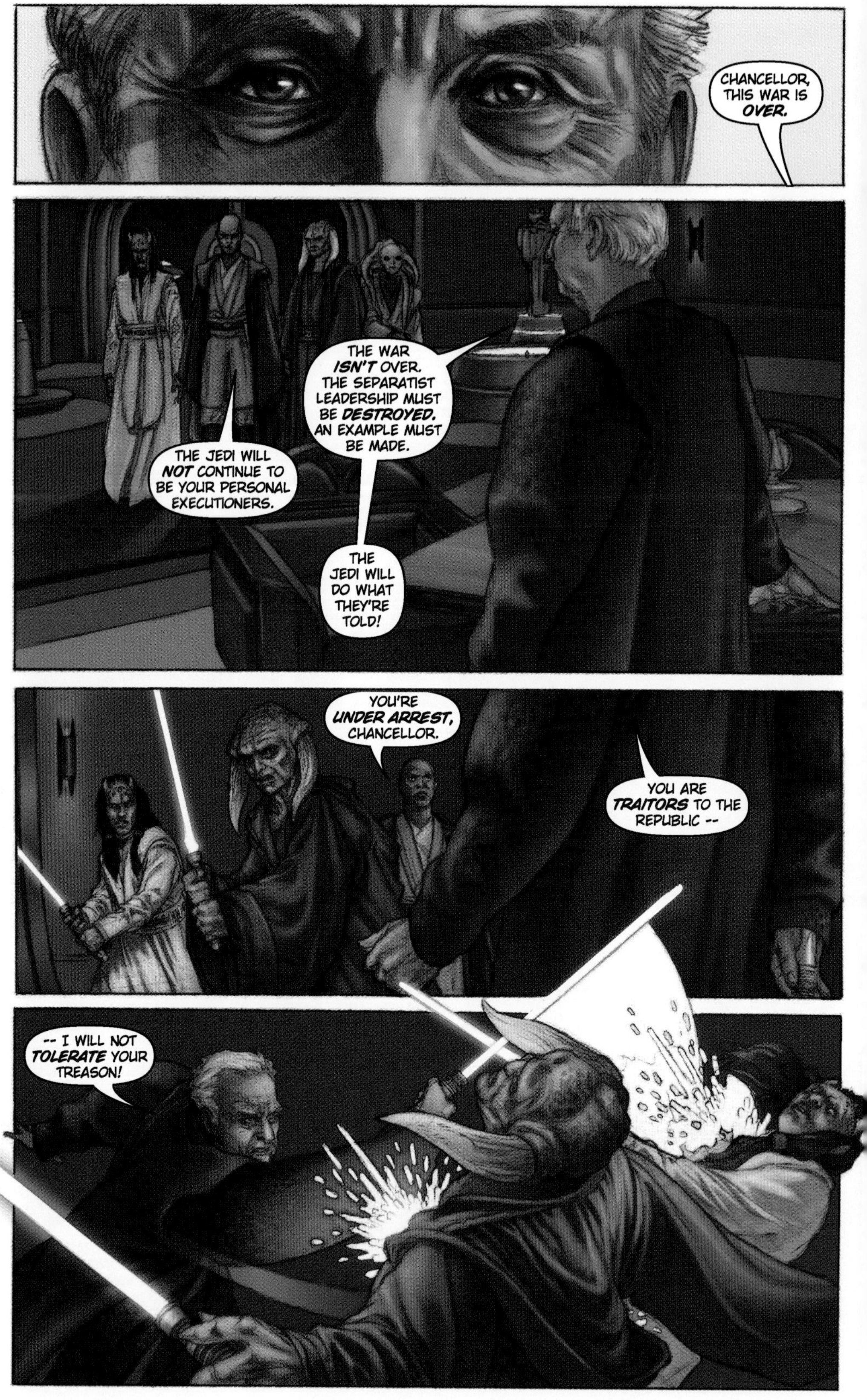
CHANCELLOR, THIS WAR IS OVER.
THE WAR ISN'T OVER. THE SEPARATIST LEADERSHIP MUST BE DESTROYED. AN EXAMPLE MUST BE MADE.
THE JEDI WILL NOT CONTINUE TO BE YOUR PERSONAL EXECUTIONERS.
THE JEDI WILL DO WHAT THEY'RE TOLD!
YOU'RE UNDER ARREST, CHANCELLOR.
YOU ARE TRAITORS TO THE REPUBLIC --
-- I WILL NOT TOLERATE YOUR TREASON!

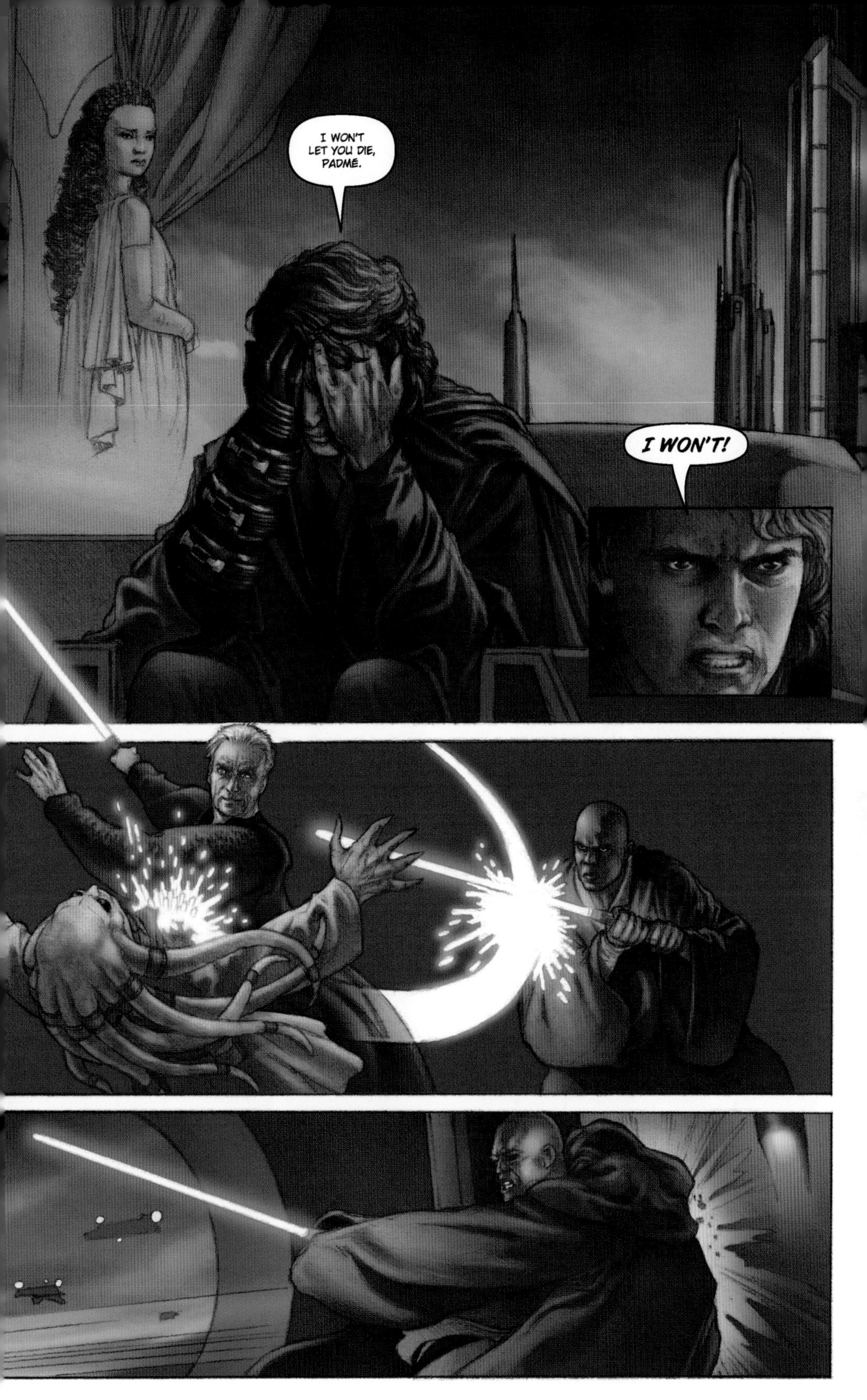

I WON'T LET YOU DIE, PADMÉ.
I WON'T!

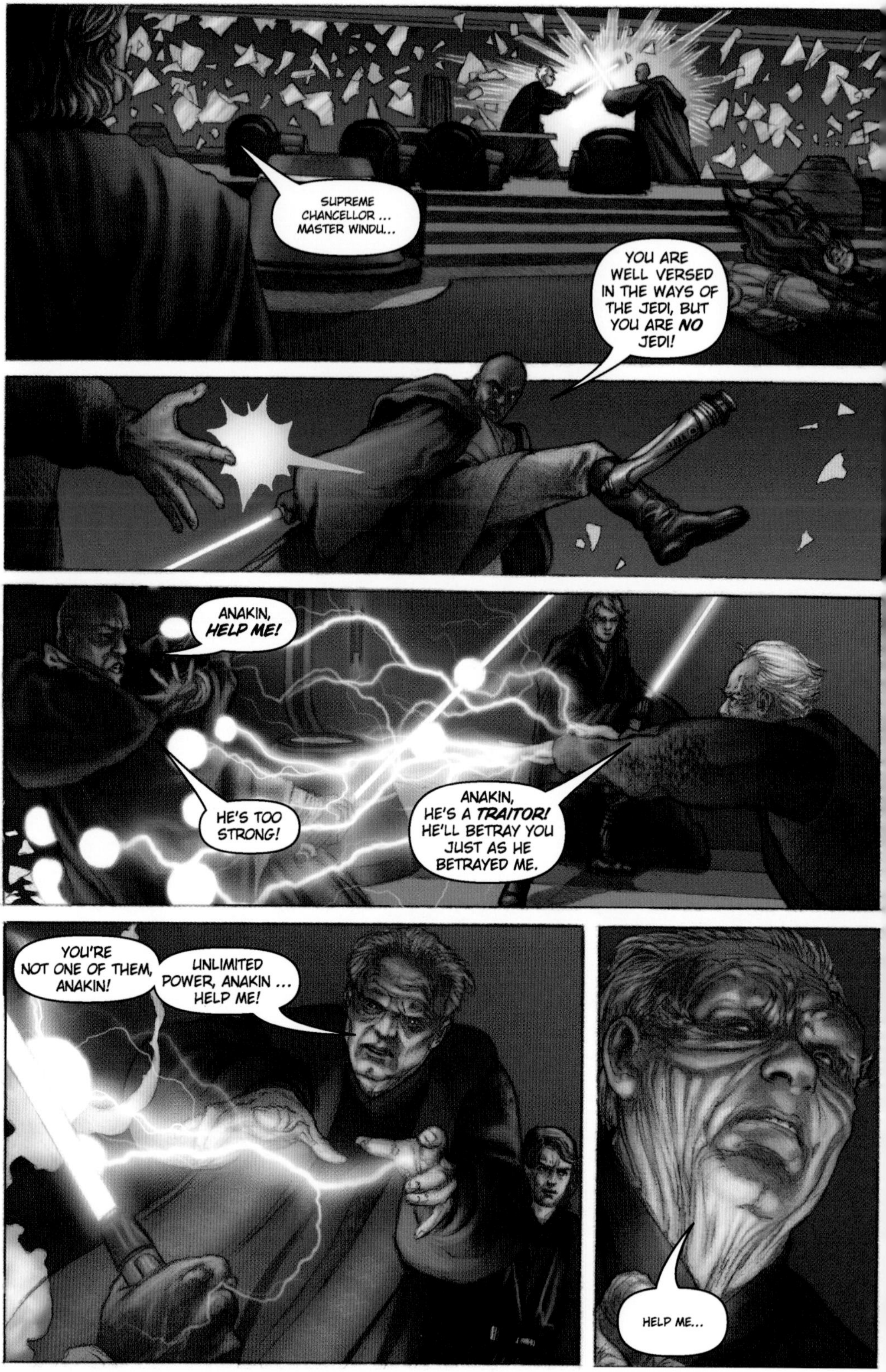
SUPREME CHANCELLOR ... MASTER WINDU...
YOU ARE WELL VERSED IN THE WAYS OF THE JEDI, BUT YOU ARE **NO** JEDI!
ANAKIN, ***HELP ME!***
HE'S TOO STRONG!
ANAKIN, HE'S A ***TRAITOR!*** HE'LL BETRAY YOU JUST AS HE BETRAYED ME.
YOU'RE NOT ONE OF THEM, ANAKIN!
UNLIMITED POWER, ANAKIN ... HELP ME!
HELP ME...

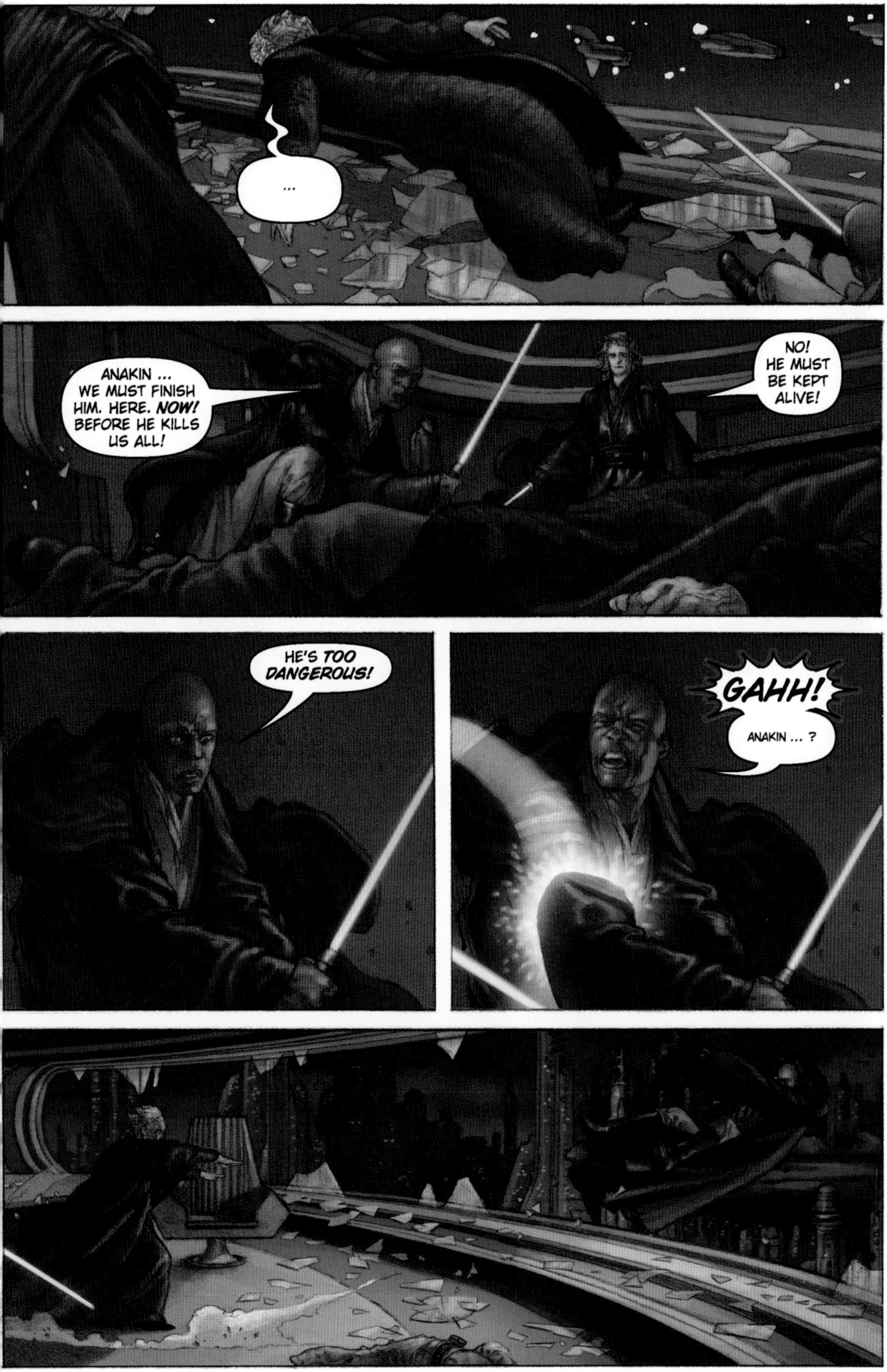
...
ANAKIN ... WE MUST FINISH HIM. HERE. NOW! BEFORE HE KILLS US ALL!
NO! HE MUST BE KEPT ALIVE!
HE'S TOO DANGEROUS!
GAHH!
ANAKIN ... ?

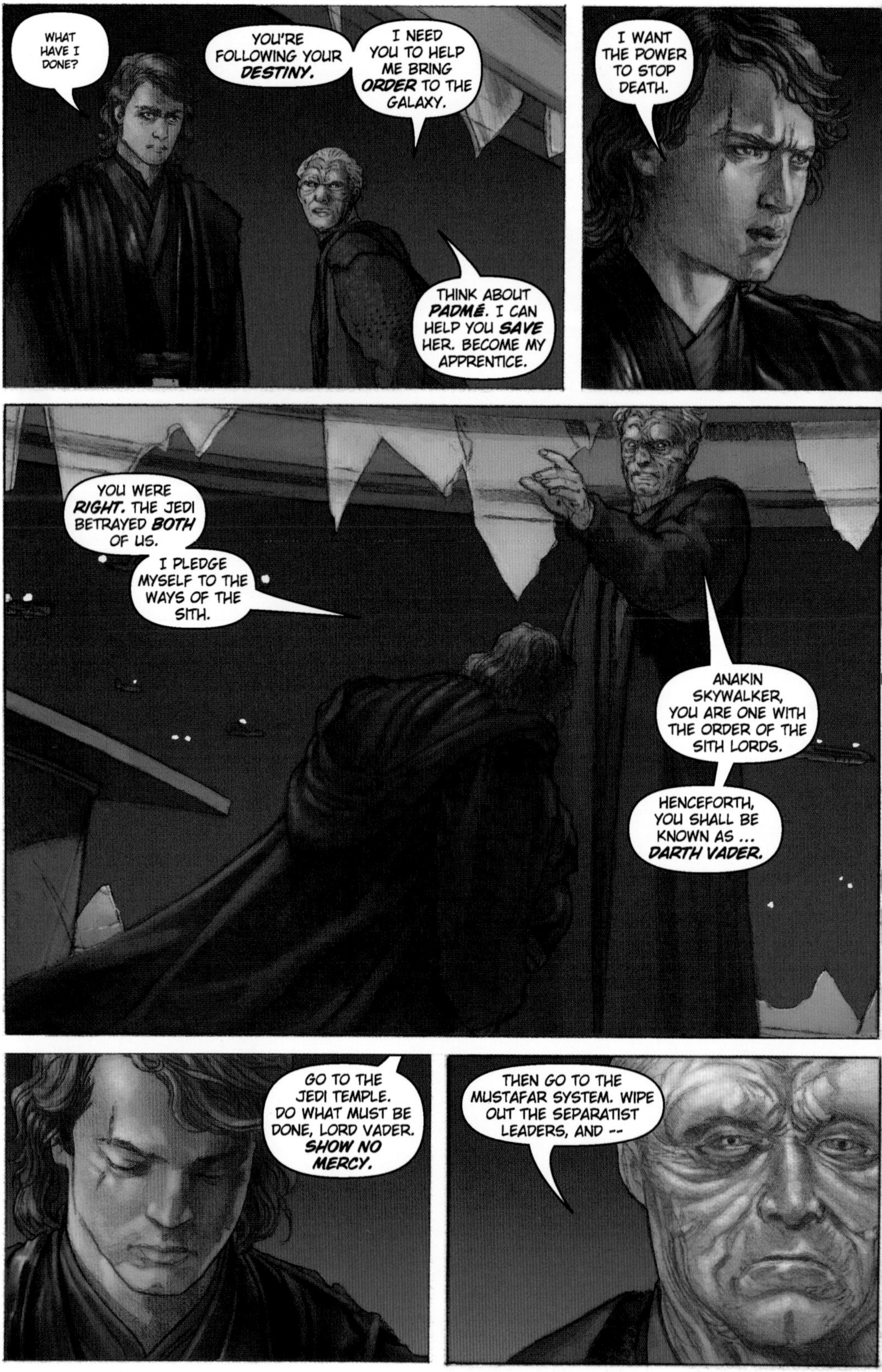
WHAT HAVE I DONE?
YOU'RE FOLLOWING YOUR DESTINY.
I NEED YOU TO HELP ME BRING ORDER TO THE GALAXY.
THINK ABOUT PADMÉ. I CAN HELP YOU SAVE HER. BECOME MY APPRENTICE.
I WANT THE POWER TO STOP DEATH.
YOU WERE RIGHT. THE JEDI BETRAYED BOTH OF US.
I PLEDGE MYSELF TO THE WAYS OF THE SITH.
ANAKIN SKYWALKER, YOU ARE ONE WITH THE ORDER OF THE SITH LORDS.
HENCEFORTH, YOU SHALL BE KNOWN AS ... DARTH VADER.
GO TO THE JEDI TEMPLE. DO WHAT MUST BE DONE, LORD VADER. SHOW NO MERCY.
THEN GO TO THE MUSTAFAR SYSTEM. WIPE OUT THE SEPARATIST LEADERS, AND --

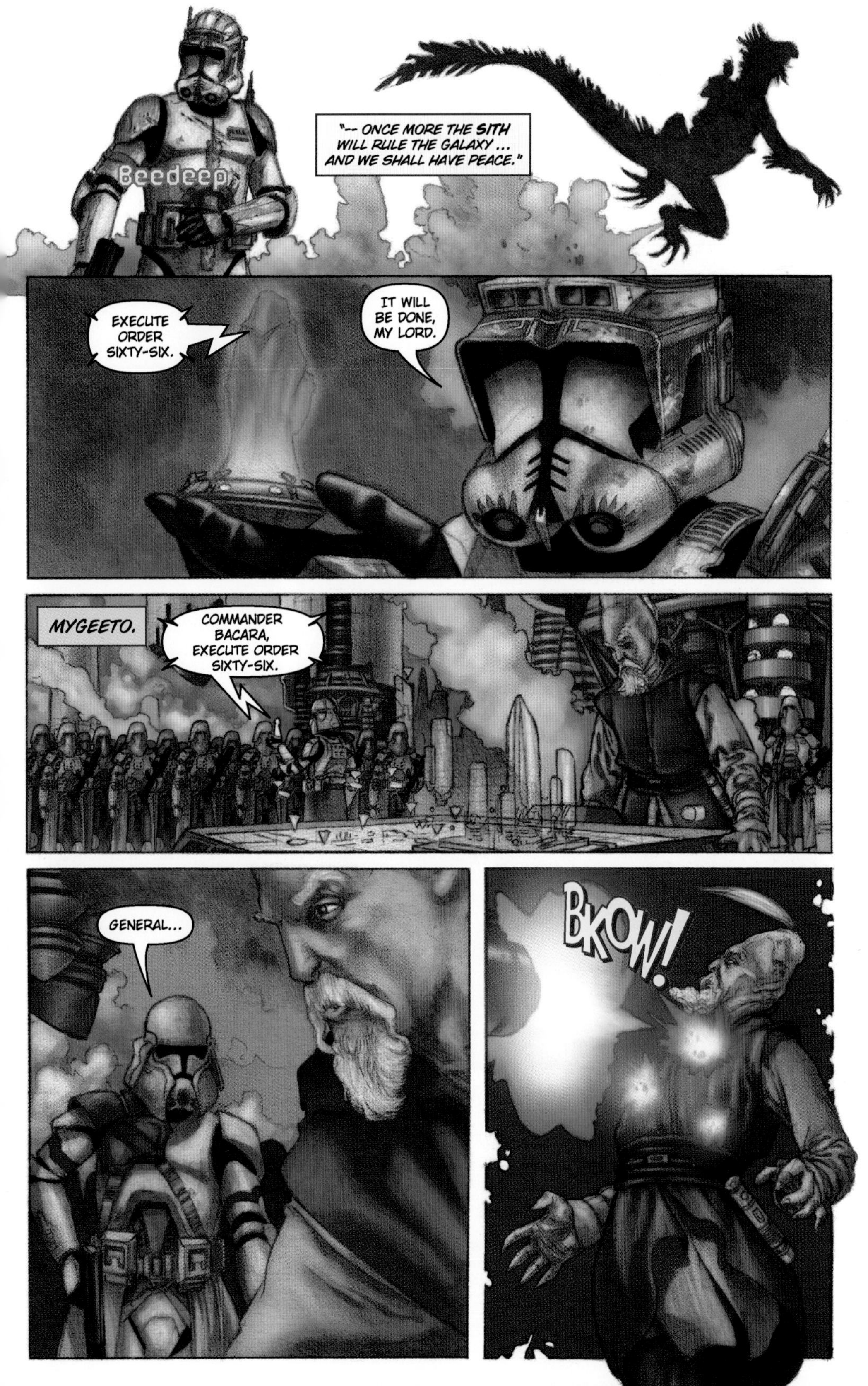
Beedeep
"-- ONCE MORE THE SITH WILL RULE THE GALAXY ... AND WE SHALL HAVE PEACE."
EXECUTE ORDER SIXTY-SIX.
IT WILL BE DONE, MY LORD.
MYGEETO.
COMMANDER BACARA, EXECUTE ORDER SIXTY-SIX.
GENERAL...
BKOW!

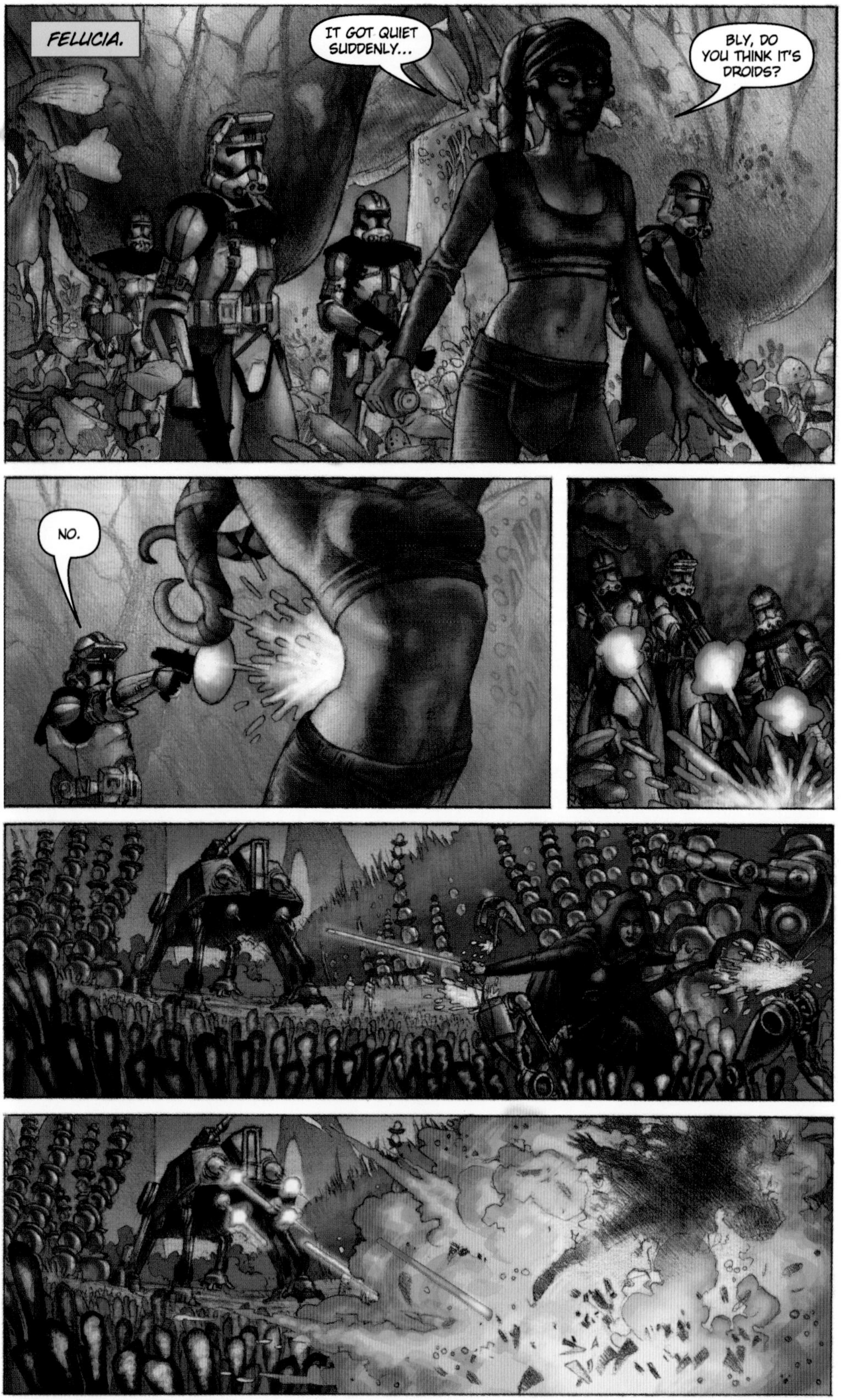
FELUCIA.
IT GOT QUIET SUDDENLY...
BLY, DO YOU THINK IT'S DROIDS?
NO.

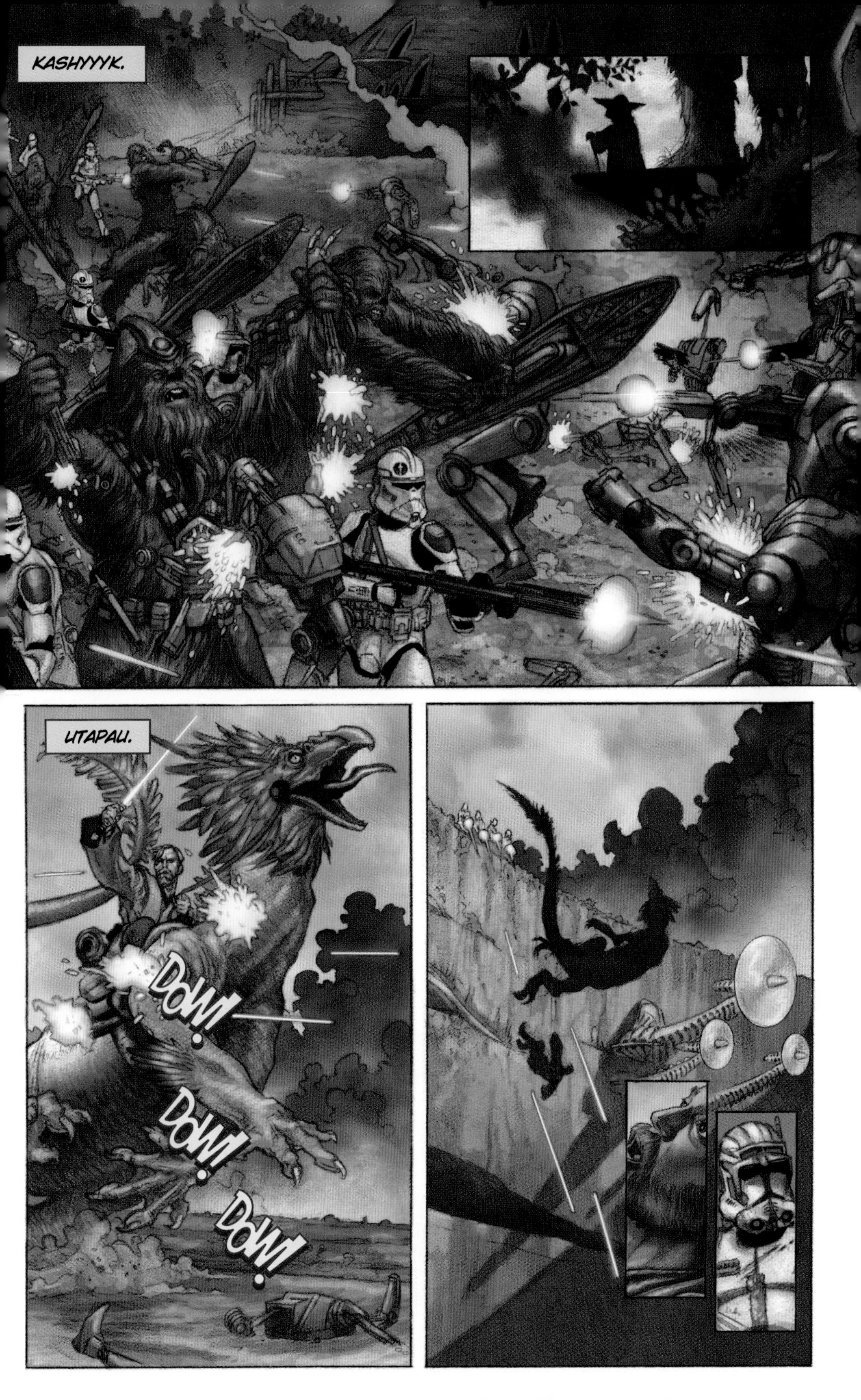
KASHYYYK.
UTAPAU.
DOW!
DOW!
DOW!

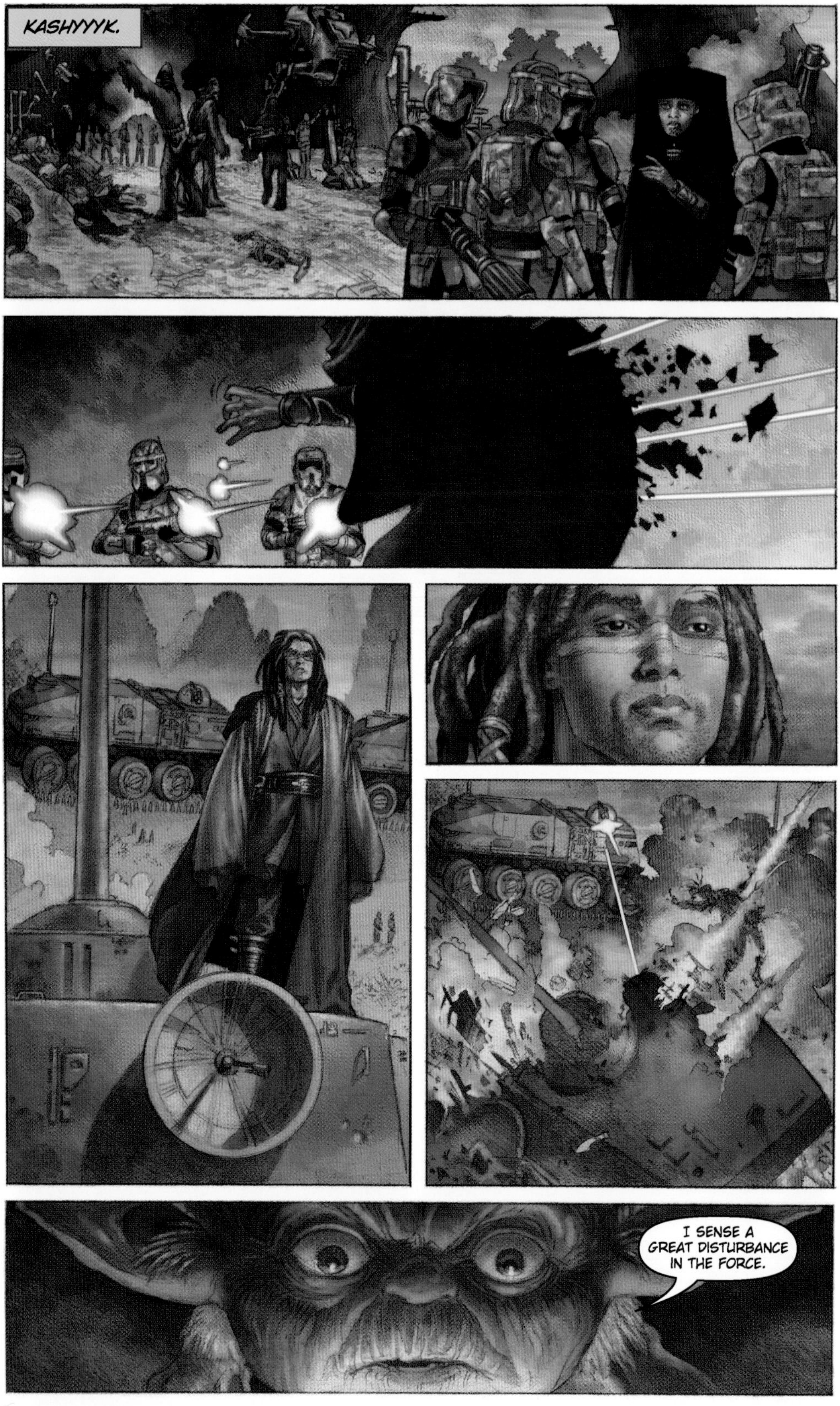
KASHYYYK.
I SENSE A GREAT DISTURBANCE IN THE FORCE.

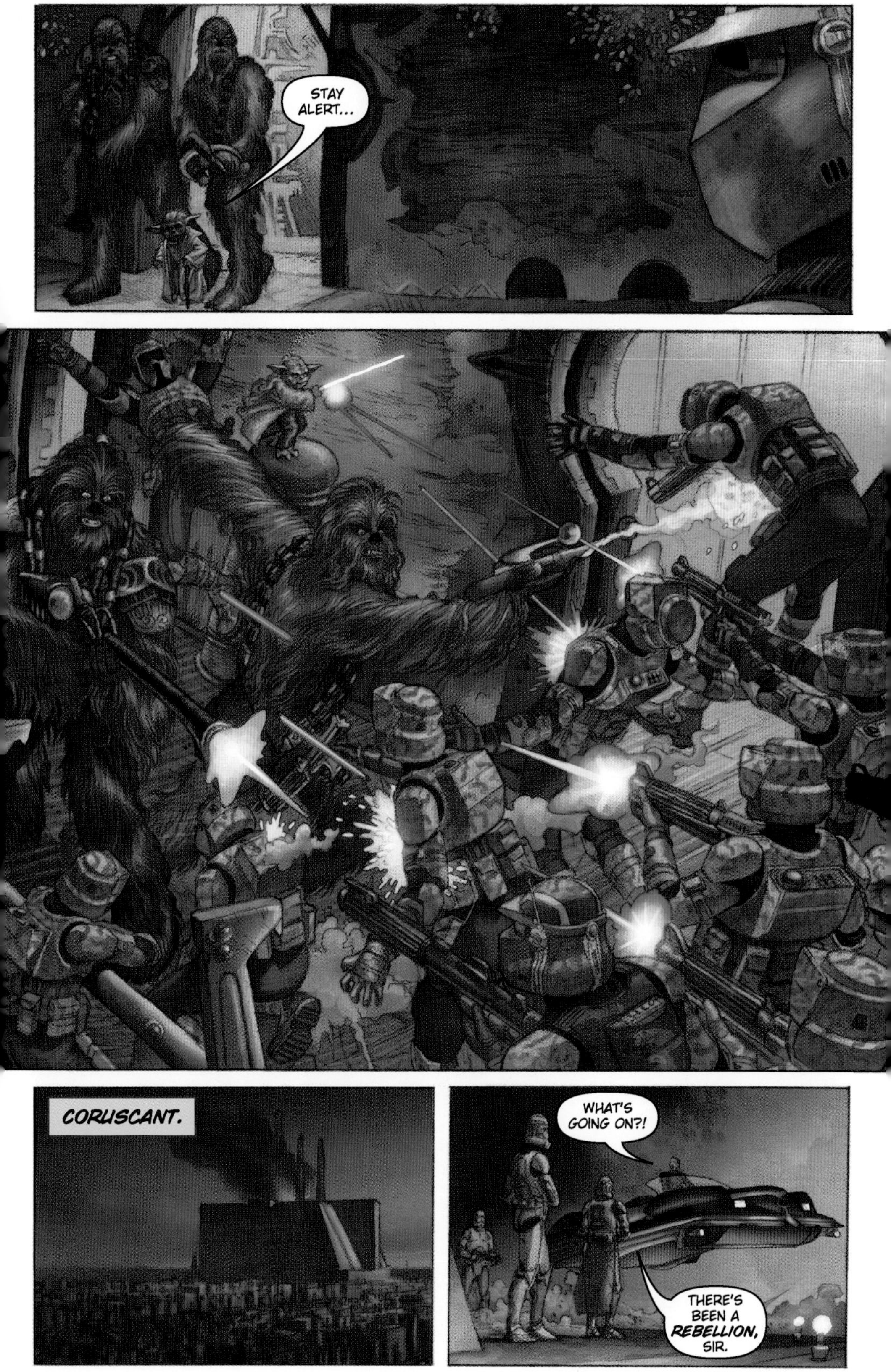
STAY ALERT...
CORUSCANT.
WHAT'S GOING ON?!
THERE'S BEEN A REBELLION, SIR.

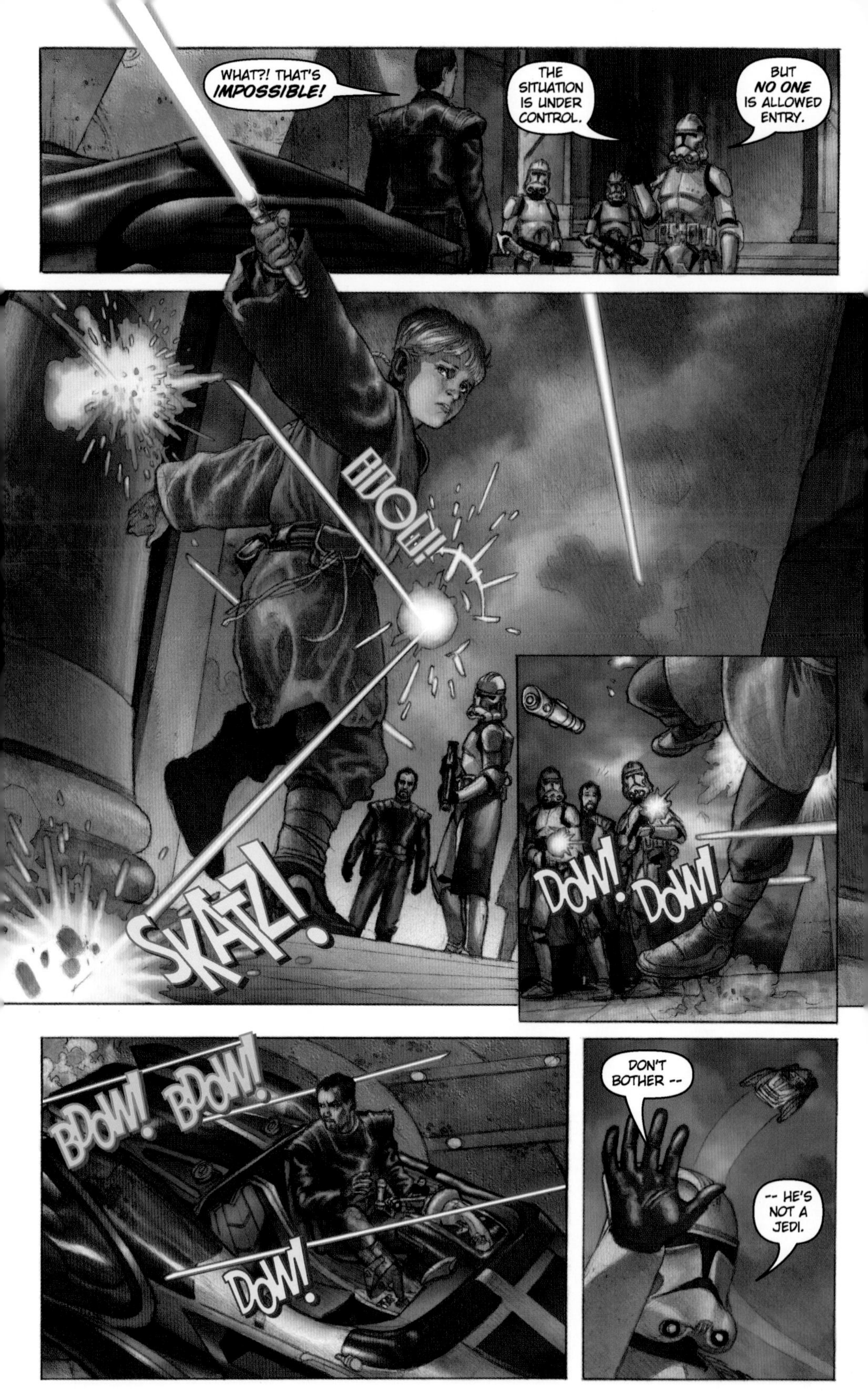
WHAT?! THAT'S IMPOSSIBLE!
THE SITUATION IS UNDER CONTROL.
BUT NO ONE IS ALLOWED ENTRY.
BDOW!
SKATZ!
DOW! DOW!
BDOW! BDOW!
DOW!
DON'T BOTHER --
-- HE'S NOT A JEDI.

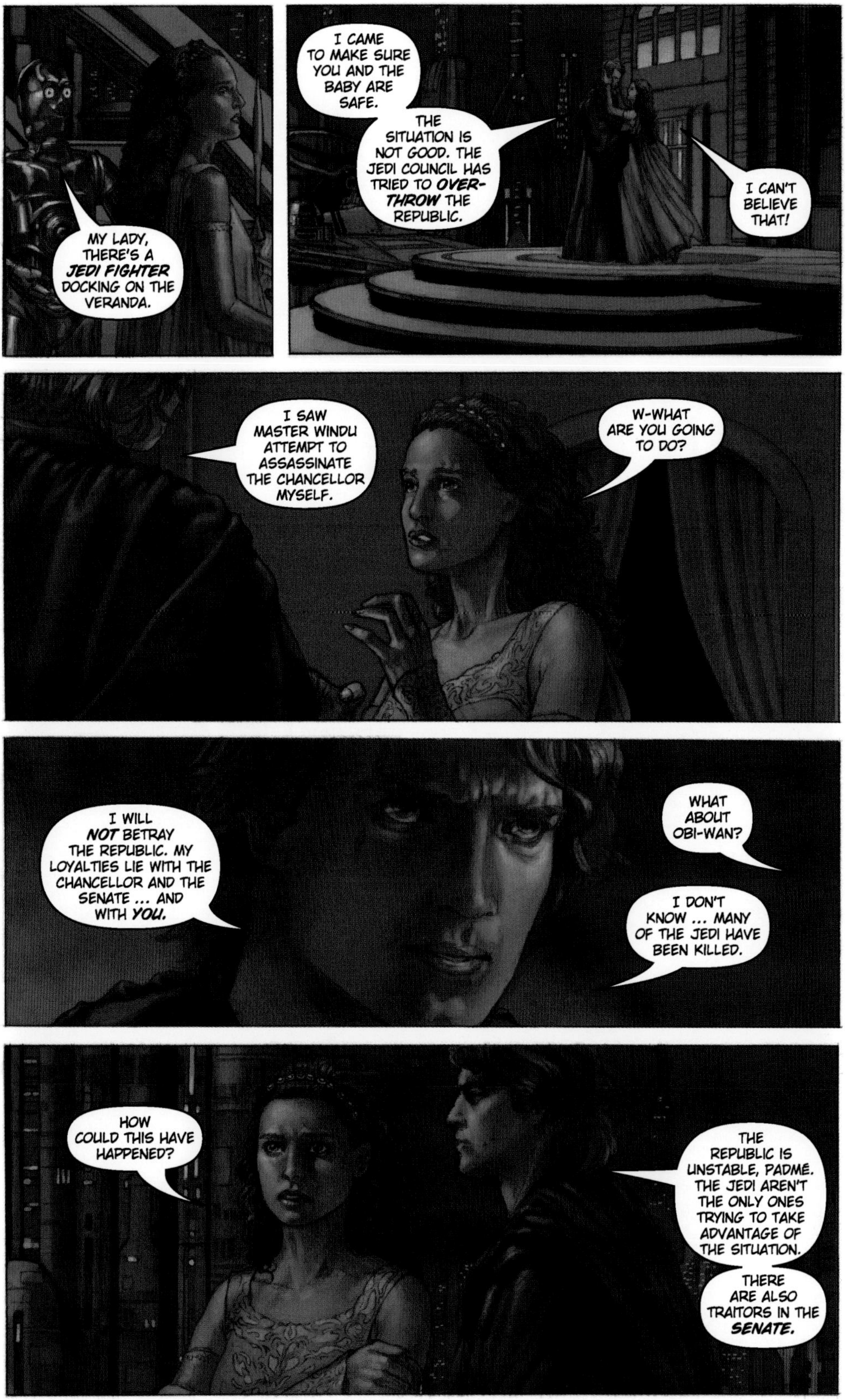
MY LADY, THERE'S A JEDI FIGHTER DOCKING ON THE VERANDA.
I CAME TO MAKE SURE YOU AND THE BABY ARE SAFE.
THE SITUATION IS NOT GOOD. THE JEDI COUNCIL HAS TRIED TO OVERTHROW THE REPUBLIC.
I CAN'T BELIEVE THAT!
I SAW MASTER WINDU ATTEMPT TO ASSASSINATE THE CHANCELLOR MYSELF.
W-WHAT ARE YOU GOING TO DO?
I WILL NOT BETRAY THE REPUBLIC. MY LOYALTIES LIE WITH THE CHANCELLOR AND THE SENATE ... AND WITH YOU.
WHAT ABOUT OBI-WAN?
I DON'T KNOW ... MANY OF THE JEDI HAVE BEEN KILLED.
HOW COULD THIS HAVE HAPPENED?
THE REPUBLIC IS UNSTABLE, PADMÉ. THE JEDI AREN'T THE ONLY ONES TRYING TO TAKE ADVANTAGE OF THE SITUATION.
THERE ARE ALSO TRAITORS IN THE SENATE.

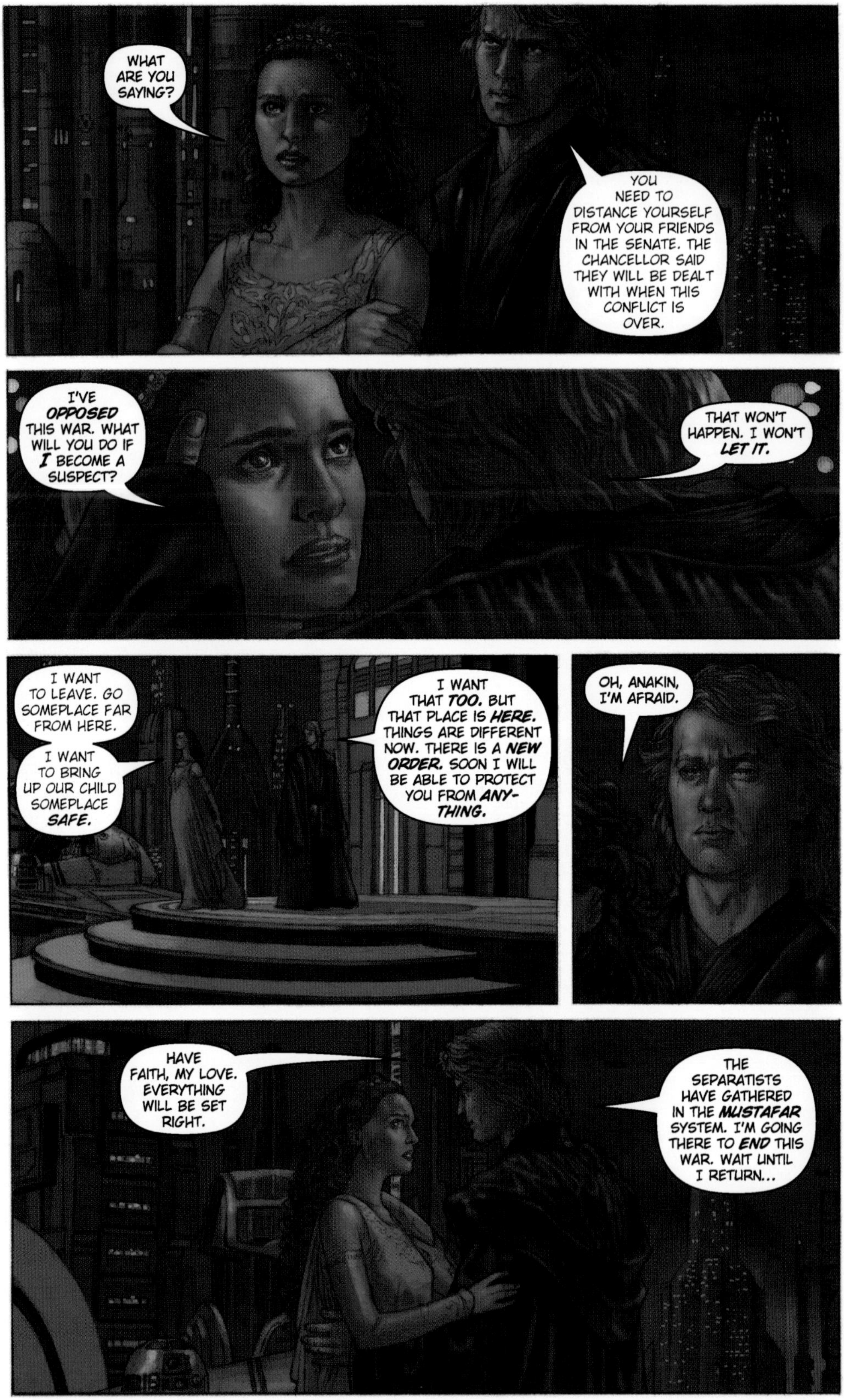
WHAT ARE YOU SAYING?
YOU NEED TO DISTANCE YOURSELF FROM YOUR FRIENDS IN THE SENATE. THE CHANCELLOR SAID THEY WILL BE DEALT WITH WHEN THIS CONFLICT IS OVER.
I'VE **OPPOSED** THIS WAR. WHAT WILL YOU DO IF ***I*** BECOME A SUSPECT?
THAT WON'T HAPPEN. I WON'T ***LET IT.***
I WANT TO LEAVE. GO SOMEPLACE FAR FROM HERE.
I WANT TO BRING UP OUR CHILD SOMEPLACE ***SAFE.***
I WANT THAT ***TOO.*** BUT THAT PLACE IS ***HERE.*** THINGS ARE DIFFERENT NOW. THERE IS A ***NEW ORDER.*** SOON I WILL BE ABLE TO PROTECT YOU FROM ***ANY-THING.***
OH, ANAKIN, I'M AFRAID.
HAVE FAITH, MY LOVE. EVERYTHING WILL BE SET RIGHT.
THE SEPARATISTS HAVE GATHERED IN THE ***MUSTAFAR*** SYSTEM. I'M GOING THERE TO ***END*** THIS WAR. WAIT UNTIL I RETURN...

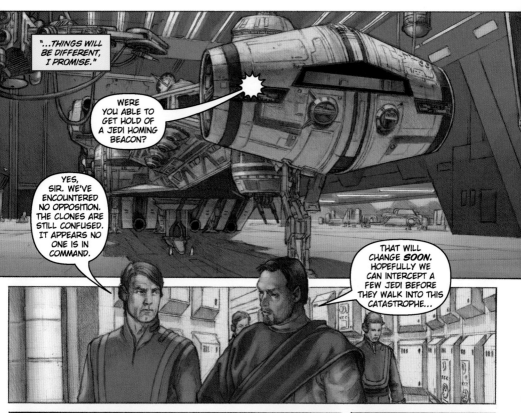

"...THINGS WILL BE DIFFERENT, I PROMISE."

WERE YOU ABLE TO GET HOLD OF A JEDI HOMING BEACON?

YES, SIR. WE'VE ENCOUNTERED NO OPPOSITION. THE CLONES ARE STILL CONFUSED. IT APPEARS NO ONE IS IN COMMAND.

THAT WILL CHANGE *SOON.* HOPEFULLY WE CAN INTERCEPT A FEW JEDI BEFORE THEY WALK INTO THIS CATASTROPHE...

CHEWBACCA AND TARFFUL, *GOOD FRIENDS* YOU ARE. FOR YOUR HELP, MUCH GRATITUDE AND RESPECT, I HAVE.

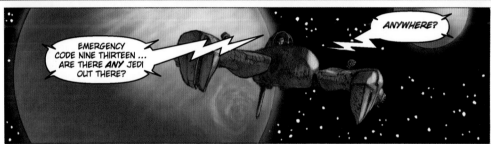

EMERGENCY CODE NINE THIRTEEN ... ARE THERE *ANY* JEDI OUT THERE?

ANYWHERE?

BZZT >FSSSSSHH< KRACKLE!

I'VE LOCKED ON! *REPEAT.*

MASTER KENOBI?

SENATOR ORGANA! MY CLONE TROOPS TURNED ON ME ... I NEED HELP.

IT APPEARS THIS AMBUSH HAS HAPPENED *EVERYWHERE.* LOCK ON TO MY COORDINATES.

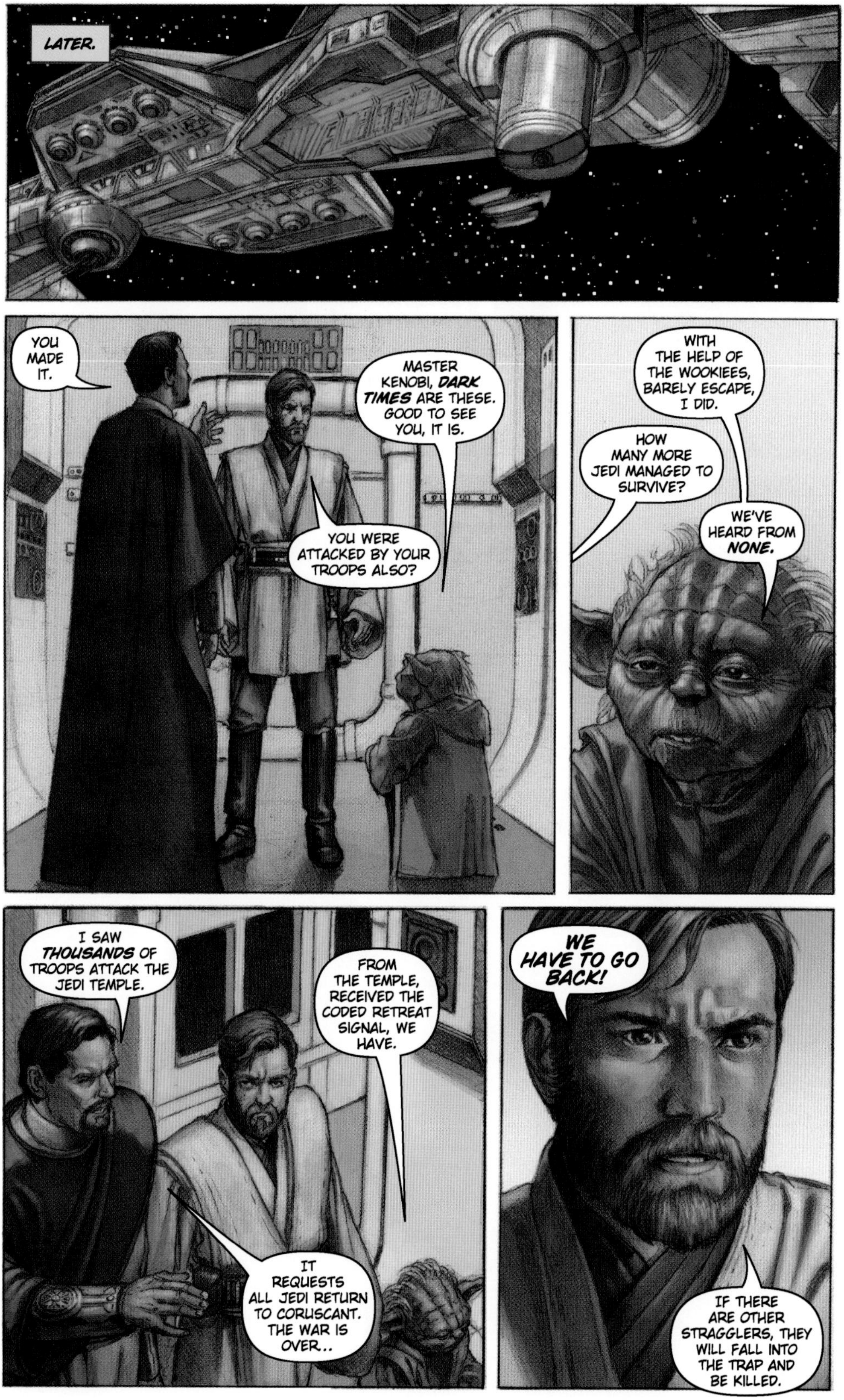
LATER.
YOU MADE IT.
MASTER KENOBI, DARK TIMES ARE THESE. GOOD TO SEE YOU, IT IS.
YOU WERE ATTACKED BY YOUR TROOPS ALSO?
WITH THE HELP OF THE WOOKIEES, BARELY ESCAPE, I DID.
HOW MANY MORE JEDI MANAGED TO SURVIVE?
WE'VE HEARD FROM NONE.
I SAW THOUSANDS OF TROOPS ATTACK THE JEDI TEMPLE.
FROM THE TEMPLE, RECEIVED THE CODED RETREAT SIGNAL, WE HAVE.
IT REQUESTS ALL JEDI RETURN TO CORUSCANT. THE WAR IS OVER..
WE HAVE TO GO BACK!
IF THERE ARE OTHER STRAGGLERS, THEY WILL FALL INTO THE TRAP AND BE KILLED.

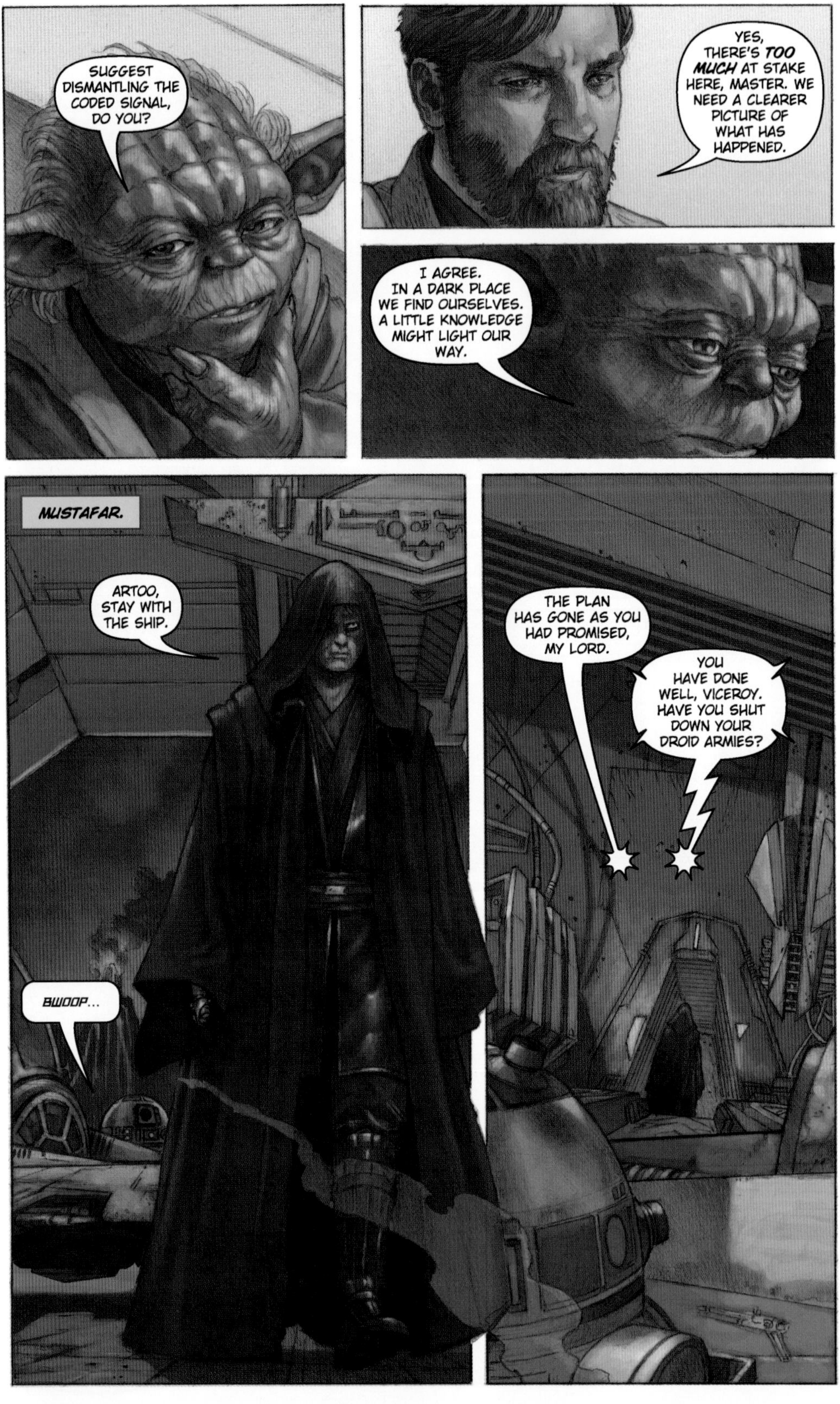
SUGGEST DISMANTLING THE CODED SIGNAL, DO YOU?
YES, THERE'S TOO MUCH AT STAKE HERE, MASTER. WE NEED A CLEARER PICTURE OF WHAT HAS HAPPENED.
I AGREE. IN A DARK PLACE WE FIND OURSELVES. A LITTLE KNOWLEDGE MIGHT LIGHT OUR WAY.
MUSTAFAR.
ARTOO, STAY WITH THE SHIP.
BWOOP...
THE PLAN HAS GONE AS YOU HAD PROMISED, MY LORD.
YOU HAVE DONE WELL, VICEROY. HAVE YOU SHUT DOWN YOUR DROID ARMIES?

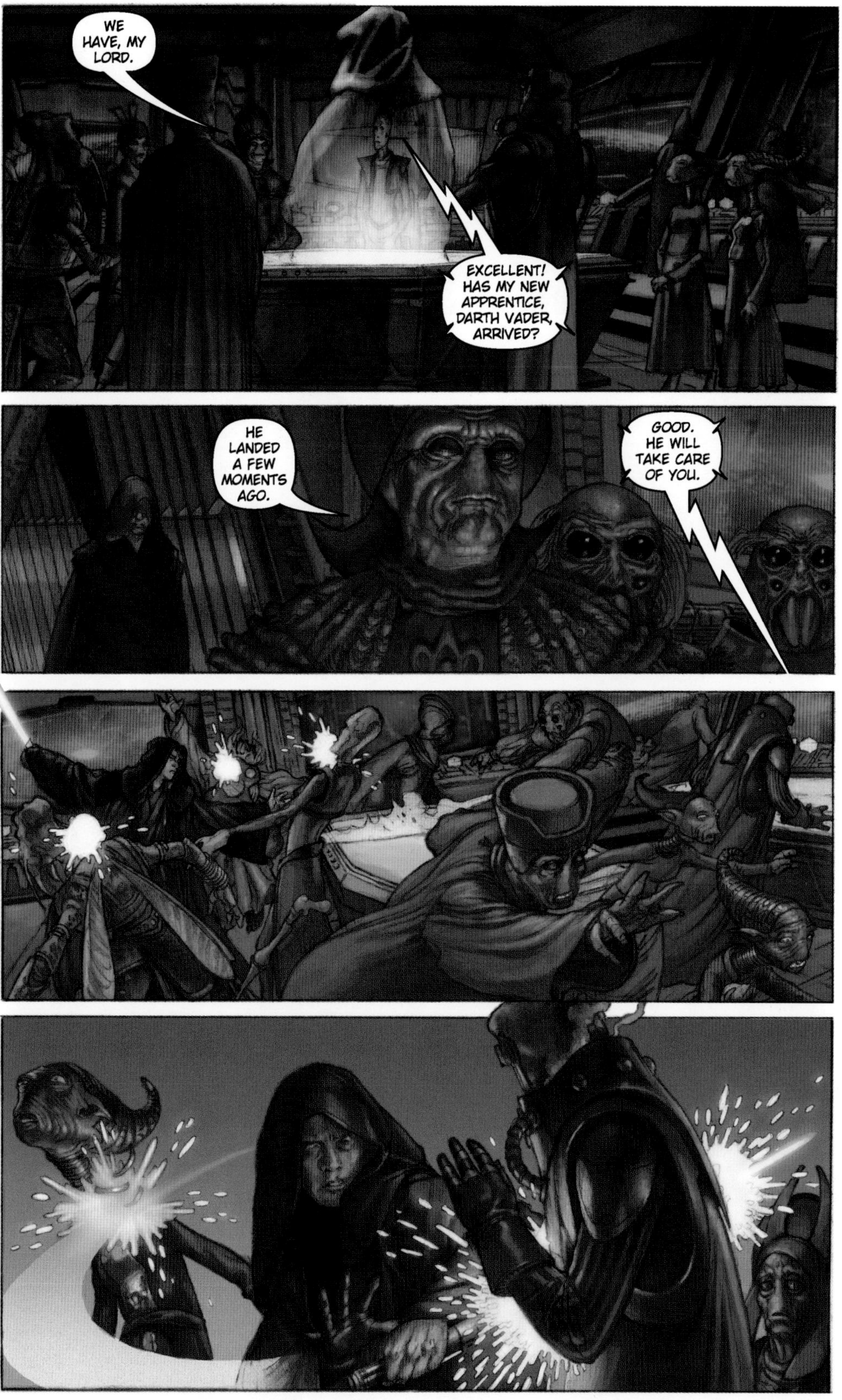
WE HAVE, MY LORD.
EXCELLENT! HAS MY NEW APPRENTICE, DARTH VADER, ARRIVED?
HE LANDED A FEW MOMENTS AGO.
GOOD. HE WILL TAKE CARE OF YOU.

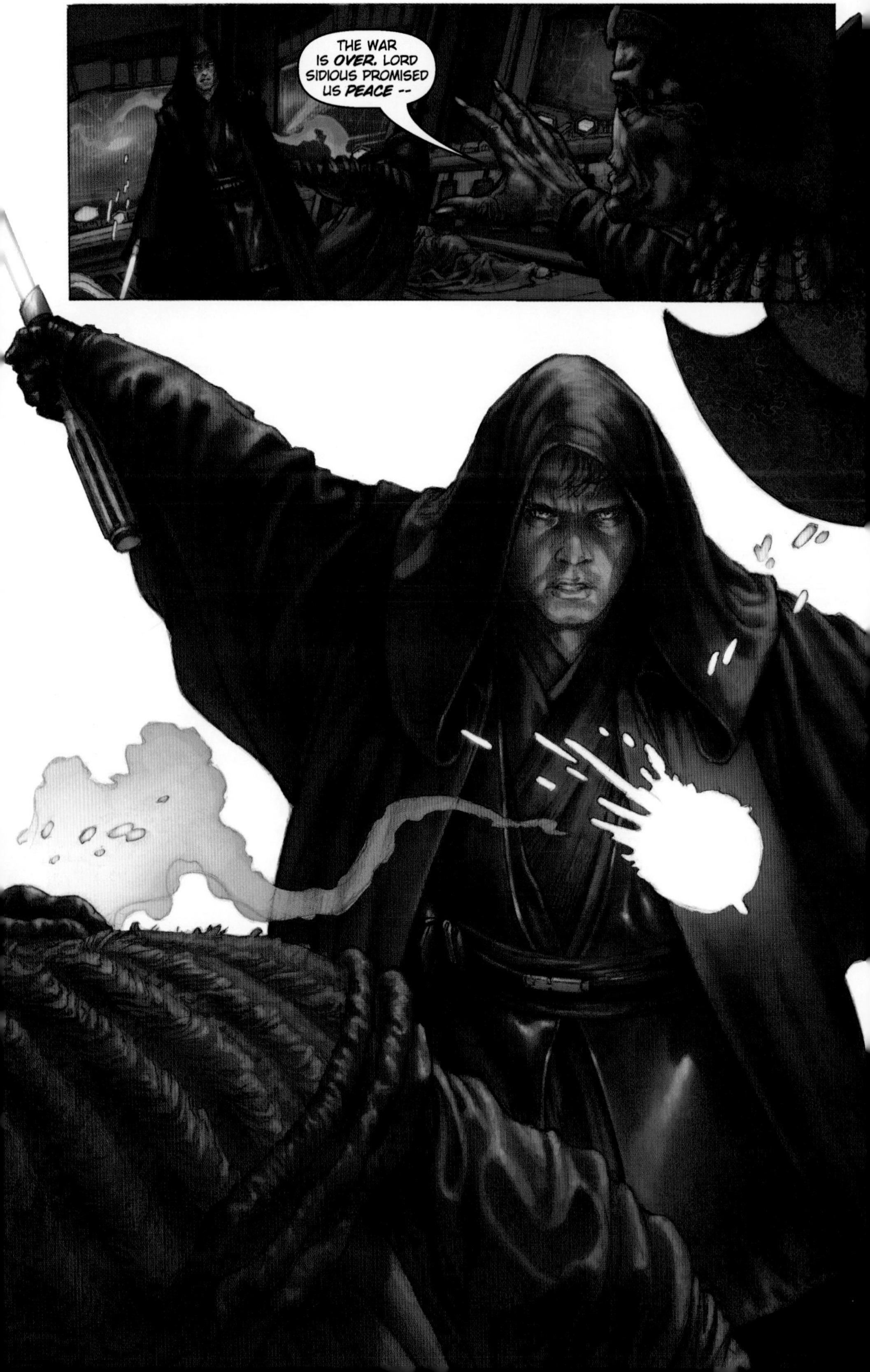
THE WAR IS OVER. LORD SIDIOUS PROMISED US PEACE --

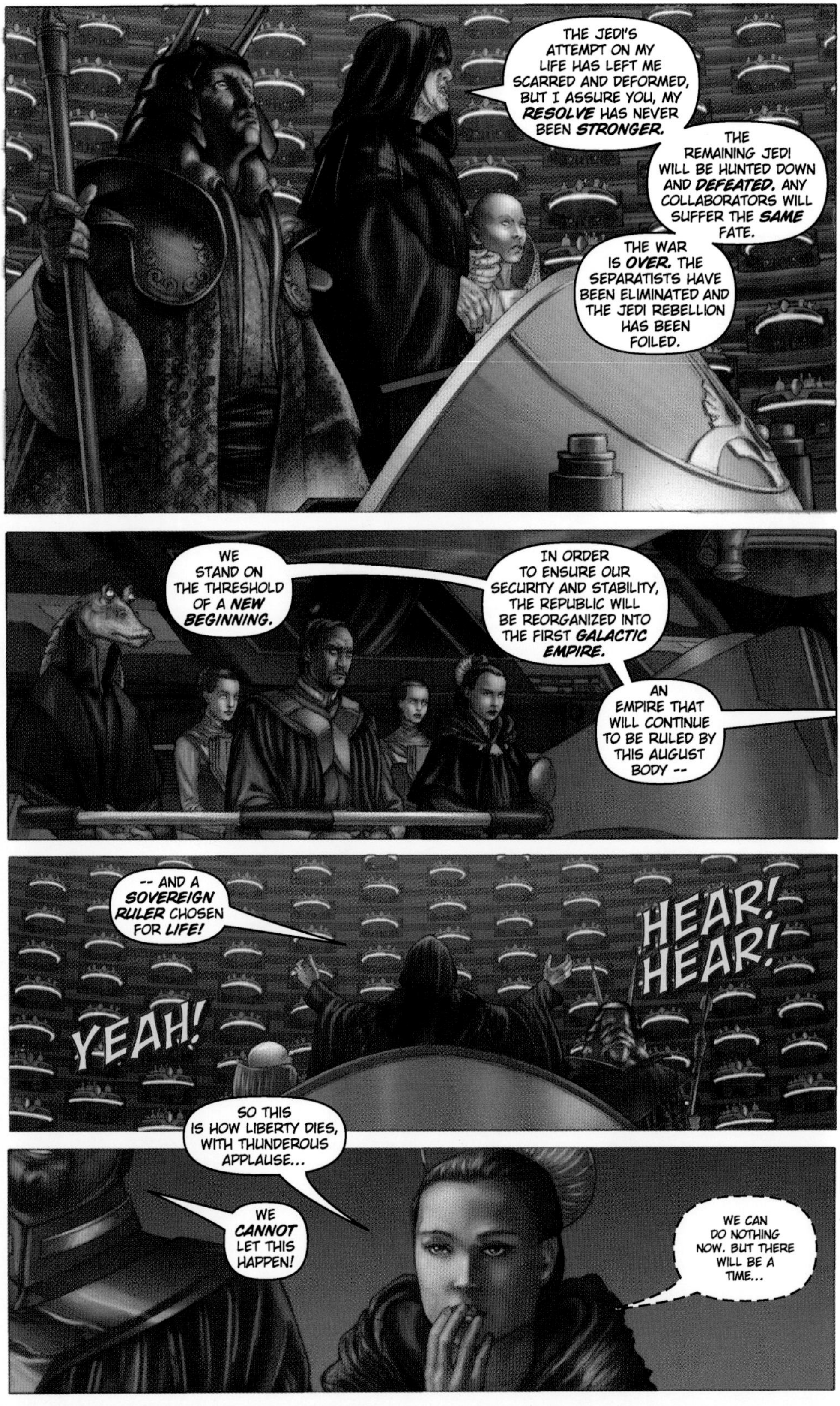
THE JEDI'S ATTEMPT ON MY LIFE HAS LEFT ME SCARRED AND DEFORMED, BUT I ASSURE YOU, MY RESOLVE HAS NEVER BEEN STRONGER.
THE REMAINING JEDI WILL BE HUNTED DOWN AND DEFEATED. ANY COLLABORATORS WILL SUFFER THE SAME FATE.
THE WAR IS OVER. THE SEPARATISTS HAVE BEEN ELIMINATED AND THE JEDI REBELLION HAS BEEN FOILED.
WE STAND ON THE THRESHOLD OF A NEW BEGINNING.
IN ORDER TO ENSURE OUR SECURITY AND STABILITY, THE REPUBLIC WILL BE REORGANIZED INTO THE FIRST GALACTIC EMPIRE.
AN EMPIRE THAT WILL CONTINUE TO BE RULED BY THIS AUGUST BODY --
-- AND A SOVEREIGN RULER CHOSEN FOR LIFE!
HEAR! HEAR!
YEAH!
SO THIS IS HOW LIBERTY DIES, WITH THUNDEROUS APPLAUSE...
WE CANNOT LET THIS HAPPEN!
WE CAN DO NOTHING NOW. BUT THERE WILL BE A TIME...

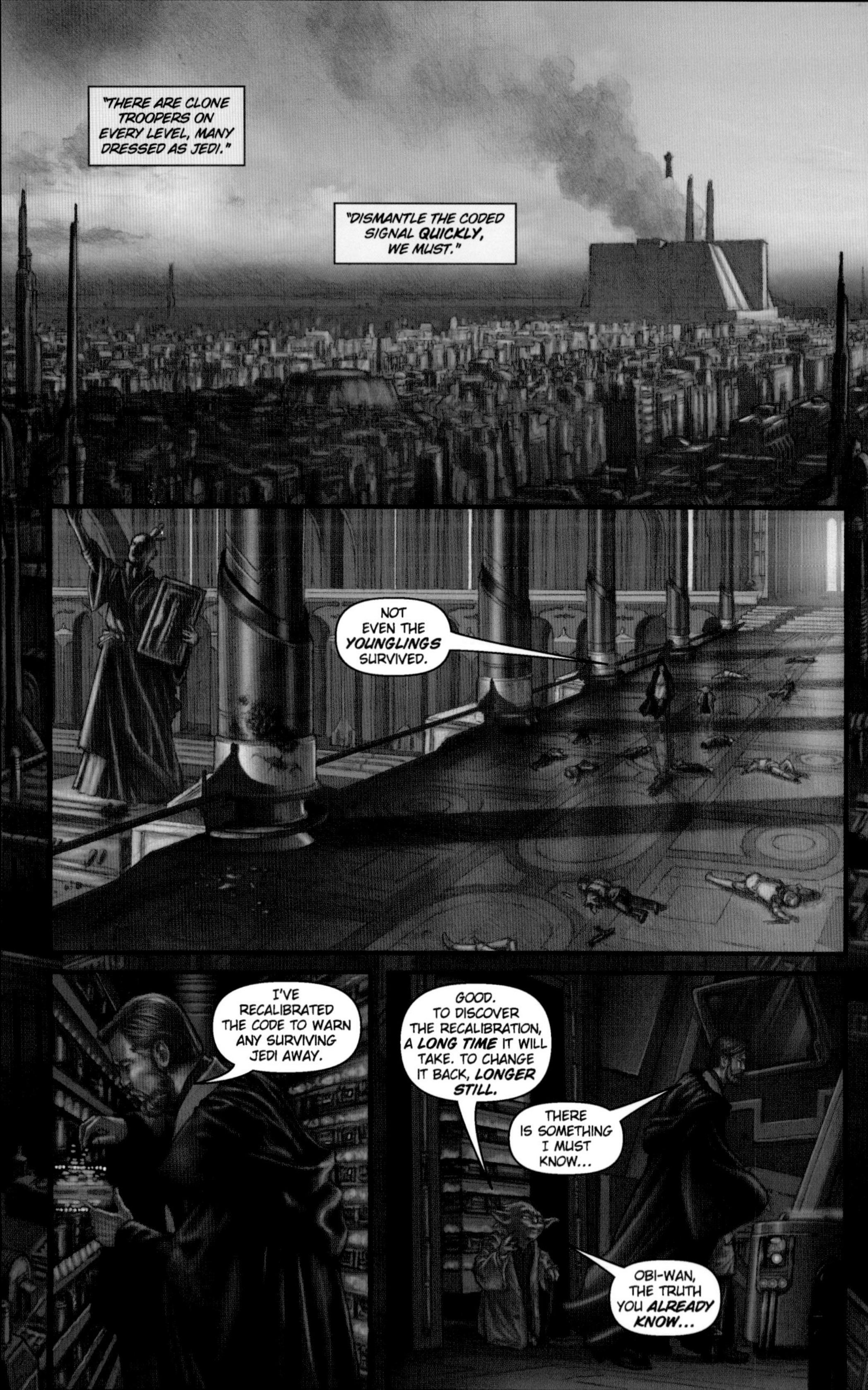
"THERE ARE CLONE TROOPERS ON EVERY LEVEL, MANY DRESSED AS JEDI."
"DISMANTLE THE CODED SIGNAL QUICKLY, WE MUST."
NOT EVEN THE YOUNGLINGS SURVIVED.
I'VE RECALIBRATED THE CODE TO WARN ANY SURVIVING JEDI AWAY.
GOOD. TO DISCOVER THE RECALIBRATION, A LONG TIME IT WILL TAKE. TO CHANGE IT BACK, LONGER STILL.
THERE IS SOMETHING I MUST KNOW...
OBI-WAN, THE TRUTH YOU ALREADY KNOW...

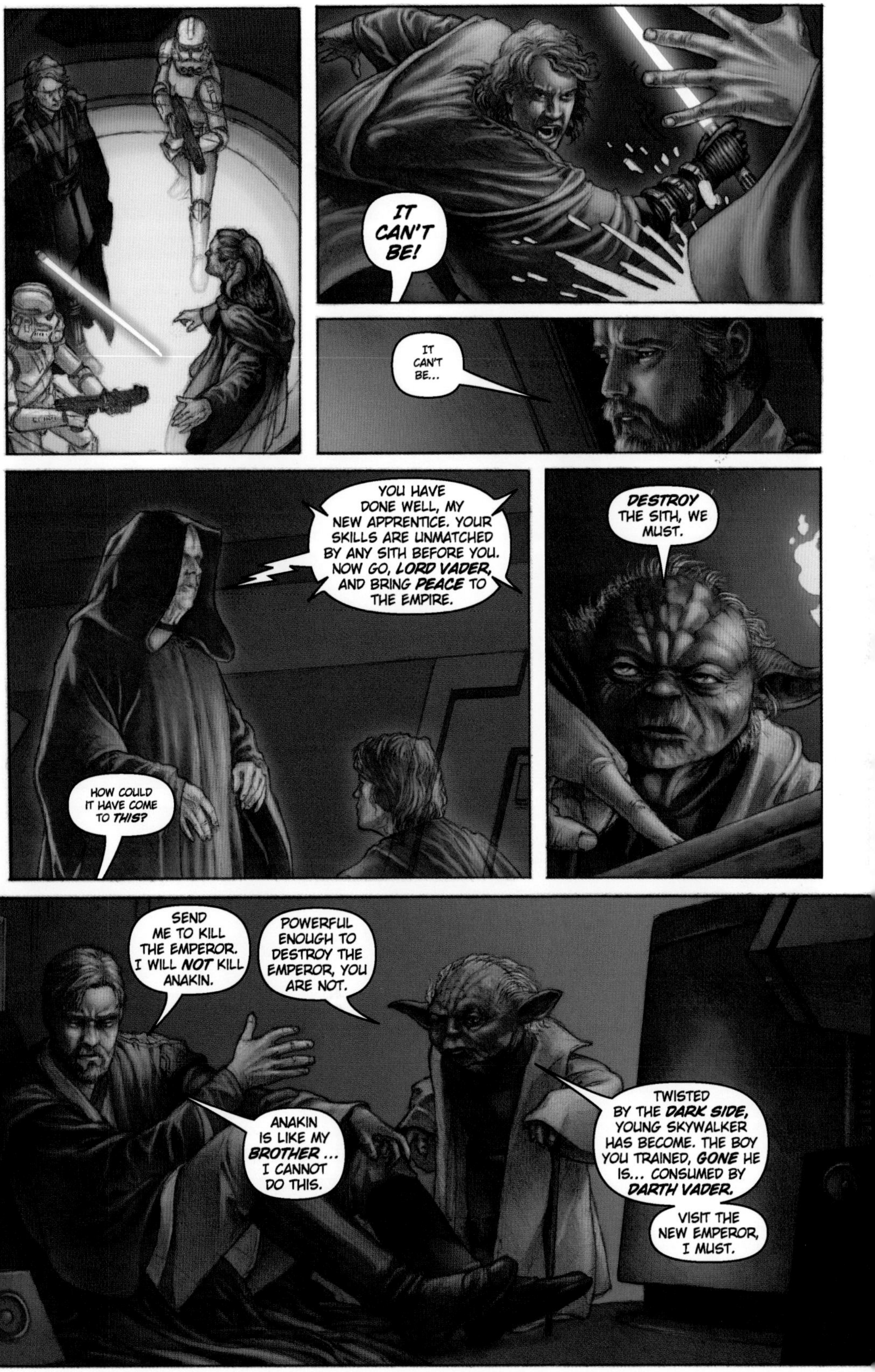
IT CAN'T BE!
IT CAN'T BE...
YOU HAVE DONE WELL, MY NEW APPRENTICE. YOUR SKILLS ARE UNMATCHED BY ANY SITH BEFORE YOU. NOW GO, LORD VADER, AND BRING PEACE TO THE EMPIRE.
HOW COULD IT HAVE COME TO THIS?
DESTROY THE SITH, WE MUST.
SEND ME TO KILL THE EMPEROR. I WILL NOT KILL ANAKIN.
POWERFUL ENOUGH TO DESTROY THE EMPEROR, YOU ARE NOT.
ANAKIN IS LIKE MY BROTHER ... I CANNOT DO THIS.
TWISTED BY THE DARK SIDE, YOUNG SKYWALKER HAS BECOME. THE BOY YOU TRAINED, GONE HE IS... CONSUMED BY DARTH VADER.
VISIT THE NEW EMPEROR, I MUST.

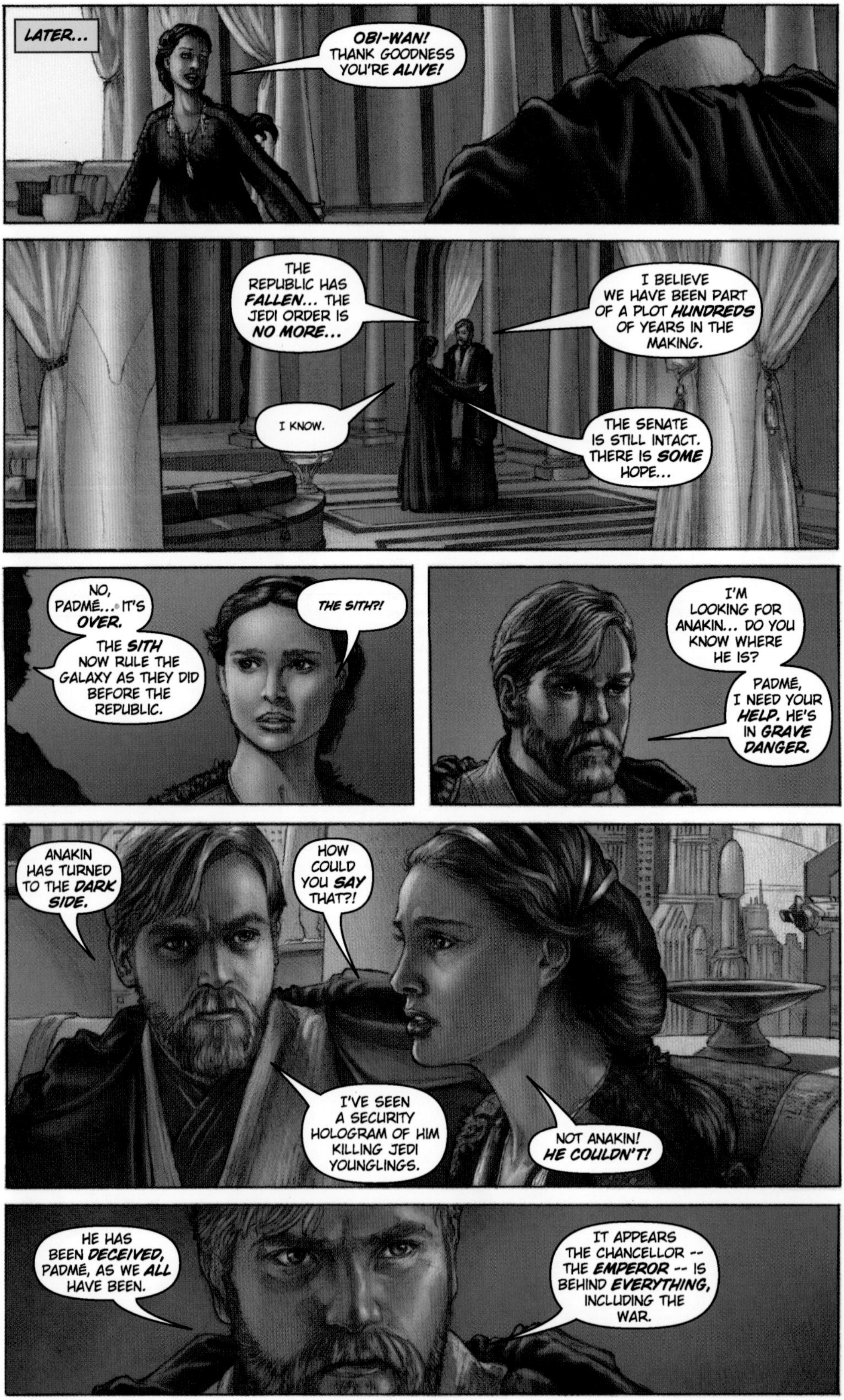
LATER...
OBI-WAN! THANK GOODNESS YOU'RE ALIVE!
THE REPUBLIC HAS FALLEN... THE JEDI ORDER IS NO MORE...
I BELIEVE WE HAVE BEEN PART OF A PLOT HUNDREDS OF YEARS IN THE MAKING.
I KNOW.
THE SENATE IS STILL INTACT. THERE IS SOME HOPE...
NO, PADMÉ... IT'S OVER.
THE SITH NOW RULE THE GALAXY AS THEY DID BEFORE THE REPUBLIC.
THE SITH?!
I'M LOOKING FOR ANAKIN... DO YOU KNOW WHERE HE IS?
PADMÉ, I NEED YOUR HELP. HE'S IN GRAVE DANGER.
ANAKIN HAS TURNED TO THE DARK SIDE.
HOW COULD YOU SAY THAT?!
I'VE SEEN A SECURITY HOLOGRAM OF HIM KILLING JEDI YOUNGLINGS.
NOT ANAKIN! HE COULDN'T!
HE HAS BEEN DECEIVED, PADMÉ, AS WE ALL HAVE BEEN.
IT APPEARS THE CHANCELLOR -- THE EMPEROR -- IS BEHIND EVERYTHING, INCLUDING THE WAR.

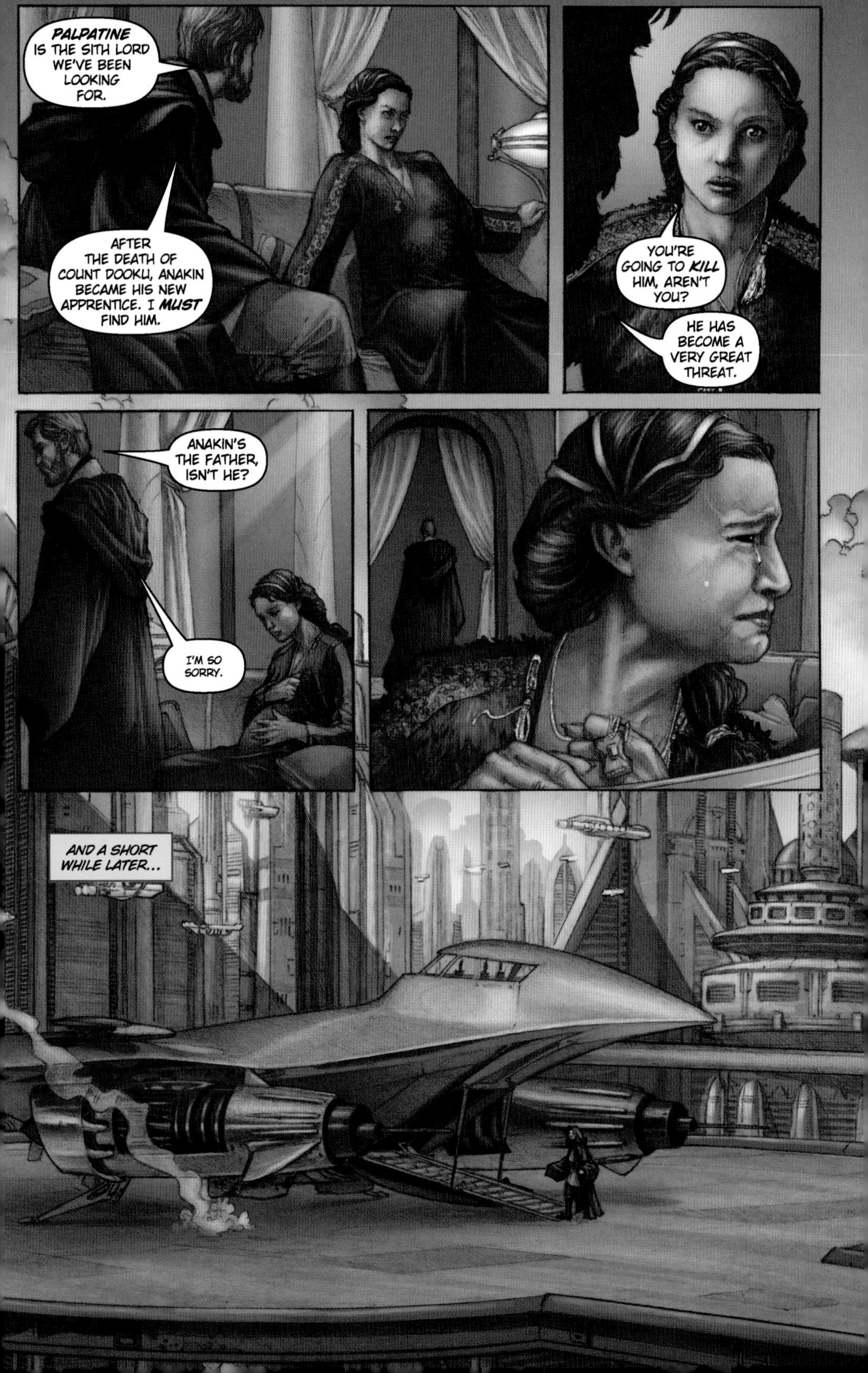
PALPATINE IS THE SITH LORD WE'VE BEEN LOOKING FOR.
AFTER THE DEATH OF COUNT DOOKU, ANAKIN BECAME HIS NEW APPRENTICE. I MUST FIND HIM.
YOU'RE GOING TO KILL HIM, AREN'T YOU?
HE HAS BECOME A VERY GREAT THREAT.
ANAKIN'S THE FATHER, ISN'T HE?
I'M SO SORRY.
AND A SHORT WHILE LATER...

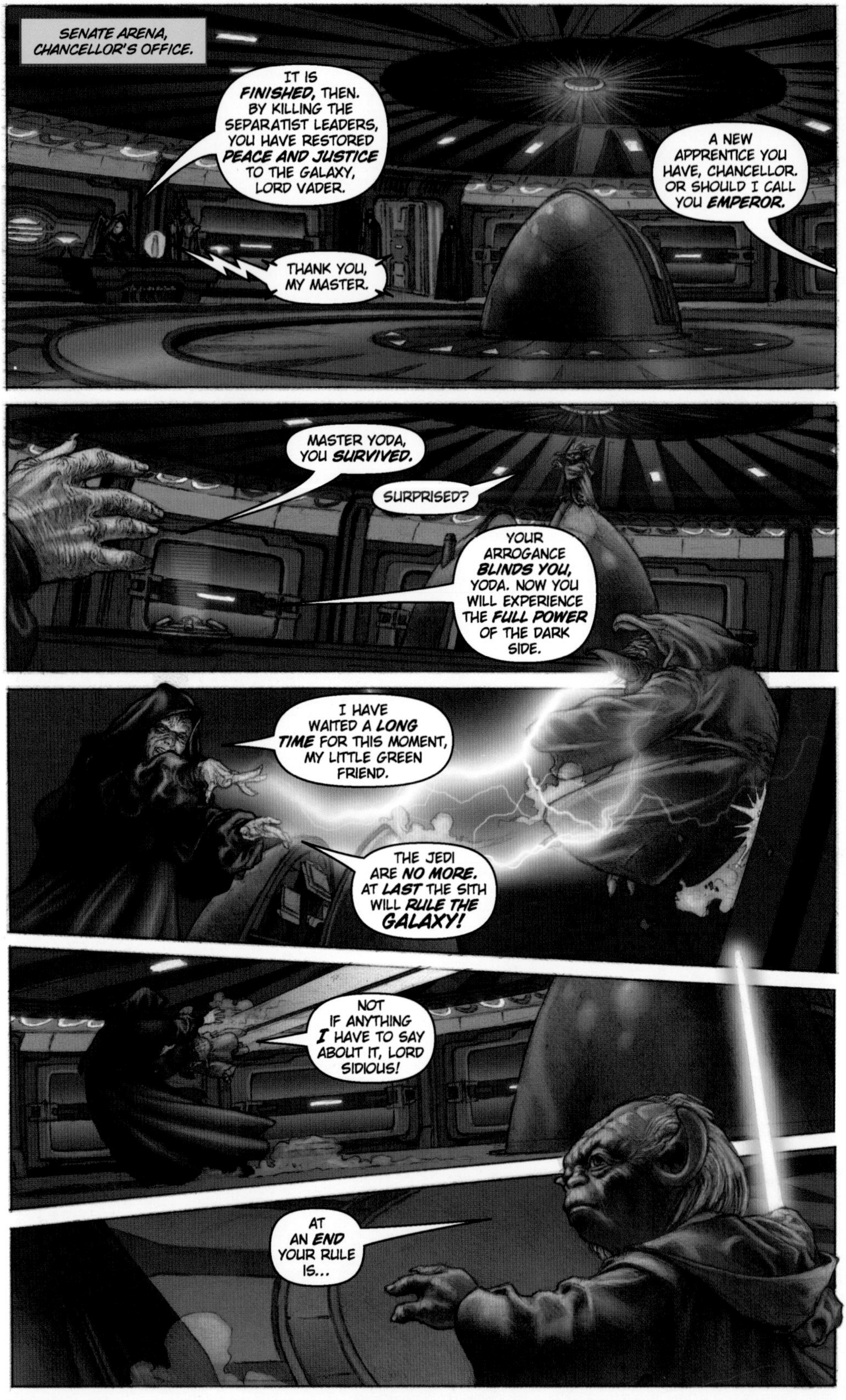
SENATE ARENA, CHANCELLOR'S OFFICE.
IT IS FINISHED, THEN. BY KILLING THE SEPARATIST LEADERS, YOU HAVE RESTORED PEACE AND JUSTICE TO THE GALAXY, LORD VADER.
THANK YOU, MY MASTER.
A NEW APPRENTICE YOU HAVE, CHANCELLOR. OR SHOULD I CALL YOU EMPEROR.
MASTER YODA, YOU SURVIVED.
SURPRISED?
YOUR ARROGANCE BLINDS YOU, YODA. NOW YOU WILL EXPERIENCE THE FULL POWER OF THE DARK SIDE.
I HAVE WAITED A LONG TIME FOR THIS MOMENT, MY LITTLE GREEN FRIEND.
THE JEDI ARE NO MORE. AT LAST THE SITH WILL RULE THE GALAXY!
NOT IF ANYTHING I HAVE TO SAY ABOUT IT, LORD SIDIOUS!
AT AN END YOUR RULE IS...

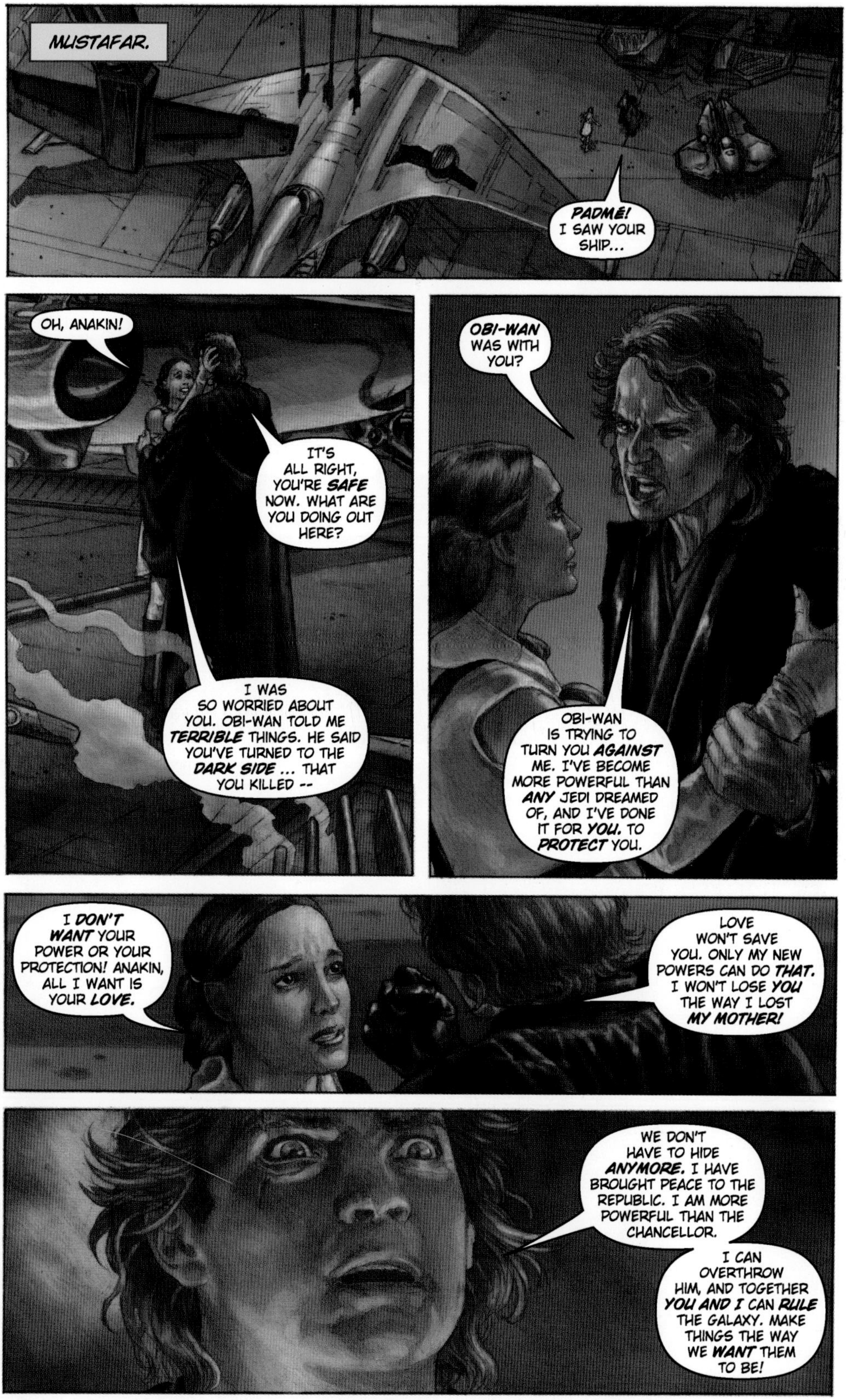

MUSTAFAR.
PADMÉ! I SAW YOUR SHIP...
OH, ANAKIN!
IT'S ALL RIGHT, YOU'RE SAFE NOW. WHAT ARE YOU DOING OUT HERE?
I WAS SO WORRIED ABOUT YOU. OBI-WAN TOLD ME TERRIBLE THINGS. HE SAID YOU'VE TURNED TO THE DARK SIDE ... THAT YOU KILLED --
OBI-WAN WAS WITH YOU?
OBI-WAN IS TRYING TO TURN YOU AGAINST ME. I'VE BECOME MORE POWERFUL THAN ANY JEDI DREAMED OF, AND I'VE DONE IT FOR YOU. TO PROTECT YOU.
I DON'T WANT YOUR POWER OR YOUR PROTECTION! ANAKIN, ALL I WANT IS YOUR LOVE.
LOVE WON'T SAVE YOU. ONLY MY NEW POWERS CAN DO THAT. I WON'T LOSE YOU THE WAY I LOST MY MOTHER!
WE DON'T HAVE TO HIDE ANYMORE. I HAVE BROUGHT PEACE TO THE REPUBLIC. I AM MORE POWERFUL THAN THE CHANCELLOR.
I CAN OVERTHROW HIM, AND TOGETHER YOU AND I CAN RULE THE GALAXY. MAKE THINGS THE WAY WE WANT THEM TO BE!

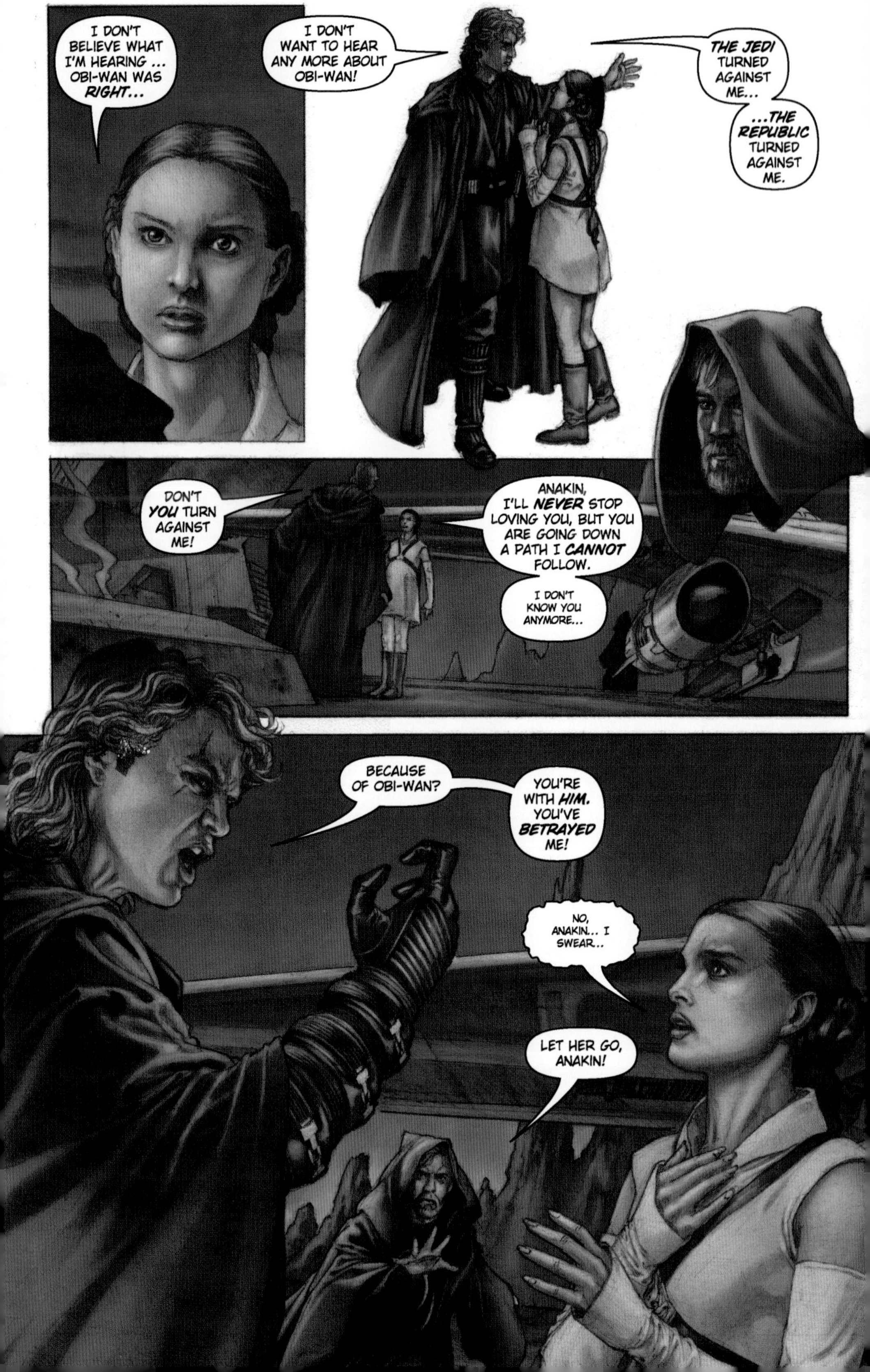
I DON'T BELIEVE WHAT I'M HEARING ... OBI-WAN WAS RIGHT...
I DON'T WANT TO HEAR ANY MORE ABOUT OBI-WAN!
THE JEDI TURNED AGAINST ME...
...THE REPUBLIC TURNED AGAINST ME.
DON'T YOU TURN AGAINST ME!
ANAKIN, I'LL NEVER STOP LOVING YOU, BUT YOU ARE GOING DOWN A PATH I CANNOT FOLLOW.
I DON'T KNOW YOU ANYMORE...
BECAUSE OF OBI-WAN?
YOU'RE WITH HIM. YOU'VE BETRAYED ME!
NO, ANAKIN... I SWEAR..
LET HER GO, ANAKIN!

WHAT HAVE YOU AND SHE BEEN UP TO?!
LET HER GO!
YOU WILL NOT TAKE HER FROM ME!
UNNH!
YOU TURNED HER AGAINST ME!
YOU DID THAT YOURSELF.
YOU'VE LET THE DARK LORD TWIST YOUR POINT OF VIEW UNTIL YOU'VE BECOME THE VERY THING YOU SWORE TO DESTROY!
DON'T LECTURE ME, OBI-WAN. I SEE THROUGH THE LIES OF THE JEDI. I DO NOT FEAR THE DARK SIDE AS YOU DO.
I HAVE BROUGHT PEACE AND SECURITY TO MY NEW EMPIRE...
YOUR NEW EMPIRE?! MY ALLEGIANCE IS TO THE REPUBLIC, ANAKIN...
IF YOU ARE NOT WITH ME --
-- THEN YOU ARE MY ENEMY!

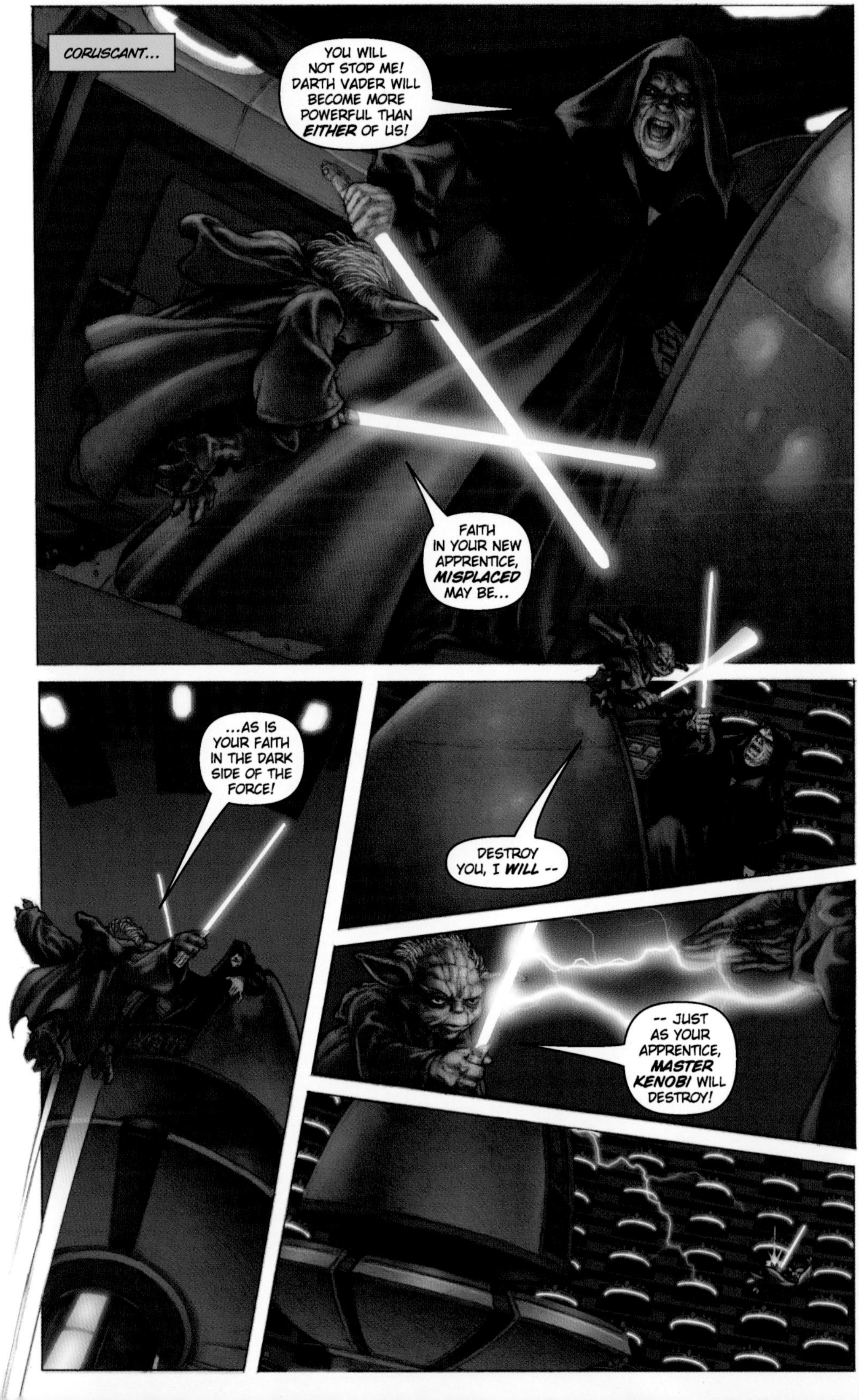
CORUSCANT...
YOU WILL NOT STOP ME! DARTH VADER WILL BECOME MORE POWERFUL THAN EITHER OF US!
FAITH IN YOUR NEW APPRENTICE, MISPLACED MAY BE...
...AS IS YOUR FAITH IN THE DARK SIDE OF THE FORCE!
DESTROY YOU, I WILL --
-- JUST AS YOUR APPRENTICE, MASTER KENOBI WILL DESTROY!

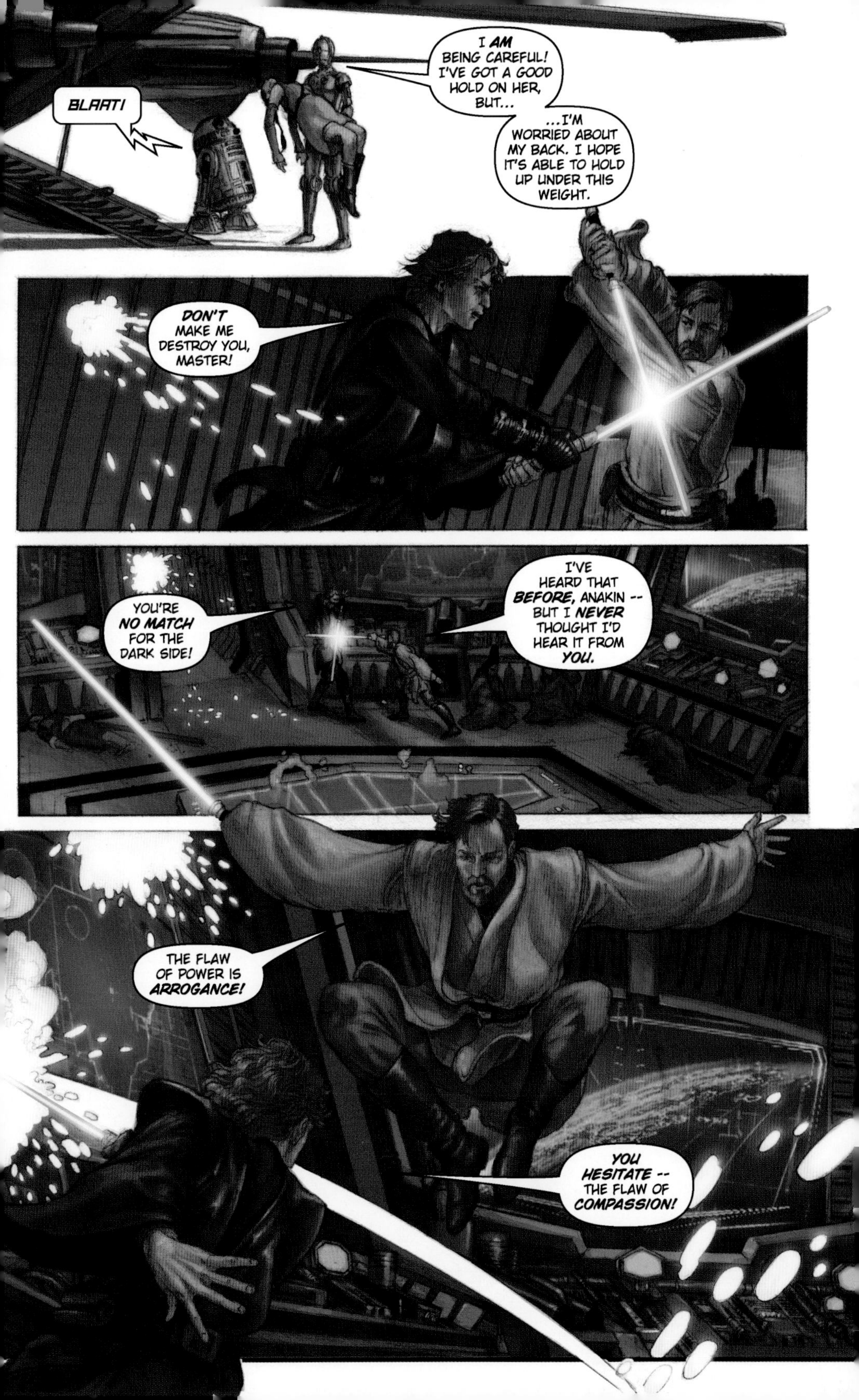

I AM BEING CAREFUL! I'VE GOT A GOOD HOLD ON HER, BUT...
BLAAT!
...I'M WORRIED ABOUT MY BACK. I HOPE IT'S ABLE TO HOLD UP UNDER THIS WEIGHT.
DON'T MAKE ME DESTROY YOU, MASTER!
YOU'RE NO MATCH FOR THE DARK SIDE!
I'VE HEARD THAT BEFORE, ANAKIN -- BUT I NEVER THOUGHT I'D HEAR IT FROM YOU.
THE FLAW OF POWER IS ARROGANCE!
YOU HESITATE -- THE FLAW OF COMPASSION!

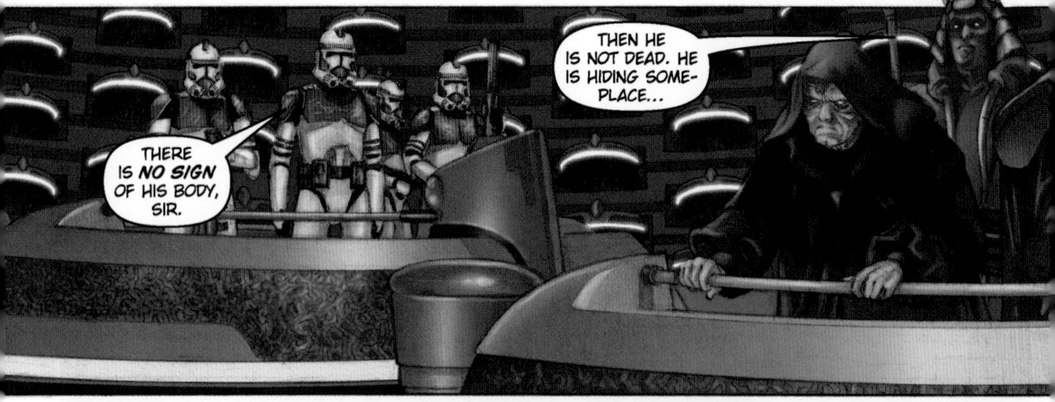
THERE IS NO SIGN OF HIS BODY, SIR.
THEN HE IS NOT DEAD. HE IS HIDING SOME-PLACE...
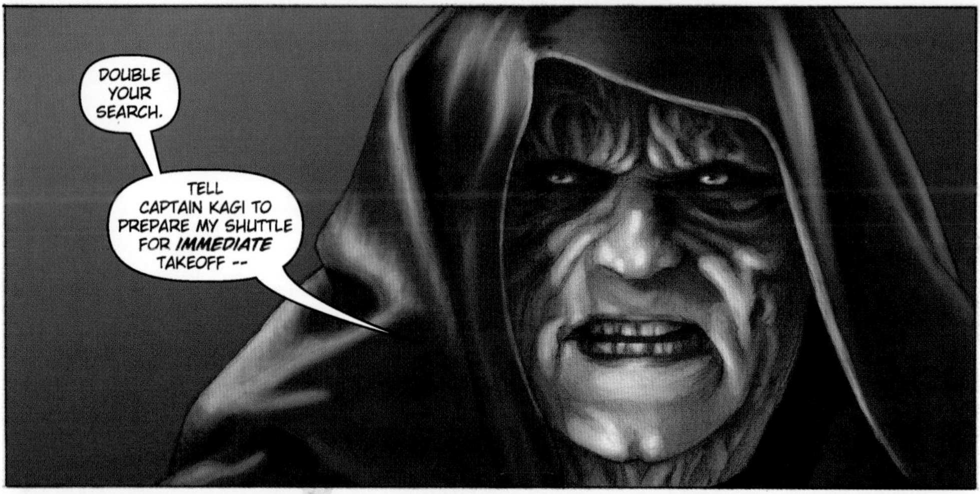
DOUBLE YOUR SEARCH.
TELL CAPTAIN KAGI TO PREPARE MY SHUTTLE FOR IMMEDIATE TAKEOFF --
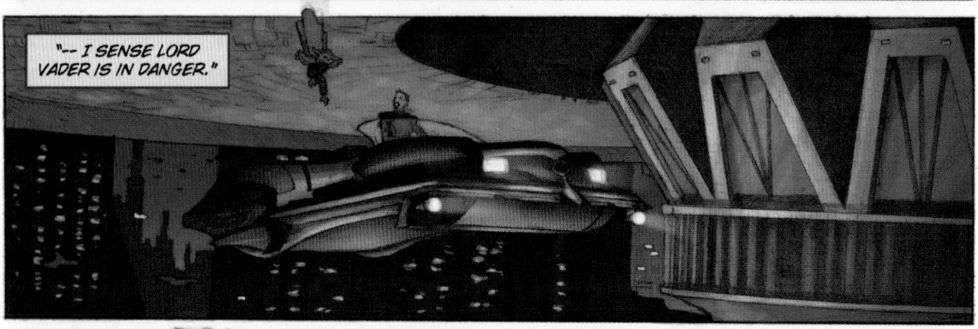
"-- I SENSE LORD VADER IS IN DANGER."
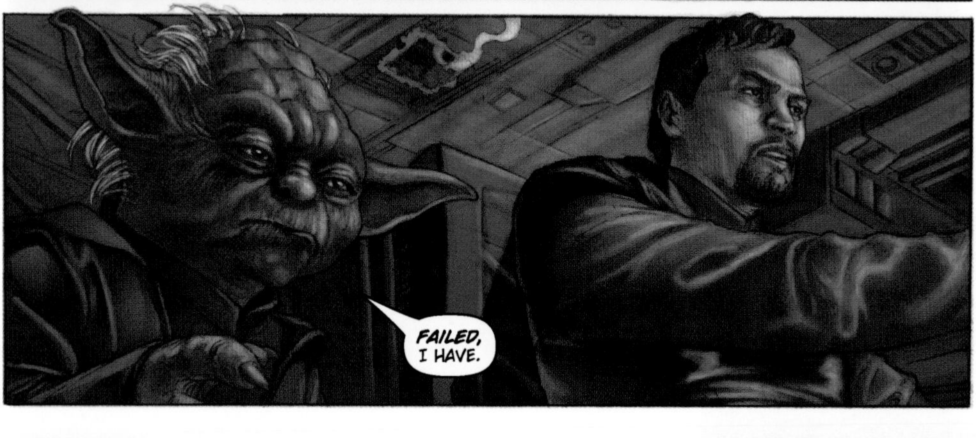
FAILED, I HAVE.

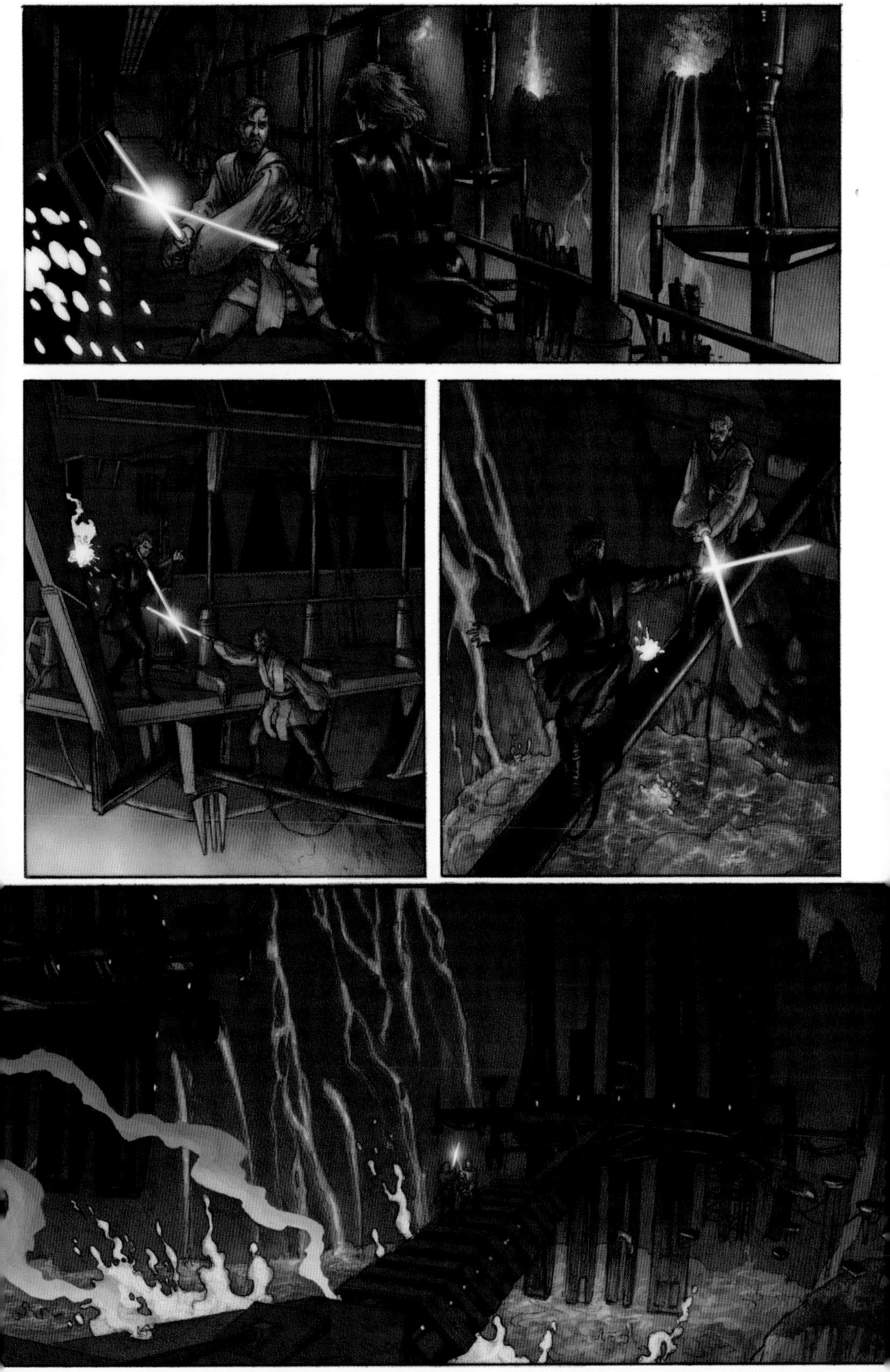

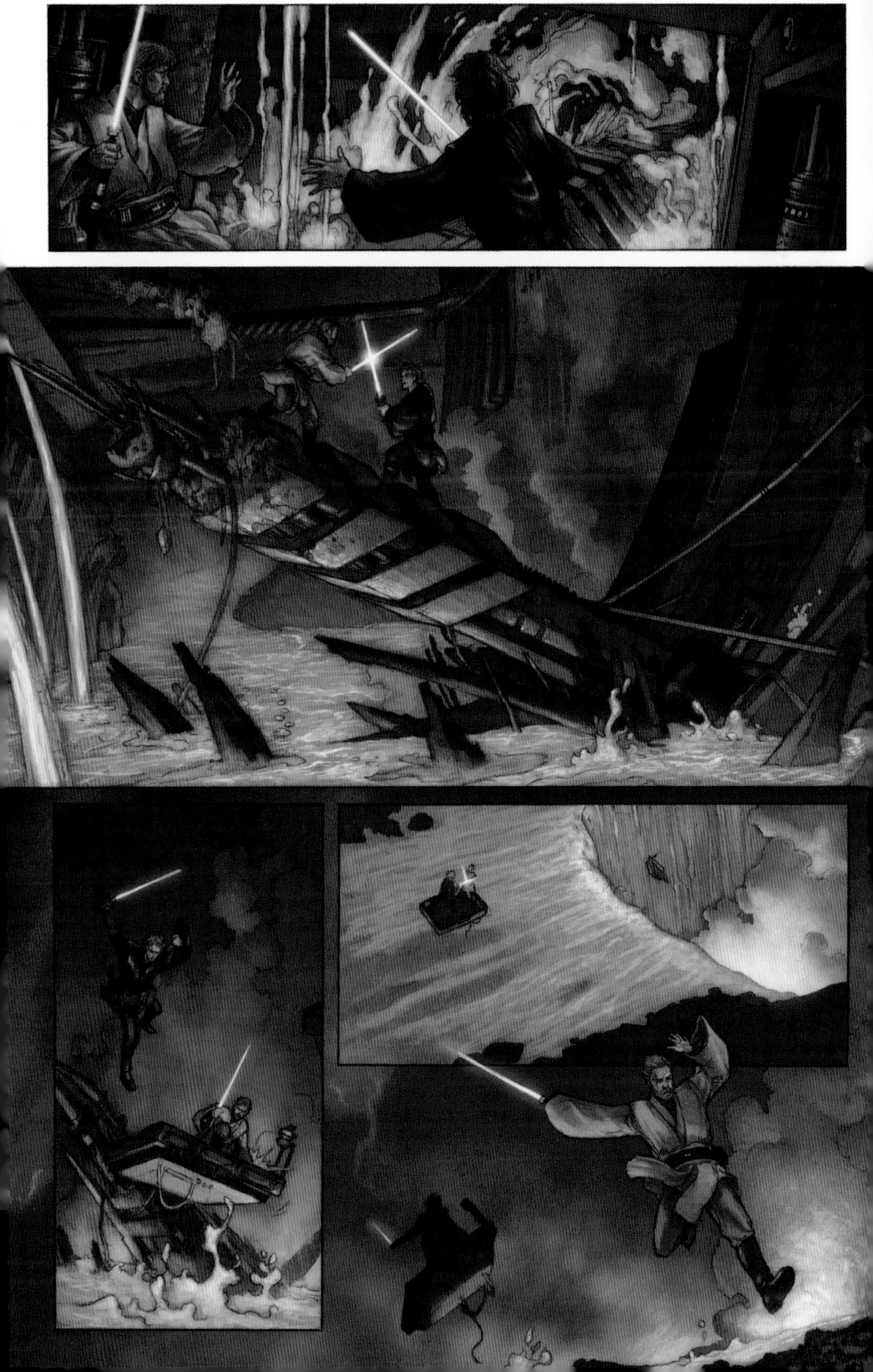

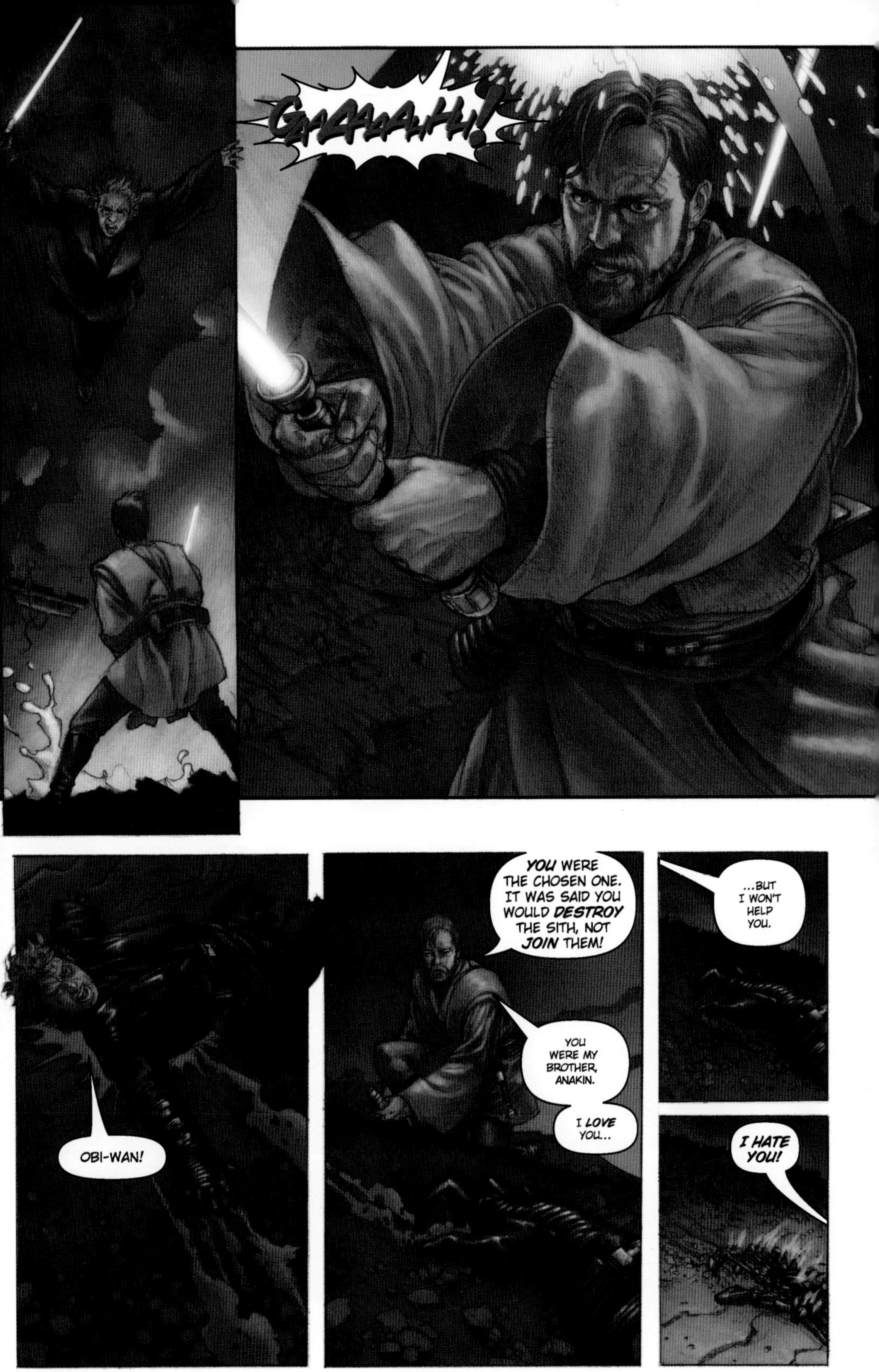
GAAAAHH!
OBI-WAN!
YOU WERE THE CHOSEN ONE. IT WAS SAID YOU WOULD DESTROY THE SITH, NOT JOIN THEM!
YOU WERE MY BROTHER, ANAKIN.
I LOVE YOU...
...BUT I WON'T HELP YOU.
I HATE YOU!

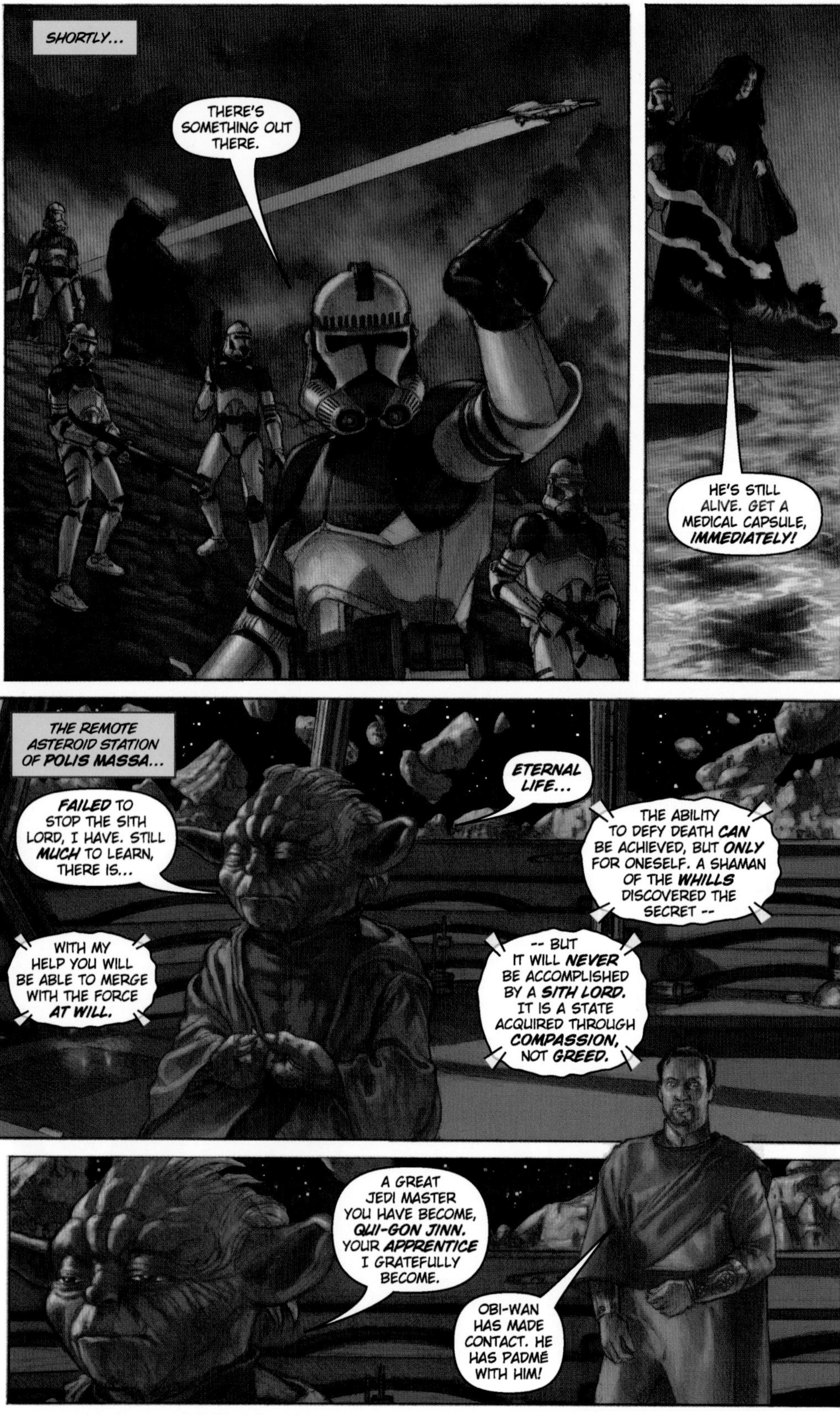
SHORTLY...
THERE'S SOMETHING OUT THERE.
HE'S STILL ALIVE. GET A MEDICAL CAPSULE, IMMEDIATELY!
THE REMOTE ASTEROID STATION OF POLIS MASSA...
FAILED TO STOP THE SITH LORD, I HAVE. STILL MUCH TO LEARN, THERE IS...
ETERNAL LIFE...
THE ABILITY TO DEFY DEATH CAN BE ACHIEVED, BUT ONLY FOR ONESELF. A SHAMAN OF THE WHILLS DISCOVERED THE SECRET --
WITH MY HELP YOU WILL BE ABLE TO MERGE WITH THE FORCE AT WILL.
-- BUT IT WILL NEVER BE ACCOMPLISHED BY A SITH LORD. IT IS A STATE ACQUIRED THROUGH COMPASSION, NOT GREED.
A GREAT JEDI MASTER YOU HAVE BECOME, QUI-GON JINN. YOUR APPRENTICE I GRATEFULLY BECOME.
OBI-WAN HAS MADE CONTACT. HE HAS PADMÉ WITH HIM!

TWINS?!
SAVE THEM WE MUST. OUR LAST HOPE, ARE THEY.
DON'T GIVE UP, PADMÉ.
IS IT A GIRL?
LEIA.
IT'S A BOY...
LUKE...
...AND A GIRL.
YOUR TWINS NEED YOU, PADMÉ. HANG ON...
OBI-WAN, THERE... IS GOOD IN HIM. I KNOW THERE IS...

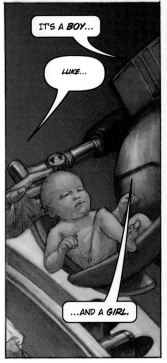

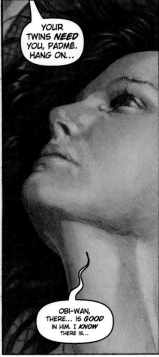

TO *NABOO*, SEND HER BODY. *PREGNANT*, SHE MUST STILL APPEAR. HIDDEN, *SAFE*, THE CHILDREN MUST BE KEPT.

SPLIT UP, THEY SHOULD BE.

WE MUST TAKE THEM SOMEPLACE WHERE THE SITH WILL NOT SENSE THEIR PRESENCE.

MY WIFE AND I WILL TAKE THE GIRL. SHE WILL BE LOVED WITH US.

AND WHAT ABOUT THE BOY?

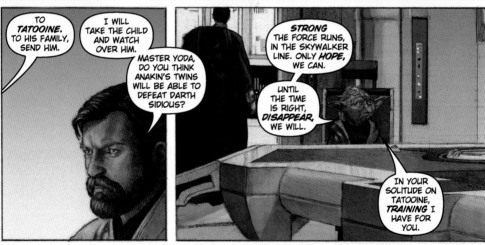

TO *TATOOINE*. TO HIS FAMILY, SEND HIM.

I WILL TAKE THE CHILD AND WATCH OVER HIM. MASTER YODA, DO YOU THINK ANAKIN'S TWINS WILL BE ABLE TO DEFEAT DARTH SIDIOUS?

STRONG THE FORCE RUNS, IN THE SKYWALKER LINE. ONLY *HOPE*, WE CAN.

UNTIL THE TIME IS RIGHT, *DISAPPEAR*, WE WILL.

IN YOUR SOLITUDE ON TATOOINE, *TRAINING* I HAVE FOR YOU.

AN OLD FRIEND HAS LEARNED THE PATH TO IMMORTALITY. ONE WHO HAS RETURNED FROM THE NETHERWORLD OF THE FORCE TO TRAIN ME --

-- YOUR OLD MASTER, *QUI-GON JINN.* HOW TO COMMUNE WITH HIM, I WILL TEACH YOU.

QUI-GON?! I WILL BE ABLE TO TALK WITH HIM?

HOW TO JOIN THE FORCE, HE WILL TRAIN YOU.

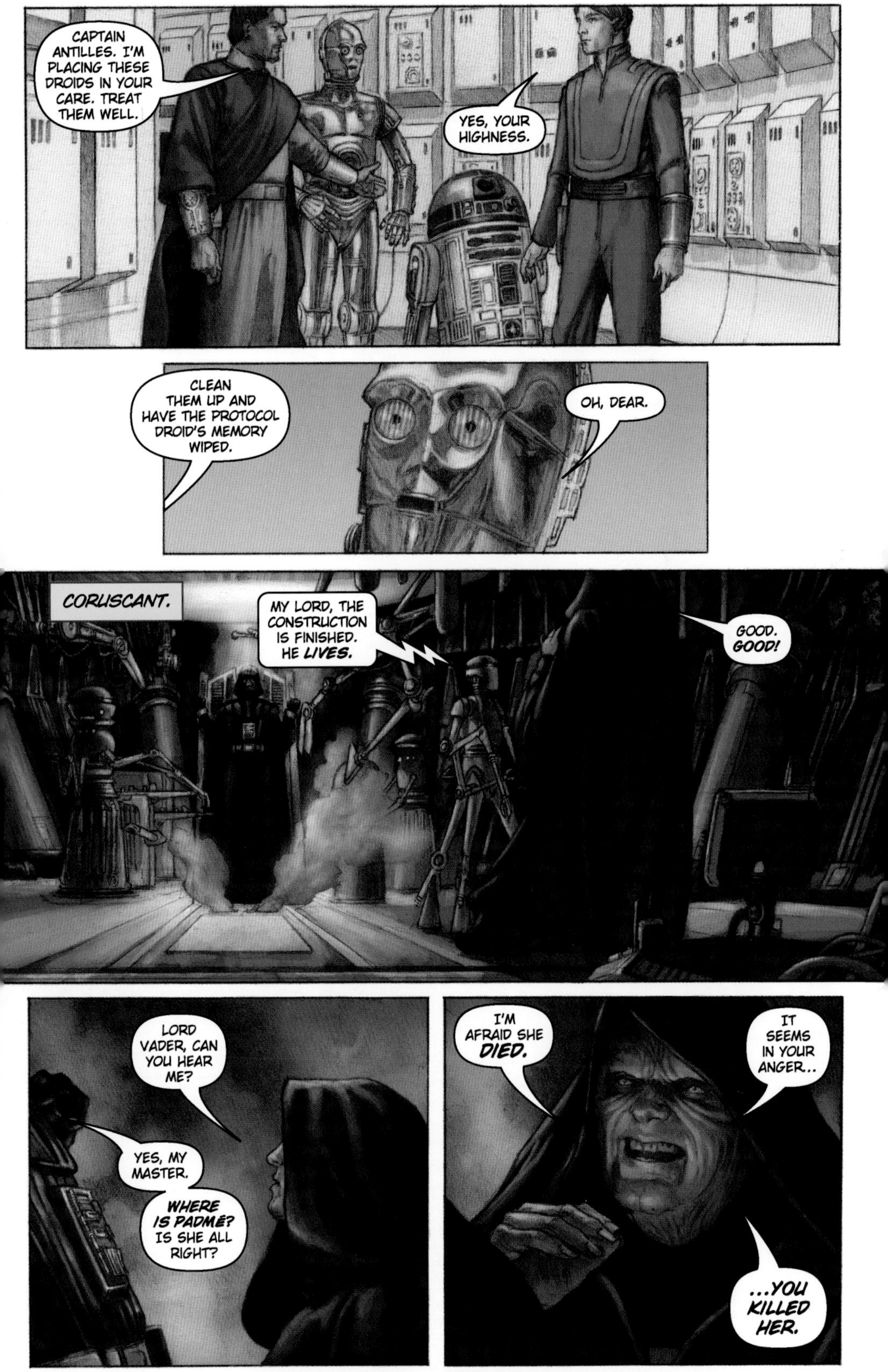
CAPTAIN ANTILLES. I'M PLACING THESE DROIDS IN YOUR CARE. TREAT THEM WELL.
YES, YOUR HIGHNESS.
CLEAN THEM UP AND HAVE THE PROTOCOL DROID'S MEMORY WIPED.
OH, DEAR.
CORUSCANT.
MY LORD, THE CONSTRUCTION IS FINISHED. HE LIVES.
GOOD. GOOD!
LORD VADER, CAN YOU HEAR ME?
YES, MY MASTER.
WHERE IS PADMÉ? IS SHE ALL RIGHT?
I'M AFRAID SHE DIED.
IT SEEMS IN YOUR ANGER...
...YOU KILLED HER.

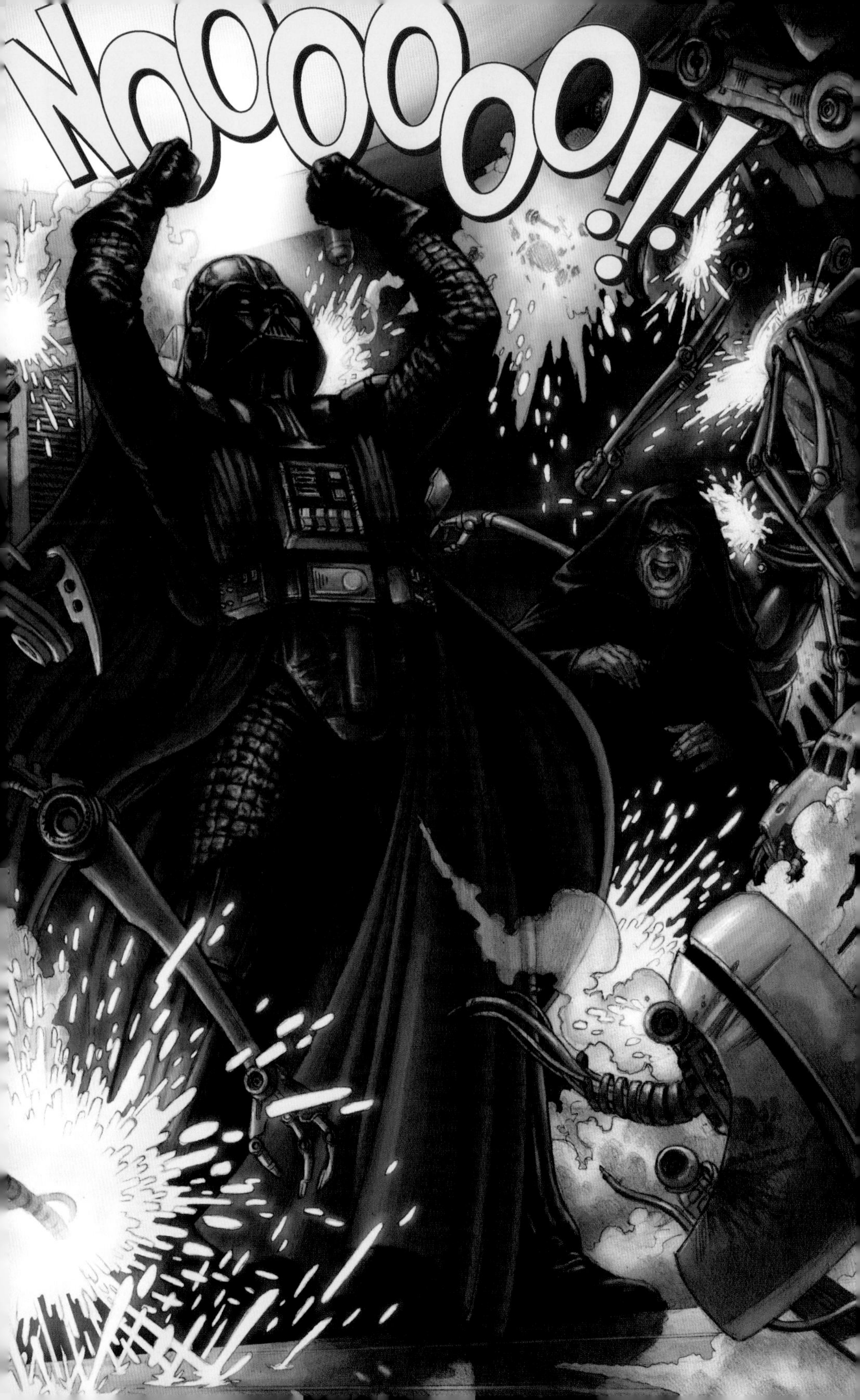
NOOOOOO!!!

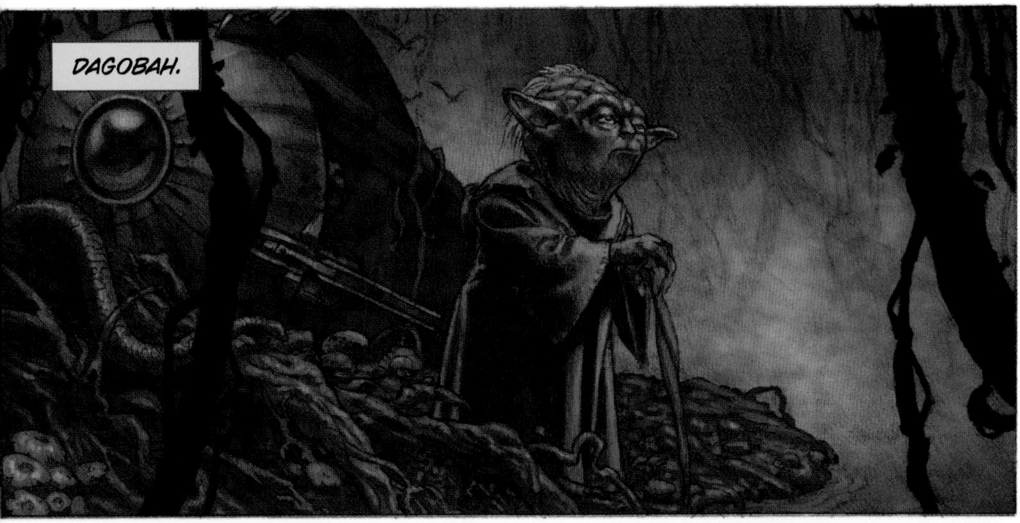
DAGOBAH.

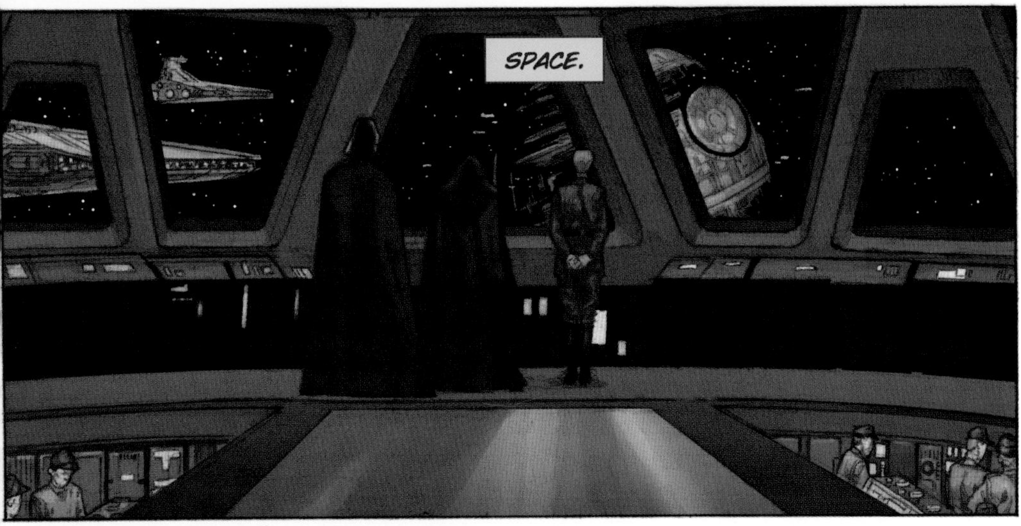
SPACE.

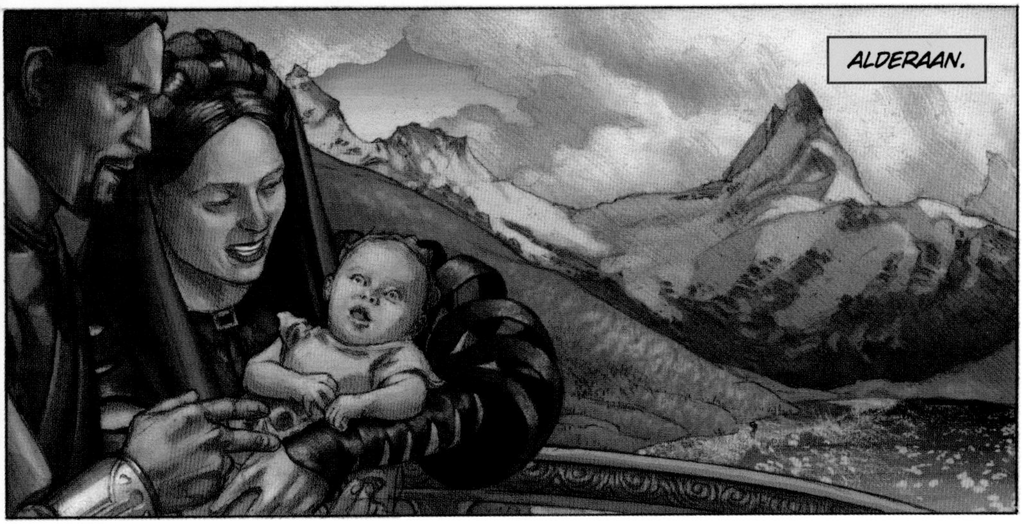
ALDERAAN.

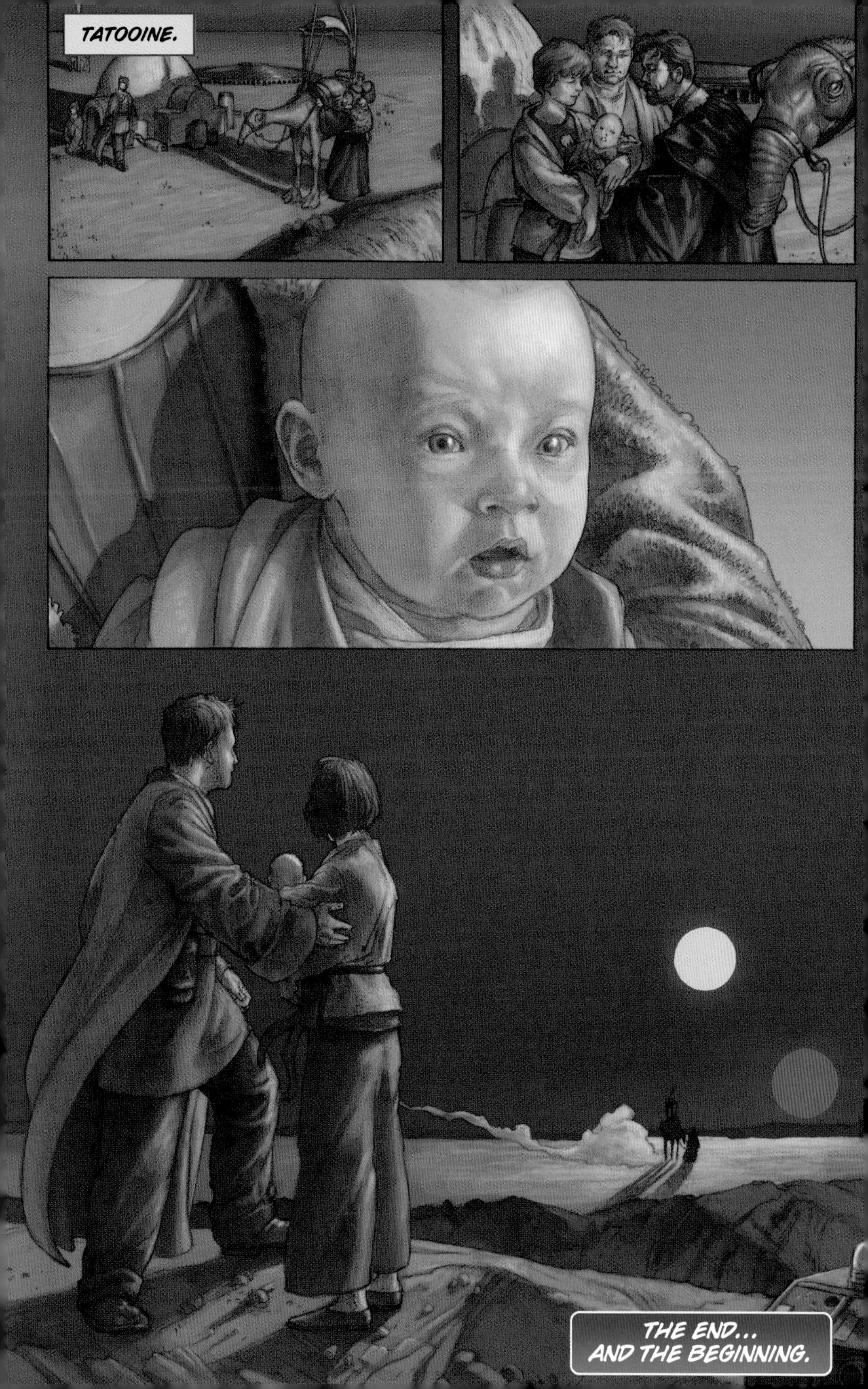
TATOOINE.
THE END...
AND THE BEGINNING.

A New Hope | Illustration by Dave Dorman

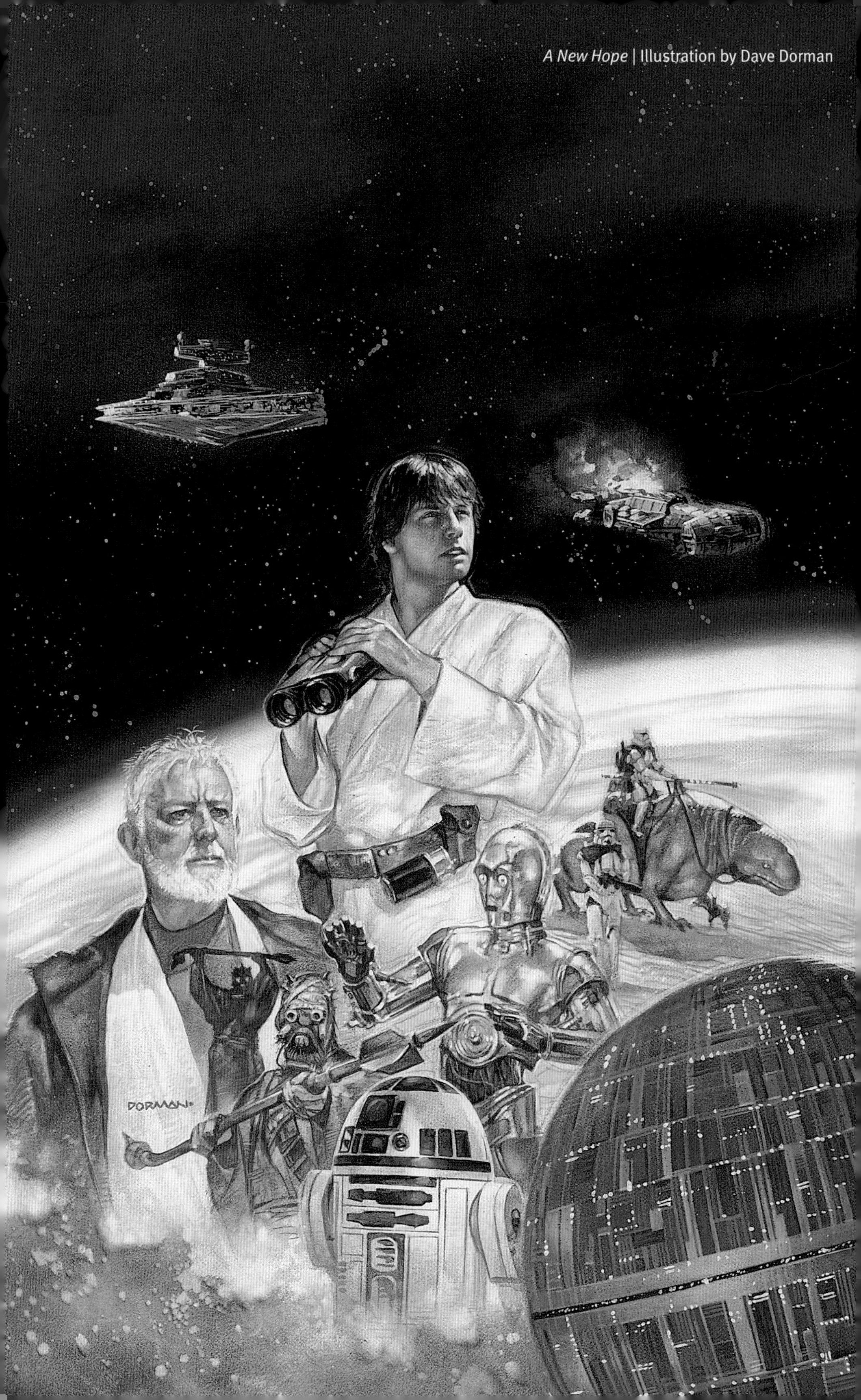
DORMAN

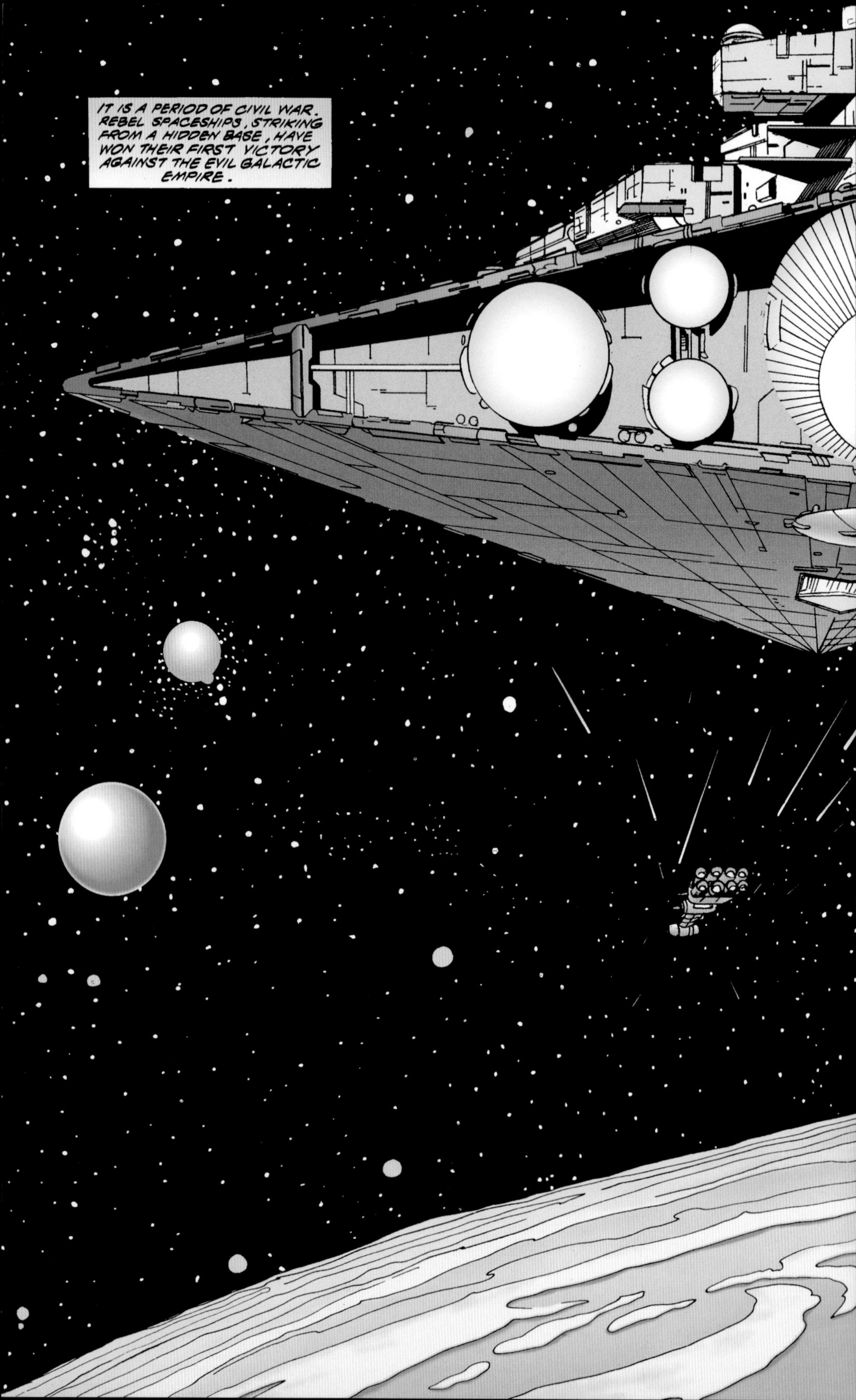
IT IS A PERIOD OF CIVIL WAR. REBEL SPACESHIPS, STRIKING FROM A HIDDEN BASE, HAVE WON THEIR FIRST VICTORY AGAINST THE EVIL GALACTIC EMPIRE.

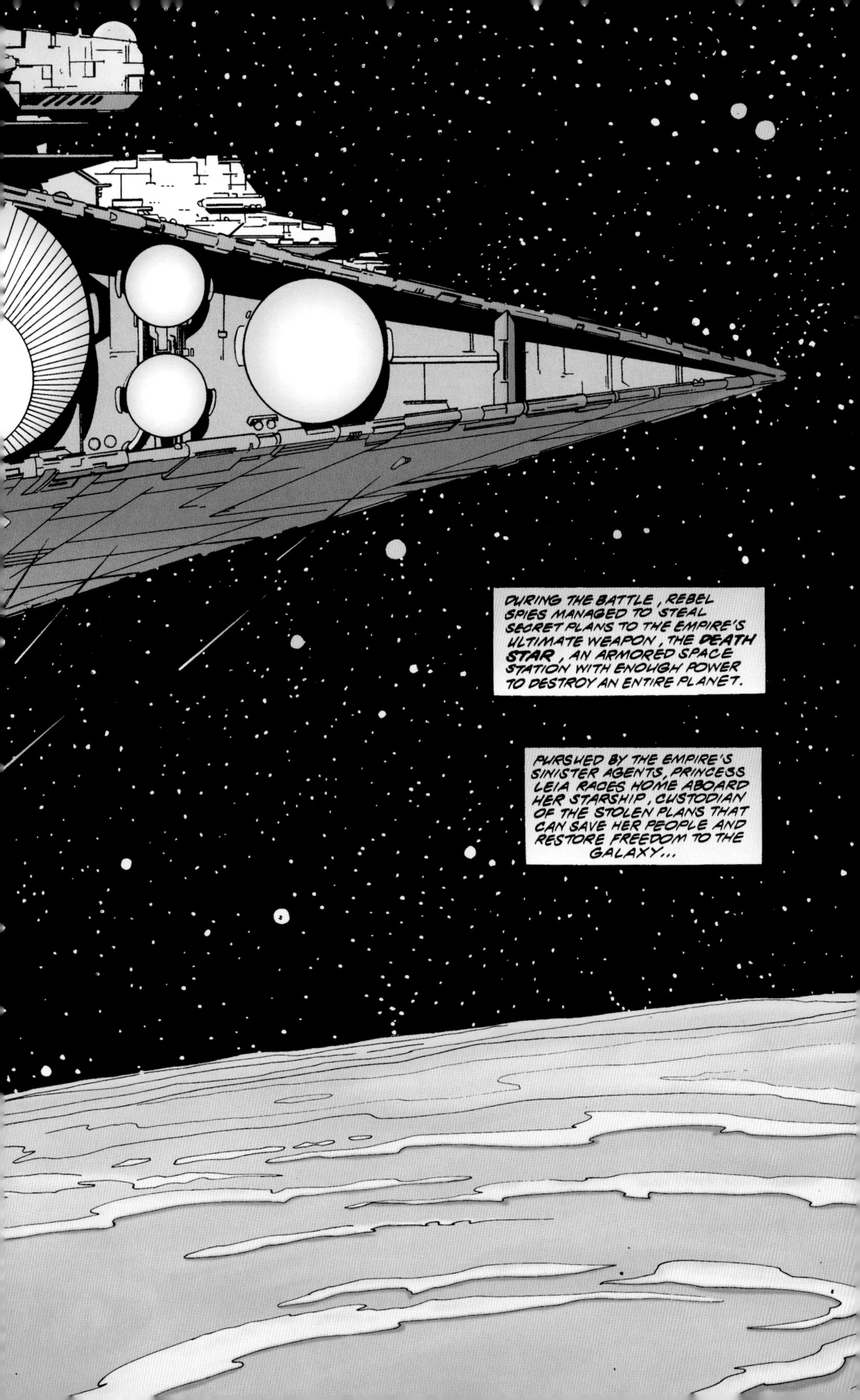
DURING THE BATTLE, REBEL SPIES MANAGED TO STEAL SECRET PLANS TO THE EMPIRE'S ULTIMATE WEAPON, THE DEATH STAR, AN ARMORED SPACE STATION WITH ENOUGH POWER TO DESTROY AN ENTIRE PLANET.
PURSUED BY THE EMPIRE'S SINISTER AGENTS, PRINCESS LEIA RACES HOME ABOARD HER STARSHIP, CUSTODIAN OF THE STOLEN PLANS THAT CAN SAVE HER PEOPLE AND RESTORE FREEDOM TO THE GALAXY...

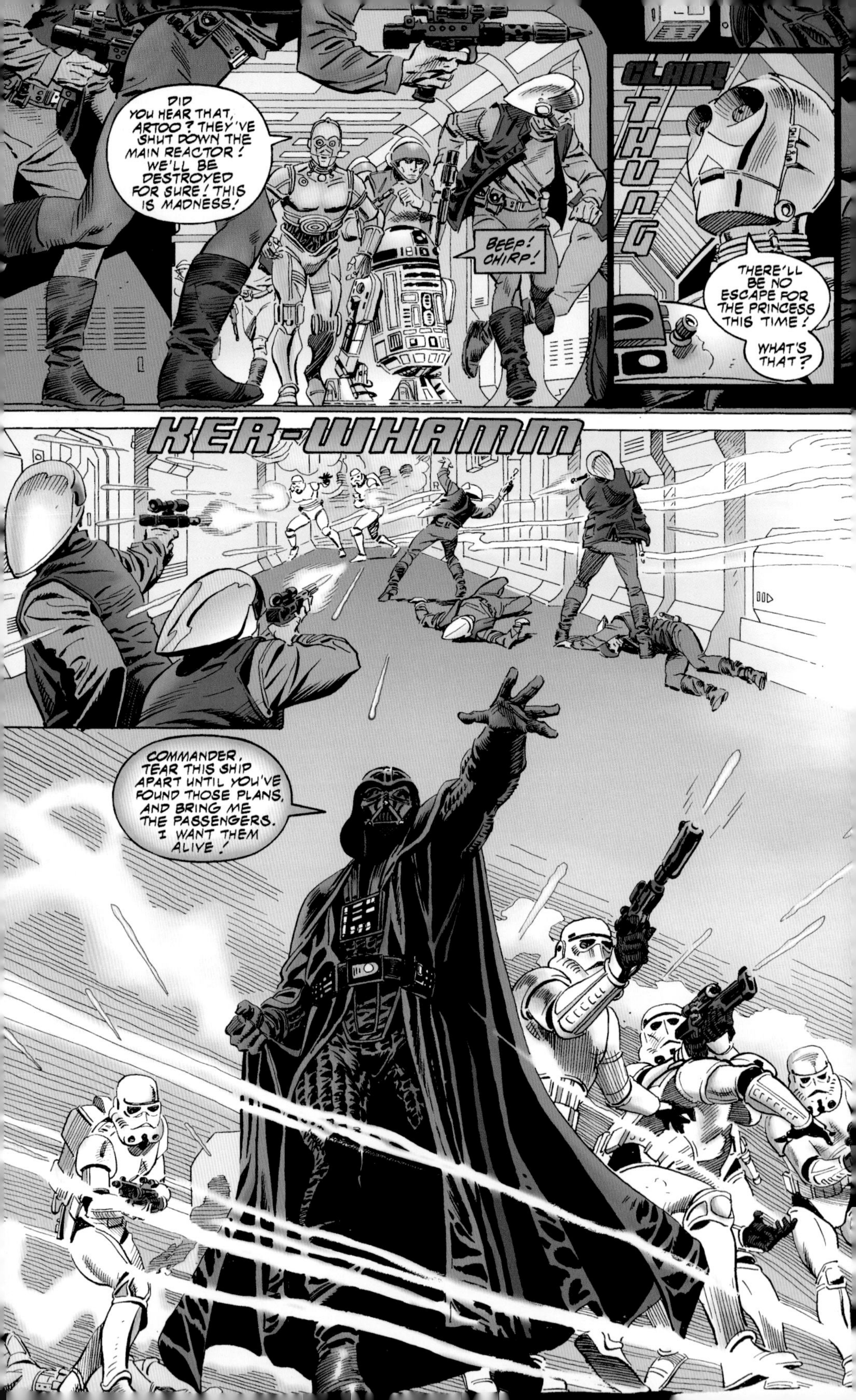

DID YOU HEAR THAT, ARTOO? THEY'VE SHUT DOWN THE MAIN REACTOR! WE'LL BE DESTROYED FOR SURE! THIS IS MADNESS!
BEEP! CHIRP!
CLANK
THUNG
THERE'LL BE NO ESCAPE FOR THE PRINCESS THIS TIME!
WHAT'S THAT?
KER-WHAMM
COMMANDER, TEAR THIS SHIP APART UNTIL YOU'VE FOUND THOSE PLANS, AND BRING ME THE PASSENGERS. I WANT THEM ALIVE!

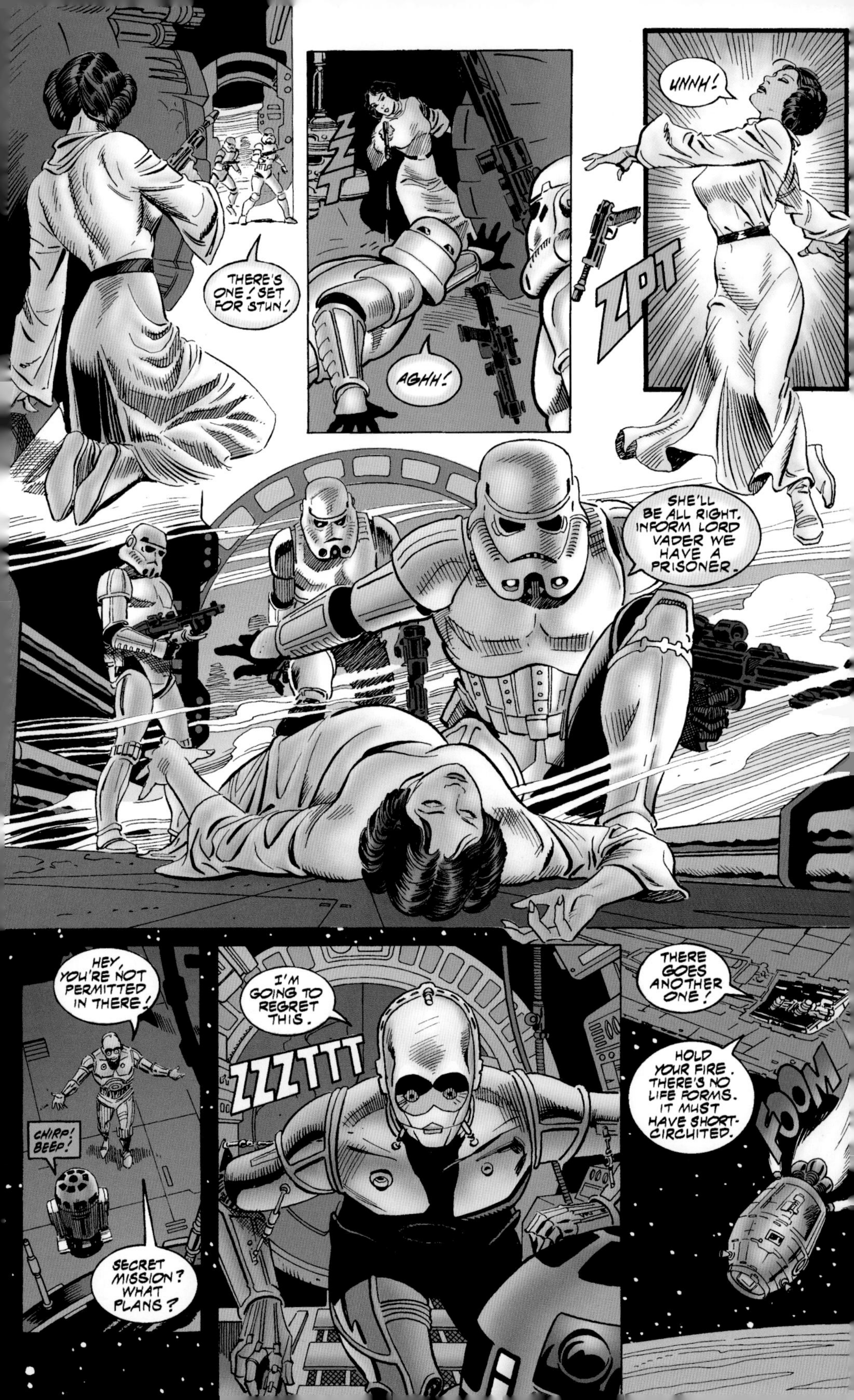
THERE'S ONE! SET FOR STUN!
ZZT
AGHH!
UNNH!
ZPT
SHE'LL BE ALL RIGHT. INFORM LORD VADER WE HAVE A PRISONER.
HEY, YOU'RE NOT PERMITTED IN THERE!
CHIRP! BEEP!
SECRET MISSION? WHAT PLANS?
I'M GOING TO REGRET THIS.
ZZZTTT
THERE GOES ANOTHER ONE!
HOLD YOUR FIRE. THERE'S NO LIFE FORMS. IT MUST HAVE SHORT-CIRCUITED.
FOOM

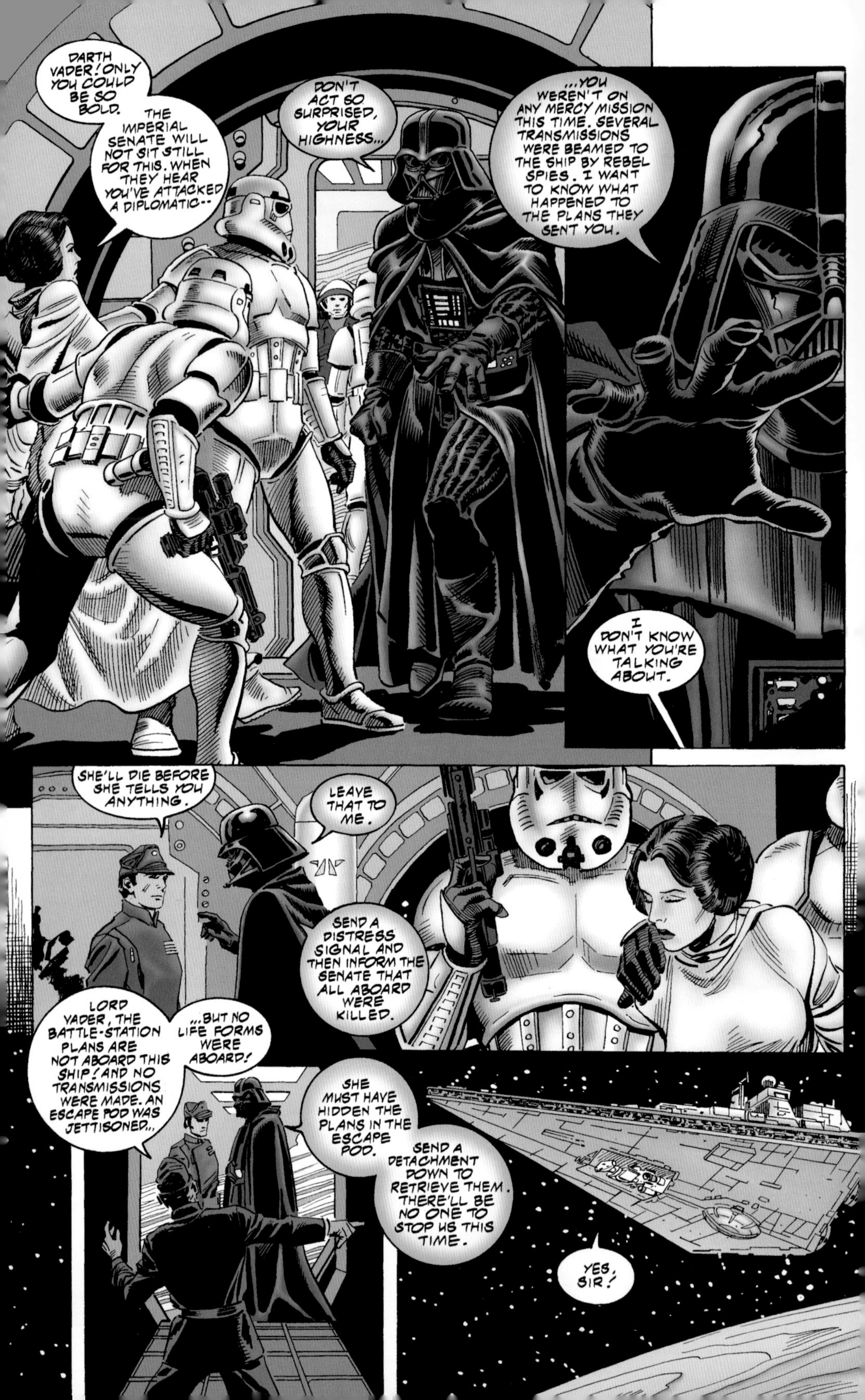

DARTH VADER! ONLY YOU COULD BE SO BOLD.
THE IMPERIAL SENATE WILL NOT SIT STILL FOR THIS. WHEN THEY HEAR YOU'VE ATTACKED A DIPLOMATIC--
DON'T ACT SO SURPRISED, YOUR HIGHNESS...
...YOU WEREN'T ON ANY MERCY MISSION THIS TIME. SEVERAL TRANSMISSIONS WERE BEAMED TO THE SHIP BY REBEL SPIES. I WANT TO KNOW WHAT HAPPENED TO THE PLANS THEY SENT YOU.
I DON'T KNOW WHAT YOU'RE TALKING ABOUT.
SHE'LL DIE BEFORE SHE TELLS YOU ANYTHING.
LEAVE THAT TO ME.
SEND A DISTRESS SIGNAL AND THEN INFORM THE SENATE THAT ALL ABOARD WERE KILLED.
LORD VADER, THE BATTLE-STATION PLANS ARE NOT ABOARD THIS SHIP! AND NO TRANSMISSIONS WERE MADE. AN ESCAPE POD WAS JETTISONED...
...BUT NO LIFE FORMS WERE ABOARD!
SHE MUST HAVE HIDDEN THE PLANS IN THE ESCAPE POD.
SEND A DETACHMENT DOWN TO RETRIEVE THEM. THERE'LL BE NO ONE TO STOP US THIS TIME.
YES, SIR!

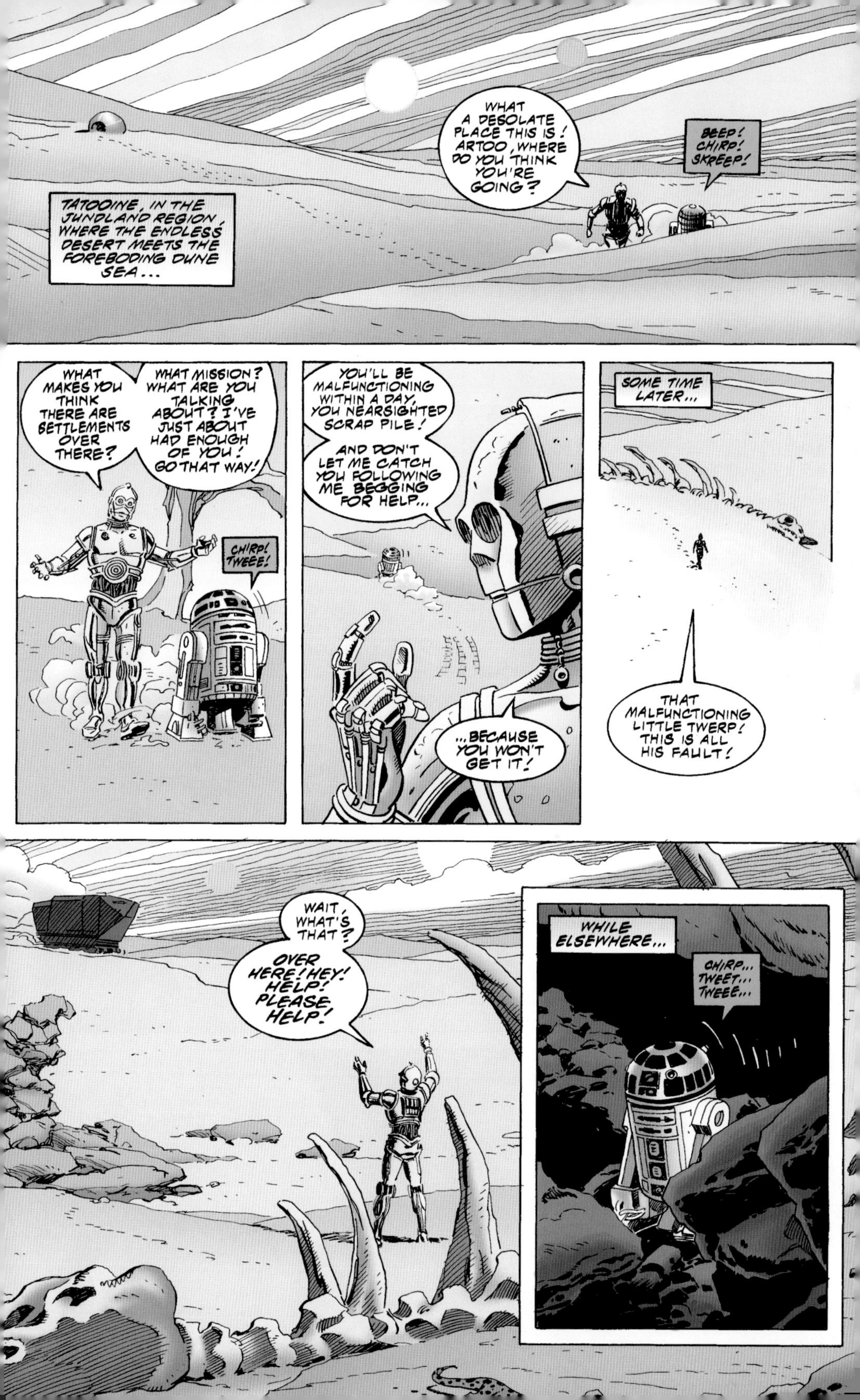
TATOOINE, IN THE JUNDLAND REGION, WHERE THE ENDLESS DESERT MEETS THE FOREBODING DUNE SEA...
WHAT A DESOLATE PLACE THIS IS! ARTOO, WHERE DO YOU THINK YOU'RE GOING?
BEEP! CHIRP! SKREEP!
WHAT MAKES YOU THINK THERE ARE SETTLEMENTS OVER THERE?
WHAT MISSION? WHAT ARE YOU TALKING ABOUT? I'VE JUST ABOUT HAD ENOUGH OF YOU! GO THAT WAY!
CHIRP! TWEEE!
YOU'LL BE MALFUNCTIONING WITHIN A DAY, YOU NEARSIGHTED SCRAP PILE!
AND DON'T LET ME CATCH YOU FOLLOWING ME BEGGING FOR HELP...
...BECAUSE YOU WON'T GET IT!
SOME TIME LATER...
THAT MALFUNCTIONING LITTLE TWERP! THIS IS ALL HIS FAULT!
WAIT, WHAT'S THAT?
OVER HERE! HEY! HELP! PLEASE HELP!
WHILE ELSEWHERE...
CHIRP... TWEET... TWEEE...

ARTOO?
ARTOO-DETOO!
IT IS YOU!

SOMEONE
WAS IN THE POD.
THE TRACKS
GO OFF IN THIS
DIRECTION.

LOOK, SIR--
DROIDS.

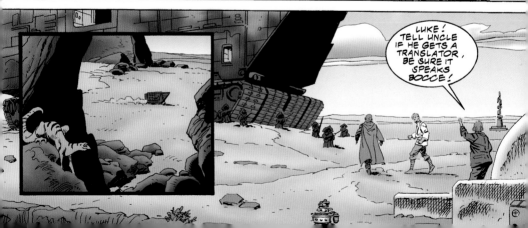

LUKE!
TELL UNCLE
IF HE GETS A
TRANSLATOR,
BE SURE IT
SPEAKS
BOCCE!

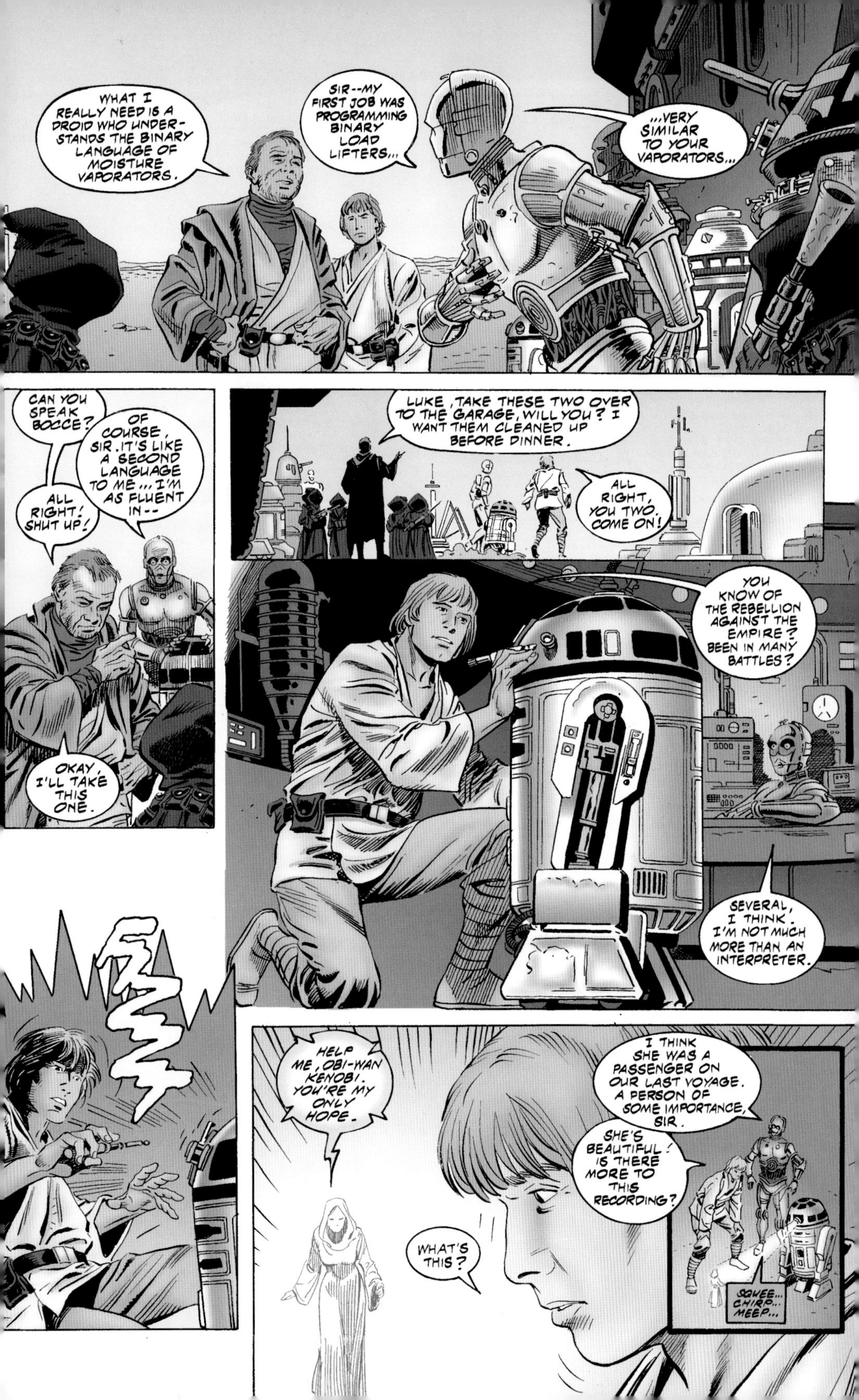
WHAT I REALLY NEED IS A DROID WHO UNDERSTANDS THE BINARY LANGUAGE OF MOISTURE VAPORATORS.
SIR--MY FIRST JOB WAS PROGRAMMING BINARY LOAD LIFTERS...
...VERY SIMILAR TO YOUR VAPORATORS...
CAN YOU SPEAK BOCCE?
OF COURSE, SIR. IT'S LIKE A SECOND LANGUAGE TO ME... I'M AS FLUENT IN--
ALL RIGHT! SHUT UP!
OKAY, I'LL TAKE THIS ONE.
LUKE, TAKE THESE TWO OVER TO THE GARAGE, WILL YOU? I WANT THEM CLEANED UP BEFORE DINNER.
ALL RIGHT, YOU TWO. COME ON!
YOU KNOW OF THE REBELLION AGAINST THE EMPIRE? BEEN IN MANY BATTLES?
SEVERAL, I THINK. I'M NOT MUCH MORE THAN AN INTERPRETER.
FZZZT
HELP ME, OBI-WAN KENOBI. YOU'RE MY ONLY HOPE.
WHAT'S THIS?
I THINK SHE WAS A PASSENGER ON OUR LAST VOYAGE. A PERSON OF SOME IMPORTANCE, SIR.
SHE'S BEAUTIFUL! IS THERE MORE TO THIS RECORDING?
SQUEE... CHIRP... MEEP...

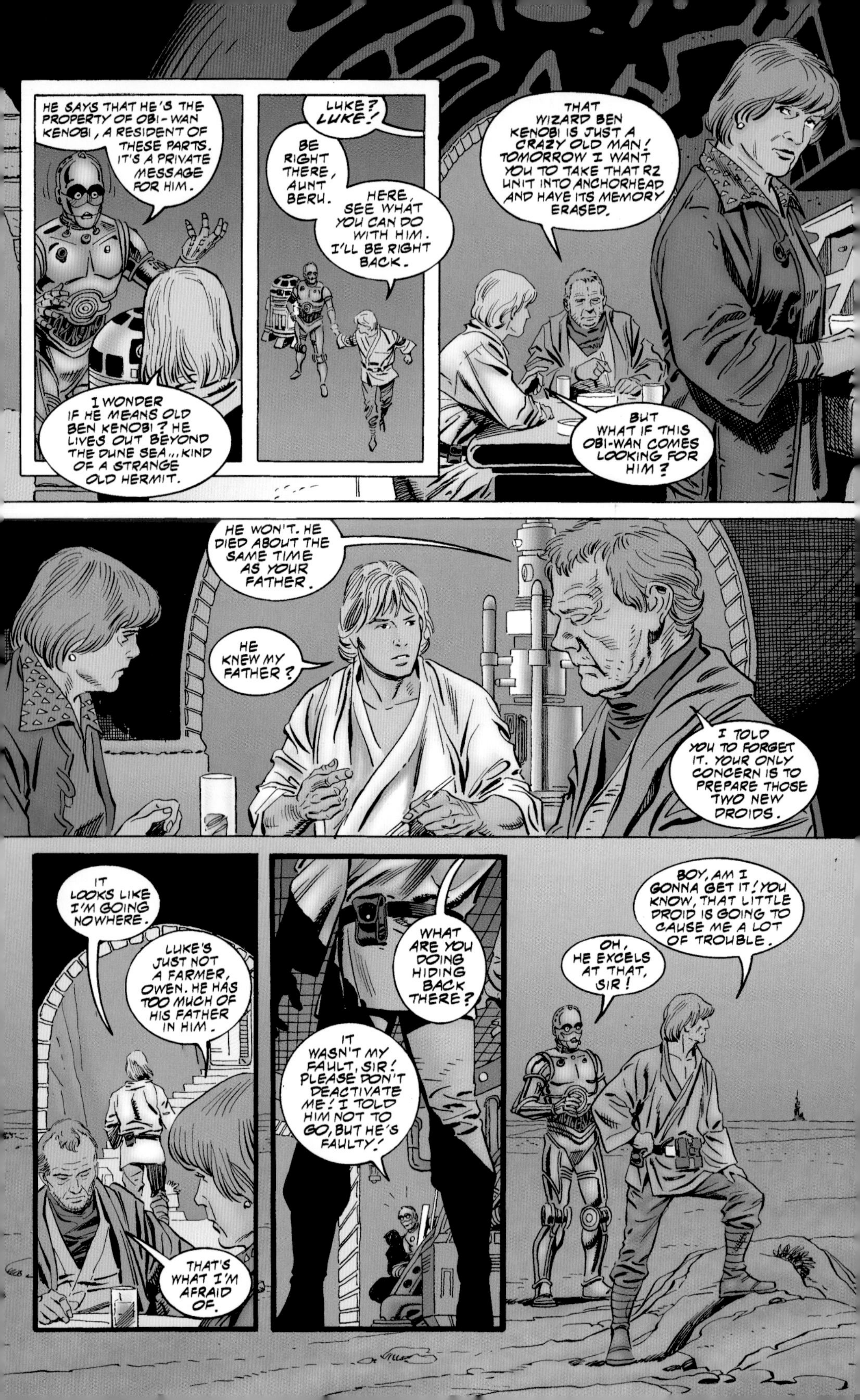
HE SAYS THAT HE'S THE PROPERTY OF OBI-WAN KENOBI, A RESIDENT OF THESE PARTS. IT'S A PRIVATE MESSAGE FOR HIM.
I WONDER IF HE MEANS OLD BEN KENOBI? HE LIVES OUT BEYOND THE DUNE SEA... KIND OF A STRANGE OLD HERMIT.
LUKE? LUKE!
BE RIGHT THERE, AUNT BERU.
HERE, SEE WHAT YOU CAN DO WITH HIM. I'LL BE RIGHT BACK.
THAT WIZARD BEN KENOBI IS JUST A CRAZY OLD MAN! TOMORROW I WANT YOU TO TAKE THAT R2 UNIT INTO ANCHORHEAD AND HAVE ITS MEMORY ERASED.
BUT WHAT IF THIS OBI-WAN COMES LOOKING FOR HIM?
HE WON'T. HE DIED ABOUT THE SAME TIME AS YOUR FATHER.
HE KNEW MY FATHER?
I TOLD YOU TO FORGET IT. YOUR ONLY CONCERN IS TO PREPARE THOSE TWO NEW DROIDS.
IT LOOKS LIKE I'M GOING NOWHERE.
LUKE'S JUST NOT A FARMER, OWEN. HE HAS TOO MUCH OF HIS FATHER IN HIM.
THAT'S WHAT I'M AFRAID OF.
WHAT ARE YOU DOING HIDING BACK THERE?
IT WASN'T MY FAULT, SIR! PLEASE DON'T DEACTIVATE ME! I TOLD HIM NOT TO GO, BUT HE'S FAULTY!
BOY, AM I GONNA GET IT! YOU KNOW, THAT LITTLE DROID IS GOING TO CAUSE ME A LOT OF TROUBLE.
OH, HE EXCELS AT THAT, SIR!

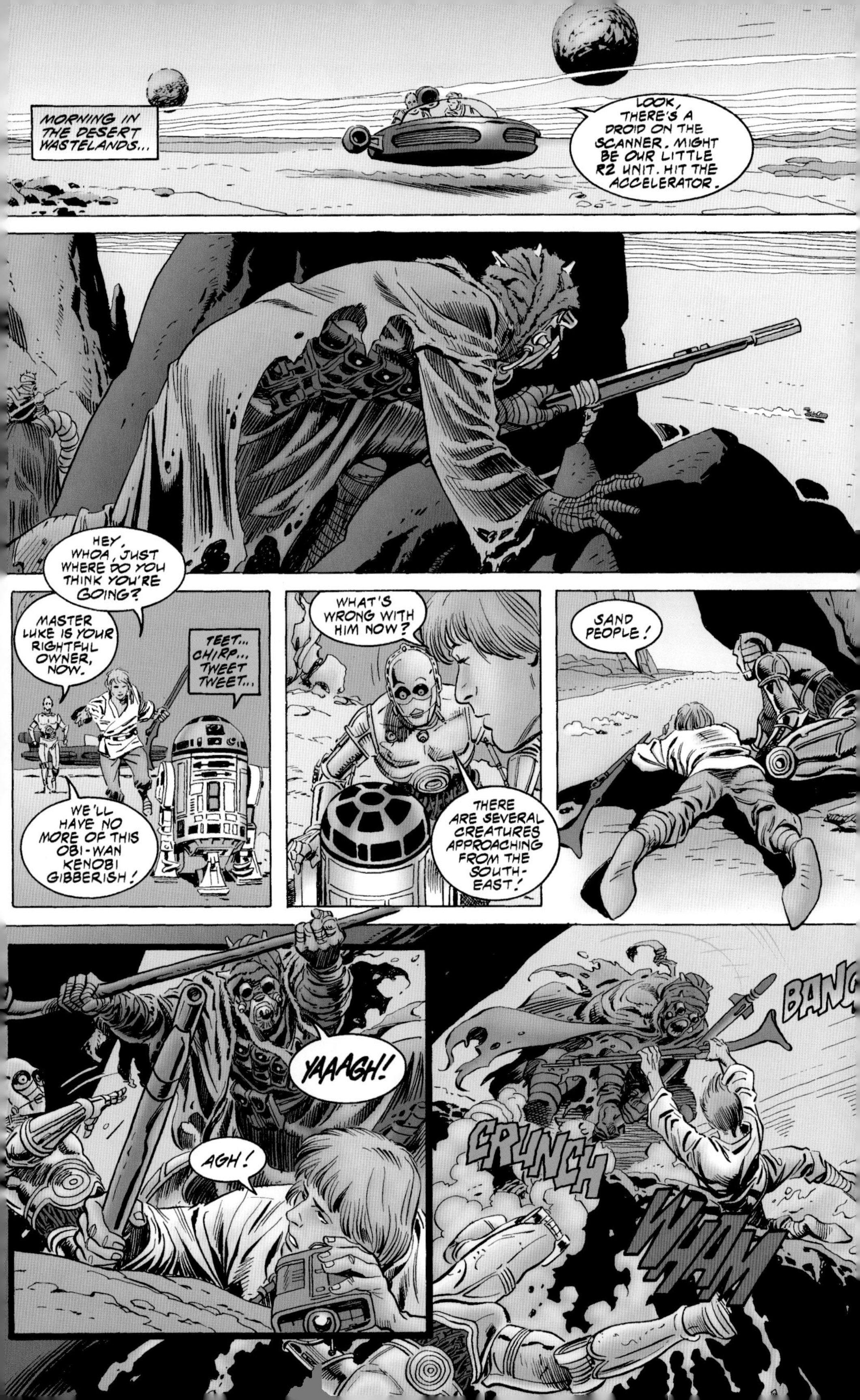
MORNING IN THE DESERT WASTELANDS...
LOOK, THERE'S A DROID ON THE SCANNER. MIGHT BE OUR LITTLE R2 UNIT. HIT THE ACCELERATOR.
HEY, WHOA, JUST WHERE DO YOU THINK YOU'RE GOING?
MASTER LUKE IS YOUR RIGHTFUL OWNER, NOW.
TEET... CHIRP... TWEET TWEET...
WE'LL HAVE NO MORE OF THIS OBI-WAN KENOBI GIBBERISH!
WHAT'S WRONG WITH HIM NOW?
THERE ARE SEVERAL CREATURES APPROACHING FROM THE SOUTH-EAST!
SAND PEOPLE!
YAAAGH!
AGH!
CRUNCH
WHAM

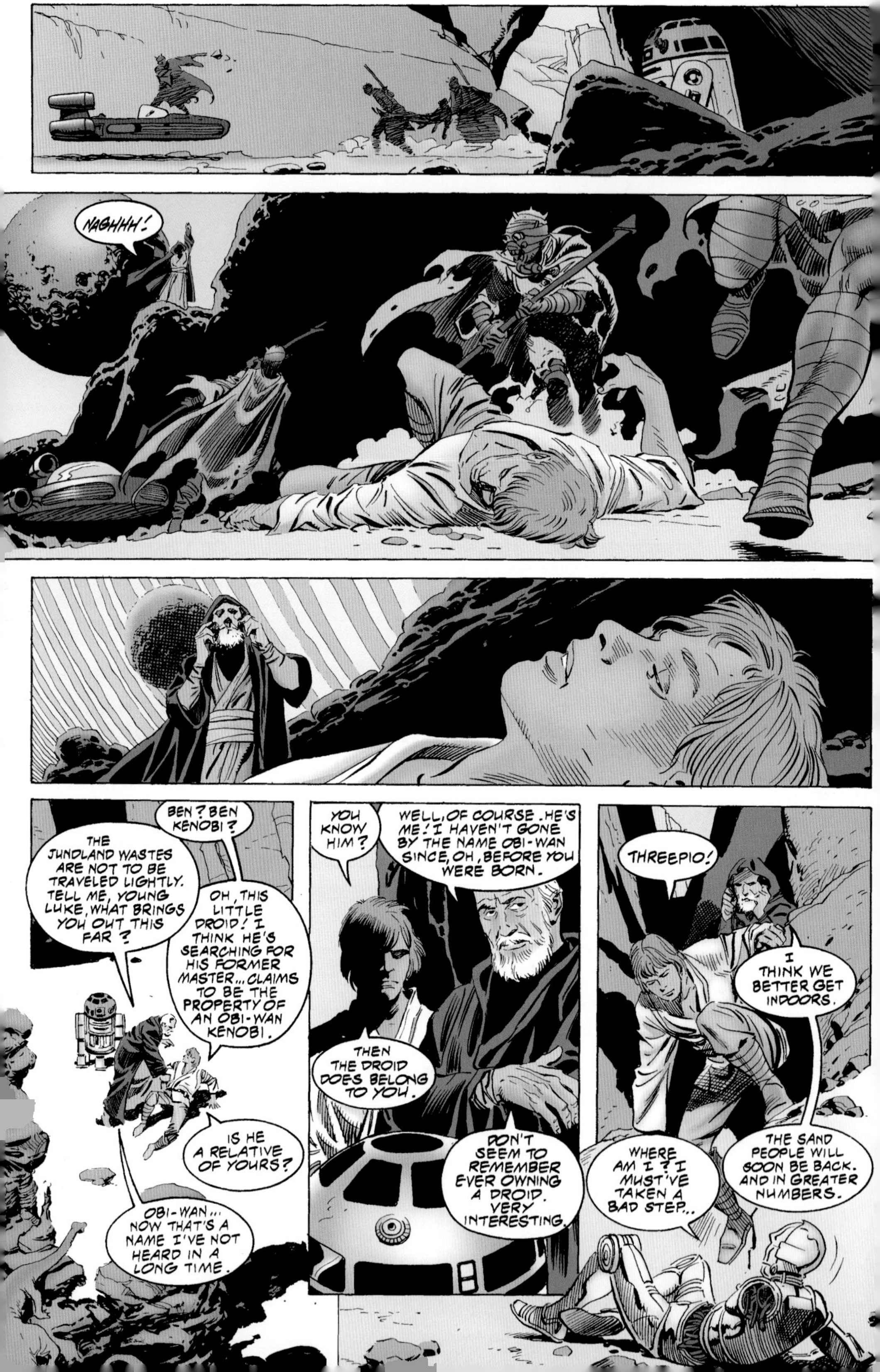
NAGHHH!
BEN? BEN KENOBI?
THE JUNDLAND WASTES ARE NOT TO BE TRAVELED LIGHTLY. TELL ME, YOUNG LUKE, WHAT BRINGS YOU OUT THIS FAR?
OH, THIS LITTLE DROID! I THINK HE'S SEARCHING FOR HIS FORMER MASTER... CLAIMS TO BE THE PROPERTY OF AN OBI-WAN KENOBI.
IS HE A RELATIVE OF YOURS?
OBI-WAN... NOW THAT'S A NAME I'VE NOT HEARD IN A LONG TIME.
YOU KNOW HIM?
WELL, OF COURSE. HE'S ME! I HAVEN'T GONE BY THE NAME OBI-WAN SINCE, OH, BEFORE YOU WERE BORN.
THEN THE DROID DOES BELONG TO YOU.
DON'T SEEM TO REMEMBER EVER OWNING A DROID. VERY INTERESTING.
THREEPIO!
I THINK WE BETTER GET INDOORS.
WHERE AM I? I MUST'VE TAKEN A BAD STEP...
THE SAND PEOPLE WILL SOON BE BACK. AND IN GREATER NUMBERS.

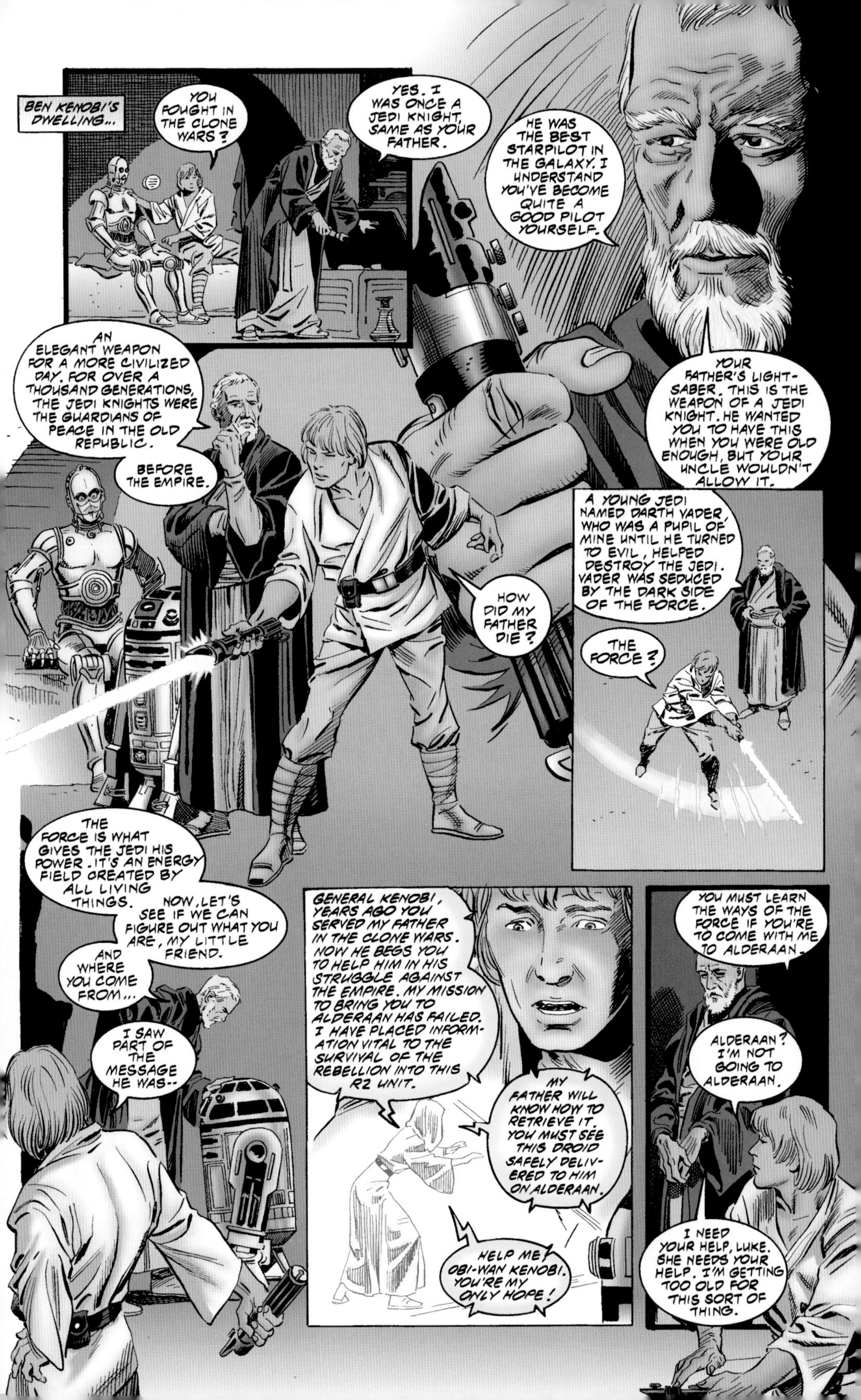
BEN KENOBI'S DWELLING...
YOU FOUGHT IN THE CLONE WARS?
YES. I WAS ONCE A JEDI KNIGHT, SAME AS YOUR FATHER.
HE WAS THE BEST STARPILOT IN THE GALAXY. I UNDERSTAND YOU'VE BECOME QUITE A GOOD PILOT YOURSELF.
YOUR FATHER'S LIGHT-SABER. THIS IS THE WEAPON OF A JEDI KNIGHT. HE WANTED YOU TO HAVE THIS WHEN YOU WERE OLD ENOUGH, BUT YOUR UNCLE WOULDN'T ALLOW IT.
AN ELEGANT WEAPON FOR A MORE CIVILIZED DAY. FOR OVER A THOUSAND GENERATIONS, THE JEDI KNIGHTS WERE THE GUARDIANS OF PEACE IN THE OLD REPUBLIC.
BEFORE THE EMPIRE.
HOW DID MY FATHER DIE?
A YOUNG JEDI NAMED DARTH VADER, WHO WAS A PUPIL OF MINE UNTIL HE TURNED TO EVIL, HELPED DESTROY THE JEDI. VADER WAS SEDUCED BY THE DARK SIDE OF THE FORCE.
THE FORCE?
THE FORCE IS WHAT GIVES THE JEDI HIS POWER. IT'S AN ENERGY FIELD CREATED BY ALL LIVING THINGS.
NOW, LET'S SEE IF WE CAN FIGURE OUT WHAT YOU ARE, MY LITTLE FRIEND.
AND WHERE YOU COME FROM...
I SAW PART OF THE MESSAGE HE WAS--
GENERAL KENOBI, YEARS AGO YOU SERVED MY FATHER IN THE CLONE WARS. NOW HE BEGS YOU TO HELP HIM IN HIS STRUGGLE AGAINST THE EMPIRE. MY MISSION TO BRING YOU TO ALDERAAN HAS FAILED. I HAVE PLACED INFORMATION VITAL TO THE SURVIVAL OF THE REBELLION INTO THIS R2 UNIT.
MY FATHER WILL KNOW HOW TO RETRIEVE IT. YOU MUST SEE THIS DROID SAFELY DELIVERED TO HIM ON ALDERAAN.
HELP ME! OBI-WAN KENOBI. YOU'RE MY ONLY HOPE!
YOU MUST LEARN THE WAYS OF THE FORCE IF YOU'RE TO COME WITH ME TO ALDERAAN.
ALDERAAN? I'M NOT GOING TO ALDERAAN.
I NEED YOUR HELP, LUKE. SHE NEEDS YOUR HELP. I'M GETTING TOO OLD FOR THIS SORT OF THING.

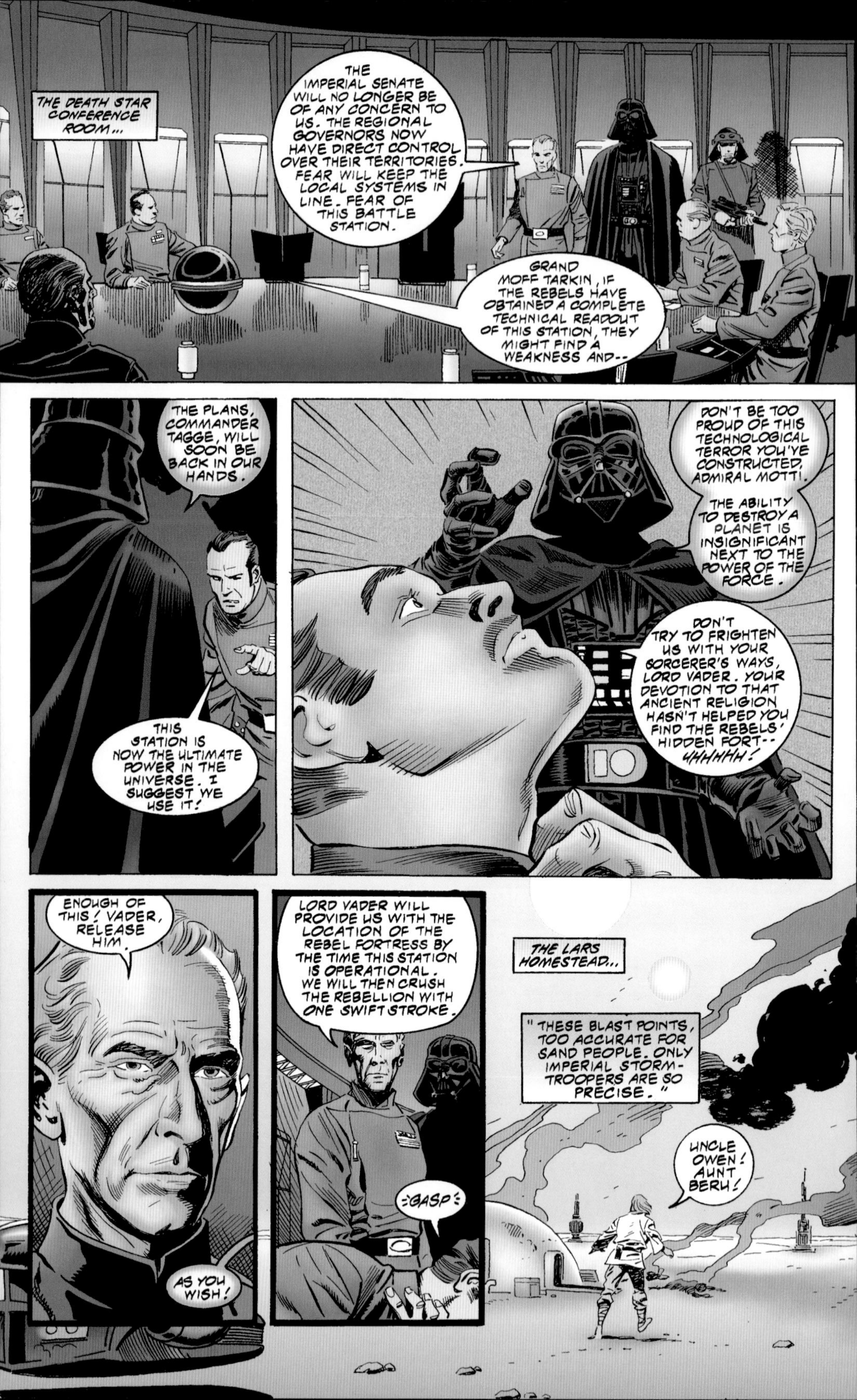
THE DEATH STAR CONFERENCE ROOM...
THE IMPERIAL SENATE WILL NO LONGER BE OF ANY CONCERN TO US. THE REGIONAL GOVERNORS NOW HAVE DIRECT CONTROL OVER THEIR TERRITORIES. FEAR WILL KEEP THE LOCAL SYSTEMS IN LINE. FEAR OF THIS BATTLE STATION.
GRAND MOFF TARKIN, IF THE REBELS HAVE OBTAINED A COMPLETE TECHNICAL READOUT OF THIS STATION, THEY MIGHT FIND A WEAKNESS AND--
THE PLANS, COMMANDER TAGGE, WILL SOON BE BACK IN OUR HANDS.
THIS STATION IS NOW THE ULTIMATE POWER IN THE UNIVERSE. I SUGGEST WE USE IT!
DON'T BE TOO PROUD OF THIS TECHNOLOGICAL TERROR YOU'VE CONSTRUCTED, ADMIRAL MOTTI.
THE ABILITY TO DESTROY A PLANET IS INSIGNIFICANT NEXT TO THE POWER OF THE FORCE.
DON'T TRY TO FRIGHTEN US WITH YOUR SORCERER'S WAYS, LORD VADER. YOUR DEVOTION TO THAT ANCIENT RELIGION HASN'T HELPED YOU FIND THE REBELS' HIDDEN FORT-- UHHHHH!
ENOUGH OF THIS! VADER, RELEASE HIM.
AS YOU WISH!
LORD VADER WILL PROVIDE US WITH THE LOCATION OF THE REBEL FORTRESS BY THE TIME THIS STATION IS OPERATIONAL. WE WILL THEN CRUSH THE REBELLION WITH ONE SWIFT STROKE.
GASP
THE LARS HOMESTEAD...
"THESE BLAST POINTS, TOO ACCURATE FOR SAND PEOPLE. ONLY IMPERIAL STORM-TROOPERS ARE SO PRECISE."
UNCLE OWEN! AUNT BERU!

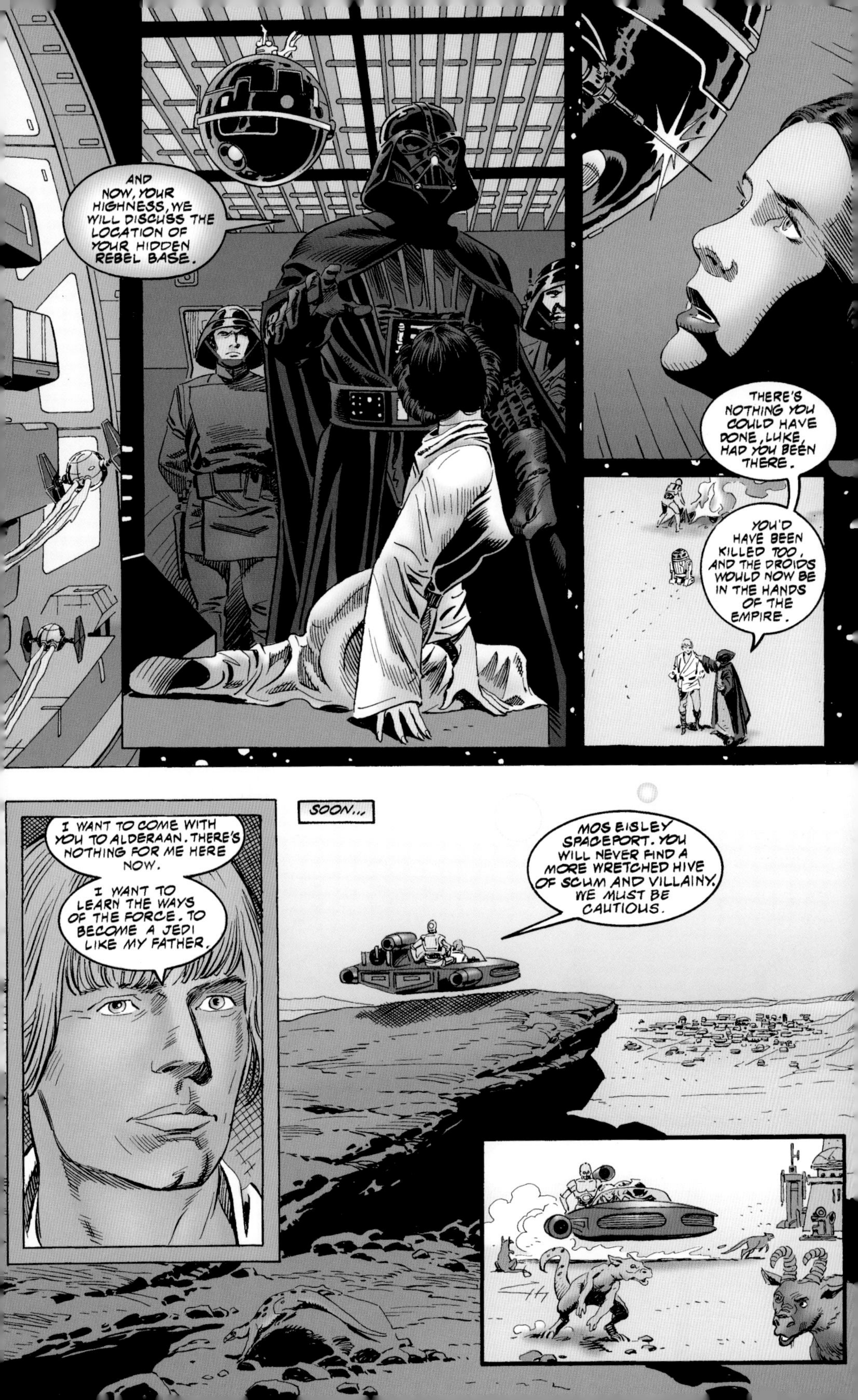
AND NOW, YOUR HIGHNESS, WE WILL DISCUSS THE LOCATION OF YOUR HIDDEN REBEL BASE.
THERE'S NOTHING YOU COULD HAVE DONE, LUKE, HAD YOU BEEN THERE.
YOU'D HAVE BEEN KILLED TOO, AND THE DROIDS WOULD NOW BE IN THE HANDS OF THE EMPIRE.
I WANT TO COME WITH YOU TO ALDERAAN. THERE'S NOTHING FOR ME HERE NOW.
I WANT TO LEARN THE WAYS OF THE FORCE. TO BECOME A JEDI LIKE MY FATHER.
SOON...
MOS EISLEY SPACEPORT. YOU WILL NEVER FIND A MORE WRETCHED HIVE OF SCUM AND VILLAINY. WE MUST BE CAUTIOUS.

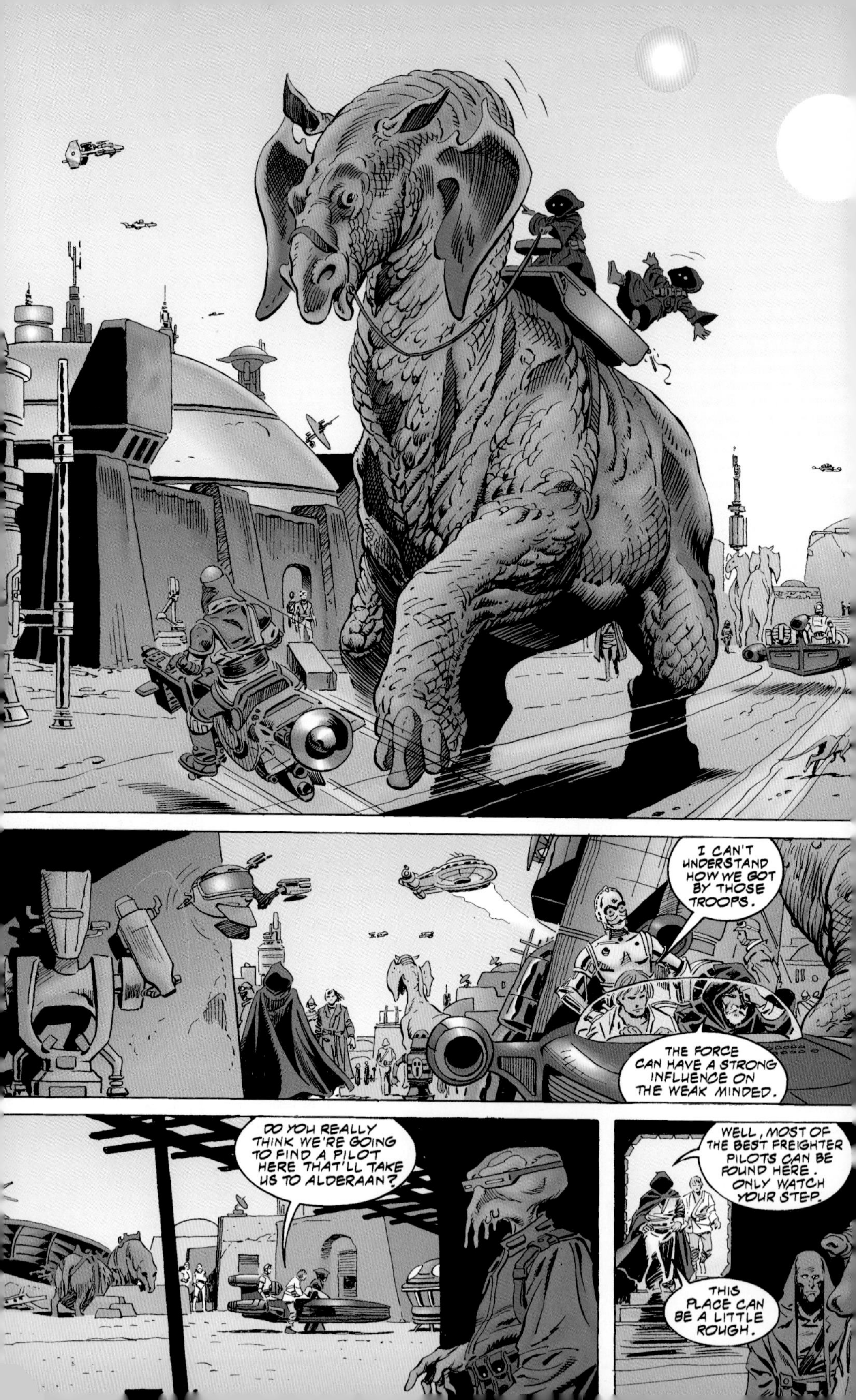
I CAN'T UNDERSTAND HOW WE GOT BY THOSE TROOPS.
THE FORCE CAN HAVE A STRONG INFLUENCE ON THE WEAK MINDED.
DO YOU REALLY THINK WE'RE GOING TO FIND A PILOT HERE THAT'LL TAKE US TO ALDERAAN?
WELL, MOST OF THE BEST FREIGHTER PILOTS CAN BE FOUND HERE. ONLY WATCH YOUR STEP.
THIS PLACE CAN BE A LITTLE ROUGH.

NEGOLA DEWAGHI WOOLDUGGER?

HE DOESN'T LIKE YOU.

I'M SORRY.

I DON'T LIKE YOU EITHER.

UH!

NO BLASTERS!

AGH!

WMMMTT

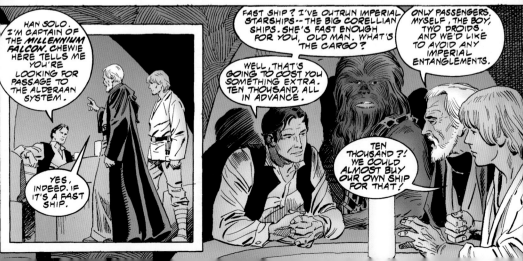

HAN SOLO. I'M CAPTAIN OF THE *MILLENNIUM FALCON*. CHEWIE HERE TELLS ME YOU'RE LOOKING FOR PASSAGE TO THE ALDERAAN SYSTEM.

YES, INDEED. IF IT'S A FAST SHIP.

FAST SHIP? I'VE OUTRUN IMPERIAL STARSHIPS-- THE BIG CORELLIAN SHIPS. SHE'S FAST ENOUGH FOR YOU, OLD MAN. WHAT'S THE CARGO?

ONLY PASSENGERS. MYSELF, THE BOY, TWO DROIDS. AND WE'D LIKE TO AVOID ANY IMPERIAL ENTANGLEMENTS.

WELL, THAT'S GOING TO COST YOU SOMETHING EXTRA. TEN THOUSAND, ALL IN ADVANCE.

TEN THOUSAND?! WE COULD ALMOST BUY OUR OWN SHIP FOR THAT!

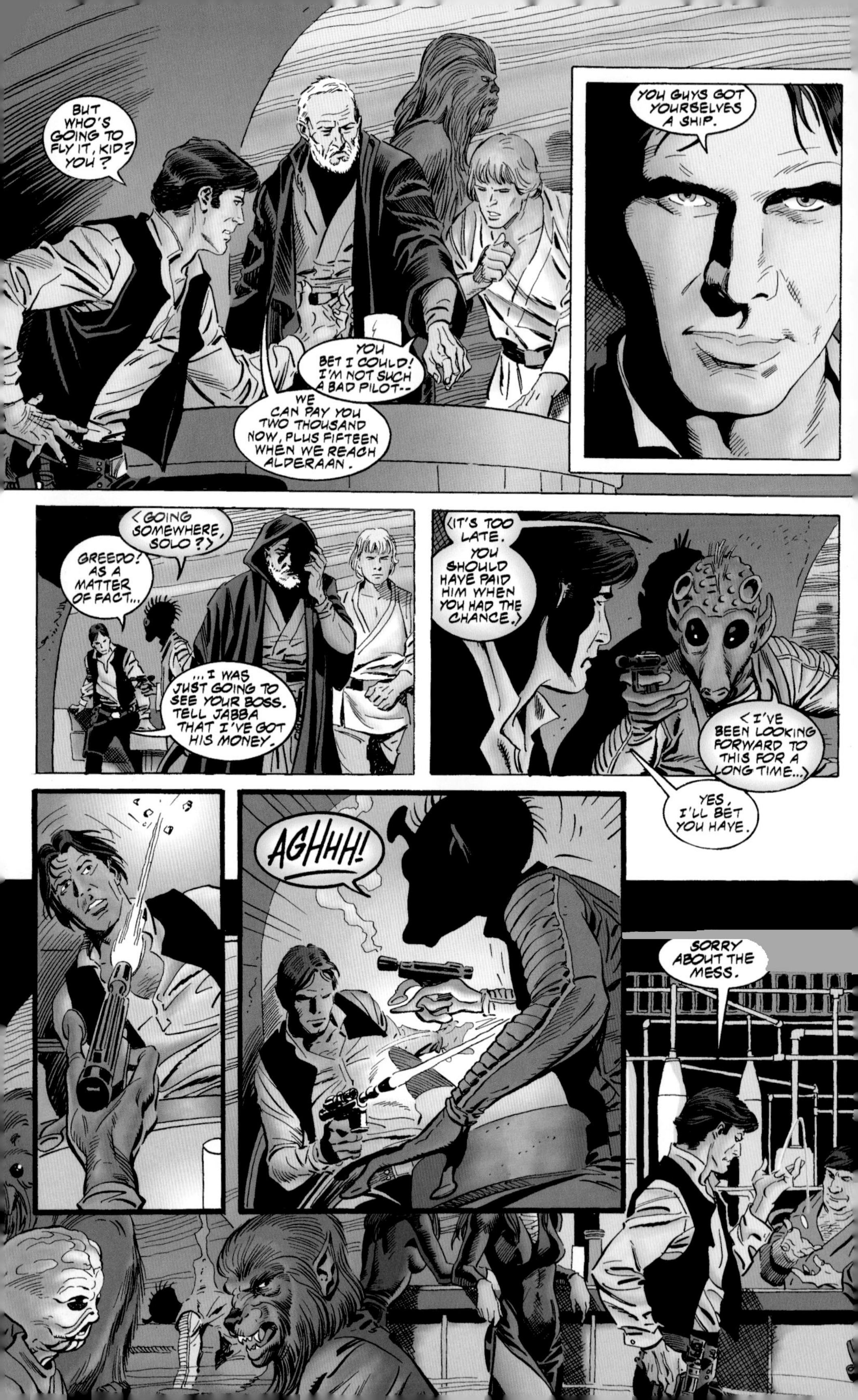
BUT WHO'S GOING TO FLY IT, KID? YOU?
YOU BET I COULD! I'M NOT SUCH A BAD PILOT--
WE CAN PAY YOU TWO THOUSAND NOW, PLUS FIFTEEN WHEN WE REACH ALDERAAN.
YOU GUYS GOT YOURSELVES A SHIP.
<GOING SOMEWHERE, SOLO?>
GREEDO! AS A MATTER OF FACT...
...I WAS JUST GOING TO SEE YOUR BOSS. TELL JABBA THAT I'VE GOT HIS MONEY.
<IT'S TOO LATE. YOU SHOULD HAVE PAID HIM WHEN YOU HAD THE CHANCE.>
<I'VE BEEN LOOKING FORWARD TO THIS FOR A LONG TIME...>
YES, I'LL BET YOU HAVE.
AGHHH!
SORRY ABOUT THE MESS.

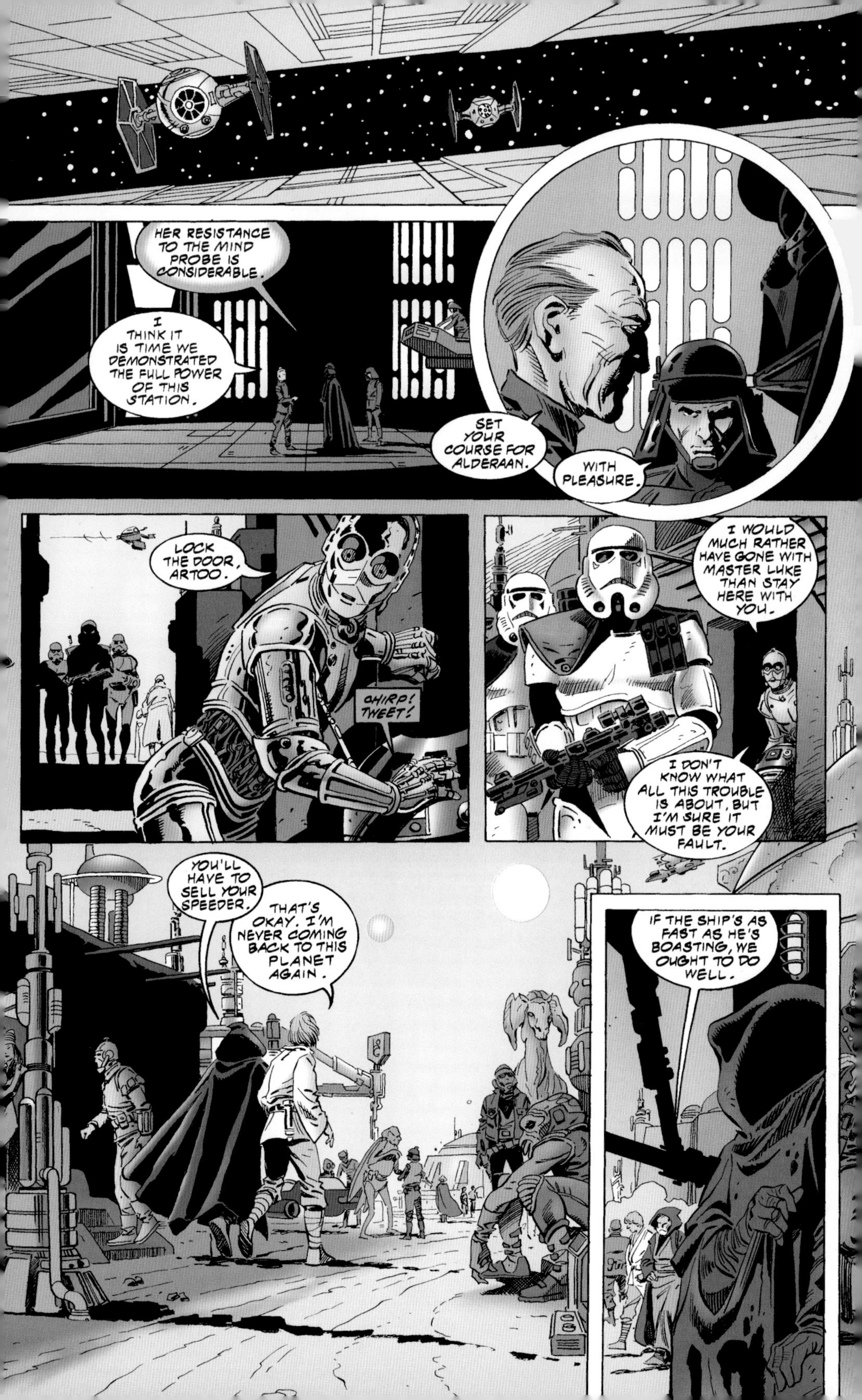
HER RESISTANCE TO THE MIND PROBE IS CONSIDERABLE.
I THINK IT IS TIME WE DEMONSTRATED THE FULL POWER OF THIS STATION.
SET YOUR COURSE FOR ALDERAAN.
WITH PLEASURE.
LOCK THE DOOR, ARTOO.
CHIRP! TWEET!
I WOULD MUCH RATHER HAVE GONE WITH MASTER LUKE THAN STAY HERE WITH YOU.
I DON'T KNOW WHAT ALL THIS TROUBLE IS ABOUT, BUT I'M SURE IT MUST BE YOUR FAULT.
YOU'LL HAVE TO SELL YOUR SPEEDER.
THAT'S OKAY. I'M NEVER COMING BACK TO THIS PLANET AGAIN.
IF THE SHIP'S AS FAST AS HE'S BOASTING, WE OUGHT TO DO WELL.

‹SOLO! COME OUT OF THERE, SOLO!›

RIGHT HERE, JABBA. I'VE BEEN WAITING FOR YOU.

‹HAVE YOU, NOW?›

YOU DIDN'T THINK I WAS GONNA RUN, DID YOU?

‹HAN, MY BOY, YOU DISAPPOINT ME. WHY HAVEN'T YOU PAID ME? WHY DID YOU FRY POOR GREEDO?›

LOOK, JABBA, NEXT TIME YOU WANT TO TALK TO ME, COME SEE ME YOURSELF. DON'T SEND ONE OF THESE TWERPS.

‹HAN, I CAN'T MAKE EXCEPTIONS. WHAT IF EVERYONE WHO SMUGGLED FOR ME DROPPED THEIR CARGO AT THE FIRST SIGN OF AN IMPERIAL STARSHIP? IT'S NOT GOOD FOR BUSINESS.›

LOOK, JABBA, EVEN I GET BOARDED SOMETIMES.

YOU THINK I HAD A CHOICE? I GOT A NICE EASY CHARTER NOW. PAY YOU BACK, PLUS A LITTLE EXTRA. I JUST NEED A LITTLE MORE TIME.

‹HAN, MY BOY, YOU'RE THE BEST. SO FOR AN EXTRA TWENTY PERCENT--›

FIFTEEN, JABBA. DON'T PUSH IT.

‹OKAY, FIFTEEN PERCENT. BUT IF YOU FAIL ME AGAIN, I'LL PUT A PRICE ON YOUR HEAD SO BIG YOU WON'T BE ABLE TO GO NEAR A CIVILIZED SYSTEM.›

JABBA, YOU'RE A WONDERFUL HUMAN BEING.

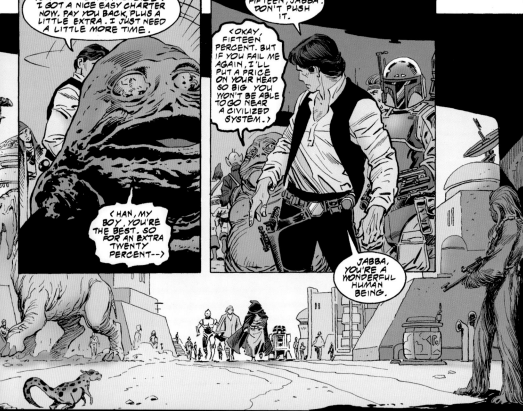

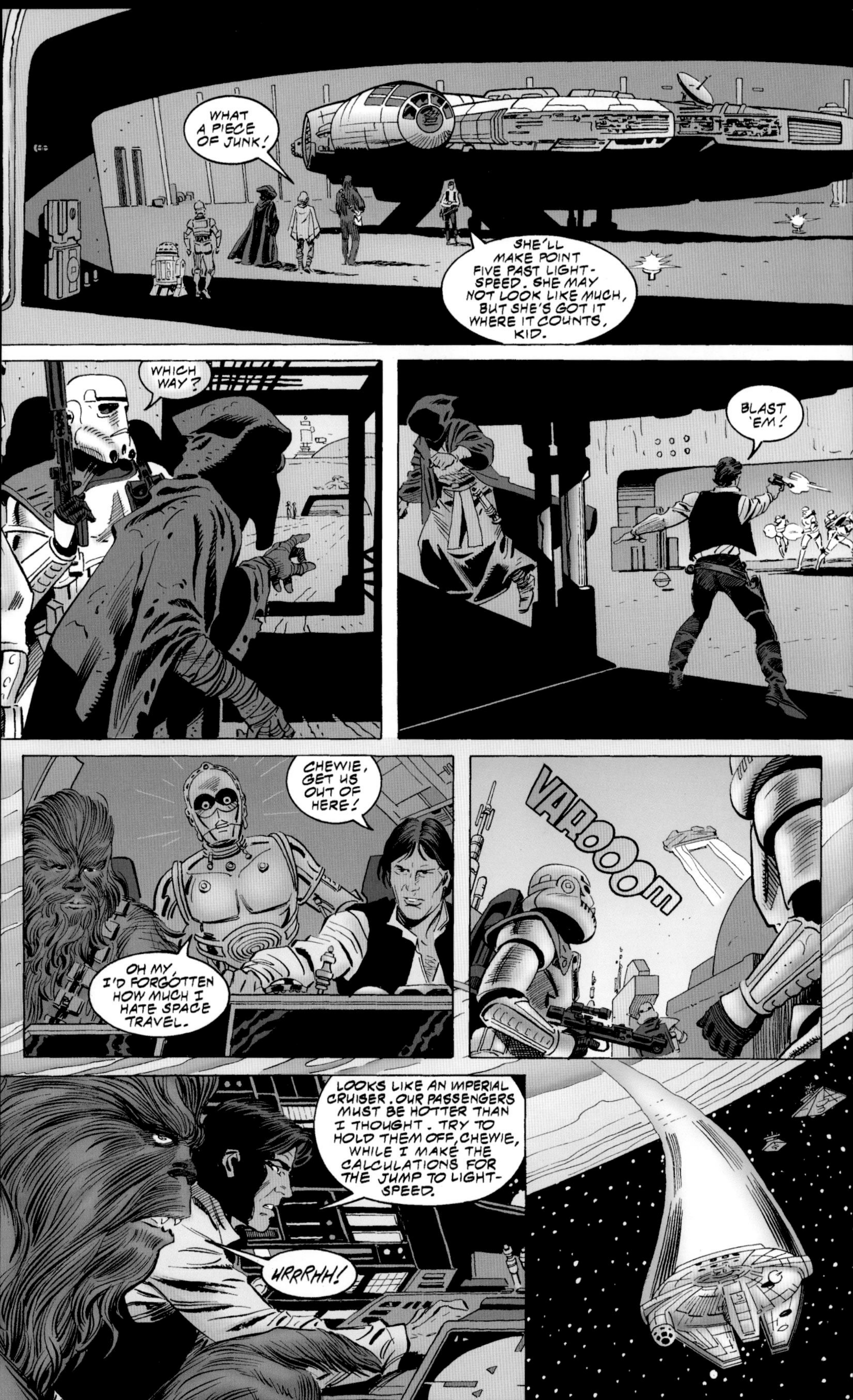
WHAT A PIECE OF JUNK!
SHE'LL MAKE POINT FIVE PAST LIGHT-SPEED. SHE MAY NOT LOOK LIKE MUCH, BUT SHE'S GOT IT WHERE IT COUNTS, KID.
WHICH WAY?
BLAST 'EM!
CHEWIE, GET US OUT OF HERE!
OH MY, I'D FORGOTTEN HOW MUCH I HATE SPACE TRAVEL.
VAROOOOM
LOOKS LIKE AN IMPERIAL CRUISER. OUR PASSENGERS MUST BE HOTTER THAN I THOUGHT. TRY TO HOLD THEM OFF, CHEWIE, WHILE I MAKE THE CALCULATIONS FOR THE JUMP TO LIGHT-SPEED.
URRRHH!

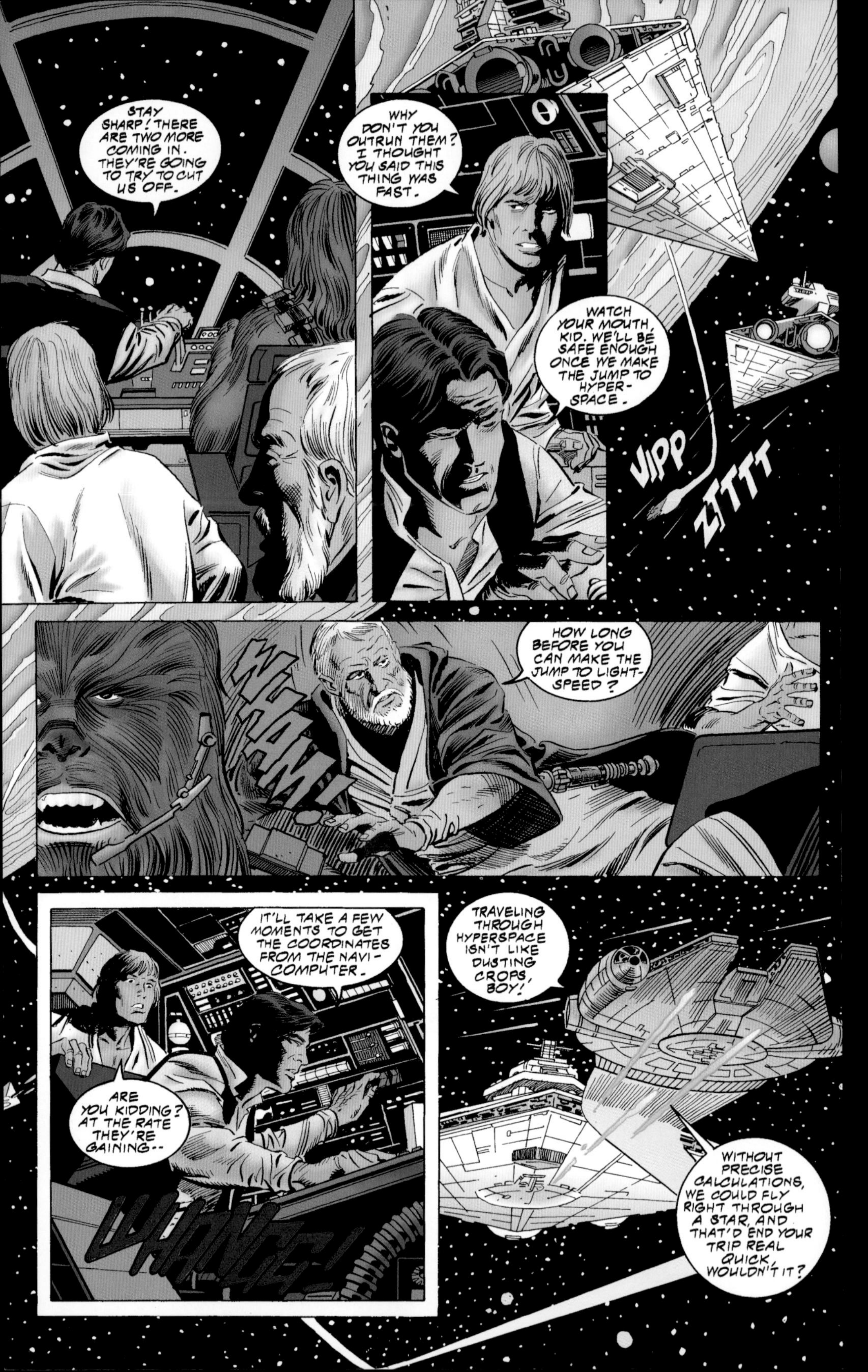
STAY SHARP! THERE ARE TWO MORE COMING IN. THEY'RE GOING TO TRY TO CUT US OFF.
WHY DON'T YOU OUTRUN THEM? I THOUGHT YOU SAID THIS THING WAS FAST.
WATCH YOUR MOUTH, KID. WE'LL BE SAFE ENOUGH ONCE WE MAKE THE JUMP TO HYPER-SPACE.
VIPP
ZTTTT
HOW LONG BEFORE YOU CAN MAKE THE JUMP TO LIGHT-SPEED?
IT'LL TAKE A FEW MOMENTS TO GET THE COORDINATES FROM THE NAVI-COMPUTER.
ARE YOU KIDDING? AT THE RATE THEY'RE GAINING--
TRAVELING THROUGH HYPERSPACE ISN'T LIKE DUSTING CROPS, BOY!
WITHOUT PRECISE CALCULATIONS, WE COULD FLY RIGHT THROUGH A STAR, AND THAT'D END YOUR TRIP REAL QUICK, WOULDN'T IT?

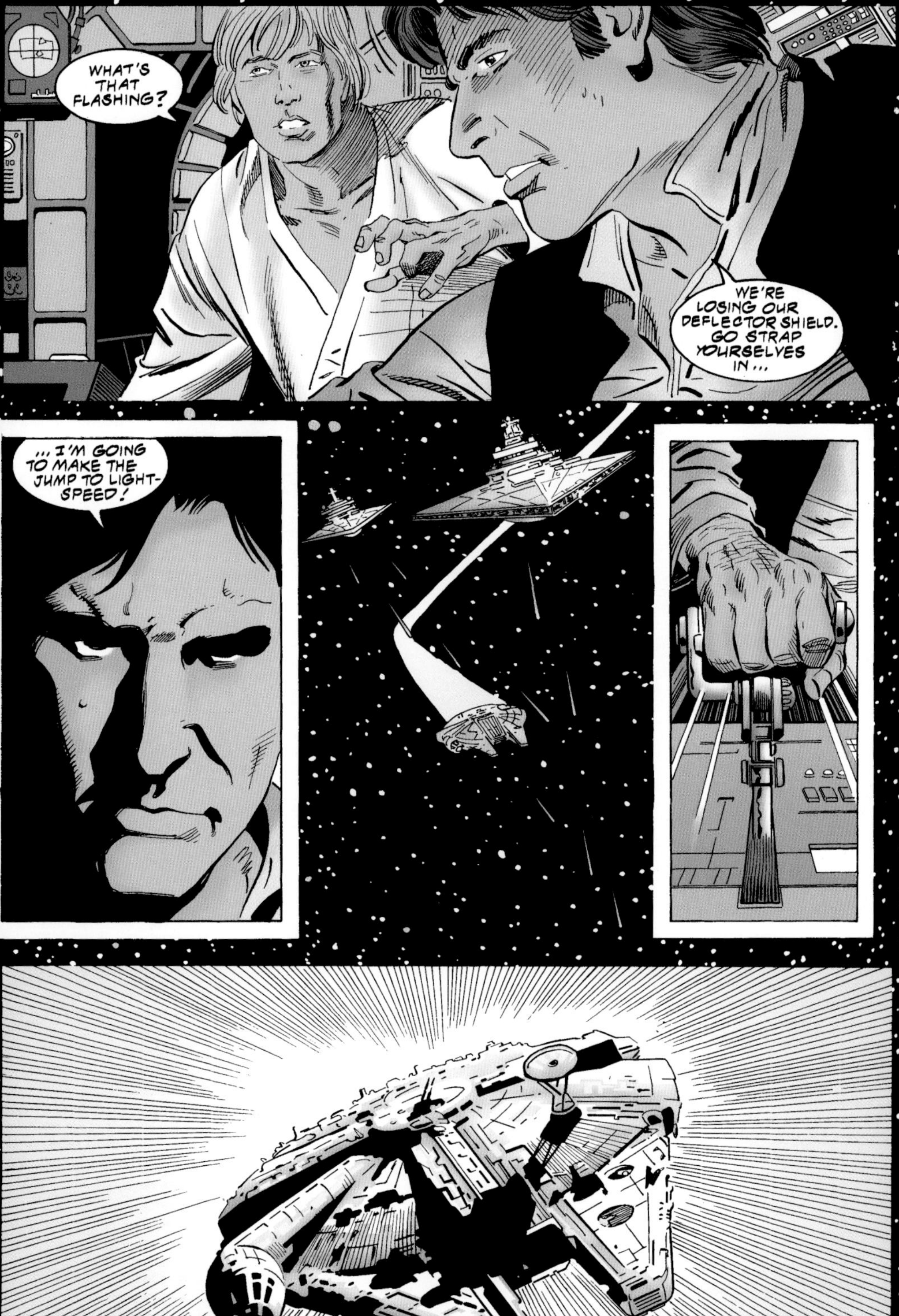
WHAT'S THAT FLASHING?
WE'RE LOSING OUR DEFLECTOR SHIELD. GO STRAP YOURSELVES IN...
...I'M GOING TO MAKE THE JUMP TO LIGHT-SPEED!
END OF PART ONE.

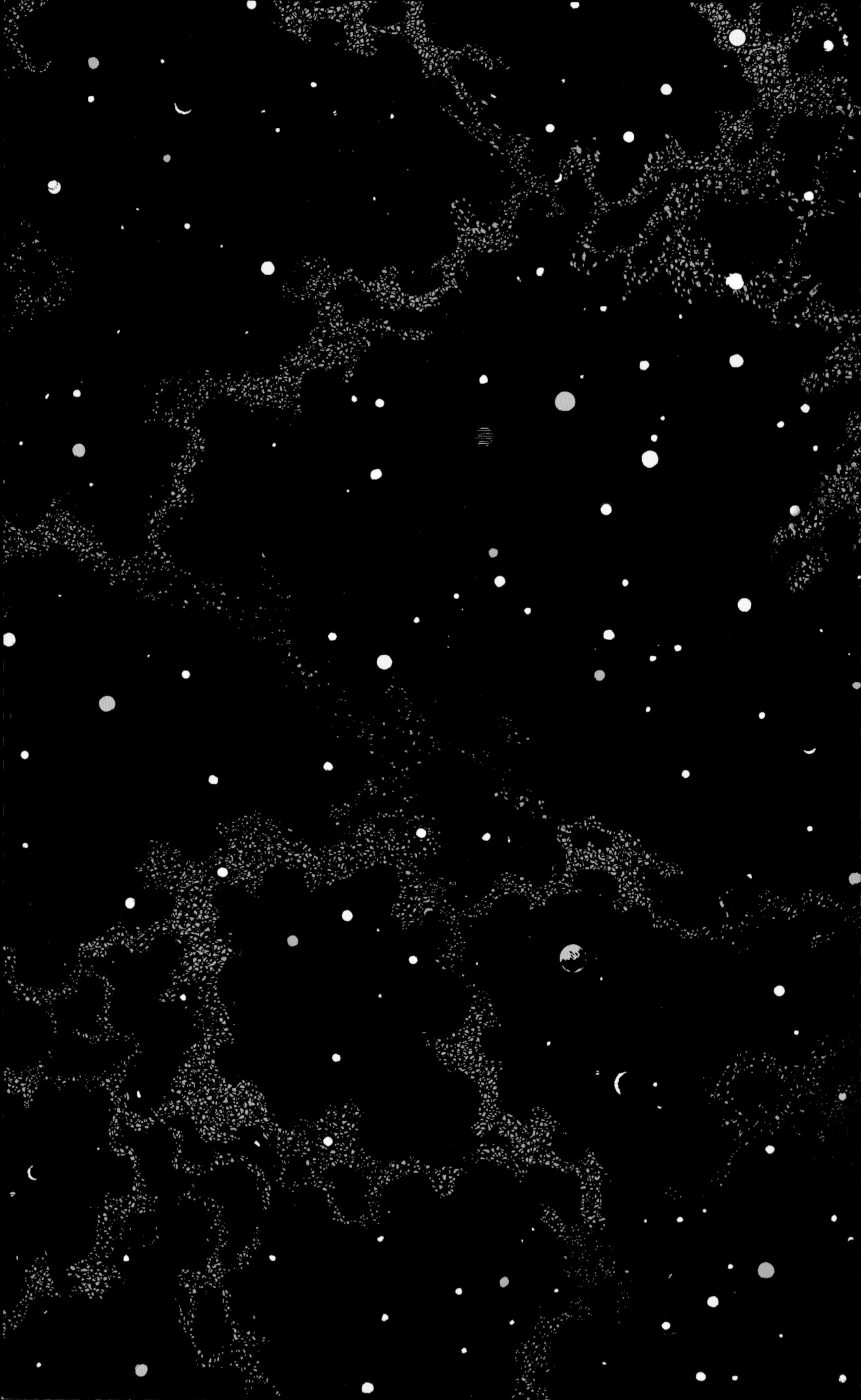

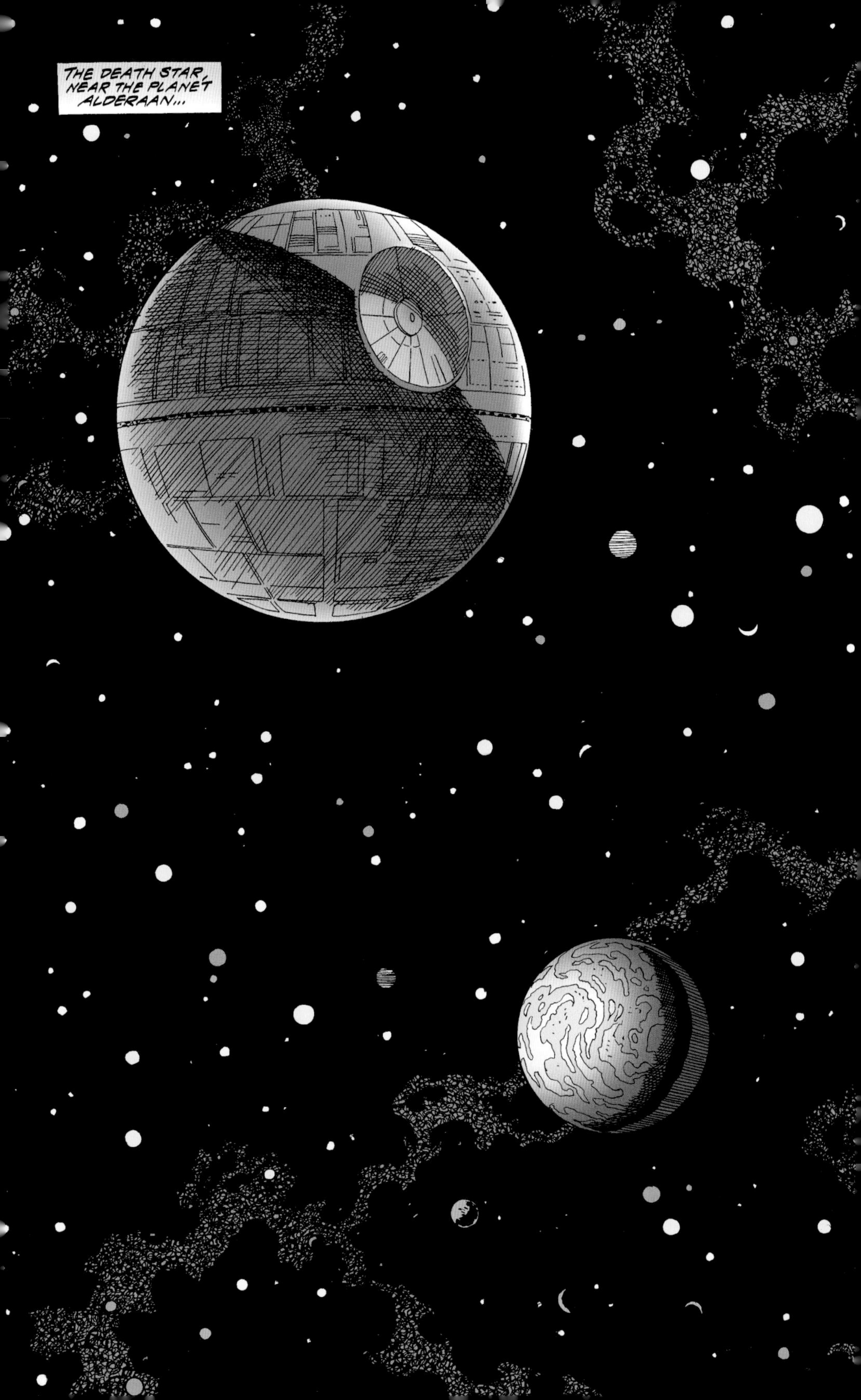
THE DEATH STAR, NEAR THE PLANET ALDERAAN...

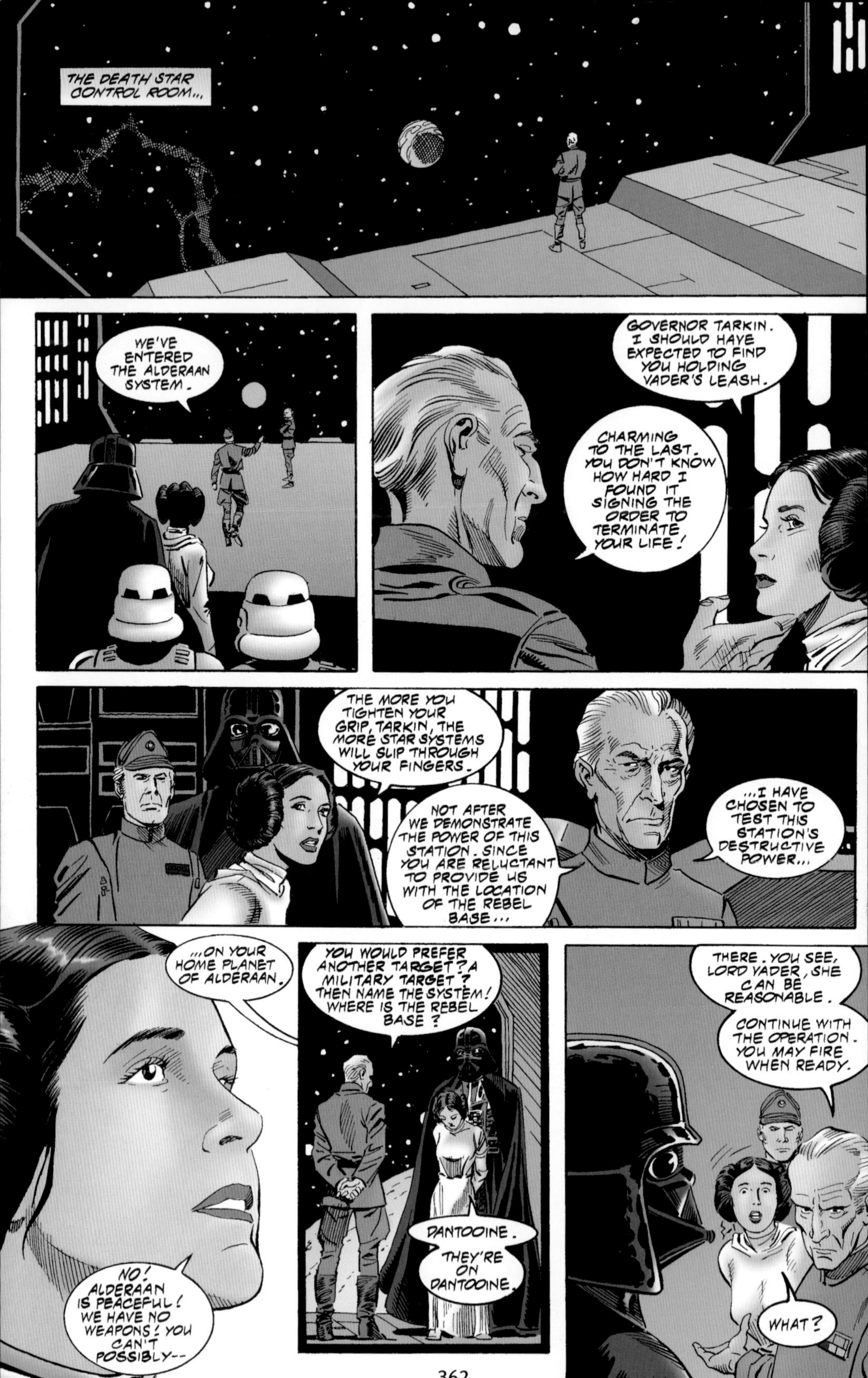
THE DEATH STAR CONTROL ROOM...
WE'VE ENTERED THE ALDERAAN SYSTEM.
GOVERNOR TARKIN. I SHOULD HAVE EXPECTED TO FIND YOU HOLDING VADER'S LEASH.
CHARMING TO THE LAST. YOU DON'T KNOW HOW HARD I FOUND IT SIGNING THE ORDER TO TERMINATE YOUR LIFE!
THE MORE YOU TIGHTEN YOUR GRIP, TARKIN, THE MORE STAR SYSTEMS WILL SLIP THROUGH YOUR FINGERS.
NOT AFTER WE DEMONSTRATE THE POWER OF THIS STATION. SINCE YOU ARE RELUCTANT TO PROVIDE US WITH THE LOCATION OF THE REBEL BASE...
...I HAVE CHOSEN TO TEST THIS STATION'S DESTRUCTIVE POWER...
...ON YOUR HOME PLANET OF ALDERAAN.
NO! ALDERAAN IS PEACEFUL! WE HAVE NO WEAPONS! YOU CAN'T POSSIBLY--
YOU WOULD PREFER ANOTHER TARGET? A MILITARY TARGET? THEN NAME THE SYSTEM! WHERE IS THE REBEL BASE?
DANTOOINE.
THEY'RE ON DANTOOINE.
THERE. YOU SEE, LORD VADER, SHE CAN BE REASONABLE.
CONTINUE WITH THE OPERATION. YOU MAY FIRE WHEN READY.
WHAT?

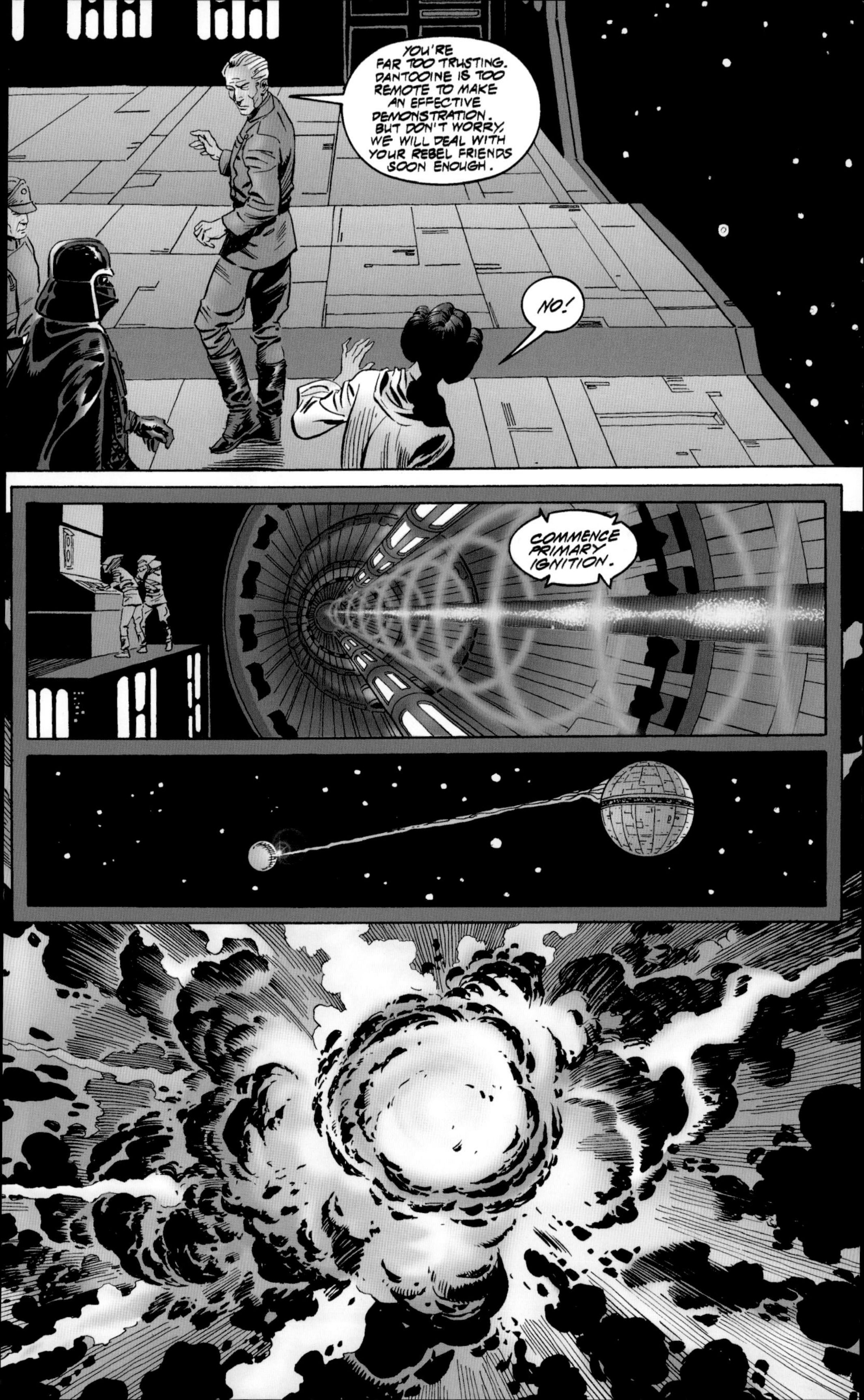
YOU'RE FAR TOO TRUSTING. DANTOOINE IS TOO REMOTE TO MAKE AN EFFECTIVE DEMONSTRATION. BUT DON'T WORRY, WE WILL DEAL WITH YOUR REBEL FRIENDS SOON ENOUGH.
NO!
COMMENCE PRIMARY IGNITION.

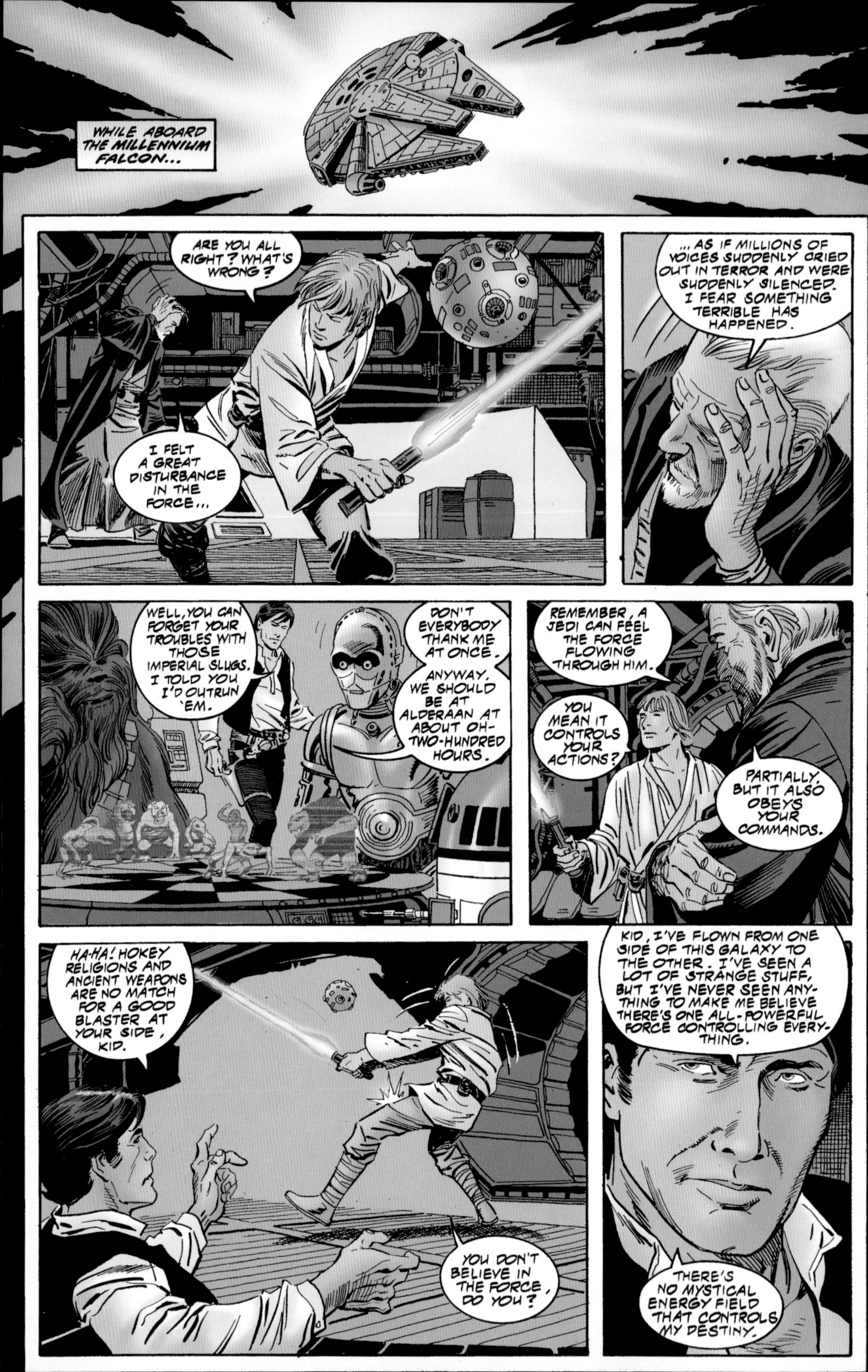
WHILE ABOARD THE MILLENNIUM FALCON...
ARE YOU ALL RIGHT? WHAT'S WRONG?
I FELT A GREAT DISTURBANCE IN THE FORCE...
...AS IF MILLIONS OF VOICES SUDDENLY CRIED OUT IN TERROR AND WERE SUDDENLY SILENCED. I FEAR SOMETHING TERRIBLE HAS HAPPENED.
WELL, YOU CAN FORGET YOUR TROUBLES WITH THOSE IMPERIAL SLUGS. I TOLD YOU I'D OUTRUN 'EM.
DON'T EVERYBODY THANK ME AT ONCE.
ANYWAY, WE SHOULD BE AT ALDERAAN AT ABOUT OH-TWO-HUNDRED HOURS.
REMEMBER, A JEDI CAN FEEL THE FORCE FLOWING THROUGH HIM.
YOU MEAN IT CONTROLS YOUR ACTIONS?
PARTIALLY, BUT IT ALSO OBEYS YOUR COMMANDS.
HA-HA! HOKEY RELIGIONS AND ANCIENT WEAPONS ARE NO MATCH FOR A GOOD BLASTER AT YOUR SIDE, KID.
YOU DON'T BELIEVE IN THE FORCE, DO YOU?
KID, I'VE FLOWN FROM ONE SIDE OF THIS GALAXY TO THE OTHER. I'VE SEEN A LOT OF STRANGE STUFF, BUT I'VE NEVER SEEN ANYTHING TO MAKE ME BELIEVE THERE'S ONE ALL-POWERFUL FORCE CONTROLLING EVERYTHING.
THERE'S NO MYSTICAL ENERGY FIELD THAT CONTROLS MY DESTINY.

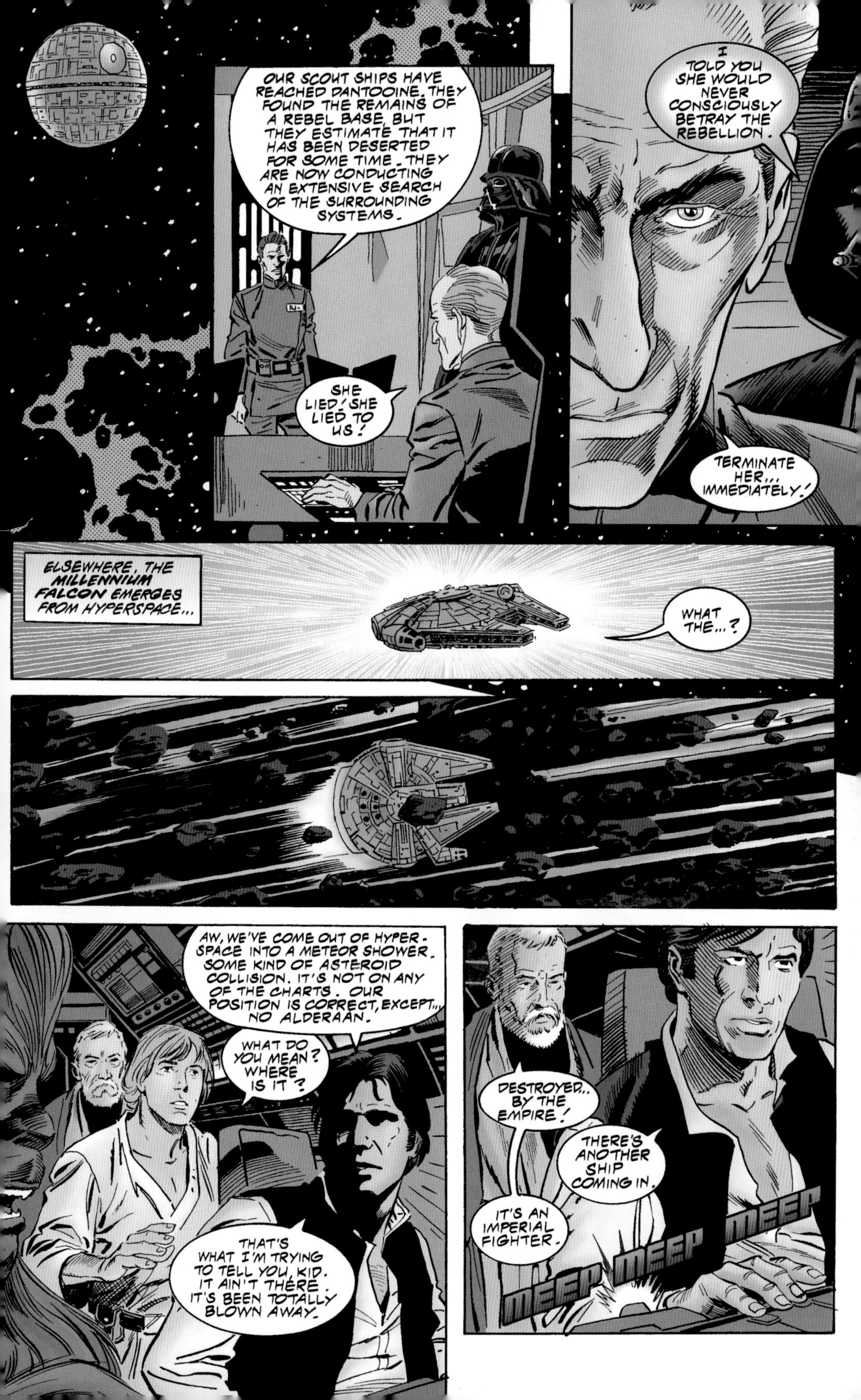
OUR SCOUT SHIPS HAVE REACHED DANTOOINE. THEY FOUND THE REMAINS OF A REBEL BASE, BUT THEY ESTIMATE THAT IT HAS BEEN DESERTED FOR SOME TIME. THEY ARE NOW CONDUCTING AN EXTENSIVE SEARCH OF THE SURROUNDING SYSTEMS.
SHE LIED! SHE LIED TO US!
I TOLD YOU SHE WOULD NEVER CONSCIOUSLY BETRAY THE REBELLION.
TERMINATE HER... IMMEDIATELY!
ELSEWHERE, THE MILLENNIUM FALCON EMERGES FROM HYPERSPACE...
WHAT THE...?
AW, WE'VE COME OUT OF HYPER-SPACE INTO A METEOR SHOWER. SOME KIND OF ASTEROID COLLISION. IT'S NOT ON ANY OF THE CHARTS. OUR POSITION IS CORRECT, EXCEPT... NO ALDERAAN.
WHAT DO YOU MEAN? WHERE IS IT?
THAT'S WHAT I'M TRYING TO TELL YOU, KID. IT AIN'T THERE. IT'S BEEN TOTALLY BLOWN AWAY.
DESTROYED... BY THE EMPIRE!
THERE'S ANOTHER SHIP COMING IN.
IT'S AN IMPERIAL FIGHTER.
MEEP MEEP MEEP

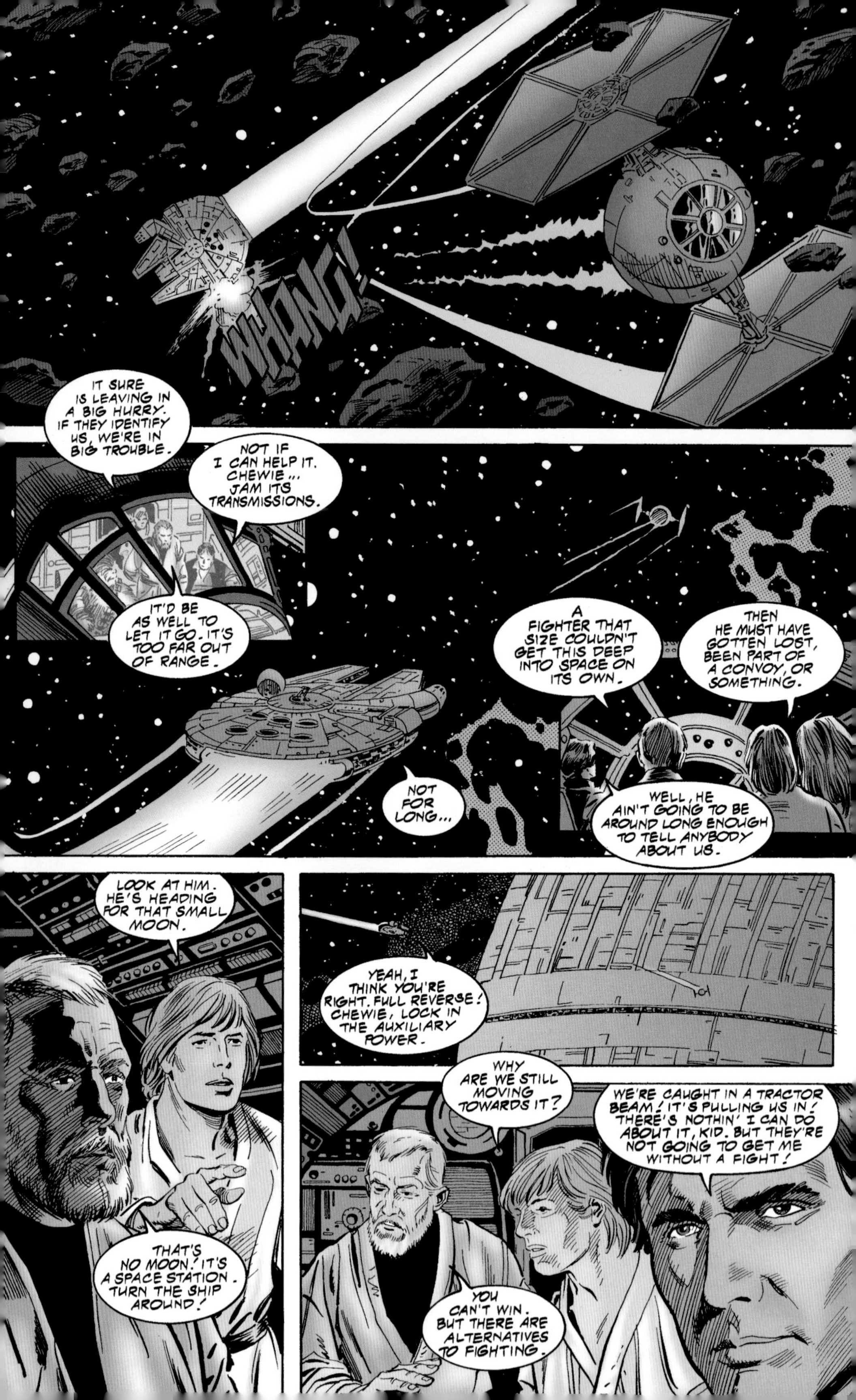
WHANG!
IT SURE IS LEAVING IN A BIG HURRY. IF THEY IDENTIFY US, WE'RE IN BIG TROUBLE.
NOT IF I CAN HELP IT. CHEWIE... JAM ITS TRANSMISSIONS.
IT'D BE AS WELL TO LET IT GO. IT'S TOO FAR OUT OF RANGE.
A FIGHTER THAT SIZE COULDN'T GET THIS DEEP INTO SPACE ON ITS OWN.
THEN HE MUST HAVE GOTTEN LOST, BEEN PART OF A CONVOY, OR SOMETHING.
NOT FOR LONG...
WELL, HE AIN'T GOING TO BE AROUND LONG ENOUGH TO TELL ANYBODY ABOUT US.
LOOK AT HIM. HE'S HEADING FOR THAT SMALL MOON.
THAT'S NO MOON! IT'S A SPACE STATION. TURN THE SHIP AROUND!
YEAH, I THINK YOU'RE RIGHT. FULL REVERSE! CHEWIE, LOCK IN THE AUXILIARY POWER.
WHY ARE WE STILL MOVING TOWARDS IT?
WE'RE CAUGHT IN A TRACTOR BEAM! IT'S PULLING US IN! THERE'S NOTHIN' I CAN DO ABOUT IT, KID. BUT THEY'RE NOT GOING TO GET ME WITHOUT A FIGHT!
YOU CAN'T WIN. BUT THERE ARE ALTERNATIVES TO FIGHTING.

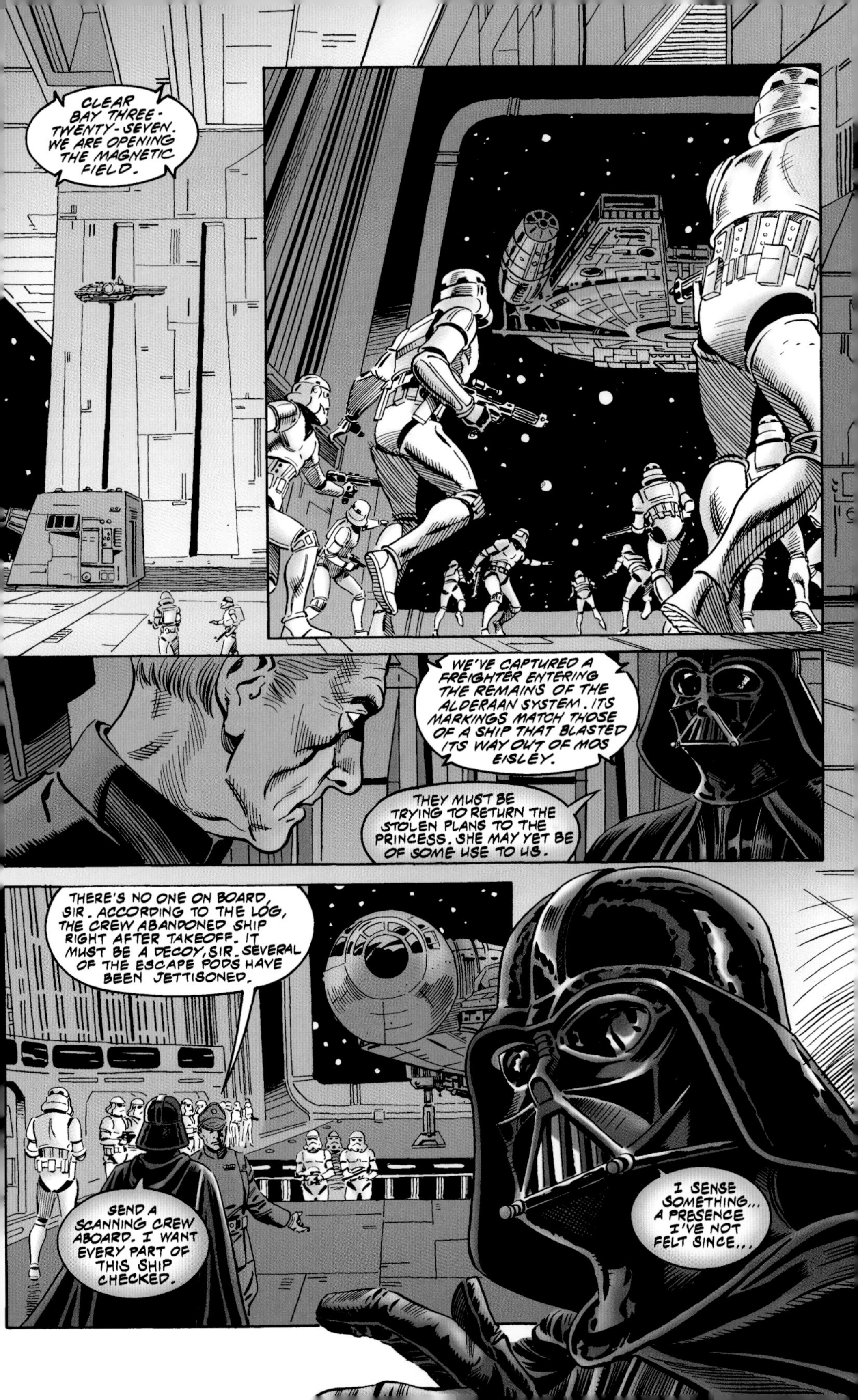
CLEAR BAY THREE-TWENTY-SEVEN. WE ARE OPENING THE MAGNETIC FIELD.
WE'VE CAPTURED A FREIGHTER ENTERING THE REMAINS OF THE ALDERAAN SYSTEM. ITS MARKINGS MATCH THOSE OF A SHIP THAT BLASTED ITS WAY OUT OF MOS EISLEY.
THEY MUST BE TRYING TO RETURN THE STOLEN PLANS TO THE PRINCESS. SHE MAY YET BE OF SOME USE TO US.
THERE'S NO ONE ON BOARD, SIR. ACCORDING TO THE LOG, THE CREW ABANDONED SHIP RIGHT AFTER TAKEOFF. IT MUST BE A DECOY, SIR. SEVERAL OF THE ESCAPE PODS HAVE BEEN JETTISONED.
SEND A SCANNING CREW ABOARD. I WANT EVERY PART OF THIS SHIP CHECKED.
I SENSE SOMETHING... A PRESENCE I'VE NOT FELT SINCE...

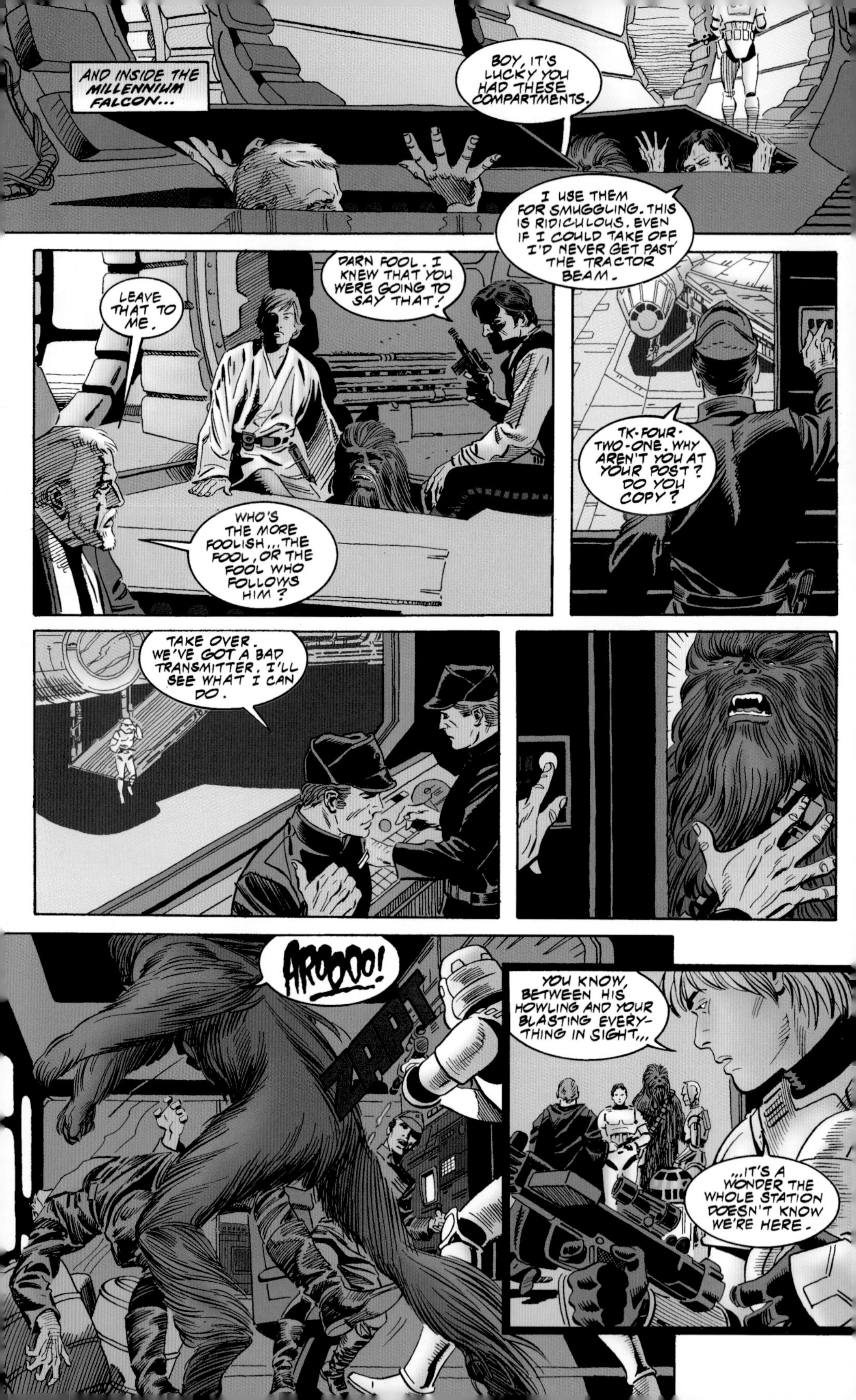
AND INSIDE THE MILLENNIUM FALCON...
BOY, IT'S LUCKY YOU HAD THESE COMPARTMENTS.
I USE THEM FOR SMUGGLING. THIS IS RIDICULOUS. EVEN IF I COULD TAKE OFF I'D NEVER GET PAST THE TRACTOR BEAM.
LEAVE THAT TO ME.
DARN FOOL. I KNEW THAT YOU WERE GOING TO SAY THAT!
WHO'S THE MORE FOOLISH... THE FOOL, OR THE FOOL WHO FOLLOWS HIM?
TK-FOUR-TWO-ONE. WHY AREN'T YOU AT YOUR POST? DO YOU COPY?
TAKE OVER. WE'VE GOT A BAD TRANSMITTER. I'LL SEE WHAT I CAN DO.
AROOOO!
ZAAT
YOU KNOW, BETWEEN HIS HOWLING AND YOUR BLASTING EVERY-THING IN SIGHT...
...IT'S A WONDER THE WHOLE STATION DOESN'T KNOW WE'RE HERE.

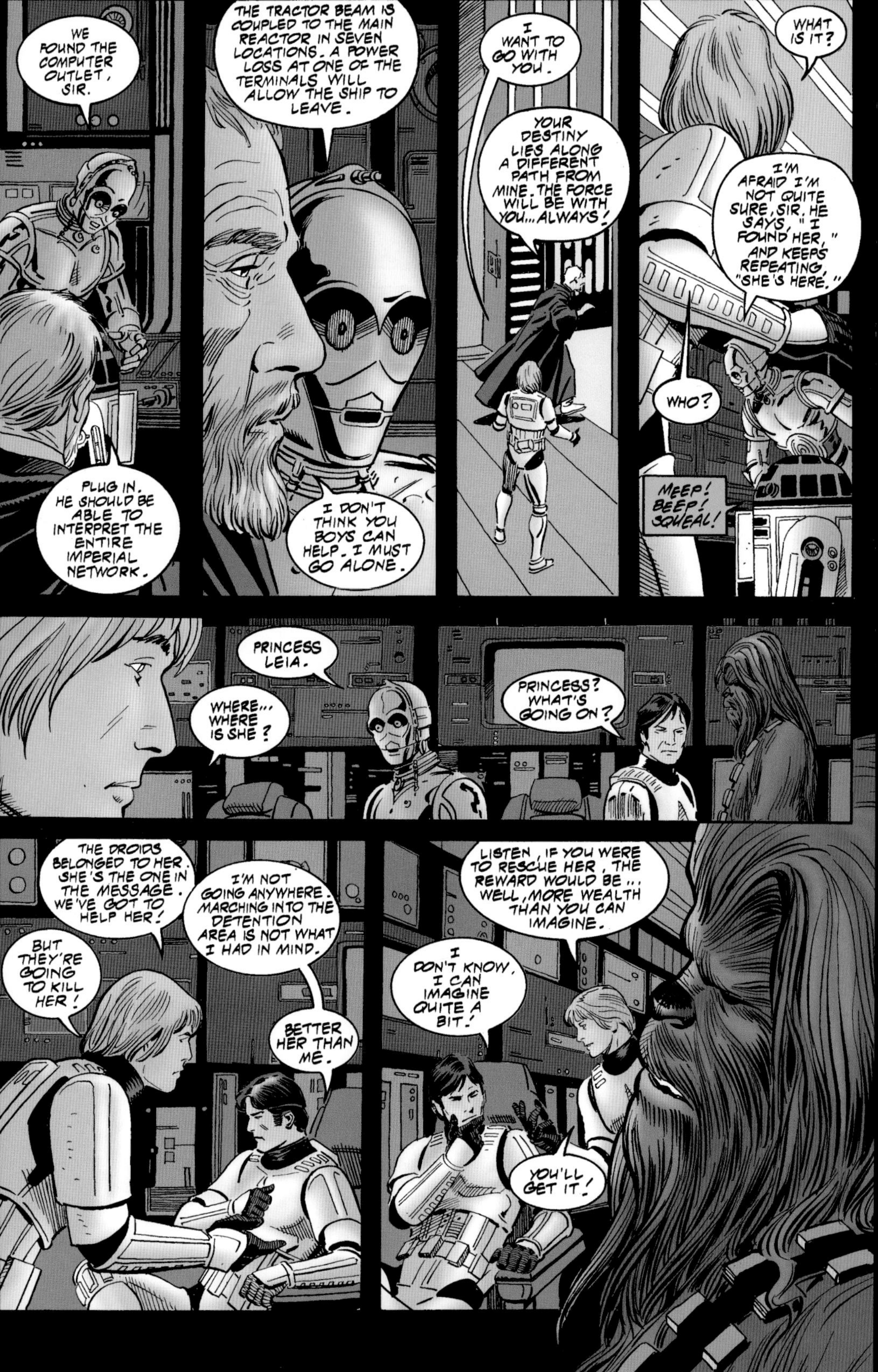

WE FOUND THE COMPUTER OUTLET, SIR.
PLUG IN. HE SHOULD BE ABLE TO INTERPRET THE ENTIRE IMPERIAL NETWORK.
THE TRACTOR BEAM IS COUPLED TO THE MAIN REACTOR IN SEVEN LOCATIONS. A POWER LOSS AT ONE OF THE TERMINALS WILL ALLOW THE SHIP TO LEAVE.
I DON'T THINK YOU BOYS CAN HELP. I MUST GO ALONE.
I WANT TO GO WITH YOU.
YOUR DESTINY LIES ALONG A DIFFERENT PATH FROM MINE. THE FORCE WILL BE WITH YOU... ALWAYS!
WHAT IS IT?
I'M AFRAID I'M NOT QUITE SURE, SIR. HE SAYS, "I FOUND HER," AND KEEPS REPEATING, "SHE'S HERE."
WHO?
MEEP! BEEP! SQUEAL!
PRINCESS LEIA.
WHERE... WHERE IS SHE?
PRINCESS? WHAT'S GOING ON?
THE DROIDS BELONGED TO HER. SHE'S THE ONE IN THE MESSAGE. WE'VE GOT TO HELP HER!
I'M NOT GOING ANYWHERE. MARCHING INTO THE DETENTION AREA IS NOT WHAT I HAD IN MIND.
BUT THEY'RE GOING TO KILL HER!
BETTER HER THAN ME.
LISTEN, IF YOU WERE TO RESCUE HER, THE REWARD WOULD BE... WELL, MORE WEALTH THAN YOU CAN IMAGINE.
I DON'T KNOW, I CAN IMAGINE QUITE A BIT!
YOU'LL GET IT!

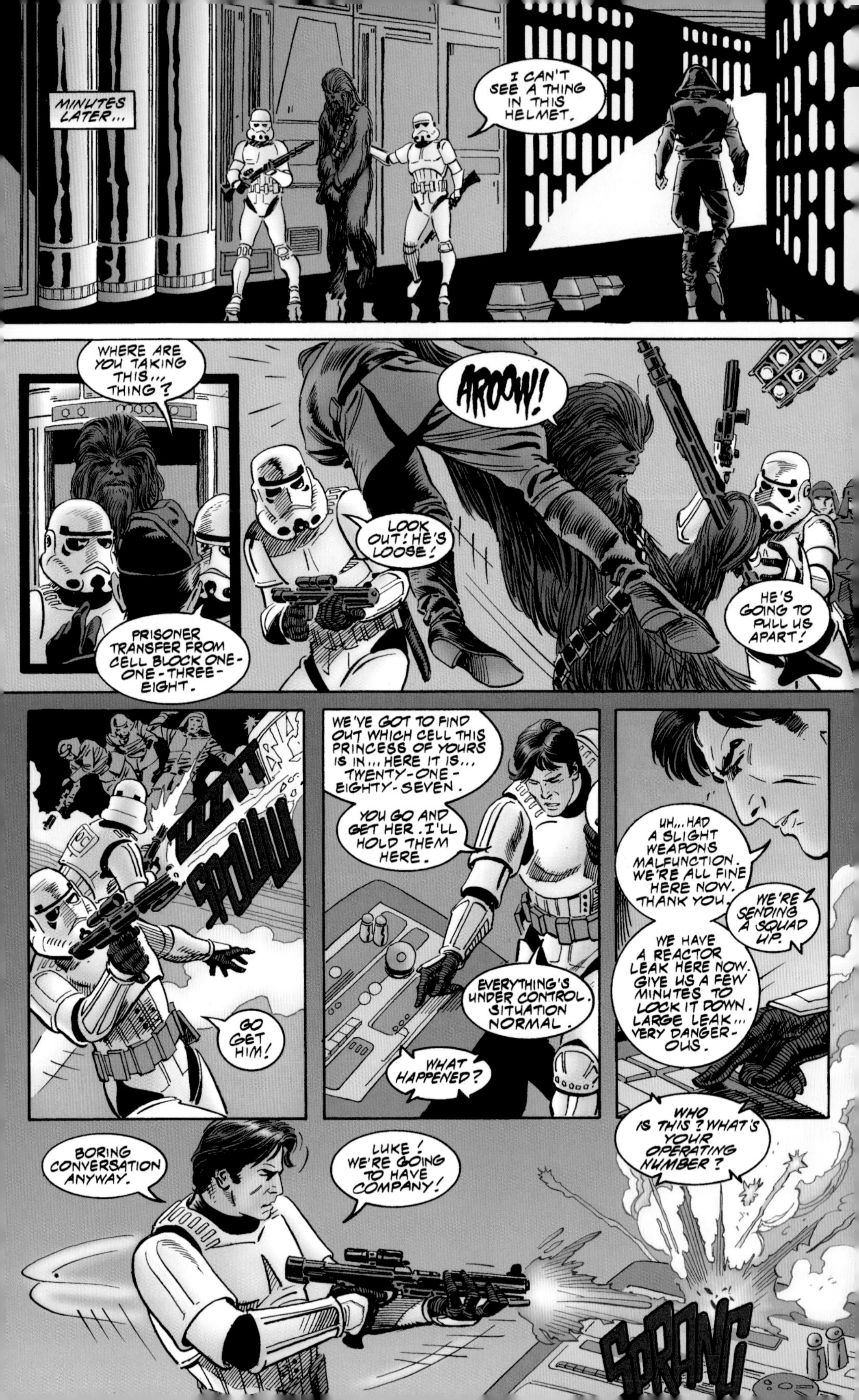

MINUTES LATER...
I CAN'T SEE A THING IN THIS HELMET.
WHERE ARE YOU TAKING THIS... THING?
PRISONER TRANSFER FROM CELL BLOCK ONE-ONE-THREE-EIGHT.
AROOW!
LOOK OUT! HE'S LOOSE!
HE'S GOING TO PULL US APART!
ZZZTTT
SPOWW
GO GET HIM!
WE'VE GOT TO FIND OUT WHICH CELL THIS PRINCESS OF YOURS IS IN... HERE IT IS... TWENTY-ONE-EIGHTY-SEVEN.
YOU GO AND GET HER. I'LL HOLD THEM HERE.
EVERYTHING'S UNDER CONTROL. SITUATION NORMAL.
WHAT HAPPENED?
UH... HAD A SLIGHT WEAPONS MALFUNCTION. WE'RE ALL FINE HERE NOW. THANK YOU.
WE'RE SENDING A SQUAD UP.
WE HAVE A REACTOR LEAK HERE NOW. GIVE US A FEW MINUTES TO LOCK IT DOWN. LARGE LEAK... VERY DANGEROUS.
WHO IS THIS? WHAT'S YOUR OPERATING NUMBER?
BORING CONVERSATION ANYWAY.
LUKE! WE'RE GOING TO HAVE COMPANY!
SPRANG

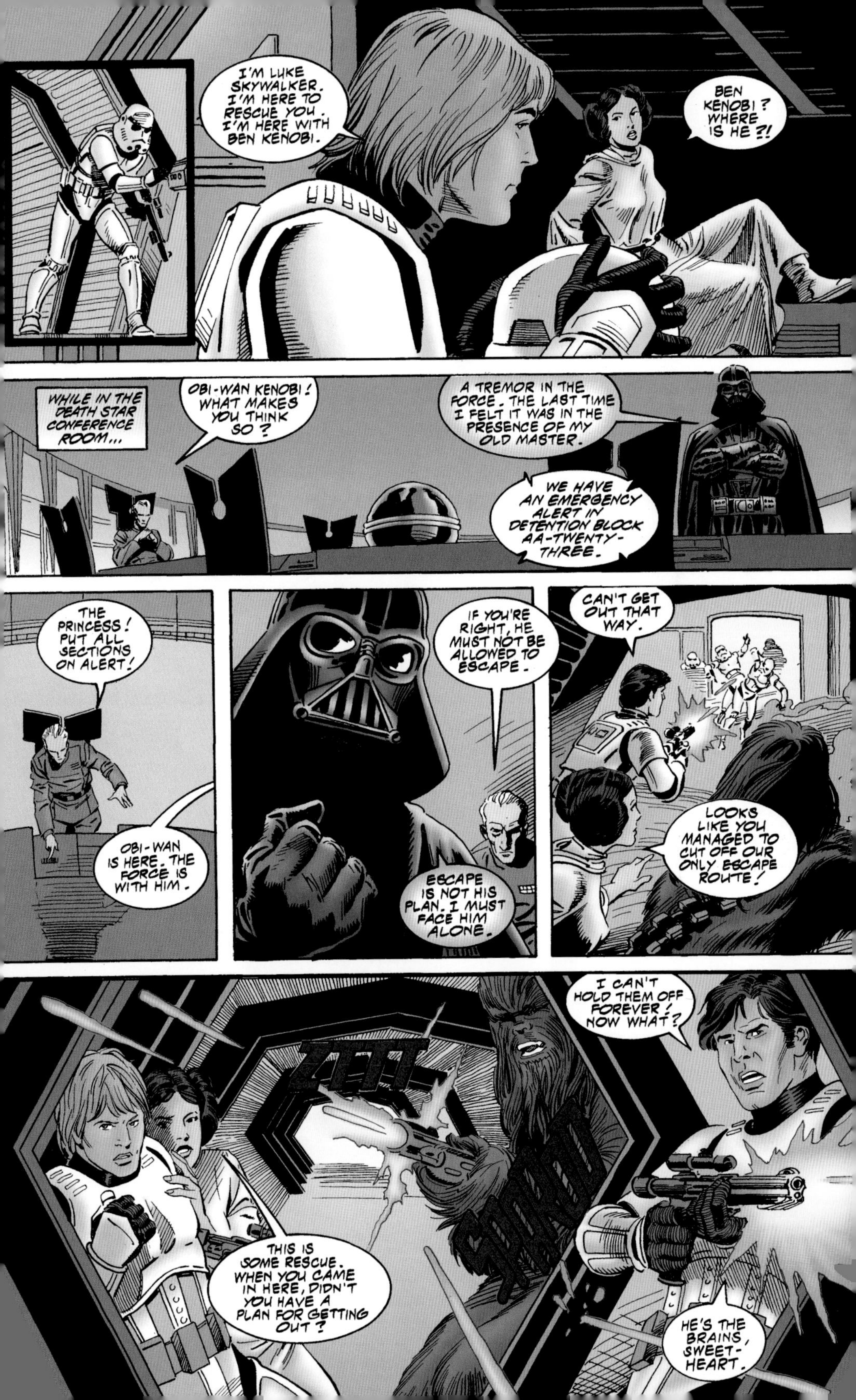
I'M LUKE SKYWALKER. I'M HERE TO RESCUE YOU. I'M HERE WITH BEN KENOBI.
BEN KENOBI? WHERE IS HE?!
WHILE IN THE DEATH STAR CONFERENCE ROOM...
OBI-WAN KENOBI! WHAT MAKES YOU THINK SO?
A TREMOR IN THE FORCE. THE LAST TIME I FELT IT WAS IN THE PRESENCE OF MY OLD MASTER.
WE HAVE AN EMERGENCY ALERT IN DETENTION BLOCK AA-TWENTY-THREE.
THE PRINCESS! PUT ALL SECTIONS ON ALERT!
OBI-WAN IS HERE. THE FORCE IS WITH HIM.
IF YOU'RE RIGHT, HE MUST NOT BE ALLOWED TO ESCAPE.
ESCAPE IS NOT HIS PLAN. I MUST FACE HIM ALONE.
CAN'T GET OUT THAT WAY.
LOOKS LIKE YOU MANAGED TO CUT OFF OUR ONLY ESCAPE ROUTE!
I CAN'T HOLD THEM OFF FOREVER! NOW WHAT?
ZZTT
THIS IS SOME RESCUE. WHEN YOU CAME IN HERE, DIDN'T YOU HAVE A PLAN FOR GETTING OUT?
HE'S THE BRAINS, SWEET-HEART.

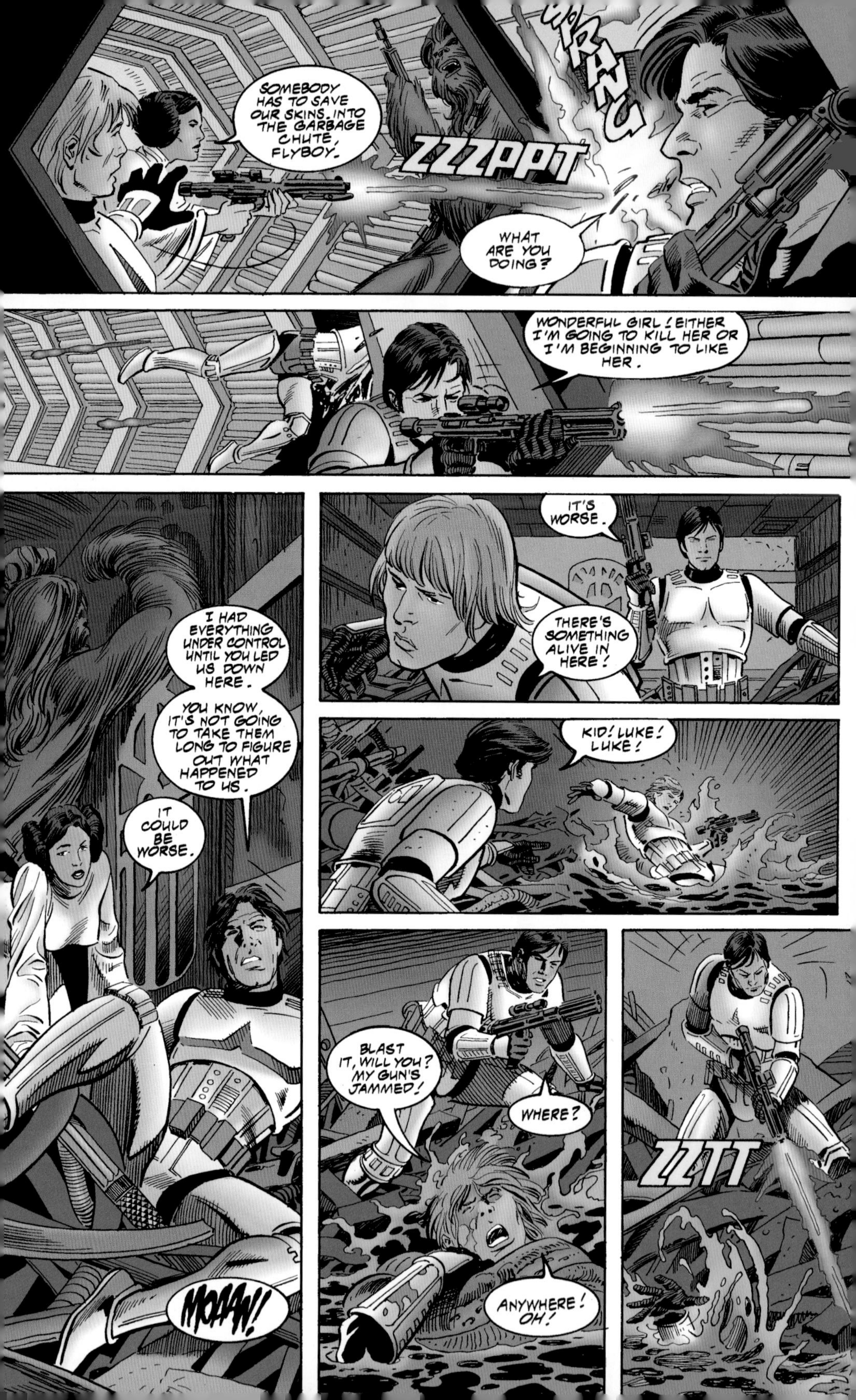
WRANG
SOMEBODY HAS TO SAVE OUR SKINS. INTO THE GARBAGE CHUTE, FLYBOY.
ZZZPPT
WHAT ARE YOU DOING?
WONDERFUL GIRL! EITHER I'M GOING TO KILL HER OR I'M BEGINNING TO LIKE HER.
I HAD EVERYTHING UNDER CONTROL UNTIL YOU LED US DOWN HERE.
YOU KNOW, IT'S NOT GOING TO TAKE THEM LONG TO FIGURE OUT WHAT HAPPENED TO US.
IT COULD BE WORSE.
MOAAN!
IT'S WORSE.
THERE'S SOMETHING ALIVE IN HERE!
KID! LUKE! LUKE!
BLAST IT, WILL YOU? MY GUN'S JAMMED!
WHERE?
ANYWHERE! OH!
ZZTT

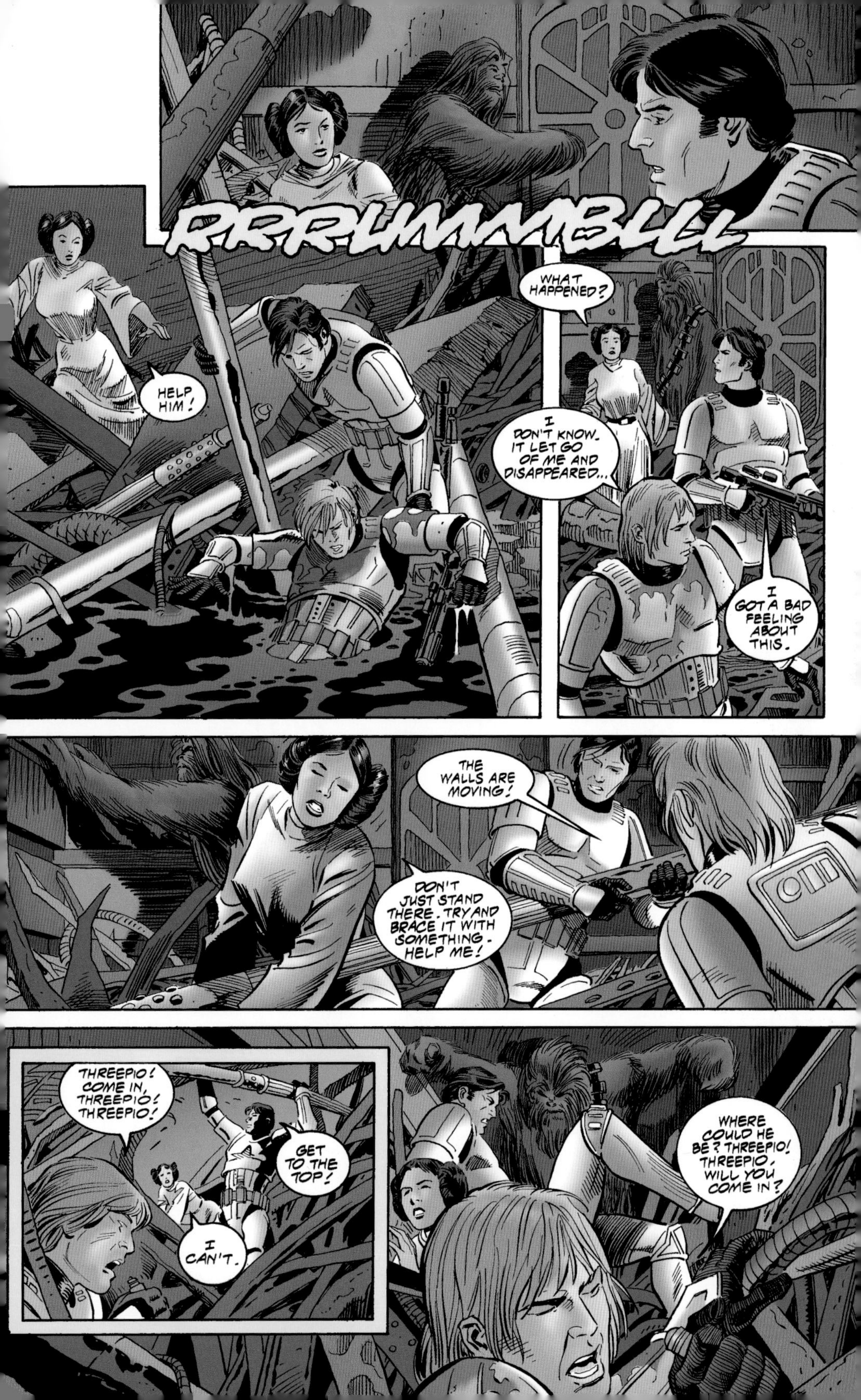
RRRUMMBLL
HELP HIM!
WHAT HAPPENED?
I DON'T KNOW. IT LET GO OF ME AND DISAPPEARED...
I GOT A BAD FEELING ABOUT THIS.
THE WALLS ARE MOVING!
DON'T JUST STAND THERE. TRY AND BRACE IT WITH SOMETHING. HELP ME!
THREEPIO! COME IN, THREEPIO! THREEPIO!
GET TO THE TOP!
I CAN'T.
WHERE COULD HE BE? THREEPIO! THREEPIO, WILL YOU COME IN?

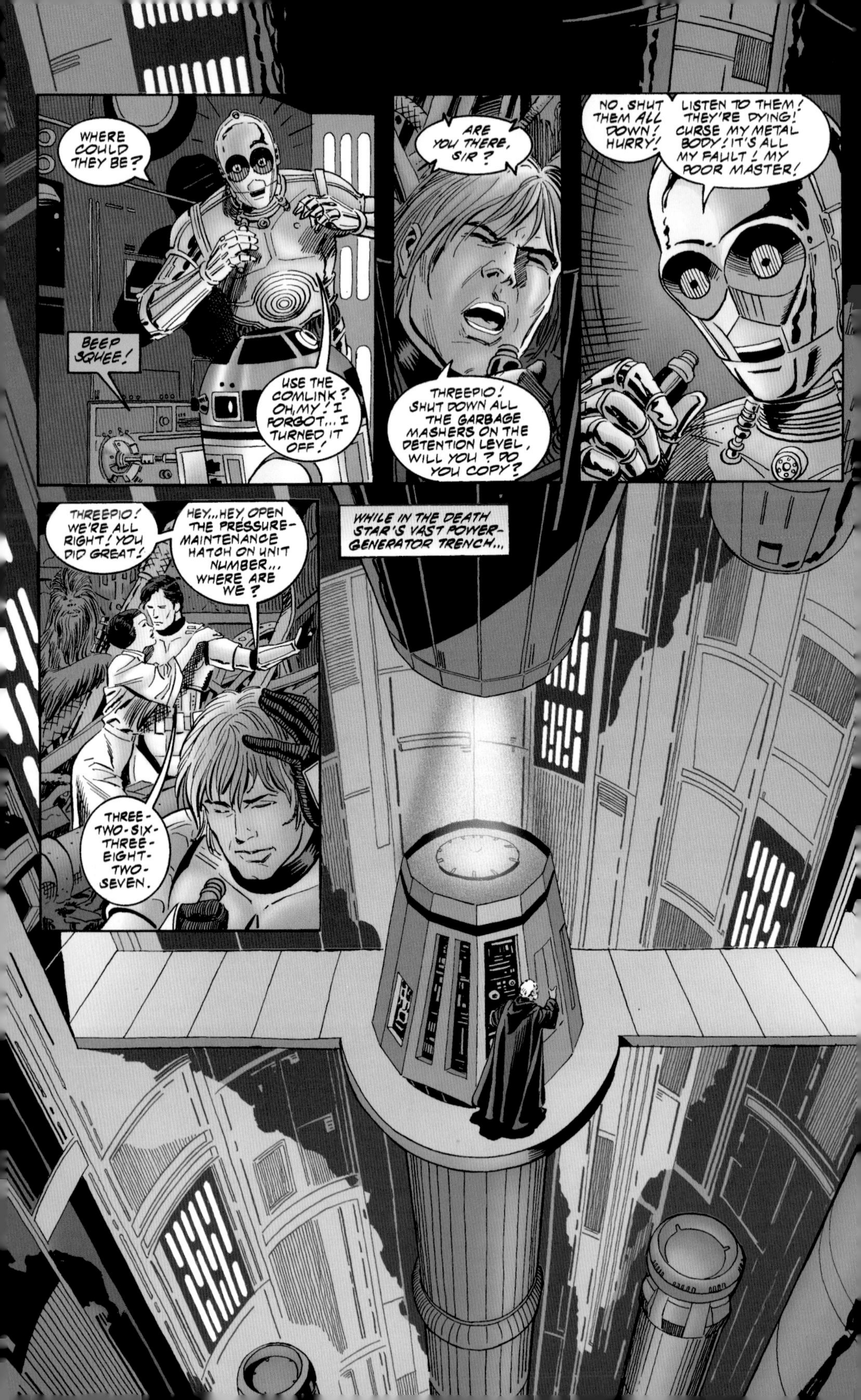
WHERE COULD THEY BE?
BEEP SQUEE!
USE THE COMLINK? OH, MY! I FORGOT... I TURNED IT OFF!
ARE YOU THERE, SIR?
THREEPIO! SHUT DOWN ALL THE GARBAGE MASHERS ON THE DETENTION LEVEL, WILL YOU? DO YOU COPY?
NO. SHUT THEM ALL DOWN! HURRY!
LISTEN TO THEM! THEY'RE DYING! CURSE MY METAL BODY! IT'S ALL MY FAULT! MY POOR MASTER!
THREEPIO! WE'RE ALL RIGHT! YOU DID GREAT!
HEY...HEY, OPEN THE PRESSURE-MAINTENANCE HATCH ON UNIT NUMBER... WHERE ARE WE?
THREE-TWO-SIX-THREE-EIGHT-TWO-SEVEN.
WHILE IN THE DEATH STAR'S VAST POWER-GENERATOR TRENCH...

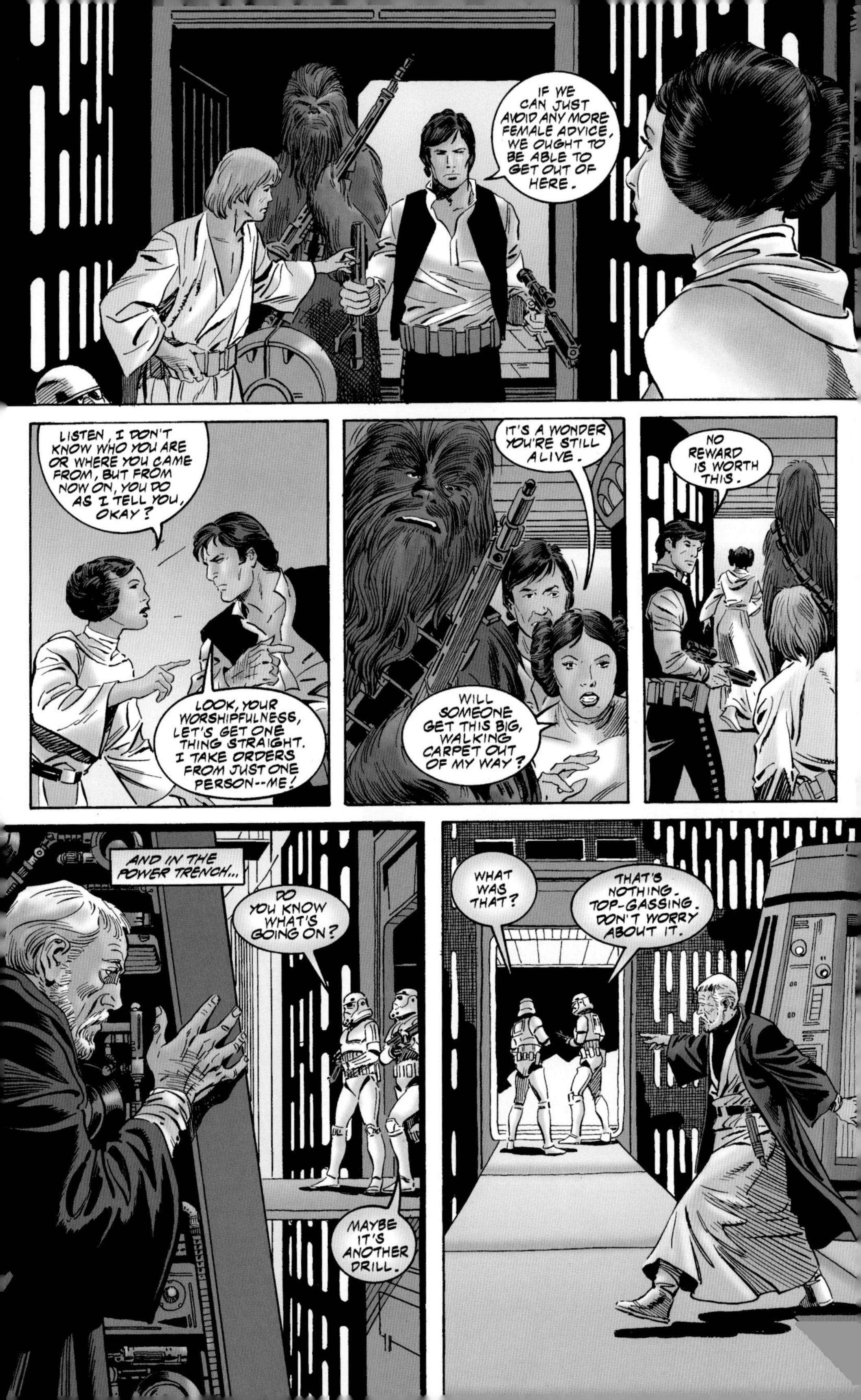
IF WE CAN JUST AVOID ANY MORE FEMALE ADVICE, WE OUGHT TO BE ABLE TO GET OUT OF HERE.
LISTEN, I DON'T KNOW WHO YOU ARE OR WHERE YOU CAME FROM, BUT FROM NOW ON, YOU DO AS I TELL YOU, OKAY?
LOOK, YOUR WORSHIPFULNESS, LET'S GET ONE THING STRAIGHT. I TAKE ORDERS FROM JUST ONE PERSON--ME!
IT'S A WONDER YOU'RE STILL ALIVE.
WILL SOMEONE GET THIS BIG, WALKING CARPET OUT OF MY WAY?
NO REWARD IS WORTH THIS.
AND IN THE POWER TRENCH...
DO YOU KNOW WHAT'S GOING ON?
MAYBE IT'S ANOTHER DRILL.
WHAT WAS THAT?
THAT'S NOTHING. TOP-GASSING. DON'T WORRY ABOUT IT.

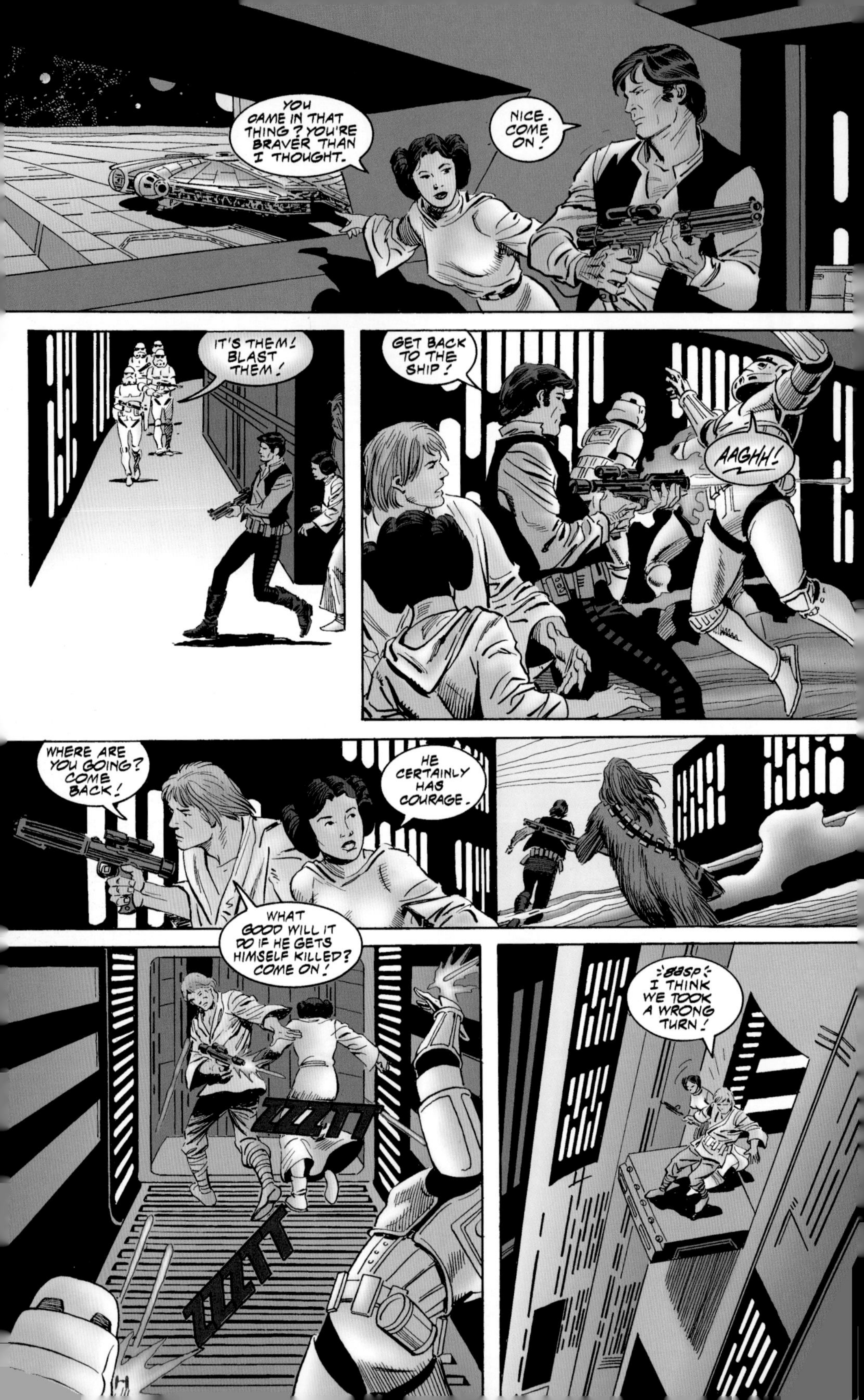
YOU CAME IN THAT THING? YOU'RE BRAVER THAN I THOUGHT.
NICE. COME ON!
IT'S THEM! BLAST THEM!
GET BACK TO THE SHIP!
AAGHH!
WHERE ARE YOU GOING? COME BACK!
HE CERTAINLY HAS COURAGE.
WHAT GOOD WILL IT DO IF HE GETS HIMSELF KILLED? COME ON!
TZZZT
TZZZT
TZZZT
BBSP
I THINK WE TOOK A WRONG TURN!

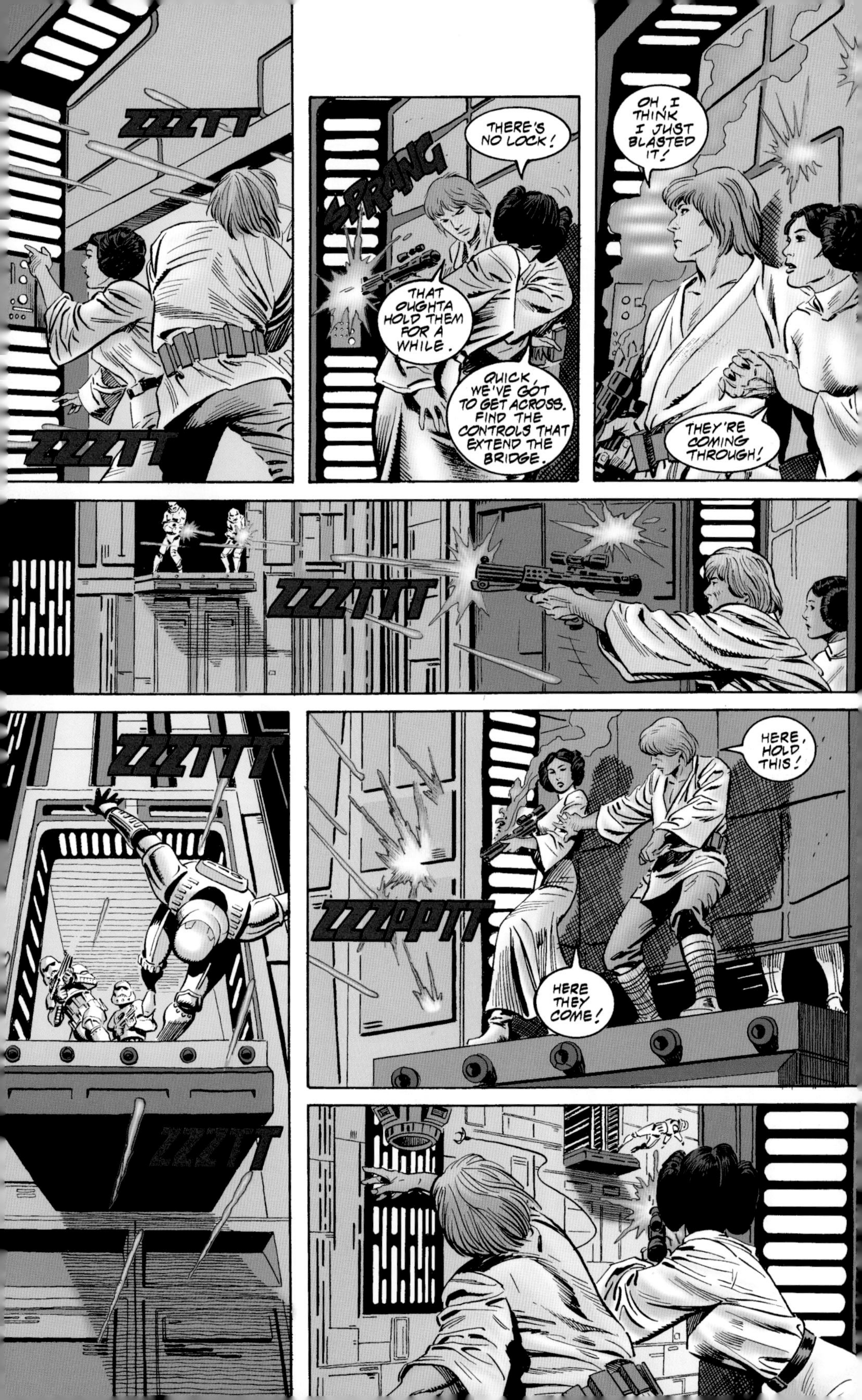
ZZZTT
ZZZTT
SPRANG
THERE'S NO LOCK!
THAT OUGHTA HOLD THEM FOR A WHILE.
QUICK, WE'VE GOT TO GET ACROSS. FIND THE CONTROLS THAT EXTEND THE BRIDGE.
OH, I THINK I JUST BLASTED IT!
THEY'RE COMING THROUGH!
ZZZTTT
ZZZTTT
ZZZTT
HERE, HOLD THIS!
ZZZAPTT
HERE THEY COME!

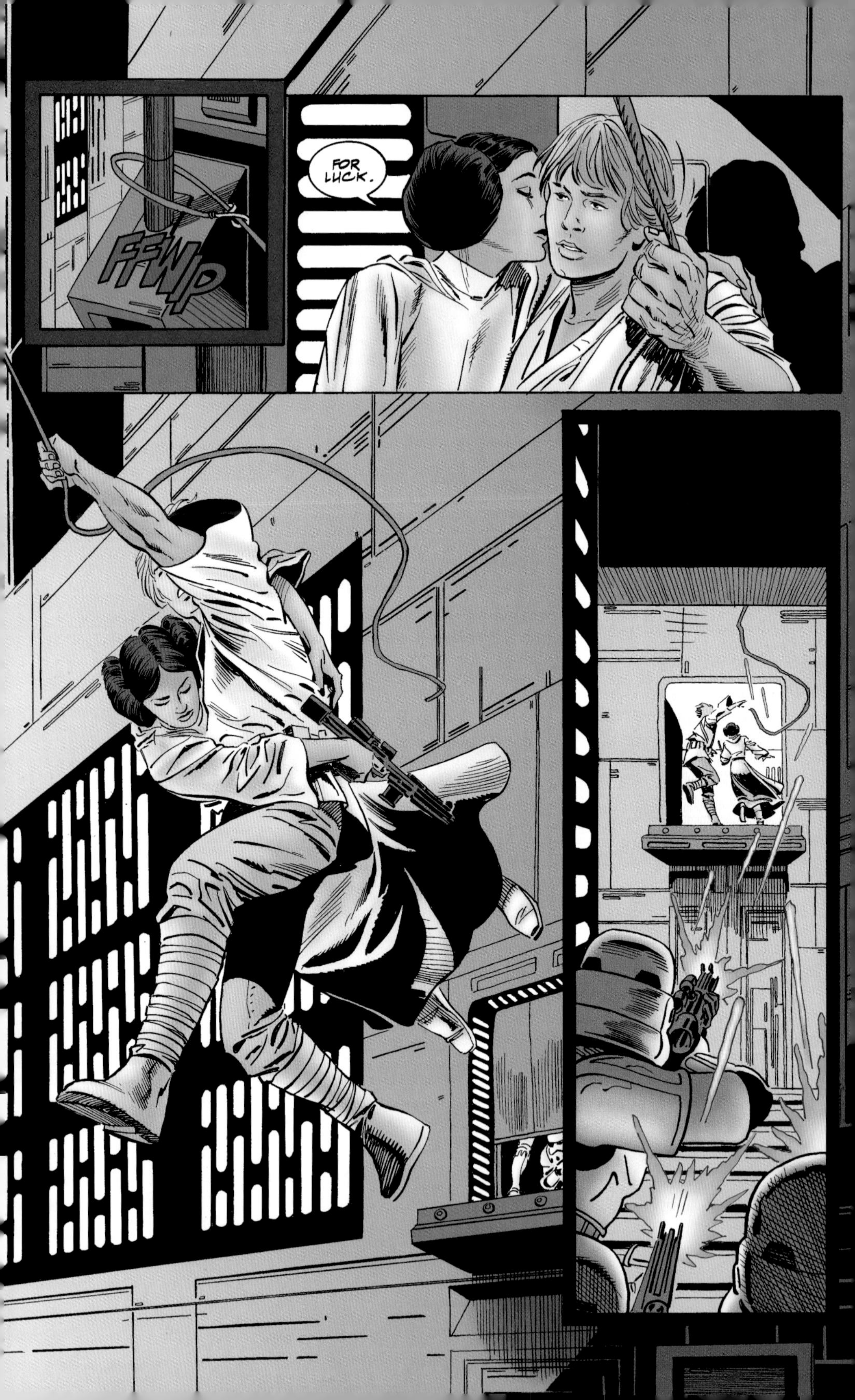
FFWIP
FOR LUCK.

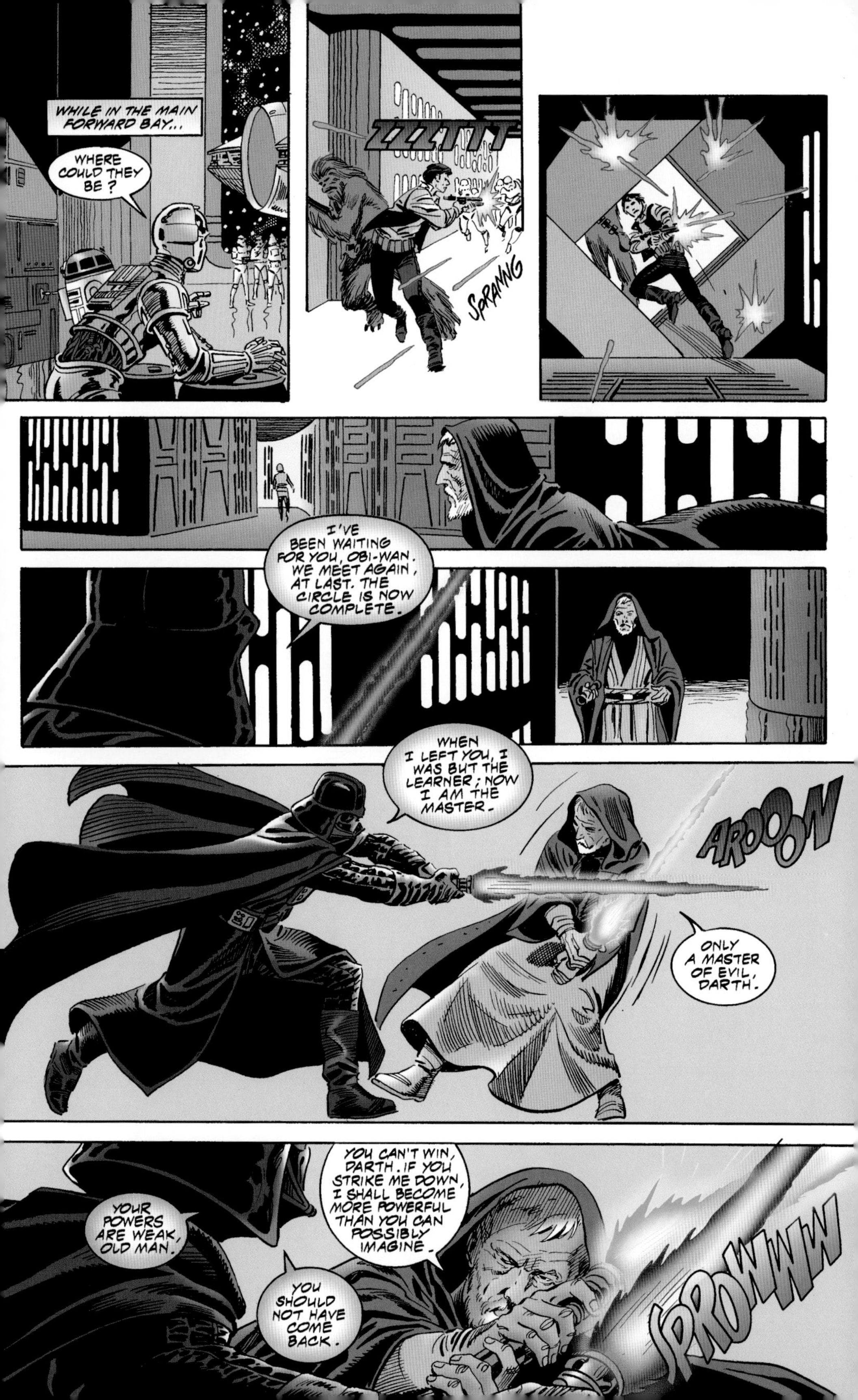
WHILE IN THE MAIN FORWARD BAY...
WHERE COULD THEY BE ?
ZZZTTT
SPRANNG
I'VE BEEN WAITING FOR YOU, OBI-WAN. WE MEET AGAIN, AT LAST. THE CIRCLE IS NOW COMPLETE.
WHEN I LEFT YOU, I WAS BUT THE LEARNER ; NOW I AM THE MASTER.
AROOOON
ONLY A MASTER OF EVIL, DARTH.
YOUR POWERS ARE WEAK, OLD MAN.
YOU CAN'T WIN, DARTH. IF YOU STRIKE ME DOWN, I SHALL BECOME MORE POWERFUL THAN YOU CAN POSSIBLY IMAGINE.
YOU SHOULD NOT HAVE COME BACK.
SPROWWW

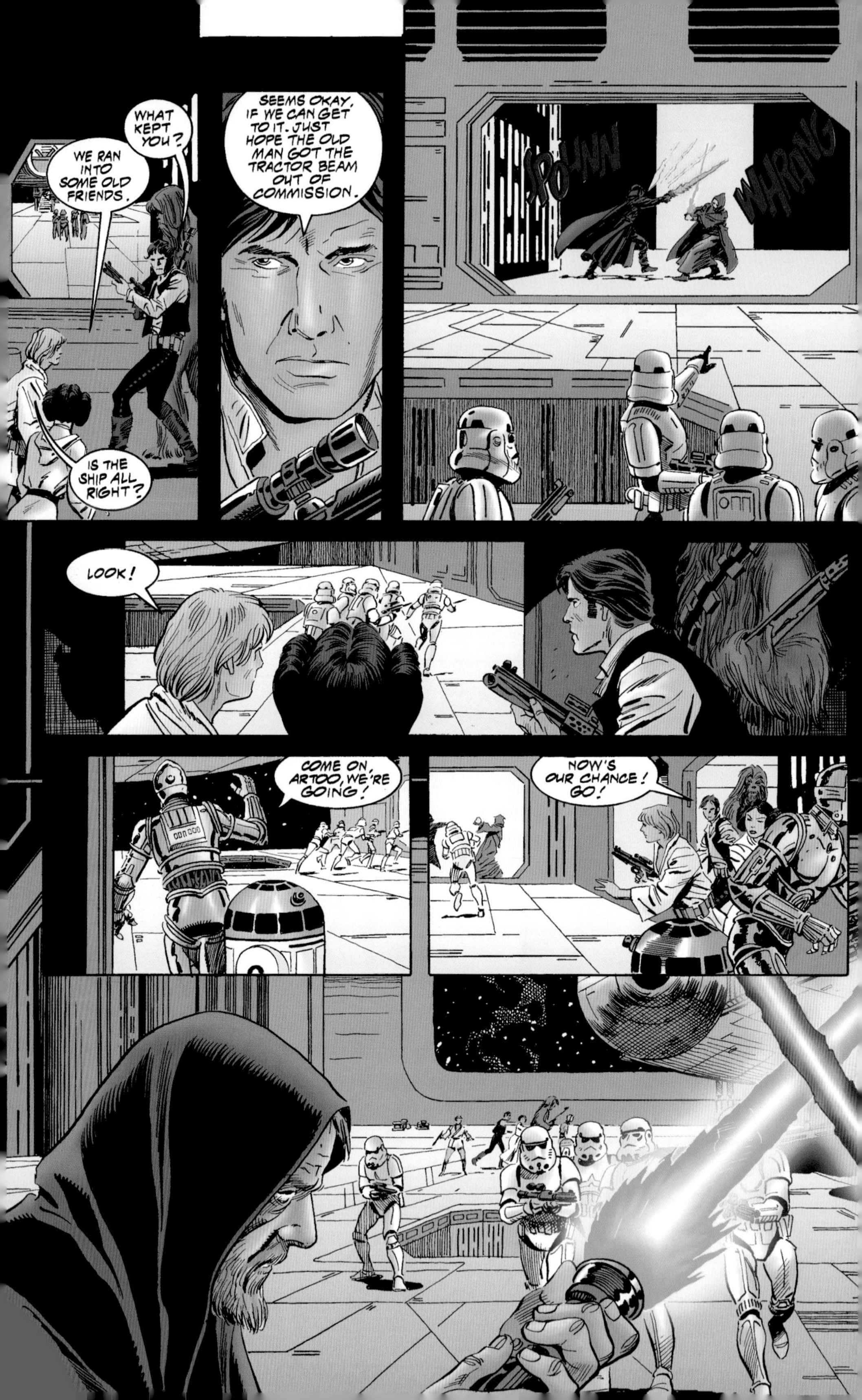
WHAT KEPT YOU?
WE RAN INTO SOME OLD FRIENDS.
IS THE SHIP ALL RIGHT?
SEEMS OKAY, IF WE CAN GET TO IT. JUST HOPE THE OLD MAN GOT THE TRACTOR BEAM OUT OF COMMISSION.
SPONN
WHRONG
LOOK!
COME ON, ARTOO, WE'RE GOING!
NOW'S OUR CHANCE! GO!

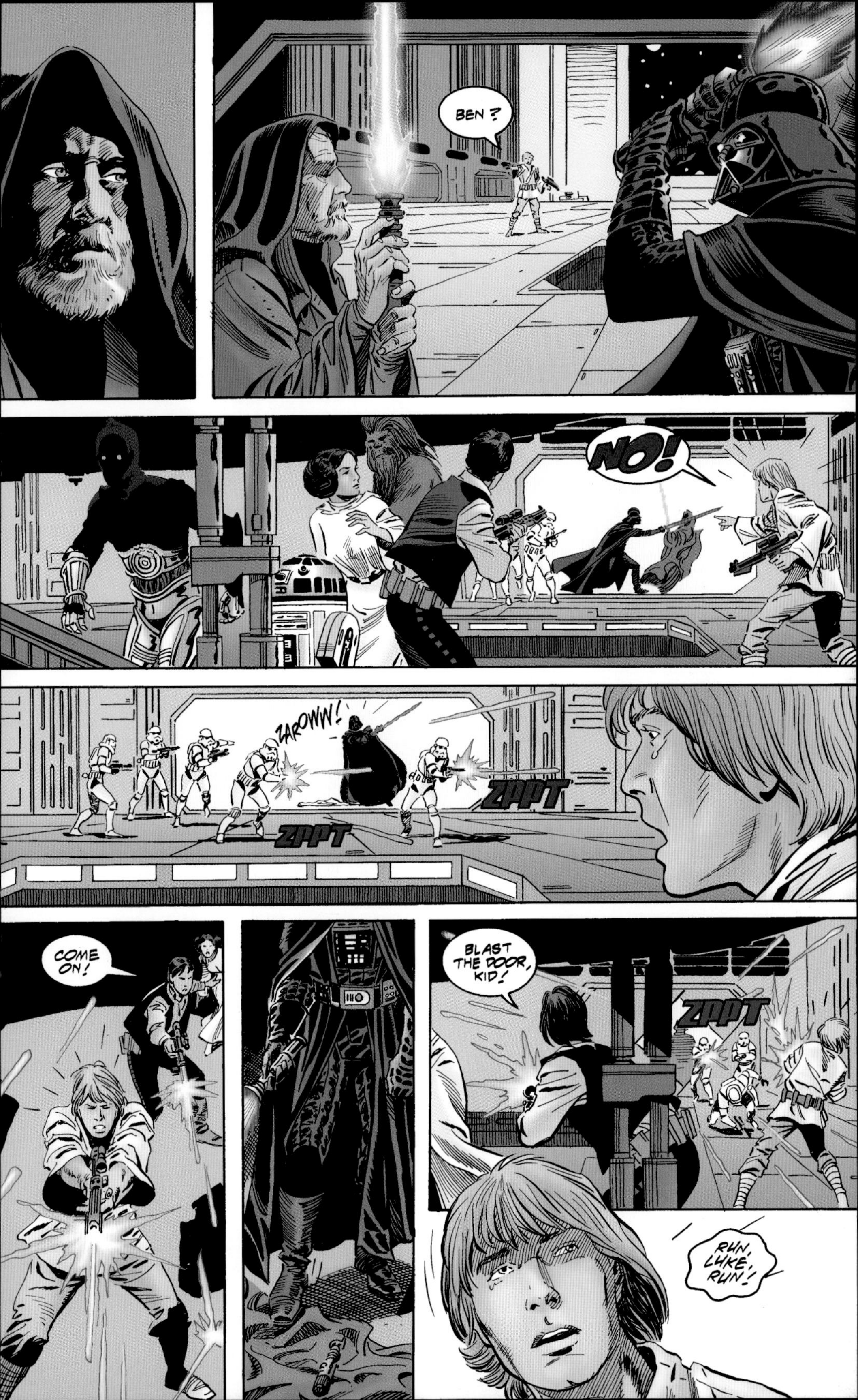
BEN ?
NO!
ZAROWW!
ZPPT
ZPPT
COME ON!
BLAST THE DOOR, KID!
ZPPT
RUN, LUKE, RUN!

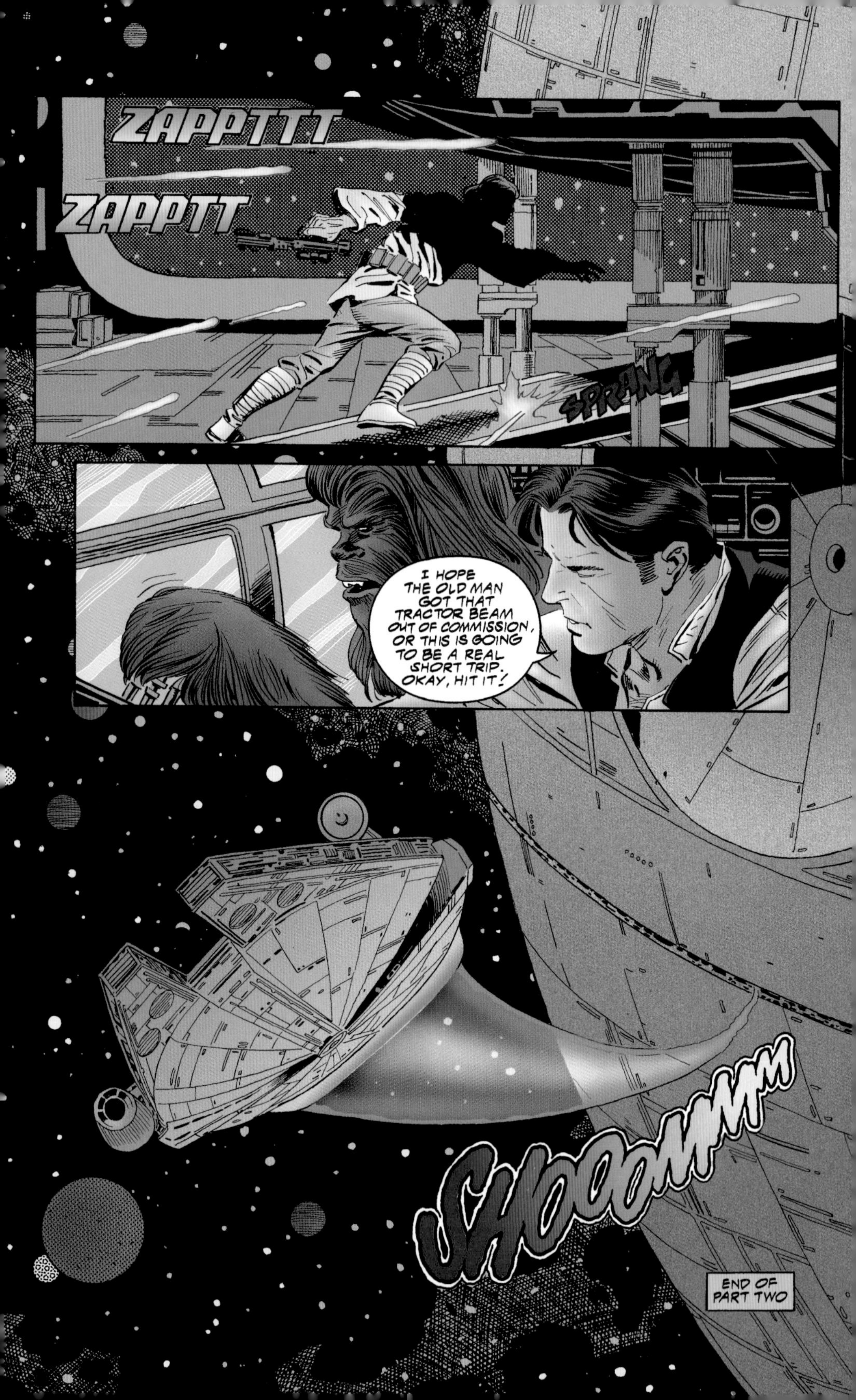
ZAPPTTT
ZAPPTT
SPRANG
I HOPE THE OLD MAN GOT THAT TRACTOR BEAM OUT OF COMMISSION, OR THIS IS GOING TO BE A REAL SHORT TRIP. OKAY, HIT IT!
SHOOOMMM
END OF PART TWO

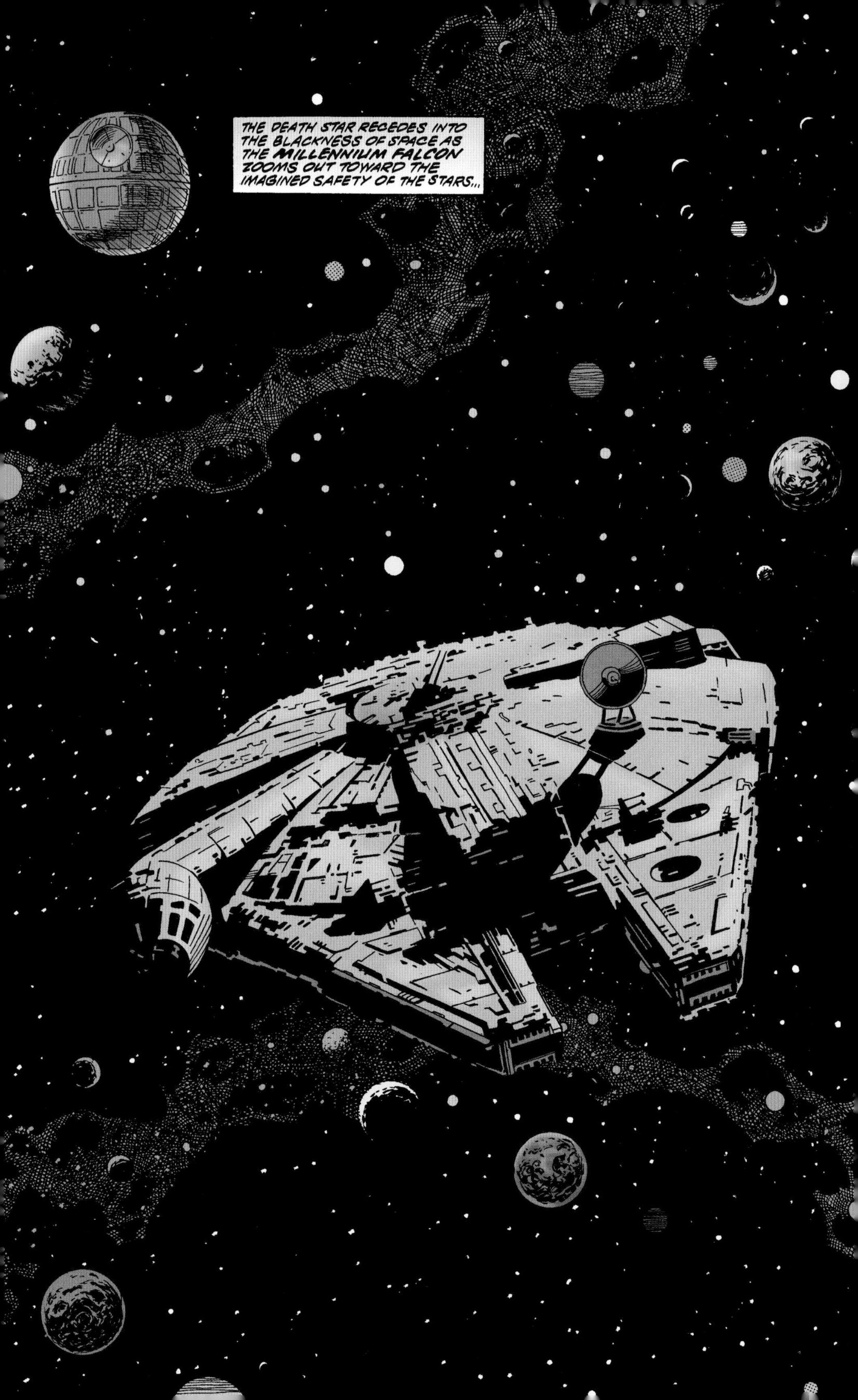
THE DEATH STAR RECEDES INTO THE BLACKNESS OF SPACE AS THE MILLENNIUM FALCON ZOOMS OUT TOWARD THE IMAGINED SAFETY OF THE STARS...

LUKE SKYWALKER, SADDENED BY THE LOSS OF OBI-WAN KENOBI, STARES OFF INTO SPACE...

WE'RE COMING UP ON THEIR SENTRY SHIPS.

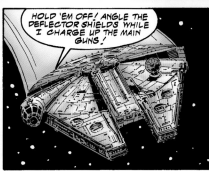

HOLD 'EM OFF! ANGLE THE DEFLECTOR SHIELDS WHILE I CHARGE UP THE MAIN GUNS!

I CAN'T BELIEVE HE'S GONE.

THERE WASN'T ANYTHING YOU COULD HAVE DONE.

COME ON, BUDDY, WE'RE NOT OUT OF THIS YET!

YOU IN, KID? OKAY, STAY SHARP!

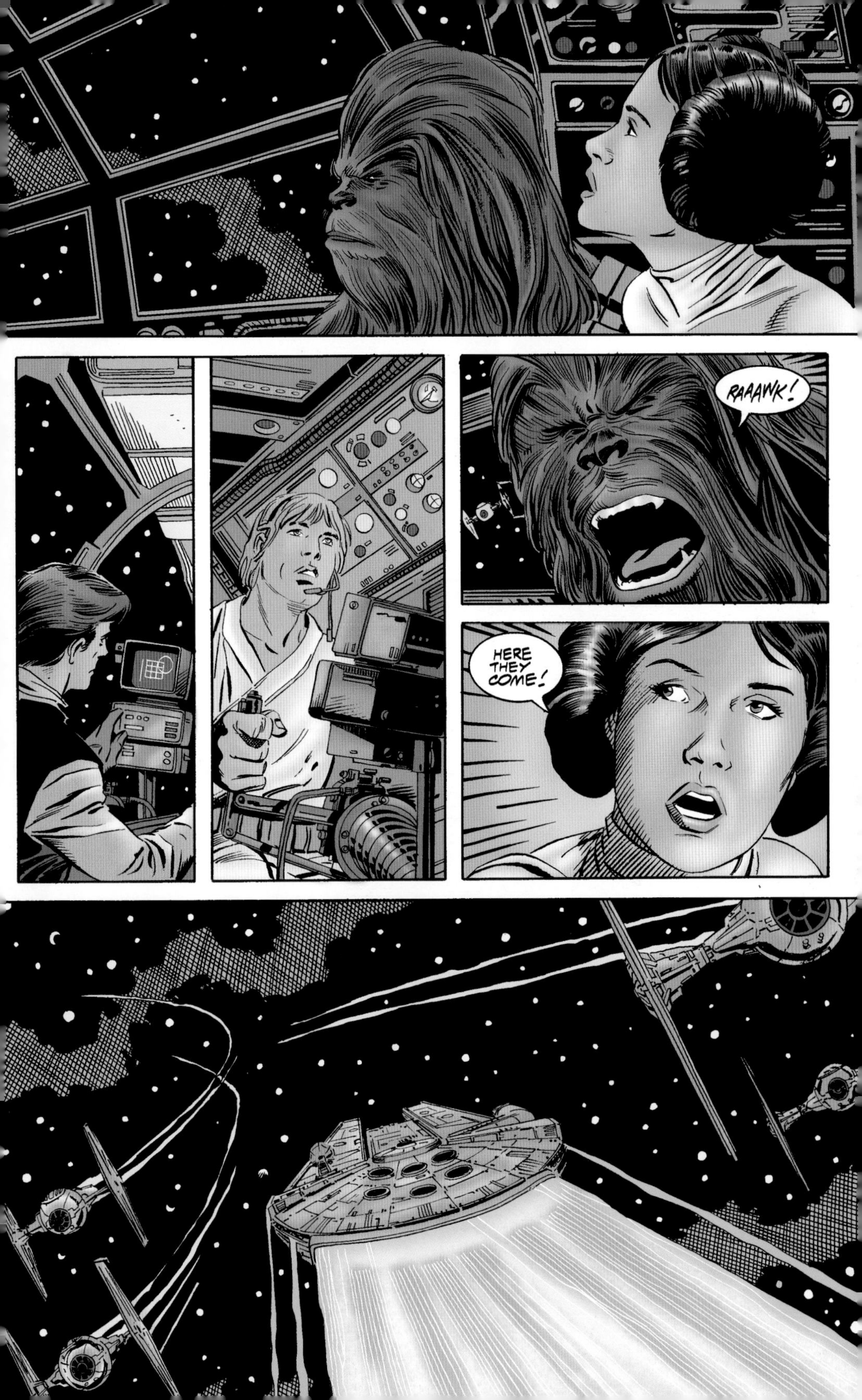
RAAAWK!
HERE THEY COME!

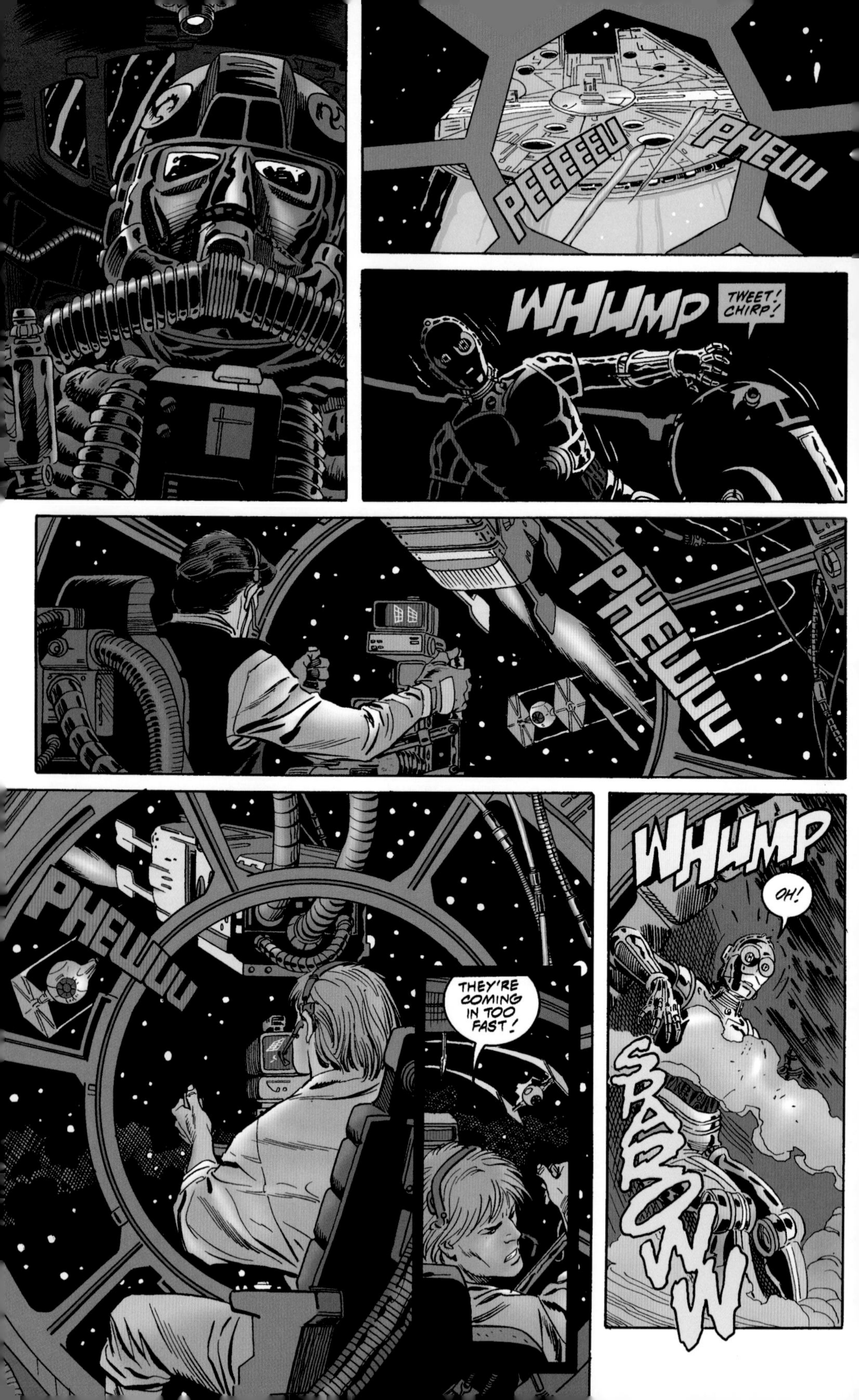
PEEEEEU
PHEUU
WHUMP
TWEET! CHIRP!
PHEUUU
PHEUUU
THEY'RE COMING IN TOO FAST!
WHUMP
OH!
SPABOWW

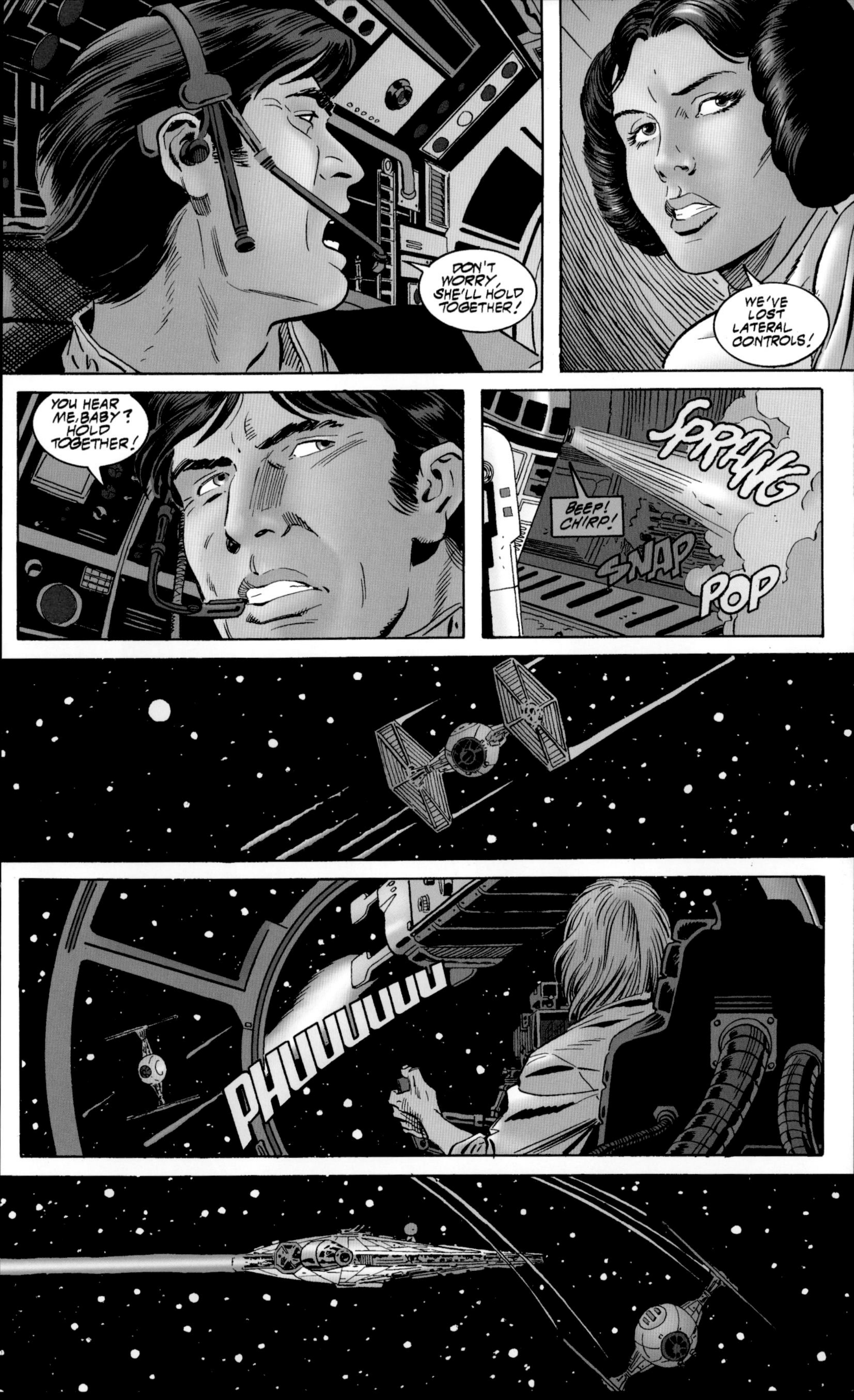
DON'T WORRY, SHE'LL HOLD TOGETHER!
WE'VE LOST LATERAL CONTROLS!
YOU HEAR ME, BABY? HOLD TOGETHER!
SPPANG
BEEP! CHIRP!
SNAP
POP
PHUUUUUU

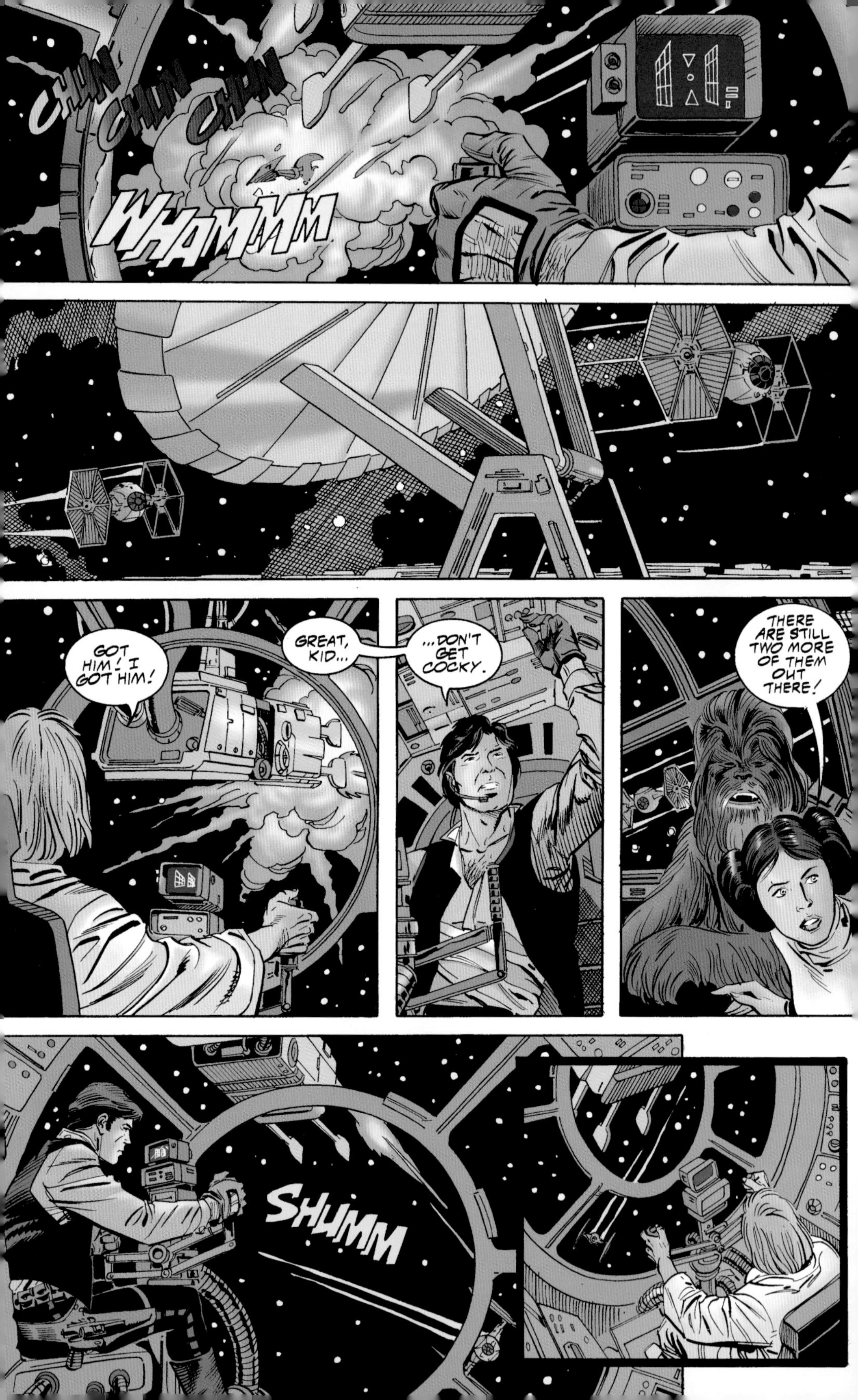
CHUN CHUN CHUN
WHAMMMM
GOT HIM! I GOT HIM!
GREAT, KID...
...DON'T GET COCKY.
THERE ARE STILL TWO MORE OF THEM OUT THERE!
SHUMM

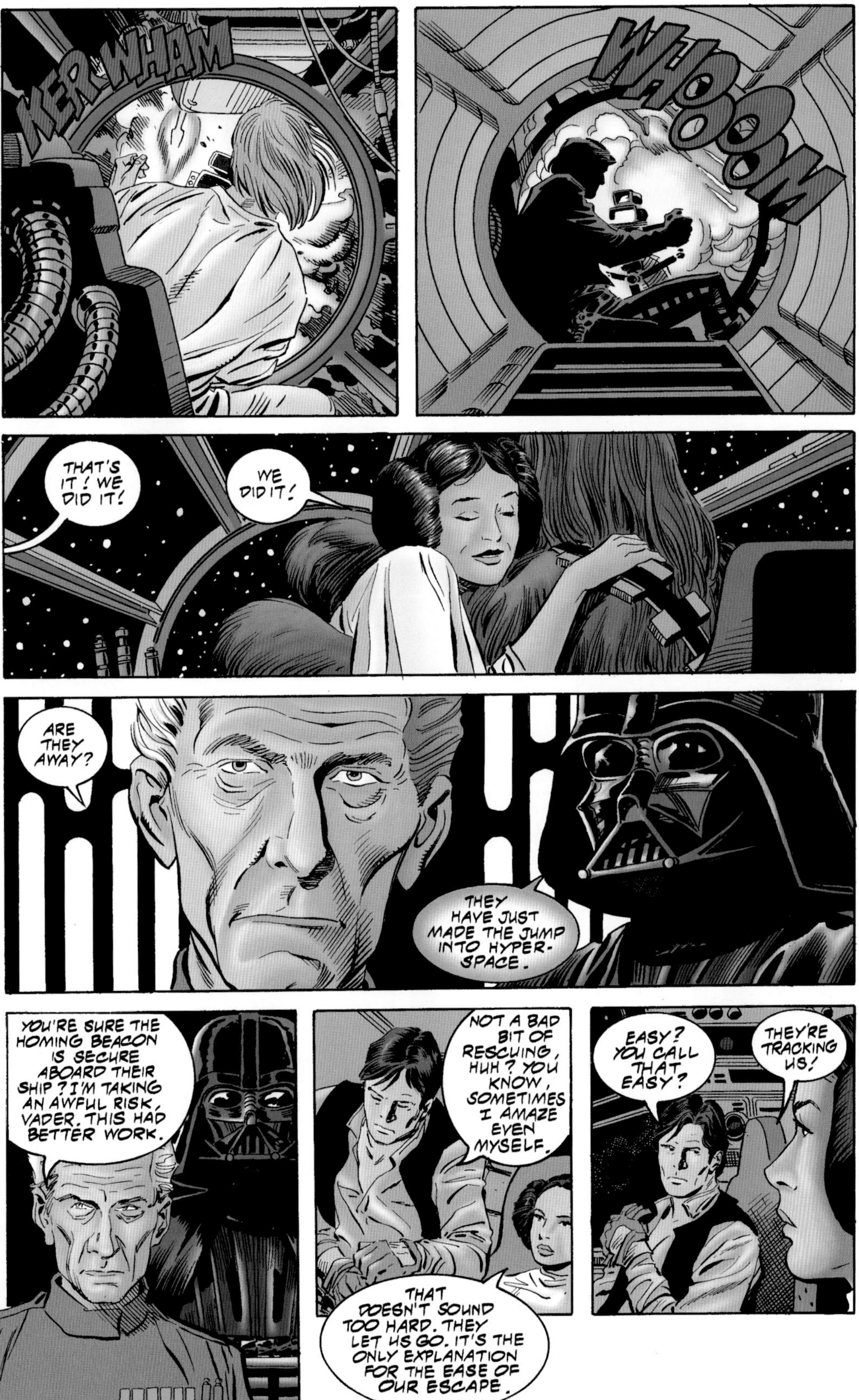
KER-WHAM
WHOOOM
THAT'S IT! WE DID IT!
WE DID IT!
ARE THEY AWAY?
THEY HAVE JUST MADE THE JUMP INTO HYPER-SPACE.
YOU'RE SURE THE HOMING BEACON IS SECURE ABOARD THEIR SHIP? I'M TAKING AN AWFUL RISK, VADER. THIS HAD BETTER WORK.
NOT A BAD BIT OF RESCUING, HUH? YOU KNOW, SOMETIMES I AMAZE EVEN MYSELF.
THAT DOESN'T SOUND TOO HARD. THEY LET US GO. IT'S THE ONLY EXPLANATION FOR THE EASE OF OUR ESCAPE.
EASY? YOU CALL THAT EASY?
THEY'RE TRACKING US!

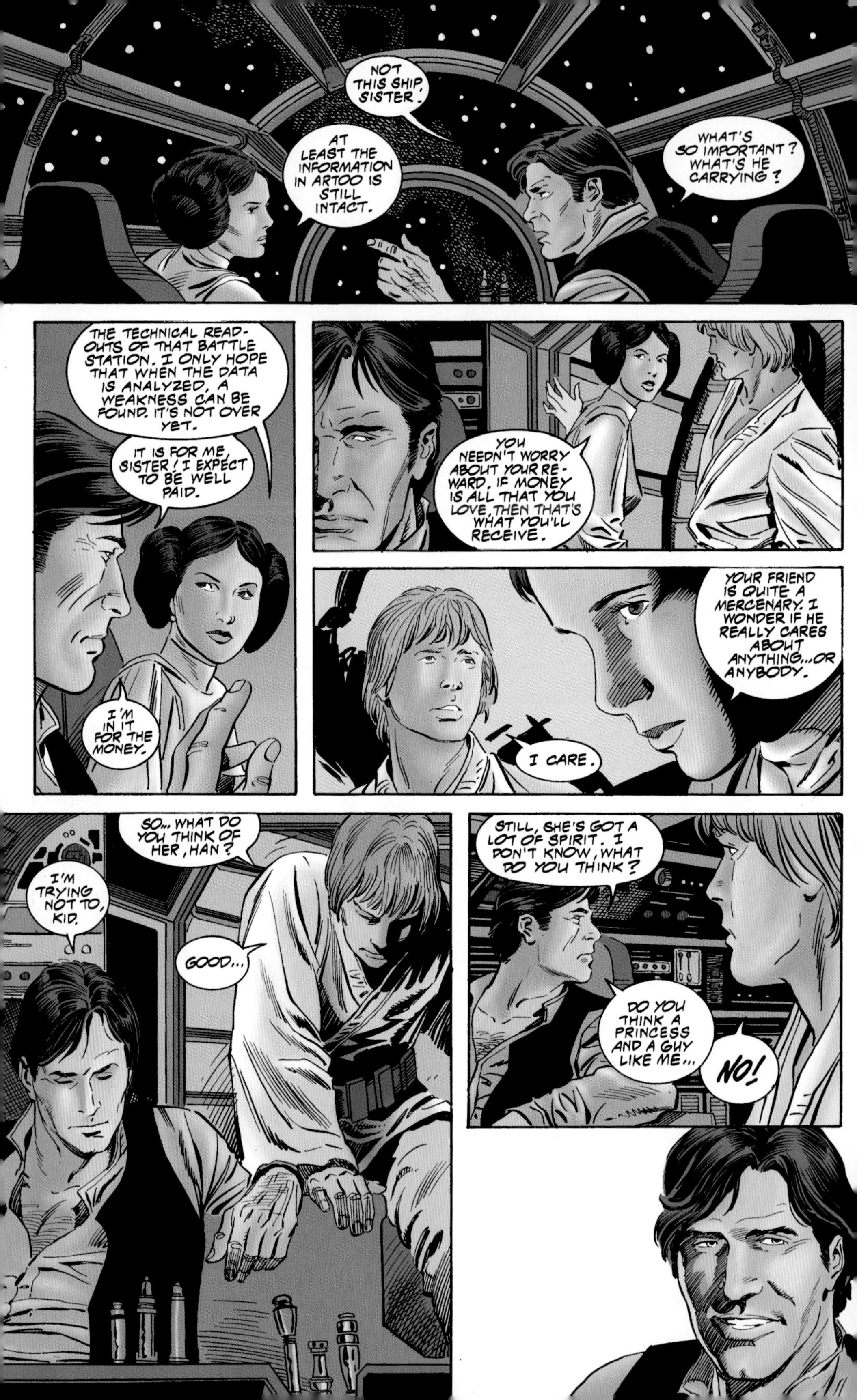

NOT THIS SHIP, SISTER.
AT LEAST THE INFORMATION IN ARTOO IS STILL INTACT.
WHAT'S SO IMPORTANT? WHAT'S HE CARRYING?
THE TECHNICAL READ-OUTS OF THAT BATTLE STATION. I ONLY HOPE THAT WHEN THE DATA IS ANALYZED, A WEAKNESS CAN BE FOUND. IT'S NOT OVER YET.
IT IS FOR ME, SISTER! I EXPECT TO BE WELL PAID.
I'M IN IT FOR THE MONEY.
YOU NEEDN'T WORRY ABOUT YOUR RE-WARD. IF MONEY IS ALL THAT YOU LOVE, THEN THAT'S WHAT YOU'LL RECEIVE.
YOUR FRIEND IS QUITE A MERCENARY. I WONDER IF HE REALLY CARES ABOUT ANYTHING...OR ANYBODY.
I CARE.
SO... WHAT DO YOU THINK OF HER, HAN?
I'M TRYING NOT TO, KID.
GOOD...
STILL, SHE'S GOT A LOT OF SPIRIT. I DON'T KNOW, WHAT DO YOU THINK?
DO YOU THINK A PRINCESS AND A GUY LIKE ME...
NO!

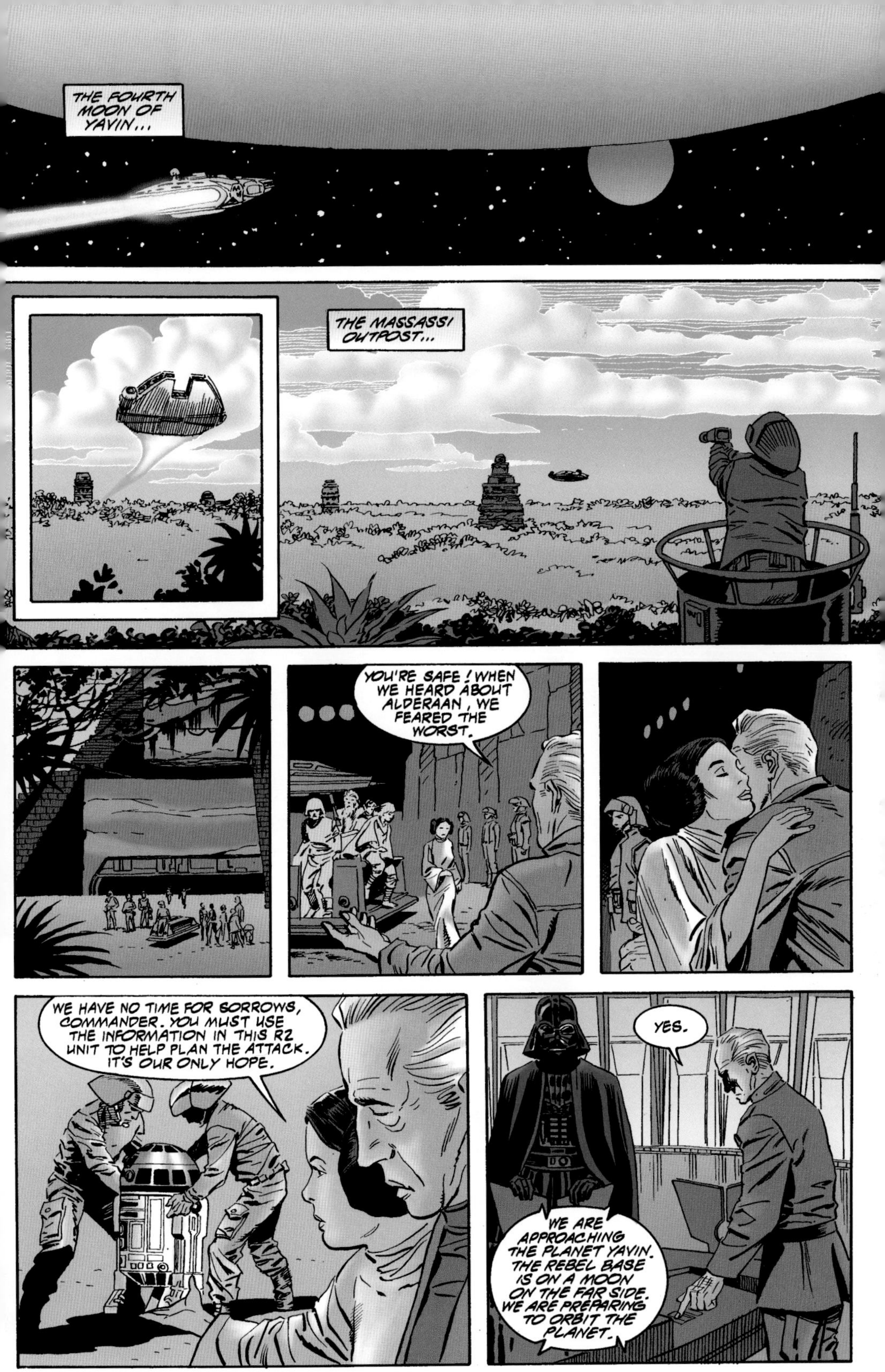
THE FOURTH MOON OF YAVIN...
THE MASSASSI OUTPOST...
YOU'RE SAFE! WHEN WE HEARD ABOUT ALDERAAN, WE FEARED THE WORST.
WE HAVE NO TIME FOR SORROWS, COMMANDER. YOU MUST USE THE INFORMATION IN THIS R2 UNIT TO HELP PLAN THE ATTACK. IT'S OUR ONLY HOPE.
YES.
WE ARE APPROACHING THE PLANET YAVIN. THE REBEL BASE IS ON A MOON ON THE FAR SIDE. WE ARE PREPARING TO ORBIT THE PLANET.

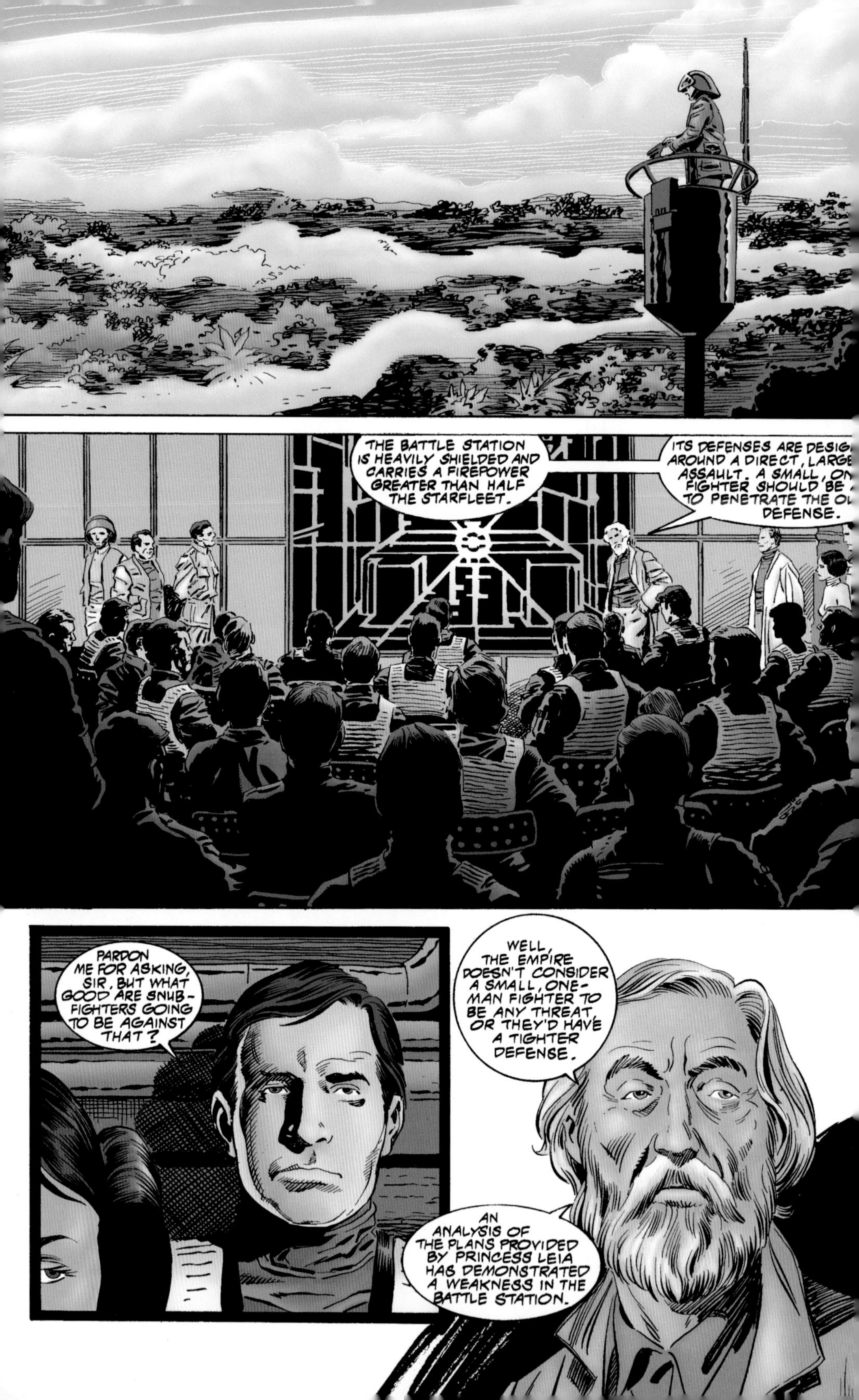
THE BATTLE STATION IS HEAVILY SHIELDED AND CARRIES A FIREPOWER GREATER THAN HALF THE STARFLEET.
ITS DEFENSES ARE DESIG AROUND A DIRECT, LARGE ASSAULT. A SMALL, ON FIGHTER SHOULD BE TO PENETRATE THE O DEFENSE.
PARDON ME FOR ASKING, SIR, BUT WHAT GOOD ARE SNUB-FIGHTERS GOING TO BE AGAINST THAT?
WELL, THE EMPIRE DOESN'T CONSIDER A SMALL, ONE-MAN FIGHTER TO BE ANY THREAT, OR THEY'D HAVE A TIGHTER DEFENSE.
AN ANALYSIS OF THE PLANS PROVIDED BY PRINCESS LEIA HAS DEMONSTRATED A WEAKNESS IN THE BATTLE STATION.

THE APPROACH WILL NOT BE EASY. YOU ARE REQUIRED TO MANEUVER STRAIGHT DOWN THIS TRENCH AND SKIM THE SURFACE TO THIS POINT...

...THE TARGET AREA IS ONLY TWO METERS WIDE. IT'S A SMALL, THERMAL-EXHAUST PORT, RIGHT BELOW THE MAIN PORT.

THE SHAFT LEADS DIRECTLY TO THE REACTOR SYSTEM.

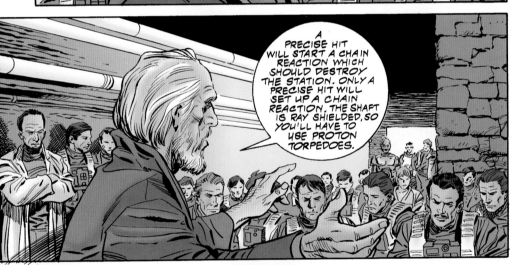

A PRECISE HIT WILL START A CHAIN REACTION WHICH SHOULD DESTROY THE STATION. ONLY A PRECISE HIT WILL SET UP A CHAIN REACTION. THE SHAFT IS RAY SHIELDED, SO YOU'LL HAVE TO USE PROTON TORPEDOES.

THAT'S IMPOSSIBLE, EVEN FOR A COMPUTER.

IT'S *NOT* IMPOSSIBLE.

I USED TO BULL'S-EYE WOMP RATS IN MY T-16 BACK HOME. THEY'RE NOT MUCH BIGGER THAN TWO METERS.

THEN MAN YOUR SHIPS! AND MAY THE FORCE BE WITH YOU!

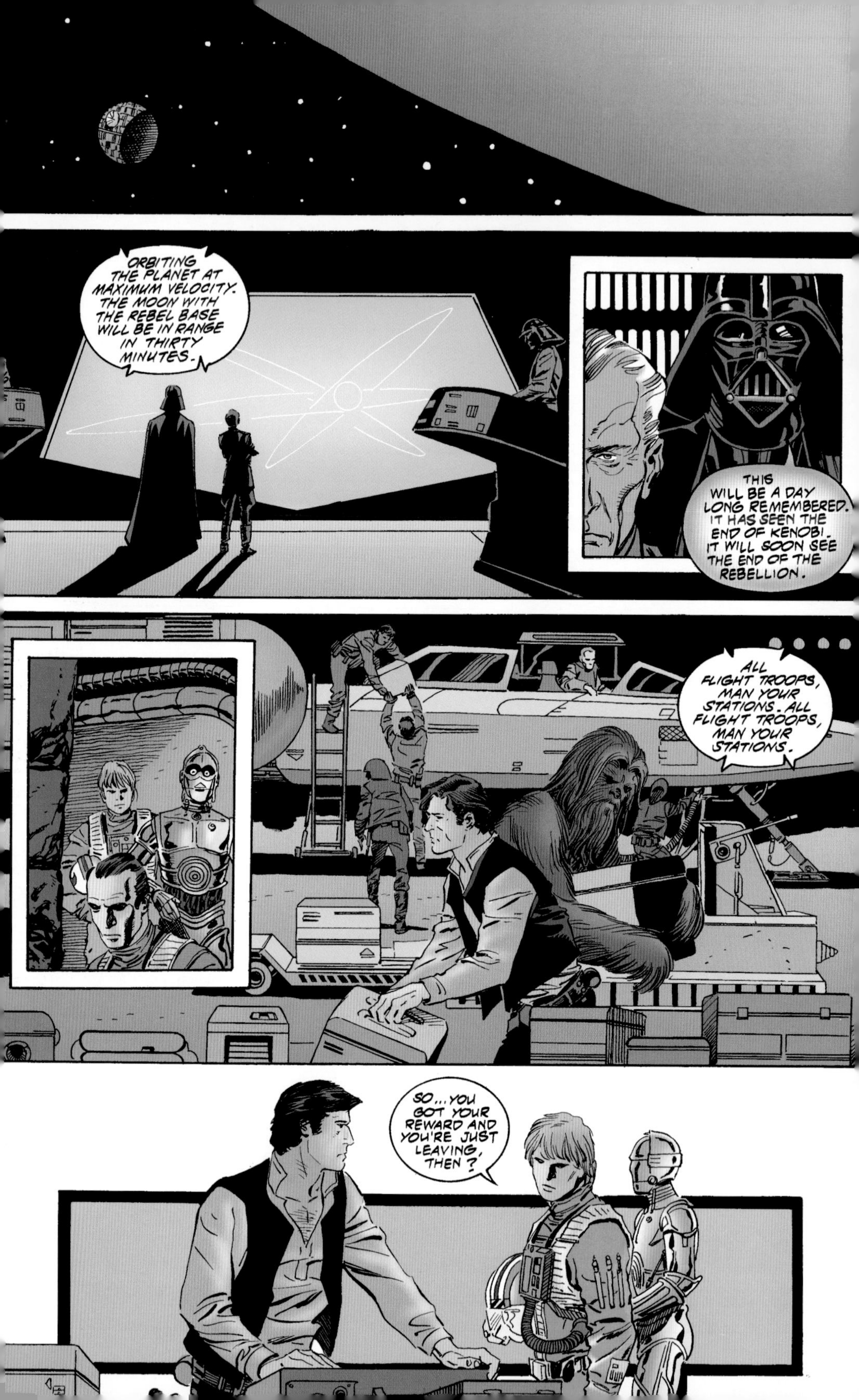

ORBITING THE PLANET AT MAXIMUM VELOCITY. THE MOON WITH THE REBEL BASE WILL BE IN RANGE IN THIRTY MINUTES.
THIS WILL BE A DAY LONG REMEMBERED. IT HAS SEEN THE END OF KENOBI. IT WILL SOON SEE THE END OF THE REBELLION.
ALL FLIGHT TROOPS, MAN YOUR STATIONS. ALL FLIGHT TROOPS, MAN YOUR STATIONS.
SO... YOU GOT YOUR REWARD AND YOU'RE JUST LEAVING, THEN?

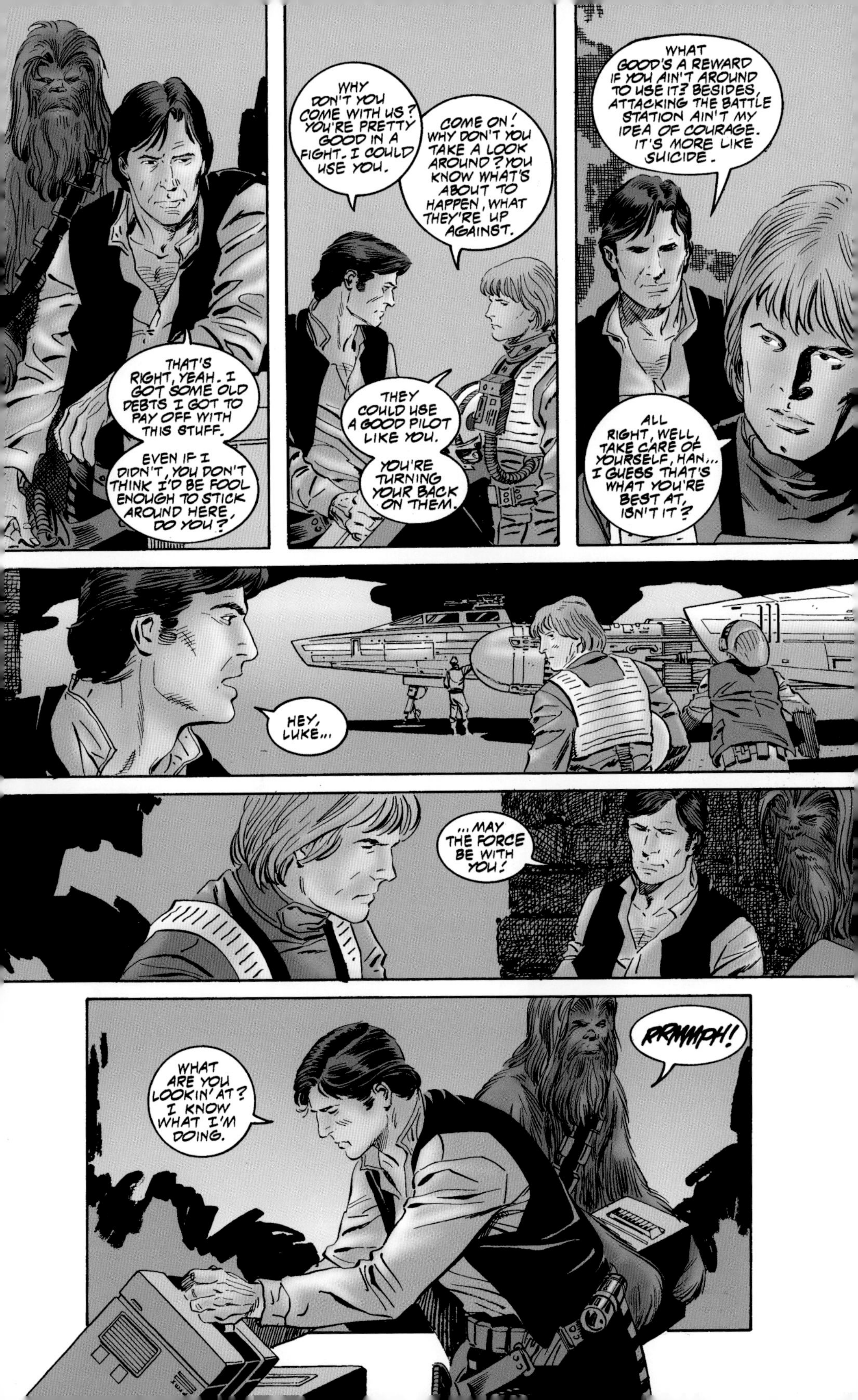
THAT'S RIGHT, YEAH. I GOT SOME OLD DEBTS I GOT TO PAY OFF WITH THIS STUFF.
EVEN IF I DIDN'T, YOU DON'T THINK I'D BE FOOL ENOUGH TO STICK AROUND HERE, DO YOU?
WHY DON'T YOU COME WITH US? YOU'RE PRETTY GOOD IN A FIGHT. I COULD USE YOU.
COME ON! WHY DON'T YOU TAKE A LOOK AROUND? YOU KNOW WHAT'S ABOUT TO HAPPEN, WHAT THEY'RE UP AGAINST.
THEY COULD USE A GOOD PILOT LIKE YOU.
YOU'RE TURNING YOUR BACK ON THEM.
WHAT GOOD'S A REWARD IF YOU AIN'T AROUND TO USE IT? BESIDES, ATTACKING THE BATTLE STATION AIN'T MY IDEA OF COURAGE. IT'S MORE LIKE SUICIDE.
ALL RIGHT, WELL, TAKE CARE OF YOURSELF, HAN... I GUESS THAT'S WHAT YOU'RE BEST AT, ISN'T IT?
HEY, LUKE...
...MAY THE FORCE BE WITH YOU!
WHAT ARE YOU LOOKIN' AT? I KNOW WHAT I'M DOING.
RRWWPH!

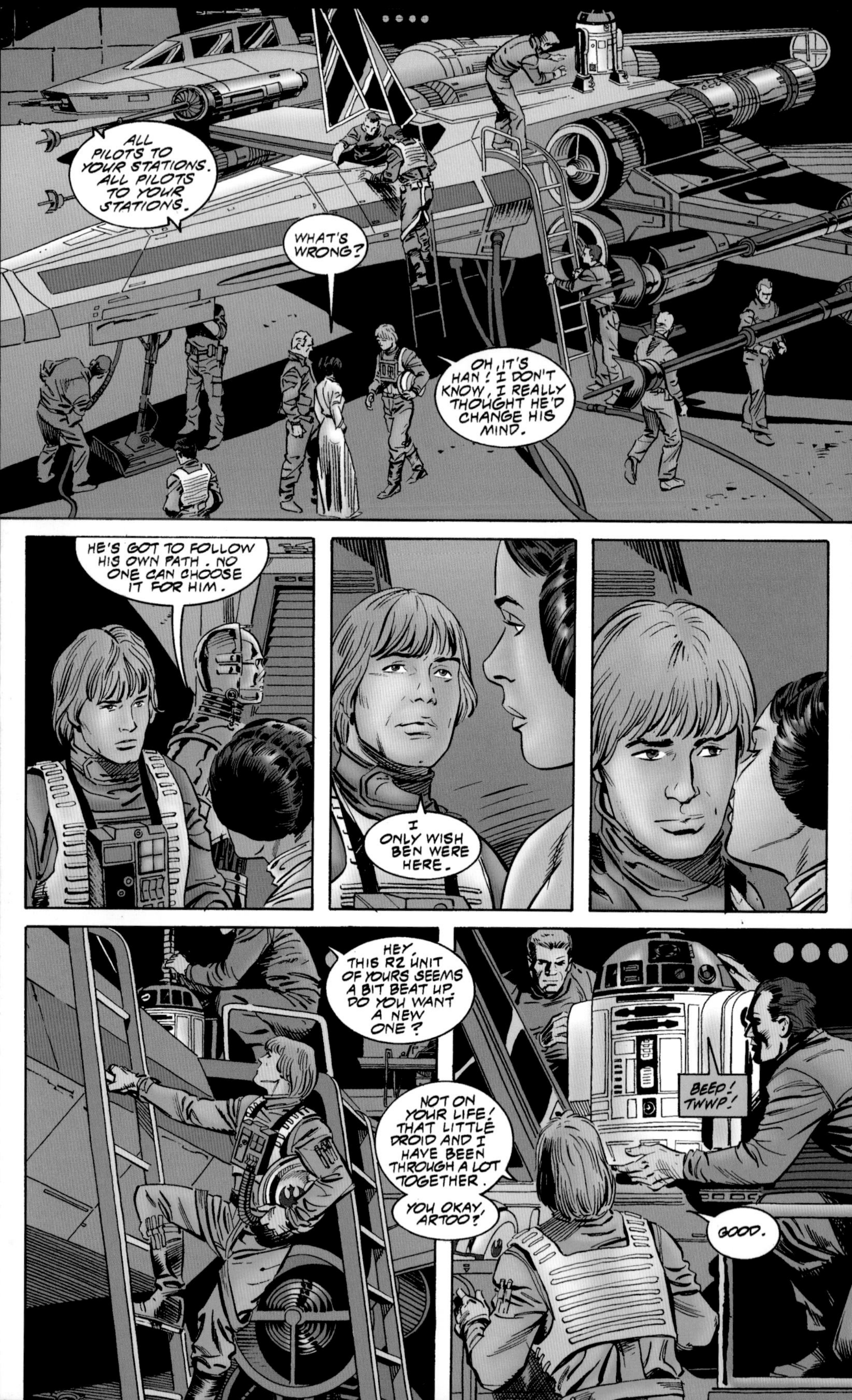
ALL PILOTS TO YOUR STATIONS. ALL PILOTS TO YOUR STATIONS.
WHAT'S WRONG?
OH, IT'S HAN! I DON'T KNOW, I REALLY THOUGHT HE'D CHANGE HIS MIND.
HE'S GOT TO FOLLOW HIS OWN PATH. NO ONE CAN CHOOSE IT FOR HIM.
I ONLY WISH BEN WERE HERE.
HEY, THIS R2 UNIT OF YOURS SEEMS A BIT BEAT UP. DO YOU WANT A NEW ONE?
NOT ON YOUR LIFE! THAT LITTLE DROID AND I HAVE BEEN THROUGH A LOT TOGETHER.
YOU OKAY, ARTOO?
BEEP! TWWP!
GOOD.

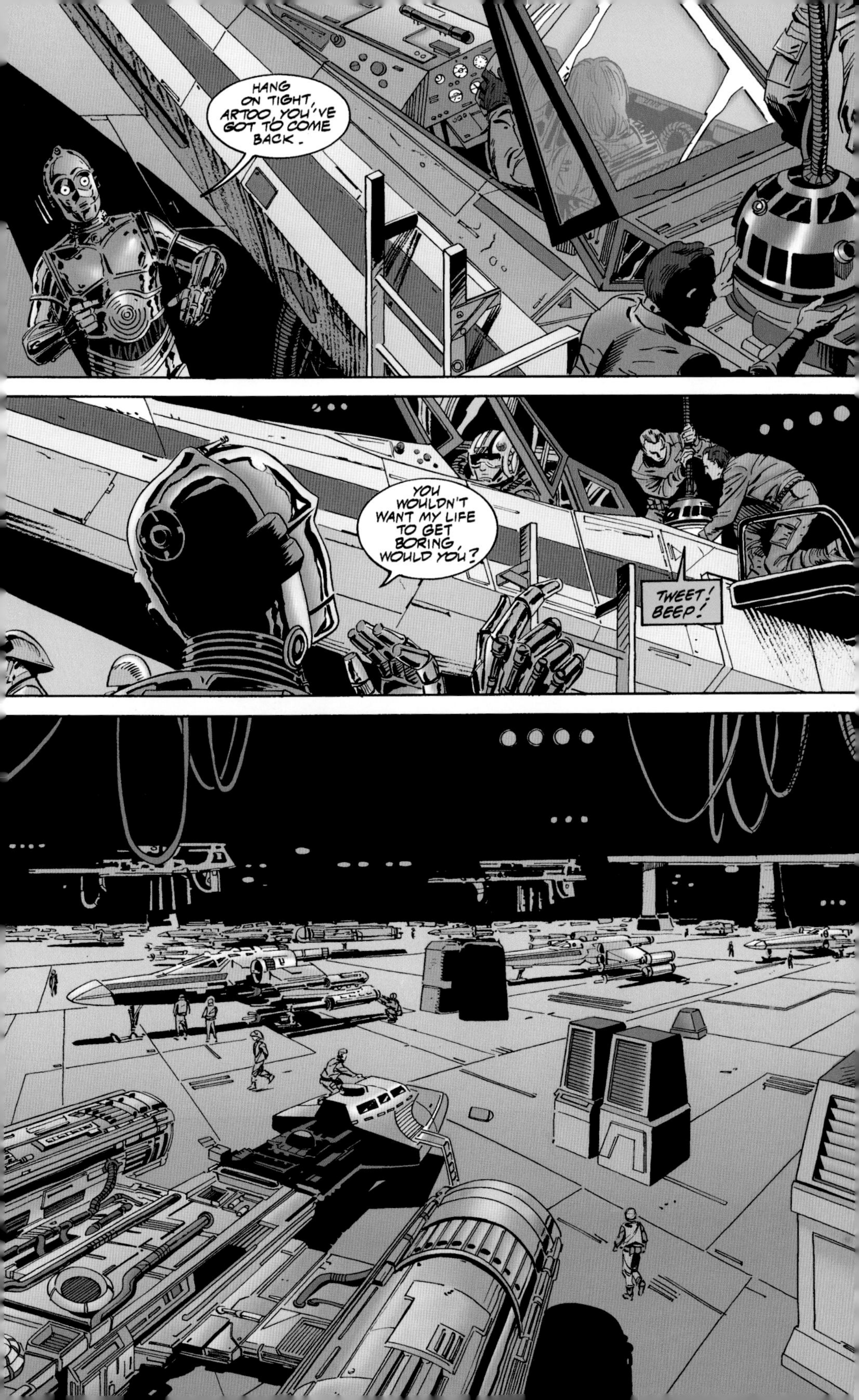
HANG ON TIGHT, ARTOO, YOU'VE GOT TO COME BACK.
YOU WOULDN'T WANT MY LIFE TO GET BORING, WOULD YOU?
TWEET! BEEP!

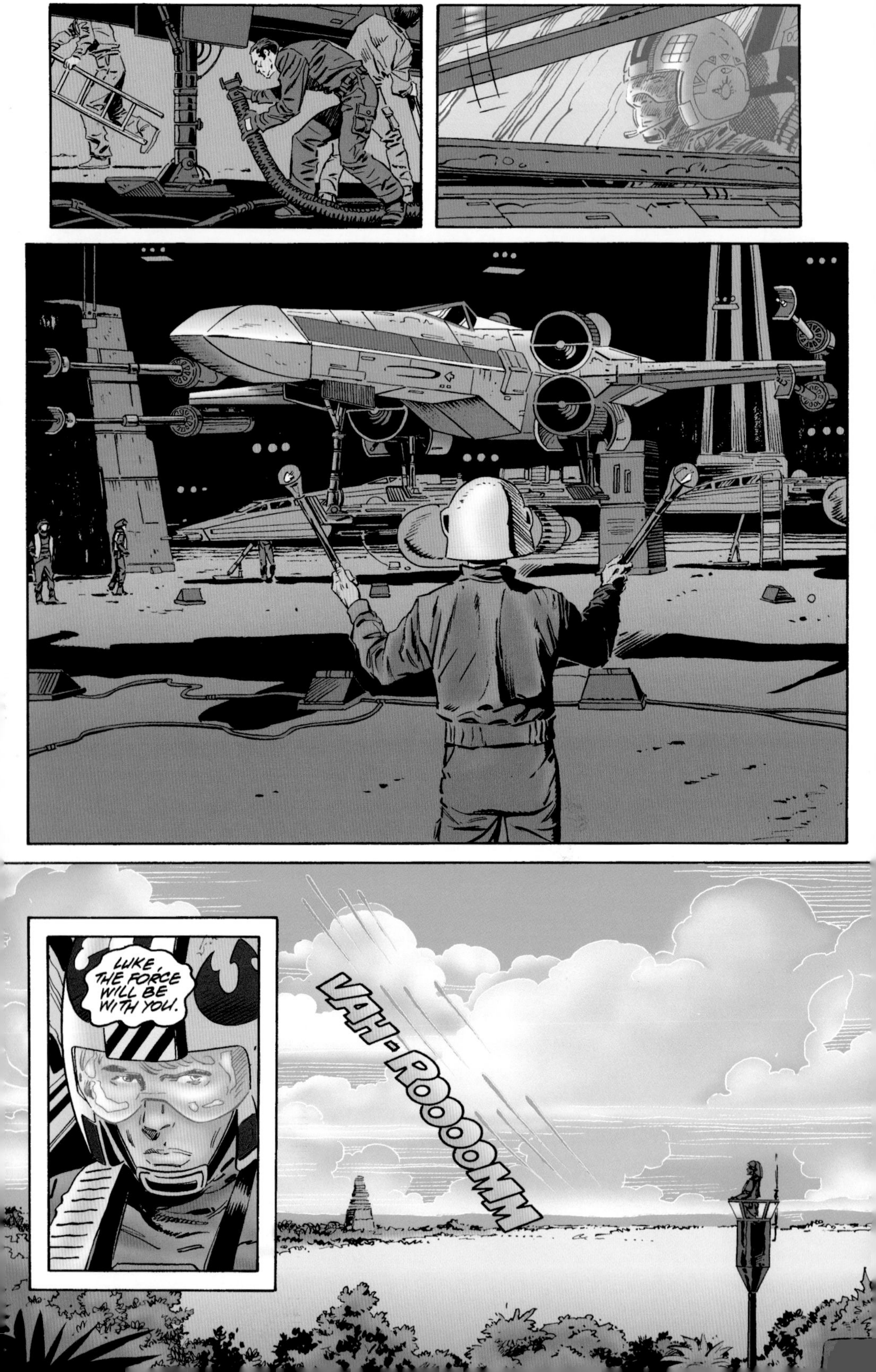

LUKE, THE FORCE WILL BE WITH YOU.
VAH-ROOOOMM

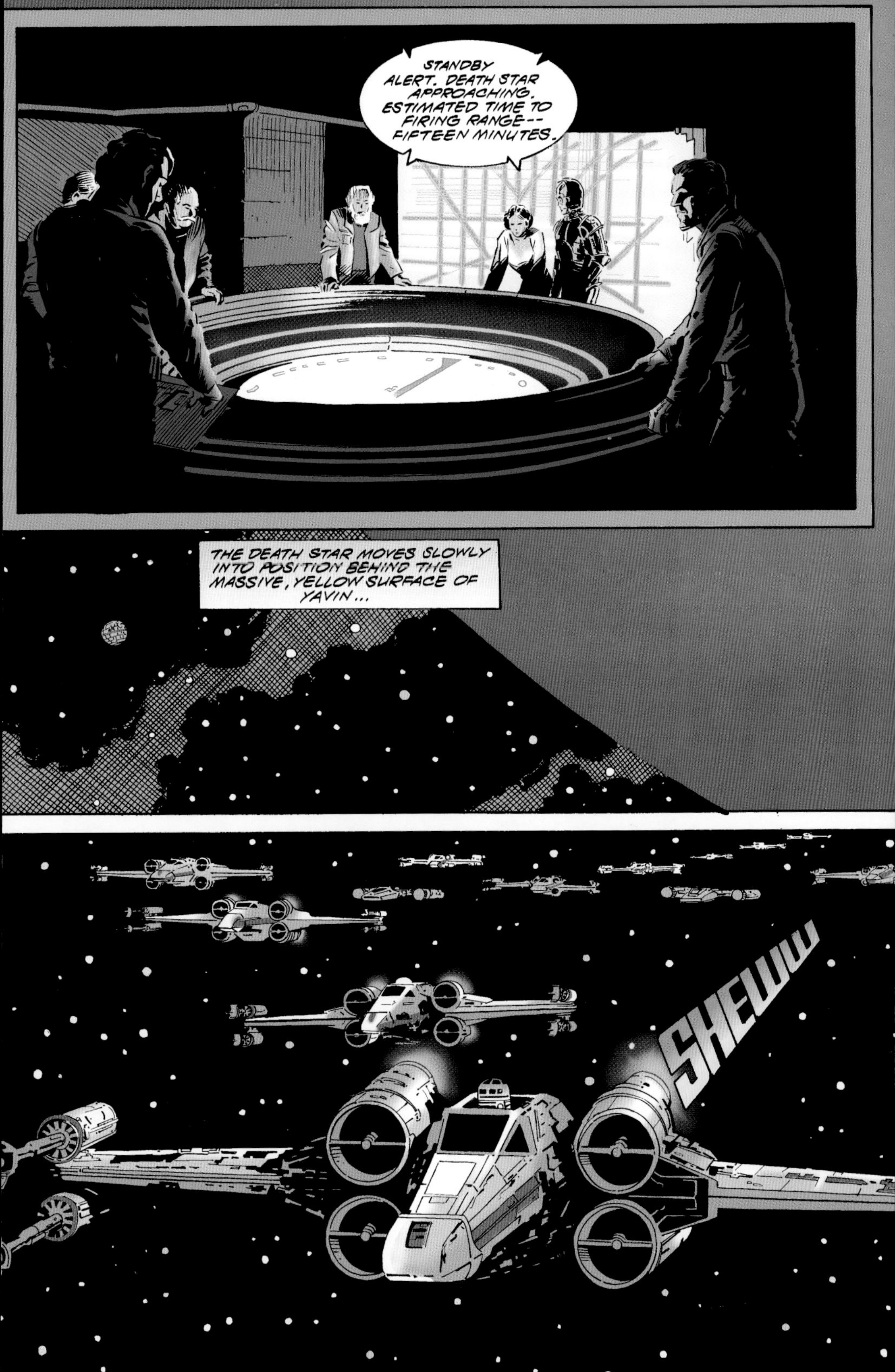
STANDBY ALERT. DEATH STAR APPROACHING. ESTIMATED TIME TO FIRING RANGE--FIFTEEN MINUTES.
THE DEATH STAR MOVES SLOWLY INTO POSITION BEHIND THE MASSIVE, YELLOW SURFACE OF YAVIN...
SHEWW

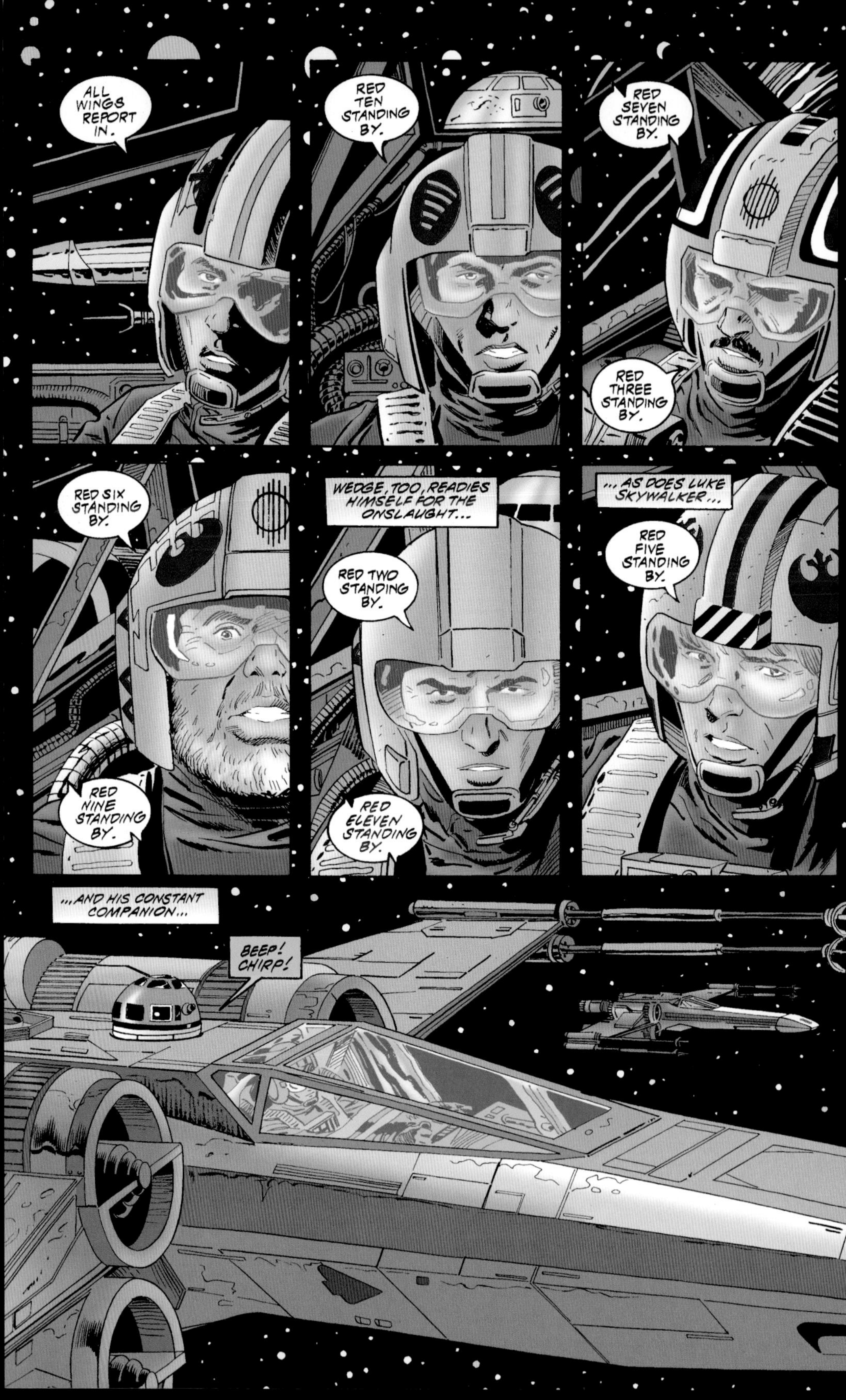
ALL WINGS REPORT IN.
RED TEN STANDING BY.
RED SEVEN STANDING BY.
RED THREE STANDING BY.
RED SIX STANDING BY.
RED NINE STANDING BY.
WEDGE, TOO, READIES HIMSELF FOR THE ONSLAUGHT...
RED TWO STANDING BY.
RED ELEVEN STANDING BY.
...AS DOES LUKE SKYWALKER...
RED FIVE STANDING BY.
...AND HIS CONSTANT COMPANION...
BEEP! CHIRP!

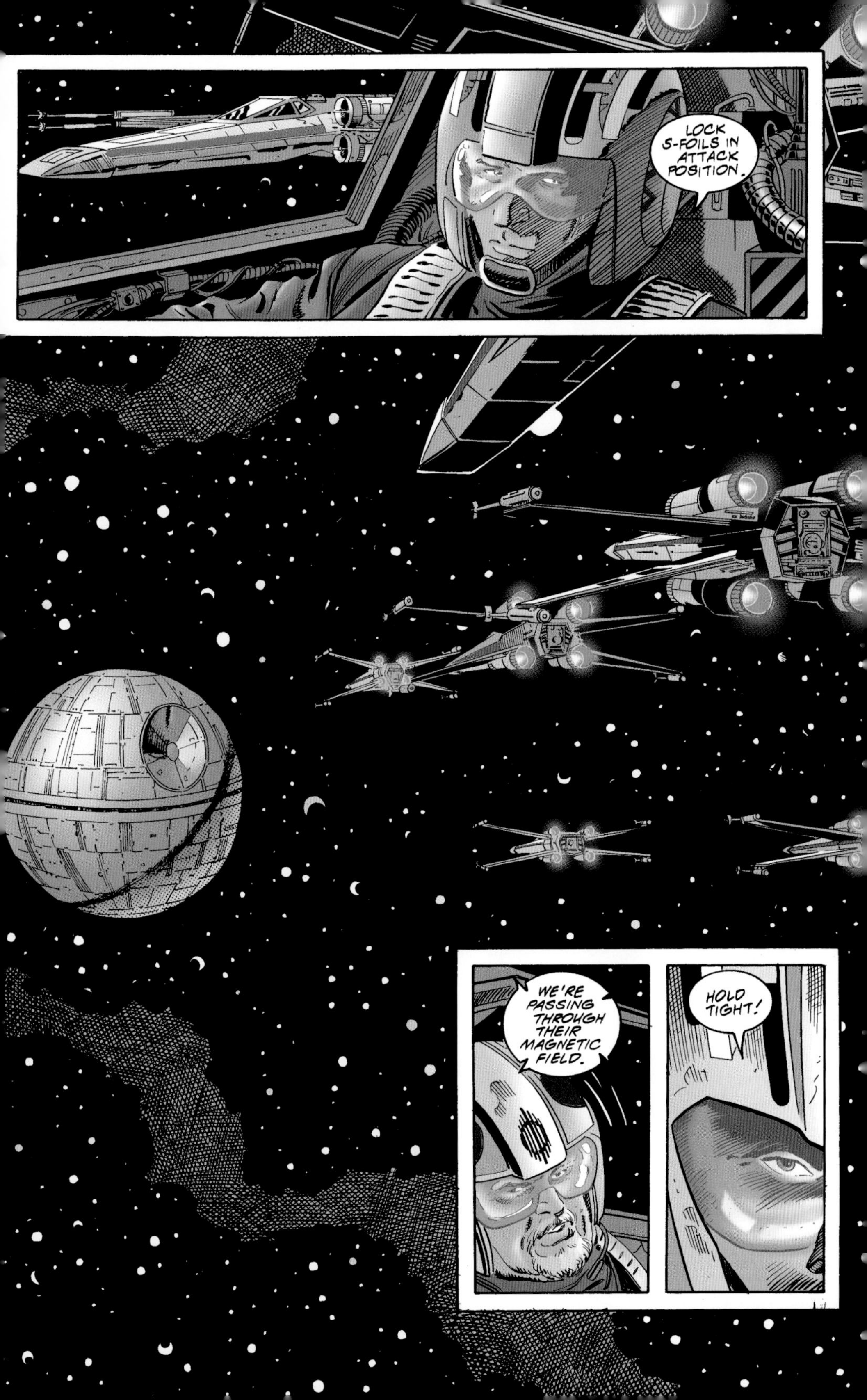
LOCK S-FOILS IN ATTACK POSITION.
WE'RE PASSING THROUGH THEIR MAGNETIC FIELD.
HOLD TIGHT!

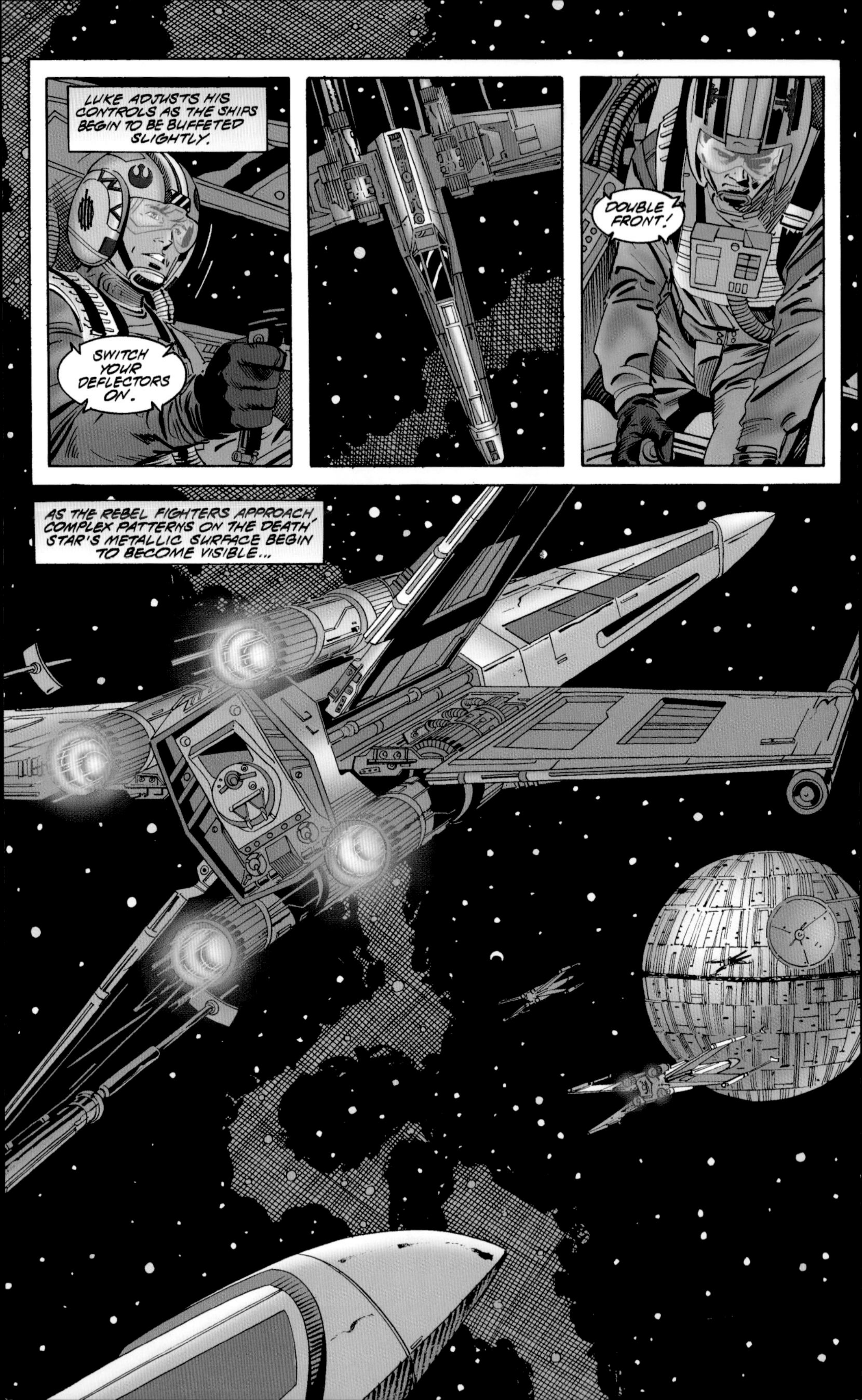
LUKE ADJUSTS HIS CONTROLS AS THE SHIPS BEGIN TO BE BUFFETED SLIGHTLY.
SWITCH YOUR DEFLECTORS ON.
DOUBLE FRONT!
AS THE REBEL FIGHTERS APPROACH, COMPLEX PATTERNS ON THE DEATH STAR'S METALLIC SURFACE BEGIN TO BECOME VISIBLE...

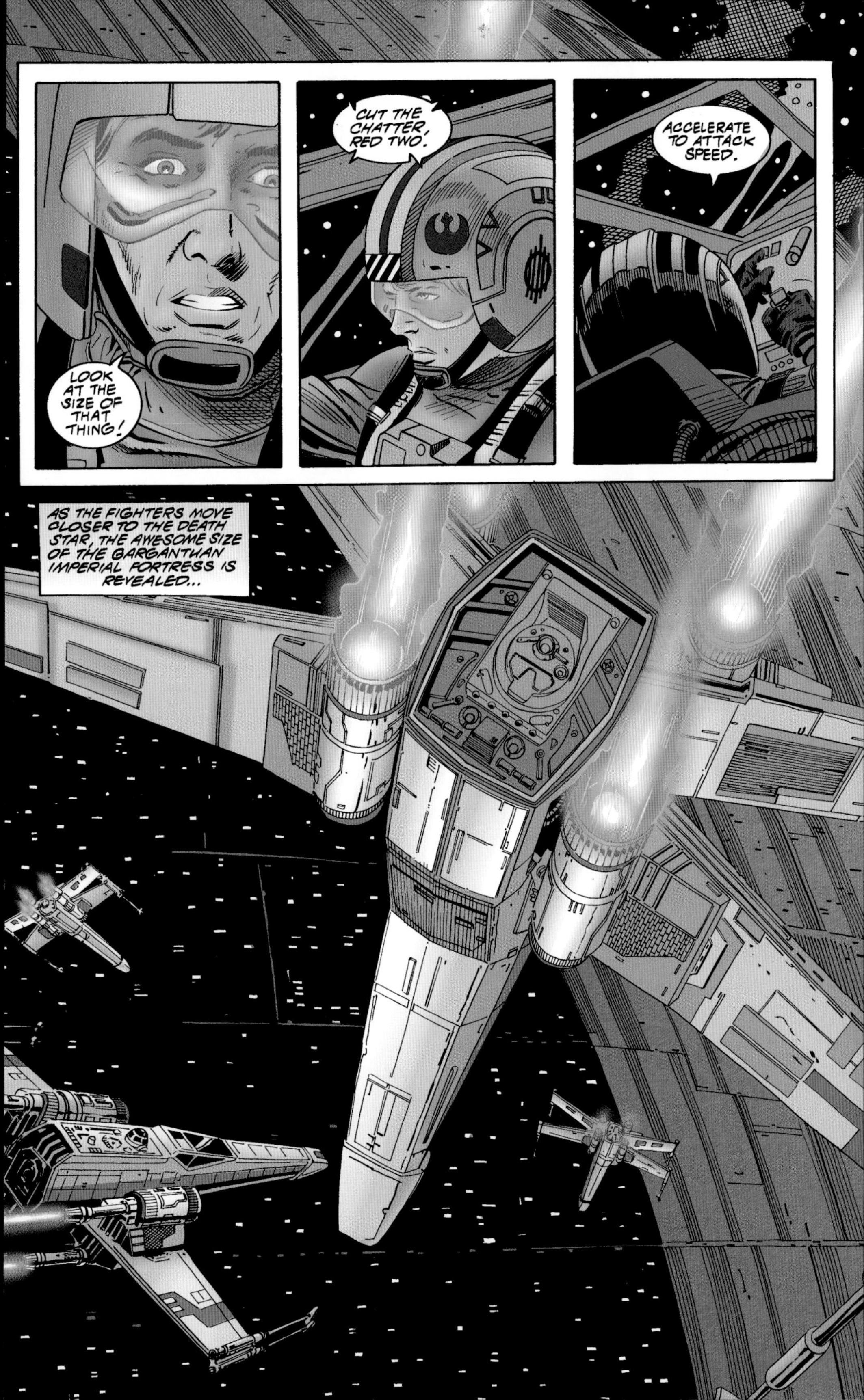
LOOK AT THE SIZE OF THAT THING!
CUT THE CHATTER, RED TWO.
ACCELERATE TO ATTACK SPEED.
AS THE FIGHTERS MOVE CLOSER TO THE DEATH STAR, THE AWESOME SIZE OF THE GARGANTUAN IMPERIAL FORTRESS IS REVEALED...

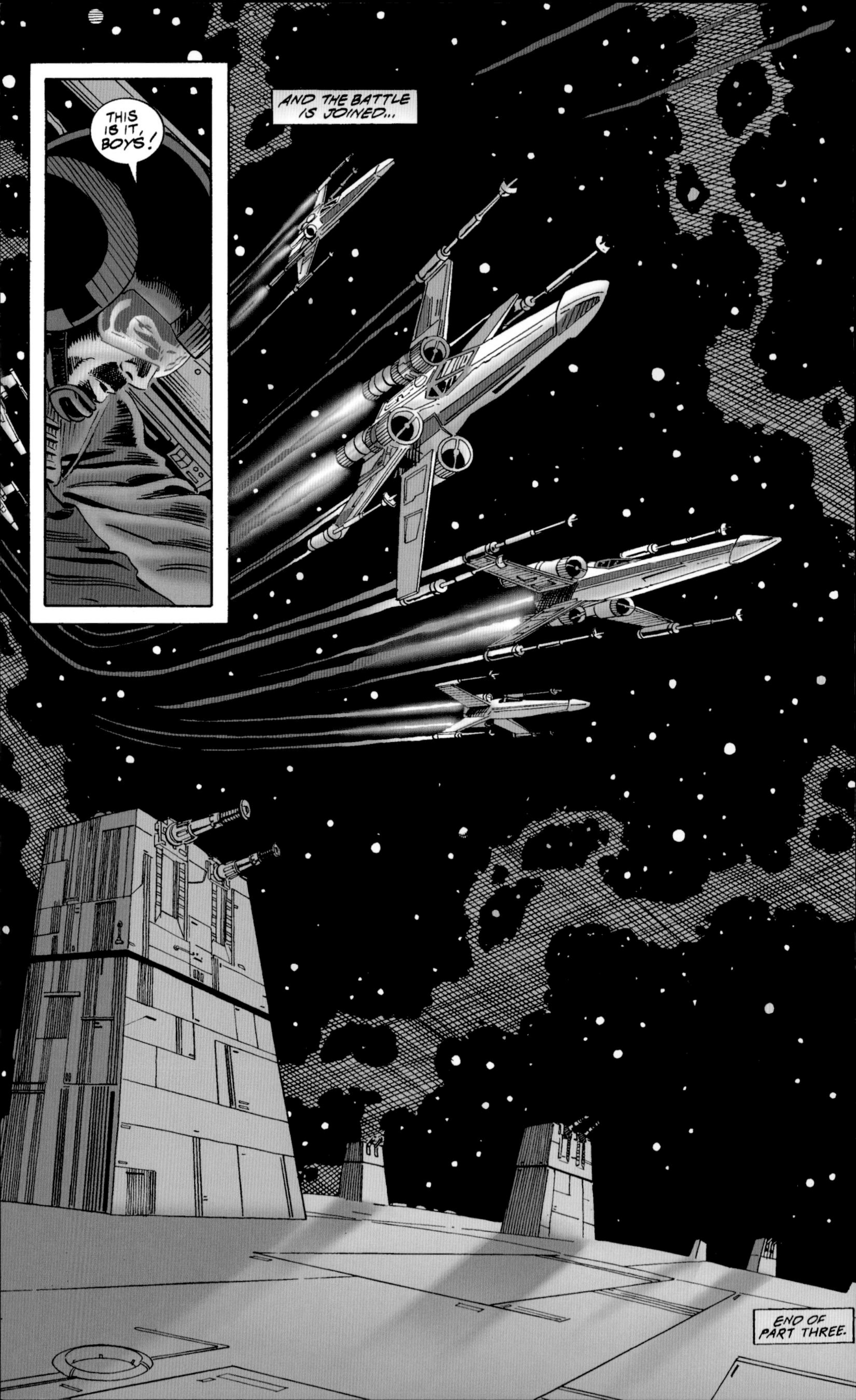
THIS IS IT, BOYS!
AND THE BATTLE IS JOINED...
END OF PART THREE.

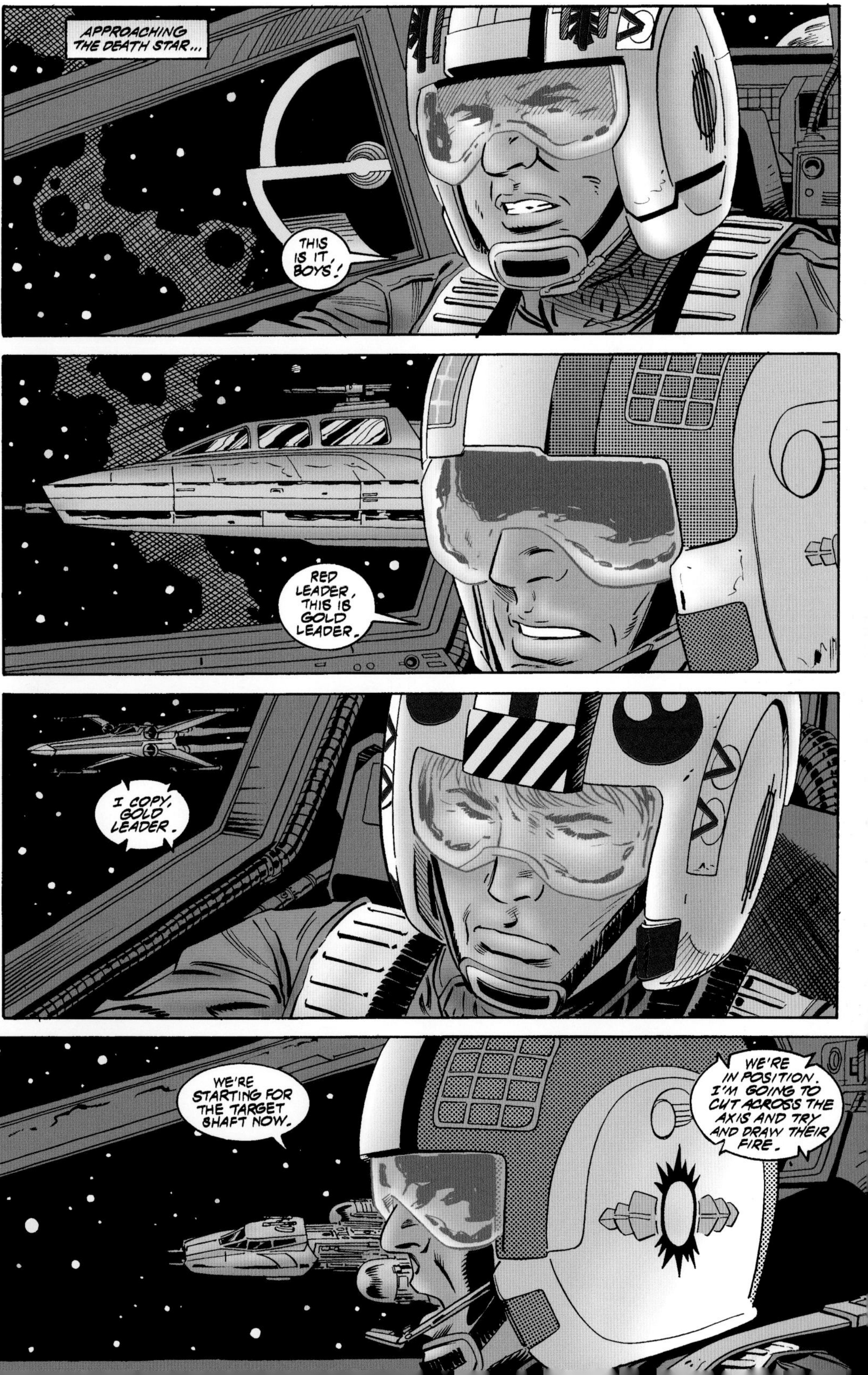
APPROACHING THE DEATH STAR...
THIS IS IT, BOYS!
RED LEADER, THIS IS GOLD LEADER.
I COPY, GOLD LEADER.
WE'RE STARTING FOR THE TARGET SHAFT NOW.
WE'RE IN POSITION. I'M GOING TO CUT ACROSS THE AXIS AND TRY AND DRAW THEIR FIRE.

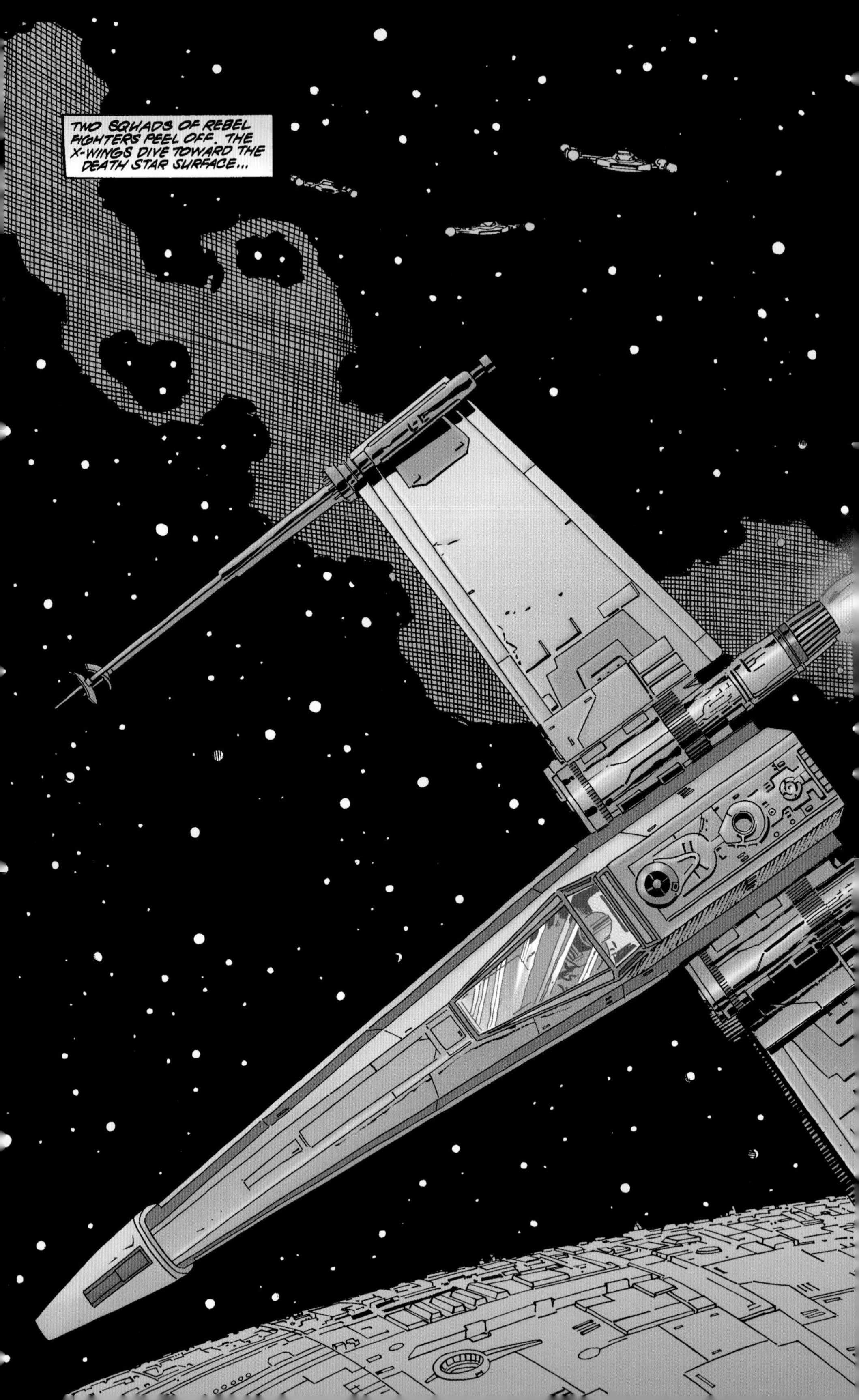
TWO SQUADS OF REBEL FIGHTERS PEEL OFF. THE X-WINGS DIVE TOWARD THE DEATH STAR SURFACE...

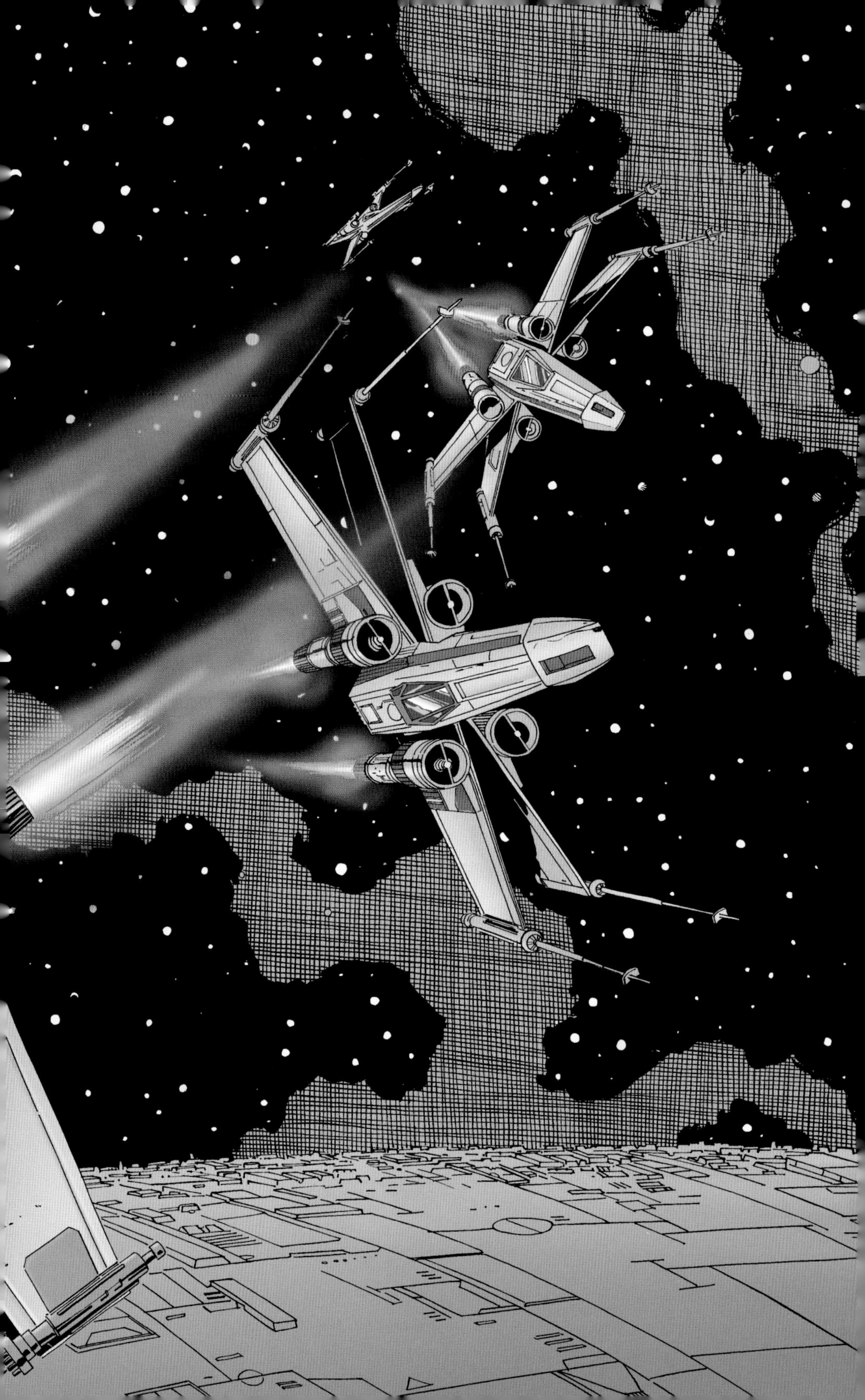

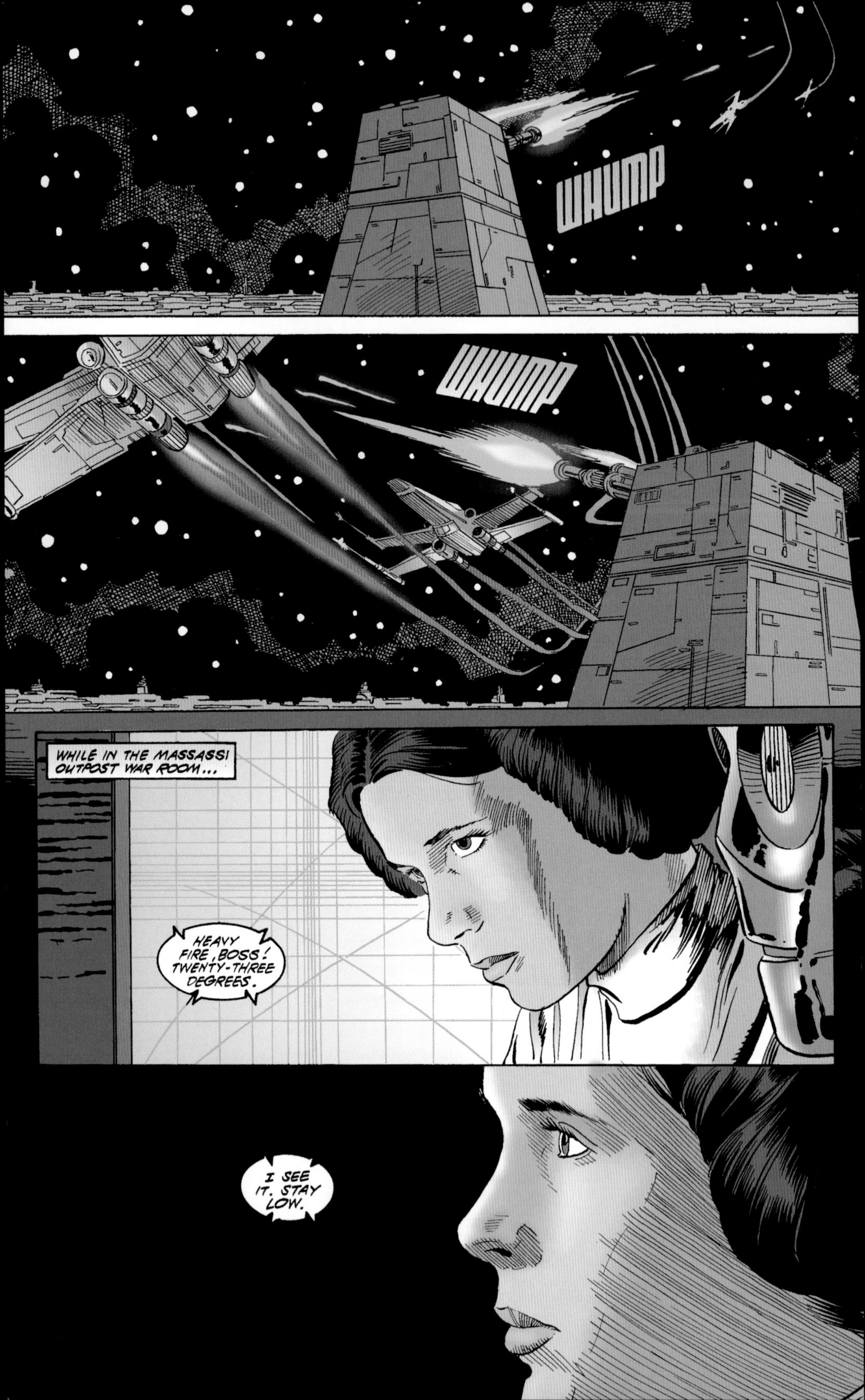
WHUMP
WHUMP
WHILE IN THE MASSASSI OUTPOST WAR ROOM...
HEAVY FIRE, BOSS! TWENTY-THREE DEGREES.
I SEE IT. STAY LOW.

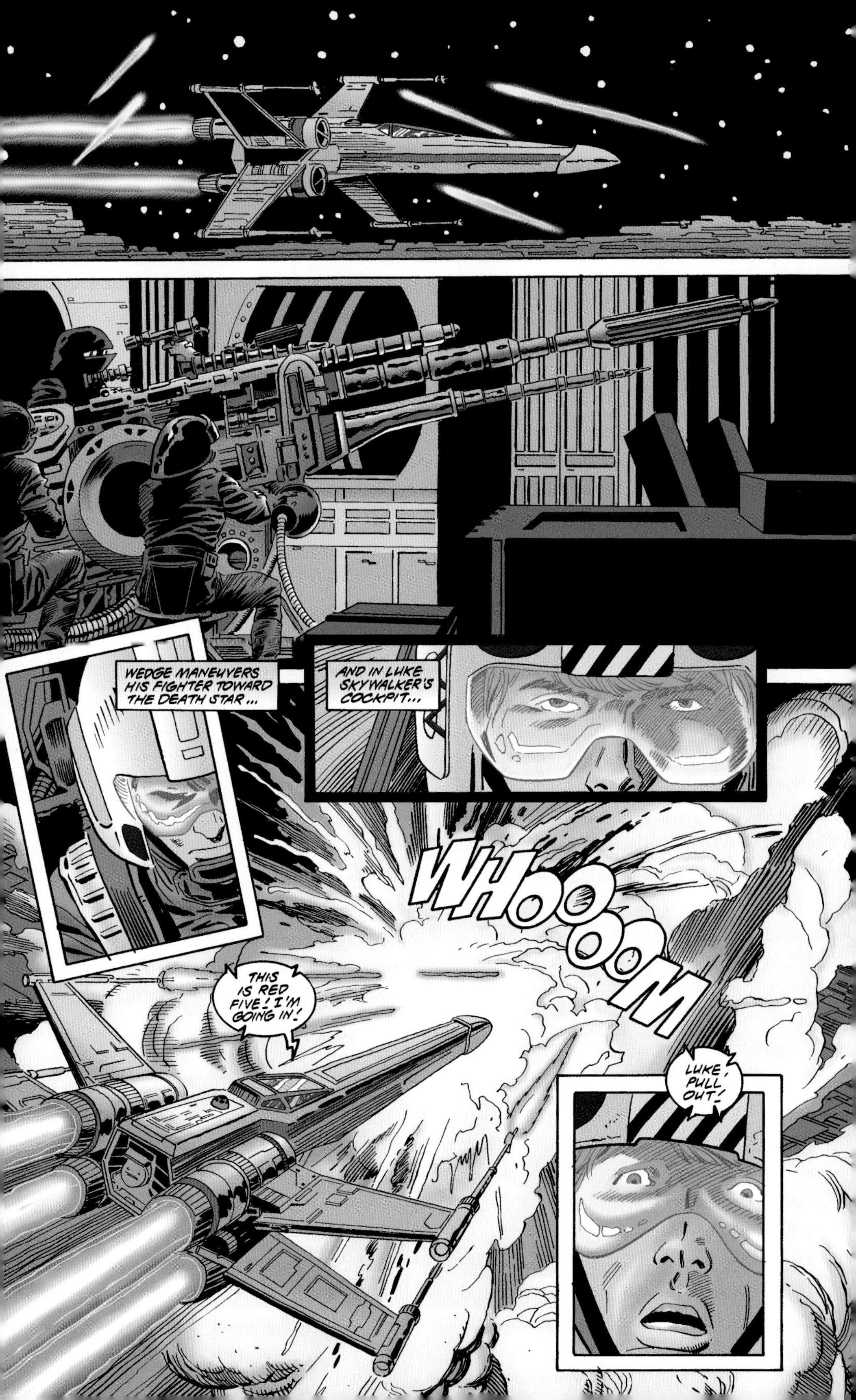

WEDGE MANEUVERS HIS FIGHTER TOWARD THE DEATH STAR...
AND IN LUKE SKYWALKER'S COCKPIT...
WHOOOOOM
THIS IS RED FIVE! I'M GOING IN!
LUKE, PULL OUT!

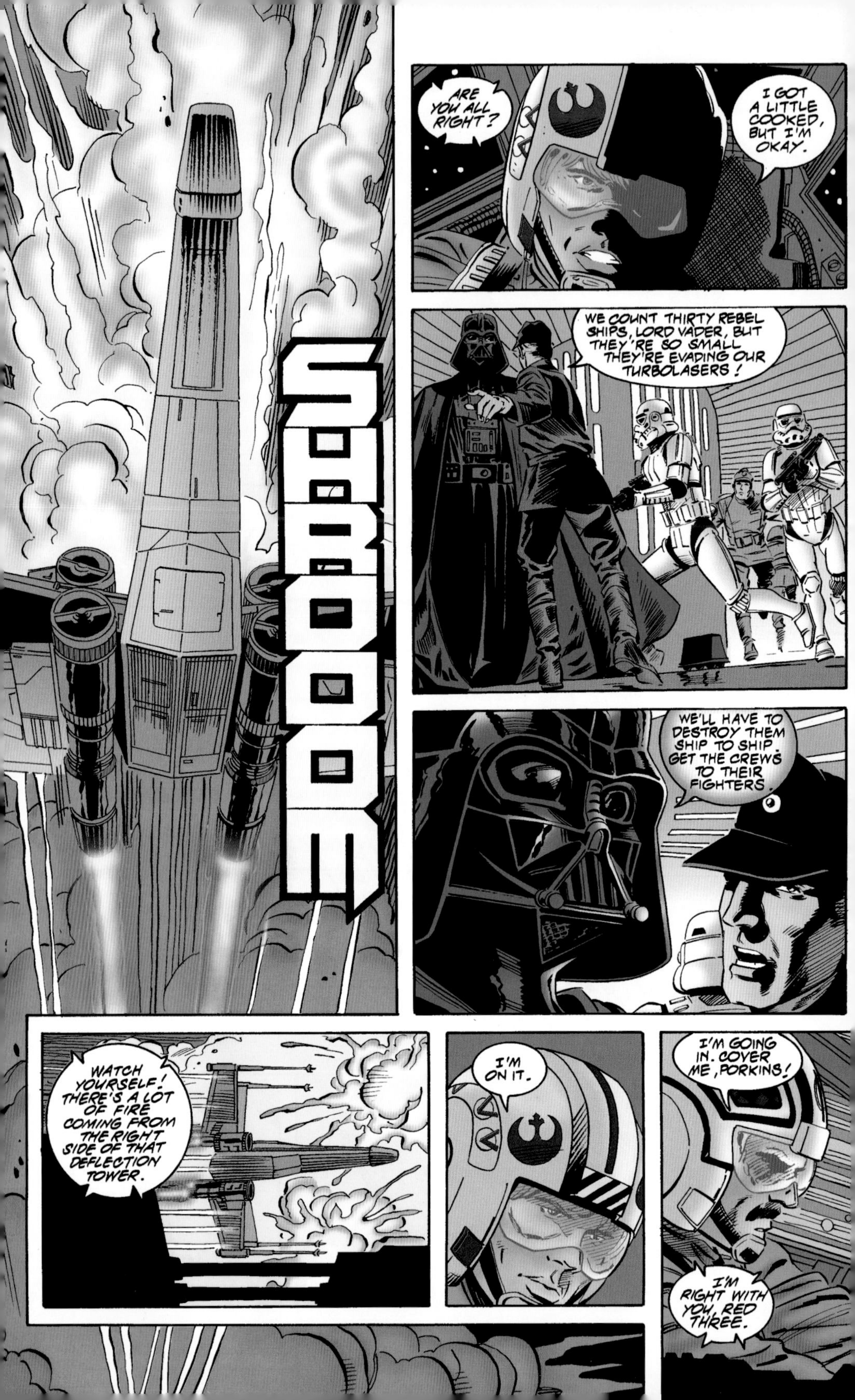

SHROOOM
ARE YOU ALL RIGHT?
I GOT A LITTLE COOKED, BUT I'M OKAY.
WE COUNT THIRTY REBEL SHIPS, LORD VADER, BUT THEY'RE SO SMALL THEY'RE EVADING OUR TURBOLASERS!
WE'LL HAVE TO DESTROY THEM SHIP TO SHIP. GET THE CREWS TO THEIR FIGHTERS.
WATCH YOURSELF! THERE'S A LOT OF FIRE COMING FROM THE RIGHT SIDE OF THAT DEFLECTION TOWER.
I'M ON IT.
I'M GOING IN. COVER ME, PORKINS!
I'M RIGHT WITH YOU, RED THREE.

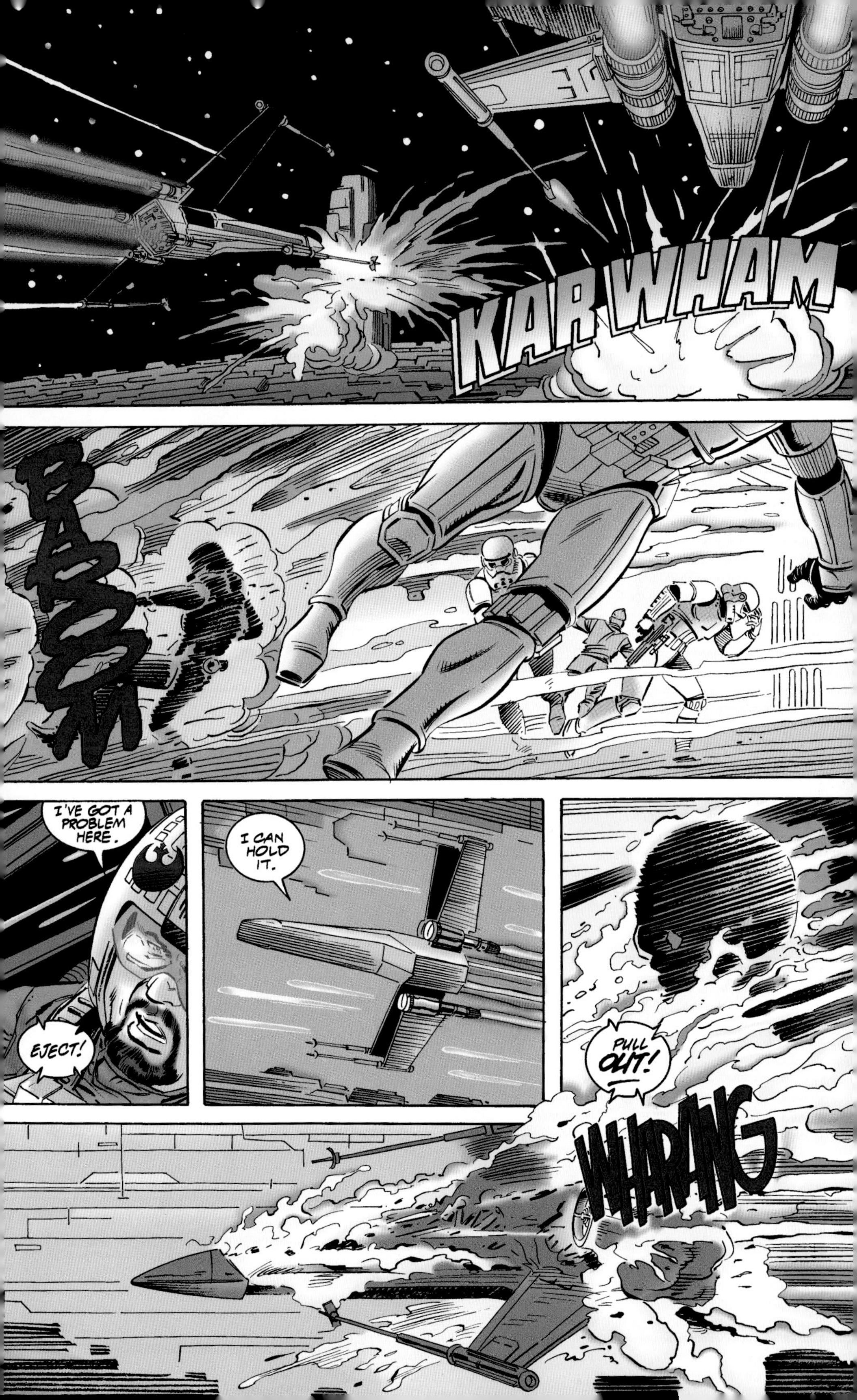
KARWHAM
BOOM
I'VE GOT A PROBLEM HERE.
EJECT!
I CAN HOLD IT.
PULL OUT!
WHRANG

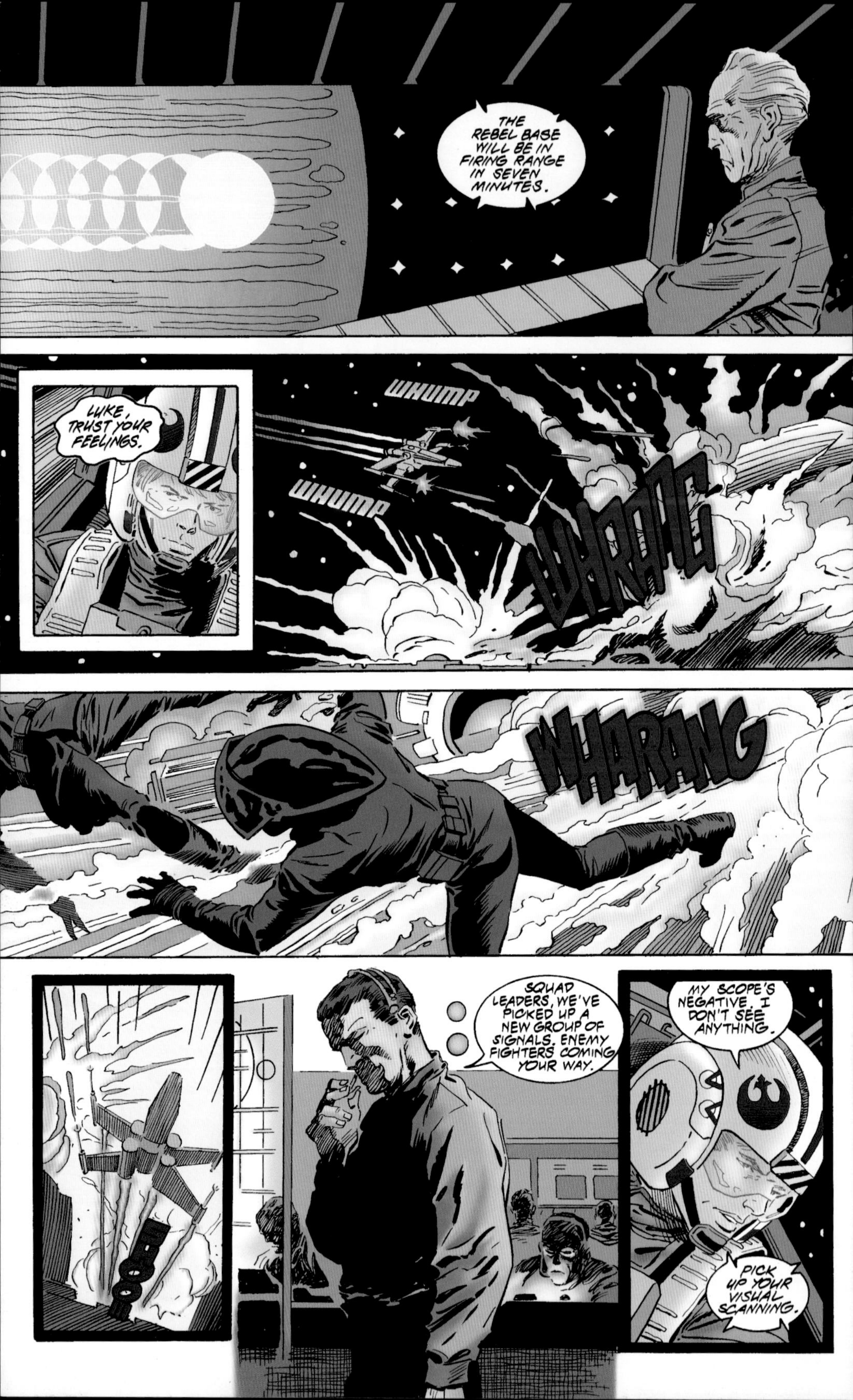
THE REBEL BASE WILL BE IN FIRING RANGE IN SEVEN MINUTES.
LUKE, TRUST YOUR FEELINGS.
WHUMP
WHUMP
WHRANG
WHARANG
SQUAD LEADERS, WE'VE PICKED UP A NEW GROUP OF SIGNALS. ENEMY FIGHTERS COMING YOUR WAY.
MY SCOPE'S NEGATIVE. I DON'T SEE ANYTHING.
PICK UP YOUR VISUAL SCANNING.

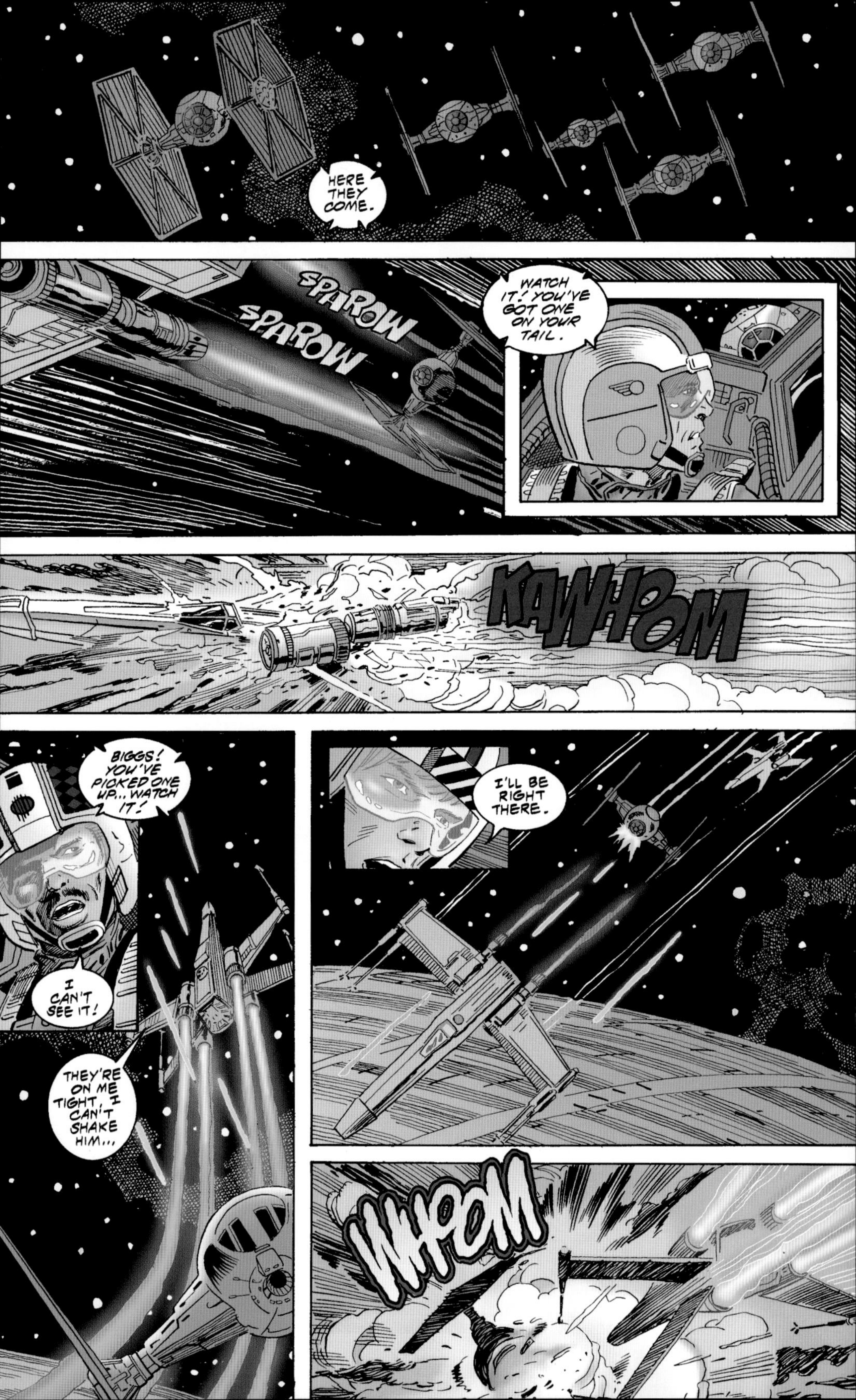
HERE THEY COME.
SPAROW
SPAROW
WATCH IT! YOU'VE GOT ONE ON YOUR TAIL.
KAWHOOM
BIGGS! YOU'VE PICKED ONE UP... WATCH IT!
I CAN'T SEE IT!
THEY'RE ON ME TIGHT, I CAN'T SHAKE HIM...
I'LL BE RIGHT THERE.
WHOOM

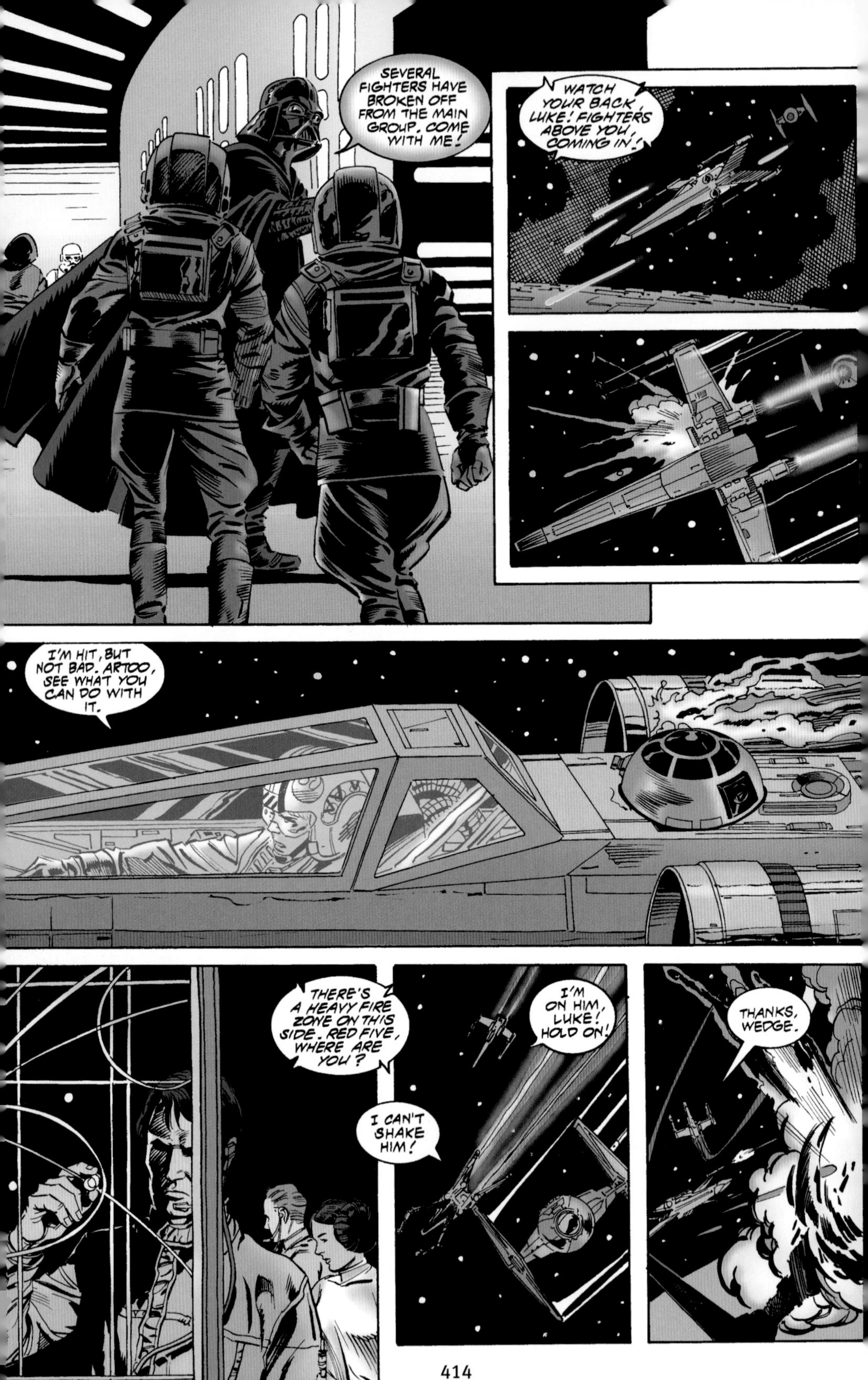
SEVERAL FIGHTERS HAVE BROKEN OFF FROM THE MAIN GROUP. COME WITH ME!
WATCH YOUR BACK, LUKE! FIGHTERS ABOVE YOU, COMING IN!
I'M HIT, BUT NOT BAD. ARTOO, SEE WHAT YOU CAN DO WITH IT.
THERE'S A HEAVY FIRE ZONE ON THIS SIDE. RED FIVE, WHERE ARE YOU?
I CAN'T SHAKE HIM!
I'M ON HIM, LUKE! HOLD ON!
THANKS, WEDGE.

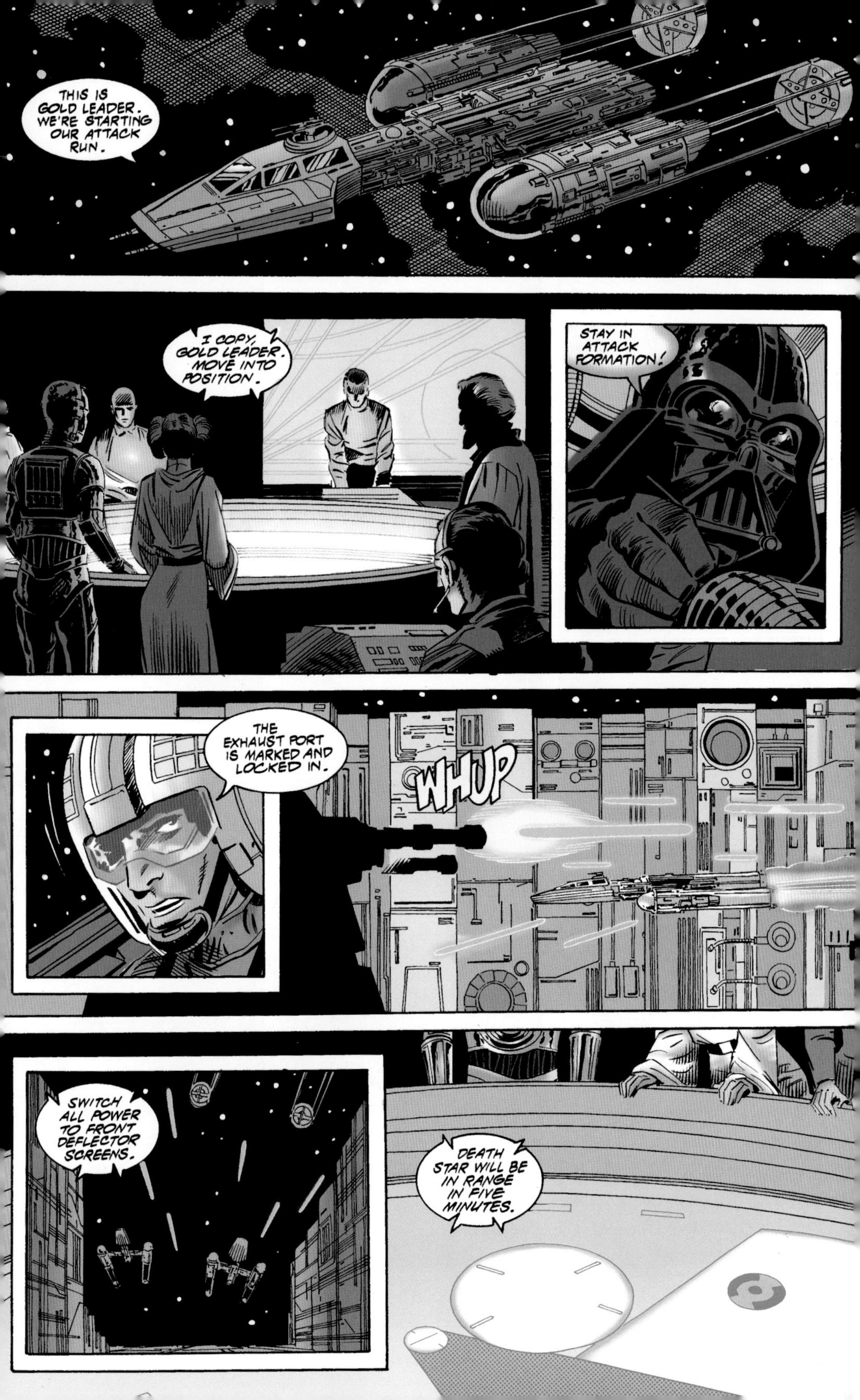
THIS IS GOLD LEADER. WE'RE STARTING OUR ATTACK RUN.
I COPY, GOLD LEADER. MOVE INTO POSITION.
STAY IN ATTACK FORMATION!
THE EXHAUST PORT IS MARKED AND LOCKED IN.
WHUP
SWITCH ALL POWER TO FRONT DEFLECTOR SCREENS.
DEATH STAR WILL BE IN RANGE IN FIVE MINUTES.

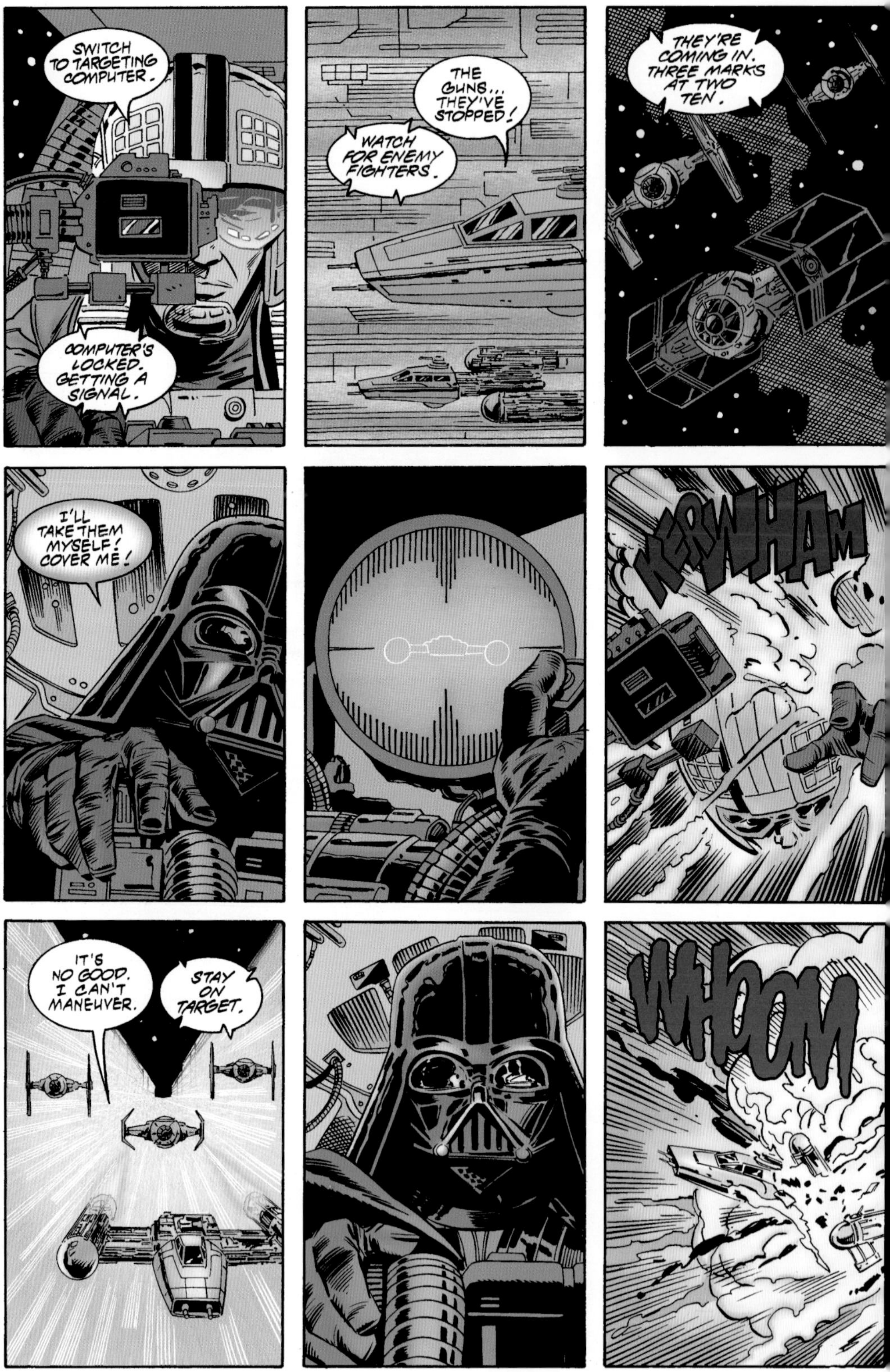
SWITCH TO TARGETING COMPUTER.
COMPUTER'S LOCKED. GETTING A SIGNAL.
THE GUNS... THEY'VE STOPPED!
WATCH FOR ENEMY FIGHTERS.
THEY'RE COMING IN. THREE MARKS AT TWO TEN.
I'LL TAKE THEM MYSELF! COVER ME!
KERWHAM
IT'S NO GOOD. I CAN'T MANEUVER.
STAY ON TARGET.
WHOOM

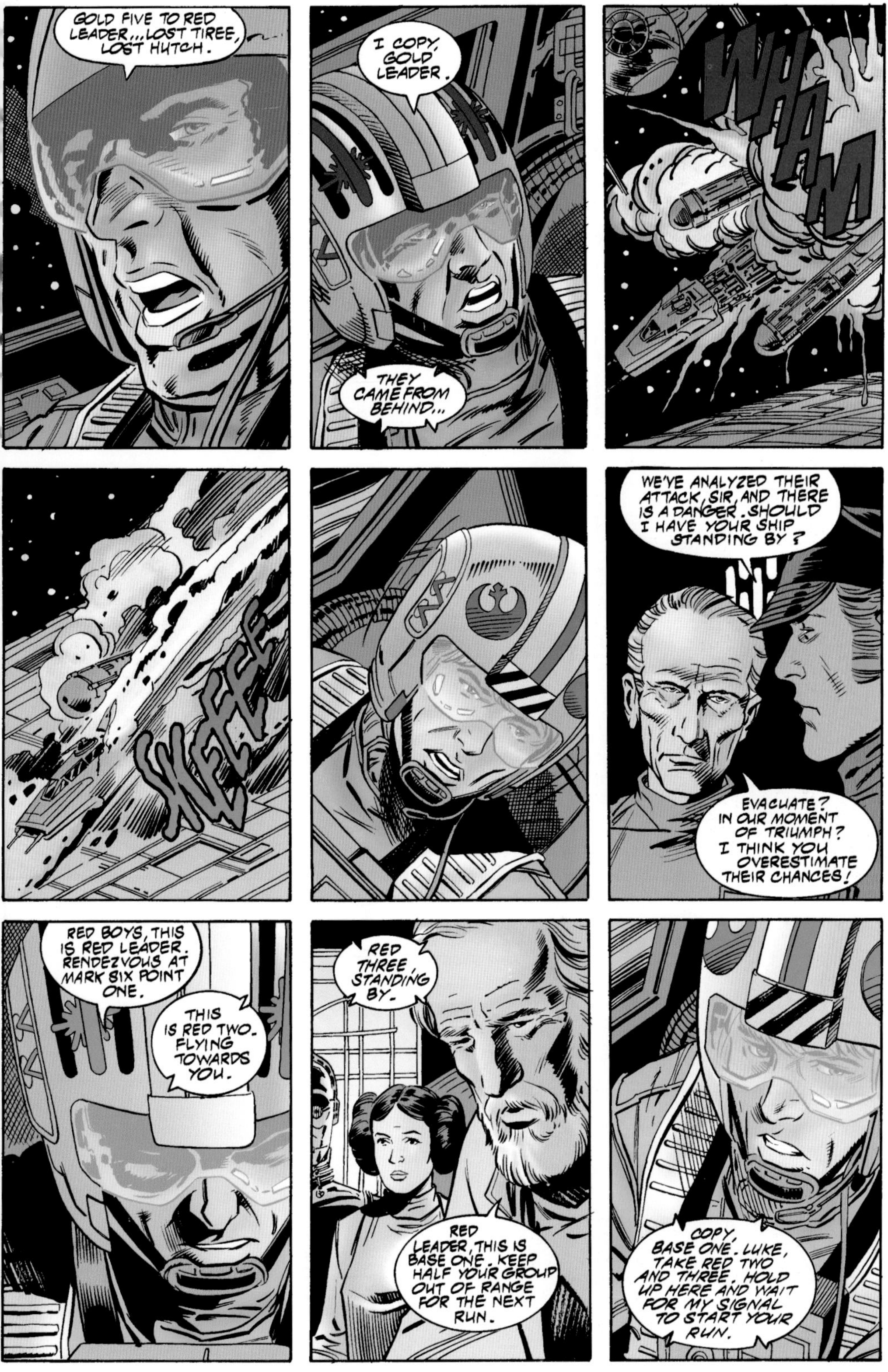

GOLD FIVE TO RED LEADER... LOST TIREE, LOST HUTCH.
I COPY, GOLD LEADER.
THEY CAME FROM BEHIND...
WHAM
WE'VE ANALYZED THEIR ATTACK, SIR, AND THERE IS A DANGER. SHOULD I HAVE YOUR SHIP STANDING BY?
EVACUATE? IN OUR MOMENT OF TRIUMPH? I THINK YOU OVERESTIMATE THEIR CHANCES!
RED BOYS, THIS IS RED LEADER. RENDEZVOUS AT MARK SIX POINT ONE.
THIS IS RED TWO. FLYING TOWARDS YOU.
RED THREE STANDING BY.
RED LEADER, THIS IS BASE ONE. KEEP HALF YOUR GROUP OUT OF RANGE FOR THE NEXT RUN.
COPY, BASE ONE. LUKE, TAKE RED TWO AND THREE. HOLD UP HERE AND WAIT FOR MY SIGNAL TO START YOUR RUN.

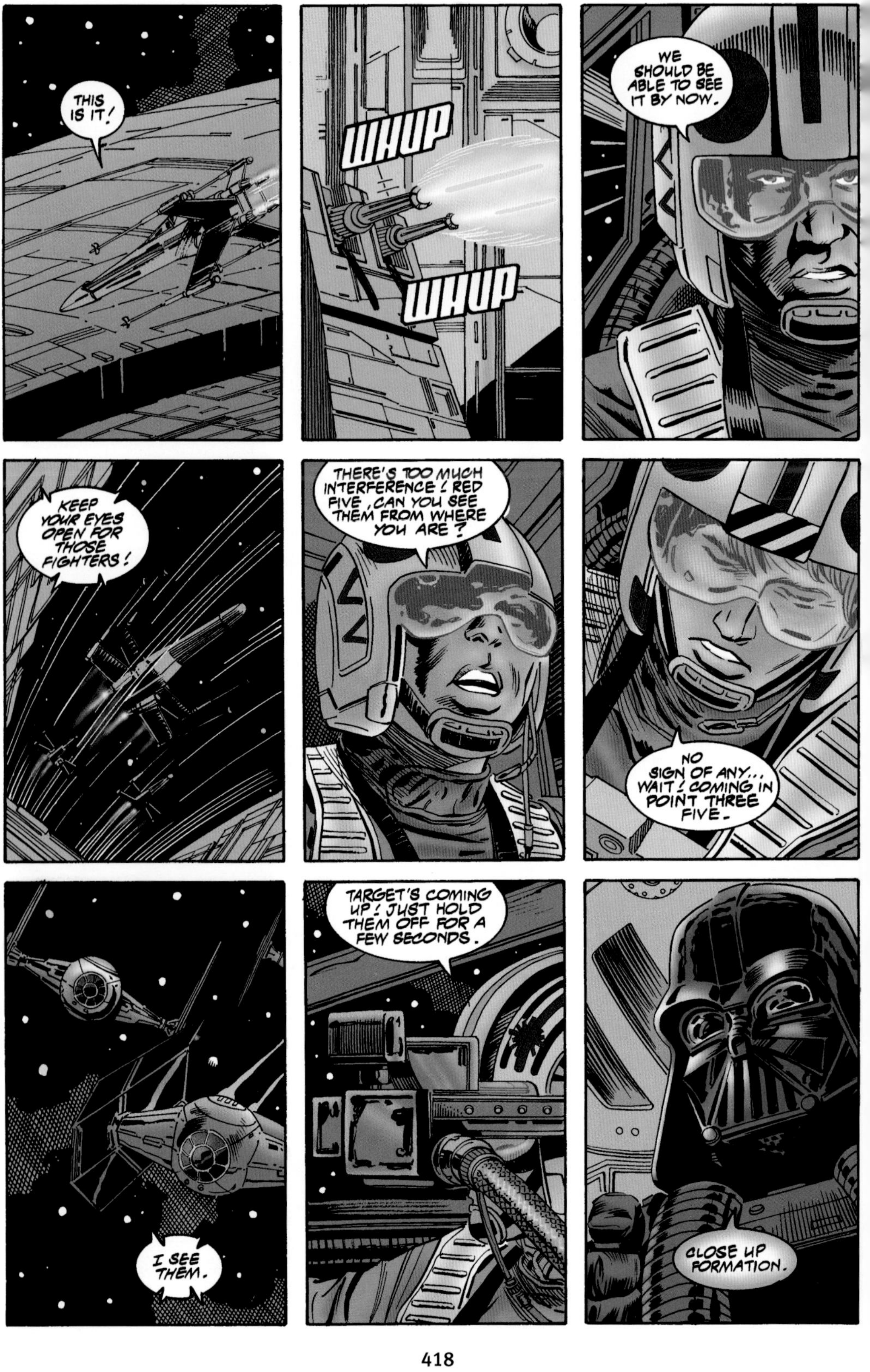
THIS IS IT!
WHUP
WHUP
WE SHOULD BE ABLE TO SEE IT BY NOW.
KEEP YOUR EYES OPEN FOR THOSE FIGHTERS!
THERE'S TOO MUCH INTERFERENCE! RED FIVE, CAN YOU SEE THEM FROM WHERE YOU ARE?
NO SIGN OF ANY... WAIT! COMING IN POINT THREE FIVE.
I SEE THEM.
TARGET'S COMING UP! JUST HOLD THEM OFF FOR A FEW SECONDS.
CLOSE UP FORMATION.

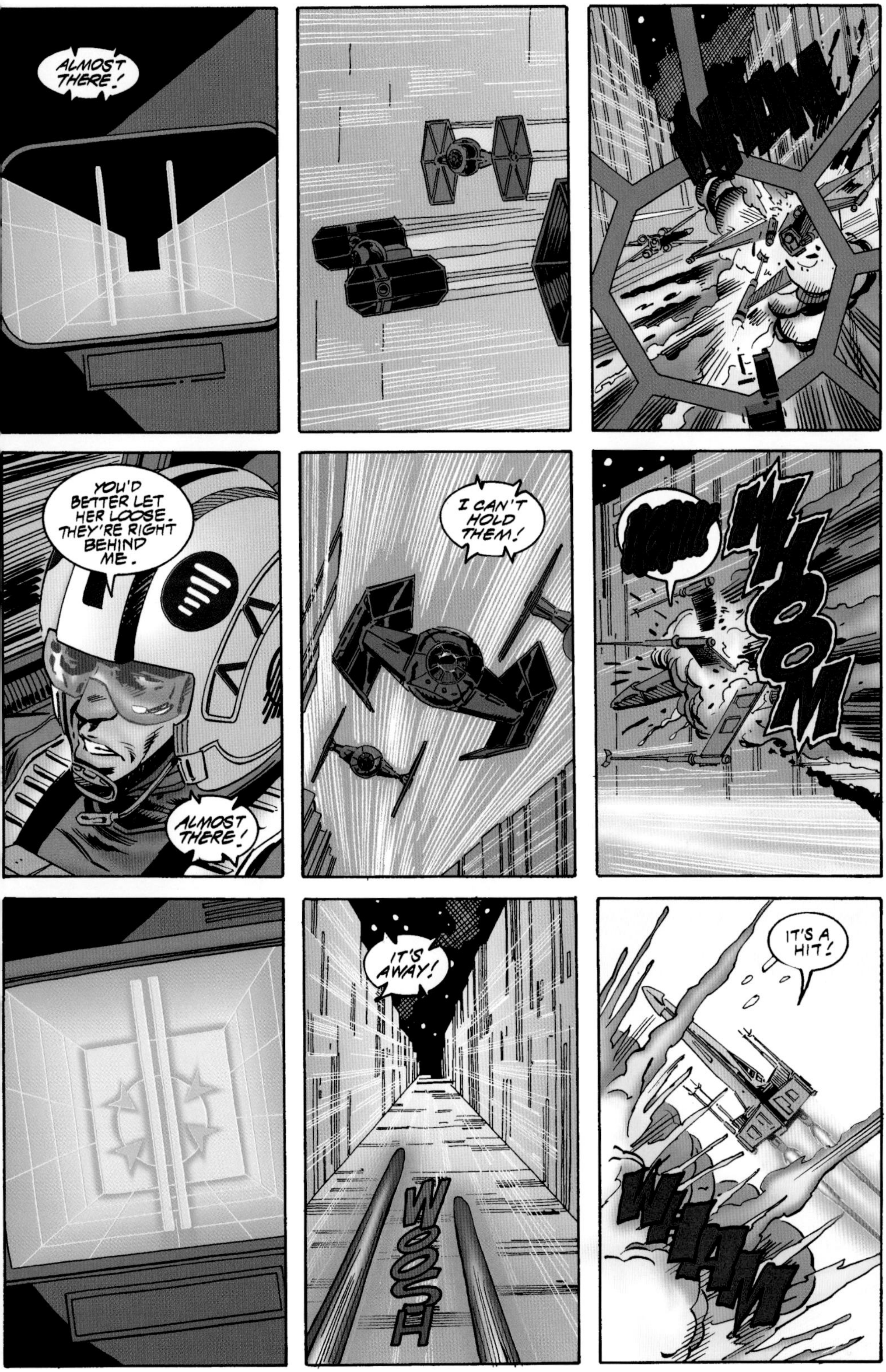
ALMOST THERE!
YOU'D BETTER LET HER LOOSE. THEY'RE RIGHT BEHIND ME.
ALMOST THERE!
I CAN'T HOLD THEM!
WHOOM
IT'S AWAY!
WOOSH
IT'S A HIT!
WHAM

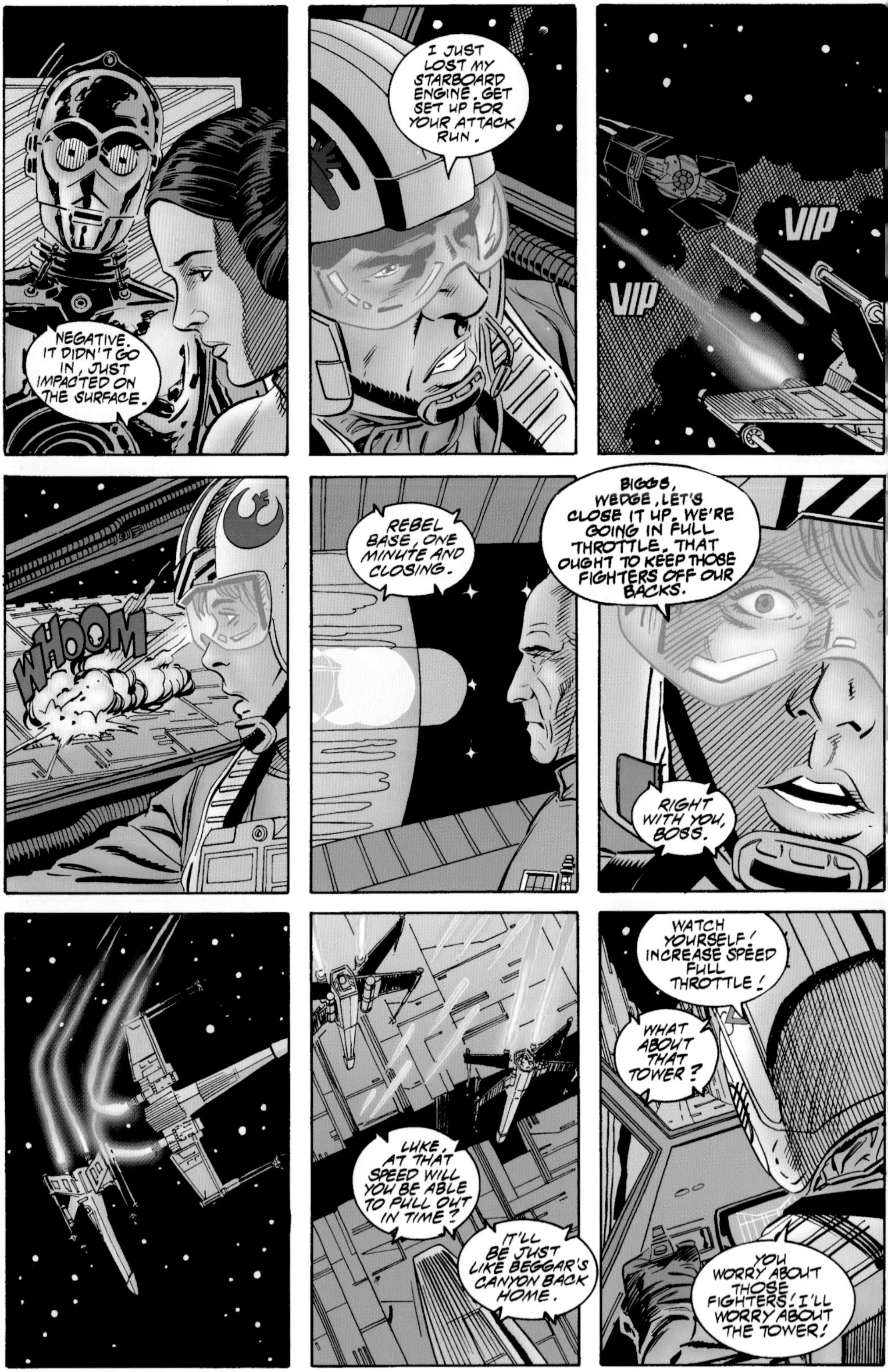
NEGATIVE. IT DIDN'T GO IN, JUST IMPACTED ON THE SURFACE.
I JUST LOST MY STARBOARD ENGINE. GET SET UP FOR YOUR ATTACK RUN.
VIP
VIP
WHOOM
REBEL BASE, ONE MINUTE AND CLOSING.
BIGGS, WEDGE, LET'S CLOSE IT UP. WE'RE GOING IN FULL THROTTLE. THAT OUGHT TO KEEP THOSE FIGHTERS OFF OUR BACKS.
RIGHT WITH YOU, BOSS.
LUKE, AT THAT SPEED WILL YOU BE ABLE TO PULL OUT IN TIME?
IT'LL BE JUST LIKE BEGGAR'S CANYON BACK HOME.
WATCH YOURSELF! INCREASE SPEED FULL THROTTLE!
WHAT ABOUT THAT TOWER?
YOU WORRY ABOUT THOSE FIGHTERS! I'LL WORRY ABOUT THE TOWER!

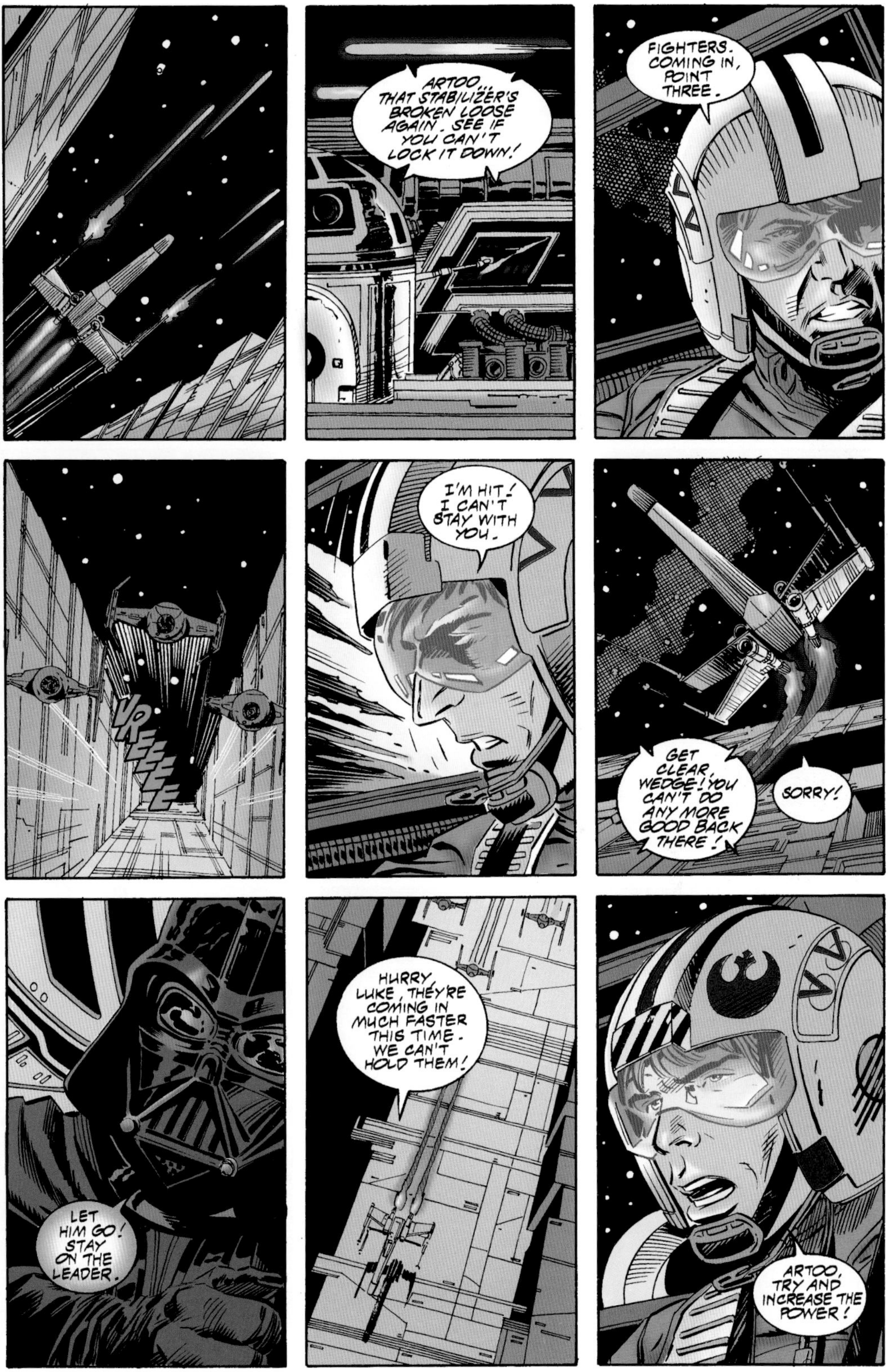
ARTOO... THAT STABILIZER'S BROKEN LOOSE AGAIN. SEE IF YOU CAN'T LOCK IT DOWN!
FIGHTERS. COMING IN, POINT THREE.
VREEEE
I'M HIT! I CAN'T STAY WITH YOU.
GET CLEAR, WEDGE! YOU CAN'T DO ANY MORE GOOD BACK THERE!
SORRY!
LET HIM GO! STAY ON THE LEADER.
HURRY, LUKE, THEY'RE COMING IN MUCH FASTER THIS TIME. WE CAN'T HOLD THEM!
ARTOO, TRY AND INCREASE THE POWER!

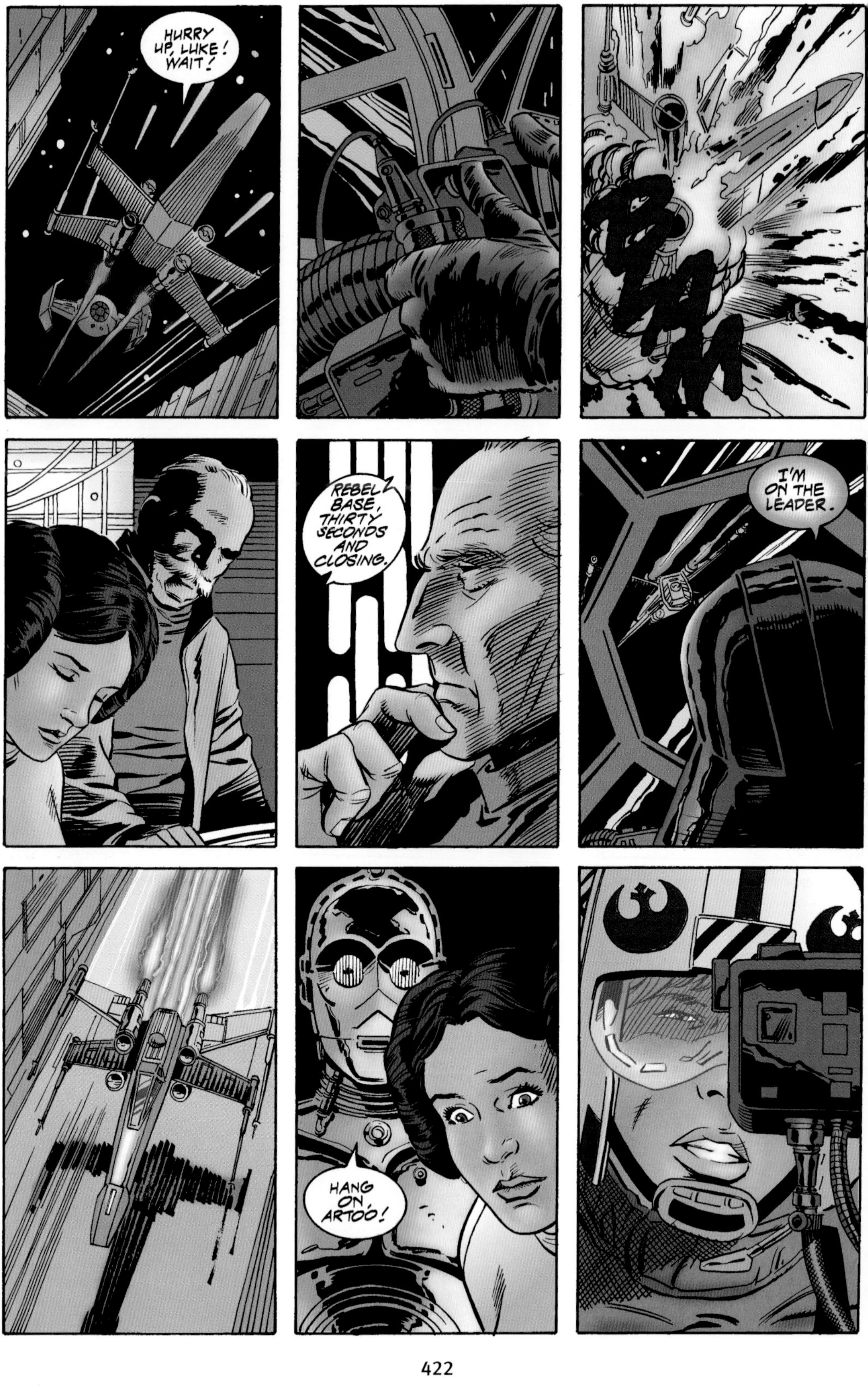
HURRY UP, LUKE! WAIT!
REBEL BASE, THIRTY SECONDS AND CLOSING.
I'M ON THE LEADER.
HANG ON, ARTOO!

USE THE FORCE, LUKE.
LET GO, LUKE.
THE FORCE IS STRONG WITH THIS ONE.
LUKE, TRUST ME.
HIS COMPUTER'S OFF.
LUKE, YOU SWITCHED OFF YOUR TARGETING COMPUTER. WHAT'S WRONG?
NOTHING. I'M ALL RIGHT.

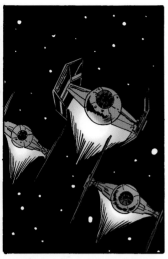

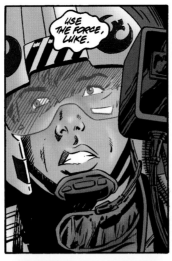

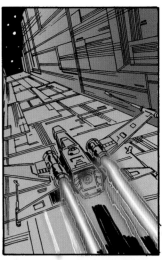

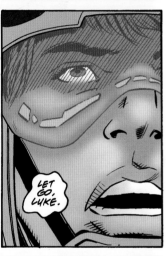

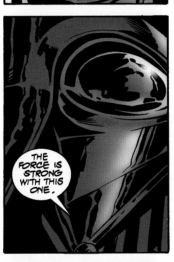

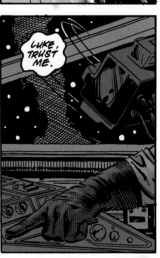

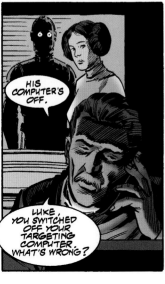

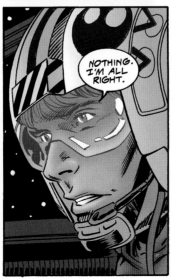

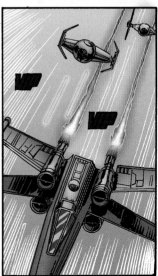

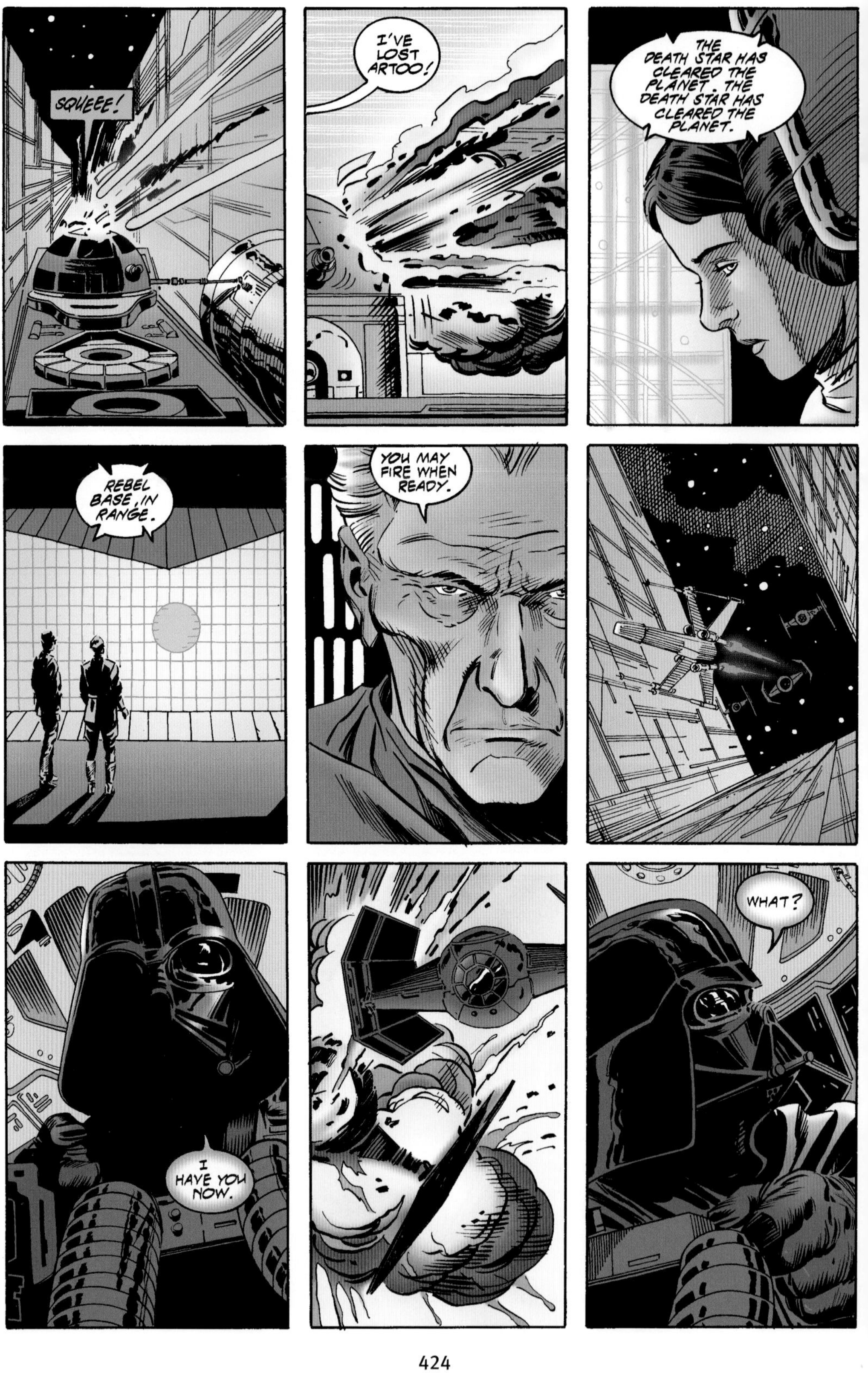
SQUEEE!
I'VE LOST ARTOO!
THE DEATH STAR HAS CLEARED THE PLANET. THE DEATH STAR HAS CLEARED THE PLANET.
REBEL BASE, IN RANGE.
YOU MAY FIRE WHEN READY.
I HAVE YOU NOW.
WHAT?

YAHOO!
KHARANG!
WHOOM
YOU'RE ALL CLEAR, KID! NOW LET'S BLOW THIS THING AND GO HOME!

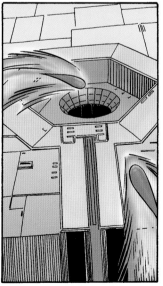

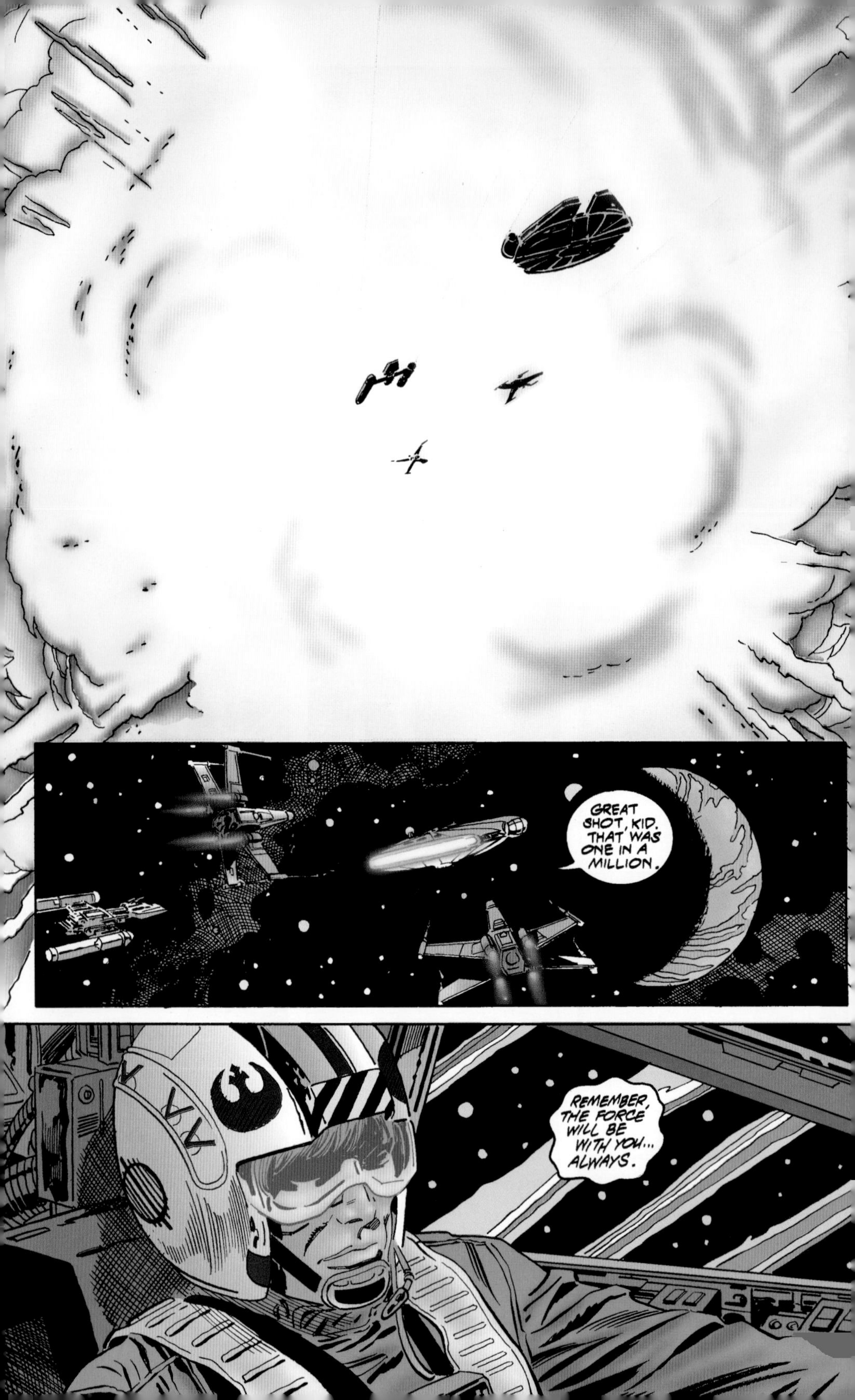
GREAT SHOT, KID. THAT WAS ONE IN A MILLION.
REMEMBER, THE FORCE WILL BE WITH YOU... ALWAYS.

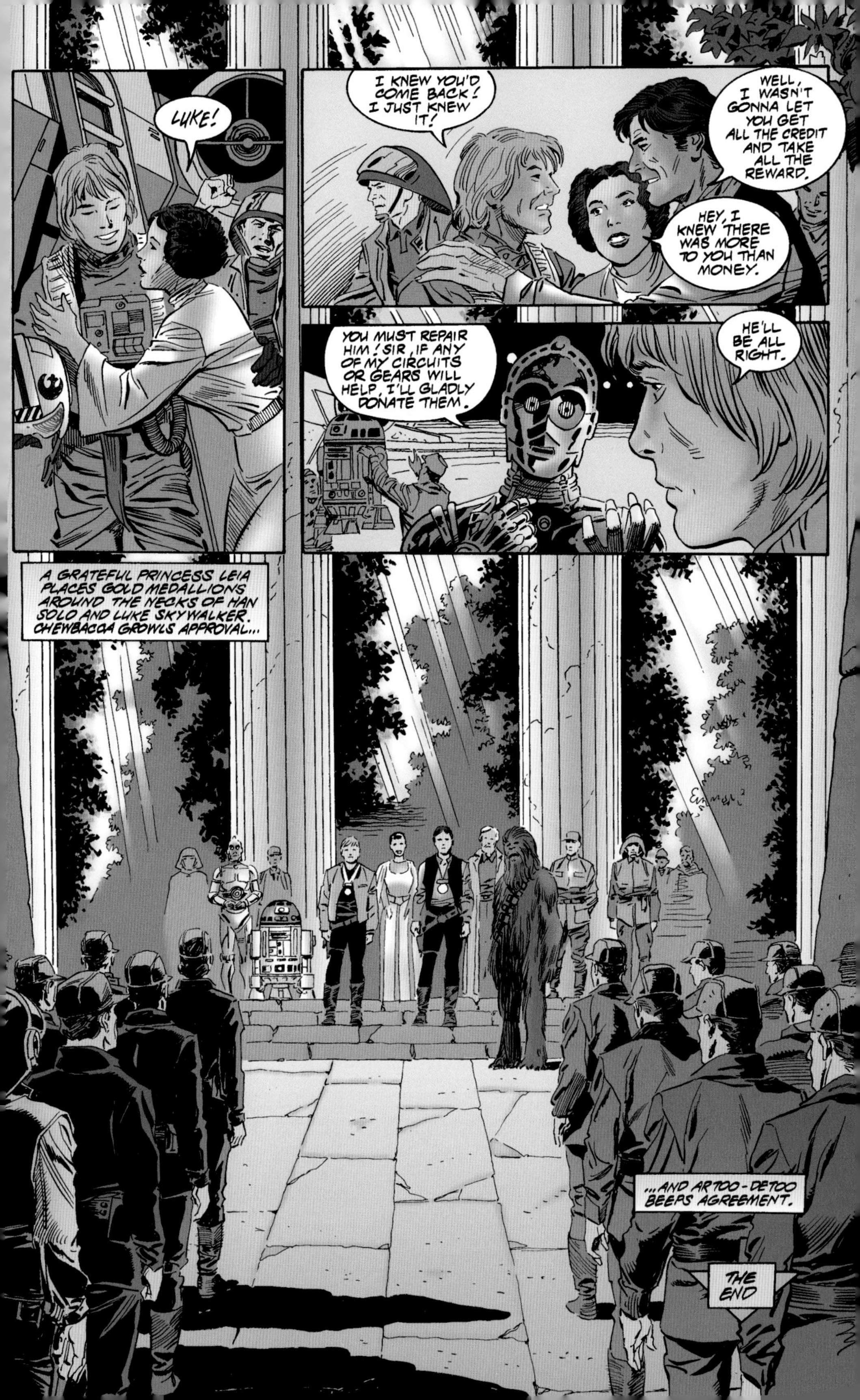
LUKE!
I KNEW YOU'D COME BACK! I JUST KNEW IT!
WELL, I WASN'T GONNA LET YOU GET ALL THE CREDIT AND TAKE ALL THE REWARD.
HEY, I KNEW THERE WAS MORE TO YOU THAN MONEY.
YOU MUST REPAIR HIM! SIR, IF ANY OF MY CIRCUITS OR GEARS WILL HELP, I'LL GLADLY DONATE THEM.
HE'LL BE ALL RIGHT.
A GRATEFUL PRINCESS LEIA PLACES GOLD MEDALLIONS AROUND THE NECKS OF HAN SOLO AND LUKE SKYWALKER. CHEWBACCA GROWLS APPROVAL...
...AND ARTOO-DETOO BEEPS AGREEMENT.
THE END

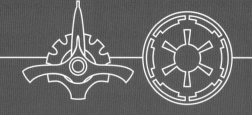

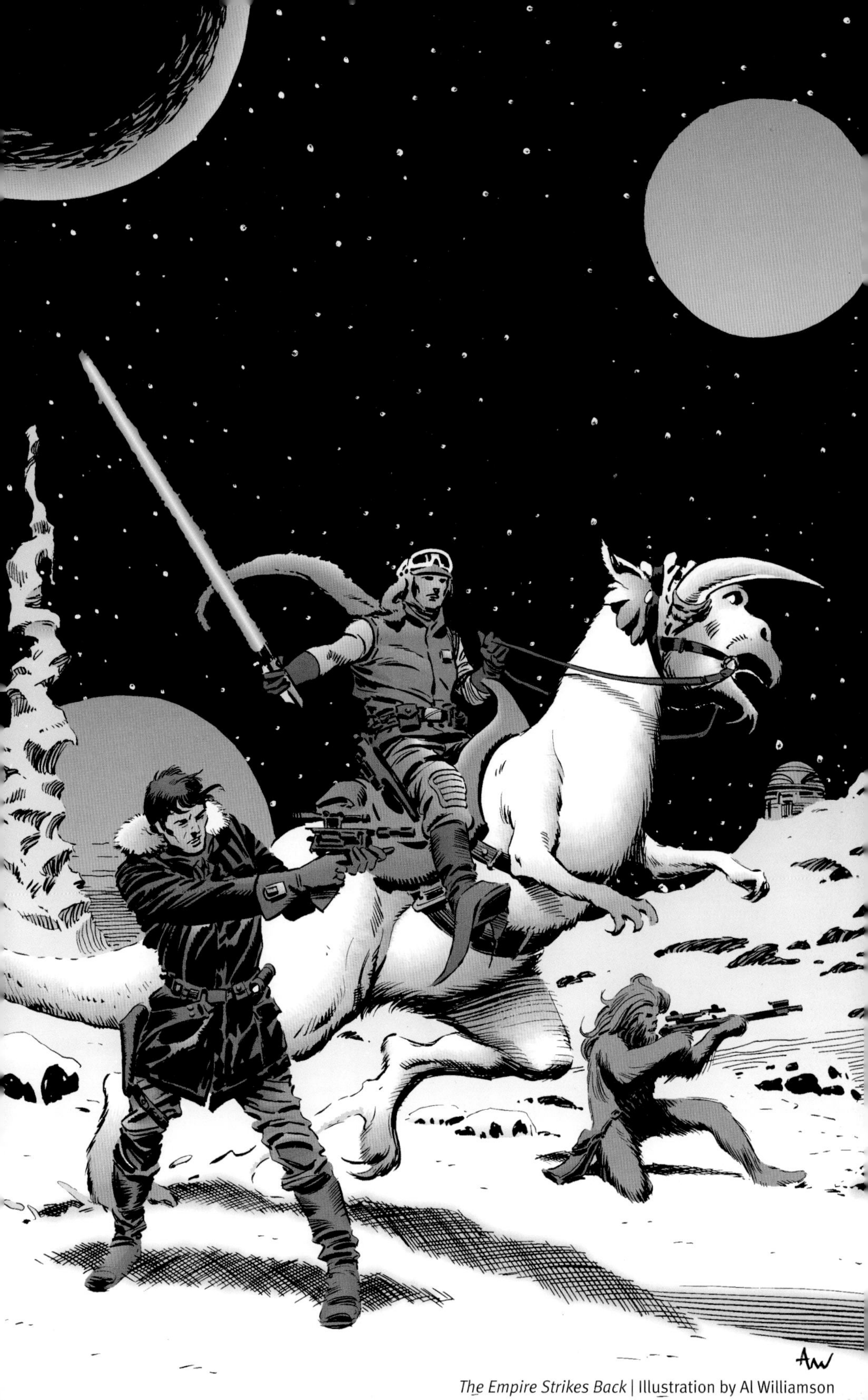

The Empire Strikes Back | Illustration by Al Williamson

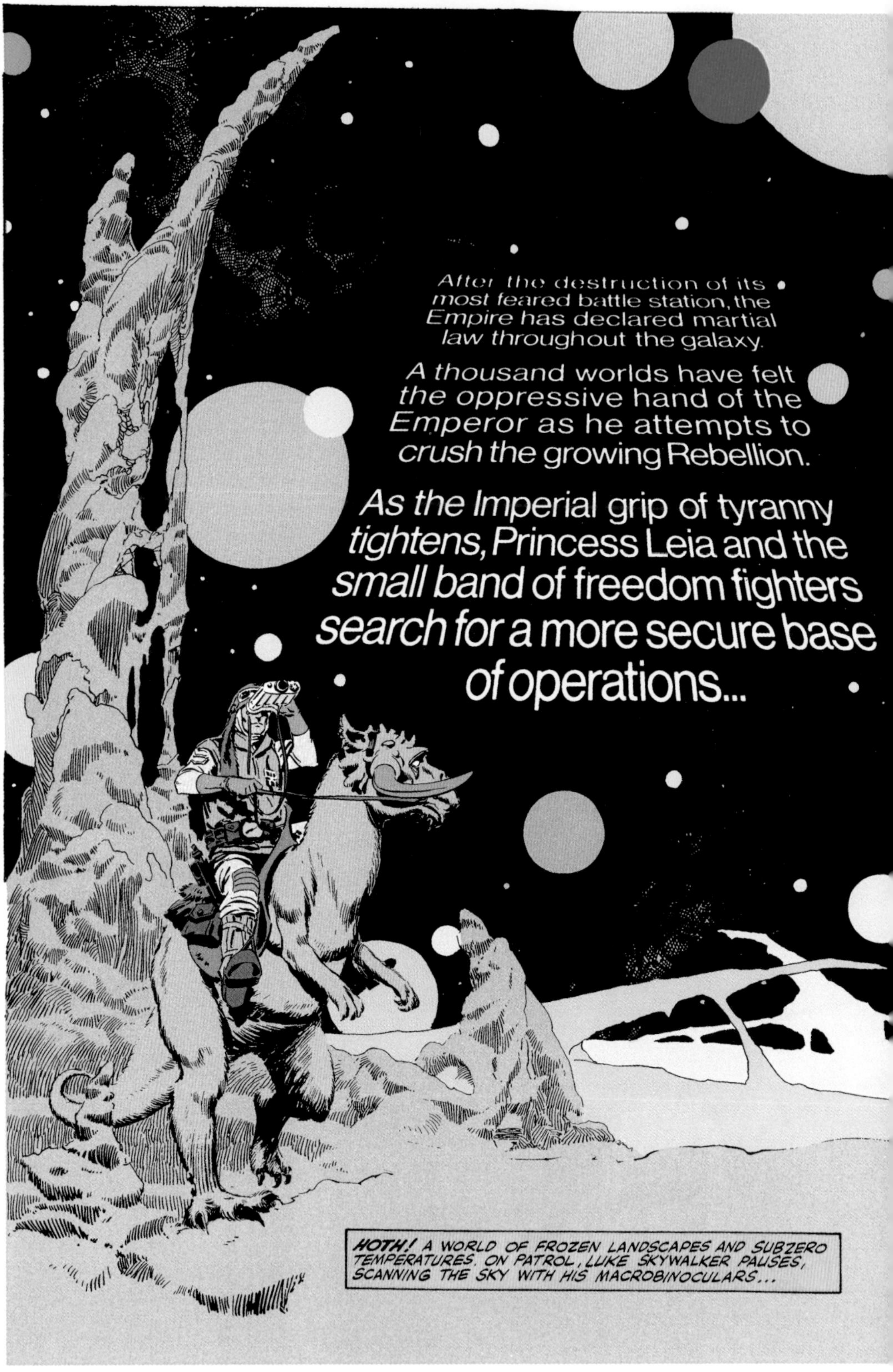

After the destruction of its most feared battle station, the Empire has declared martial law throughout the galaxy.
A thousand worlds have felt the oppressive hand of the Emperor as he attempts to crush the growing Rebellion.
As the Imperial grip of tyranny tightens, Princess Leia and the small band of freedom fighters search for a more secure base of operations...
HOTH! A WORLD OF FROZEN LANDSCAPES AND SUBZERO TEMPERATURES. ON PATROL, LUKE SKYWALKER PAUSES, SCANNING THE SKY WITH HIS MACROBINOCULARS...

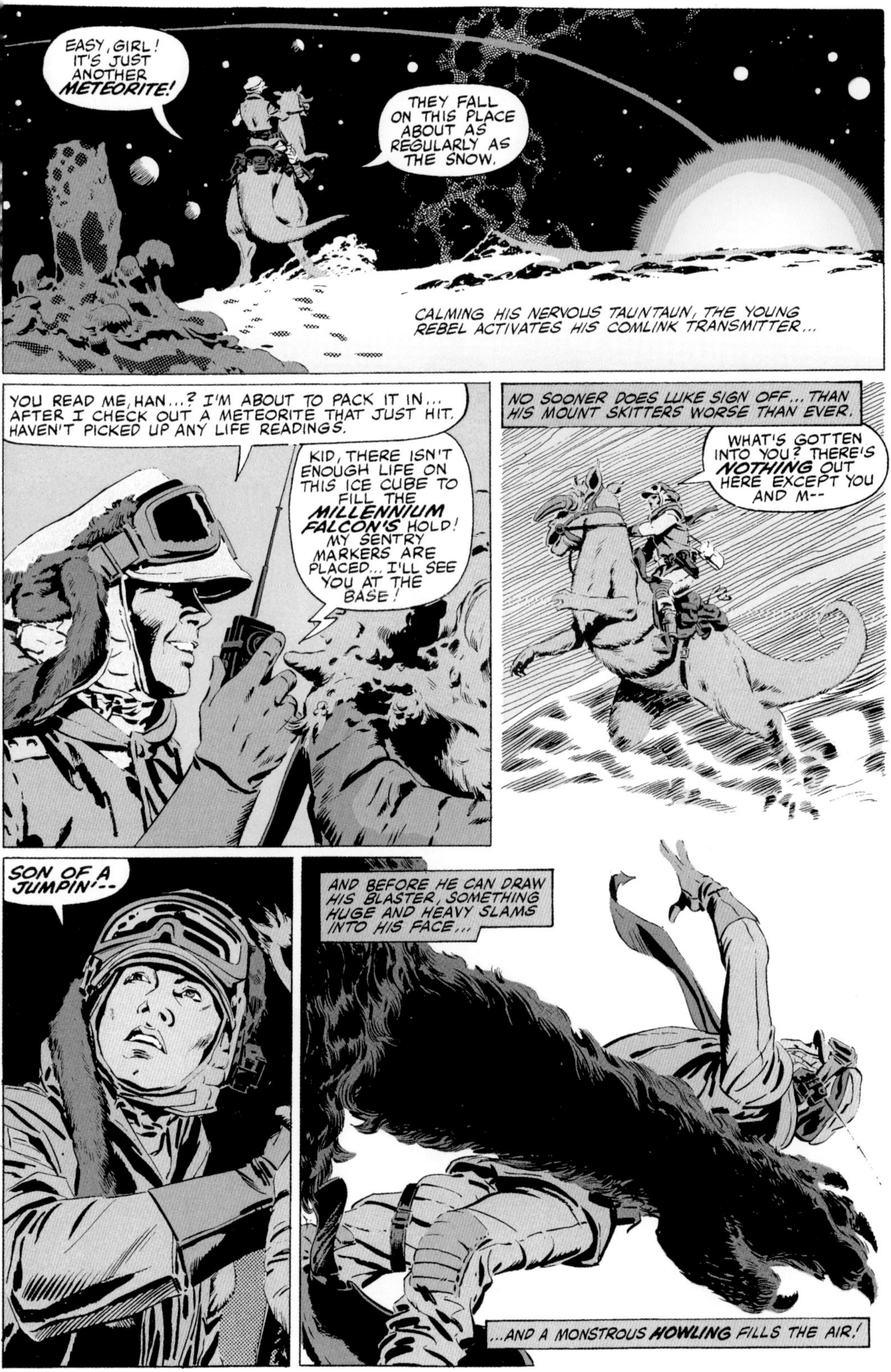
EASY, GIRL! IT'S JUST ANOTHER METEORITE!
THEY FALL ON THIS PLACE ABOUT AS REGULARLY AS THE SNOW.
CALMING HIS NERVOUS TAUNTAUN, THE YOUNG REBEL ACTIVATES HIS COMLINK TRANSMITTER...
YOU READ ME, HAN...? I'M ABOUT TO PACK IT IN... AFTER I CHECK OUT A METEORITE THAT JUST HIT. HAVEN'T PICKED UP ANY LIFE READINGS.
KID, THERE ISN'T ENOUGH LIFE ON THIS ICE CUBE TO FILL THE MILLENNIUM FALCON'S HOLD! MY SENTRY MARKERS ARE PLACED... I'LL SEE YOU AT THE BASE!
NO SOONER DOES LUKE SIGN OFF... THAN HIS MOUNT SKITTERS WORSE THAN EVER.
WHAT'S GOTTEN INTO YOU? THERE'S NOTHING OUT HERE EXCEPT YOU AND M--
SON OF A JUMPIN'--
AND BEFORE HE CAN DRAW HIS BLASTER, SOMETHING HUGE AND HEAVY SLAMS INTO HIS FACE...
...AND A MONSTROUS HOWLING FILLS THE AIR!

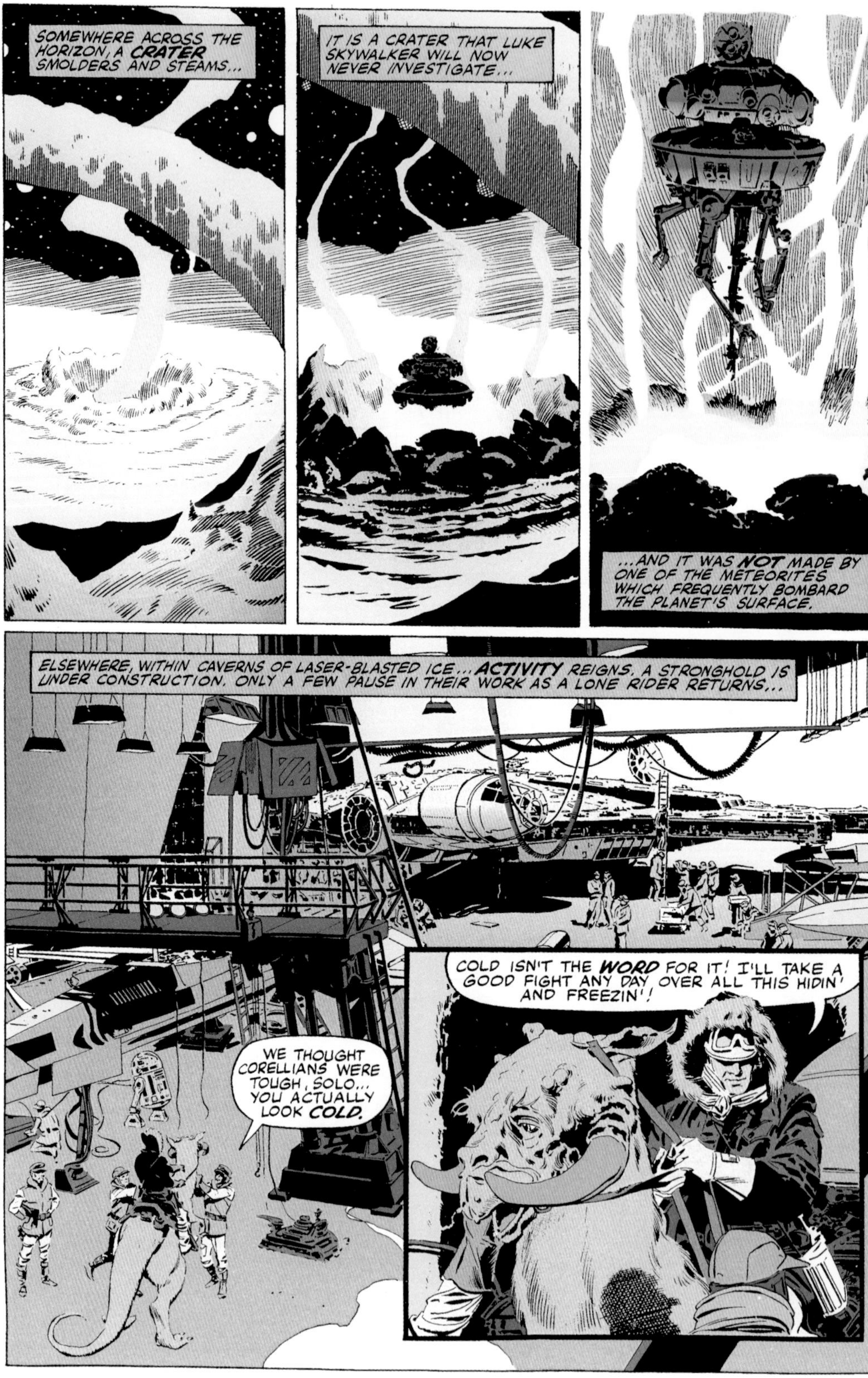

SOMEWHERE ACROSS THE HORIZON, A CRATER SMOLDERS AND STEAMS...
IT IS A CRATER THAT LUKE SKYWALKER WILL NOW NEVER INVESTIGATE...
...AND IT WAS NOT MADE BY ONE OF THE METEORITES WHICH FREQUENTLY BOMBARD THE PLANET'S SURFACE.
ELSEWHERE, WITHIN CAVERNS OF LASER-BLASTED ICE... ACTIVITY REIGNS. A STRONGHOLD IS UNDER CONSTRUCTION. ONLY A FEW PAUSE IN THEIR WORK AS A LONE RIDER RETURNS...
WE THOUGHT CORELLIANS WERE TOUGH, SOLO... YOU ACTUALLY LOOK COLD.
COLD ISN'T THE WORD FOR IT! I'LL TAKE A GOOD FIGHT ANY DAY OVER ALL THIS HIDIN' AND FREEZIN'!

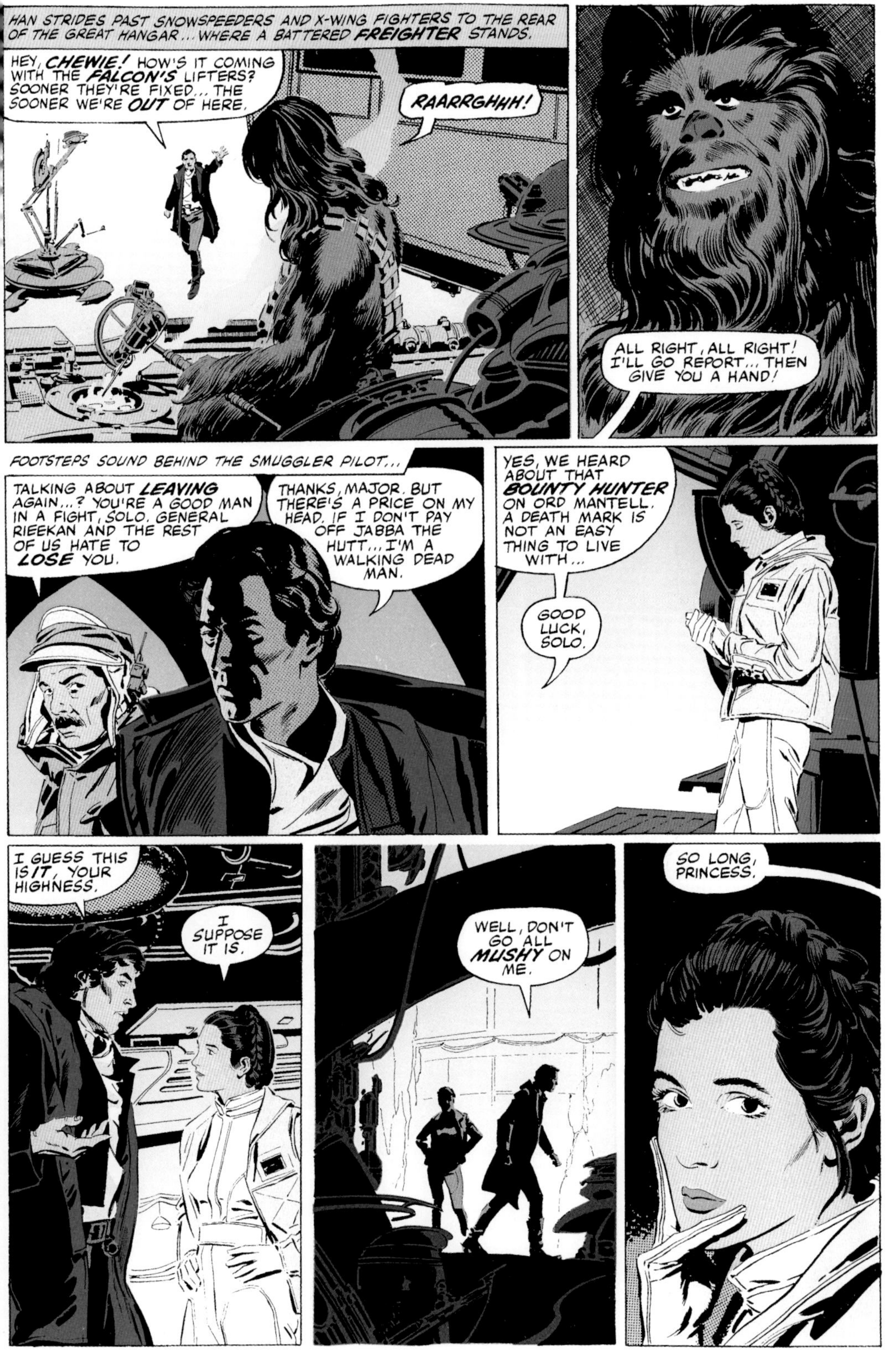
HAN STRIDES PAST SNOWSPEEDERS AND X-WING FIGHTERS TO THE REAR OF THE GREAT HANGAR... WHERE A BATTERED FREIGHTER STANDS.
HEY, CHEWIE! HOW'S IT COMING WITH THE FALCON'S LIFTERS? SOONER THEY'RE FIXED... THE SOONER WE'RE OUT OF HERE.
RAARRGHHH!
ALL RIGHT, ALL RIGHT! I'LL GO REPORT... THEN GIVE YOU A HAND!
FOOTSTEPS SOUND BEHIND THE SMUGGLER PILOT...
TALKING ABOUT LEAVING AGAIN...? YOU'RE A GOOD MAN IN A FIGHT, SOLO. GENERAL RIEEKAN AND THE REST OF US HATE TO LOSE YOU.
THANKS, MAJOR. BUT THERE'S A PRICE ON MY HEAD. IF I DON'T PAY OFF JABBA THE HUTT... I'M A WALKING DEAD MAN.
YES, WE HEARD ABOUT THAT BOUNTY HUNTER ON ORD MANTELL. A DEATH MARK IS NOT AN EASY THING TO LIVE WITH...
GOOD LUCK, SOLO.
I GUESS THIS IS IT, YOUR HIGHNESS.
I SUPPOSE IT IS.
WELL, DON'T GO ALL MUSHY ON ME.
SO LONG, PRINCESS.

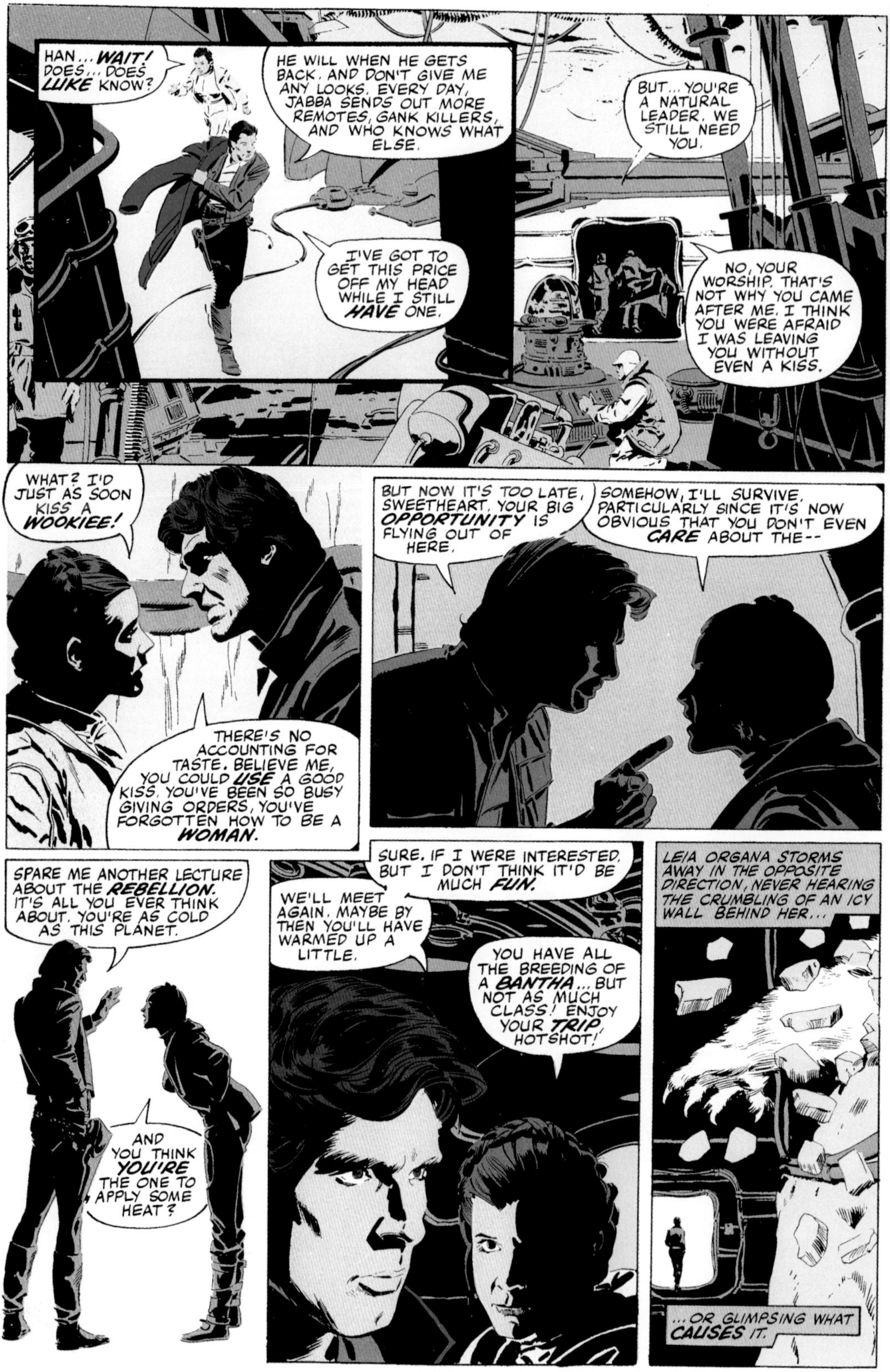

HAN... WAIT! DOES... DOES LUKE KNOW?
HE WILL WHEN HE GETS BACK. AND DON'T GIVE ME ANY LOOKS. EVERY DAY, JABBA SENDS OUT MORE REMOTES, GANK KILLERS, AND WHO KNOWS WHAT ELSE.
I'VE GOT TO GET THIS PRICE OFF MY HEAD WHILE I STILL HAVE ONE.
BUT... YOU'RE A NATURAL LEADER. WE STILL NEED YOU.
NO, YOUR WORSHIP. THAT'S NOT WHY YOU CAME AFTER ME. I THINK YOU WERE AFRAID I WAS LEAVING YOU WITHOUT EVEN A KISS.
WHAT? I'D JUST AS SOON KISS A WOOKIEE!
THERE'S NO ACCOUNTING FOR TASTE. BELIEVE ME, YOU COULD USE A GOOD KISS. YOU'VE BEEN SO BUSY GIVING ORDERS, YOU'VE FORGOTTEN HOW TO BE A WOMAN.
BUT NOW IT'S TOO LATE, SWEETHEART. YOUR BIG OPPORTUNITY IS FLYING OUT OF HERE.
SOMEHOW, I'LL SURVIVE, PARTICULARLY SINCE IT'S NOW OBVIOUS THAT YOU DON'T EVEN CARE ABOUT THE--
SPARE ME ANOTHER LECTURE ABOUT THE REBELLION. IT'S ALL YOU EVER THINK ABOUT. YOU'RE AS COLD AS THIS PLANET.
AND YOU THINK YOU'RE THE ONE TO APPLY SOME HEAT?
SURE. IF I WERE INTERESTED. BUT I DON'T THINK IT'D BE MUCH FUN.
WE'LL MEET AGAIN. MAYBE BY THEN YOU'LL HAVE WARMED UP A LITTLE.
YOU HAVE ALL THE BREEDING OF A BANTHA... BUT NOT AS MUCH CLASS! ENJOY YOUR TRIP, HOTSHOT!
LEIA ORGANA STORMS AWAY IN THE OPPOSITE DIRECTION, NEVER HEARING THE CRUMBLING OF AN ICY WALL BEHIND HER...
...OR GLIMPSING WHAT CAUSES IT.

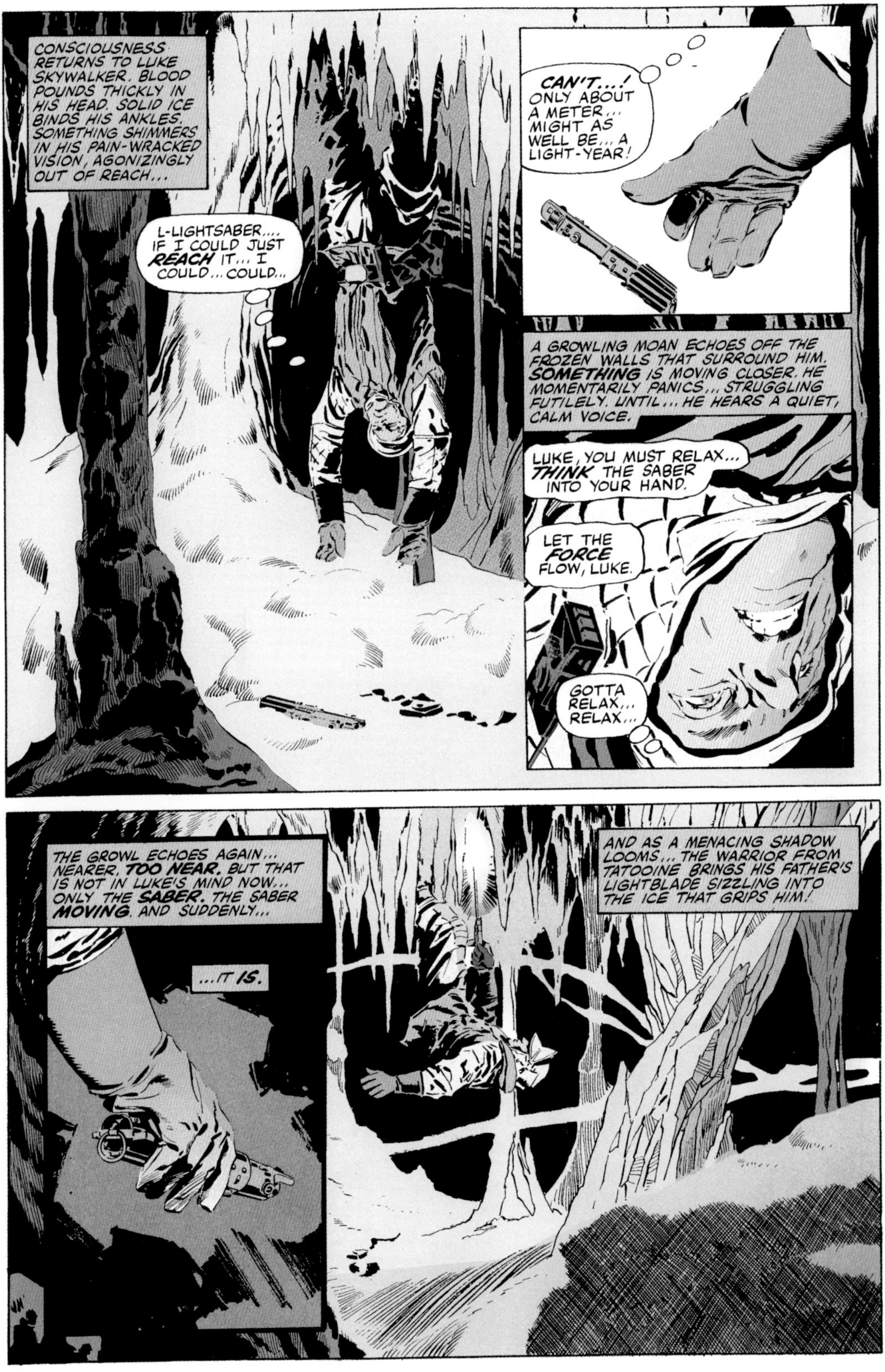
CONSCIOUSNESS RETURNS TO LUKE SKYWALKER. BLOOD POUNDS THICKLY IN HIS HEAD. SOLID ICE BINDS HIS ANKLES. SOMETHING SHIMMERS IN HIS PAIN-WRACKED VISION, AGONIZINGLY OUT OF REACH...
L-LIGHTSABER... IF I COULD JUST REACH IT... I COULD... COULD...
CAN'T...! ONLY ABOUT A METER... MIGHT AS WELL BE... A LIGHT-YEAR!
A GROWLING MOAN ECHOES OFF THE FROZEN WALLS THAT SURROUND HIM. SOMETHING IS MOVING CLOSER. HE MOMENTARILY PANICS... STRUGGLING FUTILELY. UNTIL... HE HEARS A QUIET, CALM VOICE.
LUKE, YOU MUST RELAX... THINK THE SABER INTO YOUR HAND.
LET THE FORCE FLOW, LUKE.
GOTTA RELAX... RELAX...
THE GROWL ECHOES AGAIN... NEARER. TOO NEAR. BUT THAT IS NOT IN LUKE'S MIND NOW... ONLY THE SABER. THE SABER MOVING. AND SUDDENLY...
...IT IS.
AND AS A MENACING SHADOW LOOMS... THE WARRIOR FROM TATOOINE BRINGS HIS FATHER'S LIGHTBLADE SIZZLING INTO THE ICE THAT GRIPS HIM!

LUKE *FALLS*, CRASHING HEAVILY INTO THE SNOW... AS SOMETHING *HUGE* RUSHES TOWARD HIM!

HE *ROLLS*, SLASHING OUT WITH HIS LIGHTBLADE...

...AND A SCREAM OF *PAIN* FILLS THE ICY GORGE.

IT STILL ECHOES IN HIS MIND AS HE SOMEHOW STAGGERS TO SAFETY...

...LIMPING INTO THE GATHERING GRAYNESS THAT HERALDS THE APPROACH OF SUBZERO *NIGHT* ON HOTH.

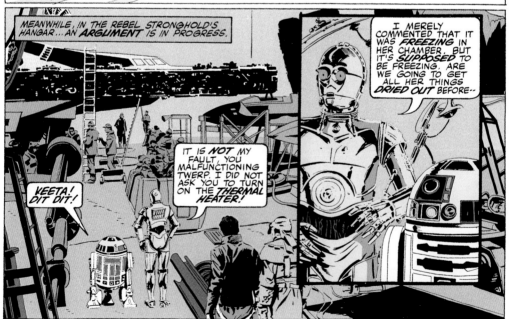

MEANWHILE, IN THE REBEL STRONGHOLD'S HANGAR... AN *ARGUMENT* IS IN PROGRESS.

KEETA! DIT DIT!

IT IS *NOT* MY FAULT, YOU MALFUNCTIONING TWERP. I DID NOT ASK YOU TO TURN ON THE *THERMAL HEATER!*

I MERELY COMMENTED THAT IT WAS *FREEZING* IN HER CHAMBER, BUT IT'S *SUPPOSED* TO BE FREEZING. ARE WE GOING TO GET ALL HER THINGS *DRIED OUT* BEFORE--

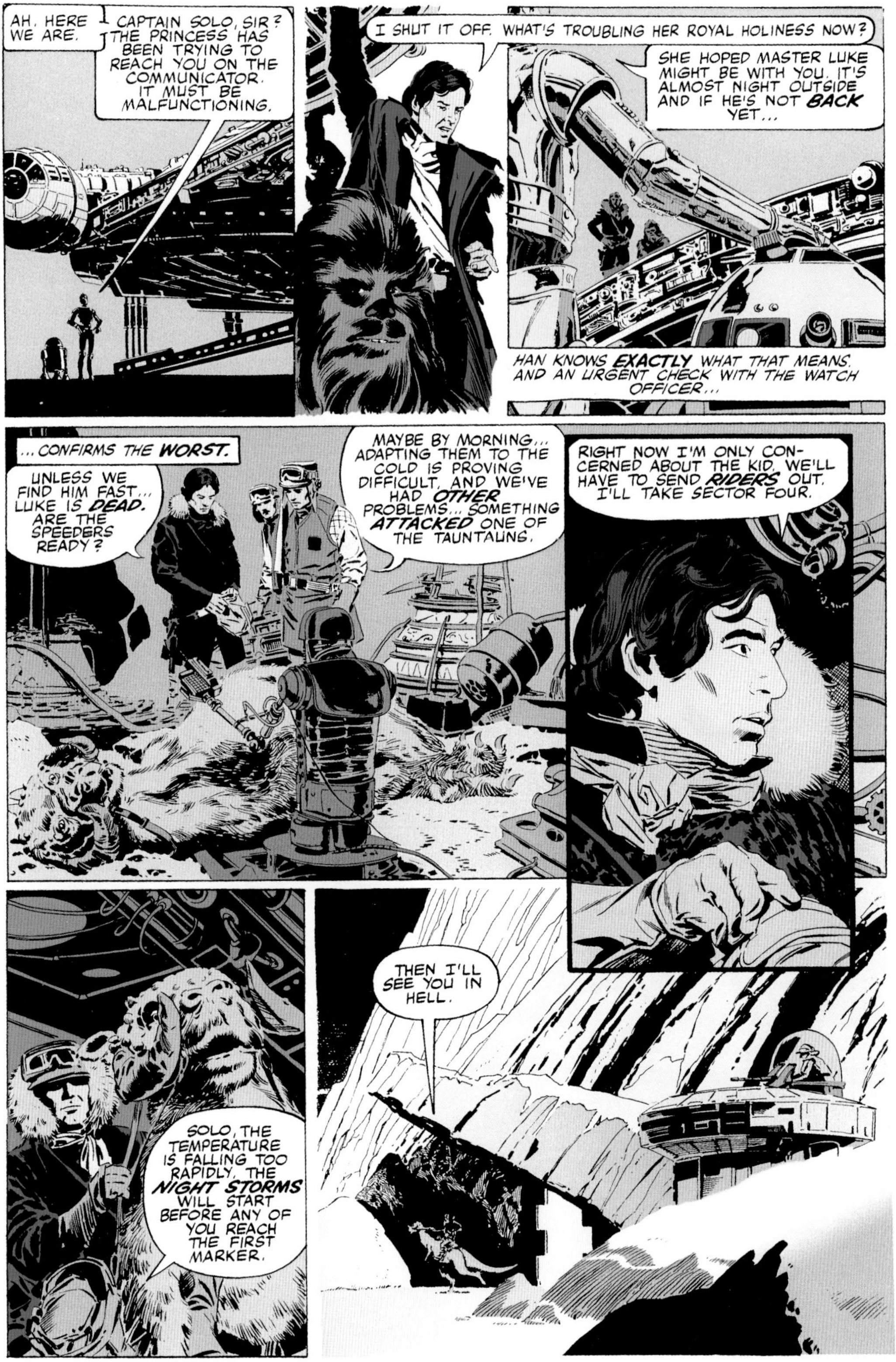
AH. HERE WE ARE.
CAPTAIN SOLO, SIR? THE PRINCESS HAS BEEN TRYING TO REACH YOU ON THE COMMUNICATOR. IT MUST BE MALFUNCTIONING.
I SHUT IT OFF. WHAT'S TROUBLING HER ROYAL HOLINESS NOW?
SHE HOPED MASTER LUKE MIGHT BE WITH YOU. IT'S ALMOST NIGHT OUTSIDE AND IF HE'S NOT BACK YET...
HAN KNOWS EXACTLY WHAT THAT MEANS. AND AN URGENT CHECK WITH THE WATCH OFFICER...
...CONFIRMS THE WORST.
UNLESS WE FIND HIM FAST... LUKE IS DEAD. ARE THE SPEEDERS READY?
MAYBE BY MORNING... ADAPTING THEM TO THE COLD IS PROVING DIFFICULT, AND WE'VE HAD OTHER PROBLEMS... SOMETHING ATTACKED ONE OF THE TAUNTAUNS.
RIGHT NOW I'M ONLY CONCERNED ABOUT THE KID. WE'LL HAVE TO SEND RIDERS OUT. I'LL TAKE SECTOR FOUR.
SOLO, THE TEMPERATURE IS FALLING TOO RAPIDLY. THE NIGHT STORMS WILL START BEFORE ANY OF YOU REACH THE FIRST MARKER.
THEN I'LL SEE YOU IN HELL.

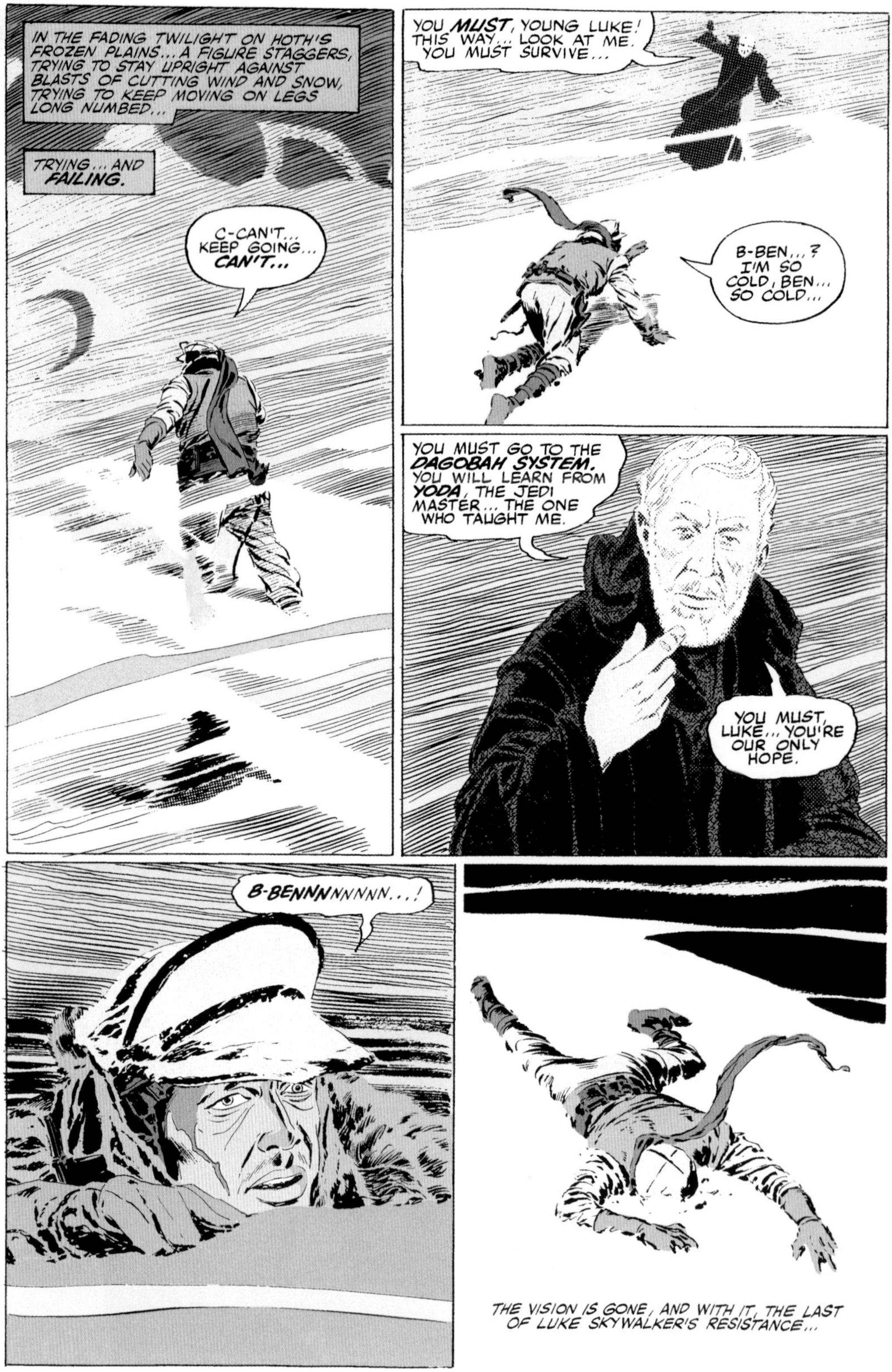
IN THE FADING TWILIGHT ON HOTH'S FROZEN PLAINS... A FIGURE STAGGERS, TRYING TO STAY UPRIGHT AGAINST BLASTS OF CUTTING WIND AND SNOW, TRYING TO KEEP MOVING ON LEGS LONG NUMBED...
TRYING... AND FAILING.
C-CAN'T... KEEP GOING... CAN'T...
YOU MUST, YOUNG LUKE! THIS WAY... LOOK AT ME. YOU MUST SURVIVE...
B-BEN...? I'M SO COLD, BEN... SO COLD...
YOU MUST GO TO THE DAGOBAH SYSTEM. YOU WILL LEARN FROM YODA, THE JEDI MASTER... THE ONE WHO TAUGHT ME.
YOU MUST, LUKE... YOU'RE OUR ONLY HOPE.
B-BENNNNNNNN...!
THE VISION IS GONE, AND WITH IT, THE LAST OF LUKE SKYWALKER'S RESISTANCE...

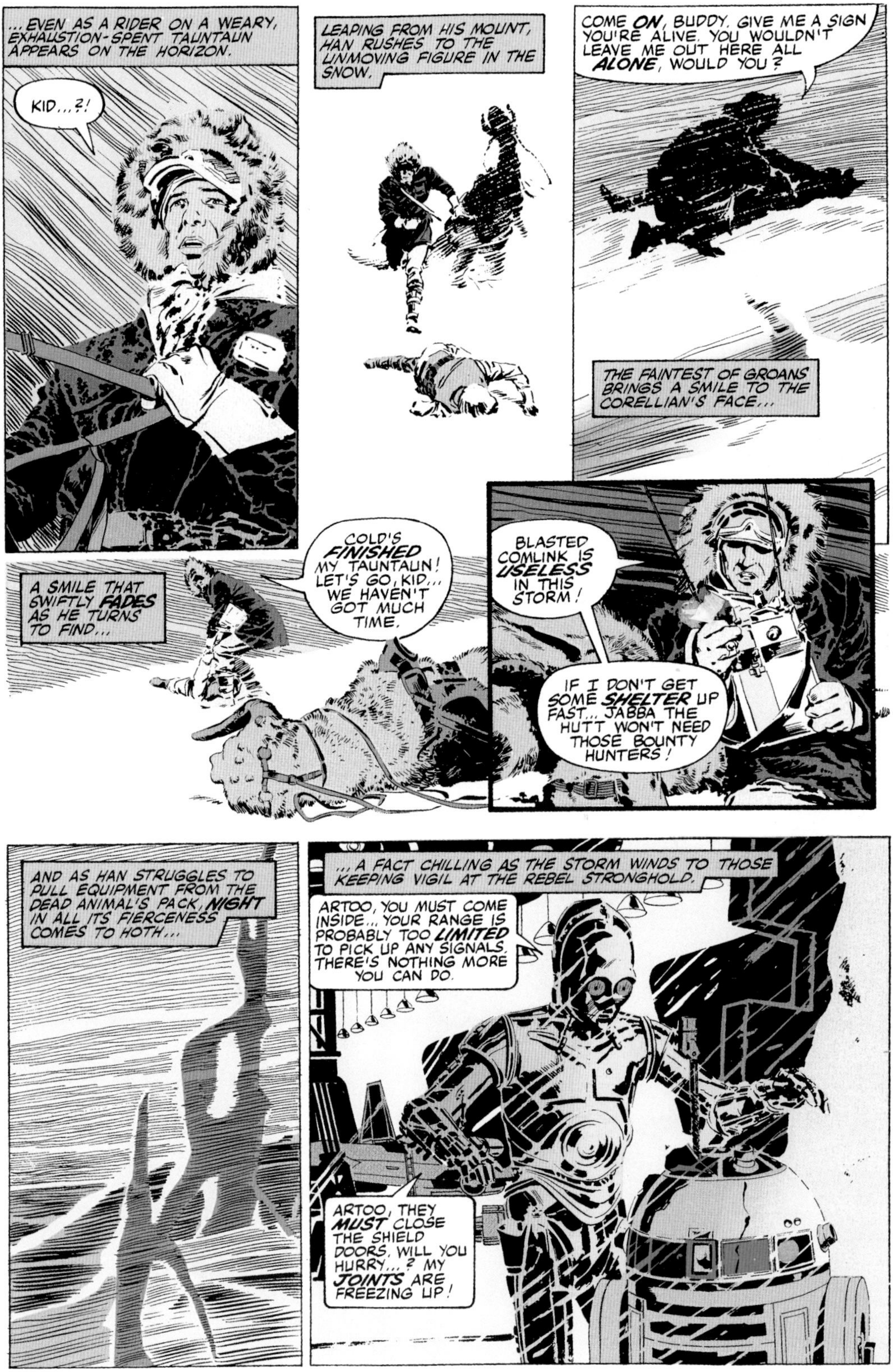
...EVEN AS A RIDER ON A WEARY, EXHAUSTION-SPENT TAUNTAUN APPEARS ON THE HORIZON.
KID...?!
LEAPING FROM HIS MOUNT, HAN RUSHES TO THE UNMOVING FIGURE IN THE SNOW.
COME ON, BUDDY, GIVE ME A SIGN YOU'RE ALIVE. YOU WOULDN'T LEAVE ME OUT HERE ALL ALONE, WOULD YOU?
THE FAINTEST OF GROANS BRINGS A SMILE TO THE CORELLIAN'S FACE...
A SMILE THAT SWIFTLY FADES AS HE TURNS TO FIND...
COLD'S FINISHED MY TAUNTAUN! LET'S GO, KID... WE HAVEN'T GOT MUCH TIME.
BLASTED COMLINK IS USELESS IN THIS STORM!
IF I DON'T GET SOME SHELTER UP FAST... JABBA THE HUTT WON'T NEED THOSE BOUNTY HUNTERS!
AND AS HAN STRUGGLES TO PULL EQUIPMENT FROM THE DEAD ANIMAL'S PACK, NIGHT IN ALL ITS FIERCENESS COMES TO HOTH...
...A FACT CHILLING AS THE STORM WINDS TO THOSE KEEPING VIGIL AT THE REBEL STRONGHOLD.
ARTOO, YOU MUST COME INSIDE... YOUR RANGE IS PROBABLY TOO LIMITED TO PICK UP ANY SIGNALS. THERE'S NOTHING MORE YOU CAN DO.
ARTOO, THEY MUST CLOSE THE SHIELD DOORS. WILL YOU HURRY...? MY JOINTS ARE FREEZING UP!

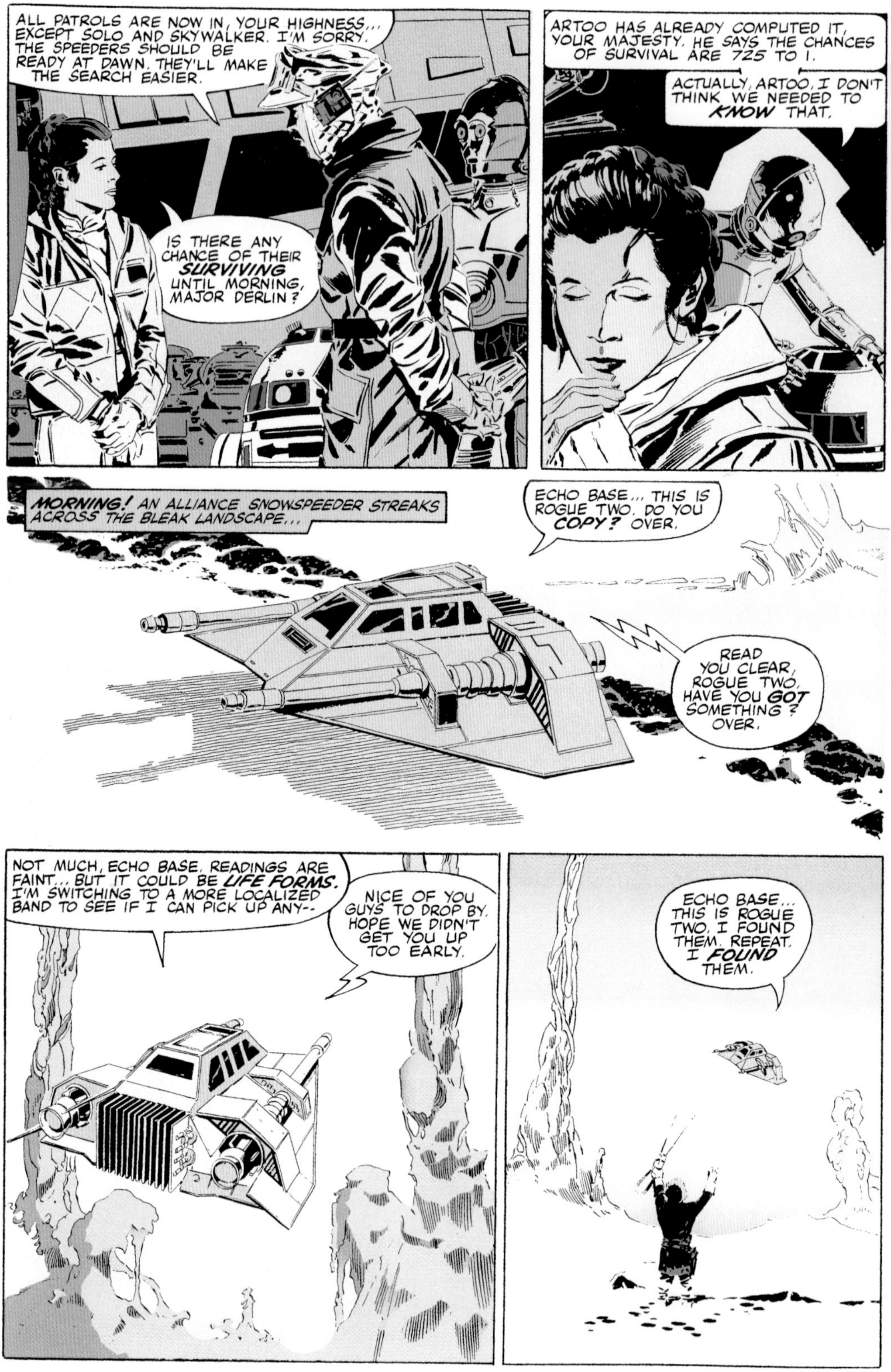
ALL PATROLS ARE NOW IN, YOUR HIGHNESS... EXCEPT SOLO AND SKYWALKER. I'M SORRY. THE SPEEDERS SHOULD BE READY AT DAWN. THEY'LL MAKE THE SEARCH EASIER.
IS THERE ANY CHANCE OF THEIR SURVIVING UNTIL MORNING, MAJOR DERLIN?
ARTOO HAS ALREADY COMPUTED IT, YOUR MAJESTY. HE SAYS THE CHANCES OF SURVIVAL ARE 725 TO 1.
ACTUALLY, ARTOO, I DON'T THINK WE NEEDED TO KNOW THAT.
MORNING! AN ALLIANCE SNOWSPEEDER STREAKS ACROSS THE BLEAK LANDSCAPE...
ECHO BASE... THIS IS ROGUE TWO. DO YOU COPY? OVER.
READ YOU CLEAR, ROGUE TWO. HAVE YOU GOT SOMETHING? OVER.
NOT MUCH, ECHO BASE. READINGS ARE FAINT... BUT IT COULD BE LIFE FORMS. I'M SWITCHING TO A MORE LOCALIZED BAND TO SEE IF I CAN PICK UP ANY--
NICE OF YOU GUYS TO DROP BY. HOPE WE DIDN'T GET YOU UP TOO EARLY.
ECHO BASE... THIS IS ROGUE TWO. I FOUND THEM. REPEAT. I FOUND THEM.

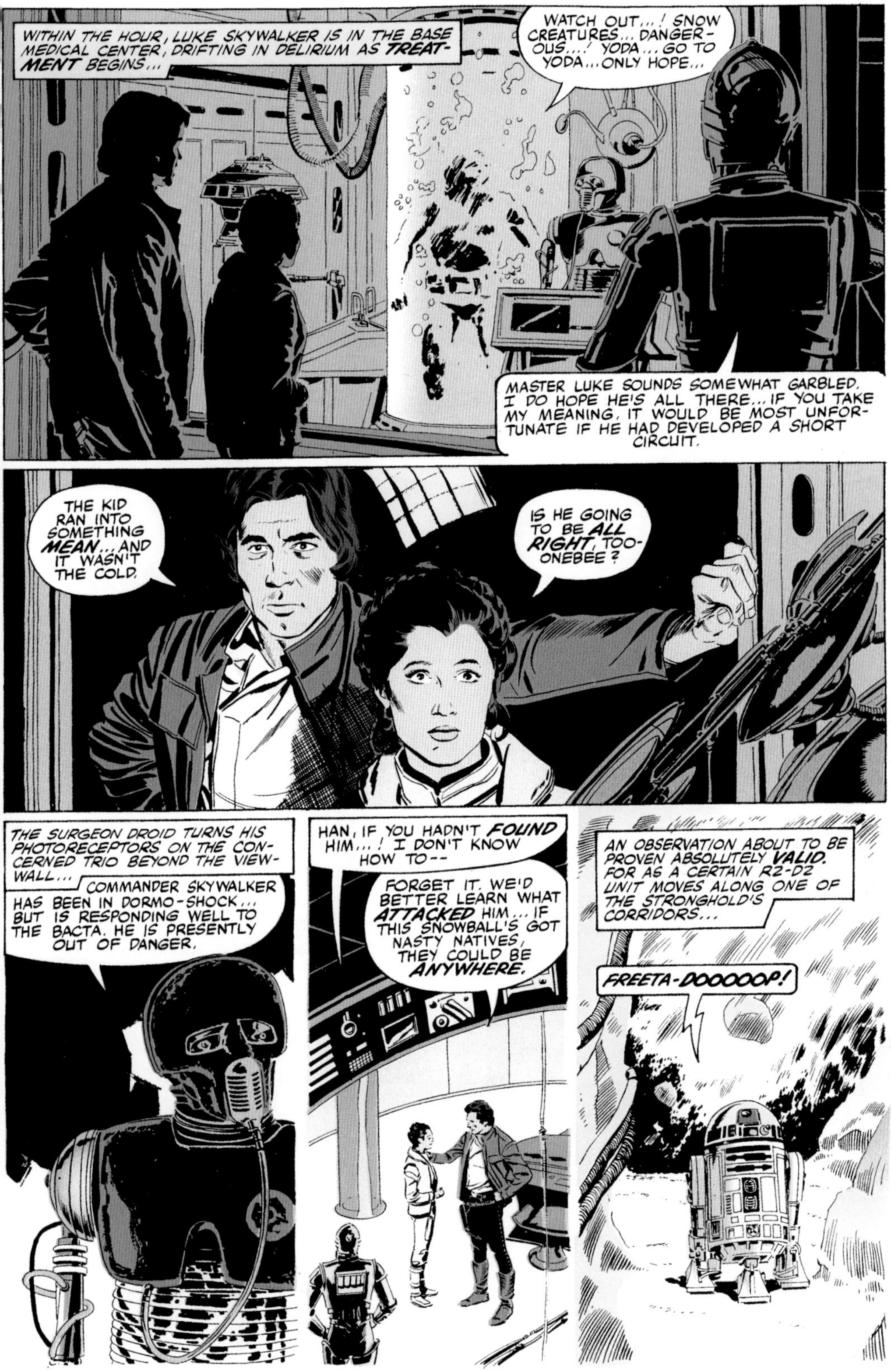
WITHIN THE HOUR, LUKE SKYWALKER IS IN THE BASE MEDICAL CENTER, DRIFTING IN DELIRIUM AS TREATMENT BEGINS...
WATCH OUT...! SNOW CREATURES... DANGEROUS...! YODA... GO TO YODA... ONLY HOPE...
MASTER LUKE SOUNDS SOMEWHAT GARBLED. I DO HOPE HE'S ALL THERE... IF YOU TAKE MY MEANING. IT WOULD BE MOST UNFORTUNATE IF HE HAD DEVELOPED A SHORT CIRCUIT.
THE KID RAN INTO SOMETHING MEAN... AND IT WASN'T THE COLD.
IS HE GOING TO BE ALL RIGHT, TOO-ONEBEE?
THE SURGEON DROID TURNS HIS PHOTORECEPTORS ON THE CONCERNED TRIO BEYOND THE VIEW-WALL...
COMMANDER SKYWALKER HAS BEEN IN DORMO-SHOCK... BUT IS RESPONDING WELL TO THE BACTA. HE IS PRESENTLY OUT OF DANGER.
HAN, IF YOU HADN'T FOUND HIM...! I DON'T KNOW HOW TO--
FORGET IT. WE'D BETTER LEARN WHAT ATTACKED HIM... IF THIS SNOWBALL'S GOT NASTY NATIVES, THEY COULD BE ANYWHERE.
AN OBSERVATION ABOUT TO BE PROVEN ABSOLUTELY VALID. FOR AS A CERTAIN R2-D2 UNIT MOVES ALONG ONE OF THE STRONGHOLD'S CORRIDORS...
FREETA-DOOOOOP!

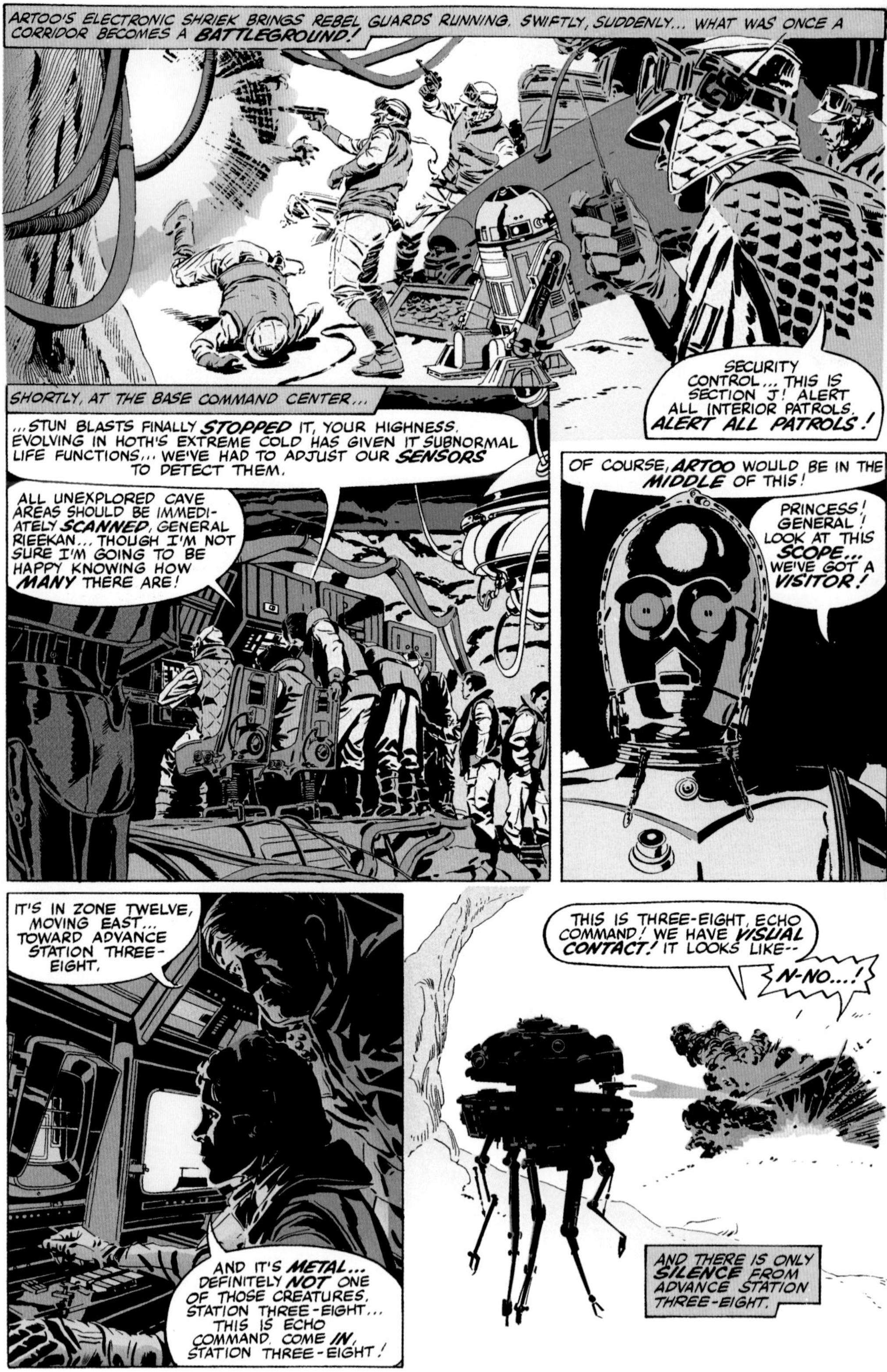
ARTOO'S ELECTRONIC SHRIEK BRINGS REBEL GUARDS RUNNING. SWIFTLY, SUDDENLY... WHAT WAS ONCE A CORRIDOR BECOMES A BATTLEGROUND!
SECURITY CONTROL... THIS IS SECTION J! ALERT ALL INTERIOR PATROLS. ALERT ALL PATROLS!
SHORTLY, AT THE BASE COMMAND CENTER...
...STUN BLASTS FINALLY STOPPED IT, YOUR HIGHNESS. EVOLVING IN HOTH'S EXTREME COLD HAS GIVEN IT SUBNORMAL LIFE FUNCTIONS... WE'VE HAD TO ADJUST OUR SENSORS TO DETECT THEM.
ALL UNEXPLORED CAVE AREAS SHOULD BE IMMEDIATELY SCANNED, GENERAL RIEEKAN... THOUGH I'M NOT SURE I'M GOING TO BE HAPPY KNOWING HOW MANY THERE ARE!
OF COURSE, ARTOO WOULD BE IN THE MIDDLE OF THIS!
PRINCESS! GENERAL! LOOK AT THIS SCOPE... WE'VE GOT A VISITOR!
IT'S IN ZONE TWELVE, MOVING EAST... TOWARD ADVANCE STATION THREE-EIGHT.
AND IT'S METAL... DEFINITELY NOT ONE OF THOSE CREATURES. STATION THREE-EIGHT... THIS IS ECHO COMMAND. COME IN, STATION THREE-EIGHT!
THIS IS THREE-EIGHT, ECHO COMMAND! WE HAVE VISUAL CONTACT! IT LOOKS LIKE--
N-NO...!
AND THERE IS ONLY SILENCE FROM ADVANCE STATION THREE-EIGHT.

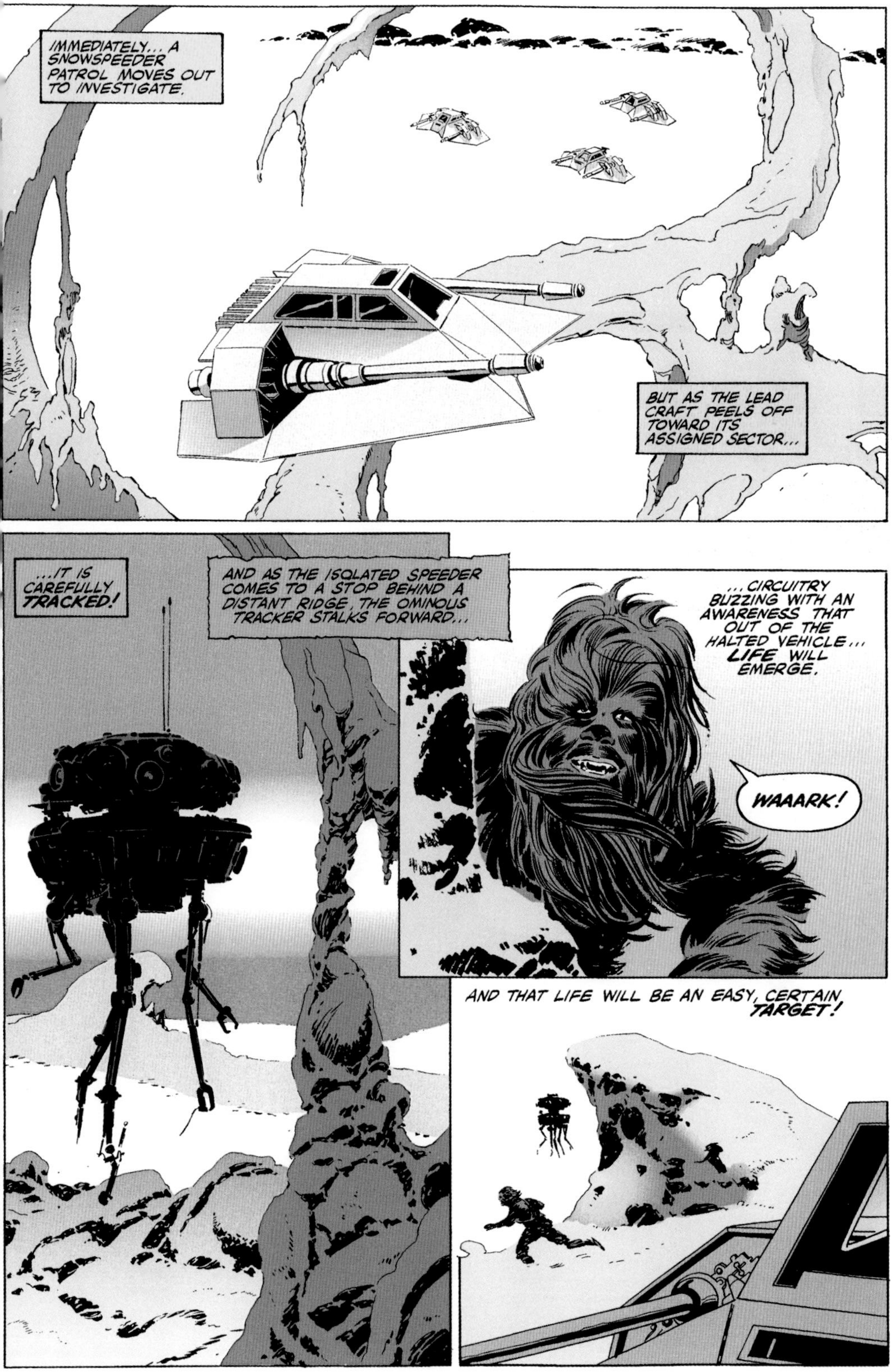
IMMEDIATELY... A SNOWSPEEDER PATROL MOVES OUT TO INVESTIGATE.
BUT AS THE LEAD CRAFT PEELS OFF TOWARD ITS ASSIGNED SECTOR...
...IT IS CAREFULLY TRACKED!
AND AS THE ISOLATED SPEEDER COMES TO A STOP BEHIND A DISTANT RIDGE, THE OMINOUS TRACKER STALKS FORWARD...
...CIRCUITRY BUZZING WITH AN AWARENESS THAT OUT OF THE HALTED VEHICLE... LIFE WILL EMERGE.
WAAARK!
AND THAT LIFE WILL BE AN EASY, CERTAIN TARGET!

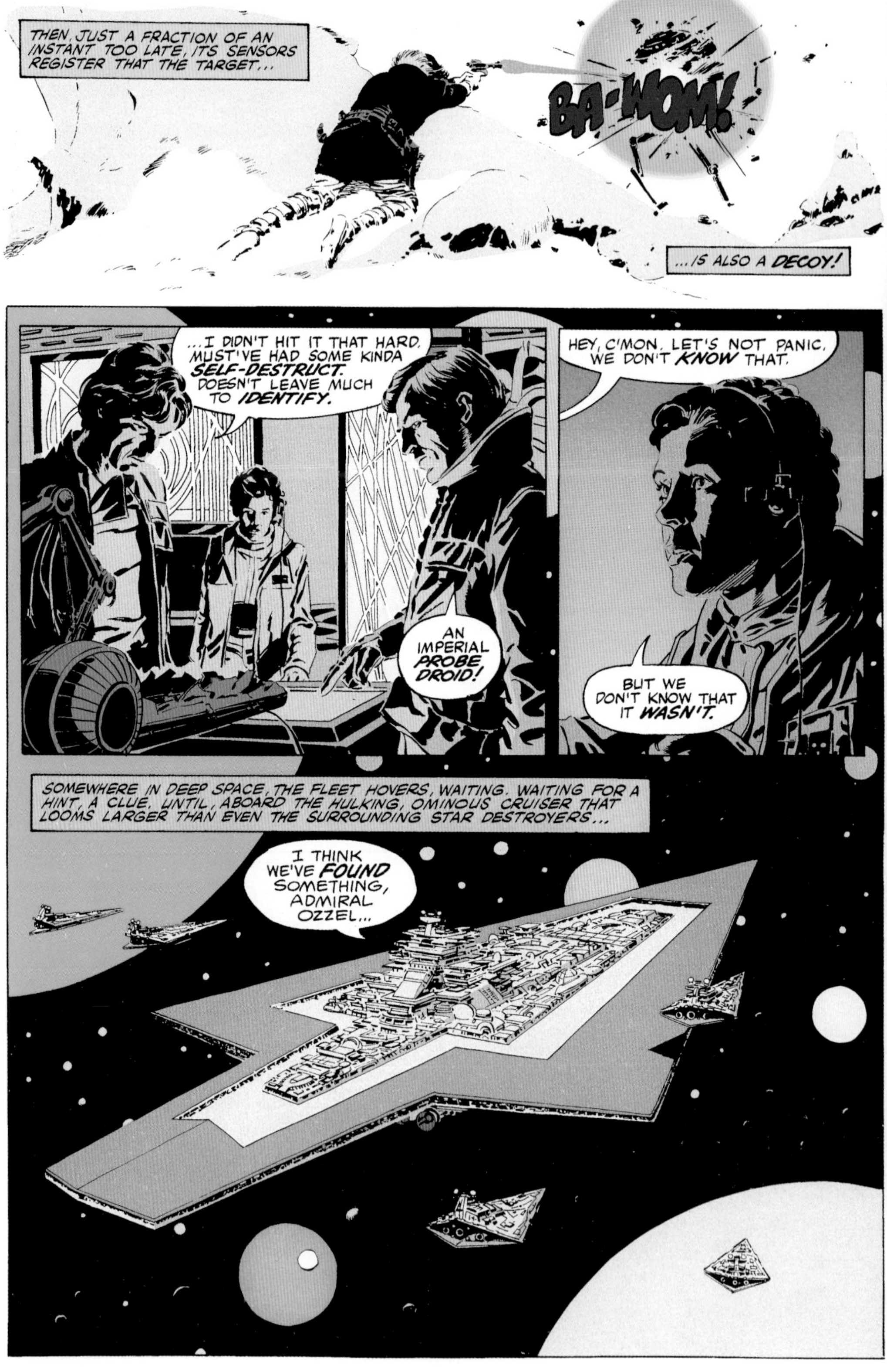
THEN, JUST A FRACTION OF AN INSTANT TOO LATE, ITS SENSORS REGISTER THAT THE TARGET...
BA-WOM!
...IS ALSO A DECOY!
...I DIDN'T HIT IT THAT HARD. MUST'VE HAD SOME KINDA SELF-DESTRUCT. DOESN'T LEAVE MUCH TO IDENTIFY.
AN IMPERIAL PROBE DROID!
HEY, C'MON, LET'S NOT PANIC. WE DON'T KNOW THAT.
BUT WE DON'T KNOW THAT IT WASN'T.
SOMEWHERE IN DEEP SPACE, THE FLEET HOVERS, WAITING. WAITING FOR A HINT, A CLUE, UNTIL, ABOARD THE HULKING, OMINOUS CRUISER THAT LOOMS LARGER THAN EVEN THE SURROUNDING STAR DESTROYERS...
I THINK WE'VE FOUND SOMETHING, ADMIRAL OZZEL...

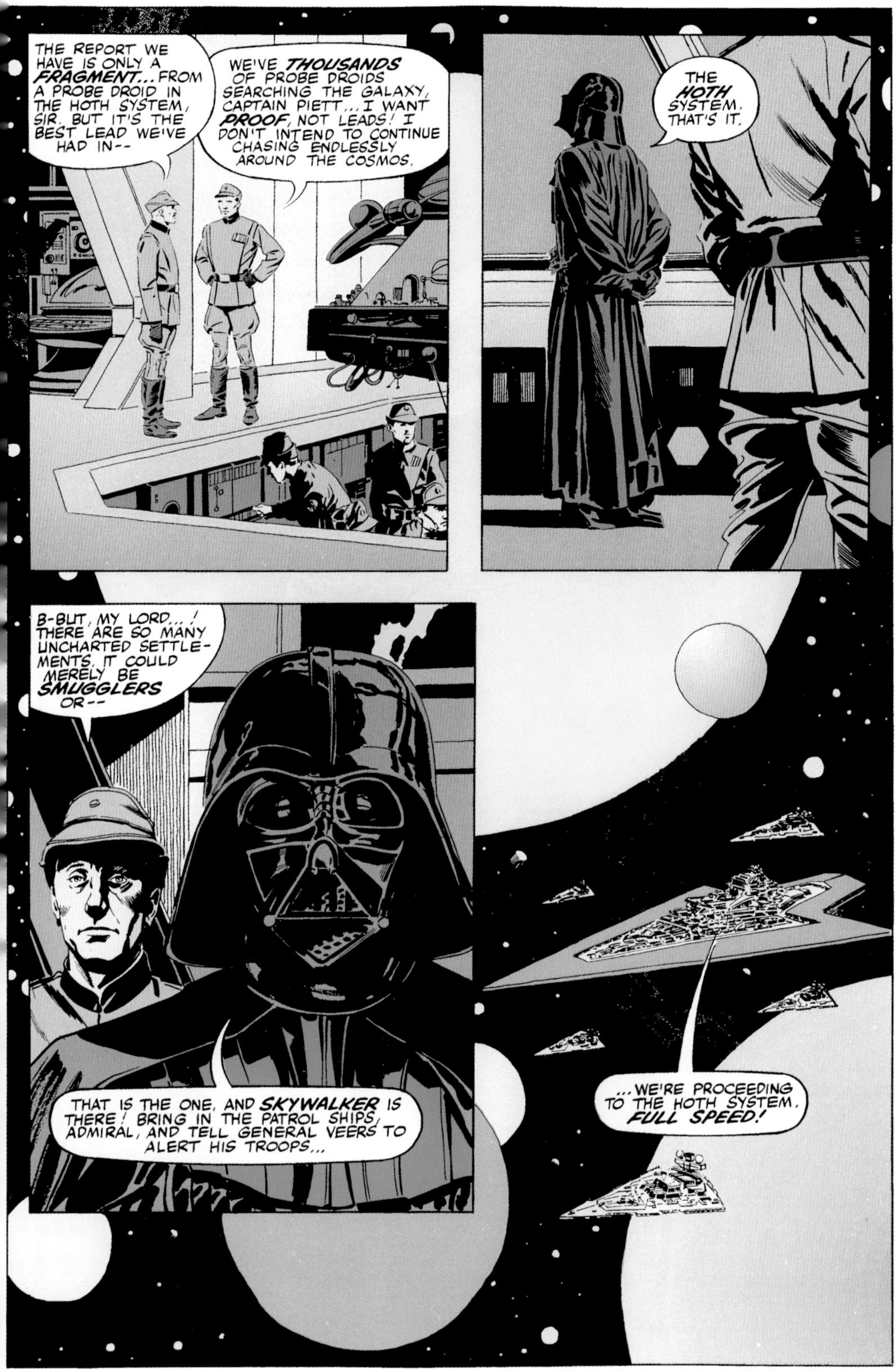
THE REPORT WE HAVE IS ONLY A FRAGMENT... FROM A PROBE DROID IN THE HOTH SYSTEM, SIR. BUT IT'S THE BEST LEAD WE'VE HAD IN--
WE'VE THOUSANDS OF PROBE DROIDS SEARCHING THE GALAXY, CAPTAIN PIETT... I WANT PROOF, NOT LEADS! I DON'T INTEND TO CONTINUE CHASING ENDLESSLY AROUND THE COSMOS.
THE HOTH SYSTEM. THAT'S IT.
B-BUT, MY LORD... ! THERE ARE SO MANY UNCHARTED SETTLEMENTS. IT COULD MERELY BE SMUGGLERS OR--
THAT IS THE ONE, AND SKYWALKER IS THERE! BRING IN THE PATROL SHIPS, ADMIRAL, AND TELL GENERAL VEERS TO ALERT HIS TROOPS...
...WE'RE PROCEEDING TO THE HOTH SYSTEM, FULL SPEED!

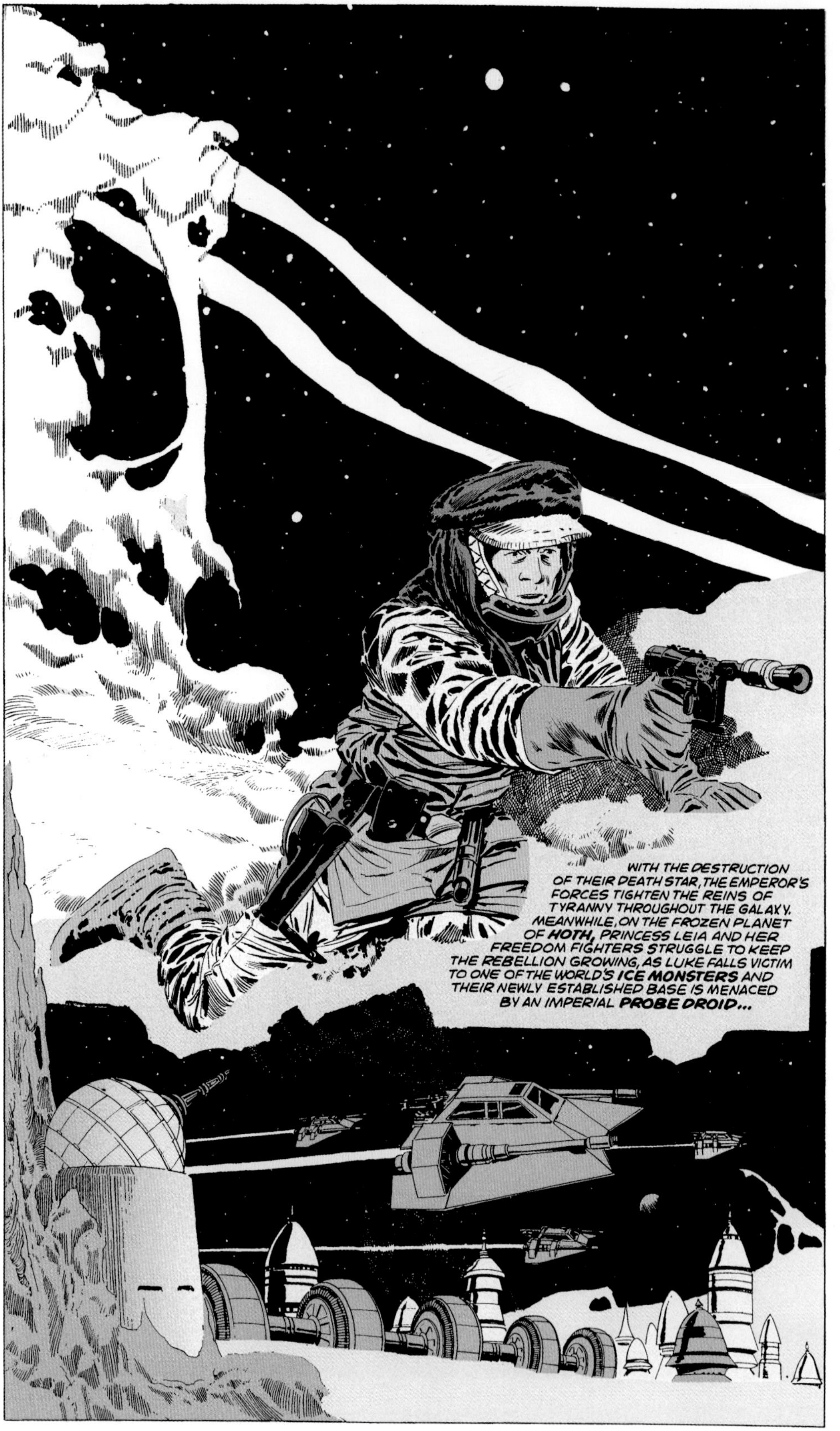
WITH THE DESTRUCTION OF THEIR DEATH STAR, THE EMPEROR'S FORCES TIGHTEN THE REINS OF TYRANNY THROUGHOUT THE GALAXY. MEANWHILE, ON THE FROZEN PLANET OF HOTH, PRINCESS LEIA AND HER FREEDOM FIGHTERS STRUGGLE TO KEEP THE REBELLION GROWING, AS LUKE FALLS VICTIM TO ONE OF THE WORLD'S ICE MONSTERS AND THEIR NEWLY ESTABLISHED BASE IS MENACED BY AN IMPERIAL PROBE DROID...

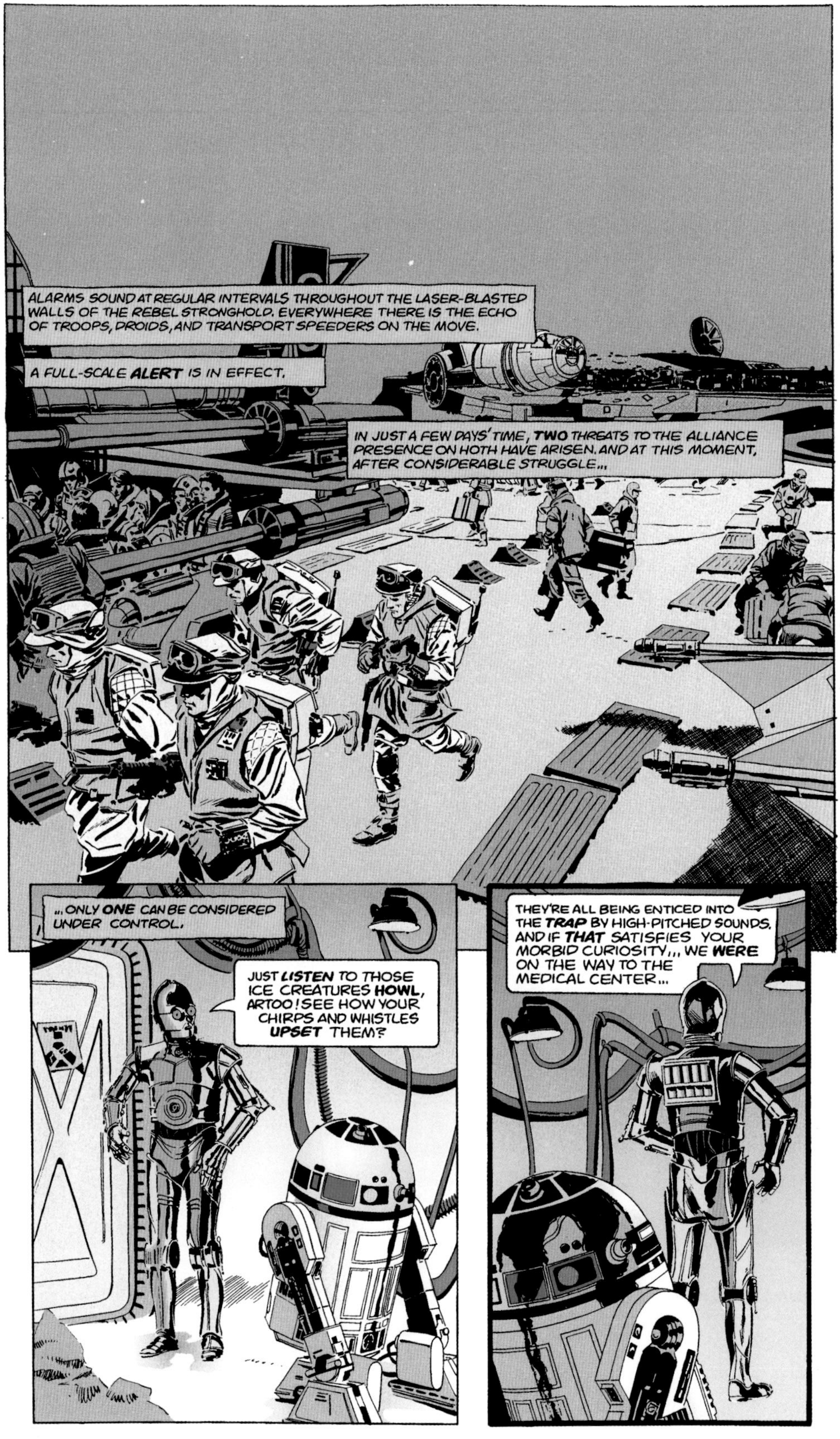
ALARMS SOUND AT REGULAR INTERVALS THROUGHOUT THE LASER-BLASTED WALLS OF THE REBEL STRONGHOLD. EVERYWHERE THERE IS THE ECHO OF TROOPS, DROIDS, AND TRANSPORT SPEEDERS ON THE MOVE.
A FULL-SCALE ALERT IS IN EFFECT.
IN JUST A FEW DAYS' TIME, TWO THREATS TO THE ALLIANCE PRESENCE ON HOTH HAVE ARISEN. AND AT THIS MOMENT, AFTER CONSIDERABLE STRUGGLE...
...ONLY ONE CAN BE CONSIDERED UNDER CONTROL.
JUST LISTEN TO THOSE ICE CREATURES HOWL, ARTOO! SEE HOW YOUR CHIRPS AND WHISTLES UPSET THEM?
THEY'RE ALL BEING ENTICED INTO THE TRAP BY HIGH-PITCHED SOUNDS. AND IF THAT SATISFIES YOUR MORBID CURIOSITY... WE WERE ON THE WAY TO THE MEDICAL CENTER...

WHERE...

HOLD STILL FOR ONE MOMENT, COMMANDER SKYWALKER...

THERE, YES...

THE BACTA ARE GROWING WELL. THOSE SCARS SHOULD BE GONE IN A DAY OR SO.

THE SURGEON DROID TOO-ONEBEE SLIDES BACK, AND LEIA ORGANA MOVES FORWARD WITH COMPASSION AND CONCERN. AND PERHAPS, SOMETHING MORE.

LUKE, DOES IT STILL **HURT** YOU?

I'M FINE, REALLY, BUT...Y'KNOW, LEIA... WHEN I WAS **LOST** OUT THERE IN THAT SNOW AND ICE AND IT LOOKED, LOOKED PRETTY **BAD**, WELL, I FELT...

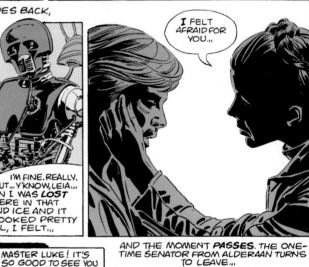

I FELT AFRAID FOR YOU...

LEIA, I DON'T REALLY KNOW HOW TO **SAY** THIS. BUT YOU **MUST** KNOW THAT YOU...WELL...YOU'RE THE **ONLY** ONE I...I...

UNCERTAIN, BUT DRAWN BY THE MOMENT, THE PRINCESS LEANS CLOSE TO THE YOUNG REBEL HERO...

MASTER LUKE! IT'S SO GOOD TO SEE YOU **FUNCTIONAL** AGAIN!

VA-DOOT BIP!

AND THE MOMENT **PASSES**. THE ONE-TIME SENATOR FROM ALDERAAN TURNS TO LEAVE...

LEIA... **WAIT!**... W-WHAT WOULD YOU THINK IF...I WENT **AWAY** FOR A WHILE? TO ANOTHER SYSTEM...A PLACE CALLED **DAGOBAH**... I'VE GOT TO--

WHAT? THAT'S JUST **FINE!** FIRST **HAN**...NOW **YOU!** I COULD GET MORE **LOYALTY** IF I RECRUITED SOME OF THOSE **ICE CREATURES** WE'VE TRAPPED!

AH! SHE'S BEING *CHARMING* AGAIN. HI, KID! YOU LOOK STRONG ENOUGH TO WRESTLE A GUNDARK!

VAAARRK!

THANKS TO *YOU,* HAN, BETWEEN THE DEATH STAR TRENCH AND RESCUING ME AFTER I WANDERED AWAY *DELIRIOUS* FROM THAT MONSTER'S LAIR... THAT'S *TWO* I OWE YOU.

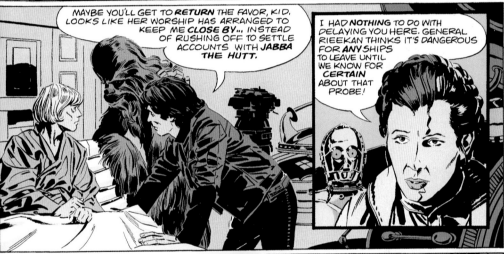

MAYBE YOU'LL GET TO *RETURN* THE FAVOR, KID. LOOKS LIKE HER WORSHIP HAS ARRANGED TO KEEP ME *CLOSE BY...* INSTEAD OF RUSHING OFF TO SETTLE ACCOUNTS WITH *JABBA THE HUTT.*

I HAD *NOTHING* TO DO WITH DELAYING YOU HERE. GENERAL RIEEKAN THINKS IT'S DANGEROUS FOR *ANY* SHIPS TO LEAVE UNTIL WE KNOW FOR *CERTAIN* ABOUT THAT PROBE!

MAKES A GOOD *STORY,* LADY... BUT I THINK YOU JUST CAN'T *BEAR* TO LET ME OUT OF YOUR SIGHT. ESPECIALLY AFTER EXPRESSING YOUR *TRUE* FEELINGS WHEN WE WERE *ALONE* THE OTHER DAY.

I *MUST* BE RIGHT OR YOU WOULDN'T BE SO *STEAMED.* LOOK THAT WAY TO *YOU,* LUKE...?

WELL... YEAH... IT DOES. KIND OF...

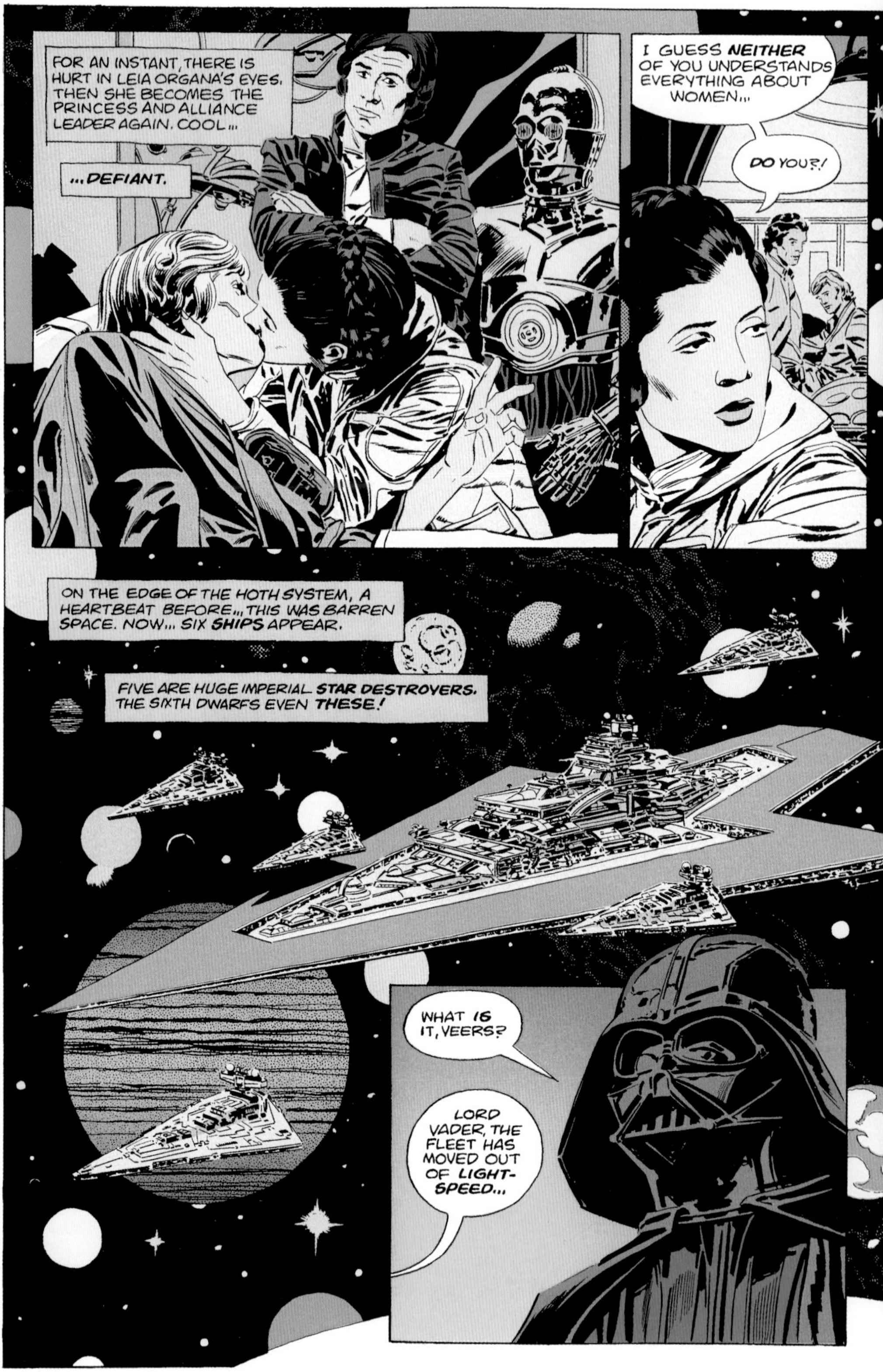

FOR AN INSTANT, THERE IS HURT IN LEIA ORGANA'S EYES. THEN SHE BECOMES THE PRINCESS AND ALLIANCE LEADER AGAIN. COOL...
...DEFIANT.
I GUESS NEITHER OF YOU UNDERSTANDS EVERYTHING ABOUT WOMEN...
DO YOU?!
ON THE EDGE OF THE HOTH SYSTEM, A HEARTBEAT BEFORE... THIS WAS BARREN SPACE. NOW... SIX SHIPS APPEAR.
FIVE ARE HUGE IMPERIAL STAR DESTROYERS. THE SIXTH DWARFS EVEN THESE!
WHAT IS IT, VEERS?
LORD VADER, THE FLEET HAS MOVED OUT OF LIGHT-SPEED...

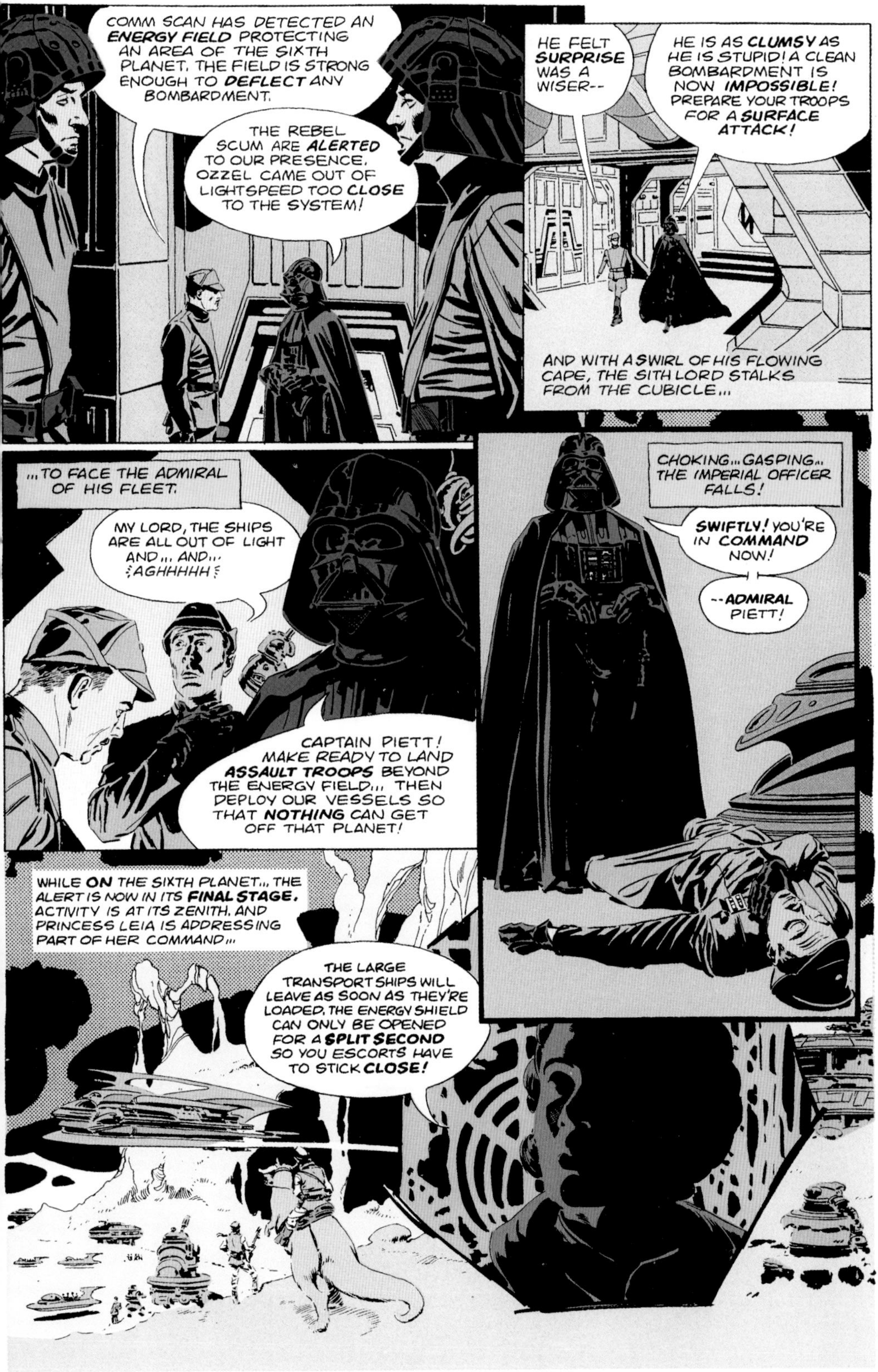
COMM SCAN HAS DETECTED AN ENERGY FIELD PROTECTING AN AREA OF THE SIXTH PLANET. THE FIELD IS STRONG ENOUGH TO DEFLECT ANY BOMBARDMENT.
THE REBEL SCUM ARE ALERTED TO OUR PRESENCE. OZZEL CAME OUT OF LIGHTSPEED TOO CLOSE TO THE SYSTEM!
HE FELT SURPRISE WAS A WISER--
HE IS AS CLUMSY AS HE IS STUPID! A CLEAN BOMBARDMENT IS NOW IMPOSSIBLE! PREPARE YOUR TROOPS FOR A SURFACE ATTACK!
AND WITH A SWIRL OF HIS FLOWING CAPE, THE SITH LORD STALKS FROM THE CUBICLE...
...TO FACE THE ADMIRAL OF HIS FLEET.
MY LORD, THE SHIPS ARE ALL OUT OF LIGHT AND... AND... AGHHHHH
CAPTAIN PIETT! MAKE READY TO LAND ASSAULT TROOPS BEYOND THE ENERGY FIELD... THEN DEPLOY OUR VESSELS SO THAT NOTHING CAN GET OFF THAT PLANET!
CHOKING... GASPING... THE IMPERIAL OFFICER FALLS!
SWIFTLY! YOU'RE IN COMMAND NOW!
--ADMIRAL PIETT!
WHILE ON THE SIXTH PLANET... THE ALERT IS NOW IN ITS FINAL STAGE. ACTIVITY IS AT ITS ZENITH. AND PRINCESS LEIA IS ADDRESSING PART OF HER COMMAND...
THE LARGE TRANSPORT SHIPS WILL LEAVE AS SOON AS THEY'RE LOADED. THE ENERGY SHIELD CAN ONLY BE OPENED FOR A SPLIT SECOND SO YOU ESCORTS HAVE TO STICK CLOSE!

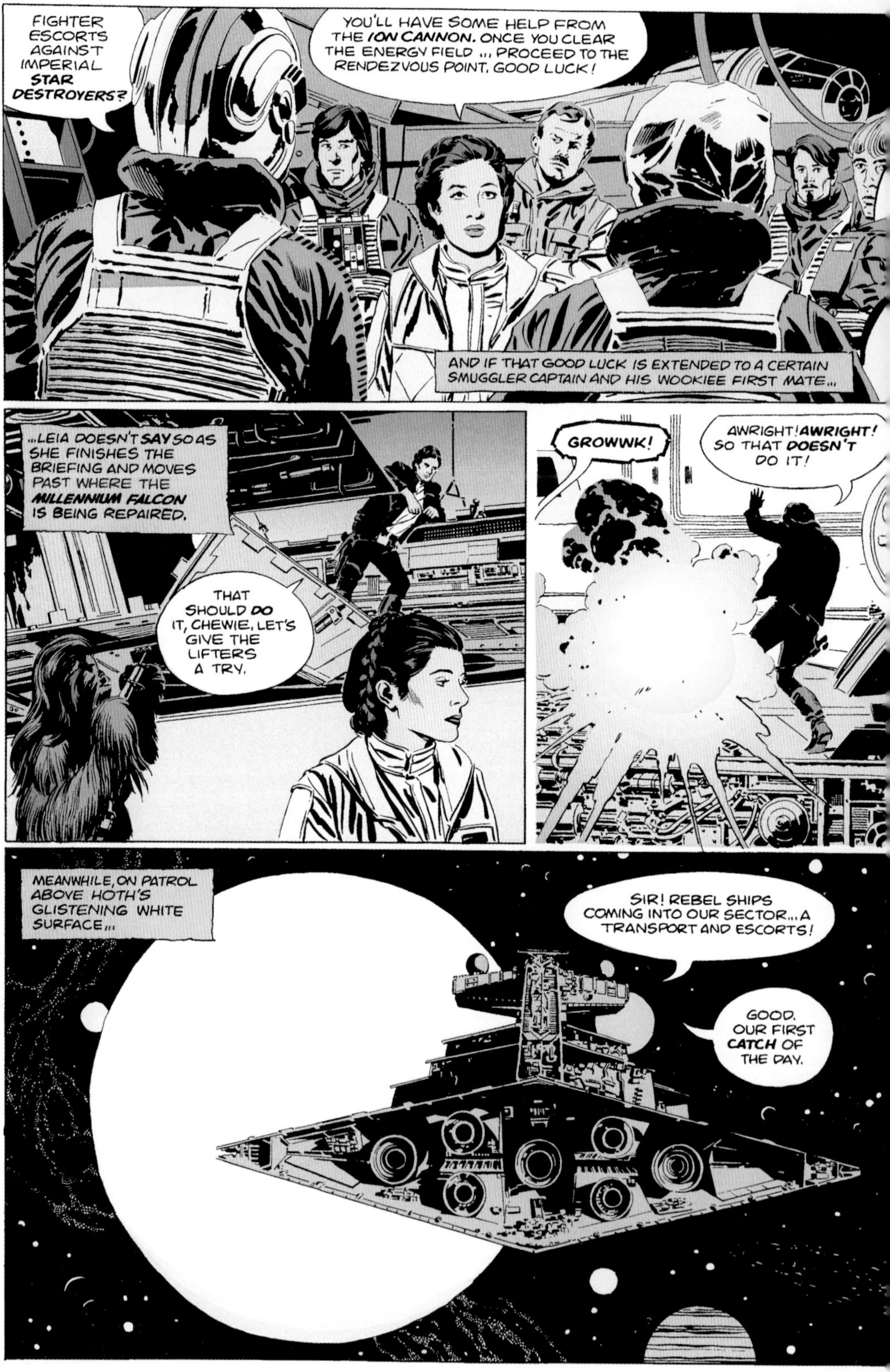

FIGHTER ESCORTS AGAINST IMPERIAL STAR DESTROYERS?
YOU'LL HAVE SOME HELP FROM THE ION CANNON. ONCE YOU CLEAR THE ENERGY FIELD ... PROCEED TO THE RENDEZVOUS POINT. GOOD LUCK!
AND IF THAT GOOD LUCK IS EXTENDED TO A CERTAIN SMUGGLER CAPTAIN AND HIS WOOKIEE FIRST MATE...
...LEIA DOESN'T SAY SO AS SHE FINISHES THE BRIEFING AND MOVES PAST WHERE THE MILLENNIUM FALCON IS BEING REPAIRED.
THAT SHOULD DO IT, CHEWIE, LET'S GIVE THE LIFTERS A TRY.
GROWWK!
AWRIGHT! AWRIGHT! SO THAT DOESN'T DO IT!
MEANWHILE, ON PATROL ABOVE HOTH'S GLISTENING WHITE SURFACE...
SIR! REBEL SHIPS COMING INTO OUR SECTOR... A TRANSPORT AND ESCORTS!
GOOD. OUR FIRST CATCH OF THE DAY.

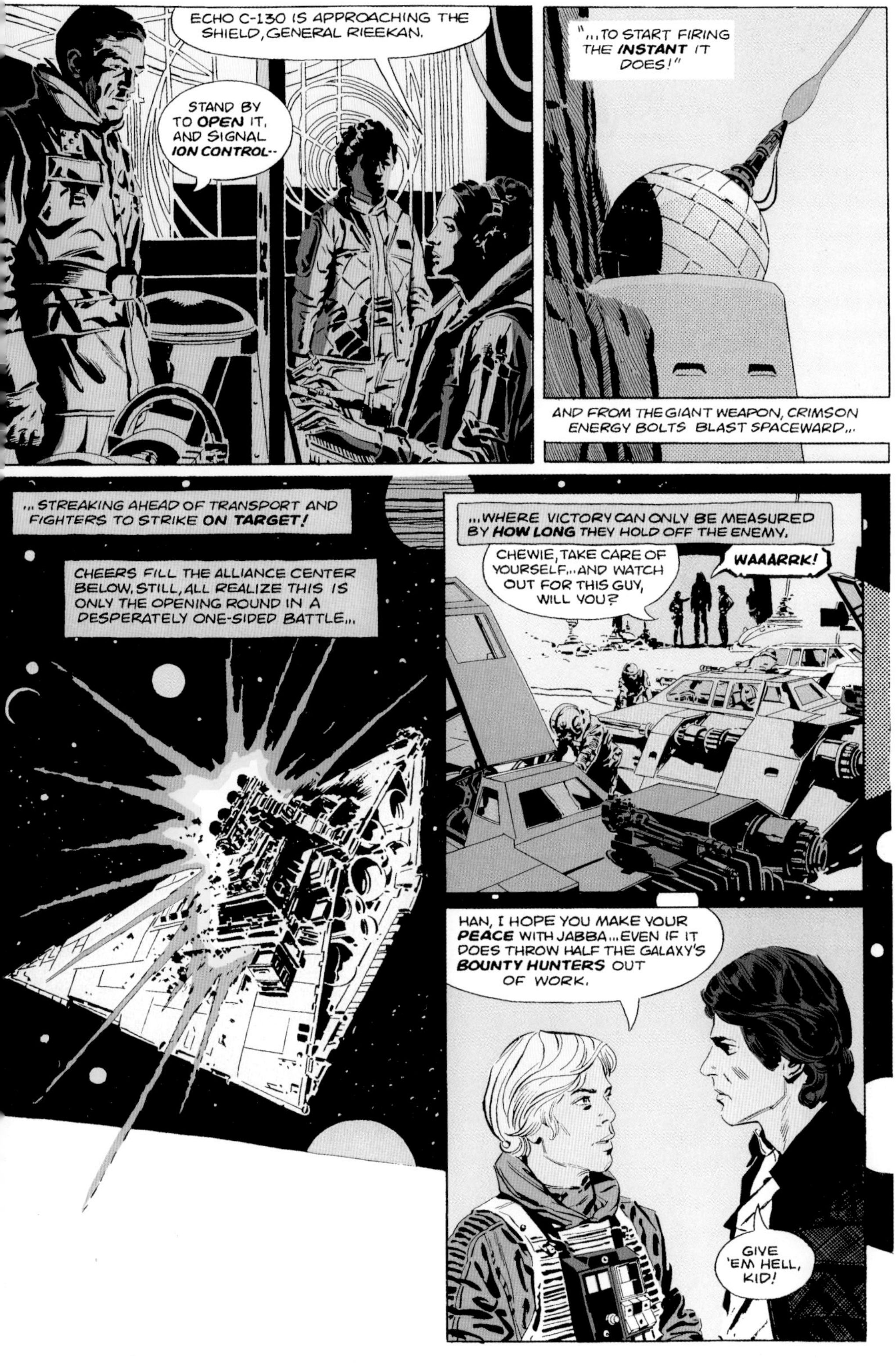
ECHO C-130 IS APPROACHING THE SHIELD, GENERAL RIEEKAN.
STAND BY TO OPEN IT, AND SIGNAL ION CONTROL--
"...TO START FIRING THE INSTANT IT DOES!"
AND FROM THE GIANT WEAPON, CRIMSON ENERGY BOLTS BLAST SPACEWARD...
...STREAKING AHEAD OF TRANSPORT AND FIGHTERS TO STRIKE ON TARGET!
CHEERS FILL THE ALLIANCE CENTER BELOW. STILL, ALL REALIZE THIS IS ONLY THE OPENING ROUND IN A DESPERATELY ONE-SIDED BATTLE...
...WHERE VICTORY CAN ONLY BE MEASURED BY HOW LONG THEY HOLD OFF THE ENEMY.
CHEWIE, TAKE CARE OF YOURSELF...AND WATCH OUT FOR THIS GUY, WILL YOU?
WAAARRK!
HAN, I HOPE YOU MAKE YOUR PEACE WITH JABBA...EVEN IF IT DOES THROW HALF THE GALAXY'S BOUNTY HUNTERS OUT OF WORK.
GIVE 'EM HELL, KID!

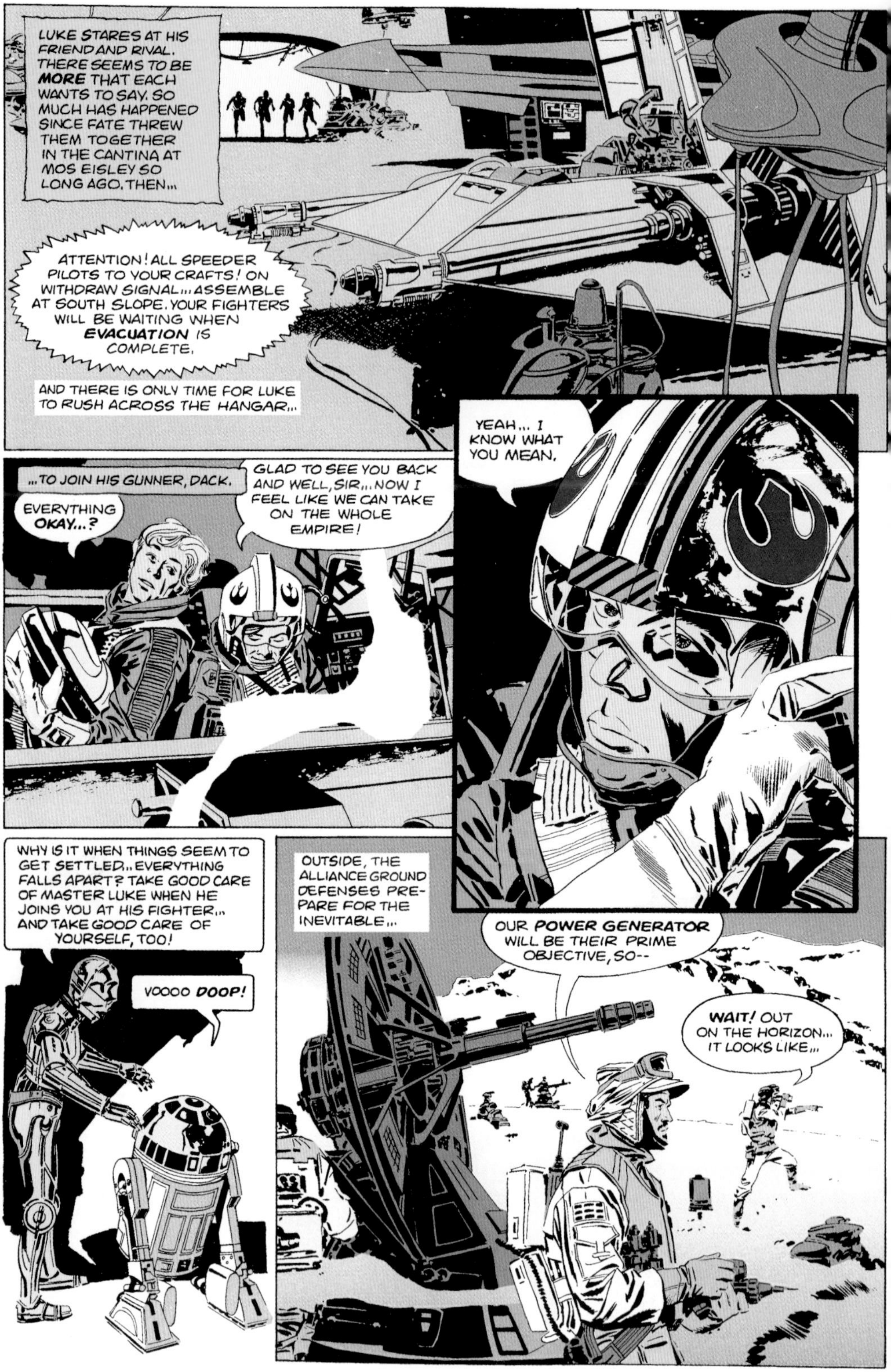
LUKE STARES AT HIS FRIEND AND RIVAL. THERE SEEMS TO BE MORE THAT EACH WANTS TO SAY. SO MUCH HAS HAPPENED SINCE FATE THREW THEM TOGETHER IN THE CANTINA AT MOS EISLEY SO LONG AGO. THEN...
ATTENTION! ALL SPEEDER PILOTS TO YOUR CRAFTS! ON WITHDRAW SIGNAL... ASSEMBLE AT SOUTH SLOPE. YOUR FIGHTERS WILL BE WAITING WHEN EVACUATION IS COMPLETE.
AND THERE IS ONLY TIME FOR LUKE TO RUSH ACROSS THE HANGAR...
...TO JOIN HIS GUNNER, DACK.
EVERYTHING OKAY...?
GLAD TO SEE YOU BACK AND WELL, SIR... NOW I FEEL LIKE WE CAN TAKE ON THE WHOLE EMPIRE!
YEAH... I KNOW WHAT YOU MEAN.
WHY IS IT WHEN THINGS SEEM TO GET SETTLED... EVERYTHING FALLS APART? TAKE GOOD CARE OF MASTER LUKE WHEN HE JOINS YOU AT HIS FIGHTER... AND TAKE GOOD CARE OF YOURSELF, TOO!
VOOOO DOOP!
OUTSIDE, THE ALLIANCE GROUND DEFENSES PREPARE FOR THE INEVITABLE...
OUR POWER GENERATOR WILL BE THEIR PRIME OBJECTIVE, SO--
WAIT! OUT ON THE HORIZON... IT LOOKS LIKE...

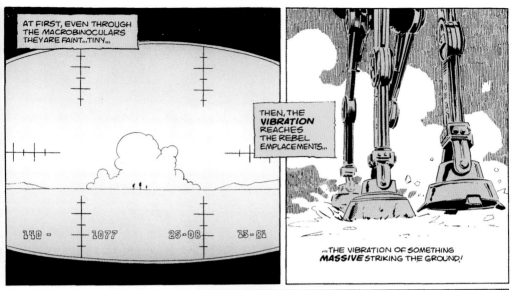

AT FIRST, EVEN THROUGH THE MACROBINOCULARS THEY ARE FAINT...TINY...

THEN, THE **VIBRATION** REACHES THE REBEL EMPLACEMENTS...

...THE VIBRATION OF SOMETHING **MASSIVE** STRIKING THE GROUND!

POINT RIDER FIVE TO ECHO DEFENSE! ENEMY CONTACT! **ENEMY CONTACT!**

IMPERIAL **WALKERS** ADVANCING ON YOUR POSITION!

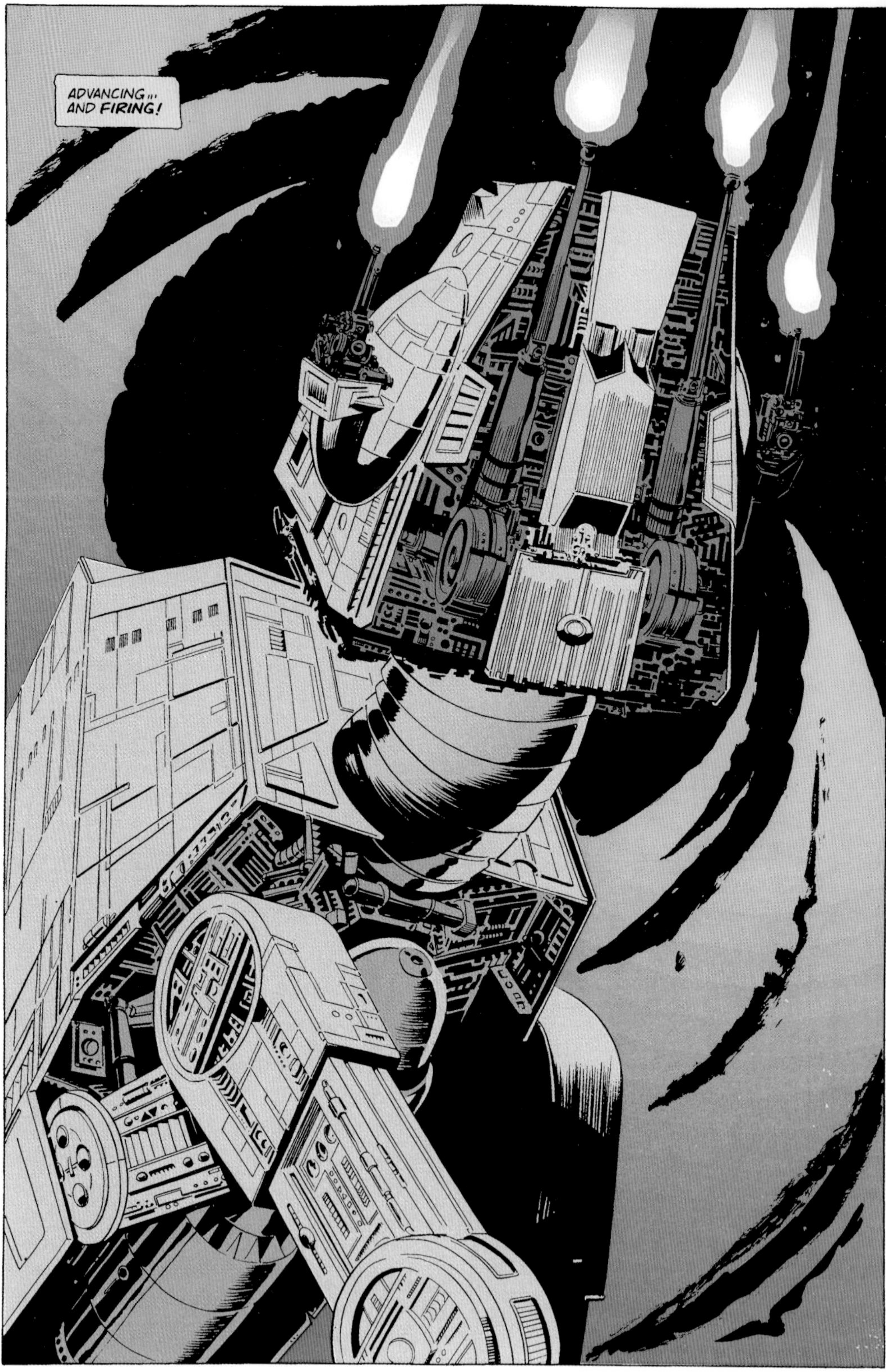
ADVANCING... AND FIRING!

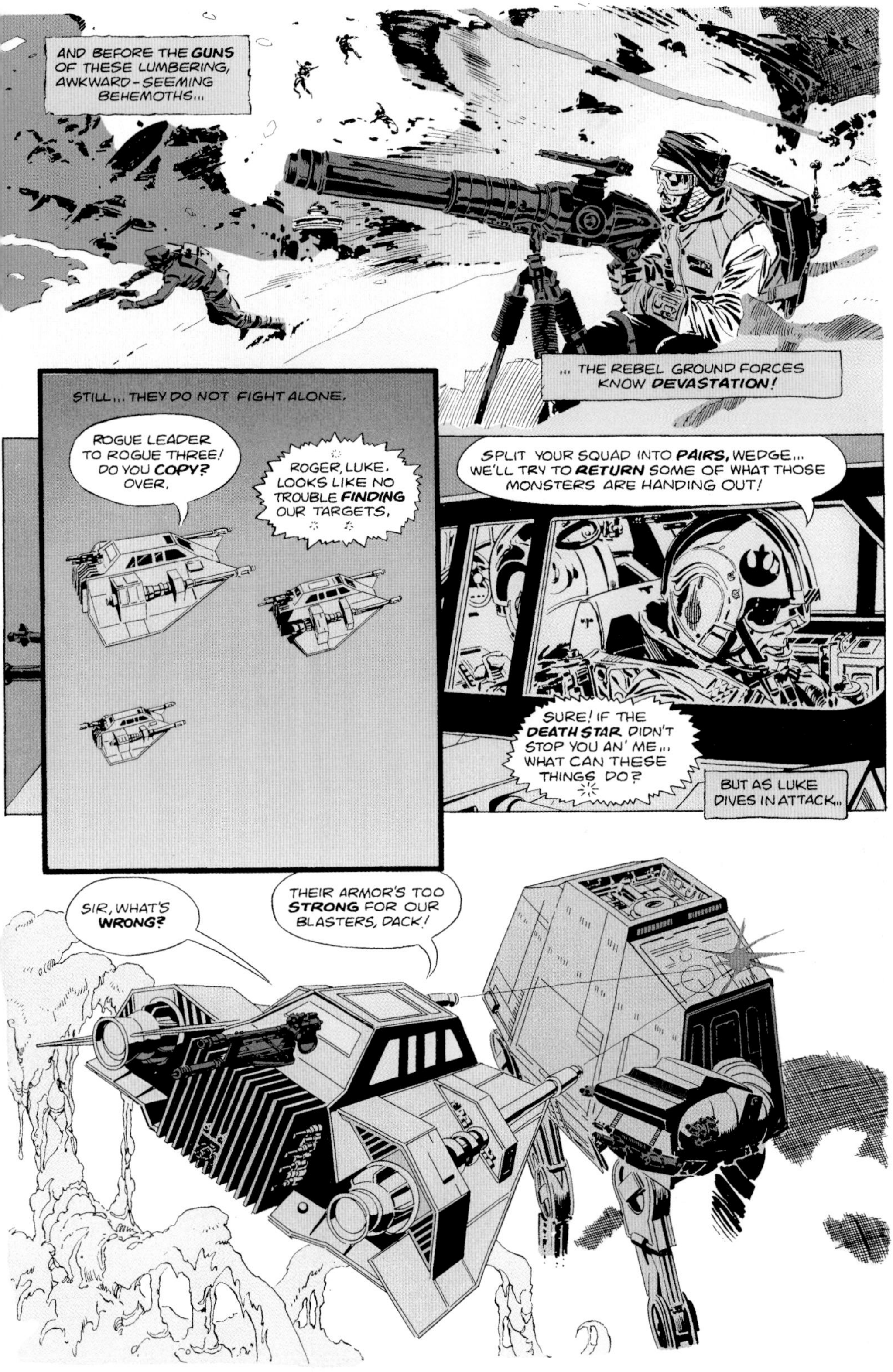
AND BEFORE THE GUNS OF THESE LUMBERING, AWKWARD-SEEMING BEHEMOTHS...
... THE REBEL GROUND FORCES KNOW DEVASTATION!
STILL... THEY DO NOT FIGHT ALONE.
ROGUE LEADER TO ROGUE THREE! DO YOU COPY? OVER.
ROGER, LUKE. LOOKS LIKE NO TROUBLE FINDING OUR TARGETS.
SPLIT YOUR SQUAD INTO PAIRS, WEDGE... WE'LL TRY TO RETURN SOME OF WHAT THOSE MONSTERS ARE HANDING OUT!
SURE! IF THE DEATH STAR DIDN'T STOP YOU AN' ME... WHAT CAN THESE THINGS DO?
BUT AS LUKE DIVES IN ATTACK...
SIR, WHAT'S WRONG?
THEIR ARMOR'S TOO STRONG FOR OUR BLASTERS, DACK!

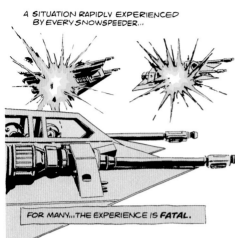

A SITUATION RAPIDLY EXPERIENCED BY EVERY SNOWSPEEDER...

FOR MANY...THE EXPERIENCE IS *FATAL.*

NO BETTER LUCK WITH *MY* GUNS, SIR!

WE'VE GOT TO CHANGE *TACTICS,* DACK. ONCE WE'RE IN THE CLEAR I'VE GOT AN IDEA WHAT TO--

BUT AS THE SNOWSPEEDER SOARS FROM THE STRIDING MECHANICAL GIANT...

WE'VE TAKEN A *HIT!* DACK, WHAT'S THE *DAMAGE* BACK THERE?

DACK...?!

THE RELENTLESS ENEMY BARRAGE IS FELT EVERY-WHERE... INCLUDING THE ALLIANCE STRONGHOLD'S ALMOST DESERTED *HANGAR.*

FIRST CHANCE WE GET... WE'RE GIVING THIS CRATE A *COMPLETE* OVERHAUL, BUT UNDER THE CIRCUMSTANCES, PAL... THAT WELD'S TIGHT ENOUGH.

IN FACT, I'D BET IT'S GONNA HOLD A LOT *LONGER* THAN THIS JOINT'S *CEILING!*

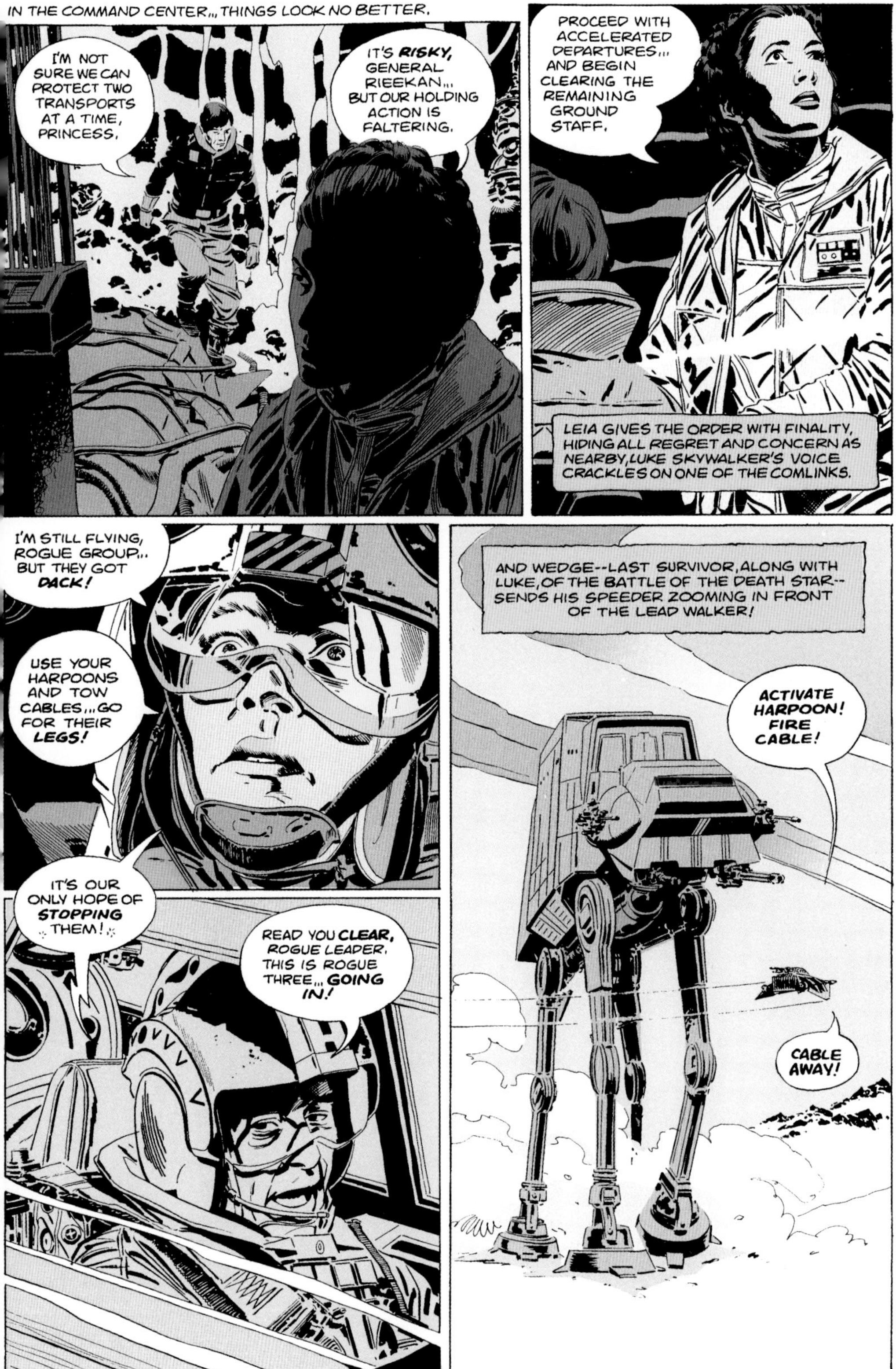

IN THE COMMAND CENTER... THINGS LOOK NO BETTER.
I'M NOT SURE WE CAN PROTECT TWO TRANSPORTS AT A TIME, PRINCESS.
IT'S RISKY, GENERAL RIEEKAN... BUT OUR HOLDING ACTION IS FALTERING.
PROCEED WITH ACCELERATED DEPARTURES... AND BEGIN CLEARING THE REMAINING GROUND STAFF.
LEIA GIVES THE ORDER WITH FINALITY, HIDING ALL REGRET AND CONCERN AS NEARBY, LUKE SKYWALKER'S VOICE CRACKLES ON ONE OF THE COMLINKS.
I'M STILL FLYING, ROGUE GROUP... BUT THEY GOT DACK!
USE YOUR HARPOONS AND TOW CABLES... GO FOR THEIR LEGS!
IT'S OUR ONLY HOPE OF STOPPING THEM!
READ YOU CLEAR, ROGUE LEADER. THIS IS ROGUE THREE... GOING IN!
AND WEDGE--LAST SURVIVOR, ALONG WITH LUKE, OF THE BATTLE OF THE DEATH STAR--SENDS HIS SPEEDER ZOOMING IN FRONT OF THE LEAD WALKER!
ACTIVATE HARPOON! FIRE CABLE!
CABLE AWAY!

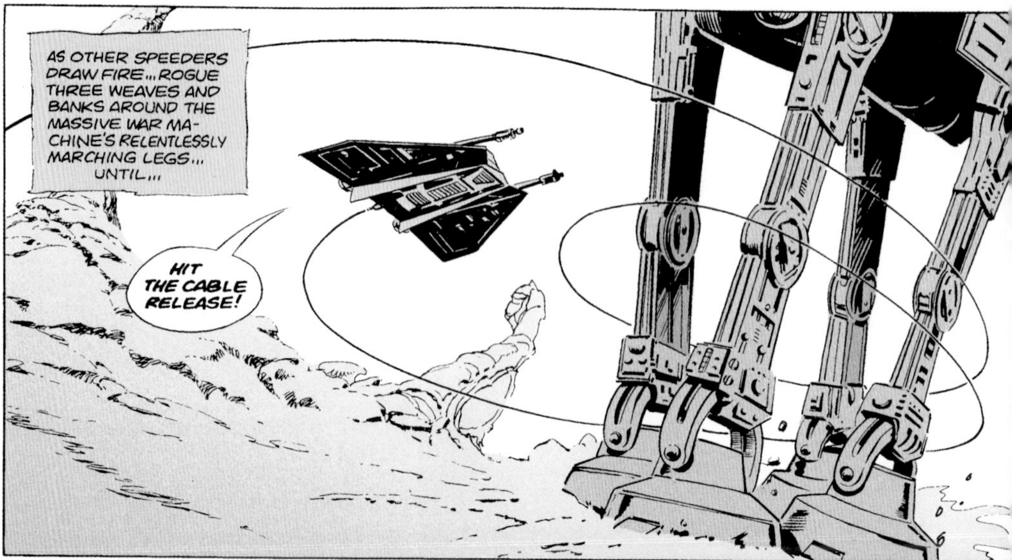
AS OTHER SPEEDERS DRAW FIRE... ROGUE THREE WEAVES AND BANKS AROUND THE MASSIVE WAR MACHINE'S RELENTLESSLY MARCHING LEGS... UNTIL...
HIT THE CABLE RELEASE!

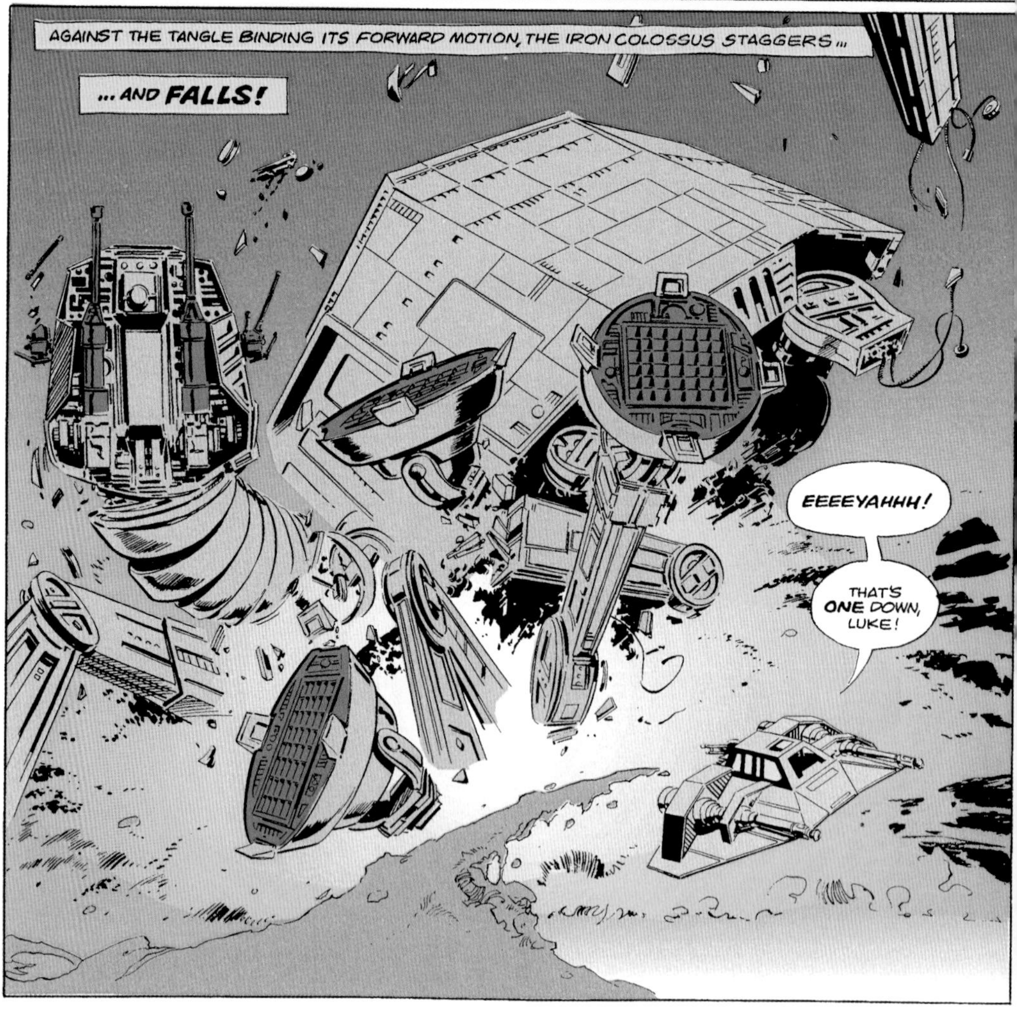
AGAINST THE TANGLE BINDING ITS FORWARD MOTION, THE IRON COLOSSUS STAGGERS...
...AND FALLS!
EEEEYAHHH!
THAT'S ONE DOWN, LUKE!

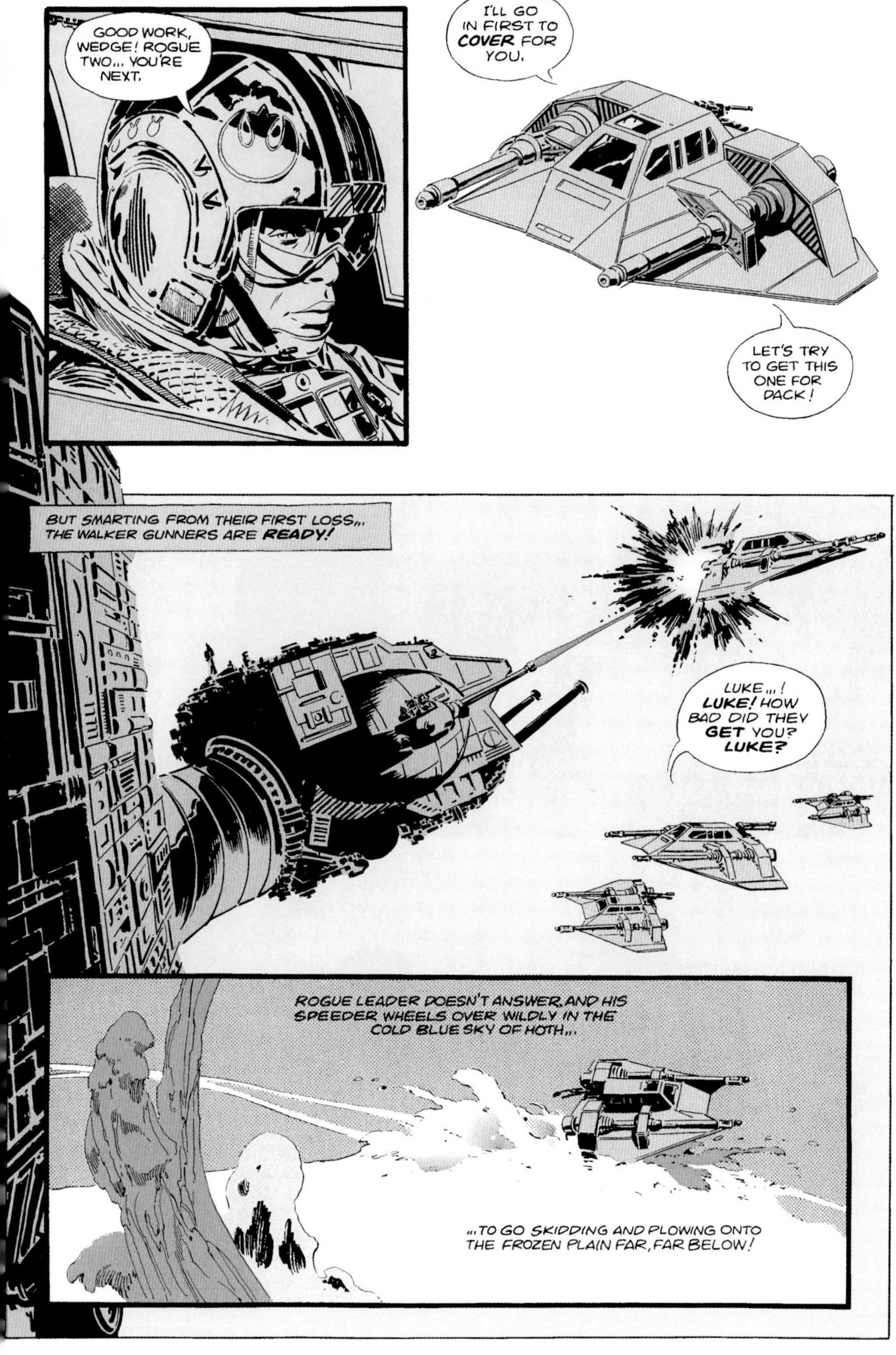
GOOD WORK, WEDGE! ROGUE TWO... YOU'RE NEXT.
I'LL GO IN FIRST TO COVER FOR YOU.
LET'S TRY TO GET THIS ONE FOR DACK!
BUT SMARTING FROM THEIR FIRST LOSS... THE WALKER GUNNERS ARE READY!
LUKE...! LUKE! HOW BAD DID THEY GET YOU? LUKE?
ROGUE LEADER DOESN'T ANSWER, AND HIS SPEEDER WHEELS OVER WILDLY IN THE COLD BLUE SKY OF HOTH...
...TO GO SKIDDING AND PLOWING ONTO THE FROZEN PLAIN FAR, FAR BELOW!

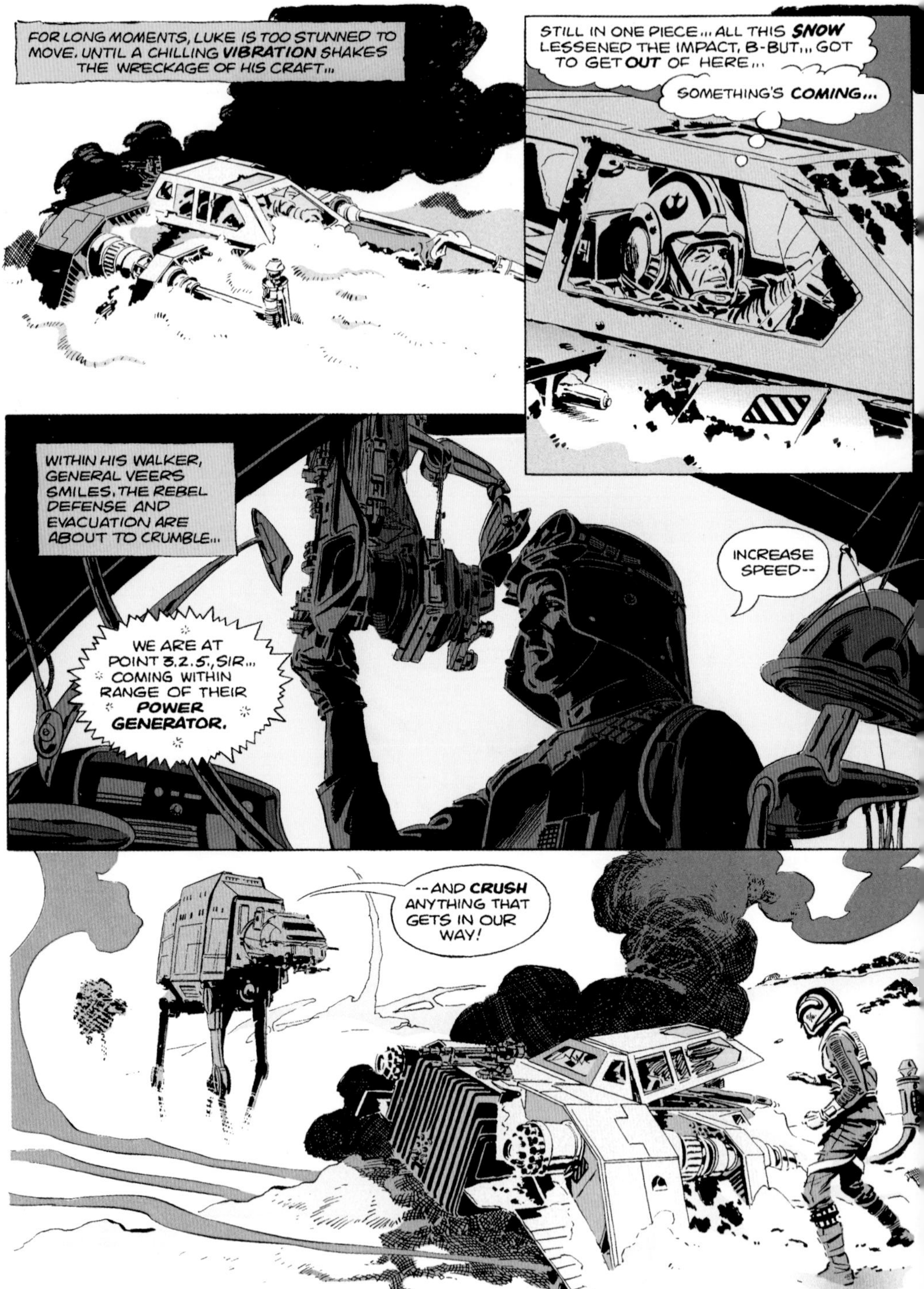
FOR LONG MOMENTS, LUKE IS TOO STUNNED TO MOVE, UNTIL A CHILLING VIBRATION SHAKES THE WRECKAGE OF HIS CRAFT...
STILL IN ONE PIECE... ALL THIS SNOW LESSENED THE IMPACT. B-BUT... GOT TO GET OUT OF HERE...
SOMETHING'S COMING...
WITHIN HIS WALKER, GENERAL VEERS SMILES. THE REBEL DEFENSE AND EVACUATION ARE ABOUT TO CRUMBLE...
WE ARE AT POINT 3.2.5., SIR... COMING WITHIN RANGE OF THEIR POWER GENERATOR.
INCREASE SPEED--
--AND CRUSH ANYTHING THAT GETS IN OUR WAY!

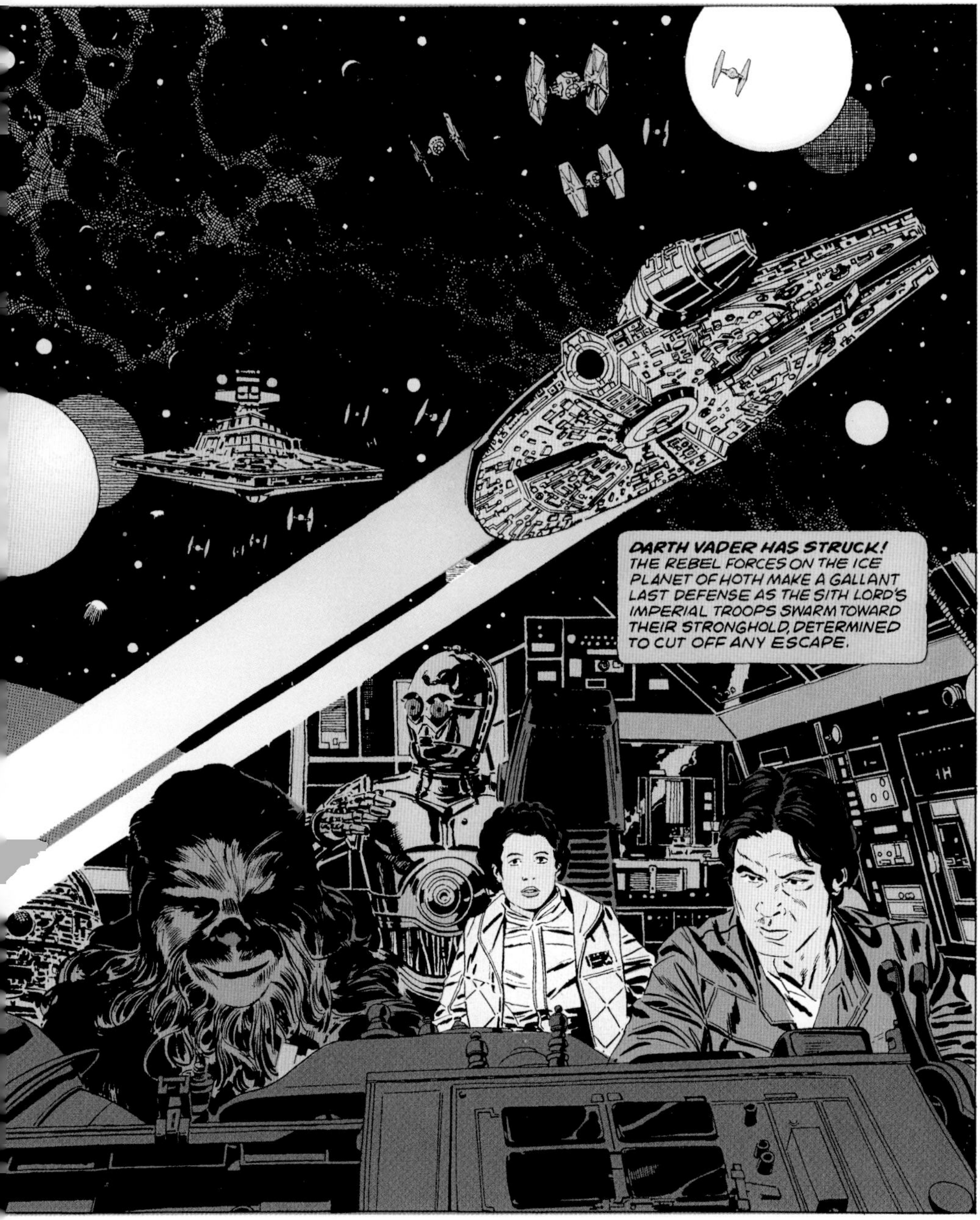
DARTH VADER HAS STRUCK! THE REBEL FORCES ON THE ICE PLANET OF HOTH MAKE A GALLANT LAST DEFENSE AS THE SITH LORD'S IMPERIAL TROOPS SWARM TOWARD THEIR STRONGHOLD, DETERMINED TO CUT OFF ANY ESCAPE.

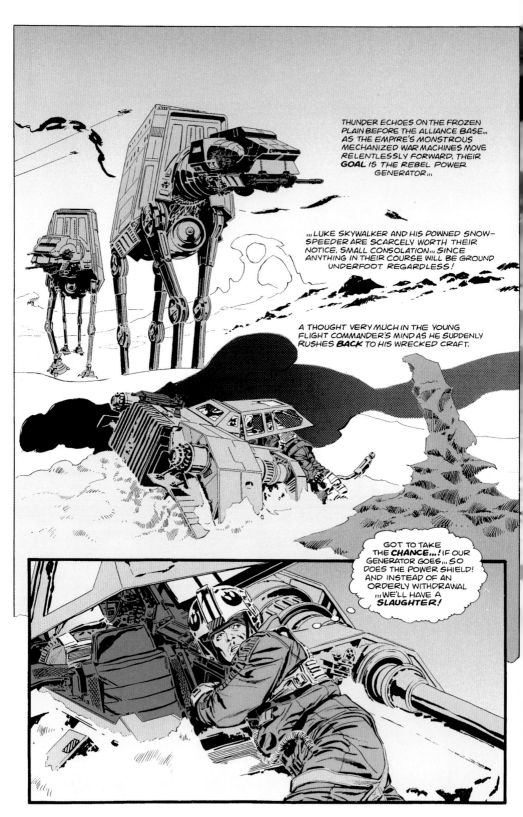

THUNDER ECHOES ON THE FROZEN PLAIN BEFORE THE ALLIANCE BASE... AS THE EMPIRE'S MONSTROUS MECHANIZED WAR MACHINES MOVE RELENTLESSLY FORWARD, THEIR *GOAL* IS THE REBEL POWER GENERATOR...

...LUKE SKYWALKER AND HIS DOWNED SNOW-SPEEDER ARE SCARCELY WORTH THEIR NOTICE, SMALL CONSOLATION... SINCE ANYTHING IN THEIR COURSE WILL BE GROUND UNDERFOOT REGARDLESS!

A THOUGHT VERY MUCH IN THE YOUNG FLIGHT COMMANDER'S MIND AS HE SUDDENLY RUSHES *BACK* TO HIS WRECKED CRAFT.

GOT TO TAKE THE *CHANCE...!* IF OUR GENERATOR GOES... SO DOES THE POWER SHIELD! AND INSTEAD OF AN ORDERLY WITHDRAWAL ...WE'LL HAVE A *SLAUGHTER!*

FIGHTING TO KEEP HIS BALANCE AS THE GROUND SHAKES BENEATH HIM, LUKE TURNS FROM THE COCKPIT WITH **TWO** OBJECTS...

...ONE IS A **HARPOON GUN.**

AND AS EVERY INSTINCT SCREAMS TO FLEE **AWAY** FROM THE GIANT SNOW WALKER...

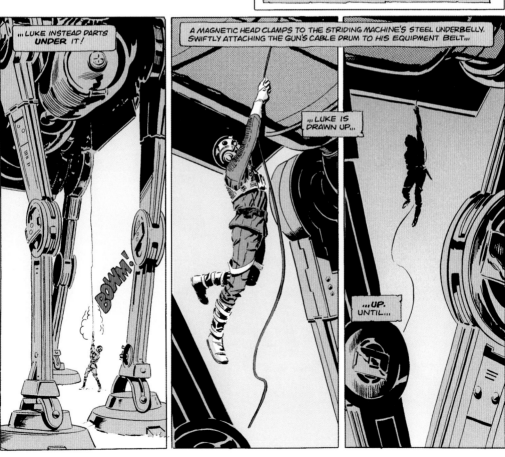

...LUKE INSTEAD DARTS **UNDER IT!**

BOWM!

A MAGNETIC HEAD CLAMPS TO THE STRIDING MACHINE'S STEEL UNDERBELLY. SWIFTLY ATTACHING THE GUN'S CABLE DRUM TO HIS EQUIPMENT BELT...

...LUKE IS DRAWN UP...

...UP. UNTIL...

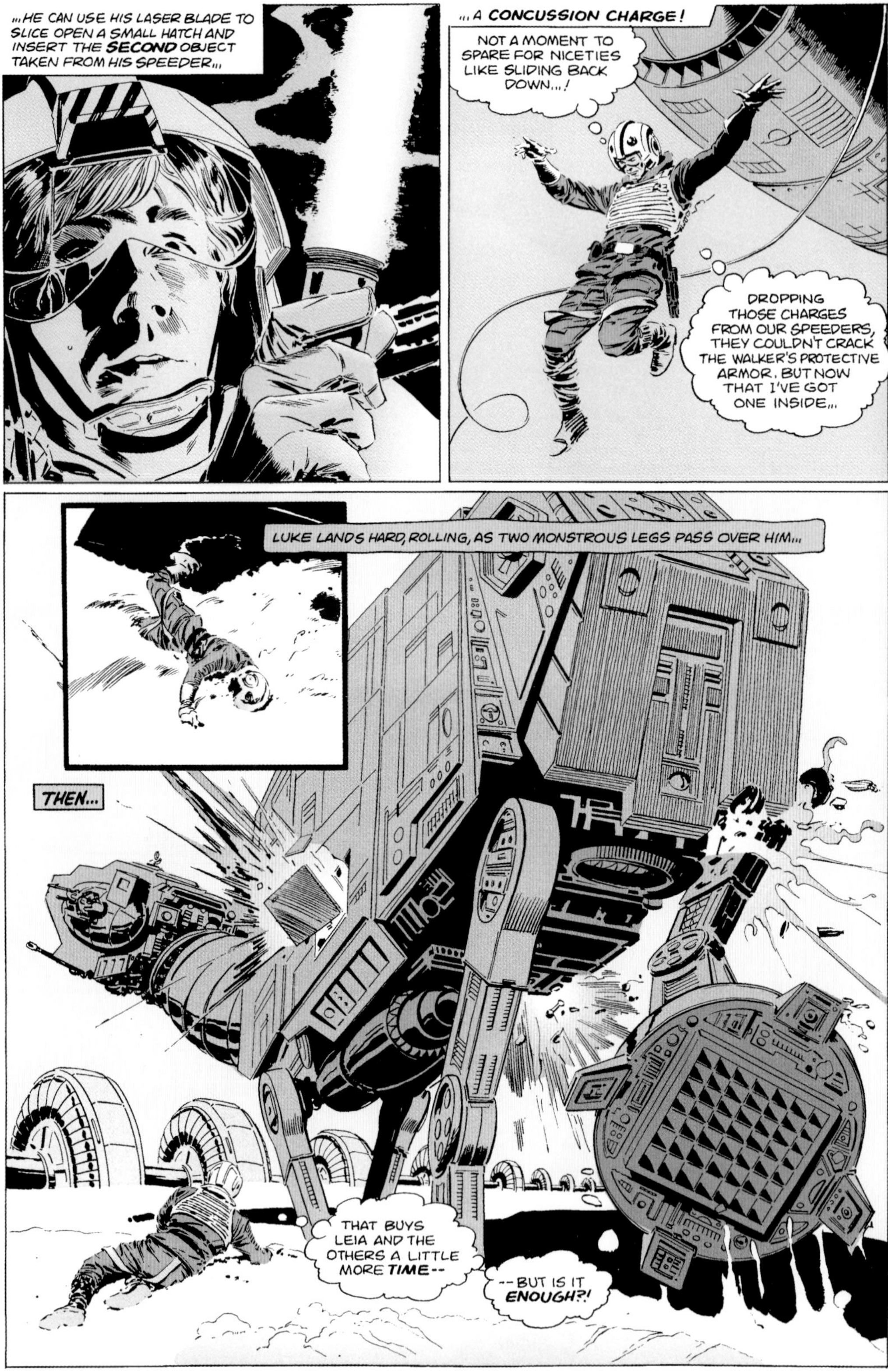

...HE CAN USE HIS LASER BLADE TO SLICE OPEN A SMALL HATCH AND INSERT THE SECOND OBJECT TAKEN FROM HIS SPEEDER...
...A CONCUSSION CHARGE!
NOT A MOMENT TO SPARE FOR NICETIES LIKE SLIDING BACK DOWN...!
DROPPING THOSE CHARGES FROM OUR SPEEDERS, THEY COULDN'T CRACK THE WALKER'S PROTECTIVE ARMOR. BUT NOW THAT I'VE GOT ONE INSIDE...
LUKE LANDS HARD, ROLLING, AS TWO MONSTROUS LEGS PASS OVER HIM...
THEN...
THAT BUYS LEIA AND THE OTHERS A LITTLE MORE TIME--
--BUT IS IT ENOUGH?!

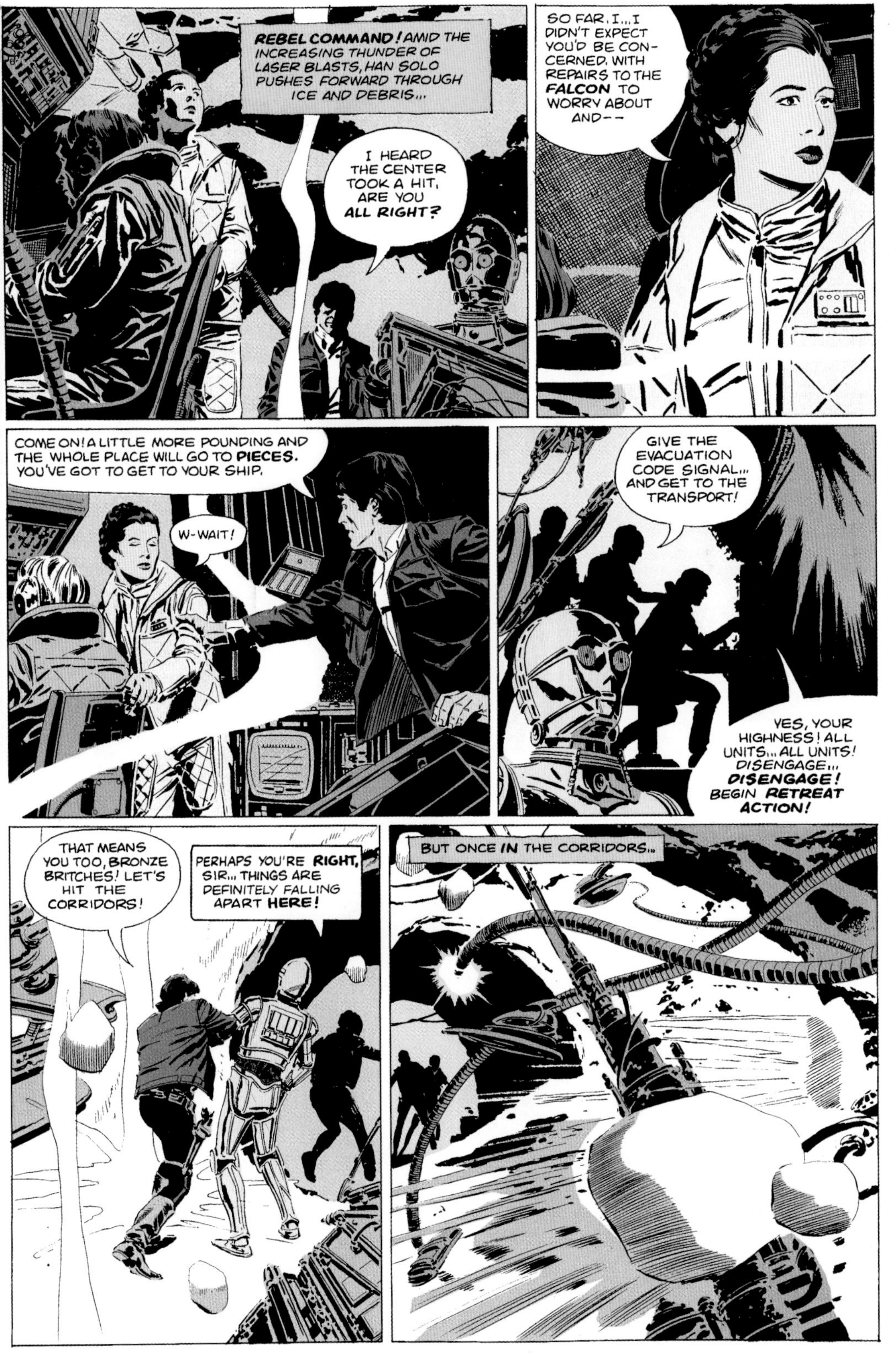
REBEL COMMAND! AMID THE INCREASING THUNDER OF LASER BLASTS, HAN SOLO PUSHES FORWARD THROUGH ICE AND DEBRIS...
I HEARD THE CENTER TOOK A HIT, ARE YOU ALL RIGHT?
SO FAR. I... I DIDN'T EXPECT YOU'D BE CONCERNED, WITH REPAIRS TO THE FALCON TO WORRY ABOUT AND--
COME ON! A LITTLE MORE POUNDING AND THE WHOLE PLACE WILL GO TO PIECES. YOU'VE GOT TO GET TO YOUR SHIP.
W-WAIT!
GIVE THE EVACUATION CODE SIGNAL... AND GET TO THE TRANSPORT!
YES, YOUR HIGHNESS! ALL UNITS... ALL UNITS! DISENGAGE... DISENGAGE! BEGIN RETREAT ACTION!
THAT MEANS YOU TOO, BRONZE BRITCHES! LET'S HIT THE CORRIDORS!
PERHAPS YOU'RE RIGHT, SIR... THINGS ARE DEFINITELY FALLING APART HERE!
BUT ONCE IN THE CORRIDORS...

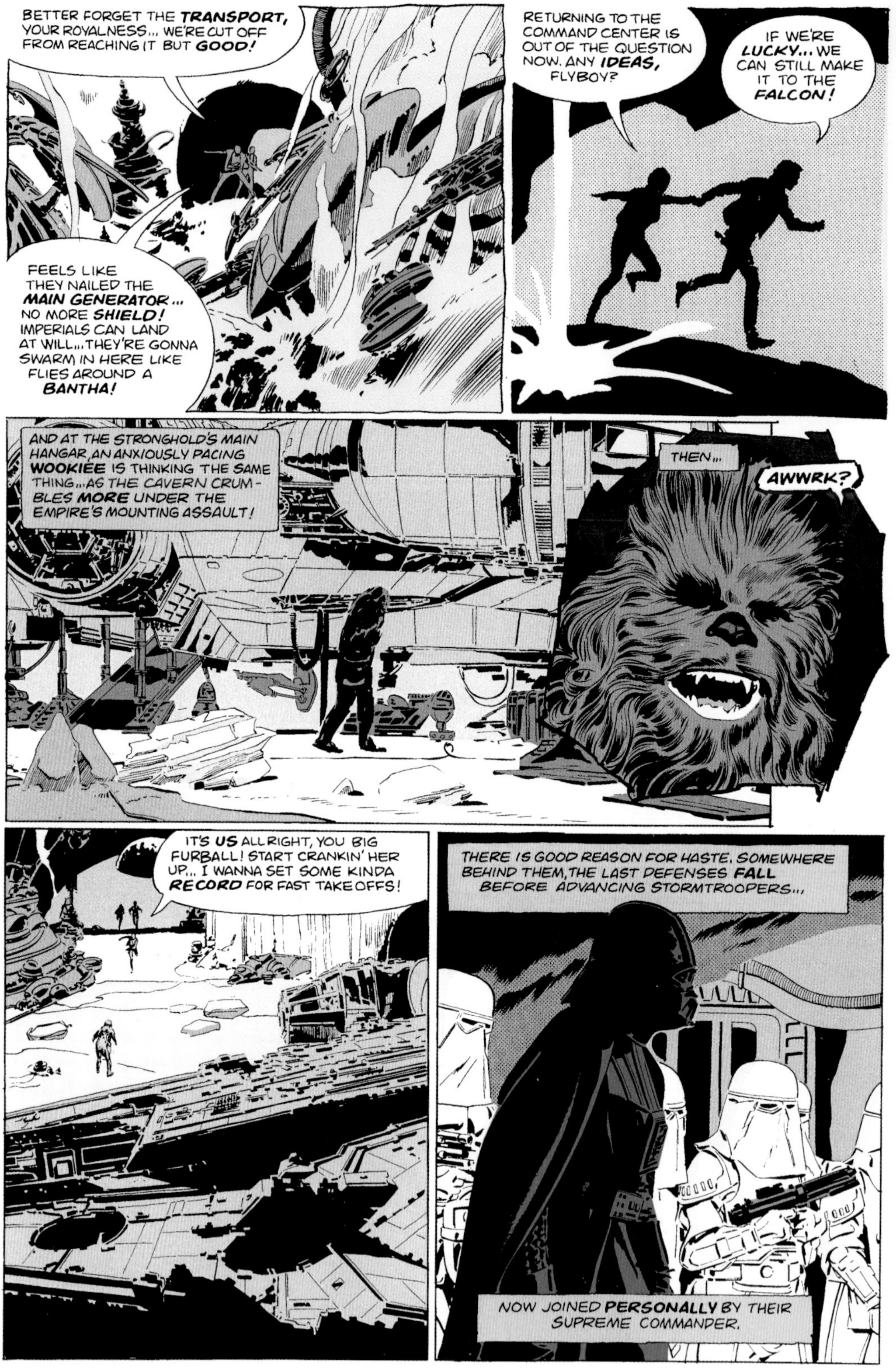

BETTER FORGET THE TRANSPORT, YOUR ROYALNESS... WE'RE CUT OFF FROM REACHING IT BUT GOOD!
FEELS LIKE THEY NAILED THE MAIN GENERATOR... NO MORE SHIELD! IMPERIALS CAN LAND AT WILL... THEY'RE GONNA SWARM IN HERE LIKE FLIES AROUND A BANTHA!
RETURNING TO THE COMMAND CENTER IS OUT OF THE QUESTION NOW. ANY IDEAS, FLYBOY?
IF WE'RE LUCKY... WE CAN STILL MAKE IT TO THE FALCON!
AND AT THE STRONGHOLD'S MAIN HANGAR, AN ANXIOUSLY PACING WOOKIEE IS THINKING THE SAME THING... AS THE CAVERN CRUMBLES MORE UNDER THE EMPIRE'S MOUNTING ASSAULT!
THEN...
AWWRK?
IT'S US ALL RIGHT, YOU BIG FURBALL! START CRANKIN' HER UP... I WANNA SET SOME KINDA RECORD FOR FAST TAKE OFFS!
THERE IS GOOD REASON FOR HASTE. SOMEWHERE BEHIND THEM, THE LAST DEFENSES FALL BEFORE ADVANCING STORMTROOPERS...
NOW JOINED PERSONALLY BY THEIR SUPREME COMMANDER.

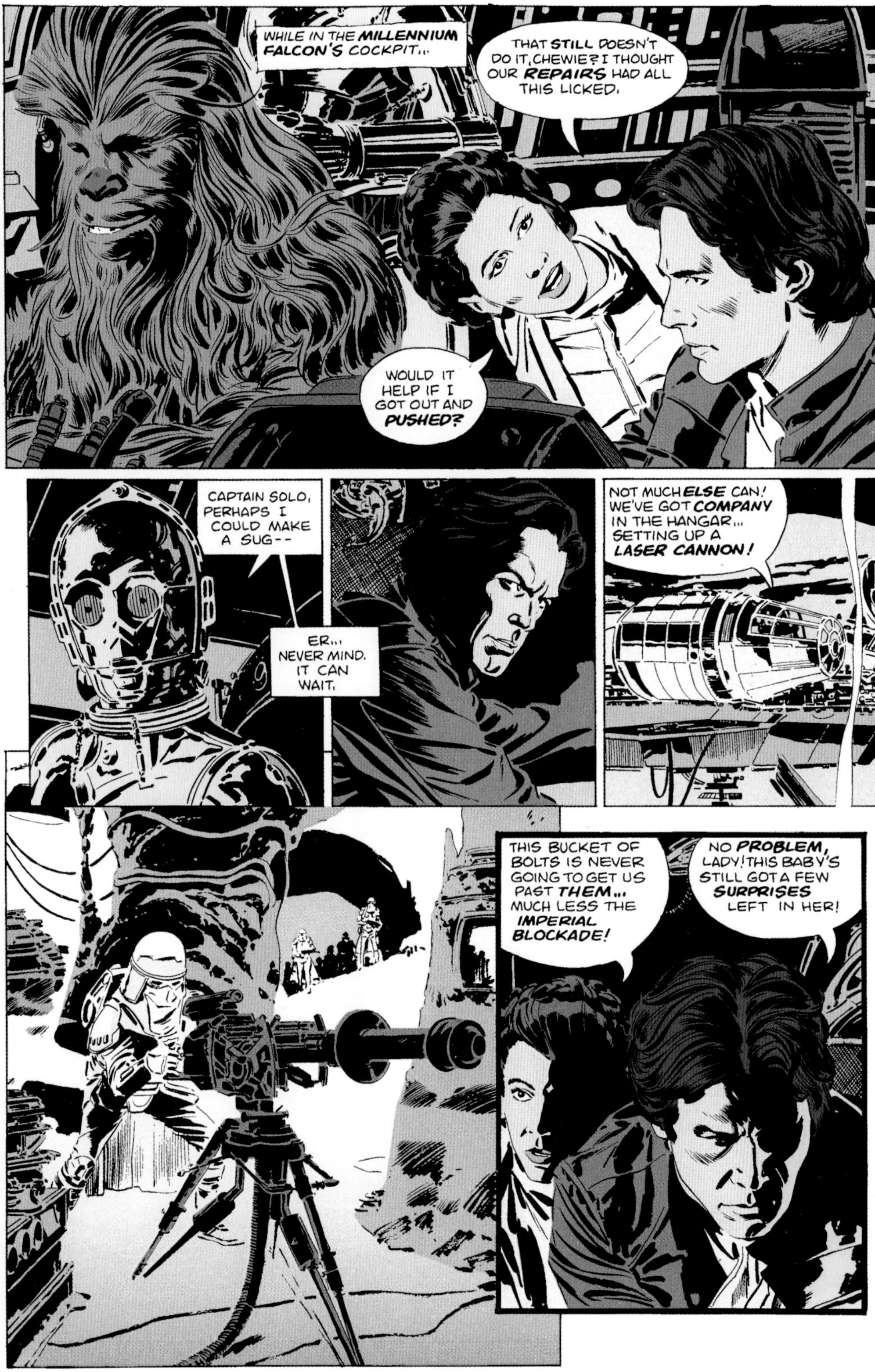
WHILE IN THE MILLENNIUM FALCON'S COCKPIT...
THAT STILL DOESN'T DO IT, CHEWIE? I THOUGHT OUR REPAIRS HAD ALL THIS LICKED.
WOULD IT HELP IF I GOT OUT AND PUSHED?
CAPTAIN SOLO, PERHAPS I COULD MAKE A SUG--
ER... NEVER MIND. IT CAN WAIT.
NOT MUCH ELSE CAN! WE'VE GOT COMPANY IN THE HANGAR... SETTING UP A LASER CANNON!
THIS BUCKET OF BOLTS IS NEVER GOING TO GET US PAST THEM... MUCH LESS THE IMPERIAL BLOCKADE!
NO PROBLEM, LADY! THIS BABY'S STILL GOT A FEW SURPRISES LEFT IN HER!

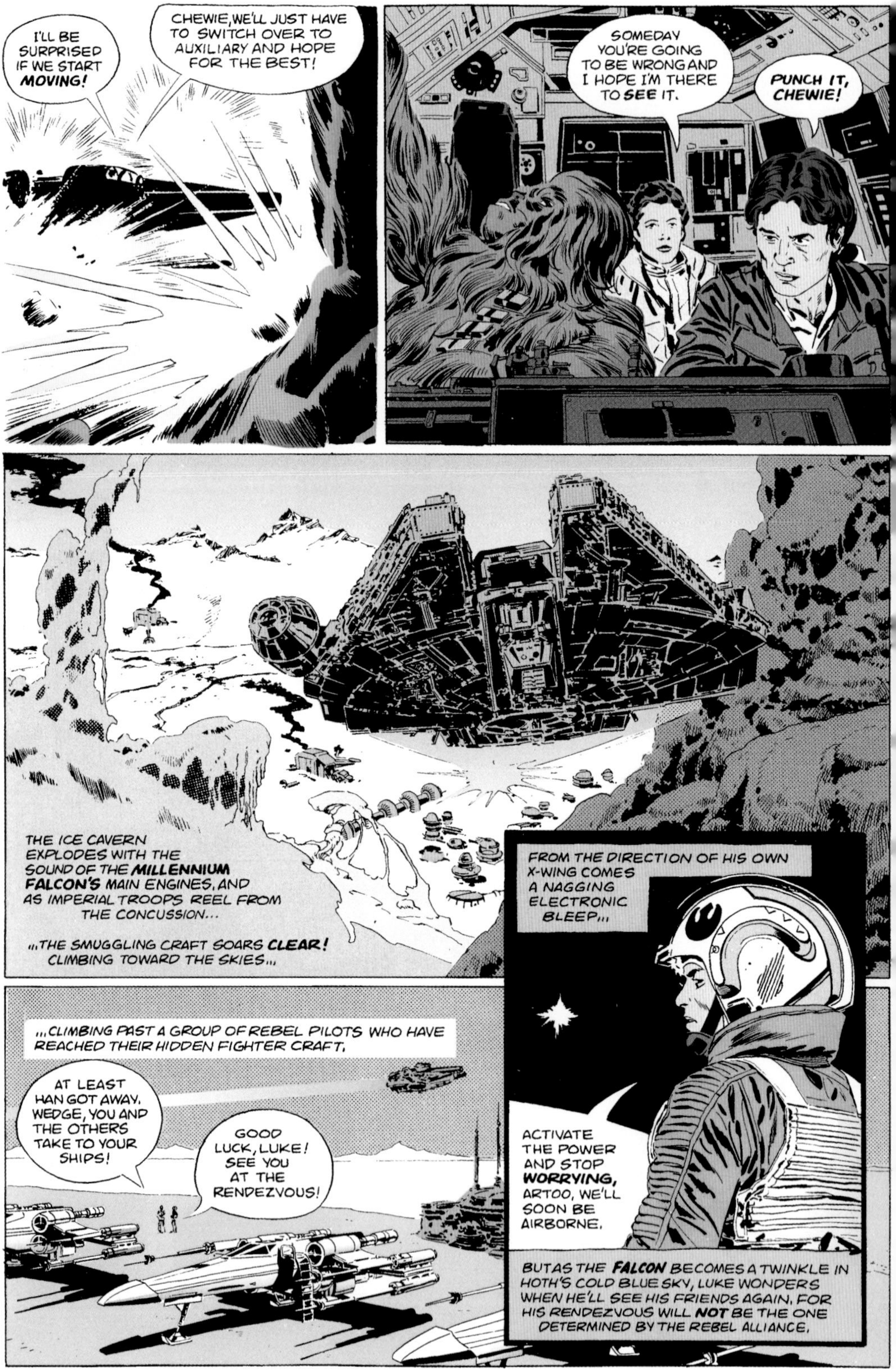

I'LL BE SURPRISED IF WE START MOVING!
CHEWIE, WE'LL JUST HAVE TO SWITCH OVER TO AUXILIARY AND HOPE FOR THE BEST!
SOMEDAY YOU'RE GOING TO BE WRONG AND I HOPE I'M THERE TO SEE IT.
PUNCH IT, CHEWIE!
THE ICE CAVERN EXPLODES WITH THE SOUND OF THE MILLENNIUM FALCON'S MAIN ENGINES, AND AS IMPERIAL TROOPS REEL FROM THE CONCUSSION...
...THE SMUGGLING CRAFT SOARS CLEAR! CLIMBING TOWARD THE SKIES...
...CLIMBING PAST A GROUP OF REBEL PILOTS WHO HAVE REACHED THEIR HIDDEN FIGHTER CRAFT.
AT LEAST HAN GOT AWAY. WEDGE, YOU AND THE OTHERS TAKE TO YOUR SHIPS!
GOOD LUCK, LUKE! SEE YOU AT THE RENDEZVOUS!
FROM THE DIRECTION OF HIS OWN X-WING COMES A NAGGING ELECTRONIC BLEEP...
ACTIVATE THE POWER AND STOP WORRYING, ARTOO, WE'LL SOON BE AIRBORNE.
BUT AS THE FALCON BECOMES A TWINKLE IN HOTH'S COLD BLUE SKY, LUKE WONDERS WHEN HE'LL SEE HIS FRIENDS AGAIN. FOR HIS RENDEZVOUS WILL NOT BE THE ONE DETERMINED BY THE REBEL ALLIANCE.

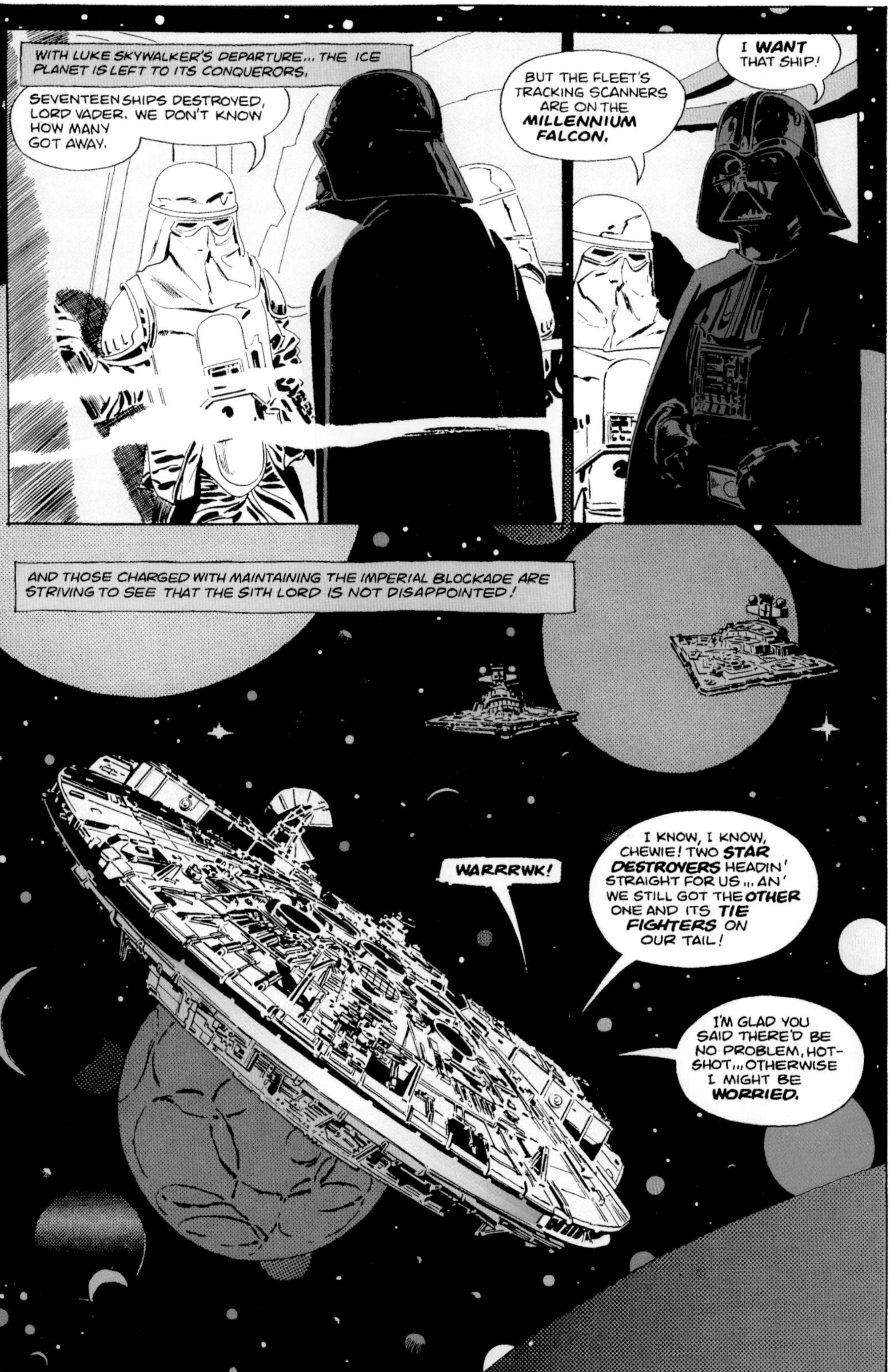

WITH LUKE SKYWALKER'S DEPARTURE... THE ICE PLANET IS LEFT TO ITS CONQUERORS.
SEVENTEEN SHIPS DESTROYED, LORD VADER. WE DON'T KNOW HOW MANY GOT AWAY.
BUT THE FLEET'S TRACKING SCANNERS ARE ON THE MILLENNIUM FALCON.
I WANT THAT SHIP!
AND THOSE CHARGED WITH MAINTAINING THE IMPERIAL BLOCKADE ARE STRIVING TO SEE THAT THE SITH LORD IS NOT DISAPPOINTED!
WARRRWK!
I KNOW, I KNOW, CHEWIE! TWO STAR DESTROYERS HEADIN' STRAIGHT FOR US... AN' WE STILL GOT THE OTHER ONE AND ITS TIE FIGHTERS ON OUR TAIL!
I'M GLAD YOU SAID THERE'D BE NO PROBLEM, HOT-SHOT... OTHERWISE I MIGHT BE WORRIED.

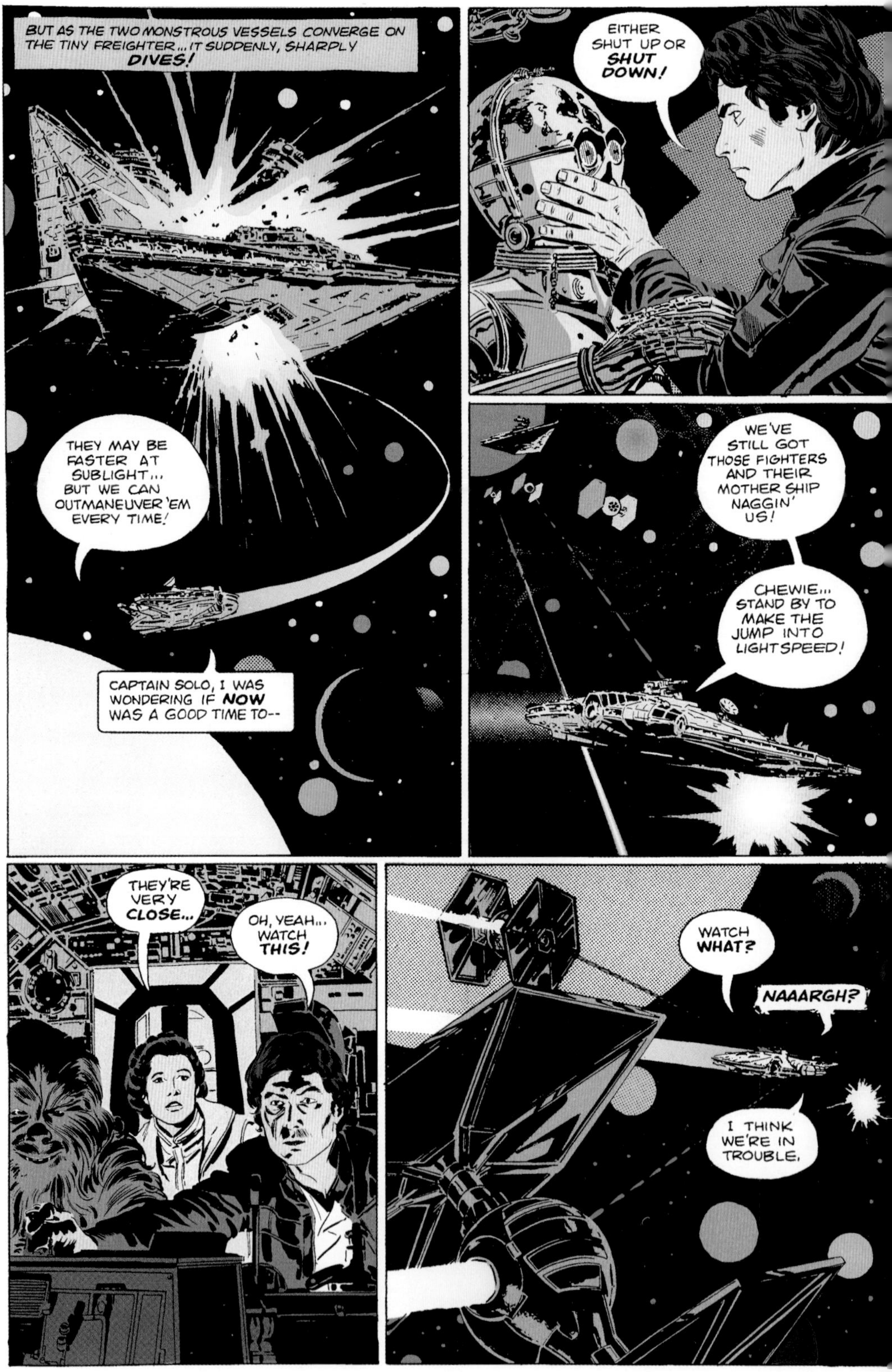
BUT AS THE TWO MONSTROUS VESSELS CONVERGE ON THE TINY FREIGHTER... IT SUDDENLY, SHARPLY DIVES!
THEY MAY BE FASTER AT SUBLIGHT... BUT WE CAN OUTMANEUVER 'EM EVERY TIME!
CAPTAIN SOLO, I WAS WONDERING IF NOW WAS A GOOD TIME TO--
EITHER SHUT UP OR SHUT DOWN!
WE'VE STILL GOT THOSE FIGHTERS AND THEIR MOTHER SHIP NAGGIN' US!
CHEWIE... STAND BY TO MAKE THE JUMP INTO LIGHTSPEED!
THEY'RE VERY CLOSE...
OH, YEAH... WATCH THIS!
WATCH WHAT?
NAAARGH?
I THINK WE'RE IN TROUBLE.

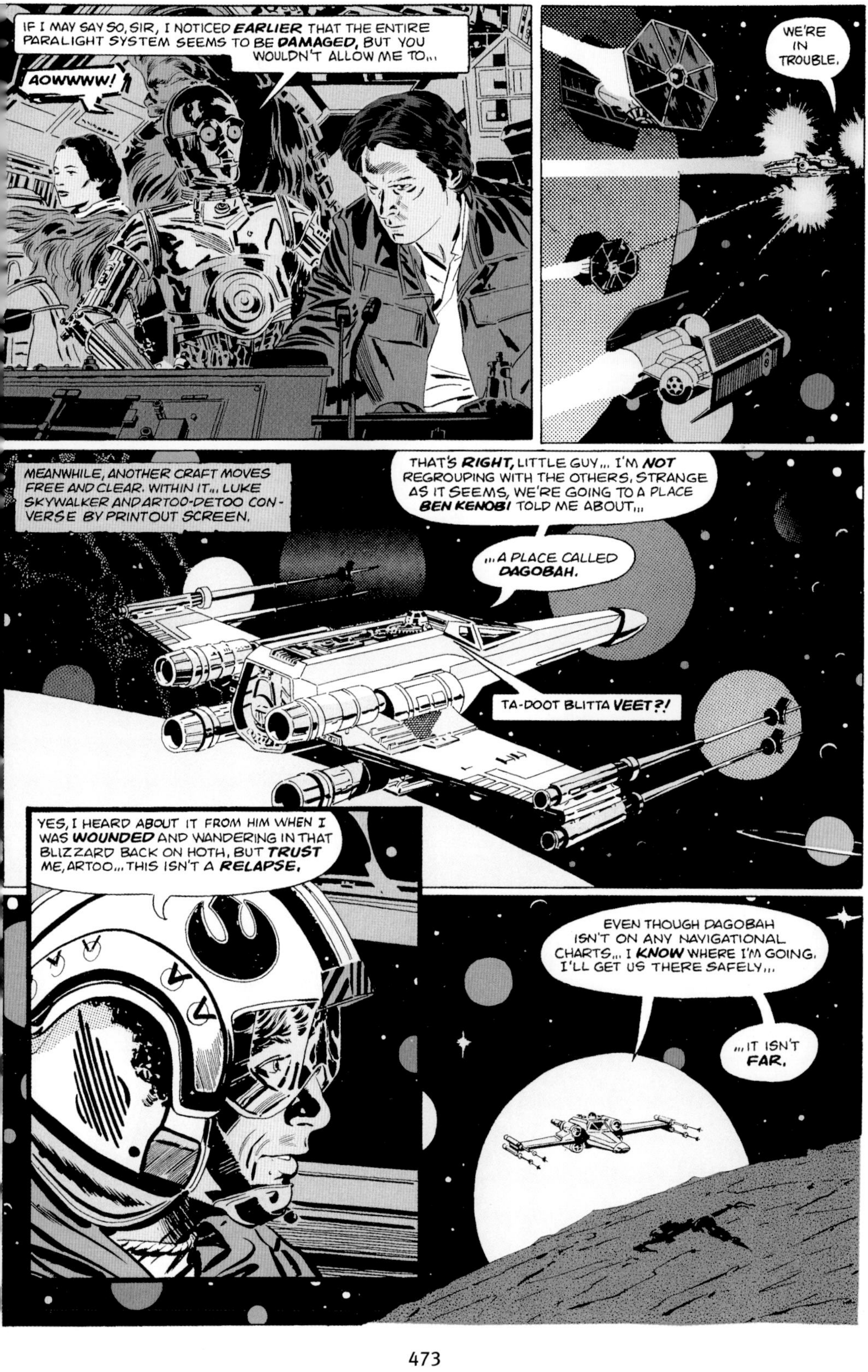

IF I MAY SAY SO, SIR, I NOTICED EARLIER THAT THE ENTIRE PARALIGHT SYSTEM SEEMS TO BE DAMAGED, BUT YOU WOULDN'T ALLOW ME TO...
AOWWWW!
WE'RE IN TROUBLE.
MEANWHILE, ANOTHER CRAFT MOVES FREE AND CLEAR. WITHIN IT... LUKE SKYWALKER AND ARTOO-DETOO CONVERSE BY PRINTOUT SCREEN.
THAT'S RIGHT, LITTLE GUY... I'M NOT REGROUPING WITH THE OTHERS. STRANGE AS IT SEEMS, WE'RE GOING TO A PLACE BEN KENOBI TOLD ME ABOUT...
...A PLACE CALLED DAGOBAH.
TA-DOOT BLITTA VEET?!
YES, I HEARD ABOUT IT FROM HIM WHEN I WAS WOUNDED AND WANDERING IN THAT BLIZZARD BACK ON HOTH, BUT TRUST ME, ARTOO... THIS ISN'T A RELAPSE.
EVEN THOUGH DAGOBAH ISN'T ON ANY NAVIGATIONAL CHARTS... I KNOW WHERE I'M GOING. I'LL GET US THERE SAFELY...
...IT ISN'T FAR.

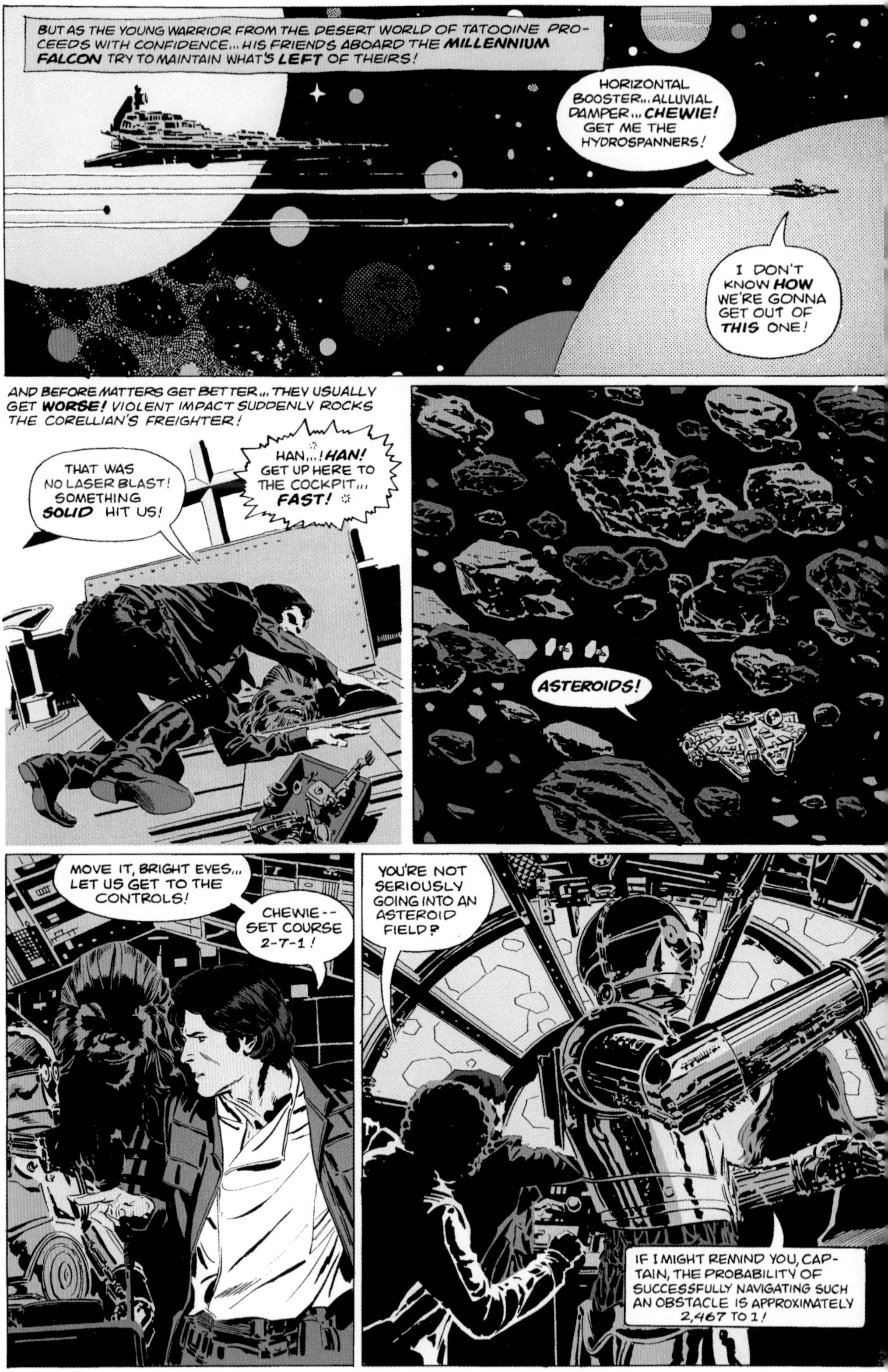
BUT AS THE YOUNG WARRIOR FROM THE DESERT WORLD OF TATOOINE PROCEEDS WITH CONFIDENCE... HIS FRIENDS ABOARD THE MILLENNIUM FALCON TRY TO MAINTAIN WHAT'S LEFT OF THEIRS!
HORIZONTAL BOOSTER... ALLUVIAL DAMPER... CHEWIE! GET ME THE HYDROSPANNERS!
I DON'T KNOW HOW WE'RE GONNA GET OUT OF THIS ONE!
AND BEFORE MATTERS GET BETTER... THEY USUALLY GET WORSE! VIOLENT IMPACT SUDDENLY ROCKS THE CORELLIAN'S FREIGHTER!
THAT WAS NO LASER BLAST! SOMETHING SOLID HIT US!
HAN...! HAN! GET UP HERE TO THE COCKPIT... FAST!
ASTEROIDS!
MOVE IT, BRIGHT EYES... LET US GET TO THE CONTROLS!
CHEWIE -- SET COURSE 2-7-1!
YOU'RE NOT SERIOUSLY GOING INTO AN ASTEROID FIELD?
IF I MIGHT REMIND YOU, CAPTAIN, THE PROBABILITY OF SUCCESSFULLY NAVIGATING SUCH AN OBSTACLE IS APPROXIMATELY 2,467 TO 1!

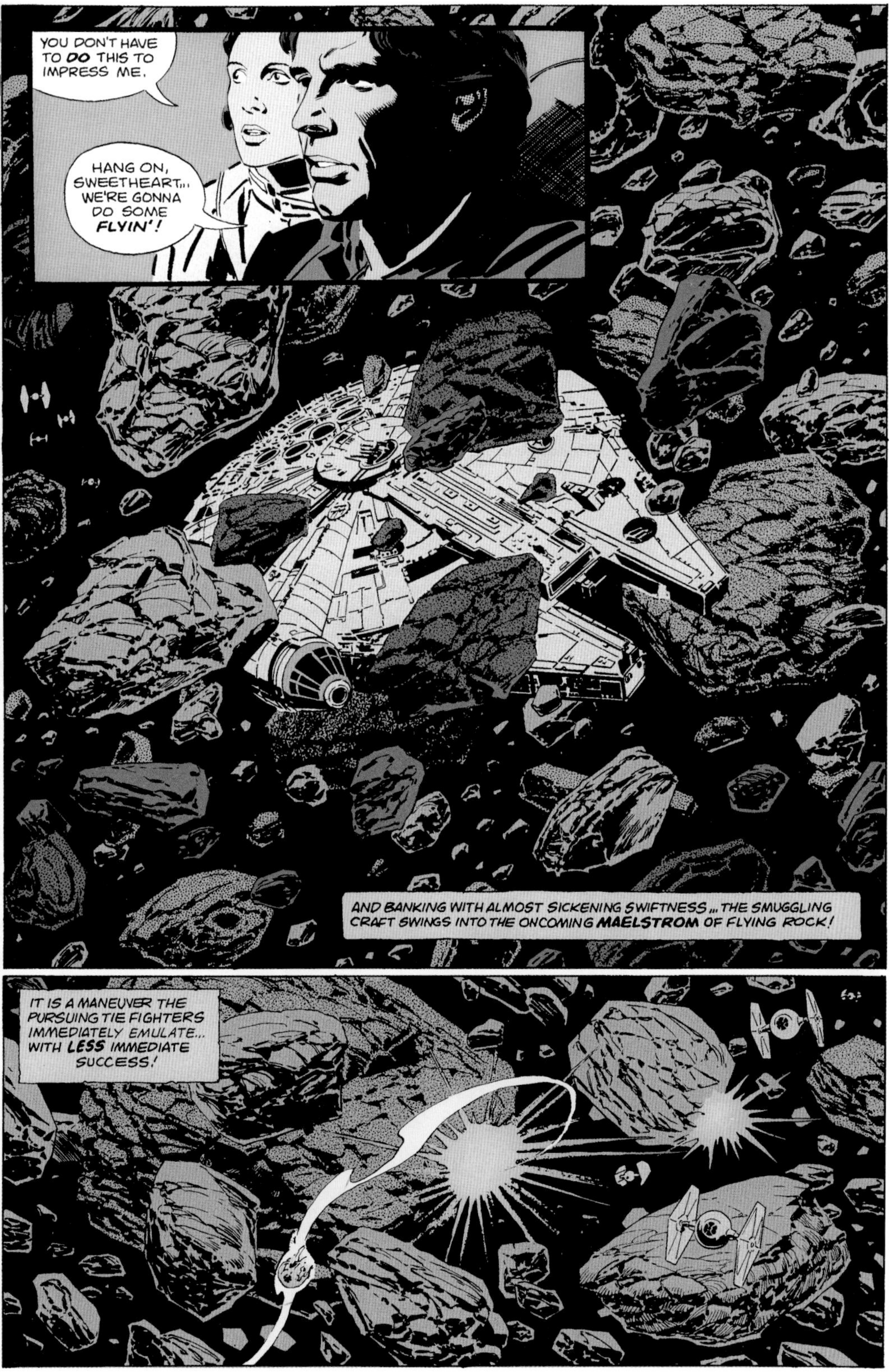

YOU DON'T HAVE TO DO THIS TO IMPRESS ME.
HANG ON, SWEETHEART... WE'RE GONNA DO SOME FLYIN'!
AND BANKING WITH ALMOST SICKENING SWIFTNESS... THE SMUGGLING CRAFT SWINGS INTO THE ONCOMING MAELSTROM OF FLYING ROCK!
IT IS A MANEUVER THE PURSUING TIE FIGHTERS IMMEDIATELY EMULATE... WITH LESS IMMEDIATE SUCCESS!

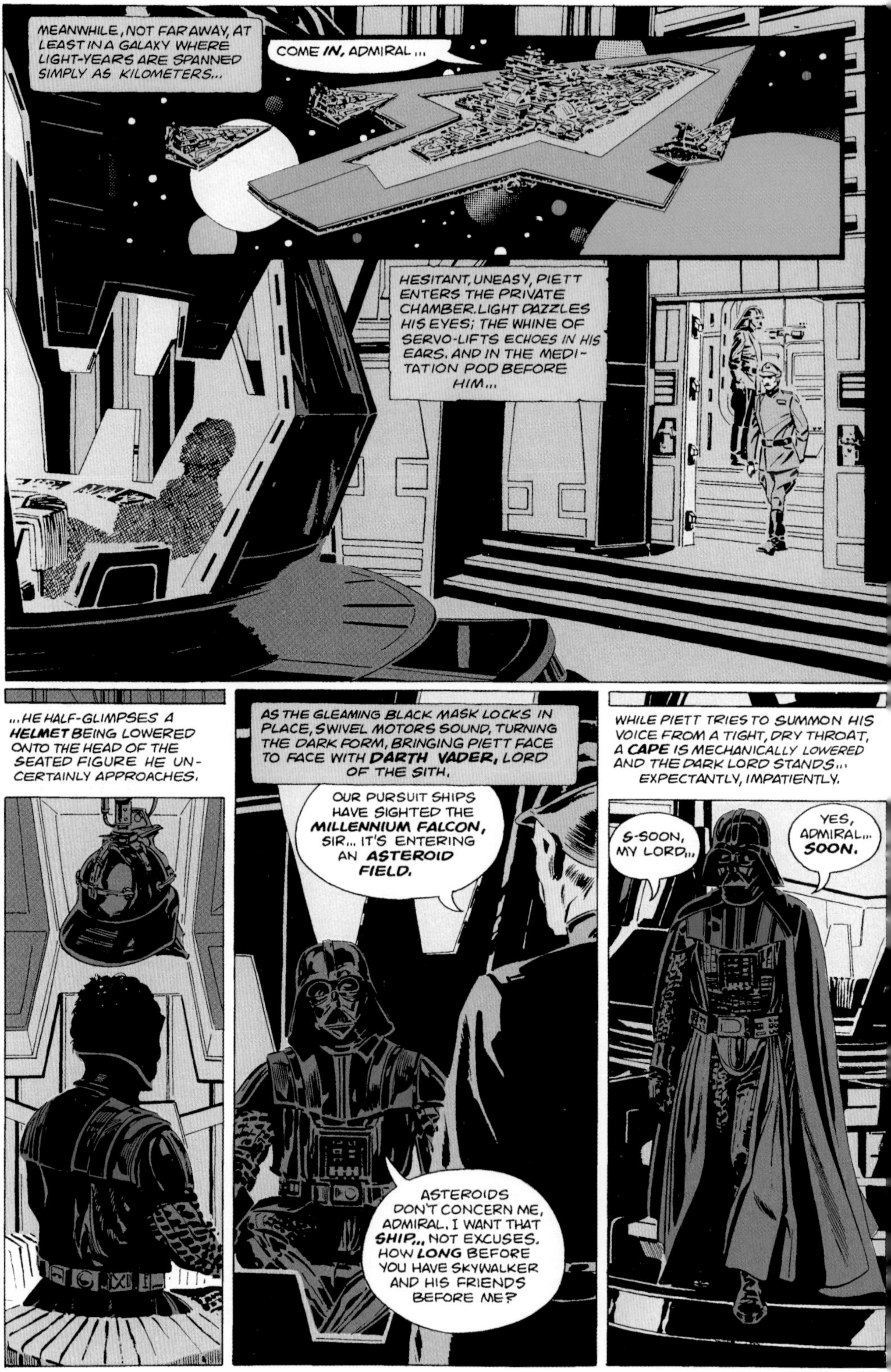
MEANWHILE, NOT FAR AWAY, AT LEAST IN A GALAXY WHERE LIGHT-YEARS ARE SPANNED SIMPLY AS KILOMETERS...
COME IN, ADMIRAL...
HESITANT, UNEASY, PIETT ENTERS THE PRIVATE CHAMBER. LIGHT DAZZLES HIS EYES; THE WHINE OF SERVO-LIFTS ECHOES IN HIS EARS. AND IN THE MEDITATION POD BEFORE HIM...
...HE HALF-GLIMPSES A HELMET BEING LOWERED ONTO THE HEAD OF THE SEATED FIGURE HE UNCERTAINLY APPROACHES.
AS THE GLEAMING BLACK MASK LOCKS IN PLACE, SWIVEL MOTORS SOUND, TURNING THE DARK FORM, BRINGING PIETT FACE TO FACE WITH DARTH VADER, LORD OF THE SITH.
OUR PURSUIT SHIPS HAVE SIGHTED THE MILLENNIUM FALCON, SIR... IT'S ENTERING AN ASTEROID FIELD.
ASTEROIDS DON'T CONCERN ME, ADMIRAL. I WANT THAT SHIP... NOT EXCUSES. HOW LONG BEFORE YOU HAVE SKYWALKER AND HIS FRIENDS BEFORE ME?
WHILE PIETT TRIES TO SUMMON HIS VOICE FROM A TIGHT, DRY THROAT, A CAPE IS MECHANICALLY LOWERED AND THE DARK LORD STANDS... EXPECTANTLY, IMPATIENTLY.
S-SOON, MY LORD...
YES, ADMIRAL... SOON.

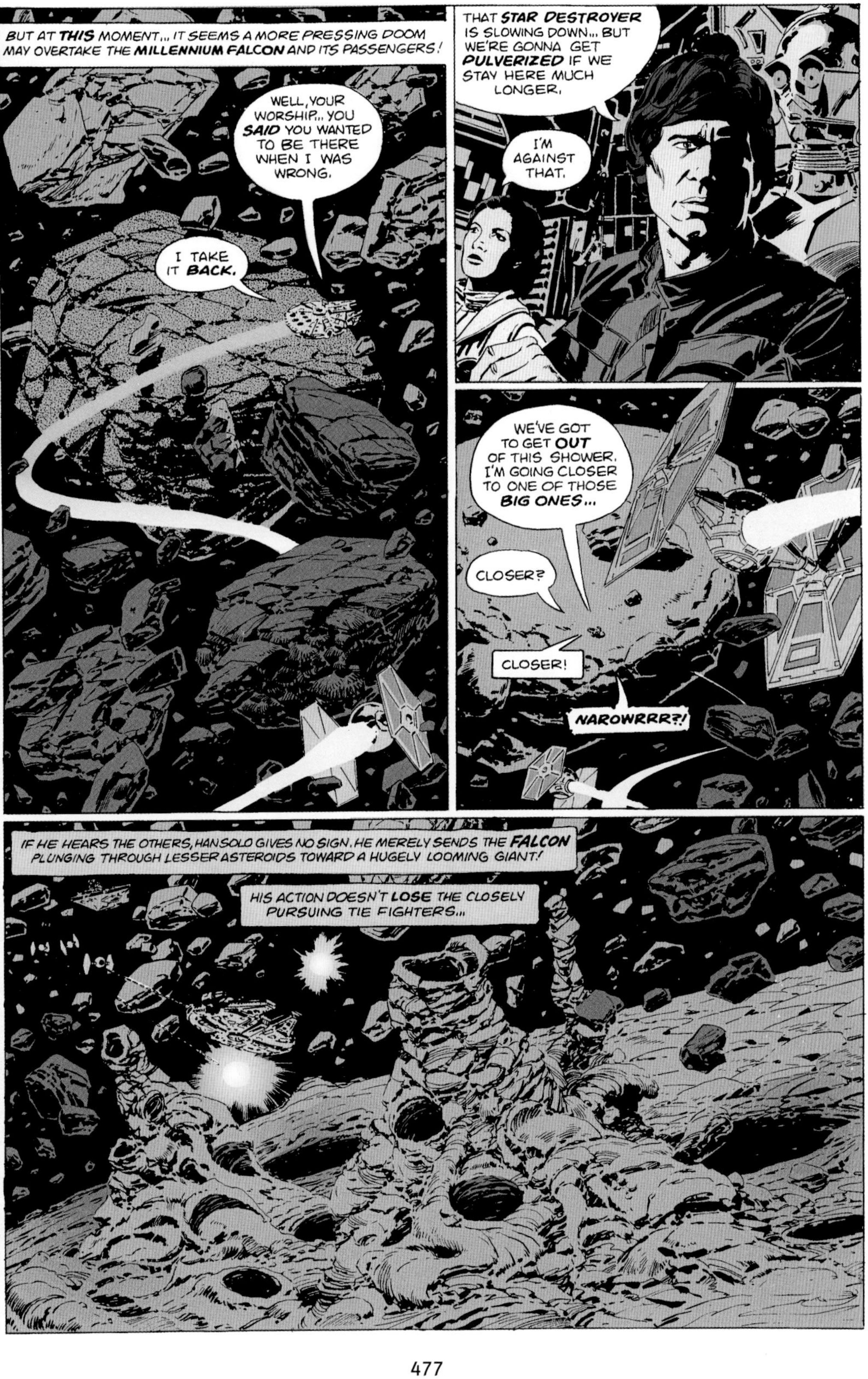
BUT AT THIS MOMENT... IT SEEMS A MORE PRESSING DOOM MAY OVERTAKE THE MILLENNIUM FALCON AND ITS PASSENGERS!
WELL, YOUR WORSHIP... YOU SAID YOU WANTED TO BE THERE WHEN I WAS WRONG.
I TAKE IT BACK.
THAT STAR DESTROYER IS SLOWING DOWN... BUT WE'RE GONNA GET PULVERIZED IF WE STAY HERE MUCH LONGER.
I'M AGAINST THAT.
WE'VE GOT TO GET OUT OF THIS SHOWER. I'M GOING CLOSER TO ONE OF THOSE BIG ONES...
CLOSER?
CLOSER!
NAROWRRR?!
IF HE HEARS THE OTHERS, HAN SOLO GIVES NO SIGN. HE MERELY SENDS THE FALCON PLUNGING THROUGH LESSER ASTEROIDS TOWARD A HUGELY LOOMING GIANT!
HIS ACTION DOESN'T LOSE THE CLOSELY PURSUING TIE FIGHTERS...

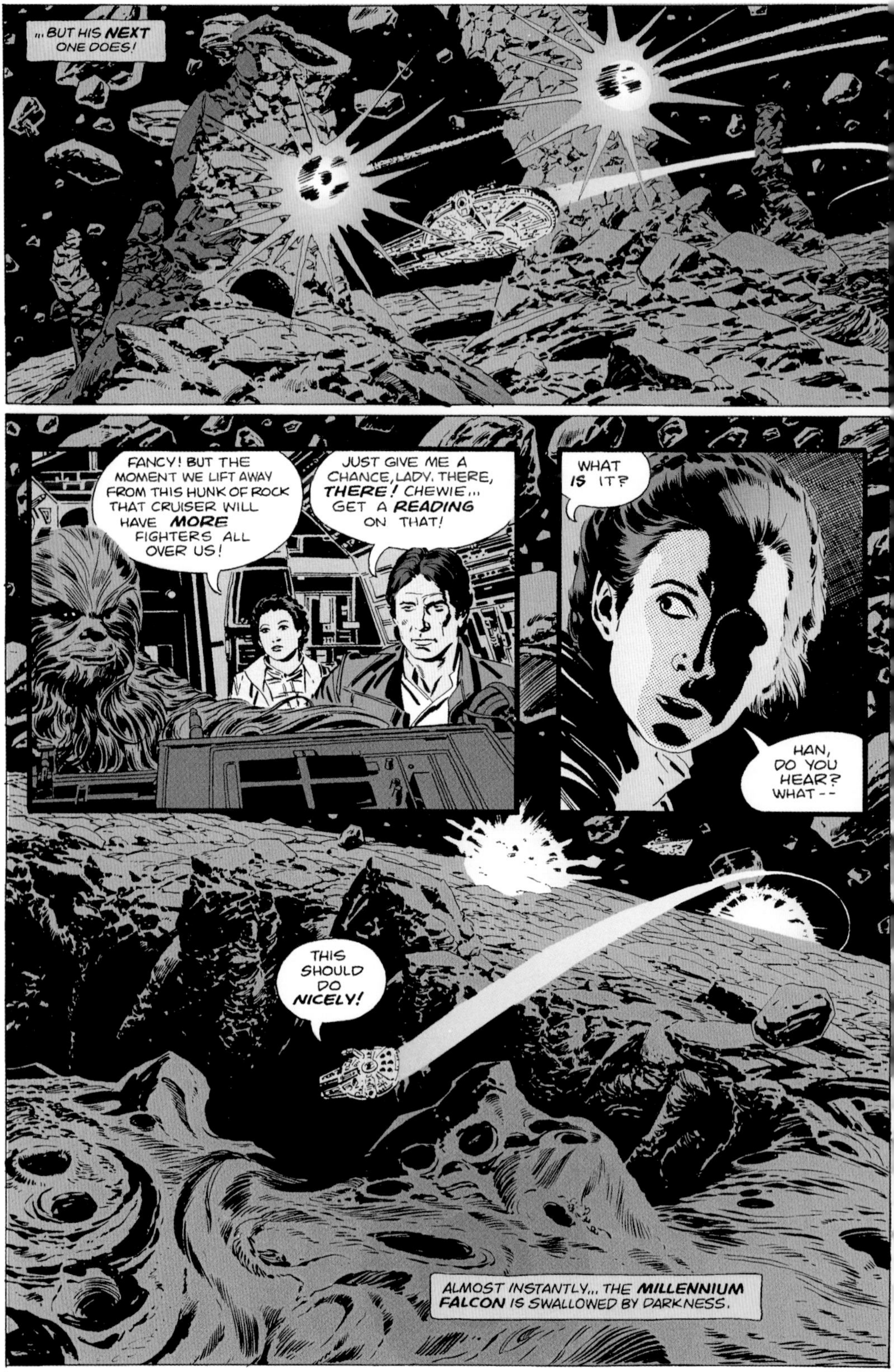
...BUT HIS NEXT ONE DOES!
FANCY! BUT THE MOMENT WE LIFT AWAY FROM THIS HUNK OF ROCK THAT CRUISER WILL HAVE MORE FIGHTERS ALL OVER US!
JUST GIVE ME A CHANCE, LADY. THERE, THERE! CHEWIE... GET A READING ON THAT!
WHAT IS IT?
HAN, DO YOU HEAR? WHAT--
THIS SHOULD DO NICELY!
ALMOST INSTANTLY... THE MILLENNIUM FALCON IS SWALLOWED BY DARKNESS.

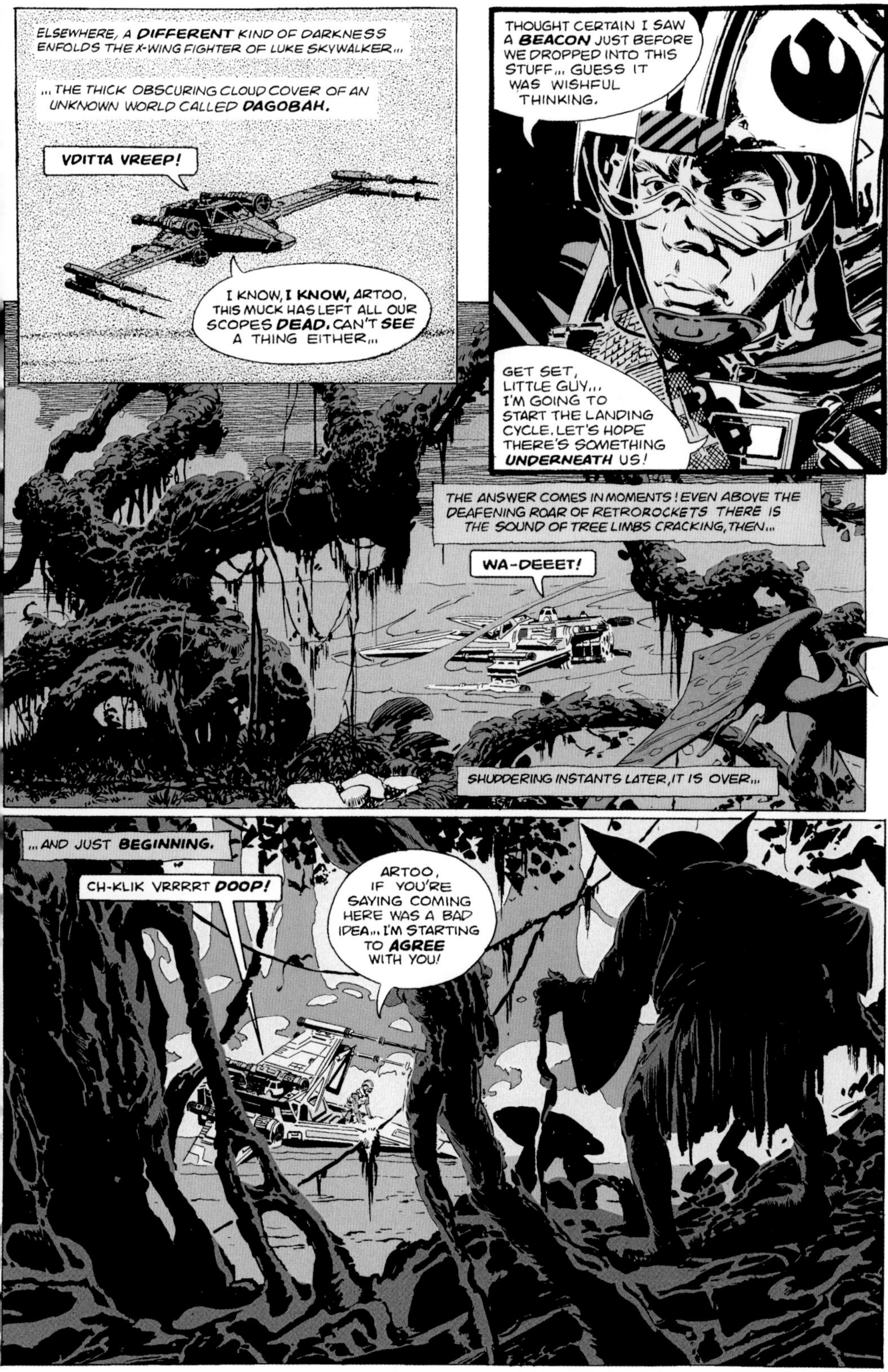
ELSEWHERE, A DIFFERENT KIND OF DARKNESS ENFOLDS THE X-WING FIGHTER OF LUKE SKYWALKER...
...THE THICK OBSCURING CLOUD COVER OF AN UNKNOWN WORLD CALLED DAGOBAH.
VDITTA VREEP!
I KNOW, I KNOW, ARTOO. THIS MUCK HAS LEFT ALL OUR SCOPES DEAD. CAN'T SEE A THING EITHER...
THOUGHT CERTAIN I SAW A BEACON JUST BEFORE WE DROPPED INTO THIS STUFF... GUESS IT WAS WISHFUL THINKING.
GET SET, LITTLE GUY... I'M GOING TO START THE LANDING CYCLE. LET'S HOPE THERE'S SOMETHING UNDERNEATH US!
THE ANSWER COMES IN MOMENTS! EVEN ABOVE THE DEAFENING ROAR OF RETROROCKETS THERE IS THE SOUND OF TREE LIMBS CRACKING, THEN...
WA-DEEET!
SHUDDERING INSTANTS LATER, IT IS OVER...
...AND JUST BEGINNING.
CH-KLIK VRRRRT DOOP!
ARTOO, IF YOU'RE SAYING COMING HERE WAS A BAD IDEA... I'M STARTING TO AGREE WITH YOU!

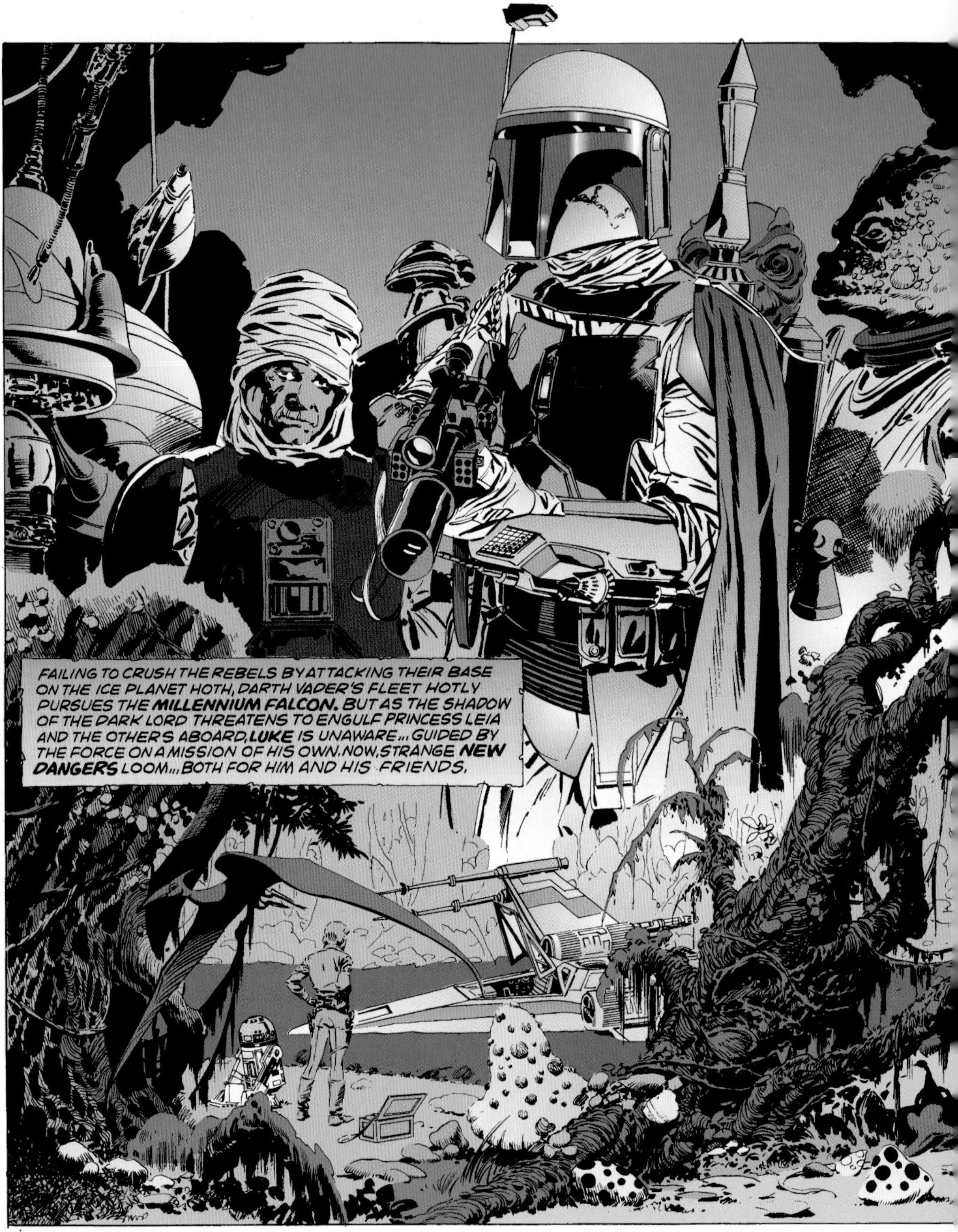
FAILING TO CRUSH THE REBELS BY ATTACKING THEIR BASE ON THE ICE PLANET HOTH, DARTH VADER'S FLEET HOTLY PURSUES THE **MILLENNIUM FALCON.** BUT AS THE SHADOW OF THE DARK LORD THREATENS TO ENGULF PRINCESS LEIA AND THE OTHERS ABOARD, **LUKE** IS UNAWARE... GUIDED BY THE FORCE ON A MISSION OF HIS OWN. NOW, STRANGE **NEW DANGERS** LOOM... BOTH FOR HIM AND HIS FRIENDS.

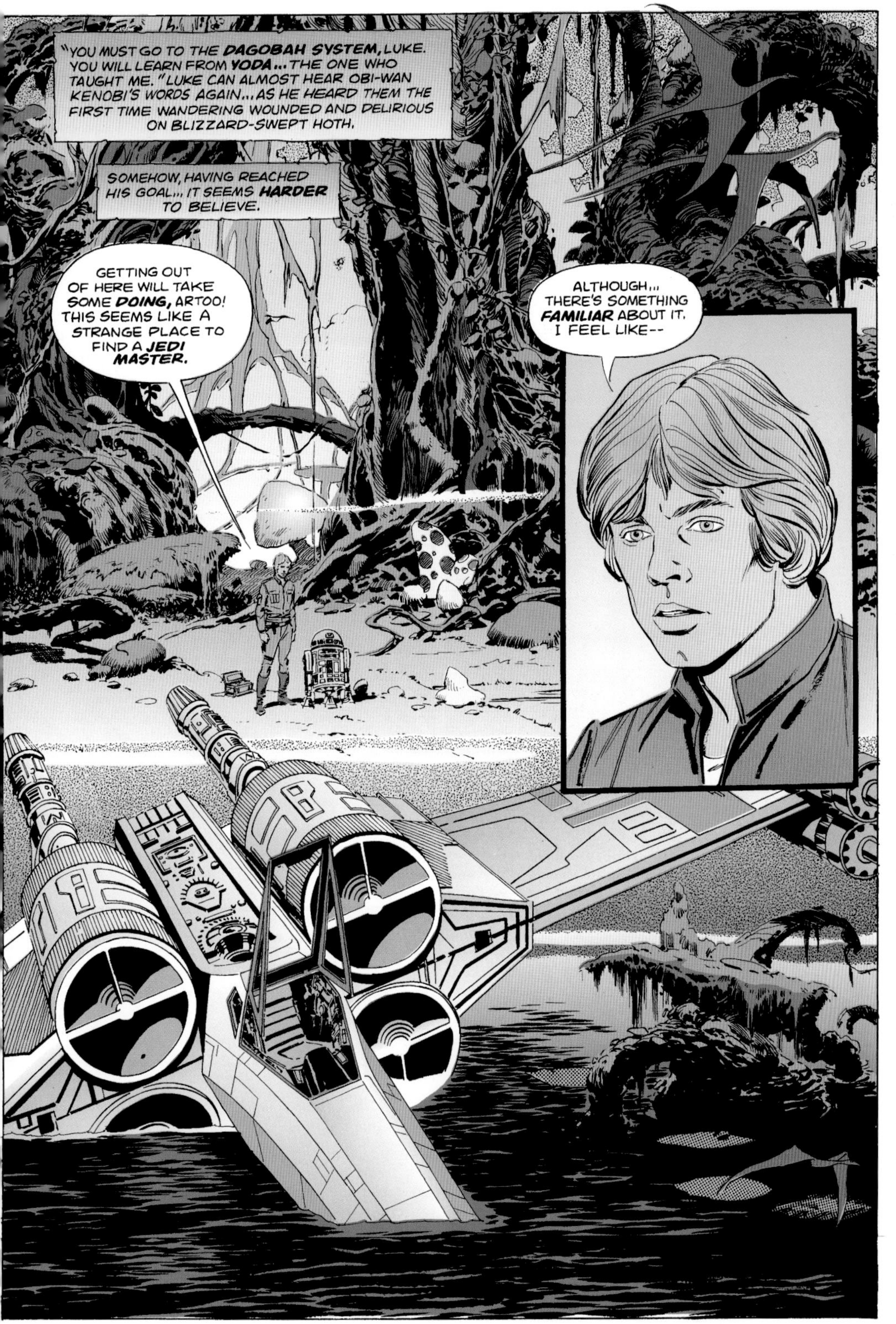
"YOU MUST GO TO THE DAGOBAH SYSTEM, LUKE. YOU WILL LEARN FROM YODA... THE ONE WHO TAUGHT ME." LUKE CAN ALMOST HEAR OBI-WAN KENOBI'S WORDS AGAIN... AS HE HEARD THEM THE FIRST TIME WANDERING WOUNDED AND DELIRIOUS ON BLIZZARD-SWEPT HOTH.
SOMEHOW, HAVING REACHED HIS GOAL... IT SEEMS HARDER TO BELIEVE.
GETTING OUT OF HERE WILL TAKE SOME DOING, ARTOO! THIS SEEMS LIKE A STRANGE PLACE TO FIND A JEDI MASTER.
ALTHOUGH... THERE'S SOMETHING FAMILIAR ABOUT IT. I FEEL LIKE--

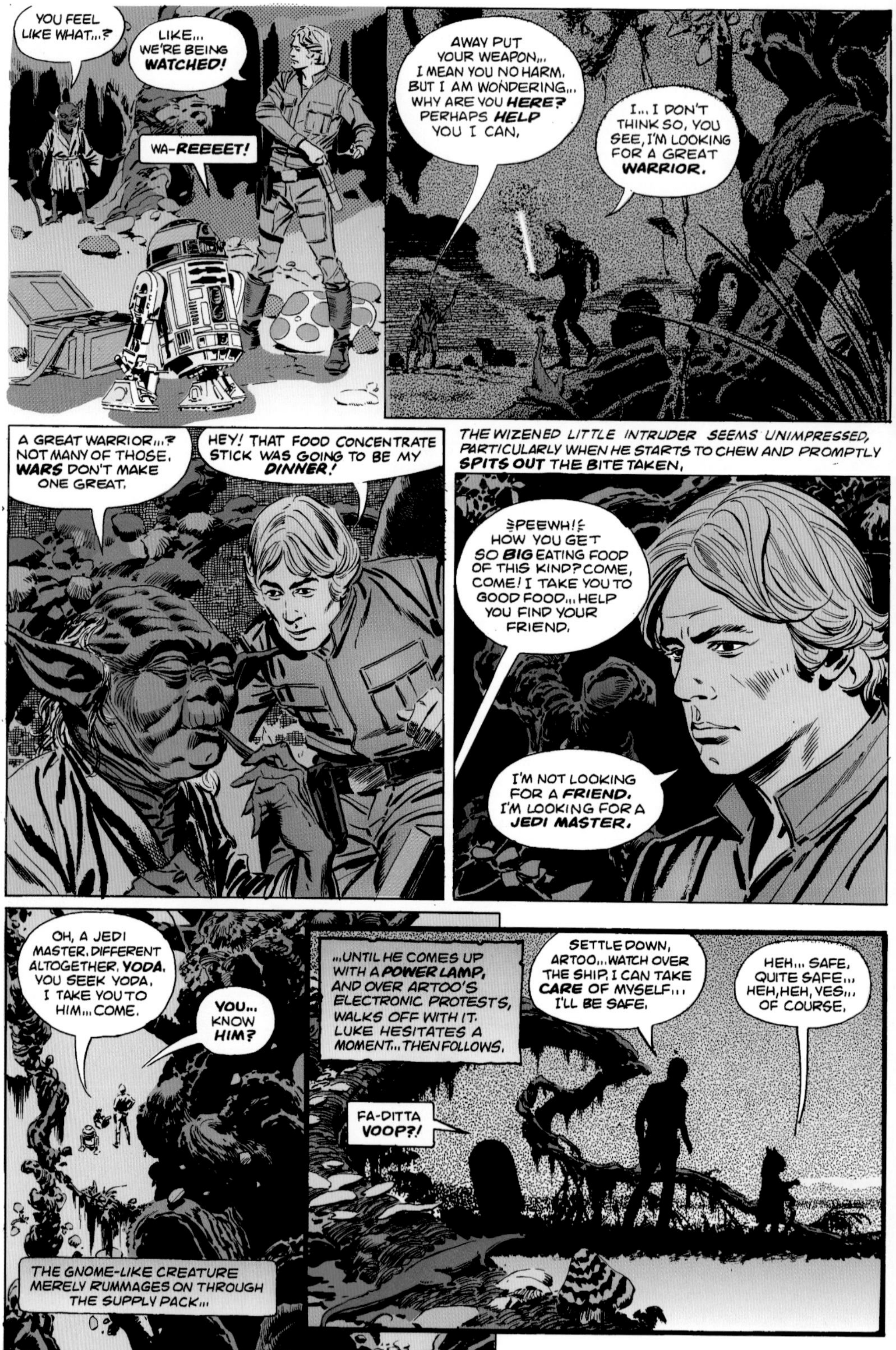
YOU FEEL LIKE WHAT...?
LIKE... WE'RE BEING WATCHED!
WA-REEEET!
AWAY PUT YOUR WEAPON... I MEAN YOU NO HARM. BUT I AM WONDERING... WHY ARE YOU HERE? PERHAPS HELP YOU I CAN.
I... I DON'T THINK SO. YOU SEE, I'M LOOKING FOR A GREAT WARRIOR.
A GREAT WARRIOR...? NOT MANY OF THOSE. WARS DON'T MAKE ONE GREAT.
HEY! THAT FOOD CONCENTRATE STICK WAS GOING TO BE MY DINNER!
THE WIZENED LITTLE INTRUDER SEEMS UNIMPRESSED, PARTICULARLY WHEN HE STARTS TO CHEW AND PROMPTLY SPITS OUT THE BITE TAKEN.
PEEWH! HOW YOU GET SO BIG EATING FOOD OF THIS KIND? COME, COME! I TAKE YOU TO GOOD FOOD... HELP YOU FIND YOUR FRIEND.
I'M NOT LOOKING FOR A FRIEND. I'M LOOKING FOR A JEDI MASTER.
OH, A JEDI MASTER. DIFFERENT ALTOGETHER. YODA. YOU SEEK YODA. I TAKE YOU TO HIM... COME.
YOU... KNOW HIM?
THE GNOME-LIKE CREATURE MERELY RUMMAGES ON THROUGH THE SUPPLY PACK...
...UNTIL HE COMES UP WITH A POWER LAMP, AND OVER ARTOO'S ELECTRONIC PROTESTS, WALKS OFF WITH IT. LUKE HESITATES A MOMENT... THEN FOLLOWS.
FA-DITTA VOOP?!
SETTLE DOWN, ARTOO... WATCH OVER THE SHIP. I CAN TAKE CARE OF MYSELF... I'LL BE SAFE.
HEH... SAFE. QUITE SAFE... HEH, HEH, YES... OF COURSE.

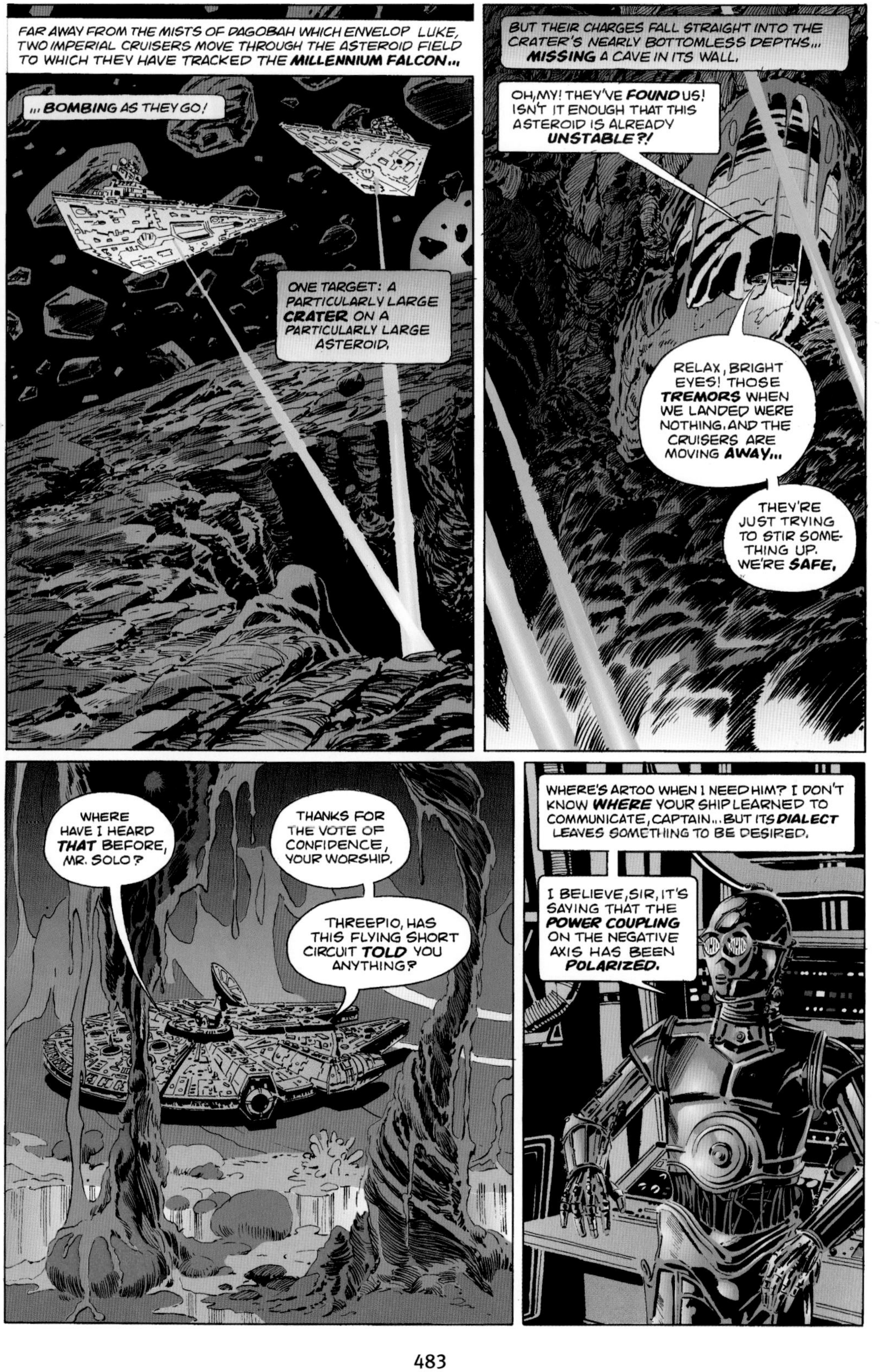
FAR AWAY FROM THE MISTS OF DAGOBAH WHICH ENVELOP LUKE, TWO IMPERIAL CRUISERS MOVE THROUGH THE ASTEROID FIELD TO WHICH THEY HAVE TRACKED THE MILLENNIUM FALCON...
...BOMBING AS THEY GO!
ONE TARGET: A PARTICULARLY LARGE CRATER ON A PARTICULARLY LARGE ASTEROID.
BUT THEIR CHARGES FALL STRAIGHT INTO THE CRATER'S NEARLY BOTTOMLESS DEPTHS... MISSING A CAVE IN ITS WALL.
OH, MY! THEY'VE FOUND US! ISN'T IT ENOUGH THAT THIS ASTEROID IS ALREADY UNSTABLE?!
RELAX, BRIGHT EYES! THOSE TREMORS WHEN WE LANDED WERE NOTHING. AND THE CRUISERS ARE MOVING AWAY...
THEY'RE JUST TRYING TO STIR SOMETHING UP. WE'RE SAFE.
WHERE HAVE I HEARD THAT BEFORE, MR. SOLO?
THANKS FOR THE VOTE OF CONFIDENCE, YOUR WORSHIP.
THREEPIO, HAS THIS FLYING SHORT CIRCUIT TOLD YOU ANYTHING?
WHERE'S ARTOO WHEN I NEED HIM? I DON'T KNOW WHERE YOUR SHIP LEARNED TO COMMUNICATE, CAPTAIN... BUT ITS DIALECT LEAVES SOMETHING TO BE DESIRED.
I BELIEVE, SIR, IT'S SAYING THAT THE POWER COUPLING ON THE NEGATIVE AXIS HAS BEEN POLARIZED.

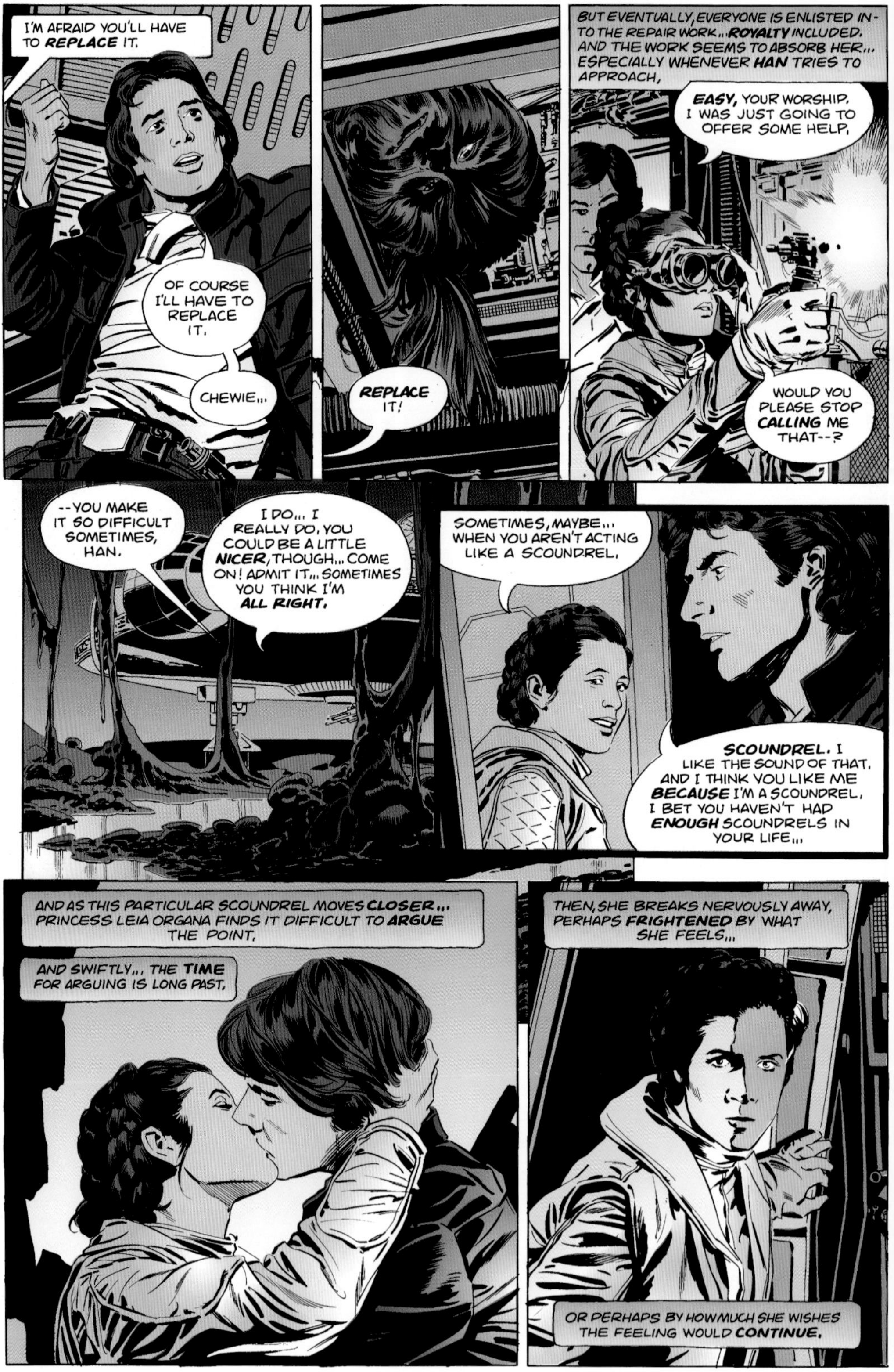
I'M AFRAID YOU'LL HAVE TO REPLACE IT.
OF COURSE I'LL HAVE TO REPLACE IT.
CHEWIE...
REPLACE IT!
BUT EVENTUALLY, EVERYONE IS ENLISTED INTO THE REPAIR WORK... ROYALTY INCLUDED. AND THE WORK SEEMS TO ABSORB HER... ESPECIALLY WHENEVER HAN TRIES TO APPROACH.
EASY, YOUR WORSHIP. I WAS JUST GOING TO OFFER SOME HELP.
WOULD YOU PLEASE STOP CALLING ME THAT--?
--YOU MAKE IT SO DIFFICULT SOMETIMES, HAN.
I DO... I REALLY DO. YOU COULD BE A LITTLE NICER, THOUGH... COME ON! ADMIT IT... SOMETIMES YOU THINK I'M ALL RIGHT.
SOMETIMES, MAYBE... WHEN YOU AREN'T ACTING LIKE A SCOUNDREL.
SCOUNDREL. I LIKE THE SOUND OF THAT. AND I THINK YOU LIKE ME BECAUSE I'M A SCOUNDREL. I BET YOU HAVEN'T HAD ENOUGH SCOUNDRELS IN YOUR LIFE...
AND AS THIS PARTICULAR SCOUNDREL MOVES CLOSER... PRINCESS LEIA ORGANA FINDS IT DIFFICULT TO ARGUE THE POINT.
AND SWIFTLY... THE TIME FOR ARGUING IS LONG PAST.
THEN, SHE BREAKS NERVOUSLY AWAY, PERHAPS FRIGHTENED BY WHAT SHE FEELS...
OR PERHAPS BY HOW MUCH SHE WISHES THE FEELING WOULD CONTINUE.

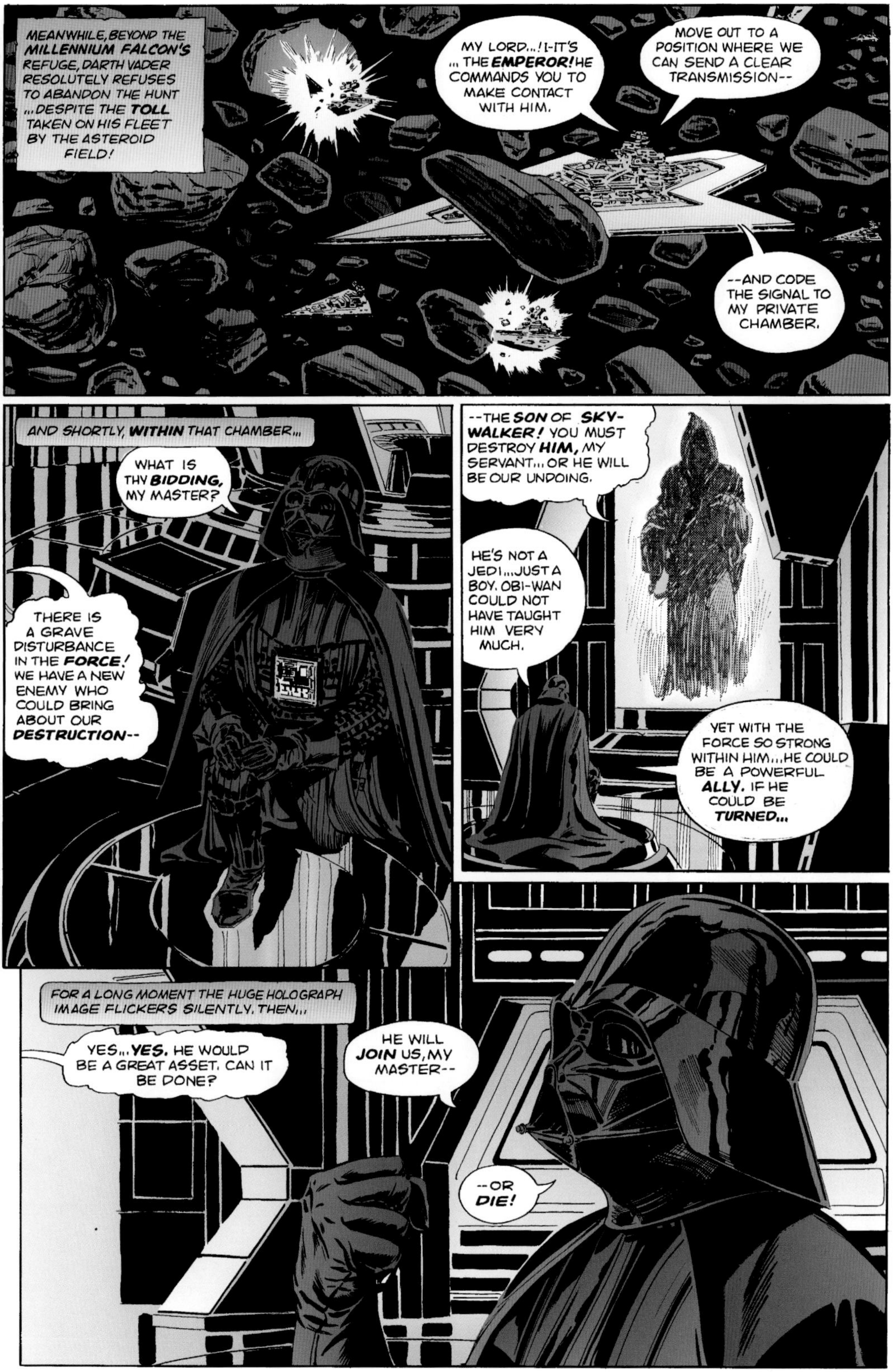

MEANWHILE, BEYOND THE MILLENNIUM FALCON'S REFUGE, DARTH VADER RESOLUTELY REFUSES TO ABANDON THE HUNT ...DESPITE THE TOLL TAKEN ON HIS FLEET BY THE ASTEROID FIELD!
MY LORD...! I-IT'S ... THE EMPEROR! HE COMMANDS YOU TO MAKE CONTACT WITH HIM.
MOVE OUT TO A POSITION WHERE WE CAN SEND A CLEAR TRANSMISSION--
--AND CODE THE SIGNAL TO MY PRIVATE CHAMBER.
AND SHORTLY, WITHIN THAT CHAMBER...
WHAT IS THY BIDDING, MY MASTER?
THERE IS A GRAVE DISTURBANCE IN THE FORCE! WE HAVE A NEW ENEMY WHO COULD BRING ABOUT OUR DESTRUCTION--
--THE SON OF SKYWALKER! YOU MUST DESTROY HIM, MY SERVANT... OR HE WILL BE OUR UNDOING.
HE'S NOT A JEDI... JUST A BOY. OBI-WAN COULD NOT HAVE TAUGHT HIM VERY MUCH.
YET WITH THE FORCE SO STRONG WITHIN HIM... HE COULD BE A POWERFUL ALLY. IF HE COULD BE TURNED...
FOR A LONG MOMENT THE HUGE HOLOGRAPH IMAGE FLICKERS SILENTLY. THEN...
YES... YES. HE WOULD BE A GREAT ASSET. CAN IT BE DONE?
HE WILL JOIN US, MY MASTER--
--OR DIE!

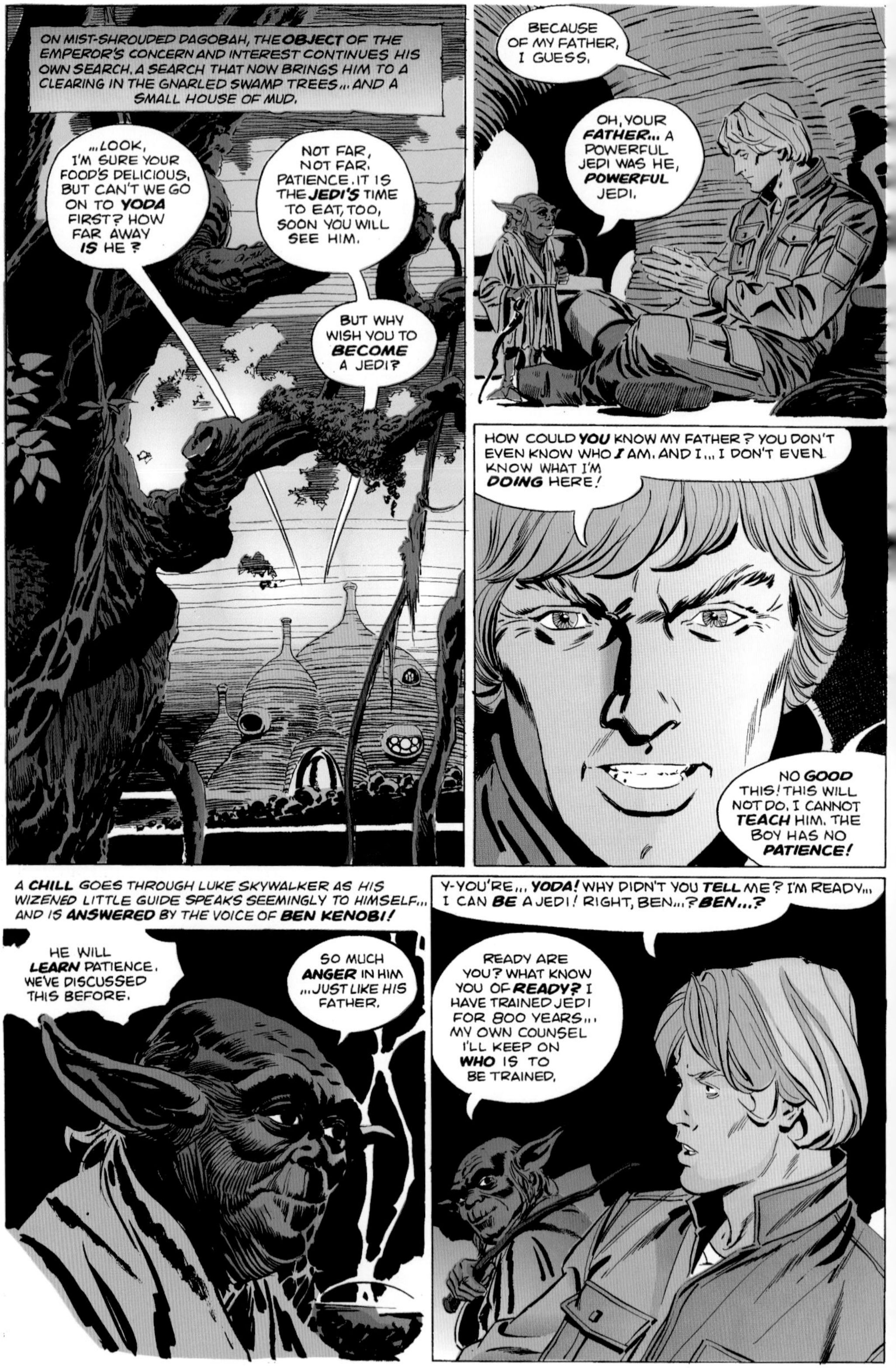
ON MIST-SHROUDED DAGOBAH, THE OBJECT OF THE EMPEROR'S CONCERN AND INTEREST CONTINUES HIS OWN SEARCH. A SEARCH THAT NOW BRINGS HIM TO A CLEARING IN THE GNARLED SWAMP TREES... AND A SMALL HOUSE OF MUD.
...LOOK, I'M SURE YOUR FOOD'S DELICIOUS, BUT CAN'T WE GO ON TO YODA FIRST? HOW FAR AWAY IS HE?
NOT FAR, NOT FAR. PATIENCE. IT IS THE JEDI'S TIME TO EAT, TOO, SOON YOU WILL SEE HIM.
BUT WHY WISH YOU TO BECOME A JEDI?
BECAUSE OF MY FATHER, I GUESS.
OH, YOUR FATHER... A POWERFUL JEDI WAS HE, POWERFUL JEDI.
HOW COULD YOU KNOW MY FATHER? YOU DON'T EVEN KNOW WHO I AM. AND I... I DON'T EVEN KNOW WHAT I'M DOING HERE!
NO GOOD THIS! THIS WILL NOT DO. I CANNOT TEACH HIM. THE BOY HAS NO PATIENCE!
A CHILL GOES THROUGH LUKE SKYWALKER AS HIS WIZENED LITTLE GUIDE SPEAKS SEEMINGLY TO HIMSELF... AND IS ANSWERED BY THE VOICE OF BEN KENOBI!
HE WILL LEARN PATIENCE. WE'VE DISCUSSED THIS BEFORE.
SO MUCH ANGER IN HIM ...JUST LIKE HIS FATHER.
Y-YOU'RE... YODA! WHY DIDN'T YOU TELL ME? I'M READY... I CAN BE A JEDI! RIGHT, BEN...? BEN...?
READY ARE YOU? WHAT KNOW YOU OF READY? I HAVE TRAINED JEDI FOR 800 YEARS... MY OWN COUNSEL I'LL KEEP ON WHO IS TO BE TRAINED.

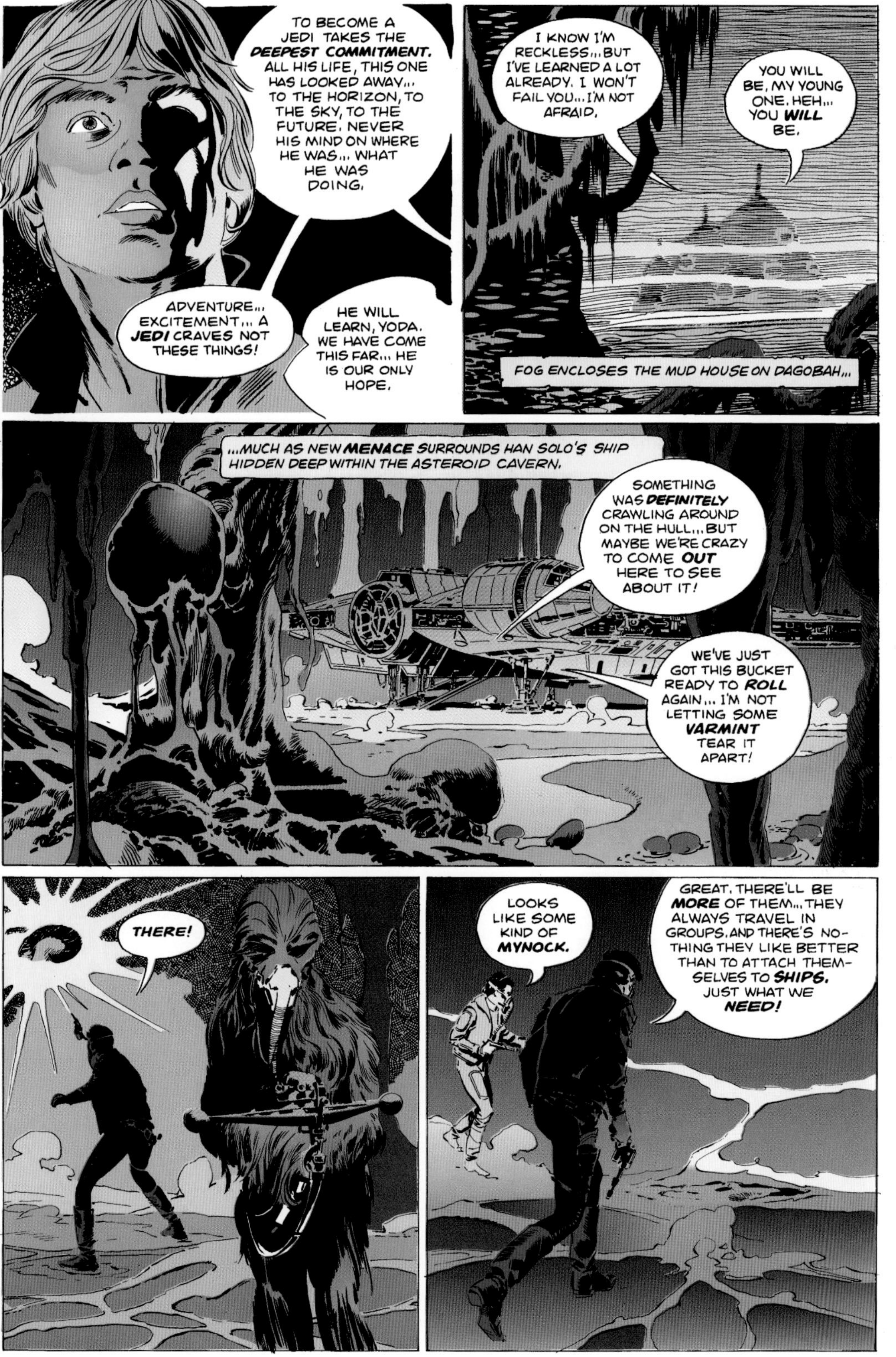

TO BECOME A JEDI TAKES THE DEEPEST COMMITMENT. ALL HIS LIFE, THIS ONE HAS LOOKED AWAY... TO THE HORIZON, TO THE SKY, TO THE FUTURE. NEVER HIS MIND ON WHERE HE WAS... WHAT HE WAS DOING.
ADVENTURE... EXCITEMENT... A JEDI CRAVES NOT THESE THINGS!
HE WILL LEARN, YODA. WE HAVE COME THIS FAR... HE IS OUR ONLY HOPE.
I KNOW I'M RECKLESS... BUT I'VE LEARNED A LOT ALREADY. I WON'T FAIL YOU... I'M NOT AFRAID.
YOU WILL BE, MY YOUNG ONE. HEH... YOU WILL BE.
FOG ENCLOSES THE MUD HOUSE ON DAGOBAH...
...MUCH AS NEW MENACE SURROUNDS HAN SOLO'S SHIP HIDDEN DEEP WITHIN THE ASTEROID CAVERN.
SOMETHING WAS DEFINITELY CRAWLING AROUND ON THE HULL... BUT MAYBE WE'RE CRAZY TO COME OUT HERE TO SEE ABOUT IT!
WE'VE JUST GOT THIS BUCKET READY TO ROLL AGAIN... I'M NOT LETTING SOME VARMINT TEAR IT APART!
THERE!
LOOKS LIKE SOME KIND OF MYNOCK.
GREAT. THERE'LL BE MORE OF THEM... THEY ALWAYS TRAVEL IN GROUPS. AND THERE'S NOTHING THEY LIKE BETTER THAN TO ATTACH THEMSELVES TO SHIPS. JUST WHAT WE NEED!

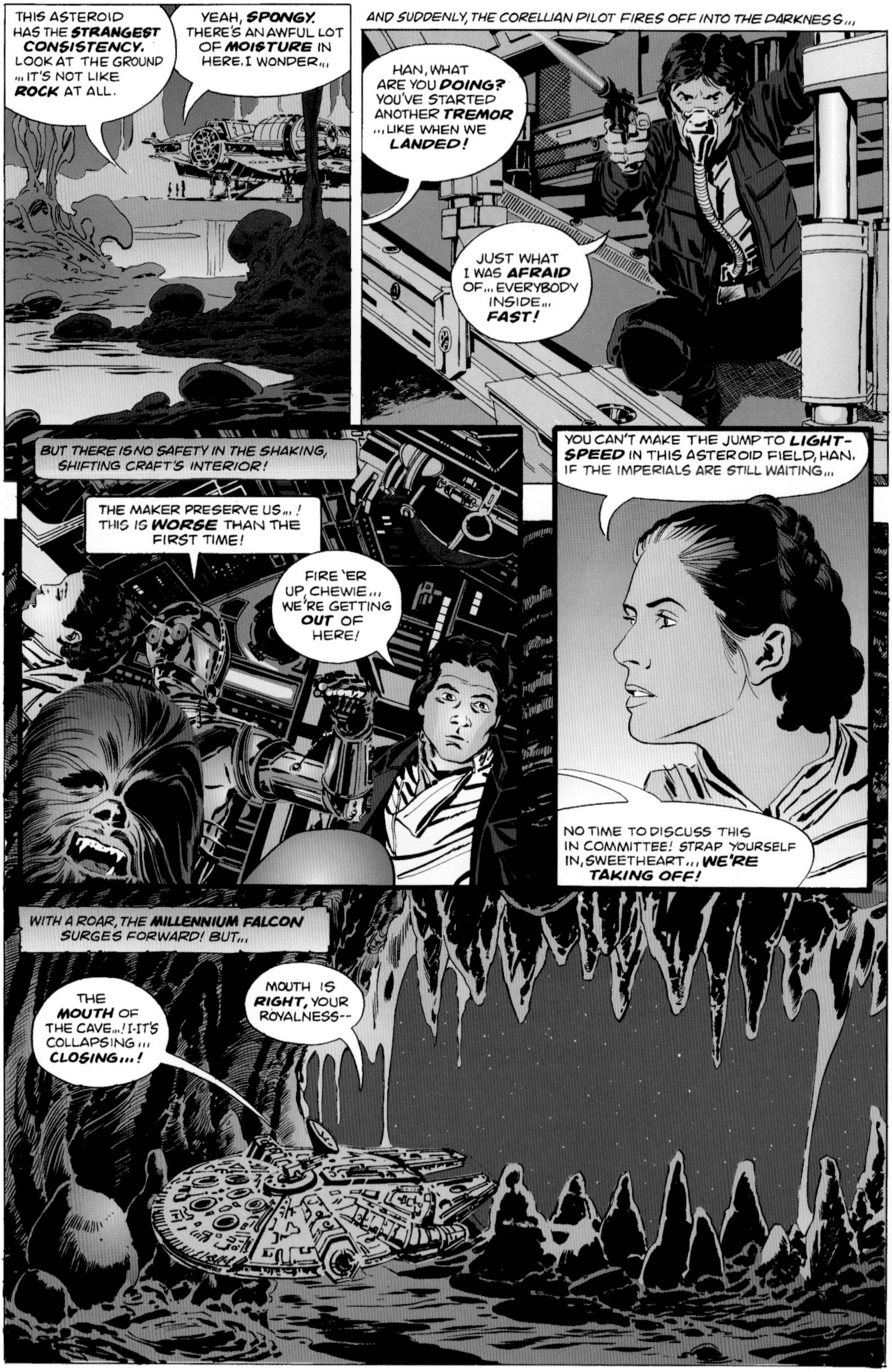
THIS ASTEROID HAS THE STRANGEST CONSISTENCY. LOOK AT THE GROUND ... IT'S NOT LIKE ROCK AT ALL.
YEAH, SPONGY. THERE'S AN AWFUL LOT OF MOISTURE IN HERE. I WONDER...
AND SUDDENLY, THE CORELLIAN PILOT FIRES OFF INTO THE DARKNESS...
HAN, WHAT ARE YOU DOING? YOU'VE STARTED ANOTHER TREMOR ... LIKE WHEN WE LANDED!
JUST WHAT I WAS AFRAID OF... EVERYBODY INSIDE... FAST!
BUT THERE IS NO SAFETY IN THE SHAKING, SHIFTING CRAFT'S INTERIOR!
THE MAKER PRESERVE US...! THIS IS WORSE THAN THE FIRST TIME!
FIRE 'ER UP, CHEWIE... WE'RE GETTING OUT OF HERE!
YOU CAN'T MAKE THE JUMP TO LIGHT-SPEED IN THIS ASTEROID FIELD, HAN. IF THE IMPERIALS ARE STILL WAITING...
NO TIME TO DISCUSS THIS IN COMMITTEE! STRAP YOURSELF IN, SWEETHEART... WE'RE TAKING OFF!
WITH A ROAR, THE MILLENNIUM FALCON SURGES FORWARD! BUT...
THE MOUTH OF THE CAVE...! I-IT'S COLLAPSING... CLOSING...!
MOUTH IS RIGHT, YOUR ROYALNESS--

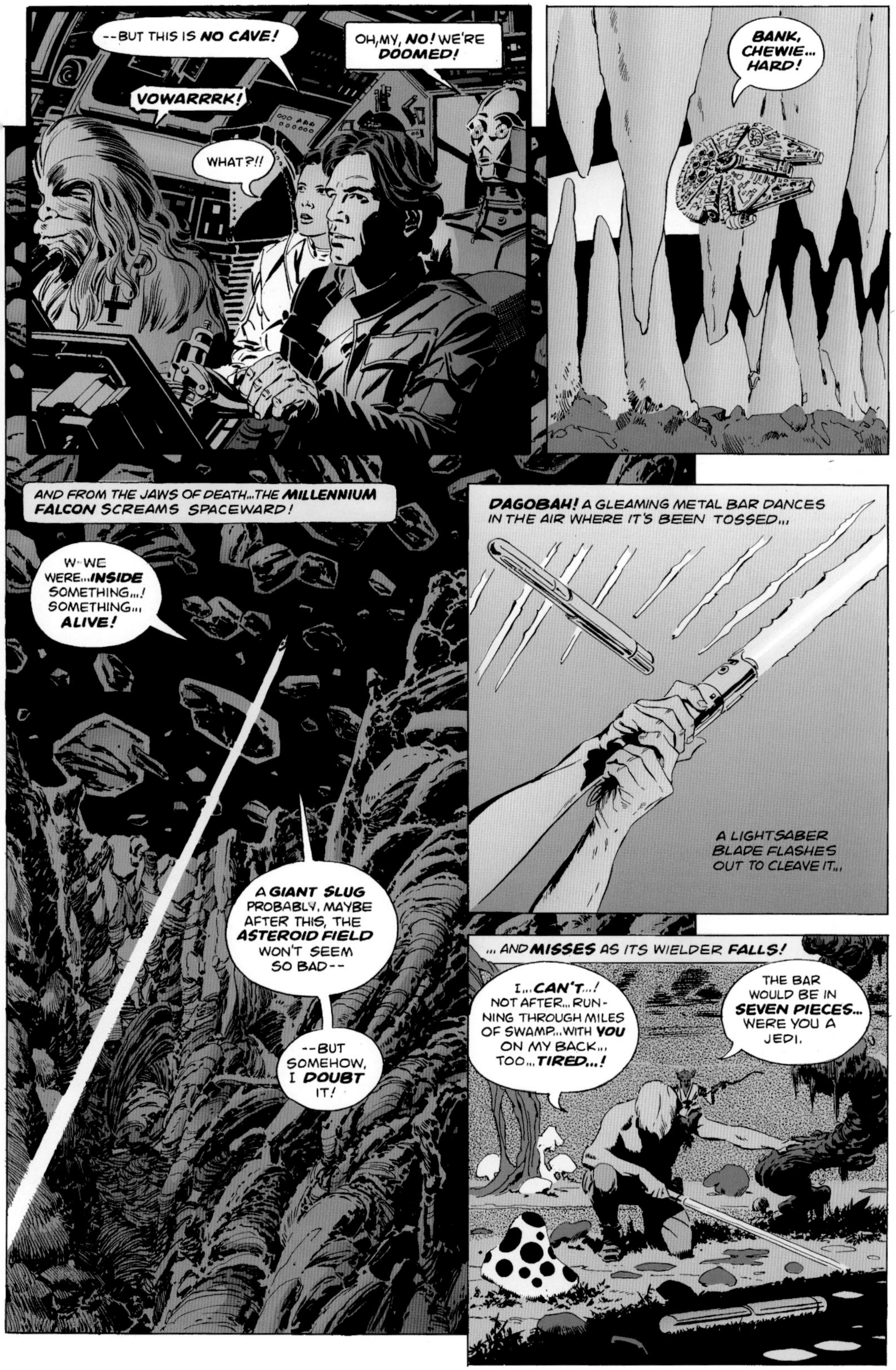
--BUT THIS IS NO CAVE!
OH, MY, NO! WE'RE DOOMED!
VOWARRRK!
WHAT?!!
BANK, CHEWIE... HARD!
AND FROM THE JAWS OF DEATH... THE MILLENNIUM FALCON SCREAMS SPACEWARD!
W-WE WERE... INSIDE SOMETHING...! SOMETHING... ALIVE!
A GIANT SLUG PROBABLY. MAYBE AFTER THIS, THE ASTEROID FIELD WON'T SEEM SO BAD--
--BUT SOMEHOW, I DOUBT IT!
DAGOBAH! A GLEAMING METAL BAR DANCES IN THE AIR WHERE IT'S BEEN TOSSED...
A LIGHTSABER BLADE FLASHES OUT TO CLEAVE IT...
...AND MISSES AS ITS WIELDER FALLS!
I... CAN'T...! NOT AFTER... RUNNING THROUGH MILES OF SWAMP... WITH YOU ON MY BACK... TOO... TIRED...!
THE BAR WOULD BE IN SEVEN PIECES... WERE YOU A JEDI.

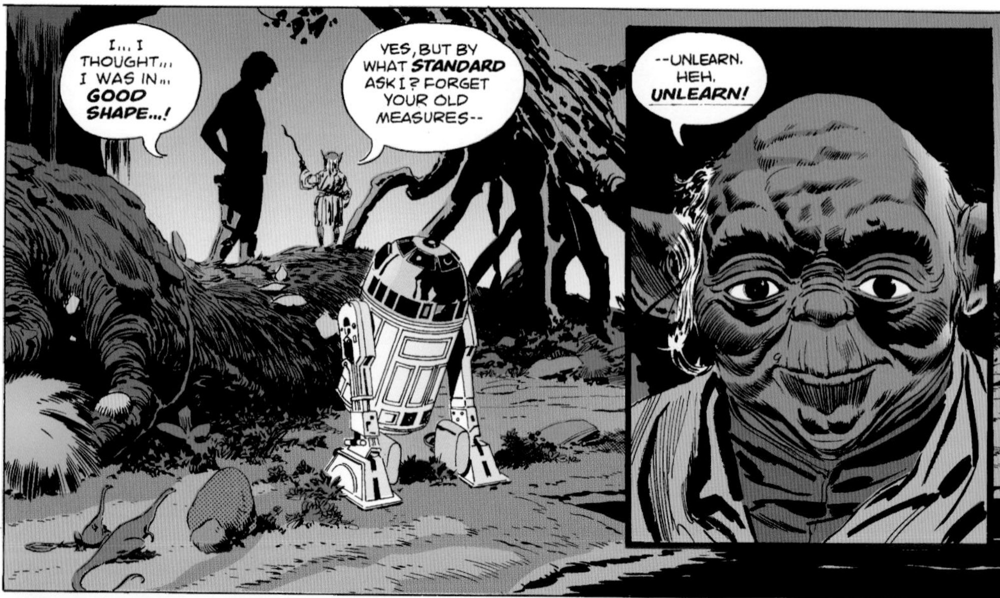
I... I THOUGHT... I WAS IN... GOOD SHAPE...!
YES, BUT BY WHAT STANDARD ASK I? FORGET YOUR OLD MEASURES--
--UNLEARN. HEH. UNLEARN!

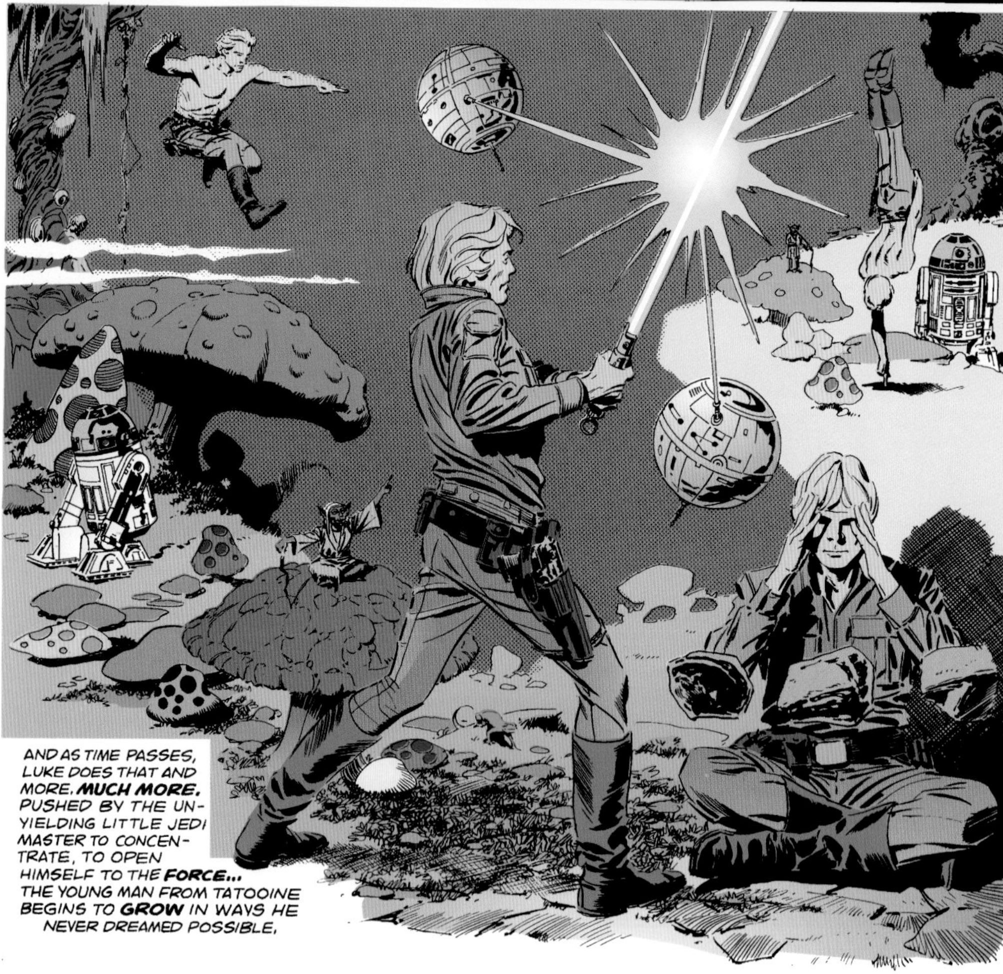
AND AS TIME PASSES, LUKE DOES THAT AND MORE. MUCH MORE. PUSHED BY THE UNYIELDING LITTLE JEDI MASTER TO CONCENTRATE, TO OPEN HIMSELF TO THE FORCE... THE YOUNG MAN FROM TATOOINE BEGINS TO GROW IN WAYS HE NEVER DREAMED POSSIBLE.

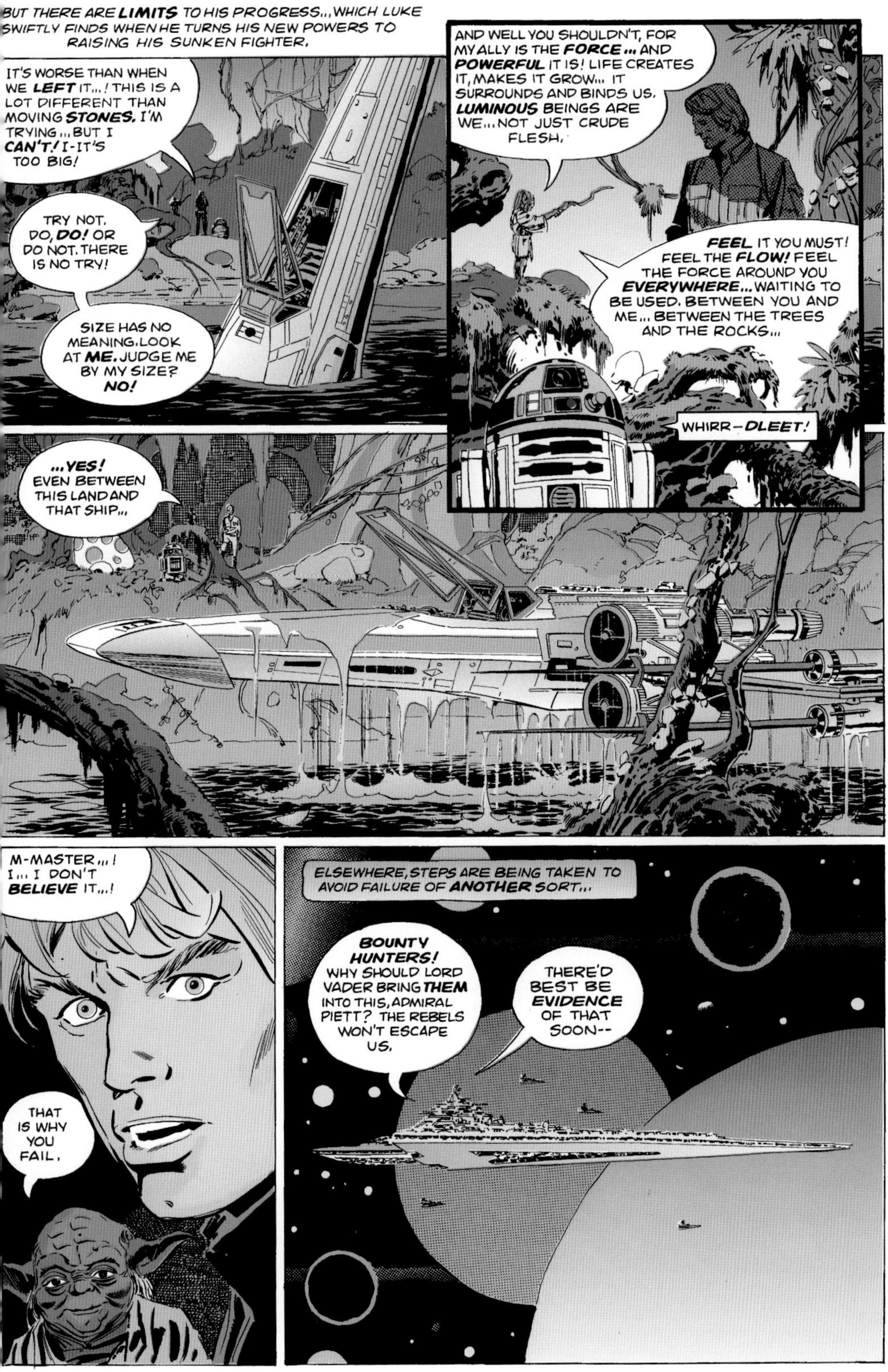
BUT THERE ARE LIMITS TO HIS PROGRESS... WHICH LUKE SWIFTLY FINDS WHEN HE TURNS HIS NEW POWERS TO RAISING HIS SUNKEN FIGHTER.
IT'S WORSE THAN WHEN WE LEFT IT...! THIS IS A LOT DIFFERENT THAN MOVING STONES. I'M TRYING... BUT I CAN'T! I-IT'S TOO BIG!
TRY NOT. DO, DO! OR DO NOT. THERE IS NO TRY!
SIZE HAS NO MEANING. LOOK AT ME. JUDGE ME BY MY SIZE? NO!
AND WELL YOU SHOULDN'T, FOR MY ALLY IS THE FORCE... AND POWERFUL IT IS! LIFE CREATES IT, MAKES IT GROW... IT SURROUNDS AND BINDS US. LUMINOUS BEINGS ARE WE... NOT JUST CRUDE FLESH.
FEEL IT YOU MUST! FEEL THE FLOW! FEEL THE FORCE AROUND YOU EVERYWHERE... WAITING TO BE USED. BETWEEN YOU AND ME... BETWEEN THE TREES AND THE ROCKS...
WHIRR-DLEET!
...YES! EVEN BETWEEN THIS LAND AND THAT SHIP...
M-MASTER...! I... I DON'T BELIEVE IT...!
THAT IS WHY YOU FAIL.
ELSEWHERE, STEPS ARE BEING TAKEN TO AVOID FAILURE OF ANOTHER SORT...
BOUNTY HUNTERS! WHY SHOULD LORD VADER BRING THEM INTO THIS, ADMIRAL PIETT? THE REBELS WON'T ESCAPE US.
THERE'D BEST BE EVIDENCE OF THAT SOON--

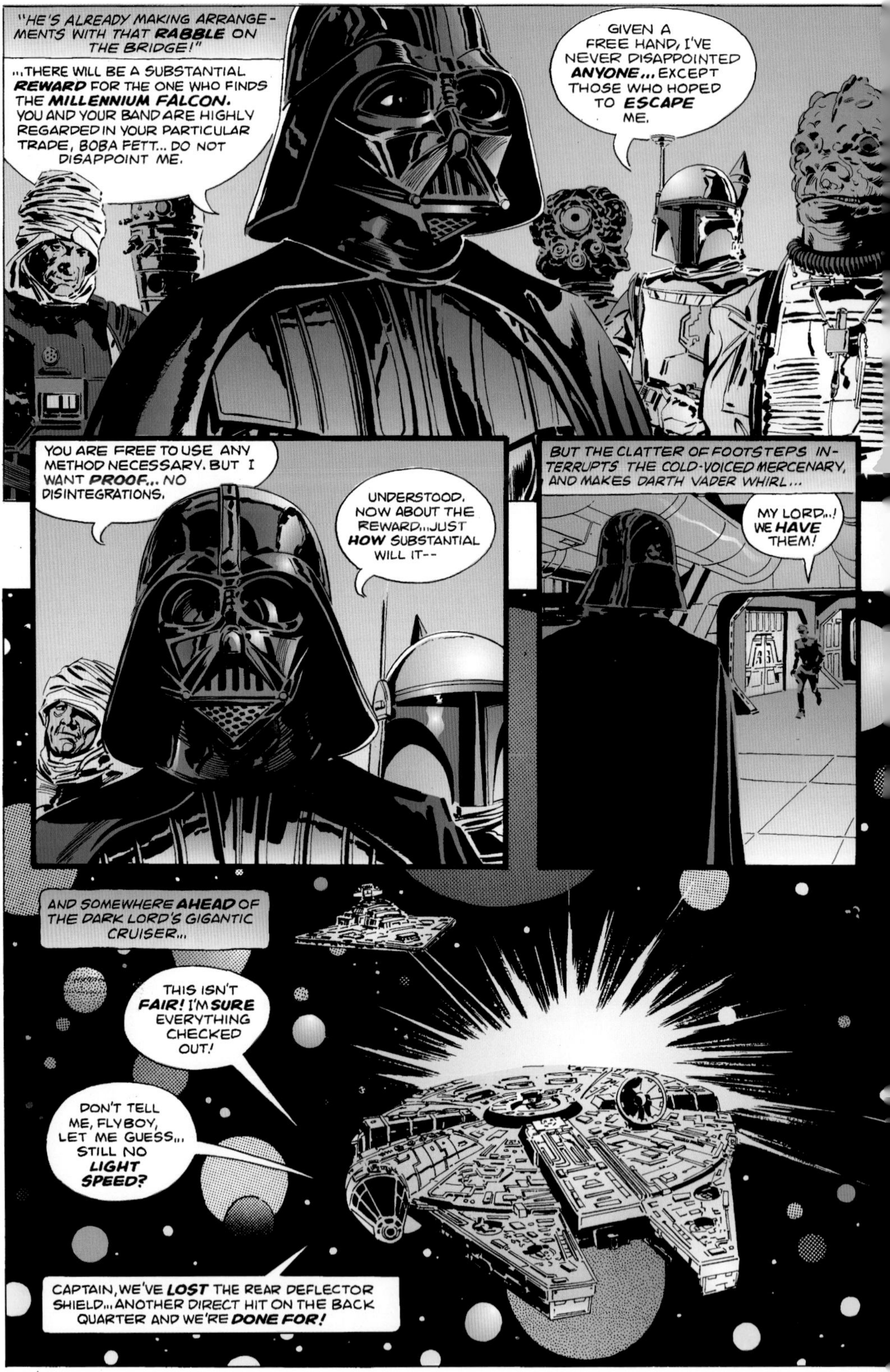
"HE'S ALREADY MAKING ARRANGE-MENTS WITH THAT RABBLE ON THE BRIDGE!"
...THERE WILL BE A SUBSTANTIAL REWARD FOR THE ONE WHO FINDS THE MILLENNIUM FALCON. YOU AND YOUR BAND ARE HIGHLY REGARDED IN YOUR PARTICULAR TRADE, BOBA FETT... DO NOT DISAPPOINT ME.
GIVEN A FREE HAND, I'VE NEVER DISAPPOINTED ANYONE... EXCEPT THOSE WHO HOPED TO ESCAPE ME.
YOU ARE FREE TO USE ANY METHOD NECESSARY. BUT I WANT PROOF... NO DISINTEGRATIONS.
UNDERSTOOD. NOW ABOUT THE REWARD...JUST HOW SUBSTANTIAL WILL IT--
BUT THE CLATTER OF FOOTSTEPS IN-TERRUPTS THE COLD-VOICED MERCENARY, AND MAKES DARTH VADER WHIRL...
MY LORD...! WE HAVE THEM!
AND SOMEWHERE AHEAD OF THE DARK LORD'S GIGANTIC CRUISER...
THIS ISN'T FAIR! I'M SURE EVERYTHING CHECKED OUT!
DON'T TELL ME, FLYBOY, LET ME GUESS... STILL NO LIGHT SPEED?
CAPTAIN, WE'VE LOST THE REAR DEFLECTOR SHIELD... ANOTHER DIRECT HIT ON THE BACK QUARTER AND WE'RE DONE FOR!

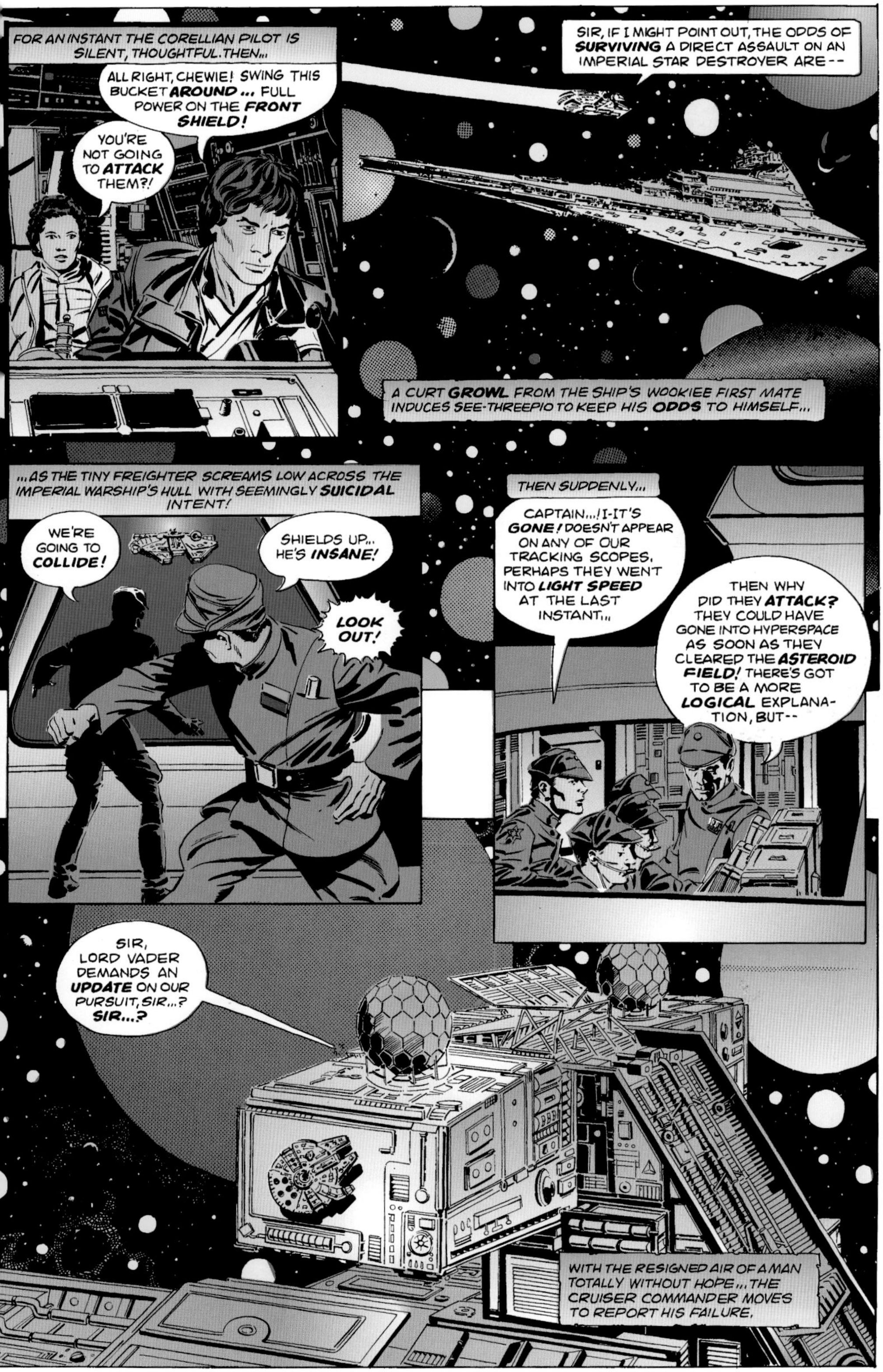
FOR AN INSTANT THE CORELLIAN PILOT IS SILENT, THOUGHTFUL. THEN...
ALL RIGHT, CHEWIE! SWING THIS BUCKET AROUND... FULL POWER ON THE FRONT SHIELD!
YOU'RE NOT GOING TO ATTACK THEM?!
SIR, IF I MIGHT POINT OUT, THE ODDS OF SURVIVING A DIRECT ASSAULT ON AN IMPERIAL STAR DESTROYER ARE--
A CURT GROWL FROM THE SHIP'S WOOKIEE FIRST MATE INDUCES SEE-THREEPIO TO KEEP HIS ODDS TO HIMSELF...
...AS THE TINY FREIGHTER SCREAMS LOW ACROSS THE IMPERIAL WARSHIP'S HULL WITH SEEMINGLY SUICIDAL INTENT!
WE'RE GOING TO COLLIDE!
SHIELDS UP... HE'S INSANE!
LOOK OUT!
THEN SUDDENLY...
CAPTAIN...! I-IT'S GONE! DOESN'T APPEAR ON ANY OF OUR TRACKING SCOPES. PERHAPS THEY WENT INTO LIGHT SPEED AT THE LAST INSTANT...
THEN WHY DID THEY ATTACK? THEY COULD HAVE GONE INTO HYPERSPACE AS SOON AS THEY CLEARED THE ASTEROID FIELD! THERE'S GOT TO BE A MORE LOGICAL EXPLANATION, BUT--
SIR, LORD VADER DEMANDS AN UPDATE ON OUR PURSUIT, SIR...? SIR...?
WITH THE RESIGNED AIR OF A MAN TOTALLY WITHOUT HOPE... THE CRUISER COMMANDER MOVES TO REPORT HIS FAILURE.

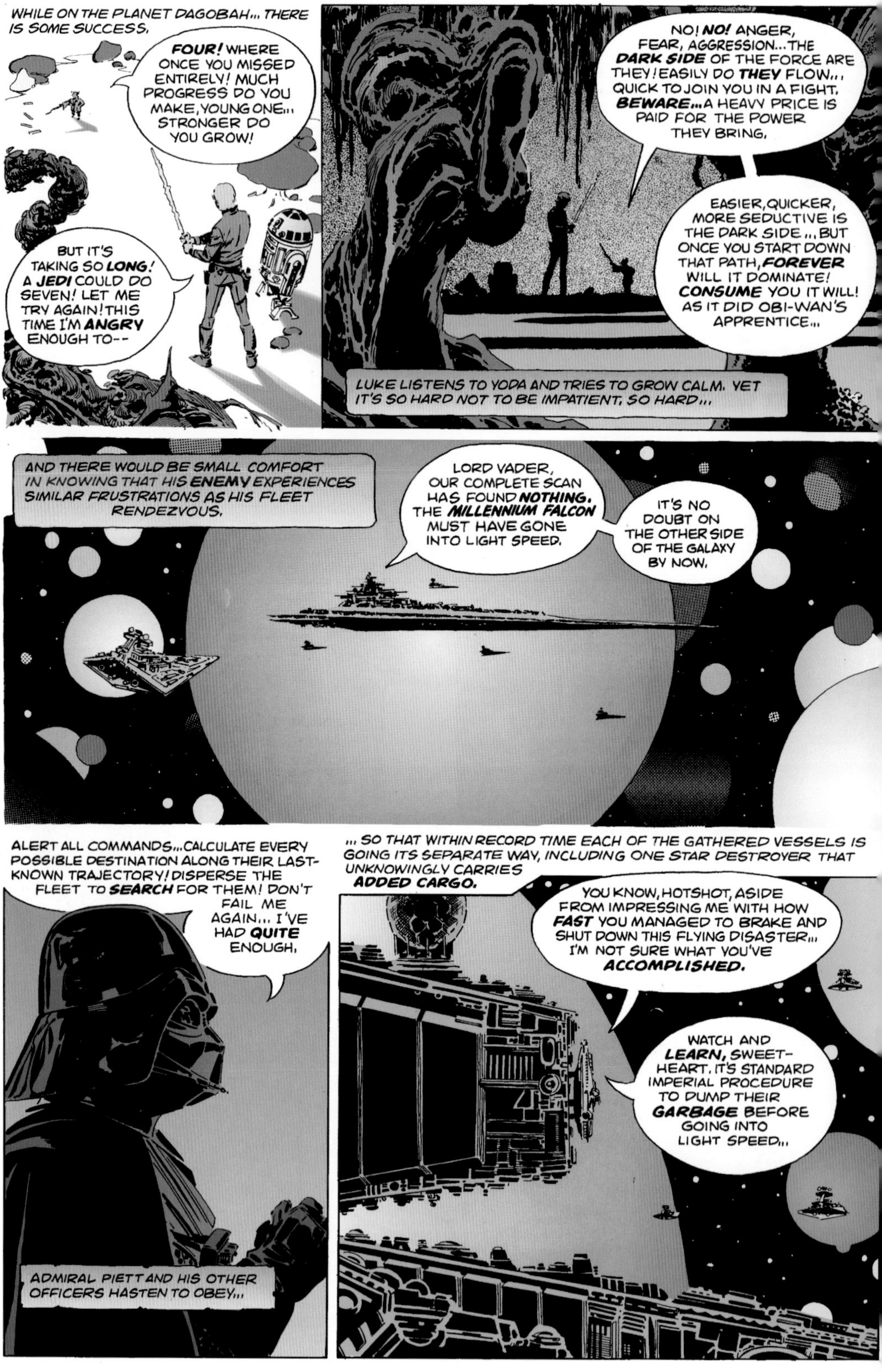
WHILE ON THE PLANET DAGOBAH... THERE IS SOME SUCCESS.
FOUR! WHERE ONCE YOU MISSED ENTIRELY! MUCH PROGRESS DO YOU MAKE, YOUNG ONE... STRONGER DO YOU GROW!
BUT IT'S TAKING SO LONG! A JEDI COULD DO SEVEN! LET ME TRY AGAIN! THIS TIME I'M ANGRY ENOUGH TO--
NO! NO! ANGER, FEAR, AGGRESSION... THE DARK SIDE OF THE FORCE ARE THEY! EASILY DO THEY FLOW... QUICK TO JOIN YOU IN A FIGHT. BEWARE... A HEAVY PRICE IS PAID FOR THE POWER THEY BRING.
EASIER, QUICKER, MORE SEDUCTIVE IS THE DARK SIDE... BUT ONCE YOU START DOWN THAT PATH, FOREVER WILL IT DOMINATE! CONSUME YOU IT WILL! AS IT DID OBI-WAN'S APPRENTICE...
LUKE LISTENS TO YODA AND TRIES TO GROW CALM. YET IT'S SO HARD NOT TO BE IMPATIENT. SO HARD...
AND THERE WOULD BE SMALL COMFORT IN KNOWING THAT HIS ENEMY EXPERIENCES SIMILAR FRUSTRATIONS AS HIS FLEET RENDEZVOUS.
LORD VADER, OUR COMPLETE SCAN HAS FOUND NOTHING. THE MILLENNIUM FALCON MUST HAVE GONE INTO LIGHT SPEED.
IT'S NO DOUBT ON THE OTHER SIDE OF THE GALAXY BY NOW.
ALERT ALL COMMANDS... CALCULATE EVERY POSSIBLE DESTINATION ALONG THEIR LAST-KNOWN TRAJECTORY! DISPERSE THE FLEET TO SEARCH FOR THEM! DON'T FAIL ME AGAIN... I'VE HAD QUITE ENOUGH.
ADMIRAL PIETT AND HIS OTHER OFFICERS HASTEN TO OBEY...
... SO THAT WITHIN RECORD TIME EACH OF THE GATHERED VESSELS IS GOING ITS SEPARATE WAY, INCLUDING ONE STAR DESTROYER THAT UNKNOWINGLY CARRIES ADDED CARGO.
YOU KNOW, HOTSHOT, ASIDE FROM IMPRESSING ME WITH HOW FAST YOU MANAGED TO BRAKE AND SHUT DOWN THIS FLYING DISASTER... I'M NOT SURE WHAT YOU'VE ACCOMPLISHED.
WATCH AND LEARN, SWEETHEART. IT'S STANDARD IMPERIAL PROCEDURE TO DUMP THEIR GARBAGE BEFORE GOING INTO LIGHT SPEED...

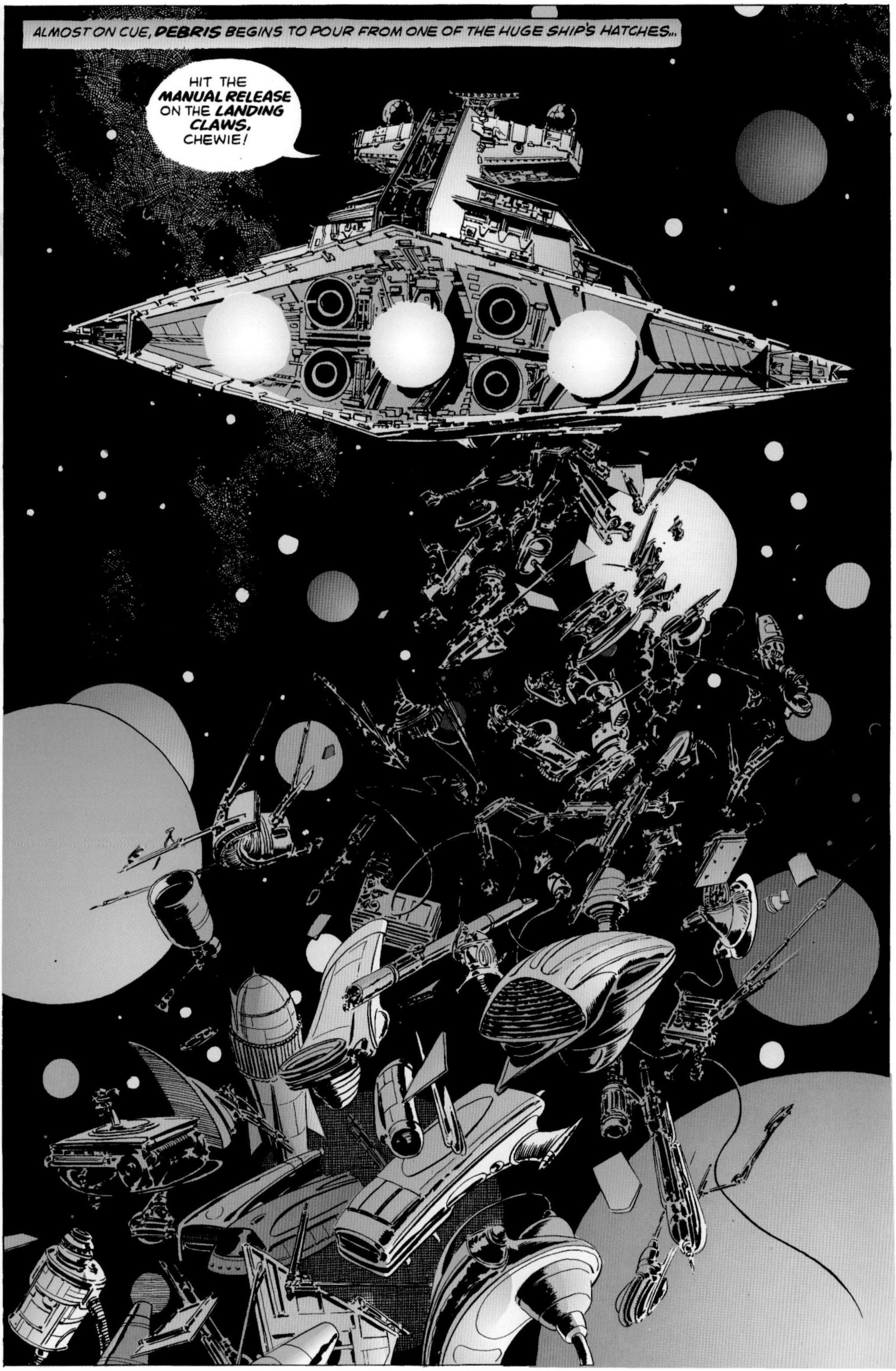
ALMOST ON CUE, DEBRIS BEGINS TO POUR FROM ONE OF THE HUGE SHIP'S HATCHES...
HIT THE MANUAL RELEASE ON THE LANDING CLAWS, CHEWIE!

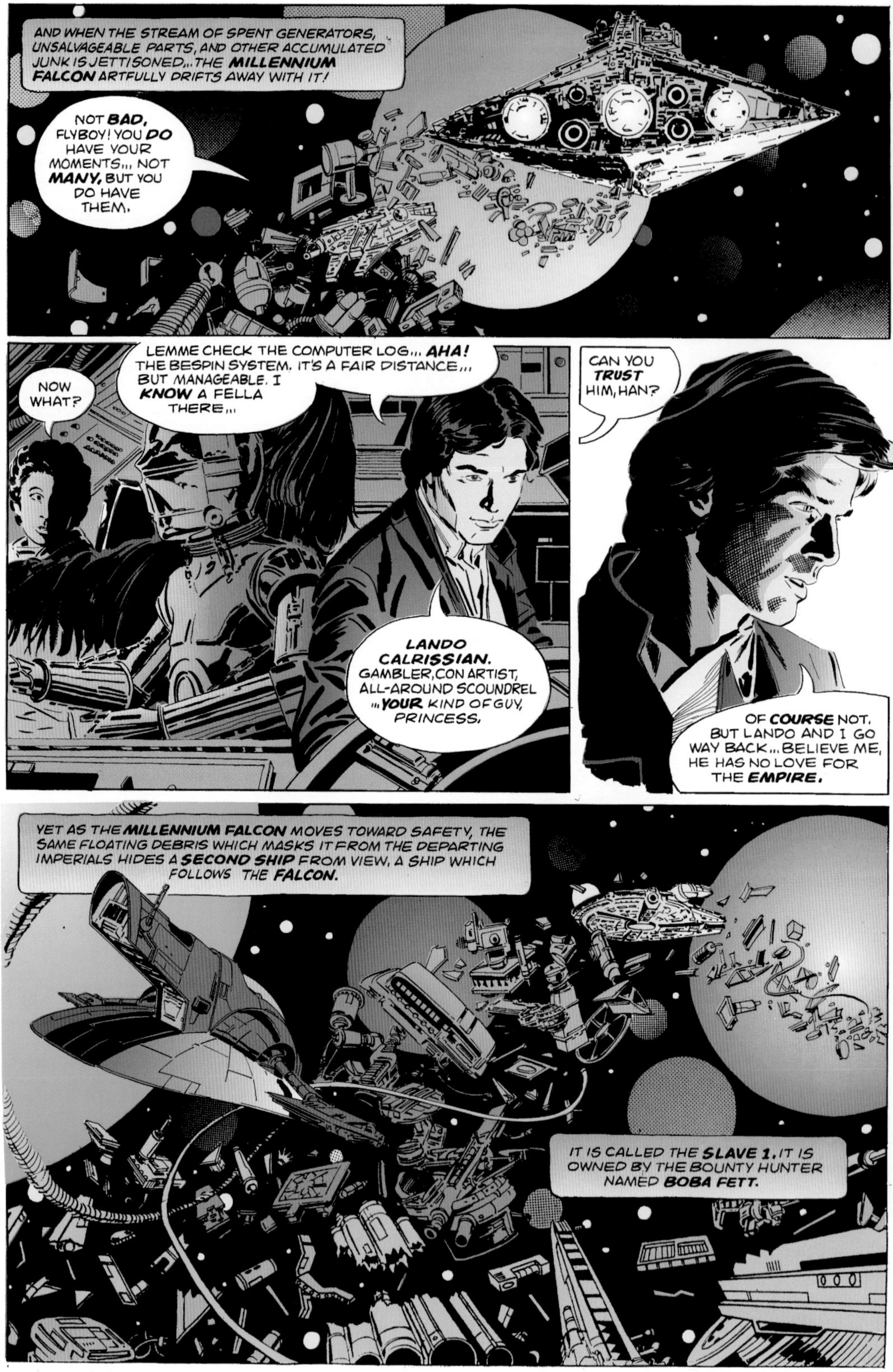
AND WHEN THE STREAM OF SPENT GENERATORS, UNSALVAGEABLE PARTS, AND OTHER ACCUMULATED JUNK IS JETTISONED... THE MILLENNIUM FALCON ARTFULLY DRIFTS AWAY WITH IT!
NOT BAD, FLYBOY! YOU DO HAVE YOUR MOMENTS... NOT MANY, BUT YOU DO HAVE THEM.
NOW WHAT?
LEMME CHECK THE COMPUTER LOG... AHA! THE BESPIN SYSTEM. IT'S A FAIR DISTANCE... BUT MANAGEABLE. I KNOW A FELLA THERE...
LANDO CALRISSIAN. GAMBLER, CON ARTIST, ALL-AROUND SCOUNDREL ...YOUR KIND OF GUY, PRINCESS.
CAN YOU TRUST HIM, HAN?
OF COURSE NOT. BUT LANDO AND I GO WAY BACK... BELIEVE ME, HE HAS NO LOVE FOR THE EMPIRE.
YET AS THE MILLENNIUM FALCON MOVES TOWARD SAFETY, THE SAME FLOATING DEBRIS WHICH MASKS IT FROM THE DEPARTING IMPERIALS HIDES A SECOND SHIP FROM VIEW, A SHIP WHICH FOLLOWS THE FALCON.
IT IS CALLED THE SLAVE 1. IT IS OWNED BY THE BOUNTY HUNTER NAMED BOBA FETT.

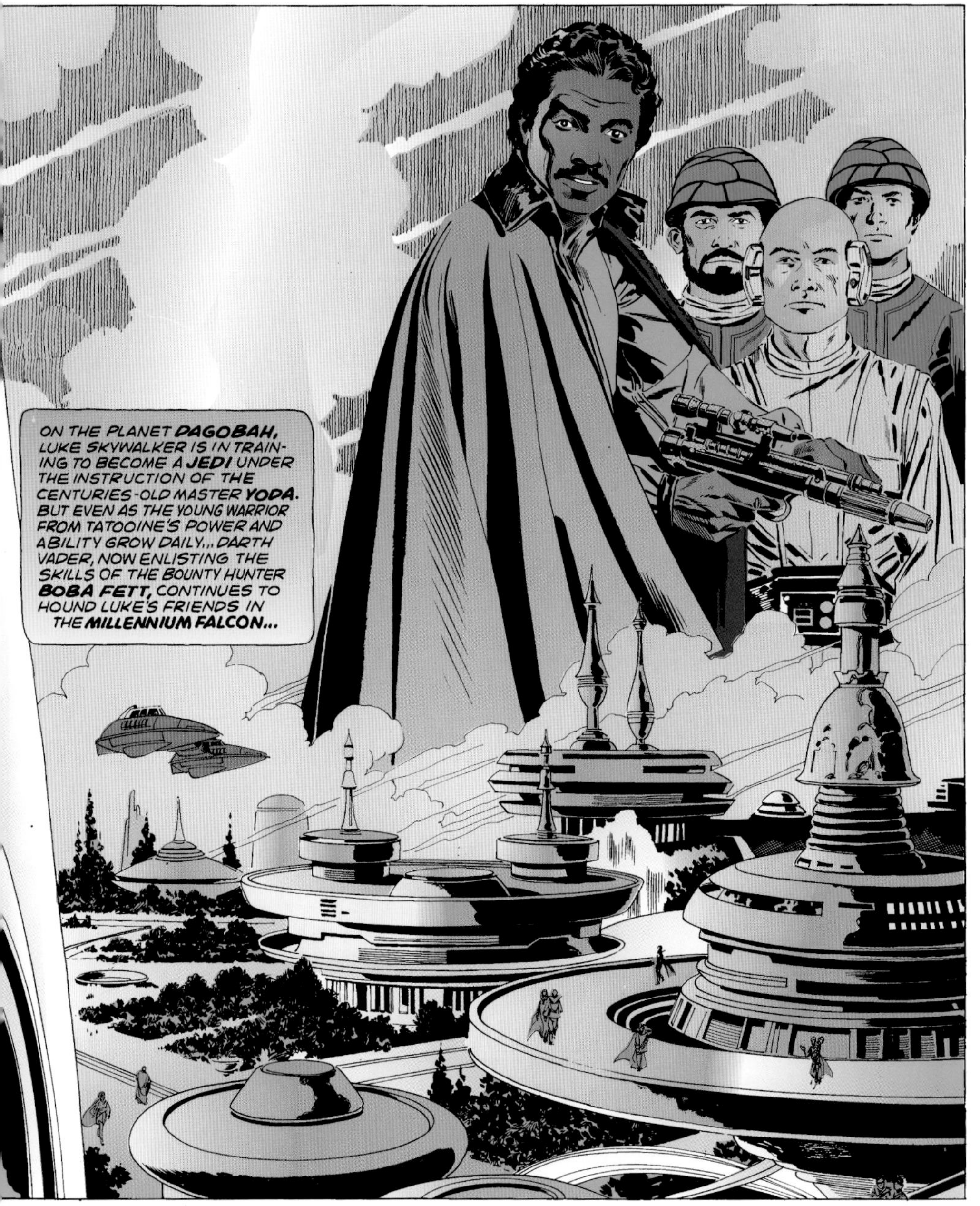
ON THE PLANET DAGOBAH, LUKE SKYWALKER IS IN TRAINING TO BECOME A JEDI UNDER THE INSTRUCTION OF THE CENTURIES-OLD MASTER YODA. BUT EVEN AS THE YOUNG WARRIOR FROM TATOOINE'S POWER AND ABILITY GROW DAILY... DARTH VADER, NOW ENLISTING THE SKILLS OF THE BOUNTY HUNTER BOBA FETT, CONTINUES TO HOUND LUKE'S FRIENDS IN THE MILLENNIUM FALCON...

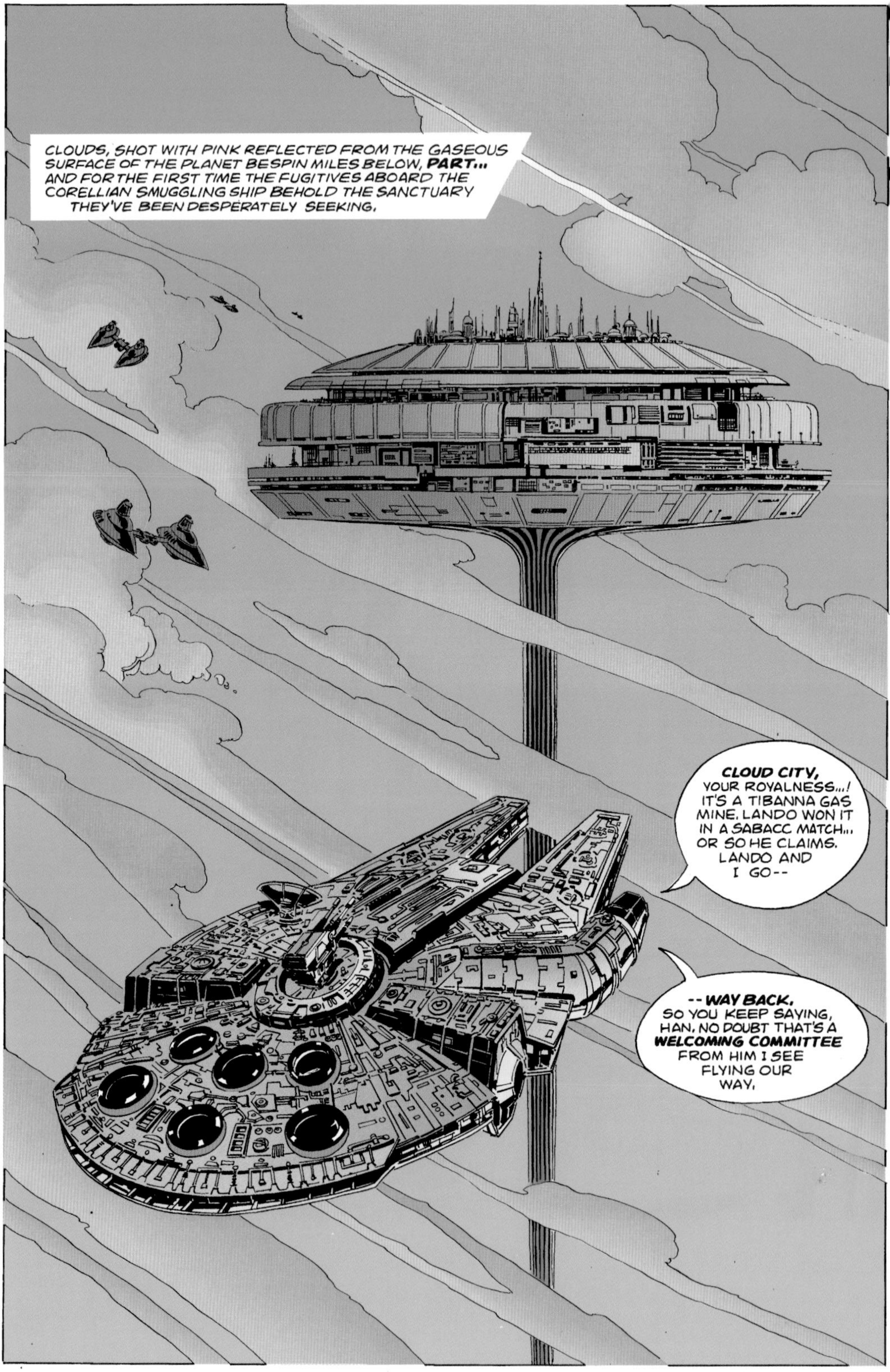
CLOUDS, SHOT WITH PINK REFLECTED FROM THE GASEOUS SURFACE OF THE PLANET BESPIN MILES BELOW, PART... AND FOR THE FIRST TIME THE FUGITIVES ABOARD THE CORELLIAN SMUGGLING SHIP BEHOLD THE SANCTUARY THEY'VE BEEN DESPERATELY SEEKING.
CLOUD CITY, YOUR ROYALNESS...! IT'S A TIBANNA GAS MINE. LANDO WON IT IN A SABACC MATCH... OR SO HE CLAIMS. LANDO AND I GO--
--WAY BACK. SO YOU KEEP SAYING, HAN. NO DOUBT THAT'S A WELCOMING COMMITTEE FROM HIM I SEE FLYING OUR WAY.

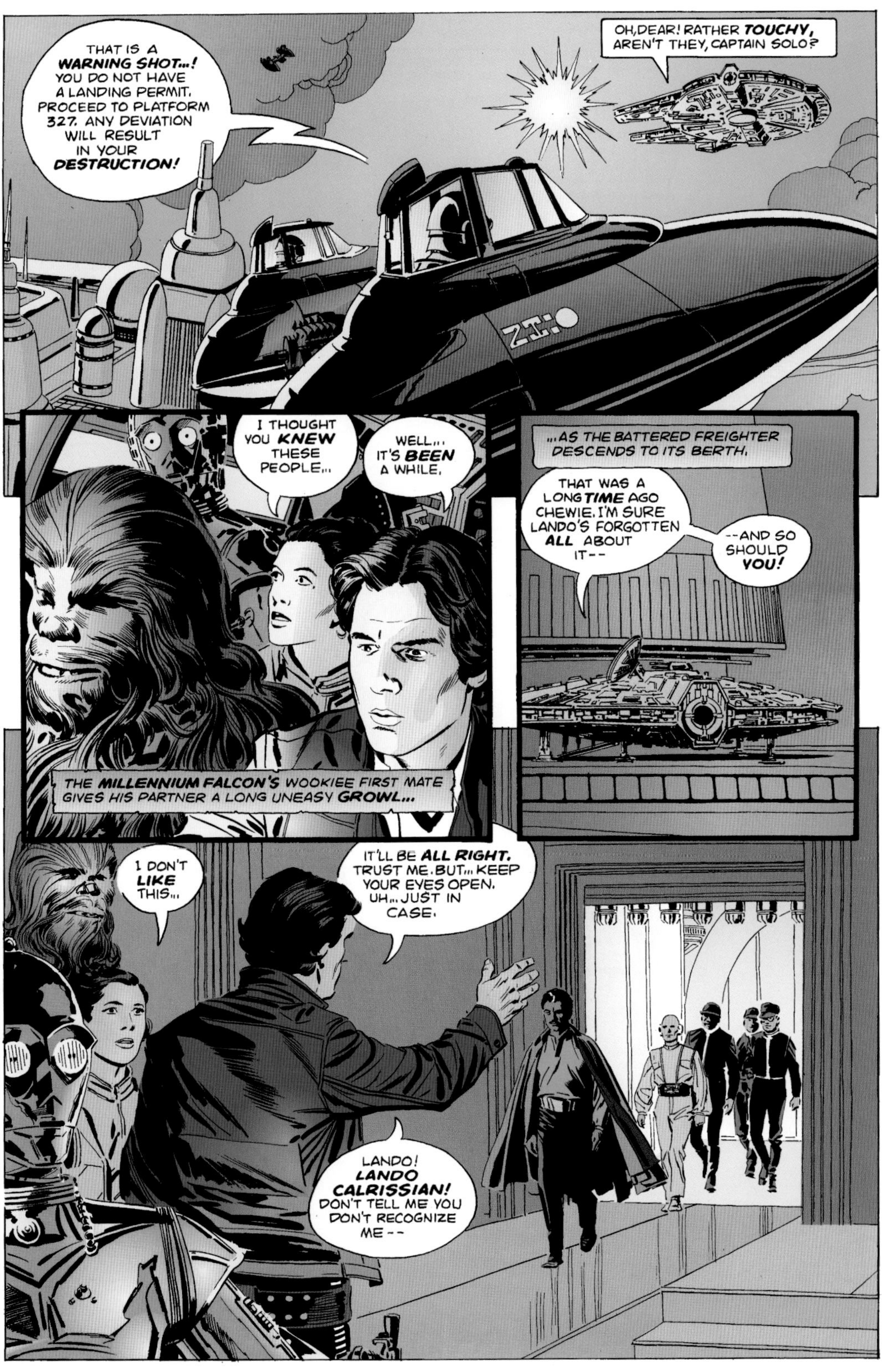
THAT IS A WARNING SHOT...! YOU DO NOT HAVE A LANDING PERMIT. PROCEED TO PLATFORM 327. ANY DEVIATION WILL RESULT IN YOUR DESTRUCTION!
OH, DEAR! RATHER TOUCHY, AREN'T THEY, CAPTAIN SOLO?
I THOUGHT YOU KNEW THESE PEOPLE...
WELL... IT'S BEEN A WHILE.
THE MILLENNIUM FALCON'S WOOKIEE FIRST MATE GIVES HIS PARTNER A LONG UNEASY GROWL...
...AS THE BATTERED FREIGHTER DESCENDS TO ITS BERTH.
THAT WAS A LONG TIME AGO CHEWIE. I'M SURE LANDO'S FORGOTTEN ALL ABOUT IT--
--AND SO SHOULD YOU!
I DON'T LIKE THIS...
IT'LL BE ALL RIGHT. TRUST ME. BUT... KEEP YOUR EYES OPEN. UH... JUST IN CASE.
LANDO! LANDO CALRISSIAN! DON'T TELL ME YOU DON'T RECOGNIZE ME--

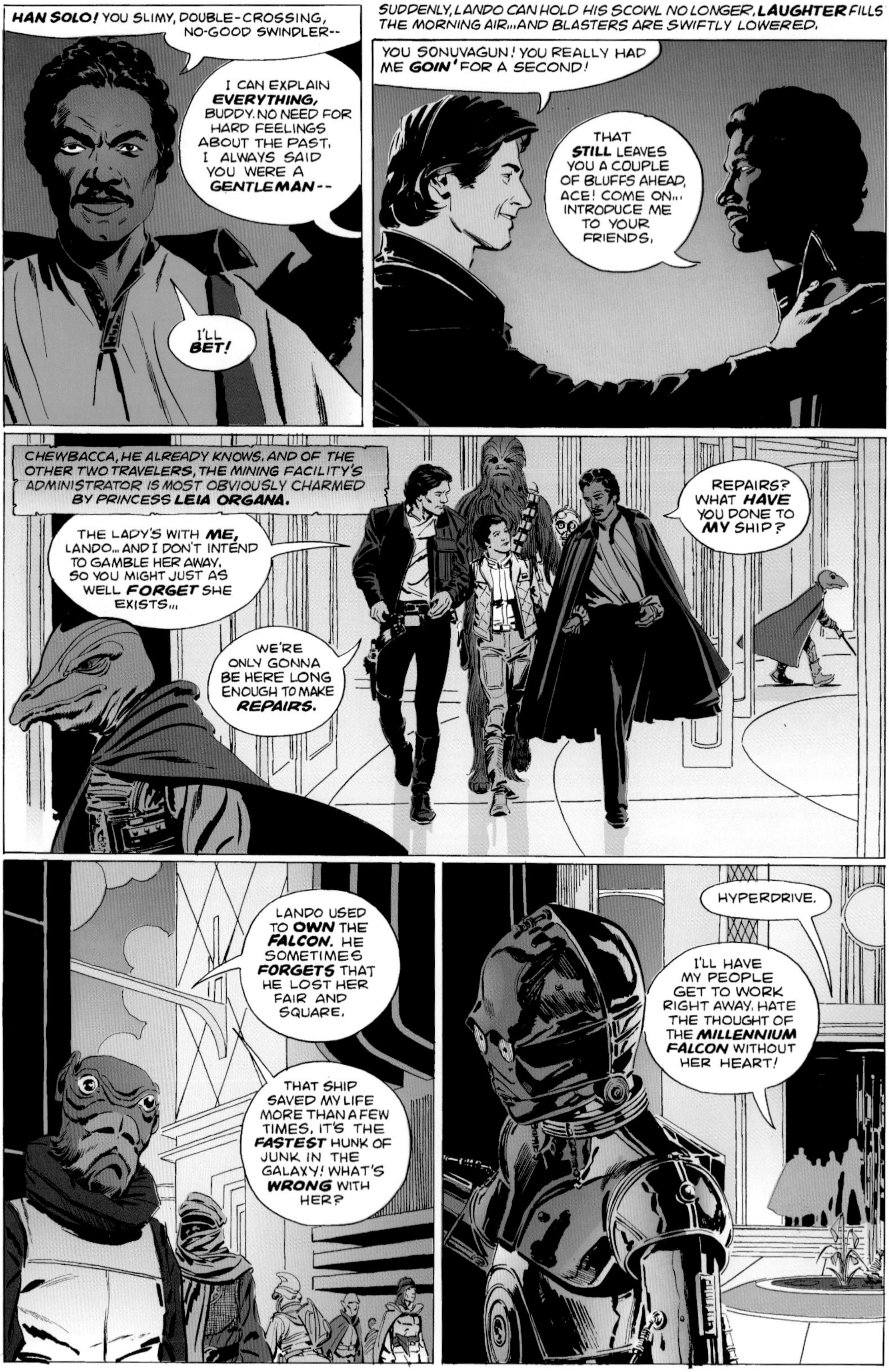
HAN SOLO! YOU SLIMY, DOUBLE-CROSSING, NO-GOOD SWINDLER--
I CAN EXPLAIN EVERYTHING, BUDDY. NO NEED FOR HARD FEELINGS ABOUT THE PAST. I ALWAYS SAID YOU WERE A GENTLEMAN--
I'LL BET!
SUDDENLY, LANDO CAN HOLD HIS SCOWL NO LONGER. LAUGHTER FILLS THE MORNING AIR... AND BLASTERS ARE SWIFTLY LOWERED.
YOU SONUVAGUN! YOU REALLY HAD ME GOIN' FOR A SECOND!
THAT STILL LEAVES YOU A COUPLE OF BLUFFS AHEAD, ACE! COME ON... INTRODUCE ME TO YOUR FRIENDS.
CHEWBACCA, HE ALREADY KNOWS, AND OF THE OTHER TWO TRAVELERS, THE MINING FACILITY'S ADMINISTRATOR IS MOST OBVIOUSLY CHARMED BY PRINCESS LEIA ORGANA.
THE LADY'S WITH ME, LANDO... AND I DON'T INTEND TO GAMBLE HER AWAY. SO YOU MIGHT JUST AS WELL FORGET SHE EXISTS...
WE'RE ONLY GONNA BE HERE LONG ENOUGH TO MAKE REPAIRS.
REPAIRS? WHAT HAVE YOU DONE TO MY SHIP?
LANDO USED TO OWN THE FALCON. HE SOMETIMES FORGETS THAT HE LOST HER FAIR AND SQUARE.
THAT SHIP SAVED MY LIFE MORE THAN A FEW TIMES. IT'S THE FASTEST HUNK OF JUNK IN THE GALAXY! WHAT'S WRONG WITH HER?
HYPERDRIVE.
I'LL HAVE MY PEOPLE GET TO WORK RIGHT AWAY. HATE THE THOUGHT OF THE MILLENNIUM FALCON WITHOUT HER HEART!

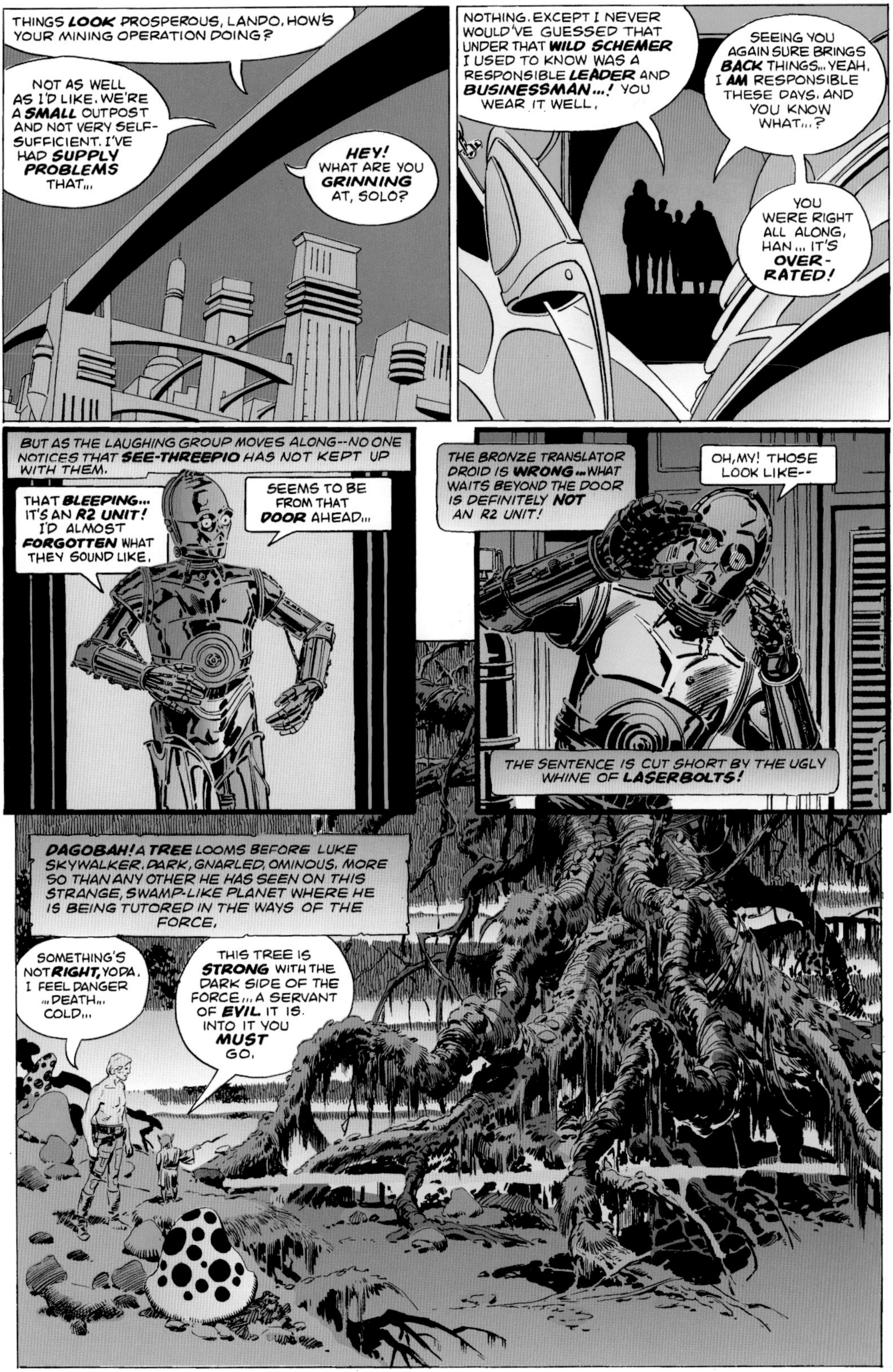

THINGS LOOK PROSPEROUS, LANDO. HOW'S YOUR MINING OPERATION DOING?
NOT AS WELL AS I'D LIKE. WE'RE A SMALL OUTPOST AND NOT VERY SELF-SUFFICIENT. I'VE HAD SUPPLY PROBLEMS THAT...
HEY! WHAT ARE YOU GRINNING AT, SOLO?
NOTHING. EXCEPT I NEVER WOULD'VE GUESSED THAT UNDER THAT WILD SCHEMER I USED TO KNOW WAS A RESPONSIBLE LEADER AND BUSINESSMAN...! YOU WEAR IT WELL.
SEEING YOU AGAIN SURE BRINGS BACK THINGS... YEAH, I AM RESPONSIBLE THESE DAYS. AND YOU KNOW WHAT...?
YOU WERE RIGHT ALL ALONG, HAN... IT'S OVER-RATED!
BUT AS THE LAUGHING GROUP MOVES ALONG--NO ONE NOTICES THAT SEE-THREEPIO HAS NOT KEPT UP WITH THEM.
THAT BLEEPING... IT'S AN R2 UNIT! I'D ALMOST FORGOTTEN WHAT THEY SOUND LIKE.
SEEMS TO BE FROM THAT DOOR AHEAD...
THE BRONZE TRANSLATOR DROID IS WRONG... WHAT WAITS BEYOND THE DOOR IS DEFINITELY NOT AN R2 UNIT!
OH, MY! THOSE LOOK LIKE--
THE SENTENCE IS CUT SHORT BY THE UGLY WHINE OF LASERBOLTS!
DAGOBAH! A TREE LOOMS BEFORE LUKE SKYWALKER. DARK, GNARLED, OMINOUS. MORE SO THAN ANY OTHER HE HAS SEEN ON THIS STRANGE, SWAMP-LIKE PLANET WHERE HE IS BEING TUTORED IN THE WAYS OF THE FORCE.
SOMETHING'S NOT RIGHT, YODA. I FEEL DANGER ...DEATH... COLD...
THIS TREE IS STRONG WITH THE DARK SIDE OF THE FORCE... A SERVANT OF EVIL IT IS. INTO IT YOU MUST GO.

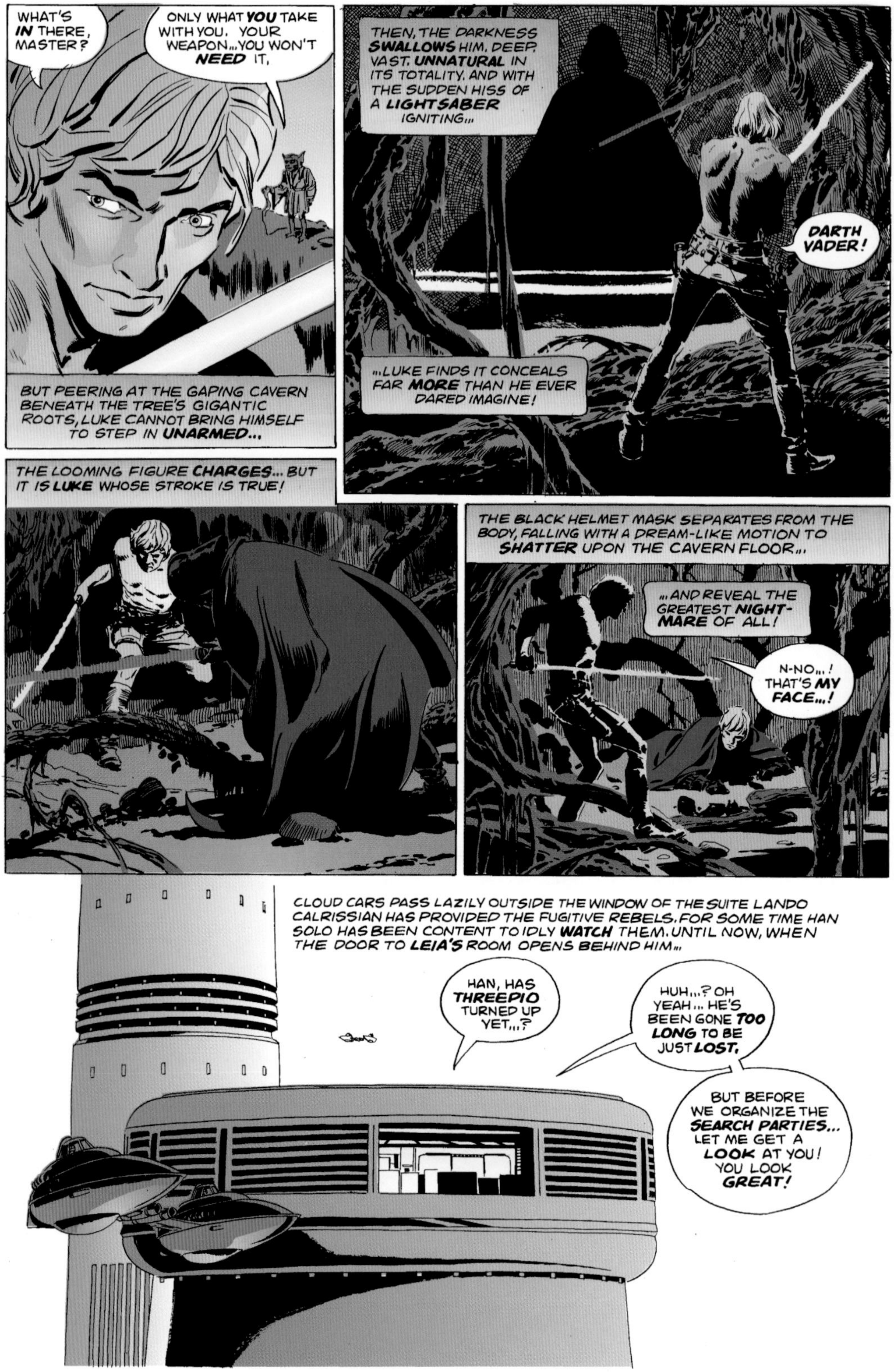
WHAT'S IN THERE, MASTER?
ONLY WHAT YOU TAKE WITH YOU. YOUR WEAPON... YOU WON'T NEED IT.
BUT PEERING AT THE GAPING CAVERN BENEATH THE TREE'S GIGANTIC ROOTS, LUKE CANNOT BRING HIMSELF TO STEP IN UNARMED...
THEN, THE DARKNESS SWALLOWS HIM. DEEP. VAST. UNNATURAL IN ITS TOTALITY. AND WITH THE SUDDEN HISS OF A LIGHTSABER IGNITING...
...LUKE FINDS IT CONCEALS FAR MORE THAN HE EVER DARED IMAGINE!
DARTH VADER!
THE LOOMING FIGURE CHARGES... BUT IT IS LUKE WHOSE STROKE IS TRUE!
THE BLACK HELMET MASK SEPARATES FROM THE BODY, FALLING WITH A DREAM-LIKE MOTION TO SHATTER UPON THE CAVERN FLOOR...
...AND REVEAL THE GREATEST NIGHTMARE OF ALL!
N-NO...! THAT'S MY FACE...!
CLOUD CARS PASS LAZILY OUTSIDE THE WINDOW OF THE SUITE LANDO CALRISSIAN HAS PROVIDED THE FUGITIVE REBELS. FOR SOME TIME HAN SOLO HAS BEEN CONTENT TO IDLY WATCH THEM. UNTIL NOW, WHEN THE DOOR TO LEIA'S ROOM OPENS BEHIND HIM...
HAN, HAS THREEPIO TURNED UP YET...?
HUH...? OH YEAH... HE'S BEEN GONE TOO LONG TO BE JUST LOST.
BUT BEFORE WE ORGANIZE THE SEARCH PARTIES... LET ME GET A LOOK AT YOU! YOU LOOK GREAT!

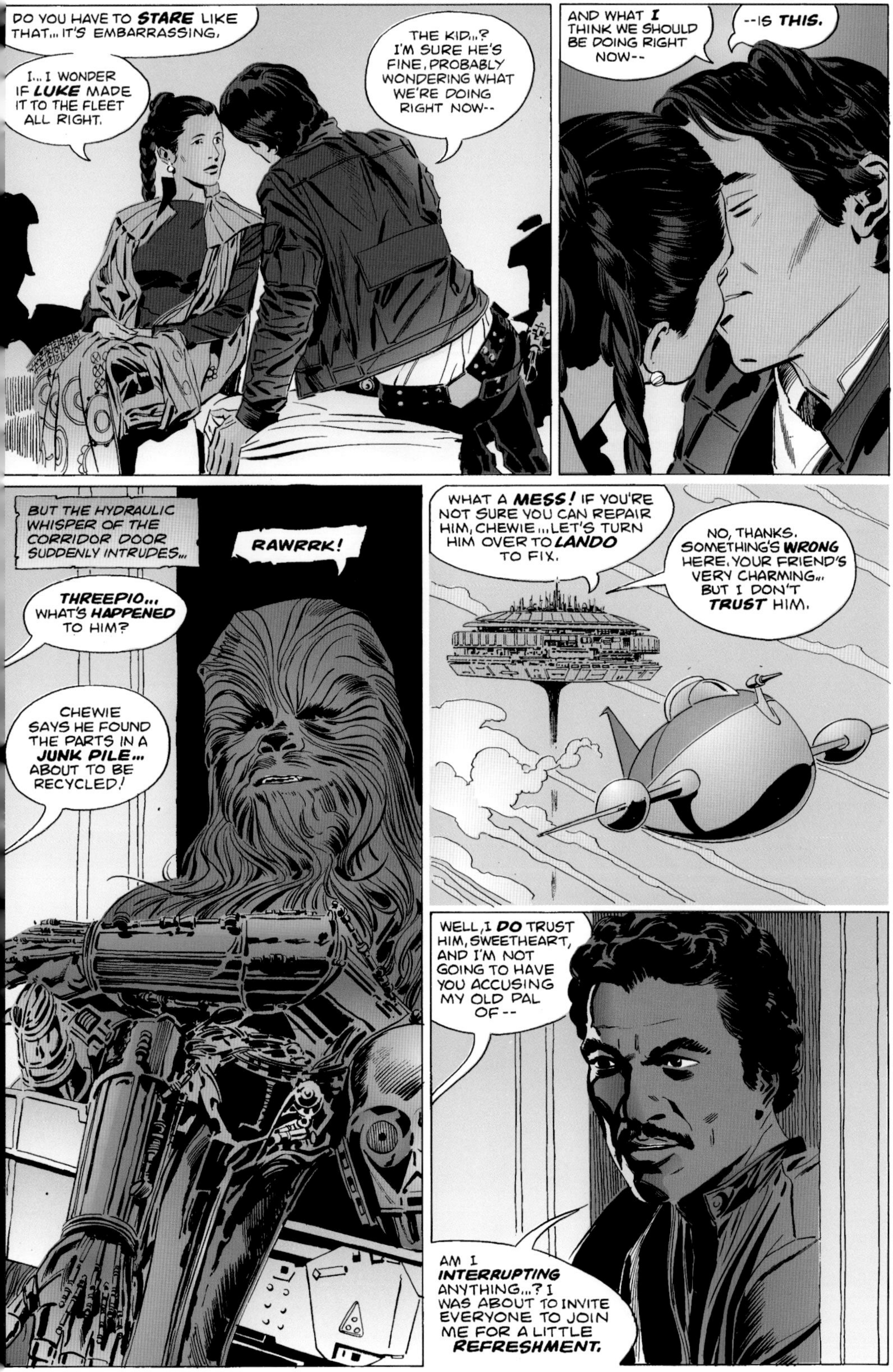
DO YOU HAVE TO STARE LIKE THAT... IT'S EMBARRASSING.
I... I WONDER IF LUKE MADE IT TO THE FLEET ALL RIGHT.
THE KID...? I'M SURE HE'S FINE. PROBABLY WONDERING WHAT WE'RE DOING RIGHT NOW--
AND WHAT I THINK WE SHOULD BE DOING RIGHT NOW--
--IS THIS.
BUT THE HYDRAULIC WHISPER OF THE CORRIDOR DOOR SUDDENLY INTRUDES...
RAWRRK!
THREEPIO... WHAT'S HAPPENED TO HIM?
CHEWIE SAYS HE FOUND THE PARTS IN A JUNK PILE... ABOUT TO BE RECYCLED!
WHAT A MESS! IF YOU'RE NOT SURE YOU CAN REPAIR HIM, CHEWIE... LET'S TURN HIM OVER TO LANDO TO FIX.
NO, THANKS. SOMETHING'S WRONG HERE. YOUR FRIEND'S VERY CHARMING... BUT I DON'T TRUST HIM.
WELL, I DO TRUST HIM, SWEETHEART, AND I'M NOT GOING TO HAVE YOU ACCUSING MY OLD PAL OF --
AM I INTERRUPTING ANYTHING...? I WAS ABOUT TO INVITE EVERYONE TO JOIN ME FOR A LITTLE REFRESHMENT.

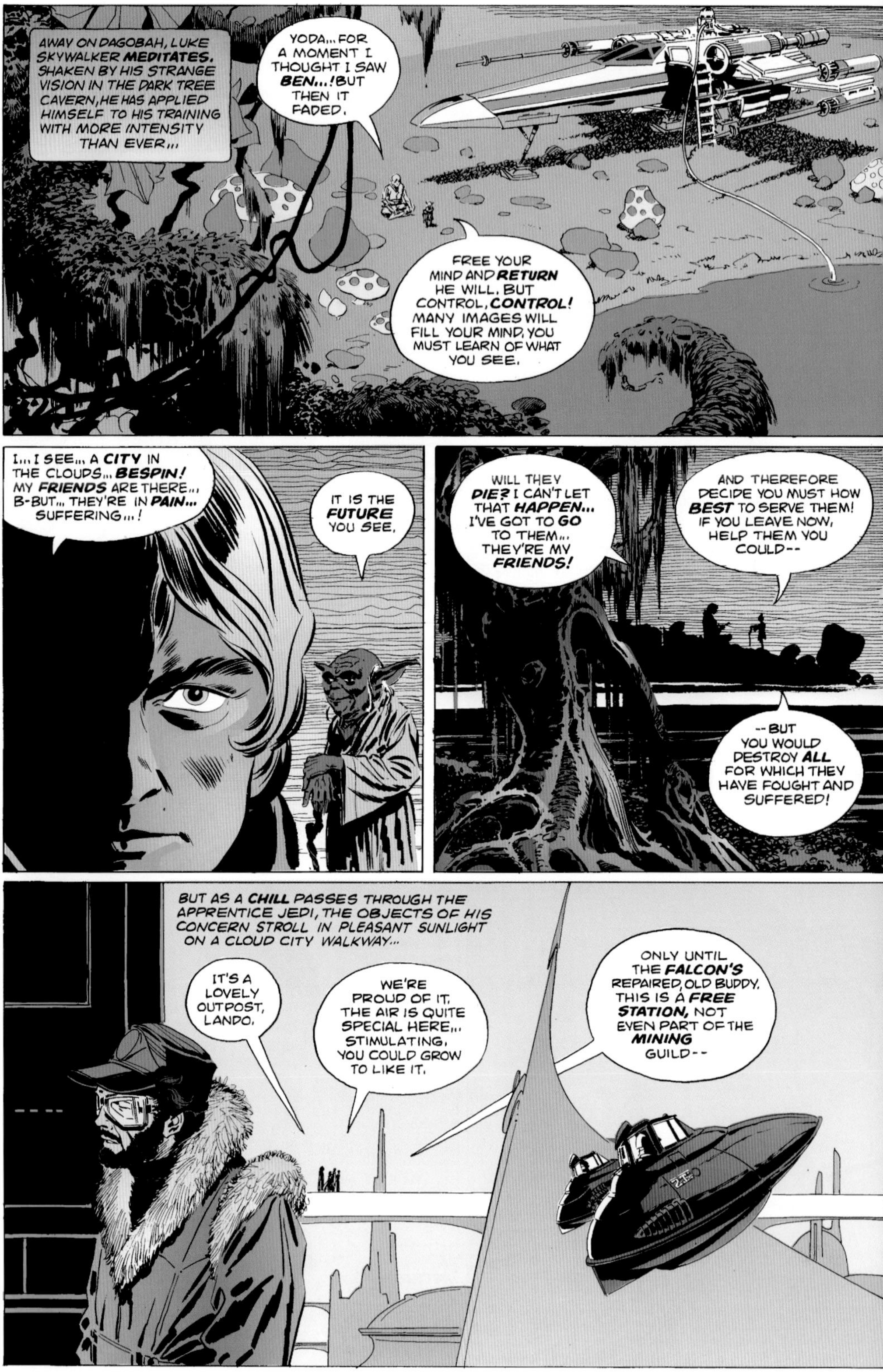
AWAY ON DAGOBAH, LUKE SKYWALKER MEDITATES. SHAKEN BY HIS STRANGE VISION IN THE DARK TREE CAVERN, HE HAS APPLIED HIMSELF TO HIS TRAINING WITH MORE INTENSITY THAN EVER...
YODA... FOR A MOMENT I THOUGHT I SAW BEN...! BUT THEN IT FADED.
FREE YOUR MIND AND RETURN HE WILL. BUT CONTROL, CONTROL! MANY IMAGES WILL FILL YOUR MIND, YOU MUST LEARN OF WHAT YOU SEE.
I... I SEE... A CITY IN THE CLOUDS... BESPIN! MY FRIENDS ARE THERE... B-BUT... THEY'RE IN PAIN... SUFFERING...!
IT IS THE FUTURE YOU SEE.
WILL THEY DIE? I CAN'T LET THAT HAPPEN... I'VE GOT TO GO TO THEM... THEY'RE MY FRIENDS!
AND THEREFORE DECIDE YOU MUST HOW BEST TO SERVE THEM! IF YOU LEAVE NOW, HELP THEM YOU COULD--
--BUT YOU WOULD DESTROY ALL FOR WHICH THEY HAVE FOUGHT AND SUFFERED!
BUT AS A CHILL PASSES THROUGH THE APPRENTICE JEDI, THE OBJECTS OF HIS CONCERN STROLL IN PLEASANT SUNLIGHT ON A CLOUD CITY WALKWAY...
IT'S A LOVELY OUTPOST, LANDO.
WE'RE PROUD OF IT. THE AIR IS QUITE SPECIAL HERE... STIMULATING. YOU COULD GROW TO LIKE IT.
ONLY UNTIL THE FALCON'S REPAIRED, OLD BUDDY. THIS IS A FREE STATION, NOT EVEN PART OF THE MINING GUILD--

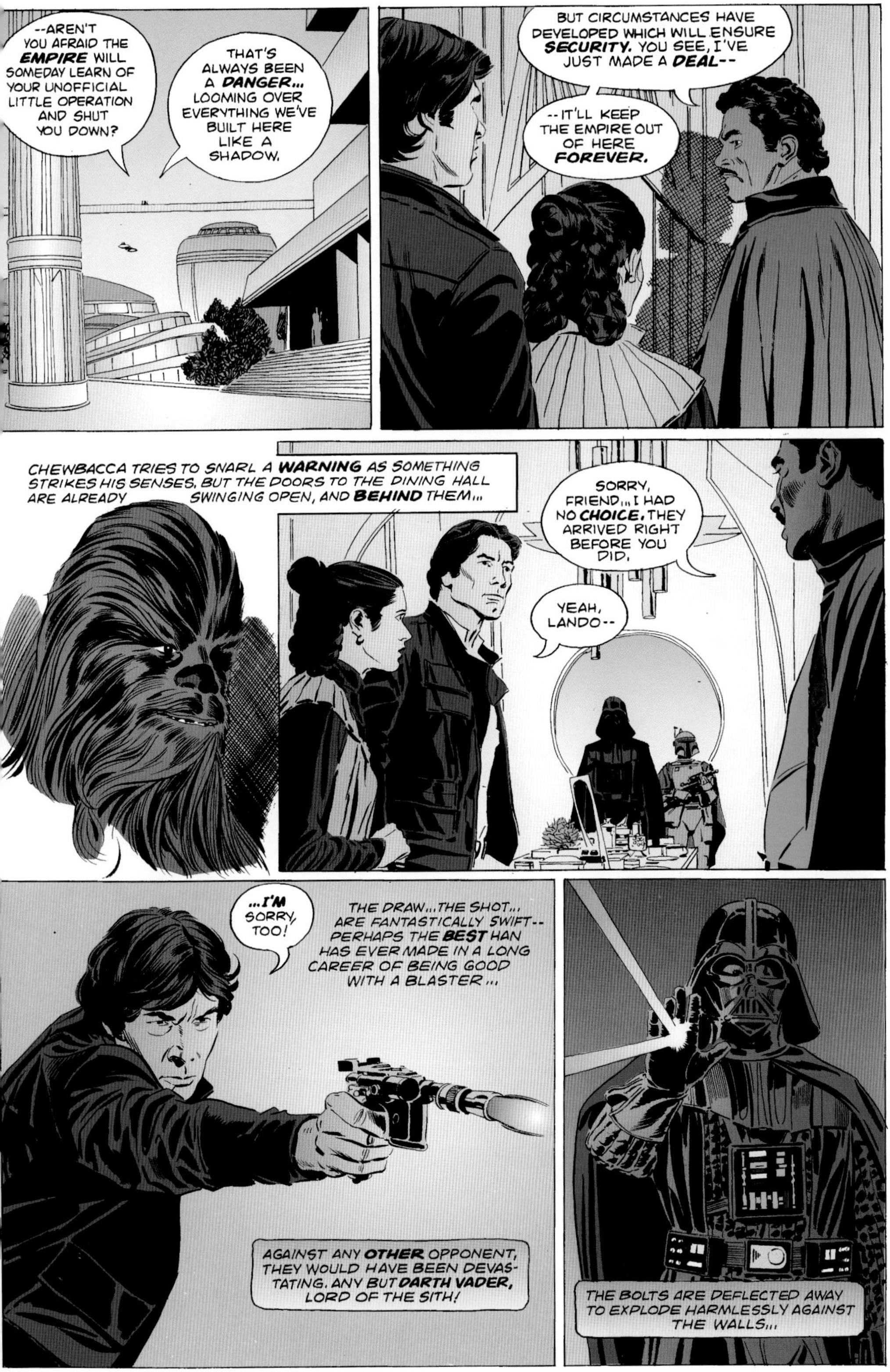
--AREN'T YOU AFRAID THE EMPIRE WILL SOMEDAY LEARN OF YOUR UNOFFICIAL LITTLE OPERATION AND SHUT YOU DOWN?
THAT'S ALWAYS BEEN A DANGER... LOOMING OVER EVERYTHING WE'VE BUILT HERE LIKE A SHADOW.
BUT CIRCUMSTANCES HAVE DEVELOPED WHICH WILL ENSURE SECURITY. YOU SEE, I'VE JUST MADE A DEAL--
--IT'LL KEEP THE EMPIRE OUT OF HERE FOREVER.
CHEWBACCA TRIES TO SNARL A WARNING AS SOMETHING STRIKES HIS SENSES, BUT THE DOORS TO THE DINING HALL ARE ALREADY SWINGING OPEN, AND BEHIND THEM...
SORRY, FRIEND... I HAD NO CHOICE. THEY ARRIVED RIGHT BEFORE YOU DID.
YEAH, LANDO--
...I'M SORRY, TOO!
THE DRAW... THE SHOT... ARE FANTASTICALLY SWIFT-- PERHAPS THE BEST HAN HAS EVER MADE IN A LONG CAREER OF BEING GOOD WITH A BLASTER...
AGAINST ANY OTHER OPPONENT, THEY WOULD HAVE BEEN DEVASTATING. ANY BUT DARTH VADER, LORD OF THE SITH!
THE BOLTS ARE DEFLECTED AWAY TO EXPLODE HARMLESSLY AGAINST THE WALLS...

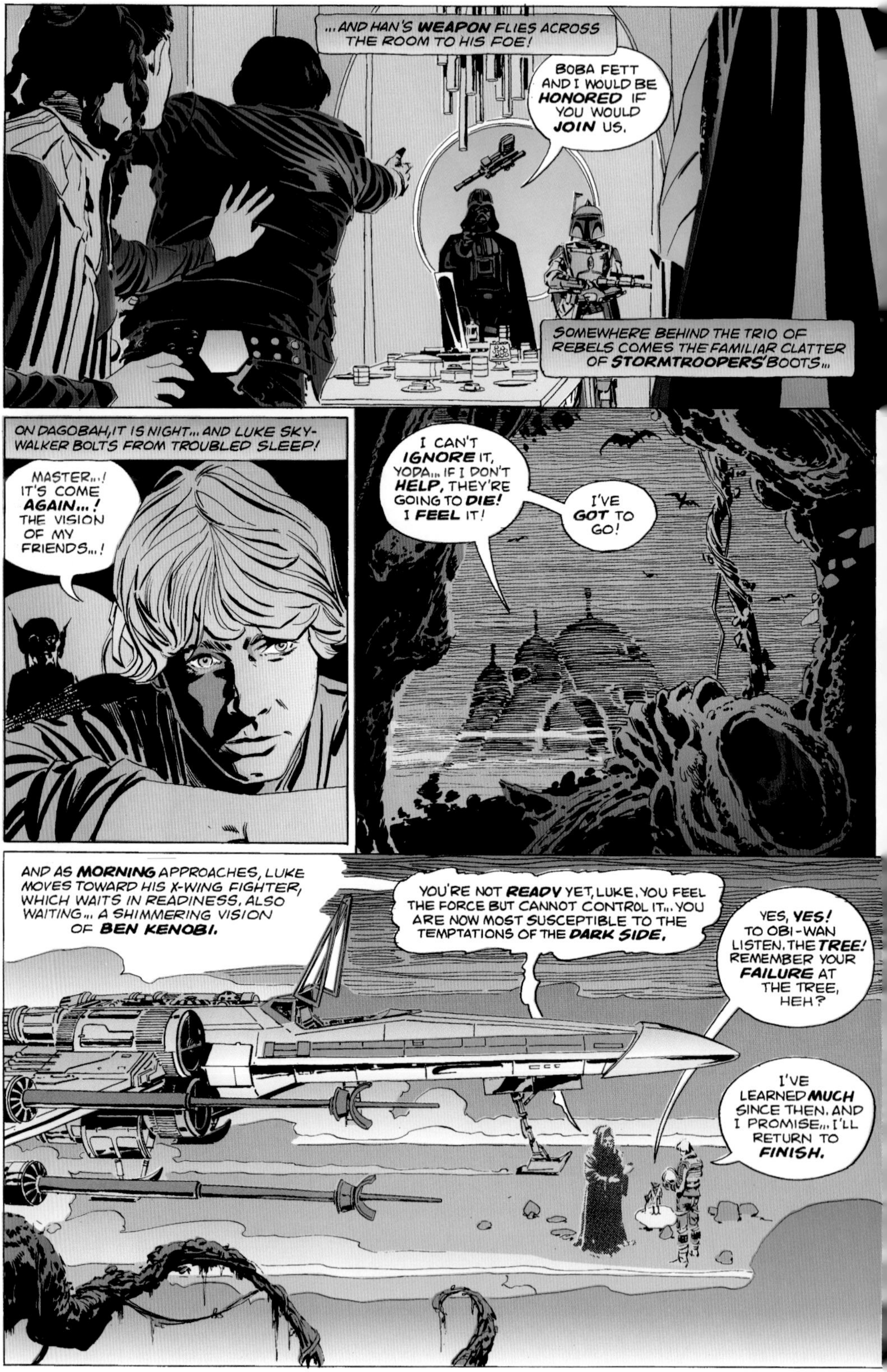
...AND HAN'S WEAPON FLIES ACROSS THE ROOM TO HIS FOE!
BOBA FETT AND I WOULD BE HONORED IF YOU WOULD JOIN US.
SOMEWHERE BEHIND THE TRIO OF REBELS COMES THE FAMILIAR CLATTER OF STORMTROOPERS' BOOTS...
ON DAGOBAH, IT IS NIGHT... AND LUKE SKY-WALKER BOLTS FROM TROUBLED SLEEP!
MASTER...! IT'S COME AGAIN...! THE VISION OF MY FRIENDS...!
I CAN'T IGNORE IT, YODA... IF I DON'T HELP, THEY'RE GOING TO DIE! I FEEL IT!
I'VE GOT TO GO!
AND AS MORNING APPROACHES, LUKE MOVES TOWARD HIS X-WING FIGHTER, WHICH WAITS IN READINESS. ALSO WAITING... A SHIMMERING VISION OF BEN KENOBI.
YOU'RE NOT READY YET, LUKE. YOU FEEL THE FORCE BUT CANNOT CONTROL IT... YOU ARE NOW MOST SUSCEPTIBLE TO THE TEMPTATIONS OF THE DARK SIDE.
YES, YES! TO OBI-WAN LISTEN. THE TREE! REMEMBER YOUR FAILURE AT THE TREE, HEH?
I'VE LEARNED MUCH SINCE THEN. AND I PROMISE... I'LL RETURN TO FINISH.

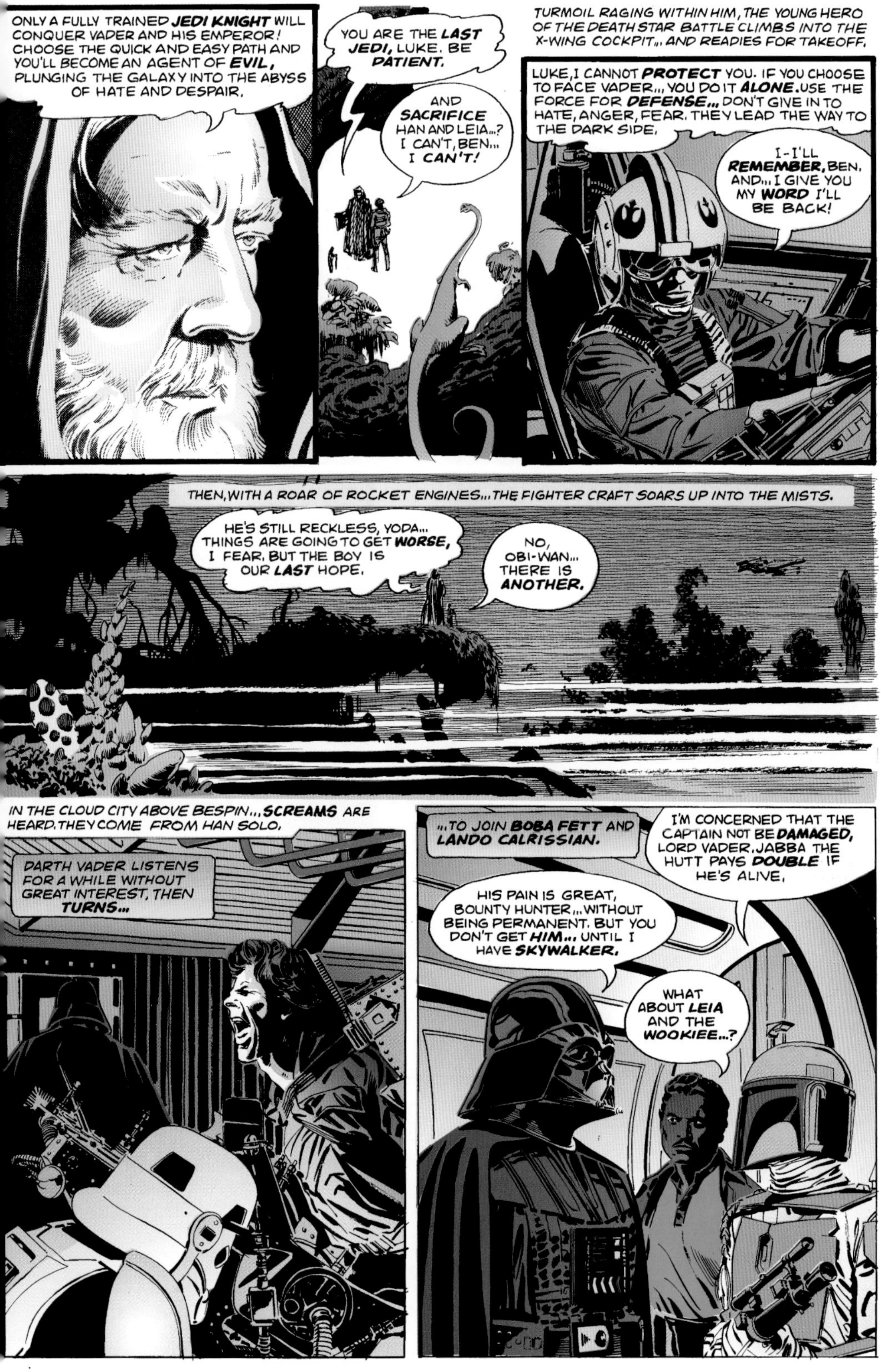
ONLY A FULLY TRAINED JEDI KNIGHT WILL CONQUER VADER AND HIS EMPEROR! CHOOSE THE QUICK AND EASY PATH AND YOU'LL BECOME AN AGENT OF EVIL, PLUNGING THE GALAXY INTO THE ABYSS OF HATE AND DESPAIR.
YOU ARE THE LAST JEDI, LUKE. BE PATIENT.
AND SACRIFICE HAN AND LEIA...? I CAN'T, BEN... I CAN'T!
TURMOIL RAGING WITHIN HIM, THE YOUNG HERO OF THE DEATH STAR BATTLE CLIMBS INTO THE X-WING COCKPIT... AND READIES FOR TAKEOFF.
LUKE, I CANNOT PROTECT YOU. IF YOU CHOOSE TO FACE VADER... YOU DO IT ALONE. USE THE FORCE FOR DEFENSE... DON'T GIVE IN TO HATE, ANGER, FEAR. THEY LEAD THE WAY TO THE DARK SIDE.
I-I'LL REMEMBER, BEN. AND... I GIVE YOU MY WORD I'LL BE BACK!
THEN, WITH A ROAR OF ROCKET ENGINES... THE FIGHTER CRAFT SOARS UP INTO THE MISTS.
HE'S STILL RECKLESS, YODA... THINGS ARE GOING TO GET WORSE, I FEAR. BUT THE BOY IS OUR LAST HOPE.
NO, OBI-WAN... THERE IS ANOTHER.
IN THE CLOUD CITY ABOVE BESPIN... SCREAMS ARE HEARD. THEY COME FROM HAN SOLO.
DARTH VADER LISTENS FOR A WHILE WITHOUT GREAT INTEREST, THEN TURNS...
...TO JOIN BOBA FETT AND LANDO CALRISSIAN.
I'M CONCERNED THAT THE CAPTAIN NOT BE DAMAGED, LORD VADER. JABBA THE HUTT PAYS DOUBLE IF HE'S ALIVE.
HIS PAIN IS GREAT, BOUNTY HUNTER... WITHOUT BEING PERMANENT. BUT YOU DON'T GET HIM... UNTIL I HAVE SKYWALKER.
WHAT ABOUT LEIA AND THE WOOKIEE...?

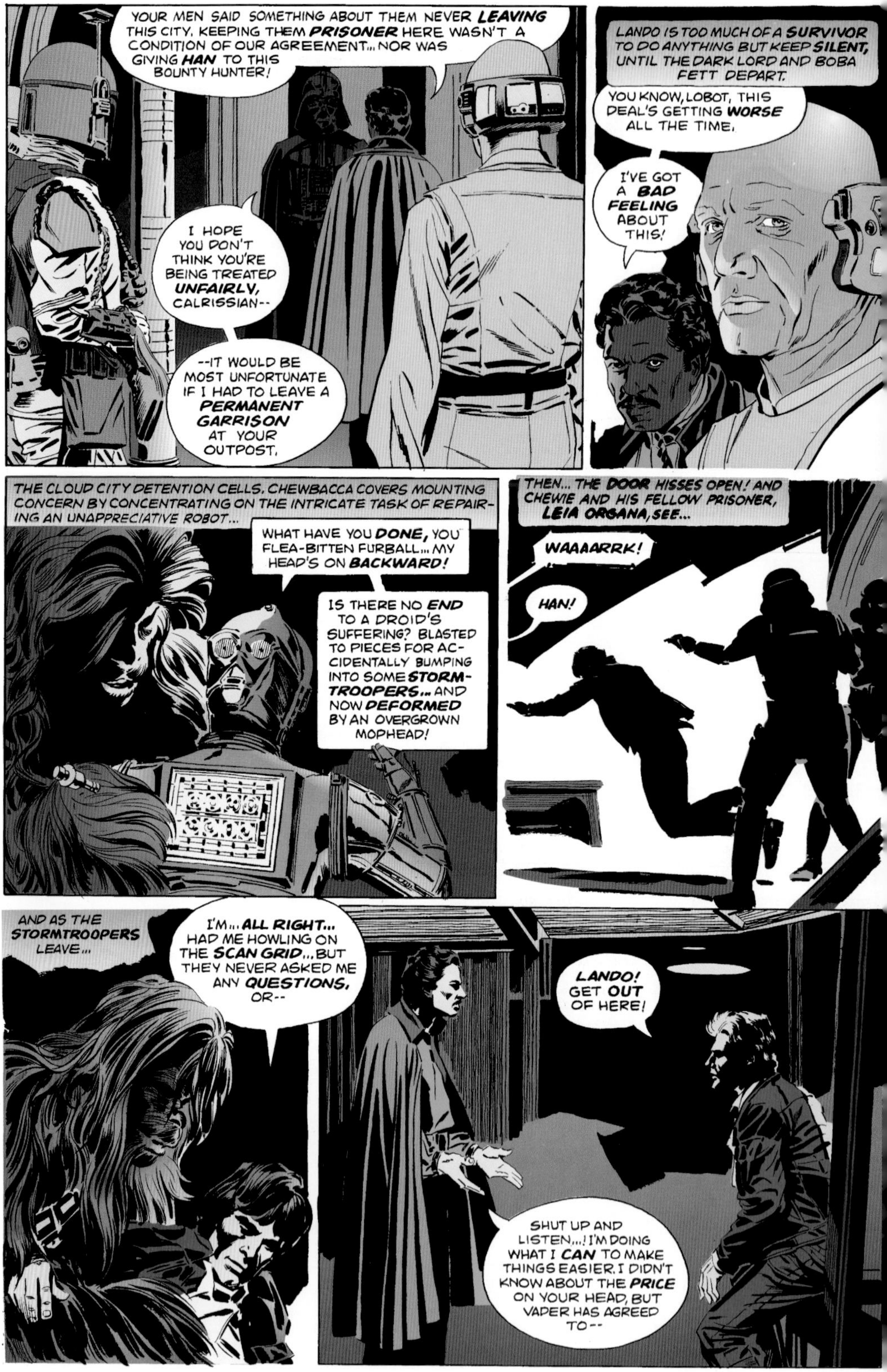
YOUR MEN SAID SOMETHING ABOUT THEM NEVER LEAVING THIS CITY. KEEPING THEM PRISONER HERE WASN'T A CONDITION OF OUR AGREEMENT... NOR WAS GIVING HAN TO THIS BOUNTY HUNTER!
I HOPE YOU DON'T THINK YOU'RE BEING TREATED UNFAIRLY, CALRISSIAN--
--IT WOULD BE MOST UNFORTUNATE IF I HAD TO LEAVE A PERMANENT GARRISON AT YOUR OUTPOST.
LANDO IS TOO MUCH OF A SURVIVOR TO DO ANYTHING BUT KEEP SILENT, UNTIL THE DARK LORD AND BOBA FETT DEPART.
YOU KNOW, LOBOT, THIS DEAL'S GETTING WORSE ALL THE TIME.
I'VE GOT A BAD FEELING ABOUT THIS!
THE CLOUD CITY DETENTION CELLS. CHEWBACCA COVERS MOUNTING CONCERN BY CONCENTRATING ON THE INTRICATE TASK OF REPAIRING AN UNAPPRECIATIVE ROBOT...
WHAT HAVE YOU DONE, YOU FLEA-BITTEN FURBALL... MY HEAD'S ON BACKWARD!
IS THERE NO END TO A DROID'S SUFFERING? BLASTED TO PIECES FOR ACCIDENTALLY BUMPING INTO SOME STORMTROOPERS... AND NOW DEFORMED BY AN OVERGROWN MOPHEAD!
THEN... THE DOOR HISSES OPEN! AND CHEWIE AND HIS FELLOW PRISONER, LEIA ORGANA, SEE...
WAAAARRK!
HAN!
AND AS THE STORMTROOPERS LEAVE...
I'M... ALL RIGHT... HAD ME HOWLING ON THE SCAN GRID... BUT THEY NEVER ASKED ME ANY QUESTIONS, OR--
LANDO! GET OUT OF HERE!
SHUT UP AND LISTEN...! I'M DOING WHAT I CAN TO MAKE THINGS EASIER. I DIDN'T KNOW ABOUT THE PRICE ON YOUR HEAD, BUT VADER HAS AGREED TO--

YOU DON'T **KNOW** MUCH IF YOU THINK DARTH VADER WANTS ALL OF US ANYTHING BUT **DEAD** BEFORE THIS THING IS OVER!

HE DOESN'T WANT YOU AT **ALL,** HAN! HE'S SETTING A **TRAP** FOR SOME YOUNG REBEL NAMED **SKYWALKER**... YOU PEOPLE ARE THE **BAIT.**

I DON'T KNOW WHAT'S SO **IMPORTANT** ABOUT THE KID, BUT THE IMPERIALS HAVE PINPOINTED THAT HE'S ON HIS **WAY**...

LUKE'S COMING **HERE**...? YOU FIXED US **ALL** PRETTY GOOD--

--FRIEND!

FOR A MOMENT IT'S A **FIGHT**... UNTIL LANDO'S GUARDS MOVE IN, CLUBBING WITH THEIR BLASTERS!

OKAY... **ENOUGH!** I'VE DONE AS MUCH AS I CAN. I WISH IT WERE MORE... BUT I'VE GOT MY **OWN** PROBLEMS.

I'VE ALREADY STUCK MY **NECK** OUT FARTHER THAN I SHOULD.

YEAH, YEAH, LANDO ... YOU'RE A REAL **HERO!**

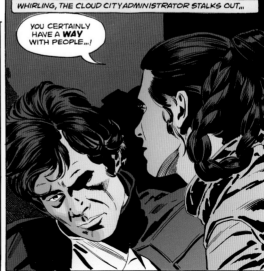

WHIRLING, THE CLOUD CITY ADMINISTRATOR STALKS OUT...

YOU CERTAINLY HAVE A **WAY** WITH PEOPLE...!

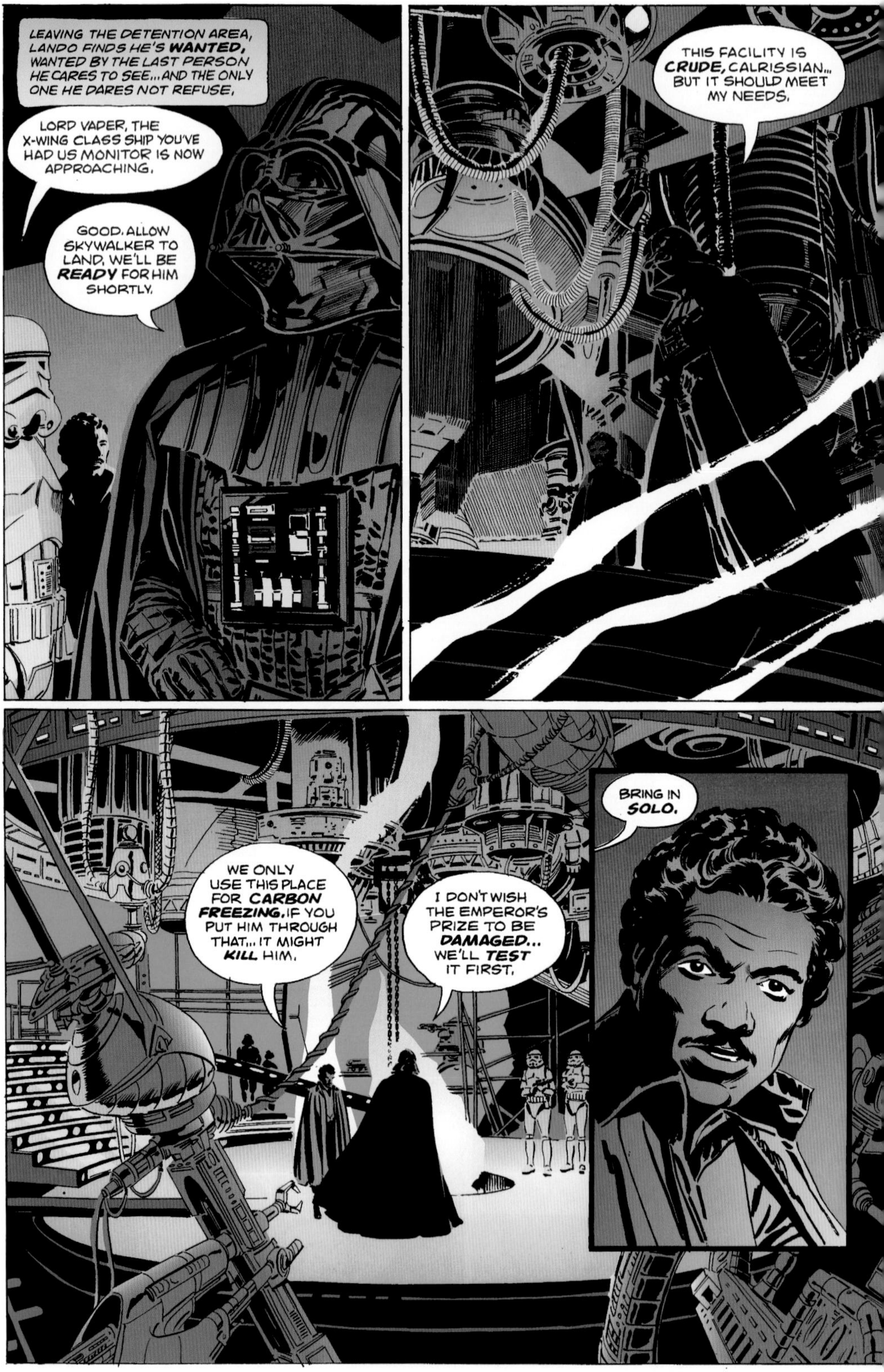
LEAVING THE DETENTION AREA, LANDO FINDS HE'S WANTED, WANTED BY THE LAST PERSON HE CARES TO SEE... AND THE ONLY ONE HE DARES NOT REFUSE.
LORD VADER, THE X-WING CLASS SHIP YOU'VE HAD US MONITOR IS NOW APPROACHING.
GOOD. ALLOW SKYWALKER TO LAND. WE'LL BE READY FOR HIM SHORTLY.
THIS FACILITY IS CRUDE, CALRISSIAN... BUT IT SHOULD MEET MY NEEDS.
WE ONLY USE THIS PLACE FOR CARBON FREEZING. IF YOU PUT HIM THROUGH THAT... IT MIGHT KILL HIM.
I DON'T WISH THE EMPEROR'S PRIZE TO BE DAMAGED... WE'LL TEST IT FIRST.
BRING IN SOLO.

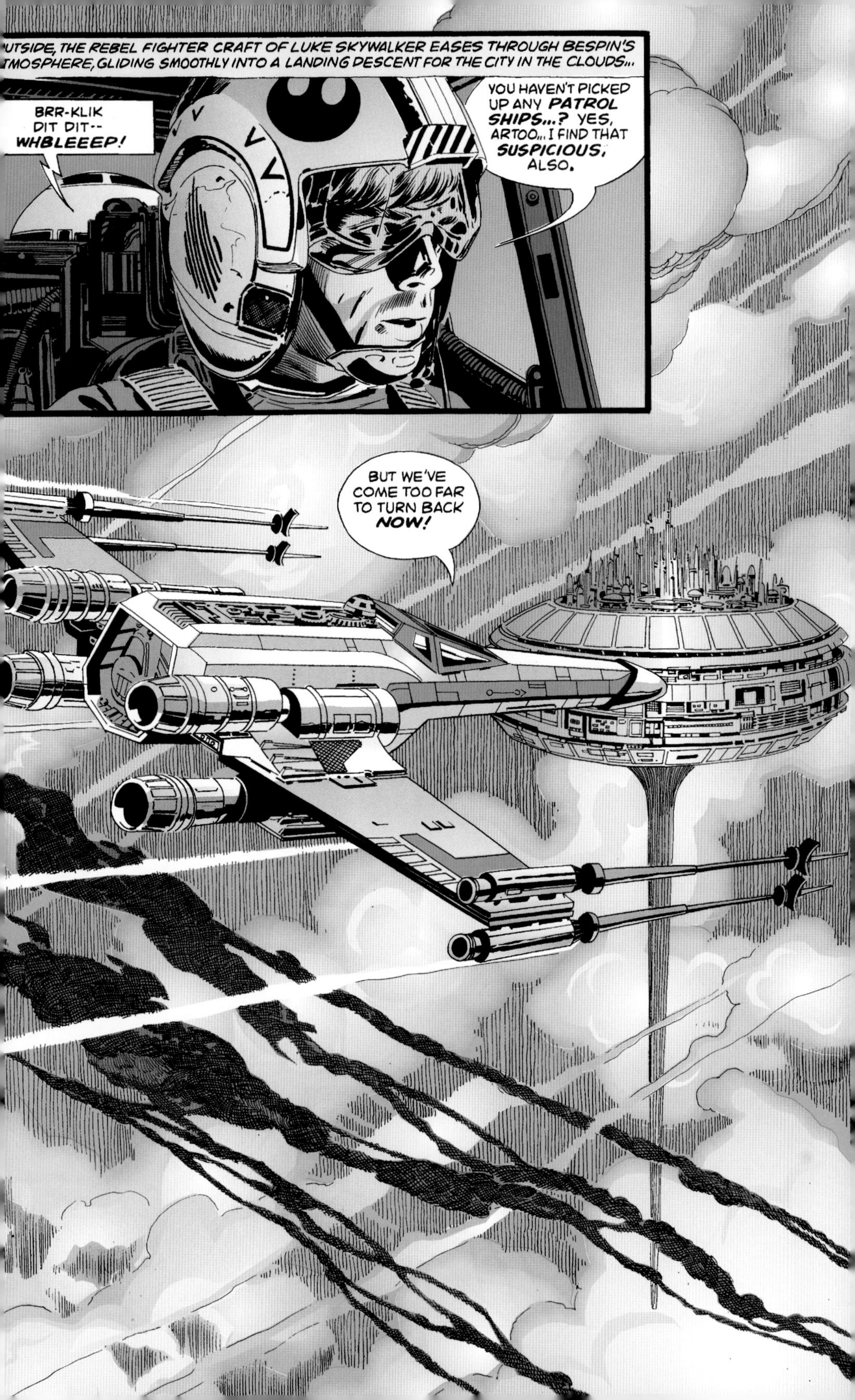

UTSIDE, THE REBEL FIGHTER CRAFT OF LUKE SKYWALKER EASES THROUGH BESPIN'S TMOSPHERE, GLIDING SMOOTHLY INTO A LANDING DESCENT FOR THE CITY IN THE CLOUDS...
BRR-KLIK DIT DIT-- WHBLEEEP!
YOU HAVEN'T PICKED UP ANY PATROL SHIPS...? YES, ARTOO... I FIND THAT SUSPICIOUS, ALSO.
BUT WE'VE COME TOO FAR TO TURN BACK NOW!

RESPONDING INSTANTLY TO THEIR LEADER'S COMMAND... STORMTROOPERS BRING HAN. TOO SOON THE TEST OF THE CARBON-FREEZING CHAMBER IS READY TO *BEGIN*... BEFORE AN AUDIENCE OF THE WILLING AND THE *UNWILLING*.

THE EMPIRE WILL *COMPENSATE* YOU FOR THE LOSS.

PUT HIM IN THE *CHAMBER!*

NO!

WHAT IF SOLO DOESN'T *SURVIVE,* LORD VADER? BEYOND WHAT YOU'RE PAYING... HE'S WORTH A *LOT* TO ME.

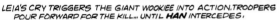

LEIA'S CRY TRIGGERS THE GIANT WOOKIEE INTO ACTION. TROOPERS POUR FORWARD FOR THE KILL... UNTIL *HAN* INTERCEDES.

THANK THE *MAKER!*

NO, BIG BUDDY, COME ON, SAVE YOUR STRENGTH FOR *ANOTHER* TIME... WHEN THE *ODDS* ARE BETTER.

NOWRRRRRAGH!

YEAH... I KNOW... I FEEL THE SAME WAY.

HAN... OH, *HAN...!* I *LOVE* YOU...! I COULDN'T TELL YOU BEFORE... BUT IT'S *TRUE.*

JUST *REMEMBER* THAT, LEIA--

--'CAUSE I'LL BE *BACK.*

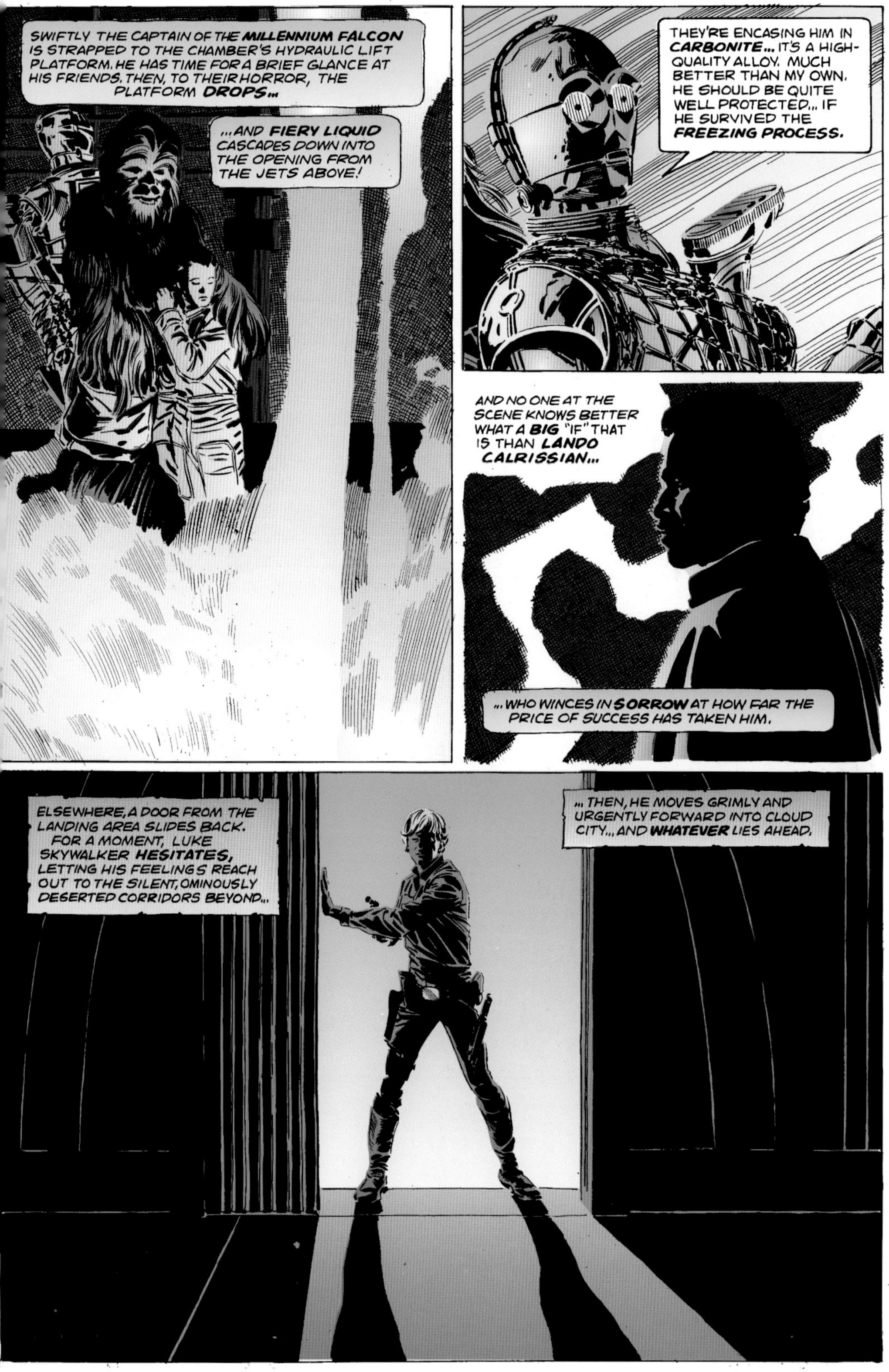
SWIFTLY THE CAPTAIN OF THE MILLENNIUM FALCON IS STRAPPED TO THE CHAMBER'S HYDRAULIC LIFT PLATFORM. HE HAS TIME FOR A BRIEF GLANCE AT HIS FRIENDS. THEN, TO THEIR HORROR, THE PLATFORM DROPS...
...AND FIERY LIQUID CASCADES DOWN INTO THE OPENING FROM THE JETS ABOVE!
THEY'RE ENCASING HIM IN CARBONITE... IT'S A HIGH-QUALITY ALLOY. MUCH BETTER THAN MY OWN. HE SHOULD BE QUITE WELL PROTECTED... IF HE SURVIVED THE FREEZING PROCESS.
AND NO ONE AT THE SCENE KNOWS BETTER WHAT A BIG "IF" THAT IS THAN LANDO CALRISSIAN...
...WHO WINCES IN SORROW AT HOW FAR THE PRICE OF SUCCESS HAS TAKEN HIM.
ELSEWHERE, A DOOR FROM THE LANDING AREA SLIDES BACK. FOR A MOMENT, LUKE SKYWALKER HESITATES, LETTING HIS FEELINGS REACH OUT TO THE SILENT, OMINOUSLY DESERTED CORRIDORS BEYOND...
...THEN, HE MOVES GRIMLY AND URGENTLY FORWARD INTO CLOUD CITY... AND WHATEVER LIES AHEAD.

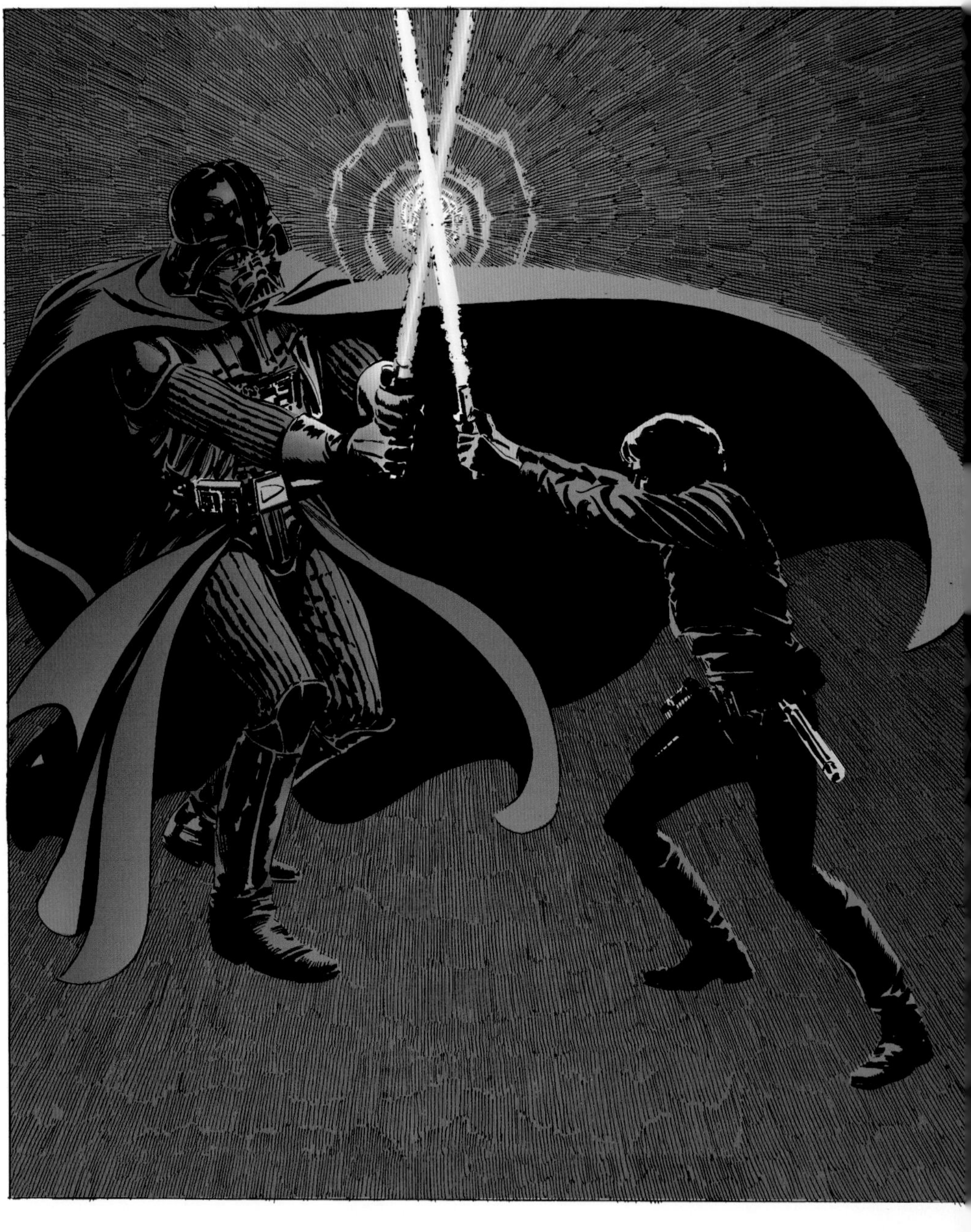

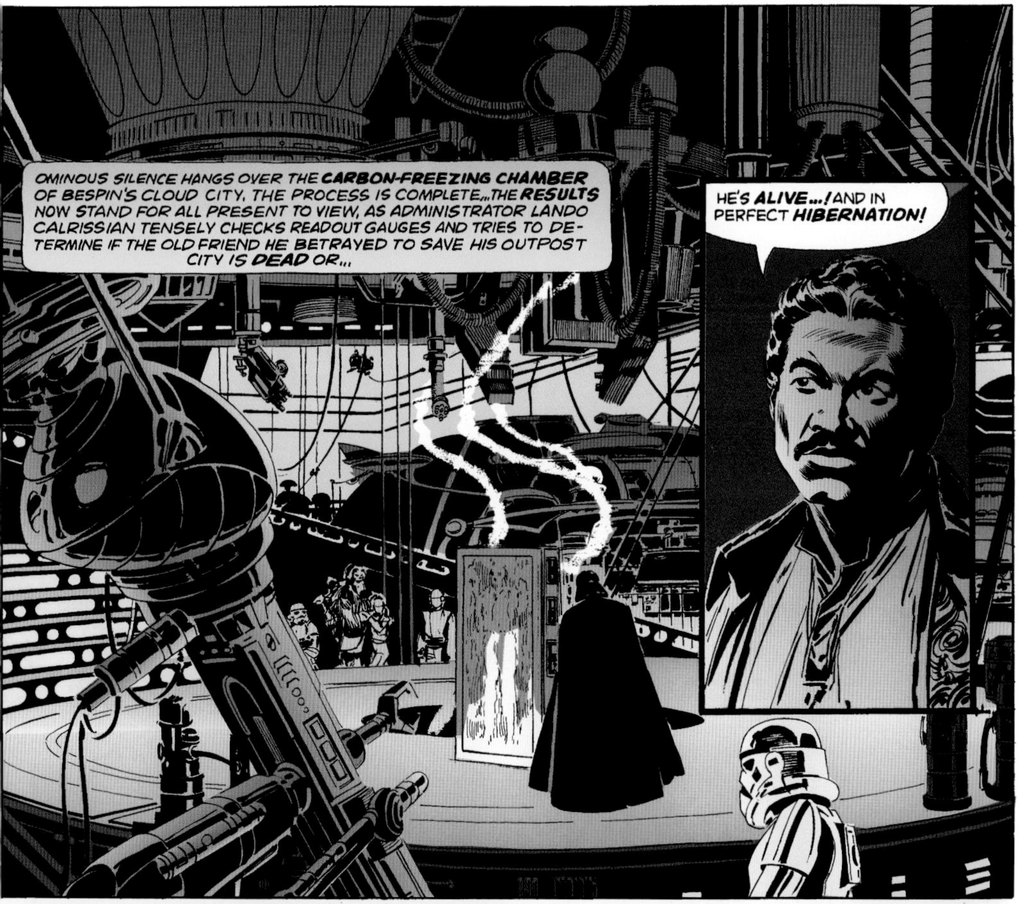
OMINOUS SILENCE HANGS OVER THE CARBON-FREEZING CHAMBER OF BESPIN'S CLOUD CITY. THE PROCESS IS COMPLETE... THE RESULTS NOW STAND FOR ALL PRESENT TO VIEW, AS ADMINISTRATOR LANDO CALRISSIAN TENSELY CHECKS READOUT GAUGES AND TRIES TO DETERMINE IF THE OLD FRIEND HE BETRAYED TO SAVE HIS OUTPOST CITY IS DEAD OR...
HE'S ALIVE...! AND IN PERFECT HIBERNATION!

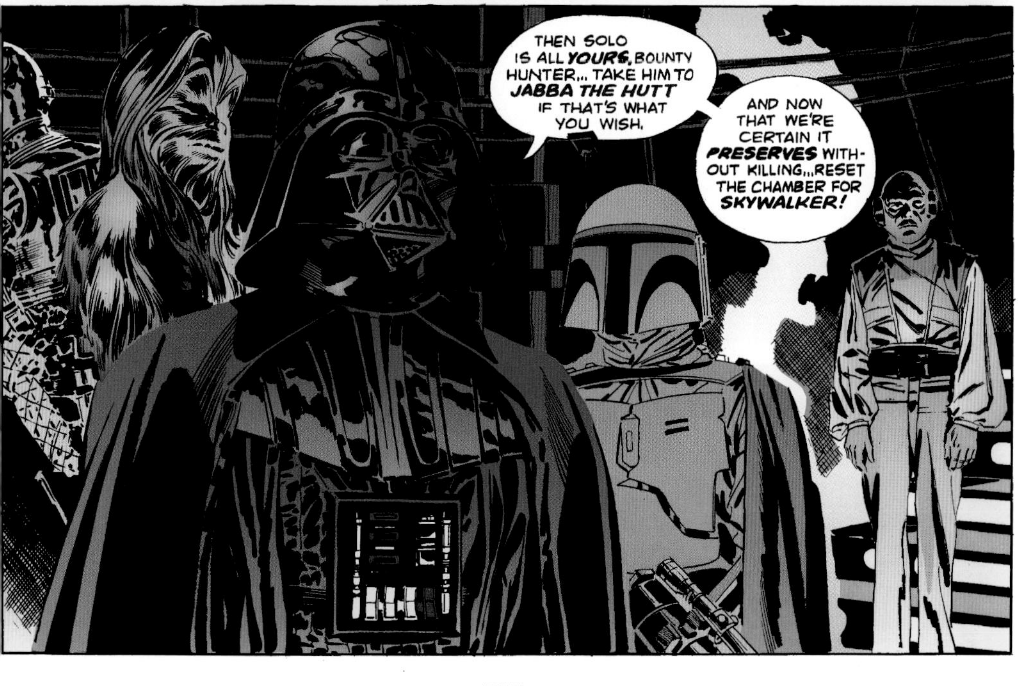
THEN SOLO IS ALL YOURS, BOUNTY HUNTER... TAKE HIM TO JABBA THE HUTT IF THAT'S WHAT YOU WISH.
AND NOW THAT WE'RE CERTAIN IT PRESERVES WITHOUT KILLING... RESET THE CHAMBER FOR SKYWALKER!

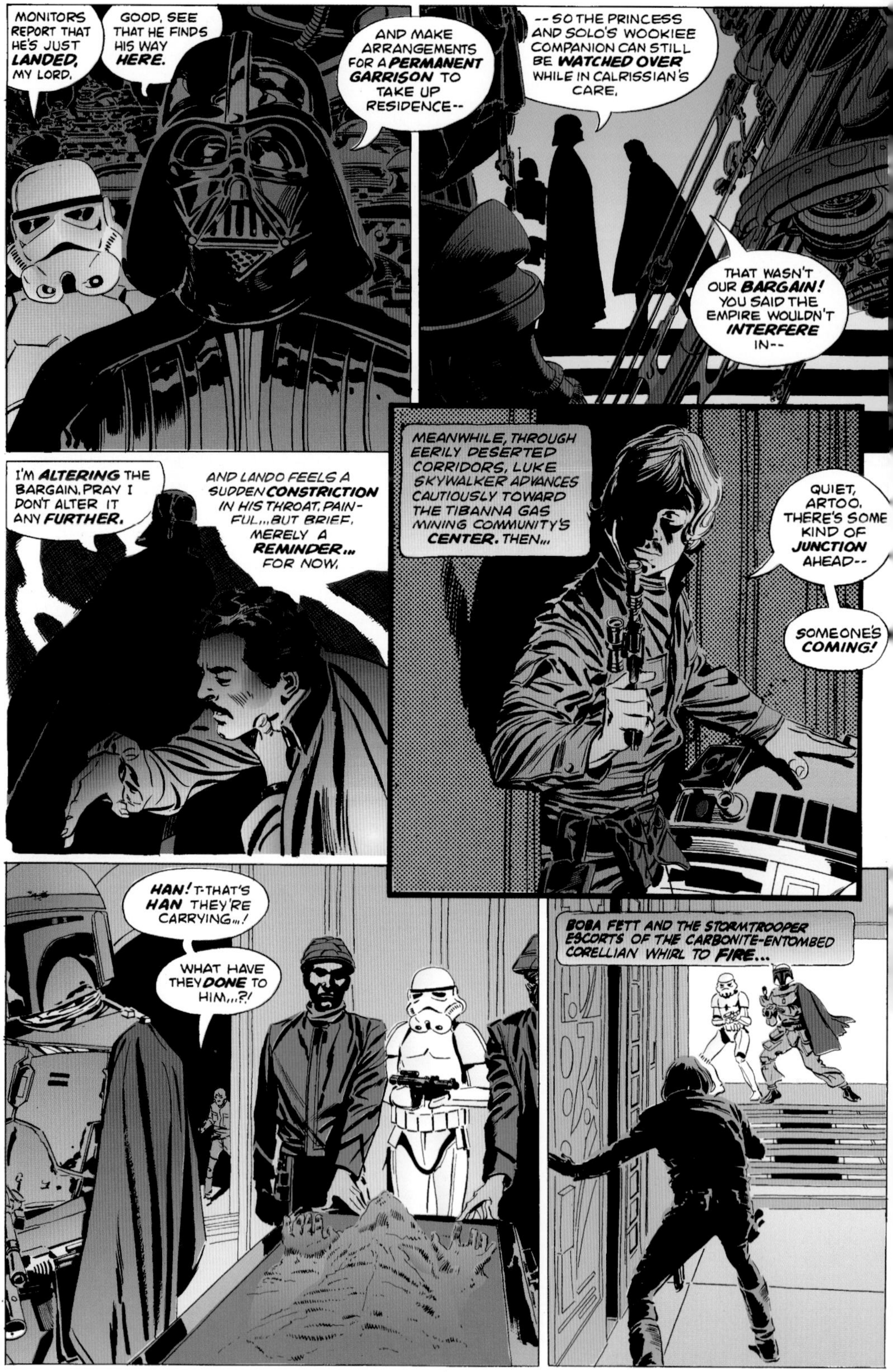
MONITORS REPORT THAT HE'S JUST LANDED, MY LORD.
GOOD, SEE THAT HE FINDS HIS WAY HERE.
AND MAKE ARRANGEMENTS FOR A PERMANENT GARRISON TO TAKE UP RESIDENCE--
--SO THE PRINCESS AND SOLO'S WOOKIEE COMPANION CAN STILL BE WATCHED OVER WHILE IN CALRISSIAN'S CARE.
THAT WASN'T OUR BARGAIN! YOU SAID THE EMPIRE WOULDN'T INTERFERE IN--
I'M ALTERING THE BARGAIN. PRAY I DON'T ALTER IT ANY FURTHER.
AND LANDO FEELS A SUDDEN CONSTRICTION IN HIS THROAT. PAINFUL... BUT BRIEF. MERELY A REMINDER... FOR NOW.
MEANWHILE, THROUGH EERILY DESERTED CORRIDORS, LUKE SKYWALKER ADVANCES CAUTIOUSLY TOWARD THE TIBANNA GAS MINING COMMUNITY'S CENTER. THEN...
QUIET, ARTOO. THERE'S SOME KIND OF JUNCTION AHEAD--
SOMEONE'S COMING!
HAN! T-THAT'S HAN THEY'RE CARRYING...!
WHAT HAVE THEY DONE TO HIM...?!
BOBA FETT AND THE STORMTROOPER ESCORTS OF THE CARBONITE-ENTOMBED CORELLIAN WHIRL TO FIRE...

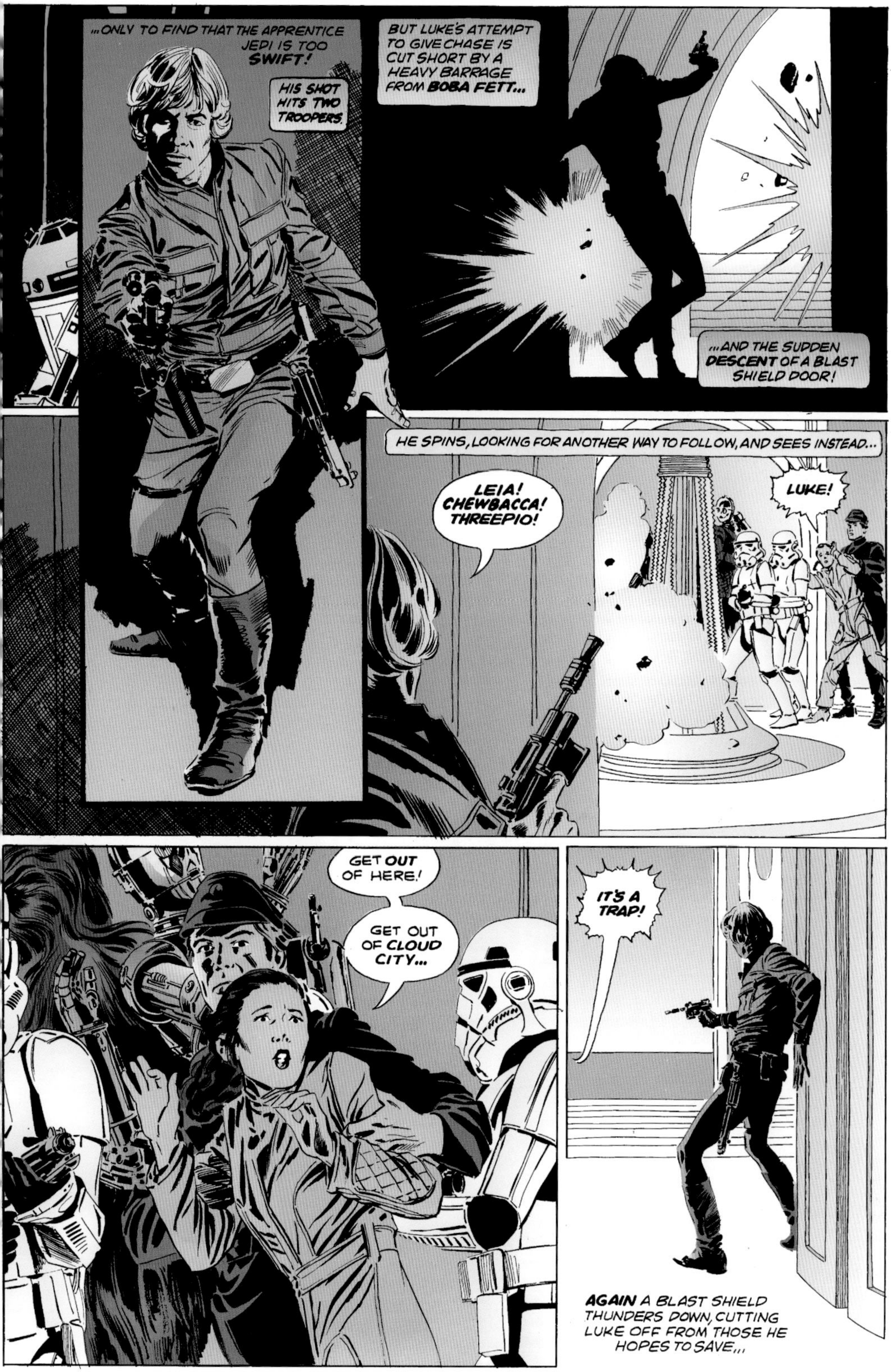
...ONLY TO FIND THAT THE APPRENTICE JEDI IS TOO SWIFT!
HIS SHOT HITS TWO TROOPERS.
BUT LUKE'S ATTEMPT TO GIVE CHASE IS CUT SHORT BY A HEAVY BARRAGE FROM BOBA FETT...
...AND THE SUDDEN DESCENT OF A BLAST SHIELD DOOR!
HE SPINS, LOOKING FOR ANOTHER WAY TO FOLLOW, AND SEES INSTEAD...
LEIA! CHEWBACCA! THREEPIO!
LUKE!
GET OUT OF HERE!
GET OUT OF CLOUD CITY...
IT'S A TRAP!
AGAIN A BLAST SHIELD THUNDERS DOWN, CUTTING LUKE OFF FROM THOSE HE HOPES TO SAVE...

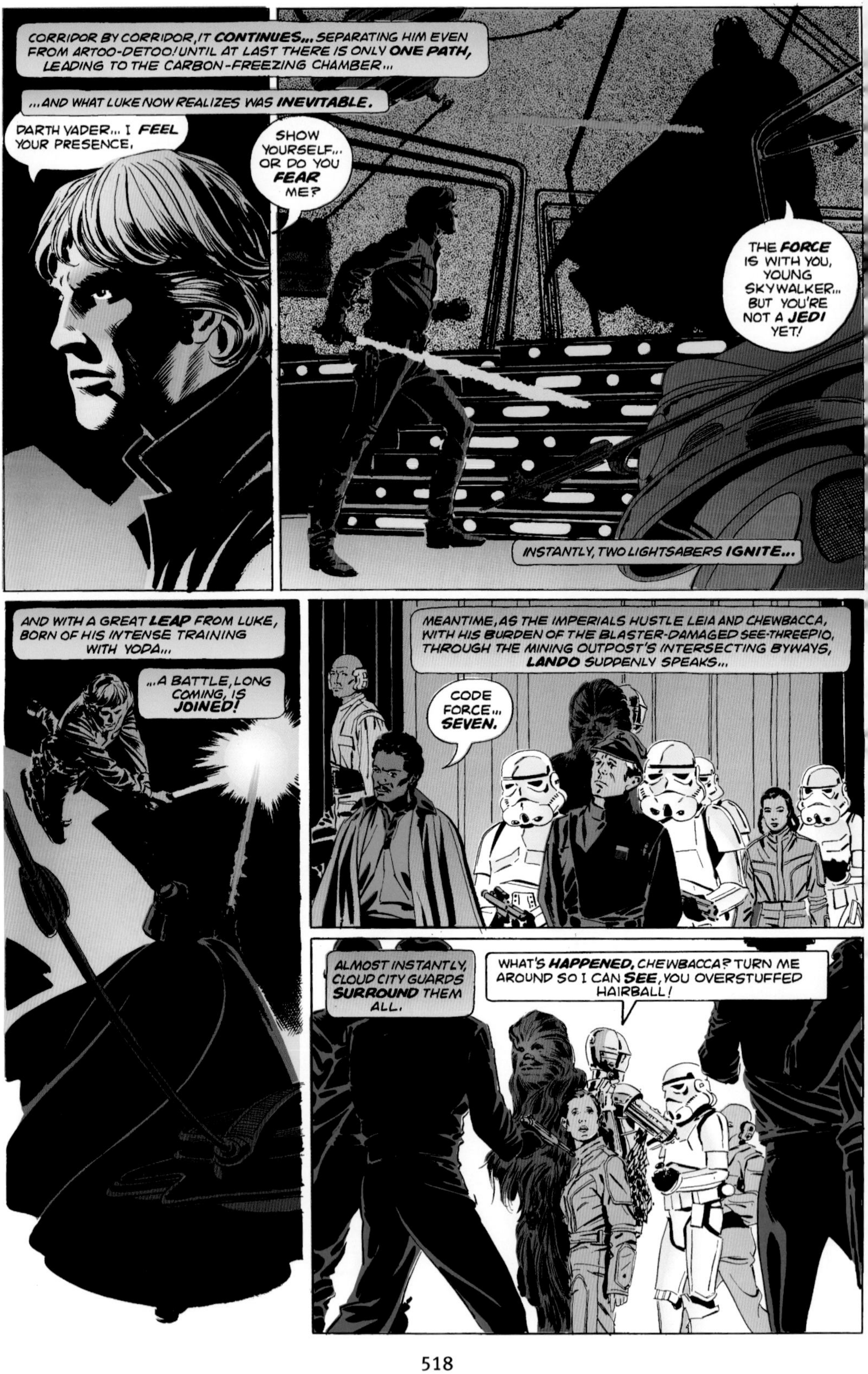
CORRIDOR BY CORRIDOR, IT CONTINUES... SEPARATING HIM EVEN FROM ARTOO-DETOO! UNTIL AT LAST THERE IS ONLY ONE PATH, LEADING TO THE CARBON-FREEZING CHAMBER...
...AND WHAT LUKE NOW REALIZES WAS INEVITABLE.
DARTH VADER... I FEEL YOUR PRESENCE.
SHOW YOURSELF... OR DO YOU FEAR ME?
THE FORCE IS WITH YOU, YOUNG SKYWALKER... BUT YOU'RE NOT A JEDI YET!
INSTANTLY, TWO LIGHTSABERS IGNITE...
AND WITH A GREAT LEAP FROM LUKE, BORN OF HIS INTENSE TRAINING WITH YODA...
...A BATTLE, LONG COMING, IS JOINED!
MEANTIME, AS THE IMPERIALS HUSTLE LEIA AND CHEWBACCA, WITH HIS BURDEN OF THE BLASTER-DAMAGED SEE-THREEPIO, THROUGH THE MINING OUTPOST'S INTERSECTING BYWAYS, LANDO SUDDENLY SPEAKS...
CODE FORCE... SEVEN.
ALMOST INSTANTLY, CLOUD CITY GUARDS SURROUND THEM ALL.
WHAT'S HAPPENED, CHEWBACCA? TURN ME AROUND SO I CAN SEE, YOU OVERSTUFFED HAIRBALL!

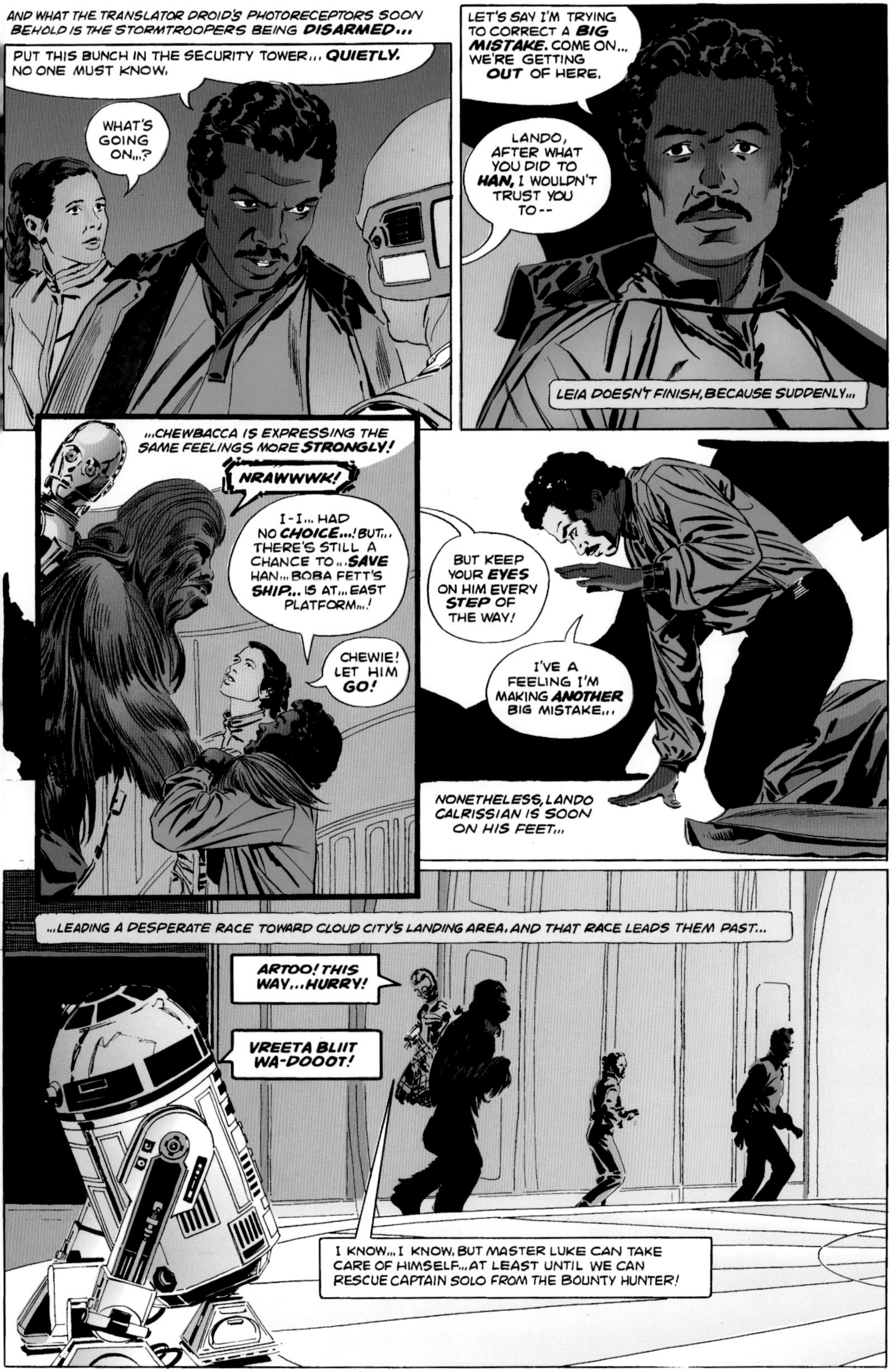
AND WHAT THE TRANSLATOR DROID'S PHOTORECEPTORS SOON BEHOLD IS THE STORMTROOPERS BEING DISARMED...
PUT THIS BUNCH IN THE SECURITY TOWER... QUIETLY. NO ONE MUST KNOW.
WHAT'S GOING ON...?
LET'S SAY I'M TRYING TO CORRECT A BIG MISTAKE. COME ON... WE'RE GETTING OUT OF HERE.
LANDO, AFTER WHAT YOU DID TO HAN, I WOULDN'T TRUST YOU TO--
LEIA DOESN'T FINISH, BECAUSE SUDDENLY...
...CHEWBACCA IS EXPRESSING THE SAME FEELINGS MORE STRONGLY!
NRAWWWK!
I-I... HAD NO CHOICE...! BUT... THERE'S STILL A CHANCE TO... SAVE HAN... BOBA FETT'S SHIP... IS AT... EAST PLATFORM...!
CHEWIE! LET HIM GO!
BUT KEEP YOUR EYES ON HIM EVERY STEP OF THE WAY!
I'VE A FEELING I'M MAKING ANOTHER BIG MISTAKE...
NONETHELESS, LANDO CALRISSIAN IS SOON ON HIS FEET...
...LEADING A DESPERATE RACE TOWARD CLOUD CITY'S LANDING AREA. AND THAT RACE LEADS THEM PAST...
ARTOO! THIS WAY... HURRY!
VREETA BLIIT WA-DOOOT!
I KNOW... I KNOW. BUT MASTER LUKE CAN TAKE CARE OF HIMSELF... AT LEAST UNTIL WE CAN RESCUE CAPTAIN SOLO FROM THE BOUNTY HUNTER!

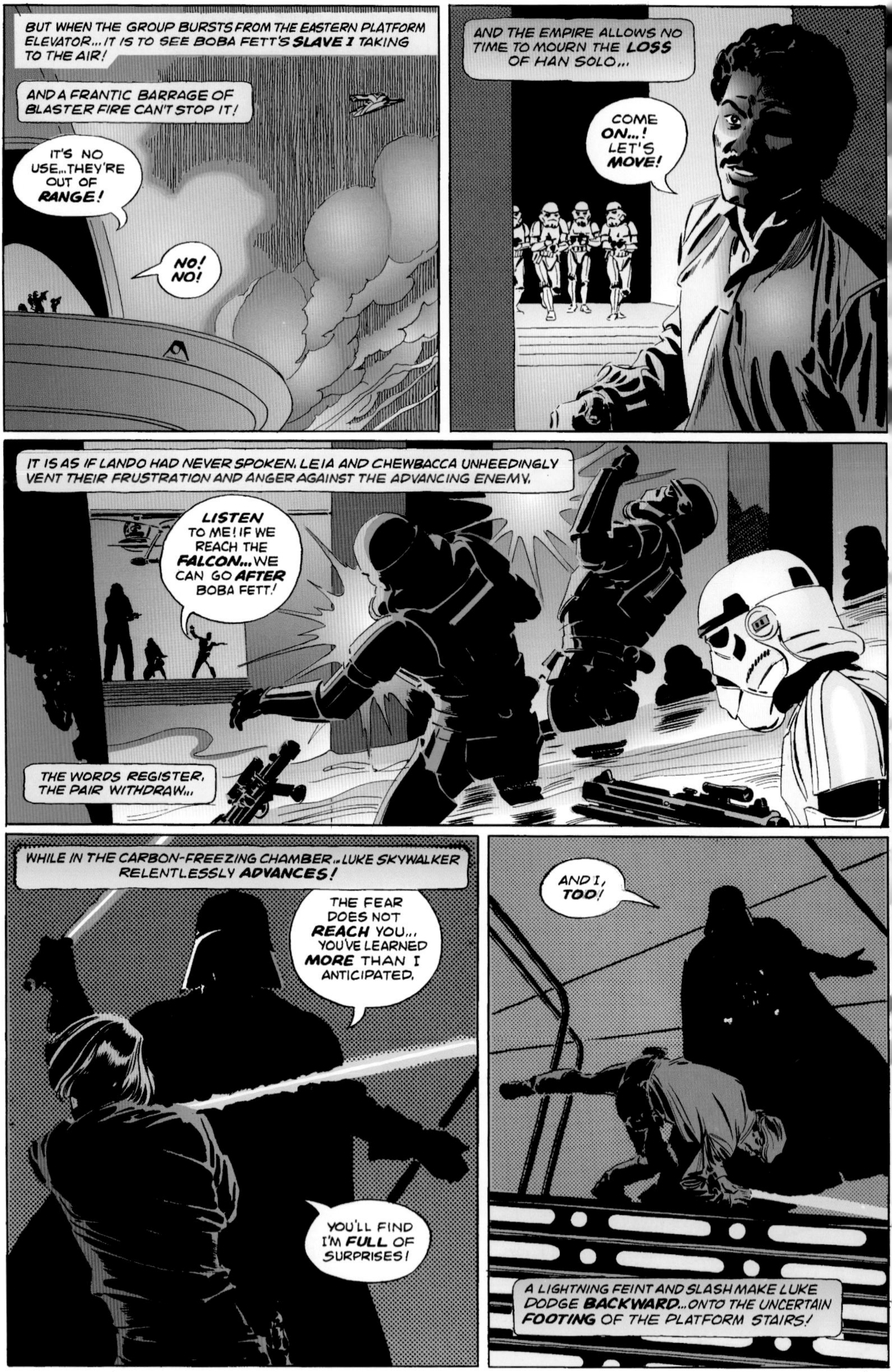

BUT WHEN THE GROUP BURSTS FROM THE EASTERN PLATFORM ELEVATOR... IT IS TO SEE BOBA FETT'S SLAVE I TAKING TO THE AIR!
AND A FRANTIC BARRAGE OF BLASTER FIRE CAN'T STOP IT!
IT'S NO USE...THEY'RE OUT OF RANGE!
NO! NO!
AND THE EMPIRE ALLOWS NO TIME TO MOURN THE LOSS OF HAN SOLO...
COME ON...! LET'S MOVE!
IT IS AS IF LANDO HAD NEVER SPOKEN. LEIA AND CHEWBACCA UNHEEDINGLY VENT THEIR FRUSTRATION AND ANGER AGAINST THE ADVANCING ENEMY.
LISTEN TO ME! IF WE REACH THE FALCON...WE CAN GO AFTER BOBA FETT!
THE WORDS REGISTER. THE PAIR WITHDRAW...
WHILE IN THE CARBON-FREEZING CHAMBER.. LUKE SKYWALKER RELENTLESSLY ADVANCES!
THE FEAR DOES NOT REACH YOU... YOU'VE LEARNED MORE THAN I ANTICIPATED.
YOU'LL FIND I'M FULL OF SURPRISES!
AND I, TOO!
A LIGHTNING FEINT AND SLASH MAKE LUKE DODGE BACKWARD...ONTO THE UNCERTAIN FOOTING OF THE PLATFORM STAIRS!

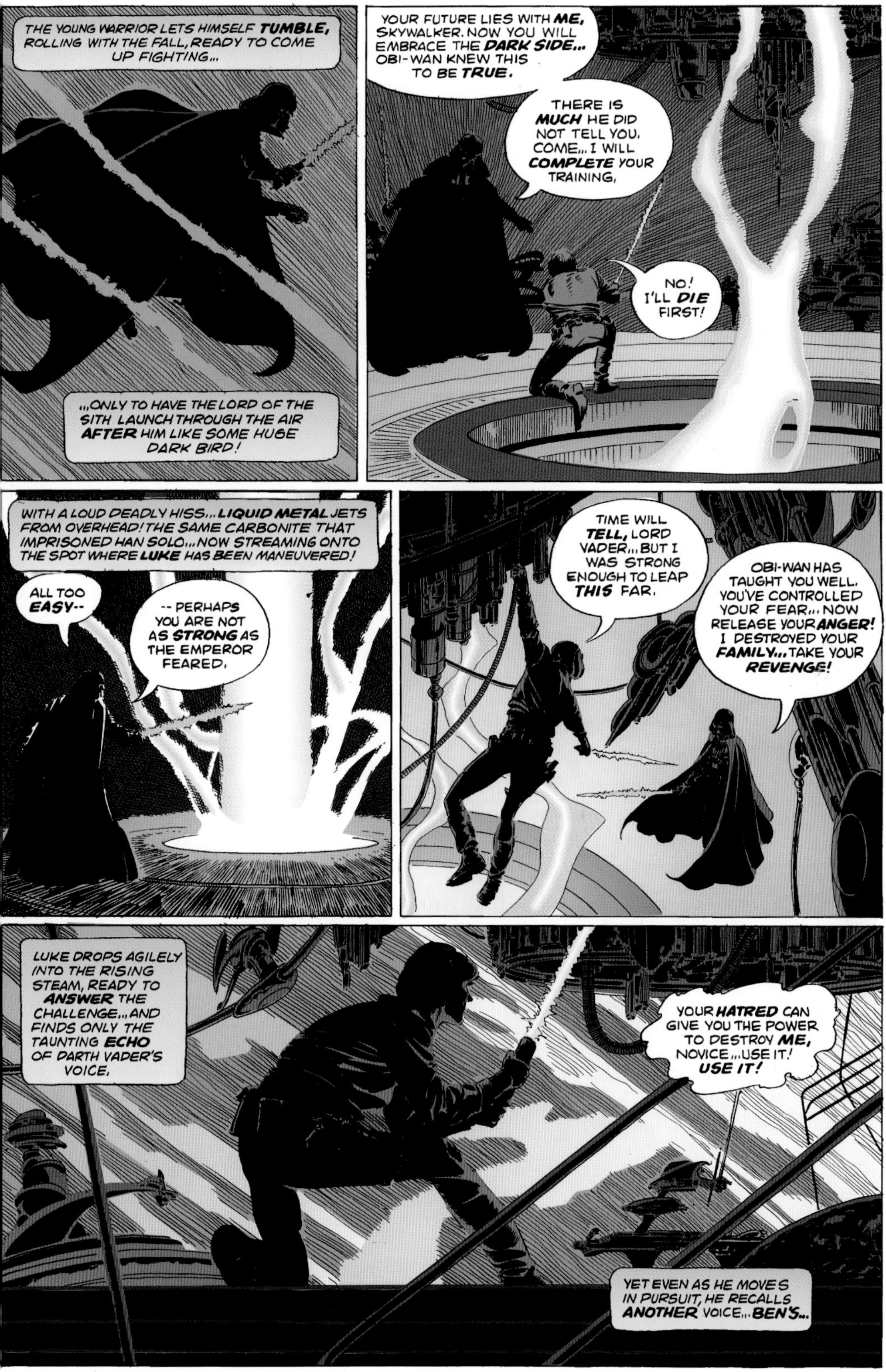
THE YOUNG WARRIOR LETS HIMSELF TUMBLE, ROLLING WITH THE FALL, READY TO COME UP FIGHTING...
...ONLY TO HAVE THE LORD OF THE SITH LAUNCH THROUGH THE AIR AFTER HIM LIKE SOME HUGE DARK BIRD!
YOUR FUTURE LIES WITH ME, SKYWALKER. NOW YOU WILL EMBRACE THE DARK SIDE... OBI-WAN KNEW THIS TO BE TRUE.
THERE IS MUCH HE DID NOT TELL YOU. COME... I WILL COMPLETE YOUR TRAINING.
NO! I'LL DIE FIRST!
WITH A LOUD DEADLY HISS... LIQUID METAL JETS FROM OVERHEAD! THE SAME CARBONITE THAT IMPRISONED HAN SOLO... NOW STREAMING ONTO THE SPOT WHERE LUKE HAS BEEN MANEUVERED!
ALL TOO EASY--
-- PERHAPS YOU ARE NOT AS STRONG AS THE EMPEROR FEARED.
TIME WILL TELL, LORD VADER... BUT I WAS STRONG ENOUGH TO LEAP THIS FAR.
OBI-WAN HAS TAUGHT YOU WELL. YOU'VE CONTROLLED YOUR FEAR... NOW RELEASE YOUR ANGER! I DESTROYED YOUR FAMILY... TAKE YOUR REVENGE!
LUKE DROPS AGILELY INTO THE RISING STEAM, READY TO ANSWER THE CHALLENGE... AND FINDS ONLY THE TAUNTING ECHO OF DARTH VADER'S VOICE.
YOUR HATRED CAN GIVE YOU THE POWER TO DESTROY ME, NOVICE... USE IT! USE IT!
YET EVEN AS HE MOVES IN PURSUIT, HE RECALLS ANOTHER VOICE... BEN'S...

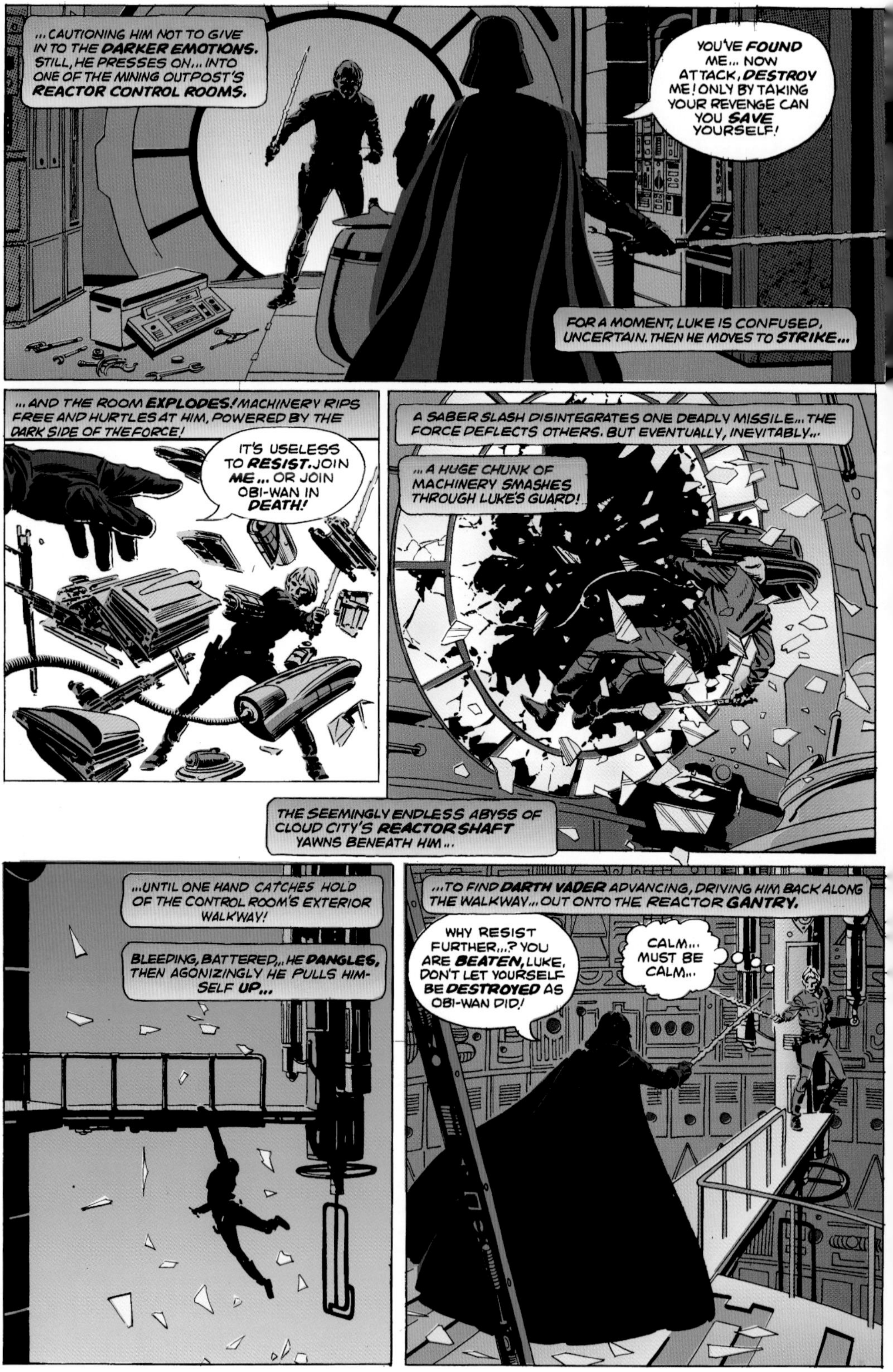
...CAUTIONING HIM NOT TO GIVE IN TO THE DARKER EMOTIONS. STILL, HE PRESSES ON... INTO ONE OF THE MINING OUTPOST'S REACTOR CONTROL ROOMS.
YOU'VE FOUND ME... NOW ATTACK, DESTROY ME! ONLY BY TAKING YOUR REVENGE CAN YOU SAVE YOURSELF!
FOR A MOMENT, LUKE IS CONFUSED, UNCERTAIN. THEN HE MOVES TO STRIKE...
...AND THE ROOM EXPLODES! MACHINERY RIPS FREE AND HURTLES AT HIM, POWERED BY THE DARK SIDE OF THE FORCE!
IT'S USELESS TO RESIST. JOIN ME... OR JOIN OBI-WAN IN DEATH!
A SABER SLASH DISINTEGRATES ONE DEADLY MISSILE... THE FORCE DEFLECTS OTHERS. BUT EVENTUALLY, INEVITABLY...
...A HUGE CHUNK OF MACHINERY SMASHES THROUGH LUKE'S GUARD!
THE SEEMINGLY ENDLESS ABYSS OF CLOUD CITY'S REACTOR SHAFT YAWNS BENEATH HIM...
...UNTIL ONE HAND CATCHES HOLD OF THE CONTROL ROOM'S EXTERIOR WALKWAY!
BLEEDING, BATTERED... HE DANGLES, THEN AGONIZINGLY HE PULLS HIMSELF UP...
...TO FIND DARTH VADER ADVANCING, DRIVING HIM BACK ALONG THE WALKWAY... OUT ONTO THE REACTOR GANTRY.
WHY RESIST FURTHER...? YOU ARE BEATEN, LUKE. DON'T LET YOURSELF BE DESTROYED AS OBI-WAN DID!
CALM... MUST BE CALM...

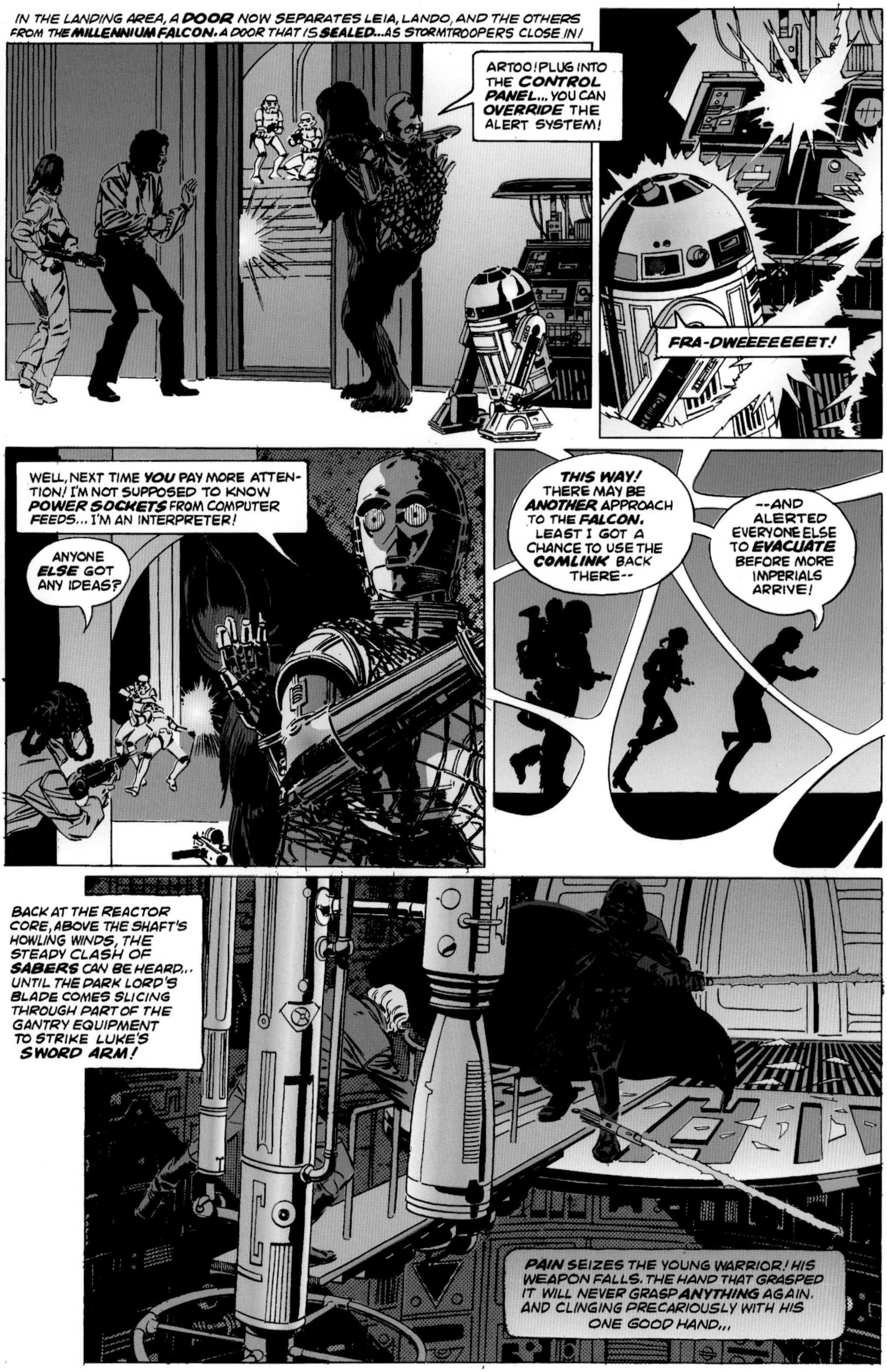
IN THE LANDING AREA, A DOOR NOW SEPARATES LEIA, LANDO, AND THE OTHERS FROM THE MILLENNIUM FALCON. A DOOR THAT IS SEALED...AS STORMTROOPERS CLOSE IN!
ARTOO! PLUG INTO THE CONTROL PANEL... YOU CAN OVERRIDE THE ALERT SYSTEM!
FRA-DWEEEEEEET!
WELL, NEXT TIME YOU PAY MORE ATTENTION! I'M NOT SUPPOSED TO KNOW POWER SOCKETS FROM COMPUTER FEEDS... I'M AN INTERPRETER!
ANYONE ELSE GOT ANY IDEAS?
THIS WAY! THERE MAY BE ANOTHER APPROACH TO THE FALCON. LEAST I GOT A CHANCE TO USE THE COMLINK BACK THERE--
--AND ALERTED EVERYONE ELSE TO EVACUATE BEFORE MORE IMPERIALS ARRIVE!
BACK AT THE REACTOR CORE, ABOVE THE SHAFT'S HOWLING WINDS, THE STEADY CLASH OF SABERS CAN BE HEARD... UNTIL THE DARK LORD'S BLADE COMES SLICING THROUGH PART OF THE GANTRY EQUIPMENT TO STRIKE LUKE'S SWORD ARM!
PAIN SEIZES THE YOUNG WARRIOR! HIS WEAPON FALLS. THE HAND THAT GRASPED IT WILL NEVER GRASP ANYTHING AGAIN. AND CLINGING PRECARIOUSLY WITH HIS ONE GOOD HAND...

...HE FACES DARTH VADER AND **DEATH.**

THERE IS NO **ESCAPE,** LUKE, DON'T MAKE ME **SLAY** YOU... **JOIN** ME, TOGETHER WE WILL BE MORE **POWERFUL** THAN THE EMPEROR--

IT WAS **MEANT** TO BE! THERE ARE **MANY** THINGS OBI-WAN HAS KEPT FROM YOU, SUCH AS WHAT HAPPENED TO YOUR **FATHER...**

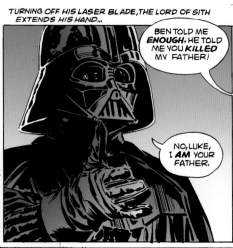

TURNING OFF HIS LASER BLADE, THE LORD OF SITH EXTENDS HIS HAND...

BEN TOLD ME **ENOUGH.** HE TOLD ME YOU **KILLED** MY FATHER!

NO, LUKE, I **AM** YOUR FATHER.

N-NO... THAT... **CAN'T** BE! I-IT'S... **IMPOSSIBLE!**

SEARCH YOUR FEELINGS, YOUNGSTER, YOU **KNOW** IT TO BE TRUE.

NO...! NO...!

LUKE, YOU CAN **DESTROY** THE EMPEROR... HE HAS **FORESEEN** THIS. WE CAN RULE THE **GALAXY** TOGETHER... **FATHER** AND **SON!** COME WITH ME... IT'S THE **ONLY** WAY.

STUNNED, LUKE PONDERS, THEN SUDDENLY REALIZES THAT HE HAS NO **CHOICE...**

...AND STEPS OFF INTO NOTHINGNESS!

NEVERRRRR

VADER STARES AS THE YOUTH VANISHES INTO THE DARKNESS. IT IS **OVER.** THE SHAFT'S CHANGING AIR CURRENTS MAY CUSHION HIM MOMENTARILY, BUT SOMEWHERE BELOW ARE **EXHAUST VENTS.** CERTAINLY THE BOY WILL BE DRAGGED INTO ONE OF THESE... AND SPEWED OUT OF CLOUD CITY **MILES** ABOVE THE GASEOUS SURFACE OF BESPIN.

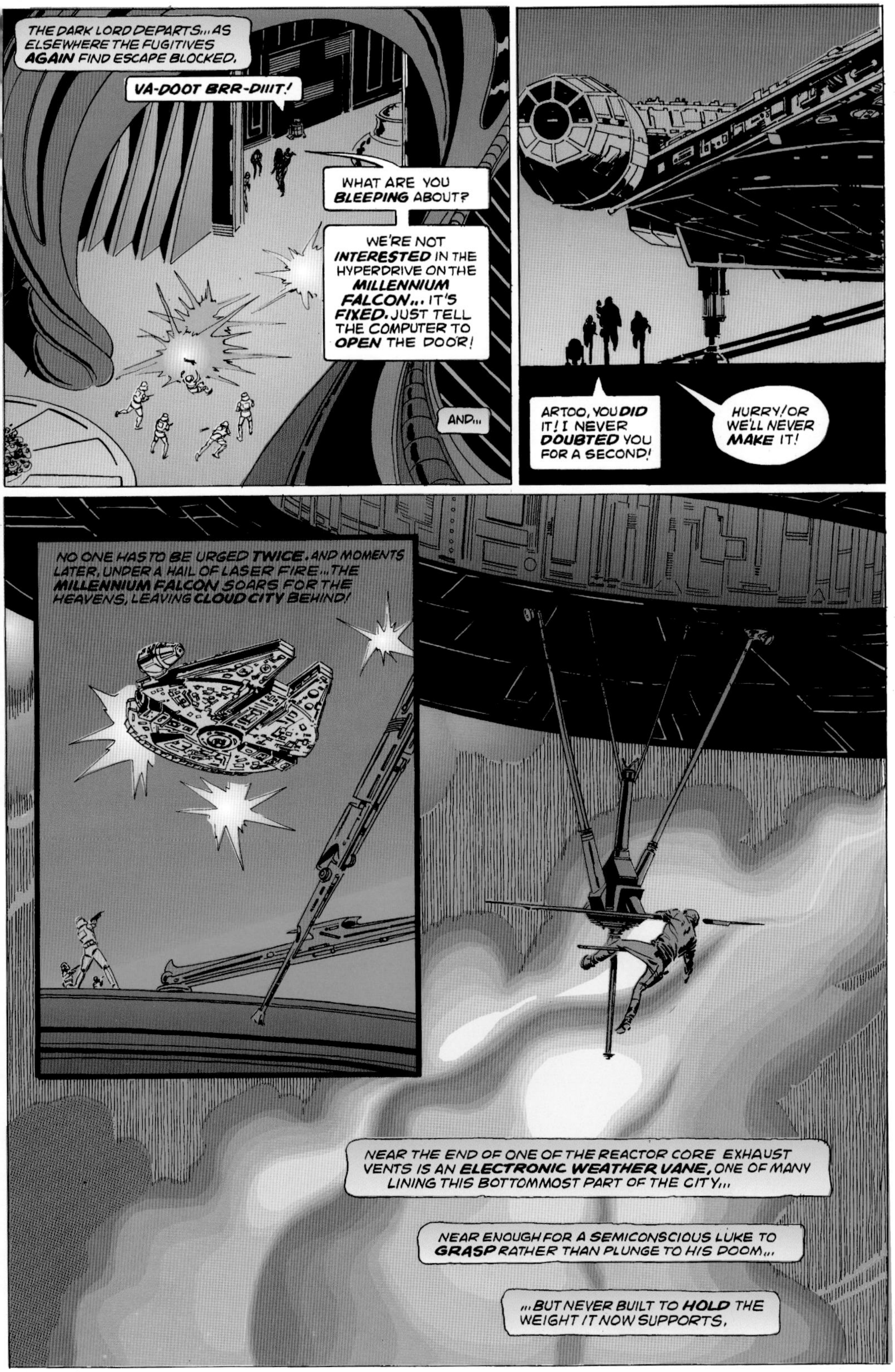

THE DARK LORD DEPARTS... AS ELSEWHERE THE FUGITIVES AGAIN FIND ESCAPE BLOCKED.
VA-DOOT BRR-DIIIT!
WHAT ARE YOU BLEEPING ABOUT?
WE'RE NOT INTERESTED IN THE HYPERDRIVE ON THE MILLENNIUM FALCON... IT'S FIXED. JUST TELL THE COMPUTER TO OPEN THE DOOR!
AND...
ARTOO, YOU DID IT! I NEVER DOUBTED YOU FOR A SECOND!
HURRY! OR WE'LL NEVER MAKE IT!
NO ONE HAS TO BE URGED TWICE. AND MOMENTS LATER, UNDER A HAIL OF LASER FIRE... THE MILLENNIUM FALCON SOARS FOR THE HEAVENS, LEAVING CLOUD CITY BEHIND!
NEAR THE END OF ONE OF THE REACTOR CORE EXHAUST VENTS IS AN ELECTRONIC WEATHER VANE, ONE OF MANY LINING THIS BOTTOMMOST PART OF THE CITY...
NEAR ENOUGH FOR A SEMICONSCIOUS LUKE TO GRASP RATHER THAN PLUNGE TO HIS DOOM...
...BUT NEVER BUILT TO HOLD THE WEIGHT IT NOW SUPPORTS.

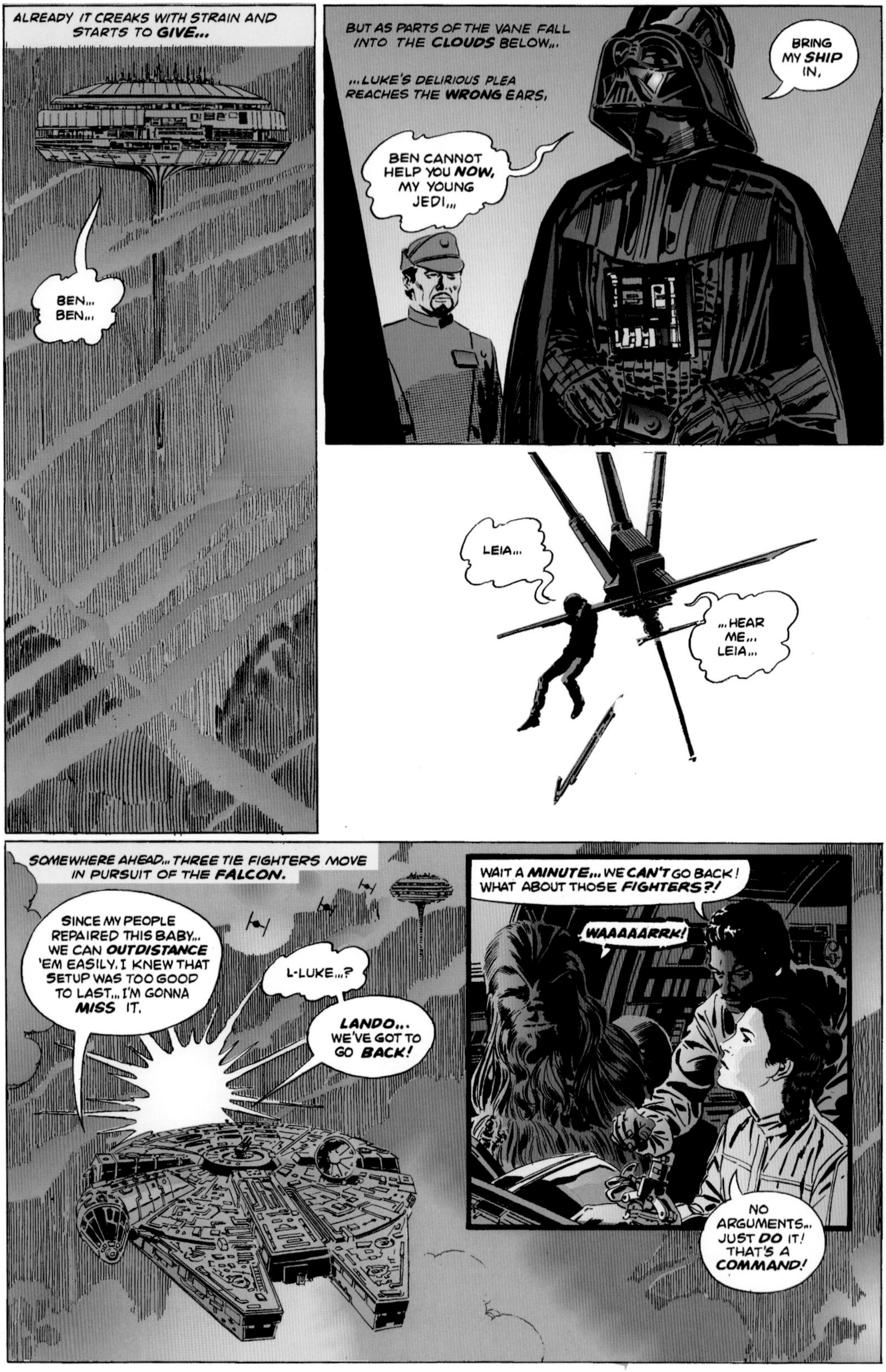

ALREADY IT CREAKS WITH STRAIN AND STARTS TO GIVE...
BEN... BEN...
BUT AS PARTS OF THE VANE FALL INTO THE CLOUDS BELOW...
...LUKE'S DELIRIOUS PLEA REACHES THE WRONG EARS.
BEN CANNOT HELP YOU NOW, MY YOUNG JEDI...
BRING MY SHIP IN.
LEIA...
...HEAR ME... LEIA...
SOMEWHERE AHEAD... THREE TIE FIGHTERS MOVE IN PURSUIT OF THE FALCON.
SINCE MY PEOPLE REPAIRED THIS BABY... WE CAN OUTDISTANCE 'EM EASILY. I KNEW THAT SETUP WAS TOO GOOD TO LAST... I'M GONNA MISS IT.
L-LUKE...?
LANDO... WE'VE GOT TO GO BACK!
WAIT A MINUTE... WE CAN'T GO BACK! WHAT ABOUT THOSE FIGHTERS?!
WAAAAARRK!
NO ARGUMENTS... JUST DO IT! THAT'S A COMMAND!

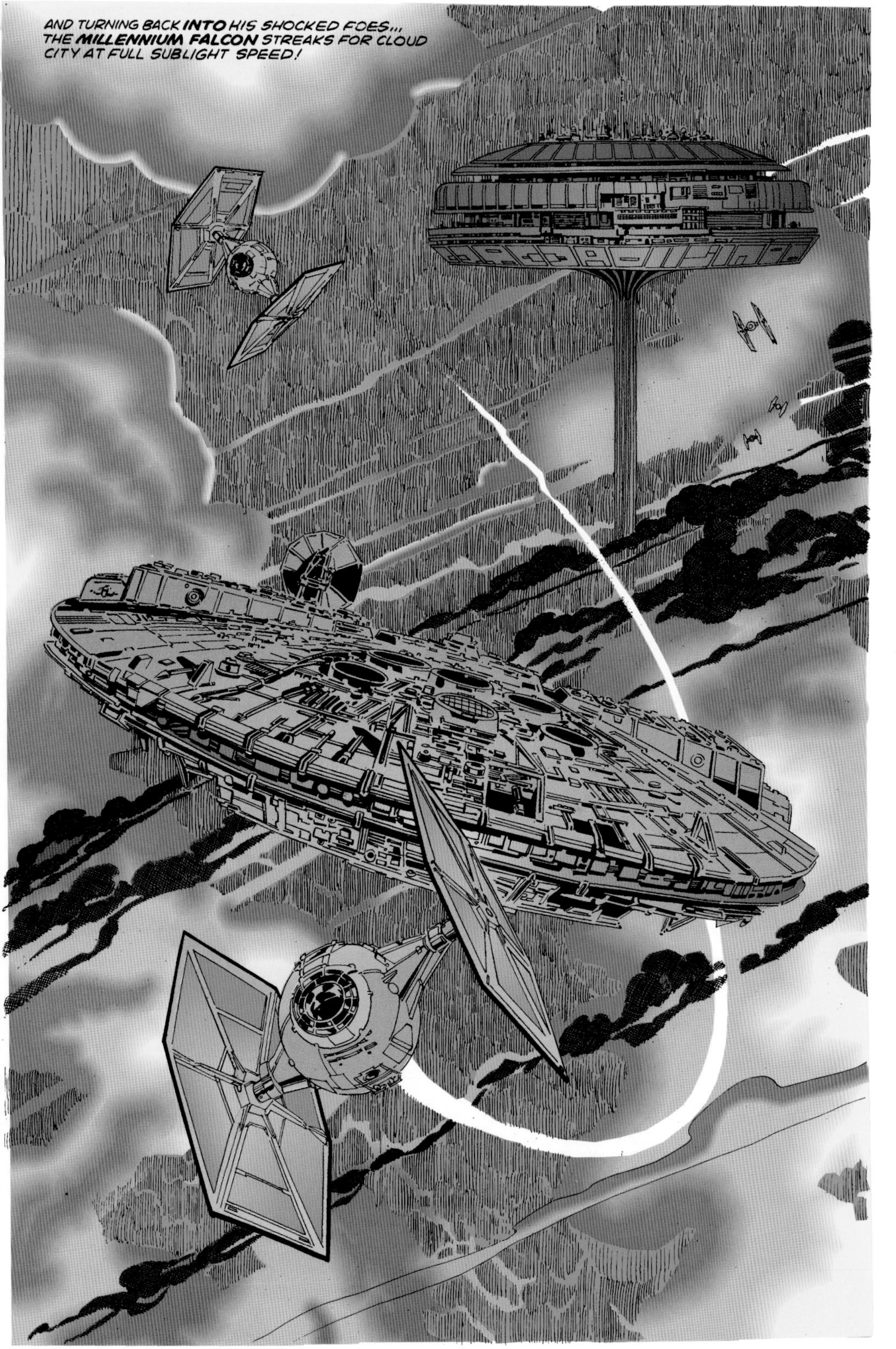
AND TURNING BACK INTO HIS SHOCKED FOES... THE MILLENNIUM FALCON STREAKS FOR CLOUD CITY AT FULL SUBLIGHT SPEED!

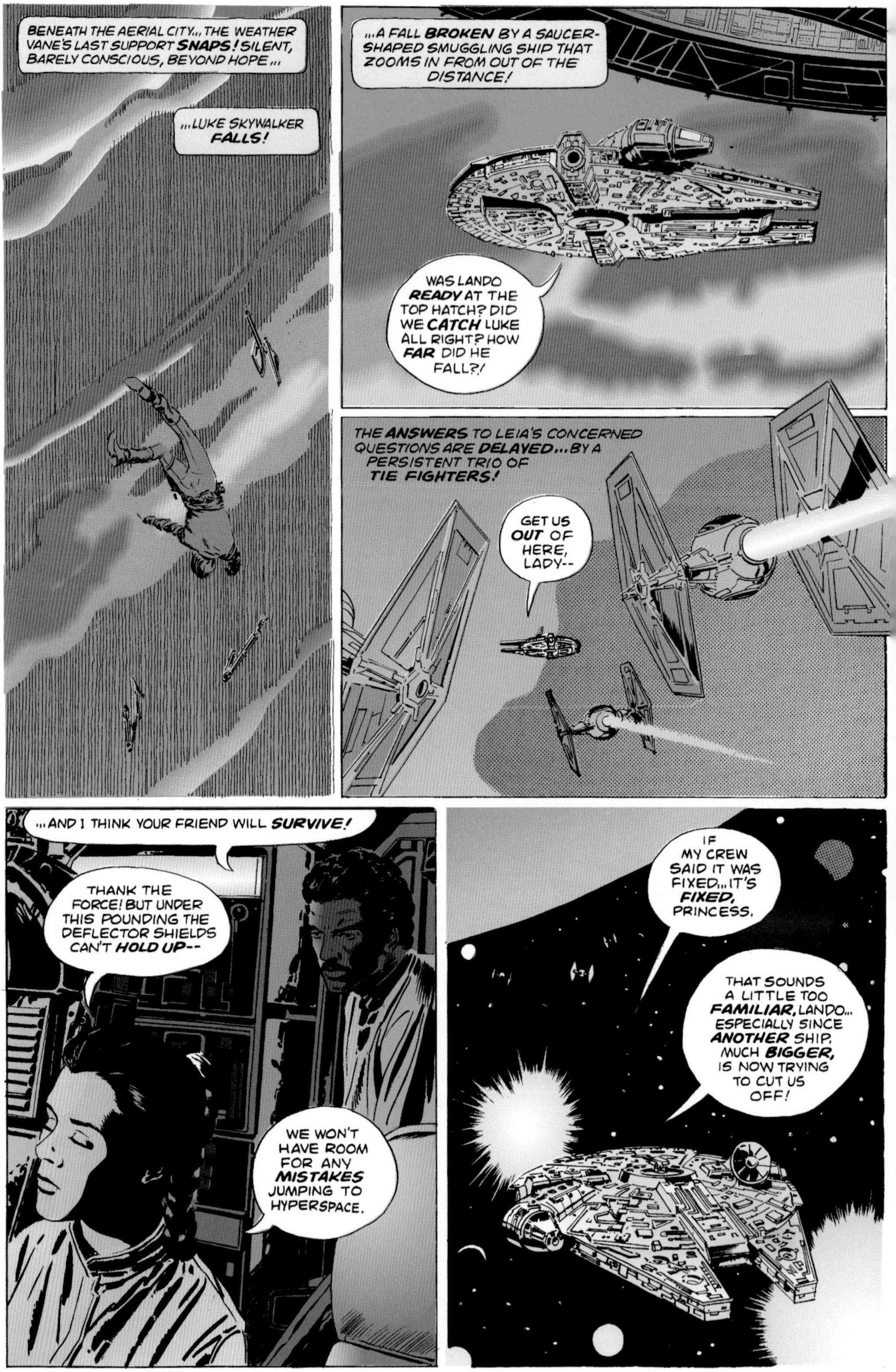
BENEATH THE AERIAL CITY... THE WEATHER VANE'S LAST SUPPORT SNAPS! SILENT, BARELY CONSCIOUS, BEYOND HOPE...
...LUKE SKYWALKER FALLS!
...A FALL BROKEN BY A SAUCER-SHAPED SMUGGLING SHIP THAT ZOOMS IN FROM OUT OF THE DISTANCE!
WAS LANDO READY AT THE TOP HATCH? DID WE CATCH LUKE ALL RIGHT? HOW FAR DID HE FALL?!
THE ANSWERS TO LEIA'S CONCERNED QUESTIONS ARE DELAYED... BY A PERSISTENT TRIO OF TIE FIGHTERS!
GET US OUT OF HERE, LADY--
...AND I THINK YOUR FRIEND WILL SURVIVE!
THANK THE FORCE! BUT UNDER THIS POUNDING THE DEFLECTOR SHIELDS CAN'T HOLD UP--
WE WON'T HAVE ROOM FOR ANY MISTAKES JUMPING TO HYPERSPACE.
IF MY CREW SAID IT WAS FIXED... IT'S FIXED, PRINCESS.
THAT SOUNDS A LITTLE TOO FAMILIAR, LANDO... ESPECIALLY SINCE ANOTHER SHIP, MUCH BIGGER, IS NOW TRYING TO CUT US OFF!

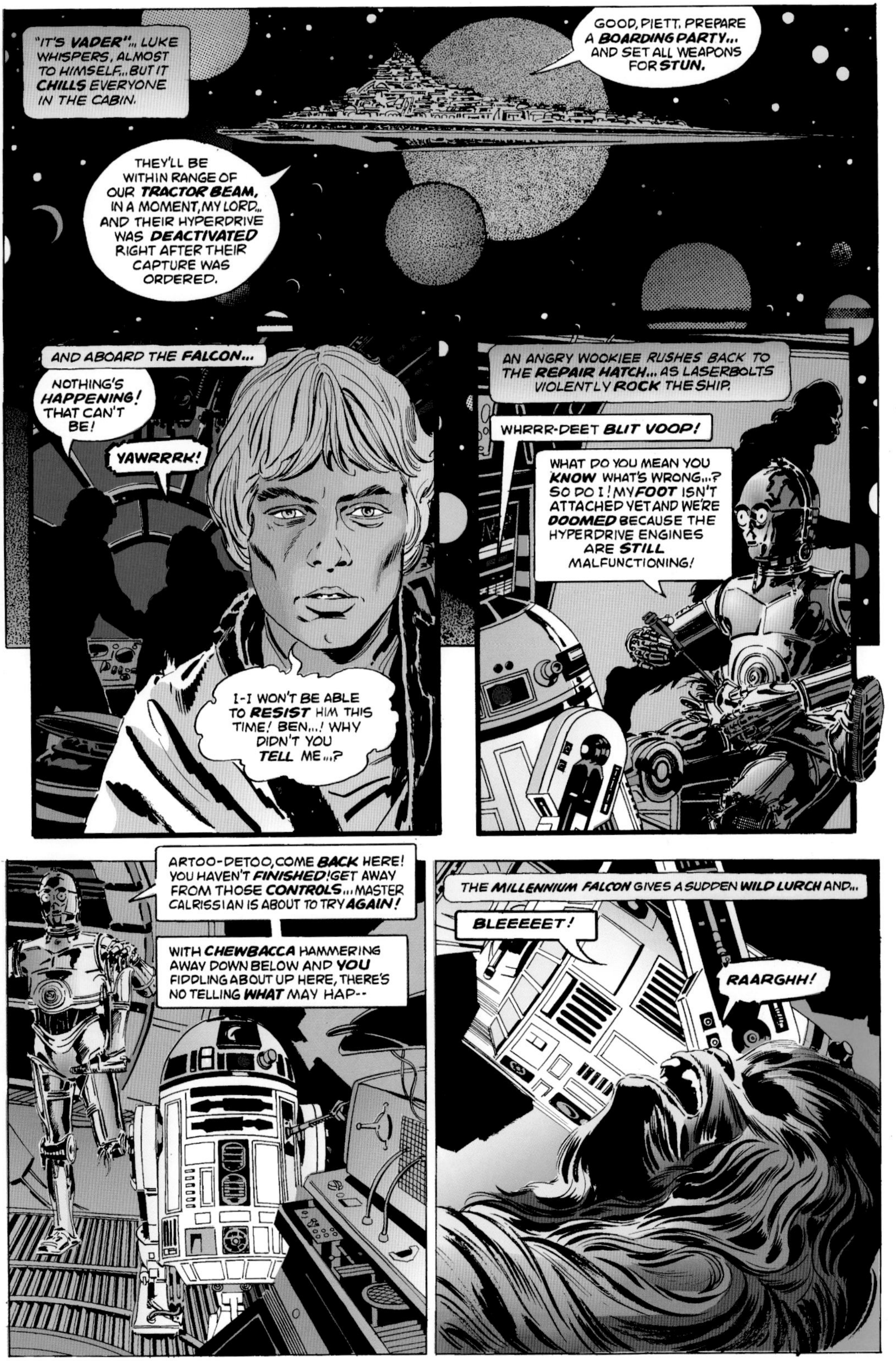
"IT'S VADER"... LUKE WHISPERS, ALMOST TO HIMSELF... BUT IT CHILLS EVERYONE IN THE CABIN.
GOOD, PIETT. PREPARE A BOARDING PARTY... AND SET ALL WEAPONS FOR STUN.
THEY'LL BE WITHIN RANGE OF OUR TRACTOR BEAM, IN A MOMENT, MY LORD... AND THEIR HYPERDRIVE WAS DEACTIVATED RIGHT AFTER THEIR CAPTURE WAS ORDERED.
AND ABOARD THE FALCON...
NOTHING'S HAPPENING! THAT CAN'T BE!
YAWRRRK!
I-I WON'T BE ABLE TO RESIST HIM THIS TIME! BEN...! WHY DIDN'T YOU TELL ME...?
AN ANGRY WOOKIEE RUSHES BACK TO THE REPAIR HATCH... AS LASERBOLTS VIOLENTLY ROCK THE SHIP.
WHRRR-DEET BLIT VOOP!
WHAT DO YOU MEAN YOU KNOW WHAT'S WRONG...? SO DO I! MY FOOT ISN'T ATTACHED YET AND WE'RE DOOMED BECAUSE THE HYPERDRIVE ENGINES ARE STILL MALFUNCTIONING!
ARTOO-DETOO, COME BACK HERE! YOU HAVEN'T FINISHED! GET AWAY FROM THOSE CONTROLS... MASTER CALRISSIAN IS ABOUT TO TRY AGAIN!
WITH CHEWBACCA HAMMERING AWAY DOWN BELOW AND YOU FIDDLING ABOUT UP HERE, THERE'S NO TELLING WHAT MAY HAP--
THE MILLENNIUM FALCON GIVES A SUDDEN WILD LURCH AND...
BLEEEEET!
RAARGHH!

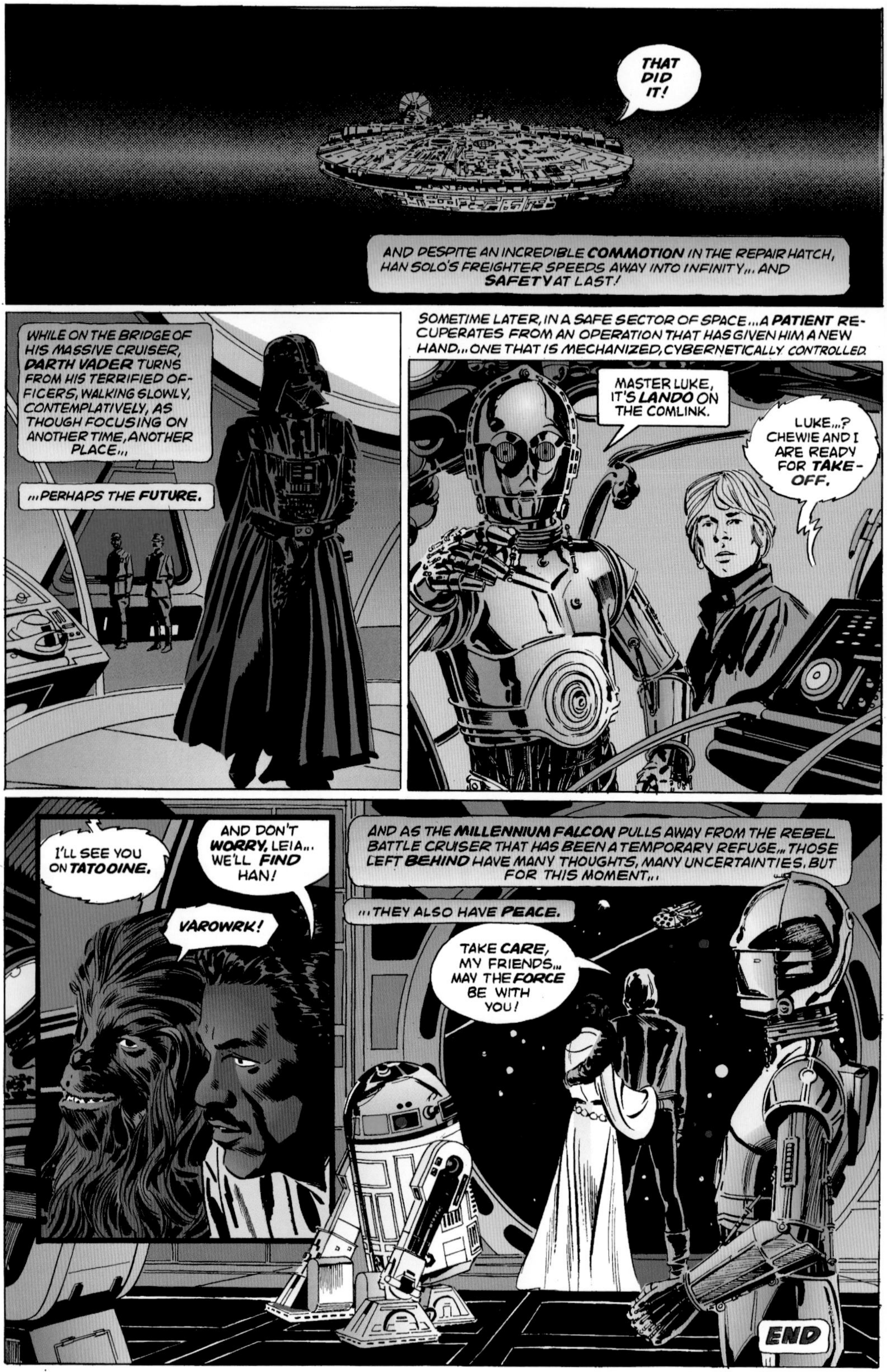
THAT DID IT!
AND DESPITE AN INCREDIBLE COMMOTION IN THE REPAIR HATCH, HAN SOLO'S FREIGHTER SPEEDS AWAY INTO INFINITY... AND SAFETY AT LAST!
WHILE ON THE BRIDGE OF HIS MASSIVE CRUISER, DARTH VADER TURNS FROM HIS TERRIFIED OF-FICERS, WALKING SLOWLY, CONTEMPLATIVELY, AS THOUGH FOCUSING ON ANOTHER TIME, ANOTHER PLACE...
...PERHAPS THE FUTURE.
SOMETIME LATER, IN A SAFE SECTOR OF SPACE...A PATIENT RE-CUPERATES FROM AN OPERATION THAT HAS GIVEN HIM A NEW HAND... ONE THAT IS MECHANIZED, CYBERNETICALLY CONTROLLED.
MASTER LUKE, IT'S LANDO ON THE COMLINK.
LUKE...? CHEWIE AND I ARE READY FOR TAKE-OFF.
I'LL SEE YOU ON TATOOINE.
AND DON'T WORRY, LEIA... WE'LL FIND HAN!
VAROWRK!
AND AS THE MILLENNIUM FALCON PULLS AWAY FROM THE REBEL BATTLE CRUISER THAT HAS BEEN A TEMPORARY REFUGE... THOSE LEFT BEHIND HAVE MANY THOUGHTS, MANY UNCERTAINTIES. BUT FOR THIS MOMENT...
...THEY ALSO HAVE PEACE.
TAKE CARE, MY FRIENDS... MAY THE FORCE BE WITH YOU!
END

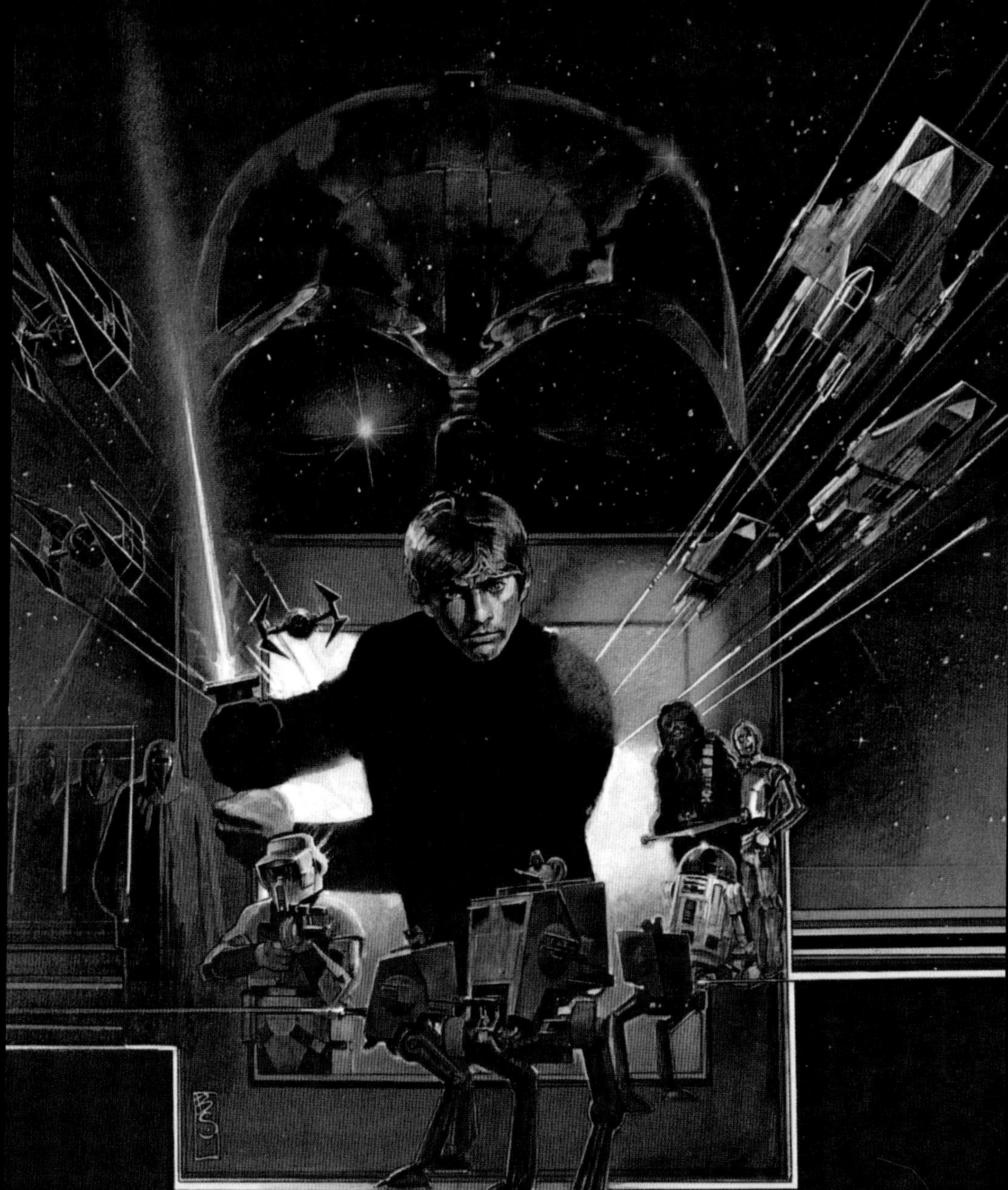

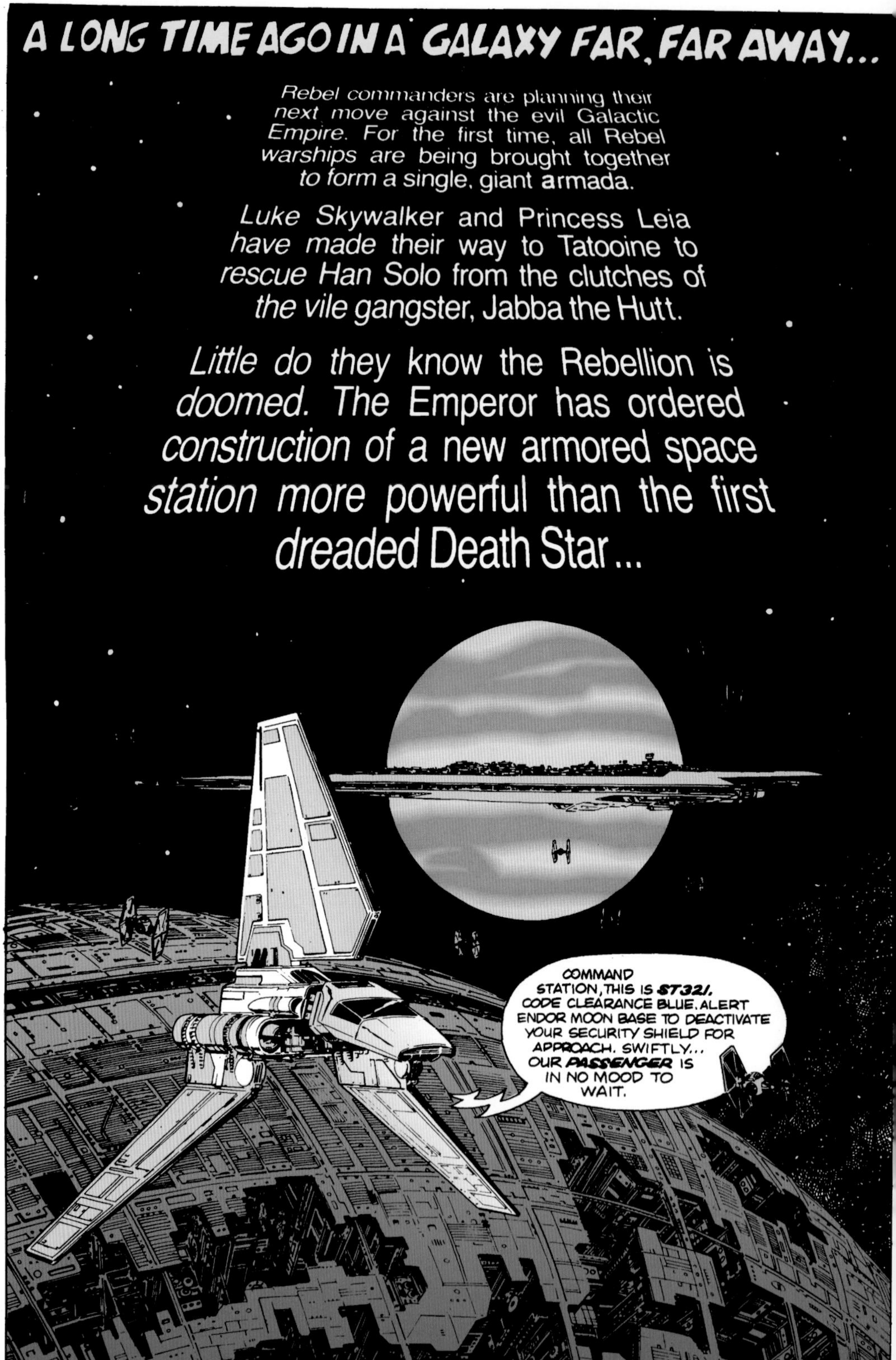
A LONG TIME AGO IN A GALAXY FAR, FAR AWAY...
Rebel commanders are planning their next move against the evil Galactic Empire. For the first time, all Rebel warships are being brought together to form a single, giant armada.
Luke Skywalker and Princess Leia have made their way to Tatooine to rescue Han Solo from the clutches of the vile gangster, Jabba the Hutt.
Little do they know the Rebellion is doomed. The Emperor has ordered construction of a new armored space station more powerful than the first dreaded Death Star...
COMMAND STATION, THIS IS ST321. CODE CLEARANCE BLUE. ALERT ENDOR MOON BASE TO DEACTIVATE YOUR SECURITY SHIELD FOR APPROACH. SWIFTLY... OUR PASSENGER IS IN NO MOOD TO WAIT.

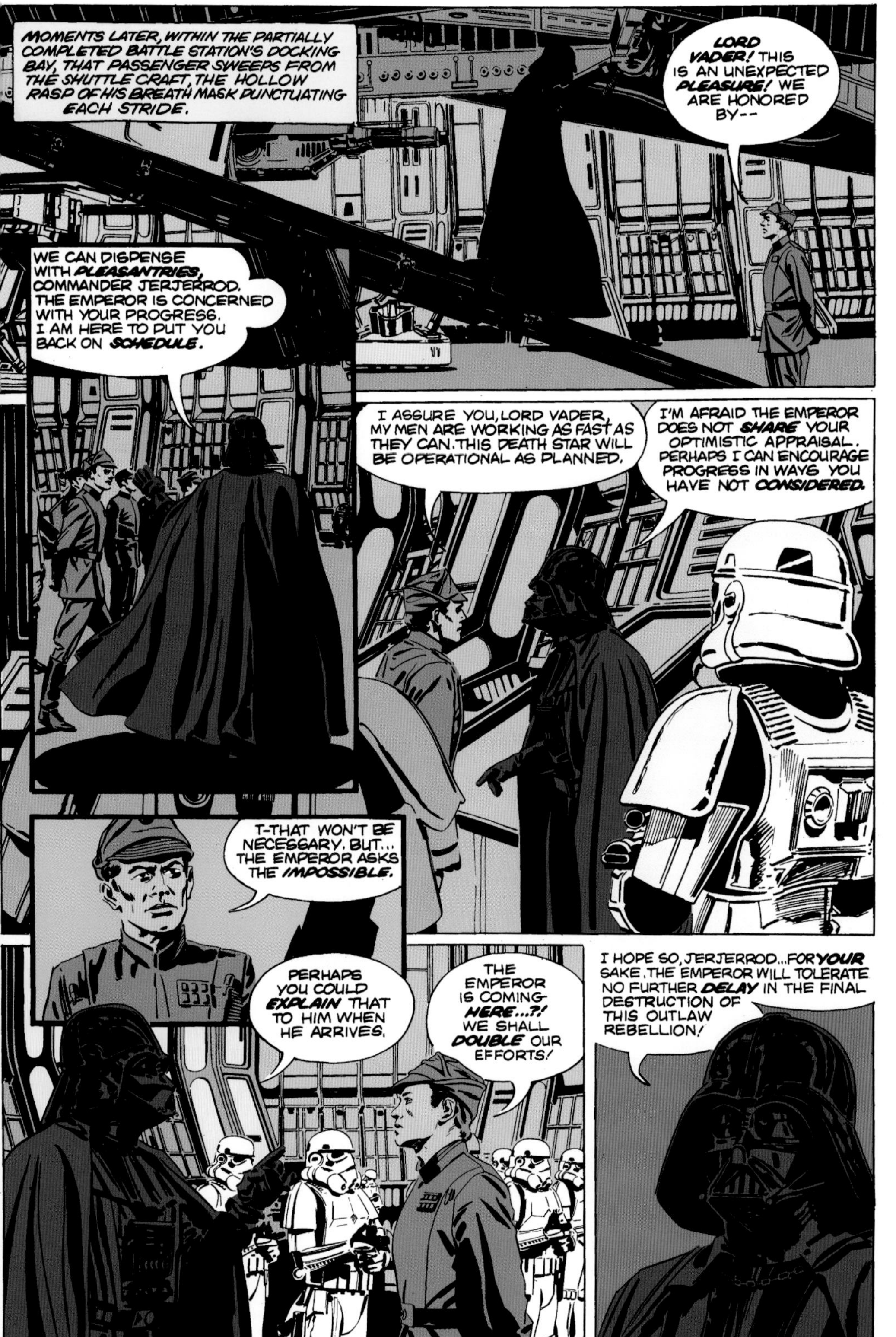
MOMENTS LATER, WITHIN THE PARTIALLY COMPLETED BATTLE STATION'S DOCKING BAY, THAT PASSENGER SWEEPS FROM THE SHUTTLE CRAFT, THE HOLLOW RASP OF HIS BREATH MASK PUNCTUATING EACH STRIDE.
LORD VADER! THIS IS AN UNEXPECTED PLEASURE! WE ARE HONORED BY--
WE CAN DISPENSE WITH PLEASANTRIES, COMMANDER JERJERROD. THE EMPEROR IS CONCERNED WITH YOUR PROGRESS. I AM HERE TO PUT YOU BACK ON SCHEDULE.
I ASSURE YOU, LORD VADER, MY MEN ARE WORKING AS FAST AS THEY CAN. THIS DEATH STAR WILL BE OPERATIONAL AS PLANNED.
I'M AFRAID THE EMPEROR DOES NOT SHARE YOUR OPTIMISTIC APPRAISAL. PERHAPS I CAN ENCOURAGE PROGRESS IN WAYS YOU HAVE NOT CONSIDERED.
T-THAT WON'T BE NECESSARY. BUT... THE EMPEROR ASKS THE IMPOSSIBLE.
PERHAPS YOU COULD EXPLAIN THAT TO HIM WHEN HE ARRIVES.
THE EMPEROR IS COMING HERE...?! WE SHALL DOUBLE OUR EFFORTS!
I HOPE SO, JERJERROD... FOR YOUR SAKE. THE EMPEROR WILL TOLERATE NO FURTHER DELAY IN THE FINAL DESTRUCTION OF THIS OUTLAW REBELLION!

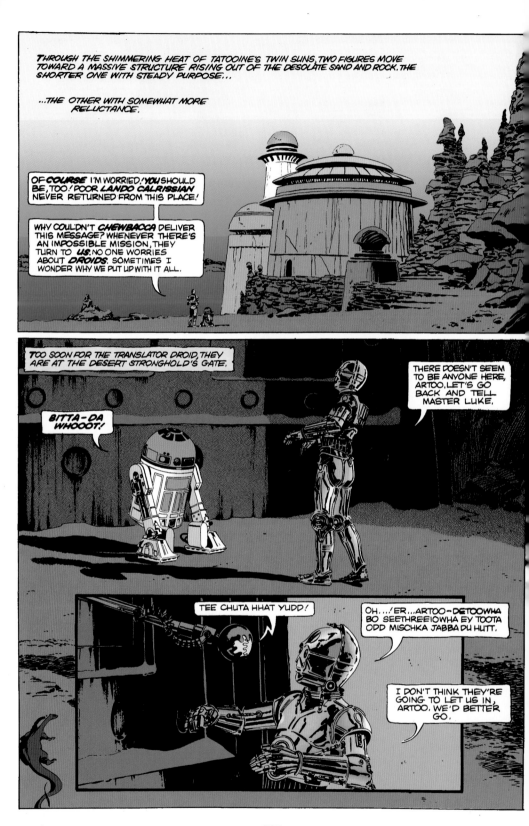

THROUGH THE SHIMMERING HEAT OF TATOOINE'S TWIN SUNS, TWO FIGURES MOVE TOWARD A MASSIVE STRUCTURE RISING OUT OF THE DESOLATE SAND AND ROCK. THE SHORTER ONE WITH STEADY PURPOSE...

...THE OTHER WITH SOMEWHAT MORE RELUCTANCE.

OF *COURSE* I'M WORRIED.' *YOU* SHOULD BE, TOO.' POOR *LANDO CALRISSIAN* NEVER RETURNED FROM THIS PLACE!

WHY COULDN'T *CHEWBACCA* DELIVER THIS MESSAGE? WHENEVER THERE'S AN IMPOSSIBLE MISSION, THEY TURN TO *US*. NO ONE WORRIES ABOUT *DROIDS*. SOMETIMES I WONDER WHY WE PUT UP WITH IT ALL.

TOO SOON FOR THE TRANSLATOR DROID, THEY ARE AT THE DESERT STRONGHOLD'S GATE.

THERE DOESN'T SEEM TO BE ANYONE HERE, ARTOO, LET'S GO BACK AND TELL MASTER LUKE.

BITTA-DA WHOOOT!

TEE CHUTA HHAT YUDD!

OH,.../ER...ARTOO-DETOOWHA BO SEETHREEIOWHA EY TOOTA ODD MISCHKA JABBA DU HUTT.

I DON'T THINK THEY'RE GOING TO LET US IN, ARTOO, WE'D BETTER GO.

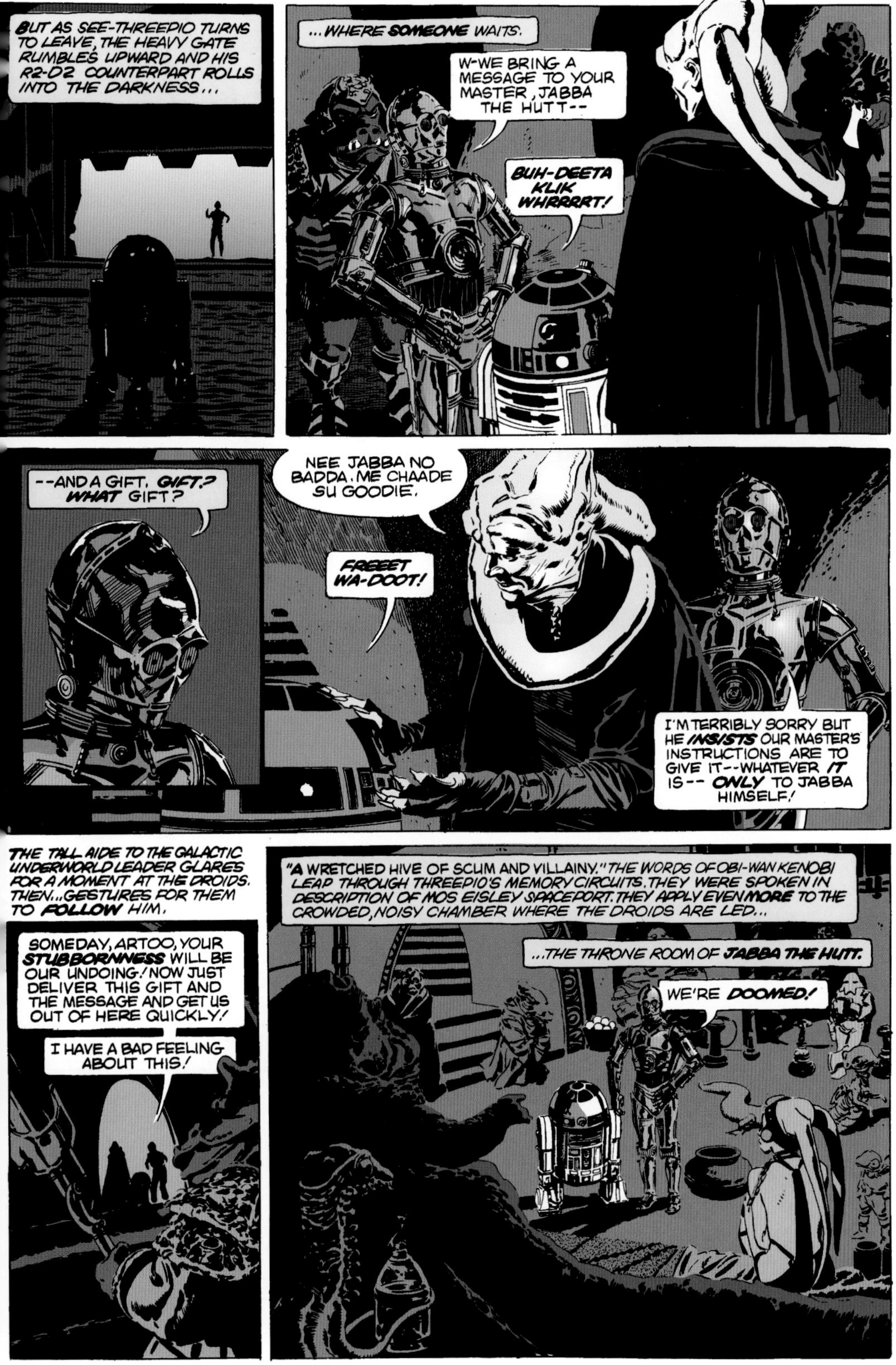

BUT AS SEE-THREEPIO TURNS TO LEAVE, THE HEAVY GATE RUMBLES UPWARD AND HIS R2-D2 COUNTERPART ROLLS INTO THE DARKNESS...
...WHERE SOMEONE WAITS.
W-WE BRING A MESSAGE TO YOUR MASTER, JABBA THE HUTT--
BUH-DEETA KLIK WHRRRRT!
--AND A GIFT. GIFT? WHAT GIFT?
NEE JABBA NO BADDA. ME CHAADE SU GOODIE.
FREEEET WA-DOOT!
I'M TERRIBLY SORRY BUT HE INSISTS OUR MASTER'S INSTRUCTIONS ARE TO GIVE IT--WHATEVER IT IS-- ONLY TO JABBA HIMSELF!
THE TALL AIDE TO THE GALACTIC UNDERWORLD LEADER GLARES FOR A MOMENT AT THE DROIDS. THEN...GESTURES FOR THEM TO FOLLOW HIM.
SOMEDAY, ARTOO, YOUR STUBBORNNESS WILL BE OUR UNDOING! NOW JUST DELIVER THIS GIFT AND THE MESSAGE AND GET US OUT OF HERE QUICKLY!
I HAVE A BAD FEELING ABOUT THIS!
"A WRETCHED HIVE OF SCUM AND VILLAINY." THE WORDS OF OBI-WAN KENOBI LEAP THROUGH THREEPIO'S MEMORY CIRCUITS. THEY WERE SPOKEN IN DESCRIPTION OF MOS EISLEY SPACEPORT. THEY APPLY EVEN MORE TO THE CROWDED, NOISY CHAMBER WHERE THE DROIDS ARE LED...
...THE THRONE ROOM OF JABBA THE HUTT.
WE'RE DOOMED!

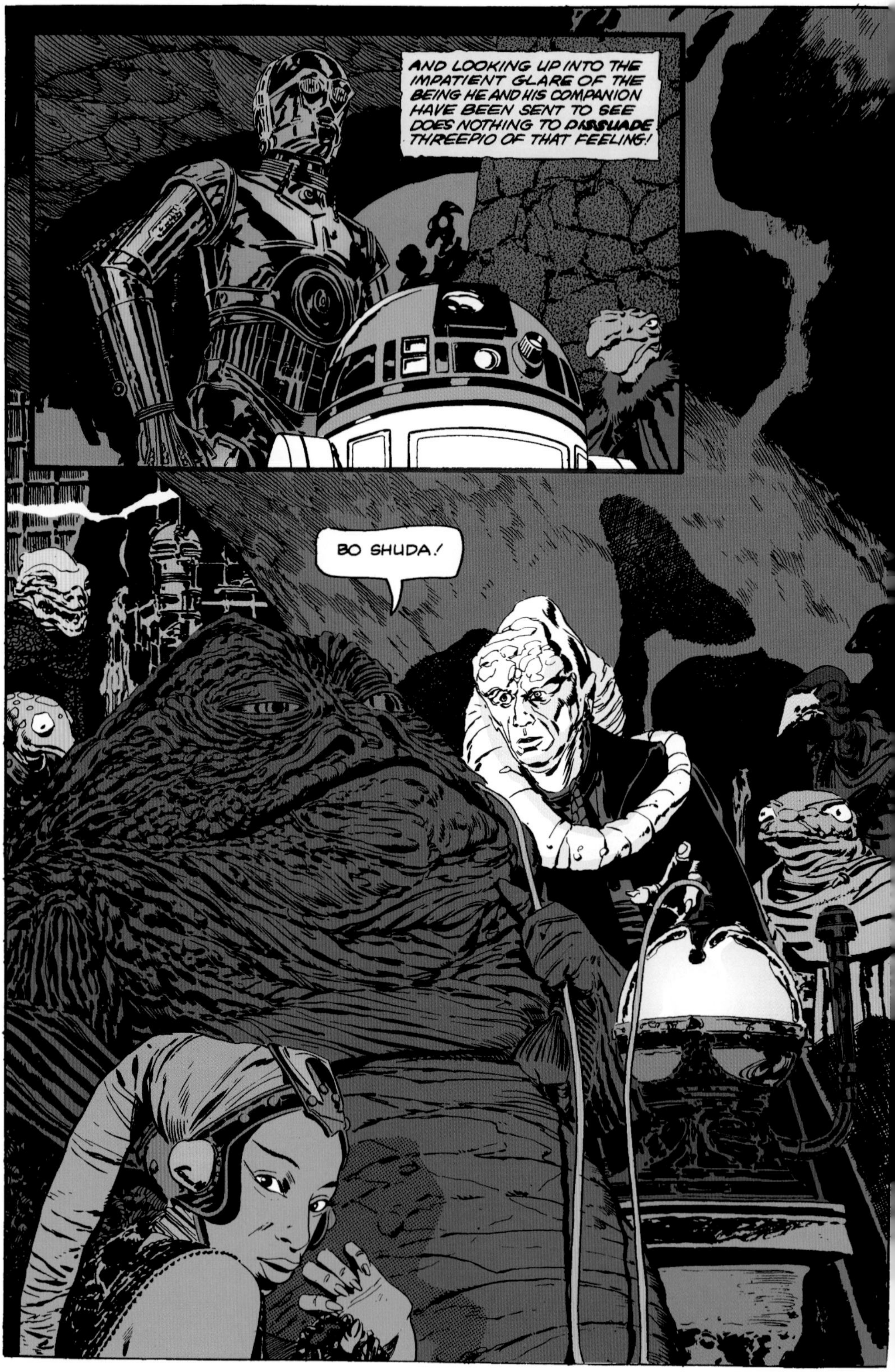
AND LOOKING UP INTO THE IMPATIENT GLARE OF THE BEING HE AND HIS COMPANION HAVE BEEN SENT TO SEE DOES NOTHING TO DISSUADE THREEPIO OF THAT FEELING!
BO SHUDA!

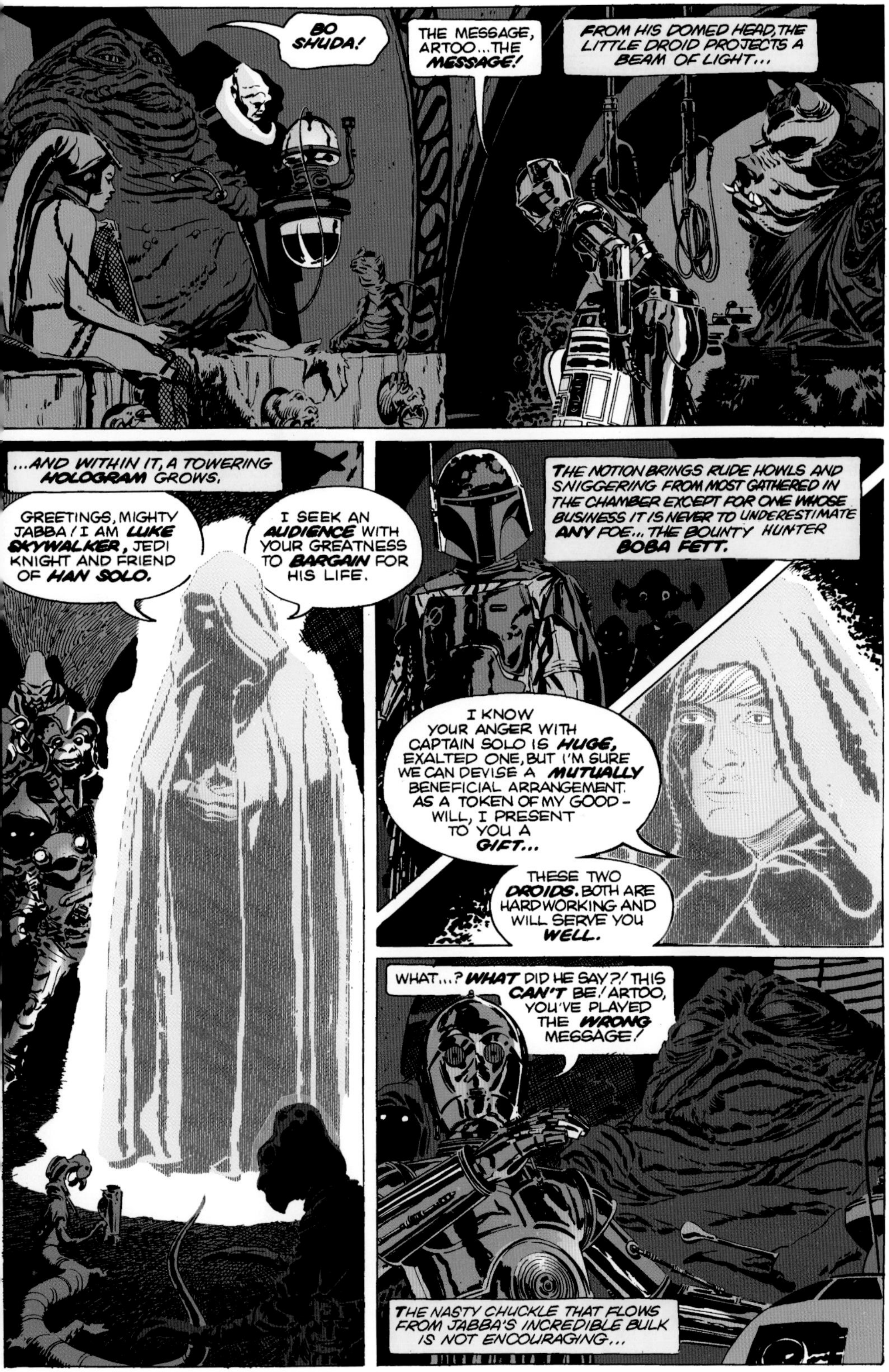
BO SHUDA!
THE MESSAGE, ARTOO...THE MESSAGE!
FROM HIS DOMED HEAD, THE LITTLE DROID PROJECTS A BEAM OF LIGHT...
...AND WITHIN IT, A TOWERING HOLOGRAM GROWS.
GREETINGS, MIGHTY JABBA! I AM LUKE SKYWALKER, JEDI KNIGHT AND FRIEND OF HAN SOLO.
I SEEK AN AUDIENCE WITH YOUR GREATNESS TO BARGAIN FOR HIS LIFE.
THE NOTION BRINGS RUDE HOWLS AND SNIGGERING FROM MOST GATHERED IN THE CHAMBER EXCEPT FOR ONE WHOSE BUSINESS IT IS NEVER TO UNDERESTIMATE ANY FOE... THE BOUNTY HUNTER BOBA FETT.
I KNOW YOUR ANGER WITH CAPTAIN SOLO IS HUGE, EXALTED ONE, BUT I'M SURE WE CAN DEVISE A MUTUALLY BENEFICIAL ARRANGEMENT. AS A TOKEN OF MY GOOD-WILL, I PRESENT TO YOU A GIFT...
THESE TWO DROIDS. BOTH ARE HARDWORKING AND WILL SERVE YOU WELL.
WHAT...? WHAT DID HE SAY?! THIS CAN'T BE! ARTOO, YOU'VE PLAYED THE WRONG MESSAGE!
THE NASTY CHUCKLE THAT FLOWS FROM JABBA'S INCREDIBLE BULK IS NOT ENCOURAGING...

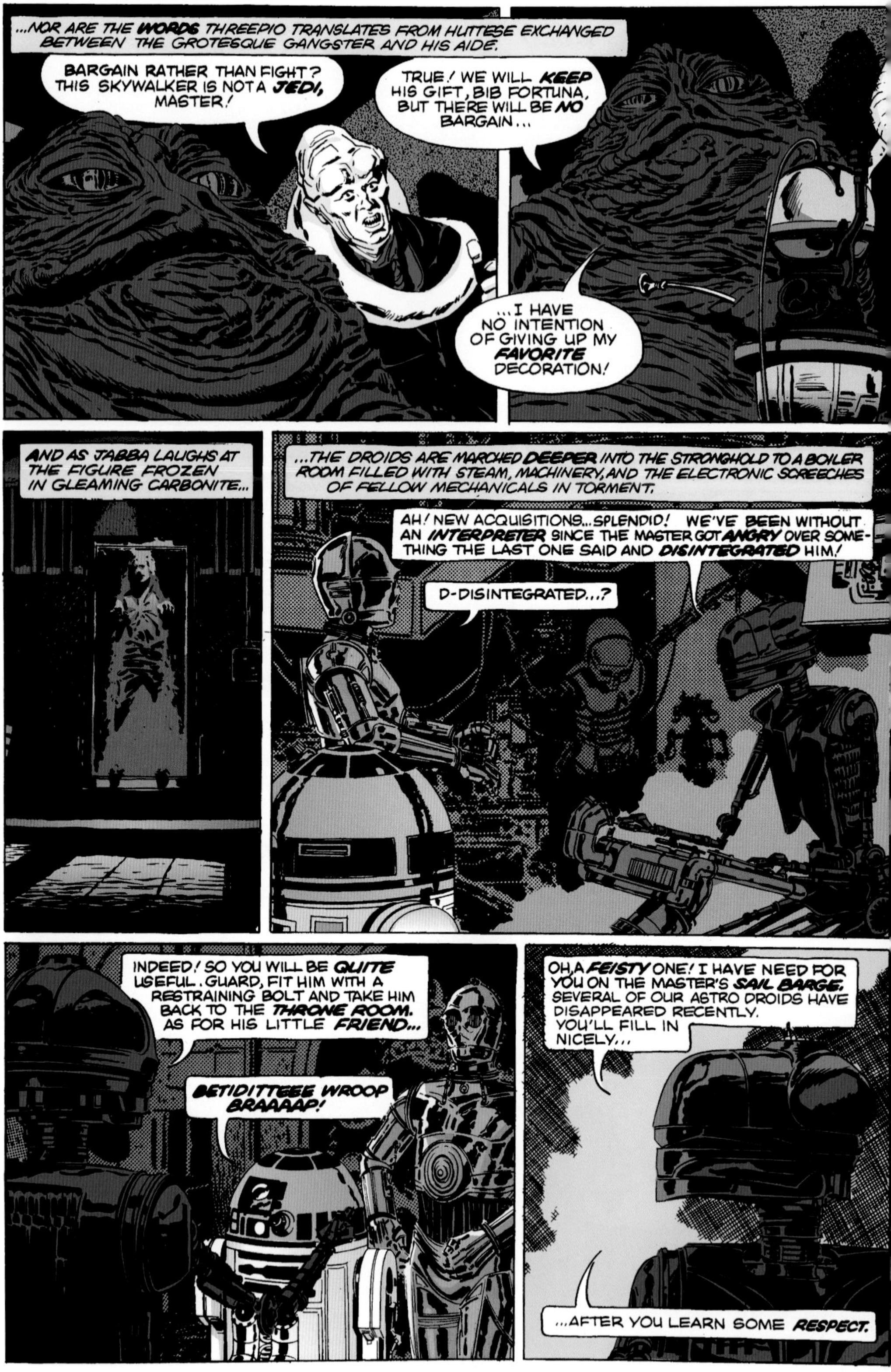
...NOR ARE THE WORDS THREEPIO TRANSLATES FROM HUTTESE EXCHANGED BETWEEN THE GROTESQUE GANGSTER AND HIS AIDE.
BARGAIN RATHER THAN FIGHT? THIS SKYWALKER IS NOT A JEDI, MASTER!
TRUE! WE WILL KEEP HIS GIFT, BIB FORTUNA, BUT THERE WILL BE NO BARGAIN...
...I HAVE NO INTENTION OF GIVING UP MY FAVORITE DECORATION!
AND AS JABBA LAUGHS AT THE FIGURE FROZEN IN GLEAMING CARBONITE...
...THE DROIDS ARE MARCHED DEEPER INTO THE STRONGHOLD TO A BOILER ROOM FILLED WITH STEAM, MACHINERY, AND THE ELECTRONIC SCREECHES OF FELLOW MECHANICALS IN TORMENT.
AH! NEW ACQUISITIONS...SPLENDID! WE'VE BEEN WITHOUT AN INTERPRETER SINCE THE MASTER GOT ANGRY OVER SOMETHING THE LAST ONE SAID AND DISINTEGRATED HIM!
D-DISINTEGRATED...?
INDEED! SO YOU WILL BE QUITE USEFUL. GUARD, FIT HIM WITH A RESTRAINING BOLT AND TAKE HIM BACK TO THE THRONE ROOM. AS FOR HIS LITTLE FRIEND...
BETIDITTEEE WROOP BRAAAAP!
OH, A FEISTY ONE! I HAVE NEED FOR YOU ON THE MASTER'S SAIL BARGE. SEVERAL OF OUR ASTRO DROIDS HAVE DISAPPEARED RECENTLY. YOU'LL FILL IN NICELY...
...AFTER YOU LEARN SOME RESPECT.

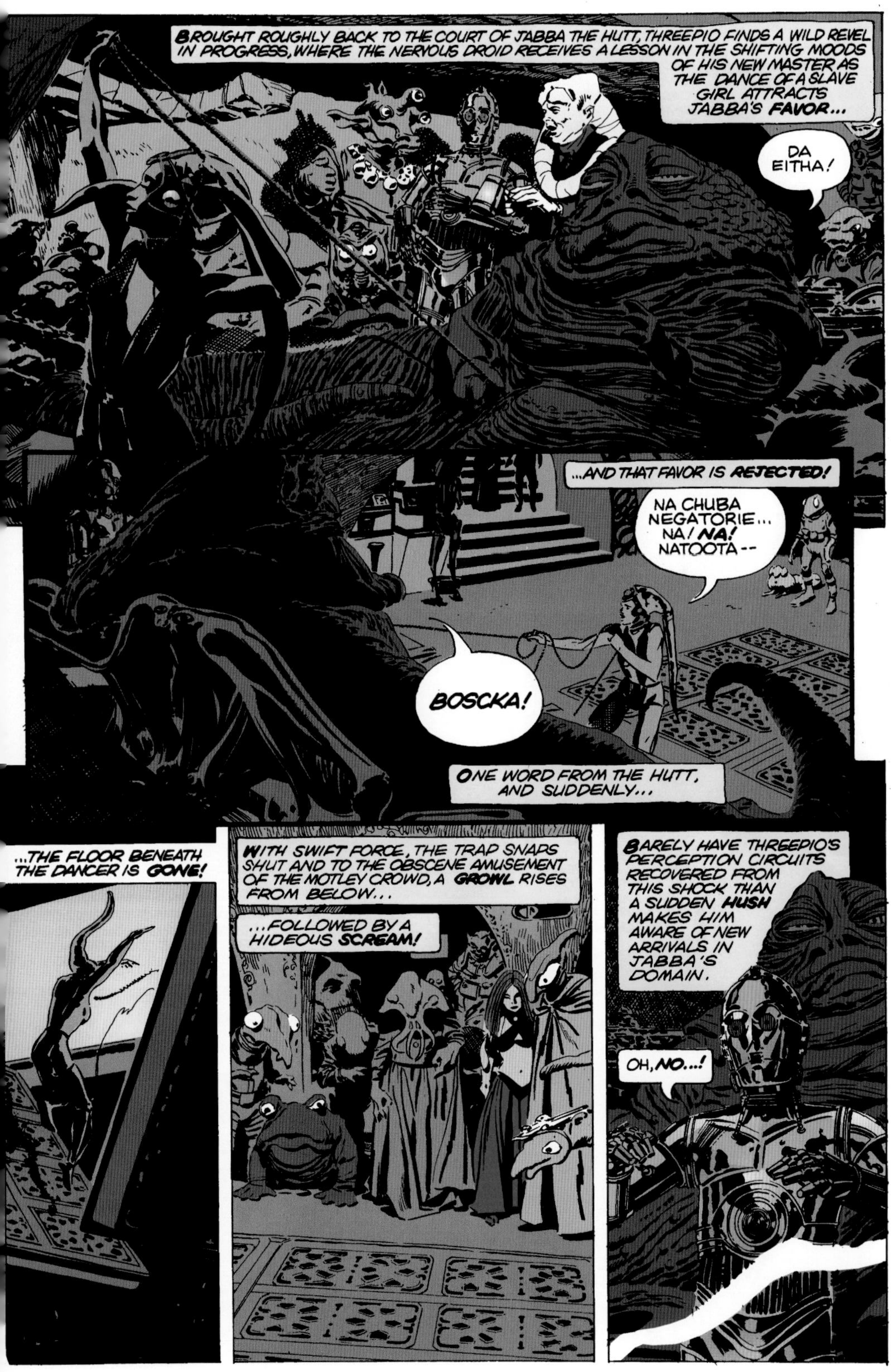
BROUGHT ROUGHLY BACK TO THE COURT OF JABBA THE HUTT, THREEPIO FINDS A WILD REVEL IN PROGRESS, WHERE THE NERVOUS DROID RECEIVES A LESSON IN THE SHIFTING MOODS OF HIS NEW MASTER AS THE DANCE OF A SLAVE GIRL ATTRACTS JABBA'S FAVOR...
DA EITHA!
...AND THAT FAVOR IS REJECTED!
NA CHUBA NEGATORIE... NA! NA! NATOOTA--
BOSCKA!
ONE WORD FROM THE HUTT, AND SUDDENLY...
...THE FLOOR BENEATH THE DANCER IS GONE!
WITH SWIFT FORCE, THE TRAP SNAPS SHUT AND TO THE OBSCENE AMUSEMENT OF THE MOTLEY CROWD, A GROWL RISES FROM BELOW...
...FOLLOWED BY A HIDEOUS SCREAM!
BARELY HAVE THREEPIO'S PERCEPTION CIRCUITS RECOVERED FROM THIS SHOCK THAN A SUDDEN HUSH MAKES HIM AWARE OF NEW ARRIVALS IN JABBA'S DOMAIN.
OH, NO...!

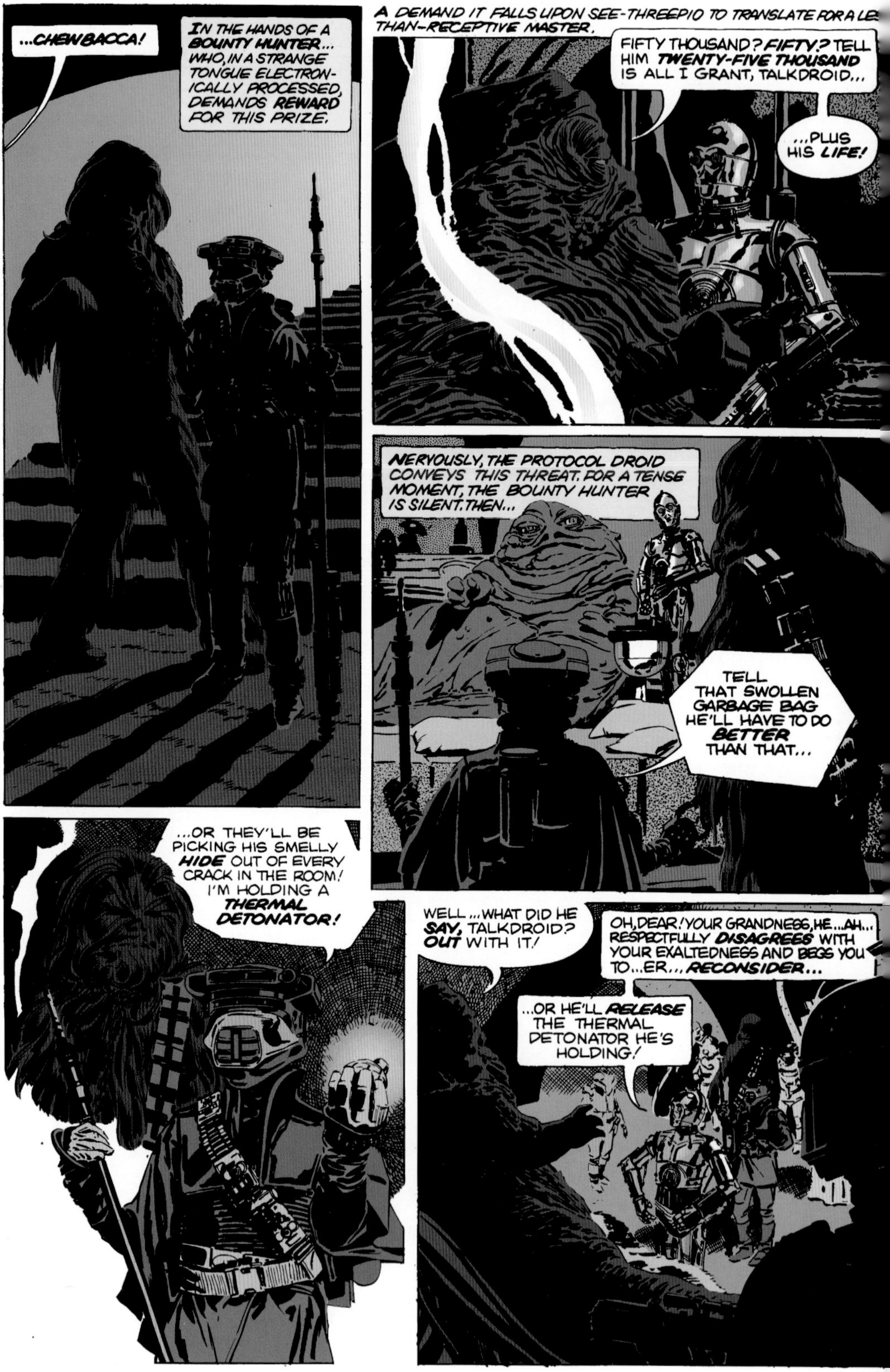

...CHEWBACCA!
IN THE HANDS OF A BOUNTY HUNTER... WHO, IN A STRANGE TONGUE ELECTRONICALLY PROCESSED, DEMANDS REWARD FOR THIS PRIZE.
A DEMAND IT FALLS UPON SEE-THREEPIO TO TRANSLATE FOR A LE THAN-RECEPTIVE MASTER.
FIFTY THOUSAND? FIFTY? TELL HIM TWENTY-FIVE THOUSAND IS ALL I GRANT, TALKDROID...
...PLUS HIS LIFE!
NERVOUSLY, THE PROTOCOL DROID CONVEYS THIS THREAT. FOR A TENSE MOMENT, THE BOUNTY HUNTER IS SILENT. THEN...
TELL THAT SWOLLEN GARBAGE BAG HE'LL HAVE TO DO BETTER THAN THAT...
...OR THEY'LL BE PICKING HIS SMELLY HIDE OUT OF EVERY CRACK IN THE ROOM! I'M HOLDING A THERMAL DETONATOR!
WELL ...WHAT DID HE SAY, TALKDROID? OUT WITH IT!
OH, DEAR! YOUR GRANDNESS, HE...AH... RESPECTFULLY DISAGREES WITH YOUR EXALTEDNESS AND BEGS YOU TO...ER... RECONSIDER...
...OR HE'LL RELEASE THE THERMAL DETONATOR HE'S HOLDING!

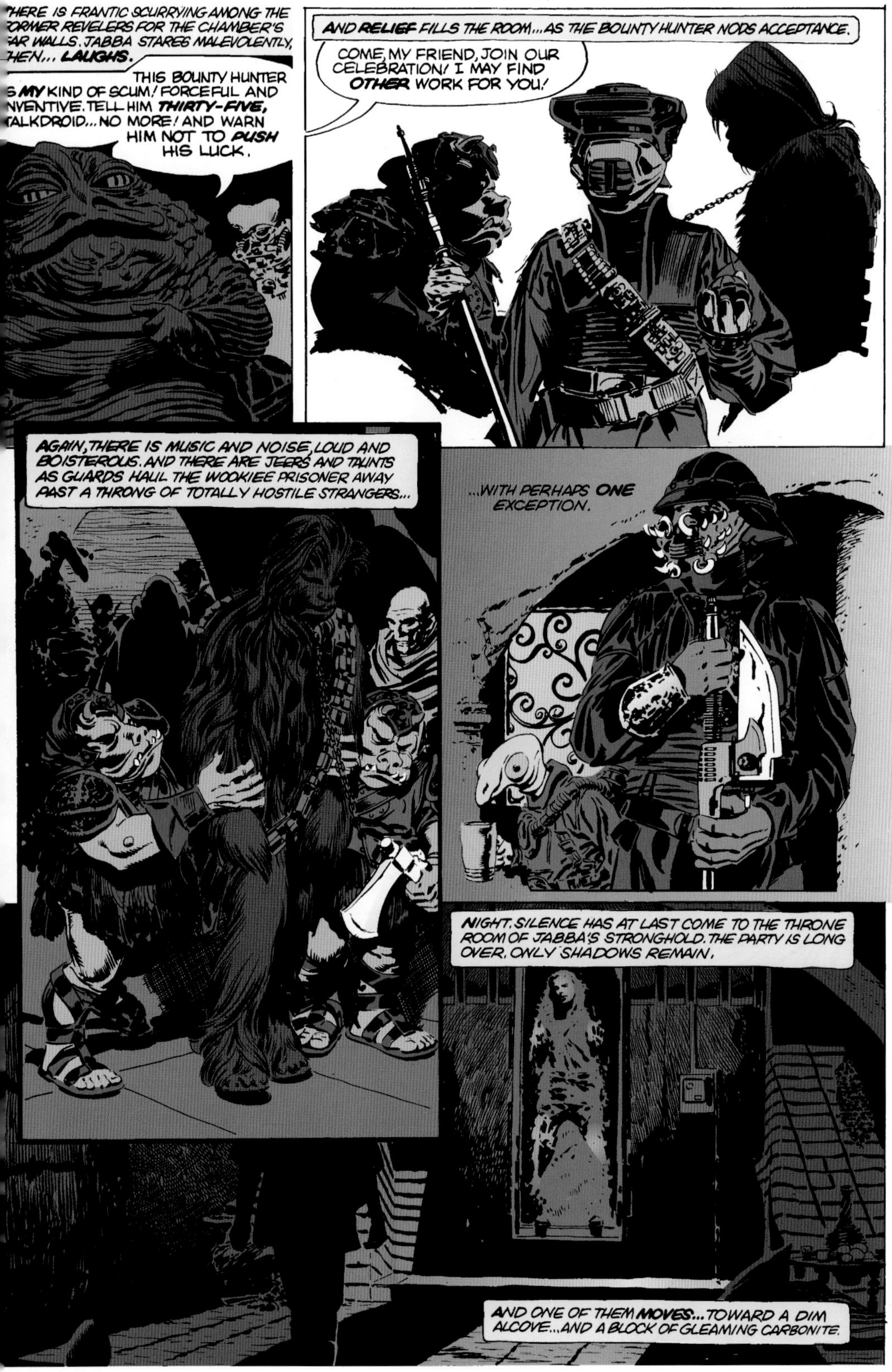

THERE IS FRANTIC SCURRYING AMONG THE FORMER REVELERS FOR THE CHAMBER'S FAR WALLS. JABBA STARES MALEVOLENTLY, THEN... LAUGHS.
THIS BOUNTY HUNTER IS MY KIND OF SCUM! FORCEFUL AND INVENTIVE. TELL HIM THIRTY-FIVE, TALKDROID... NO MORE! AND WARN HIM NOT TO PUSH HIS LUCK.
AND RELIEF FILLS THE ROOM... AS THE BOUNTY HUNTER NODS ACCEPTANCE.
COME, MY FRIEND, JOIN OUR CELEBRATION! I MAY FIND OTHER WORK FOR YOU!
AGAIN, THERE IS MUSIC AND NOISE, LOUD AND BOISTEROUS. AND THERE ARE JEERS AND TAUNTS AS GUARDS HAUL THE WOOKIEE PRISONER AWAY PAST A THRONG OF TOTALLY HOSTILE STRANGERS...
...WITH PERHAPS ONE EXCEPTION.
NIGHT. SILENCE HAS AT LAST COME TO THE THRONE ROOM OF JABBA'S STRONGHOLD. THE PARTY IS LONG OVER. ONLY SHADOWS REMAIN.
AND ONE OF THEM MOVES... TOWARD A DIM ALCOVE... AND A BLOCK OF GLEAMING CARBONITE.

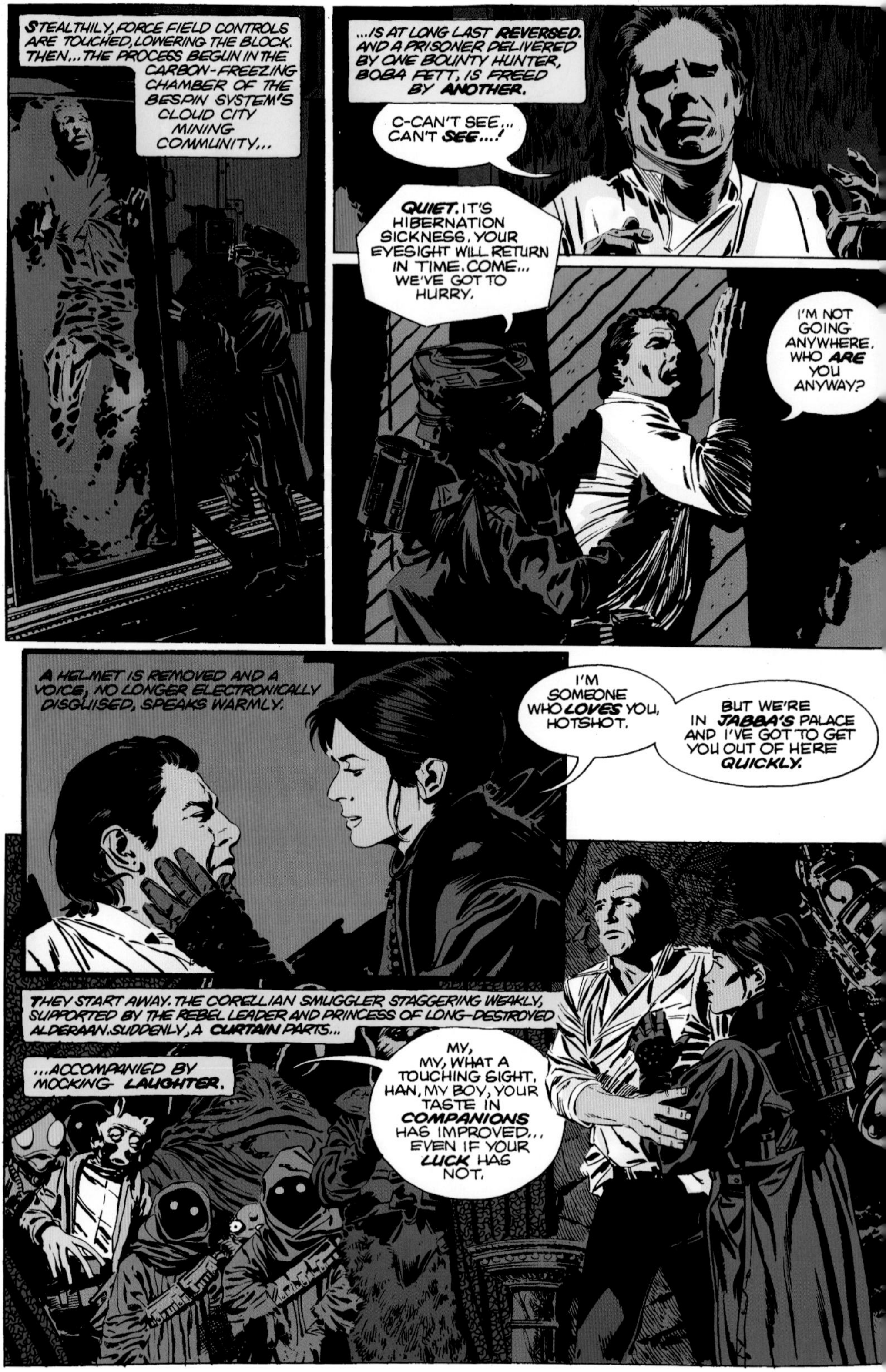
STEALTHILY, FORCE FIELD CONTROLS ARE TOUCHED, LOWERING THE BLOCK. THEN... THE PROCESS BEGUN IN THE CARBON-FREEZING CHAMBER OF THE BESPIN SYSTEM'S CLOUD CITY MINING COMMUNITY...
...IS AT LONG LAST REVERSED. AND A PRISONER DELIVERED BY ONE BOUNTY HUNTER, BOBA FETT, IS FREED BY ANOTHER.
C-CAN'T SEE... CAN'T SEE...!
QUIET. IT'S HIBERNATION SICKNESS. YOUR EYESIGHT WILL RETURN IN TIME. COME... WE'VE GOT TO HURRY.
I'M NOT GOING ANYWHERE. WHO ARE YOU ANYWAY?
A HELMET IS REMOVED AND A VOICE, NO LONGER ELECTRONICALLY DISGUISED, SPEAKS WARMLY.
I'M SOMEONE WHO LOVES YOU, HOTSHOT.
BUT WE'RE IN JABBA'S PALACE AND I'VE GOT TO GET YOU OUT OF HERE QUICKLY.
THEY START AWAY. THE CORELLIAN SMUGGLER STAGGERING WEAKLY, SUPPORTED BY THE REBEL LEADER AND PRINCESS OF LONG-DESTROYED ALDERAAN. SUDDENLY, A CURTAIN PARTS...
...ACCOMPANIED BY MOCKING LAUGHTER.
MY, MY, WHAT A TOUCHING SIGHT. HAN, MY BOY, YOUR TASTE IN COMPANIONS HAS IMPROVED... EVEN IF YOUR LUCK HAS NOT.

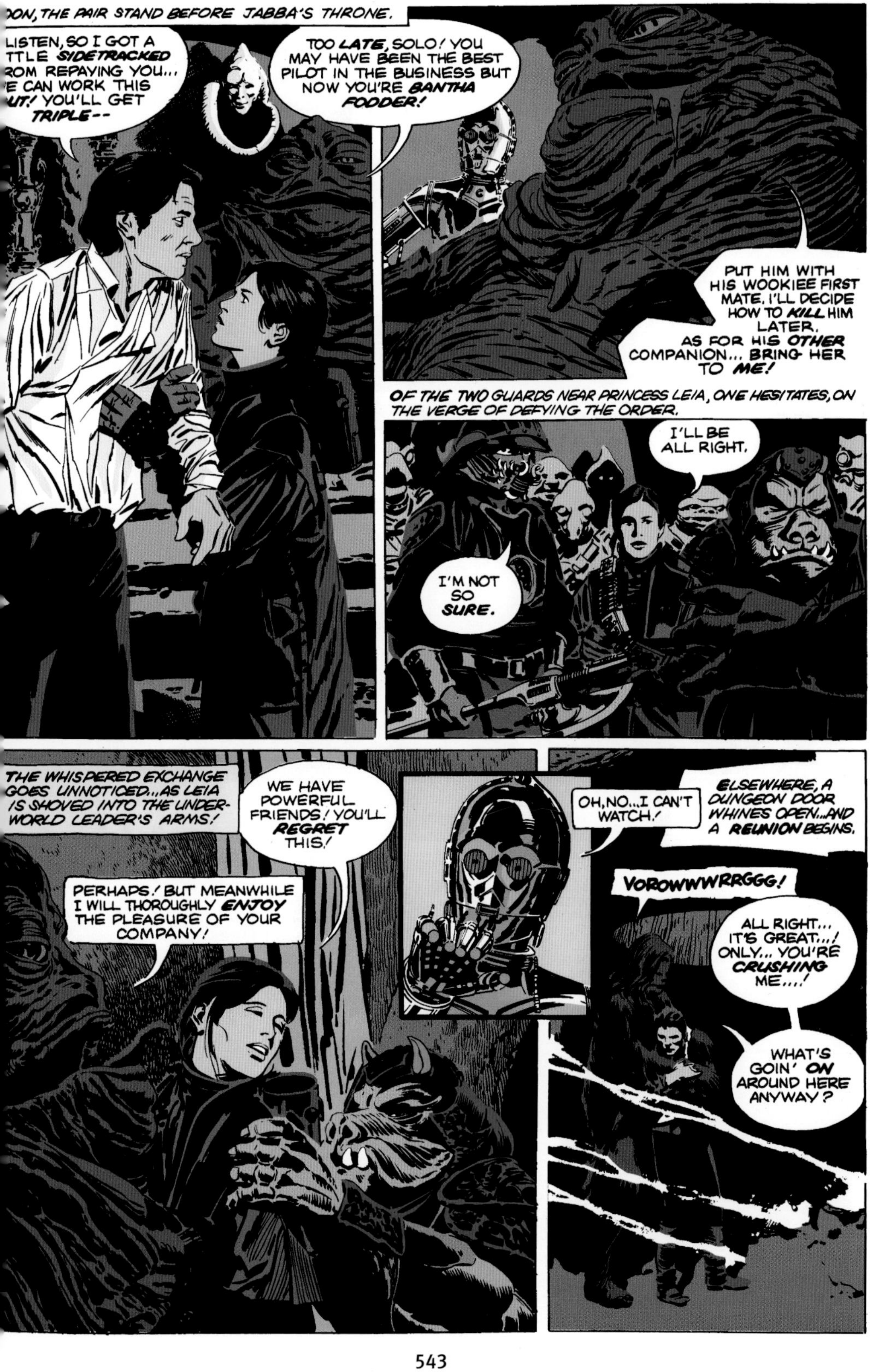

OON, THE PAIR STAND BEFORE JABBA'S THRONE.
LISTEN, SO I GOT A TTLE SIDETRACKED ROM REPAYING YOU... 'E CAN WORK THIS UT! YOU'LL GET TRIPLE--
TOO LATE, SOLO! YOU MAY HAVE BEEN THE BEST PILOT IN THE BUSINESS BUT NOW YOU'RE BANTHA FODDER!
PUT HIM WITH HIS WOOKIEE FIRST MATE. I'LL DECIDE HOW TO KILL HIM LATER.
AS FOR HIS OTHER COMPANION... BRING HER TO ME!
OF THE TWO GUARDS NEAR PRINCESS LEIA, ONE HESITATES, ON THE VERGE OF DEFYING THE ORDER.
I'LL BE ALL RIGHT.
I'M NOT SO SURE.
THE WHISPERED EXCHANGE GOES UNNOTICED...AS LEIA IS SHOVED INTO THE UNDER-WORLD LEADER'S ARMS!
WE HAVE POWERFUL FRIENDS! YOU'LL REGRET THIS!
PERHAPS! BUT MEANWHILE I WILL THOROUGHLY ENJOY THE PLEASURE OF YOUR COMPANY!
OH, NO...I CAN'T WATCH!
ELSEWHERE, A DUNGEON DOOR WHINES OPEN...AND A REUNION BEGINS.
VOROWWWRRGGG!
ALL RIGHT... IT'S GREAT...! ONLY... YOU'RE CRUSHING ME...!
WHAT'S GOIN' ON AROUND HERE ANYWAY?

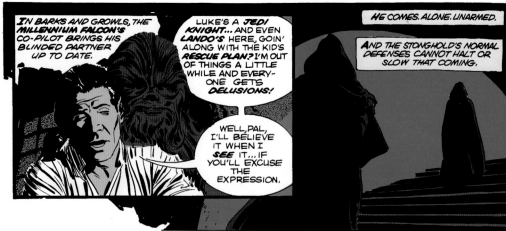

IN BARKS AND GROWLS, THE MILLENNIUM FALCON'S CO-PILOT BRINGS HIS BLINDED PARTNER UP TO DATE.

LUKE'S A *JEDI KNIGHT*... AND EVEN *LANDO'S* HERE, GOIN' ALONG WITH THE KID'S *RESCUE PLAN?* I'M OUT OF THINGS A LITTLE WHILE AND EVERYONE GETS *DELUSIONS!*

WELL, PAL, I'LL BELIEVE IT WHEN I *SEE* IT... IF YOU'LL EXCUSE THE EXPRESSION.

HE COMES. ALONE. UNARMED.

AND THE STONGHOLD'S NORMAL DEFENSES CANNOT HALT OR SLOW THAT COMING.

YOU WILL TAKE ME TO JABBA *NOW*. YOU SERVE HIM *WELL*. YOU ARE SURE TO BE *REWARDED*.

I WILL TAKE YOU TO JABBA NOW. I SERVE HIM WELL. I AM SURE TO BE REWARDED.

TUMULT GREETS LUKE SKYWALKER'S APPEARANCE IN THE THRONE ROOM, BUT HE REMAINS CALM... EVEN AT THE SIGHT OF THE *REPLACEMENT* NOW CHAINED IN THE PLACE OF JABBA'S DANCING GIRL.

I TOLD YOU *NOT* TO ADMIT HIM! BIB FORTUNA, YOU'RE A WEAK-BRAINED FOOL!

JEDI *MIND TRICKS* WILL NOT WORK ON ME, BOY. I AM NOT AFFECTED BY YOUR HUMAN THOUGHT PATTERN. I WAS KILLING YOUR KIND WHEN BEING A JEDI *MEANT* SOMETHING!

I'M *TAKING* CAPTAIN SOLO AND HIS FRIENDS, JABBA. YOU CAN PROFIT... OR BE *DESTROYED*. IT'S YOUR CHOICE. I WARN YOU NOT TO *UNDERESTIMATE* MY POWERS.

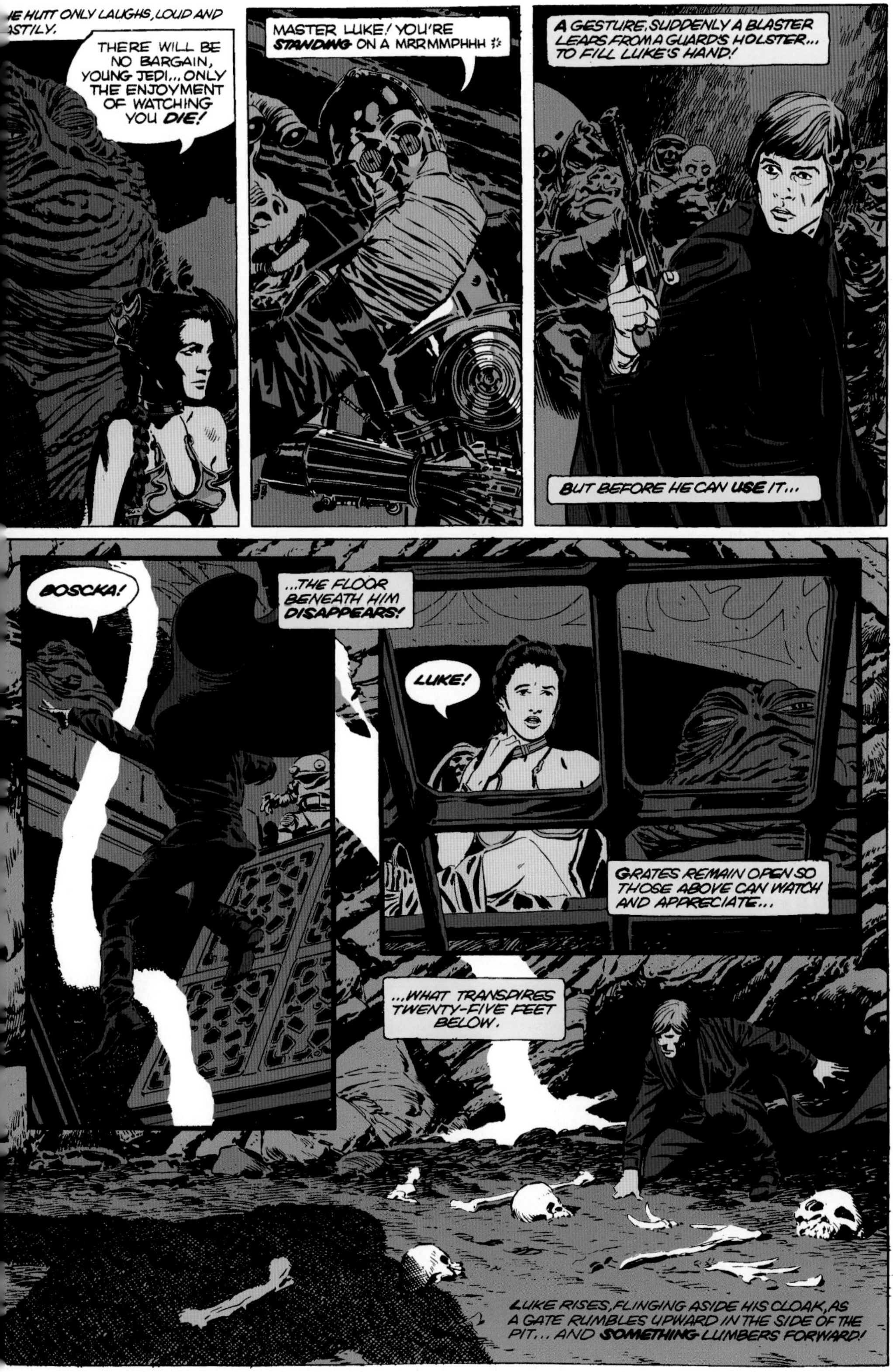

...HE HUTT ONLY LAUGHS, LOUD AND ...ASTILY.
THERE WILL BE NO BARGAIN, YOUNG JEDI... ONLY THE ENJOYMENT OF WATCHING YOU DIE!
MASTER LUKE! YOU'RE STANDING ON A MRRMMPHHH
A GESTURE. SUDDENLY A BLASTER LEAPS FROM A GUARD'S HOLSTER... TO FILL LUKE'S HAND!
BUT BEFORE HE CAN USE IT...
BOSCKA!
...THE FLOOR BENEATH HIM DISAPPEARS!
LUKE!
GRATES REMAIN OPEN SO THOSE ABOVE CAN WATCH AND APPRECIATE...
...WHAT TRANSPIRES TWENTY-FIVE FEET BELOW.
LUKE RISES, FLINGING ASIDE HIS CLOAK, AS A GATE RUMBLES UPWARD IN THE SIDE OF THE PIT... AND SOMETHING LUMBERS FORWARD!

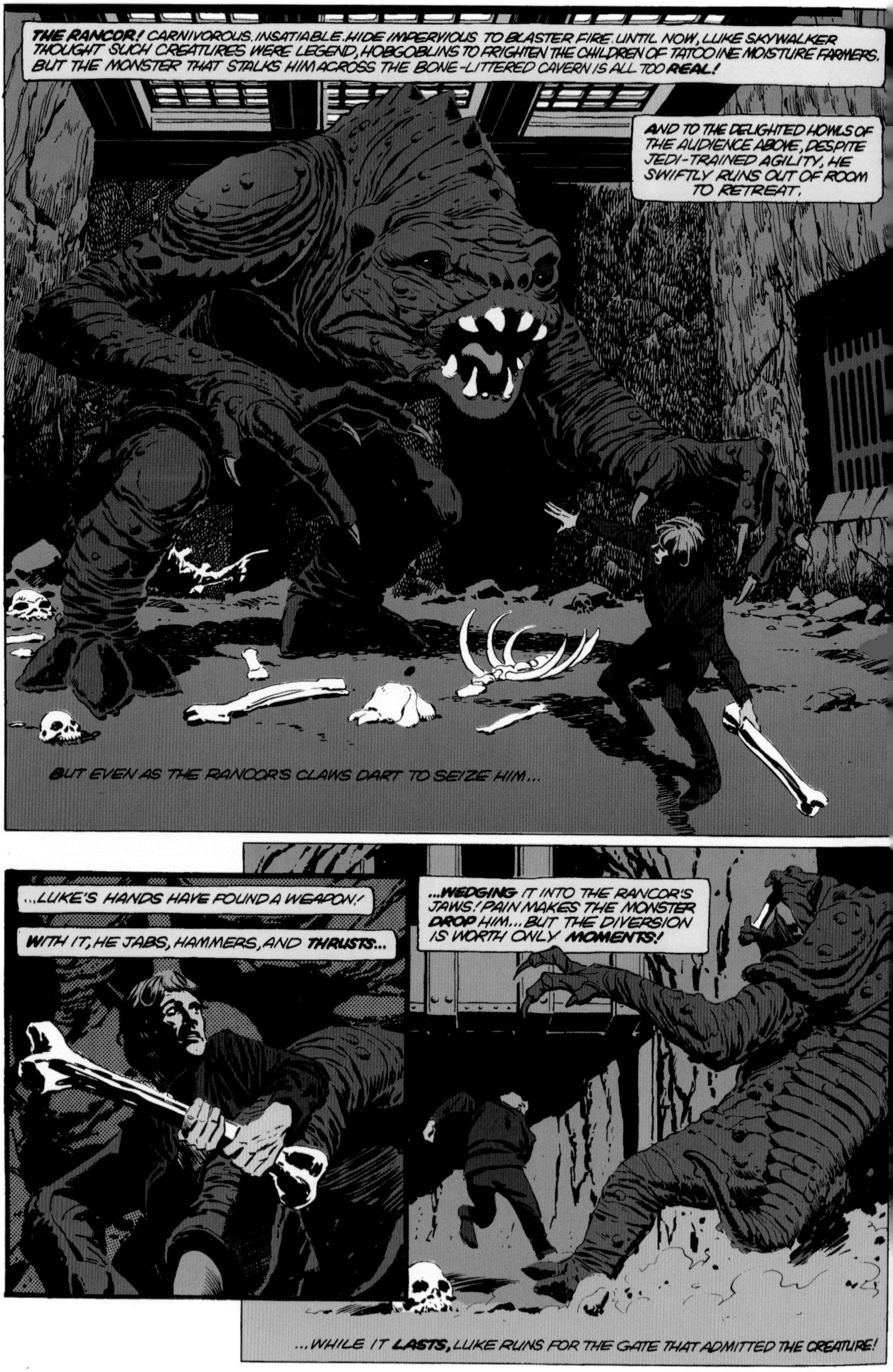
THE RANCOR! CARNIVOROUS. INSATIABLE. HIDE IMPERVIOUS TO BLASTER FIRE. UNTIL NOW, LUKE SKYWALKER THOUGHT SUCH CREATURES WERE LEGEND, HOBGOBLINS TO FRIGHTEN THE CHILDREN OF TATOOINE MOISTURE FARMERS. BUT THE MONSTER THAT STALKS HIM ACROSS THE BONE-LITTERED CAVERN IS ALL TOO REAL!
AND TO THE DELIGHTED HOWLS OF THE AUDIENCE ABOVE, DESPITE JEDI-TRAINED AGILITY, HE SWIFTLY RUNS OUT OF ROOM TO RETREAT.
BUT EVEN AS THE RANCOR'S CLAWS DART TO SEIZE HIM...
...LUKE'S HANDS HAVE FOUND A WEAPON!
WITH IT, HE JABS, HAMMERS, AND THRUSTS...
...WEDGING IT INTO THE RANCOR'S JAWS! PAIN MAKES THE MONSTER DROP HIM... BUT THE DIVERSION IS WORTH ONLY MOMENTS!
...WHILE IT LASTS, LUKE RUNS FOR THE GATE THAT ADMITTED THE CREATURE!

...UT PAST THE GATE, THE WAY TO SAFETY IS **BARRED**...AND THE ATE'S CONTROLS LIE **BEYOND** THOSE BARS! AS THE RANCOR, NGRIER THAN EVER, COMES SNARLING AFTER HIM...

...LUKE HURLS A **SKULL** SCOOPED FROM THIS HOLDING CAVE'S FLOOR...

...SHATTERING THE CONTROL PANEL AND BRINGING THE MASSIVE GATE THUNDERING DOWN ONTO THE GREAT BEAST'S HEAD!

THE RANCOR **DIES**...

..BUT THE TRIUMPH IS **BRIEF**, GRABBED BY OUTRAGED GUARDS, LUKE SOON FINDS HIMSELF FACING THE HUTT AGAIN. ONLY THIS TIME...HAN AND CHEWBACCA ARE BROUGHT TO **JOIN** HIM.

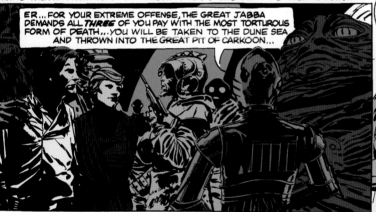

ER...FOR YOUR EXTREME OFFENSE, THE GREAT JABBA DEMANDS ALL **THREE** OF YOU PAY WITH THE MOST TORTUROUS FORM OF DEATH...YOU WILL BE TAKEN TO THE DUNE SEA AND THROWN INTO THE GREAT PIT OF CARKOON...

THAT DOESN'T SOUND TOO BAD...

...NESTING PLACE OF THE ALL-POWERFUL **SARLACC**! IN ITS BELLY, YOU WILL FIND A NEW DEFINITION OF SUFFERING AS YOU SLOWLY ARE **DIGESTED** FOR A THOUSAND YEARS!

ON SECOND THOUGHT, WE COULD **PASS** ON THAT.

YOU SHOULD HAVE BARGAINED, JABBA... THIS IS THE LAST MISTAKE YOU'LL EVER MAKE!

TELL THAT TO THE **SARLACC**, YOUNG JEDI! **TAKE THEM AWAY!**

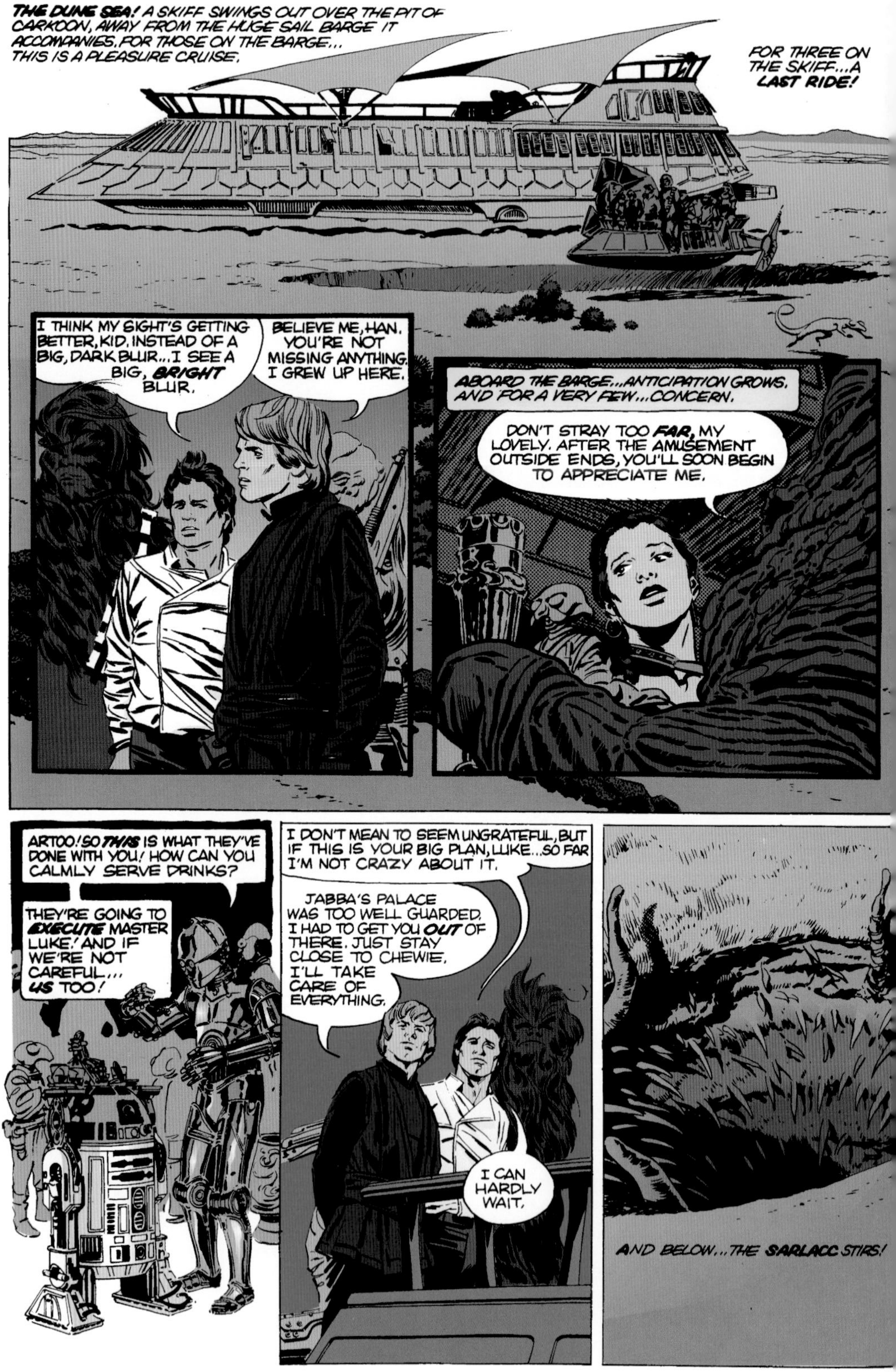
THE DUNE SEA! A SKIFF SWINGS OUT OVER THE PIT OF CARKOON, AWAY FROM THE HUGE SAIL BARGE IT ACCOMPANIES. FOR THOSE ON THE BARGE... THIS IS A PLEASURE CRUISE.
FOR THREE ON THE SKIFF...A LAST RIDE!
I THINK MY SIGHT'S GETTING BETTER, KID. INSTEAD OF A BIG, DARK BLUR...I SEE A BIG, BRIGHT BLUR.
BELIEVE ME, HAN. YOU'RE NOT MISSING ANYTHING. I GREW UP HERE.
ABOARD THE BARGE...ANTICIPATION GROWS. AND FOR A VERY FEW...CONCERN.
DON'T STRAY TOO FAR, MY LOVELY. AFTER THE AMUSEMENT OUTSIDE ENDS, YOU'LL SOON BEGIN TO APPRECIATE ME.
ARTOO! SO THIS IS WHAT THEY'VE DONE WITH YOU! HOW CAN YOU CALMLY SERVE DRINKS?
THEY'RE GOING TO EXECUTE MASTER LUKE! AND IF WE'RE NOT CAREFUL... US TOO!
I DON'T MEAN TO SEEM UNGRATEFUL, BUT IF THIS IS YOUR BIG PLAN, LUKE...SO FAR I'M NOT CRAZY ABOUT IT.
JABBA'S PALACE WAS TOO WELL GUARDED. I HAD TO GET YOU OUT OF THERE. JUST STAY CLOSE TO CHEWIE. I'LL TAKE CARE OF EVERYTHING.
I CAN HARDLY WAIT.
AND BELOW...THE SARLACC STIRS!

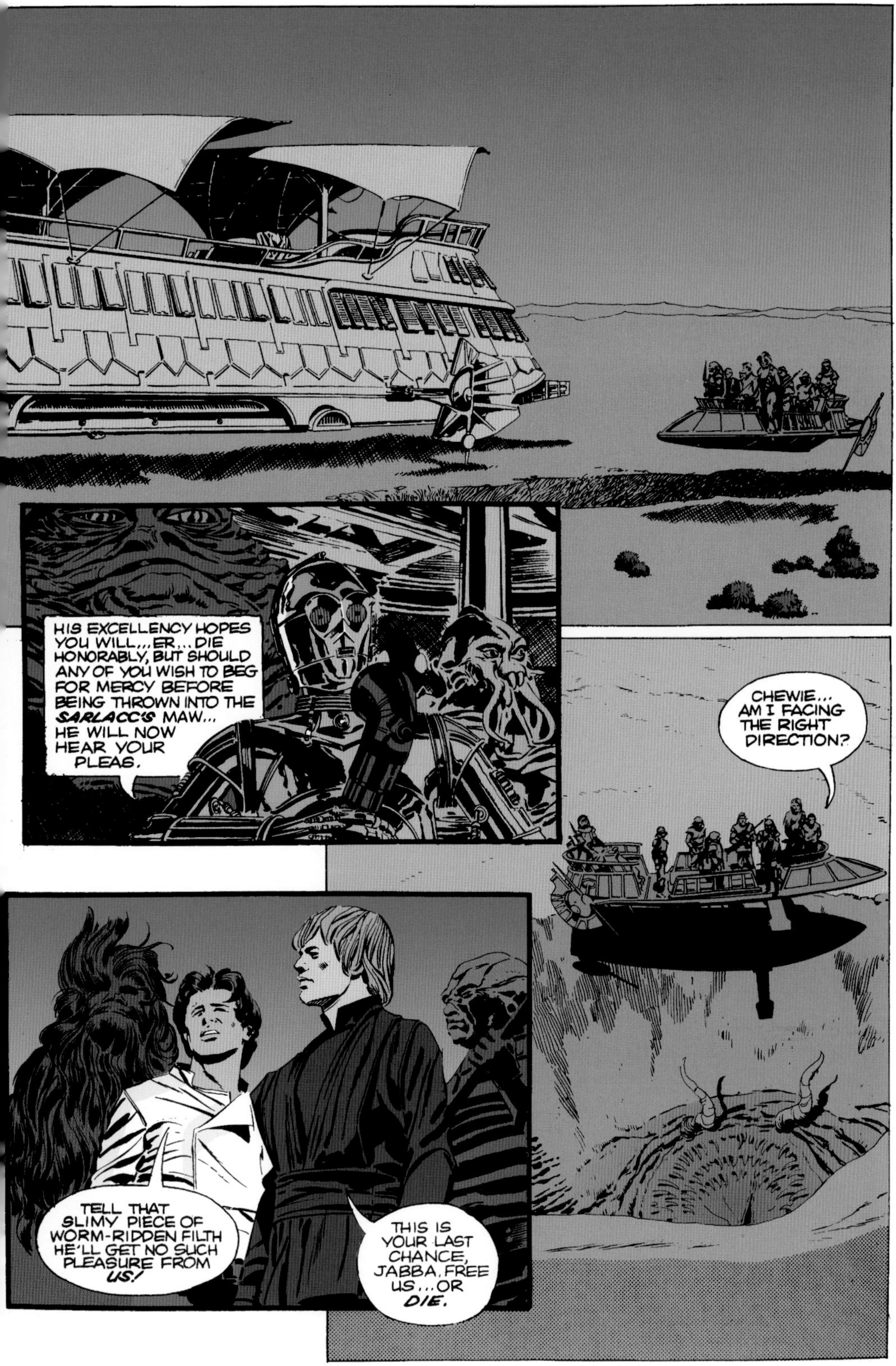
HIS EXCELLENCY HOPES YOU WILL,,,ER,..DIE HONORABLY, BUT SHOULD ANY OF YOU WISH TO BEG FOR MERCY BEFORE BEING THROWN INTO THE SARLACC'S MAW... HE WILL NOW HEAR YOUR PLEAS.
CHEWIE... AM I FACING THE RIGHT DIRECTION?
TELL THAT SLIMY PIECE OF WORM-RIDDEN FILTH HE'LL GET NO SUCH PLEASURE FROM US!
THIS IS YOUR LAST CHANCE, JABBA. FREE US...OR DIE.

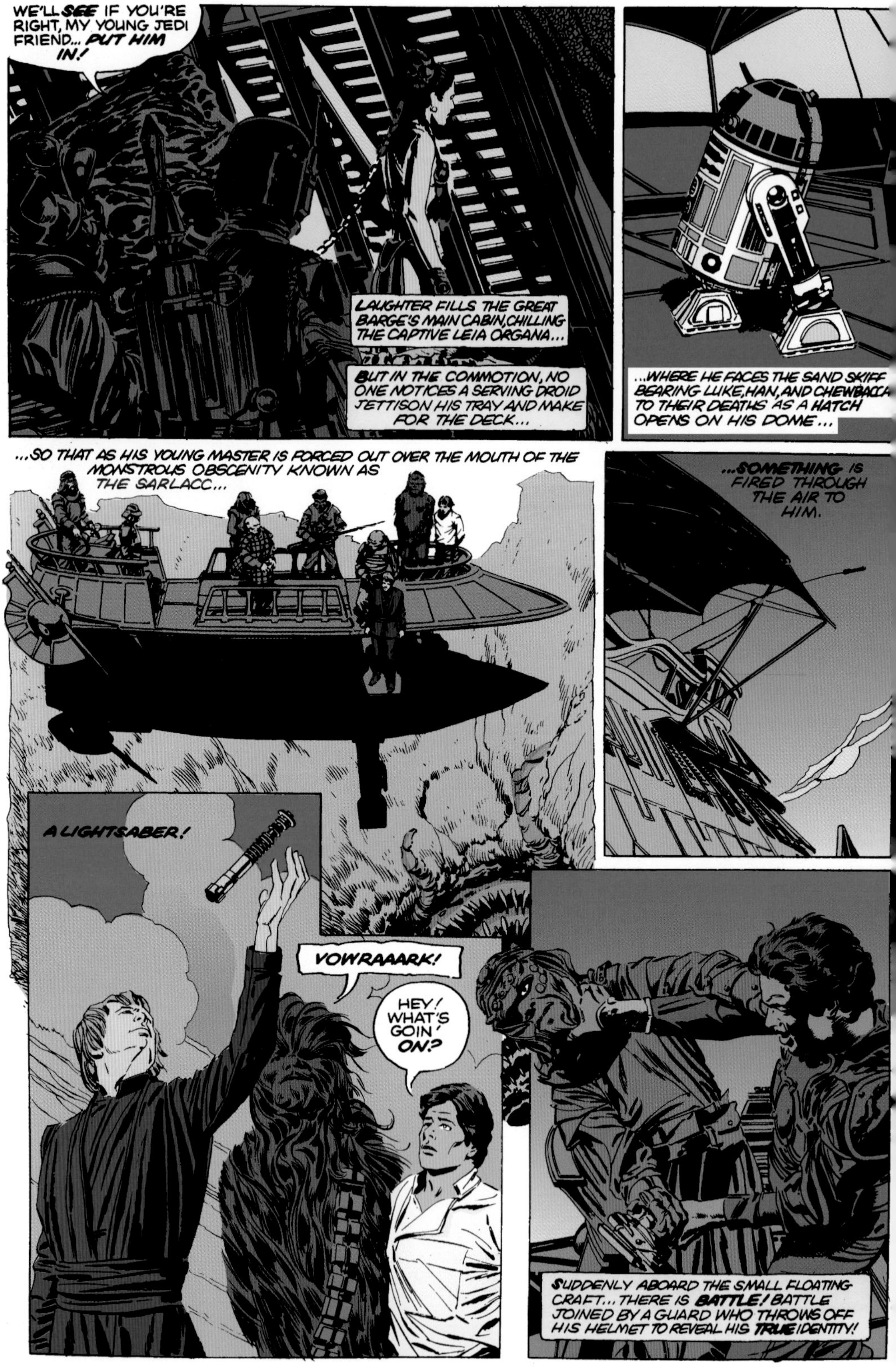
WE'LL SEE IF YOU'RE RIGHT, MY YOUNG JEDI FRIEND... PUT HIM IN!
LAUGHTER FILLS THE GREAT BARGE'S MAIN CABIN, CHILLING THE CAPTIVE LEIA ORGANA...
BUT IN THE COMMOTION, NO ONE NOTICES A SERVING DROID JETTISON HIS TRAY AND MAKE FOR THE DECK...
...WHERE HE FACES THE SAND SKIFF BEARING LUKE, HAN, AND CHEWBACCA TO THEIR DEATHS AS A HATCH OPENS ON HIS DOME...
...SO THAT AS HIS YOUNG MASTER IS FORCED OUT OVER THE MOUTH OF THE MONSTROUS OBSCENITY KNOWN AS THE SARLACC...
...SOMETHING IS FIRED THROUGH THE AIR TO HIM.
A LIGHTSABER!
VOWRAAARK!
HEY! WHAT'S GOIN' ON?
SUDDENLY ABOARD THE SMALL FLOATING CRAFT... THERE IS BATTLE! BATTLE JOINED BY A GUARD WHO THROWS OFF HIS HELMET TO REVEAL HIS TRUE IDENTITY!

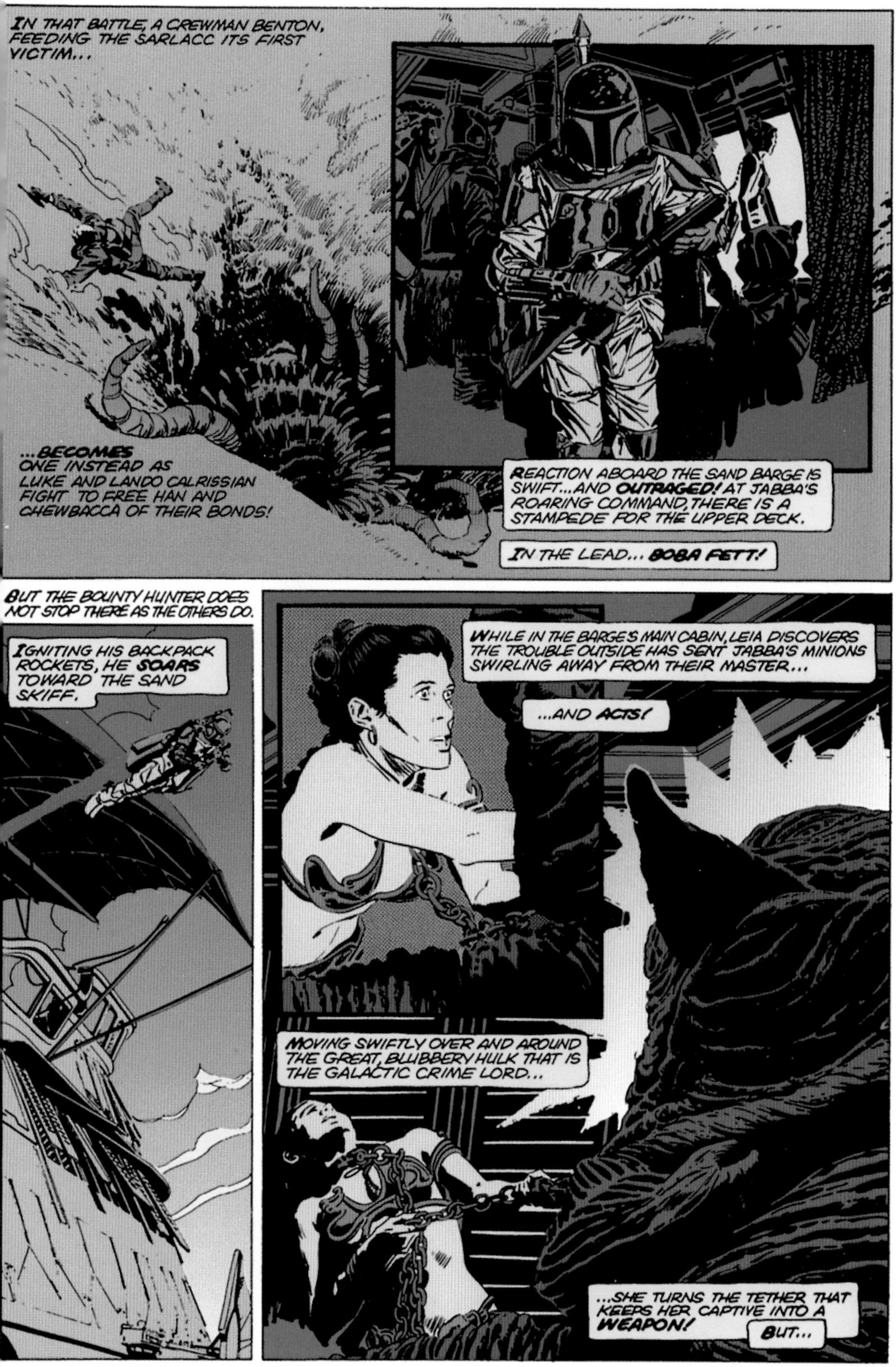
IN THAT BATTLE, A CREWMAN BENTON, FEEDING THE SARLACC ITS FIRST VICTIM...
...BECOMES ONE INSTEAD AS LUKE AND LANDO CALRISSIAN FIGHT TO FREE HAN AND CHEWBACCA OF THEIR BONDS!
REACTION ABOARD THE SAND BARGE IS SWIFT...AND OUTRAGED! AT JABBA'S ROARING COMMAND, THERE IS A STAMPEDE FOR THE UPPER DECK.
IN THE LEAD... BOBA FETT!
BUT THE BOUNTY HUNTER DOES NOT STOP THERE AS THE OTHERS DO.
IGNITING HIS BACKPACK ROCKETS, HE SOARS TOWARD THE SAND SKIFF.
WHILE IN THE BARGE'S MAIN CABIN, LEIA DISCOVERS THE TROUBLE OUTSIDE HAS SENT JABBA'S MINIONS SWIRLING AWAY FROM THEIR MASTER...
...AND ACTS!
MOVING SWIFTLY OVER AND AROUND THE GREAT, BLUBBERY HULK THAT IS THE GALACTIC CRIME LORD...
...SHE TURNS THE TETHER THAT KEEPS HER CAPTIVE INTO A WEAPON!
BUT...

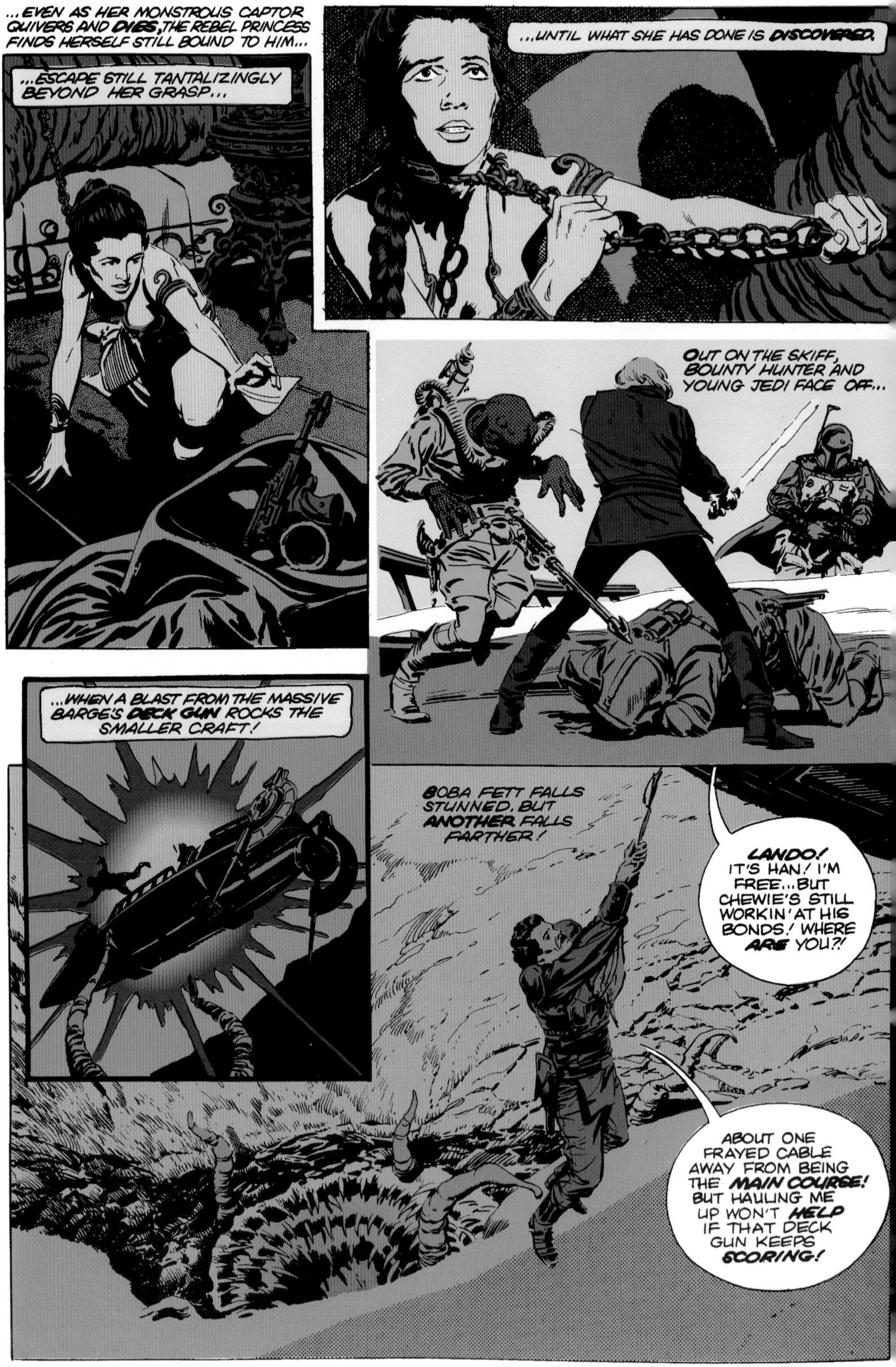

...EVEN AS HER MONSTROUS CAPTOR QUIVERS AND DIES, THE REBEL PRINCESS FINDS HERSELF STILL BOUND TO HIM...
...ESCAPE STILL TANTALIZINGLY BEYOND HER GRASP...
...UNTIL WHAT SHE HAS DONE IS DISCOVERED.
OUT ON THE SKIFF, BOUNTY HUNTER AND YOUNG JEDI FACE OFF...
...WHEN A BLAST FROM THE MASSIVE BARGE'S DECK GUN ROCKS THE SMALLER CRAFT!
BOBA FETT FALLS STUNNED, BUT ANOTHER FALLS FARTHER!
LANDO! IT'S HAN! I'M FREE...BUT CHEWIE'S STILL WORKIN' AT HIS BONDS! WHERE ARE YOU?!
ABOUT ONE FRAYED CABLE AWAY FROM BEING THE MAIN COURSE! BUT HAULING ME UP WON'T HELP IF THAT DECK GUN KEEPS SCORING!

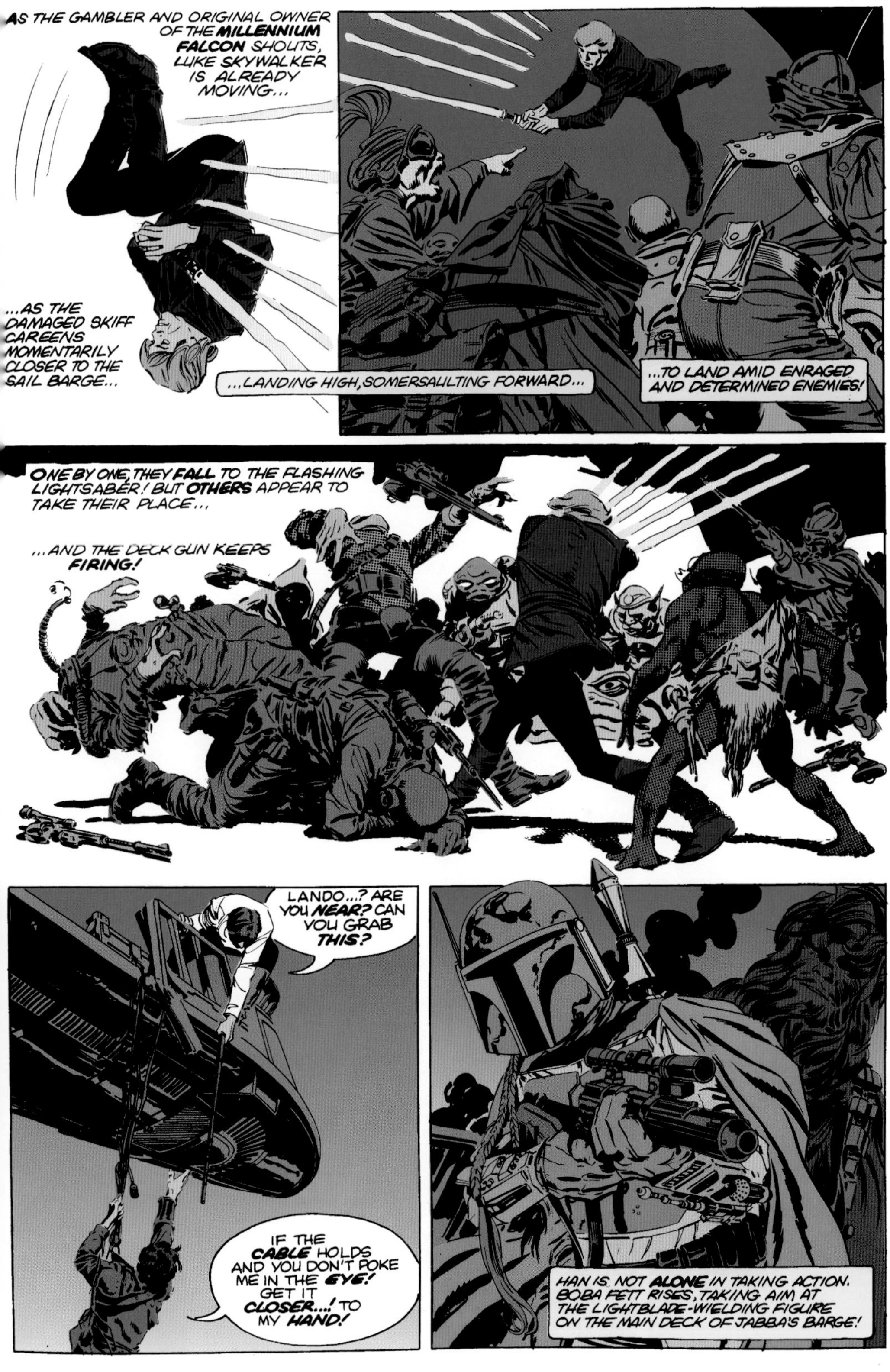
AS THE GAMBLER AND ORIGINAL OWNER OF THE MILLENNIUM FALCON SHOUTS, LUKE SKYWALKER IS ALREADY MOVING...
...AS THE DAMAGED SKIFF CAREENS MOMENTARILY CLOSER TO THE SAIL BARGE...
...LANDING HIGH, SOMERSAULTING FORWARD...
...TO LAND AMID ENRAGED AND DETERMINED ENEMIES!
ONE BY ONE, THEY FALL TO THE FLASHING LIGHTSABER! BUT OTHERS APPEAR TO TAKE THEIR PLACE...
...AND THE DECK GUN KEEPS FIRING!
LANDO...? ARE YOU NEAR? CAN YOU GRAB THIS?
IF THE CABLE HOLDS AND YOU DON'T POKE ME IN THE EYE! GET IT CLOSER...! TO MY HAND!
HAN IS NOT ALONE IN TAKING ACTION. BOBA FETT RISES, TAKING AIM AT THE LIGHTBLADE-WIELDING FIGURE ON THE MAIN DECK OF JABBA'S BARGE!

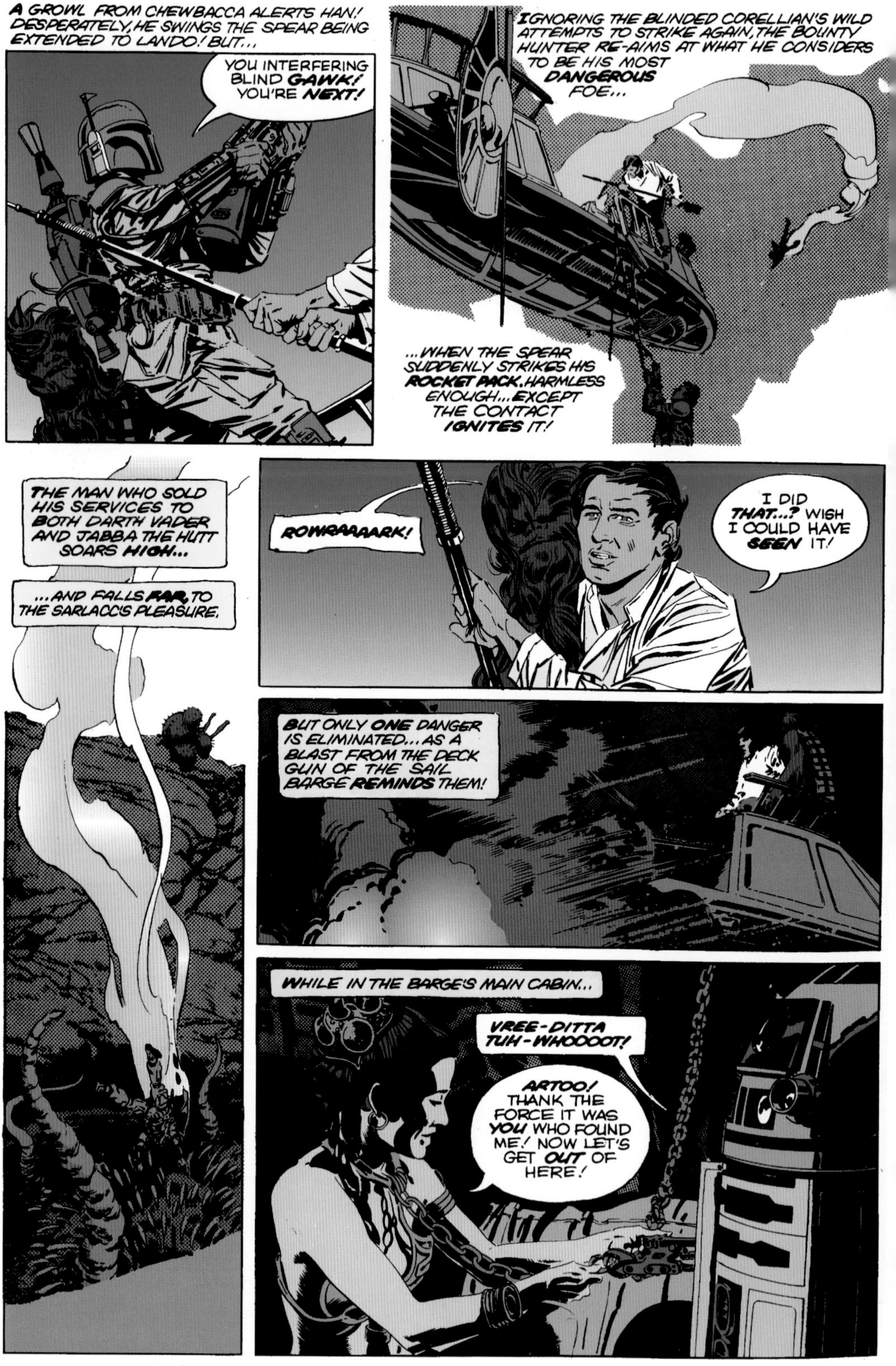
A GROWL FROM CHEWBACCA ALERTS HAN! DESPERATELY, HE SWINGS THE SPEAR BEING EXTENDED TO LANDO! BUT...
YOU INTERFERING BLIND GAWK! YOU'RE NEXT!
IGNORING THE BLINDED CORELLIAN'S WILD ATTEMPTS TO STRIKE AGAIN, THE BOUNTY HUNTER RE-AIMS AT WHAT HE CONSIDERS TO BE HIS MOST DANGEROUS FOE...
...WHEN THE SPEAR SUDDENLY STRIKES HIS ROCKET PACK. HARMLESS ENOUGH... EXCEPT THE CONTACT IGNITES IT!
THE MAN WHO SOLD HIS SERVICES TO BOTH DARTH VADER AND JABBA THE HUTT SOARS HIGH...
...AND FALLS FAR, TO THE SARLACC'S PLEASURE.
ROWRAAAARK!
I DID THAT...? WISH I COULD HAVE SEEN IT!
BUT ONLY ONE DANGER IS ELIMINATED... AS A BLAST FROM THE DECK GUN OF THE SAIL BARGE REMINDS THEM!
WHILE IN THE BARGE'S MAIN CABIN...
VREE-DITTA TUH-WHOOOOT!
ARTOO! THANK THE FORCE IT WAS YOU WHO FOUND ME! NOW LET'S GET OUT OF HERE!

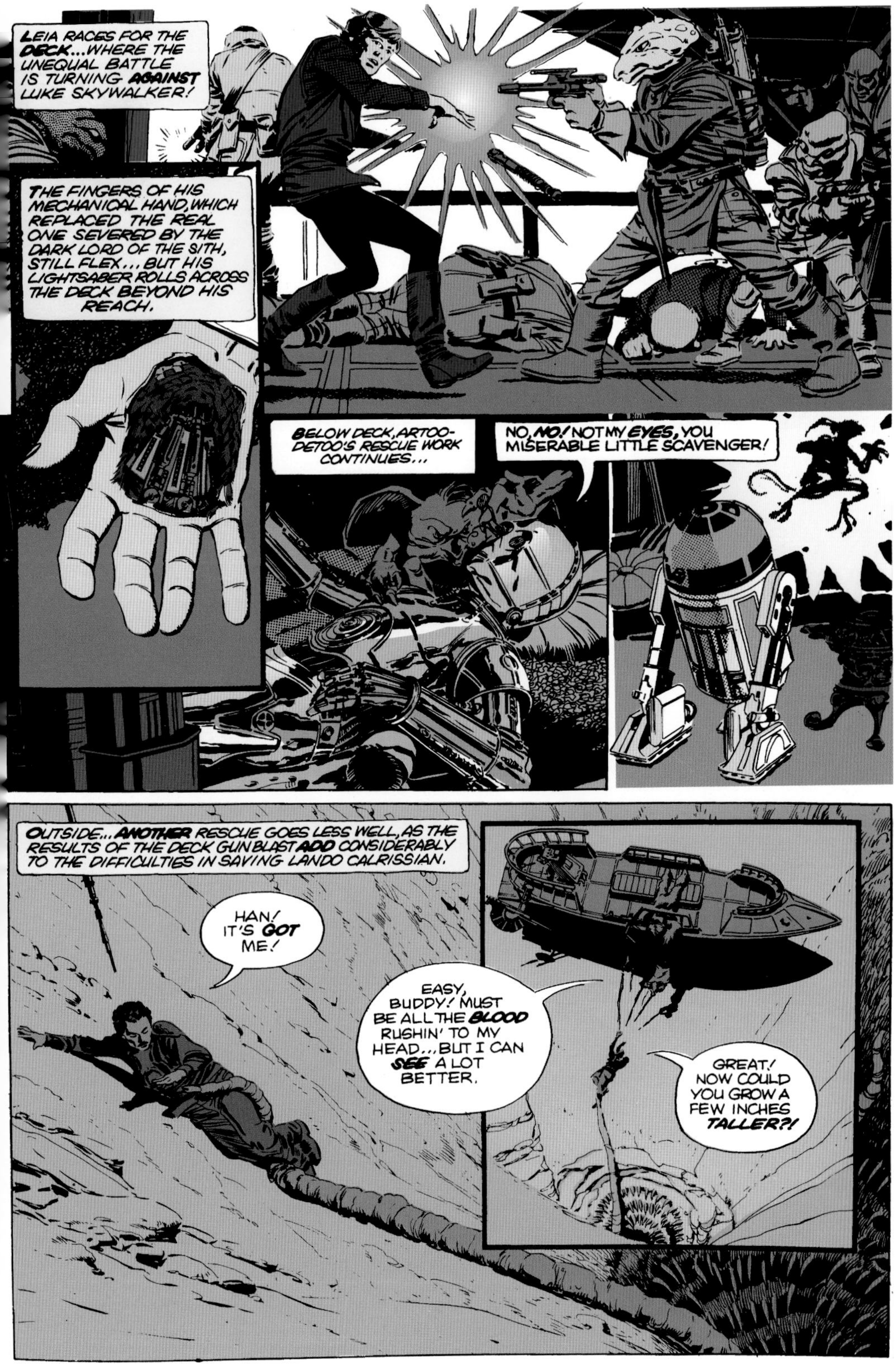
LEIA RACES FOR THE DECK...WHERE THE UNEQUAL BATTLE IS TURNING AGAINST LUKE SKYWALKER!
THE FINGERS OF HIS MECHANICAL HAND, WHICH REPLACED THE REAL ONE SEVERED BY THE DARK LORD OF THE SITH, STILL FLEX... BUT HIS LIGHTSABER ROLLS ACROSS THE DECK BEYOND HIS REACH.
BELOW DECK, ARTOO-DETOO'S RESCUE WORK CONTINUES...
NO, NO! NOT MY EYES, YOU MISERABLE LITTLE SCAVENGER!
OUTSIDE... ANOTHER RESCUE GOES LESS WELL, AS THE RESULTS OF THE DECK GUN BLAST ADD CONSIDERABLY TO THE DIFFICULTIES IN SAVING LANDO CALRISSIAN.
HAN! IT'S GOT ME!
EASY, BUDDY! MUST BE ALL THE BLOOD RUSHIN' TO MY HEAD... BUT I CAN SEE A LOT BETTER.
GREAT! NOW COULD YOU GROW A FEW INCHES TALLER?!

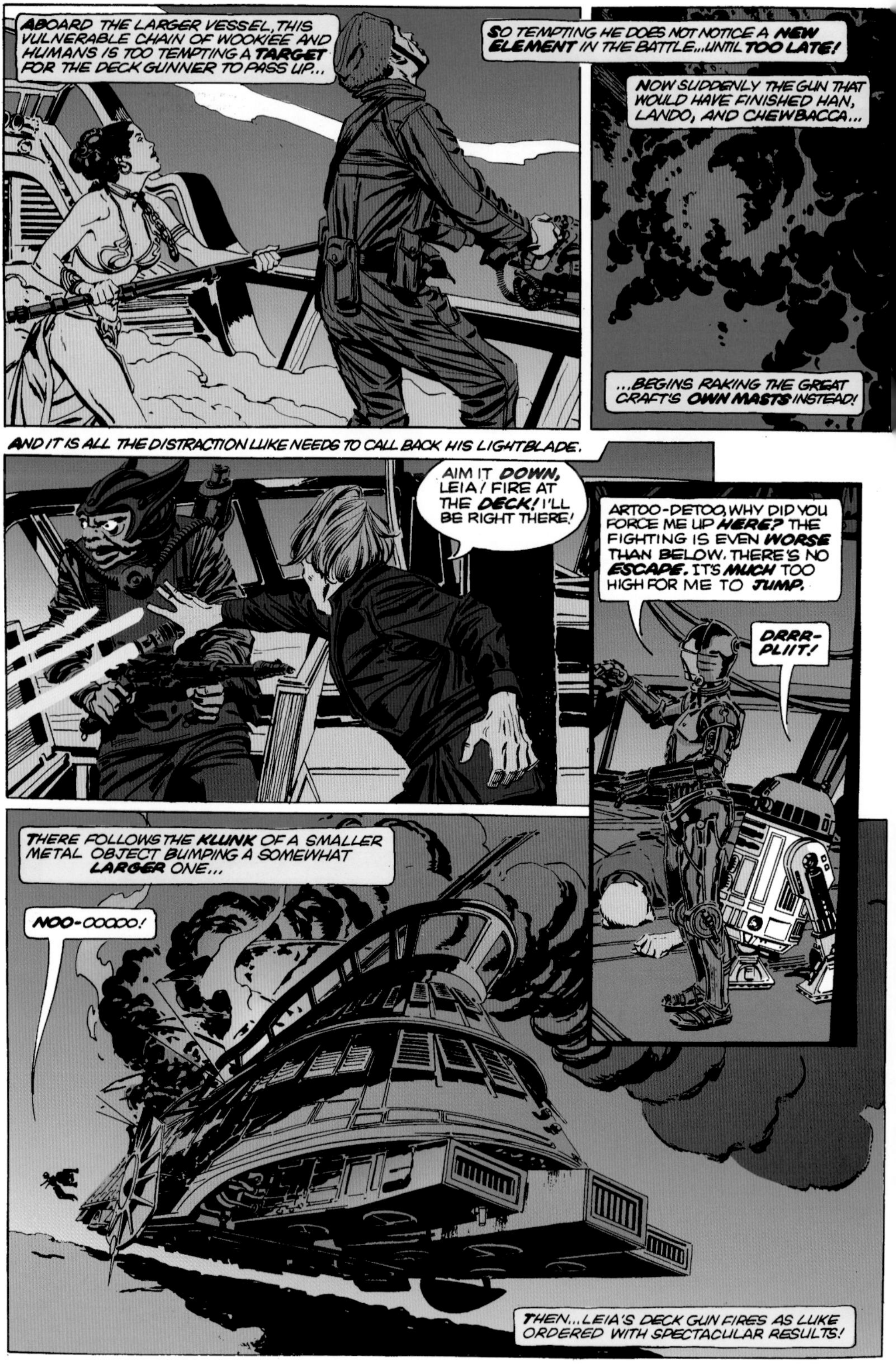
ABOARD THE LARGER VESSEL, THIS VULNERABLE CHAIN OF WOOKIEE AND HUMANS IS TOO TEMPTING A TARGET FOR THE DECK GUNNER TO PASS UP...
SO TEMPTING HE DOES NOT NOTICE A NEW ELEMENT IN THE BATTLE...UNTIL TOO LATE!
NOW SUDDENLY THE GUN THAT WOULD HAVE FINISHED HAN, LANDO, AND CHEWBACCA...
...BEGINS RAKING THE GREAT CRAFT'S OWN MASTS INSTEAD!
AND IT IS ALL THE DISTRACTION LUKE NEEDS TO CALL BACK HIS LIGHTBLADE.
AIM IT DOWN, LEIA! FIRE AT THE DECK! I'LL BE RIGHT THERE!
ARTOO-DETOO, WHY DID YOU FORCE ME UP HERE? THE FIGHTING IS EVEN WORSE THAN BELOW. THERE'S NO ESCAPE. IT'S MUCH TOO HIGH FOR ME TO JUMP.
DRRR-PLIIT!
THERE FOLLOWS THE KLUNK OF A SMALLER METAL OBJECT BUMPING A SOMEWHAT LARGER ONE...
NOO-OOOOO!
THEN...LEIA'S DECK GUN FIRES AS LUKE ORDERED WITH SPECTACULAR RESULTS!

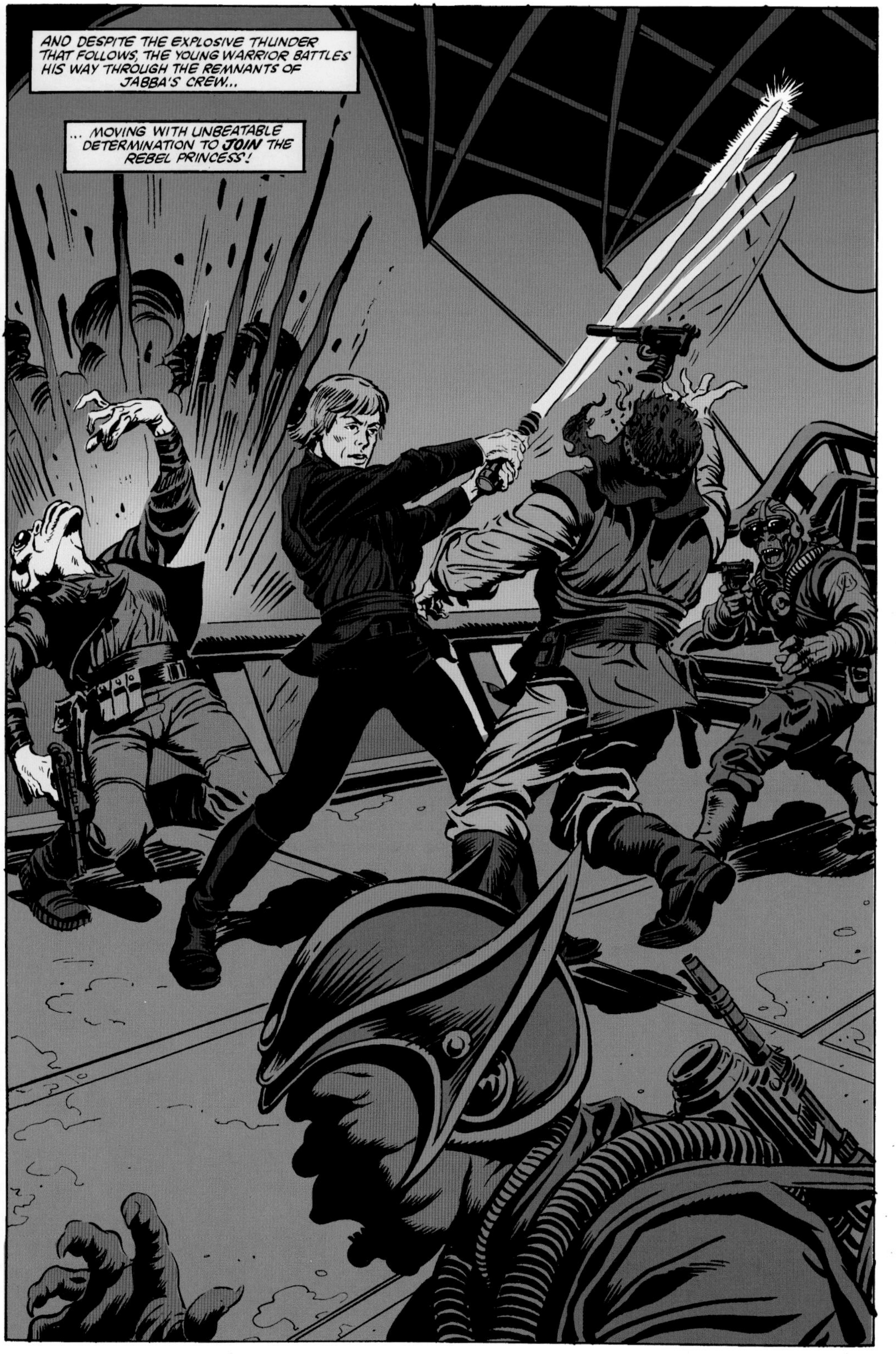
AND DESPITE THE EXPLOSIVE THUNDER THAT FOLLOWS, THE YOUNG WARRIOR BATTLES HIS WAY THROUGH THE REMNANTS OF JABBA'S CREW...
... MOVING WITH UNBEATABLE DETERMINATION TO JOIN THE REBEL PRINCESS!

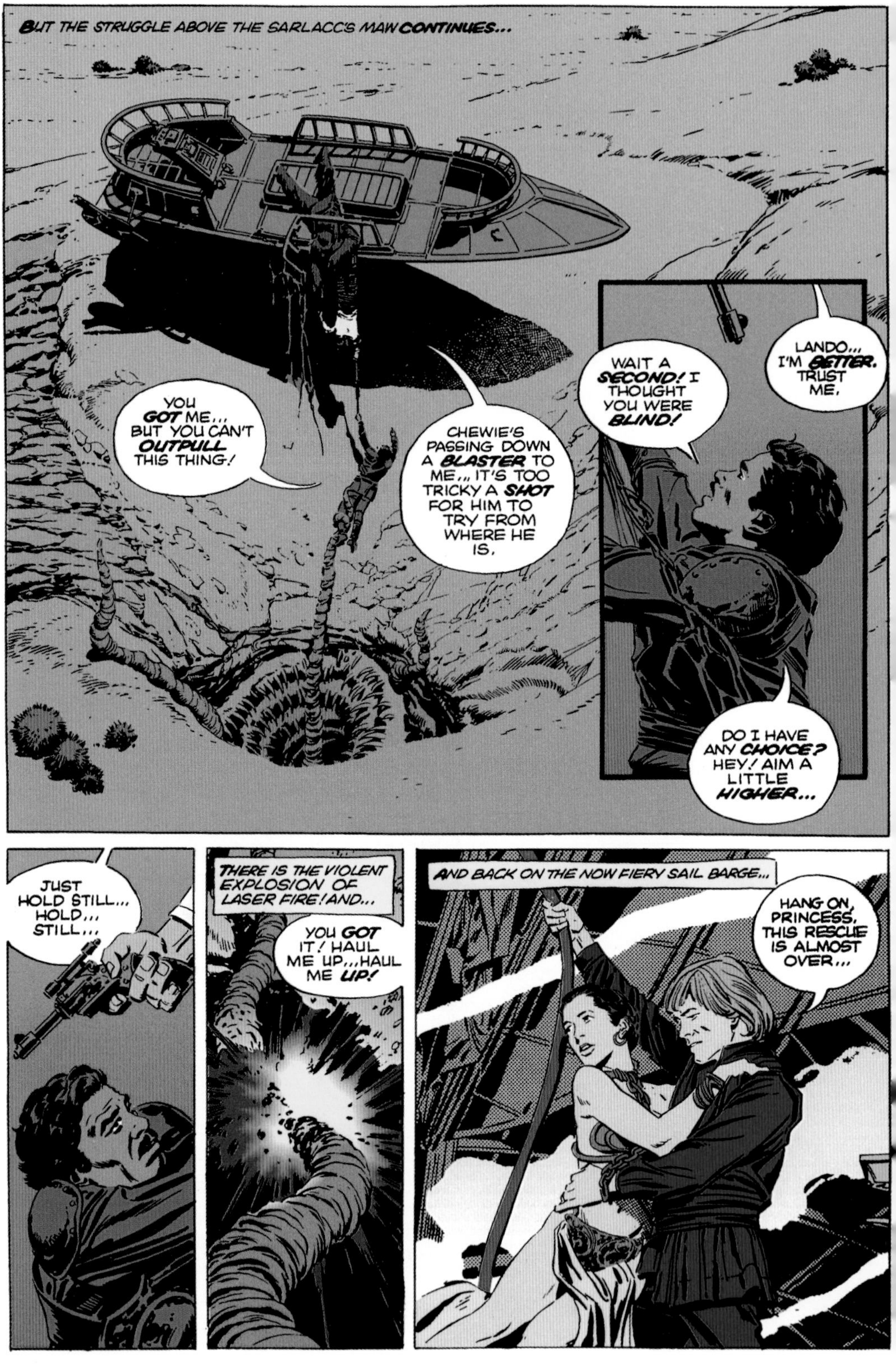
BUT THE STRUGGLE ABOVE THE SARLACC'S MAW CONTINUES...
YOU GOT ME... BUT YOU CAN'T OUTPULL THIS THING!
CHEWIE'S PASSING DOWN A BLASTER TO ME... IT'S TOO TRICKY A SHOT FOR HIM TO TRY FROM WHERE HE IS.
WAIT A SECOND! I THOUGHT YOU WERE BLIND!
LANDO... I'M BETTER. TRUST ME.
DO I HAVE ANY CHOICE? HEY! AIM A LITTLE HIGHER...
JUST HOLD STILL... HOLD... STILL...
THERE IS THE VIOLENT EXPLOSION OF LASER FIRE! AND...
YOU GOT IT! HAUL ME UP... HAUL ME UP!
AND BACK ON THE NOW FIERY SAIL BARGE...
HANG ON, PRINCESS, THIS RESCUE IS ALMOST OVER...

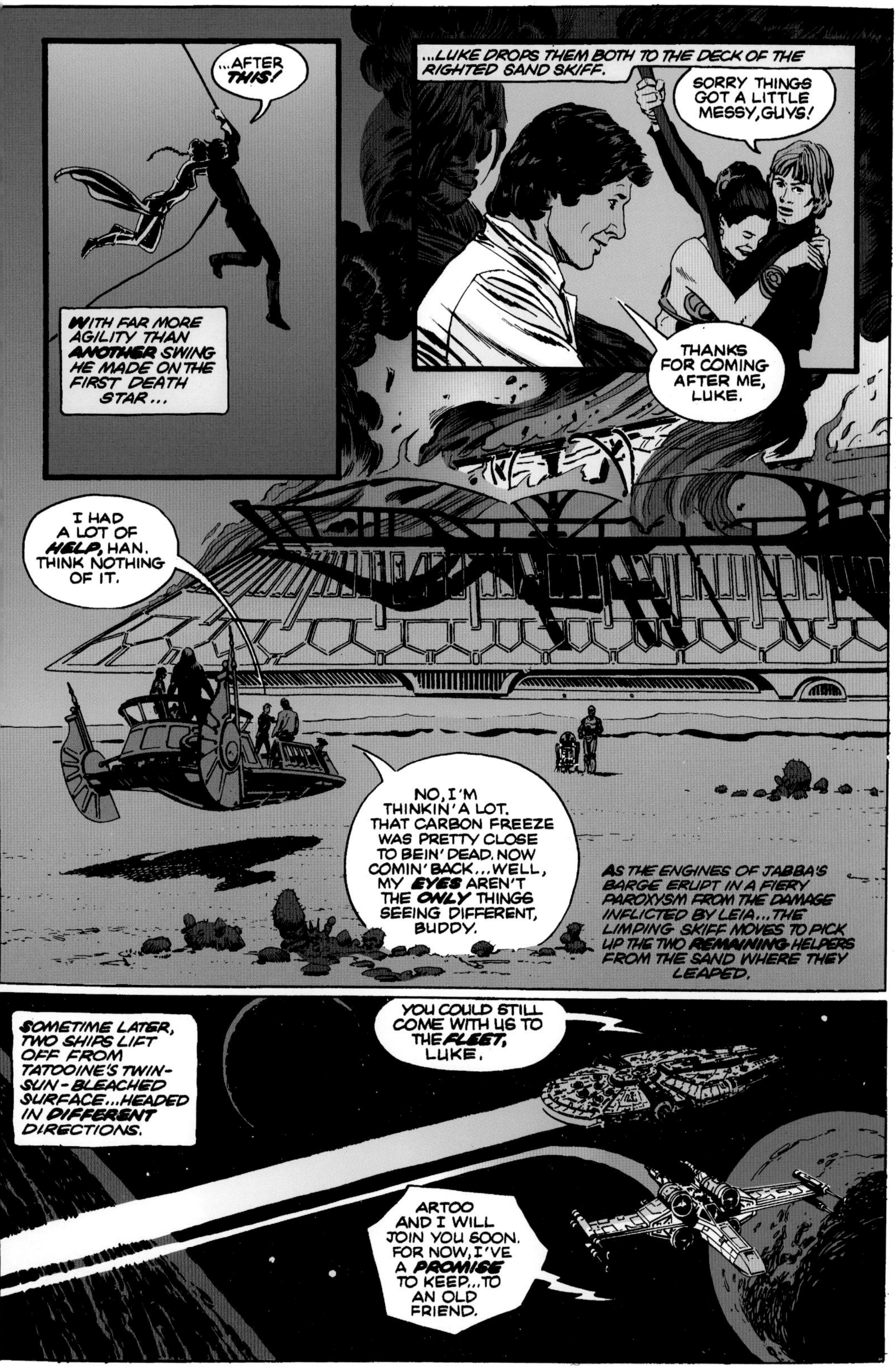
...AFTER THIS!
WITH FAR MORE AGILITY THAN ANOTHER SWING HE MADE ON THE FIRST DEATH STAR...
...LUKE DROPS THEM BOTH TO THE DECK OF THE RIGHTED SAND SKIFF.
SORRY THINGS GOT A LITTLE MESSY, GUYS!
THANKS FOR COMING AFTER ME, LUKE.
I HAD A LOT OF HELP, HAN. THINK NOTHING OF IT.
NO, I'M THINKIN' A LOT. THAT CARBON FREEZE WAS PRETTY CLOSE TO BEIN' DEAD. NOW COMIN' BACK... WELL, MY EYES AREN'T THE ONLY THINGS SEEING DIFFERENT, BUDDY.
AS THE ENGINES OF JABBA'S BARGE ERUPT IN A FIERY PAROXYSM FROM THE DAMAGE INFLICTED BY LEIA... THE LIMPING SKIFF MOVES TO PICK UP THE TWO REMAINING HELPERS FROM THE SAND WHERE THEY LEAPED.
SOMETIME LATER, TWO SHIPS LIFT OFF FROM TATOOINE'S TWIN-SUN-BLEACHED SURFACE... HEADED IN DIFFERENT DIRECTIONS.
YOU COULD STILL COME WITH US TO THE FLEET, LUKE.
ARTOO AND I WILL JOIN YOU SOON. FOR NOW, I'VE A PROMISE TO KEEP... TO AN OLD FRIEND.

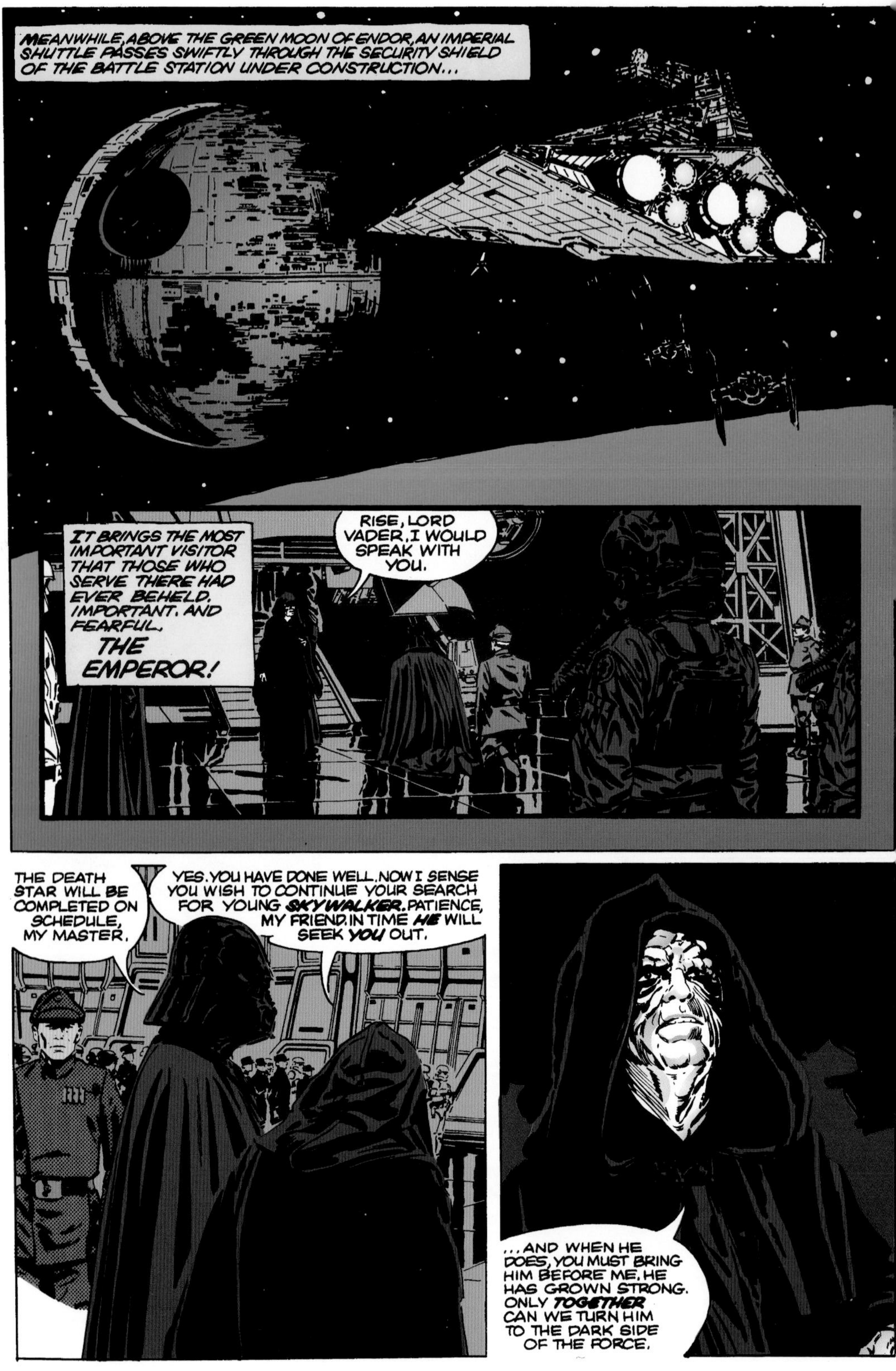
MEANWHILE, ABOVE THE GREEN MOON OF ENDOR, AN IMPERIAL SHUTTLE PASSES SWIFTLY THROUGH THE SECURITY SHIELD OF THE BATTLE STATION UNDER CONSTRUCTION...
IT BRINGS THE MOST IMPORTANT VISITOR THAT THOSE WHO SERVE THERE HAD EVER BEHELD. IMPORTANT. AND FEARFUL. THE EMPEROR!
RISE, LORD VADER. I WOULD SPEAK WITH YOU.
THE DEATH STAR WILL BE COMPLETED ON SCHEDULE, MY MASTER.
YES. YOU HAVE DONE WELL. NOW I SENSE YOU WISH TO CONTINUE YOUR SEARCH FOR YOUNG SKYWALKER. PATIENCE, MY FRIEND. IN TIME HE WILL SEEK YOU OUT.
...AND WHEN HE DOES, YOU MUST BRING HIM BEFORE ME. HE HAS GROWN STRONG. ONLY TOGETHER CAN WE TURN HIM TO THE DARK SIDE OF THE FORCE.

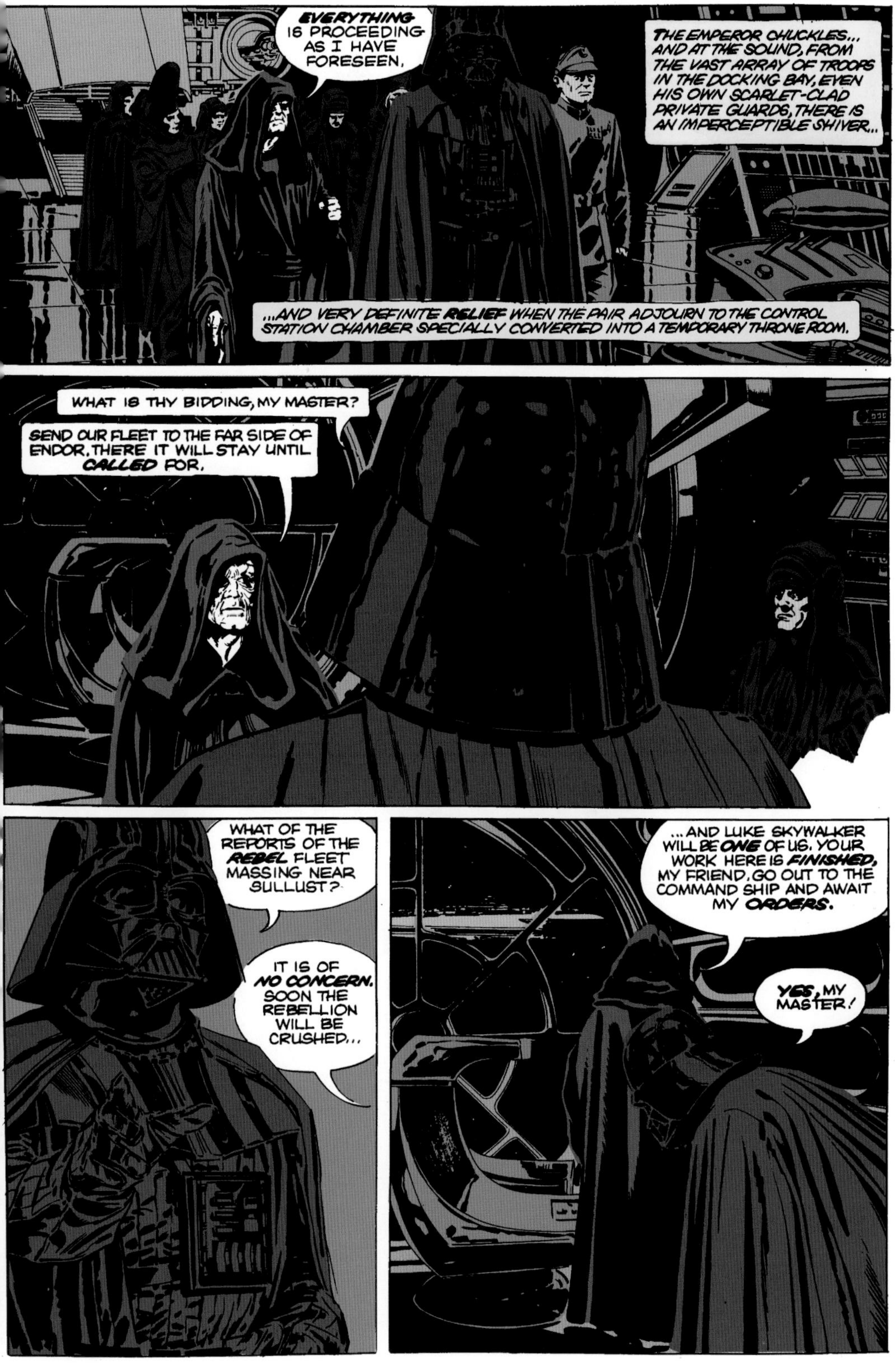
EVERYTHING IS PROCEEDING AS I HAVE FORESEEN.
THE EMPEROR CHUCKLES... AND AT THE SOUND, FROM THE VAST ARRAY OF TROOPS IN THE DOCKING BAY, EVEN HIS OWN SCARLET-CLAD PRIVATE GUARDS, THERE IS AN IMPERCEPTIBLE SHIVER...
...AND VERY DEFINITE RELIEF WHEN THE PAIR ADJOURN TO THE CONTROL STATION CHAMBER SPECIALLY CONVERTED INTO A TEMPORARY THRONE ROOM.
WHAT IS THY BIDDING, MY MASTER?
SEND OUR FLEET TO THE FAR SIDE OF ENDOR. THERE IT WILL STAY UNTIL CALLED FOR.
WHAT OF THE REPORTS OF THE REBEL FLEET MASSING NEAR SULLUST?
IT IS OF NO CONCERN. SOON THE REBELLION WILL BE CRUSHED...
...AND LUKE SKYWALKER WILL BE ONE OF US. YOUR WORK HERE IS FINISHED, MY FRIEND. GO OUT TO THE COMMAND SHIP AND AWAIT MY ORDERS.
YES, MY MASTER!

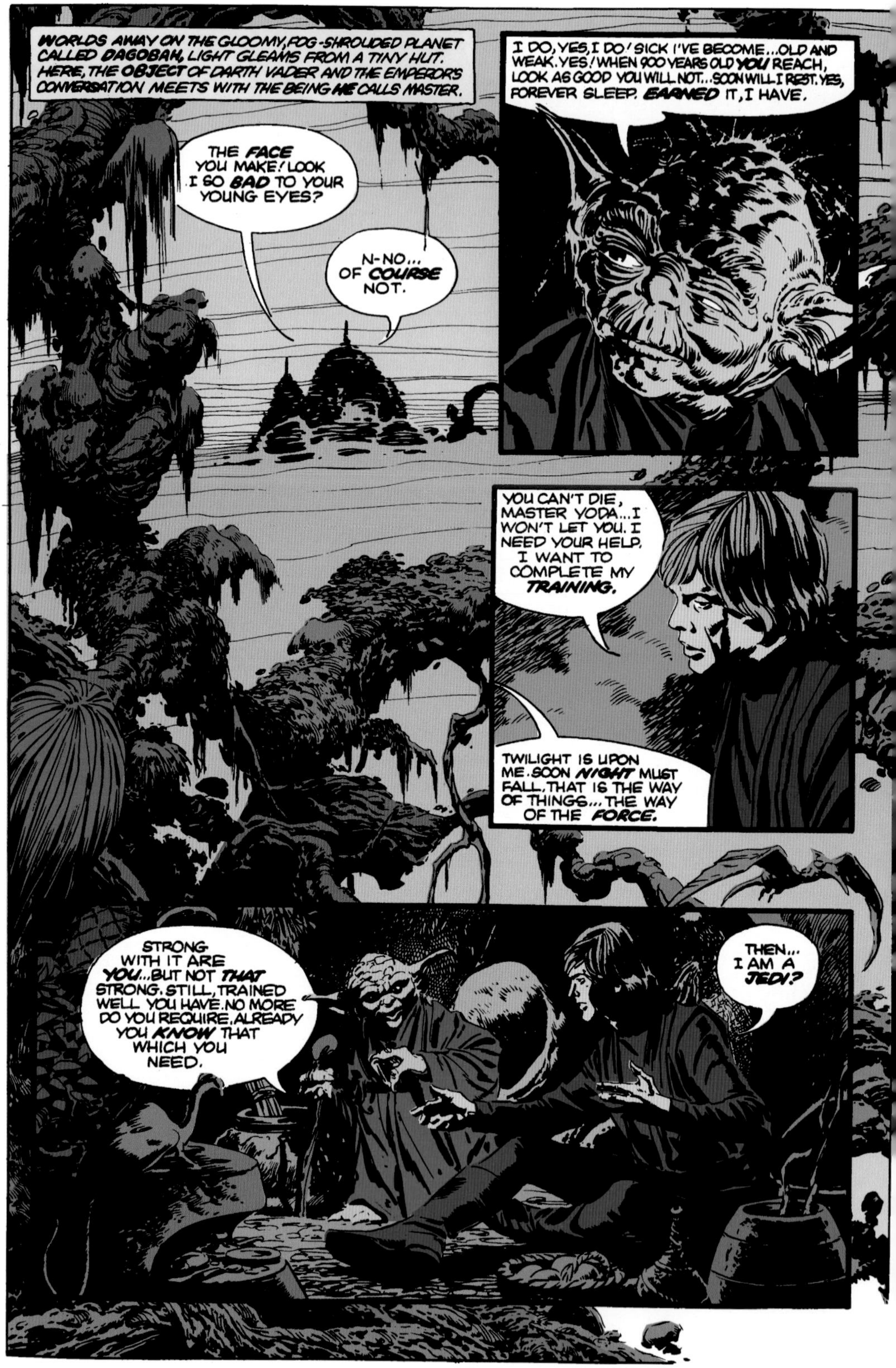
WORLDS AWAY ON THE GLOOMY, FOG-SHROUDED PLANET CALLED DAGOBAH, LIGHT GLEAMS FROM A TINY HUT. HERE, THE OBJECT OF DARTH VADER AND THE EMPEROR'S CONVERSATION MEETS WITH THE BEING HE CALLS MASTER.
THE FACE YOU MAKE! LOOK I SO BAD TO YOUR YOUNG EYES?
N-NO... OF COURSE NOT.
I DO, YES, I DO! SICK I'VE BECOME... OLD AND WEAK. YES! WHEN 900 YEARS OLD YOU REACH, LOOK AS GOOD YOU WILL NOT... SOON WILL I REST. YES, FOREVER SLEEP. EARNED IT, I HAVE.
YOU CAN'T DIE, MASTER YODA... I WON'T LET YOU. I NEED YOUR HELP. I WANT TO COMPLETE MY TRAINING.
TWILIGHT IS UPON ME. SOON NIGHT MUST FALL. THAT IS THE WAY OF THINGS... THE WAY OF THE FORCE.
STRONG WITH IT ARE YOU... BUT NOT THAT STRONG. STILL, TRAINED WELL YOU HAVE. NO MORE DO YOU REQUIRE. ALREADY YOU KNOW THAT WHICH YOU NEED.
THEN... I AM A JEDI?

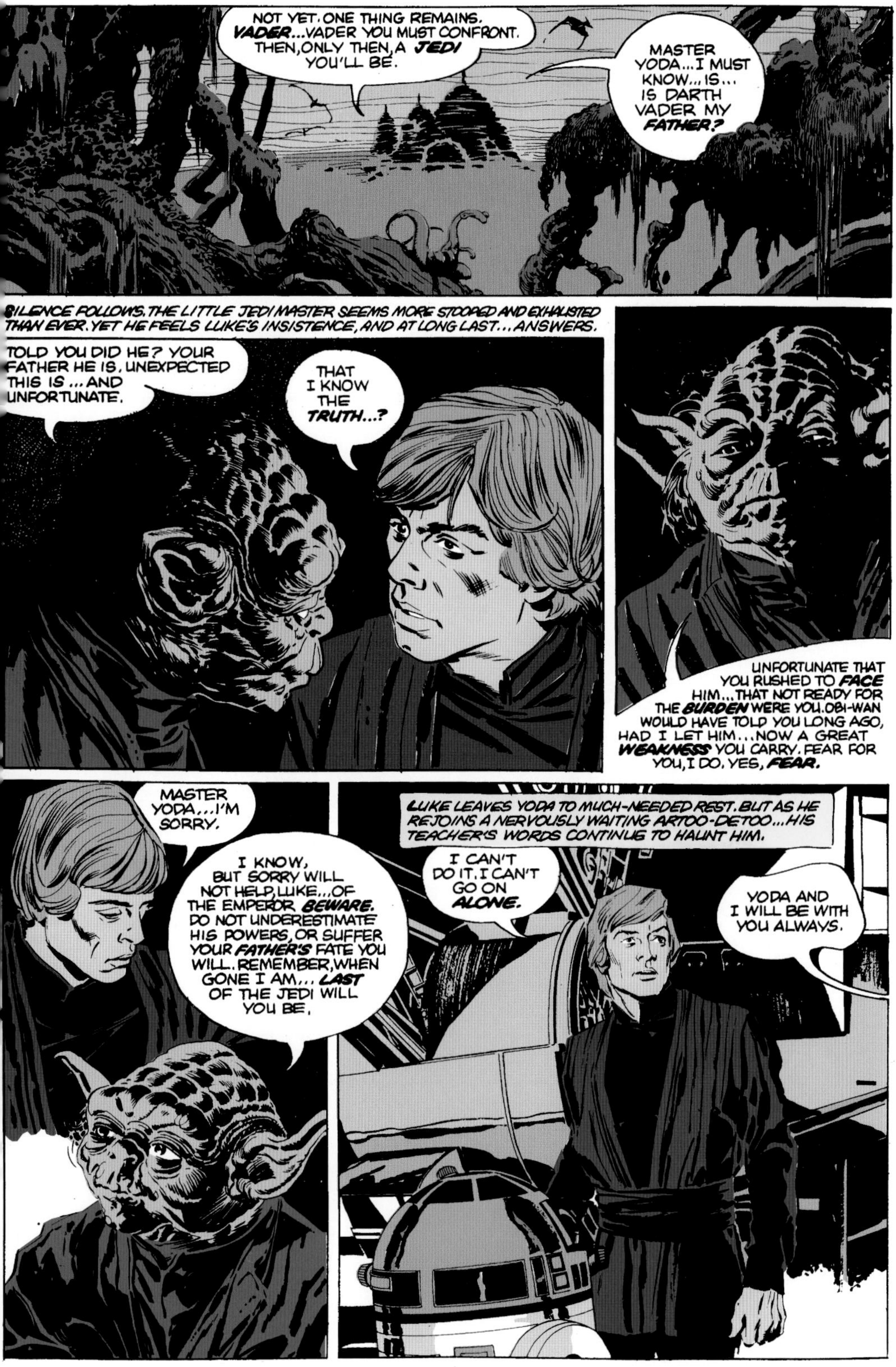
NOT YET. ONE THING REMAINS. VADER...VADER YOU MUST CONFRONT. THEN, ONLY THEN, A JEDI YOU'LL BE.
MASTER YODA...I MUST KNOW...IS... IS DARTH VADER MY FATHER?
SILENCE FOLLOWS. THE LITTLE JEDI MASTER SEEMS MORE STOOPED AND EXHAUSTED THAN EVER. YET HE FEELS LUKE'S INSISTENCE, AND AT LONG LAST... ANSWERS.
TOLD YOU DID HE? YOUR FATHER HE IS. UNEXPECTED THIS IS ...AND UNFORTUNATE.
THAT I KNOW THE TRUTH...?
UNFORTUNATE THAT YOU RUSHED TO FACE HIM...THAT NOT READY FOR THE BURDEN WERE YOU. OBI-WAN WOULD HAVE TOLD YOU LONG AGO, HAD I LET HIM...NOW A GREAT WEAKNESS YOU CARRY. FEAR FOR YOU, I DO. YES, FEAR.
MASTER YODA...I'M SORRY.
I KNOW, BUT SORRY WILL NOT HELP, LUKE...OF THE EMPEROR BEWARE. DO NOT UNDERESTIMATE HIS POWERS, OR SUFFER YOUR FATHER'S FATE YOU WILL. REMEMBER, WHEN GONE I AM... LAST OF THE JEDI WILL YOU BE.
LUKE LEAVES YODA TO MUCH-NEEDED REST. BUT AS HE REJOINS A NERVOUSLY WAITING ARTOO-DETOO...HIS TEACHER'S WORDS CONTINUE TO HAUNT HIM.
I CAN'T DO IT, I CAN'T GO ON ALONE.
YODA AND I WILL BE WITH YOU ALWAYS.

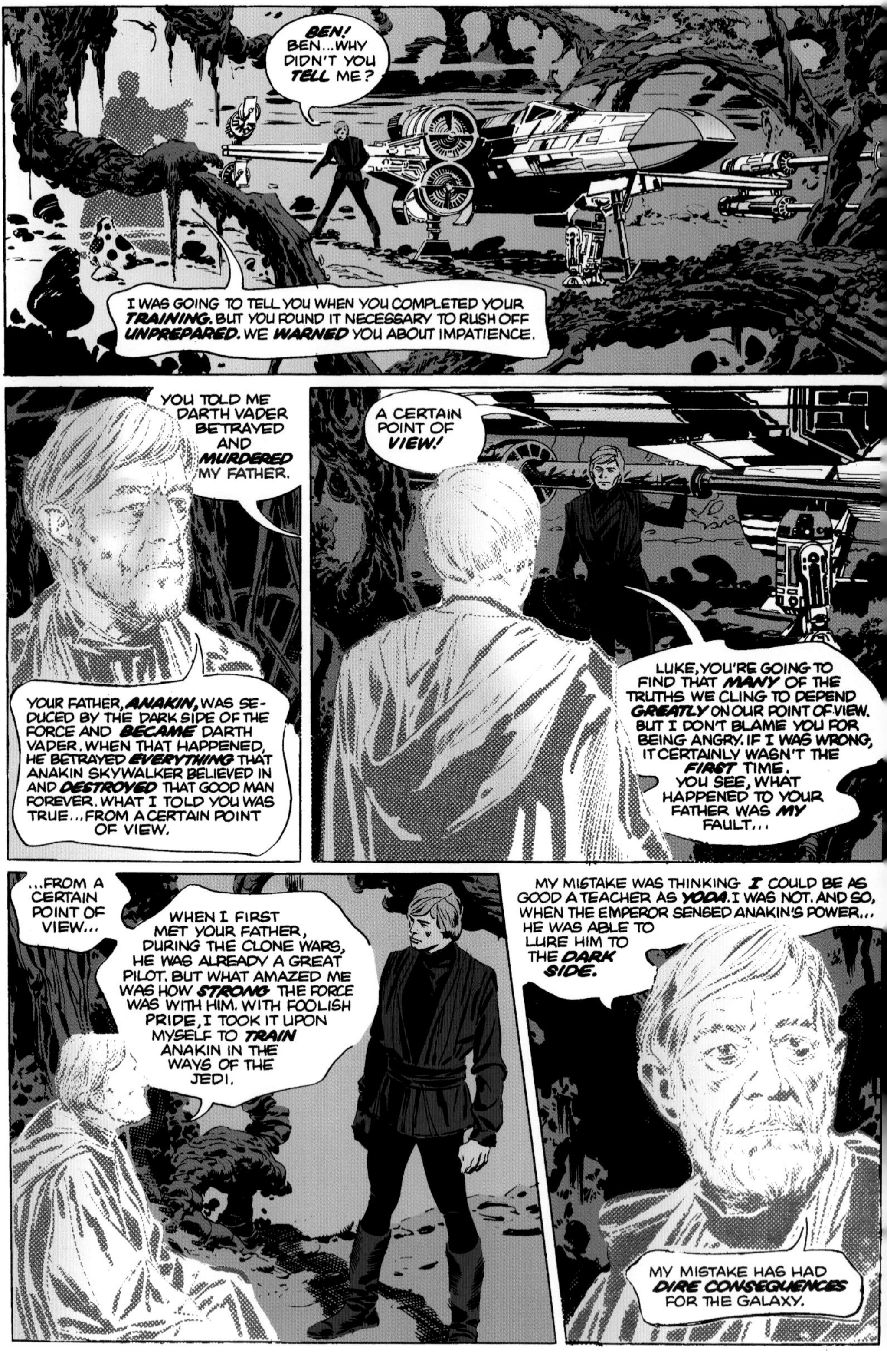
BEN! BEN...WHY DIDN'T YOU TELL ME?
I WAS GOING TO TELL YOU WHEN YOU COMPLETED YOUR TRAINING. BUT YOU FOUND IT NECESSARY TO RUSH OFF UNPREPARED. WE WARNED YOU ABOUT IMPATIENCE.
YOU TOLD ME DARTH VADER BETRAYED AND MURDERED MY FATHER.
YOUR FATHER, ANAKIN, WAS SEDUCED BY THE DARK SIDE OF THE FORCE AND BECAME DARTH VADER. WHEN THAT HAPPENED, HE BETRAYED EVERYTHING THAT ANAKIN SKYWALKER BELIEVED IN AND DESTROYED THAT GOOD MAN FOREVER. WHAT I TOLD YOU WAS TRUE...FROM A CERTAIN POINT OF VIEW.
A CERTAIN POINT OF VIEW!
LUKE, YOU'RE GOING TO FIND THAT MANY OF THE TRUTHS WE CLING TO DEPEND GREATLY ON OUR POINT OF VIEW. BUT I DON'T BLAME YOU FOR BEING ANGRY. IF I WAS WRONG, IT CERTAINLY WASN'T THE FIRST TIME. YOU SEE, WHAT HAPPENED TO YOUR FATHER WAS MY FAULT...
...FROM A CERTAIN POINT OF VIEW...
WHEN I FIRST MET YOUR FATHER, DURING THE CLONE WARS, HE WAS ALREADY A GREAT PILOT. BUT WHAT AMAZED ME WAS HOW STRONG THE FORCE WAS WITH HIM. WITH FOOLISH PRIDE, I TOOK IT UPON MYSELF TO TRAIN ANAKIN IN THE WAYS OF THE JEDI.
MY MISTAKE WAS THINKING I COULD BE AS GOOD A TEACHER AS YODA. I WAS NOT. AND SO, WHEN THE EMPEROR SENSED ANAKIN'S POWER... HE WAS ABLE TO LURE HIM TO THE DARK SIDE.
MY MISTAKE HAS HAD DIRE CONSEQUENCES FOR THE GALAXY.

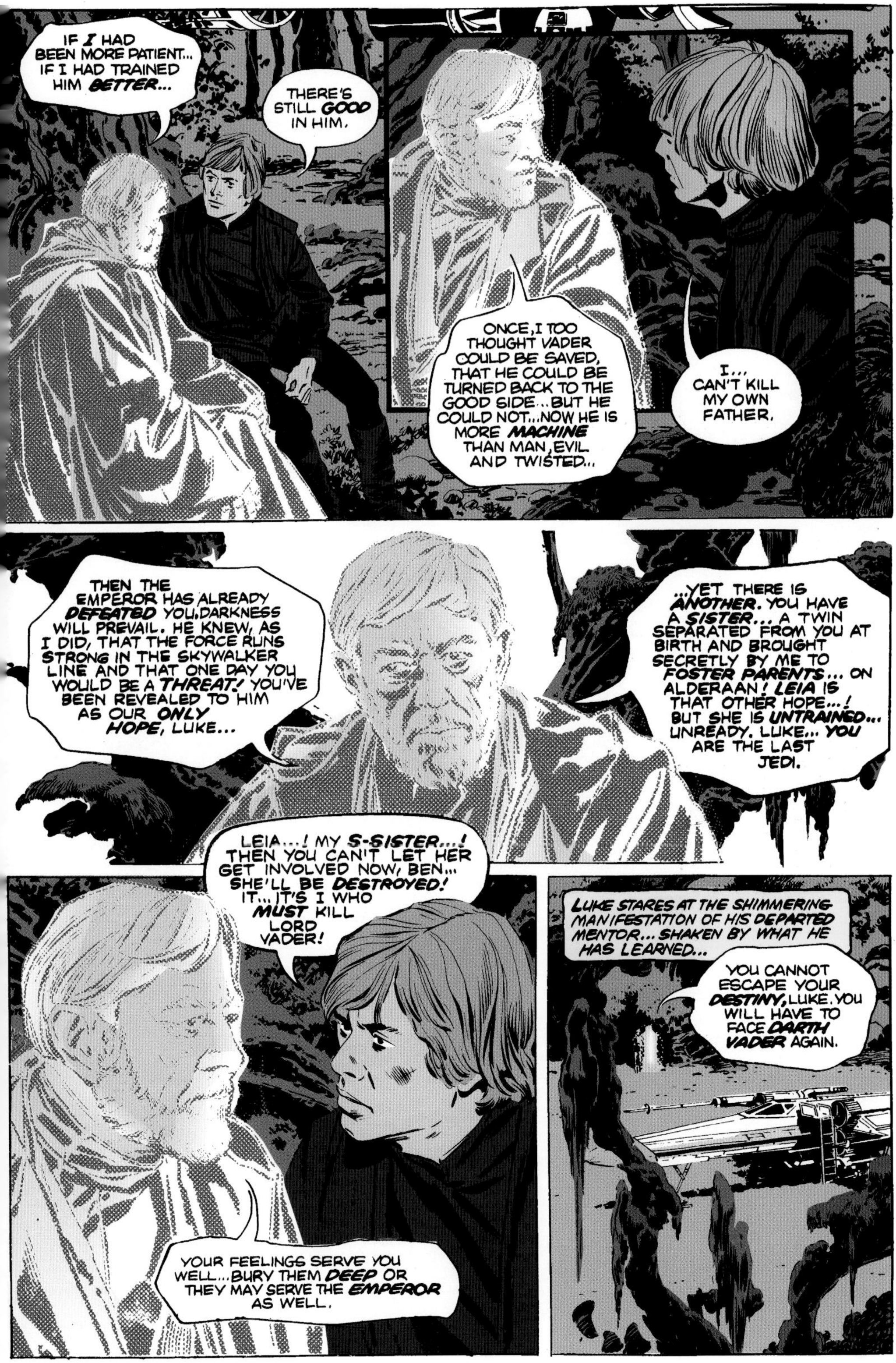
IF I HAD BEEN MORE PATIENT... IF I HAD TRAINED HIM BETTER...
THERE'S STILL GOOD IN HIM.
ONCE, I TOO THOUGHT VADER COULD BE SAVED, THAT HE COULD BE TURNED BACK TO THE GOOD SIDE... BUT HE COULD NOT... NOW HE IS MORE MACHINE THAN MAN, EVIL AND TWISTED...
I... CAN'T KILL MY OWN FATHER.
THEN THE EMPEROR HAS ALREADY DEFEATED YOU. DARKNESS WILL PREVAIL. HE KNEW, AS I DID, THAT THE FORCE RUNS STRONG IN THE SKYWALKER LINE AND THAT ONE DAY YOU WOULD BE A THREAT! YOU'VE BEEN REVEALED TO HIM AS OUR ONLY HOPE, LUKE...
...YET THERE IS ANOTHER. YOU HAVE A SISTER... A TWIN SEPARATED FROM YOU AT BIRTH AND BROUGHT SECRETLY BY ME TO FOSTER PARENTS... ON ALDERAAN! LEIA IS THAT OTHER HOPE...! BUT SHE IS UNTRAINED... UNREADY. LUKE... YOU ARE THE LAST JEDI.
LEIA...! MY S-SISTER...! THEN YOU CAN'T LET HER GET INVOLVED NOW, BEN... SHE'LL BE DESTROYED! IT... IT'S I WHO MUST KILL LORD VADER!
YOUR FEELINGS SERVE YOU WELL... BURY THEM DEEP OR THEY MAY SERVE THE EMPEROR AS WELL.
LUKE STARES AT THE SHIMMERING MANIFESTATION OF HIS DEPARTED MENTOR... SHAKEN BY WHAT HE HAS LEARNED...
YOU CANNOT ESCAPE YOUR DESTINY, LUKE. YOU WILL HAVE TO FACE DARTH VADER AGAIN.

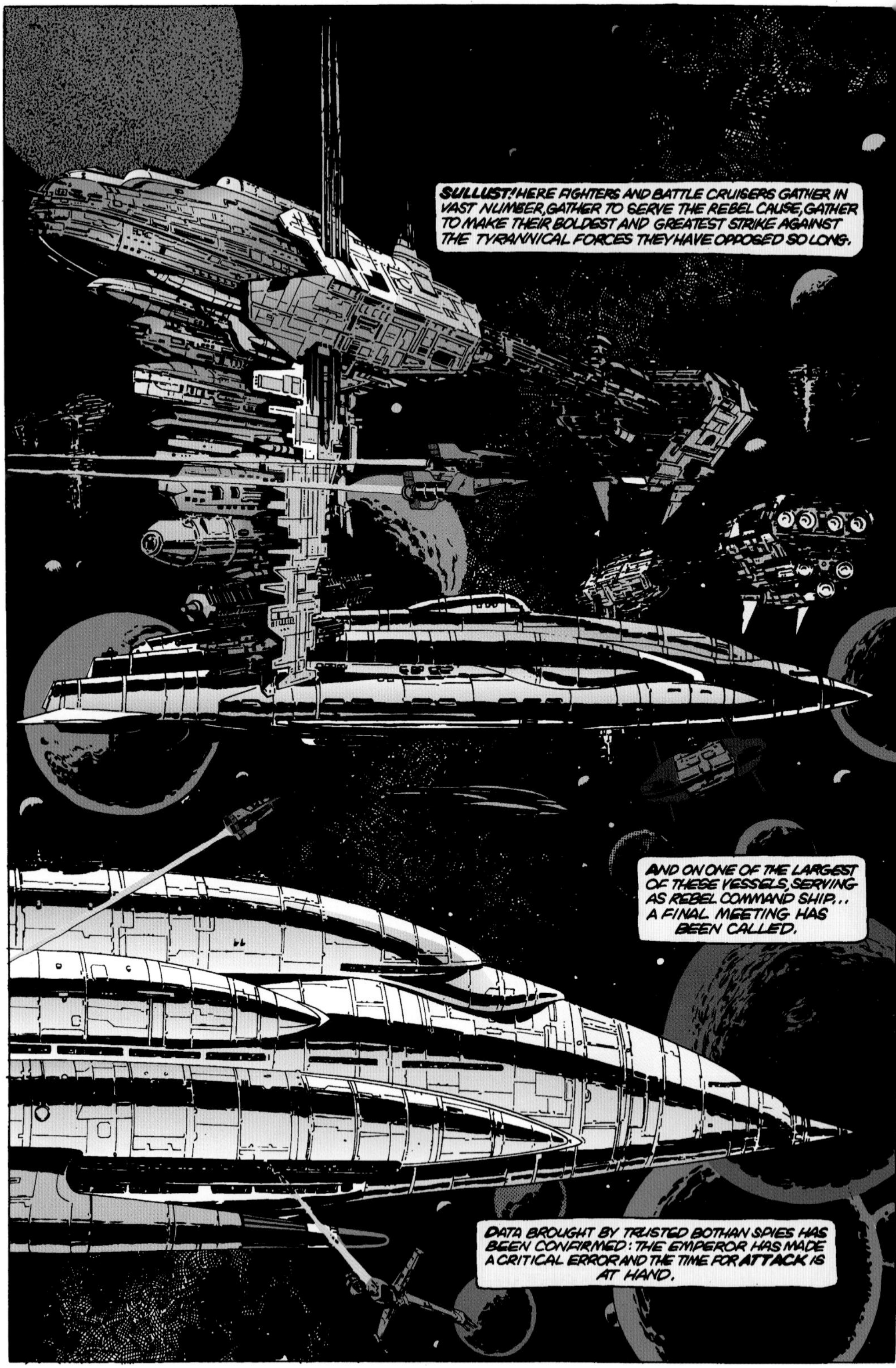
SULLUST! HERE FIGHTERS AND BATTLE CRUISERS GATHER IN VAST NUMBER, GATHER TO SERVE THE REBEL CAUSE, GATHER TO MAKE THEIR BOLDEST AND GREATEST STRIKE AGAINST THE TYRANNICAL FORCES THEY HAVE OPPOSED SO LONG.
AND ON ONE OF THE LARGEST OF THESE VESSELS, SERVING AS REBEL COMMAND SHIP... A FINAL MEETING HAS BEEN CALLED.
DATA BROUGHT BY TRUSTED BOTHAN SPIES HAS BEEN CONFIRMED: THE EMPEROR HAS MADE A CRITICAL ERROR AND THE TIME FOR ATTACK IS AT HAND.

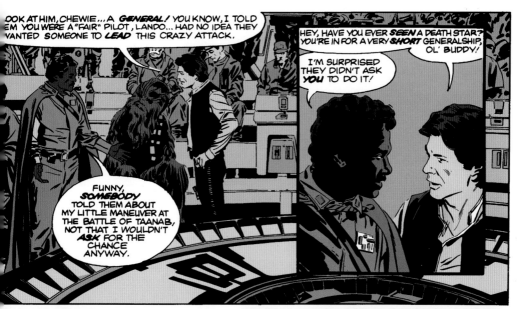

OOK AT HIM, CHEWIE...A *GENERAL!* YOU KNOW, I TOLD EM YOU WERE A "FAIR" PILOT, LANDO... HAD NO IDEA THEY VANTED *SOMEONE* TO *LEAD* THIS CRAZY ATTACK.

HEY, HAVE YOU EVER *SEEN* A DEATH STAR? YOU'RE IN FOR A VERY *SHORT* GENERALSHIP, OL' BUDDY!

I'M SURPRISED THEY DIDN'T ASK *YOU* TO DO IT!

FUNNY, *SOMEBODY* TOLD THEM ABOUT MY LITTLE MANEUVER AT THE BATTLE OF TAANAB, NOT THAT I WOULDN'T *ASK* FOR THE CHANCE ANYWAY.

MAYBE THEY DID, BUT *I'M* NOT CRAZY. *YOU'RE* THE RESPECTABLE ONE, REMEMBER?

HAN'S STAYING ON THE COMMAND SHIP WITH ME. WE'RE *BOTH* GRATEFUL FOR WHAT YOU'RE DOING, LANDO...AND *PROUD.*

THEN, THE CHAMBER GROWS DARK AND HUSHED, AS A HOLOGRAPHIC IMAGE OF AN IMPERIAL CONSTRUCTION APPEARS...AND MON MOTHMA, SUPREME LEADER OF THE REBEL ALLIANCE, BEGINS TO SPEAK.

THIS IS THE EMPEROR'S NEW *BATTLE STATION*...ITS WEAPONS SYSTEMS ARE NOT YET *OPERATIONAL.* WITH THE IMPERIAL FLEET SPREAD THROUGHOUT THE GALAXY, VAINLY ATTEMPTING TO *ENGAGE* US...

IT IS RELATIVELY *UNPROTECTED.* MOST IMPORTANT, OUR SPY NETWORK HAS LEARNED THE *EMPEROR* IS PERSONALLY *OVERSEEING* THE CONSTRUCTION.

WHEN THE EXCITEMENT OF THIS INFORMATION DIES DOWN, ADMIRAL ACKBAR OF THE ALLIANCE'S MON CALAMARI ALLIES TAKES THE PODIUM.

THIS DEATH STAR IS NOT *ENTIRELY* WITHOUT DEFENSES. IT IS PROTECTED BY AN *ENERGY SHIELD* GENERATED FROM THE NEARBY MOON OF *ENDOR.*

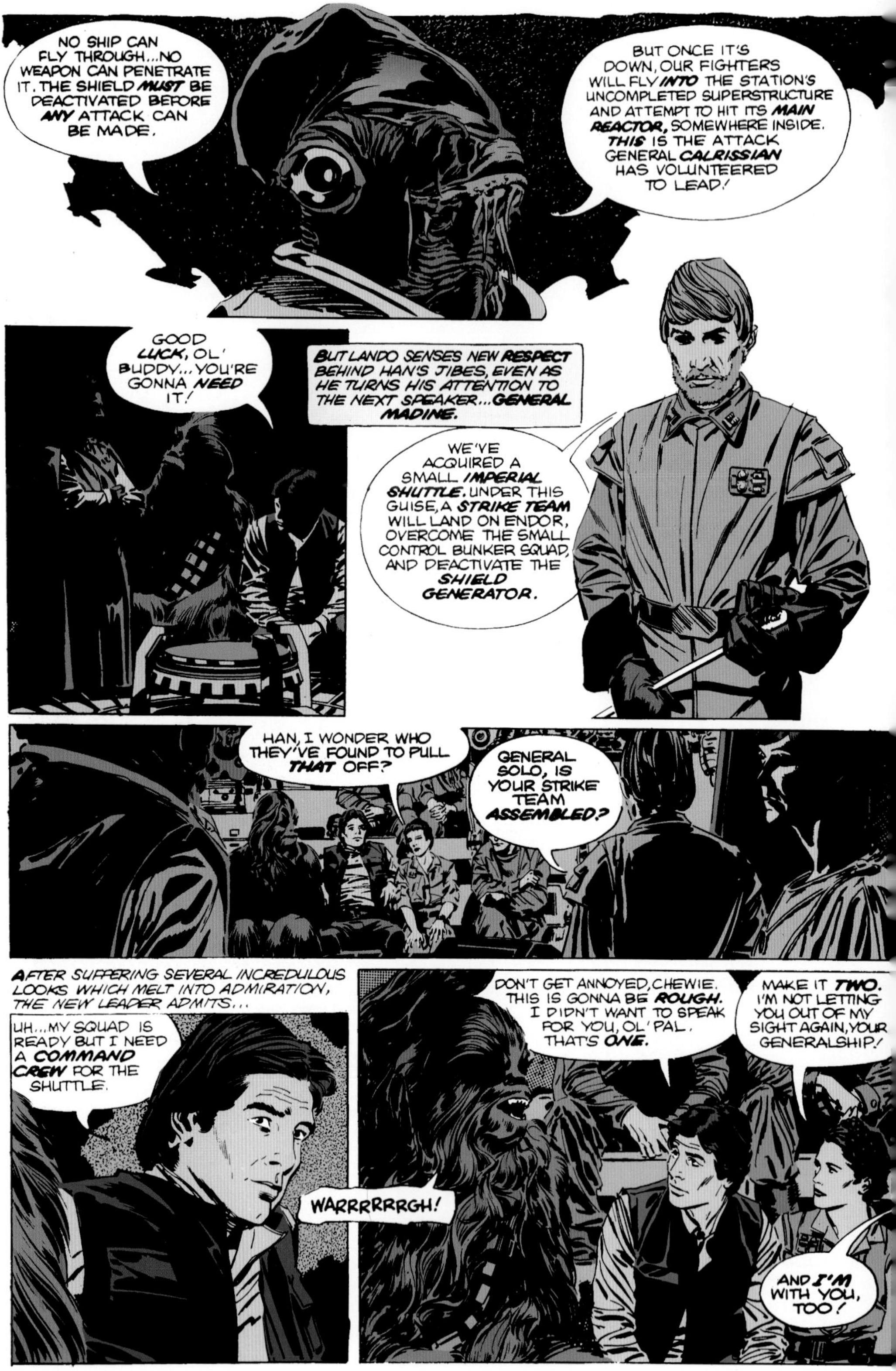
NO SHIP CAN FLY THROUGH...NO WEAPON CAN PENETRATE IT. THE SHIELD MUST BE DEACTIVATED BEFORE ANY ATTACK CAN BE MADE.
BUT ONCE IT'S DOWN, OUR FIGHTERS WILL FLY INTO THE STATION'S UNCOMPLETED SUPERSTRUCTURE AND ATTEMPT TO HIT ITS MAIN REACTOR, SOMEWHERE INSIDE. THIS IS THE ATTACK GENERAL CALRISSIAN HAS VOLUNTEERED TO LEAD!
GOOD LUCK, OL' BUDDY...YOU'RE GONNA NEED IT!
BUT LANDO SENSES NEW RESPECT BEHIND HAN'S JIBES, EVEN AS HE TURNS HIS ATTENTION TO THE NEXT SPEAKER...GENERAL MADINE.
WE'VE ACQUIRED A SMALL IMPERIAL SHUTTLE. UNDER THIS GUISE, A STRIKE TEAM WILL LAND ON ENDOR, OVERCOME THE SMALL CONTROL BUNKER SQUAD, AND DEACTIVATE THE SHIELD GENERATOR.
HAN, I WONDER WHO THEY'VE FOUND TO PULL THAT OFF?
GENERAL SOLO, IS YOUR STRIKE TEAM ASSEMBLED?
AFTER SUFFERING SEVERAL INCREDULOUS LOOKS WHICH MELT INTO ADMIRATION, THE NEW LEADER ADMITS...
UH...MY SQUAD IS READY BUT I NEED A COMMAND CREW FOR THE SHUTTLE.
WARRRRRRGH!
DON'T GET ANNOYED, CHEWIE. THIS IS GONNA BE ROUGH. I DIDN'T WANT TO SPEAK FOR YOU, OL' PAL. THAT'S ONE.
MAKE IT TWO. I'M NOT LETTING YOU OUT OF MY SIGHT AGAIN, YOUR GENERALSHIP!
AND I'M WITH YOU, TOO!

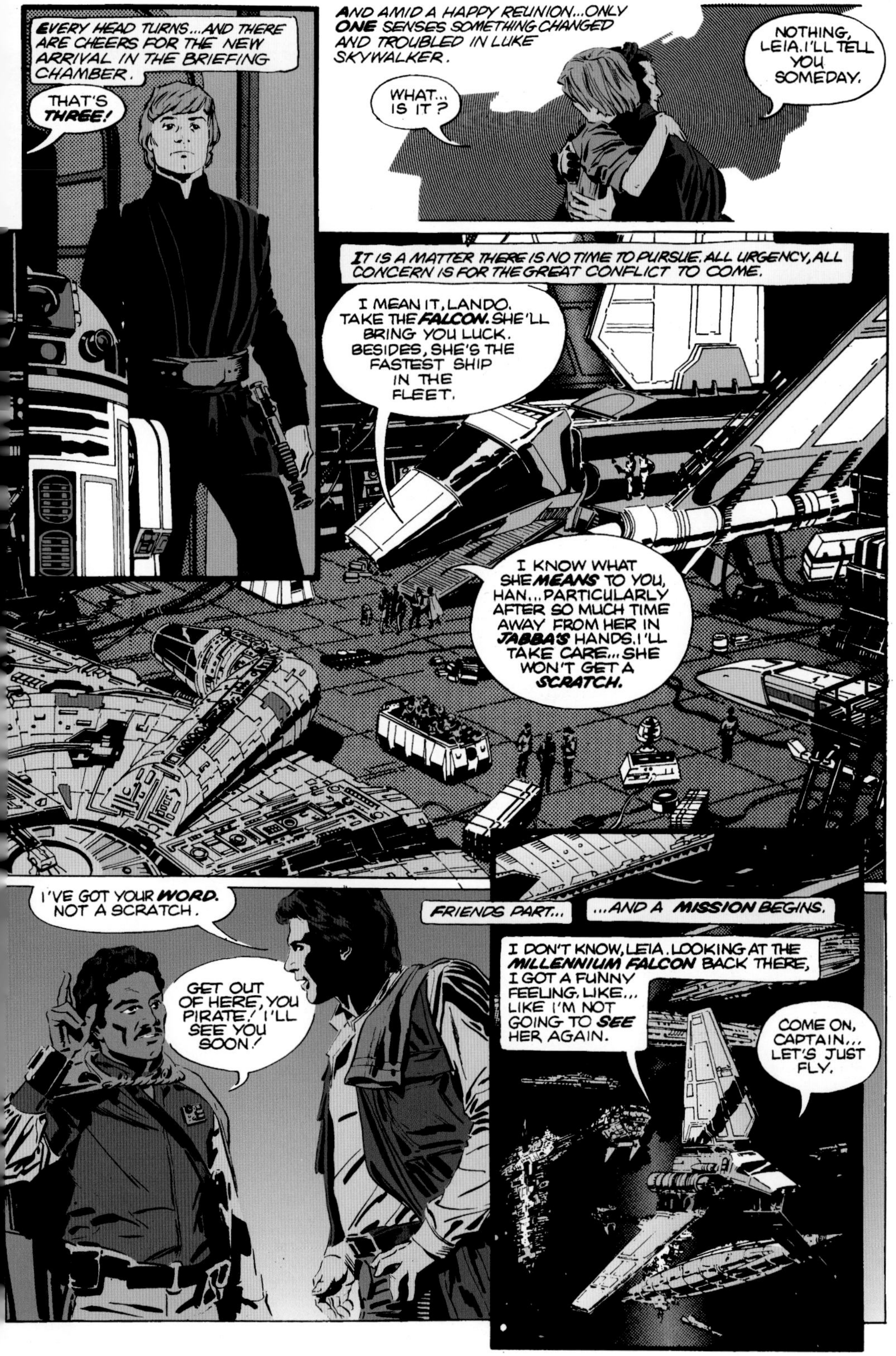
EVERY HEAD TURNS...AND THERE ARE CHEERS FOR THE NEW ARRIVAL IN THE BRIEFING CHAMBER.
THAT'S THREE!
AND AMID A HAPPY REUNION...ONLY ONE SENSES SOMETHING CHANGED AND TROUBLED IN LUKE SKYWALKER.
WHAT... IS IT?
NOTHING, LEIA. I'LL TELL YOU SOMEDAY.
IT IS A MATTER THERE IS NO TIME TO PURSUE. ALL URGENCY, ALL CONCERN IS FOR THE GREAT CONFLICT TO COME.
I MEAN IT, LANDO. TAKE THE FALCON. SHE'LL BRING YOU LUCK. BESIDES, SHE'S THE FASTEST SHIP IN THE FLEET.
I KNOW WHAT SHE MEANS TO YOU, HAN...PARTICULARLY AFTER SO MUCH TIME AWAY FROM HER IN JABBA'S HANDS. I'LL TAKE CARE...SHE WON'T GET A SCRATCH.
I'VE GOT YOUR WORD. NOT A SCRATCH.
GET OUT OF HERE, YOU PIRATE! I'LL SEE YOU SOON!
FRIENDS PART...
...AND A MISSION BEGINS.
I DON'T KNOW, LEIA. LOOKING AT THE MILLENNIUM FALCON BACK THERE, I GOT A FUNNY FEELING. LIKE... LIKE I'M NOT GOING TO SEE HER AGAIN.
COME ON, CAPTAIN... LET'S JUST FLY.

HAN SOLO DOES THAT... DESPITE COMPLAINTS FROM CHEWBACCA THAT THE EMPIRE DOESN'T DESIGN ITS SHUTTLES WITH WOOKIEE
IN MIND, DESPITE MECHANIZED BICKERING BETWEEN SEE-THREEPIO AND ARTOO-DETOO, AND DESPITE HIS OWN EARLY UNEASINES
SOON, PERHAPS TOO SOON, THEY ARE APPROACHING THEIR DESTINATION...

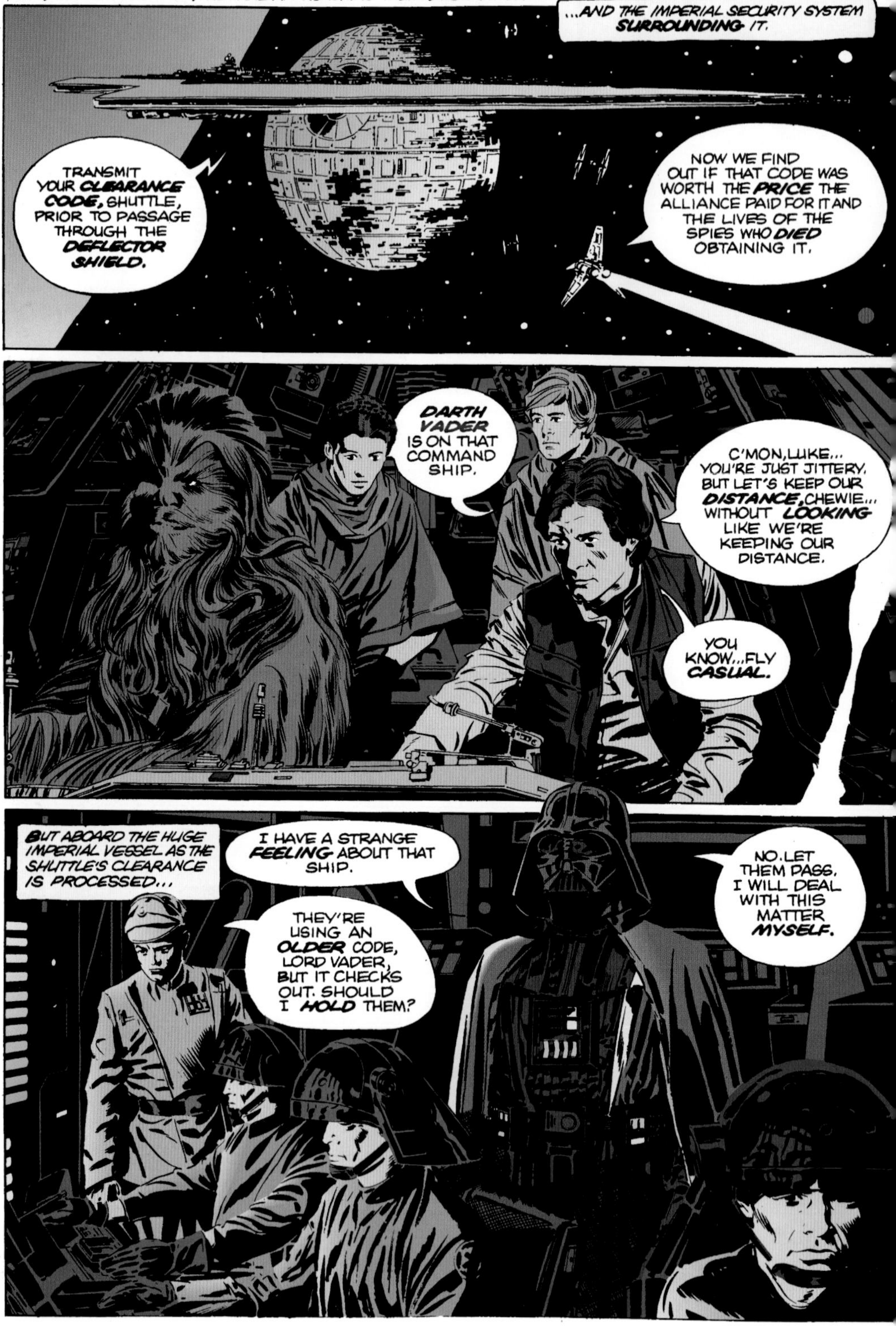
...AND THE IMPERIAL SECURITY SYSTEM SURROUNDING IT.
TRANSMIT YOUR CLEARANCE CODE, SHUTTLE, PRIOR TO PASSAGE THROUGH THE DEFLECTOR SHIELD.
NOW WE FIND OUT IF THAT CODE WAS WORTH THE PRICE THE ALLIANCE PAID FOR IT AND THE LIVES OF THE SPIES WHO DIED OBTAINING IT.
DARTH VADER IS ON THAT COMMAND SHIP.
C'MON, LUKE... YOU'RE JUST JITTERY. BUT LET'S KEEP OUR DISTANCE, CHEWIE... WITHOUT LOOKING LIKE WE'RE KEEPING OUR DISTANCE.
YOU KNOW... FLY CASUAL.
BUT ABOARD THE HUGE IMPERIAL VESSEL AS THE SHUTTLE'S CLEARANCE IS PROCESSED...
I HAVE A STRANGE FEELING ABOUT THAT SHIP.
THEY'RE USING AN OLDER CODE, LORD VADER, BUT IT CHECKS OUT. SHOULD I HOLD THEM?
NO. LET THEM PASS. I WILL DEAL WITH THIS MATTER MYSELF.

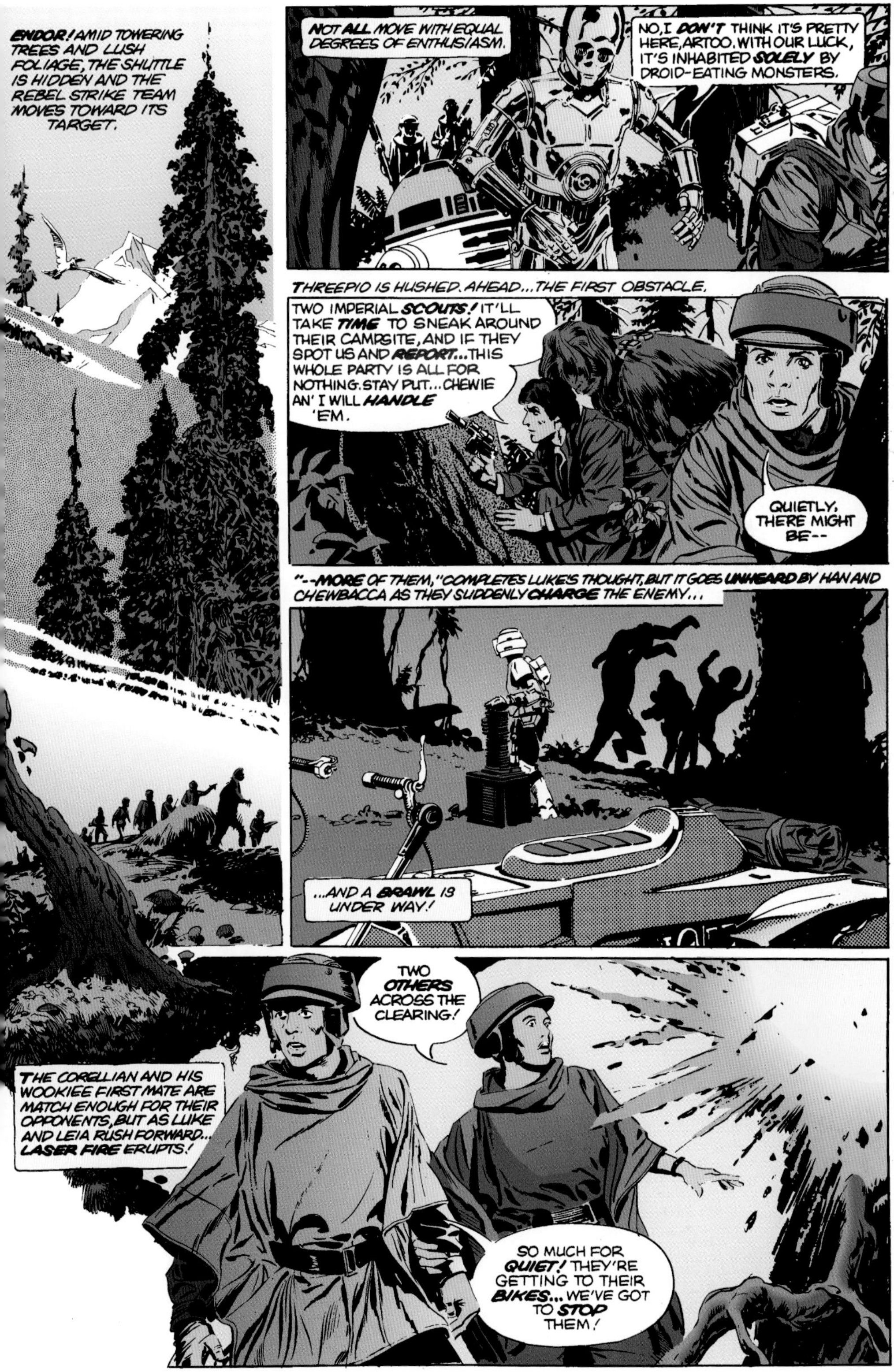

ENDOR! AMID TOWERING TREES AND LUSH FOLIAGE, THE SHUTTLE IS HIDDEN AND THE REBEL STRIKE TEAM MOVES TOWARD ITS TARGET.
NOT ALL MOVE WITH EQUAL DEGREES OF ENTHUSIASM.
NO, I DON'T THINK IT'S PRETTY HERE, ARTOO. WITH OUR LUCK, IT'S INHABITED SOLELY BY DROID-EATING MONSTERS.
THREEPIO IS HUSHED. AHEAD... THE FIRST OBSTACLE.
TWO IMPERIAL SCOUTS! IT'LL TAKE TIME TO SNEAK AROUND THEIR CAMPSITE, AND IF THEY SPOT US AND REPORT... THIS WHOLE PARTY IS ALL FOR NOTHING. STAY PUT... CHEWIE AN' I WILL HANDLE 'EM.
QUIETLY. THERE MIGHT BE--
"--MORE OF THEM," COMPLETES LUKE'S THOUGHT, BUT IT GOES UNHEARD BY HAN AND CHEWBACCA AS THEY SUDDENLY CHARGE THE ENEMY...
...AND A BRAWL IS UNDER WAY!
THE CORELLIAN AND HIS WOOKIEE FIRST MATE ARE MATCH ENOUGH FOR THEIR OPPONENTS, BUT AS LUKE AND LEIA RUSH FORWARD... LASER FIRE ERUPTS!
TWO OTHERS ACROSS THE CLEARING!
SO MUCH FOR QUIET! THEY'RE GETTING TO THEIR BIKES... WE'VE GOT TO STOP THEM!

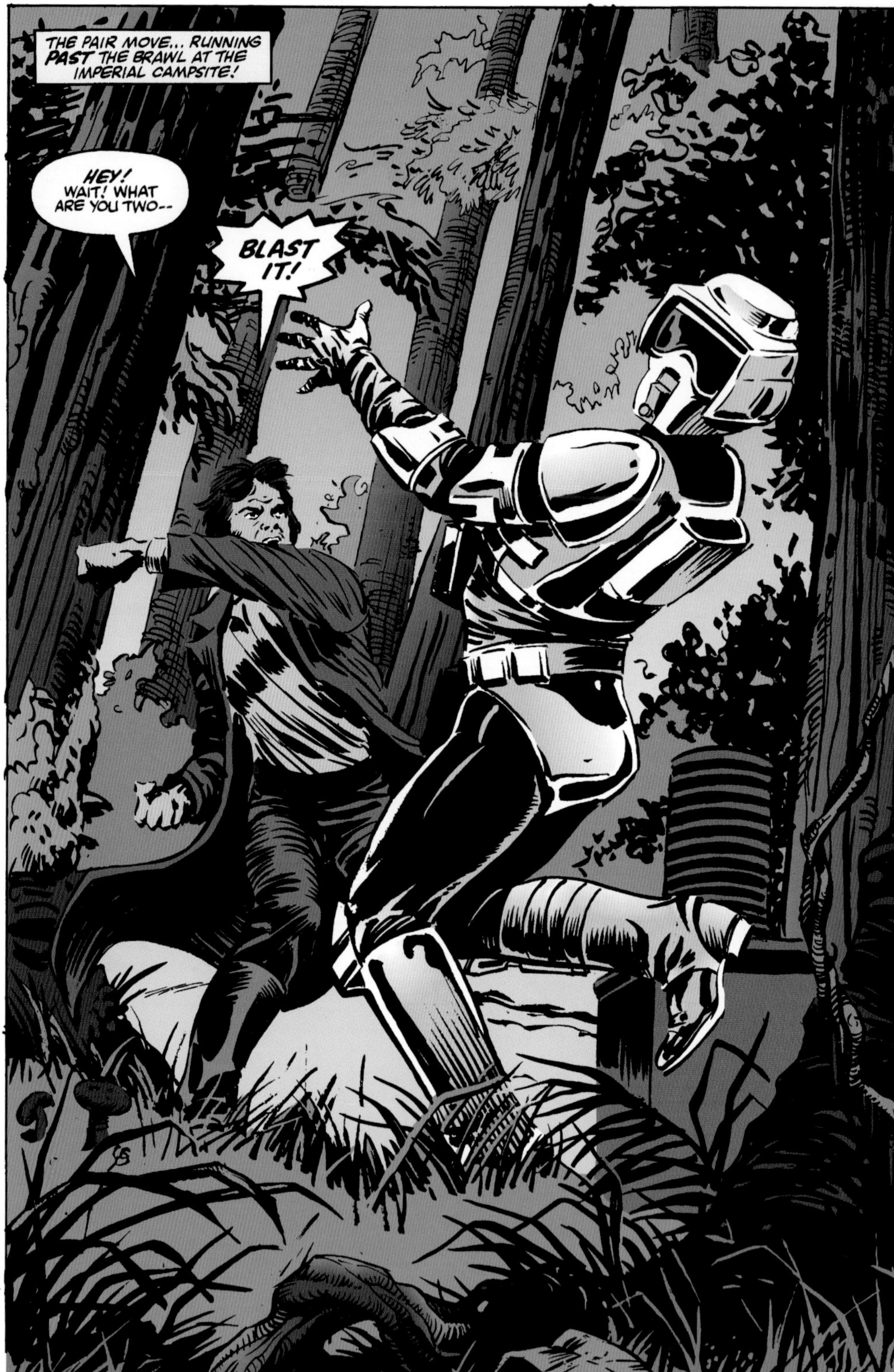
THE PAIR MOVE... RUNNING PAST THE BRAWL AT THE IMPERIAL CAMPSITE!
HEY! WAIT! WHAT ARE YOU TWO--
BLAST IT!

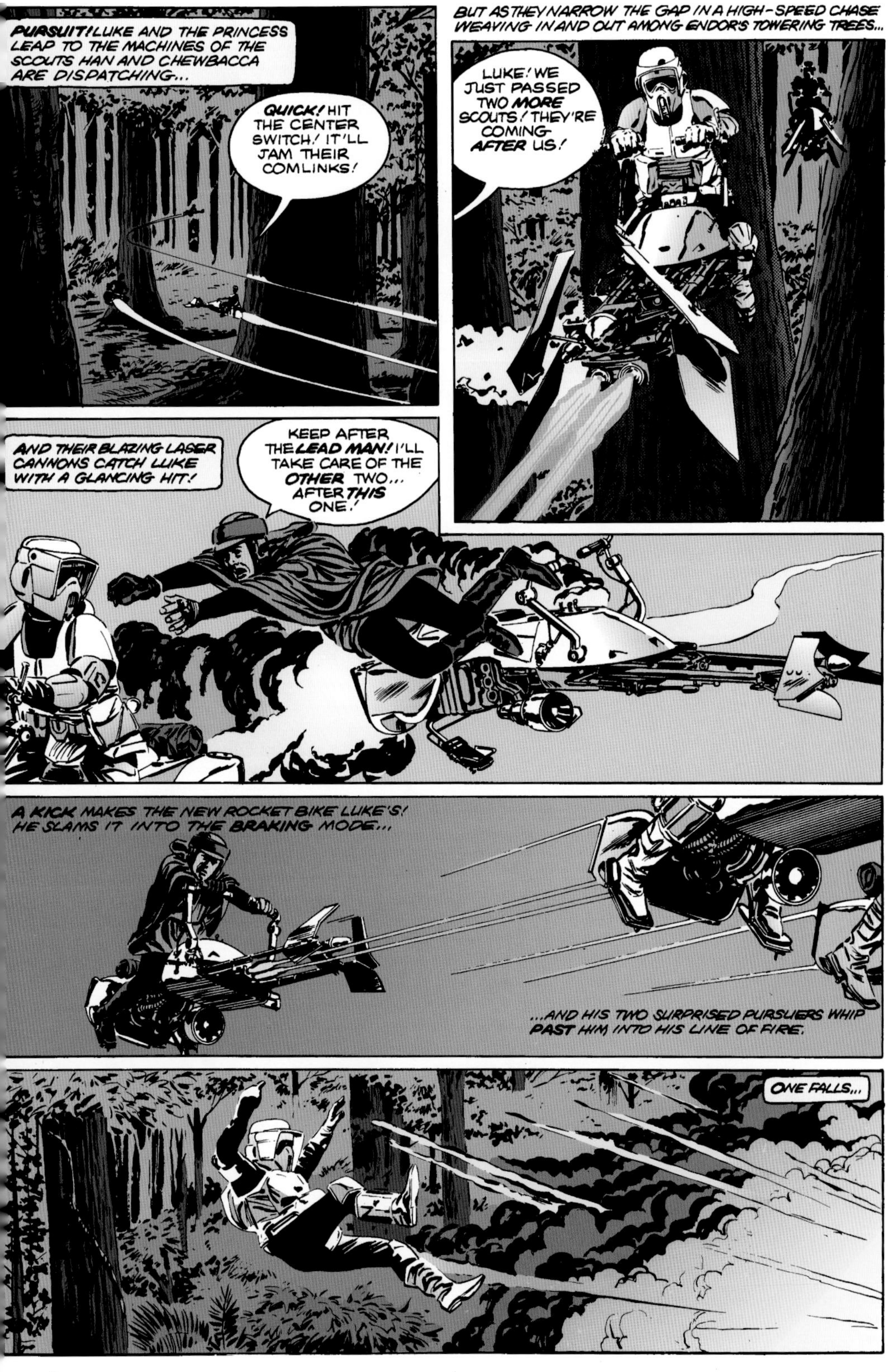
PURSUIT! LUKE AND THE PRINCESS LEAP TO THE MACHINES OF THE SCOUTS HAN AND CHEWBACCA ARE DISPATCHING...
QUICK! HIT THE CENTER SWITCH! IT'LL JAM THEIR COMLINKS!
BUT AS THEY NARROW THE GAP IN A HIGH-SPEED CHASE WEAVING IN AND OUT AMONG ENDOR'S TOWERING TREES...
LUKE! WE JUST PASSED TWO MORE SCOUTS! THEY'RE COMING AFTER US!
AND THEIR BLAZING LASER CANNONS CATCH LUKE WITH A GLANCING HIT!
KEEP AFTER THE LEAD MAN! I'LL TAKE CARE OF THE OTHER TWO... AFTER THIS ONE!
A KICK MAKES THE NEW ROCKET BIKE LUKE'S! HE SLAMS IT INTO THE BRAKING MODE...
...AND HIS TWO SURPRISED PURSUERS WHIP PAST HIM INTO HIS LINE OF FIRE.
ONE FALLS...

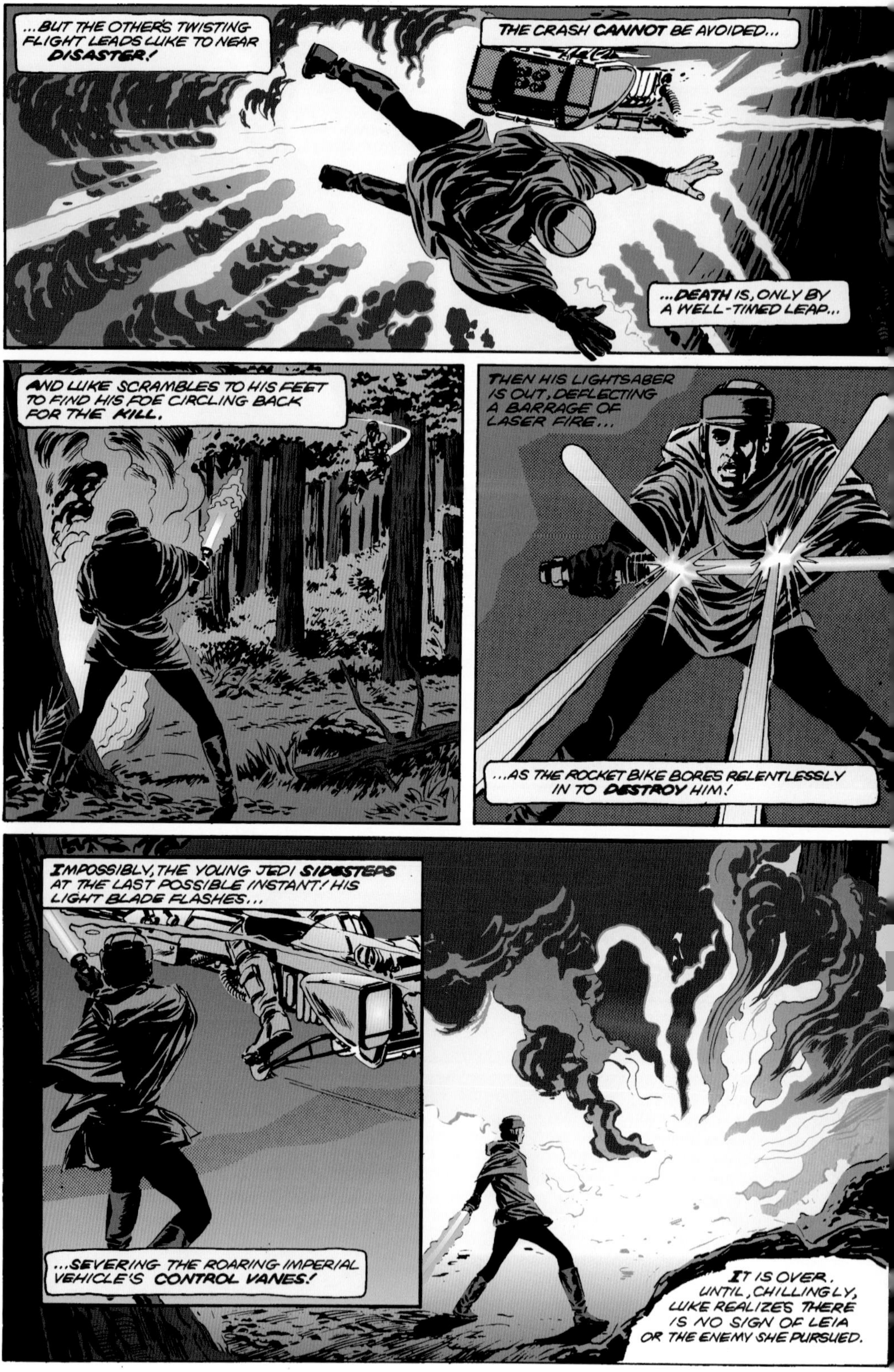
...BUT THE OTHER'S TWISTING FLIGHT LEADS LUKE TO NEAR DISASTER!
THE CRASH CANNOT BE AVOIDED...
...DEATH IS, ONLY BY A WELL-TIMED LEAP...
AND LUKE SCRAMBLES TO HIS FEET TO FIND HIS FOE CIRCLING BACK FOR THE KILL.
THEN HIS LIGHTSABER IS OUT, DEFLECTING A BARRAGE OF LASER FIRE...
...AS THE ROCKET BIKE BORES RELENTLESSLY IN TO DESTROY HIM!
IMPOSSIBLY, THE YOUNG JEDI SIDESTEPS AT THE LAST POSSIBLE INSTANT! HIS LIGHT BLADE FLASHES...
...SEVERING THE ROARING IMPERIAL VEHICLE'S CONTROL VANES!
IT IS OVER. UNTIL, CHILLINGLY, LUKE REALIZES THERE IS NO SIGN OF LEIA OR THE ENEMY SHE PURSUED.

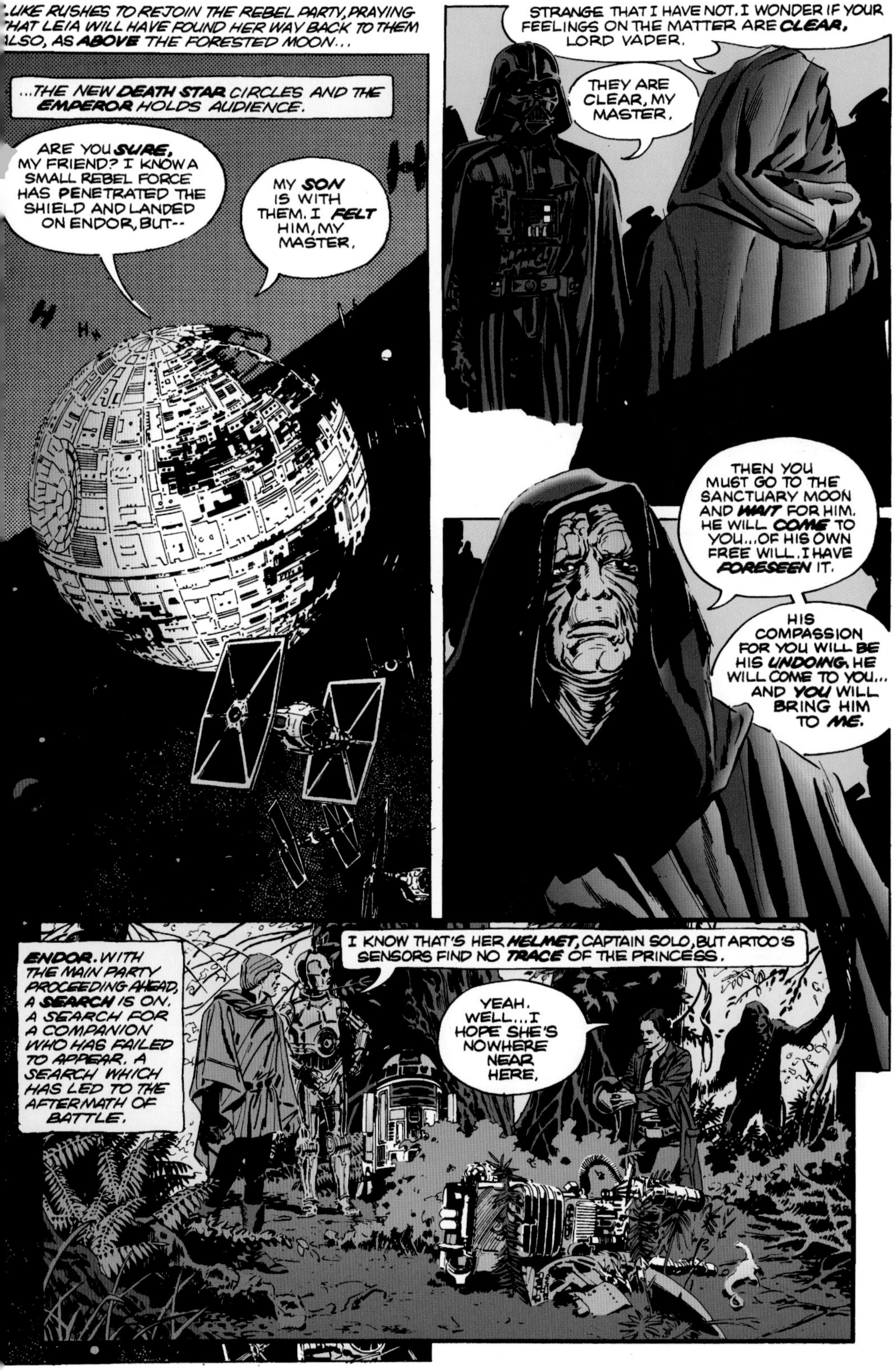
LUKE RUSHES TO REJOIN THE REBEL PARTY, PRAYING THAT LEIA WILL HAVE FOUND HER WAY BACK TO THEM ALSO, AS ABOVE THE FORESTED MOON...
...THE NEW DEATH STAR CIRCLES AND THE EMPEROR HOLDS AUDIENCE.
ARE YOU SURE, MY FRIEND? I KNOW A SMALL REBEL FORCE HAS PENETRATED THE SHIELD AND LANDED ON ENDOR, BUT--
MY SON IS WITH THEM. I FELT HIM, MY MASTER.
STRANGE THAT I HAVE NOT. I WONDER IF YOUR FEELINGS ON THE MATTER ARE CLEAR, LORD VADER.
THEY ARE CLEAR, MY MASTER.
THEN YOU MUST GO TO THE SANCTUARY MOON AND WAIT FOR HIM. HE WILL COME TO YOU...OF HIS OWN FREE WILL. I HAVE FORESEEN IT.
HIS COMPASSION FOR YOU WILL BE HIS UNDOING. HE WILL COME TO YOU... AND YOU WILL BRING HIM TO ME.
ENDOR. WITH THE MAIN PARTY PROCEEDING AHEAD, A SEARCH IS ON. A SEARCH FOR A COMPANION WHO HAS FAILED TO APPEAR. A SEARCH WHICH HAS LED TO THE AFTERMATH OF BATTLE.
I KNOW THAT'S HER HELMET, CAPTAIN SOLO, BUT ARTOO'S SENSORS FIND NO TRACE OF THE PRINCESS.
YEAH. WELL...I HOPE SHE'S NOWHERE NEAR HERE.

AS THE SEARCH WIDENS...

LEIA DEFINITELY SURVIVED THE WRECK... HERE ARE TWO *MORE* IMPERIALS SHE RAN INTO...

FROM THE *LOOKS* OF THEM, SHE SEEMS TO HAVE DONE ALL RIGHT. BUT WHERE IS SHE *NOW?*

THEN...SOMETHING IN THE AIR SENDS HAN'S WOOKIEE PARTNER CHARGING THROUGH THE HEAVY FOLIAGE! THE OTHERS FOLLOW TO FIND...

FOOD? I DON'T GET IT. DID SOMEBODY HANG IT OUT TO *CURE,* OR--

CHEWBACCA! *WAIT!* DON'T TOUCH--

NICE *WORK,* FUZZBALL! THINKIN' WITH YOUR *STOMACH...!* OLDEST TRAP IN THE GALAXY...AND *WE'RE* IN IT!

EASY, HAN, LET'S SEE...CAN ANYBODY REACH MY *LIGHTSABER?* THREEPIO...?

I FEAR NOT, MASTER LUKE, BUT PERHAPS *ARTOO* CAN CUT WITH--

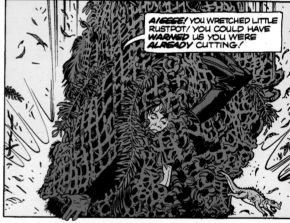

AIEEEE! YOU WRETCHED LITTLE *RUSTPOT!* YOU COULD HAVE *WARNED* US YOU WERE *ALREADY* CUTTING!

BUT AS EFFECTS OF THE FALL WEAR OFF...A NEW REALIZATION DAWNS.

OH, DEAR...I THINK WE'VE *FOUND* THE ONES WHO SET THE TRAP...OR *THEY'VE* FOUND US!

AND THE SIGHT OF THE GOLDEN DROID BRINGS EXCITEMENT TO THE SMALL SPEAR-WIELDING CREATURES...

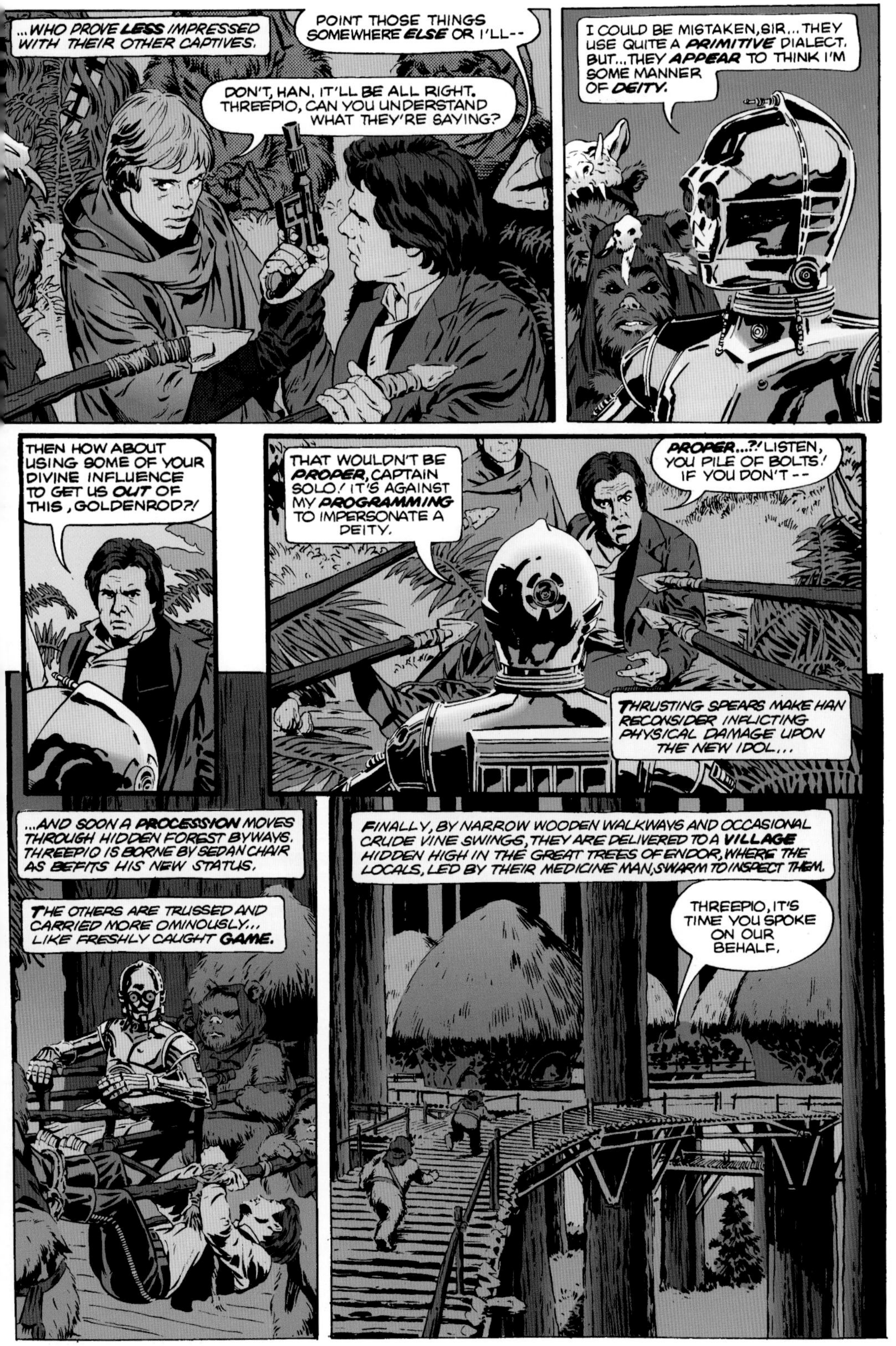

...WHO PROVE LESS IMPRESSED WITH THEIR OTHER CAPTIVES.
POINT THOSE THINGS SOMEWHERE ELSE OR I'LL--
DON'T, HAN. IT'LL BE ALL RIGHT. THREEPIO, CAN YOU UNDERSTAND WHAT THEY'RE SAYING?
I COULD BE MISTAKEN, SIR... THEY USE QUITE A PRIMITIVE DIALECT. BUT...THEY APPEAR TO THINK I'M SOME MANNER OF DEITY.
THEN HOW ABOUT USING SOME OF YOUR DIVINE INFLUENCE TO GET US OUT OF THIS, GOLDENROD?!
THAT WOULDN'T BE PROPER, CAPTAIN SOLO! IT'S AGAINST MY PROGRAMMING TO IMPERSONATE A DEITY.
PROPER...?! LISTEN, YOU PILE OF BOLTS! IF YOU DON'T --
THRUSTING SPEARS MAKE HAN RECONSIDER INFLICTING PHYSICAL DAMAGE UPON THE NEW IDOL...
...AND SOON A PROCESSION MOVES THROUGH HIDDEN FOREST BYWAYS. THREEPIO IS BORNE BY SEDAN CHAIR AS BEFITS HIS NEW STATUS.
THE OTHERS ARE TRUSSED AND CARRIED MORE OMINOUSLY... LIKE FRESHLY CAUGHT GAME.
FINALLY, BY NARROW WOODEN WALKWAYS AND OCCASIONAL CRUDE VINE SWINGS, THEY ARE DELIVERED TO A VILLAGE HIDDEN HIGH IN THE GREAT TREES OF ENDOR, WHERE THE LOCALS, LED BY THEIR MEDICINE MAN, SWARM TO INSPECT THEM.
THREEPIO, IT'S TIME YOU SPOKE ON OUR BEHALF.

THE RESULTS ARE NOT ENCOURAGING. FIREWOOD IS STACKED UNDER HAN SOLO.

WELL? WHAT DID THEY SAY?

I'M RATHER EMBARRASSED, CAPTAIN. IT APPEARS *YOU* ARE TO BE THE *MAIN COURSE* AT A BANQUET IN *MY* HONOR. THE MEDICINE MAN IS QUITE OFFENDED I SHOULD SUGGEST OTHERWISE.

LOOK, BRIGHT EYES, YOU'D BETTER *TELL* THAT SAWED-OFF LITTLE--

TELL THEM YOU ARE ALL *MY* FRIENDS, THREEPIO... AND MUST BE SET FREE!

LEIA! H-HOW...?

ONE OF THESE LITTLE FOLK-- THE *EWOKS*--FOUND ME AFTER MY *RUN-IN* WITH THE IMPERIALS. I GUESS HE WAS *IMPRESSED* SINCE THE EWOKS DON'T LIKE THEM EITHER!

BUT SHARING MUTUAL ENEMIES IS NOT ENOUGH TO DISSUADE THE MEDICINE MAN FROM HONORING TH' TRIBE'S NEW DEITY.

THREEPIO, TELL THEM IF THEY DON'T DO AS YOU WISH, YOU'LL BECOME *ANGRY* AND USE YOUR *MAGIC.*

SIR...? *WHAT* MAGIC? I COULDN'T--

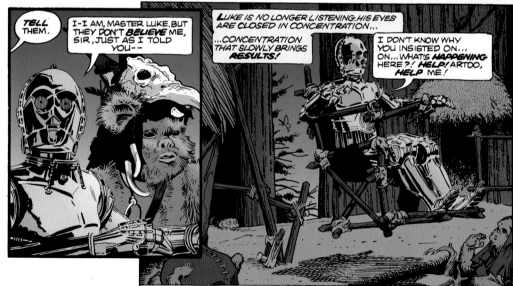

TELL THEM.

I-I AM, MASTER LUKE, BUT THEY DON'T *BELIEVE* ME, SIR, JUST AS I TOLD YOU--

LUKE IS NO LONGER LISTENING. HIS EYES ARE CLOSED IN CONCENTRATION...

...CONCENTRATION THAT SLOWLY BRINGS *RESULTS!*

I DON'T KNOW WHY YOU INSISTED ON... ON... WHAT'S *HAPPENING* HERE?! *HELP!* ARTOO, *HELP* ME!

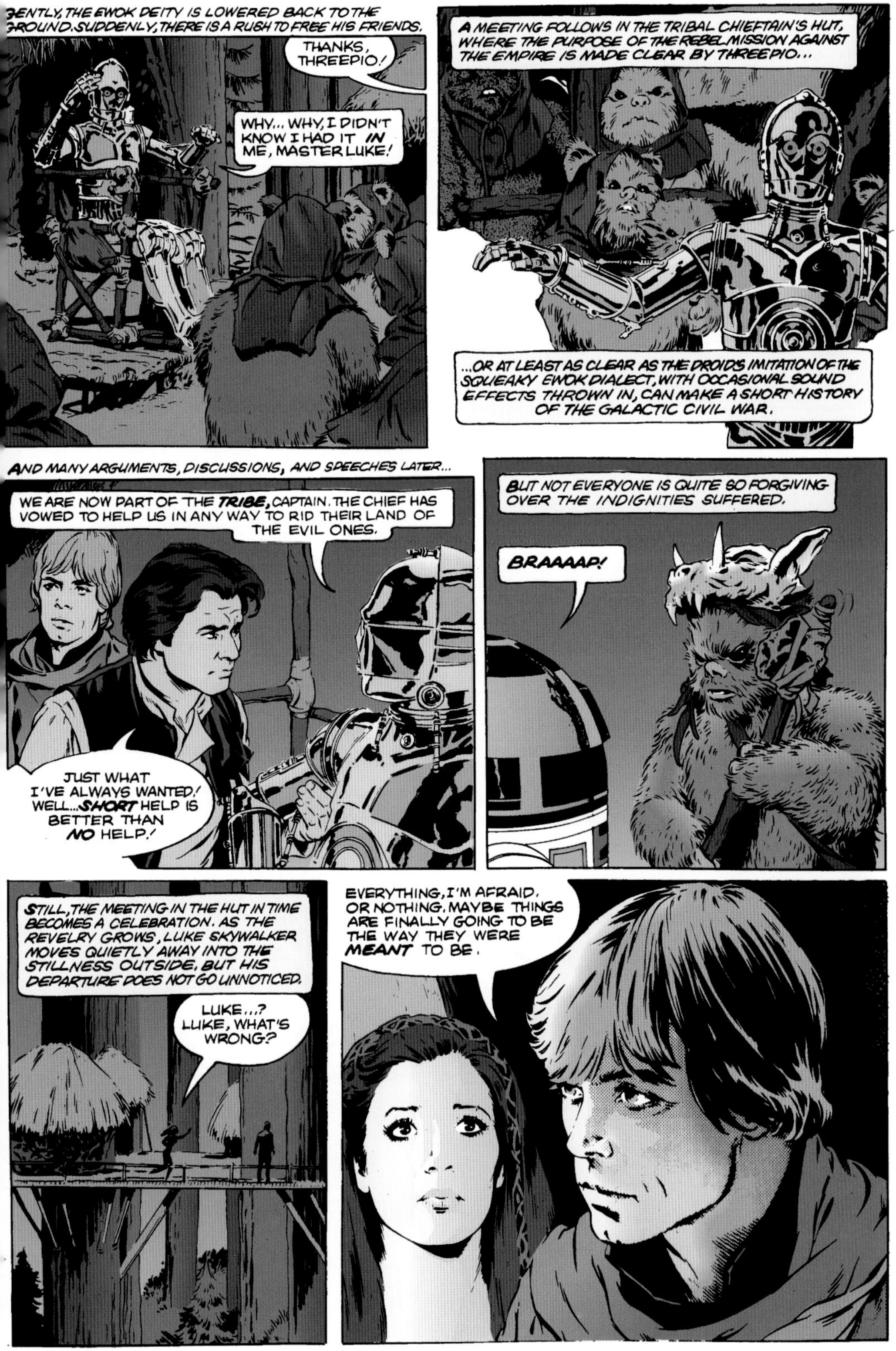
GENTLY, THE EWOK DEITY IS LOWERED BACK TO THE GROUND. SUDDENLY, THERE IS A RUSH TO FREE HIS FRIENDS.
THANKS, THREEPIO!
WHY... WHY, I DIDN'T KNOW I HAD IT IN ME, MASTER LUKE!
A MEETING FOLLOWS IN THE TRIBAL CHIEFTAIN'S HUT, WHERE THE PURPOSE OF THE REBEL MISSION AGAINST THE EMPIRE IS MADE CLEAR BY THREEPIO...
...OR AT LEAST AS CLEAR AS THE DROID'S IMITATION OF THE SQUEAKY EWOK DIALECT, WITH OCCASIONAL SOUND EFFECTS THROWN IN, CAN MAKE A SHORT HISTORY OF THE GALACTIC CIVIL WAR.
AND MANY ARGUMENTS, DISCUSSIONS, AND SPEECHES LATER...
WE ARE NOW PART OF THE TRIBE, CAPTAIN. THE CHIEF HAS VOWED TO HELP US IN ANY WAY TO RID THEIR LAND OF THE EVIL ONES.
JUST WHAT I'VE ALWAYS WANTED! WELL... SHORT HELP IS BETTER THAN NO HELP!
BUT NOT EVERYONE IS QUITE SO FORGIVING OVER THE INDIGNITIES SUFFERED.
BRAAAAP!
STILL, THE MEETING IN THE HUT IN TIME BECOMES A CELEBRATION. AS THE REVELRY GROWS, LUKE SKYWALKER MOVES QUIETLY AWAY INTO THE STILLNESS OUTSIDE, BUT HIS DEPARTURE DOES NOT GO UNNOTICED.
LUKE...? LUKE, WHAT'S WRONG?
EVERYTHING, I'M AFRAID. OR NOTHING. MAYBE THINGS ARE FINALLY GOING TO BE THE WAY THEY WERE MEANT TO BE.

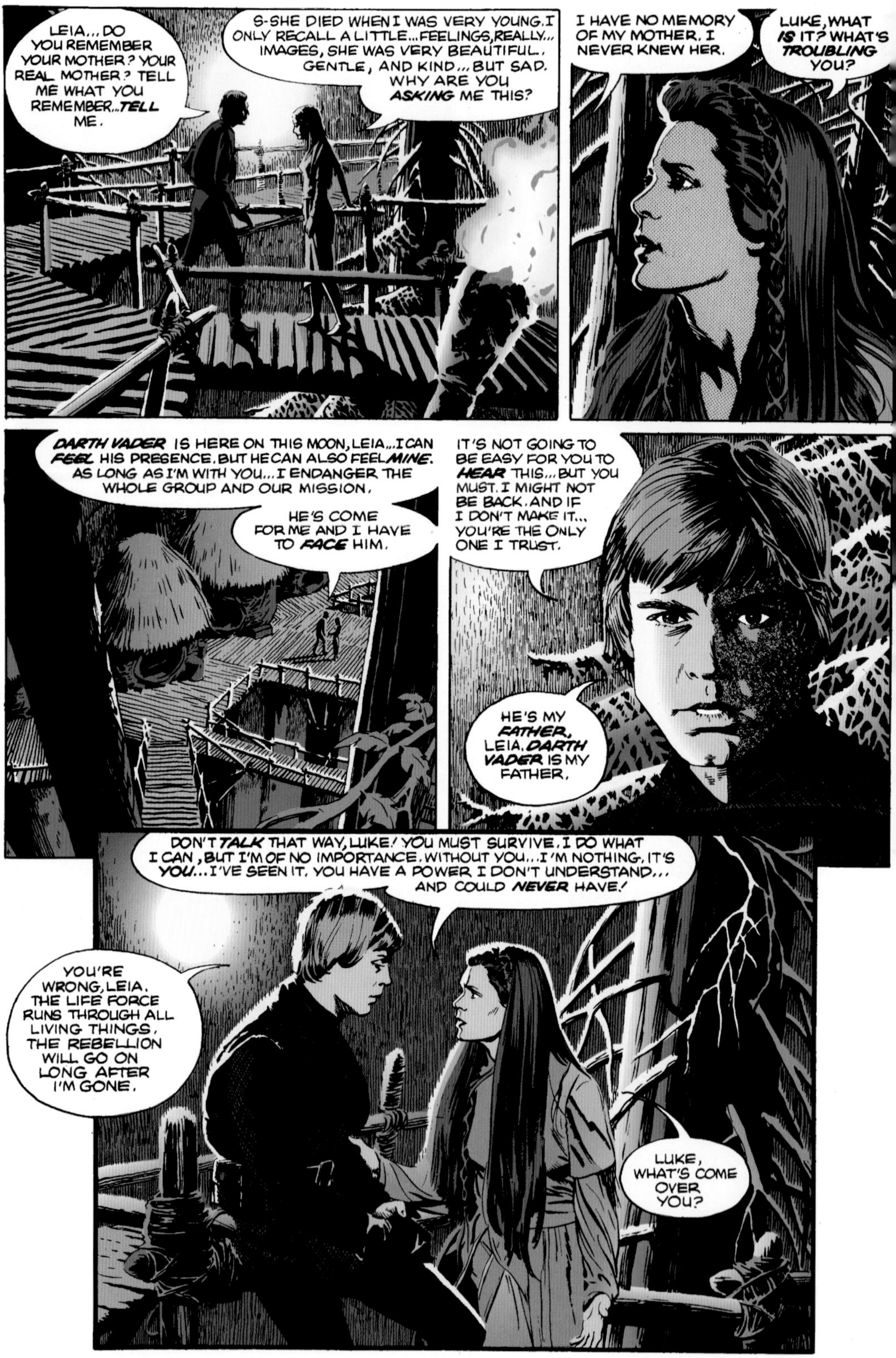
LEIA... DO YOU REMEMBER YOUR MOTHER? YOUR REAL MOTHER? TELL ME WHAT YOU REMEMBER...TELL ME.
S-SHE DIED WHEN I WAS VERY YOUNG. I ONLY RECALL A LITTLE... FEELINGS, REALLY... IMAGES, SHE WAS VERY BEAUTIFUL, GENTLE, AND KIND... BUT SAD. WHY ARE YOU ASKING ME THIS?
I HAVE NO MEMORY OF MY MOTHER. I NEVER KNEW HER.
LUKE, WHAT IS IT? WHAT'S TROUBLING YOU?
DARTH VADER IS HERE ON THIS MOON, LEIA... I CAN FEEL HIS PRESENCE. BUT HE CAN ALSO FEEL MINE. AS LONG AS I'M WITH YOU... I ENDANGER THE WHOLE GROUP AND OUR MISSION.
HE'S COME FOR ME AND I HAVE TO FACE HIM.
IT'S NOT GOING TO BE EASY FOR YOU TO HEAR THIS... BUT YOU MUST. I MIGHT NOT BE BACK. AND IF I DON'T MAKE IT... YOU'RE THE ONLY ONE I TRUST.
HE'S MY FATHER, LEIA. DARTH VADER IS MY FATHER.
DON'T TALK THAT WAY, LUKE! YOU MUST SURVIVE. I DO WHAT I CAN, BUT I'M OF NO IMPORTANCE. WITHOUT YOU... I'M NOTHING. IT'S YOU... I'VE SEEN IT. YOU HAVE A POWER I DON'T UNDERSTAND... AND COULD NEVER HAVE!
YOU'RE WRONG, LEIA. THE LIFE FORCE RUNS THROUGH ALL LIVING THINGS. THE REBELLION WILL GO ON LONG AFTER I'M GONE.
LUKE, WHAT'S COME OVER YOU?

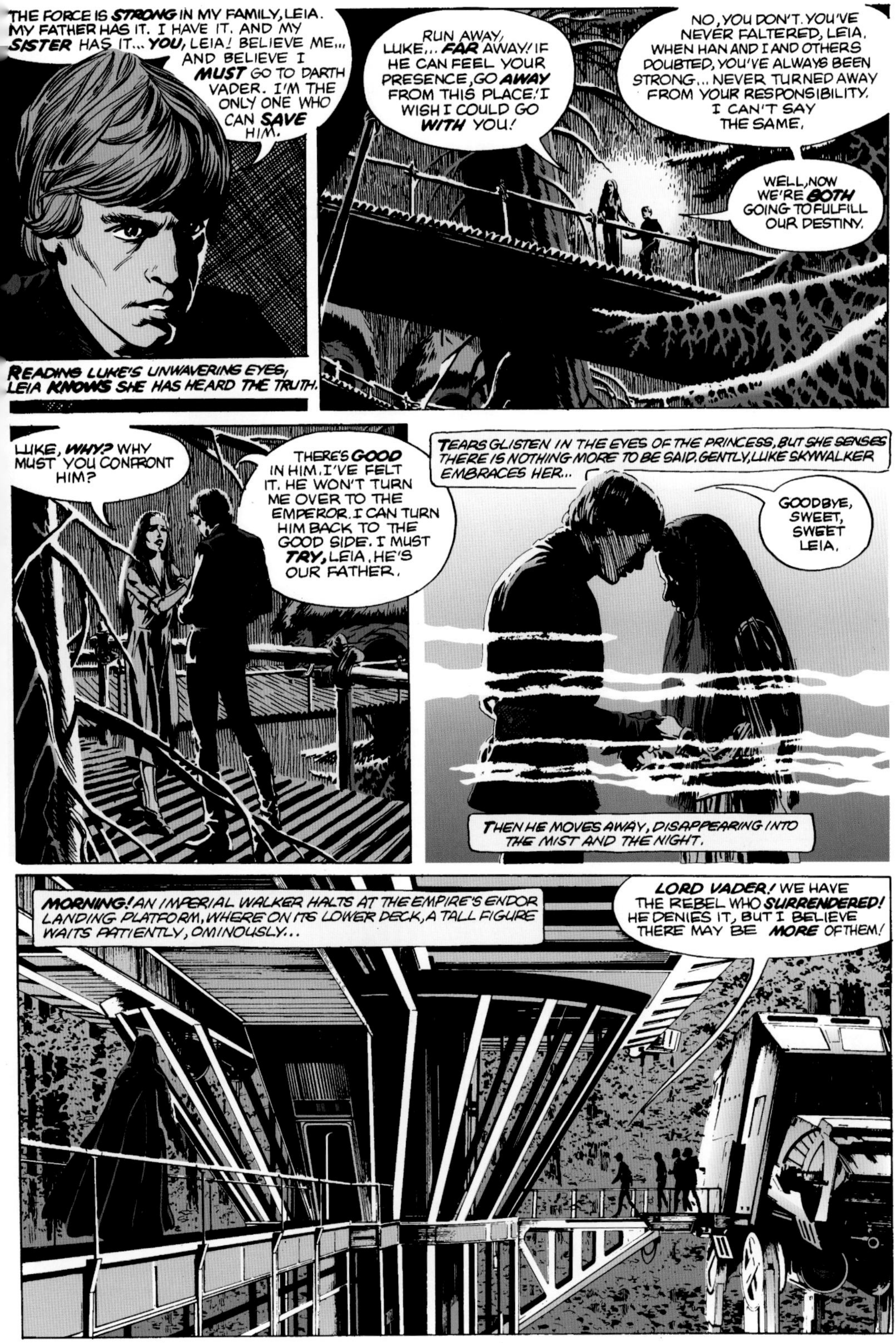
THE FORCE IS STRONG IN MY FAMILY, LEIA. MY FATHER HAS IT. I HAVE IT. AND MY SISTER HAS IT... YOU, LEIA! BELIEVE ME... AND BELIEVE I MUST GO TO DARTH VADER. I'M THE ONLY ONE WHO CAN SAVE HIM.
READING LUKE'S UNWAVERING EYES, LEIA KNOWS SHE HAS HEARD THE TRUTH.
RUN AWAY, LUKE... FAR AWAY! IF HE CAN FEEL YOUR PRESENCE, GO AWAY FROM THIS PLACE! I WISH I COULD GO WITH YOU!
NO, YOU DON'T. YOU'VE NEVER FALTERED, LEIA. WHEN HAN AND I AND OTHERS DOUBTED, YOU'VE ALWAYS BEEN STRONG... NEVER TURNED AWAY FROM YOUR RESPONSIBILITY. I CAN'T SAY THE SAME.
WELL, NOW WE'RE BOTH GOING TO FULFILL OUR DESTINY.
LUKE, WHY? WHY MUST YOU CONFRONT HIM?
THERE'S GOOD IN HIM. I'VE FELT IT. HE WON'T TURN ME OVER TO THE EMPEROR. I CAN TURN HIM BACK TO THE GOOD SIDE. I MUST TRY, LEIA. HE'S OUR FATHER.
TEARS GLISTEN IN THE EYES OF THE PRINCESS, BUT SHE SENSES THERE IS NOTHING MORE TO BE SAID. GENTLY, LUKE SKYWALKER EMBRACES HER...
GOODBYE, SWEET, SWEET LEIA.
THEN HE MOVES AWAY, DISAPPEARING INTO THE MIST AND THE NIGHT.
MORNING! AN IMPERIAL WALKER HALTS AT THE EMPIRE'S ENDOR LANDING PLATFORM, WHERE ON ITS LOWER DECK, A TALL FIGURE WAITS PATIENTLY, OMINOUSLY...
LORD VADER! WE HAVE THE REBEL WHO SURRENDERED! HE DENIES IT, BUT I BELIEVE THERE MAY BE MORE OF THEM!

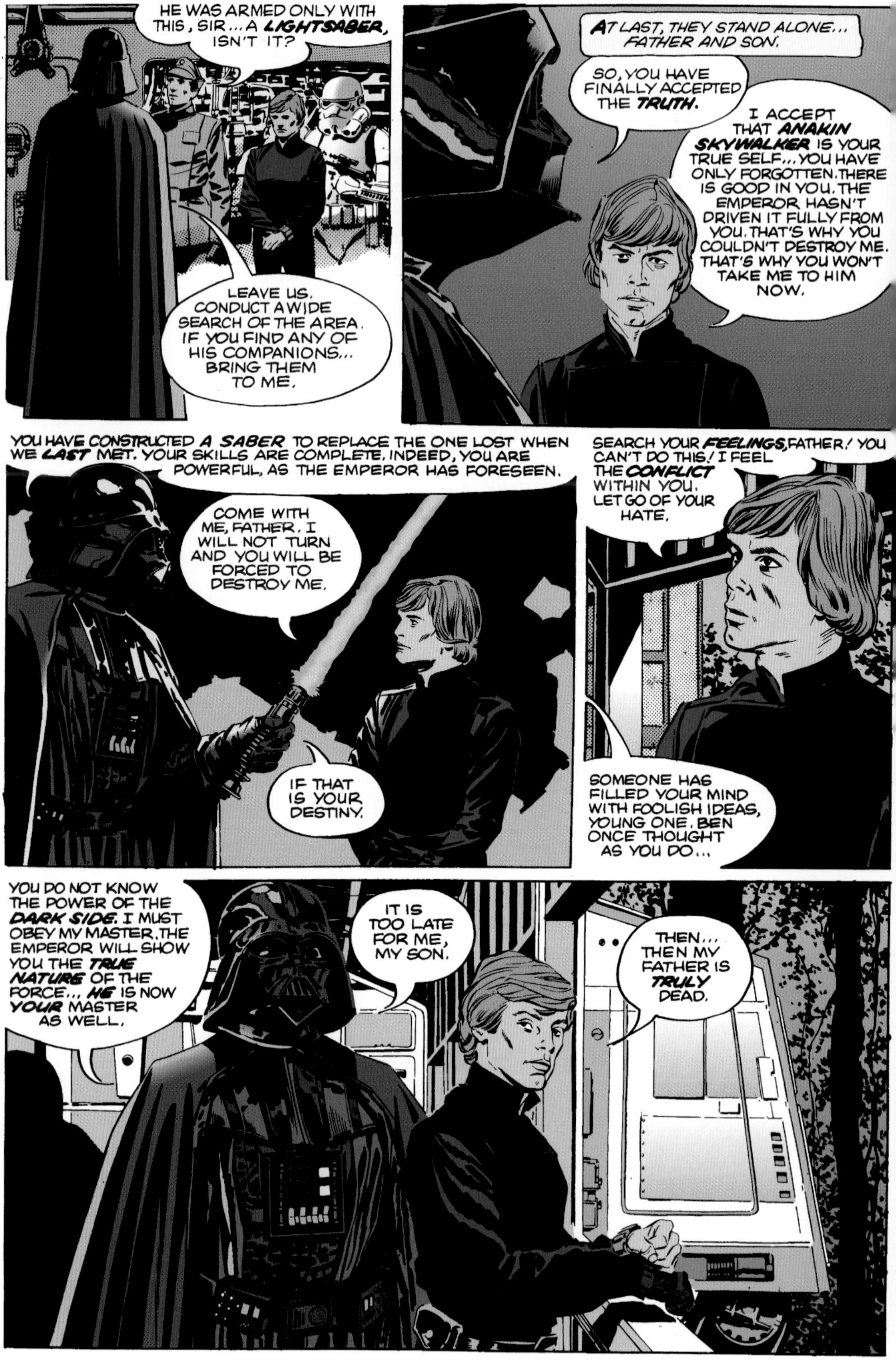
HE WAS ARMED ONLY WITH THIS, SIR... A LIGHTSABER, ISN'T IT?
LEAVE US. CONDUCT A WIDE SEARCH OF THE AREA. IF YOU FIND ANY OF HIS COMPANIONS... BRING THEM TO ME.
AT LAST, THEY STAND ALONE... FATHER AND SON.
SO, YOU HAVE FINALLY ACCEPTED THE TRUTH.
I ACCEPT THAT ANAKIN SKYWALKER IS YOUR TRUE SELF... YOU HAVE ONLY FORGOTTEN. THERE IS GOOD IN YOU. THE EMPEROR HASN'T DRIVEN IT FULLY FROM YOU. THAT'S WHY YOU COULDN'T DESTROY ME. THAT'S WHY YOU WON'T TAKE ME TO HIM NOW.
YOU HAVE CONSTRUCTED A SABER TO REPLACE THE ONE LOST WHEN WE LAST MET. YOUR SKILLS ARE COMPLETE. INDEED, YOU ARE POWERFUL, AS THE EMPEROR HAS FORESEEN.
COME WITH ME, FATHER. I WILL NOT TURN AND YOU WILL BE FORCED TO DESTROY ME.
IF THAT IS YOUR DESTINY.
SEARCH YOUR FEELINGS, FATHER! YOU CAN'T DO THIS! I FEEL THE CONFLICT WITHIN YOU. LET GO OF YOUR HATE.
SOMEONE HAS FILLED YOUR MIND WITH FOOLISH IDEAS, YOUNG ONE. BEN ONCE THOUGHT AS YOU DO...
YOU DO NOT KNOW THE POWER OF THE DARK SIDE. I MUST OBEY MY MASTER. THE EMPEROR WILL SHOW YOU THE TRUE NATURE OF THE FORCE... HE IS NOW YOUR MASTER AS WELL.
IT IS TOO LATE FOR ME, MY SON.
THEN... THEN MY FATHER IS TRULY DEAD.

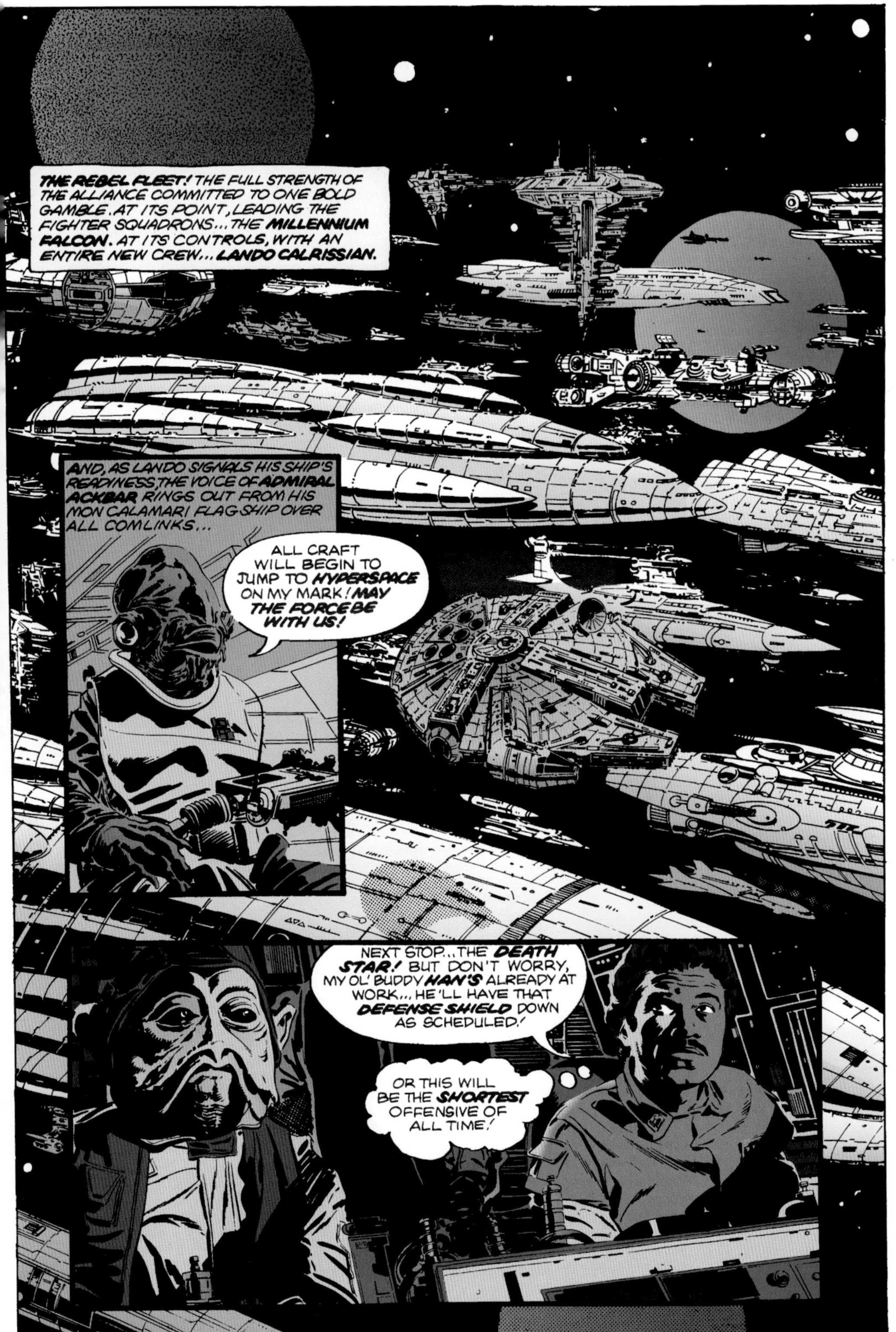
THE REBEL FLEET! THE FULL STRENGTH OF THE ALLIANCE COMMITTED TO ONE BOLD GAMBLE. AT ITS POINT, LEADING THE FIGHTER SQUADRONS... THE MILLENNIUM FALCON. AT ITS CONTROLS, WITH AN ENTIRE NEW CREW... LANDO CALRISSIAN.
AND, AS LANDO SIGNALS HIS SHIP'S READINESS, THE VOICE OF ADMIRAL ACKBAR RINGS OUT FROM HIS MON CALAMARI FLAG-SHIP OVER ALL COMLINKS...
ALL CRAFT WILL BEGIN TO JUMP TO HYPERSPACE ON MY MARK! MAY THE FORCE BE WITH US!
NEXT STOP... THE DEATH STAR! BUT DON'T WORRY, MY OL' BUDDY HAN'S ALREADY AT WORK... HE'LL HAVE THAT DEFENSE SHIELD DOWN AS SCHEDULED!
OR THIS WILL BE THE SHORTEST OFFENSIVE OF ALL TIME!

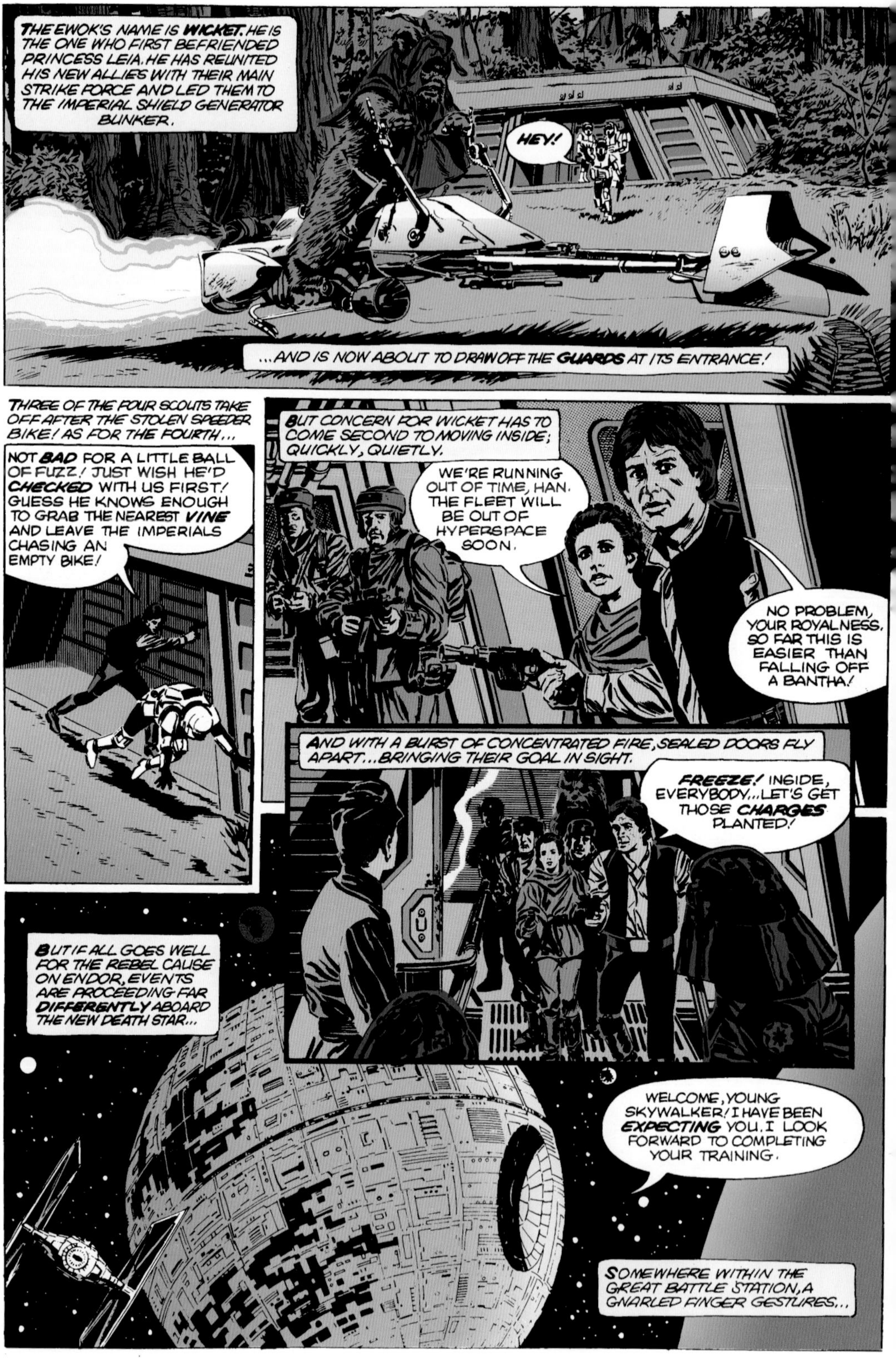
THE EWOK'S NAME IS WICKET. HE IS THE ONE WHO FIRST BEFRIENDED PRINCESS LEIA. HE HAS REUNITED HIS NEW ALLIES WITH THEIR MAIN STRIKE FORCE AND LED THEM TO THE IMPERIAL SHIELD GENERATOR BUNKER.
HEY!
...AND IS NOW ABOUT TO DRAW OFF THE GUARDS AT ITS ENTRANCE!
THREE OF THE FOUR SCOUTS TAKE OFF AFTER THE STOLEN SPEEDER BIKE! AS FOR THE FOURTH...
NOT BAD FOR A LITTLE BALL OF FUZZ! JUST WISH HE'D CHECKED WITH US FIRST! GUESS HE KNOWS ENOUGH TO GRAB THE NEAREST VINE AND LEAVE THE IMPERIALS CHASING AN EMPTY BIKE!
BUT CONCERN FOR WICKET HAS TO COME SECOND TO MOVING INSIDE; QUICKLY, QUIETLY.
WE'RE RUNNING OUT OF TIME, HAN. THE FLEET WILL BE OUT OF HYPERSPACE SOON.
NO PROBLEM, YOUR ROYALNESS. SO FAR THIS IS EASIER THAN FALLING OFF A BANTHA!
AND WITH A BURST OF CONCENTRATED FIRE, SEALED DOORS FLY APART... BRINGING THEIR GOAL IN SIGHT.
FREEZE! INSIDE, EVERYBODY... LET'S GET THOSE CHARGES PLANTED!
BUT IF ALL GOES WELL FOR THE REBEL CAUSE ON ENDOR, EVENTS ARE PROCEEDING FAR DIFFERENTLY ABOARD THE NEW DEATH STAR...
WELCOME, YOUNG SKYWALKER! I HAVE BEEN EXPECTING YOU. I LOOK FORWARD TO COMPLETING YOUR TRAINING.
SOMEWHERE WITHIN THE GREAT BATTLE STATION, A GNARLED FINGER GESTURES...

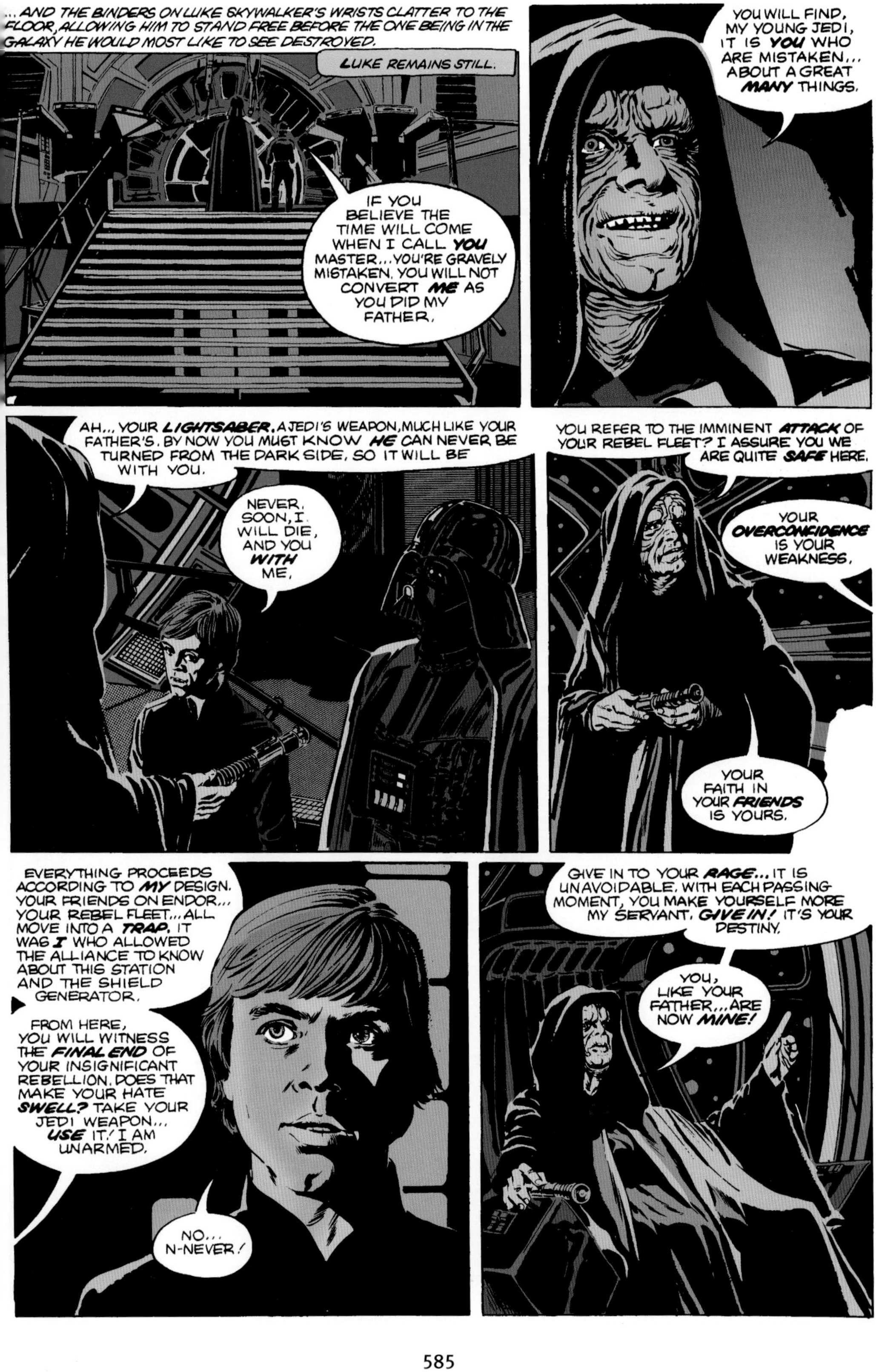
...AND THE BINDERS ON LUKE SKYWALKER'S WRISTS CLATTER TO THE FLOOR, ALLOWING HIM TO STAND FREE BEFORE THE ONE BEING IN THE GALAXY HE WOULD MOST LIKE TO SEE DESTROYED.
LUKE REMAINS STILL.
IF YOU BELIEVE THE TIME WILL COME WHEN I CALL YOU MASTER... YOU'RE GRAVELY MISTAKEN. YOU WILL NOT CONVERT ME AS YOU DID MY FATHER.
YOU WILL FIND, MY YOUNG JEDI, IT IS YOU WHO ARE MISTAKEN... ABOUT A GREAT MANY THINGS.
AH... YOUR LIGHTSABER. A JEDI'S WEAPON, MUCH LIKE YOUR FATHER'S. BY NOW YOU MUST KNOW HE CAN NEVER BE TURNED FROM THE DARK SIDE, SO IT WILL BE WITH YOU.
NEVER. SOON, I WILL DIE, AND YOU WITH ME.
YOU REFER TO THE IMMINENT ATTACK OF YOUR REBEL FLEET? I ASSURE YOU WE ARE QUITE SAFE HERE.
YOUR OVERCONFIDENCE IS YOUR WEAKNESS.
YOUR FAITH IN YOUR FRIENDS IS YOURS.
EVERYTHING PROCEEDS ACCORDING TO MY DESIGN. YOUR FRIENDS ON ENDOR... YOUR REBEL FLEET... ALL MOVE INTO A TRAP. IT WAS I WHO ALLOWED THE ALLIANCE TO KNOW ABOUT THIS STATION AND THE SHIELD GENERATOR.
FROM HERE, YOU WILL WITNESS THE FINAL END OF YOUR INSIGNIFICANT REBELLION. DOES THAT MAKE YOUR HATE SWELL? TAKE YOUR JEDI WEAPON... USE IT! I AM UNARMED.
NO... N-NEVER!
GIVE IN TO YOUR RAGE... IT IS UNAVOIDABLE. WITH EACH PASSING MOMENT, YOU MAKE YOURSELF MORE MY SERVANT. GIVE IN! IT'S YOUR DESTINY.
YOU, LIKE YOUR FATHER... ARE NOW MINE!

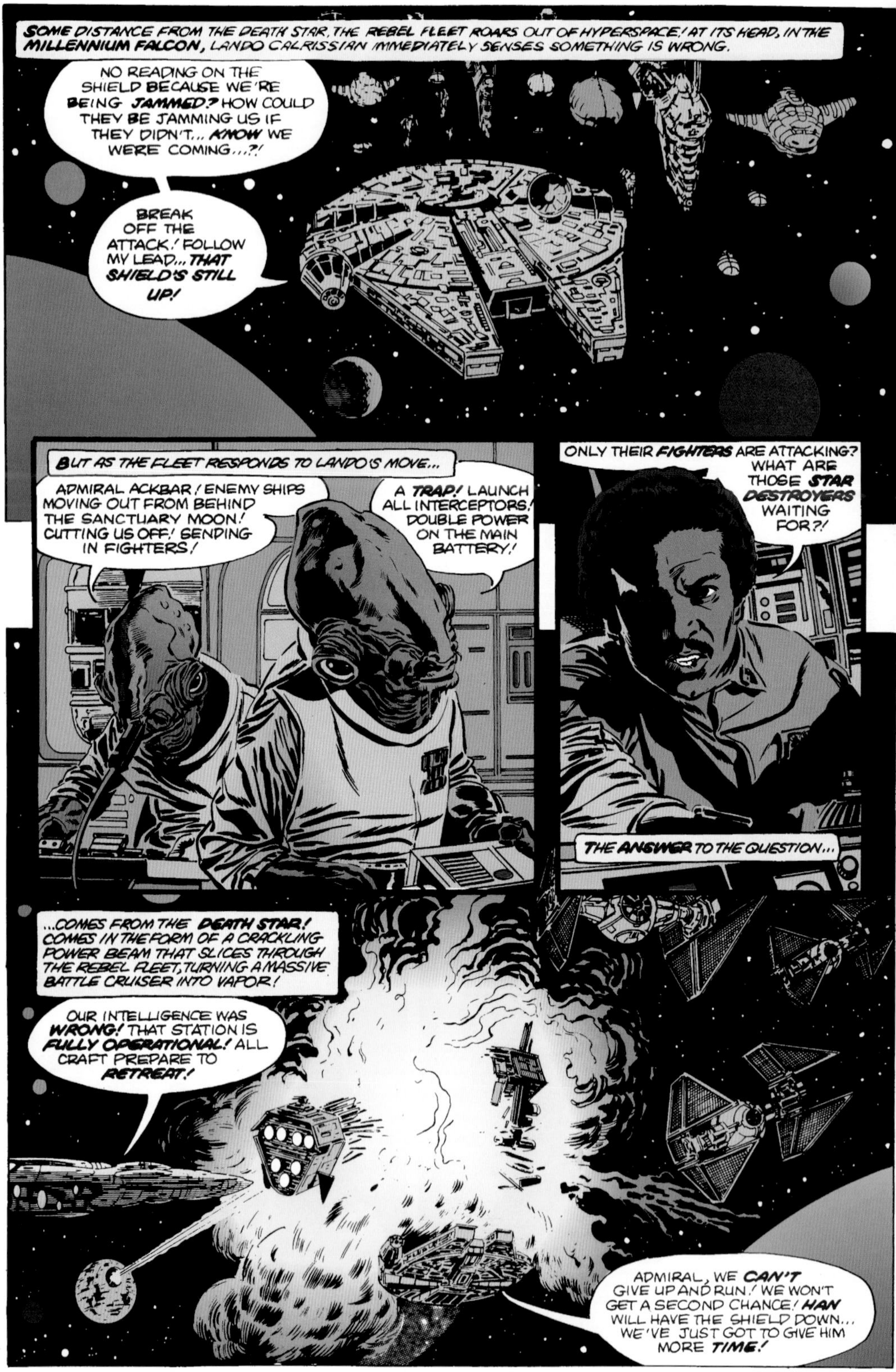
SOME DISTANCE FROM THE DEATH STAR, THE REBEL FLEET ROARS OUT OF HYPERSPACE! AT ITS HEAD, IN THE MILLENNIUM FALCON, LANDO CALRISSIAN IMMEDIATELY SENSES SOMETHING IS WRONG.
NO READING ON THE SHIELD BECAUSE WE'RE BEING JAMMED? HOW COULD THEY BE JAMMING US IF THEY DIDN'T... KNOW WE WERE COMING...?!
BREAK OFF THE ATTACK! FOLLOW MY LEAD... THAT SHIELD'S STILL UP!
BUT AS THE FLEET RESPONDS TO LANDO'S MOVE...
ADMIRAL ACKBAR! ENEMY SHIPS MOVING OUT FROM BEHIND THE SANCTUARY MOON! CUTTING US OFF! SENDING IN FIGHTERS!
A TRAP! LAUNCH ALL INTERCEPTORS! DOUBLE POWER ON THE MAIN BATTERY!
ONLY THEIR FIGHTERS ARE ATTACKING? WHAT ARE THOSE STAR DESTROYERS WAITING FOR?!
THE ANSWER TO THE QUESTION...
...COMES FROM THE DEATH STAR! COMES IN THE FORM OF A CRACKLING POWER BEAM THAT SLICES THROUGH THE REBEL FLEET, TURNING A MASSIVE BATTLE CRUISER INTO VAPOR!
OUR INTELLIGENCE WAS WRONG! THAT STATION IS FULLY OPERATIONAL! ALL CRAFT PREPARE TO RETREAT!
ADMIRAL, WE CAN'T GIVE UP AND RUN! WE WON'T GET A SECOND CHANCE! HAN WILL HAVE THE SHIELD DOWN... WE'VE JUST GOT TO GIVE HIM MORE TIME!

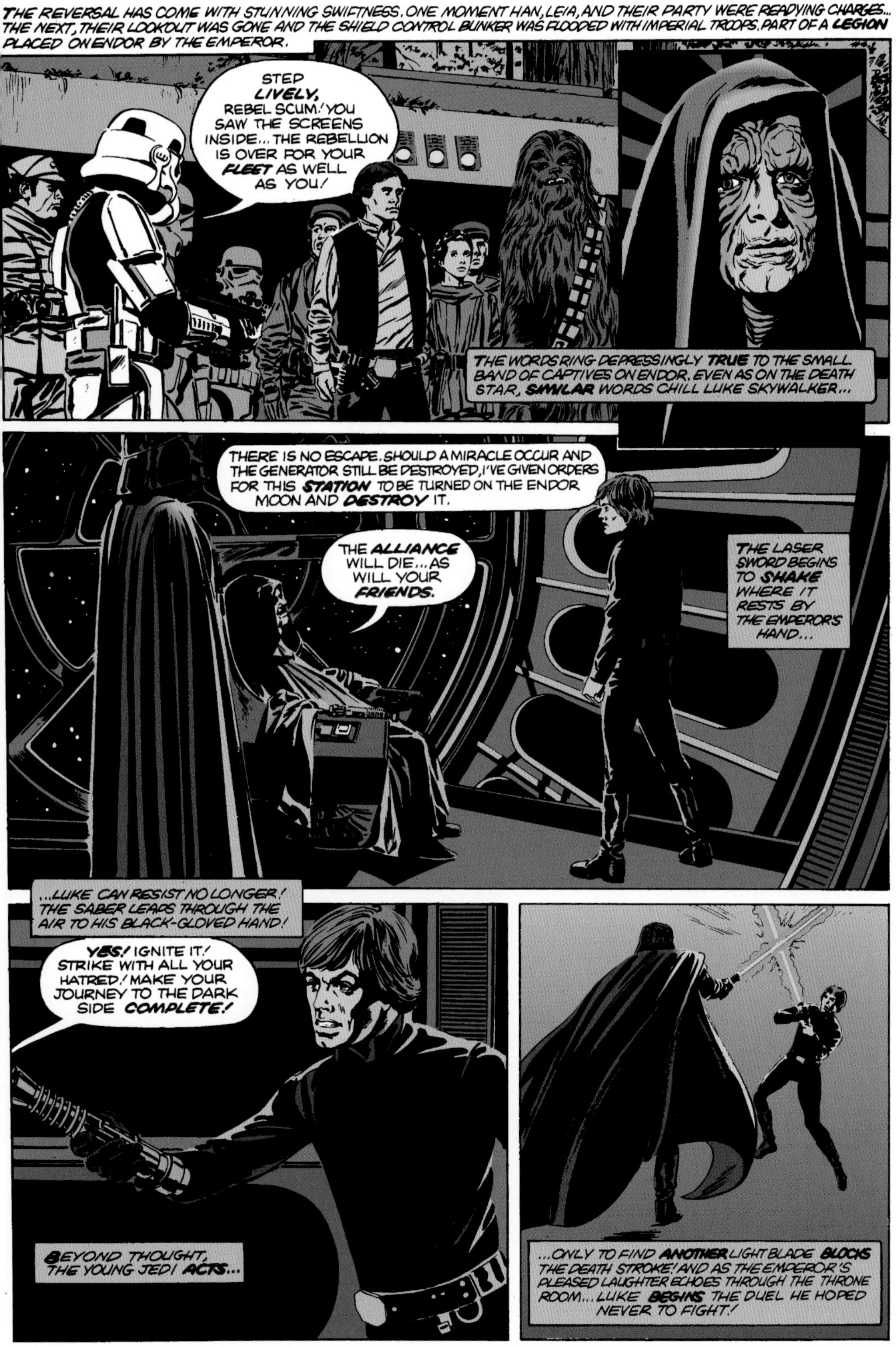
THE REVERSAL HAS COME WITH STUNNING SWIFTNESS. ONE MOMENT HAN, LEIA, AND THEIR PARTY WERE READYING CHARGES... THE NEXT, THEIR LOOKOUT WAS GONE AND THE SHIELD CONTROL BUNKER WAS FLOODED WITH IMPERIAL TROOPS, PART OF A LEGION PLACED ON ENDOR BY THE EMPEROR.
STEP LIVELY, REBEL SCUM! YOU SAW THE SCREENS INSIDE... THE REBELLION IS OVER FOR YOUR FLEET AS WELL AS YOU!
THE WORDS RING DEPRESSINGLY TRUE TO THE SMALL BAND OF CAPTIVES ON ENDOR, EVEN AS ON THE DEATH STAR, SIMILAR WORDS CHILL LUKE SKYWALKER...
THERE IS NO ESCAPE. SHOULD A MIRACLE OCCUR AND THE GENERATOR STILL BE DESTROYED, I'VE GIVEN ORDERS FOR THIS STATION TO BE TURNED ON THE ENDOR MOON AND DESTROY IT.
THE ALLIANCE WILL DIE... AS WILL YOUR FRIENDS.
THE LASER SWORD BEGINS TO SHAKE WHERE IT RESTS BY THE EMPEROR'S HAND...
...LUKE CAN RESIST NO LONGER! THE SABER LEAPS THROUGH THE AIR TO HIS BLACK-GLOVED HAND!
YES! IGNITE IT! STRIKE WITH ALL YOUR HATRED! MAKE YOUR JOURNEY TO THE DARK SIDE COMPLETE!
BEYOND THOUGHT, THE YOUNG JEDI ACTS...
...ONLY TO FIND ANOTHER LIGHT BLADE BLOCKS THE DEATH STROKE! AND AS THE EMPEROR'S PLEASED LAUGHTER ECHOES THROUGH THE THRONE ROOM... LUKE BEGINS THE DUEL HE HOPED NEVER TO FIGHT!

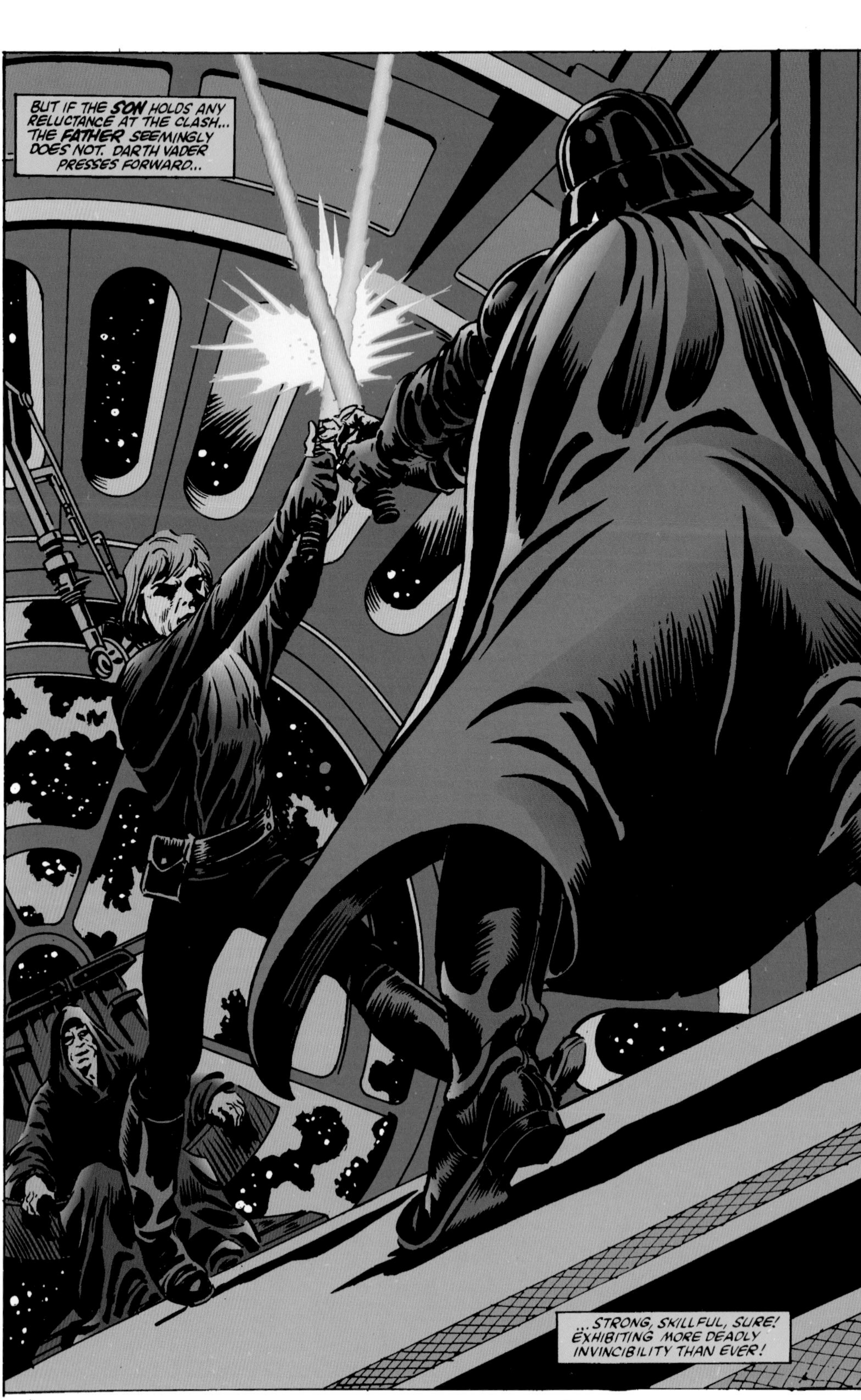
BUT IF THE SON HOLDS ANY RELUCTANCE AT THE CLASH... THE FATHER SEEMINGLY DOES NOT. DARTH VADER PRESSES FORWARD...
...STRONG, SKILLFUL, SURE! EXHIBITING MORE DEADLY INVINCIBILITY THAN EVER!

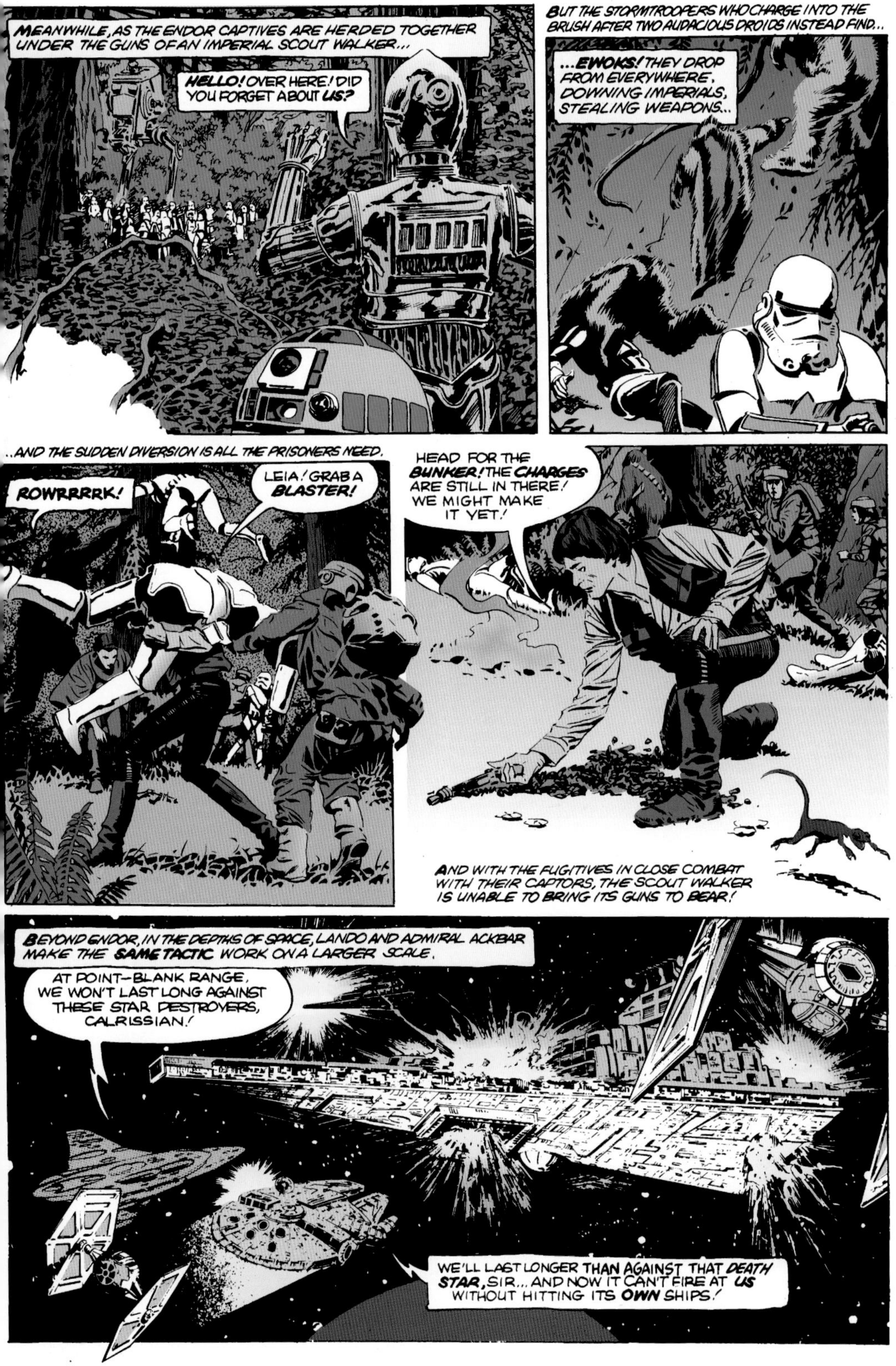
MEANWHILE, AS THE ENDOR CAPTIVES ARE HERDED TOGETHER UNDER THE GUNS OF AN IMPERIAL SCOUT WALKER...
HELLO! OVER HERE! DID YOU FORGET ABOUT US?
BUT THE STORMTROOPERS WHO CHARGE INTO THE BRUSH AFTER TWO AUDACIOUS DROIDS INSTEAD FIND...
...EWOKS! THEY DROP FROM EVERYWHERE, DOWNING IMPERIALS, STEALING WEAPONS...
..AND THE SUDDEN DIVERSION IS ALL THE PRISONERS NEED.
ROWRRRRK!
LEIA! GRAB A BLASTER!
HEAD FOR THE BUNKER! THE CHARGES ARE STILL IN THERE! WE MIGHT MAKE IT YET!
AND WITH THE FUGITIVES IN CLOSE COMBAT WITH THEIR CAPTORS, THE SCOUT WALKER IS UNABLE TO BRING ITS GUNS TO BEAR!
BEYOND ENDOR, IN THE DEPTHS OF SPACE, LANDO AND ADMIRAL ACKBAR MAKE THE SAME TACTIC WORK ON A LARGER SCALE.
AT POINT-BLANK RANGE, WE WON'T LAST LONG AGAINST THESE STAR DESTROYERS, CALRISSIAN!
WE'LL LAST LONGER THAN AGAINST THAT DEATH STAR, SIR... AND NOW IT CAN'T FIRE AT US WITHOUT HITTING ITS OWN SHIPS!

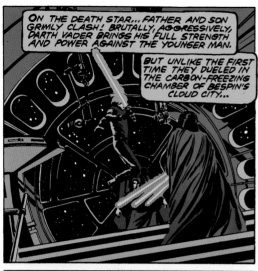

ON THE DEATH STAR... FATHER AND SON GRIMLY CLASH! BRUTALLY, AGGRESSIVELY, DARTH VADER BRINGS HIS FULL STRENGTH AND POWER AGAINST THE YOUNGER MAN.

BUT UNLIKE THE FIRST TIME THEY DUELED IN THE CARBON-FREEZING CHAMBER OF BESPIN'S CLOUD CITY...

...THIS IS A BATTLE OF EQUALS.

THE YOUNG JEDI HAS GROWN IN THE INTERIM...

...AND IF THERE IS ANY TRUE ADVANTAGE, IT SEEMS TO HAVE SHIFTED TO HIM.

THAT'S IT! USE YOUR AGGRESSIVE FEELINGS, BOY! ATTACK! ATTACK! LET THE HATE FLOW THROUGH YOU!

BUT THE EMPEROR'S WORDS AWAKEN LUKE TO SOMETHING TERRIBLE RISING WITHIN HIM. HE STOPS... AND LOWERS HIS LIGHT-SABER.

I...I WILL NOT FIGHT YOU, FATHER. HERE... TAKE MY WEAPON.

HE DARK LORD, RISING FROM WHERE HE STUMBLED, CATCHES THE SWORD AS IT ROLLS TO HIM, ATTACHING IT TO HIS BELT.

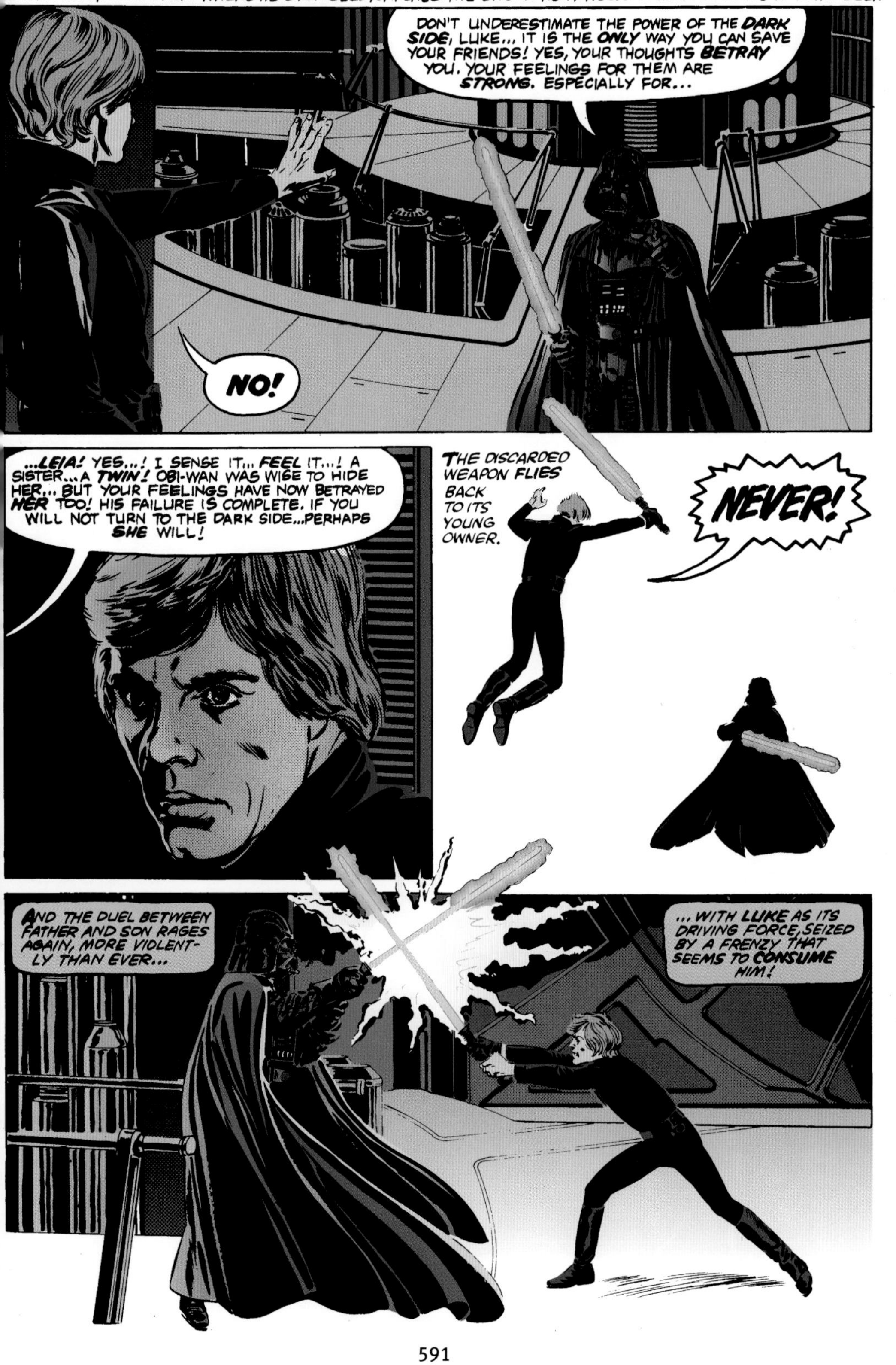
DON'T UNDERESTIMATE THE POWER OF THE DARK SIDE, LUKE... IT IS THE ONLY WAY YOU CAN SAVE YOUR FRIENDS! YES, YOUR THOUGHTS BETRAY YOU. YOUR FEELINGS FOR THEM ARE STRONG. ESPECIALLY FOR...
NO!
...LEIA! YES...! I SENSE IT... FEEL IT...! A SISTER...A TWIN! OBI-WAN WAS WISE TO HIDE HER... BUT YOUR FEELINGS HAVE NOW BETRAYED HER TOO! HIS FAILURE IS COMPLETE. IF YOU WILL NOT TURN TO THE DARK SIDE...PERHAPS SHE WILL!
THE DISCARDED WEAPON FLIES BACK TO ITS YOUNG OWNER.
NEVER!
AND THE DUEL BETWEEN FATHER AND SON RAGES AGAIN, MORE VIOLENTLY THAN EVER...
... WITH LUKE AS ITS DRIVING FORCE, SEIZED BY A FRENZY THAT SEEMS TO CONSUME HIM!

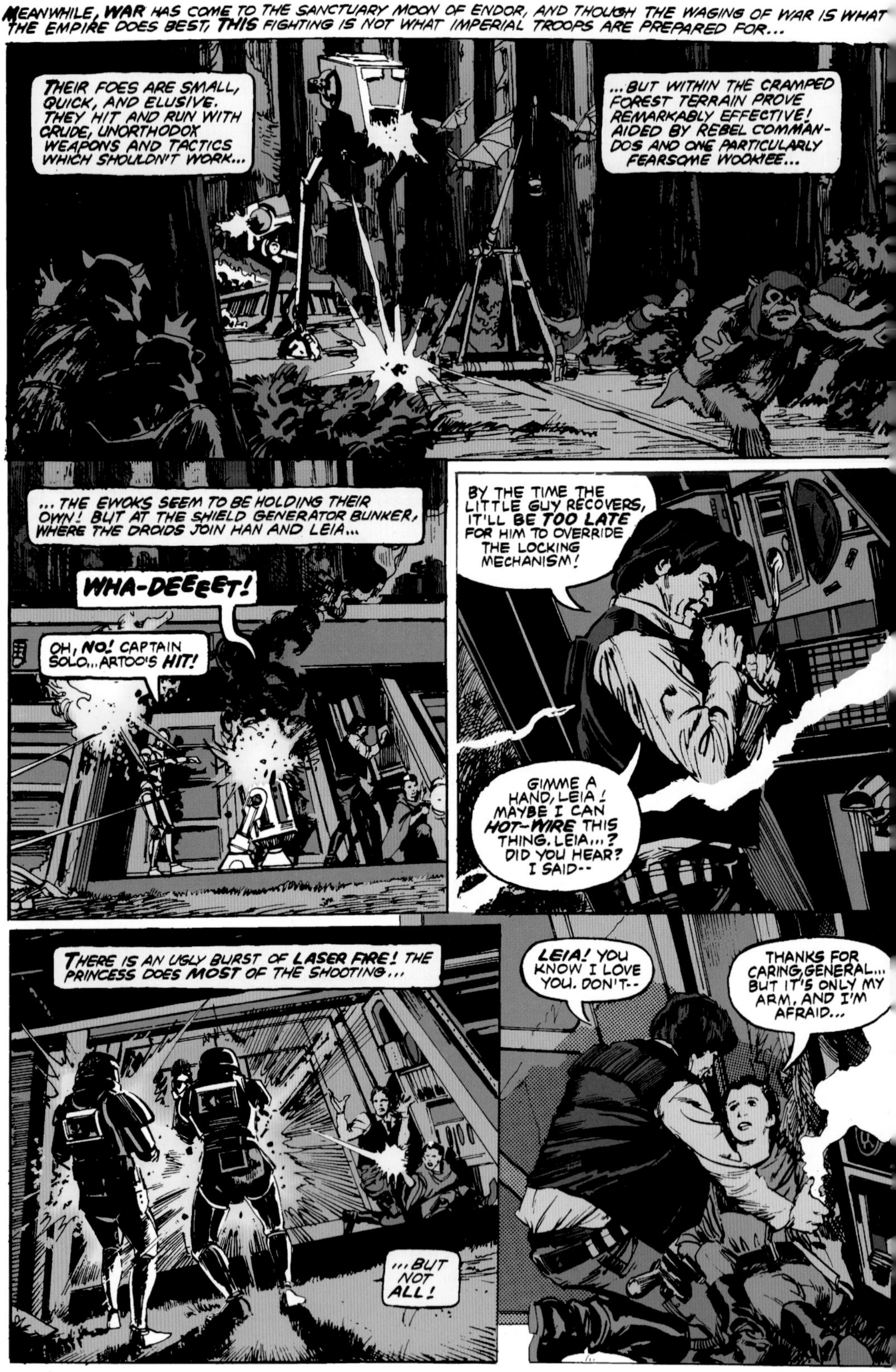
MEANWHILE, WAR HAS COME TO THE SANCTUARY MOON OF ENDOR, AND THOUGH THE WAGING OF WAR IS WHAT THE EMPIRE DOES BEST, THIS FIGHTING IS NOT WHAT IMPERIAL TROOPS ARE PREPARED FOR...
THEIR FOES ARE SMALL, QUICK, AND ELUSIVE. THEY HIT AND RUN WITH CRUDE, UNORTHODOX WEAPONS AND TACTICS WHICH SHOULDN'T WORK...
...BUT WITHIN THE CRAMPED FOREST TERRAIN PROVE REMARKABLY EFFECTIVE! AIDED BY REBEL COMMANDOS AND ONE PARTICULARLY FEARSOME WOOKIEE...
...THE EWOKS SEEM TO BE HOLDING THEIR OWN! BUT AT THE SHIELD GENERATOR BUNKER, WHERE THE DROIDS JOIN HAN AND LEIA...
WHA-DEEEET!
OH, NO! CAPTAIN SOLO...ARTOO'S HIT!
BY THE TIME THE LITTLE GUY RECOVERS, IT'LL BE TOO LATE FOR HIM TO OVERRIDE THE LOCKING MECHANISM!
GIMME A HAND, LEIA! MAYBE I CAN HOT-WIRE THIS THING. LEIA...? DID YOU HEAR? I SAID--
THERE IS AN UGLY BURST OF LASER FIRE! THE PRINCESS DOES MOST OF THE SHOOTING...
...BUT NOT ALL!
LEIA! YOU KNOW I LOVE YOU. DON'T--
THANKS FOR CARING, GENERAL... BUT IT'S ONLY MY ARM, AND I'M AFRAID...

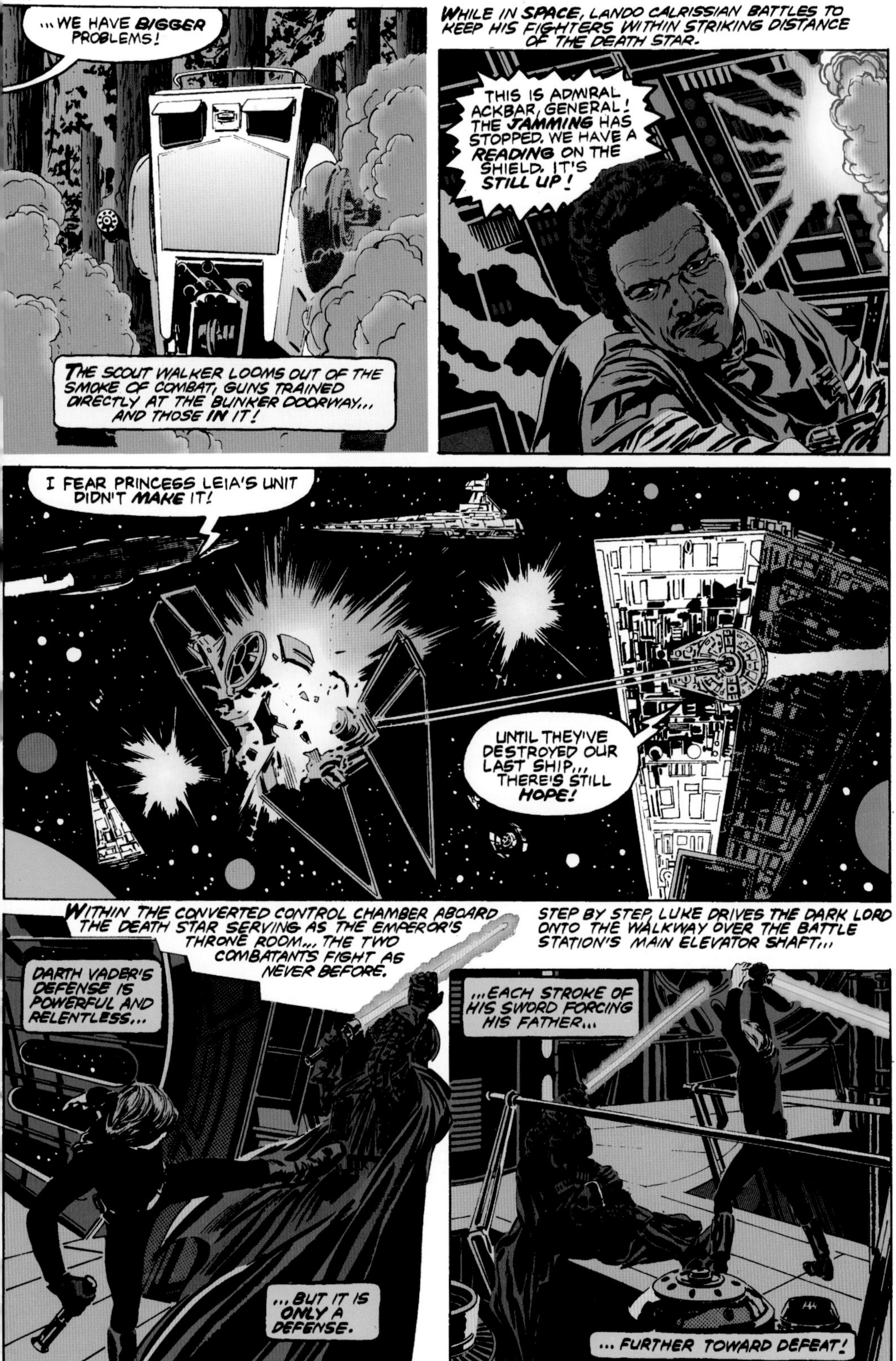

...WE HAVE BIGGER PROBLEMS!
THE SCOUT WALKER LOOMS OUT OF THE SMOKE OF COMBAT, GUNS TRAINED DIRECTLY AT THE BUNKER DOORWAY... AND THOSE IN IT!
WHILE IN SPACE, LANDO CALRISSIAN BATTLES TO KEEP HIS FIGHTERS WITHIN STRIKING DISTANCE OF THE DEATH STAR.
THIS IS ADMIRAL ACKBAR, GENERAL! THE JAMMING HAS STOPPED. WE HAVE A READING ON THE SHIELD. IT'S STILL UP!
I FEAR PRINCESS LEIA'S UNIT DIDN'T MAKE IT!
UNTIL THEY'VE DESTROYED OUR LAST SHIP... THERE'S STILL HOPE!
WITHIN THE CONVERTED CONTROL CHAMBER ABOARD THE DEATH STAR SERVING AS THE EMPEROR'S THRONE ROOM... THE TWO COMBATANTS FIGHT AS NEVER BEFORE.
DARTH VADER'S DEFENSE IS POWERFUL AND RELENTLESS...
...BUT IT IS ONLY A DEFENSE.
STEP BY STEP, LUKE DRIVES THE DARK LORD ONTO THE WALKWAY OVER THE BATTLE STATION'S MAIN ELEVATOR SHAFT...
...EACH STROKE OF HIS SWORD FORCING HIS FATHER...
...FURTHER TOWARD DEFEAT!

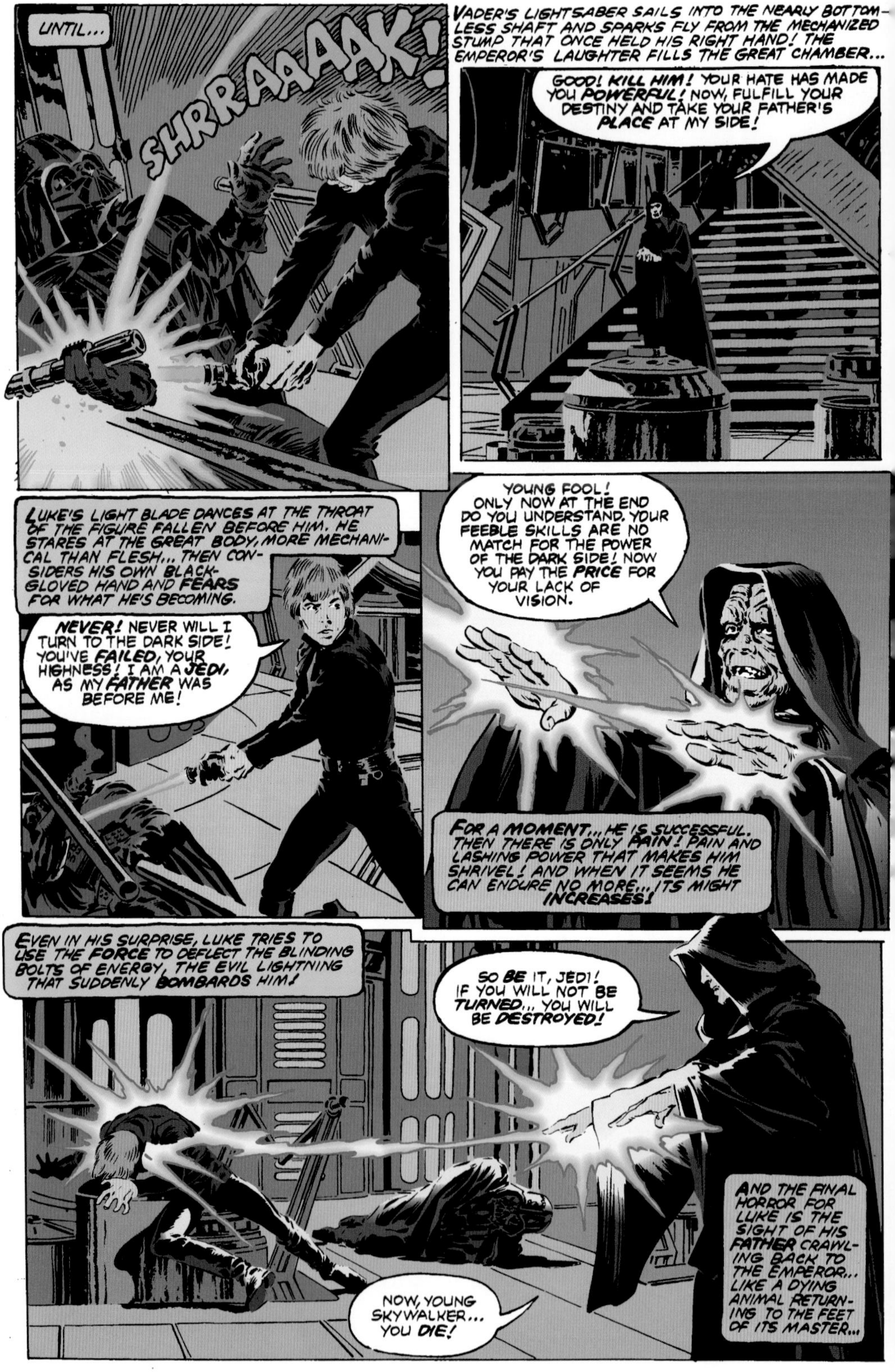
UNTIL...
SHRRAAAAK!
VADER'S LIGHTSABER SAILS INTO THE NEARLY BOTTOMLESS SHAFT AND SPARKS FLY FROM THE MECHANIZED STUMP THAT ONCE HELD HIS RIGHT HAND! THE EMPEROR'S LAUGHTER FILLS THE GREAT CHAMBER...
GOOD! KILL HIM! YOUR HATE HAS MADE YOU POWERFUL! NOW, FULFILL YOUR DESTINY AND TAKE YOUR FATHER'S PLACE AT MY SIDE!
LUKE'S LIGHT BLADE DANCES AT THE THROAT OF THE FIGURE FALLEN BEFORE HIM. HE STARES AT THE GREAT BODY, MORE MECHANICAL THAN FLESH... THEN CONSIDERS HIS OWN BLACK-GLOVED HAND AND FEARS FOR WHAT HE'S BECOMING.
NEVER! NEVER WILL I TURN TO THE DARK SIDE! YOU'VE FAILED, YOUR HIGHNESS! I AM A JEDI, AS MY FATHER WAS BEFORE ME!
YOUNG FOOL! ONLY NOW AT THE END DO YOU UNDERSTAND. YOUR FEEBLE SKILLS ARE NO MATCH FOR THE POWER OF THE DARK SIDE! NOW YOU PAY THE PRICE FOR YOUR LACK OF VISION.
FOR A MOMENT... HE IS SUCCESSFUL. THEN THERE IS ONLY PAIN! PAIN AND LASHING POWER THAT MAKES HIM SHRIVEL! AND WHEN IT SEEMS HE CAN ENDURE NO MORE... ITS MIGHT INCREASES!
EVEN IN HIS SURPRISE, LUKE TRIES TO USE THE FORCE TO DEFLECT THE BLINDING BOLTS OF ENERGY, THE EVIL LIGHTNING THAT SUDDENLY BOMBARDS HIM!
SO BE IT, JEDI! IF YOU WILL NOT BE TURNED... YOU WILL BE DESTROYED!
NOW, YOUNG SKYWALKER... YOU DIE!
AND THE FINAL HORROR FOR LUKE IS THE SIGHT OF HIS FATHER CRAWLING BACK TO THE EMPEROR... LIKE A DYING ANIMAL RETURNING TO THE FEET OF ITS MASTER...

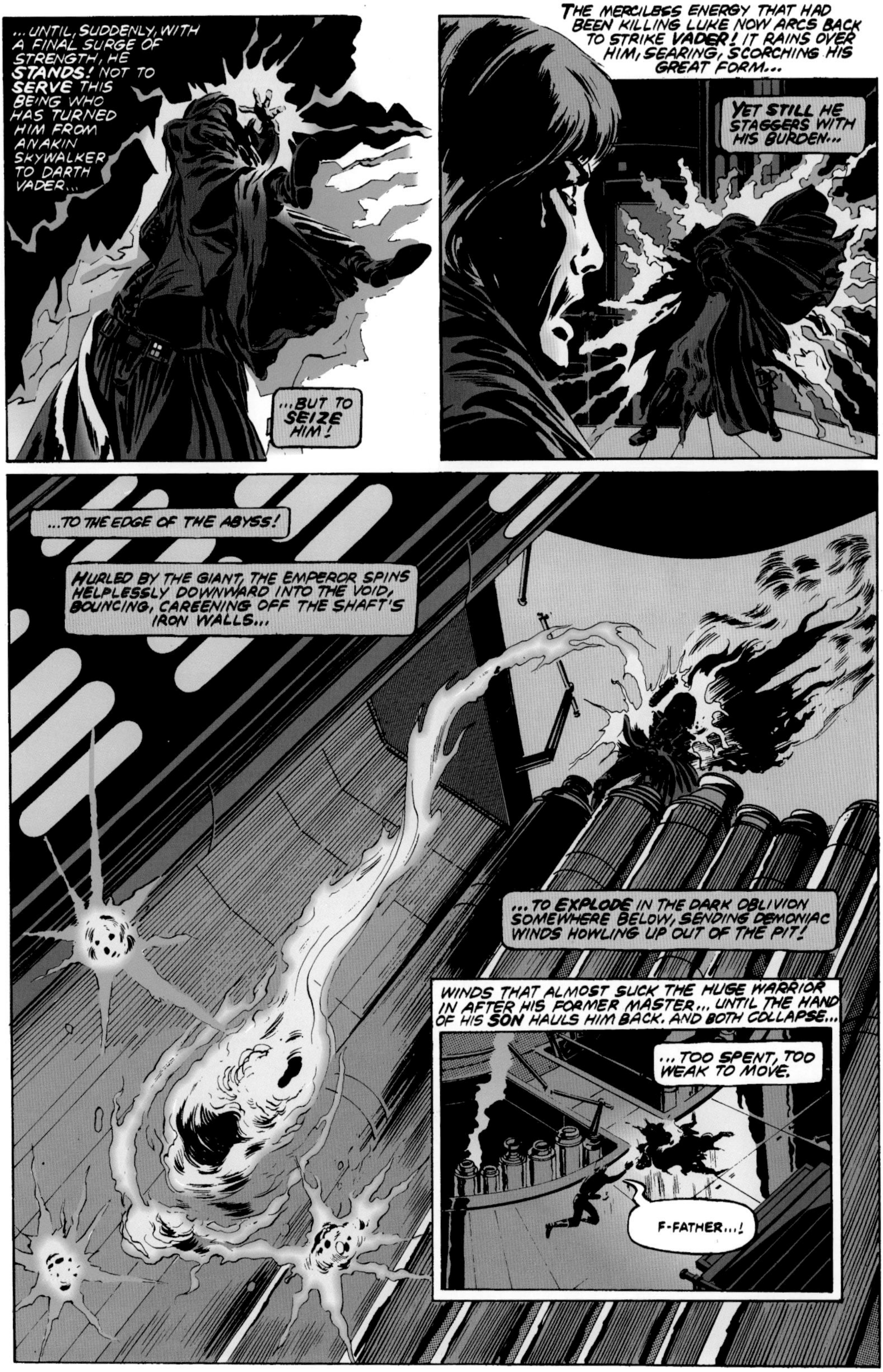
...UNTIL, SUDDENLY, WITH A FINAL SURGE OF STRENGTH, HE STANDS! NOT TO SERVE THIS BEING WHO HAS TURNED HIM FROM ANAKIN SKYWALKER TO DARTH VADER...
...BUT TO SEIZE HIM!
THE MERCILESS ENERGY THAT HAD BEEN KILLING LUKE NOW ARCS BACK TO STRIKE VADER! IT RAINS OVER HIM, SEARING, SCORCHING HIS GREAT FORM...
YET STILL HE STAGGERS WITH HIS BURDEN...
...TO THE EDGE OF THE ABYSS!
HURLED BY THE GIANT, THE EMPEROR SPINS HELPLESSLY DOWNWARD INTO THE VOID, BOUNCING, CAREENING OFF THE SHAFT'S IRON WALLS...
...TO EXPLODE IN THE DARK OBLIVION SOMEWHERE BELOW, SENDING DEMONIAC WINDS HOWLING UP OUT OF THE PIT!
WINDS THAT ALMOST SUCK THE HUGE WARRIOR IN AFTER HIS FORMER MASTER... UNTIL THE HAND OF HIS SON HAULS HIM BACK. AND BOTH COLLAPSE...
...TOO SPENT, TOO WEAK TO MOVE.
F-FATHER...!

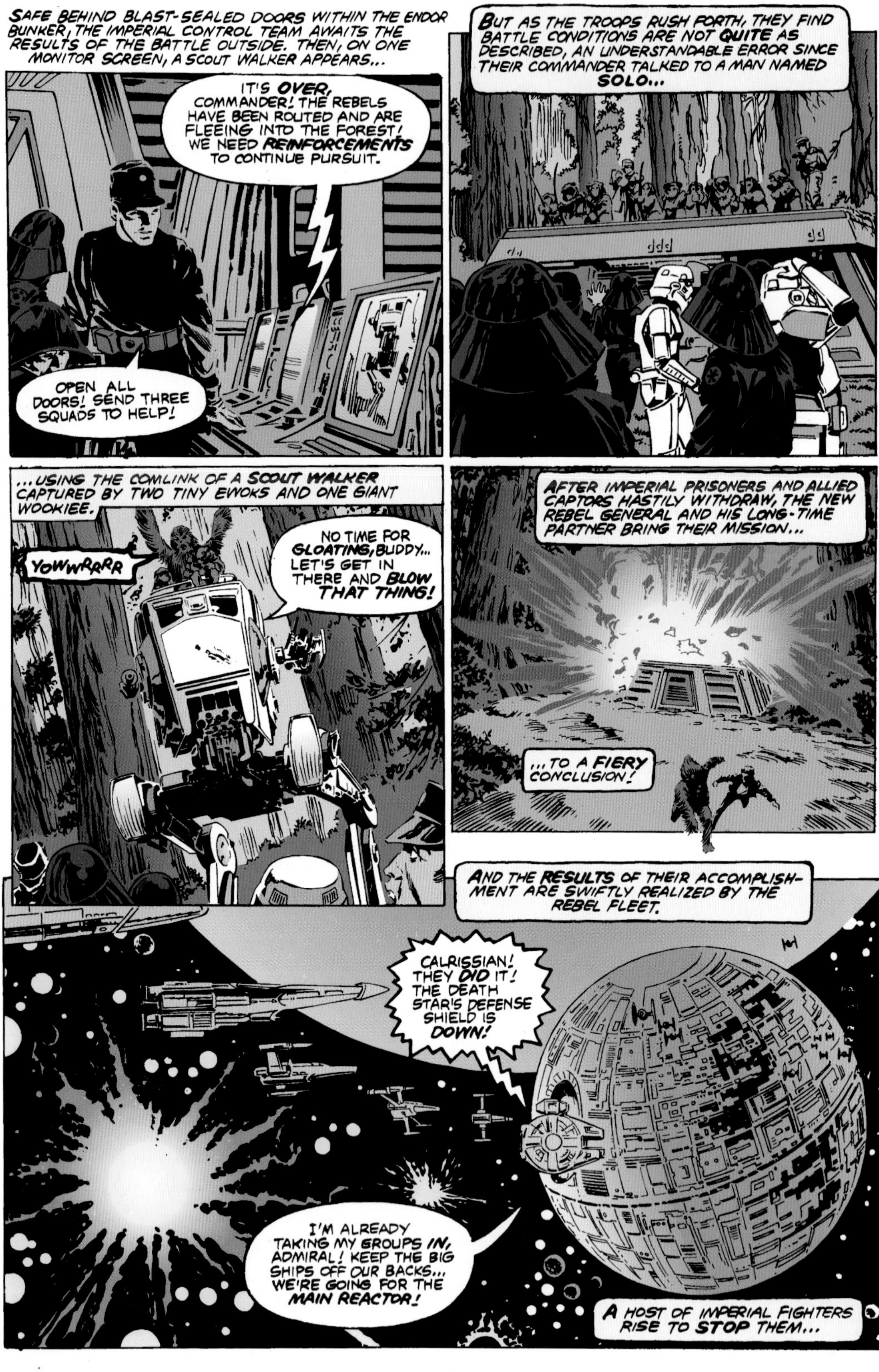
SAFE BEHIND BLAST-SEALED DOORS WITHIN THE ENDOR BUNKER, THE IMPERIAL CONTROL TEAM AWAITS THE RESULTS OF THE BATTLE OUTSIDE. THEN, ON ONE MONITOR SCREEN, A SCOUT WALKER APPEARS...
IT'S OVER, COMMANDER! THE REBELS HAVE BEEN ROUTED AND ARE FLEEING INTO THE FOREST! WE NEED REINFORCEMENTS TO CONTINUE PURSUIT.
OPEN ALL DOORS! SEND THREE SQUADS TO HELP!
BUT AS THE TROOPS RUSH FORTH, THEY FIND BATTLE CONDITIONS ARE NOT QUITE AS DESCRIBED, AN UNDERSTANDABLE ERROR SINCE THEIR COMMANDER TALKED TO A MAN NAMED SOLO...
...USING THE COMLINK OF A SCOUT WALKER CAPTURED BY TWO TINY EWOKS AND ONE GIANT WOOKIEE.
YOWWRRRR
NO TIME FOR GLOATING, BUDDY... LET'S GET IN THERE AND BLOW THAT THING!
AFTER IMPERIAL PRISONERS AND ALLIED CAPTORS HASTILY WITHDRAW, THE NEW REBEL GENERAL AND HIS LONG-TIME PARTNER BRING THEIR MISSION...
...TO A FIERY CONCLUSION!
AND THE RESULTS OF THEIR ACCOMPLISHMENT ARE SWIFTLY REALIZED BY THE REBEL FLEET.
CALRISSIAN! THEY DID IT! THE DEATH STAR'S DEFENSE SHIELD IS DOWN!
I'M ALREADY TAKING MY GROUPS IN, ADMIRAL! KEEP THE BIG SHIPS OFF OUR BACKS... WE'RE GOING FOR THE MAIN REACTOR!
A HOST OF IMPERIAL FIGHTERS RISE TO STOP THEM...

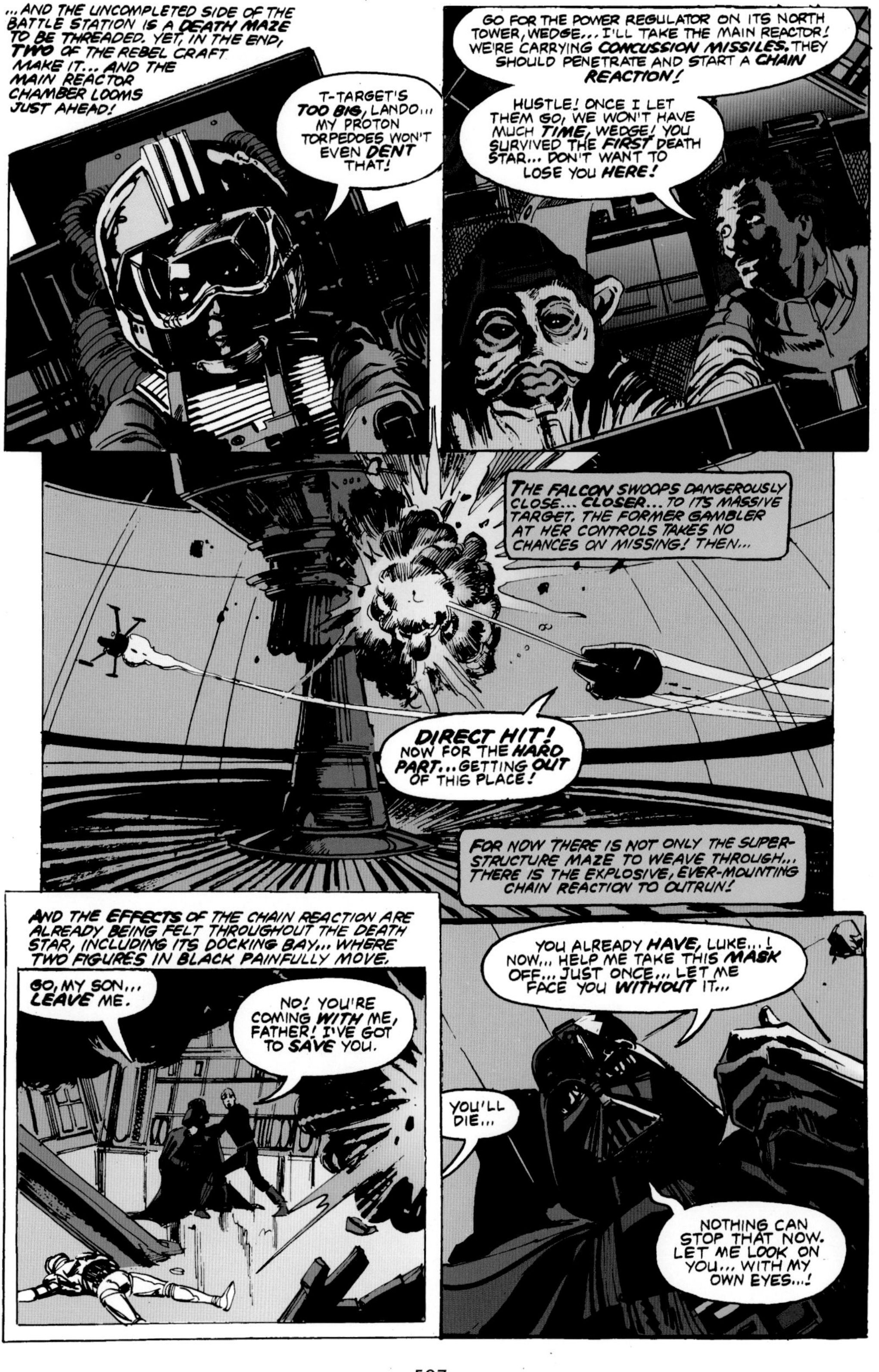
...AND THE UNCOMPLETED SIDE OF THE BATTLE STATION IS A DEATH MAZE TO BE THREADED. YET, IN THE END, TWO OF THE REBEL CRAFT MAKE IT... AND THE MAIN REACTOR CHAMBER LOOMS JUST AHEAD!
T-TARGET'S TOO BIG, LANDO... MY PROTON TORPEDOES WON'T EVEN DENT THAT!
GO FOR THE POWER REGULATOR ON ITS NORTH TOWER, WEDGE... I'LL TAKE THE MAIN REACTOR! WE'RE CARRYING CONCUSSION MISSILES. THEY SHOULD PENETRATE AND START A CHAIN REACTION!
HUSTLE! ONCE I LET THEM GO, WE WON'T HAVE MUCH TIME, WEDGE! YOU SURVIVED THE FIRST DEATH STAR... DON'T WANT TO LOSE YOU HERE!
THE FALCON SWOOPS DANGEROUSLY CLOSE... CLOSER... TO ITS MASSIVE TARGET. THE FORMER GAMBLER AT HER CONTROLS TAKES NO CHANCES ON MISSING! THEN...
DIRECT HIT! NOW FOR THE HARD PART... GETTING OUT OF THIS PLACE!
FOR NOW THERE IS NOT ONLY THE SUPER-STRUCTURE MAZE TO WEAVE THROUGH... THERE IS THE EXPLOSIVE, EVER-MOUNTING CHAIN REACTION TO OUTRUN!
AND THE EFFECTS OF THE CHAIN REACTION ARE ALREADY BEING FELT THROUGHOUT THE DEATH STAR, INCLUDING ITS DOCKING BAY... WHERE TWO FIGURES IN BLACK PAINFULLY MOVE.
GO, MY SON... LEAVE ME.
NO! YOU'RE COMING WITH ME, FATHER! I'VE GOT TO SAVE YOU.
YOU ALREADY HAVE, LUKE...! NOW... HELP ME TAKE THIS MASK OFF... JUST ONCE... LET ME FACE YOU WITHOUT IT...
YOU'LL DIE...
NOTHING CAN STOP THAT NOW. LET ME LOOK ON YOU... WITH MY OWN EYES...!

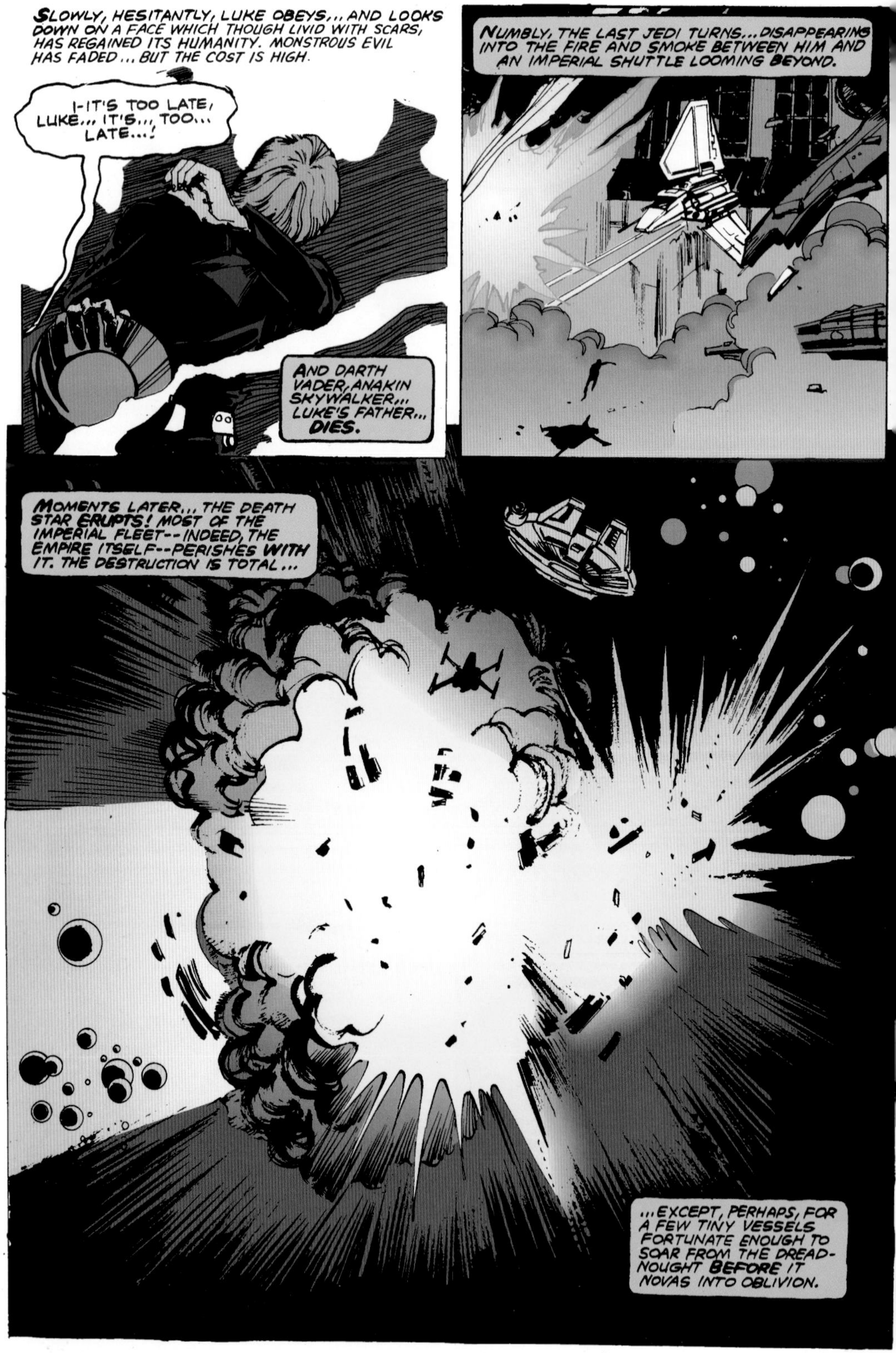
SLOWLY, HESITANTLY, LUKE OBEYS... AND LOOKS DOWN ON A FACE WHICH THOUGH LIVID WITH SCARS, HAS REGAINED ITS HUMANITY. MONSTROUS EVIL HAS FADED... BUT THE COST IS HIGH.
I-IT'S TOO LATE, LUKE... IT'S... TOO... LATE...!
AND DARTH VADER, ANAKIN SKYWALKER... LUKE'S FATHER... DIES.
NUMBLY, THE LAST JEDI TURNS... DISAPPEARING INTO THE FIRE AND SMOKE BETWEEN HIM AND AN IMPERIAL SHUTTLE LOOMING BEYOND.
MOMENTS LATER... THE DEATH STAR ERUPTS! MOST OF THE IMPERIAL FLEET--INDEED, THE EMPIRE ITSELF--PERISHES WITH IT. THE DESTRUCTION IS TOTAL...
...EXCEPT, PERHAPS, FOR A FEW TINY VESSELS FORTUNATE ENOUGH TO SOAR FROM THE DREAD-NOUGHT BEFORE IT NOVAS INTO OBLIVION.

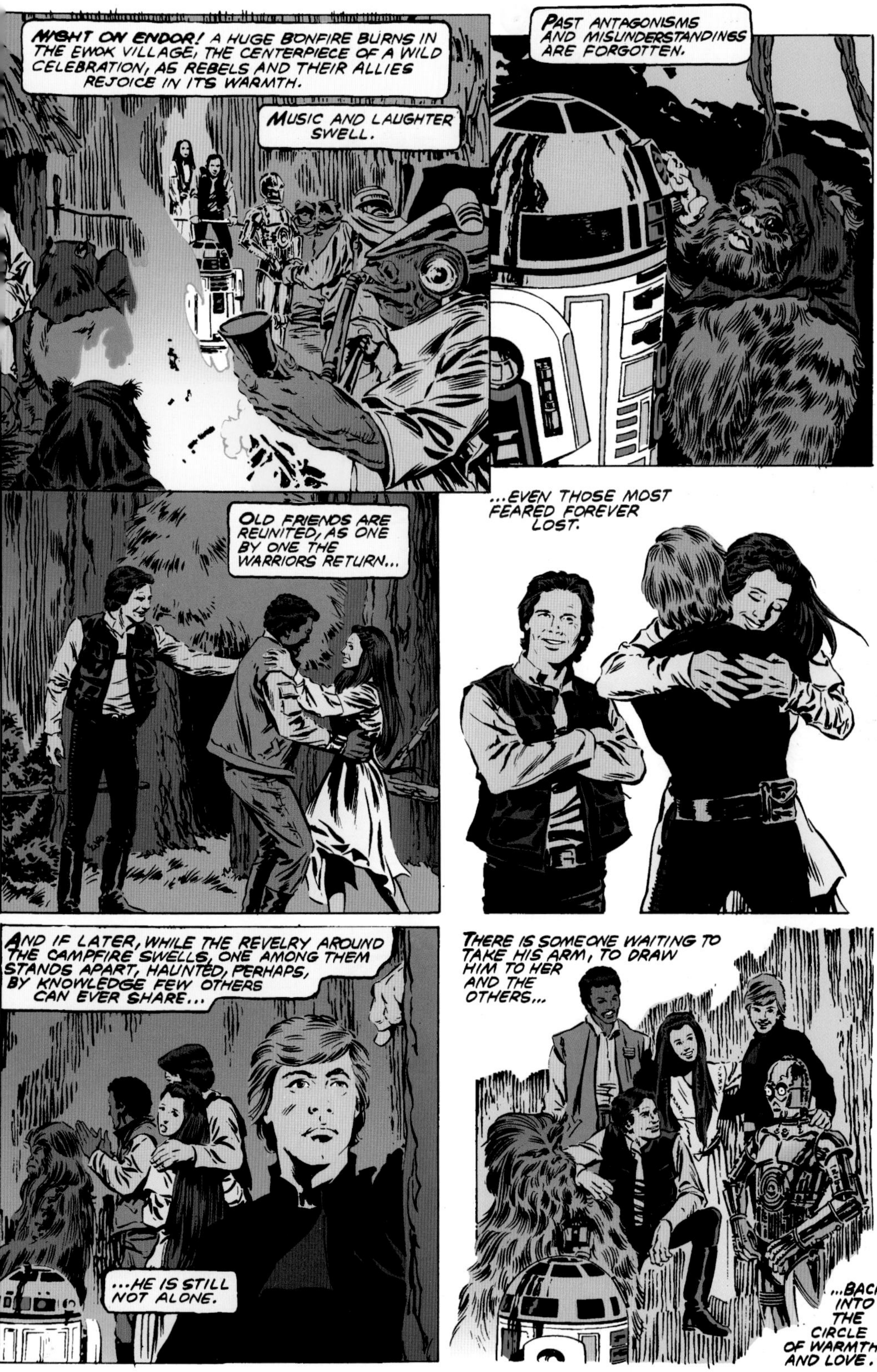
NIGHT ON ENDOR! A HUGE BONFIRE BURNS IN THE EWOK VILLAGE, THE CENTERPIECE OF A WILD CELEBRATION, AS REBELS AND THEIR ALLIES REJOICE IN ITS WARMTH.
MUSIC AND LAUGHTER SWELL.
PAST ANTAGONISMS AND MISUNDERSTANDINGS ARE FORGOTTEN.
OLD FRIENDS ARE REUNITED, AS ONE BY ONE THE WARRIORS RETURN...
...EVEN THOSE MOST FEARED FOREVER LOST.
AND IF LATER, WHILE THE REVELRY AROUND THE CAMPFIRE SWELLS, ONE AMONG THEM STANDS APART, HAUNTED, PERHAPS, BY KNOWLEDGE FEW OTHERS CAN EVER SHARE...
...HE IS STILL NOT ALONE.
THERE IS SOMEONE WAITING TO TAKE HIS ARM, TO DRAW HIM TO HER AND THE OTHERS...
...BACK INTO THE CIRCLE OF WARMTH AND LOVE.

STAR WARS GRAPHIC NOVEL TIMELINE (IN YEARS)

Omnibus: Tales of the Jedi—5,000–3,986 BSW4
Knights of the Old Republic—3,964–3,963 BSW4
The Old Republic—3653, 3678 BSW4
Knight Errant—1,032 BSW4
Jedi vs. Sith—1,000 BSW4
Omnibus: Rise of the Sith—33 BSW4
Episode I: The Phantom Menace—32 BSW4
Omnibus: Emissaries and Assassins—32 BSW4
Twilight—31 BSW4
Omnibus: Menace Revealed—31–22 BSW4
Darkness—30 BSW4
The Stark Hyperspace War—30 BSW4
Rite of Passage—28 BSW4
Honor and Duty—22 BSW4
Blood Ties—22 BSW4
Episode II: Attack of the Clones—22 BSW4
Clone Wars—22–19 BSW4
Clone Wars Adventures—22–19 BSW4
General Grievous—22–19 BSW4
Episode III: Revenge of the Sith—19 BSW4
Dark Times—19 BSW4
Omnibus: Droids—5.5 BSW4
Boba Fett: Enemy of the Empire—3 BSW4
Underworld—1 BSW4
Episode IV: A New Hope—SW4
Classic Star Wars—0–3 ASW4
A Long Time Ago . . . —0–4 ASW4
Empire—0 ASW4
Rebellion—0 ASW4
Boba Fett: Man with a Mission—0 ASW4
Omnibus: Early Victories—0–3 ASW4
Jabba the Hutt: The Art of the Deal—1 ASW4
Episode V: The Empire Strikes Back—3 ASW4
Omnibus: Shadows of the Empire—3.5–4.5 ASW4
Episode VI: Return of the Jedi—4 ASW4
Omnibus: X-Wing Rogue Squadron—4–5 ASW4
Heir to the Empire—9 ASW4
Dark Force Rising—9 ASW4
The Last Command—9 ASW4
Dark Empire—10 ASW4
Boba Fett: Death, Lies, and Treachery—10 ASW4
Crimson Empire—11 ASW4
Jedi Academy: Leviathan—12 ASW4
Union—19 ASW4
Chewbacca—25 ASW4
Invasion—25 ASW4
Legacy—130–137 ASW4

Old Republic Era
25,000 – 1000 years before
Star Wars: A New Hope

Rise of the Empire Era
1000 – 0 years before
Star Wars: A New Hope

Rebellion Era
0 – 5 years after
Star Wars: A New Hope

New Republic Era
5 – 25 years after
Star Wars: A New Hope

New Jedi Order Era
25+ years after
Star Wars: A New Hope

Legacy Era
130+ years after
Star Wars: A New Hope

Vector
Crosses four eras in the timeline

Volume 1
Knights of the Old Republic Volume 5
Dark Times Volume 3
Volume 2
Rebellion Volume 4
Legacy Volume 6

BSW4 = before *Episode IV: A New Hope*. ASW4 = after *Episode IV: A New Hope*.